WHAT OTHERS ARE SAYING ABOUT THIS BOOK .....

"A handbook that compiles as much information as possible on people, places, technology, statistics, and automotive history has been put together for the car enthusiast. This readable reference can be a quick guide for car buffs, writers and anyone affiliated with the automotive industry who might want to look up a term, a date, or a car-related word. Organized in alphabetical order, and by subject, the book includes simple definitions of terms, places, associations. It also features an automotive time line and summary index."
-- **Automotive News.**

"Our observations of the contents of the book indicate, that, indeed, your long-term efforts have yielded a unique reference which contains a wealth of information that has not otherwise been gathered in one reference work. The entries which refer to our Corporation and its car models are an especially interesting aspect of the publication." -- **Vice President, major US car manufacturer, Detroit, MI.**

"I was impressed by your book and by you. I admire your courage to commit yourself in such a meaningful way to using your talents." -- **B.L., Librarian, Seattle, WA.**

"I've been working in the automotive business for over 25 years and I've never seen anything like this. I thought I knew most everything pertaining to cars, until I started reading this book". -- **S.F., Forth Worth, TX.**

"One of the most interesting reference books I have ever read. I can open the book to any page and find something interesting about automobiles. It's easy to get caught up reading page after page like a novel. It's amazing that it was the work of one man." -- **R.B., Boise, ID.**

"I've been in automotive repair for many years and enjoy working on cars and collecting automotive books. I have books covering a lot of the subjects contained in this book, but they are in many volumes and don't cover the field as completely, especially for a one-volume reference." -- **J.S., San Diego, CA.**

"I tried one of the unusual car service tips to diagnose a stubborn car problem and it worked !" -- **S.D., Seattle, WA.**

"Good information" -- **Marcia Miller, Librarian, Sidney, NE.**

"Instantly essential to automotive journalism. Suggest you plan updates, including contributions from readers." -- **Daniel S. Broun, free-lance writer, West Nyack, NY.**

"This encyclopedic dictionary with more than 14,000 entries appears to cover every possible word, phrase, name, and personality related to both the historical and contemporary automotive industry. The entries are arranged in alphabetical order followed by a brief definition or discussion of 5 to 200 words. Adequate cross-references lead to alternative and additional terms. At first glance, one may not be enticed to consult this book because of its physical appearance, but after reading only a few entries, the car enthusiast will hardly be able to lay it down. Abbreviations for international license plates are included as well as car models, people in the industry, and race car drivers. Eighty four separate entries under magazine give names and brief, one sentence annotations for each. Also included are entries that pertain to automotive repair and maintenance. Under sound will be found banging, knocking, rumbling, whining, and whooshing followed by the possible reasons for such a sound. The same is true under car service tip and engine problem, where one can find such subheadings as air bypass valve test, wheel drag test, acceleration causes cutout, and won't start. In this respect the book becomes a troubleshooting manual. A chronology, Automotive Time Line, of important events in the automotive industry is an appendix.

The type and crowded pages may not be pleasing to the eye, but the wealth of automotive information here more than makes up for this deficiency. This would be an appropriate reference book for public libraries, and academic libraries may want it for its historical information." -- **Reference Books Bulletin**

A New Approach

IMAGINE all the different kinds of automotive/related information scattered in countless places. Is it possible to bring it together into a readable form ? The author thinks so.

AUTOMOTIVE REFERENCE is the first laymen/professional book designed to embrace the world of auto/related information as it currently exists. Extensive research, experience, writing, and a new method of organizing information was required to make this the most complete reference of its kind in the automotive industry.

Automotive Reference is.....

USED BY	USED AS A	A SOURCE COVERING ....
● Do-it-yourselfers ● Car buyers/sellers	● Textbook ● Encyclopedia/dictionary	● Con games ● Jargon

● Teachers
● Students
	● Car repair/maint manual	● con man/repairman
		  ● dealer/salesman/racer
		  ● advertiser/insurance

● Libraries
● Schools
	● Troubleshooter
	
	● Parts describer
		● law enforcement/foreign
		  ● old car/auction/tire
		  ● radar/oil business
		  ● customizer/etc

● Racing fans
● Car collectors
● Car historians
● Car customizers
	● Source
	  ● car language/jargon
	  ● car make/model/year
	  ● car manufacturer
		● Language – terms/phrases/
		  abbreviations/slang/etc
		● Parts/products/suppliers
		● Problems

● Mechanics
● Partsmen
● Car salesmen
● Car industry workers
● Engineers
	● Guide
	  ● consumer protection
	  ● petroleum products
	  ● racing/race tracks
	  ● performance equipment
		● engine/starting/clutch
		  ● electrical/transmission
		  ● fluid leak/paint coat
		  ● brake/car handling/etc
		● Makes/models/producers
		● Performance/racing equip

● Repair shops
● Service stations
● Service departments
	● customizing cars
	  ● car products
	  ● famous car people
	  ● road help/situations
	  ● antique cars
		● Tips
		  ● saving gas/driving
		  ● car service work
		  ● road situation/towing
		● Tire wear patterns

● Car advertisers
● Automotive publishers
● Auto parts stores
	● insurance
	  ● warranty/guarantee
	  ● contract/leasing
	  ● product manufacturer
	  ● car publications
	  ● driver education
	  ● oil companies
		● Petroleum products – gas/
		  oil/grease/additive/etc
		● Race cars/drivers
		● Land speed records
		● People/places/history
		● Sounds/smells/vibrations

● Types
  ● body style/frame
  ● engine/clutch/brake
  ● transmission/steering
  ● suspension/carburetor
  ● tire/ignition system
  ● magneto/generator/etc
● Sensors/gauges
● Troubleshooting – tests/
  methods
● Latest electronic parts
● Companies
  ● car manufacturers
  ● petroleum/car products
● Insurance
● Warranties/guarantees
● Contracts/leases
● Car customizing
● Car publications
● Car industry jobs

AND MUCH, MUCH MORE ! ! !

AUTOMOTIVE REFERENCE

A New Approach – To The World of Auto/Related Information

1987 Edition

**Whitehorse
Boise, Idaho**

G. J. DAVIS

AUTOMOTIVE REFERENCE

A New Approach - To The World of Auto/Related Information

By G.J. Davis

Publisher

Whitehorse
P.O. Box 6125
Boise, Idaho 83707, U.S.A.

Copyright Information

Copyright - c1987 by G. J. Davis
First Printing - March 1987
Printed and Bound - In the United States of America.

Library of Congress Cataloging-in-Publication Data

Davis, G. J. (Greg J.), 1949-
    Automotive reference.

    1. Automobiles--Dictionaries. 2. Automobiles--
Handbooks, manuals, etc. I. Title.
TL9.D28 1987   629.2'222'0321   87-8113
ISBN 0-937591-01-7 Hardcover
ISBN 0-937591-00-9 Softcover

THE AUTHOR'S STORY

G.J. Davis let his imagination run wild. He wondered -- what if ? -- over 20 years ago, and it never went away. What if he could somehow assemble and organize the world of automotive and related information into one efficient reference ? With such an accomplishment, his long standing interest in cars would be benefited in countless ways. A part of his life would become more enjoyable and easier to control, as well as the life of others sharing in his dream.

The dream began as a thought, grew and matured from countless personal life experiences, and finally became real when he committed himself to a non-stop research and writing effort until completed.

Yet, writing the book was not enough. He wanted it done right. Complete control of his creation would insure his thoughts and ideas would not be lost at the hands of someone else. So, he resolved to research, organize, write, edit, and then oversee the book's printing, assemblage, and distribution. It required using his background in engineering, auto mechanics, technical writing, and other areas to make it happen. It also required ending one career, starting another, and making certain sacrifices as do all worthy pursuits in life.

AUTOMOTIVE REFERENCE represents the author's years of: locating, selecting, and reading countless car books; researching the automotive information field; finding solutions to countless car problems; doing endless hours of car repair work; learning how the automotive industry works; and talking and learning from countless people associated with cars in all walks of life.

AUTOMOTIVE REFERENCE is: the only book of its kind.

ACKNOWLEDGEMENT

Those Contributing to the 1987 Edition

Many people and organizations contributed to the preparation of this book. They provided me with support, inspiration, guidance, and editing. My deepest thanks go to: my wife Sandy, my parents, my brothers, and my friends - June, Daryl, and Jackie.

DISCLAIMER

DEDICATION

This book is dedicated to all who hunger for knowledge. We
each chart our destiny by what we know. May the world
inside this book illuminate, educate, and help those whose
path it graces.

This book is specifically

        dedicated to .... Sandy,

           and

               to .... Max and Segundo.

HOW TO USE THIS BOOK

Welcome to the world of automotive and related information !

The information in this book is organized in a unique way to make finding
people, places and things easy.   In general, each term is entered according to
its name alone or its name and subject category.   For example, the term engine
and the different types of engines are entered as follows:

        engine -
        engine(diesel) -
        engine(fuel injected) -
        engine(in line) -

The book's system of organizing information is covered in detail in Section B
of the Appendix, Book Organization.   Topics covered include: term formats;
descriptors; primary, secondary, and tertiary subjects, special character
usage, cross referencing, capitalization, and entry of a person's name.

A quick overview of the information contained in this book can be found in
Section C of the Appendix, Term Summary.   It lists those terms in the book for
which there are two or more related types.   For example, there are 57
different types of engines covered.

A very comprehensive chronological list of significant events in automotive
history is contained in Section A of the Appendix, Automotive Time Line.

TABLE OF CONTENTS

DESCRIPTION	PAGE

TERMS

APPENDIX

NUMERIC

1/4 inch drive – One quarter inch square opening in a socket wrench. It is the smallest size used in socket wrenches.

1/4 mile – Type of race performed at race tracks by two competing racing vehicles. Course length is a straight 1/4 mile from start to finish. Vehicles usually compete by accelerating from a standing start to the maximum speed possible within the distance.

3/8 inch drive – Three eighths inch square opening in a socket wrench. This size is the most common size used for general automotive work.

1/2 inch drive – One half inch square opening in a socket wrench. This size is used for heavy duty work and on impact sockets.

3/4 inch drive – Three quarter inch square opening in a socket wrench. This size is used for heavy duty turning applications such as in truck and construction equipment applications.

2 door – Car with two side doors for passenger access.

2 Dr – Abbreviation for two door.

2S – Abbreviation for two door sedan.

2-tone – Abbreviation for two color paint job on car body.

2 way stop – Two street intersection with traffic flow regulated by the placement of stop signs for one street direction.

2WD – Abbreviation for two wheel drive.

3 across seating – Bench car seat capacity of three people sitting side by side.

3 speed – Transmission built with three forward speeds and one reverse speed.

4X2 – Abbreviation for four wheel vehicle with two wheel drive.

4X4 – Abbreviation for four wheel vehicle with four wheel drive.

4 banger – Four cylinder engine.

4 door – Car with four doors.

4 Dr – Abbreviation for four door.

4S – Abbreviation for four door sedan.

4 speed – Transmission with four forward speeds and one reverse speed.

4 way stop – Four-way intersection where all cars must stop before proceding.

4WD – Abbreviation for four wheel drive.

4wd – Abbreviation for four wheel drive.

4whd – Abbreviation for four wheel drive.

5 mph bumper – Car bumper designed to absorb impacts up to 5 mph without damaging a car body or frame.

5 speed – Transmission with five forward speeds and one reverse speed.

5th wheel – Trailer hitch mounted in the middle of a truck bed for towing large trailers. Also, it refers to a large trailer with such a hitch.

5 year/50,000 mile coverage – Clause used in a new car warranty to guarantee a car's engine and powertrain to be free of defects in material and workmanship for a period of 5 years or 50,000 miles whichever occurs first. It commonly takes effect when a 12 month/12,000 mile coverage stipulation expires. Engine parts and accessories are usually not covered and include: carburetor, ignition system, starter motor and solenoid, coil, distributor, alternator, radiator, and power steering and brakes.

6 cylinder engine – See engine(six cylinder).

8 cylinder engine – See engine(eight cylinder).

8 tr – Abbreviation for eight track tape.

10 to 2 position – Driver's left and right hand positioning on a steering wheel located in 10 and 2 o'clock positions respectively. It provides good steering control of the car.

10W/40 – See oil(10W/40).

12 month/12,000 mile coverage – Clause used in a new car warranty to guarantee a entire car and/or its engine and powertrain to be free of defects in material and workmanship for a period of 12 months or 12,000 miles whichever occurs first.

12V – Abbreviation for 12 volts, the normal voltage level of a car's electrical system.

18 wheeler – Semi-truck with 18 wheels.

30 day guarantee – See guarantee(30 day).

49 state car – See federal version.

50-50 guarantee – See guarantee(50-50).

90 days same as cash – Selling incentive used to increase sales. Buyer agrees to make necessary minimum payments within 90 days. If the payments are made, all finance charges are refunded.

100-point car - Car judged at a car exhibit to be essentially perfect in all judging categories. Such cars are rare.

360 - See donut.

A

A(1) - See A-Bone.

A(2) - Abbreviation for Austria found usually on an international license plate.

AAA - Abbreviation for American Automobile Association. It is the ruling body for car racing in the United States.

AABM - Abbreviation for Association of American Battery Manufacturers.

AAMCO - American car repair business chain engaged in car transmission repair.

AAP - Abbreviation for auxiliary accelerator pump.

A-arm - A-shaped pivoting suspension link used to attach a car's wheel assembly to a car frame. It differs from a control arm in that no strut rod is used and two mounting points are used with a large spacing. Most late model cars now use lower control arms with strut rods. See also control arm.

Abbot - American car produced from 1909-1918 by Abbot Motor Car Co. (1909-1915) in Michigan, Consolidated Car Co. (1916) in Michigan, and Abbot Corp. in Ohio (1916-1918).

Abbot-Cleveland - American car produced in 1917.

Abbot-Detroit - American car produced in 1909-1918 by Abbot Motor Car Co. in Michigan (1909-1915), Consolidated Car Co. in Michigan (1916), and Abbot Corp. in Ohio (1916-1918).

Abbot-Downing - American car produced in 1919.

ABC - American car produced from 1906-1910 by Autobuggy Manufacturing Co. (1906-1908), ABC Motor Vehicle Manufacturing Co. (1908-1910), both in Missouri.

ABC Steamer - American steam powered car produced in 1901.

Abenaque - American car produced in 1900.

Abendroth & Root - American car produced from 1907-1913.

Able - American car produced in 1916.

abnormal tire wear - Tire tread worn unevenly or too quickly.

A-bone - Model A Ford.

Abresh-Cramer - American car produced from 1910-1911.

ABS - Abbreviation for antilocking braking system.

absolute pressure - Pressure measured relative to zero, and not atmospheric pressure. For example, a pressure of 30 psi absolute is 30-14.6 or 15.4 psi above atmospheric pressure. See also gage pressure, and sensor(manifold absolute pressure).

ABV - Abbreviation for air bypass valve.

A/C - Abbreviation for air conditioning.

AC(1) - Abbreviation for air conditioning.

AC(2) - Abbreviation for alternating current.

AC(3) - American line of spark plugs.

Acadia - American car produced in 1904 by Ernest Kelly in Delaware.

Acadian - American car produced in 1962 by General Motors.

Acadian Beaumont - American car produced from 1963-1970 by General Motors Corp. in Michigan.

Acaslon - American car produced from 1915-1926.

acc - Abbreviation for accessories.

accessories - Optional equipment added to cars for convenience, comfort, appearance, performance, etc.

accessory load - Electrical current flow required to operate a car accessory. Typical loads include: radio 0.5-2 amps, heater 6-8, headlights 6-20, windshield wipers 2-4, alternator field windings 3-5, air conditioner 10-15, and conventional ignition 2-5.

Accel - American line of performance automotive products.

acceleration clause - Clause used in a loan agreement specifying all future loan payments may be immediately due (the loan balance) if payments are not made when due.

accelerator - Long rectangular floor pedal used to control a car's speed by varying the amount of fuel and air entering an engine. It is located on the driver's side and is connected by linkage to a carburetor's throttle plate. It is also known as a gas pedal.

accelerator linkage - Throttle linkage.

accelerator pump - Small diaphragm pump, in a carburetor, used to supply additional gasoline to an intake manifold when an accelerator is depressed quickly.

accelerator pump circuit - See carburetor circuit(accelerator pump).

accelerator pump discharge nozzle - See pump jet.

accelerator pump plunger rod - Rod directly attached to an accelerator pump diaphragm. Accelerator pump linkage moves this rod to pump fuel.

accelerator pump rocker arm - Pivoting arm used in some accelerator pump linkages.

accelerator pump vent - Small passageway used in certain carburetors to prevent fuel from being drawn out of an accelerator pump circuit due to the vacuum created by airflow in a carburetor airway. It is usually located just above the accelerator jet.

accelerator's stuck - Condition created when gas pedal linkage binds and keeps a carburetor throttle open. The engine usually races. If there is no nearby traffic, first try tapping the accelerator pedal a few times. If it still remains stuck, do the following: turn the ignition switch to off (not lock), put the car in neutral, brake to a stop off the roadway, locate the binding, and eliminate it before driving again. Possible binding causes include: sticky throttle plate shaft, broken return springs, unlubricated throttle cable lining, melted throttle cable lining due to broken engine ground strap causing electrical current to flow to ground through lining, and unlubricated linkage bushings and/or pivot points.

accelerator vacuum switch - See vacuum switch(ball type).

accelerometer - See sensor(detonation).

accent stripes - Small painted lines applied to a finished car body. They are typically applied to accent certain body contours. See also pinstripes.

accept delivery - To finalize purchase of a new car at a dealership, and drive it off the lot.

accident - Situation created when one or more cars become damaged by colliding with other cars or nearby objects. An accident may or may not involve injuries to driver and passengers of each car. If an accident occurs, do the following: stop; assist people who are injured; make sure someone calls the police and an ambulance, if needed; exchange information with other drivers (license numbers, insurance companies, etc); don't argue with people at scene of accident or try to assign blame; take a picture of the accident; identify any witnesses; and file an accident report. If you hit an unattended vehicle, try to locate the owner or leave a note, and then notify the police.
  Accidents create grim statistics in the United States. More than 50,000 people die every year from traffic accidents. To date traffic deaths outnumber American deaths in all the wars Americans have ever fought. Auto related death and injury cost averages 20-30 billion annually.

accident citation - Traffic citation issued to a driver involved in an accident who violated a law.

accident report - Report filed at a police station providing details of a car accident.

accumulator - Battery.

ACCUS - Abbreviation for Automobile Competition Committee for the United States.

A/C distributor duct - Section of air conditioning duct used to distribute air to two or more air conditioning outlet ducts.

Ace - American car produced from 1920-1922 by Apex Motor Corp. in Pennsylvania.

Ace Truck - American truck produced from 1919-1923.

acetylene headlamp - Headlamp powered by acetylene gas. It was popular on cars in the early 1900s.

acetylene painting - Custom painting technique used to apply smoke from an acetylene torch to a panel area in different design patterns.

ACF - American car produced in 1926.

AC generator - See alternator.

acid - Chemical compound formulated to liberate hydrogen ions in a water solution. The electrolyte solution in lead storage batteries is about 20 percent sulfuric acid.

Ackerman Principle - Turning principle devised to cause the outer ends of steering arms to bend slightly inward resulting in the inside wheel turning more sharply than the outer wheel. It causes the outer wheel to toe out when turning.

Acme - American car produced from 1902-1910 by Acme Motor Car Co. in Pennsylvania (1902-1910), and Acme Motor Buggy Manufacturing Co. in Minnesota (1908-1909). Also, a Canadian car produced from 1910-1911.

AC motor - See motor(AC).

Acorn - American car produced in 1910.

Acorn Truck - American truck produced in 1925.

acoustical tuning - Tuning done to a racing engine's header exhaust system by determining individual pipe diameters necessary to allow the exhaust gas pressure wave to travel at a speed sufficient to create a proper suction wave moving back up the pipe. If the suction wave is properly timed, residual gases will be sucked out of the engine cylinder at the right time improving performance. See also inertia tuning.

acquittal - Court verdict reached clearing a person of charges (not guilty).

acrylic - Colorless, strong smelling acid created by oxidizing acrolein which is a decomposition product of glycerol and glycerides.

acrylic enamel - See paint(acrylic enamel).

acrylic resin - Transparent thermoplastic resin formed by polymerizing esters of acrylic or metaacrylic acid.

acrylic resin paint - See paint(acrylic resin).

active material - Chemical substance attached to a battery plate. It reacts with the sulfuric acid, and is usually lead peroxide on the positive plates and metallic lead on the negative plates.

actual miles - See original miles.

Adams - American car produced in 1906-1907, 1911, and 1924.

Adams-Farwell - American car produced from 1903-1913 by the Adams Company in Iowa.

adapter - See adapter plate.

adapter plate - Plate used to mate a different transmission and/or engine together. It is sandwiched between the transmission bell housing and rear engine mounting surface, and contains the necessary bolt hole pattern to bolt the two together. It is often required when a car engine is swapped for a different type. See also engine swapping.

adapter type carburetor - See carburetor(adapter type).

additive - Powder, solution, or other material added to gasoline, water, antifreeze, oil, grease, brake fluid, gear oil, transmission fluid, and other substances to help a product perform better.

additive(additive restorer) - Engine coolant additive used to supplement antifreeze additives to increase its life. Two year changing of antifreeze no longer necessitates using this additive.

additive(alcohol) - Alcohol compound added to gasoline to absorb condensed moisture in a fuel system. Water in a fuel system tends to corrode certain parts and slow or clog fuel flow. Alcohol mixes with and absorbs the water which will then pass through a gas filter, carburetor, and be used by an engine. Alcohol also helps boost a fuel's octane rating. See also gasohol.

additive(anti-icing) - Gasoline additive used to suppress carburetor icing on the throttle plate.

additive(antiknock) - Gasoline additive used to increase the octane number of gas.

additive(anti oxidant) - Gasoline additive used to provide storage stability by inhibiting oxidation and gum formation.

additive(anti rust) - Gasoline additive used to prevent rust in gasoline handling systems.

additive(anti scuff) - Oil additive used to minimize metal to metal contact between moving parts under heavy loads.

additive(anti wear) - Important oil additive used to increase the oil coating action on engine part surfaces to minimize metal to metal contact. Without this additive, engine wear would increase significantly. It is in most quality oils.

additive(battery) - Additive(s) used in battery electrolyte to improve battery performance, longevity, inhibit sulphation, etc. It is controversial.

additive(combustion chamber cleaner) - Gasoline additive used remove carbon buildup from combustion chambers.

additive(corrosion inhibitor) - Oil additive used to inhibit engine parts corrosion from water, gas, dirt, etc. Without it, engine part surfaces are more prone to reacting to contaminants and corroding. Also, an antifreeze additive used for the same purpose.

additive(degummer) - Gasoline additive used to remove gum buildup in the fuel delivery system.

additive(detergent/dispersant-1) - Oil additive used to keep sludge and varnish deposits in suspension and from forming. Without it, deposits tend to form and build up in an engine. The detergent keeps the high temperature deposits from accumulating. The dispersant keeps low temperature sludge from accumulating by keeping it in suspension until the oil is changed. See also oil(detergent/dispersant) and oil(Heavy Duty).

additive(detergent/dispersant-2) - Gasoline additive used to remove or reduce deposit formation in carburetor or fuel injector parts, and intake manifold in order to maintain accurate fuel metering.

additive(diesel fuel) - Diesel additive(s) used to improve fuel characteristics such as fluidity at low temperature (prevent gelling), storage stability, and ignitability (cetane rating).

additive(dye) - Gasoline additive used to indicate presence of antiknock compounds and identify makes and grades of gasoline.

additive(extreme pressure) - Oil additive used maintain lubrication film between moving surfaces exposed to heavy loads or pressures such as bearings. Many of today's hot running engines cause most of it to be depleted in engine oil after just 3,000 miles.

additive(foam inhibitor) - Oil additive used to minimize foam formation from rotating engine parts. Without this additive, oil would tend to turn into foam and deprive engine parts of lubrication.

additive(lead scavenger) - Gasoline additive used to prevent buildup of lead deposits in the combustion chamber and on the valves by combining with the lead antiknock compounds during the combustion process.

additive(leak sealer) - Engine coolant additive used to seal cooling system leaks usually in the radiator. It is mixed into some antifreeze mixtures.

additive(metal deactivator) - Gasoline additive used to improve storage stability by inhibiting gum formation resulting from the catalytic action of certain metals.

additive(oil) - Additive mixed with an engine oil to improve various characteristics. Today's car engines have lubrication requirements regular mineral oils cannot satisfy. Those requirements include: higher engine rpm, higher compression, heavy bearing loads, corrosion, rusting, sludge formation, etc. Oils are now blended with a variety of additives to help meet these requirements.

additive(octane booster) - Gasoline additive used to increase octane number of gasoline. Some are not safe to use in unleaded cars as they can damage catalytic convertors and oxygen sensors.

additive(oxidation inhibitor-1) - Oil additive used to reduce oil oxidation. Without it, a hot engine will oxidize oil and cause deposits to begin forming.

additive(oxidation inhibitor-2) - Antifreeze additive used to minimize rust formation in coolant system.

additive(radiator) - Additive(s) used in engine coolant to lubricate water pumps, restore antifreeze additive strength, and/or seal leaks. Most are found in antifreeze mixtures.

additive(rear axle) - Gear oil additive used to reduce friction.

additive(rust inhibitor) - Oil additive used to prevent formation of rust from any water in the engine. Without it, engine part surfaces, cooling and condensing with water, would rust more readily. Also, an antifreeze additive used for the same purpose.

additive(scavenger) - Gasoline additive used to remove the combustion products of antiknock compounds.

additive(tetraethyl lead) - Gasoline additive used in gasoline to minimize engine knock, and help lubricate valve seats and heads made of softer metal than the metal in use today.

additive(transmission-automatic) - Transmission fluid additive used usually to stop internal leaks around seals.

additive(transmission-manual) - Transmission oil additive used usually to reduce friction.

additive(upper cylinder lubricant) - Gasoline additive used to lubricate upper cylinder area and control intake system deposits.

additive(viscosity index improver) - Oil additive used to reduce viscosity change in oil with temperature change. Without it, certain oils would thin out too much at higher temperatures and not adequately lubricate engine parts.

additive(water pump lubricant) - Engine coolant additive used to lubricate water pump bushing. It is usually contained in most antifreeze mixtures.

additive(windshield washer) - Water additive used to increase detergency.

add mark - Indicator mark used on an oil or transmission dipstick to indicate the minimum safe oil level. When it is reached, oil should be added until it reaches the full mark. If oil falls below the mark, less oil will be available for lubrication causing it to: contaminate faster, get hotter, oxidize faster, etc. If the level falls too low (usually off the dipstick), engine damage can occur from lack of oil. See also full mark.

add on - Interest rate of a sales contract.

add-ons - High-profit items installed by a car seller and not the factory.

Adelphia - American car produced in 1921.

Adette - American car produced in 1947.

adhesion limitation - Clause used in a loan agreement placing specific restrictions on the distance a car can be driven.

adiabatic compression - Compression of an air/fuel mixture without any heat transfer to or from the compressed mixture.

adjustable wrench - Open end wrench built with an adjustable opening. Different types include: adjustable end (crescent) wrench, monkey wrench, and stillson (pipe) wrench.

adjuster - See insurance adjuster.

adjuster tube - Threaded tube used to increase or decrease a tie rod's length for adjusting toe-in or toe-out. It is located on the wheel end of a tie rod.

adjust the bands and linkage - To adjust brake band clearances and linkage in an automatic transmission.

adjust the valves - To adjust the valve clearance of each intake and exhaust valve in an engine.

Admiral - American car produced in 1914.

Adria - American car produced from 1921-1922 by Adria Motor Car Corp. in New

York.

Adrian - American car produced from 1902-1903.

Advance - American car produced from 1909-1911 by Advance Motor Vehicle Co. in Ohio.

advance - Measurement made to determine piston head distance from the top of its compression stroke. It is expressed in degrees of crankshaft rotation and is the point at which a spark plug ignites a cylinder's air/fuel mixture.

advance(centrifugal) - Adjustment made to ignition timing according to distributor shaft rotational speed. It is accomplished by a centrifugal advance mechanism, mounted in the distributor. See also advance mechanism(centrifugal).

advance(excessive) - Ignition timing set to ignite an air/fuel mixture too early. An upward traveling piston meets expanding pressure tending to force the piston back down before reaching the top. This is hard on a piston and can cause: piston damage, cylinder wall galling, broken rings, poor fuel economy, and lower power. See also retard.

advance(ignition) - See advance(spark).

advance(spark) - Ignition timing setting used to control when a spark plug receives an electrical spark to ignite an air/fuel mixture being compressed in an engine cylinder. It is measured in degrees of crankshaft rotation before a piston reaches the top of its compression stroke. Ignition timing adjusts itself during engine operation to protect an engine and maximize performance. Adjustments are made with centrifugal and vacuum advance mechanisms installed on the distributor.

More spark advance is needed when the following conditions exist: low power demand, high speed/high power demand, cold engine, bigger cylinder bores, less volatile fuel, rich fuel mixture, low compression ratio, higher altitudes, and high octane fuel rating.

Less spark advance is needed when these conditions exist: high power demand, low speed/low demand, warm engine, smaller cylinder bores, more volatile and/or lower octane fuel, lower altitude, lean fuel mixture, high compression ratio, and lower octane fuel rating.

Factors determining spark advance, in general, include: location of spark plug, shape of combustion chambers, distribution of air/fuel mixture to the cylinders, fuel grade, air density, combustion chamber surface roughness, carbon accumulation rate in combustion chambers, and valve location. See also advance(vacuum), advance(centrifugal), and advance(excessive).

advance(vacuum) - Adjustment made to ignition timing according to intake manifold vacuum. It is accomplished by a vacuum advance mechanism mounted on the distributor body. See also advance mechanism(vacuum).

advance curve - A curve plotted on a graph to show a particular distributor advance rate for centrifugal weights or for a vacuum advance unit. The graph usually shows degrees advance vs. engine rpm. Specification books depict various advance curves and usually reference them according to a number stamped on the distributor body.

advance diaphragm - Vacuum operated diaphragm mounted on a distributor to advance spark when an engine is accelerated. See also retard diaphragm, advance mechanism(vacuum), and distributor(exhaust emission control).

advance mechanism - Device mounted on a distributor to adjust ignition timing during engine operation.

advance mechanism(centrifugal) - Device used to adjust spark advance by using movable weights acting under centrifugal force. It typically consists of: a weight base, two pivoting weights, weight springs, and plate adjusting mechanism. The weights rotate with a distributor shaft and are usually mounted underneath a distributor point plate. As the shaft rotates faster, the weights are forced farther out, advancing the distributor cam. Increasing engine speed increases the centrifugal advance portion of spark advance to a specified limit. See also car service tip(centrifugal advance test).

advance mechanism(vacuum) - Device used to adjust spark advance by using intake manifold vacuum. It typically consists of: a diaphragm assembly linked to a distributor point plate, and tubing to a carburetor and/or intake manifold. Maximum vacuum advance usually occurs when a throttle is opened slightly. Minimum advance usually occurs when a throttle is closed or wide open.

advance stop - Surface, in a vacuum advance mechanism, used to limit movement of a diaphragm. See also retard stop.

advancing the spark - To adjust ignition timing so a spark occurs earlier in a piston's compression cycle. See also retarding the spark.

adverse driving conditions - Road conditions encountered making driving more dangerous. They include heavy rain, snowing, ice, slush, high winds, etc.

AEA - Abbreviation for Automotive Electric Association.

AEC - American car produced from 1913-1914 by Anger Engineering Company in Wisconsin.

AERA - Abbreviation for Automotive Engine Rebuilders Association.

Aero - American car produced in 1921.

Aerocar - American car produced in 1906-1908 and 1921 by Aerocar Co. in Michigan, and Sheldon F. Reese Co. in South Dakota, respectively. Also, an American car produced beginning in 1948 by Aerocar in Washington. It was a four passenger car built with attachable wings for flying.

aerodynamic drag - Resistance to movement created when a body moves through an air stream.

aerodynamics - Air flow behavior and the forces it exerts as it passes around a moving car.

aerofoil - Air flow device used to produce a downward force. It can be in the form of a fixed spoiler or a movable wing.

Aerolus - Experimental model of a 200 passenger air-cushioned car based on the Levacar concept. It was built by Ford in 1961.

Aerostar - American car produced from 1986 to date by Ford Motor Company in Michigan.

Aero Type - American car produced in 1921.

Aetna - American car produced in 1915 and 1922.

A frame - Steel framework shaped like a letter "A" and used for lifting heavy loads. A frames were commonly used for hoisting engines out of cars. Portable hoists are more convenient now.

afterburn - A mild form of exhaust backfiring created by small quantities of fuel igniting in the exhaust system. It is generally audible as repeated popping sounds in the exhaust pipe or muffler. See also backfiring.

afterburning - See backfiring.

aftermarket accessory - Accessory item not normally added to cars by the manufacturers. Such items include: extra gauges, trailer hitches, seat covers, chrome wheels, high lift suspension kit, etc.

aftermarket add on - Non-standard equipment accessory added to a car.

after-run - See dieseling.

after sale service - Policy offered by a merchant specifying after sale service or help on a product. It is a typical sales and future business tactic.

aged finish - Car topcoat exposed to the atmosphere for some time causing it to become dull. The dullness is created by conditions destroying the original smooth surface such as: dust scratching, wash water containing harsh chemicals, and oxidation of paint.

aggressive - Characteristic of a car built with reinforced side, front, and rear body structures.

aggressive salesmanship - Ability possessed by a successful salesman to aggressively sell a product.

aggressive tread pattern - Tire tread constructed with prominent tire elements. For example, a snow or off-road tire has a very aggressive tread pattern. The pattern creates significant noise and increased wear at highway speeds.

Ahrens-Fox - American car produced from 1911-1933.

AI - Abbreviation for air injection.

AIA - Abbreviation for American Insurance Association.

AIC - American car produced in 1913.

ailing engine - Engine in poor operating condition.

AIR - Abbreviation for air injection reactor.

air(1) - Mixture of gases found in the atmosphere. The major gases from 0-13 miles up are: nitrogen (78%), oxygen (21%), carbon dioxide (.03%), argon (.95%), neon (.0018%), helium (.0005%), krypton (.0001%), xenon (.000009%), and water vapor. The percent values shown are by volume.

air(2) - Abbreviation for air conditioning.

air adjustable shock - Shock absorber designed for adjustment by adding additional air pressure.

air bag - Inflatable bag installed in a car's dashboard or steering wheel to protect the driver in the event of a head on collision. Some bags are also mounted for front seat passengers. The bag inflates, usually with nitrogen, in a fraction of a second when crash sensors are activated.

air brush - Small paint spraying device used to apply small precise amounts of paint. Air brushes are popular for artwork, pinstriping, etc.

air bypass valve - See anti-backfire valve.

air cap - Cap-like device mounted on a spray gun to atomize exiting paint.

air capacity - See volumetric efficiency.

Air-Car - Experimental car built by Curtis-Wright Corporation in 1959 to travel on a 6-12 inch air cushion. It was powered by a 300 horsepower engine.

air check - To check air pressure in one or more car tires.

air cleaner - Device used to remove dust, dirt, and other foreign airborne material from air as it is drawn into an engine. Today's air cleaners are commonly made of treated paper. Other types include foam and oil bath.

air cleaner(foam) - Air cleaner built to use a foam element lightly coated with oil. It is not popular on cars. When the element becomes dirty, it is washed in a solvent, coated lightly with fresh oil, and replaced. Maintenance intervals depend on the type of driving.

air cleaner(oil bath) - Air cleaner built to trap air contaminants in oil. In general, it is constructed with an oil reservoir at the base with a two-stage air cleaner above it. Air coming into the housing moves down across the oil where dust is trapped, and then upward through the air cleaner. This filter requires less frequent maintenance than the oil wetted mesh type. Cleanup is recommended every 4-6,000 miles and consists of: draining and refilling the oil reservoir, cleaning filtering mesh in solvent, and recoating mesh with oil.

air cleaner(oil wetted mesh) - Early type air cleaner built to trap air particles with a copper mesh screen coated with oil. It is probably the least efficient. When in use, it quickly clogs up with dust, restricting air flow, and yet it still allows many of the finer particles in air to pass through. This filter requires frequent maintenance, usually recommended at 1-2,000 mile intervals. The filter is cleaned in a solvent, like kerosene, and then recoated with engine oil.

air cleaner(paper element) - Most popular air cleaner used today. It consists of a treated paper element resting in an air cleaner body, and lasts 5-10,000 miles depending on the type of driving. The element is usually replaced rather than cleaned.

air cleaner body - Housing positioned over a carburetor intake. It forces all air entering an engine to pass through an air filter. It typically consists of: an air filtering element, necessary hoses, air inlet, and temperature-controlled air gate.

air cleaner restriction - Air flow restriction in an air cleaner caused by a dirty filter or obstruction.

air cleaner rod attachment - Metal strap and rod assembly attached to a carburetor air horn usually to attach an air cleaner body to a carburetor.

air cleaner snorkel - See air inlet.

air compressor - Machine designed to compress air.

air compressor(diaphragm type) - Air compressor designed to compress air with a diaphragm and valve assembly. It usually runs continuously, generates air pressure in the 30-45 psi range, outputs relatively small quantities of air, and has no storage tank. It is commonly used with airbrush equipment.

air compressor(piston type) - Air compressor designed to compress air with a reciprocating piston and valve assembly. It usually runs intermittently, generates air pressures in the 80-200 psi range (depending on model), outputs larger quantities of air, and uses a storage tank.

air conditioner - Heat transfer device used to regulate air temperature and humidity. The primary components of a car air conditioner include: compressor, condenser coil, receiver/dryer, sight glass, expansion valve, evaporator coil, controls, refrigerant, and various tubes and fittings. The compressor is usually powered with a drive belt, connecting crankshaft and compressor pulleys. See also car service tip(air conditioner).

air conditioner distributor - A ductwork fitting used in air conditioning ductwork to divide air flow.

air conditioner problem - Condition created when a car's air conditioning system is not functioning properly.

air conditioner problem(air-intermittently cool) - Air does not stay consistently cool. Possible causes include: compressor clutch that slips or has high coil resistance, faulty blower motor and/or switch, faulty temperature control, sticking evaporator control valve, bad circuit breaker, and moisture in system.

air conditioner problem(air-not cool enough) - Air receives little cooling. Possible causes include: compressor clutch slippage, slow blower motor, faulty evaporator control valves, low refrigerant level, excess moisture and/or air in system, faulty expansion control valve, and clogged evaporator coils and/or receiver-dryer screen.

air conditioner problem(air-too cold) - Air is too cold. Possible causes include: malfunctioning temperature control and air not properly distributed.

air conditioner problem(air-warm) - No cool air is produced. Possible causes include: compressor that has malfunctioning clutch, worn pulley, and malfunctioning valves; low on refrigerant; blown fuse; malfunctioning blower motor; break in electrical circuit; and receiver-drier screen clogged.

air conditioner problem(compressor leaking oil) - Compressor leaks oil. Possible causes include: damaged compressor due to operating with low charge, contamination in system, and defective system component(s).

air conditioner problem(noisy) - Operating air conditioner is noisy. Possible causes of the noise include: loose and/or worn compressor parts, compressor mounting bracket, blower motor, and drive belt; low or high refrigerant level; faulty or slipping clutch; stuck compressor discharge valve, and moisture in system. See also sound(hissing), sound(rumbling-2), and sound(knocking-4).

air conditioner speed-up solenoid - See speed-up solenoid.

air conditioner thermostatic switch - Switch used to detect discharge air temperature and adjust conditioning effect as required.

air conditioning performance test - Test performed on an air conditioner to determine its ability to cool air properly.

air conditioning service - Service work performed on a car air conditioner. A repair shop usually performs the following work: inspect the air conditioner's operation; inspect hoses, fittings, and lines for cracks; perform pressure and leak tests; check cooling capacity of system; and add refrigerant, if needed, to bring system up to normal operating capacity. Extra work or charges typically include: replacing any parts, excess quantity of refrigerant, evacuating entire system, and overhauling compressor.

air cooled engine - See engine(air cooled).

air dam(1) - Carburetor air intake design used to help route and slightly pressurize air. A typical installation includes an air collection box mounted behind the grille on the left or right side with tubing running to the air cleaner.

air dam(2) - See spoiler.

air distributor manifold - Pipe arrangement used to distribute air from an air pump to an area outside each individual exhaust valve inside the exhaust manifold. See also exhaust emission control system(exhaust system).

air dryer - Filtering device used to remove oil and water from air. It is commonly used to filter air before it enters a spray gun.

air file - See air tool(file).

air filter - See air cleaner.

air flow meter - See sensor(air flow).

air foil - See spoiler.

air/fuel mixture - Mixture of air and atomized fuel routed to an engine through a carburetor. A carburetor adds fuel to incoming air by sucking and/or pumping it into the incoming air. See also air/fuel ratio.

air/fuel mixture screw - Screw mounted at the base of a carburetor for adjusting an air/fuel mixture entering an intake manifold when a car is idling. It also contributes to the mixture as a car comes off idle. When adjusted too low (turned in too far), an engine starves for fuel, sounds like it's stumbling, and tends to stall or start accelerating poorly. When adjusted too high, fuel is wasted and pollution of the engine becomes excessive. The screw directly regulates an engine's carbon monoxide and hydrocarbon emissions and should be adjusted as low as possible.

air/fuel ratio - Ratio defined as volume of air to volume of fuel metered into an engine for combustion. An engine at normal operating temperature typically uses the following air/fuel ratios: normal driving @ 16-17:1, and acceleration @ 12-14:1. See also fuel mixture. An overly rich mixture causes: poor fuel economy, reduced power, slow throttle response, hard starting, and increased pollution. An overly lean mixture causes: hesitation under acceleration, rough idling, and poor fuel economy.

air gap - Two surfaces separated by a small gap of empty space. Air gaps are used: to control electric current flowing across spark plug electrodes, distributor points, voltage regulator points, and various relay points; and to maintain space between rotating and stationary parts of motors and generators.

air gate - Hinged plate, in an air cleaner's air inlet, used to control the flow of normal and preheated air into a carburetor.

air horn - Circular flanged surface located at the entrance to a carburetor air passageway. The air cleaner base rests on it. The air horn often refers to the entire top of the carburetor.

air injection - Air pumped under pressure directly into the downstream side of each exhaust valve, or into a thermal reactor. The air helps gases, exiting the combustion chambers, burn more completely before reaching the atmosphere. Air injection can create problems like increased backpressure and backfiring due to increased burning of overrich exhaust mixtures on deceleration. Air bypass valves are used to minimize the problem. See also exhaust emission control system and air pump.

air injection reactor - System built to inject air directly into downstream side of exhaust valves to help reduce emissions. Air helps reduce level of carbon monoxide and unburned hydrocarbons. See also thermal reactor, pulse air injection reactor, and emission control system(combustion-air injection).

air injection system - Engine driven air pump and air supply lines used to deliver air near the exhaust valves on the downstream side. The air combines with exiting unburned hydrocarbons to more completely burn them. End result is lower unburned hydrocarbons and a warmer exhaust system. See also anti-backfire valve.

air inlet - Air intake opening mounted on a carburetor's air cleaner body. It is a rectangular or oval shaped duct usually extending 6-12 inches from the body. On today's cars, the inlet is usually equipped with a warm air inlet and a temperature and vacuum controlled air gate controlling the flow of preheated and normal air under different driving conditions. Some designs also use a fresh air duct for routing outside air from the grille area directly to the air cleaner. See also hot air inlet and hot air stove.

air in the brakes - Condition caused by air leaking into a brake system and mixing with brake fluid. Air, being compressible, often causes brakes to feel sluggish when applied. Air can only be removed by bleeding the brakes.

air intake vent - Device used to control air flow into a car.

air inversion - Atmospheric condition caused when a layer of warm air traps cooler air near the earth's surface preventing it from normally rising.

air lock - Air trapped in liquid restricting fluid movement. See also vapor lock.

Airphibian - American car produced from 1950-1956 by Continental in Connecticut. It was a combination car/airplane with a top speed of 120 mph in the air and 55 on the road. It was fully licensed by the Federal Aviation Agency and offered for sale.

air pressure gauge - Handheld or remote gauge designed to read air pressure.

air pump - Pump used to supply high-volume low-pressure air to an engine exhaust manifold. Air is pumped to the downstream side of exhaust valves in order to help emerging exhaust gases burn more completely. It is usually a centrifugal pump driven by a belt like an alternator. See also air injection.

air regulator - Device used to control air flow around a throttle valve in a fuel injected engine. It is typically used to supply additional air when an engine is cold to maintain adequate rpm, and is controlled by a coolant temperature sensor.

air respirator - Air filter worn over the mouth. A good quality respirator is very important when spray painting a car.

air scoop - Device used to direct outside air to a specific part of a car such as a carburetor, brake drum, rotor, interior, and oil cooler. See also hood scoop.

Airscoot - American car produced in 1947.

air sensor plate - Plate used in the intake portion of certain fuel injection systems to maintain precise injection of fuel.

air shock - Shock absorber designed to provide additional support when pressurized with air. Common design is an inflatable rubber cylinder used in place of a coil spring.

air spring - Device designed to create spring action with pressurized air.

air supply pump - See air pump.

air suspension - Car suspension system built with shock absorbers designed to provide additional support by when pressurized with air. Also, it refers to a car suspension using air rather than metal springs.

air tool - Tool powered by compressed air.

air tool(chisel) - Tool used to apply variable hammering action to removable chisels.

air tool(die grinder) - Tool used to provide high speed rotation for grinding.

air tool(drill) - Air powered electric drill.

air tool(file) - Air powered rectangular file used to smooth large body panel areas covered with plastic filler.

air tool(impact wrench) - Tool used to provide rotational impact action against nuts and bolts.

air tool(ratchet) - Tool used to replace a socket ratchet.

air tool(spray gun) - See spray gun.

air vacuum control valve - Vacuum operated solenoid valve used to control a mode-and-blend door in a car's climate control system regulating flow of outside air into heating and air conditioning ductwork.

air valve - Vacuum-operated valve used in the secondary bore of certain carburetor designs above the throttle plate to control air flow. It remains closed even when the secondary throttle plate is open, until sufficient suction builds up below the valve to open it. A spring or weight is usually used to control opening.

air valve carburetor - See carburetor(air valve).

air vent - See air vent.

Airway - American car produced in 1949-1950 by T.P. Hall Engineering Co. in California. It carried two passengers, weighed 775 lbs, used an air cooled engine, and reportedly got 45 mpg.

Ajax - American car produced in 1901-1903, 1914, 1920-1921, and 1925-1926.

Ajax Electric - American electric car produced from 1901-1903 by Ajax Motor Vehicle Co. in New York.

Akron - American car produced in 1901 and 1912-1913.

AL - Abbreviation for Albania found usually on an international license plate.

Alamobile - American car produced in 1902.

Aland - American car produced from 1916-1917 by Aland Motor Car Co. in Michigan.

alarm system - Alarm device used to prevent car theft. Alarms are designed to activate from: car movement, someone touching the car, opening the trunk, starting the ignition, etc. A secondary alarm system is often installed as a backup to a primary.

Albany - American car produced from 1907-1908 by Albany Automobile Co. in Indiana.

ALCL - Abbreviation for assembly line computer link.

ALCL diagnostic connector - Terminal connection used to access and activate an ECM's trouble code generator in order to determine the source of an engine problem. See also trouble code and self-diagnostic mode.

Alco - American car produced from 1905-1913 by American Locomotive Automobile Co. (1905-1908), and American Locomotive Co. (1908-1913), both in Rhode Island.

alcohol - Fuel produced by distillation of wood or grain products, or derived from natural gas. The two major types of alcohol are ethanol and methanol. Ethanol is made from grain products while methanol is made from wood products or natural gas. Most methanol today is derived from natural gas. Alcohol is used today as: a fuel additive, and with benzol to fuel racing cars. Alcohol's main advantages include: fairly high octane rating, greater internal cooling, and slower burning (permits turbocharging). Disadvantages include: corrosive; reacts with aluminum, lead, magnesium, and some rubbers and plastics; dilutes oil excessively; raises vapor pressure; and affinity for water (causes alcohol to separate from gasoline). Alcohol's affinity for water can cause the inside of mild steel fuel tanks and fuel line to rust, and corrode the metals in fuel pumps and carburetors. Manufacturers claim the corrosion problem is minimized by using concentrations of 10 percent or less as well as certain anti-corrosive agents. See also additive(alcohol), gasohol, and GTBA.

Alco Truck - American truck produced from 1910-1914.

ALDL - Abbreviation for assembly line diagnostic lead.

Aldo - American car produced from 1910-1911 by Albaugh-Dover Co. in Illinois.

Aldrich - American car produced from 1897-1898.

Alena - American car produced in 1922.

Alexander Brothers - Car customizer brothers from Detroit known for producing futuristic car designs.

Algonquin - American car produced in 1913.

alignment - Positioning separate objects (such as wheels) into a correct relationship with each other.

alignment angle - See wheel alignment angle.

alignment problem - See wheel alignment problem.

alignment rack - Special platform used to check and adjust the various wheel alignment angles of a car's front end.

alki - Alcohol mixture used as a racing fuel. It helps boost engine rpm and keep an engine cool at high rpm. It is usually mixed with nitromethane.

alky - See alki.

All American - American car produced in 1919 and 1923.

Allard - Car line produced from 1981 to date by Allard Motor Co. in Ontario.

all around mechanic - Mechanic skilled in doing the different types of repair work required on a car.

all disks - Abbreviation for disk brakes on all four wheels.

Alleghany - American car produced in 1908.

Allen - American car produced from 1913-1922 by Allen Iron & Steel Co. in Pennsylvania (1913-1914), and Allen Motor Co. in Ohio (1914-1922).

Allen & Clark - American car produced from 1908-1909.

Allen Cyclecar - American car produced in 1914.

Allen-Kingston - American car produced from 1907-1910 by Allen-Kingston Motor Car Co. in New York.

allen wrench - L-shaped handle, with hex cross section, used for turning hex screws and nuts, set screws, etc.

alley - Side street located between two main streets.

Allfour - American car produced in 1919.

Allis-Chalmers - American car produced from 1914-1917.

Allison, Bobby - He won the Daytona 500 Race in 1978 and 1982 averaging 159.7 and 154.0 mph. Cars driven were a Ford and Buick. He also became the NASCAR Grand National Champion in 1983.

Allith - American car produced in 1908.

allowance buyer - Potential car customer interested only in the money given for their trade-in car.

alloy(1) - Metal composed of two or more metals. For example, stainless steel is an alloy of steel and chromium.

alloy(2) - See mag wheel.

alloy wheel - See mag wheel. Also, it refers to any non-steel wheel.

All Power - American car produced from 1917-1921.

all season - Designation used to describe a product, service, etc. designed for use during any season of the year.

all season tire - See tire(all season).

AllState - American car produced from 1952-1953 by Kaiser-Frazer Corp. in Michigan. It was a mail-order car made for Sears-Roebuck.

All-Steel - American car produced from 1915-1916 by All-Steel Car Co. in Missouri.

all way stop - Intersection provided with stop signs on all approaching roads.

all weather cap - Distributor cap designed to work under wet conditions.

Alma - American car produced in 1913.

Alpena - American car produced from 1910-1914 by Alpena Motor Car Co. in Michigan.

Alpha Romeo - Car line produced from 1910 to date by Alfa Romeo SpA in Italy. The 1932 Alpha Romeo was a racing car with a top speed of over 100 mph. It won most international races back then. More recent models include: Alphasud (1971 to date), Alfetta, Berlina, Alfasix (1979 to date), Giulietta (1954-1962; 1976 to date), Spider, Guilia, GTV, Arna, and Alpha.
   The U.S. representative is headquartered in Englewood Cliffs, New Jersey.

Alpha Romeo Type 158 - Alpha Romeo race car almost unbeatable until 1951.

Alpine Renault - Car line produced from 1955 to date by Automobiles Alpine in France. Recent models include: Alpine, Mille Miles, and Dauphine. Factories also exist in Bulgaria, Brazil, Mexico, and Spain.

Alsace - American car produced from 1919-1920 by Automotive Products Co. in New York.

Alstel - See All-Steel.

Alter - American car produced from 1914-1917 by Alter Motor Car Co. in Michigan.

alternating current - Electric current defined by directional flow reversal in a circuit at regular intervals. See also direct current.

alternator - Electrical generator designed to produce alternating current, then transform it into direct current. It differs from a DC generator in the following ways: a magnetic field rotates in the center, voltage is generated in stationary outer coils of wire, and alternating current is produced before it is rectified. The rotating magnetic field windings or rotor receive current from brushes riding on two bearing-like surfaces, known as slip rings, mounted at one end of a rotor. Voltage is generated in three separate coils of wire, known as a stator, mounted around the circumference of the alternator housing. Alternating current output from stator windings is transformed into direct current by use of rectifiers or diodes. Two are used for each stator winding.
   Primary parts of an alternator consist of: a housing, stator, rotor, slip ring and brush assembly, rectifier and heat sink assembly, support bearings, and drive pulley.
   Alternator advantages include: producing more current at low speed, low current requirement (2-3 amps typically) for brushes powering the rotating magnetic field, no brush arcing due to low current and use of slip rings, long brush and slip ring life, and voltage generated in stationary coils.
   Most cars today use alternators.

alternator charging test - See car service tip(alternator charging test).

Altha Electric - American electric car produced from 1900-1901.

Altham - American car produced 1896-1901.

altimeter - Instrument designed to measure height above a reference level such as sea level. It measures the difference in air pressure.

aluminum - Silvery metal used on cars because it is lightweight, easily machined, and resistant to corrosion. Car uses include: fittings, master hydraulic brake cylinder, alternator body, water pump body, cylinder head, valve cover, intake manifold, carburetor body, and custom wheels.

aluminum balancer - Harmonic balancer made from aluminum for lightness.

aluminum head - Engine cylinder head made from aluminum.

ALV - Abbreviation for autonomous land vehicle.

Alxo - American car produced in 1905.

AM - Abbreviation for amplitude modulation. See also AM radio.

AMA - Abbreviation for Automobile Manufacturers Association.

amalgam - Combination, mixture, or blend.

Amalgamated - American car produced from 1917-1919 by Amalgamated Machinery Corp. in Illinois.

Ambassador - American car produced from 1922-1926 by Yellow Cab Manufacturing Co. in Illinois. Also, an American car produced from 1956-1974 by American Motors Corp. in Michigan.

ambient air - Outside air surrounding a car.

ambulance - Car equipped to carry sick or wounded people to medical facilities.

AMC - Abbreviation for American Motors Corporation.

Amco - American car produced from 1919-1920 by American Motors in New York.

America - American car produced in 1911.

American - American car produced from 1902-1903, 1914, and 1916-1924 by American Motor Carriage Co. in Ohio (1902-1903), American Cyclecar Co. in Washington and Michigan (1914), American Motor Vehicle Co. in Indiana (1916-1920), and American Motors Corp. and Bessemer-American Motor Corp. in New Jersey (1916-1924). Also, an American car produced from 1960-1972 by

American Motors Corp. in Michigan.

American Austin - American car produced form 1930-1934 by American Austin Car Co. in Pennsylvania.

American Auto - American car produced in 1904.

American Auto Vehicle - American car produced in 1907.

American Bantam - See Bantam.

American Beauty - American car produced in 1915-1916 and 1920-1921.

American Berliet - American car produced from 1905-1907.

American Chocolate - American car produced from 1903-1906.

American Coulthard - American car produced from 1905-1907.

American Electric - American electric car produced from 1899-1902 by American Electric Vehicle Co. in Illinois (1899-1902), and New Jersey (1902).

American Fiat - American car produced in 1915.

American Gas - American car produced in 1895.

American Juvenile Electric - American electric car produced in 1907.

American Knight - American car produced in 1919.

American LaFrance Truck - American truck produced in 1910.

American Mercedes - American car produced from 1905-1907 by Daimler Mfg. Co. in New York. It was an exact copy of Mercedes built under U.S. license.

American Mors - American car produced from 1906-1909 by St. Louis Motor Car Co. in Missouri.

American Motor - American car produced in 1902-1903 and 1905-1906.

American Motors - American car line produced from 1968 to date by American Motors Corp. in Michigan.

American Motor Sleigh - American car produced in 1905.

American Motor Truck - American truck produced from 1906-1911.

American Napier - American car produced in 1904.

American Petroleum Institute - Organization known for setting motor oil formulation standards.

American Populaire - American car produced in 1904.

American Power Carriage - An American car produced in 1900.

American Simplex - American car produced from 1906-1910 by Simplex Motor Co. in Massachusetts.

American Six - American car produced from 1916-1917.

American Southern - American car produced in 1921.

American Steamer - American steam car produced from 1922-1924 by American Steam Truck Co. in Illinois.

American Steam Car - American steam car produced from 1929-1931 by the American Steam Automobile Co. in Massachusetts.

American Steamer - American steam car produced from 1922-1924 by the American Steam Truck Co. in Illinois.

American Tri-Car - American car produced in 1912.

American Underslung - American car produced from 1906-1914 by the American Motor Car Co. in Colorado.

American Voiturette - American car produced in 1899.

American Waltham - American car produced from 1898-1899 by the American Waltham Mfg. Co. in Massachusetts.

American Wire Gauge - Numbering system devised to equate a series of whole numbers to specific wire diameters and areas. Numbers generally range from 0000 to 36. Corresponding wire diameters and areas are .4600 to .0050 inches and 211,600 to 25.0 square mils respectively. See also gauge number.

Americar - American car produced by Willys from 1940-1942.

Ames - American car produced in 1898. Also, an American car produced from 1910-1915 by Carriage Woodstock Co (1910-1911), and Ames Motor Car Co. (1912-1915), both in Kentucky.

Amesbury - American car produced in 1898.

AM/FM - Abbreviation for AM/FM radio.

AM/FM cassette - Combination audio cassette and AM/FM radio unit used for listening to radio stations or playing music on cassettes. It is commonly available as a new car option or an aftermarket product.

AM/FM radio - Radio designed to receive and audibly produce AM and FM radio signals.

Amhurst - Canadian car produced in 1912.

Amilcar - French sports car produced in the 1920s. It was light weight and sat two people.

ammeter gauge - See gauge(ammeter).

AMOCO Corporation - A U.S. petroleum company headquartered in Chicago, Illinois. It was formerly called Standard Oil Of Indiana. See also petroleum company.

Amos - American car produced in 1913.

Amoskegg Fire Engine - American fire engine truck produced from 1897-1906.

amp - See ampere.

amperage - Electric current flow rate measured in an electrical circuit.

ampere - Unit of measurement used to specify electric current flow rate in an electrical circuit.

ampere-hour capacity - Unit of measurement used to specify a battery's ability to produce a specified electric current flow during a specified time period.
amp gauge - See gauge(ammeter).
Amplex - American car produced from 1910-1915 by Amplex Mfg Co. and Amplex Motor Car Co., both in Indiana.
AM radio - Radio designed to receive and audibly produce AM radio signals.
Ams-Sterling - American car produced in 1917.
AMX - American car produced by American Motors from 1964-1977 and 1980 to date by American Motors Corp. in Michigan.
Anchor - American car produced from 1909-1911 by Anchor Buggy Co. and Anchor Motor Car Co., both in Ohio.
anchors - Brakes.
AND - Abbreviation for Andorra found usually on an international license plate.
Anderson - American car produced in 1907-1909 and 1916-1926 by Anderson Carriage Mfg. Co. in Indiana, and Anderson Motor Co. in South Carolina respectively.
Anderson Electric - American car produced from 1907-1919.
Andover - American car produced from 1914-1917.
Andretti, Mario - He became the Grand Prix world champion in 1978 driving a Lotus-Ford. In 1969, he won the Indianapolis 500 Race driving an average of 156.9 mph in an STP Oil Treatment Special. In 1967, he won the Daytona 500 Race averaging 146.9 mph in a Ford.
Andrews - American car produced in 1895.
angle parking - Parking a car at an angle to a curb.
Anglia - American car produced from 1959-1968 by Ford Motor Car Co. in Michigan.
Anhut - American car produced from 1909-1910 by Anhut Motor Car Co. in Michigan.
aniline oil - Ingredient used in some gasoline additives. It must be handled carefully as it can readily be absorbed through the skin.
Anna - American car produced in 1912.
Ann Arbor - American car produced from 1911-1912 by Huron River Mfg. Co. in Michigan.
annealing - Process defined as the heating and slow cooling of metal to impart certain properties.
Annhauser-Bush Truck - American truck produced in 1905.
annual fuel cost - Money spent driving a car one year.
annual percentage rate - The basic interest rate paid when money is borrowed.
anode - Electrode positioned to receive electric current flow. In a battery, for example, it is a negative electrode or negative outside terminal.
anodize - To plate or coat a metal electrolytically with a protective substance. Aluminum surfaces are commonly anodized.
Ansted - American car produced from 1926-1927 by Ansted Motors in Indiana.
Ant - Abbreviation for antique.
antenna - An arrangement of wires, rods, etc., used to send and receive electromagnetic waves. Antennas are used on cars primarily to receive radio and/or CB signals.
Anthony - American car produced in 1897.
anti-backfire valve - Vacuum-operated valve used in an air injection system to divert air flowing to exhaust air ports directly to: an intake manifold, air cleaner, or the atmosphere (depending on design) whenever a car decelerates. It prevents fuel-rich unburned gases from getting additional air, possibly igniting, and causing backfiring in an exhaust system. See also air injection system, emission control system(combustion-air injection), and car service tip(air bypass valve test).
anti-dieseling solenoid - See idle stop solenoid.
anti-dive - Resistance to front-end dive built into a car's suspension system.
antifreeze - Chemical mixed with a car engine's cooling water to dramatically lower the solution's freezing point, allowing a car to be operated in cold weather. Other antifreeze properties help guard against corrosion and lubricate internal cooling system parts. The most common antifreeze compounds are methyl alcohol, ethyl alcohol, and ethylene glycol. Alcohols were used in the past with ethyl alcohol being the most popular then. Alcohols tend to evaporate while ethylene glycol does not. All three compounds offer similar freezing protection with about the same concentration of water to about 30 below zero. The freezing point of pure methyl alcohol, ethyl alcohol, and ethylene glycol is -144.2, -174.6, and -92 degrees Fahrenheit respectively. When an antifreeze solution is made with protection to -20 degrees Fahrenheit, both alcohols lower the boiling point to 180 degrees while ethylene glycol raises it to 223 degrees Fahrenheit. As a reference, water boils at 212 degrees Fahrenheit.
antifreeze concentration - The percentage of antifreeze contained in an engine's coolant. The normal mixture used today is a 50/50 concentration of water and antifreeze (ethyl glycol). Such a concentration provides

protection from -30 to 265 degrees Fahrenheit when the system is pressurized
12-15 lbs. Using more than 60 percent antifreeze in engine coolant is not
recommended because heat absorption will decrease. Pure antifreeze can
absorb only 85 percent of the heat pure water can. See also radiator cap and
boiling point.

antifreeze hydrometer - Instrument designed to measure a coolant solution's
specific gravity and thus its antifreeze content.

antifreeze protection - Difference measured between the freezing point of
water and an antifreeze solution to indicate cold weather protection.

antifreeze solution - Mixture of water and antifreeze used in an engine's
cooling system. An antifreeze solution is used to keep engine coolant fluid
at temperatures colder than water's freezing point of 32 degrees Fahrenheit.

antifriction bearing - See bearing(antifriction).

antiknock compound - Substance added to fuel giving it the ability to burn
with little or no detonation in an internal combustion engine. See also
detonation.

Antiknock Index - The octane rating number displayed on most gasoline pumps.
It is determined by taking the average of the antiknock values determined in
tests using the Research and Motor Octane Number Methods. See also octane
rating, Research Octane Number Method, and Motor Octane Number Method.

antiknock quality - Ability specified of a fuel to resist or eliminate the
tendency to detonate before burning in a combustion chamber. See also octane
rating, detonation, and preignition.

anti-lift - Resistance to rear end lift built into a car's suspension system.

anti-lock braking system - An assemblage of brake components, sensors, and a
hydraulic pressure adjuster designed to control a car's slippage on roads
during hard braking. The system typically works by adjusting hydraulic
pressure to any wheel which sensors determine is turning much faster or
slower than road speed.

anti-percolation vent - See anti-percolator.

anti-percolator - Device located at the top of a carburetor float bowl chamber
to vent gas vapors and thereby minimize vapor locking during hot weather.
Methods used include: vent direct to atmosphere, vent to venturi area, and a
valve controlling venting from discharge nozzle area.

Antique Automobile Club of America - The oldest and largest club in the United
States devoted to car history, restoration, preservation, and maintenance.

antique car - Car generally classified as built upto 1935. See also brass era
car, vintage car, contemporary car, milestone car, special interest car,
classic car, contemporary classic car, pre-war car, and post-war car.

anti-roll bar - Bar connected between the front or rear of a car and the
suspension to limit body roll when cornering.

anti-roll strut - See torque rod.

anti-rust - Property of a substance or product designed to resist or eliminate
formation of rust.

anti-skid - Resistance to wheel lockup built into a car's braking system. It
usually adjusts hydraulic brake pressure when wheels are about to lockup.
See also anti-lock braking system.

anti-smog device - Device used to reduce or eliminate certain exhaust
emissions.

anti-squat - Resistance to rear end dive built into a car's suspension system.

anti-stall dashpot - Adjustable diaphragm-like device used to keep carburetor
throttle from closing too quickly and stalling an engine. It is more of a
concern on automatic transmission cars where letting off the gas quickly at
low speed causes the transmission to lower engine speed to idle almost
immediately. Without an anti-stall dashpot, the engine would momentarily
receive too much fuel and flood out or die. Standard transmission cars,
however, are in gear and have the forward momentum to get through the stall
period, or the clutch can simply be disengaged.
  Dashpot designs range from external to internally mounted carburetor
devices.

antistatic shield - See static shield.

anti-surge cap - Gas tank cap designed to allow air entry into a fuel tank,
but under certain conditions not back out. For example, the cap will seal on
a hot day when gas warms up and partly pressurizes the tank.

anti-sway bar - Continuous steel bar formed into a shape for attaching to both
sides of a rear axle and to the left and right side of a car's frame. It is
also used in front ends where left and right sway bar sides are attached to
the car body and the sway bar ends are attached to lower control arms via
vertical anti-sway links. Anti-sway bars are designed to reduce body rolling
and swaying, reduce wheel drop in holes, wheel hopping, fish tailing, loss of
traction, etc. See also Panhard rod.

anti-sway bar link - Short vertical rod installed with one end attached to a
sway bar and the other end to a front wheel lower control arm.

anti-theft sensor - Device used to sense some aspect of illegal car entry.
Sensors are available today that can detect: car body motion; interior

movement of people; doors, trunk lids, and hoods opening; glass breakage; and changes in electrical system voltage.

anti-theft system - Assemblage of parts, controls, and sensors used to deter theft of a car. See also anti-theft sensor.

antiwear - Property exhibited by a lubricant able to maintain a good lubricant film under different engine operating conditions. See also additive(anti-wear).

Apal - Belgian Car line produced from 1964 to date by A.P.A.L.S.a.r.l.

aperture - Opening or hole.

apex - Inside point of a curve.

Apex - American car produced from 1920-1922.

apex seal - Seal mounted at each apex of a rotor in a rotary engine. It is a rotary engine's version of a piston ring.

API - Abbreviation for American Petroleum Institute.

API designation - Specification used to designate what types of service are suitable for an automotive gear lubricant.

API designation(API-GL-1) - Gear lubricant suitable for use: in worm gear and spiral bevel gear axles, and manual transmissions subjected to mild operating conditions. Various additives may be used to improve the lubricant's characteristics. Extreme pressure additives and frictional modifiers are not allowed.

API designation(API-GL-2) - Gear lubricant suitable for use in worm gear axles operating under conditions not suitable for API-GL-1 lubricants.

API designation(API-GL-3) - Gear lubricant suitable for use in manual transmissions and spiral bevel axles. Speed and load conditions are moderately severe. It requires lubricant to have load carrying capacities greater than API-GL-1, but less than API-GL-4.

API designation(API-GL-4) - Gear lubricant suitable for multipurpose gear usage (differentials, manual transmissions, etc.) in cars operating under high speed-low torque or low speed-high torque conditions.

API designation(API-GL-5) - Gear lubricant suitable for multipurpose gear usage (differentials, manual transmissions, etc.) in cars operating under high speed-low torque, low speed-high torque, and high speed-shock load conditions.

API letter symbols - See API service category.

API service category - Category used to classify an engine oil according to its performance and intended use. It is usually preceded by the words -- API Service. The "S" category prefix refers to service stations, new car dealers, garages, etc. type applications. The "C" category prefix refers to commercial car fleets, contractor usage, farmers, etc. type applications. Oils can have one or more categories such as API Service SF or API Service SF/CC. See also equipment manufacturers specifications.

API service category(CA) - Category used for Light Duty Diesel Engine Service. It covers diesel engines and certain specified gasoline engines operated under mild to moderate conditions using high quality diesel fuel. Formulation requirements include: protection against bearing corrosion, and deposit formation (in certain naturally aspirated engines). It was a popular oil in the late 1940s and early 1950s. It should not be used in today's cars unless specified by the manufacturer.

API service category(CB) - Category used for Moderate Duty Diesel Engine Service. It covers diesel engines operated under mild to moderate conditions using lower quality diesel fuel. Formulation requirements call for greater protection against the following than for the CA category: wear and deposit formation. Other formulation requirements include: protection against bearing corrosion and high temperature deposit formation in naturally aspirated diesel engines using a higher sulfur content fuel.

API service category(CC) - Category used for Moderate Duty Diesel and Gasoline Engine Service. It covers certain turbocharged, supercharged, and naturally aspirated diesel engines and certain naturally aspirated and turbocharged gasoline engines operated under moderate to severe conditions. Formulation requirements include: protection against bearing corrosion and high temperature deposits in diesel engines; and protection against low temperature deposits, rust, and corrosion in gasoline engines. It was first marketed in 1961.

API service category(CD) - Category used for Severe Duty Diesel Engine Service. It covers certain turbocharged, supercharged, and naturally aspirated diesel engines operated under severe conditions and using diesel fuel of varying quality and sulfur content. Formulation requirements include: protection against wear, high temperature deposit formation, and bearing corrosion. It was first marketed in 1955.

API service category(SA) - Category used for Utility Gasoline and Diesel Engine Service. It covers older engines operating under mild conditions. There are no performance requirements. These type oils should not be used in an engine unless specifically recommended by the car manufacturer.

API service category(SB) - Category used for Minimum Gasoline Engine Service.

It covers engines operating under mild conditions requiring only minimum protection. These oils have been in use since the 1930s. Their only formulation requirements are: anti-scuff capability, resistance to bearing corrosion, and resistance to oil oxidation. This type oil should not be used unless specified.

API service category(SC) - Category used for 1964 Gasoline Engine Warranty Maintenance Service. It covers car and some truck gasoline engines from 1964-1967 still under manufacturer warranty. Formulation requirements include: resistance to deposit formation at high and low temperatures, wear, rust and corrosion.

API service category(SD) - Category used for 1968 Gasoline Engine Warranty Maintenance Service. It covers cars and some truck gasoline engines from 1968-1970, and some 1971 and later car (where specified) still under manufacturer warranty. Formulation requirements call for greater protection of the following than for SC category: protection against deposit formation at high and low temperatures, wear, rust, and corrosion. This oil is suitable for use as an SC Oil.

API service category(SE) - Category used for 1972 Gasoline Engine Warranty Maintenance Service. It covers cars and some trucks from 1972 on and certain 1971 cars still under manufacturer warranty. Formulation requirements call for greater protection against the following than for SC or SD categories: oil oxidation, high temperature deposits, rust, and corrosion. This oil is suitable for use as an SC or SD oil.

API service category(SF) - Category used for 1980 Gasoline Engine Warranty Maintenance Service. It covers cars and some trucks from 1980 on still under manufacturer warranty. Formulation requirements call for greater protection against the following than for the SE category: oxidation stability and anti-wear. Other formulation requirements meeting the SF category include: protection against deposit formation, rust, and corrosion. This oil is suitable for use as an SC, SD, or SE oil.

API service classification - See API service category.

API service symbol - Circular symbol commonly seen on the top of oil cans. It specifies the lubricant's: viscosity rating, API service categories, any energy conserving features of the oil, product name, part number, and manufacturer warranty statement.

A pillar - One of two metal posts used to support the front of a car roof and the windshield. It runs from a forward roof corner to a cowl area and provides a lateral mounting area for a windshield. Successive pillars rearward are labeled B, C, and D (on station wagons).

Apollo - American car produced from 1906-1907 by Chicago recording Scale Co. in Illinois, 1962-1964 by Apollo Int. Corp. in California, and 1964-1979 by Buick Division of General Motors Corp. in Michigan.

A post - Vertical metal post located where a front car door attaches. Upward extension of the post is an A pillar.

apparent viscosity - Ratio of a fluid or semifluid material defined as the shear stress to the shear rate occurring at a specified shear rate and temperature. It is commonly used to describe the flow property of a grease. It usually increases with shear rate for grease.

appeal - To ask a higher court to review a decision made by a lower court.

appearance recondition - To make a car look better rather than run better.

appearing in court - To go before a judge regarding a legal matter.

Appel - American car produced in 1909.

Apperson - American car produced from 1902-1926 by Apperson Bros. Automobile Co. (1902-1924), and Apperson Automobile Co. (1924-1926), both in Indiana.

Apperson, Edgar - He formed the Haynes-Apperson Auto Company and then the Apperson Brothers Motor Car Company with his brother Elmer. The latter company manufactured the Apperson Jack Rabbit car. Edgar was the first member of the Automotive Hall of Fame in 1946.

Apperson, Elmer - He was Edgar Apperson's brother and worked with him as a partner.

Apple - American car produced in 1909. Also, an American car produced from 1917-1918 by W.A. Apple Motor Car Co. in Ohio.

Appleton - American car produced in 1922.

applique - Decorative feature applied to a basic interior or exterior panel. Different types include: metal, plastic, or a combination. Surface finishes include: bright, brushed, textured, or painted.

apportioning valve - Valve used on some skid-control cars to regulate hydraulic brake fluid pressure to a brake cylinder based on a car's forward weight shift.

apprentice - Person assigned for a specified period of time to a master craftsman in order to learn a craft or trade. Person is usually a member of a union, and is bound by a legal agreement during the apprenticeship period.

apprenticeship - To accept an apprentice assignment from a union.

APR - Abbreviation for annual percentage rate.

apron - See running board.

Arabian – American car produced in 1917.
Arbenz – American car produced from 1911-1918 by Argbenz Car Co. in Ohio.
arc – Electricity flow across two conductive electrodes separated by an air gap. It produces an intense light and releases a great deal of heat.
Arcadia – American car produced in 1911.
arcing – Jumping of electrical current across a air gap between two conductors.
ARCO – Abbreviation for Atlantic Richfield Co.
arc welding – See welding(arc).
Ardsley – American car produced from 1905-1906 by Ardsley Motor Car Co. in New York.
Arfons, Art – An Ohio farmer, he set a world land speed record in 1964 and 1965 driving a Green Monster J-79 Jet car. Speeds were 536.7 and 576.6 mph.
argent finish – Silvery aluminum-pigmented paint characterized as having approximately the same color and luster as brushed or satin chrome, aluminum or steel.
Argo – American car produced from 1914-1916 by Argo Motor Co. in Michigan.
Argo-Case – American car produced in 1905.
Argo Electric – American electric car produced from 1912-1914 by Argo Electric Vehicle Co. in Michigan.
Argo Gas – See Argo.
Argonne Four – American car produced from 1919-1920 by Argonne Motor Co. in New Jersey.
Argyll – British car line produced from 1976 to date by Minnow Fish Carburetters.
Ariel – American car produced from 1905-1907 by Ariel Co. in Massachusetts and Connecticut.
Aries – American car produced from 1980 to date by Dodge Division of Chrysler Corp. in Michigan.
Ariston – American car produced in 1906.
Aristos – American car produced in 1913.
arm – See A-arm.
Armac – American car produced in 1905.
armature(electrical-1) – Circular soft steel casting mounted on a shaft containing copper windings for generating power. An armature forms the core of a motor, generator, etc., and is surrounded by field magnets. It generates power by rotating in a magnetic field created by field magnets.
armature(electrical-2) – Soft iron bar attached to the poles of a magnet to minimize magnetic power loss.
armature(electrical-3) – Vibrating device used in an electrical relay to control current flow.
armature(model) – Car structure composed of a metal I-beam frame, wheels, and a wood or styrofoam structure. It is used as a car model base to support clay and is made approximately three inches under the proposed finished clay shape size.
armature and field grounded circuit test – See car service tip(armature and field grounded circuit test).
armature and field open circuit test – See car service tip(armature and field open circuit test).
armature reaction – Effect an armature's magnetic field has on a magnetic field created by generator's field coils. An armature's magnetic field is created by flow of current in armature coils.
Armleder – American car produced in 1914.
armored car – Vehicle covered with armor plate, bullet proof glass, puncture proof tires, etc.
armored collar – Anti-car theft device made in the form of a steel plate to lock up a steering column and cover an ignition switch.
Armstrong – American line of tires.
Arnold, Billy – He won the Indianapolis 500 Race in 1930 driving an average of 100.4 mph in a Miller Hartz Special.
Arnold Electric – American car produced in 1895.
Arnolt – American car produced from 1953-1964 by S.H. Arnolt in Illinois.
Aro – Romanian car line produced from 1971 to date by Uzina Mecanica Muscel.
around the bend – To specify a location around a curve in a road out of present sight.
arraignment – Appearance made before a judge to be told of the charges made against you and to enter a guilty or not guilty plea.
ARRC – Abbreviation for American Road Race of Champions.
arrest – To seize or take a person into custody under authority of law.
arrest bond – See bail bond.
Arrow – American car produced in 1914. Also, a Japanese car imported from 1971-1980 for Plymouth Division of Chrysler Corp. in Michigan.
arterial – Main road or highway linked with many branch roads. Also, it refers to a branch road.
artmobile – Trailer truck used to house, display, and transport an art

collection.
Artzberger – American car produced in 1904.
asbestos – Naturally occurring fibrous mineral characterized by being highly
 resistant to burning, and not conducting to heat or electricity. It is commonly
 used as an ingredient in brake linings.
Ascari, Alberto – He was an Italian driver who won the Grand Prix world
 championship in 1952 and 1953 driving a Ferrari.
ash content – Amount of ash contained in an oil's formulation. It determines
 an oil's detergency. See also additive(detergent-dispersant-1).
Ashland Oil, Inc – A U.S. petroleum company headquartered in Ashland,
 Kentucky. See also petroleum company.
Ashville – American car produced from 1914-1915 by Ashville Light Car Co. in
 North Carolina.
ASIA – Abbreviation for Automotive Service Industry Association.
as is – Condition of a product or service bought or sold. For example, a car
 sold "as is" is a car sold with a buyer understanding he accepts it with all
 its present known and unknown problems. Used cars are usually sold this way,
 and such cars should be thoroughly inspected before purchasing.
asking price – The highest amount of money a seller can hope to attain on the
 sale of a car. It is usually a somewhat arbitrary figure and can be
 bargained lower. See also list price.
ASME – Abbreviation for American Society of Mechanical Engineers.
aspect ratio – See tire aspect ratio.
Aspen – American car produced from 1976 to date by Dodge Division of Chrysler
 Corp. in Michigan.
asperity – Roughness or harshness.
asphalt – Brown or black tarlike substance found in a natural state or derived
 from evaporating petroleum. It is a variety of bitumen. Also, it refers to
 a mixture asphalt with sand and gravel for use in roofing and pavement.
asphalt base oil – See oil(asphalt base).
asphalt eater – Hard to beat dragster.
asphaltite – Naturally occurring purer form of asphalt.
asphalt jungle – Crowded city characterized by people struggling to survive in
 an atmosphere of predatory behavior.
asphalt slicks – Racing tire built with smooth tread for maximum traction on
 pavement.
asphaltum – See asphalt.
aspirator valve – Valve used to control the flow of air through piping from an
 air cleaner to an exhaust manifold. The air is added to the exhaust to
 reduce carbon monoxide and hydrocarbon emissions. A faulty valve can cause:
 hose deterioration between valve and air cleaner, burn marks on air cleaner
 paper element, exhaust backfiring problems, and increased emissions. See
 also emission control system(combustion-aspirator).
assembly line – Workers, tools, and machines organized in a line for the
 purpose of assembling a product in a series of specific, successive stages.
assembly line diagnostic lead – Electric terminal installed in some cars to
 allow service centers to hook up testing equipment to monitor engine
 functions and/or on-board computer operation.
assemblyline service – Auto repair business set up to run cars through as
 quickly as possible to maximize profits. Such businesses usually do poor
 quality work and leave motorists highly dissatisfied.
assigned risk – Insurance policy issued to a driver with a poor driving
 record. See also auto insurance fund and automobile insurance plan.
assistant sales manager – See sales serviceman.
Assys – Abbreviation for assemblies.
asymmetrical tread – See tire tread(asymmetrical).
Aster – American car produced from 1906-1907.
ASTM – Abbreviation for American Society for Testing Materials.
Aston – American car produced from 1908-1909 by Aston Motor Car Co. in
 Connecticut.
Aston Martin – British car line produced from 1922 to date. The most recent
 company is Aston Martin Lagonda (1975 to date). The U.S. representative is
 Aston Martin Lagonda headquartered in New Rochelle, New York.
Astor – American car produced in 1925.
Astra – American car produced in 1920.
Astre – American car produced from 1975-1980 by Pontiac Division of General
 Motors Corp. in Michigan.
astro roof – Car roof constructed of metal and vinyl components.
ASV – Abbreviation for air switching valve.
A/T – Abbreviation for automatic transmission. See also M/T.
AT – Abbreviation for automatic transmission. See also ST.
ATA – Abbreviation for American Trucking Association.
Atco – American car produced in from 1920-1922.
at cost – Cost figured by a dealer to sell a car and break even. It can be
 very deceptive since a dealer will typically take what a manufacturer charges

him and add on such items as: advertising, car preparation, dealer overhead, and sales commissions. See also margin of profit, list price, and dealer preparation.

Atlantic - American car produced in 1915.

Atlantic Richfield Co - A U.S. petroleum company headquartered in Los Angeles, California. See also petroleum company.

Atlas(1) - American car produced from 1907-1913 by Atlas Motor Car Co. in Massachusetts.

Atlas(2) - American line of tires produced by Atlas Supply Company.

Atlas-Knight - American car produced from 1911-1913 by Atlas Motor Car Co. in Massachusetts.

Atlas Truck - American truck produced in 1918.

atmospheric engine - See engine(atmospheric).

atmospheric pressure - Air pressure evident at sea level (14.7 psi) due to its weight.

atmospheric vent - Vent used to dissipate vapors to the atmosphere. Vents are used in carburetors, transmissions, differential housings, etc.

Atterbury Truck - American truck produced in 1915.

attorney's fees - Monetary charges made by an attorney for services rendered.

AT - Abbreviation for Automatic transmission.

ATF - Abbreviation for automatic transmission fluid.

ATV - Abbreviation for all terrain vehicle.

A type generator circuit - Common generator circuit associated with a regulator. It consists of a regulator resistance lying between generator field coils and ground when regulator points are open. See also B type generator circuit.

Auburn - American car produced from 1900-1937 by the Auburn Motor Car Co. in Massachusetts. It was one of America's most famous cars. Also, an American car produced beginning in 1967 by Auburn-Cord Duesenberg Co. in Oklahoma. It was a 1936 Auburn Speedster replica with a high performance late model engine.

auction - Public sale used to sell items one by one to highest competitive bidder. Cars sold at an auction are usually consigned to the auction company. Car owners pay a fee regardless of whether the car sells or not. See also shill bidder.

auction(no reserve) - Auction characterized by no minimum bid requirement on items sold.

auction(reserve) - Auction characterized by a minimum bid requirement on all items sold. In the case of cars, the minimum bid is supposedly only known by the auctioneer and the car owner. Most auctions are this type.

auction car rating code - Set of single letter codes used to describe the condition of cars being auctioned. Letters used include: M, E, R, U, G, F, and P. See also auto condition code.

auction company - Company hired to auction off items.

auction program - Listing of items sold in an auction. Each item usually has a reference number.

Audi - West German car line produced from 1910-1939 and 1965 to date. The most recent company is Audi N.S.U. (1969 to date).

Auglaize Truck - American truck produced in 1912.

Aultman - American steam car produced from 1901-1902 by Altman Co. in Ohio.

Aunt Eulalia - See Porsche-Lohner Chaise.

Aurora(1) - American car produced from 1906-1908 by Aurora Motor Co. in Illinois, and in 1858 by Father Alfred Juliano. Also, an experimental station wagon built by Ford in 1964.

Aurora(2) - Canadian car line produced from 1980 to date by Aurora Cars Ltd. in Ontario.

AUS - Abbreviation for Australia found usually on an international license plate.

Austin(1) - American car produced in 1901-1921 by Austin Automobile Co. in Michigan. Also, an American car produced in 1930.

Austin(2) - British car line produced from 1906 to date. The most recent company is Light Medium Cars Division, B.L. Cars Ltd. Recent models include: Mini City, Mini Mayfair, Mini Miner, Metro, Maestro, and Montego.

Austin Healey - British car line produced from 1953-1971 by Austin Motor Co. Ltd. Popular models included: Sprite and Midget.

Austin, Herbert - He was a British car manufacturer who produced the cheap successful Austin Seven car in 1922.

Austin Seven - British car produced by car manufacturer Herbert Austin in 1922. It became the first successful baby car in Europe. It was a cheap little car making motoring possible for everybody.

Austin Steamer - American steam car produced in 1894.

auto(1) - See automobile.

auto(2) - Abbreviation for automatic transmission.

auto accessory shop - Automotive business engaged in selling car accessories and related parts.

Auto-Acetylene - American car produced in 1899.
auto and equipment show - Community event organized to publicly display cars
   and related equipment.
Autobianchi - Italian car line produced from 1957 to date by Sezione
   Autobianchi (1968 to date).
auto body - Outer car shell built to sit over the wheels and enclose the
   passenger, engine, and trunk compartments.
auto body shop - Auto repair business engaged in repairing structural damage,
   restoring car body contours, and refinishing body surfaces. There are
   generally three business types known as: a new car dealership, established
   non-dealer shops, and cut-rate shops. The latter should be avoided as the
   work is usually hurried, and poor quality.
auto broker - A person or organization engaged as an agent or intermediary in
   the buying and selling cars. See also Montgomery Ward Auto Club, United Auto
   Brokers, and Nationwide Auto Brokers.
Auto-Bug - American car produced in 1909-1910 by Auto-Bug Co. in Ohio.
Autobuggy - American car produced in 1906.
Auto Buying Guide - Popular annual publication produced by Consumers Union
   containing results of new car testing on such subjects as safety, repair
   records, and economy.
AUTOCAP - Abbreviation for Automotive Consumer Action Panels. Panels are set
   up in certain states to resolve disputes between car buyers and car dealers.
Autocar - American car produced from 1897-1911 by Pittsburgh Motor Vehicle Co.
   (1897-1899), and Auto Car Co. (1900-1911), both in Pennsylvania. A 1901
   model was the first multi-cylinder shaft drive car produced in America.
Autocar Truck - American truck produced in 1908.
auto club - Club organized to promote certain automotive activities.
auto condition code - Set of code words commonly used to describe the
   condition of a car. They are frequently heard at auto auctions. The words
   include: concours, outstanding, parts car, recoverable, sound, and
   serviceable. See also auction car rating code.
autocross - Timed competition runs made maneuvering cars through a specific
   course.
Autocycle - American car produced in 1907.
auto detailing - See car detailing.
auto diagnostic center - Auto repair business engaged in using sophisticated
   electronic and other test equipment to determine car problems. Most of these
   businesses are franchised.
Auto Dynamic - American car produced in 1901.
Autodynamics - Company organized in 1964 to build racing cars.
Autoette - American car produced from 1910-1913 by Manistee Motor Car Co. in
   Michigan.
Auto Fore Car - American car produced in 1900.
Auto-Go - American car produced in 1900.
Autohorse - American car produced from 1917-1921.
auto insurance fund - See assigned risk. See also automobile insurance plan.
Auto-King - American car produced in 1900.
auto log - Book used to record maintenance and service work done to a car.
auto lube center - Auto repair business engaged in checking and changing the
   fluids in cars. Most of these businesses are franchised.
automated assembly line - Assembly line built to minimize use of human labor
   through the extensive use of machinery, computers, robots, etc.
Automatic - American car produced in 1906 and 1921.
automatic - See automatic transmission.
automatic choke - Carburetor choke designed to automatically open and thereby
   meter the proper air/fuel mixture as an engine warms up.
automatic choke thermostat - Device designed to open a choke plate as engine
   temperature increases. See also spring(bimetallic).
automatic clutch - See clutch(automatic).
automatic inlet valve - Inlet valve opened by atmospheric pressure. It
   required no mechanic controls by was not very efficient. It was used on
   early engines.
automatic level control - Assemblage of parts and controls used to regulate
   the height of a car body above each wheel. Most common system employs
   air adjustable shock absorbers at each wheel. An on board air compressor
   supplies air, when needed, to each shock absorber.
automatic overdrive transmission - See transmission(automatic overdrive).
automatic steering effect - Effect expressed by a car's front wheels tending
   to continue traveling in a straight line when released from a turn. It is
   controlled by wheel alignment angles.
automatic transmission - See transmission(automatic).
automatic transmission fluid - See oil(automatic transmission).
auto mechanic - See job(auto mechanic).
automobile - Car powered by a self-contained engine and meant for traveling on
   roads and streets. It usually has four wheels.

automobile company lobby — Special interest group supported by one or more automobile companies for the purpose of influencing automotive legislation introduced or being voted on by government administrators in order to benefit automobile companies involved.

Automobile Forecarriage — American car produced in 1900.

automobile hospital — Auto repair business.

automobile insurance plan — See assigned risk. See also auto insurance fund.

automobile mechanic — See job(auto mechanic).

automobile museum — Building used to preserve and exhibit older popular, classic, valuable, etc. cars.

automobile trade — Auto business or skill pursued as a livelihood.

Automobile Voiturette — American car produced in 1900.

automotive — Moving by use of its own power. Also, it pertains to the design, operation, manufacture, and sale of automobiles.

automotive bodywork — Repair work done to restore a damaged car body to its original shape and appearance.

automotive engineer — See job(automotive engineer).

automotive inspection and readjustment program — See emission inspection program.

Automotor — American car produced from 1901-1904 by Automotor Co. in Massachusetts.

Auto Motor — American car produced in 1912.

auto parts — Any of the various parts found on an automobile.

auto pilot — See speed control system.

auto recall — Announcement made by a car manufacturer to owners of a specific car regarding a possible defect needing correction. The recall usually instructs an owner to take the car to the nearest dealer where the problem will be taken care of for free. A recall letter to a car owner usually follows the announcement. See also recall letter.

Auto Red Bug — See Red Bug.

auto repair business — Business engaged in doing specific kinds of car repair and/or maintenance work. There are several types including: new car dealership, large independent general repair shop, shop franchised by a national company, small independent shop run by a few individuals, gas station with repair bays, auto diagnostic center, auto lube center, muffler shop, and tire center.

auto repair racket — Any of the numerous dishonest auto repair schemes, tricks, and business activities perpetrated by auto repair businesses. See also con game.

auto repair shark — See con man.

auto repair trade organization — Organization set up to promote a specific aspect of the auto repair trade.

auto repair garage — See auto repair business.

auto reverse deck — Audio cassette tape player designed to play both sides of a tape without removing it.

Auto-Tricar — American car produced in 1914.

Autotwo — American car produced in 1900.

Auto Union — German car produced in the 1930s. The 1938 three liter model was a formidable racing car. It had a rear mounted 12 cylinder engine supercharged to 500 HP, and won the Italian Grand Prix that year.

Auto Vehicle — American car produced in 1903.

auto wagon — Early term used for a truck.

auxiliary acceleration pump — Extra acceleration pump used in the carburetor of certain lean burning engines to meter extra fuel during acceleration when engine is cold. It is usually controlled by a thermal valve. See also thermal valve(2).

auxiliary discharge nozzle — See secondary discharge nozzle.

auxiliary gas tank — Extra gas tank used to increase a car's driving range.

auxiliary idle ports — See off-idle ports.

available cash — The total money amount available to a car buyer. It includes: equity, pocket money, and car loan money.

Available Truck — American truck produced in 1910.

Avanti — American car produced by Studebaker from 1962-1966.

Avanti II — American car produced from 1965 to date by Avanti Motor Corp. in Indiana.

avant-train — Two-wheeled power unit used on horse-drawn vehicles built in the 1890s to convert them to cars. It consisted of an: engine, transmission, final drive, steering wheel, and other controls. It was the first example of front wheel drive.

average — Used car characterized as still in good condition despite signs of wear.

Average Man's Runabout — American car produced from 1907-1908 by Adams Automobile Co. in Kansas.

Avery — American car produced in 1921.

Avery Tractor — American car produced in 1942.

Avery Truck – American truck produced from 1912-1916.
axial – In the same direction or parallel to an axis of rotation.
axis – Line around which a rotating body turns.
axle – Solid metal rod, pin, bar, or shaft built to rotate wheels, gears, etc. Today's rear wheel drive cars use two axles that extend from the differential housing. The end of each axle has a flange for attaching a wheel.
axle(dead) – Axle used to attach and support a wheel, but not drive it. For example, front wheel drive cars use dead axles for the rear wheels.
axle(De Dion) – Swing axle used on rear wheels in which a differential and associated axles float. The axle shafts use universal joints at each end. Wheels pivot on control arms. A leaf spring is mounted underneath a differential and attaches to control arms to provide support and relative movement. It was first used on the 1890s French De Dion-Bouton steam cars and is still used on several recent sports cars.
axle(Elliot steering) – Front axle beam used with ends straddling or forming pivot points for a wheel spindle.
axle(full floating) – Axle used to drive a rear wheel, but not support any car weight. It can be removed with the wheel intact. Floating describes how the rear end carries the axle shaft.
axle(live) – Wheel axle supported by inner and outer axle shaft bearings and used to drive a rear wheel. It was used years ago, but didn't hold up well and is not used today.
axle(low pivot swing) – Rear axle arrangement used with a differential housing attached to a car frame by means of a pivot mount.
axle(one quarter floating) – See axle(semi-floating).
axle(semi-floating) – Axle used to drive a rear wheel, hold it on, and support its share of a car's weight. It is a popular axle in use today.
axle(swing) – Axle used to pivot each axle shaft independently at the differential. Universal joints are located in the differential housing. The end of each axle attaches to a respective universal joint. This design permits a differential housing to remain stationary while allowing the wheels and axles to move up and down. See also axle(trans).
axle(swinging half) – Drive axle located running from one wheel to a transmission housing.
axle(three quarter floating) – Axle used to drive a rear wheel and hold it on, but not support it. A common problem with this design is a broken axle would cause the wheel to separate from the car taking one part of the axle with it.
axle(trans) – Swing axle built to incorporate a differential, transmission, and bell housing into one unit. The whole assembly mates up to an engine flywheel. An input transmission shaft runs from an engine over a differential gear assembly to the transmission assembly. Transmission output is then typically routed to a pinion drive. A Volkswagen Beetle car uses this type of axle.
axle carrier – Rear end housing.
axle ratio – See gear ratio.
axle shaft – See axle.
axle stand – Support stand used to hold an axle at a higher elevation off the ground for service work. It typically consists of a triangular base with an adjustable vertical tube containing a fitting on one end to hold the shaft in place.
axle windup – Condition created when torque transmitted to axle shafts tends to rotate an axle housing about its centerline. Rotation will cause a driveline yoke coupled to a transmission output shaft to move in or out along the mating splines. See also sound(clunking-2).

B

B - Abbreviation for Belgium found usually on an international license plate.
babbitt - Bearing material composed of various alloys of tin, antimony, and copper. It is used as an antifriction lining for bearings.
Babcock - American car produced from 1909-1913 by H.H. Babcock Co. in New York.
Babcock Electric - American electric car produced from 1906-1912 by Babcock Electric Carriage Co. in New York.
Babs V-12 - English car driven by J.G. Perry Thomas to a 1926 world land speed record of 171.0 mph at Pendine, Wales.
Baby - Nickname used for small Austin Seven car produced in the 1920s.
Bachelles Electric - American electric car produced in 1901.
back-end gross - Car dealer profit made on the sale of add-ons, financing, insurance, etc. See also front-end gross.
backfire - Air/fuel mixture ignited in an intake manifold or exhaust system.
  Intake backfiring usually occurs when intake and/or exhaust valves leak. When intake valves leak, backfire is caused by fuel mixture ignition carrying a flame front through the leaky valve(s) into the intake manifold where fuel vapors are ignited. When exhaust valves leak, backfire is caused by fuel mixture leaking into the hot interior of the exhaust manifold, igniting, and carrying the flame front back into the combustion chamber and on to the intake manifold through open intake valves (usually occurs on high mileage car during hard acceleration). Intake backfiring can also be caused by: ignition crossfire; improper valve timing due to worn camshaft, loose timing chain, wrong timing relationship between camshaft and crankshaft, shifted valve timing due to timing chain jumping camshaft or crankshaft gear teeth, and/or improper valve clearances; and missing exhaust cam lobe(s). It is a dangerous condition that can cause a carburetor fire if conditions are right.
  Exhaust backfiring is usually caused by unburned fuel igniting near the exhaust valves due to high heat, air received from an air pump, or a faulty anti-backfire valve (causes backfiring during deceleration or letting foot off gas). On today's cars, it is usually due to a faulty emission control system. See also afterburn.
backfiring - Condition created when an engine backfires.
Backhus - American car produced in 1925.
backing up - To move a car backwards or to the rear. All backing up should be done slowly as it is dangerous.
backlash - Clearance or play measured between two parts. Gear backlash is very important, especially in critical areas like differentials. If not properly set, gears will quickly become damaged or worn out.
backlight - Rear window mounted opposite a windshield. It is also known as a back window.
backout valve - Valve used in an automatic transmission to prevent certain operations from occurring simultaneously. More than one is sometimes used.
backpressure - Exhaust gas pressure created in an exhaust system due to a choking effect caused by airflow resistance. It prevents free flow of exhaust gases from an engine. All exhaust systems generate some backpressure. As backpressure increases, the quantity of burned gases not completely expelled from engine cylinders increases due to decreased airflow. Leftover gases dilute and slow the flow of the incoming air/fuel mixture, reduce an engine's power output, and overheat exhaust valves. The end result is increased fuel consumption since an engine must generate more power to compensate for lost power due to decreased airflow and fuel dilution. Excessive backpressure will cause an engine to start up OK, but quickly lose power, idle poorly and/or stall.
  An engine must have relatively low resistance to air flow in both the intake and exhaust sides to run properly. If exhaust gases cannot be expelled, an engine will only run momentarily.
  Back pressure can be reduced by: using better mufflers, headers, larger exhaust pipes, dual exhaust, and making sure there are no dents or restrictions in the system.
backrest - The vertical portion of a seat used to support a passenger's back.
backup lights - See light(backup).
backup light switch - Electrical switch operated by transmission linkage to activate a car's backup lights when reverse gear is used.
back window - See backlight.
backyard mechanic - See job(backyard mechanic).
Bacon - American car produced in 1905.

Bacon, Roger - He was an English scientist/philosopher who believed, in the 13th century, in cars powered by means other than animals. He also believed that such vehicles existed in ancient times.
bad connection - Electrical connection poorly made resulting in a circuit that is intermittently open or has high resistance.
Badger - American car produced from 1908-1912 by Four Wheel Drive Auto Co. (1908-1910), and Badger Motor Car Co. (1910-1912), both in Wisconsin.
bad ground - Electrical circuit poorly attached to ground resulting in intermittent operation or high resistance.
bad news - Car in poor running condition. Also, it sometimes refers to a car in good running condition.
bad weather - Adverse weather created by changing atmospheric conditions.
baffle - Device used to divert or regulate a flow of liquids, gases, or sound waves.
baffle plate - See choke housing plate.
bail - Property deposited with a law enforcement agency as security that a person released from custody will return at an appointed time. It is usually in the form of money. See also jump bail, out on bail, bail him out, and stand bail.
bail bond - A money or property bond offered to insure a defendants appearance at a future appointed court date and thus allow his release from jail. It is usually offered by the defendant charged with an offense, or by other persons or organizations acting on his behalf. See also bond.
bail bondsman - Person prepared to take responsibility for a jailed person being released and appearing in court at an appointed time by furnishing a bail bond to a law enforcement agency.
Bailey - American car produced from 1907-1915 by Bailey Automobile Co. (1907-1910), and S.R. Bailey & Co. (1907-1915), both in Massachusetts.
Bailey Klapp - American car produced in 1915.
Bailey Perking - American car produced in 1907.
bail him out - Bail provided to a law enforcement agency to release someone held in custody.
bailiff - Person responsible for maintaining order in a courtroom.
Bailon, Joe - Popular car customizer known for excellent bodywork.
bail's been set - Bail set by a court of law for a person charged with an offense.
bait and switch - See con game(bait and switch).
Baja 500 - Five hundred mile cross country race held annually in Baja California for cars and trucks.
Baja 1000 - One thousand mile cross country race held annually in Baja California for cars and trucks.
baked enamel finish - Paint finish applied on new cars at the factory. The car body is painted with an enamel paint then placed in a drying room at elevated temperature to cure and harden the paint. The end result is a hard durable finish superior to air dry finishes.
Baker-Bell - American car produced in 1913.
Baker, Buck - He became the NASCAR Grand National Champion in 1956 and 1957.
Baker, Buddy - He won the Daytona 500 Race in 1980 averaging 177.6 mph in an Oldsmobile.
Baker Electric - American electric car produced from 1899-1916 by Baker Motor Vehicle Co. in Ohio.
Baker & Elberg Electric - American electric car produced in 1894.
Baker R & L Electric - American electric car produced from 1915-1920.
Baker-Steam - American steam car produced from 1917-1924 by Baker Steam Motor Car Co. in Colorado.
Baker Steamer - American steam car produced from 1921-1923.
balance - A state of equilibrium. See also wheel balance.
balance(bubble) - See balance(static).
balance(dynamic) - Method used to balance rotating objects such as tires to minimize vibration. The object is balanced so the mass centerline and physical centerline are in the same plane. Tires are dynamically balanced on a wheel with a wheel on or off a car depending on balancing equipment available. Most tire shops today use the dynamic balancing method. Dynamic balancing is recommended for highway driving. See also tire balancer(dynamic) and tire balancer(static).
balance(spin) - See balance(dynamic).
balance(static) - Method used to balance stationary objects such as tires to minimize vibration. The object is balanced so the mass centerline and physical centerline are in the same plane at rest. Static balancing is not popular today because it does not allow for change in a tire shape and hence balance at higher speeds. See also tire balancer(static) and balance(dynamic).
balance(wheel) - Wheel and tire assembly balanced in weight around its circumference. Most are not, hence the need for tire balancing equipment. An unbalanced tire may appear round and turn true when rotated slowly, but

can vibrate greatly when faster tire rotation brings centrifugal force into play. See also unbalanced tire, static unbalance, and dynamic unbalance.

balanced & blueprinted - Process used to modify a stock engine into a performance engine, and balance the weight distribution of all moving engine parts in order to minimize vibrations.

balance vent tube - Vent tube positioned from a carburetor's float bowl top to its airway. It is used on some carburetors to bleed off gas vapor accumulations in a float bowl during hot temperatures.

balance weights - Weights positioned and attached at specified locations around the circumference of a wheel rim to even out a tire and wheel's weight distribution when rotating.

Balboa - American car produced in 1925.

Baldner - American car produced from 1901-1903 by Baldner Motor Vehicle Co. in Ohio.

bald tire - See tire(bald).

Baldwin - American car produced from 1899-1902 by Baldwin Automobile Mfg. Co. in Pennsylvania.

balk ring - Friction pawl or plunger used to ease the engagement of transmission gears.

Ball - American car produced in 1902.

ball and socket joint - Joint formed by a ball held in a socket allowing limited movement in all directions. Such joints are common in front end steering and suspension systems.

Ballard - American car produced in 1894.

ballast - Weight added to a car to meet racing requirements.

ballast resistor - Resistor constructed of a special type of wire which raises or lowers voltage according to the wire's heat. See also ignition coil resistor.

ball bearing - See bearing(ball). See also race.

ball joint - Flexible ball-and-socket joint commonly used as a steering or suspension linkage connector on an independent front suspension. It consists of a hard rubber ball mounted in a lubricated socket housing with a tapered and threaded steel stud. Some joints are lubricated for life while others have zerc fittings for periodic lubrication. Each front wheel assembly usually has two. See also ball and socket joint.

ball joint(friction) - See ball joint(upper).

ball joint(load bearing) - See ball joint(lower).

ball joint(lower) - Ball joint used to attach the lower part of a steering knuckle to a lower control arm. It carries most of the wheel load.

ball joint(upper) - Ball joint used to attach the upper part of a steering knuckle to an upper control arm. It steadies the upper end of the wheel spindle.

ball joint steering knuckle - Steering knuckle attached to and pivoting on a ball joint. See also steering knuckle.

balloon note - Agreement in a finance contract used to require a buyer to pay off a balance due at the end of a contract in one lump sum. This type of agreement is used to lower monthly payments. In the case of a new car loan, a car dealer usually hopes you cannot pay the lump sum when it is due. If that happens, the loan can be refinanced with possibly even another balloon note. It's a common ploy to get more money out of you.

Baltimore - American car produced in 1900.

Balzer - American car produced from 1894-1900 by Stephen M. Balzer (1894-1898), and Balzer Motor Carriage Co. (1898-1900), both in New York.

band - See brake band.

Bandag - American line of retread tires.

bang shift hydro - Automatic transmission built to be held in any gear when racing.

banked turn - Road curve tilted upward from inner to outer edge. Banked turns allow higher speeds since the tilt transfers part of the outward centrifugal force generated in a turn downward.

Banker - American car produced in 1905.

Banker Bros - American car produced in 1896.

Banker Electric - American car produced in 1905.

Banker Juvenile Electric - American electric car produced in 1905.

Banner - American car produced in 1915.

Banner Boy Buckboard - American car produced in 1958 by Banner Welder in Wisconsin. It was sold in kit form with plans for $399.

Bantam - American car produced in 1914. Also, an American car produced from 1935-1941 by American Bantam Car Co. in Pennsylvania. They also designed and built the first Jeep vehicle for the U.S. Army in 1940, but were not able to deliver in large quantities. Willys-Overland Co. got the order.

banzai - To drive a car all out or operate an engine at its maximum performance.

Baras, Paul - He set a world land speed record of 104.5 mph in 1904 driving a Darracq 4 Cylinder.

Barbarino - American car produced from 1924-1925 by Barbarino Motor Car Corp. in New York.

barbershopping - See con game(barbershopping).

Barby - American car produced in 1910.

Bardahl - American line of additives produced by Bardahl MFG Corporation.

bare block - Engine block furnished without the following parts: crankshaft, connecting rods, pistons, camshaft, valvegear, and no cylinder head(s).

bargaining power - Bargaining skills used to bluff and fool customers. Also, the ability to decide on a good price and convince another into thinking it is your maximum offer.

Barker - American car produced in 1912.

Barley - American car produced from 1922-1924 by Barley Motor Car Co. in Michigan.

Barlow - American car produced in 1922.

Barnes - American car produced from 1907-1912 by Barnes Mfg. Co. in Ohio.

Barnhart - American car produced in 1905.

Barracuda - American car produced from 1962-1981 by Plymouth Division of Chrysler Corp. in Michigan.

barrel - See engine cylinder. Also, it refers to a carburetor airway.

barrel cylinder - Separate cylinder bolted onto a crankcase. It is most commonly found on air cooled engines.

Barrett & Perret Electric - American car produced in 1895.

Barrie - Canadian car produced from 1919-1920.

Barris, George - Popular car customizer known for radical styling and starting new trends. He was known as the King of the Kustomizers.

Barris, Sam - Car customizer associated with his brother George.

Barrows - American electric car produced from 1897-1898 by Barrow's Vehicle Co. in Connecticut.

Barrows Motor Vehicle - American car produced in 1897.

Bartholomew - American car produced from 1901-1920.

Bartlett - Canadian car produced from 1914-1917.

Barton - American car produced in 1903.

Barver - American car produced in 1925.

base coat - See paint(base coat).

base price - Price of a new car without any of the available options.

bash - Car event such as a race, car show, rally, etc.

basic timing - The ignition timing of an engine set without the influences of vacuum, centrifugal, on-board computer, and other ignition advance modifying controls. It is also known as static timing.

basket case - Car characterized by being partially or completely disassembled.

Basson's Star - American car produced in 1956. It was a three-wheeled minicar with a fiberglass body selling for $999.

Bateman - American car produced in 1917.

Bates - American car produced from 1903-1905 by Bates Automobile Co. in Massachusetts.

bath - See taking a bath.

BAT terminal - Electrical terminal marked with BAT designation. It usually refers to a terminal receiving voltage from the battery, and is a common sight on a regulator, or an ignition coil primary input.

BATT - Abbreviation for battery. See also ignition coil terminal and BAT.

battered car - Used car with extensive body damage.

battery - Electrochemical device used to produce and store electrical energy in chemical form. A battery produces energy by initiating chemical reactions, when a load is placed across the terminals. The amount of electrical energy a battery can store is determined by the quantity of chemical substances in a battery. In general, more battery plates increase storage capacity. Lead acid battery is the most common type. It consists of a container filled with sulfuric acid in which a number of positive and negative plates are immersed. The negative plates are composed of pure sponge lead while the positive plates contain a high percentage of lead dioxide. These compounds cause electrons (current) to flow from one plate to the other depending on the demand placed on the battery.

battery(6 volt) - Battery designed to produce six volts of electricity by using three two volt cells in its construction. Six volt cells have more plates in them than 12 volt cells. It is not common in today's cars.

battery(12 volt) - Battery designed to produce twelve of electricity by using six two volt cells in its construction. It is the battery commonly used in today's cars.

battery(antimonial lead) - See battery(lead acid).

battery(calcium/lead alloy) - Lead acid battery designed using a calcium/lead alloy to minimize gassing tendency during charging mode. Maintenance free batteries use this design to minimize water consumption.

battery(charged) - Battery condition created when a battery has stored the maximum amount of electrical energy possible.

battery(discharged) - Battery condition created when all the stored electrical energy has been consumed.

battery(dry) – Battery designed to use an electrolyte in paste rather than liquid form. Flashlight batteries are an example.

battery(dry charged) – Battery shipped from a manufacturer with no electrolyte and with cell elements initially charged with special equipment. It retains its charge as long as moisture does not get into the cells. It is made ready for use by simply filling cells with electrolyte.

battery(dual voltage) – Battery designed to house two six volt batteries in one case. It allows an engine to be started with twelve volts and revert back to six when running. It is often used on six volt cars to increase cranking speed and avoid replacing all the accessories and lights.

battery(lead acid) – Most common car battery used. It consists of a container filled with sulfuric acid in which a number of positive and negative plates are immersed. Negative plates are usually composed of pure sponge lead while positive plates contain a high percentage of lead dioxide. Gassing readily occurs during charging causing this type of battery to use larger quantities of water during its operation.

battery(maintenance free) – Battery designed to minimize loss of electrolyte and other battery compounds over its life. Vent plugs are designed to condense any vapors generated back into the battery. This type battery does not allow easy adjustment or observation of fluid level.

battery(no fill) – See battery(maintenance free).

battery(oxygen recombination) – A sealed lead acid battery designed to prevent the generation of hydrogen and oxygen gases during the charging mode. Advantages include: no liquid electrolyte allowing it to operate in any position, terminals corrode very little due to no battery gases, more resistant to vibration, spillproof (no liquid electrolyte), higher cold cranking amps per pound resulting in lighter battery, lower internal resistance, less susceptible to deep discharge damage, and long life. Disadvantages include: higher cost, and reserve capacity more limited.

battery(sealed) – Battery filled with electrolyte and sealed at the factory.

battery(silver zinc) – Experimental battery designed to use zinc and silver compounds.

battery(sodium sulfur) – Experimental battery designed using sodium and sodium sulfur compounds. It produces 15-20 times as much power per pound as lead acid batteries. The main disadvantage is the battery must be kept at 800 degrees Fahrenheit to function.

battery(wet type) – Battery built to store and dispense electrical energy by using positive and negative plates immersed in a liquid electrolyte. Lead acid and maintenance free batteries are wet types.

battery bridge – Structure positioned at the bottom of a battery's case permitting plates to rest off the bottom so sediment can settle below them.

battery box – Box designed to protectively house a battery.

battery cables – High current insulated electrical wires used to carry current flow from a car's battery to the electrical system. Positive cable runs from the positive post of a battery to the starter relay. One or more smaller wires also run from the positive post to power other parts of a car's electrical circuit and provide a path for generator current to reach a battery. Negative cable grounds a battery to the frame of a car, providing a complete circuit for electricity flow in a car. It is not necessary that the negative cable be insulated since it is connected to ground. See also positive ground system and negative ground system.

battery case – Container designed to hold a battery's components. Older ones were made of hard rubber or asphalt. Today, it is usually made of plastic.

battery cell – Compartment located in a battery. It contains one set of positive plates, and one set of negative plates, submerged in an electrolyte. Electricity is produced chemically when positive and negative terminals are connected to a load. Plates are usually composed of a lead alloy and electrolyte is usually sulfuric acid and distilled water. A twelve volt battery typically has six cells. Each cell produces approximately two volts.

battery cell connector – Conductive strap used to connect one cell to another electrically. Cell connectors give a battery its total voltage drop, usually 6 or 12 volts. They are composed of lead in most cases. Older batteries had external connectors. In today's batteries, the connectors are inside underneath a cell cover.

battery cell cover – Battery case top designed to seal a battery's inside components from the outside.

battery cell divider – Wall inside a battery designed to separate one cell from another.

battery charging – Process used to restore a battery's energy by passing a direct electrical current through a battery in the reverse direction. During charging, the following chemical reactions take place: lead sulfate on both plates splits up into lead and sulfate parts, water splits up into hydrogen and oxygen parts, sulfate and hydrogen combine to form sulfuric acid in the electrolyte, lead and oxygen combine to form lead peroxide on one plate, and

lead and sulfate split apart to leave behind pure lead on one plate. The end
result is: the specific gravity of the electrolyte increases due to a
decrease of available water and the increase of sulfuric acid in the
electrolyte, and the positive and negative plate materials become lead
peroxide and pure lead respectively.
  Charge rate should not allow electrolyte temperature to exceed 125 degrees
or else battery damage can result. Badly sulfated or fully discharged
batteries should be charged at slower rates. In general, a safe charging
rate is one ampere for each positive plate in a cell. See also active
material, reverse charge, and battery discharging.

battery components – Various items used in construction of a battery. See
  also battery plate, battery bridge, battery sediment chamber, battery fill
  level, battery rubber separator, battery cell cover, battery terminal post,
  battery vent plug, battery plate strap, battery case, and battery cell
  connector.

battery corrosion – Deterioration of battery terminals and other metal on the
  top of a battery caused by the corrosive nature of battery acid. It can be
  minimized by coating affected parts with grease or some of the protective
  sprays. No-maintenance batteries vent less acid fumes and thus have less
  corrosion problems.

battery cover – See battery hold down.

battery discharging – Process used to draw electric current from a battery.
  During discharging, the following chemical reaction takes place: lead
  peroxide on the positive plate splits up into lead and oxygen parts, sulfuric
  acid splits up into hydrogen and sulfate, oxygen and hydrogen combine to form
  water, and lead and sulfate combine to form lead sulfate on both plates. The
  end result is: the specific gravity of the electrolyte decreases due to an
  increase of available water and the decrease of sulfuric acid, and both
  plates store lead peroxide.
  Lead acid batteries are not really designed to repeatedly discharge much
  more than 25 percent of their charged capacity. Deep discharging shortens
  battery life unless it is specifically designed for it. Car battery life is
  maximized when the battery is kept in a charged up state. See also active
  material.

battery electrolyte – See electrolyte.

battery explosion – Explosion caused when hydrogen gas in battery cells is
  ignited by a spark. It most commonly occurs when jumping starting a car.
  One of the batteries will have cells with a low fluid level that has allowed
  hydrogen gas to accumulate. If jumper cables are not connected correctly, a
  shower of sparks will be created at one of the terminals. Such sparks can
  easily ignite gas fumes migrating out of one of the battery cell vents. An
  explosion will send battery acid and shrapnel-like pieces of battery
  components flying through the air.

battery fill level – Electrolyte level maintained in a battery case.
  Conventional batteries usually have upper and lower level markings.

battery grid – Metal framework of a battery plate used to hold active
  material.

battery group – Classification used by battery manufacturers and retailers to
  place a certain size battery in a specific group designation facilitating
  ordering and selling of batteries to customers.

battery hold down – Metal bracket and clamp assembly used to hold a battery
  firmly in position. Metal bracket is positioned around the top edge of a
  battery and anchored with long threaded bolts attached to a car frame.

battery hydrometer – Instrument designed to determines a battery's state of
  charge by measuring the specific gravity of an electrolytic solution.

battery is dead – Condition caused when most or all of the electrical energy
  stored in a battery is gone. A car with a dead battery can be started from
  another car with jumper cables. Once started, the car's own charging system
  will start recharging the battery. It typically takes an hour or more of
  driving or running an engine to get the charge back up significantly.

battery leads – See battery cables.

battery plate – Positive or negative plate located in a battery. Plate is
  shaped into a rectangular pattern with connectors located at the top for
  transmitting electricity out of the cell. Plate composition is typically
  lead peroxide or sponge lead with other lead compounds being used for special
  applications.

battery plate strap – Connector located at the top of the cell joining all
  negative or positive plates together into one unit. It is responsible for
  keeping all plates evenly separated, and for transferring electrical energy
  to cell connectors.

battery posts – See battery terminal posts.

battery rating – Method used to rate the endurance or stored power of a
  battery.

battery rating(20 hour) – See battery rating(ampere hour).

battery rating(ampere hour) – Battery rated according to the number of amperes of current flow it can sustain over a period of time. The period is usually 20 hours. A 200 ampere-hour battery should sustain a current flow of 10 amperes for 20 hours. In general, the more plates in a battery cell, the higher the ampere-hour rating.

battery rating(cold cranking) - Method used to rate a battery's engine starting ability at low temperature. At a specified low temperature, a battery is discharged at a high rate for a specified time period to measure beginning and ending voltages.

battery rubber separator - Thin rubber sheet placed between battery plates to keep them separated.

battery sediment chamber - Space located in the bottom of each cell where debris settles as battery plates slowly wear out.

battery specific gravity - Battery electrolyte solution density measured relative to water. In a discharged state, specific gravity will be near 1.00. In a fully charged state, it averages 1.25-1.29. See also electrolyte.

battery's dead - See electrical problem(dead battery).

battery separator - Sheet of plastic, rubber, or other nonconductive material sandwiched between a positive and negative plate of a battery to keep them from contacting each other and grounding out a battery.

battery's shot - Battery no longer capable of storing and/or holding a charge.

battery strap - Lead bar used to connect positive or negative plates. Older batteries used external straps.

battery sulfation - Condition created when a lead acid battery's plates become covered with a thick layer of lead sulfate. It is due to a battery being in an undercharged state for a significant period of time. Areas of a battery remaining sulfated for a long time usually lose the ability to chemically revert during the charging process. A sulfated battery must be slowly charged to completely remove the sulfate. See also battery charging.

battery terminal posts - Electrical connectors located on top or side of a battery. Every battery has a positive and negative post. Positive post is connected to the positive side of all battery cells, and negative to the negative side. All electrical current flows in and out of a battery through these two posts. See also negative terminal and positive terminal.

battery tester - Electrical instrument used to determine the health of a fully charged battery. A high discharge across the battery posts is performed for 15-20 seconds. The battery should be able to sustain a current flow of at least three times the ampere-hour rating and not drop below 9.5 volts for a 12 volt battery.

battery testing - Test performed to test the condition of a battery. The most common are: using a battery hygrometer, and measuring cell voltage under static and high discharge conditions.

battery vapor - Highly acidic vapor generated by all lead acid batteries when charging. The vapors oxidize many different types of materials such as lead, steel, and paint. Oxidation appears as a powdery substance on the battery terminals, battery hold down covers, etc. Protection against oxidation requires coating exposed items with a protective material. See also battery washers.

battery vent plug - Cap pressed or screwed into a cell opening to contain battery cell fluids and allow vapors to escape.

battery voltmeter - Electrical instrument used to test individual cell voltages. It consists of two prongs which are inserted into a cell opening contacting the cell's two poles. See also high discharge voltage check.

battery washers - Chemically treated felt washers placed on battery posts underneath battery connectors to minimize corrosion.

battery water - Water used in a battery's electrolyte solution. Mineral free water is advised such as distilled water. Small amounts of iron, manganese, chlorides, and other compounds found in tap water will shorten a battery's life.
    If a battery loses an excessive amount of water, it may be an indication the voltage regulator is charging the battery at too high a rate.

BAT wire - Wire attached to BAT terminal on regulators, some ignition coils, etc.

Bauer - American car produced in 1914 and 1925.

Bauroth - American car produced in 1899.

Bayard - American car produced in 1903.

Bay State - American car produced from 1906-1907 and 1922-1923 by Bay State Automobile Co., and R.H. Long Co. respectively, both in Massachusetts.

BBB - Abbreviation for Better Business Bureau.

BDAC - American car produced in 1904.

BDC - Abbreviation for Bottom Dead Center.

bds - Abbreviation for boards.

Beach - American Formula Vee race car produced beginning in 1962 by Competition Components in Florida.

Beacon - American car produced in 1933.

Beacon Flyer - American car produced in 1908.
bead - See tire bead.
bead breaker - Device used to break a tubeless tire bond with the rim.
bead molding - Molding characterized by a small cross section.
bead wire - Wire molded into the bead of a tire. It is used to strengthen a tire bead, help seal a tire around the rim surface, and keep a tire on a wheel during different driving conditions. Bead wire is usually a multi-strand high tensile steel type.
Bean - Car manufactured in Dudley, England. It became popular in the 1920s, but later became a casualty of mass production by other car makers.
bear - Police officer.
Beardsley - American car produced from 1901-1902.
Beardsley Electric - American electric car produced from 1915-1917 by Beardsley Electric Co. in California.
bearing - Device or surface used to support machine parts and allow them to slide or rotate. All bearings use some form of lubrication to minimize friction.
bearing(annular ball) - Ball bearing designed with non-adjustable inner and outer races.
bearing(antifriction) - Bearing designed to roll by means of balls or rollers. It usually consists of rollers or balls that are contained and roll on inner and outer races.
bearing(axle shaft) - Bearing mounted on an axle shaft. Today's cars usually use sealed ball bearings on rear axle shafts.
bearing(ball) - Circular antifriction bearing constructed of hardened steel balls placed between an inner and an outer race. The inner and outer race rotate independently when the balls roll. Sealed ball bearings have rubber seals between the inner and outer races keeping grease from leaking out.
bearing(camshaft) - Bearing used to support a camshaft. It is usually a one piece type with several being used. Worn camshaft bearings are usually determined by the degree of oil clearance.
bearing(crankshaft) - Insert type bearing used to support a crankshaft journal. Several are used.
bearing(insert) - Pre-formed bearing made to close specifications and simply inserted where needed. It is usually constructed in two semi-circular pieces. Most main and connecting rod bearings use this type today. The shell is usually made of steel or bronze with the bearing material made of an alloy of metals such as lead, copper, tin, cadmium, etc.
bearing(integral) - Bearing poured (cast) into place. It is not common in today's cars. Such bearings are still used on machinery with large journal surfaces carrying heavy loads.
bearing(needle) - Antifriction bearing designed using a large number of small diameter rollers with proportionally long lengths.
bearing(rod) - Insert type bearing used in a connecting rod's upper and lower ends to support a piston pin or crank pin journal, respectively.
bearing(roller) - Bearing designed with cylindrical rollers moving between two races.
bearing(sealed) - Bearing designed with flexible seals between inner and outer races to contain grease for extended periods of time.
bearing(slip in) - Bearing lining made to very close tolerances usually in two pieces. Crankshaft and lower connecting rod bearings are examples of slip in types. See also bearing(insert).
bearing(tapered roller) - Two-piece bearing designed using a series of hardened steel rollers caged together and operating between tilted inner and outer races.
bearing(wheel) - Bearing used to support a wheel shaft. On cars, a rear axle shaft uses a sealed ball bearing, while a front axle shaft uses two tapered roller bearings.
bearing clearance - Space specified between a shaft or surface and a bearing surface. It is used for containing lubricating oil or grease to minimize friction between surfaces.
bearing lubrication - Film of lubricant used to coat bearing surfaces to minimize metal to metal contact or friction.
bearing preloading - Procedure used to slightly overtighten bearings in order to minimize shaft end play. Pinion drives are commonly installed this way.
bearing race - Smooth hardened surface designed for bearing rollers or balls to ride on. Ball and roller bearings typically have the bearing race and balls as one integral unit. Tapered roller bearings are usually in two pieces, a roller and outer bearing race assembly, and a separate inner bearing race. A rough or cracked bearing race surface will quickly damage balls or rollers requiring bearing replacement. Race surface damage is usually caused by grease contamination, and/or breaking balls or rollers from improper installation or overloading the bearing.
beater - Rough car or junker.
beat the deal - Offer made by a business with better terms than a competitor.

Beau Chamberlain - American car produced in 1901.
Beaumont - See Acadian Beaumont.
beauty bolts - Large round bright bolt heads located on bumper surfaces. Also, it refers to similar bolts heads used on wood grained station wagon panels.
Beaver - American car produced from 1916-1923 by Beaver State Motor Co. in Oregon.
be-back - Potential car customer promising to return tomorrow. They seldom do.
Beck - American car produced in 1921.
bed - Rectangular cargo area of a truck formed by the two side walls, tailgate, and rear cab wall.
bed depth - Vertical truck bed length measured from the bed surface to a side wall top edge.
Bedelia - American car produced in 1909.
bed length - Horizontal truck bed length measured parallel to truck length from the rear cab wall to the tailgate.
bed width - Horizontal truck bed width measured perpendicular to truck length between the two side walls.
Beebe - American car produced in 1906.
Beech Creek - American car produced from 1915-1919.
Beetle - Popular West German economy car produced from 1936-1979 by Volkswagen.
Beggs - American car produced from 1918-1923 by Beggs Motor Car Co. in Missouri.
BEI - Abbreviation for breakerless electronic ignition.
Beijing - Chinese car line produced from 1968 to date by Beijing Motor Vehicle Factory in China.
Beisel - American car produced in 1914.
BEL - American car produced in 1921.
Belair - American car produced from 1955-1976 by Chevrolet Division of General Motors Corp. in Michigan.
Belden - American car produced from 1908-1911 by Belden Motor Car Co. in Pennsylvania.
Bell - American car produced in 1907 and 1911-1923.
bellcrank - A lever or rocker used for transmitting motion between two arms meeting at right angles to a pivot point.
Bellefontaine - American car produced in 1908.
bell housing - Aluminum or cast iron housing designed to surround and protect a flywheel and clutch assembly area. It is situated between the back of an engine and the front of a transmission.
bell mouth - Condition caused when the edge of a circular opening becomes larger in diameter. Engine cylinders become bell mouthed due to wear from piston rings. Brake drums sometimes develop this condition. The only remedy is usually replacement or machining the opening to a larger diameter.
belly band - Lightweight frame crossmember mounted underneath a transmission.
belly pan - Protective metal covering used to protect the entire underside of a car.
Belmobile - American car produced in 1912.
Belmont - American car produced from 1909-1912 by Belmont Motor Car Co. in Connecticut and Belmont Motor Vehicle Co. in New York. Also, an American car produced in 1916.
belt(1) - Reinforced rubber belt used to drive engine accessories such as alternators, air pumps, and air compressors. Belts should be regularly checked for proper tension and replaced at least every two years.
belt(2) - See tire belt.
belt drive - Method used to transfer power to a rear axle on early cars using leather belts running from a countershaft.
belted bias tire - See tire(belted bias).
beltline - Line established by the intersection car body panels with the lower edge of car windows.
belt overload - Condition created when a good properly tensioned belt, matched to the pulleys it is driving, cannot turn the accessories without slipping. A squealing sound is usually generated constantly, intermittently, or during acceleration. If such is the case, a double pulley arrangement may be the only feasible solution. See also sound(squealing-5).
Belvedere - American car produced from 1957-1977 by Plymouth Division of Chrysler Corp. in Michigan.
Bemmel & Burnham - American car produced in 1908.
bench racing - Talking rather than driving a good race.
bench seat - Seat built to span the width of a car's interior. It is constructed in two pieces, a seat and a back. See also bucket seat.
Bendix(1) - See starter drive(Bendix).
Bendix(2) - American car produced from 1907-1910 by the Bendix Co. in Illinois and Indiana.

Bendix drive - See starter drive(Bendix).
Bendix spring - See spring(Bendix).
Benham - American car produced from 1914-1917 by Benham Mfg. Co. in Michigan.
Ben-Hur - American car produced from 1916-1918 by Ben Hur Motor Co. in Ohio.
Benner - American car produced from 1908-1910 by Benner Motor Car Co. in New York.
Benson - American car produced in 1901.
bent eight - V8 engine. See also engine(V type).
Bentley - British car line produced from 1920 to date by Bentley Motors. Recent models include: Eight, Mulsanne, and Continental.
Benton - American car produced in 1913.
Benton Harbor Motor Carriage - American car produced in 1896.
bent stovebolt - Chevrolet V-8 engine.
Benz - One of the first successful motorcars ever built. It was actually a tricycle, and was successfully tested in 1885.
Benz 4 Cylinder Blitzen Benz - German car driven by Bob Burmon to a 1911 world land speed record of 141.4 mph at Daytona, Florida.
benzol - Highly volatile liquid hydrocarbon produced by refining coal tar. It is used in combination with alcohol as a fuel for racing engines. Properties include: high octane rating, and low boiling point.
Berg - American car produced from 1902-1905 by Berg Automobile Co. in Ohio (1902-1904), and Worthington Automobile Co. in New York (1905).
Bergdoll - American car produced from 1908-1913 by L.J. Bergdoll Motor Co. in Pennsylvania.
Berkley - American car produced in 1907.
Berkshire - American car produced from 1905-1913.
Berliet - American car produced in 1905.
berlina - An enclosed luxury car built with small windows for privacy from the outside.
Bertolet - American car produced from 1908-1912 by Dr J.M. Bertolet (1908-1909), Bertolet Motor Car Co. (1909-1912), both in Pennsylvania.
Berwick Electric - American electric car produced in 1904.
Bessemer Truck - American truck produced in 1922.
Best - American car produced in 1900.
best of show - Award presented at a car exhibit for the most outstanding car.
best probable difference figure - Estimate made by a car salesman of the lowest price a customer will likely agree to when trading a car in.
best races rule - Method used to figure a championship in racing by adding up points accumulated from a driver's best runs in a specified number of races.
Bethlehem - American car produced in 1906-1908 and 1917.
Better Business Bureau - Independent agency organized to protect its dues paying business members and keep unreliable businesses out of town. They are best known for answering public inquiries on the reliability of companies. It is not usually very informative about complaints or too willing to step in on your behalf.
Betz - American car produced in 1919.
Beverly - American car produced from 1905-1907.
Bewis - American car produced in 1915.
Bewman - American car produced in 1912.
Beyster-Detroit - American car produced from 1910-1911.
bezel - Sloping surface or edge of an object such as a blade chisel. Also, a grooved rim or ring used to hold a transparent cover in place.
BF - American car produced in 1912.
B F Goodrich - U.S. tire manufacturing company.
BG(1) - Abbreviation for buggy.
BG(2) - Abbreviation for Bulgaria found usually on an international license plate.
bhp - Abbreviation for brake horsepower.
bialbero - Twin camshaft.
bias - Acute angle measured where tire fabric cords intersect a tire tread centerline.
bias ply tire - See tire(bias ply).
Bi-Autogo - American car produced in 1913.
Bi-Car - American car produced in 1912.
bid - Offer made to secure a contract.
Biddle - American car produced from 1915-1923 by Biddle Motor Car Co. in Pennsylvania.
Biddle-Crane - American car produced from 1922-1923.
Biddle-Murray - American car produced from 1906-1908.
bid on the repair work - Offer made to perform specified repair work for a set fee.
bid rigging - Illegal pricing maneuver used by a body repair business to persuade you to let them do the body repair work on a car. They will solve the need for three bids, required by an insurance adjuster, by offering to prepare two other repair bids having their competitor's costs on them. They

are usually phony and doctored so the costs are higher than their own.
Biederman Truck – American truck produced in 1921.
big arm – Long piston stroke.
big cam – See camshaft(big).
big cam-small head – Engine component mismatch caused by using a long duration camshaft with a cylinder head containing small intake and exhaust valves. The combination restricts air flow too much in the rpm range where the cam is designed to produce maximum power. The net result is an engine losing low end power with no increase in upper engine rpm.
Big Daddy – See Garlits, Don.
big end – Big end of connecting rod. Also, it refers to the finish area of a quarter mile race track.
big end bearing – Connecting rod bearing attached to a crankshaft.
big foot – Large tire designed for off-road use on 4 wheel drive trucks.
big Rs – High engine rpm.
big rumper – Big high performance engine.
big time kiddie car – See midget racer.
big wienie – Best or hard to beat race driver.
bilk – To defraud or cheat.
Billiken – American car produced 1914.
bill of exchange – A written authorization used to direct that a sum of money be paid to a specified person.
bill of lading – A written receipt given to a customer by a shipper acknowledging that goods are accepted for transportation.
bill of sale – Document used to transfer the ownership of personal property from a seller to a buyer. It usually contains the following: buyer and seller's names, addresses, etc.; description of item being sold; purchase price; and date.
bill padding – Questionable charges added to a repair or towing bill's original fee.
Billy – American car produced in 1910.
Bimel – American car produced in 1911 and 1915-1917.
bimetallic – Material made of two different metal substances. See also spring(bimetallic).
binder(1) – Basic ingredient found in paint. It is non-volatile, carries paint pigment, and makes a paint coating durable, shiny, and tough.
binder(2) – See brake.
binnacle – Dashboard gauge area.
Binney-Burnham – American car produced from 1901-1902 by Binney & Burnham in Massachusetts.
binocular vision – Aspect of eye vision characterized when objects brought together before a person's eyes fuse together properly. If they don't, a person may misjudge car speed, distances, etc. A simple test is to bring a pointed finger from each hand together in front of you until they touch. If you have difficulty with this, you should probably see an eye specialist.
Birch – American car produced from 1917-1923 by Birch Motor Cars in Illinois.
Bird – American car produced from 1896-1897.
bird dog – Person involved in seeking out and sending a car salesman potential customers. He usually receives a commission for each referral. A salesman will often have several bird dogs in jobs where they contact lots of people. They may even drive a nice car sold to them by the salesman as a further selling tactic. Bird dogs are usually registered with a car dealer rather than a salesman, since salesmen come and go.
Birmingham – American car produced from 1921-1922 by Birmingham No-Axle Motor Corp. in New York.
Birnell – American car produced in 1911.
Biscayne – American car produced from 1958-1976 by Chevrolet Division of General Motors Corp. in Michigan.
biscuit – Rectangular area sewn on a door panel or seat.
Bison – Experimental turbine powered freight hauler built by General Motors in 1964 for carrying containerized cargo.
bite – Amount of traction on a race course surface.
biting edges – Rubber edges created in a tire tread design. Each edge provides tire traction when contacting a road surface. More biting edges usually mean better tire traction, but also a shorter tire life, so manufacturers work to strike a balance with the number of biting edges, tread rubber compound, etc.
Bitter – West German car line produced from 1973 to date by Bitter & Co. KG.
bkts – Abbreviation for bucket seats.
Black – American car produced in 1891. Also, a car produced from 1903-1909 by Black Mfg. Co. in Illinois.
black and white – Police car.
black box – Electronic module designed to control one or more car functions such as: timing, fuel metering, emissions, fastening seat belts, and closing doors. It is also known as an on-board computer and a control unit. Though

usually reliable, the device can be sensitive to failure due to: heat, dirty connectors, polarity reversal, incorrect current flow, poor ground, and missing or disconnected spark plug cables (no high voltage current flow). A faulty black box will usually prevent a car from being started.

Black Crow - American car produced in 1907 and 1909.

Black Diamond - American car produced from 1904-1905.

Blackhawk - American car produced from 1902-1903 and 1929-1931 by Clark Mfg. Co. in Illinois, and Stutz Motor Car Co. of America respectively.

black flag - See flag(black).

Blackstone - American car produced in 1916.

blacktop - Bituminous substance used to pave roads, parking lots, etc. Also, it refers to asphalt.

blackwall - Tire sidewall molded with no white band.

blacky carbon - Gasoline.

blade - Thin sharp ridge defined in body metal, or an applique.

Blair - American car produced in 1911.

Blaisdell - American car produced in 1903.

Blaisdell Electric - American car produced in 1906.

blanket overhaul - Non-specific engine overhaul work authorized by a customer. It usually leads to a padded repair bill, since exact work was not specified. See also con game(extra repair work) and con game(padding the bill).

Blazer - American car produced from 1967 to date by Chevrolet Division of General Motors Corp. in Michigan.

Bleach - Liquid bleach poured under rear tires for burnout.

Bleach box - Area located away from starting line for performing burnouts.

bleed down - Loss of fuel in a carburetor when engine stops. It usually causes difficult starting. Possible causes include: stuck needle valve, heat soak, vapor lock, low boiling point gas, and cracked carburetor float bowl.

bleeding(1) - See paint coat problem(bleeding).

bleeding(2) - Ability of a grease to release oil from within its structure.

bleeding the brakes - Process used to remove air from brake lines of a hydraulic brake system.

bleeding the brakes(manual method) - Most common method used to bleed brake lines. It usually requires two people, one doing brake pumping and the other observing air in fluid exiting a brake cylinder. Air is removed by pumping brake fluid through a brake cylinder bleeder screw. Only one is open at any time. The farthest one is opened first. A short plastic tube is attached to an open bleeder screw. Fluid moves through the tube to a clear glass or plastic jar where bubbles in the fluid can be observed. Pumping the brake pedal and replenishing the master brake cylinder reservoir continues until no more bubbles are observed. The bleeder screw is closed and the process repeated for the next farthest brake cylinder.

bleeding the brakes(pressure method) - Method used to bleed brakes requiring one person and specialized equipment. A pressurized tank is used containing brake fluid. It is connected to a brake master cylinder. Brake fluid is forced into a brake system at a controlled rate eliminating the need for brake pumping. Each bleeder screw is then opened and closed, as in the manual method, until all air is removed.

Blemline - American car produced in 1898.

blending - Custom painting technique used to make subtle transitions from one color to another on a panel. An airbrush usually produces the best results. See also shading.

blew a head gasket - Engine condition created when a cylinder head gasket ruptures causing loss of pressure to one or more cylinders and possible fluid leakage. Possible causes include: loose, improperly torqued, or broken head bolts; excessive compression ratio; poor gasket material; improper gasket installation; and excessive heat and pressure build-up in combustion chamber due to excessive spark advance. The only remedy is removal of cylinder head and replacement of gasket.

blew a rod - Engine condition created when a connecting rod separates from a piston. Most common cause is lack of lubrication in which a piston freezes against a cylinder wall and the connecting rod pulls itself out of the bottom of the piston. When it becomes free, the continued rotation of the crankshaft will cause the rod to bind against the bottom of the cylinder wall and crack or rupture it. The result is usually a ruined engine block. A rod going bad makes a noticeable rattling or knocking sound when a car is accelerated or when it is decelerated from a high speed.

blindgating - To tailgate a lead car far enough away to stop if it stops, but not far enough to miss an obstacle in the road it swerves to miss.

blinding reflection - Eye vision problem created by bright light reaching a driver's eyes and impairing his vision. It can come from trailing car headlights that shine in mirrors, approaching car headlights, sun reflections off bodies of water, glass surfaces, etc. The best solution at night is to block or look away from the light. In the daytime, sun glasses and a sun visor are effective.

blind quarter – Wide C pillar or roof quarter used to enclose rear seat area.
blind spot – Rear viewing areas blocked from a driver's vision by side and rear portions of car and mirror limitations. Cars, located in these areas, cannot usually be seen through rear or side view mirrors. It is usually a good practice to glance at those areas before making a traffic maneuver.
blinkey – Timing light located at a race track's finish line.
blips – Small ornamentation design used in series such as several identical ports, windsplits, and bars. They can be aligned horizontally or vertically on a car body surface.
blip the throttle – To quickly and partly open a throttle and then close it. It is done periodically on certain high performance engines when they are idling to avoid gas fouling of spark plugs.
Bliss – American car produced in 1906.
Blitzen Benz – See Benz 4 Cylinder Blitzen Benz.
blizzard – Violent windstorm characterized by dry driving snow and intense cold.
blk – Abbreviation for black interior.
blk/blk – Abbreviation for black interior and exterior.
BLM – American car produced from 1906-1907 by Breese, Lawrence, & Moulton Motor Car & Equipment Co. in New York.
block – Cast steel part of an engine designed to contain the cylinders, pistons, and crankshaft.
Block Bros – American car produced in 1905.
block drain tap – Threaded plug or brass valve mounted at the base of a cylinder water jacket area. When removed or opened, engine block water drains. This is done to thoroughly flush cooling system or to drain a block before removing it from a car.
block heater – Heating device used to heat and circulate coolant water through an engine block when an engine is stopped during cold weather. It keeps an engine from getting cold and hard to start.
blocking ring – See synchronizer ring.
block prep – Preparations made to an engine block before assembling engine parts. It includes all machine work, and making sure the following parts and any internal passageways are washed and clean: engine block, pistons, connecting rods, crankshaft, and main bearing caps.
Blomstrom – American car produced from 1907-1909 by Blomstrom Mfg. Co. in Michigan.
Blood – American car produced from 1903-1905 by Blood Brothers Auto & Machine Co. in Michigan.
blood bank – Finance company.
blow – Engine failure.
blow by – Condition caused when exhaust gases escape past piston rings into the crankcase. Gases escape at ring end gaps and behind the rings (all rings leak somewhat), and consist mostly of unburned gasoline. In the crankcase, blowby dilutes oil with gasoline reducing its lubricating capacity, and also causes the formation of sludge, acids, varnish, and other contaminants that are especially harmful to crankshaft and connecting rod bearing metal. Amount of blowby is an indicator of engine wear.
blowby eliminator valve – See PCV valve.
blower – See supercharger.
blower motor – Motor used to operate a car's heater fan.
blower pressure gauge – Gauge designed to read intake manifold pressure. It is used in conjunction with a supercharger or turbocharger.
blowing out an engine – Process used to help remove accumulation of combustion chamber and spark plug deposits. See also car service tip(blowing out an engine).
blown(1) – See engine(supercharged).
blown(2) – Badly damaged engine.
blown engine – See engine(supercharged).
blown gasser – Supercharged gasoline engine.
blown head gasket – See blew a head gasket.
blow off valve – Valve used in superchargers to limit boost.
blowout – Condition created when a tire suddenly loses air while driving. Possible causes include: excess tire pressure, hitting an obstruction, broken tire bead, and large puncture. When a front blowout occurs, a car will tend to pull to the blow out side. A rear blow out will cause a car to weave. Blow out tires are often damaged beyond repair.
blow out – To sell a car to a wholesaler.
blowup – Small blob of paint deposited onto a paint surface then fanned into a larger thin circle with air. It is created like freak drops but with less air force and more distance. See also blowup painting.
blowup painting – Custom painting technique used to create a panel of blowups in a specific design. See also freak drop painting.
Bluebird – See Napier V-12 Bluebird.
Bluebird Gas Turbine – English car driven by Donald Campbell to a 1964 world

land speed record of 403.1 mph at Lake Eyre, Australia.
Bluebird V-12 - English car driven to a world land speed record in 1931, 1932, 1933, and 1935. Speeds were 246.1, 254.0, 272.5, 276.8 and 301.1 mph. Locations were Daytona, Florida (1931, 1932, and 1933); and Bonneville, Utah. Malcom Campbell was the driver.
blue book - Book published yearly listing wholesale and retail value of used cars. It is usually made available only to qualified car dealers, and is an important book for car salesmen. See also NADA.
blue bomb - Car using too much oil. See also smoker.
blue dots - Purple taillights.
Blue Flame - American rocket car built by United States Institute of Gas Technology. It ran on liquefied gas and hydrogen peroxide, and broke the world land speed record in 1970, traveling 630.3 mph on the Utah Salt Flats near Bonneville, Utah.
blue glow - See blue spark.
blueprinted - Stock engine modified into a performance engine.
blueprinting - Process used to build a performance engine. See also balanced and blueprinted.
blue smoke - Bluish tinted smoke emitted by a car when excess quantities of oil reach the combustion chambers and burn. It is usually due to worn engine components such as pistons, piston rings, cylinder walls, and valve guides. A plugged catalytic converter can cause blue smoke, but only at startup. See also exhaust.
blue spark - Color emitted by high voltage sparks in a car's ignition circuit.
Blue Streak - American car produced in 1908.
Bluffelimber - American car produced in 1901.
Blumberg - American car produced in 1918.
blushing - See paint coat problem(blushing).
BMC Sports - American car produced in 1952 by British Motor Car Co. in California.
BMW - West German car line produced from 1928 to date. The U.S. representative is BMW of North America, headquartered in Montvale, New Jersey.
    Also, it refers to an American electric car produced from 1949 to date by Boulevard Machine Works in California.
BO - Abbreviation for best offer.
Board - American car produced in 1912.
boattail - Any cylindrical object characterized by a diameter that decreases in size along its axis. It is commonly done to reduce aerodynamic drag.
bobbed - Cut shorter such as shortened fenders.
Bobbi-Car - American car produced from 1945-1947 by Bobbi Motor Car Corp. in California and Alabama.
Bobcat - American car produced from 1971 to date by Mercury Division of Ford Motor Co. in Michigan.
Bobsy - Small American racing car produced beginning in 1962 by C.W. Smith Engineering Co. in Ohio.
bob-weight - Weight located at the end of a clutch pressure plate release lever to adjust the rpm at which the plate stops slipping and locks up.
Bocar - American car produced from 1958-1960 by Bocar Mfg. Co. in Colorado.
body - See auto body.
body cancer - Car body panel rust spots.
body cords - Cords of material used in a tire carcass to increase its strength.
body filler - See solder(plastic).
body lift kit - Assemblage of parts designed to raise a car or truck body. Popular kits lift the back half of a car or truck's body.
body panel - Metal shape used to cover part of a car body such as a fender, quarter panel, hood, and door panel.
body plies - See tire body plies.
body prep - Work done to prepare a car body for painting.
body putty - See solder(plastic).
body repair shop - See auto body shop.
body roll - Condition created when cornering a car which tends to cause rotation about the centerline of the car.
body rot - See body cancer.
body shape - Outline of a car body.
body style - Type of body shape such as sedan, convertible, coupe, truck, etc.
body style(2+2) - Car body built with two front seats and two smaller back seat for children, luggage, etc.
body style(all weather touring car) - Touring car body style built with fixed or windup windows. It was replaced by the closed car body styles in the early 1930s.
body style(berlina) - See berlina.
body style(bustleback) - See body style(sedan). Sometimes, it refers to a notchback.

body style(closed car) - Car body built with a top, front, back, and sides to protect passengers from the weather.
body style(coke bottle) - Car body built narrower in the middle section than over the front and rear wheels.
body style(convertible) - Car body constructed with a folding or removable top and rollup windows.
body style(convertible coupe) - See body style(convertible).
body style(convertible sedan) - See body style(convertible).
body style(coupe) - Enclosed car body built with two doors and a shorter body and smaller interior than a same model sedan.
body style(cyclecar) - Small car body built to carry one or two passengers. They were first introduced in 1913. Though their market rapidly expanded, the popularity was short lived. Few of the small economy vehicles remained on the market after 1915.
body style(dos-a-dos) - Car body built to carry four passengers in two seats mounted back to back.
body style(double phaeton) - Phaeton car body built with two seats to carry four passengers.
body style(drophead coupe) - A convertible.
body style(fastback) - Enclosed car body built with a long slanting rear roof. See also body style(liftback).
body style(five passenger closed car) - Enclosed car body built with usually four doors and having room for two passengers in front and three in back.
body style(four door hardtop) - See body style(four door sedan).
body style(four door sedan) - Enclosed car body built with four doors for entering and leaving. It offers reasonable roll-over protection and easy access for all passengers. Drawbacks include more areas around doors for rattles, leaks, squeaks, etc. to develop.
body style(hardtop) - Enclosed car body built with a rigid metal top having no center posts between side windows.
body style(hardtop convertible) - Enclosed body style resembling a convertible but with a non-removable roof. It was a 1950s term that is now termed a hardtop. Also, it refers to a car body design using a hardtop built to retract into a trunk.
body style(hatchback) - Enclosed car body built with a rear-mounted door opening upwards to provide access to a car's rear deck area. The rear window is mounted in the door.
body style(King of the Belgians) - Luxurious open style touring car.
body style(landau) - Enclosed sedan car body built with a short convertible back or the appearance of one. On early cars, it referred to a car body style using a roof folding in two parts. It permitted a roof to be open at the front, back, or both.
body style(landaulet) - Enclosed car body built so the rear could be opened. Also, an expensive car body mounted on Austin cars in the early 1900s to give wealthy car owners the comforts of home. Also, a small version of a landau.
body style(liftback) - Enclosed car body built with a long slanting rear mounted door opening upwards to provide access to a car's rear deck area. The rear window is mounted in the door.
body style(limousine) - Enclosed car body built with a glass division between the driver and passenger compartments. It also refers to a luxurious car driven by chauffeur.
body style(monocoque) - Car body built in one piece with all components attached to it. It is used on racing cars, is expensive to build, and is very strong.
body style(notchback) - Car body built with a roof line dropping abruptly to the rear deck area. It makes the rear window almost vertical.
body style(open car) - Car body built with no roof or side windows. Some had windshields.
body style(permanent top phaeton) - Open car body style built with a permanent roof.
body style(phaeton) - An open car body built to carry two passengers. See also body style(double phaeton) and body style(triple phaeton).
body style(roadster) - Car built with an open car body. It usually has one seat for seating one or two people, a large trunk, and often a rumble seat.
body style(Roi de Belges) - Luxurious touring car body style named after Belgium's King Leopold II.
body style(runabout) - Lightweight open two passenger car built in the early 1900s.
body style(saloon) - See body style(sedan).
body style(sedan) - Enclosed car body constructed with two or four doors and seating four or more people on two full width seats.
body style(side entrance tonneau) - See body style(touring car).
body style(sociable) - Car body introduced in 1915 by Packard, Kline, Winton and others with an aisle between the front and back seats.
body style(sports sedan) - Two door high performance version of a sedan.

body style(spyder) – Lightweight open two-seat sports car.
body style(station wagon) – Enclosed car body constructed with one or more rows of folding seats behind the driver area, no separate luggage compartment, and an open area accessible through a tailgate.
body style(surrey) – Open car body built to carry four passengers. It usually has a fringed top.
body style(three door hatchback) – Enclosed car body built with three doors, two as passenger doors and one as a rear trunk door. The rear seat usually folds down to extend the storage area. They are popular for those who want the room of a station wagon without having to buy one. Drawbacks are difficulty in entering and exiting from the rear seat area.
body style(tonneau) – Car body built to carry four passengers with rear seat access from a rear door. Also, it refers to an open car body with a front bench seat and semi-circular rear seat. Parts of the rear seat were often built into the rear door(s). See also tonneau.
body style(torpedo) – Touring car body style built with a continuous surface running from hood, to windshield, to roof, to trunk area. The tops of the car seats were even with the top of the car sides. It first appeared around 1910 and looked like a bathtub on wheels. The dashboard was brought closer to the driver, the sides were extended upward, and the driver and passengers sat lower to the ground.
body style(torpedo tourer) – See body style(torpedo).
body style(town car) – Car body built with an enclosed passenger compartment and an open driver's compartment or one with a sliding roof.
body style(tourer) – See body style(touring car).
body style(touring car) – Open car body built with seats for at least four passengers. Early cars usually had roofs but no side protection against the weather. Subsequent models used removable side curtains or screens. It was produced until about 1930. See also body style(all weather touring car).
body style(tricycle) – Early open car body built with three wheels and a frame of steel tubing. See also body style(cyclecar).
body style(triple phaeton) – Phaeton car body built with three seats to carry six passengers.
body style(truck) – Car body constructed with a passenger compartment and separate box structure used to haul loads. Passenger compartment usually consists of two bucket seats or one bench seat.
body style(tulip phaeton) – See body style(Roi de Belges).
body style(two door hardtop) – Enclosed car body built with two doors and a rigid metal top having no center posts between side windows.
body style(two door sedan) – Enclosed car built with two doors for entering and exiting and a separate trunk area. It usually provides reasonable protection in roll-over accidents. Entrance and exit from the vehicle is more controlled, an advantage with children. Primary drawback is entering and leaving the back seat area.
body style(unit body) – Car body built with the body, floor, and frame as one unit. It is a lighter and more rigid structure.
body style(van) – Car body constructed with a large covered cargo area for moving furniture, supplies, animals, etc.
body style(victoria) – Open car body built with two seats and a large folding car top.
body style(vis-a-vis) – Car body built to carry four passengers with two seats facing each other.
body style(voiturette) – Early touring-type car body built with no hood.
body style(wagonette) – Car body built to carry at least six passengers with the rear seats facing each other and accessible from the rear.
body superstructure – Car body resting on a car's chassis.
body type – See body style.
body water drain – Drain hole designed to drain water from a car body panel area and minimize rust formation. For example, water flows down a side window and drains out the bottom of a door through a body water drain. Cars have several drain holes.
body work – Work performed to repair and restore a car body to its original shape.
bogging the engine – See lugging the engine.
Boggs – American car produced in 1903.
boiling over – Engine condition created when coolant temperature reaches its boiling point causing excess pressure and steam formation. Radiator cap will release some of the pressure as steam. Removing a cap during a boil over is not wise. It would cause excessive steam and water release and possible injury to the person removing it. It is usually best to let an engine cool down.
boiling point – Temperature reached when a fluid begins to change into a vapor or gaseous state. The fluid typically bubbles. A fluid's boiling point can be increased by pressurizing it. For engine coolant, each 1 pound increase in pressure increases the boiling point by 3 degrees Fahrenheit. Radiator

caps usually pressurize an engine's cooling system to 15 lbs. At this
pressure, a 50-50 concentration of water and antifreeze has a boiling point
of 265 degrees. See also radiator cap and antifreeze concentration.
Boisselot - American car produced in 1901.
BOL - Abbreviation for Bolivia found usually on an international license
plate.
Bolide - American car produced beginning in 1969 by Bolide Motor Car Corp. in
New York.
Bollee - Three wheeled car built 1897 with only one wheel in back.
Bollee - American car produced in 1908.
Bollstrom - American car produced in 1920.
bolster - Seat portion designed to roll over or form the uppermost part of a
seat's back or its leading edge.
Bolte - American car produced in 1901.
bomb - Hot rod.
bond - Written promise executed to guarantee fulfillment of an obligation to
an affected party if the promise cannot be kept. The obligation may be to
pay specified sums of money or to do or not do certain things. See also bail
bond.
bonded brake lining - Brake lining attached to a brake shoe or disc pad by an
adhesive compound.
bondo - See solder(plastic).
bondo board - Hand held sanding board used to sand a car body surface.
bonnet - Hood.
bonnet louvres - Series of parallel hood slits used to route air into an
engine compartment.
Bonneville - American car produced from 1955 to date by Pontiac Division of
General Motors Corp. in Michigan.
bonus car - Selling tactic used to move a car sitting on a lot for sometime by
offering a cash bonus or discount if a buyer pays in cash. A salesman will
use the cash enticement to steer potential customers to the car.
boost - Intake manifold pressure supplied by a supercharger or turbocharger.
booster - Mechanical or hydraulic device used in brake, and/or steering
systems to increase force applied by an operator.
booster cables - See jumper cables.
boosting a car - See jump start.
boost pressure sensing port - Opening located near the entrance to an intake
manifold on turbocharger equipped car. It is used to determine amount of
boost or pressure in the manifold. The pressure is either measured by a
sensor or routed via a line to controls which regulate boost via a wastegate.
boost venturi - Small venturi located at the discharge end of a carburetor's
main or secondary discharge nozzle. Some carburetor designs have a second
boost venturi located beneath the first one. See also venturi.
boot(1) - See tire.
boot(2) - Car trunk.
boot cover - Cover used to conceal area around base of a transmission shift
lever.
Booth - American car produced in 1896.
Borbein - American car produced from 1903-1907 by H.F. Borbein & Co., and
Borbein Automobile Co., both in Missouri.
bore - Inside diameter of an engine cylinder.
bored - Cutting or machining cylinder wall to desired ID.
bored and stroked - Engine modified with increased bore and stroke length.
bore diameter - See bore.
Borg-Warner - American line of automotive products.
Borland Electric - American electric car produced in 1903-1914 by Borland
Grannis Co. in Illinois.
Borland-Grannis - American car produced from 1912-1916.
Bosch - German line of automotive products.
boss(1) - Raised part of a flat surface.
boss(2) - High quality or close to perfection.
Boss(1) - American car produced from 1903-1907 by Boss Knitting Machine Works
in Pennsylvania.
Boss(2) - Large displacement Ford performance engine.
Boston - American car produced in 1900.
Boston Electric - American electric car produced from 1906-1907 by Concord
Motor Car Co. in Massachusetts.
Boston & Amesbury - American car produced in 1904.
Boston-Haynes Apperson - American car produced in 1898.
Boston High Wheel - American car produced in 1907.
bottled gas - Mixture of propane, butane, and other gases pressurized into
liquid form.
bottom end - Engine components located below the cylinder head.
bottom end rebuild - Process used to rebuild a worn engine's components below
the cylinder head.

bottom hose - Lower radiator hose used to circulate coolant from radiator to water pump.

bottoming piston - To push a piston to the bottom or innermost part of a cylinder bore.

bounce - Condition created when a valve does not remain tightly closed after cam lobe pressure has been removed. Also, it refers to point bounce in a distributor.

bounce test - See car service tip(bounce test).

Bourassa 6 - Canadian car produced from 1899-1926 by H.E. Bourassa in Quebec.

Bour-Davis - American car produced from 1915-1922 by Bour-Davis Co. in Louisiana.

Bourne - American car produced in 1917.

Bournville - American car produced from 1921-1922.

Bouton, George - He invented the trembler ignition coil in 1895. See also trembler coil ignition.

Bowling Green - American car produced in 1912.

Bowman - American car produced from 1921-1922 by Bowman Motor Car Co. in Kentucky.

box - Enclosed housing used to contain gears and shafts transferring motion from one shaft to another. Examples include: transmission, steering box, and differential.

box end wrench - Wrench constructed with a socket-like opening at one or both ends. It is designed to reduce wrench slippage from a nut or bolt.

box on wheels - Early car.

Boyd - American car produced in 1911.

Boynton - American car produced in 1922.

B pillar - Metal roof post positioned behind an A pillar. It is an upward extension of a B post.

B post - Vertical metal post positioned at the rear edge of a front door latch.

BR(1) - Abbreviation for Brougham.

BR(2) - Abbreviation for Brazil found usually on an international license plate.

bra - Flexible covering placed over the front of a hood to protect the paint surface from chipping, scratches, etc. Material is usually made out of Naugahyde, an imitation leather.

Brabham, Jack - He became the Grand Prix world champion in 1959, 1960 and 1966 driving a Cooper-Climax (1959 and 1960), and Brabham-Repco.

Bradfield - American car produced in 1929.

Bradford - American car produced in 1920.

Bradley - American car produced from 1920-1921 by Bradley MotorCar Co. in Illinois. Also, America's largest kit car maker in business from 1972 to date by Bradley Automotive in Minnesota.

brake - Device designed to slow and stop the rotation of a wheel using friction. Without brakes, you would not be able to safely stop a moving car in many cases. The ability to stop makes brakes the most important system on a car. See also brake(disc), brake(drum), and brake(power), etc.

brake(air) - Brake designed to use air pressure instead of fluid pressure to operate brake shoes or pads. Air brake systems are more complicated and expensive, but are more effective for heavy duty braking such as on large trucks.

brake(anti-skid) - Brake designed to maintain braking force in a pulsing fashion just below point at which wheel loses traction. Wheel speed sensor sends information to a microprocessor which controls fluid pressure to each brake cylinder.

brake(center plane) - Brake designed to use two brake shoes each with their own brake cylinder and pivot points.

brake(disc) - Brake designed to operate by pressing friction pads against a rotating steel disc. One piston brake cylinder is mounted on each side of a disc to press pads against it. Pads are usually square or rectangular in shape and constantly but lightly ride the disc surface. Disc brakes are common on the front wheels of today's cars with drum brakes on the back. They are much less prone to brake fading.

brake(drum) - Brake designed to operate by pressing two semi-circular brake shoes against a circular brake drum. Primary components within a drum typically include: two brake shoes, brake cylinder, two brake springs, brake shoe hold down spring and clips assemblies, brake adjusting screw, star wheel adjuster, and parking brake extension lever.

brake(dual) - Brake system designed with disc brakes in front and drum brakes in back.

brake(electric) - Brake designed to operate by using electric components to move brake shoes or pads. Electric brake systems are still experimental.

brake(emergency) - Backup braking system used on a car should the primary braking system fail. It is also used to keep a car from rolling when stationary. A hand lever or foot-operated brake pedal is used to lockup one or more brakes, or a transmission shaft via a cable and/or linkage assembly. Most cars use the rear wheel drum brakes. Some older cars used a brake drum assembly positioned around a transmission output shaft.

brake(hydraulic) - Brake designed to be activated by hydraulic fluid moving under pressure from a master cylinder to a brake cylinder. It is the most popular braking method because fluids are generally incompressible throughout a braking system.

brake(manual) - See brake(hydraulic).

brake(mechanical) - Brake designed to be activated by a mechanical linkage that connects a brake to a brake pedal. Some emergency brakes have a brake pedal that works this way. See also brake(emergency).

brake(power) - Hydraulic brake designed to apply additional fluid pressure through a power brake unit working with a master brake cylinder. When a driver pushes a brake pedal, a power brake unit exerts extra pressure on a master brake cylinder push rod. See also brake unit.

brake(self adjusting) - Brake designed to adjust its shoes or pads as they wear to maintain constant clearances during their life.

brake adjuster - Adjustable device designed to expand the bottom of two brake shoes. Some are self-adjusting while others require periodic adjustment due to brake lining wear. It is very important to periodically adjust brakes which are not self-adjusting. Rear brakes getting too far out of adjustment can cause the braking system to do most of its braking with the front wheels, a dangerous situation. The brake pedal may still even feel normal. Rule of thumb is check and adjust brake shoes every 5,000 miles. See also star wheel adjuster.

brake adjustment - Adjustment made to a brake shoe to maintain proper clearance with brake drum.

brake anchor pin - Heavy steel pin located in the top of a brake drum housing. Upper end of two brake shoes rest against it when they are not used. It is used to keep brake shoes properly positioned.

brake backing plate - Steel plate used to attach a wheel's brake shoes and associated braking components. Backing plate keeps brake shoes stationary when applied to a wheel's brake drum which causes friction and slows the rotation of a wheel according to the force applied at the brake pedal. Backing plate is usually circular.

brake band - Adjustable circular band faced with friction material and used in an automatic transmission to control rotation of a planetary gear set drum. Gear change usually occurs in an automatic transmission when one planetary gear set-clutch-drum assembly stops rotating and another begins.

brake band(front) - Brake band positioned around the front planetary gear set drum (usually reverse and high gear) of an automatic transmission.

brake bleeding - See bleeding the brakes.

brake booster - See brake booster unit.

brake booster unit - Device used to assist in increasing the force applied to a brake master cylinder. See also car service tip(brake booster test).

brake booster unit(air suspended type) - Diaphragm assembly mounted onto a master brake cylinder to help increase braking effort. It works by exposing both sides of the sealed diaphragm to atmospheric pressure. When a push rod is depressed, one side of the diaphragm receives vacuum from the intake manifold and the pressure imbalance helps push the push rod harder.

brake booster unit(vacuum suspended type) - Diaphragm assembly mounted onto a master brake cylinder to help increase braking effort. It works by exposing both sides of the sealed diaphragm to intake manifold vacuum. When a push rod is depressed, one side of the diaphragm receives vacuum from the intake manifold and the other side receives atmospheric air. The pressure imbalance helps push the push rod harder.

brake cable - Cable assembly used to connect parking brake lever to mechanism actuating rear brakes.

brake cable return spring - Spring used to return parking brake mechanism to its original position when not applied.

brake caliper - See caliper assembly.

brake chatter - Braking condition caused when brake linings are unevenly worn or not centered. It usually causes pedal vibration.

brake cylinder - Small cylinder designed to push brake shoes toward a brake drum under hydraulic pressure from a master brake cylinder. It consists primarily of: a cylinder housing, two pistons, two cups, return spring, two rubber boots, and bleeder screw.

brake cylinder hone - See hone(brake).

brake disc - See brake rotor.

brake drum - Circular cast iron housing used to contain brake shoes and provide a friction surface for them to contact to slow down a car. Drum is attached to a wheel hub located on the end of a rear axle. Cast iron drums have a higher coefficient of friction and are more resistant to galling. Some are finned to increase heat dissipation which improves braking ability.

brake drum reconditioning - Process used to restore a brake drum to operating

condition by machining the brake shoe bearing surface until it becomes smooth
and round. Many drums have an oversize limit of 0.060 inches. Going beyond
the limit causes the following: weakens the drum, causes drum to flex during
braking, and overheats drum due to less metal which causes more brake fade
and shorter lining life.

brake drum scoring - Condition created when a braking surface on a brake drum
becomes grooved and uneven. It is usually due to dirt and debris in a brake
drum, and/or running linings down until brake shoe metal contacts a drum
surface.

brake drum turning - See brake drum reconditioning.

brake dual master cylinder - See brake master cylinder(dual).

brake effectiveness - Brake performance measured by how well a brake system
stops a car. Factors affecting performance include: pressure applied to
brake linings, area of brake lining, size of brake drum or rotor, condition
of braking surface, and coefficient of friction of brake lining and tire.

brake fade - Loss of braking power caused by a decrease in brake lining
coefficient of friction. It is generally caused by excessive heat which
develops when the brake lining and braking surface remain in contact for
significant periods of time. Brake temperature can get over 700 degrees
Fahrenheit.

brake fluid - Special hydraulic fluid used in a brake system to operate brake
pads and/or shoes. It usually has the following properties: a high boiling
point, low freezing point, won't swell or soften rubber parts, is compatible
with different metals in brake system, won't cause rust or corrosion, acts as
lubricant to moving parts, allows some water infiltration, and will mix with
other hydraulic brake fluids. When a brake pedal is depressed, brake fluid
is pumped to brake cylinders at each wheel. They control brake lining
movement against the friction surfaces being used. The amount of pedal
pressure determines amount of fluid pumped and thus the degree of braking
action. It's a good idea to change the brake fluid in the brake system any
time a hydraulic component such as a wheel cylinder is replaced.

brake flushing - Process used to remove all brake fluid and debris from a
brake system.

brake friction - Friction developed between a brake shoe or pad and a braking
surface.

brake horsepower - See horsepower(brake)

brake hose - Flexible high pressure rubber hose used to transfer brake fluid
in parts of a brake system where a rigid brake line would be subjected to
flexing. Short sections of hose are used at both front wheels.

brake job - See brake service.

brake lights - See light(brake).

brake light switch - Electrical switch operated by a brake pedal to activate
tail lights when brakes are applied.

brake line - Rigid high pressure metal tubing used in a braking system to
transfer brake fluid to brake cylinders at each wheel.

brake lining - Friction producing material attached to a brake shoe or pad.
Braking occurs when the lining is pressed against a braking surface. The two
main types of lining materials include organic and metallic. Organic lining
material is most popular and contains materials such as: asbestos, powdered
resins, rubber compounds, fillers, and fine metal wire. Metallic lining
material includes: powdered iron or copper, and inorganic fillers.

brake lining(asbestos) - Lining material made with asbestos fibers in a resin
compound. It is a common lining material that has been around for a long
time. One disadvantage is the generation of asbestos dust, a known health
hazard, as the linings wear.

brake lining(fiberglass) - Lining material made with fiberglass strands in a
resin compound.

brake lining(semi-metallic) - Lining material made with steel fibers and
graphite in a resin compound. It is designed to work at higher braking
temperatures than non-metallic linings. It usually out-wears the non-
metallic lining material.

brake lining attachment - Method used to attach a brake lining to a brake shoe
or pad. Older methods used recessed rivets. Today's brake linings are
usually bonded with some type of adhesive. Bonded linings have a longer life
since more lining thickness is available for wear.

brake master cylinder - Device used to store and pump hydraulic fluid under
pressure to a brake system's wheel cylinders. It primarily consists of: a
housing with integral cylinder bore and reservoir, push rod, filler cap,
piston, caps, spring, rubber boot, and fluid outlet fitting. See also brake
master cylinder(dual).

brake master cylinder(diagonal) - Master cylinder built with two separate
reservoirs and pistons. It is commonly used on front wheel drive cars to
provide safe braking in the event one of the pistons or brake cylinders
fails. One piston forces fluid to a front disc brake cylinder and a
diagonally opposite rear brake wheel cylinder. The other piston works for

the other two diagonally opposite brakes.

brake master cylinder(dual) - Master cylinder built with two separate reservoirs and pistons. One piston forces fluid to the rear brake cylinders, while the other forces fluid to the front. A dual master cylinder has the advantage of allowing two of the brakes to still function if one of the pistons fails. Most cars today use this type of master cylinder. See also brake master cylinder.

brake pad - Brake lining used in disc brakes. It consists of a flat square or rectangular metal backing plate with brake lining material bonded to its surface. As a general rule of thumb, pads should be replaced when the lining thickness equals the metal backing plate thickness. See also brake lining.

brake pad retainer - Pin used in a disc brake caliper to hold the brake pads in a specified position. Some calipers use two. See also spring(anti rattle).

brake pedal - Floor pedal used in the driver's foot area to activate a car's braking system. It is usually positioned to the left of a gas pedal.

brake pedal problem (low) - Condition created when a brake pedal moves a substantial distance before becoming firm. Possible causes include: pedal out of adjustment, air in the brake lines, and brake shoes out of adjustment due to wear or binding star wheel adjuster.

brake pedal problem(sinks to floor) - Condition created when an applied brake pedal slowly sinks all the way to the floor. Possible causes include: leaking wheel cylinder or master cylinder, cracked or torn primary cup in master cylinder, and lack of fluid in the hydraulic system.

brake pedal problem(spongy) - Condition created when a brake pedal gives under pressure. It is usually caused by air in a hydraulic system. Pedal will firm up when air is removed. Air may have entered from loose fittings, empty reservoir, or from out of adjustment brake linings causing excessive piston movement in the brake cylinders.

brake pedal travel - Distance traveled by a brake pedal from rest until it becomes firm due to hydraulic pressure. Most brake pedals are adjusted to travel about an inch.

brake problem - Condition caused when a car's braking system is not operating properly.

brake problem(brake pedal oscillates) - Applied brake pedal moves up and down. Possible causes include: brake drum out of round, rotor warped, and rotor braking surfaces not parallel.

brake problem(brake pedal requires excessive pressure) - Brake pedal must be pushed hard for adequate braking. Possible causes include: linings are covered with oil, grease, and/or water; brake drums scored; linings making partial contact due to wrong size, being out of adjustment, incorrect anchor pin location, and defective booster.

brake problem(brake pedal spongy) - See brake pedal(spongy).

brake problem(brake pedal sinks to floor) - See brake pedal(sinks to floor).

brake problem(brake pedal travel excessive) - Brake pedal must be pushed almost to the floor before braking occurs. Possible causes include: low fluid level in master brake cylinder, normal brake lining wear, brake linings out of adjustment due to wear or faulty brake adjuster, and master brake cylinder push rod out of adjustment.

brake problem(brake pedal vibration) - See brake problem(brakes chatter).

brake problem(brakes chatter) - Applied brakes emit a chattering sound. Possible causes include: loose brake linings, brake drum scored or machined poorly, brake shoes not centered, and/or warped brake drum and/or rotor.

brake problem(brakes drag-all) - All brake linings remain in contact with the braking surfaces without the brake pedal being pushed. Indications are similar to brake problem(brakes drag-one). Possible causes include: master brake cylinder push rod improperly adjusted, and malfunctioning master brake cylinder.

brake problem(brakes drag-one) - Brake linings in one or more wheels remain in contact with the braking surface. Indications are: reduced power, car pulls to one side, grinding noise, and/or brake smell. Possible causes include: damaged or loose wheel bearing; broken, worn, or disconnected brake spring; parking brake engaged or out of adjustment; parking brake cable stuck; and malfunctioning master brake cylinder.

brake problem(brakes fade) - Braking power of a car lessens as the brakes remain applied. Possible causes include: malfunctioning master brake cylinder, linings only partially contacting braking surface, fluid vapor lock, and brake drums and/or rotors too thin causing excessive heat build up. See also brake problem(brakes weak) and brake fade.

brake problem(brakes grab) - Brake shoe linings tend to bind up as they contact a brake drum. Possible causes include: brake shoes worn out of adjustment, and linings become grease-soaked.

brake problem(brakes lock) - Brake shoes tend to stick against a braking surface causing skidding. It needs to be corrected right away to avoid further damaging brake components. Possible causes include: shoes out of adjustment and/or worn down to metal; unequal brake line pressure, retraction springs, and anchor pin adjustments, and car weight distribution (worn/broken suspension equipment). See also brake problem(brakes locked).

brake problem(brakes locked) – Brake linings get stuck against a braking surface. This most commonly happens when brake shoes get out of adjustment, worn down to metal, or too hot. When lockup occurs, try moving the car backwards momentarily. If this doesn't work let the brakes cool. If they are still frozen, the brake drum(s) will have to be pulled, and the problem corrected. Never drive with locked brakes.

brake problem(brakes rattle) – See sound(rattling-7).

brake problem(brakes screech) – Brake linings emit a harsh high-pitched sound every time brakes are applied. It is usually caused when brake linings, worn away to the metal backing plates, contact the braking surfaces. Linings in this condition need to be replaced immediately and rotors and drum checked to see if they need resurfacing.

brake problem(brakes squeak) – Brakes emits a sharp high-pitched sound when applied. Possible causes include: linings covered with oil, brake fluid, grease, or dirt; linings damaged due to heat, and/or defect; linings wrong size or type; loose brake parts; and rough and/or uneven braking surfaces.

brake problem(brakes squeal) – Brake linings emit a prolonged high-pitched sound upon contacting a braking surface. Possible causes include: linings soaked with grease, oil, or brake fluid; glazed linings; linings worn down to metal mounting surface; spring steel wear sensors contacting braking surface due to worn pads or shoes; brake component(s) improperly installed, brake drum and shoe diameters different; and pads vibrating (front disc).

brake problem(brakes weak) – Brakes do not slow car down quick enough. Possible causes include: front or rear brake line fluid pressure gone, air in lines, brake shoes and/or pads oil or grease soaked, and faulty brake master cylinder.

brake problem(car dives) – Car's front end moves rapidly downward upon applying the brakes. It is usually due to brakes grabbing too quickly. Possible causes include: reversed primary and secondary brake shoes, and shoes out of adjustment, incorrect anchor pin location, and excess front brake pressure due to clogged proportioning valve. See also brake problem(brakes grab).

brake problem(lining wear uneven) – Linings do not wear evenly. Possible causes include: grease or oil on linings, brake drum scoring, linings out of adjustment, anchor pin in wrong position, linings are wrong size, and brake drum machined too large in diameter for linings.

brake problem(pedal pushing) – Brake pedal oscillates when pressed. Possible causes include: warped rotor and/or brake drum, non-parallel rotor friction surfaces, and non-circular drum surfaces.

brake problem(pulls to one side) – Car pulls to one side upon applying the brakes. It is primarily due to wheel brakes generating different coefficients of friction. Possible causes include: brake linings covered with grease or oil, brake drum scoring, and improper tire pressures, corroded piston in wheel cylinder and/or brake caliper, and faulty metering valve. See also brakes are pulling to the right, and brakes are pulling to the left.

brake problem(power braking lost) – Power brake equipped car loses its power braking effect. Brakes feel sluggish or more like manual brakes. Possible causes include: malfunctioning brake booster unit; and plugged, broken, and/or disconnected vacuum line.

brake problem(power braking lost after startup) – Power brake loses its effect after startup, but then regains it when car is started again. Possible causes include: sticking or faulty vacuum check valve in brake booster supply line.

brake problem(rotor grooves) – Disc brake rotor develops deep grooves. Possible causes include: brake caliper improperly mounted, rusted or corroded caliper parts, caliper pistons sticking, and use of poor quality pads.

brakes pull – See brake problem(brakes pull).

brake reaction rod – See strut rod.

brake rebuild – Process used to overhaul a brake system to return it to normal operating condition. Work typically consists of: inspecting braking system operation; inspecting and/or replacing brake linings, brake cylinders, and fluid seals; bleeding brake lines; and adjusting newly installed parts.

brake reline – Brake system overhauled by installing new brake shoes or new linings on existing brake shoes or pads. Most car owners replace brake shoes. Old ones are turned in for recycling. New brake pads are commonly used as they are not generally recycled when they wear out.

brake rotor – Circular metal disc used to provide a braking surface for brake pads. It is constructed with two flat machined surfaces and attached to a wheel hub. A brake caliper straddles the rotor and presses brake pads against the flat rotor surfaces when the brake pedal is pushed.

brake rotor parallelism – Degree to which a front disc brake's two rotor braking surfaces are parallel to each other. If they are not, a pulsating

sensation can be sent up the steering column and felt in the brake pedal.
brakes are dragging – See brake problem(brakes drag).
brakes are grabbing – See brake problem(brakes grab).
brakes are locking up – See brake problem(brakes lock).
brakes are pulling to the left – Condition created opposite to: brakes are pulling to the right.
brakes are pulling to the right – Condition created when a car veers to the right upon applying the brakes. It is caused by brakes on the right side of a car generating greater friction, and thus slowing down the right wheels faster. It is usually due to uneven or rougher braking surfaces on the right side. See also brake test(pulling to one side).
brakes are shot – Brake linings worn down to the metal mounting surfaces.
brakes are spongy – See brake pedal(spongy).
brakes are squealing – See brake problem(brakes squeal).
brake screeching – See brake problem(brakes screech).
brake service – Service work performed on a brake system. It typically includes: inspecting front and rear wheel brakes for proper operation, locating possible problems, and performing certain repair, maintenance, and replacement work. Most shops offer to do the following for a certain rate: install new disc pads and shoes, resurface front rotors and rear brake drums, if necessary, adjust emergency brake, and repack front wheel bearings. Other problems, like leaking brake cylinders, air in the brake lines, and bad wheel bearings, will cost extra to remedy.
brakes grab – See brake problem(car dives), and brake problem(brakes grab).
brake shield – Circular metal covering mounted behind brake shoes. It meshes with a brake drum, protects brake parts, and provide a surface for attaching them.
brake shoe – Curved metal plate covered on one side with a brake lining material. It slows car movement by causing friction between a brake lining and braking surface. See also brake pad.
brake shoe(leading) – Brake shoe positioned to face the front of a car. It usually has a longer brake lining surface since it provides more of the braking.
brake shoe(primary) – See brake shoe(leading).
brake shoe(secondary) – See brake shoe(trailing).
brake shoe(self energizing) – Brake shoe designed to develop a wedging effect, when applied. It increases the braking force applied by a wheel cylinder.
brake shoe(trailing) – Brake shoe positioned to face the rear of a car. It usually has a shorter brake lining and provides less of the braking effort.
brake shoe action – The way brake shoes operate.
brake shoe grinder – Machine used to sand the surface of brake shoe linings. It is used: when new linings have been installed on shoes, if shoes are bent or warped, or if drum has been machined slightly larger in diameter.
brake shoe heel – Lower brake shoe end designed to rest on an anchor pin.
brake shoe toe – Upper brake shoe end located opposite the anchor pin.
brakes locked – See brake problem(brakes locked).
brakes need to be relined – Condition created when a car's brake linings are worn mostly away requiring replacement or relining.
brake spring – Spring used to return brake shoes together when they are no longer used for braking. Most brake shoe sets use two springs.
brake swept area – Area of braking surface contacted by brake linings.
brake system – Assemblage of parts used to provide a means for stopping a car in motion. The parts typically consist of: a brake pedal, master cylinder, brake lines, differential valve, metering valve, proportioning valve, brake cylinders, brake shoes and/or disc pads, brake drums and/or rotors, and emergency brake linkage.
brake temperature – Temperature of brake linings and surrounding parts. If it becomes too high, brake linings, drums or rotors, and brake fluid can be damaged, and tires can catch fire. Factors affecting brake temperature include: car weight, speed, adjustment of brakes, type of linings, balance of braking, driver braking habits, and proper operation of brake parts.
brake test – See car service tip(brake test).
brake unit – See brake booster unit.
brake wear – Amount of brake lining worn away from use. Observed lining wear will indicate if a brake is operating properly. Brake shoe linings worn thin in the middle indicate: shoes are too small for drum, or are warped. Shoe linings worn thin at one end usually indicate shoes not adjusted properly for wear.
brake wheel cylinder – See brake cylinder.
braking – Process used to slow down a car with its braking system.
braking distance – Distance required to stop a car without losing traction, once the brakes are applied. At 60 mph, the following approximate braking distances apply: dry pavement-350 feet, gravel-550 feet, wet pavement-600 feet, packed snow-800 feet, ice or sleet-1800 feet. An important point to remember is that as a car's speed doubles, the braking distance at least

triples.
braking efficiency - Brake system's ability to effectively stop a car in motion under different driving conditions.
brain bucket - Safety helmet.
Bramwell - American car produced from 1902-1904 by Bramwell Motor Co. in Massachusetts, and Springfield Automobile Co. in Ohio.
Bramwell-Robinson - American car produced in 1899-1901 by John T. Robinson & Co. in Massachusetts.
branch road - Secondary road linked to a main road, highway, or freeway. See also arterial.
Brasie - American car produced from 1914-1917 by Brasie Motor Car Co. in Minnesota.
Brasie Truck - American truck produced from 1915-1916.
brass era car - Car generally built from 1913-1919. See also vintage car, contemporary car, milestone car, special interest car, classic car, contemporary classic car, pre-war car, and post-war car.
braze - See brazing.
Brazier - American car produced from 1902-1904 by H. Bartol Brazier in Pennsylvania.
brazing - Process used to join two equal or dissimilar metal surfaces together with a metal alloy material melting above 800 degrees Fahrenheit and below the melting point of parent metals. It produces a stronger joint than soldering and equals some welded joints. Brazing process has been around a long time being used by jewelers, blacksmiths, tradesmen, aerospace industry, etc. See also brazing alloy.
brazing alloy - Metal alloy used in the brazing process. Most common type is brass, a mixture of copper and zinc. Many other types are available for joining a wide variety of metals together. Different chemical elements used include: copper, zinc, nickel, chromium, phosphorus, silver, gold, aluminum, silicon, and magnesium.
brazing flux - See flux(brazing).
brazing solder - See solder(hard).
brazing welding - See brazing. Also, it refers to brazing where more filler metal is used in a joint.
breach of contract - Contract violation created when a person has violated one or more of the clauses of a contract he has signed. An example would be a person who buys a new car and then does not maintain the car according to the contract provisions. Another example, would be a repair order in which the car owner agrees to pay for services performed by a repair shop and one of the two parties does not live up to the agreement. When such a violation occurs, the contract is breached and the clauses of the contract pertaining to contract violations come into play to allow the injured party recovery of his losses.
breach of warranty - Warranty violation created when a product or service violates one or more clauses of its respective warranty. Affected person then has specific rights that come into play.
breakdown - Condition created when a car can no longer be operated due to a mechanical or electrical malfunction.
breakdown tip - Useful information given to help someone deal with a car breakdown more knowledgeably, economically, efficiently, and/or safely. See also road situation tip.
breaker arm - See distributor point arm.
breaker cam - See distributor cam.
breakerless electronic ignition - Ignition system designed to operate and generate high voltage current to spark plugs without use of breaker points.
breaker plate - See distributor point plate.
breaker point arcing - See distributor point arcing.
breaker points - See distributor points.
breaker strip - Rubber strip applied on top of tire cord fabric.
break-in - See break in period.
breaking the bead - To separate a tire bead from its contact with a wheel rim. Special bead breaking equipment is used to perform the task. See also spreading the bead.
break in period - Length of time and/or mileage specified by a manufacturer for the purpose of smoothing the rough edges of new or reconditioned moving parts to properly conform to each other and reduce friction. During this period, certain car operation and maintenance procedures are followed. One of the most important aspects of a break-in is properly seating an engine's pistons and rings against the cylinder walls. See also car maintenance tip(break in period).
breather cap - Special cap installed somewhere on a valve cover to allow accumulating crankcase gases to be vented off into the atmosphere.
breathing capacity - See volumetric efficiency.
breath test - Test used to determine the percentage of alcohol in a person's blood, usually by exhaling into a breath testing device. It is often used to

test drivers suspected of intoxication. A driver has the right to refuse
such a test, but risks getting his license suspended.
Brecht – American car produced from 1901-1903 by Brecht Automobile Co. in
Missouri.
Breedlove, Craig – He set a world land speed record in 1963, 1964, and 1965
driving a Spirit of America J-47 Jet (1963 and 1964), and Spirit of America
Sonic 1. Speeds were 407.5, 526.3, and 600.6 mph.
Breedlove, Lee – She was Craig Breedlove's wife and is known for setting the
fastest land speed record for a woman in 1965. She reached 308.6 mph in the
Spirit of America Sonic 1 after her husband set a record of 600.6 mph at the
Bonneville Salt Flats in Utah.
Breer Steam Car – American steam car produced in 1900.
Breeze & Lawrence – American car produced in 1905.
Bremac – American car produced in 1932.
Brennan – American car produced from 1907-1908 by Brennan Motor Mfg. Co. in
New York.
Brew-Hatcher – American car produced from 1904-1905 by Brew & Hatcher Co. in
Ohio.
Brewster – American car produced from 1915-1925 and 1934-1936 by Brewster &
Co. in New York, and Springfield Mfg. Co. in Massachusetts respectively.
Brewster-Knight – See Brewster (1915-1925).
Brg – Abbreviation for British racing queen.
BRG – Abbreviation for bearing.
Bricklin – Canadian car line produced from 1974-1975 by Bricklin Motor Corp.
in New Brunswick.
Bricklin, Malcolm – He was heir to a national hardware store chain, and helped
bring the Suburu line of cars to the U.S. in the early 1970s. He also
started a company in the early 1970s to build a gull wing fiberglass car,
known as the Bricklin. Only a few were produced in New Brunswick, Canada
before the venture failed.
brickyard – Nickname used for Indianapolis race track when it was surfaced
with brick in 1909.
bridge – Structure built over a river, roadway, canyon, etc. to provide a
means for people or traffic to cross.
Bridgeport – American car produced in 1922.
Bridgestone – Line of tires originally produced in Japan, but now also
produced in the United States.
Briggs – American car produced in 1933.
Briggs-Detroiter – American car produced from 1910-1918.
Briggs & Stratton – American car produced from 1919-1923 by Briggs & Stratton
Co. in Wisconsin.
Brighton – American car produced in 1896 and 1914.
brights are on – Car operated with its lights on high beam.
Brightwood – American car produced in 1912.
bring back – See residual value.
bringing a suit against the dealer – To file a suit against a car dealer for
alleged wrongdoing.
Brintel – American car produced in 1912.
Briscoe – American car produced from 1914-1921 by Briscoe Motor Corp. in
Michigan.
Briscoe, Benjamin – He founded the Briscoe Manufacturing Company in 1887 and
was involved in the organization of several other auto companies. He
organized the United States Motor Company, a coalition of some 130 other
firms, in 1912.
Briscoe, Frank – Founder and president of Brush Runabout Company.
Bristol – American car produced in 1902-1903 and 1908. Also, a British car
line produced from 1947 to date by Bristol Cars Ltd. (1949 to date). Recent
models include: Britannia, Brigand, Beaufighter, and Beaufort.
British Motor Corporation – Company formed in 1952 by the merger of Austin and
Morris car manufacturers. It is called British Leyland today. The Austin
and Morris car names are still used today.
British Thermal Unit – English unit of heat measurement commonly used to
measure heat quantity. One BTU is the quantity of heat required to raise the
temperature of one pound of water one degree Fahrenheit. It is also equal to
252 calories.
brks – Abbreviation for brakes.
broadside – To strike the side of one car with the side of another.
Broc Electric – American electric car produced from 1909-1916 by Broc Carriage
& Wagon Co. in Ohio.
Brock – American car produced from 1920-1921.
Brock Six – Canadian car produced in 1921.
Brockville-Atlas – Canadian car produced from 1910-1915 by Brockville Atlas
Auto Co. in Ontario.
Brockway Truck – American truck produced in 1912.
Brodesser Truck – American truck produced in 1909.

Brogan – American car produced from 1946-1948 by B & B Specialty Co. in Ohio.
broke – Car sidelined out out of a competition due to mechanical failure.
broke down – Car rendered inoperable due to a mechanical malfunction.
broken piston – Piston damaged due to an engine malfunction. Damage symptoms include: cracks, vaporized hole in piston top, and rod pulled out of piston.
broken rings – Piston rings broke in one or more places around the circumference. Possible causes include: excessive advance, poor lubrication, ring sticking, and poor quality.
broker – Agent engaged in acting as an intermediary or middleman in: buying and selling products, negotiating contracts, etc.
brokerage – A broker's business or office.
Bronco – American car produced from 1966 to date by Ford Motor Co. in Michigan.
Bronco II – American car produced from 1983 to date by Ford Motor Co. in Michigan.
bronze – Metal alloy composed mostly of copper and tin.
Brook – American car produced from 1920-1921.
Brooklands Race Track – First racing circuit built especially for racing cars in 1907. It was located in Surrey, England. It was paved in concrete and the turns were banked.
Brooks – American car produced in 1908. Also, a Canadian steam car produced from 1923-1926 by Brooks Steam Motors Ltd. in Ontario. It was next in popularity to a Stanley steam car.
Brook-Spacke – American car produced from 1920-1921 by Spacke Machine & Tool Co. in Indiana..
Brougham – Limousine built with the driver's seat unenclosed. It also refers to an electrically powered car built like a coupe.
Brown – American car produced in 1899-1900, 1909, 1912, 1914, 1916, and 1922.
Brownie – American car produced from 1916-1917 by J.O. Carter in Missouri.
Brownie – Popular auxiliary transmission used on older trucks.
Browniekar – American car produced from 1908-1910.
Brown Steamer – American steam car produced in 1888.
Brown's Touring Cart – American car produced in 1898.
Brown-Burtt – American car produced in 1904.
Brownell – American car produced in 1910.
Brownie – American car produced in 1915.
Browniekar – American car produced from 1908-1910 by Omar Motor Co. in New York.
Brunn – American car produced from 1906-1910.
Brunner Truck – American truck produced in 1910.
Brunswick – American car produced in 1916.
brush – Electrical component made of carbon with a wire lead. It is used to transfer electrical current from a commutator, slip ring, or other rotating surface contacted. Motors, alternators, generators, and other devices commonly use from two to four brushes. Each brush is usually rectangular in shape.
brushed finish – Surface finished with a fine directional pattern. It is usually done on aluminum, stainless steel, or chrome plate, but can be simulated in plastic.
brush holder – Device used to hold a brush in place against rotating surfaces. Brushes are most common in starters, DC generators, and alternators.
brush holder(grounded) – Brush holder connected to ground. It provides a ground connection for generator windings.
brush holder(insulated) – Brush holder insulated from ground. It holds a brush transferring voltage out of the generator or into a starter.
brushes – See brush.
Brush Runabout – American car produced from 1907-1913 by Brush Motor Car Co. and Brush Runabout Co., both in Michigan.
Brush Truck – American car produced in 1907.
Bryan – American steam car produced from 1918-1923 by Bryan Steam Motors in Indiana. Six were made.
Bryan, Jim – He won the Indianapolis 500 Race in 1958 driving an average of 133.8 mph in a Belond AP Special.
BS – Abbreviation for Bahamas found usually on an international license plate.
BT – Abbreviation for boattail.
BTC – See BTDC.
BTDC – Abbreviation for Before Top Dead Center. It is used to specify how many degrees before the top of a compression stroke a spark plug will ignite an air/fuel mixture. Larger number means a piston is further down in a cylinder when a fuel mixture is ignited. A higher number increases an engine's power, but also puts extra strain on the engine components.
BTU – Abbreviation for British Thermal Unit.
B type generator circuit – Common generator circuit associated with a regulator. Regulator resistance is inserted before current reaches generator field coils when regulator points are open. See also A type generator

circuit.
bubble - Last racing position in a qualifying line-up.
bubble balance - See tire balancer(static) and balance(static).
bubble balancer - Tool used to balance tires. It consists of a flat circular platform with a circular level in the center. A tire is balanced by laying it flat on the platform and attaching appropriate lead weights around the rim of a tire until the bubble indicator shows a tire is balanced or level. This method of tire balancing is not as popular or accurate as the spin balancing method used today.
Buck - American car produced in 1925.
Buckaroo - American car produced in 1957.
buckboard - Four wheeled wagon built with an open carriage and one or more seats mounted on a board floor. The floor ends rested directly on axles.
bucket - See bucket seat.
bucket seat - Seat designed for one passenger. It is often contoured to provide lateral support and usually reclines in different positions.
bucket tappet - Tappet shaped like an inverted bucket. It holds the base of a valve spring and provides a contact surface for a cam lobe.
Buckeye - American car produced from 1905-1917.
Buckeye Gas Buggy - American car produced in 1895.
bucking field coil - Field coil designed to contain a separate winding of wire wound in a reverse direction and shunted across armature coil leads. Its purpose is to help regulate generator voltage by opposing a normal magnetic field. The effect increases with speed enough so that at high speed it can cancel out the effect of residual field coil magnetism. See also reverse field winding, and generator(bucking field).
buckled plates - Warped or bent battery plates.
Buckles - American car produced in 1914.
buckle up - To fasten seat belts.
Buckmobile - American car produced from 1903-1905 by Buckmobile Co. (1903-1904), and Black Diamond Automobile Co. (1904-1905), both in New York.
bucks - Hundred dollar increments in the selling field. Also, it refers to racing prize money.
bucks up - To have plenty of money.
Buddie - American car produced in 1921.
Buddy - American car produced in 1925.
Budene - Synthetic rubber developed by Goodyear in 1961. It greatly increased tire life.
Buffalo - American car produced from 1900-1902 by Buffalo Automobile & Auto-Bi Co. in New York.
Buffalo Electric - American electric car produced from 1901-1906 and 1912-1915 by Buffalo Electric Vehicle Carriage Co., and Buffalo Electric Vehicle Co. respectively, both in New York.
buffer - Electric tool used to spin a buffing wheel.
buffeting - Repeated beating effect.
Buffington - American car produced in 1900.
buffing wheel - Circular flexible wheel covered with cloth, leather, fur, etc. It is used to polish a coating applied to a surface such as wax. See also buffer.
Buffman - American car produced in 1900.
Buffum - American car produced from 1901-1907 by H.H. Buffum & Co. in Massachusetts.
Bug - American car produced in 1914. Also, a name used for the Volkswagen Beetle car.
Bugati - One of the most successful lines of racing cars produced in history. Each car was made with precision parts. The first Bugati was produced in 1909 by Ettore Bugati, a talented designer. Unlike other racing cars of its time, the Bugati could be fitted with accessories for use on the road. Many of the cars are still around today with some on display in museums and others being driven occasionally in special events.
Bugati, Ettore - He produced one of the most successful racing car lines in history beginning in 1909.
Bugati Type 35 - Racing car produced in 1924. It was one of the most successful in history. It was powered by an 8 cylinder engine, yet unlike other racing cars of its day it could be retrofitted for use on the roads.
bug catcher - Air scoop used on a hood over a supercharger.
bug deflector - Screen or plexiglass panel mounted at the front edge of a hood to protect hood and/or radiator from build-up of insects. See also rock deflector.
Bugetta - American car produced beginning in 1969 by Bugetta in California.
Buggyaut - American car produced in 1909.
Buggycar - American car produced from 1907-1909 by Buggy-Car Co. in Ohio.
bug lights - See light(fog).
Bugmobile - American car produced in 1909.
bug screen - Screen mounted on the front of a car to minimize accumulation of

bugs and insects on car hood and radiator area.

Buick – American car line produced from 1903 to date by Buick Motor Car Co. now a division of General Motors in Michigan.

Buick, David Dunbar – He founded the Buick Manufacturing Company in 1902, the Buick manufacturing Company in 1903. His controlling interests were bought in 1904 by William Durant. He played an integral part in developing a method for applying enamel paint to cast iron surfaces, and perfected a valve-in-head engine.

Buick Motor Company – American manufacturing company formed in 1903.

built-in eye – Small circular window device mounted on the top of maintenance free batteries and used to display its state of charge by color. Green indicates a good state of charge, black indicates a discharged state, and yellow indicates battery replacement.

bulb – Glass housing designed to contain the filament of an incandescent electric light.

bulky cargo – Cargo material with large dimensions.

Bull Dog – American car produced in 1924.

bullet muffler – See muffler(bullet).

bullnosing – To replace a hood ornament with a smooth low profile metal strip.

bum a ride – To get a ride free of charge from another.

bumblebee(1) – Small foreign car.

bumblebee(2) – Potential car customers interested only in looking at all the new cars at the different dealerships.

bumble paint band – Band of paint usually located around the nose (grille) of a car.

bump – Upward wheel movement caused by a road irregularity.

bumper – Device used on the front and back of a car for absorbing some of the shock of a collision.

bumper bar – See bumper.

bumper clearance – Gap located between a car bumper and body panels.

bumper guards – Vertical protective bars mounted on a car bumper. They are usually made of metal or rubber.

bumper jack – Device used to raise one corner of a car for changing a tire. It attaches to a car's bumper.

bumping(1) – Sales tactic used to get a potential car customer to increase his offer on a car.

bumping(2) – Time trials which allow drivers having non-qualifying times a chance to produce a better time. If the time improves sufficiently, a qualifying driver can be bumped from the starting line-up.

bump steer – Slight steering wheel movement generated when wheels move up and down. Normal production cars have small amounts of front and rear bump steer.

bumpstick – Engine camshaft.

bump stops – Rubber stops mounted in various places in suspension systems to prevent metal to metal contact or limit movement of the various components.

bum ticket – Undeserved traffic ticket.

Bundy Steam Wagon – American steam car produced in 1895.

burden of proof – Legal requirement requiring the complaining party to prove the truth of the charges made.

Burdick – American car produced from 1909-1910 by Burdick Motor Co. in Wisconsin.

Burford – American car produced in 1916.

Burg – American car produced from 1910-1913 by L. Burg Carriage Co. in Illinois.

Burman, Bob – He set a world land speed record of 141.4 mph in 1911 driving a Benz 4 Cylinder Blitzen Benz.

burn – See combustion.

burned up a camshaft – To damage a camshaft beyond repair. Possible causes include: poor cam design, soft cam metal, use of oil lacking in extreme pressure protection. A cam failure requires tearing down an engine to remove all the cam metal particles, replace all worn parts, and thoroughly clean all oil passageways.

burning out – To take off fast enough from rest for drive tires to lose traction. On pavement, the tires squeal and leave rubber marks behind. Burning out is hard on tires and the driveline and may make the car difficult to control.

burning rubber – To break tire traction on pavement to leave rubber marks.

burning up the clutch – To overheat the clutch friction linings and metal disc due to excessive slippage or slippage under pressure. Heat destroys the friction material, distorts the disc, and may damage the flywheel and pressure plate surfaces. The only remedy is a new clutch plate, and other affected parts.

burnout – To spin rear tires rapidly in puddles of liquid bleach. It cleans the tire tread and heats it up for maximum traction. It is performed just before a race.

Burns – American car produced from 1908-1911 by Burns Bros. in Maryland.
Burroughs – American car produced in 1914.
Burrowes – American car produced from 1905-1908 by E.T. Burrowes Co. in Maine.
Burrows – American car produced in 1914.
Burtt – American car produced from 1917-1923.
Bus – American car produced in 1917.
bus – Large vehicle designed to carry many passengers.
Bush – American car produced from 1916-1924 by Bush Motor Co. in Illinois. It was a mail-order car.
Bushbury – American car produced in 1897.
bushing(1) – Hollow cylinder used as a bearing for a shaft. Bushings are made out of softer metal than the shaft they support. They are used for light or intermittent loads. Some have lubrication impregnated in the metal while others are lubricated with grease or oil. Most small motors use a bushing at one end. Starter and blower motors are examples.
bushing(2) – Shady practice used by a car salesman where the price given for a trade-in is set and then later lowered, and/or a deposit is made and the car being sold is later increased in price.
business district – Territory comprised primarily of businesses fronting on the roads within the district.
business license – License granted by a state licensing board allowing a business to operate. Licenses can be revoked for many reasons including: unfitness, filing false information, violating license rules and regulations, not furnishing required bonds, charging excessive interest, false advertising, etc.
Bushnell – American car produced in 1912.
Busser – American car produced in 1915.
buster – Low sales commission.
bustleback – See body style(bustleback).
busy road – Road with heavy traffic.
butane – Gaseous methane series hydrocarbon compound derived from natural gas or produced in the process of refining petroleum products. It has a melting and boiling point of -217 and 31 degrees Fahrenheit respectively. Butane is an ingredient in LP gas.
Butler – American car produced in 1914.
butterfly – Two pieces of wood joined together in the shape of a cross and used to carry clay.
butterfly valve – Pivoting metal plate used to control the flow of air into a carburetor. It is so named for resembling a butterfly's wings. See also choke plate and throttle plate.
buttons – Push button transmission equipped car.
buy at once – Sales tactic used to discourage comparison shopping. A number of techniques are used by salesman.
buying on time – Selling tactic used to increase sales. It allows people to purchase merchandise by making regular installment payments until paid off. Money is usually loaned. Loans today are available from many sources. They include: credit cards, saving and loan institutions, banks, finance companies, etc.
Buzmobile – American car produced in 1917.
b/w – Abbreviation for black and white.
bye run – Single run made during race eliminations to even up the number of runs each contestant makes. They are made when an uneven number of car are qualified to enter the next level of competition.
by pass – Valve used to divert the flow of a liquid or gas through an alternate passageway.
by-pass air bleed – See idle by-pass air bleed.
bypass hose – Engine cooling system hose used to circulate coolant in an engine block while the thermostat is closed.
bypass oil filter – See oil filter(bypass).
bypass valve – See thermal valve(2).
Byrider – American electric car produced from 1908-1909 by Byrider Electric Auto Co. in Ohio.
Byron – American car produced in 1912.
Byron, Red – He became the NASCAR Grand National Champion in 1949.
by the numbers – To tune-up a car and/or set any of the engine controls according to the manufacturer's specifications.
BZT – American car produced in 1914.

C

C - Abbreviation for Cuba found usually on an international license plate.
CA - See API service category(CA).
cab(1) - Car available for public hire.
cab(2) - Truck's enclosed passenger compartment.
cabover - Tractor built with the engine underneath the cab. See also conventional.
cabriolet - Early car built with a roof that folded down like today's convertibles. See also CB(4).
cadence braking - Method used to quickly slow down a car without locking up the wheels by quickly and repeatedly hitting the brake pedal.
Cadillac - American Car line produced from 1903 to date by Cadillac Automobile Co. (1903-1905), and Cadillac Motor Car Co. (1905 on), both in Michigan.
Cadillac Automobile Company - American car manufacturing company formed in 1903.
cadmium test - Procedure used to test individual cell voltages of a battery with inside cell connectors. Tester consists of cadmium tube prods placed in electrolyte solution of each cell. A voltmeter is used to read the difference in cell voltages.
CAFE - Abbreviation for corporate average fuel economy.
Calais - American car produced from 1965 to date by Cadillac Motor Car Co. in Michigan. Also, an American car produced from 1980 to date by Oldsmobile Division of General Motors Corp. in Michigan.
calendar - The scheduled order, date, and time of court cases.
calibrate - To determine or adjust the measuring scale of an instrument in order to achieve an accurate read-out.
calibration shim - Shim of a specified thickness.
Caliente - American car produced from 1957-1964 by Mercury Division of Ford Motor Co. in Michigan.
California - American car produced in 1913.
California Cyclecar - American car produced in 1914.
Californian - American car produced from 1920-1921 by California Motor Car Corp. in California.
California Top - Solid top designed for attaching to a car in the event of inclement weather. The top had windows. It was popular on early cars.
caliper(1) - Adjustable tool used to measure inside and outside diameters, and then compare it to a measuring scale to determine actual distance.
caliper(2) - See caliper assembly.
caliper alignment - Alignment made to a caliper assembly so all friction pad surfaces maintain the same clearance.
caliper assembly - Disc brake cylinder assembly designed to sit on top of a rotor and press two brake pads against it. It consists primarily of: caliper housing, two pistons and seals, rubber boots, and fluid inlet and transfer fittings.
caliper housing - Cast metal structure used to contain the various caliper components necessary to force two disc pads against a rotor.
caliper splash shield - Metal cover positioned over the top of a caliper assembly. It is used to help keep dirt, and debris from migrating into a caliper assembly.
Call - American car produced in 1911.
Caloric - American car produced in 1904.
Calvert - American car produced in 1927.
cam(1) - Curved teardrop shaped surface found on a camshaft and used to move another component as the shaft rotates. The top of the teardrop shape is the farthest point from the centerline of the shaft, and represents the area on the cam where the greatest deflection occurs. On a camshaft, each cam opens a valve for a specified duration. The design of a cam on a normal engine is usually a compromise between quiet operation and efficiency. On racing engines, where noise is not important, cams are shaped to open a valve fast and high, keep it open longer, then close it rapidly. Racing cams cause an engine to idle poorly and wear out faster. Cam shape is defined by: heel diameter, ramp, flank, toe, and lift.
   Most of a cam's wear occurs on the lift side of the lobe.
cam(1-harmonic shape) - See cam(triple curve).
cam(1-multiple curve) - Cam constructed with many different curves. It provides maximum flexibility in controlling valve movement.
cam(1-multi sine wave) - See cam(multiple curve).
cam(1-parabolic) - See cam(multiple curve).

cam(1-triple curve) – Cam constructed with three curved surfaces on the lift portion. It is used on older engines with simpler lifting requirements.

cam(2) – See camshaft.

cam angle – See dwell angle. See also cam lobe displacement angle.

Camaro – American car produced from 1967 to date by Chevrolet Division of General Motors Corp. in Michigan.

camber – See wheel alignment angle(camber).

camber adjustment eccentric – Adjustable device located near an upper ball joint for regulating a tire's camber angle. See also wheel alignment angle(camber).

cam clearance ramp – Portion of a cam's profile located on the lower portion of each cam flank. It is designed to take up any play in tappets before actual valve opening begins.

cam deceleration ramp – Portion of a cam's profile located on either side of a cam nose. It is the rounded part of the nose curving into the cam flank.

cam eater – Engine known for wearing out camshafts prematurely.

camelback – Strip of rubber material, with a tread pattern, bonded to a tire's worn tread area. Surface is prepared by truing and roughening it. See also tire(recap).

camel's hair cloth – Material used to cover friction surfaces of brakes linings. It was employed before the introduction of asbestos linings.

camera case finish – Grainy leather-like finish used in car interiors. The name is derived from dark grained leathers used on expensive cameras.

Cameron – American car produced from 1902-1921.

cam felt – Small piece of grease-lubricated felt used to continuously lubricate a distributor cam surface. It is usually mounted on a small bracket assembly.

cam flank – Elongated portion of a cam's profile located along either side of the cam toe. It determines how long the valves stay open wide.

cam follower – See tappet.

cam heel – Portion of a cam's profile located opposite the can toe.

cam heel diameter – Diameter of circular portion of a cam.

cam leading flank – Cam flank used to open a valve.

cam lift – Distance measured from outside the circular core of a cam shape to the top or toe of a cam. It determines how wide a valve opens.

cam lobe – See cam.

cam lobe displacement angle – Angle measured between an engine cylinder's intake and exhaust cam lobe centerlines. Changing this angle affects the amount of valve overlap.

cam nose – See cam toe.

Campbell – American car produced from 1918-1919 by Campbell Motor Car Co. in New York.

Campbell, Donald – He set a world land speed record of 403.1 mph in 1964 driving a Bluebird Gas Turbine.

Campbell, Malcolm – He set a world land speed record in 1924, 1925, 1927, 1928, 1931, 1932, 1933, and 1935. Cars driven were a Sunbeam V-12 (1924 and 1925), Napier V-12 Bluebird, Napier-Campbell Bluebird, and Bluebird V-12 (1931, 1932, 1933, and 1935). Speeds were 146.2, 150.8, 174.9, 207.0, 246.1, 254.0, 272.5, and 301.1 mph.

camper – Motor vehicle or trailer equipped for camping out. See also camper shell.

camper shell – Enclosed structure built to mount on a truck bed. It contains items for camping such as: beds, stove, heater, ice box, sink, etc.

cam plate – See distributor cam plate.

cam ramp – Lower side of the teardrop portion of a cam shape. It determines how quickly and smoothly the valve opens and closes.

camshaft – Metal shaft fabricated with a number of cams, or elliptical lobes of hardened metal for operating valves and some other operating parts of an internal combustion engine. It is driven by and rotates the same direction as an engine crankshaft through gearing and a drive chain (or belt). In four stroke engines, a camshaft completes one revolution (opening and closing all valves once) for every two crankshaft revolutions.

A worn camshaft can cause such engine problems as: irregular engine cranking speed, hard starting, and fluctuation in compression check readings when repeated.

camshaft(big) – Camshaft designed with long duration cam lobes.

camshaft(flat tappet hydraulic) – Camshaft designed with lobe contact controlled by hydraulic lifters.

camshaft(flat tappet mechanical) – Camshaft designed with lobe contact controlled by adjustable rocker arms.

camshaft(full) – See camshaft(high lift).

camshaft(high lift) – Camshaft designed with longer intake and exhaust valve cam lobes to permit valves to open higher, faster, and longer.

camshaft(modified) – Any camshaft design modified from original intake and exhaust cam lobe profiles. Modifications impart certain desired engine performance characteristics. In general, cam lobe modifications remove torque from one end of an engine's power curve and add it to the other.

camshaft(performance) - Camshaft modified to provide increased engine performance over a stock camshaft.

camshaft(race) - See camshaft(high lift).

camshaft(roller tappet mechanical) - Camshaft designed with lobe contact controlled by rollers mounted on the valve lifter ends.

camshaft(semi race) - Camshaft modified with cam lift approaching a race camshaft.

camshaft(three quarter) - Camshaft designed with cam lift equal to 75 percent of a race camshaft.

camshaft advance - Camshaft installed so it causes valves to open and close a specified number of degrees sooner than normal. It increases cylinder pressure, improves mid-range performance, but decreases top-end power. Advancing a camshaft requires advancing ignition timing a like amount. See also camshaft retard.

camshaft bearings - Bearings used to support a camshaft. They are usually one piece insert types. Some cylinder heads have no camshaft bearings, but instead rely on the softer aluminum metal of bearing blocks.

camshaft gear - Gear mounted on the front of a camshaft. A steel roller chain connects the camshaft gear to a crankshaft gear to maintain the proper valve timing relationship during engine operation. See also camshaft pulley.

camshaft phasing - See camshaft timing.

camshaft pulley - Serrated pulley mounted on the front of a camshaft. A heavy duty serrated belt connects the pulley to a crankshaft pulley to maintain the proper valve timing relationship during engine operation. See also cog belt and camshaft gear.

camshaft retard - Camshaft installed so it causes valves to open and close a specified number of degrees later than normal. It decreases cylinder pressure and mid-range performance, but improves top-end power. Retarding camshaft timing requires retarding ignition timing a like amount. See also camshaft advance.

camshaft sprocket - See camshaft gear.

cam swap - To remove an engine cam and replace it with another usually modified cam.

cam timing - Rotating relationship established between a camshaft and a crankshaft, allowing intake and exhaust valves to open and close at the proper time.

cam timing belt - See timing belt.

cam toe - The top or tapered end of a cam's profile opposite the cam heel.

cam trailing flank - Cam flank used to close a valve.

cam wear - Amount of change in machined surface dimensions from new. Cam wear is more of a problem in today's cars because they are asked to work harder. Increased wear factors include: higher valve spring pressure, hotter oil and engine temperatures, new cam profiles, and metal alloys used. One of the least expensive ways to improve cam life is by regularly changing oil every 3-5,000 miles.

cam weight base - See distributor cam plate.

can - Racing fuel using a high percentage of nitromethane.

Canada - American car produced in 1900-1901 and 1911.

Canadian - Canadian car produced in 1921.

Canadian Baby Car - Canadian car produced in 1914.

Canadian Motors - Firm engaged in building various electric vehicles in Canada in the early 1900s.

canister purge system - See vapor recovery system.

Cannon - American car produced in 1902-1926 by Burtt Mfg. Co. in Michigan.

cant - Tilt or angle of an object. Cant of a wheel is the angle of a wheel. It also refers to a slang language among beggars and thieves. See also caster and camber.

can't get it started - Inability to start a car engine.

Cantone - American car produced in 1905.

Cantono - American electric car produced from 1904-1907 by Cantono Electric Tractor Co. in Ohio.

CAP - Abbreviation for clean air package. See also emission control system(combustion-ignition/induction).

cap(1) - Highest feasible sales commission for a car.

cap(2) - Tractor roof.

capac - Abbreviation for capacity.

capacitive discharge - See ignition system(capacitor discharge).

capacitor - Electrical device used to store electrical energy. Capacitors are commonly used in a primary ignition circuit to provide a clean cutoff of current when the distributor points open, and absorb surges of high voltage electricity emanating from an ignition coil and moving toward distributor points. It minimizes arcing across contact points when they separate and thereby greatly increases their life. Though commonly replaced with points, capacitors are usually fine and can last the life of a car. Capacitors are also used to help minimize electrical noise reaching car stereo systems. They can be thought of as electrical shock absorbers.

A bad or poorly grounded capacitor can cause: contact points to pit and burn after a short period of time (wrong size capacitor can also cause this), weak or no spark, and/or missing at high speeds. See also distributor point pitting.

cap electrode - High voltage spark plug cable terminal used in a distributor cap.

Capital - American car produced in 1902, 1912, and 1920.

cap latch - Latch used to attach a distributor cap to a distributor body. Some designs use an L-shaped rod, but most caps are held in place with flexible spring clips.

cap oiler - Small reservoir passageway used to meter lubricant to a bushing or bearing surface. It usually has a hinged cap to keep oil in and dirt and other contaminants out. The passageway may or may not have an absorbent material in it. It is commonly found on older DC generators and starter motors.

cap ply - Belt of rubber used between a tire's belts and the tread.

Capri - American car produced from 1960-1986 by Mercury Division of Ford Motor Co. in Michigan.

Caprice - American car produced from 1965 to date by Chevrolet Division of General Motors Corp. in Michigan.

Caps - American car produced in 1905.

captain's chair - Plush bucket seat used in vans. Features include: reclining backrest, floor swiveling, and armrests.

captive agent - See exclusive agent.

car - Any vehicle supported on wheels. The term is derived from the ancient Celtic term for wagon or cart.

car accident - See accident.

car ailment - Car problem caused by some mechanical or electrical malfunction.

Caravan - American car produced from 1984 to date by Dodge Division of Chrysler Corp. in Michigan.

caravan - A group of vehicles traveling together.

Caravelle - American car produced from 1980 to date by Plymouth Division of Chrysler Corp. in Michigan.

carb - See carburetor.

carb cleaner - Compound used to clean the air passageway of a carburetor. Also, it refers to a liquid compound used to immerse carburetor parts in to clean all the internal passageways.

car body - See auto body.

Carbon - American car produced in 1902.

carbon - Common nonmetallic element characterized by being a good conductor of electricity. It also forms into a hard and/or soft black material in those parts of an engine where fuel combustion and exhaust gases occur. Such places include: combustion chamber, spark plug tips, under piston rings, under valve heads, and in an exhaust system.

carbon arc torch - Torch used to create intense heat electrically. It consists of two carbon electrodes separated by a small air gap. When energized, electric current flows down one electrode and jumps the air gap to the other electrode creating intense heat.

carbon and valve work - See con game(carbon and valve work).

carbon build-up - See carbon deposit.

carbon deposit - Carbon material deposited in different parts of an engine and exhaust system as a result of the combustion process. If combustion chambers have excessive build-up, the only sure cure is removing and cleaning the head(s). It's also a good idea to do a valve job and valve stem seal replacement at the same time. Latest findings indicate carbon deposits may increase fuel economy slightly by increasing compression ratio and insulating chamber against heat loss. Engines with significant carbon build-up in the combustion chambers often lose significant fuel economy when scraped clean.

carbon dioxide - Gas characterized by being colorless, odorless, non-combustible, and about 1.5 times as heavy as air. It is the most common oxide of carbon. Common occurrences include: during decay processes or when carbon bearing fuels are burned. See also air.

carbon monoxide - Gas characterized by being colorless, tasteless, odorless, and highly poisonous. It is commonly produced by the incomplete combustion of gasoline hydrocarbons and is always present in car exhaust. A concentration of 1/2 of 1 percent can cause death in less than 2 minutes. A poorly tuned car can emit CO concentrations of 3-7 percent, indicating how dangerous car exhaust can be in a confined place. A leaky exhaust system can cause migration of the gas into a car. Symptoms of carbon monoxide poisoning include: headaches, drowsiness, and nausea. It is explosive in the right concentrations, and makes a good fuel, burning with a pale blue flame.

carbon monoxide poisoning - See carbon monoxide.

carbon pile tester – Heavy duty variable resistor used to simulate a steady electrical load. It is commonly used to determine how well a battery holds a charge. See also car service tip(battery load test).

carbon residue – By-product of an incomplete combustion process created when oxygen is limited. It is derived from a fuel's gum content and its heavier fractions.

carbon tracking – Small conductive path of carbon formed in one or more hairline cracks of a distributor cap. Such paths can cause improper routing of high voltage and resultant misfiring.

carborundum – Hard abrasive substance composed of silicon carbide and used in grinding wheels, and stones.

carbs – Carburetors.

carburetor – Fuel and air metering device used to transform liquid gasoline into fuel vapor, mix it with the proper amount of air, and then supply it to engine cylinders in the proper proportions needed for combustion. Because an engine requires fuel vapor to run and a carburetor meters liquid fuel, no carburetor is highly efficient in metering vapor into an engine. It has been estimated that 60-70 percent of the heat energy in gasoline is not transformed into power even with the best carburetor designs. In general, about 1/3 of a fuel's energy becomes usable power, 1/3 becomes exhaust heat, and 1/3 is dissipated as heat into the engine's cooling system.
In general, a carburetor will efficiently and economically run an engine under different conditions if it contains the following circuits in good working order: low speed (idle), high speed (main), power, accelerator pump, float, and choke.

carburetor(adapter type) – Carburetor designed to meter gasoline and LPG gas. It is usually a conventional gasoline carburetor retrofitted to allow switching between gasoline and LPG gas.

carburetor(air valve) – Carburetor built with an air inlet valve controlled by a weight or spring. The valve opens according to engine demand. See also air valve, carburetor(constant depression), and carburetor(constant vacuum).

carburetor(blow through) – Carburetor designed to withstand pressure from a supercharger or turbocharger.

carburetor(center) – Carburetor mounted in the middle of an intake manifold between a front and rear carburetor. See also carburetor(front) and carburetor(rear).

carburetor(clean air) – Carburetor designed to provide more precise metering of fuel under different engine operating conditions. Various engine sensors and other controls are often used to directly or indirectly control fuel metering.

carburetor(constant depression) – See carburetor(air valve).

carburetor(constant vacuum) – See carburetor(air valve).

carburetor(double barrel) – Carburetor designed with two separate air passageways. Two barrel carburetors are of two types. One type uses both barrels to serve an entire engine's operating requirements. This carburetor will normally have each barrel serving half the engine cylinders. The other type uses one barrel to supply the engine's light to medium load requirements, and the other barrel to supply top speed or full throttle operation. In this design, each barrel feeds all the engine cylinders.

carburetor(downdraft) – Carburetor designed for air movement downward through the venturi area to the throttle plate. It allows a fuel mixture to reach an intake manifold regardless of air velocity. There is considerable flexibility in design. It is the most popular design for car engines.

carburetor(feedback) – Carburetor designed to meter fuel according to signals sent by an on-board computer monitoring various engine functions. The quantity of fuel metered is typically controlled by a device such as a mixture control solenoid.

carburetor(four barrel) – Carburetor designed with two primary and two separate secondary air passageways. It is common on larger V-8 engines.

carburetor(front) – One of two or more carburetors mounted on an intake manifold. It is positioned toward the front of the engine. See also carburetor(center) and carburetor(rear).

carburetor(multiple) – Engine equipped with two or more carburetors.

carburetor(rear) – One of two or more carburetors mounted on an intake manifold. It is positioned toward the rear of the engine. See also carburetor(center) and carburetor(front).

carburetor(sidedraft) – Carburetor designed for air movement sideways through the venturi area to the throttle plate. It is used where space is at a premium.

carburetor(single barrel) – Carburetor designed with one air passageway reaching the intake manifold. The one barrel serves all of an engine's driving requirements. They are common on 4 and 6 cylinder engines.

carburetor(spread bore) – Four barrel carburetor built with small primary and large secondary bore diameters. Small primary bores provide: good throttle response, air/fuel mixing, and better low to mid-range fuel economy and drivability. Large secondary bores provide good air/fuel flow to allow engine to develop higher horsepower when needed.

carburetor(triple) - Engine equipped with three carburetors.

carburetor(two barrel) - Carburetor designed with one primary and one secondary air passageway. It is common on smaller displacement car engines.

carburetor(updraft) - Carburetor designed for air movement upward through the venturi area to the throttle plate. It allows a carburetor to be placed lower on one side of an engine and to even have gravity feed of fuel. It was an early carburetor design that is not popular now.

carburetor airway - See carburetor barrel.

carburetor barrel - Specially shaped tube in the carburetor designed to mix air and gasoline vapor.

carburetor body - Overall carburetor unit. Carburetors typically have three pieces that make up a body. They include: carburetor top (air horn), main body, and throttle body.

carburetor circuit - Fuel passageway(s) and/or device(s) within a carburetor used to control the flow of fuel to a carburetor air passageway under different operating conditions. A typical carburetor usually has the following circuits: idle, acceleration, main, power, high speed, float, and choke.

carburetor circuit(accelerator pump) - Circuit used to briefly send additional fuel directly into a carburetor airway via a small pump when a throttle is rapidly opened. It is necessary because the rapid opening of a throttle causes an air/fuel mixture to momentarily go lean, developing a flat spot. The mixture goes lean because the fuel has more mass than air, and is not able to immediately catch up with increased air flow.

carburetor circuit(choke) - Circuit used to operate a movable butterfly type plate near the top of a carburetor for the purpose of increasing gas flow into an engine when cold. The choke causes this by restricting airflow into the carburetor throat which creates a higher vacuum sucking more fuel into an intake manifold. See also choke.

carburetor circuit(cruising) - See carburetor circuit(high speed).

carburetor circuit(float) - Circuit built in a carburetor to maintain a fuel reservoir at a constant level. It consists of: a reservoir to store fuel, a float and needle valve assembly to regulate fuel flow into the reservoir, and jets in the reservoir base to regulate fuel flow to the air passageway. There is usually an external sight glass for observing the fuel level. If the fuel level is below normal, the engine will tend to starve for fuel. If the level is too high, too much fuel will be sucked into the engine. See also float level.

carburetor circuit(high speed) - Circuit built in a carburetor to supply additional fuel to an engine running at high engine rpm. It is designed to supplement the fuel delivered by the main carburetor circuit. It primarily consists of those parts and controls regulating fuel flow into the main discharge nozzle in a carburetor airway.

carburetor circuit(idle) - See carburetor circuit(low speed).

carburetor circuit(low speed) - Circuit used to supply the proper amount of fuel to an engine at idle and slight off-idle conditions. It usually consists of: a fuel passageway leading from the float bowl, a fuel flow screw, a fuel-cut solenoid valve to stop fuel flow when an engine is stopped, an air bleed to mix air with the fuel, and an idle mixture screw to adjust the fuel flow rate below the throttle plate. This circuit controls the car's emissions at idle.
 In most carburetors, the idle system never stops feeding small quantities of fuel, even at high speed.

carburetor circuit(main) - Circuit used to supply the necessary amount of fuel to an engine beyond off-idle conditions. Fuel flows out through the main discharge nozzle when the airflow increases in the carburetor venturi.

carburetor circuit(power) - Circuit used to supply additional fuel or fuel and air to an engine when intake vacuum drops to zero (full throttle condition). On single barrel carburetors, it usually consists of some type of vacuum-operated power valve opening under zero vacuum to send additional fuel to the main discharge nozzle in the carburetor airway. On two barrel carburetors, extra fuel and air is supplied by opening a secondary throttle plate.

carburetor cleaner - Spray type cleaner formulated to dissolve grease, dirt, rust, varnish, etc. on a carburetor's outside surface, linkage, choke plate, and interior airway(s). See also carburetor cleaning solution.

carburetor cleaning solution - Solution formulated to quickly dissolve, grease, dirt, and gum deposits on all carburetor exterior surfaces and interior passageways. It is commonly sold in gallon containers with a parts tray for immersing carburetor parts. See also carburetor cleaner.

carburetor controls - Various controls mounted on a carburetor for controlling fuel flow in the air passageway. They include: choke, primary throttle, fast idle, secondary throttle, throttle position solenoid, and anti-stall dashpot.

carburetor fire - See engine problem(carburetor fire).

60
carburetor flooding

carburetor flooding - See engine problem(carburetor flooding).
carburetor fuel bowl vent line - Fuel vapor vent line running from a
   carburetor float bowl vent to a charcoal canister. It routes any vapors
   that build up in the carburetor bowl to a charcoal canister when the engine
   stops. See also purge line, vapor recovery system, and fuel tank vent line.
carburetor fuel standoff - See intake reversion.
carburetor heat - Heat supplied to an intake manifold area directly below a
   carburetor in order to improve fuel vaporization and distribution to the
   engine cylinders. See also heat riser valve.
carburetor icing - See engine problem(carburetor icing).
carburetor is not idling - See engine problem(not idling).
carburetor linkage - The various levers, shafts, cams, etc. mounted on a
   carburetor to control air and fuel flow into an engine under different load
   conditions. The choke and throttle plate linkage should never be lubricated
   since they operate best when dry. Oil will cause a build-up of contaminants.
   A good choke cleaner can be used to clean the various linkages.
carburetor problem - Condition created when a carburetor does not perform as
   designed. Common carburetor problems include: wrong float level, float
   leaking, air horn loose, defective fuel-cut solenoid, defective throttle
   position solenoid, faulty choke operation, wrong metering block gasket,
   accelerator pump out of adjustment, accelerator pump discharge nozzle plugged
   or wrong size, ruptured accelerator pump diaphragm, missing accelerator pump
   weight, wrong type or size air cleaner, needle valve and seat wrong size
   and/or stuck open, idle mixture screw(s) out of adjustment, vacuum lines
   improperly connected, carburetor parts with wrong numbers, over-carburetion
   (too large a carburetor), carburetor overheating, and faulty secondary
   operation. See also engine problem.
carburetor rebuild - Process used to rebuild a carburetor by disassembling it,
   cleaning it, and assembling it with new gaskets and parts.
carburetor repair kit - Kit composed of repair parts and gaskets for
   overhauling a carburetor. It usually includes the necessary instructions for
   doing the overhaul work.
carburetor spacer - Spacer block mounted between the intake manifold and the
   carburetor base. It is usually made of insulated material and may contain
   connections for circulating hot water circulation, or receiving crankcase
   vapors via a PCV system.
carburetor starter switch - See vacuum switch(ball type).
carburetor synchronizer - Tool used to measure air flow into a carburetor. It
   is used to balance air flow into engines having multiple carburetors.
carburetor throat - See carburetor barrel.
carburetor top - Carburetor top used to cover a main body. It covers the
   float bowl area and usually contains the choke assembly.
carburetor unloader - Linkage set up between a carburetor's choke shaft and
   throttle shaft allowing a choke to open when a gas pedal is pushed to the
   floor. It allows an engine, flooded with gas, to admit air into the intake
   manifold and clear excess gas from the cylinders when it is cranked again.
carburetor unloader cam - A cam-like plate mounted on a throttle shaft
   linkage. It moves an arm running to a choke shaft for opening a choke plate
   when a gas pedal is pushed to the floor.
carburetor vacuum - See spark ported vacuum.
car buyer - Person interested in purchasing a car.
car company - Business engaged in manufacturing cars. Car companies are in
   business to sell cars not repair them.
car classification - Method used by car dealers for classifying a car's
   appearance and mechanical state. There are usually four different
   classification known as: tough, fair, clean, sharp. A car dealer will be
   interested in purchasing a used car only if it can be moved up at least one
   category.
car classification(clean) - Used car characterized by needing only minor
   repair work before being resold. It usually has the following
   characteristics: small dents, scratches, and surface rust bumps; original
   paint or new paint with little or no wear due to scratches, chips, rust,
   oxidation, etc.; used interior appearance with worn upholstery, carpeting,
   and floor mats; evenly worn tires with 50 percent life left; clean engine;
   wiring slightly worn with some cracking apparent; trunk is dirty but
   otherwise in good shape; and minor mechanical repairs needed.
car classification(fair) - Used car characterized by needing repair work done
   in several areas. It usually has the following characteristics: several
   areas with dents, scratches, damage, and surface rust; faded paint with
   chipping, scratches, and rust discoloration; worn interior appearance with
   worn and faded upholstery, carpeting, and paneling; tires that are 50-75
   percent worn out, mismatched; dirty engine; indications of oil leakage;
   cracked wiring; dirty trunk that needs thorough cleaning; and significant
   mechanical repairs needed such as new suspension springs, worn steering
   joints, new brake linings, etc.

car classification(rough) - Used car characterized by needing a great deal of repair work. It usually has the following characteristics: large and small dents, scratches, damaged and/or rusted out areas; needs to be repainted; interior very worn requiring extensively cleaning with upholstery, carpeting, and kick panel replacements; unevenly worn and mismatched tires with less than 25 percent life; very dirty engine with significant oil leakage; cracked and worn wiring; dirty and worn trunk; and major mechanical problems in areas such as the engine, transmission, rear end, steering system, etc.

car classification(sharp) - Used car characterized by needing no repair work and ready for immediate resale. It usually has the following characteristics: original paint; no dents, scratches, or rusting; interior looks new with little wear and no upholstery rips or tears; tires are not recaps, have even tread wear, and are less than half worn out; clean engine; wiring in good condition; and clean trunk with no tearing of cover mat or other signs of wear.

car computer - Electronic device designed to monitor several engine and other functions, and display them at a central console. Remote sensors are installed to typically read: inside/outside temperature, water temperature, oil pressure, engine rpm, fuel consumption, etc. Each is usually powered electrically and changes a resistance value according to changes in what it is measuring. Other measurements include: time, date, and distance traveled.

cardan joint - Universal joint designed with yokes at right angles.

cardan shaft - See driveline. It was an early term used to differentiate between a shaft drive versus chain drive car.

car dealer - Individual or company engaged in selling new and/or used cars. Guidelines for selecting a dealer include checking the following: their reputation; length of time in business; standing with the Better Business Bureau; size and variety of car selections; completeness of repair and maintenance facilities; quality and fairness of repair work; location in your area; use of any misleading advertising; flexibility in allowing test drives; completeness in offering all financing details; and patience and desire to make you a satisfied customer.

car defect - Condition caused when one or more car parts are defective within a warranty period. See also recall.

Car De Luxe - American car produced from 1906-1910 by De Luxe Motor Car Co. in Michigan (1906), and Ohio (1906-1910).

car design - Car layout defined according to its shape, components, size, parts arrangement, etc.

car designer - See job(car designer)

car detailer - See job(car detailer).

car detailing - Finish and/or cleaning work done to a car. For example, a newly painted surface finished and/or protected by color sanding, waxing, rubbing, etc. See also job(car detailer).

car doctor - Car repairman skilled in making a used car look like new. Such repairmen often specialize in one area of repair work, and are often associated with a car theft ring. See also con game(doctored car).

car drifts - Condition created when a car, driven in a straight line, tends to drift to the right or left when a driver's hands are removed from a steering wheel. It is indicative of front end alignment problems. See also wheel alignment problem.

card masking - Custom painting technique used to create a geometrical pattern on a panel with a group of small cardboard shapes (squares, triangles, etc.) whose edges are sprayed and moved repeatedly and randomly.

Cardway - American car produced from 1923-1925 by Frederick Cardway in New York.

car exports - Cars manufactured in the United States and shipped to foreign countries to sell.

Carey - American car produced in 1906.

car flipped - Condition created when a car turns upside down. It can happen in the following circumstances: car is turned sharply on pavement at higher speed, car goes over an embankment, car skids then turns sideways at higher speed, and car is struck sideways by another car.

cargo box - See truck bed.

cargo coil - See coil spring.

cargo restraining net - Net installed in the trunk area of some cars to help restraint loose cargo such as groceries.

cargo side walls - Vertical side walls of a truck bed running parallel to the length of a truck.

car got dinged - Car struck by another car, person, etc., causing a dent in one of a car's body panels.

car handling problem - Condition created when a car does not operate properly while being driven. It usually refers to how a car rides and steers.

car handling problem(brakes weak) - See brake problem(brakes weak).

car handling problem(drifts to one side) - Car, driven in a straight line, drifts to the left or right. One indication is driving a car on a level straight road, removing hands from the steering wheel, and watching the car almost immediately start drifting. Cars in proper alignment with good tires are designed to track straight. Possible causes include: car unevenly loaded; different tire sizes and/or tire pressures; tire belt separation or shifting; front brakes dragging; front wheel bearings too tight; bent wheel spindle, steering knuckle, steering arm, rear axle housing, car underbody, and control arm; uneven wheel alignment; loose tie strut bushings; suspension springs broken or sagging; frame out-of-line; and malfunctioning shock absorber(s).

car handling problem(engine doesn't run smoothly) – See engine problem.

car handling problem(front drive axle drops) – One of the front drive axles of a front wheel drive car disconnects usually when cornering. Possible causes include: faulty axle retainers, engine shifted due to car damage, low transaxle oil level, shaft improperly installed, and worn side gears.

car handling problem(hard ride) – Car rides as though there is no cushioning of road bumps and irregularities. Possible causes include: tires are wrong size, type, and/or too high in pressure; incorrect caster angle; overloaded car; unevenly loaded car; suspension springs broken or sagging; tight steering gear; worn out or malfunctioning shock absorbers; steering linkage parts binding or lack lubrication; and front suspension parts binding or lack of lubrication.

car handling problem(hard power steering) – Power steering equipped car becomes hard to steer when turning. Possible causes include: fluid leaking internally or externally, containing air, or low in volume or pressure; loose drive belt; front suspension too low; frozen or tight steering shaft bushings; steering gear out of adjustment; and malfunctioning pressure control valve.

car handling problem(hard power steering-one direction) – Power steering equipped car becomes hard to steer in one direction. It is often a cold component problem with no symptoms in the summer or when the car has been driven for awhile. Possible causes include: shrunk power steering unit seals due to low temperature.

car handling problem(hard steering) – Car with manual steering turns hard. Possible causes include: steering box low on oil; front and/or rear wheel alignment off; and bent, damaged, or binding steering rack.

car handling problem(loose steering) – Manual steering has excessive play in steering wheel. Possible causes include: loose or worn tie rod ends and/or steering shaft coupling, and loose steering gear and/or box.

car handling problem(moves in park) – Automatic transmission equipped car continues to move when stopped and put in park. Possible causes: linkage out of adjustment, linkage components missing, linkage obstruction such as ice (winter time problem only).

car handling problem(power steering loss) – Power steering equipped car loses its power steering ability. Possible causes include: low fluid level, loose drive belt, fluid leaking internally and/or mixed with air.

car handling problem(pulls to one side on acceleration) – Car moves left or right when accelerated. Possible causes include: one low profile front tire slightly smaller in diameter, loose components in drivetrain and/or front suspension, and rear drive tires of different diameters used with a limited slip differential.

car handling problem(pulls to one side when braking) – See brake problem(pulls to one side).

car handling problem(reverse movement difficult) – Automatic transmission equipped car is difficult to backup when shifted into reverse. Possible causes include: transmission shift valve in reverse circuit sticking, converter clutch valve engaging due to pressure leaks, and faulty converter clutch due to loose pump body bolts.

car handling problem(rough ride) – See car handling problem(hard ride).

car handling problem(tire squeal on turns) – One or more tires squeal as tires are turned. It usually happens on dry pavement at higher speeds and is not intentional. Possible causes include: poor driving habits, different tire sizes; low pressure in tires; bent wheel spindle shaft, steering knuckle, steering knuckle arm, and control arm; tires toe-in too much; and worn or loose shock absorbers.

car handling problem(wanders) – Car drifts in both directions as it is driven. Possible causes include: excessive steering wheel play due to worn, damaged, or loose steering linkage; different tire sizes and/or pressures; tight or loose front wheel bearings and/or ball joints; malfunctioning shock absorbers; steering gear and/or box loose; broken suspension spring; car unevenly loaded or overloaded; idler arm bushing tight; and wheel alignment angles out of adjustment. Possible causes in power steering equipped cars include the previous as well as the following: air in power steering fluid, and out of adjustment pressure control valve.

car handling problem(wheel shimmy) – Front wheel(s) vibrates. One indicator is a vibration increasing with road speed. Another is vibration felt in the steering wheel. Possible causes include: radial and/or lateral runout of wheel, hub, or tire; unbalanced tires; separated tire belt; loose wheel bearing nut; unequal and/or incorrect tire pressures; worn out shock absorbers; caster angle too small; toe-in setting off; loose or worn out ball joints; loose or worn out control arm bushings; steering linkage pivot points loose or worn out; steering gear meshing loose; steering gear box not tightly anchored to frame; malfunctioning stabilizer bar (sway bar); loose or worn out tie strut bushings; worn U-joints on front axles of front wheel drive cars; front and rear axles not tracking properly; wheel spindle inclination angle incorrect; and aggressive and/or oversize tire tread design.

car handling problem(wheel tramp) – See car handling problem(wheel shimmy).

Carhart Steamer – American steam car produced in 1872.

Carhartt – American car produced from 1910-1911 by Carhartt Automobile Co. in Michigan.

car hop – Waiter serving food to customers in cars at a drive-in restaurant.

car inspection – Inspection performed to carefully go over a car looking for possible safety and mechanical problems that need to be fixed. Also, it refers to having a car's emission level checked on an annual basis.

car is acting up – Condition created when a car begins malfunctioning mechanically in some way.

car is missing – Condition created when an engine is not firing on all cylinders. Possible causes are usually in the ignition system and include: one or more fouled spark plugs, grounded or broken spark plug wires, cracked or dirty distributor cap, and malfunctioning ignition coil.

car is overheating – Condition created when a car's cooling system is not able to keep an engine's temperature within limits. Overheating can be caused by overloading an engine in high temperature weather, a stuck thermostat, loss of coolant, using pure antifreeze, or a broken fan belt. If steam starts coming from the hood area, pull over and stop the car for 30-45 minutes, then release the radiator cap to check the coolant level. If some steam starts escaping just let it bleed off till gone, then remove the cap. If the coolant is not low, it may be a broken fan belt, or a stuck thermostat. If the fan belt is broke, don't count on driving for more than 5 minutes or you may ruin the engine. Be careful when checking the radiator to protect your hands and face from steam. See also overheating.

car key – Key used to lock or unlock car doors and trunk, and to start and stop engine.

car length – Length of a car. It is commonly used as a measurement for specifying safe driving distance to be maintained between a leading car and a trailing car traveling at a certain speed. The rule of thumb is 1, 2, and 3-5 car lengths per 10 mph on dry pavement, wet or gravel roads, and snowy roads respectively.

car lot – Area located at a new or used car dealership's place of business where cars offered for sale are displayed.

Carlson – American car produced from 1904-1910.

car maintenance – Work performed to keep a car in a state of good repair.

Carnation Cyclecar – American car produced from 1912-1914 by American Voiturette Co. in Michigan.

Carnegie – American car produced from 1915-1916.

car noise – See sound.

car of the year – Advertising slogan used to draw attention usually to a new car being offered for sale.

Carolina stocker – Stock car raced with an illegal engine size and/or other performance equipment.

Carpenter Electric – American car produced in 1985.

car pool – Several people formed into a group to transport themselves to and from work in one car in order to reduce commuting costs and pollution. Passengers usually take turns driving their own cars, and everyone is picked up and dropped off.

car pooler – Person riding to work with others in one car.

car pooling – To car pool.

car pooling(casual) – Relatively new car pooling phenomenon used to quickly and economically get to work. Car poolers "bum a ride" at bus stops or street corners during rush hour with cars planning to travel in a car pool lane but needing additional passengers in order to qualify. It is a resourceful way of getting around traditional transportation services.

car pool lane – Specially marked lane, usually on a freeway, restricted for use only by vehicles carrying a specified minimum number of passengers. For cars, the figure is usually two or three people. Motorcycles are usually permitted. The lanes act as an encouragement for people to car pool, and thus help cut down on the number of cars transporting people.

carport – Shelter built for a car consisting of a roof extending from the side of an existing building. It may or may not have walls.

car purchase – To purchase a car for the purpose of owning it. Prospective car buyers should keep the following in mind: carefully road test and inspect any car you are serious about buying; if necessary, get a qualified mechanic to examine the car you are interested in; check with the Better Business Bureau regarding a dealer's reputation; determine a dealer's willingness to make you a satisfied customer before and after the sale; be able to pay for one third of the car or consider a cheaper one; consider other finance agencies besides the dealer in order to find the best credit deal; if necessary, consult an expert in financing; carefully read the sales contract, making sure it has everything in it to your satisfaction (see sales contract); carefully read the new car warranty and determine what is and is not covered; obtain copies of all papers you sign; and never sign any papers you don't understand or that don't have all the necessary information to your satisfaction.

car queer – Person who frequently dreams of buying a new car and who likes spending a lot of time in auto stores.

car ramp – One of two portable ramps used to elevate one end of a car by driving a car's wheels up on them. It usually provides an elevation of 6-12 inches.

car restorer – See job(car restorer).

carriage – Wheeled vehicle designed for carrying passengers.

Carrico – American car produced in 1909.

Carrison – American car produced in 1908.

Carroll – American car produced from 1912-1920 by Carroll Motor Car Co. in Pennsylvania. Also, an American car produced from 1920-1922 by Carroll Automobile Co. in Ohio.

Carroll Six – American car produced from 1920-1921.

car roof – Car body panel used to form the roof of a car. It usually consists of a steel member structure, covered with sheet metal, and supported at four corners.

carrying charges – Charge made for carrying an account. It is usually computed as a percentage of the principal owed.

carry the wheels – See wheelie.

car salesman – See job(car salesman).

car sense – Common sense known in the care, servicing, and operation of a car.

car service tip – Useful information given to help someone diagnose a car problem and/or perform a certain aspect of car service and maintenance work more knowledgeably, economically, or efficiently.

car service tip(air bypass valve test) – If an air pump equipped car backfires during deceleration, a faulty bypass valve is often the problem. To check the valve perform the following test: mount a vacuum gauge in vacuum line running to valve, start the engine, let it idle, and observe vacuum reading. If vacuum is under 15 inches, check for leaks in vacuum line. If vacuum is strong, the valve is probably faulty.

car service tip(air cleaner warm air test) – A vacuum motor and air temperature sensor must both operate properly to maintain a proper air temperature flowing into a carburetor. To test both for operability perform the following test: remove any duct from end of air inlet, start a cold engine, observe position of gate valve in inlet (should be up), observe position of gate valve as engine reaches operating temperature (should go down). If the valve doesn't move, check for binding and vacuum in vacuum motor's hose when engine is running. If there is vacuum to the motor and no binding, the vacuum motor or the temperature sensor is bad. The motor should hold a vacuum of 10-15 inches for at least 5 minutes. If it won't, the motor is bad. If it will, the temperature sensor is bad.

car service tip(air cleaner with oily emulsion) – An emulsion of oil and water sometimes collects in an air cleaner's base. It is usually due to improper crankcase venting. Possible causes include: wrong size or partially clogged PCV valve; clogged crankcase breather screen; partially clogged breather hose; PCV parts connected improperly or leaking; and piston rings stuck, cracked, broken, and/or worn.

car service tip(air conditioner-adding compressor oil) – Method used to add compressor lubricant oil to an air conditioning system. It is added through a manifold gauge set. In most cases, the existing refrigerant does not have to be discharged. The oil circulates throughout the system with the refrigerant. A typical amount in a car system is 10 ounces.

car service tip(air conditioner-charging system) – Method used to add refrigerant to an air conditioning system. It is done through a manifold gauge set. The manner in which the freon is added will depend on the amount of refrigerant existing in the system. It is added as the engine is running at a specified rpm and load setting.

car service tip(air conditioner-discharging system) – Method used to remove refrigerant from an air conditioning system. It is done gradually through a manifold gauge set into an open container or rag. If the discharge is too rapid, the compressor oil will tend to discharge as well.

car service tip(air conditioner-evacuating system) – Method used to remove moisture, air, and other contaminants from an air conditioning system, by the use of a vacuum pump. It is connected through a manifold gauge set and typically runs for half an hour. The removal of moisture is especially important since moisture causes rust, forms ice at the expansion valve, and combines with other contaminants and compounds to form system clogging sludge.

car service tip(air conditioner check) – An air conditioner can quickly be checked for proper operation by: running it at the coldest setting and highest blower speed, and measuring the output temperature. It should be at least 20 degrees below the surrounding air temperature. Also, the inlet side of the evaporator should be very cold to the touch. If the lower temperature and cold feel are not apparent, the system is likely to be: low on refrigerant, or suffering from one or more leaks.

car service tip(air conditioner leak) – A leak in a car's AC circuit can be hard to locate. Substitute a 14 oz. can of leak detector for R12 on the next recharge. A colored residue will be left wherever the Freon escapes. Some AC systems cannot use leak detectors as they will plug certain system filtering screens.

car service tip(air conditioner removal) – An air conditioner can often remain charged when an engine is removed. The compressor is removed from the motor and tied or wired to the side of the engine compartment. A piece of wood is used to protect the condenser from engine collisions while it is being removed.

car service tip(air filter check) – The life left in a paper element air filter can easily be checked with a trouble light. Simply place the light in the center of the element. If light readily passes through and there are no tears, holes, or oil stains, the filter can continue to be used.

car service tip(alternator charging test) – Test performed with a voltmeter to determine whether an alternator is charging or not. With the engine shutoff, check the voltage drop across the battery terminals. It should be 12 volts. With the engine running, it should be 13–14 volts.

car service tip(aluminum radiator leak) – A leak in an aluminum radiator can be repaired with epoxy compounds formulated for such radiators. To seal the leak, dry the ruptured area, spread the cooling fins away, clean area around the leak, warm area with a heat lamp, mix and apply epoxy, and let cure for two hours leaving heat lamp 12 inches from area.

car service tip(antifreeze condition test) – Acidity of an engine's coolant is one way of determining when the antifreeze is worn out (additives depleted). To determine acid level, perform the following test with a voltmeter: remove the radiator cap, set voltmeter to low DC voltage scale, touch the ground lead to ground, immerse the other lead in the coolant water in the top of the radiator, and observe the voltmeter reading. If it exceeds 0.80 volts, the coolant needs to be changed and the system flushed.

car service tip(armature and field grounded circuit test) – Test used on a generator or starter motor to determine if armature or field windings are grounding to an armature shaft or housing. Test is done by checking each armature winding and field coil winding for continuity to ground.

car service tip(armature and field open circuit test) – Test used on a generator or starter motor to determine if armature or field windings have any breaks. Armature windings are checked by examining the commutator for possible burn spots. Field windings are checked by individually testing circuits for continuity.

car service tip(automatic transmission cooler lines) – Periodic inspection of the two cooler lines for dents, bending, or abrasions will help prevent costly automatic transmission damage and lengthen its life. The lines route transmission fluid to and from a radiator in front of the car to help keep it cool.

car service tip(automatic transmission overfilled) – Most automatic transmissions don't have a drain plug. If too much fluid has been added, remove the excess by: loosening one of the oil cooler line fittings at the radiator or transmission, placing a pan underneath, starting the engine in park, allowing a suitable amount to drain out, stopping the engine, and tightening the fitting. Check the fluid level. If still too high, repeat the above procedure.

car service tip(automatic transmission filter & oil change) – Changing an automatic transmission's oil and filter requires removing the transmission pan. It should be done very carefully as there may be valves, o-rings, and gaskets in addition to the filter that will need to be replaced in a certain way. Remove the pan slowly observing where everything fits together, and what components are held in place by the filter. It makes good sense to use new o-rings and filter gaskets. Transmission fluid undergoing heavy use should be replaced at least every 15,000 miles.

car service tip(ball joint wear test) – Worn ball joints can often be spotted by performing the following test: jack tire off the ground, lift tire straight up and down by hand or with a lever setup underneath the tire, and observe movement. A second test involves grabbing the tire at the bottom and trying to move it in or out. If either test produces noticeable movement, a loose or worn ball joint is indicated. If the lower ball joint is being replaced, it is usually wise to replace the corresponding upper joint on cars so equipped.

car service tip(battery charge indicator) - No-maintenance batteries are equipped with built-in charge indicators. When clear, the battery is low. Jump starting such a battery can be dangerous as it will be filled with hydrogen gas and a spark could cause an explosion.

car service tip(battery charging) - Cars built to run with on-board computers require an extra precautionary step when charging the battery. Be sure to disconnect both battery cables completely before attaching energized battery charger clamps. Failure to do so may cause an electrical surge to flow to the computer and damage it. See also jump start.

car service tip(battery cleaning) - Car batteries occasionally need to have the top surface cleaned to minimize build-up of conductive salts from electrolyte vapors. An effective cleaner is a solution of baking soda used as follows: make sure the cell caps are in place; pour the solution over the posts, the entire top surface of the battery, and any battery holddown equipment; and then rinse with regular water.

car service tip(battery post corrosion) - Battery posts corrode primarily from escaping electrolyte vapors. Corrosion can be minimized by using battery washers, or coating posts with grease, silicon sprays, etc.

car service tip(battery load test-1) - A quick test can be performed to determine a battery's ability to hold a charge. A carbon pile tester (a heavy duty resistor) is used to simulate a steady load of about 1/2 the CCA rating for 15-20 seconds. The voltage should not drop below 9.5 volts during the test period.

car service tip(battery load test-2) - A quick test can be performed to determine a battery's ability to hold a charge by using the starter if it's in good condition. To perform the test: connect a voltmeter across the battery, remove the ignition coil wire, and crank the engine for 15-20 seconds observing the voltage. If the voltage drops below 10 volts, repeat the test after charging up the battery again. If it falls below 10 volts again, the battery probably needs replacing.

car service tip(bearing cap marks) - Two number markings are used to identify each connecting rod and main bearing cap assembly. The numbers are stamped on opposite side of an outside face common to both. The matching numbers indicate the relative position of a bearing. When reassembling such parts, it is very important that the numbers match up. It is also important that both matching numbers face each other. Failure to follow both of these precautions can cause engine damage due to plugging oil passageways, and assembling parts that bind or have excessive clearances.

car service tip(belt driven accessory stuck) - If the accessory remains stuck after loosening the adjusting nut, loosen the pivot mounting bolt. Don't use force with a pry bar or other tool. It could cause damage.

car service tip(bleeder screw cap replacement) - Bleeder screw caps often get lost on hydraulic brake systems. They are found on wheel cylinders, and disc brake cylinders. To fashion a replacement, cut a short length of plastic tubing somewhat smaller in diameter than the bleeder screw shaft. Apply a dab of silicone sealant to one end, let it dry, and install.

car service tip(blower motor test) - A simple test can be performed to determine if a heater's blower motor is defective. After checking for a good fuse and good motor ground wire connection, proceed as follows: remove hot wire on blower motor, and connect a jumper wire from the battery to the blower's hot terminal. If the motor runs, the circuit leading to the motor is faulty. If the motor does not run, the motor is defective.

car service tip(blowing out an engine) - Short trip driving causes combustion chamber and spark plug deposits to build-up. An effective method of removing build-up is to run an engine through a series of full throttle accelerations on a regular basis (every couple weeks of active driving). The procedure is performed as follows: locate a road with little traffic and highway speed limits, warm engine up, bring car to complete stop (still idling), accelerate rapidly (burning rubber not necessary) to speed limit, and then slow to a stop. The acceleration and braking should be repeated half a dozen times.

car service tip(boiling fuel test) - A simple test can be performed on an operating engine to determine if poor idling is due to fuel boiling in the carburetor. First, start the car and run the engine until it reaches operating temperature and the idling becomes rough. Then with the engine running take a small stream of cool running water and direct or spray it toward the carburetor body. If the problem disappears, fuel was boiling. Solving a boiling fuel problem requires: using higher boiling point fuel, installing heat shields around the carburetor, providing cooling air to the carburetor area, and/or insulating the fuel delivery system as much as possible in the engine compartment area. See also heat soak and gasoline(winter).

car service tip(bounce test) – Test used to determine shock absorber wear. First, perform the test with a car at rest as follows. Push one corner of the car down sharply. The car should bounce back to its original position, and then remain stable. Repeat this test with each wheel. If there is a continued up and down motion, the affected shock absorber probably needs to be replaced. Some shock absorber designs require a secondary test. It involves driving your car at a speed of 5-10 mph where there is no traffic. Repeatedly tap the brakes. If a car bounces back and forth, shock wear is indicated. When replacing shocks, do it in pairs, front and/or back.

car service tip(brake adjustment) – Rear wheel brakes equipped with self-adjusters can be adjusted for wear as follows: put car in reverse, begin rolling, apply the brakes, and repeat. When the brake pedal returns to normal, the adjustment is complete.

car service tip(brake booster test) – A power brake system can quickly be checked for proper operation by performing a simple test of the vacuum-assisted power brake unit. The test consists of: turning off the engine, pumping the brake pedal several times (it gets hard when the vacuum reserve has been removed), stepping on the pedal and holding, restarting engine, and observing pedal movement. If the unit is operating normally, the pedal will drop slightly. If there is no movement or excess movement, look for problems in the booster unit.

car service tip(brake light malfunction) – Non-functioning brake lights with good bulbs and fuse may be caused by a faulty brake light switch. To check remove the switch cover and connect a wire between the cover's two contacts. If the brake lights operate, a faulty switch is indicated. If the lights don't operate, look for a loose connection or wire.

car service tip(brake squeaking) – Brakes sometimes squeak, when applied, due to brake lining mounting surface rubbing against a disc piston or drum backing plate. Apply a small amount of high temperature grease to the back of a brake disc or the high points of a drum backing plate.

car service tip(brake test-cool) – Test performed by a car evaluator to determine a car's stopping distance and applied pedal pressure when the brake linings are cold. It is usually performed at 60 mph.

car service tip(brake test-hot) – Test performed by a car evaluator to determine a car's stopping distance and applied pedal pressure when the brake linings are hot. It is usually performed at 60 mph.

car service tip(brake test-individual wheel) – Test performed on each wheel to determine proper operation of respective brake components. Place the car on secure jack stands, put the transmission in neutral, and remove the parking brake. Each wheel is then checked for the following: free rotation of wheel, brake lining thickness and surface contamination, brake cylinder leakage, condition of brake components, proper assembly and operation of brake and parking brake (rear wheel) components, and free movement of brake adjusters (rear brake).

car service tip(brake test-parking) – Test used to determine proper operation of a parking brake. It proceeds as follows: engage brake fully while at rest, then try driving the car forward. A functioning brake should greatly impede forward movement. If it doesn't, look for binding linkage, and/or brake out of adjustment.

car service tip(brake test-pedal fade) – Test used to determine a brake system's ability to maintain constant pressure when the brake pedal is pressed. It consists of: starting engine, and pressing brake pedal firmly and holding for one minute. If the pedal gives, there is a leak in the master cylinder, one or more of the brake cylinders, and/or line leakage. If pedal feels spongy, there is air in the brake fluid. See also brake pedal(spongy).

car service tip(brake test-power) – Test used to determine the proper operation of a power brake unit. It usually proceeds as follows. The engine is stopped. Brake pedal is pumped several times to rid the system of any vacuum. Pedal is then held down and the engine started. A properly operating unit will cause a pedal to move downward a little when intake manifold vacuum reaches a power brake unit. If the pedal effect is not achieved, the following may be the cause: leaking vacuum lines, dented or leaking vacuum cylinder, and malfunctioning power brake unit.

car service tip(brake test-pulling to one side) – Test used to determine if equal braking force is applied to all wheels. The test consists of: driving car with steering wheel grasped loosely, applying brakes, and noticing any steering wheel or car movement to either side. Movement indicates greater braking friction on the respective side. See also brake problem(pulls to one side).

car service tip(brake test-stopping) – Test used to determine if car slows properly to a stop. The test consists of: driving car preferably at highway speed, slowing car rapidly (not quite skidding), and noticing if pedal remains firm.

car service tip(break in period) – Breaking in an engine properly is important for long engine life. Sufficient time and proper driving habits will allow all the moving parts to properly seat. An engine needs at least 25 to 50 short warm-ups to achieve this. Popular recommendations include: warm engine up as normal, accelerate moderately, vary driving speed the first 2,000 miles between 45 and 60 mph, change oil according to manufacturer or at 1-2,000 miles for the first time, drive 2-3,000 thousand miles before taking any long trips, and avoid heavy loads for several thousand miles. Some engines require 5-6,000 miles before they are fully broke in and fuel economy reaches the designed level.

car service tip(broken valve springs) - Valve springs can break for a number of reasons. They include: spring coil binding due to excess compression (improper valve clearance or mismatched cam), valve float setting spring length shorter, and moisture on valve springs.

car service tip(buffing protective finish) - To avoid ruining a car's finish remember the following: tip pad slightly back opposite to the movement direction; avoid downward force; work a small area moving the buffer constantly; do edges, corners, and hard to reach areas by hand.

car service tip(car vibration test) - A car vibration occurring while a car is in motion at a certain speed can be narrowed down to the wheels or the drivetrain by performing two tests.

The first is a car motion test. Begin by checking the engine for any loose accessory (air pump, power steering pump, air conditioner, etc.), accessory mounting bracket, and mounting bolts. If no looseness is found, perform the following steps: connect a tachometer to the engine if there is none and route it inside the car, start the engine, close all the windows, drive on a straight level stretch of road, increase speed until the vibration appears, note the rpm, increase speed a ways beyond the vibration, shift car into neutral, let car slow down without braking through the rpm during which vibration occurred, and observe if the vibration is still there.

The second is a stationary test. It consists of: bringing car to rest, putting car in neutral, increasing engine speed until vibration rpm is reached, observing any vibration, and slowing down then shutting off engine.

If the vibration occurs during the speedup and slowdown part of the motion test, it is probably due to unbalanced tires with radial runout. If no vibration occurred during the slow down part of the test, vibration is likely in the engine, motor mounts, exhaust system, transmission, driveline, and/or differential.

If vibration occurs during the stationary test, engine and/or motor mount vibration is indicated. If not, transmission, driveline, exhaust system, and/or differential (transaxle in front wheel drive cars) vibration is indicated. See also vibration(engine) and vibration(transaxle).

car service tip(catalytic converter clogged) - A clogged converter restricts the flow of exhaust gases. An engine will lose power according to the degree of clogging. A totally clogged converter will not allow an engine to start. Factors contributing to clogging include: infrequent tune-ups, rich fuel mixture, and use of leaded fuel. See also car service tip(restricted exhaust test), vacuum gauge reading(exhaust-restricted), engine problem(power gradually lost), and backpressure.

car service tip(centrifugal advance maintenance) - Preventive maintenance on the centrifugal advance mechanism can keep it operating properly. It should be inspected, cleaned, and lubricated at least once a year. Maintenance consists of: removing assembly from distributor; cleaning the parts of all dirt; lubricating the weights, springs, and other moving surfaces with light oil.

car service tip(centrifugal advance test) - A simple test can be performed to determine the proper operation of a centrifugal advance unit in a distributor. Proceed as follows with the engine off: remove the cap, grab the rotor, twist the rotor in the direction it rotates, and release. If the centrifugal weights are connected and operating properly, the rotor will spring back into position.

car service tip(charging system test) - A simple test can be performed to determine the overall state of the charging system. Connect a voltmeter to the battery terminals. Start the car and set the idle at 2,000 rpm. If voltage is between 13-15 volts, battery charging is usually occurring normally. Lower voltage indicates battery is discharging due problems such as: grounds, faulty alternator, loose alternator belt, corroded terminals, and/or faulty regulator. High voltage causes overcharging, shortens battery life, and requires frequent battery water refills. It is usually due to a faulty regulator.

car service tip(choke element test) - A simple test can be performed to determine if an electric choke element is faulty. Disconnect the electrical lead to the element. Measure the voltage at the element terminal. If the voltage is at least 12 volts, a faulty element is indicated. If voltage is under 12 volts, a break or short in the choke element electrical circuit is likely.

car service tip(choke operation test) - The following test will isolate a problem in the choke circuit. With the engine cold proceed as follows: remove the air cleaner cover, clean the choke linkage and choke plate, depress and release the gas pedal, watch the choke plate close off the carburetor airway, start the engine, watch the choke plate open slightly, and watch the choke plate open fully by the time the engine is warm. If the choke does not operate properly, usually only two problems are possible. One, the choke linkage is dirty or binding. And two, the choke element is faulty. See also car service tip(choke element test).

car service tip(clutch release test) - To quickly test for a bad release bearing perform the following test: start the engine, put the car in neutral, depress the clutch pedal an inch or so until the release bearing begins to contact the clutch pressure plate release fingers, and listen to any noise coming from the transmission area. A grinding noise indicates a bad throwout bearing. The sound will be heard as long as the bearing is spinning.

car service tip(cold heater) - Heater blows cold air regardless of speed setting. Other symptoms may include: water vapor exiting from vents, and ice formation. Possible causes include: plugged heater core; restricted coolant flow due to faulty heater control valve; plugged heater hoses; air in heater circuit; and faulty A/C circuit exerting continuous cooling effect.

car service tip(collapsed lower radiator hose) - See radiator hose.

car service tip(collapsed upper radiator hose) - See radiator hose.

car service tip(compression leak into coolant test) - See car service tip(pressure leak into coolant test).

car service tip(condensation on windshield) - Water condensing on the inside surface of a car's windshield usually indicates a coolant leak in the heater core.

car service tip(cooling system pressure test) - Test performed on a cooling system to check for possible leaks. With the engine shut down, a pressure tester is used that attaches to the radiator cap. Air is pumped into the system until 15-18 psi is reached. Read the pressure reading and watch to see if the pressure drops after several minutes. If there is a drop, coolant is leaking externally or internally. Possible external leak causes include: leaky radiator core, upper tank, and/or lower tank; leaky heater core; loose hose clamps; cracked upper, lower, or heater hoses; bad water pump seal; leaky core plugs; and leaky heater control valve. Possible internal leak causes include: leaky head gasket, cracked block, and cracked cylinder head.

car service tip(cowling leakage test) - Locating a leak in a cowling area can be simplified by using a proper approach. First determine if the leak is water or antifreeze. Antifreeze is slippery and has a distinct smell. Next take a garden hose to the bottom of the cowl structure and thoroughly wet the area. Stop and look for leaks. Repeat the process slowly moving up the cowl wall.

car service tip(cranking vacuum test) - Test performed to determine the vacuum producing ability of an engine. Poor vacuum can indicate: badly worn pistons, rings, and/or cylinder walls; leaking or improperly timed valves; faulty EGR valve; and leaking intake manifold due to large vacuum leak, faulty gaskets, and/or cracked manifold. To perform the test do the following: connect a vacuum gauge to an intake manifold source below the carburetor, open the choke assembly, crank the engine with the throttle plate in closed position, and observe the vacuum reading. A low or zero vacuum reading indicates a problem.

car service tip(cranking voltage test) - Measuring voltage drop across battery terminals, when a starter is engaged, is helpful in diagnosing the health of a starting system. First, make sure the battery is in good condition and charged up, then proceed as follows: connect voltmeter leads to battery terminals, observe voltage drop, disconnect and ground ignition coil high voltage lead, and crank engine (5-10 seconds) observing voltage drop and listening to cranking speed. Voltage should stay above 4.5 and 9 volts, and cranking speed should be 120-150 and 160-180 rpm for 6 and 12 volt systems respectively.

Low readings indicate excessive starter load or starter problems. See also car service tip(starter relay test), car service tip(starting system test), car service tip(starter draw test), and car service tip(headlight test).

car service tip(cutout test) - An engine plagued with cutting out is often due to a pickup coil lead breaking internally when rotated. The pickup coil needs replacing if disconnecting and plugging the vacuum advance hose transforms a stalling car into one that idles OK, or transforms one that idles OK but cuts out on acceleration into one that idles and accelerates OK.

car service tip(cylinder firing order) - Engine cylinders fire in a specific sequence. If the spark plug wires have been removed or installed improperly, the correct sequence can be established in the following manner: shut off engine; determine number one cylinder firing position (See car service tip(cylinder firing position)); remove distributor cap, rotate engine in running direction (usually clockwise) to cylinder one's TDC position; observe distributor rotor movement during engine rotation; determine firing sequence from owner's manual, stamping on engine block, or possible markings on distributor cap beside each tower; install number one spark plug wire; and install remaining wires according to firing sequence and the direction of rotor rotation.

car service tip(cylinder firing position) - The firing position of an engine's number one cylinder can be determined as follows: remove the cylinder's spark plug, remove the ignition coil high voltage lead, place a thumb or finger tightly over spark plug hole, bump or slowly rotate engine until pressure is felt on finger. Pressure indicates piston is on the compression stroke with spark plug getting ready to fire as piston reaches the top. TDC can be observed by shining a light into the plug hole and slowly rotating engine until upward piston movement stops.

The correct firing or TDC position of the number one cylinder is needed to: to properly install a timing chain or belt for accurate valve timing, to time an engine, to re-establish spark plug wire order when they have been removed, etc. See also car service tip(cylinder firing order).

car service tip(cylinder head gasket failure-diesel) - A head gasket failing prematurely on a diesel engine can be due to the following: warped head, gasket and head not properly installed and/or torqued, incorrect head gasket, head bolts working loose, incorrect head bolts, and rich fuel mixture being injected too early.

car service tip(cylinder head gasket failure-gasoline) - A head gasket failing prematurely on a gasoline engine can be due to the following: faulty head gasket; head gasket and head not properly installed and/or torqued; head warped; incorrect head gasket; excessive cylinder pressure due to milled head, incorrect pistons, carbon build-up; excessive ignition advance; and head bolts working loose or incorrect.

car service tip(cylinder head installation and removal) - Proper installation and removal of a cylinder head will avoid warping it. The head should be cool before removing it. Head bolts should be removed one at a time, starting with the farthest one first, then its opposite diagonal counterpart, and so on. When reinstalling, position head gasket then position cylinder head. Install all head bolts in cylinder head until snug. Tighten bolts in three torque stages until specified torque is achieved. Tightening sequence is the reverse of the removal sequence. When the engine has warmed up, check the torque readings again and adjust as necessary.

car service tip(cylinder head warpage test) - Cylinder head warpage can be determined by a simple test. Proceed as follows: turn the head's mating surface upwards, take a good quality straight edge as long as the head and lay it on edge parallel and then diagonally from corner to corner, try to slide a 0.005 inch thickness gauge under the edge anywhere. If the gauge fits anywhere, milling the head is probably necessary. A warped head can cause: head gasket failure, and coolant or oil leakage into combustion chamber.

car service tip(cylinder knock test) - See car service tip(engine knock test).

car service tip(damaged wiper pivot shaft) - In time, many wiper pivot shaft splines get damaged and lose their gripping ability. The result is a slipping wiper blade assembly. Removing and replacing the shaft can be time consuming and expensive. An alternate easier solution requires drilling a small hole through the wiper blade collar and shaft. A cotter or other type pin is then inserted into the hole.

car service tip(damp ignition test) - Hard starting in wet weather often indicates moisture is getting into the ignition wiring somewhere. To locate secondary wiring leakage, fill a spray bottle with mater, soak each of the following areas one at a time and try starting the engine: ignition coil tower, distributor cap, individual spark plug leads, and spark plugs. If the engine starts harder or not at all, the last soaked area is probably the problem area.

car service tip(dieseling test) - Dieseling can often be caused by electrical current leaking from instruments or other accessories into the ignition circuit. To verify this perform the following test when the car is dieseling: grab the high voltage wire running from the ignition coil to distributor cap with a thick doubled over rag, and disconnect it. If the dieseling stops, current is flowing into the ignition circuit when the ignition switch is off and must be tracked down.

car service tip(diesel fuel bacteria) - Bacteria can grow in diesel fuel if rust and oxygen are present. The bacteria can form into a gummy substance; and plug up tank filters, fuel lines, pump, and injectors.

car service tip(dipstick appearance) The appearance of oil on the end of a dipstick can indicate possible internal problems. For engine oil, a creamy black or milky white coating indicates water in the crankcase. For automatic transmission oil, a dark brown coating and/or a burnt oil smell indicate overheated transmission fluid due to low level, and long use and/or hard driving conditions such as pulling heavy loads.

car service tip(dirty diesel fuel) - Dirty diesel fuel can be very dangerous
if not filtered. It can plug certain fuel metering parts causing too much
fuel to be injected. Such a situation may generate excessive combustion
pressures that can blow a head gasket; break cylinder head bolts; and/or
damage pistons, connecting rods, bearings, crank pins. In short, dirty
unfiltered diesel fuel can quickly destroy a diesel engine. Owners of diesel
engines should get in the habit of regularly changing any water and/or fuel
filters, and avoiding cheap fuel is possible.

car service tip(dirty diesel oil) - Diesel lubricating oil quickly turns black
due to carbon and other combustion products. If the oil is specifically
designed for lubricating a diesel engine, the contaminants will not be
harmful provided the oil is changed on schedule. Contaminants interact with
oil additives and most noticeably reduce anti-scuff oil properties. When
anti-scuffing decreases, moving engine parts suffer. Parts bearing heavy
loads such as cam lobes can quickly wear or gall. To minimize wear problems:
use diesel lubricating oil recommended for the engine, and change oil and oil
filter at regular intervals (3,000 miles recommended).

car service tip(distributor cap inspection) - When inspecting the cap, check
for the following: corroded, broken, or cracked cap towers; corroded, burned,
or badly worn spark plug terminals and/or rotor tip; carbon paths inside or
outside the distributor body; proper rotor contact spring tension; and cracks
in base.

car service tip(distributor cap loose) - A loose distributor can be the cause
of a car not starting. Possible causes include: not properly attached,
broken or loose spring clips, explosion from fuel vapors flowing into cap
area through ruptured vacuum advance unit and igniting from a spark. See
also engine problem(cranks but won't start).

car service tip(distributor point test) - A quick test can be performed to
determine if conventional distributor points are corroded. Proceed as
follows: check for strong spark by removing the high voltage ignition coil
lead at the distributor, hold it close to ground, crank engine a few seconds,
look for strong spark. If there is no spark or a weak one: remove
distributor cap, rotate engine until points close, separate points with a
piece of paper, turn ignition switch to "on" position, hold ignition coil
lead close to ground, short across points with a screwdriver, and observe
spark. If there is a strong bluish spark, the points are corroded. See also
breakdown tip(points corroded).

car service tip(driveline imbalance) - Even a minor driveline imbalance on
rear wheel drive cars can cause vibration problems. The following procedure
will often eliminate the vibration: jack up the rear wheels securely so they
are free to turn, block the front wheels, get someone sit in driver's seat
and run car the equivalent of 40-50 mph, crawl under car near driveline
midpoint, slowly bring a piece of white chalk or other light marker toward
the driveline until it just touches it, shutoff engine, attach one stainless
steel hose type clamp around driveline at chalk mark, adjust clamp so screw
is positioned opposite where mark is strongest, tighten clamp, run engine to
a higher rpm (50-70 mph), and observe change or elimination of vibration.
Sometimes it requires two clamps. If two clamps won't cure the vibration
even after rotating them and rerunning engine, the driveline may have a major
imbalance or the vibration could be coming from the engine.

car service tip(ECM failures) - Often times repeated failure of an electronic
control module is due to dirty or poor connections. Make sure the
connections are clean, and fit tightly together.

car service tip(EGR valve test) - A faulty EGR valve can cause a number of
engine problems. Malfunction is usually due to its exhaust metering valve
not operating at all or properly. To test with the car in motion: stop the
car, remove the vacuum hose connection and plug it, then drive the car. If
the EGR valve was operating properly, the car will now tend to hesitate, idle
roughly, accelerate poorly, etc. To test with the car stationary: start the
engine, put on protective gloves, reach behind the valve and touch the
diaphragm, accelerate and decelerate the engine, and feel the diaphragm move
up and down respectively. If no movement is detected, remove the vacuum
hose, accelerate the engine to 2-3,000 rpm, and check for vacuum in the line.
No vacuum means a plugged, kinked, or leaking hose. Vacuum means EGR
components upstream from the vacuum connection are faulty. A valve stuck
open will cause the engine to stumble and idle rough while cold. A valve
stuck closed will increase pinging tendency. See also thermal valve and
exhaust gas recirculation valve.

car service tip(electrical connections) - Electrical connections can be tight
and still conduct little or no electricity due to corrosion causing high
resistance. Suspect terminal connections should be cleaned of all oxidation
and other coatings down to bare metal. Battery terminals are especially
prone to corrosion.

car service tip(empty float bowl test) - An engine will not start if the
carburetor's float bowl is empty. To make this determination, conduct the

following test: remove the air cleaner top, look into the carburetor airway, move the carburetor linkage as if accelerating the engine, and watch for fuel squirting into the carburetor airway. If no fuel squirts (from the accelerator pump), the float bowl is empty. An empty float bowl indicates a fuel delivery problem, vapor locking, heat soak, or fuel foaming. See also engine problem(cranks but won't start).

car service tip(engine knock test) - A few quick checks and two simple tests can be performed on an engine to determine if a knocking sound is coming from one or more of the engine cylinders. The quick checks consist of: examining the oil pan bottom for dents (connecting rod hitting bottom), removing transmission cover plate, and examining torque convertor bolts for tightness. The first test determines if any belt driven components are the cause. Proceed as follows: remove all accessory belts, start the engine, and listen for the knock. If it's still there, it's time to test the engine. The second test is done as follows: reconnect the belts, start the engine, listen for the knocking sound, remove one spark plug lead at a time with insulated pliers and ground it (stop and restart electronic ignition cars to avoid possible damage), listen for a noticeable change in sound, and then reconnect the wire. A faulty cylinder will change in sound, because no pressure is exerted on the piston head due to a grounded spark plug.

Connecting rod knock is usually loudest: during acceleration, at higher speeds, when an engine changes from pulling to coasting, and in the crankcase area. Loose pistons are usually loudest: when engine is cold and idling, and near the cylinder head. Loose piston pins are usually loudest during deceleration, and near the cylinder head. See also sound(knocking-7), sound(knocking-9), car service tip(power balance test), and mechanic's stethoscope.

car service tip(exhaust leak into coolant test) - See car service tip(pressure leak into coolant test).

car service tip(exhaust system leakage test) - A rumbling throaty sound during engine operation can be due to an exhaust system leak. Leakage is usually due to corrosion, and/or loose pipe connections. To verify leakage perform the following test: start the car, let the engine idle for a few minutes, then stuff a rag into the tailpipe. If the engine quits, there are no sizable leaks in the exhaust system. If the engine continues to run, the gases are leaking out and can usually be traced down by locating the source of the sound.

car service tip(fan belt slippage test) - A fan belt slips when it is too loose or worn. To check for wear perform the following test with the engine shut off: tighten belt to proper tension, and try to rotate alternator or generator fan by hand. If the fan can be turned, the belt is worn and should be replaced.

car service tip(fan clutch test) - Proper operation of a fan equipped with a clutching mechanism can be tested as follows: keep car at rest, open hood, start engine when cold, listen to fan noise, warm engine up to operating temperature, listen for roaring sound caused by clutch engagement, observe fan operation, and stop engine. If the fan does not begin spinning at a higher speed and produce a louder sound, the clutch is defective.

car service tip(fluid changes) - Changing the various car fluids at regular intervals will prolong the life of the respective components. Popular change intervals are as follows: engine oil every 2-4,000 miles or 3 months, manual or automatic transmission oil every 25-40,000 miles or once a year, differential oil every 25-40,000 miles or once a year, brake fluid every 2 years in mild climate and every year in harsh climate, and engine coolant every year. See also car service tip(antifreeze condition test).

car service tip(flywheel test) - See sound(bumping-intermittent).

car service tip(free play test-brake pedal) - A properly adjusted brake pedal and brake system should allow a driver's foot to slip behind the pedal when it is fully applied.

car service tip(free play test-clutch pedal) - A properly adjusted clutch pedal will travel usually one inch before encountering resistance (throw out bearing contacting pressure plate).

car service tip(free play test-fan belt) - A properly tensioned V-belt should deflect no more than 1/2 inch from its centerline when pushed on with a thumb.

car service tip(free play test-parking brake) - A parking brake handle or pedal should move about 1/2 its total range when properly adjusted.

car service tip(free play test-steering linkage) - A car's steering wheel should have no more than 1/2-1 inch of free rotational movement in either direction before the wheels respond. Excessive free play indicates wear in the steering linkage, or a steering gearbox out of adjustment.

car service tip(fuel foaming) - Some cars are more prone to fuel foaming causing stalling, starting, and reduced power problems. One remedy is installing a pressure regulator as near to the carburetor as possible. Set the device at 3-4 psi. The increased pressure will help to keep the fuel in a liquid state. A car equipped with a fuel bypass may require modification of the bypass to restrict flow back to the gas tank and maintain pressure at the carburetor inlet. A small restriction orifice will need to be installed. Orifice diameter will depend on a fuel pump's pressure and flow rate values. Try starting with a 0.050 inch diameter orifice and enlarge it until the desired pressure is maintained at the carburetor inlet.

car service tip(headlights on one beam) - Headlights operate on low or high only. It is often due to a defective dimmer switch.

car service tip(headlight test) - One quick way of diagnosing starting system problems is by performing a test using the car's headlights. Make sure the battery is charged up and in good condition beforehand. The test consists of: turning on headlights, and then operating the starter.

If lights go out and starter doesn't operate, electrical connections between the starter and battery have high resistance and need cleaning. This includes: corroded battery terminals; poor ground strap; and paint on starter, bellhousing, or ground strap mounting surface.

If the lights dim significantly and engine cranks slowly, something is causing the starter to bear a heavy load. Possible causes include: engine oil too heavy (especially in cold engine), tight clearances in new or rebuilt engine, excessive spark advance due to wrong setting or faulty distributor advance mechanism, loose pole shoe in starter dragging against turning armature, and short in starter wiring.

If lights remain bright and starter doesn't operate, there is a break in the wiring somewhere in the starting system. Possible breaks can occur in: starter relay, ignition switch due to worn or corroded contacts, primary wiring running from battery to ignition switch or from switch to starter relay, starter motor field windings, armature windings (due to breaks or worn out brushes), and neutral switch on automatic transmission. See also car service tip(starter relay test).

car service tip(heater circulation test) - Low heater output is either due to low coolant level, and/or a blockage. If the coolant level is OK, a blockage can often be determined as follows: warm engine up, locate two heater hoses, feel temperature of both hoses. If they are both the same temperature, circulation is probably OK. If one is cooler than the other, a blockage is indicated. Possible causes include: faulty heater control valve, clogged heater core, and kink or obstruction in heater hose.

car service tip(heater control valve test) - The valve controls the flow of coolant through the heater core. Some are controlled by vacuum while others are controlled by a cable assembly. Check coolant level and top off, if necessary, before performing the test. For vacuum type valves, test as follows: warm up engine and leave running, remove vacuum hose to valve and cover with a finger, switch heat temperature lever from cold to hot, observe change in vacuum, reconnect vacuum hose, repeat lever movement, and check for heat output in both positions. Vacuum should come on or off depending on the valve type. If it does and no heat is produced regardless of lever setting, bypass the valve with a short hose length. If heater now works, the valve is defective. If it doesn't, the core is clogged or there is an obstruction in one of the heater hoses. For manual type valves, test as follows: check to see cable is connected at lever and valve, move lever from cold to hot (should be some resistance), observe cable movement at valve, and check heat output. If no heat is produced, a blockage exists in the heater core, valve, or heater hoses. To eliminate the valve, perform the bypass test as with the vacuum type valve.

car service tip(heater core clogged) - A heater core obstruction can sometimes be cleared if the heater hoses are reversed for a few days. The hoses are then placed back in their original positions.

car service tip(heater core leakage test) - See car service tip(radiator leakage test).

car service tip(high voltage terminal oxidation) - High voltage wires are prone to oxidation at their connector ends. Silicone grease can be applied to such terminals when new or cleaned to minimize oxidation and corrosion. The silicone grease coats the surface and also provides good electrical conductivity.

car service tip(holding bolts in place) - Bolts can be temporarily held in position by taping the heads with tape or using U-shaped clips made from paper clips. If the clips are used, position them so they face outward for removal and remove them before tightening the bolts. This procedure also works well for holding gaskets in place.

car service tip(idle stop solenoid test) - See car service tip(speed up solenoid test).

car service tip(ignition coil test) - A bad coil can cause: hard or inconsistent starting, cutting out under acceleration, and missing at high speed. The following detailed tests can be performed to pinpoint the problem.

First, check to make sure battery, battery ground strap, spark plugs, high voltage cables, timing, points, distributor cap, and distributor rotor are in good shape.

Test for strong spark as explained in car service tip(ignition coil output test). If a little or no spark occurs, continue testing.

Test for primary winding continuity as follows: remove distributor cap, place a piece of paper between points, connect one side of a 12 volt test light to ground, and connect the other lead first to one primary terminal then the other. If the ignition switch primary terminal (BAT, +, or SW) lights, current is reaching the coil. If the distributor primary terminal (CB, DIST, or -) lights, the primary winding is OK, if it doesn't, a break or short exists in the winding and the coil must be replaced. If continuity checks out, continue testing.

Test for burned points (conventional) as follows: place a piece of paper between points, remove ignition coil high voltage cable at distributor end and hold within 1/2 inch of ground, and take a clean screwdriver and jump or short the points. If a strong blue spark appears, the points are dirty, pitted, wet, etc. and need to be cleaned or replaced. If no spark appears, continue testing.

Test for grounded points, bad condenser, and faulty secondary windings as follows: turn off ignition switch, disconnect distributor primary wire at the primary terminal, attach a test wire from the terminal to a ground (acts as a temporary set of points), turn ignition switch to on position, disconnect high voltage ignition coil at distributor end and hold within 1/2 inch of ground, remove test wire from its ground connection and observe spark. If a spark appears, the points are probably grounded and/or the condenser is bad. If no spark occurs, the ignition coil's secondary windings are probably bad.

If the above tests check out and spark is still weak or non-existent, check for reversed coil polarity. See also car service tip(ignition coil reversed polarity test).

car service tip(ignition coil output test) - A quick and often reliable test of an ignition coil's output can be performed as follows: remove the high voltage coil wire at the distributor cap and place its terminal about 1/2 inch from ground, crank the engine briefly observing the spark jumping repeatedly to ground. It should be a strong spark with a bluish color emitting a cracking sound. If it is intermittent or yellow and weak looking, you may have a bad coil unless the points are corroded, the condenser is bad, the battery voltage is low, or the ignition coil's output wire has excessive resistance.

car service tip(ignition coil reversed polarity test) - To quickly test for reversed polarity perform the following test: shutoff engine, remove one of the spark plug leads, start the engine and hold the spark plug lead about 1/2 inch from a ground, place a sharpened lead pencil point midway between the plug lead and ground, and observe which side the spark flashes on. If it flashes between the pencil and the spark plug lead, the polarity is reversed. If it flashes on the ground side, polarity is correct.

car service tip(ignition coil voltage test) - Weak spark can be due to low primary voltage reaching the ignition coil or a bad resistor. The following simple test can be performed: check battery voltage to make sure it is around 12.5 volts, disconnect high voltage coil wire at the distributor and ground it, connect voltmeter leads at the positive terminal and to ground, crank the engine briefly observing the voltage, leave ignition switch in "on" position briefly and observe voltage reading. The first reading should be 5-7 volts (12V system). If less, the resistor is probably bad with high or infinite resistance which can be checked with an ohm meter. The second reading should be close to the battery voltage. If it isn't, there is resistance in the primary circuit between the ignition coil and the battery. See also ignition coil resistor.

car service tip(leaded to unleaded engine) - Engines using leaded fuel are steadily decreasing in number. The EPA has mandated the removal of all lead from gas in the near future. Engines designed to run on leaded fuel may need the following modifications to run on unleaded gas: use gasohol, change to hard exhaust valves and valve seats when a valve fails, lower compression ratio, install water injection, and avoid running engine hard. The primary problem with no lead is lack of lubrication for the exhaust valves.

car service tip(leaf spring squeaking) - Leaf springs squeak when lubrication between leaves disappears. Separate the leaf ends and apply a good grease or better yet install Teflon pads.

car service tip(light socket replacement) - Older two wire light sockets can be replaced, when they become rusty or corroded, with newer three wire sockets (extra wire is a ground wire).

car service tip(lug nuts too tight) - Removing too-tight lug nuts requires extra leverage. To increase lug wrench leverage, slide a section of pipe over the lug wrench end or improvise and use any other hollow tube-like item such as a bumper jack.

car service tip(main bearing replacement in car) - If the oil pan can be removed, one or more main bearings can be replaced without removing the engine. Proceed as follows: drain oil, remove oil pan, loosen all bearing cap bolts one turn, remove desired main bearing cap and lower bearing insert, make a small T-shaped piece of wire thinner than bearing or bend a cotter pin into the shape, insert wire into oil hole on journal, slowly rotate crankshaft in direction that will unseat bearing insert locating lug, rotate crank until upper insert falls out, remove wire, lubricate new insert liberally, insert by hand as far as possible in the opposite direction it came out, rotate crankshaft if necessary in other direction to seat bearing lug into its recess, install new lower lubricated insert, install bearing cap, tighten bolts to one turn of being snug, repeat above procedure for next bearing, tighten all cap bolts when finished till snug by hand, torque all bolts to specification, install oil pan, and add engine oil.

car service tip(metric nut and bolt numbers) - Metric nuts and bolt heads are stamped with numbers indicating their relative strength. When replacing a nut and/or bolt, be sure replacements have equal or greater strength.

car service tip(neutral switch test) - On automatic transmission cars, a starter that won't operate can often be due to a faulty neutral switch. To check the switch perform the following test: place transmission in neutral, locate switch, bypass it with a short jumper wire to ground, and turn ignition switch to start position. If the starter works, the switch is bad.

car service tip(oil change) - See oil change.

car service tip(oil filler cap residue) - A milky residue found in an oil filler cap or crankcase breather hose and/or filter is usually due to water in the oil. Possible causes: head gasket leaking, PCV valve faulty or improperly sized, crankcase breather hose leaking, and engine repeatedly driven short distances without a chance to warm up and drive off water vapors accumulating in crankcase due to condensation on cold metal surfaces.

car service tip(oil filter oil) - Temporary rod knock can be minimized after an oil change by filling the center of a full flow oil filter with fresh oil before installing it. The knocking sound is due to the rod bearings momentarily starving for oil.

car service tip(oil filter test) - A dirty or plugged oil filter can cause unfiltered oil to bypass it and flow directly to moving parts. To determine if oil is flowing through a filter: warm engine up to operating temperature, put a glove on, grasp the filter, and observe its warmth. If it's hot, oil is flowing through it OK. If it's cool or only warm, a blockage exists in the filter requiring immediate replacement.

car service tip(overfilled reservoir) - Fluid can easily be removed from a directly accessible overfilled reservoir by using a turkey baster or a pump from any hand spray dispenser.

car service tip(parking brake adjustment) - Proper adjustment is checked by jacking the rear wheels off the ground and engaging the parking brake halfway. If the rear wheels cannot be turned by hand, the brake is properly adjusted. If they can, adjust the cable adjuster. On cars without self-adjusting rear brakes, you may need to adjust the brake shoes for wear first. See also car service tip(free play test-parking brake).

car service tip(parts identification) - When doing any car work requiring disassembly and reassembly of many parts, it's a good idea to identify all the items removed. A tag attached to each item works well. Tag information should include: part description, its use, and where it connects. Items to tag include: all disconnected electrical wires; groupings of nuts, bolts, screws, etc. used for one item (such as transmission mounting bolts); hoses; pipes; sensors; switches; valves; bearings; gears; bushings; clamps; terminal on electrical devices; etc. Items can be placed in a plastic sack or can. Most people will usually forget where at least some of the components go. Identifying them takes a little more time, but will save many hours of frustration when the reassembly process begins, and possibly prevent damage due to leaving items off and/or assembling them improperly.

car service tip(PCV system test) - An easy test can be performed to determine what PCV system components are faulty. First eliminate hoses as a cause by cleaning all PCV hoses, checking them for any leaks or cracks, and replacing faulty hoses. Next clean or replace the PCV filter. Now remove the PCV valve with the engine off and shake it. If it doesn't rattle, the valve is clogged or not working and needs to be replaced. If it does rattle, start the engine, connect the valve and hosing to the carburetor, cover the valve's inlet end with a thumb. If there is no vacuum, replace the valve.

car service tip(pinging test) - Pinging under acceleration is often due to a vacuum advance unit not retarding the spark quick enough. To check for this, perform the following test: start engine, drive on an uncrowded road over 30 mph, accelerate lightly for 10-15 seconds, listen for pinging, floor accelerator for 10-15 seconds, and listen for pinging. If engine pings under light load but not under a heavy load, the vacuum advance system is probably not doing its job. See also pinging and engine problem(acceleration causes pinging-1).

car service tip(power balance test) – Test performed to initially determine if any engine cylinder has power producing problems. To perform the test: start engine, hook up a tachometer, remove one spark plug lead at a time with insulated pliers or a heavy rag, and observe drop in rpm. Rpm should drop 25-50 rpm. Little or no drop in engine rpm indicates a weak cylinder. Possible causes include: carburetion due to lean fuel mixture; ignition due wrong timing, weak spark, no spark, and/or fouled spark plug; and mechanical due to burned exhaust valve, improperly adjusted valves, broken piston rings, blown head gasket, and/or ventilated piston.

car service tip(power brake test) – See car service tip(brake booster test).

car service tip(power steering pump removal) – A power steering pump can retain its fluid when an engine is removed. To accomplish this, remove the pump from the engine, and tie it off to one side of the engine compartment. Also, a board or heavy rag should be placed over the pump to protect against engine collisions during the removal process.

car service tip(power steering test) – Hard power steering problems can be readily diagnosed by a process of elimination. Check each possible problem in the following order: low tire pressure, abnormal tread wear pattern, power steering belt for wear and proper tension, reservoir for proper fluid level, and pump bracket for tightness. Now raise the front wheels off the ground, and check the following possible problem areas: steering linkage pivot points for binding then lubricate; binding steering shaft column; start engine and turn steering fully in one direction and then the other, observing degree of stiffness; and remove pitman arm from steering gear box, grab a front wheel, and check turning stiffness.

If freeing the pitman arm from the steering gearbox makes the front wheels easy to turn, the problem probably lies in the power steering pump or the steering gearbox. The pump can be checked for proper fluid pressure output by using a power steering test valve and gauge tool. If pressure is up to specifications, the steering gearbox is binding. If pressure is below specifications, the pump is bad probably due to flow control and/or sticking pressure valves. The valves can be removed, cleaned, and polished smooth.

car service tip(pressure leak into coolant test) – Pressure built up in an engine's combustion chambers can leak into surrounding coolant jackets if the head gasket is not sealed or cracks exist in the cylinder walls or cylinder head. The hot gases can help overheat an engine. To determine if gases are leaking, perform the following test: shut off engine, disconnect water pump drive belt, remove thermostat, make sure block is full of water, start engine and accelerate it, and look for any bubbles appearing in coolant near thermostat. Presence of bubbles indicates a leaking head gasket and/or cracks between combustion chamber and coolant passageways (in head or block).

car service tip(radiator corrosion) – Interior radiator corrosion can be due to several factors. They include: heavily mineralized water, electrolysis, using little or no antifreeze in the water. There is little you can do with a heavily corroded radiator except replace it. Some cooling systems more prone to corrosion may require a water filter to help minimize the problem. Certain types are also designed to minimize electrolysis. An antifreeze with an oxidation inhibitor is good protection.

car service tip(radiator leakage test) – A simple pressure test can be performed on a radiator to find any leaks. The following items are needed: hose clamps, and a proper diameter and length of bicycle tubing containing the valve stem. To perform the test: attach the tube with hose clamps to the upper and lower radiator hose outlets, screw the radiator cap on tight, close the drain valve, pressurize the radiator to 10-15 pounds by adding compressed air through the valve stem, immerse the radiator in a tank of water, and look for escaping air bubbles.

car service tip(rear transmission seal leak) – Oil leaking out the back of a transmission is usually due to a bad oil seal or worn extension housing bushing. A worn bushing will destroy an oil seal from sideways shaft movement. To check for excess side play, try to move the driveline up and down near the end of the transmission. If there is excessive play, remove the driveline, examine the driveline yoke and extension housing bushing for signs of wear, and replace any worn parts. Other possible causes include: wrong size seal or bushing, improperly installed oil seal, too much oil in transmission, and crack in end of housing.

car service tip(removing broken axle shaft) – A broken rear axle shaft can be removed by making a wire tool. Attach a loop of flexible wire slightly larger than the axle shaft diameter at 90 degrees to a 1-3 foot length of strong straight wire. To remove the broken shaft portion in the rear axle housing slip the loop over the shaft end, then gently pull the straight wire out maintaining tension on the loop.

car service tip(removing broken bolt) – A broken bolt or stud can be removed by using a screw extractor, or by welding a nut and bar of scrap steel to the broken face.

car service tip(removing damaged screw heads) – Phillips, blade, and other screwheads can easily become damaged. Suggested ways to remove them include: using an impact wrench, sandwiching screwdriver into slot with steel wool or a grinding compound to help fill irregularities and increase grip, and drilling out head and removing with a screw extractor.

car service tip(removing tie rod end) - One effective way of removing the tapered end of a tie rod from its housing is to loosen the retaining nut, then use two hammers on the housing. One hammer remains in contact with the housing while the other taps it with light to medium blows from the opposite direction. If this fails try carefully striking the threaded stud with a rubber or non-metallic hammer.

car service tip(restricted exhaust test) - Restrictions in an exhaust system cause power loss and reduced fuel economy. To locate the restriction do the following: connect vacuum gauge to intake manifold; inspect exhaust system for signs of denting; start engine; observe vacuum reading by accelerating engine to 2-3,000 rpm and holding for several seconds; begin removing exhaust system components one at a time from tailpipe towards exhaust manifold; and perform vacuum reading after each component is removed. When the restricted part has been removed, the vacuum reading will stay high. See also car service tip(catalytic converter clogged), vacuum gauge reading(exhaust-restricted), and engine problem(power gradually lost).

car service tip(retard solenoid test) - A retard solenoid can be tested as follows: warm engine up to operating temperature, connect dwell-tachometer gauge, disconnect ground wire at carburetor, and observe engine idle speed. If speed increases noticeably, the solenoid is OK. If not, the carburetor ground and/or the solenoid is bad.

car service tip(rewaxing test) - The amount of wax left on a surface can be tested as follows: pour a small quantity of water on a flat panel and observe water beading pattern. If small drops or beads form, an adequate amount of wax is still left.

car service tip(shock absorber bushings) - Overtightened rubber bushings shorten a shock absorber's life. In general, tighten bushings until their outside diameter matches the retainer nut diameter.

car service tip(shock absorber test) - To determine shock wear simply push down on the respective fender firmly. The car should rebound slowly upwards and then dissipate to a stop. A continued up and down bouncing-like movement usually indicates a shock absorber is not doing its job and needs to be replaced. If a bad shock absorber is suspected, follow it up with a road test to confirm.

car service tip(slow starting test) - A simple test can be performed to rule out a car's ignition system as a reason for slow starting. First, verify that the engine turns over slowly. Next, remove the high voltage wire between the ignition coil and the distributor cap. Crank the engine again. If it rotates at its normal speed, a problem exists in the ignition system such as excessive advance and ignition cross fire. See also starting problem(engine cranks slowly).

car service tip(spark plug boot removal) - To remove a spark plug cable end: twist the boot until it turns easily, then pull on the boot and not the wire.

car service tip(spark plug deposit removal) - An engine can act as a good spark plug cleaner, cleaning plugs while they are operating. The following process is often effective short of removing and cleaning the plugs: warm up the engine, drive car accelerating engine (don't floor board it) to rpm where missing occurs, then slow engine rpm until missing disappears and drive at that speed for a few miles. The procedure is repeated several times. If the engine misses at higher speeds each time, the cleaning job is working.

car service tip(spark plug installation) - When installing spark plugs, a few simple steps will allow easy installation and removal, and minimize damage to spark plug and engine block threads. The procedure consists of: thoroughly cleaning threads, setting correct gap, coating threads with a small amount of oil, starting the plug carefully by hand to avoid thread damage, tightening plug until hand tight, and tightening an additional 1/4 turn for gasket seated plugs and 1/16 turn for taper seated plugs.

car service tip(spark plug removal) - The following steps will simplify removing spark plugs and prevent dirt from entering the combustion chamber: loosen plug with ratchet (if tight, use penetrating oil), unscrew a couple turns, blow compressed air or blow through a tube to clean dirt away from the plug base, and remove the plug.

car service tip(spark plug cable test) - Excessive resistance in a spark plug cable is often the cause of misfiring or plug fouling due to weak or non-existent spark. Test each cable with an ohmmeter. Resistance should average 10-15,000 ohms per foot, averaging 20,000 ohms for a typical cable length. The cable should be replaced if resistance: is significantly higher than other comparable length cables, is infinite, or changes when cable is wiggled (exception is carbon impregnated cable).

car service tip(speedometer needle bounce) - Needle bounce is often due to a speedometer cable needing lubrication. To lubricate it: remove the cable from its housing, coat it with a proper lubricant, and reinstall.

car service tip(speed up solenoid test) - A simple test can be performed to determine if a speed-up solenoid is defective. The solenoid usually opens a throttle plate slightly to avoid stalling when an air conditioner is turned on. The test consists of: turning ignition switch to accessories mode, turn on air conditioner, and watch for movement of plunger end of solenoid as power wire is removed. If no movement is observed, check for voltage to the solenoid wire terminal. Voltage indicates a defective solenoid. No voltage indicates a break or short in the wiring powering the solenoid.

car service tip(spring sag adjustment) - Sometimes one car spring will sag more than another. The sag can be caused by defects in the spring, or constantly overloading the spring in question. The sag can cause: improper tracking, uneven tire wear, and car handling problems. A sag can be repaired by replacing it or by shimming the spring back to proper height. Either is considered acceptable and will provide a lasting solution.

car service tip(starter draw test) - A measurement of a starter's current flow when cranking can help determine certain engine problems. First, determine the starter's normal current draw from spec sheets. Then perform the following test: attach voltmeter leads across the battery, attach a clamp-on type high amperage ammeter to starter cable running from the battery's positive post, remove and ground the ignition coil high voltage cable, turn ignition switch to start position and hold for 15 seconds, and observe voltmeter and ammeter reading during cranking. A too-high current flow indicates a faulty starter, heavy oil, or a tight engine. A too-low current flow indicates a weak battery (low voltage) or excess resistance in the starting circuit. See also car service tip(headlight test).

car service tip(starter drive jammed) - A starter drive will sometimes jam in the engaged position. To release the jam on a manual transmission car: stop the engine, put transmission in high gear, and rock car forward and backward (more). Possible causes include: worn or non-lubricated starter drive, and missing shims between starter and engine block (depending on design).

car service tip(starter no load test) - See no-load test.

car service tip(starter relay test) - A starter relay can quickly be checked with a voltmeter for proper operation by performing two tests.

First, test for voltage reaching the relay from the ignition switch as follows: attach positive voltmeter lead to small terminal of relay and negative lead to ground, turn ignition switch to "start" position, and observe voltage reading. It should be 12 or more volts. A smaller or zero reading indicates resistance or a break somewhere in the circuit from the relay to the ignition switch to the battery.

Second, test for voltage drop across the heavy terminals as follows: connect the positive voltmeter lead to the battery terminal and the negative lead to the starter terminal, observe voltage drop with ignition switch in "off", and then "start" position. The drop should be close to 12.5 and 0 volts respectively. A high reading in the "start" position indicates burned or worn contacts, or a short in the solenoid windings. In the latter case, no clicking sound will be heard when the relay is engaged. See also car service tip(headlight test).

car service tip(starting system test) - A quick test can be performed to determine whether a starting circuit or a starter is the cause for a no-start condition. The battery voltage should be 12.5 volts. First try the ignition switch in start position. If there is no response, turn the ignition switch off, get a short piece of heavy gauge (#8-10) insulated wire, and jump (connect) the two heavy duty terminals of the starter relay or solenoid. If the starter cranks OK, there is excessive resistance or a break in the starter wiring circuit leading up to and including the relay or solenoid. If the starter does not operate, a faulty starter is likely due to an internal ground, shorted windings, etc. See also engine problem(won't start), starting problem(starter won't operate), starting problem(engine cranks slowly), car service tip(headlight test), car service tip(starter relay test), and car service tip(cranking voltage test).

car service tip(starting test) - A common engine problem is an engine turning over OK, but very hard to start if at all. This can occur when it's cold and/or hot. It can be due to several things, but is usually due to flooding, a lean fuel mixture, weak or non-existent spark, or a large vacuum leak in the intake manifold. The following tests will track down the source of the problem.

To check for flooding, perform the following: remove air cleaner top, observe any presence of raw gas smell, observe float level through sight glass, and operate throttle linkage looking for fuel squirting into carburetor airway. High float level will cause excessive quantities of fuel to enter intake manifold and must be corrected. If the float level is OK and fuel squirts into airway, try starting engine by doing the following: open throttle linkage fully by hand and look into carburetor airway to see if choke plate is open, hold choke plate open if it isn't, push gas pedal to the floor and hold it, crank engine until it starts (maximum of 30 seconds to avoid starter overheating), and avoid over revving engine when it starts. It if won't start, let it sit for awhile and try again.

To check for lean fuel mixture, perform the following: remove air cleaner top, operate throttle linkage looking for fuel squirting into carburetor airway, and observe float level through sight glass. If no fuel squirts and float level is low, fuel is not getting to the carburetor due problems such as heat soak; vapor lock; clogged fuel pickup filter; empty fuel tank; low float level; sticking needle float valve; clogged main jet(s); leaking, broken, or clogged fuel line; and clogged fuel filter.

To check for weak or non-existent spark, first check coil output by: shutting off engine, removing distributor end of high voltage ignition coil and placing about 1/2 inch from ground, cranking engine, and watching for repetitive strong bluish spark arcing to ground. Next, check voltage to coil by connecting voltmeter to positive coil terminal and ground, cranking engine, and watching for a voltage reading close to battery voltage (12.5V). Finally, check coil ballast resistor by shutting engine off, turning ignition switch to on mode, measuring voltage drop across resistor, turning ignition switch off, and measuring resistance across resistor. Bluish spark indicates a strong spark. Low voltage will cause a weak or no-spark condition and indicates a weak battery or a resistance problem in circuit between battery and coil. Excessive voltage drop or resistance across ballast resistor will allow engine to start but not run. Other possible weak or no-spark causes include: faulty black box, high resistance in ignition coil and/or condenser due to heat, excess resistance in spark plug and/or ignition coil cable, fouled spark plugs, and points not separating.

To check for vacuum leak, check all hoses connected to manifold, check for open EGR valve, and then run a cranking vacuum test.

It is usually a good idea to also check ignition timing with a timing light during engine cranking, and rule out excessive spark advance or retard. See also car service tip(cranking vacuum test), engine problem(cranks but won't start), and car service tip(headlight test).

car service tip(static timing) – Static timing is a common method of setting spark advance on certain foreign cars. The procedure consists of the following: shut off engine, connect a 12 volt test light with one lead to ground and the other to the ignition coil's distributor terminal, turn engine until timing mark lines up with pointer, loosen distributor, rotate distributor in cam rotation direction until light goes out, rotate distributor in opposite direction until light just comes on, and then tighten distributor body.

When rotating engine to the timing mark position, be sure to use the normal engine rotation direction. This allows any slack in the distributor shaft gearing and the timing chain to be taken properly into consideration for an accurate spark advance setting.

car service tip(switch test) – Proper operation of an electrical switch can be determined by performing a simple test. Proceed as follows: turn switch on, connect voltmeter across terminals of switch, and read voltage drop. Switches are designed to carry the current flow with a very small voltage drop. Reading should be less than or equal to 2/10 of a volt. A higher reading indicates worn, corroded, or pitted contacts; or a higher current flow than switch was designed to carry. If the switch can be disassembled, repairs can often be made by cleaning up contacts. If it is sealed, a new one will have to be purchased.

car service tip(thermostat test) – The proper operation of a thermostat can be tested in the following way: remove thermostat from engine, place in a pan of water with a thermometer, heat water, observe temperature at which thermostat begins to open, watch to see if thermostat fully opens, cool water, watch to see if thermostat fully closes. The opening temperature should be within 5 degrees Fahrenheit of the temperature stamped on the thermostat.

car service tip(tie rod end wear test) – A worn tie-rod end can create excess play in the steering linkage and the steering wheel. If left uncorrected, the linkage could break causing complete loss of steering control. To test for wear: grab the tie rod end and move it up and down, then rotate it back and forth. There should be no noticeable movement in the tie-rod socket. If there is, replace it.

car service tip(timing belt check) – To insure maximum belt life and avoid possible engine damage, a car's timing belt should be periodically checked. Begin by removing the belt cover and spark plugs. Then slowly rotate the engine crankshaft using a socket wrench and ratchet. As the belt moves, check the inside surface for signs of unusual wear, broken or loose reinforcing strands, oil on the belt, and missing belt teeth. Replace belt if there is any sign of damage. See also timing belt.

car service tip(tire belt separation) – Belt separation or shifting in a tire can cause a car traveling at slow speeds to pull to one side. Belt separation can be checked by jacking up a car and spinning each tire. If a tire wobbles from side to side, belt problems are likely. When in doubt, substitute a good tire and drive the car to see if the pulling condition persists.

car service tip(tire rotation-radial) - Radial tires should be rotated from front to rear on the same side only. Rubber pulls radial steel belts in one direction. If the tire is placed on the opposite side, the pull is reversed and tends to cause belt separation and heat build-up from friction. When belts separate from the rubber, the tire becomes out of balance and has to be replaced.

car service tip(tire storage) - When storing tires off a car for a period of time, the following applies: reduce wheel-mounted tire pressure to half; place in cool, dry, dark area; and avoid standing tire on tread as it can create a permanent flat spot. See also car storage.

car service tip(torque converter installation) - To properly install an automatic transmission torque convertor, proceed as follows: slide convertor carefully into place, rotate it slowly until it is fully seated with outside edge flush with edge of bell housing, run piece of string across convertor face to two opposing bell housing bolt holes to temporarily hold convertor in place during transmission installation, mate up transmission to engine, install two or more transmission mounting bolts and tighten until a small gap remains, remove string, check for free movement of convertor by slow spinning it, install remaining mountings bolts and tighten until bell housing is snug against engine block, install and torque convertor to flywheel attachment bolts, and torque bell housing bolts.

car service tip(transmission modulator test) - The diaphragm in a transmission modulator can be checked by performing the following test. Insert a cotton swab or pipe cleaner into the open end of the modulator's diaphragm. If wetness is detected, the diaphragm is probably ruptured and the modulator must be replaced.

car service tip(turn signals flashing one side) - Turn signals will sometimes work on only one side. This is usually not the fault of the flasher unit as it is used to operate both sides. Possible causes include: short in wiring, bad connection, faulty bulb, and corroded bulb socket.

car service tip(U joint installation) - The caps on a U-joint can all be held safely in place until installed by wrapping them with a piece of masking tape.

car service tip(valve seal replacement) - Valve stem seals can be replaced without removing an engine's cylinder head. The procedure involves pressurizing one engine cylinder at a time (at top of the compression stroke) with compressed air so its respective valves will not slide into the combustion chamber when the springs and keepers are removed. Stem replacement for one cylinder is performed as follows: let the engine cool; remove the valve cover; remove all spark plugs; bring piston to the top of its compression stroke; insert threaded compressed air fitting into spark plug hole for pressurizing; pressurize and maintain at 20-40 psi; compress intake valve spring with spring compressor tool; remove valve keepers, valve spring retainer, and compressed valve spring; remove and replace valve stem seal; install compressed valve spring, valve spring retainer, and keepers; uncompress valve spring; and repeat valve stem replacement process for exhaust valve. The valve stem seals for each cylinder are done this way.

car service tip(valve spring direction) - Some valve springs are constructed with the coils more closely wound together at one end. If this is the case, be sure the more tightly coiled end is closest to the combustion chamber.

car service tip(vibration damper removal) - Vibration damper attachment bolts are usually hard to remove because the engine rotates as the bolt is turned. Engine rotation (usually clockwise when viewed from front) can be used unscrew the bolt by attaching a breaker bar and socket to the bolt, resting the bar on the car frame. Remove the ignition coil high voltage lead to the distributor cap, then bump the starter momentarily. The bolt should be loosened.

car service tip(vacuum advance test-1) - The ignition system's vacuum advance unit can be checked for proper operation by performing three tests.

The first test determines if the unit is getting vacuum. It consists of: disconnecting vacuum hose at vacuum advance unit, connecting a vacuum gauge to vacuum hose, starting engine, and running engine at idle and higher rpm observing vacuum reading. Depending on vacuum source used, high vacuum will be supplied at idle or at higher rpm. A vacuum of 15-22 inches indicates proper operation. No vacuum indicates clogged or leaking hose, or a plugged carburetor port.

The second test determines if the vacuum advance unit is defective. It consists of: attaching a hand vacuum pump to unit, applying at least 15 inches of vacuum to unit, and observe any vacuum loss for 1-2 minutes. If vacuum drops, the pump is working, and the connections are tight; the unit is faulty and must be replaced.

The third test determines if the distributor base plate moves in response to the unit. It consists of: shutting off engine, removing the distributor cap, applying vacuum to the unit with a hand pump, and observing base plate movement. If the vacuum is OK and no movement is observed, the plate is binding.

car service tip(vacuum advance test-2) - A faulty vacuum advance unit can often be determined with the following quick test: shut off engine, remove distributor cap, move breaker plate to full advance, cover vacuum hose with finger, release breaker plate, observe plate movement, and remove finger from hose after a few seconds. With the vacuum hose end covered, the plate should only move slightly before stopping. When your finger is removed, the breaker plate should rapidly move back to its retarded position. If the plate cannot be held, the vacuum diaphragm or the chamber housing is leaking, requiring replacement.

car service tip(valve spring test) - The condition of valve springs can be quickly checked for by placing them up in a straight row on a flat surface. Place a straightedge across the top of the springs and look for any different spring lengths. A spring should be replaced if it is: 1/16 inch or more shorter, deviates significantly from being perpendicular to surface, and/or contains any cracks.

car service tip(voltage drop test) - A voltage drop test is frequently used to determine amount of resistance in an electrical device when it is operating. A voltage drop higher than specifications indicates excessive resistance and probable replacement of the part tested. The test is made by: setting a voltmeter to the proper voltage range, attaching its leads to the input and output sides of the device, operating device, observing voltage drop, and comparing drop with device specifications.

car service tip(water in oil) - Water can be detected in oil by taking a sample and heating it on a stove to water boiling temperature (212 deg F). If water is present, it will disappear.

car service tip(wax application) - When applying wax to a car surface, a light application of corn starch on top of the wax will allow a high gloss to be buffed without streaking or smearing. See also car service tip(rewaxing test), and oiling.

car service tip(wet carpet) - Wet carpeting especially on the passenger side in the front seat is a common indicator of a coolant leak emanating from a heater core, heater control valve, and/or heater hose section.

car service tip(wheel alignment inspection) - See wheel alignment.

car service tip(wheel bearing inspection) - Proper inspection of a wheel bearing requires washing the bearing and detachable outer race (if there is one) in kerosene or other suitable solvent. Once clean, carefully check the following: rollers or balls to see if any are missing, have pit marks, are broken, or badly worn; and race surface for scratches and pit marks. If the bearing is a ball type, there should be very little play or wobble between the inner and outer race. If the play is excessive, bearing replacement is required.

car service tip(wheel bearing wear test) - Worn, damaged, or loose wheel bearings can be determined by a quick test. Proceed as follows: jack tire off the ground, grasp tire at the top and bottom with your hands, push and pull wheel at top and bottom, observe any movement, place one hand on top of wheel, rotate wheel slowly then faster listening for any grinding or whining sound. If the wheel can be moved the bearing wear or looseness is indicated. If the bearing whines or grinds on rotation, it will probably have to be replaced.

car service tip(wheel shimmy test) - Shimmy in a car's front end can be caused by an unbalanced tire. The following test is usually effective in finding such a tire: inflate all tires at least 5 pounds above maximum tire pressure rating when cold, drive car briefly and compare shimmy. If it's worse, one of the tires is at fault. Return one tire at a time to its original pressure and test drive. The procedure is repeated for each tire. When the shimmy changes, the last tire deflated is the culprit. See also shimmy and car handling problem(wheel shimmy).

car service tip(wheel side play test) - Tire side play usually indicates worn or loose steering linkage components. To check, perform the following: jack tire off the ground, grab the front and back of the tire with your hands, rock the tire, and observe any movement. Most cars have a small amount. If significant, worn or loose steering linkage components are indicated. Inspect joints, adjustment clamps, bushings, pitman arm, steering box mounting, and steering gear adjustment to locate problem.

car service tip(wheel cylinder check) - Any time brake shoes are inspected is a good time to check wheel cylinders for damage. To check: remove the dust covers and look for any leakage, rust, dirt, water, etc.

car service tip(wheel drag test) - To test for wheel drag proceed as follows: jack drive off the ground, slowly rotate tire, listen for grinding growling sounds caused by worn or damaged bearings, and feel any indications of tire dragging. Dragging can be caused by worn or damaged bearings, sticking caliper pistons or wheel cylinder (depending on brake type), warped rotor or drum, and rough braking surface.

car service tip(windshield fogging) - A windshield remaining fogged during defroster use is usually due to a leaky heater core or heater control valve.

car service work - Work performed on a car to fix a problem or do preventive maintenance.

car sick - To become nauseated from riding in a car, bus, etc.

car's on fire - Burning car. The most common fire is an engine fire. Fires can be started inside from burning material such as cigarettes, etc. An engine or inside fire should be extinguished quickly. A fire near a gasoline tank is very dangerous and should only be handled by professionals. If such is the case, get all passengers far away from the car, call the fire department, and wait for their help. See also engine fire, carburetor fire, and backfire.

car storage - Car placed in an area conducive to preserving all its parts when it is not being used. There are basically two types of car storage: short-term and long-term. Short-term storage is considered 2-3 months, and long-term anything beyond that.

Short term storage can be done by simply storing a car in a heated garage, building, etc. with almost no maintenance. The following should be done before leaving it: set up battery either in or out of car so it can be periodically trickle charged; fill all fluid reservoirs to capacity; and add gasoline additives to tank to combat water, gum formation. When starting the engine after storage, allow it to crank for 30-60 seconds without starting (remove ignition coil wire) to build up oil pressure. Another acceptable short-term storage method is to start the car once a week and warm it up for 15-30 minutes.

Long term storage is much more elaborate than short-term. The following steps are commonly performed: put car up on blocks (take weight off wheels); flush all fluid reservoirs, then refill them; fill cooling system with pure antifreeze; add water and gum remover additives to gas tank; pour 2-4 tablespoons of oil down an open carburetor throat while cranking the engine; remove battery and set up a charger for periodic trickle charging; treat all vinyl material with a vinyl preservative; loosen and/or remove all V-belts; coat rubber window stripping with a protective material; wax car body paint; soak all transmission, carburetor, and other movable linkages with a light oil; leave windows slightly cracked; place a box of baking soda or other odor absorbing product in car; remove any floors mats covering carpeting; and cover car only with a breathable cover or not at all.

CART - Abbreviation for Championship Auto Racing Teams. It is a body formed to regulate certain aspects of racing Indianapolis cars.

Carter(1) - American car produced in 1916.

Carter(2) - Line of American carburetors and other automotive equipment.

Cartercar - American car produced from 1906-1916 by Motor Car Co. (1906-1908), and Cartercar Co. (1908-1916), both in Michigan.

Cartermobile - American car produced from 1924-1925 by Carter Motor Car Co. in Washington D.C.

Carter Twin Engine - American car produced from 1907-1908 by Carter Motor Car Co. in Washington D.C. and Maryland.

Carthage - American car produced in 1924.

car theft - See stolen car.

car thief - Person skilled in stealing cars.

car top - See roof.

car transport - Vehicle used to transport cars. A tow truck.

car transport(flatbed) - Vehicle designed to carry a car on a movable tilting flatbed built onto the back of the vehicle. See also towing system(flatbed).

car transport(no-tow) - See car transport(flatbed).

car transport(roll-back) - See car transport(flatbed).

car transport(tilt-bed) - See car transport(flatbed).

car transport(wheel lift) - Vehicle designed to carry a car with an extendible stinger and dual claw assembly. See also towing system(wheel lift).

car vibration - See vibration(car).

car wanders - Condition created when a car drifts to the left and right during driving. Possible causes include: wear or loose parts in the steering linkage, bad front end alignment, wear or loose parts in the suspension system, and low or uneven tire pressure.

car wash - Business engaged in washing and polishing cars.

car weight balance - Car balance determined by the distribution of weight to each of the wheels. It is primarily a car design problem.

CAS - Abbreviation for cleaner air system.

CASC - Abbreviation for Formula Atlantic Canadian Automobile Sports Clubs.

Casco - American car produced in 1926.

Case - American car produced from 1910-1927 by J.I. Case Threshing Machine Co. in Wisconsin.

case harden - To harden the surface of a metal such as steel. See also heat treatment and annealing.

Casey - American car produced in 1920.

cash difference - The difference in value between a trade-in car and the selling price of the car desired.

casing head gasoline - Natural gasoline composed of lighter petroleum products obtained by condensing oil well natural gas.

cass - Abbreviation for cassette tape. See also c tape.

Cass - American car produced in 1915.

castellated nut - Nut designed with a series of slots cut into one end to receive a cotter pin and thereby prevent the nut from turning.

caster - See wheel alignment angle(caster).

caster and camber gauge - Gauge designed to measure front wheel castor and camber angles.

casting - Shape formed by pouring or spraying a plastic or liquid substance into a mold and letting the material harden. Also, it refers to the process itself.

casting plug - See freeze plug.

cast iron - Alloy composed of iron and over 2% carbon. It is used for engine blocks, differential housings, and transmission cases. It can be readily molded into complex shapes at low cost.

castle - See castellated nut.

casual car pooling - See car pooling(casual).

Catalina - American car produced from 1955 to date by Pontiac Division of General Motors Corp. in Michigan.

catalyst - Substance used to cause or accelerate a chemical change.

catalytic converter - Small muffler-like device installed in an exhaust system ahead of the muffler, and designed to use heat and chemical changes to reduce the harmful emissions of automobile exhaust. Hydrocarbons and carbon monoxide are converted into water vapor and carbon dioxide, and NOx emissions are kept low. A converter usually requires some kind of catalyst to cause the reactions to occur. The most common catalysts are high temperature and platinum.
   Catalytic converter cars run on unleaded gas. The lead compounds in leaded gas can ruin a catalytic converter in short order and plug it up. A plugged converter creates excessive backpressure, decreases engine performance and fuel economy, and gets too hot (sometimes glows dull red from 800-2,000 degree heat).
   Catalytic converters are sensitive to unburned hydrocarbons. Large amounts of raw gasoline entering a converter can severely shorten its life. Electronic ignition systems, on-board computers, various sensors, etc. help avoid this problem in today's cars by eliminating misfiring and keeping fuel mixtures lean. See also smell(rotten egg).

catalytic converter(dual bed) - Converter designed with two honeycomb structures to reduce emissions. One contains platinum and rhodium, and the other contains platinum and palladium. Rhodium is used to help reduce nitrogen oxides.

catalytic converter(monolithic) - Converter designed with a ceramic honeycomb structure containing platinum and palladium to help catalyze hydrocarbons and carbon monoxide.

catalytic converter(three way) - Converter designed to reduce three kinds of exhaust emissions: unburned hydrocarbons, carbon monoxide, and various oxides of nitrogen.

catch a tow - To get closely behind another car to take advantage of reduced air drag. It is a common racing maneuver used in racing, and actually helps lessen the drag somewhat on the lead car.

catching lights - To drive so as to arrive at each traffic light as it turns green.

catch tank - Tank used to connect overflow of liquids. The cooling systems on today's cars use overflow tanks to minimize evaporation and contain antifreeze when it expands due to heat.

catch the bus - To be at a bus stop when a bus arrives.

cathode - Electrode used to send current. In a battery, for example, it is a positive electrode or the positive outside terminal.

Cato - American car produced in 1907.

catwalk - Depressed surface usually located between a fender and a raised area of a hood or deck.

Cavac - American car produced in 1910.

Cavalier - American car produced in 1913 and 1925. Also, an American car produced from 1980 to date by Chevrolet Division of General Motors Corp. in Michigan.

cavitation - See pump cavitation.

Caward-Dart - American car produced in 1924.

Cawley - American car produced in 1917.

CB(1) - Abbreviation for contact breakers. See also ignition coil terminal.

CB(2) - American car produced from 1917-1918 by Carter Brothers Motor Co. in

Maryland.
CB(3) – See API service category(CB).
CB(4) – Abbreviation for cabriolet.
CB(5) – Abbreviation for citizen's band radio.
CC(1) – See API service category(CC).
CC(2) – Abbreviation for cyclecar.
cc – Abbreviation for cubic centimeter. It is a metric measure of volume, and is commonly used to describe foreign car engine displacement. A 1600cc engine, for example, would be approximately 98 cubic inches.
CCA number – Abbreviation for cold cranking ampere number.
CCA rating – Maximum battery output in amperes specified at a certain cold temperature such as 0 degrees Fahrenheit. See also car service tip(battery load test).
CCC – Abbreviation for computer command control.
CCC tester – Instrument used to interpret CCC signals and determine the engine problem. See also computer command control, trouble code, and self-diagnostic mode.
ccing – Process used to determine combustion chamber volume in cubic centimeters. A clear plastic plate is placed over the combustion chamber and temporarily sealed. Fluid is then inserted through a calibrated tube until flow stops. The difference in fluid height is used to determine volume. Ccing is often used to help equalize combustion chamber volumes in racing engines.
C clip – Metal clip shaped like a "C" for fitting into a recess cut in a shaft. It is commonly used to hold things, mounted on a shaft, in place.
CCMC – Abbreviation for Committee of Common Market Automobile Constructors.
CCS – Abbreviation for controlled combustion system.
CCV – Abbreviation for closed crankcase ventilation.
CD(1) – Abbreviation for capacitive discharge.
CD(2) – See API service category(CD).
CD add on unit – Capacitive discharge ignition device added to replace conventional breaker points in a distributor with a magnetic pulse pick up unit.
C De L – American car produced in 1913.
CDN – Abbreviation for Canada found usually on an international license plate.
CDT – Abbreviation for Central Daylight Time.
CEC – Abbreviation for combination emission control. See also emission control system(combustion-combination emission control), and CEC valve.
CECO – American car produced in 1914.
CEC valve – Electrically operated solenoid valve used to control exhaust emissions when an engine is decelerating by temporarily opening throttle valve a slight amount and allowing vacuum to flow to the vacuum advance unit. The net effect is to lean the fuel mixture and more completely burn it. The solenoid is usually built with a double-ended shaft. One end is tapered to meter vacuum from a carburetor vacuum port, and the other end has an adjustable screw head to contact the throttle lever for adjusting throttle valve opening. See also emission control system(combustion-combination emission control), and CEC.
Celebrity – American car produced from 1980 to date by Chevrolet Division of General Motors Corp. in Michigan.
cell – See battery cell.
cell connector – Lead strap used to connect the negative terminal of one battery cell to the positive of another. Older batteries had connectors outside the battery.
Cella I – Experimental scale model electrochemical car built by De Soto in 1959. It converted liquid fuel directly into electrical energy to power a car.
Celsius – Swedish astronomer named Anders Celsius (1701-1744), who developed the Celsius temperature scale. It is also known as the Centigrade scale. See also degree(Celsius).
Celt – American car produced in 1927.
Centaur – American car produced from 1902-1903.
center electrode – Spark plug electrode(center).
Center for Auto Safety – Consumer group organized in 1967 by Ralph Nader to put pressure on the Department of Transportation and the auto industry to strengthen safety standards. A few of their functions include: accepting and organizing complaint letters, putting pressure on the auto industry to emphasize safety rather than styling, acting on the consumer's behalf by filing briefs with the National Highway Traffic Safety Administration, and participating in Department of Transportation rule making. Be sure to send any complaint letter you generate to this group.
centerline – Any line bisecting a plane figure or an axis of rotation.
center line(highway) – Line painted down the middle of a road to mark the center of a road and keep traffic safely separated.
center link – See drag link.

center of gravity - Point specified in a body where weight is evenly distributed.

center pivot radius rod - Rod used to limit horizontal movement of usually a rear axle. It is attached at three points forming a triangular shape: to the axle near each wheel, and in the center of the car underbody usually to a cross member. See also wishbone.

center steering linkage - Steering system designed to use two tie rods connected to steering arms and to a central idler arm. The idler arm operates by using a drag link connected to a pitman arm.

center tower - See center tower terminal.

center tower terminal - High voltage terminal positioned in the center of a distributor cap. It receives the high voltage impulse from an ignition coil. The impulse is then distributed to different spark plug terminals through the distributor rotor.

centigrade - Temperature measurement scale. Water freezing and boiling temperatures are 0 and 100 degrees respectively. See also degree(centigrade).

Central - American car produced from 1905-1906 by Central Automobile Co. in Rhode Island.

Central Steam - American steam car produced from 1905-1906.

centrifugal advance - See advance(centrifugal).

centrifugal advance weights - Movable weights mounted underneath a distributor point plate. They move outward when engine speed increases and thereby alter ignition advance. See also advance(centrifugal).

centrifugal clutch - Clutch designed to expand a friction device on a driving shaft with centrifugal force until it is locked to a drum on a driven shaft.

centrifugal force - Force created which tends to pull an object away from a center when rotated about it. In addition, the force increases by the square of the rotating speed. For example, a weight on a tire exerts a force of 5 pounds at 20 mph. At 40 mph, a 20 pound force is exerted, and at 60 mph the force becomes 45 pounds. A car driving around a turn experiences this force. The faster you take the turn the more centrifugal force is exerted on the car. If the speed is too high, the centrifugal force will exceed the friction between the tires and the road causing the car to lose traction. Unbalanced tires also display the effects of centrifugal force. Such tires have an uneven mass distribution around the circumference. The centrifugal force, therefore, is not evenly distributed. This causes a back and forth movement to develop whose strength is dependent on the degree of unequal mass distribution.

centrifugal weights - Movable weights mounted on a distributor shaft for the purpose of advancing ignition timing, as speed increases, to a certain limit. The strength of the springs determine the speed of centrifugal advance. See also advance curve.

Centurion - American car produced from 1965-1970 by Buick Division of General Motors Corp. in Michigan.

Century - American steam car produced from 1899-1903 by Century Motor Vehicle Co. in New York. Also, an American car produced in 1927. Also, an American car produced from 1955 to date by Buick Division of General Motors Corp. in Michigan.

Century Electric - American car produced from 1911-1915 by Century Motor Co. (1911-1913), and Century Electric Car Co. (1913-1915), both in Michigan.

Century Steam - American car produced in 1901.

Ceres - Three-wheeled car produced from 1983 to date by Creative Cars Corporation in Illinois. Its fuel economy is estimated to be 62 and 50 mpg in highway and city driving.

certificate - A document used to serve as evidence as to the status, qualification, truth, etc. of something.

Certificate of Adequacy - Certificate posted on used cars sold by dealers stating a car is "in condition to give satisfactory service on the highway at the time of delivery". See also warranty of serviceability.

Certificate of Non-Operation - Certificate used to specify that a vehicle was not moved, operated, abandoned on a highway, or otherwise used in a manner that would require collecting any registration fees due. See also Non-Use Affidavit.

Certificate of Origin - Certificate used to specify the original owner of an imported car. The owner is usually the manufacturer.

Certificate of Ownership - Certificate used to specify the owner of a piece of property.

Certificate of Title - Certificate used to specify the owner of a car, boat, trailer, etc.

cetane number - See cetane rating.

cetane rating - Number used to specify the ignition quality of a diesel fuel. How it ignites determines engine starting and running characteristics. It specifies the time delay from injection to ignition of the fuel. Higher cetane rating means quicker fuel ignition. Diesels operating in cold weather need high cetane fuel in order to ignite in cold air and cold cylinders. Low cetane fuel often creates operating problems including: hard starting, white smoke, engine knock, and harmful engine deposits. The minimum rating for number 1 and 2 diesel fuel is supposed to be 40. Cetane ratings are not usually posted on service station pumps. See also distillation range.

CF – American car produced in 1908.

cfm – Abbreviation for cubic feet per minute.

CGV – American car produced in 1903.

CH – Abbreviation for Switzerland found usually on an international license plate.

Chadwick – American car produced from 1904-1916 by L.S. Chadwick (1904-1906), Fairmount Engineering Co. (1906-1907), and Chadwick Engineering Works (1907-1916), all in Pennsylvania.

chain drive – Drive axle powered by a chain running from a transmission output. It was used on early cars until around 1914.

Chalfant – American car produced from 1906-1912 by Chalfant Motor Car Co. in Pennsylvania.

chalk – Powdery substance formed as a result of paint oxidation.

Challenger – American car produced from 1962-1977 by Dodge Division of Chrysler Corp. in Michigan.

Chalmers – American car produced from 1908-1924 by Chalmers Motor Car Co. in Michigan. It was one of the most popular cars in its time.

Chalmers-Detroit – American car produced from 1908-1910.

Chalmers, Hugh – He ran the Chalmers Motor Company. In 1913, he challenged the success of the Ford Model T by backing the Saxon Motor Company. The venture was not successful.

chamfer – Flat surface beveled or angled off from an adjacent surface.

chamois – Cloth made of soft leather. It is commonly used to dry a car's paint surface with minimum abrasion.

Champ – American car produced from 1978-1983 by Plymouth Division of Chrysler Corp. in Michigan.

Champion(1) – American car produced from 1908-1909 and 1916-1923 by Famous Mfg. Co. in Illinois (1908-1909), Champion Auto Equipment Co. in Indiana (1916-1917), and Direct Drive Motor Co. and Champion Motors Corp. in Pennsylvania (1917-1923).

Champion(2) – American line of spark plugs produced by Champion Spark Plug Co.

Champion Electric – American car produced in 1899.

Chandler – American car produced from 1913-1929 by Chandler Motor Car Co. in Ohio. It reached its greatest production in 1920 with an output of 20,000.

Change of Ownership – See Notice of Transfer.

change of venue – Transfer made of a court case to another court jurisdiction.

change the motor – To remove an existing engine and reinstall a rebuilt, new, or different type engine.

changing lanes – Process of moving from one traffic lane to another.

changing plugs – Removing spark plugs and installing new or reconditioned ones.

channeling – Process used to spread, lower, and reattach a car body to its frame.

channellock pliers – Plier designed with a movable pivot point. It allows two opposing jaws to remain parallel to each other at different distances.

Chapin, Roy – He organized and headed the Hudson Motor Company. He also served as Secretary of Commerce in 1932 under President Herbert Hoover.

Chapman – American electric car produced from 1899-1901 by Belknap Motor Co. in Maine.

Chapman strut – Shock absorber and coil spring assembly built very similar to a MacPherson strut. It is used to support rear wheels with pivoting axles.

character line – Line used in auto styling to define a basic shape resulting in an intersection of planes.

charcoal canister – Canister filled with activated carbon and used to temporarily store gasoline vapors from a fuel tank. When an engine is running, any accumulated vapors are drawn into an engine purging the charcoal.

charge – Process used to put electrical energy back into each battery cell by reversing the flow of electrical current. Process reverses the chemical action that has taken place in a cell. It raises the specific gravity putting electrolyte absorbed in the plates back into solution.

charged battery – See battery(charged).

Charger – American car produced from 1962 to date by Dodge Division of Chrysler Corp. in Michigan.

charging circuit – Electrical circuit used in a car to direct charging current from an alternator or generator to a battery via a regulator.

charging the battery – Process used to restore electrical energy to each battery cell by reversing the flow of electricity into each cell.

charging the system – See air conditioner(charging the system).

Charles-Town-About – American car produced from 1958-1959. It was a prototype electric car similar in appearance to a Volkswagen Karmann Ghia.

chart - Condition created when a customer agrees to the highest allowable interest rate on a loan, and also agrees to buy accident, health, and life insurance policies.

Charter - American car produced in 1903 by James A. Charter in Illinois. It reportedly ran on an equal mixture of gas and water. The mixture was injected into a combustion chamber with the gas igniting and converting the water into superheated steam. The result was a longer and smoother explosion.

Charter Oak - American car produced from 1916-1917 by Eastern Motors Syndicate in Connecticut.

chase - To repair or straighten damaged threads.

Chase - American car produced from 1907-1912 by Chase Motor Truck Co. in New York. It could be converted from a car to a light truck.

chassis - Undercarriage of a car designed to contain all the parts and components necessary to support a car and power it. Generally, the chassis refers to everything on the car except the body.

chassis lubrication - To lubricate all movable chassis points requiring periodic greasing.

Chatauqua - American car produced from 1913-1914 by Chatauqua Cyclecar Co. in New York.

Chatham - Canadian car produced from 1907-1908.

chauffeur - Driver skilled in operating a car for someone else.

chauffeurs license - See license(chauffeur).

cheaters - Street tires formulated with racing-rubber compounds.

check engine light - See warning light(check engine).

Checker - American taxicab car produced from 1923 to date by Checker Motors Corp. in Michigan. Also, an American car produced beginning in 1959 by the same company.

checkered flag - See flag(checkered).

checking the map - To check a road map for directions.

check under the hood - Procedure followed to perform a quick engine check. Items checked typically include: level of engine oil, transmission oil, coolant, and windshield washer fluid; tightness and wear of belts, and wear and leakage of radiator and heater coolant. Service station attendants commonly ask drivers if they would like their engine checked. It is wise to be wary of such requests as slick attendants can cause all kinds of problems when you are not watching all for the purpose of obtaining more business. See also con game(check under the hood).

check valve - Valve designed to permit one-way flow of a fluid or gas. Valving mechanism is usually shaped like a ball. When flow moves in the right direction, material moves around the ball. When the flow reverses, the material forces the ball against its seat and stops the flow.

cheese grater file - Rough edge file used for removing plastic filler before it fully hardens.

Chelsea - American car produced in 1901-1904 and 1914.

chemical compound - Substance composed of two or more chemical elements in the form of a solid, liquid, or gas.

chemical cubic inches - See nitrous oxides.

chemical element - Solid, liquid, or gaseous substance broken down into its simplest form.

Cherokee - Car produced from 1984 to date by American Motors Corp. in Ohio.

cherry - See cream puff.

Chevelle - American car produced from 1964 to date by Chevrolet Division of General Motors Corp. in Michigan.

Chevette - American car produced from 1976-1987 by Chevrolet Division of General Motors Corp. in Michigan.

Chevrolet - American car line produced from 1911 to date by Chevrolet Motor Co., now a division of General Motors in Michigan. Additional plants exist in Brazil and South Africa.

Chevrolet, Gaston - He won the Indianapolis 500 Race in 1920 driving an average of 88.6 mph in a Monroe.

Chevrolet, Louis - He designed the first Chevrolet car models for the Chevrolet Car Company in 1911. He also became president of Frontenac Motor Company which made a racing version of the Model T Ford.

Chevrolet Motor Company - Company organized in the 1910s and responsible for producing a popular low priced car in 1916, one year before being acquired by General Motors Corporation.

Chevrolet Truck - American truck produced from 1918 to date.

Chevron Corporation - A U.S. petroleum company headquartered in San Francisco, California. It was formerly called Standard Oil Company of California. See also petroleum company.

chevy - Chevrolet engine.

Chevy - Chevrolet car.

Chevy II - American car produced from 1962-1979 by Chevrolet Division of

General Motors Corp. in Michigan.

Chicago – American car produced in 1899-1905, 1907-1910, and 1917.

Chicagoan – American car produced from 1952-1954 by Triplex Industries in Illinois. Only 15 of the sports car were made.

Chicago Commercial – American car produced from 1905-1907.

Chicago Electric – American car produced from 1912-1914.

Chicago Motor Buggy – American car produced in 1908.

Chicago Steamer – American steam car produced in 1905.

chicane – Jog in a race track designed to cut car speeds, make track safer, allow cars to compete more evenly, and make race more exciting to spectators. It is usually placed in a straightaway and consists of a sharp right followed by a sharp left or vice versa.

Chief – American car produced from 1908-1909 and 1947.

Chieftain – American car produced from 1955-1960 by Pontiac Division of General Motors Corp. in Michigan.

chilled iron – Cast iron formed with a hardened surface.

Chiltons – Line of automotive books, manuals, etc. See also Motor, Hanes, and Mitchell(2).

chizler – Chrysler engine.

chock – Triangular shaped block placed in front of a tire to keep it from rolling.

choke(1) – Assemblage of parts used to operate a movable butterfly type plate near the top of a carburetor for the purpose of increasing gas flow into an engine when cold. The choke causes this by restricting airflow into the carburetor throat which creates a higher vacuum sucking more fuel into an intake manifold. Choke parts consist of: a butterfly valve plate, choke shaft, choke housing, choke coil, heat transfer parts, and associated linkage. A faulty system can cause: poor fuel economy, stalling, flooding, and hard starting.

choke(1-automatic) – Choke designed to open a butterfly plate automatically as the engine warms up. Most modern cars have automatic chokes. It usually opens as a result of coolant circulating around a bimetallic spring that changes the position of the butterfly plate as the water gets warmer.

choke(1-crossover) – Automatic choke designed with a thermostatic coil mounted away from a choke shaft near an exhaust manifold. A rod links the coil to a choke shaft lever for controlling choke plate movement.

choke(1-electric) – Automatic choke designed to use an electromagnet and a thermostat for controlling the position of a choke plate during different engine operating conditions. It was used on earlier model cars.

choke(1-exhaust heated) – Automatic choke designed to use engine exhaust for heating a choke coil and thus determine choke plate positioning.

choke(1-manual) – Choke designed for manual control of the butterfly plate.

choke(1-spring loaded) – Choke designed with a spring-loaded plate permitting a slight opening during starting.

choke(1-water heated) – Automatic choke designed to use engine coolant temperature for heating a choke coil.

choke(2) – Electrical device used to generate an inductance.

choke circuit – See carburetor circuit(choke).

choke coil(1) – Bimetallic spring located in a choke housing. It controls the movement of a choke shaft and attached plate by uncoiling as it warms.

choke coil(2) – See choke(2).

choke coil lever – Lever mounted on a choke shaft and inside a choke housing. It transfers bimetallic spring movement to a choke shaft.

choke control rod – See fast idle cam link.

choke element – See choke coil(1).

choke housing – Enclosed circular body mounted at the end of a choke shaft to control movement of a choke plate as an engine warms ups. It contains a bimetallic spring, other linkage parts, and a hot air or water chamber. Exhaust air or hot water is routed to a chamber which heats up a bimetallic spring and moves a choke shaft.

choke housing plate – Circular plate located in a choke housing separating a bimetallic choke coil from other parts.

choke is on – Choke butterfly valve in closed position.

choke is stuck – Condition created when a butterfly plate in a carburetor starts binding usually due to accumulation of resins, gums, and other compounds built up on the surfaces of a carburetor's air passageway. One quick fix involves spraying the passageway with a carburetor cleaner. A more lasting solution requires removing the plate assembly, cleaning and lubricating the moving surfaces, and replacing it.

choke lever – Lever mounted on a choke shaft of some carburetors. It is used to control the position of a choke plate during engine warm-up through linkage to a fast idle cam.

choke on time – Time elapsed before choke plate is fully open.

choke operating lever – See choke coil lever.

choke piston – Small piston used in the choke housing of some carburetors to assist or counteract a choke coil's action and thus a choke plate during different engine operating conditions. It operates on intake manifold vacuum.

choke plate - Butterfly valve portion of a choke used to regulate gas flow into an intake manifold when an engine is cold. It is located higher up in a primary air passageway above the throttle plate.

choke shaft - Shaft mounted horizontally in the upper part of a carburetor airway. Choke plate is attached to it.

choke the carburetor - To close the choke of a carburetor.

choke vacuum break - Device used to open a choke plate slightly when a cold engine is started. Faulty operation can cause: poor fuel economy and stalling.

choke valve - See choke plate.

choking(carburetor) - Using a choke.

choking(exhaust) - See backpressure.

chopped car - See half-breed.

chopped flywheel - Flywheel modified by milling off metal to reduce weight and inertia, and improve acceleration.

chopping - Process used to shorten a car's overall length. It consists of: cutting it in two, removing the necessary metal, and rewelding the body and frame back together. Also, it refers to lowering a car's overall height by dropping its roofline. The latter process consists of: removing the glass, cutting the roof supports, removing the necessary metal, readjusting and rewelding the supports, and installing new glass.

chop shop - Car business engaged in disassembling stolen cars, selling the parts to repair shops, and often constructing half breed cars. A legal chop shop is a dismantler or auto wrecker. See also con game(chop shop).

Christie - American car produced from 1904-1910 by Christie Front Motor Drive Co. in New York.

Christman - American car produced from 1901-1902.

christmas club - Car sales technique used where a car buyer is convinced the first car payment is being made by the dealer when in actuality it is being made by the customer.

christmas tree - Multi-light device used to start drag races. It consists of a series of vertically arranged lights that come on in sequence from top to bottom. When the lowest light is activated, the race begins. It can also activate the lights on one side slower to allow a faster car to compete against a slower one.

Christopher - American car produced from 1908-1910.

chrome - Metal coating plated onto a metal surface. It is characterized by being hard and shiny. It is compounded with chromium and other chemical elements such as nickel and copper.

chrome fitting - Fitting plated with chrome.

chrome plated - Surface plated with chrome.

chromies - Simulated magnesium or chrome racing wheels used on stock cars for a custom look.

chromium steel - See stainless steel.

chrondeks - Drag racing electronic timing system.

Chrysler - American car line produced from 1923 to date by Chrysler Corp. in Michigan.

Chrysler Corporation - Company formed in 1928 to sell Dodges, Desotos, Plymouths, and Chryslers. Today, it is headquartered in Detroit, Michigan. See also Iacocca, Lee.

Chrysler, Walter - He was instrumental in the success of several Auto companies in the 1910s and 1920s. He saved the Maxwell-Chalmers Company in 1924 by introducing new Chrysler model cars which paved the way for the success of the company that evolved into the Chrysler Corporation.

chuck hole - Hole or depression formed in a road. See also pothole.

chuggle - Drivability problem associated with late model cars equipped with automatic transmissions using lock-up converters. One symptom is usually a thunking sound during shifting with momentary engine miss.

Church - American car produced in 1901-1903, 1910-1911, and 1914.

Church-Field - American electric car produced from 1912-1913 by Church-Field Motor Co. in Michigan.

chute - Straightaway on a racing track. Also, it refers to a safety chute used to slow down dragsters and other high speed racing cars.

CI - Abbreviation for Ivory Coast found usually on an international license plate.

cid - Abbreviation for cubic inch displacement.

Ciera - American car produced from 1982 to date by Oldsmobile Division of General Motors Corp. in Michigan.

cigarette lighter - Electrical heating device used to light cigarettes.

Cimarron - American car produced from 1980 to date by Cadillac Motor Car Co. in Michigan.

Cincinnati - American car produced from 1903-1905 by Cincinnati Automobile Co.

in Ohio.

Cino - American car produced from 1909-1913 by Cincinnati Automobile Co. in Ohio.

Circa-Hermann - American car produced in 1914.

circle painting - See blowup painting.

circuit - Path used to transfer electric current from its source to various components and connections, and back to the source again.

circuit breaker - Protective device used in an electrical circuit to interrupt current flow if it becomes excessive. Most circuit breakers can be reset to trip a circuit indefinitely.

circuit(closed) - Electrical circuit characterized by uninterrupted current flow.

circuit(open) - Electrical circuit characterized by an open break preventing current flow.

circuit(parallel) - Electrical circuit characterized as having a beginning (positive) and ending (negative) point in common with other circuits.

circuit(series) - Electrical circuit characterized as having the end (negative) of one circuit connected to the beginning (positive) of another circuit, one or more times, forming a single path for the current flow.

circular mil - Unit of area equal to the area of a circle one mil (1/1,000 of an inch) in diameter.

citation - See traffic citation.

Citation - American car produced from 1979 to date by Chevrolet Division of General Motors Corp. in Michigan.

Cities Service Company - A U.S. petroleum company headquartered in Tulsa, Oklahoma. It is now a subsidiary of Occidental Petroleum Corp. See also petroleum company.

citizen's arrest - Arrest made of a person, violating or suspected of violating some law, by a private citizen.

Citroen - French car line produced from 1919 to date by Citroen SA. It is one of France's most popular family cars. Many Citroens were used during World War II in France. Recent models include: Axel, BX, CX, GSA, LNA, Mehari, Visa, and Z CV.

city speeds - Speed traveled by cars in cities.

city truck - Truck driven more for show than its intended purpose. It is often customized with such items as Mag wheels, fancy paint job, nice interior, etc.

CL - Abbreviation for Sri Lanka found usually on an international license plate.

Cla-Holme - American car produced in 1923.

claim check - Part of a ticket stub given to assure only one person can claim an item left.

Clappps Motor Carriage - American car produced in 1898.

Clark - American steam car produced from 1900-1909 by Edward S. Clark Steam Automobiles in Massachusetts. Also, an American car produced from 1910-1912 by Clark Motor Car Co. in Indiana, and Clark & Co. in Michigan.

Clark-Carter - See Cutting.

Clark Electric - American electric car produced in 1912.

Clark-Hatfield - American car produced from 1908-1909 by Clark-Hatfield Auto Co. in Wisconsin.

Clark, Jim - He was a British driver who became the Grand Prix world champion in 1963 and 1965 driving a Lotus-Climax. He also won the Indianapolis 500 Race in 1965 driving an average of 150.7 mph in a Lotus.

Clarkmobile - American car produced from 1903-1906 by Clarkmobile Co in Michigan (1903-1906), and Deere-Clark Motor Car Co. in Illinois (1906).

Clarkspeed - American car produced in 1926.

Clark Steamer - American steam car produced in 1901.

clash box - Transmission prone to clashing gears by its design. See also transmission(sliding gear).

clashing gears - See gear clashing.

class action lawsuit - See lawsuit(class action).

Class D - Drag racing classification used at many drag strips for manufactured sports cars under 1500 cc.

Class E - Drag racing classification used at many drag strips for manufactured sports cars over 1500 cc.

Class F - Drag racing classification used at many drag strips for stock cars under 200 cu.in.

Class G - Drag racing classification used at many drag strips for pre-war stock cars over 200-300 cu.in.

Class H - Drag racing classification used at many drag strips for stock cars over 300 cu.in.

Classic - American car produced from 1916-1917 by Classic Motor Car Corp. in Illinois. Also, an American car produced from 1957-1972 by American Motors Corp. in Michigan.

classic car - Car generally classified as built from 1925-1948. See also brass era car, vintage car, antique car, contemporary car, milestone car, special interest car, contemporary classic car, pre-war car, and post-war car.

Class J - Drag racing classification used at many drag strips for modified or converted cars built after 1942.

Class K - Drag racing classification used at many drag strips for modified or converted cars built before 1942.

Class M - Drag racing classification used at many drag strips for modified roadsters (hot rods) or cars without standard fenders.

Class N - Drag racing classification used at many drag strips for cars without bodies, but with roll bar.

Class P - Drag racing classification used at many drag strips for all types of cars not classified in other categories.

clay buck - See armature(model).

clean car - See car classification(clean).

clean deal - Car customer characterized by having no trade-in and needing no financing when buying a car.

cleaned - To get cheated, conned, rooked, etc.

cleaning terminals - To clean battery terminals.

cleaning the engine - To clean an engine of dirt, grease, oil, etc. Steam, an engine degreaser, or soap and hot water are most commonly used.

Clear & Dunham - American car produced in 1905.

clearance - Specified amount of space located between two surfaces as between a piston and a cylinder wall, a set of contact of points, etc. See also gap.

clearance light - See light(clearance).

clearance ramp - See cam clearance ramp.

clear coat - See paint(clear coat).

Cleburne - American car produced in 1912.

Clegg Steamer - American steam car produced in 1885.

Clement Talbot - Sports car built in the 1930s.

Clendon - American car produced in 1908.

Clenet - American car produced from 1976 to date by Clenet Coachworks in California.

Clermont - American car produced in 1903.

Clermont Steamer - American steam car produced in 1922.

Cletrac Truck - American truck produced in 1922.

Cleveland - American car produced from 1904-1909 and 1919-1926 by Cleveland Motor Car Co., and Cleveland Automobile Co., respectively, both in Ohio.

Cleveland Cyclecar - American car produced in 1913.

Cleveland Electric - American electric car produced from 1899-1901 by Cleveland Machine Screw Co. in Ohio.

clevis - U-shaped piece of iron designed with holes at the ends for inserting a shaft or pin. A universal joint is actually two clevis devices held together by a cross shape pin.

climate control - See climate control system.

climate control setting(A/C position) - Air flow setting used to direct outside air through operating evaporator for cooling, then on to dash outlet ducts.

climate control setting(bi level position) - Air flow setting used to direct outside air through non-operating evaporator, then on to split air flow at heater core so warm air can flow to defroster and lower ducts and ambient air can flow to dash ducts.

climate control setting(defrost position) - Air flow setting used to direct outside air through non-operating evaporator, then on to heater core so warm air can flow to defroster ducts.

climate control setting(heater position) - Air flow setting used to direct outside air through non-operating evaporator, then on to heater core so warm air can flow to defroster and lower ducts.

climate control setting(off position) - Air flow setting used to direct outside air through non-operating evaporator, then on to lower ducts for ventilating interior with ambient air.

climate control setting(vent position) - Air flow setting used to direct outside air through operating evaporator for cooling, then on to all interior outlet ducts except the defroster.

climate control system - Assemblage of parts and controls designed to regulate warm and cold air temperature in different parts of the car's interior. Such systems often operate a car's air conditioner off and on throughout the year to dehumidify the air. An elaborate duct system is often used to direct warm and/or cool air to several outlets for comfort.

Climax - American car produced in 1907.

Climber - American car produced from 1919-1923 by Climber Motor Corp. in Arkansas.

clinometer - See gauge(clinometer).

Clinton - Canadian car line produced in 1912.

clipped car - See half breed.

Clipper - American car produced from 1955-1956 by Studebaker-Packard Corp. in Michigan.

clipping(1) - Practice followed by a car repair shop where a customer is charged for parts that are never installed.

clipping(2) - See half breed.

cln - Abbreviation for clean.

clock - To record the speed of another car.

clocking - Turning back the odometer on a used car to register lower miles. See con game(turning back the odometer).

clockwise - Rotation to the right or in the direction of clock hands.

close a deal - See closing the deal.

closed crankcase ventilation - See emission control system(crankcase-closed type).

close deal - Car sale made with a minimal profit for a salesman.

closed loop mode - On-board computer mode used when a car's engine is warm. It sets the fuel metering system up for a normal fuel mixture and interprets the various engine sensors accordingly. See also open loop mode.

closed model - Car built with passenger compartment enclosed by a top and windows. It usually refers to sedans, coupes, etc.

closer - A car dealer employee whose sole job is convincing and getting potential car buyers to sign a sales contract or buyer's order.

close ratio transmission - See transmission(close ratio).

closing - See closing the deal.

closing the deal - To complete the sale of a car or other product.

close out sale - Sale at a new car dealership conducted to get rid of last year's models.

Cloud 9 - Experimental car designed for the far off future.

Cloud 9 Studio - Car manufacturer's studio used for research and development of experimental cars and ideas for the far off future.

cloud point - Temperature reached when wax crystals begin appearing in a diesel fuel. Initial wax crystal appearance makes the fuel cloudy or hazy. Wax can clog a fuel delivery system. Cloud point always occurs at a higher temperature than the pour point.

Cloughley - American car produced from 1902-1903 by Cloughley Motor Vehicle Co. in Kansas.

clover leaf - Freeway intersection built to route traffic approaching from four different directions into any other direction without stopping. It is shaped like a square with a cross and a circle in each quadrant of the cross.

clown suit - Car clay model design built with a different profile for each side. It allows two designs to be produced on one model.

Cloyd - American car produced in 1911.

cltch - Abbreviation for clutch.

Club Car - American car produced from 1910-1911 by Club Car Co. in New York.

clunker - Rough car or junker.

cluster gear - See gear(transmission countershaft).

cluster gears - See gear(transmission countershaft).

clutch - Assemblage of components used to engage or disengage power flow from an engine to a transmission. On a manual transmission car, it consists primarily of: a clutch plate, pressure plate, throw out bearing, and clutch release fork. Clutch plate is the component actually transferring power. It is sandwiched between a flywheel and a clutch pressure plate, and is meshed to rotate with a transmission shaft. Strong springs built into a pressure plate press a clutch plate against flywheel and pressure plate surfaces. When a driver presses a clutch pedal, a throw out bearing moves along a transmission shaft, contacts pressure plate springs, and depresses them disengaging the clutch plate. At that point, the engine and transmission are disconnected. A manually operated clutch is used only on manual transmission cars.

clutch(5 plate) - Early clutch designed to engage and disengage 2 clutch plates against three pressure plates. It was considered the first multiple disc clutch.

clutch(automatic) - Clutch designed to engage a clutch plate when certain conditions have been met. One design engages a plate when a transmission is placed in gear.

clutch(band) - Early clutch designed to engage and disengage a circular band against an inner hub surface mounted on a flywheel. Automatic transmissions use brake bands in a similar, but reverse, manner to clutch planetary gear sets (they contract to engage).

clutch(centrifugal) - Clutch designed to engage a clutch plate when engine rpm increases beyond a certain point.

clutch(cone-1) - Early clutch designed to engage and disengage a large diameter cone-shaped wheel covered with friction lining.

clutch(cone-2) - Oil operated clutch used in an automatic transmission to help operate reverse gear.

clutch(dog) - Clutching mechanism used on earlier manual transmissions and some racing transmissions for engaging and disengaging gears. It consists of a circular collar or flange that moves to engage another one attached to a gear. It cannot be slipped and has only an in or out position. See also clutch(synchronizing).

clutch(forward) – Clutch used at the input shaft end of an automatic transmission to drive the ring gear of the first planetary gear set when engaged.

clutch(hydraulic) – Clutch designed to engage and disengage a clutch plate by moving a clutch release fork with a hydraulically operated slave cylinder. Depressing a clutch pedal pumps hydraulic fluid from a clutch master cylinder into a hydraulic line and on to the slave cylinder.

clutch(lockup) – Clutch used in an automatic transmission to keep a gear engaged. They are often controlled by engine vacuum. See also transmission problem(automatic-excessive shifting).

clutch(magnetic) – Clutch designed to use magnetic principles for engaging two surfaces rotating independently of each other. One design uses a medium of fine magnetizable metal and dry lubricant attracted to a gap between two rotating surfaces according to the magnetic strength induced. The magnetic strength determines the amount of slippage. This type clutch is popular on air compressors.

clutch(multiple disc) – Clutch designed to use a series of friction discs and pressure plates to engage and disengage engine power.

clutch(neutral) – Oil operated clutch used in automatic transmissions to help control power flow.

clutch(overrunning) – Clutch mechanism used to provide friction or drive force in one direction only. If the driving torque is removed or reversed, the clutch slips. It is commonly found in starter drives and overdrive units. On a starter, the clutch is part of a starter drive unit. It consists of a clutch and drive pinion gear assembly that provides positive engaging and disengaging of a starter drive pinion gear and flywheel ring gear. It drives the drive pinion gear in one direction only. See also free wheel unit.

clutch(overrunning-mechanically operated) – Overrunning clutch designed to engage when a starter pedal is depressed or through the spinning action of a starter shaft.

clutch(overrunning-solenoid operated) – Overrunning clutch designed to engage when a lever transfers motion from a starter mounted solenoid.

clutch(roller) – Overrunning clutch designed to use a series of rollers placed in ramps providing drive power in one direction and slip in the other. It is used in automatic transmissions and overdrive units.

clutch(sprague) – Overrunning clutch designed to use sprague segments instead of rollers. It is used in place of brake bands in some automatic transmissions.

clutch actuating rod – Adjustable rod attached to the clutch release fork and a lever or slave cylinder. The clutch pedal free play and distance of clutch throw out bearing to clutch pressure plate spring is made with the rod. See also clutch pedal free play, and clutch adjustment.

clutch adjustment – Adjustment made to clutch linkage as a clutch plate facing material wears. Facing wear causes a clutch pressure plate to move closer to a flywheel. In turn, the pressure plate release levers or diaphragm springs move closer to the throw out bearing. Periodic adjustment of clutch pedal free play is necessary to keep the throw out bearing the proper distance away. See clutch pedal free play.

clutch cable – Cable used to connect a clutch pedal to a clutch release fork.

clutch condition – Amount of life left in a clutch.

clutch cover – Clutch pressure plate covering. See clutch pressure plate.

clutch diaphragm spring – Circular piece of spring steel used to push a pressure plate against a clutch plate in some clutch designs.

clutch disc – See clutch plate.

Clutch-Flite – Chrysler Torque-Flite automatic transmission modified to use a conventional clutch and flywheel assembly in place of the converter.

clutch free play – Clearance maintained between a clutch throw out bearing and a clutch pressure plate's release springs. Excess free play will cause a clutch to drag. Little or no free play will greatly decrease the bearing's life. In general, a clutch pedal is adjusted to have a one inch movement before it firms up (bearing starts spinning).

clutch fork – See clutch release fork.

clutch housing – See bell housing.

clutching medium – Compound of fine magnetizable metal and dry lubricant used in magnetic clutches to regulate the amount of slippage between two independently rotating surfaces. See also clutch(magnetic).

clutch interlock – Device used in manual transmissions to prevent shifting into low or reverse by mistake. It was first introduced by Ford in 1961.

clutch is burned out – See clutch is shot.

clutch is gone – See clutch is shot.

clutch is shot – Clutch plate characterized by linings that are loose, worn away, or broken; broken clutch plate coil springs; warped metal disc; and damaged or stripped splines. See also clutch problem(short life).

clutch linkage – Assemblage of levers, cables, and other parts used to transfer clutch pedal motion to a clutch. Some cars use mechanical linkage from a clutch pedal to a clutch release fork. Other cars use a hydraulic system. It consists of: a slave cylinder operating a release fork, a fluid line, and hydraulic master cylinder that transfers movement from the clutch pedal into fluid pressure.

clutch master cylinder – Hydraulic cylinder and reservoir unit connected to a car's clutch pedal for converting clutch pedal movement into fluid pressure for use by a slave cylinder used to move a clutch release fork.

clutch off – To rapidly engage a clutch for rapid acceleration.

clutch overhaul – Process used to overhaul a clutch. Work performed includes: examining a clutch and associated components, making the necessary repairs, and returning it to proper operating condition. Clutch overhaul requires removal of a transmission. It is usually a good idea to have a clutch plate and throw out bearing replaced even if they are not worn out. This is due to the time and expense of removing and installing the transmission.

clutch pedal – Foot operated pedal on the driver's side operating the clutch linkage. It is almost always positioned to the left of a brake pedal.

clutch pedal clearance – See clutch pedal free travel.

clutch pedal free travel – Distance a clutch pedal can move from its stationary position before a clutch throw out bearing actually contacts a pressure plate. One inch is the most common adjustment. See also clutch free play.

clutch plate – Metal disc covered with friction material and splined to a transmission input shaft. It permits engine and transmission to rotate at different speeds when disengaged. It consists of: a circular metal plate and reinforced splined hub, friction facing, and coil springs. It resides between the flywheel and the clutch pressure plate. Power is transferred from the engine to the transmission as long as the clutch plate, pressure plate, and flywheel remain in contact with each other. Contact is controlled by a clutch pressure plate.

clutch plate(damped) – Plate designed to cushion or smooth engaging of engine and transmission. Springs are positioned around the inner part of the plate to accomplish this.

clutch plate(undamped) – Plate designed for minimum slippage. No springs or cushioning devices are used. It is not suitable for street use, but is popular for racing.

clutch plate coil spring – One of several small coil springs mounted near the hub of a clutch plate to help cushion its engagement.

clutch plate lining – Material bonded or riveted to both sides of a clutch's metal disc along the outer 1-2 inches. It allows the clutch plate to slip against the clutch pressure plate and the engine's flywheel. The material is designed to provide friction, minimize heat build-up, and minimize wear between itself and the surface it contacts. Linings composed of ceramic and sintered metal are considered very durable.

clutch pressure plate – Device used to bolt onto a flywheel and squeeze a clutch plate against itself and the flywheel. It consists primarily of: a clutch cover, pressure plate, pressure springs, and release levers. The squeezing pressure is released when the pressure plate backs away from the clutch plate. This happens by pushing the clutch pedal which causes the throw out bearing against the pressure plate release levers. The clutch pressure plate is needed only in cars with manual transmissions for shifting gears. The two types generally used in cars are lever and diaphragm.

clutch pressure plate(intermediate) – Pressure plate used between two clutch plates. Some larger horsepower engines use two clutch plates which requires an extra or intermediate clutch pressure plate to separate them.

clutch problem – Condition created when a clutch does not operate properly.

clutch problem(chattering) – See sound(chattering) and clutch problem(grabbing).

clutch problem(dragging clutch plate) – Clutch plate does not fully disengage. Possible causes include: clutch plate facing greasy, oily, warped, loose and/or broken; splined hub binding; pressure plate and/or cover warped; binding pilot bearing; release bearing retainer binding on input shaft; and clutch housing and or clutch assembly out of alignment.

clutch problem(grabbing) – Clutch plate does not engage smoothly but tends to grab or bind abruptly or chatter and grab less abruptly no matter how slowly clutch is released. Possible causes include: clutch plate facing greasy, oily, worn, or glazed; binding clutch plate hub, shaft splines, pressure plate pivot points, pressure plate release levers, clutch pedal, and clutch linkage; out of alignment clutch housing and/or clutch assembly; worn pilot bearing, and engine and/or transmission mounts with loose bolts, loose rubber, or spongy rubber.

clutch problem(grinding) – See sound(grinding-3).

clutch problem(no power transfer) - Clutch is not able to transfer power from an engine to a transmission. Possible causes include: clutch plate hub no longer attached; clutch plate facings gone; binding clutch plate hub; broken pressure plate springs; out of adjustment pressure plate release levers; and too little free play in clutch pedal.

clutch problem(rattling) - See sound(rattling-1).

clutch problem(short life) - Clutch plate wears out long before its expected life. Possible causes include: clutch plate and/or pressure plate wrong size imposing too small a load on clutch plate friction surfaces, pressure plate springs weak, clutch plate linings poor quality, clutch release bearing adjusted too tight, clutch plate oil soaked, and poor driving habits. A short clutch plate life usually generates substantial heat on the clutch linings, and pressure plate and flywheel contact surfaces. Such heat can cause a flywheel to crack, and a pressure plate to crack and/or distort. See also cracked flywheel.

clutch problem(slipping) - Engaged clutch plate slips on flywheel and/or pressure plate surfaces. Main symptom is engine speed increasing without car speed increase when car is accelerated. It needs to be taken care of right away or flywheel and pressure plate surfaces will become damaged. Possible causes include: warped pressure plate, and clutch plate; binding pressure plate release levers, and pressure plate pivot points; too little clutch pedal free play; weak or damaged pressure plate springs; clutch plate facing oily, greasy, and/or worn; pressure plate release springs out of adjustment (due to worn pressure plate); and out of alignment clutch housing and/or clutch assembly.

clutch problem(squeaking) - See sound(squeaking).

clutch problem(vibration) - See vibration(clutch/transmission).

clutch release - See clutch throw out bearing.

clutch release bearing - See clutch throw out bearing.

clutch release fingers - Clutch pressure plate release spring. The spring is actually a series of spines positioned radially around a plate. When the throw out bearing pushes against them, the clutch plate slides between the flywheel and the pressure plate. At this point, a gear in a transmission can be changed.

clutch release fork - Lever mounted on the transmission bell housing transmitting clutch linkage motion to a clutch throw out bearing.

clutch semi-centrifugal release fingers - Release spring of a clutch pressure plate attached to a weight. At high rpm, the weight causes a pressure plate to exert extra pressure on a clutch plate to avoid slippage.

clutch shaft - See transmission input shaft.

clutch spring - Spring used with an overrunning clutch in a starter drive.

clutch throw out bearing - Sealed roller bearing used to disengage a clutch plate from a flywheel and clutch pressure plate. It encircles and slides on a transmission input shaft. It does not rotate when not in use. When a driver pushes a clutch pedal down, the throw out bearing contacts and bears down on the rotating pressure plate spring(s) or levers, which frees the clutch plate from the flywheel and pressure plate surfaces. Once free, the transmission can be shifted safely from one gear to another. See also riding the clutch and transmission problem(bearing noise).

clutch throw out fork - Device shaped like a two pronged fork for straddling and moving a clutch throw out bearing toward a clutch pressure plate when a clutch pedal is depressed. See also clutch release fork.

Clyde - American car produced in 1919.

Clydesdale Truck - American truck produced in 1914.

Clymer - American car produced in 1908.

Clymer Publications - American publisher of automotive books.

CO(1) - Abbreviation for carbon monoxide.

CO(2) - Abbreviation for Columbia found usually on an international license plate.

c/o - Abbreviation for care of.

coach builder - Person or business engaged in building early cars.

coast-down - Slowing down part of car driving (without braking) or engine rpm. See also run-up.

coasting - To allow a car to continue moving without used of any power. It is usually done with a car in neutral.

coasting control valve - Valve used in an automatic transmission to time the operation of certain transmission components in certain coasting and downshifting situations.

Coates-Goshen - American car produced from 1908-1910 by Coates-Goshen Automobile Co. in New York.

Coats Steam Car - American steam car produced from 1922-1923 by Coates Steam Motors in Ohio.

Cobb, John R - He set a world land speed record in 1938, 1939, and 1947 driving his Railton W-12 Mobil Special. Speeds were 350.2, 369.7, and 394.2 mph.

cobbled – Production car modified with experimental or design components. Also, it refers to a component or model put together quickly.

Cobra – See Shelby Cobra.

cobwebbing – Custom painting technique used to make a car panel take on a light thread-like appearance in different patterns. Paint is applied in a thin stream generated by high air pressure. Air pressure and distance determine how stringy the pattern will be. A three foot distance is common. Cobwebbing leaves a rough textured surface.

cockpit – The driver seat.

cocoa mat – Floor mat made out of coarsely woven reed-like material.

coefficient of friction – Measurement made of the friction developed between two objects in physical contact with each other. It is measured by dividing the force required to move an object on a surface by its weight. For example, if it takes 40 pounds of force to move a 100 pound object, the coefficient of friction would be 0.40. Any change in the condition of a surface changes the coefficient of friction. Lubrication, for example, would decrease it.

coercivity – Resistance of magnetic material to demagnetization.

Coey – American car produced from 1913-1917 by Coey Motors Co. in Illinois in the Flyer and Bear models.

cog – Transmission or rear end gear.

cog belt – Toothed belt. It is commonly used to drive a camshaft from a crankshaft.

Coggswell – American car produced in 1911.

coil – See ignition coil.

coil cap – High voltage output end of an ignition coil. Cap contains primary and secondary terminal fittings.

coil resistor – See ignition coil resistor.

coil spring – See spring(coil).

coil spring adjuster – Device mounted between the coils of a coil spring increasing the load capacity of the spring. Several are usually used to keep the spring's action balanced during compression and expansion.

coil terminal – See ignition coil terminal.

coil wire – High voltage wire positioned running from a high voltage ignition coil outlet to the center tower terminal of a distributor cap.

coke bottle – Double swell used in a plan view contour. See also body style(coke bottle).

Colburn – American car produced from 1906-1911 by Colburn Automobile Co. in Colorado.

Colby – American car produced from 1911-1914 by Colby Motor Car Co. in Iowa.

cold – See soft.

cold-blooded – Characteristic of an engine warming up too slowly. Possible causes include: low temperature thermostat, thermostat stuck open, improper choking when cold, carburetor hot air system leaks, restrictions in exhaust passageways, and bad intake manifold exhaust heat control.

cold canvas – See cold spearing.

cold cranking amps – See battery rating(cold cranking).

cold engine – Engine block at same temperature as surrounding air.

cold filter plugging point – Test used as an alternative to a cloud point test to determine the temperature when fuel will no longer flow through a specified test filter. It is used primarily outside the U.S.

cold manifold – Intake manifold designed to function without heat from exhaust gases.

cold plug – See spark plug(cold).

cold soak – Condition of an engine shutoff and allowed to cool down for several hours.

cold spearing – Selling tactic used by car salesman where new prospects are located by calling phone numbers in a telephone book. It is usually done as a last resort when business is slow.

cold start a car – To start and run a car engine while cold and minimize wear and tear. The best general method is to: start the engine, let oil pressure normalize for about a minute, drive away slowly, and go through the transmission gears gradually keeping engine rpm low until operating temperature is reached. Placing a light load on an engine will warm it up quickly and not harm the engine. Driving a cold engine fast is very hard on all the moving parts and will cause it to wear out prematurely. Maximum engine life is attained through proper maintenance, good driving habits, and running an engine as much as possible at operating temperature.

cold start valve – Fuel injector used to inject fuel at the entrance to an intake manifold. It is used primarily on fuel injected engines to supply additional fuel when the engine is cold. It is controlled by a coolant temperature sensor that turns it off when a certain water temperature has been reached. See also air regulator.

cold weather package – Specified new car modifications designed to equip a car for cold weather driving. Such items might include: winter tires, studs on tires, enhanced exhaust heat collection system, high temperature thermostat, engine block heater, heavy duty battery, heavy duty radiator, adjustable radiator shield, high percentage antifreeze mix, etc.

Cole – American car produced from 1909-1925 by Cole Motor Car Co. in Indiana.

Coleman – American car produced in 1933.

Coleman Truck – American truck produced in 1928.

collateral – Property used to secure or guarantee a loan.

collector box – Short section of larger diameter pipe used to bring all the header pipes off one exhaust manifold into one pipe. It is usually fitted with a flat flange for attaching a secondary collector.

Collier – American car produced in 1917.

Collinet – American car produced in 1921.

Collins – American car produced from 1920-1921.

Collins Electric – American car produced in 1901.

Colly – American car produced in 1901.

Colonial – American electric car produced in 1912. Also, an American car produced from 1917-1922 by Colonial Automobile Co. in Indiana (1917-1921), Mechanical Development Corp. in California (1920), and Colonial Motors Co. in Massachusetts (1921-1922).

Colonial Electric – American car produced from 1912-1913 and 1917-1918.

Colony Park – American car produced from 1957-1977 by Mercury Division of Ford Motor Co. in Michigan.

color fogging – Custom painting technique used where a car panel's color is blended in lighter and darker shades.

color perception – Ability to see different colors. A person with poor color perception is handicapped, but can compensate.

color sanding – Process used where a new lacquer paint coating is sanded to open up paint pores and speed the drying process.

Colt – American car produced in 1907. Also, an American car produced in 1958. Also, a Japanese car imported from 1971 to date for Dodge Division of Chrysler Corp. in Michigan.

Colt Truck – American truck produced in 1908.

Columbia – American car produced from 1907-1924 by Electric Vehicle Co. in Connecticut (1907-1909), and Columbia Motor Car Co. in Connecticut (1909-1913).

Columbia-Dauman – American car produced in 1900.

Columbia Electric – American electric car produced in 1897-1907 by Pope Mfg. Co. (1897-1899), Columbia Automobile Co. (1899), Columbia & Electric Vehicle Co. (1900), and Electric Vehicle Co. (1901-1907), all in Connecticut. Also, an American electric car produced by Columbia Electric Vehicle Co. in Michigan (1914-1918).

Columbia Gas – American car produced in 1900.

Columbia-Knight – American car produced in 1911.

Columbia Motor Carriage – American car produced in 1897.

Columbia & Riker – American car produced in 1901.

Columbia Steamer – American steam car produced in 1900.

Columbia Taxicab – American car produced in 1915.

Columbia Truck – American truck produced from 1916-1920.

Columbia Wagonette – American car produced in 1901.

Columbus – American car produced from 1903-1913 by Columbus Buggy Co. in Ohio.

Columbus Electric – American electric car produced in 1906.

column shift – Transmission shift lever mounted on a steering wheel column.

column shift control lever – See column shift.

combination crown – Shape characterized by high and low crowns. Fenders and door panels are good examples. See also reverse crown.

combination wrench – Wrench designed with an open and box end opening at opposite ends.

combustion – Process created when a material combines rapidly with oxygen generating both light and heat. Combustion of fuel is called fire. Most fuels burn with a flame. An engine produces power by creating combustion of a fuel mixture in the engine cylinders. See also oxidation and fire.

combustion analyzer – See exhaust gas analyzer.

combustion chamber – Small volume at the top of an engine cylinder used to initiate combustion of a fuel mixture. The chamber is formed by the top of the cylinder, the cylinder wall, and the piston head when the piston reaches the top of its stroke. The combustion chamber and an air/fuel mixture create a source of power in an engine. Temperature in the chamber approaches 2,000 degrees Fahrenheit when combustion occurs.

combustion efficiency – Measure made of how efficiently an engine burns an air/fuel mixture to generate power. Increased engine efficiency results in lower emissions and more usable power.

combustion leak tester – Test device used to sample vapors in upper radiator tank for presence of exhaust fumes.

combustion stages – Different stage of a combustion process produced in an internal combustion engine. There are three generally recognized stages,

known as formation, growing, and propagation. In the formation stage, a
spark appears at a spark plug electrode gap. It becomes the nucleus of a
flame front, expanding slowly with no measurable heat-produced pressure.
Next is the growing stage. The nucleus begins to expand sending out its
flame front, like tentacles, into different parts of a combustion chamber.
Heat begins to build with its attendant rise in pressure and temperature.
The third and final stage is propagation. It is here where most of the
burning and its effects take place. The air/fuel mixture becomes fully
engulfed by a strong flame front. The rapid burning generates a great deal
of heat and subsequent pressure. The propagation stage is what creates the
pressure necessary to force the piston downward.

come on - Inducement or lure.

Comet - American car produced from 1906-1908, 1914-1915, 1917-1922, and 1946-
1948 by Hall Auto Repair Co. in California (1906-1908), Economy Cyclecar Co.
and Comet Cyclecar Co. in Indiana (1914-1915), Comet Automobile Co. in
Illinois (1917-1922), and General Development Co. in New York (1946-1948).
Also, an American car produced from 1960-1977 by Mercury Division of Ford
Motor Co. in Michigan.

Comet Electric - American car produced in 1921.

coming off the choke - The opening of an engine's choke plate.

Commander - American car produced from 1921-1922.

Commer - American car produced in 1912.

Commerce - American car produced in 1924.

Commercial - American car produced in 1902-1909 and 1927.

commission - Percentage of money received from sales of products and/or
services. It is given to the salesman responsible. Some salesman receive
only commission for wages while others receive a base salary plus commission.
Commission provides an incentive to sell since the more you sell the more you
make. Unfortunately, it pressures salesman into selling you products or
services you may not need, and therefore encourages dishonesty.

Commodore - American car produced from 1921-1922.

Commonwealth - American car produced from 1917-1922 by Commonwealth Motors Co.
in Illinois. Also, an American car produced in 1903.

commutating zone - See neutral point.

commutator - Enlarged circular area located at one end of a motor armature
where current flow in and out of armature coils is transferred. It is
insulated from an armature shaft. Its circumference is divided into bar-like
segments insulated from each other. Each segment is a positive or negative
side of one of the armature coils. Brushes ride on the commutator surface to
transfer current produced from armature coils. When a commutator surface
wears out, the armature must usually be replaced. See also armature,
brushes, and commutator bars.

commutator bars - Rectangular segments located on a commutator surface. Each
commutator bar is one half of an armature coil circuit. They are insulated
from each other.

Commuter - American car produced from 1950-1977 by Mercury Division of Ford
Motor Co. in Michigan.

commuter - Person traveling regularly. It usually refers to a person who
spends a significant amount of time each day traveling to and from work by
car, train, subway, etc.

commuter traffic - Traffic composed primarily of cars commuting to and from
work.

commuting - Traveling on a regular basis to and from two places, usually home
and work, in a car, bus, train, subway, car pool, etc.

commuting to work - See commuting.

compact - Car designed with a longer wheelbase (typically 100-111 inches)
and longer body than a sub-compact. Price usually ranges from $6-9,000.
Weight is less than 3,000 lbs. Gas mileage is somewhat lower than a sub-
compact with more room being offered.

compact snow and ice - Dangerous road condition characterized by snow and ice
compacted onto its surface.

companion flange - See pinion drive flange.

compensating nozzle - Fuel discharge nozzle mounted in a carburetor venturi
area to meter a constant flow of fuel into an engine. It helps a main
discharge nozzle provide a more constant fuel flow. When engine speed is
high, a compensating nozzle will deliver less fuel than at low speed.

compensating port - Brake master cylinder opening designed to allow fluid flow
back to the reservoir.

competition disc - Smooth flat hubcap used on racing cars.

competitor - Person, business, team, etc. striving to outdo a rival.

complaint letter - Letter written by a car owner dissatisfied with the outcome
of work done to his car. It is usually written as a last recourse to an
unresolvable car problem. The letter should be factual and well organized
without threats or name calling. It should contain the following
information: owner's name, address, telephone number; year and make of car;

repair shop name and location; repair order or warranty repair number; description of the problem; sequence of events that took place to try correcting the problem including dates; what the dispute has cost the owner in money, time lost from work, repairs made elsewhere, any legal counsel, etc.; copies of documents pertaining to the problem such as repair orders, correspondence with repair shop, etc.; and conduct of repair shop in resolving the problem. The completed letter should be sent to: the owner of the repair shop, relevant consumer groups and government agencies, and the action column of local newspaper. Remember to keep copies of the letters you send out. Such letters help to expose a company's reputation through subsequent publicity making them particularly effective.

compound - Mixture of two or more substances.

Compound - American car produced from 1904-1908 by Eisenhuth Horseless Vehicle Co. in Connecticut.

compound carburetor - Two carburetors mounted on an engine's intake manifold. Second carburetor is activated when the accelerator is pushed to the floor. It was introduced by Buick in 1940.

compounding - Rubbing or polishing type compound applied to a paint surface in order to help blend new paint into scratches, remove blemishes, or remove paint oxidation.

compression - Process used to force something into a smaller space, length, etc. Compressing a gaseous mixture increases pressure and temperature.

compression(cylinder) - Compression created when reducing the volume within a cylinder. This is done by pushing a piston to the top of a sealed cylinder. When an air/fuel mixture is reduced, the pressure and temperature build up. It serves to help drive a piston back down when the mixture is ignited. During engine operation, combustion chamber pressures, developed from spark ignition to the tail end of combustion, can range from 100-600 psi.

compression(spring) - Compression created when reducing a spring's length.

compression braking - See downshifting.

compression check - Procedure followed to check the pressure each engine cylinder is capable of producing. Compression check can provide a good indication of the general condition of an engine's valves, rings, and cylinders. An engine is first prepared by warming it up to operating temperature, then stopping the engine. Spark plugs are then removed, the carburetor throttle plate is blocked wide open, the distributor coil lead from the ignition coil is removed, and a remote starter switch is installed. A compression gauge is inserted into one of the spark plug holes and the engine cranked until the gauge no longer climbs (about 5-10 revolutions). Each engine cylinder is tested the same way.

compression check(low adjacent cylinders) - Compression measured as low readings on two adjacent cylinders. It is usually caused by a head gasket with a poor seal between two cylinders. A subsequent vacuum reading can help pinpoint this condition. The remedy is to remove the cylinder head and replace the gasket.

compression check(pressure variance) - Compression measured where one or more cylinder pressures vary by 15 percent or more. Generally, a cylinder pressure variance of 5-10 percent is considered normal. When the variance is greater, problems usually exist with one or more of the following areas: cylinders, rings, and valves. A further check on wide variations can be made by squirting a teaspoonful of oil into low cylinders and check the compression again. If the compression improves significantly, the rings are at fault indicating cylinder wear or broken rings. If there is no significant improvement, then one or both valves are not sealing well enough due to burnt edges on the valve face and/or seat. An engine that has been well cared for and exhibits cylinder pressure variances of over 15 percent is usually due for a valve job, especially if the valves have 50-100,000 miles running time on them.

compression gauge - Instrument used to test cylinder pressure of an engine.

compression ignition - Combustion of an air/fuel mixture caused by the heat generated from compressing the mixture. No spark is required. Diesel engines are based on this concept.

compression ratio - Numerical ratio based on engine cylinder volume at the bottom and top of a piston stroke.

compression stroke - Part of a piston's cycle used to compress an air/fuel mixture in an engine cylinder.

compression test - See compression check.

compressor(air) - Motor/engine assembly designed to take surrounding air, raise it to a higher pressure, and store it in a tank for use.

compressor(refrigeration) - Sealed electric motor/engine assembly designed to take refrigerant and raise it to a higher pressure and temperature. The pressurized gas then flows to a condenser for cooling into a liquid. See also air conditioner.

compressor bearing - See bearing(compressor).

compressor oil - Oil used in an air conditioning system to lubricate a compressor. It stays mixed with the refrigerant. See also air conditioner(adding compressor oil).

compressor pulley - Pulley mounted on a compressor. It is used to drive a compressor via a belt running to a crankshaft pulley.

compressor seal - One of several seals in a compressor designed to prevent leakage of refrigerant under pressure.

compulsory insurance law - Law enacted requiring a registered car to have a certain minimum amount of car insurance.

computer command control - On-board computer used in conjunction with various engine sensors, on some cars, to control an engine's air/fuel ratio. The computer receives signals from the sensors, interprets them, and adjusts the amount of fuel metered to keep it as close to ideal as possible. On carburetor cars, fuel quantity is typically metered by a mixture control solenoid. On fuel injected cars, fuel quantity is metered by changing an injector's open time. A computer and/or sensor malfunction will activate a check engine or similar warning light. See also check engine light and CCC tester.

computer controlled coil ignition - Solid state ignition system used on some cars to control spark timing without the use of a distributor. Crankshaft and camshaft sensors send signals to an on-board computer signaling when to energize one or more ignition coils and thus generate spark. Other engine sensors come into play modifying the spark advance based on variables such as engine load, car speed, water temperature, etc.

computerized wheel balancing - Tire balancing performed by mounting a tire and wheel assembly on a spin balancing machine. See also tire balancer(dynamic).

con - To swindle, trick, or fool. See also con game.

concentric - Two or more circles sharing a common center. The inside and outside diameter of a tire is an example of two concentric circles.

Concord - American car produced in 1916. Also, an American car produced from 1969 to date by American Motors in Michigan.

concours(1) - An assemblage or gathering of people, cars, etc.

concours(2) - Auto condition code word used to specify a car restored to meet exacting requirements usually for a competition. It is usually in excellent condition.

cond - Abbreviation for condition.

condensation - Moisture in the air deposited on a cool surface when the conditions are right. Airborne moisture vapor turns to liquid when it condenses onto a surface. See also condense.

condense - Process used to turn a vapor back into a liquid. Car air conditioners rely on this process in order to operate.

condenser(ignition) - See capacitor.

condenser(refrigeration) - Unit in a car's air conditioning system designed to cool hot compressed refrigerant from a vapor to a liquid. The condenser is usually a small radiator mounted near or in front of a car's coolant radiator.

conditional sales contract - See sales contract.

conditioner - See air conditioner.

conditioning the crank - Process used to recondition a crankshaft involving: cleaning, magnafluxing, chamfering the oil holes, deburring the crank, grinding the crank undersize, and polishing the journals.

Condor Truck - American truck produced in 1929.

conduction(heat) - Heat transferred from one object to another when objects are in physical contact.

conduction(electrical) - Electricity transferred from one point to another within a conductor.

conductor - Substance characterized by its ability to transmit electricity. See also insulator.

cone clutch - Clutch designed with cone-shaped moving frictional surfaces.

Conestoga - American car produced in 1918.

confidence game - See con game.

confidence man - See con man.

con game - Plan carried out to get money or property from another person by lying, cheating, deceiving, etc.

In the car repair business, there are some general guidelines to follow to protect yourself. They are: get to know your car by studying owner and/or shop manuals, find a regular mechanic you can depend on, learn to describe your car problems clearly, stay around your car at unfamiliar repair businesses or service stations, be suspicious of misleading or dramatic car problem claims (like your engine is shot), get more than one estimate of repair work in writing on each repair shop's form, allow only work specified on a repair order to be done, ask to see all parts replaced, ask to see all new or rebuilt parts in their original packaging, and have your car inspected thoroughly before taking a trip. Also, getting the complete name and address of the potential con man will often reveal his true intentions. If he is reluctant to give that information take your business elsewhere. See also mechanics lien.

con game(air conditioner malfunction) - Repair shop diagnoses lack of cold air output from a car air conditioning system as due to a bad air conditioner compressor. You are then usually charged for: removing and replacing the compressor, the cost of the compressor, evacuating and recharging the system, and cost of freon used. In most cases, lack of cold air output is due to a low freon level from a leak in the system and not a bad compressor. The best defense is to get several estimates and have the system checked for leaks.

con game(alternator grounding) - Attempt made to sell an alternator. A service attendant gets under the hood and causes a faulty alternator reading by bending alternator output wires until they ground out. It will cause the generator light to come on or a car's ammeter gauge (if it has one) to show a steady discharge. The tip-off here should be the condition of the car when driven in. If the symptoms described above occur, your best bet is to drive to another station or remedy the problem yourself. Good defense is never allow a stranger to examine an engine unless he is closely watched.

con game(auctioning repossessed car) - Repossessor takes possession of a car and gets the owner to dispute the repossession charges. He then arranges for an auction and sells the repossessed car.

con game(auctioning repaired car) - Repair shop talks a customer into signing a blank repair order, then pads the repair bill so much a customer refuses to pay. The repair shop then places a mechanic's lien on the car, arranges an auction at the shop, and often buys the car for little more than the lien. The end result is they now own the car for the cost of the repair work. Good defense is never leave your car to be worked on without a signed repair order in your possession specifying the work to be done and the cost of the work.

con game(automatic transmission overhaul) - Transmission repair shop mechanic tries to convince a customer his automatic transmission problems require overhauling the unit. If allowed to do the work, he may just make adjustments to the bands and/or replace some low priced parts. You will still be charged for an entire overhaul. If you get into such a situation, insist that the mechanic show you the problem or defective parts before the unit is put back together, and ask for the bad parts before you pay for the work. Good defense is to get the problem diagnosed and cost estimated in writing by several shops, then review each shop's attitude before deciding where to have the work done.

con game(bail reduction) - Person, arrested in an accident, is released on reduced bail if he agrees to have his car repaired by a moonlighting patrolman or at a certain local repair shop. The game works for the benefit of both parties. The police get kickbacks and the repair shop gets business. This game has been exposed and proven in the past and may still exist in certain locales today.

con game(bait and switch) - Illegal or unfair selling scheme commonly practiced where a seller gets customers by advertising non-existent merchandise at very good prices and then attempts to talk a customer into more expensive goods. Another variation is a dealer who will accept a deposit on a car selling for a very good price only to later announce that it has been sold. The dealer will then try to talk you into a different car at a higher price.

con game(bad points) - Repair shop diagnoses poor engine performance as being due to bad points in a distributor. Upon removing them, you will be told they are burned out or shot. They may use the color of the points (black is a common color for many points that are designed to resist wear) to convince you. If you agree, you may even get talked into a tune-up.

con game(barbershopping) - Mechanic or service station attendant tries to make you believe your tires and/or other car parts will fail shortly if not replaced immediately. See also con game(skinning the dude).

con game(bargain advertising) - Car repair business advertises parts, accessories or repairs at bargain prices to entice customers into bringing in their cars for servicing. Once the customer agrees to some car work, the repairman will perform the work and try to convince the car owner of other problems that have been "uncovered" and need immediate attention. Another ploy will be to convince the customer that the bargain is not really as good as a slightly more expensive part or repair job. Good defense is have just the specified work done or take your business elsewhere.

con game(board meeting) - Several repair shop workers gather around a car to confer on what problems it may have. This tactic is used to intimidate you into believing your car has several problems beyond the obvious that must be taken care of. Good defense is to state you will get another opinion elsewhere before authorizing any additional work to be done.

con game(brake rebuild) - Auto repair shop does tires, shock, and/or brake work to your car, and then tries to convince you your brake system is in need of repair or requires extra repair work. This is a common gimmick to get extra work. The best defense is to get more than one estimate of the work needed if you suspect the work is not necessary.

con game(carbon and valve work) - Repair shop tries to convince a customer that part of his car problems are due to excessive carbon build up in the combustion chamber and around the valves. If the customer agrees, the repair shop usually does little more than clean up the outside of the engine, yet still charges you as if they pulled the head and cleaned it. The customer has no way of knowing if the work has been done unless the engine head is pulled. Good defense is to get several estimates of the car problem.

con game(carburetor rebuild) - Common scheme practiced where a repair shop tries to convince a customer that a carburetion problem such as rough idling, fast idling, stalling, hard starting, etc. can only be cured by completely rebuilding or replacing the carburetor. If the shop goes the rebuild route, they may just make a few adjustments or at most replace a few minor parts. In most cases, the carburetor will not be removed. If they go the replacement route, they may still do only minor adjustment and/or repair on the existing carburetor. Whether they do adjustment, minor repair, or actual replacement of the carburetor, the cost will be high. You will be told that either the carburetor had to be removed and completely rebuilt or removed and replaced.

   Carburetors are one of the few devices on cars that rarely wear out and need to be replaced if properly cared for. Fuel filters insure that they never get very dirty internally. A carburetor usually only gets dirty in the air passageway from gum and varnish compounds in the fuel. It does not greatly affect the carburetor's performance. Statements like worn out jets, floats, passageways, choke plates, gaskets, full of water, etc. should be taken with a grain of salt. If you must rely on someone else's judgement in this area, be sure to get several opinions. If you elect to have the work done, be sure to put a distinguishing mark on your carburetor and insist that all the used parts be saved for you to see. The mark will allow you to see if a claimed carburetor replacement was actually made.

   If a carburetor is not repairable and must be replaced, it is better to purchase a new one instead of a rebuild.

con game(check your battery) - Service station attendant offers to check your battery. If you agree, he will then proceed to put a little dish detergent, an alka seltzer tablet, or other compound which causes bubbling and frothing in one or more of the battery cells. The bubbling and frothing action is enough to frighten most motorists making them ripe for a new battery purchase on the spot. Good defense includes: closely watch any battery check, have a reliable business check your battery, or do it yourself.

con game(check your tires) - Service station attendant tries to convince you there is something wrong with one or more of your tires. They will usually ask to check your tires for you. Air will be let out of usually one tire to convince you it's leaking and needs to be repaired. If you agree, they will remove the tire, probably puncture it when you are not looking with a nail or sharp object, and then try to convince you the tire is shot and needs to be replaced. Good defense includes: closely watch any tire checks, or check your own tires.

con game(chop shop) - Car business disassembles stolen cars and sells the parts to repair shops. The purpose is to make a good profit on parts that are in high demand, difficult to obtain, or expensive. See also con game(parts switching).

con game(collapsed plugs) - Car repair business diagnoses one of your car problems as being due "collapsed" spark plugs. It usually works this way. You bring the car in for diagnosis. The repairman removes one of the spark plugs and, while you are not looking, bends the side electrode down until it touches the center electrode. You are then told something to the effect that high compression engines suffer this kind of problem due to high combustion chamber pressure bending the spark plug points. If you agree, they will sell you a new set of spark plugs and install them. Your old spark plugs will likely be cleaned and sold as new ones to their next victim.

con game(changing antifreeze) - Repair shop charges for installing new antifreeze and flushing out a car's cooling system, yet all they really do is drain and refill it. It usually works in the following way. The shop will drain the coolant from the engine by opening the drain valve at the bottom of the radiator, and will not drain the engine block. This usually removes enough liquid so that sufficient antifreeze can be added for the desired cold weather protection. They will then refill the system with new or used coolant, or just water and proceed to tell you the work is done. A proper job requires a thorough flushing of the car's cooling system and then adding the right quantity of new antifreeze. Flushing is required in order to effectively remove contaminants, rust scale, debris, etc., that have accumulated throughout the coolant passageways. It requires draining the radiator and engine block, and refilling the system several times. When the drained coolant looks clear, the process can be stopped. At each refilling, the car should be brought up to operating temperature. Good defense is to remain and observe the work being done. Be suspicious of shops that don't want you to hang around or watch the work they do.

con game(dealer insurance) — Dealer has a kickback arrangement with an insurance company for every car buyer who elects to buy the required car insurance from the dealer. The dealer will make his pitch on why the insurance might be better or perhaps even offer some kind of discount. If you agree, the dealer receives a fee from the insurance company for selling the insurance policy. The buyer should carefully evaluate what the dealer is offering with other policies that are available. If you agree to the dealer policy, make sure you have liability protection.

con game(doctored car) — Used car dealer performs an elaborate face-lift on a used car to make the car look like new and thereby get a higher selling price. Changes may include: turning back the odometer, changing worn pedals, replacing the carpeting, repainting the car, repainting the engine block, deodorizing the car with a new car smell, etc. Good defense is careful inspection of the vehicle, checking ownership papers, and checking serial numbers, engine block numbers, etc.

con game(double coding) — Car salesman attempts to sell something twice to a customer on a sales sheet in order to rectify an earlier mistake or close a deal.

con game(double dipping) — Car salesman arranges a car buyer's downpayment from two loan companies to increase his cut. Also, it refers to arranging two downpayment loans for a car buyer when only one is needed by calling a loan in twice on the same day to a bank. It is not legal, but the deal is often closed before the bank and finance company have a chance to check on it. See also spastic.

con game(escalating insurance) — Insurance agency adds new coverage or increases limits to your existing car insurance at renewal time in order to increase premium payments. When questioned, they will often say the company has recommended the increased coverage based on studies. Good defense is to carefully check your insurance policy at renewal time, and agree only to the insurance you need.

con game(escalating work estimate) — See con game(extra repair work).

con game(exhaust manifold replacement) — Repair shop tries to convince you the exhaust system problems or noises are due to a faulty, cracked, or worn out exhaust manifold. This is rarely the case. Noise around the exhaust manifold is usually due to a loose manifold or a gasket that has worn out or gotten burned. Tightening the nuts and bolts or replacing the gasket is usually all that is necessary. If you are not knowledgeable in this area of your car get several opinions before committing to any repairs.

con game(extra repair work) — Very common con practiced at auto repair shops in which the owner of a car is told during the repair process that other repairs are badly needed to make the car safe to drive. A phone call is usually made later in the day by the mechanic in which the customer is informed that other items have "been discovered" that need repair or replacement. Many drivers fall for this scare tactic and proceed to have unnecessary repairs done. The smart owner will allow only specified repairs to be made, and will insist the service manager accompany him on a short test drive of the car making sure the repairs are satisfactory before paying the bill. New car dealers are often the worst offenders of this type of con game.

A good defense includes: get more than one estimate of needed work and compare estimates, learn about the different types of repair shops, have only the estimated work done, and become more informed about cars. See also auto repair business.

con game(face lifting stolen car) — New car is stolen, and a second older car is purchased and then junked to provide a new identity for the stolen car. The old car's papers and motor numbers are transferred to the stolen car, and after other modification work, the stolen car can be sold. This is a common practice in car theft rings.

con game(fan belt) — Repair shop tries convincing you a fan belt problem indicates more serious problems exist. Problem areas mentioned will usually include one or more of the following; the battery, generator, alternator, or voltage regulator. Your best defense is to get a second opinion, or better yet first check the fan belt for slippage and wear yourself when you have electrical problems. See also fan belt.

con game(free diagnosis) — Car repair business advertises free diagnosis of specific car problems to lure customers to their business. In actuality, the diagnosis winds up costing money if the customer agrees to it. It works as follows. When a potential customer arrives, he is told the trouble can only be determined by removing, disassembling, and inspecting the parts in question which is done free. If the customer agrees, the parts are removed and the parts problem is determined. It is at this point that the trouble begins. If the customer wants the work done elsewhere, the business will refuse to put the parts back in for free. This is done as an inducement to get the business. Good defense includes: get more than one estimate of work needed before allowing any work, and get free diagnosis including disassembly and assembly in writing.

con game(free examination) - See con game(free diagnosis).

con game(free products or services with work done) - Attempt made to drum up business when a car repair business advertises free services or parts included with work they do or other parts they sell. A typical example is a tire business where the customer is offered free wheel balancing, mounting of tires, front end alignment, etc. with each set of tires purchased. If you agree to it, you will be pressed hard by a salesman to buy a more expensive set of tires. If you give in, their plan has worked.

con game(freeway runner) - Service station sends out drivers to pull up alongside traveling cars and, in a friendly fashion, indicate to the driver there is something wrong with one or more of their tires. If successful, the driver pulls over and the pitch is made to drive it to a nearby service station to fix the problem. If there was no vibration while driving the car and the tire appears OK, a good defense is to simply refuse the help and continue on your way.

con game(front end alignment) - Repair shop or alignment center tries to convince you that car symptoms such as wheel vibration, thumping, and cup-like depressions in the tread are due to the front end being out of alignment. These are all symptoms of wheels out of balance which is usually much less expensive to fix. The most obvious proof of the need for front end alignment is in the tire tread wear pattern. If the tread has worn more on one side, a front end alignment is indicated. When in doubt, get a second opinion.

con game(gas overcharging) - Service station charges you extra for gasoline pumped by using one of the following tactics: not clearing the pump dollar and gallons numbers from last use; using charges made on another pump; pumping gas then clearing pump while you are in restroom or away from your car (now you don't know what it cost), and charging a padded higher price; and by not giving you cash discount on your purchase.

con game(guaranteed for the life of your car) - Car repair business guarantees certain car parts for the life of a car with no cost for replacement if ever needed. In actuality, these businesses often have a service charge for the replacement work and will often charge for new fittings they insist are needed such as: new muffler clamps, rubber supports, nuts and bolts, gaskets, etc.

con game(half breed car) - Car repair business welds the opposite ends of two same model cars together in order to make a good used car. Often both cars are wrecked, and can be purchased for a small investment at a wrecking yard. Such cars are dangerous being structurally weaker than the original.

con game(hard starting car-bad battery) - Repair shop diagnoses your car starting problem as due to a defective battery. They will then test each cell with a battery tester and supposedly find one or more bad cells. Usually, the bad cell reading was obtained by reversing tester leads. You will then be given a sales pitch on buying one of their batteries which may be rebuilt.

con game(hard starting car-faulty starter) - Repair shop attempts to convince you your car is hard to start because of a faulty starter. There are many reasons why a car may be hard to start. The most common, however, is insufficient battery voltage or a bad solenoid. The solenoid is the heavy duty switch used to route battery current to a starter when it is used. It can easily be diagnosed by shorting across its terminals to see if the starter works. Shops like to replace starters because they can remove and replace them quickly yet still charge you a lot for labor and a new starter. Best defense is to get several estimates of work needed, and/or conduct the above described test yourself.

con game(highball) - New car dealership tries to convince a prospective car buyer to trade in his old car and buy a new car at a phony price agreed to in a sales contract. Subsequently, the buyer is told the new car will cost more due to an oversight on the salesman's part or that "discovered" problems with the trade in lower its value. In this case, the salesman who got you to sign the contract is probably not an officer of the company and thus the contract is not binding. The dealer has the option to back out of the contract at any time. It is important that the sales contract be signed by an officer of the company and that you get in writing everything the car is suppose to have for options or work done to it before delivery. Most people give in and finally agree to the dealer's terms to avoid the hassle. See also sales contract.

con game(high reading odometer) - Scheme perpetrated at some car rental agencies where the odometer is set to register more miles than are actually driven in order to increase rental income. Despite legislation to control it, the practice still goes on. There is little the motorist can do unless you can prove the car odometer is off. If you measure the odometer reading against some actual road mileage posts, you may be able to deduct the percentage difference.

con game(honker) - Service station attendant uses a sharp instrument, known as a honker, to slash tires, fan belts, hoses, etc. when you are not looking in order to get business. See also con game(skinning the dude).

con game(last year's model) - New car dealership tries to sell you a previous year model car as the current year model. They simply update the model year of the car. Be aware of this when buying. If you suspect this activity, check the serial number of the car with the manufacturer, and/or the door latch post for a sticker that carries the month and year of manufacture. It is usually mounted on the driver's side. If you get caught with an earlier year model, you may be paying as much as one year's depreciation too much for it.

con game(lifetime muffler) - Muffler or other repair shop tries to convince you to buy one of their mufflers based on a "guaranteed for as long as you own your car" claim. The guarantee will cover the muffler, but not the clamps, extra piping, and hanger, etc., all of which add up. Also, installation fees are often made for replacing a bad muffler, and foreign cars may be not even have the muffler guaranteed. Inquire about the type of mufflers used, the limitations of the guarantee, etc. Ask what your cost would be if it had to be replaced. If the shop is evasive take your business elsewhere before you even start with them. Shop around.

con game(loading the deal) - New car dealership gets a customer to order a "standard" car, only to substitute a car with extra features later on. This con usually works in the following manner. The buyer comes in to take delivery and finds that the "standard" car he ordered will not be available for quite some time, but another same model car was received from the factory with a number of extras. The salesman's pitch comes on at this time to the effect: he will sell the extras at cost and it will only increase the monthly payments a small amount. He knows you are anxious to get your new car. If you agree to the deal, he increases his sales commission by selling you extra goods you didn't ask for.

con game(low balling) - See con game(bargain advertising).

con game(make ready) - New car dealer increases his profit on each new car sold by not performing the final inspection before delivering to the buyer. Factories usually give dealers an allowance, varying from $50 to $100, to inspect a car for problems missed at the factory before turning it over to the customer. Rather than spend the money, dealers will often rely on the factory's inspection. If the buyer subsequently brings the car back with problems, the dealer can then, at his option, choose whether to work on it or not. Often, dealers will drag their feet on the repair work and keep the car in the shop for a significant period of time. Most people don't have the time for this and so minor problems are often taken to repair shops. When buying a new car, make sure the sales contract specifies the car was inspected by the dealer and is delivered trouble free.

con game(metal shavings in rear end) - Mechanic, working on the rear end of your car, shows you metal shavings he claims are caused by worn out parts. He may say the differential gears are worn out, or a sealed bearing is going out. Insist on seeing the source of the problem. If the mechanic cannot show you more shavings, bad gears, a bad wheel bearing, etc., then decline replacing those components which don't seem bad, and have the unit put back together.

con game(metal shavings in transmission) - Mechanic, working on your transmission, shows you metal shavings he claims are caused by worn out gears, bearings, and other moving parts which need to be replaced. Insist on seeing the affected transmission parts and gearbox, and examine both carefully. There should be more of the shavings in the gearbox and some of the gear teeth should be broken off or severely worn. If there are bad bearings, they will be loose and/or noisy when rotated by hand. If they cannot show you more shavings, bad gears, or bad bearings, then decline the gear replacement and have the unit put back together.

con game(missing items) - New car dealership or repair shop deliberately leaves specified items off a car in order to increase profit. Such items can include undercoating, clear coating the car's paint, special tires, wheel balancing, transmission oil cooler, etc. Good defense is check to make sure the order items are on the car and specified in the sales contract or repair bill before signing.

con game(model year updating) - Shady practice used by many car dealers in which last year's models are updated so a 1984, for example, becomes a 1985. A prospective buyer should determine the actual car year before purchasing just to be safe. This can be done with serial numbers, etc. See also con game(last year's model).

con game(muffler replacement) - Muffler shop tries to convince a car owner that both mufflers (muffler and resonator) on a car so equipped must be replaced when one is bad. It is uncommon for both mufflers to go bad at the same time. The shop may also try to push replacement of other exhaust system

components. The best defense is to replace only what is necessary.
con game(new car extras) - New car dealer increases his profit on a sale by
selling a new car with actual or imaginary extra accessories. It usually
works the following way. The buyer orders the standard car he wants.
Sometime later, he is told the car has come in. When the buyer goes to pick
up the car, he learns it "mistakenly" came with extras and he will either
have to pay for them or have the standard car ordered again. Most buyers
will fall for this trick and pay the extra rather than wait for another car
to arrive. The buyer has the right to refuse acceptance of the car. The
salesman, however, knows he's got you over a barrel because you are anxious
to take delivery of your new car.
     Another "extras con" can happen to people who pay cash. The extras usually
don't exist. The salesman mentions they do in order to sell the car for a
little more. This helps to make up for loss of finance charges due to no
loan. Before signing any sales contract, check to make sure the extras are
on the car and work.
     If a decision is made to buy a car with the extras, make sure they are
specified in the sales contract, they exist, the extra brand names are
specified, and they operate before accepting the car. See also sales
contract and road test.
con game(new car parts substitution) - New car arrives with cheaper parts
substituted for more expensive ones. More expensive items could include
heavy duty radiator, heavy duty shock absorbers, special rear end, power
steering, etc. Good defense is make sure the options specified are on the
car and are spelled out clearly in the sales contract before signing it.
con game(no down payment) - New or used car dealership offers a car for sale
with no down payment as a sales ploy. To the unwary buyer, it sounds like a
good deal. Those who agree usually wind up paying far more than the original
purchase price of the car due to financing terms in favor of the dealer. The
terms are usually a fixed number of payments, and no option to pay off the
loan early. The end result is the buyer pays a great deal of interest
besides the principal on the loan. A car buyer should very carefully read
any finance contract, understand what the options are, and what the total
price of the car will actually be when it is finally paid for. Other
considerations include: repercussions of late payments, existence of balloon
payments, car insurance requirements, and title holder.
con game(oil switch) - Car parts and supplies business puts cheap bulk oil in
expensive oil containers and charges accordingly.
con game(one owner rental car) - Used car dealer buys rental cars, fixes them
up, and then sells them as one-owner cars. Part of the fix up process may
involve rolling back the odometer to show low miles, another selling point.
Dealers doing this may send the car to a professional to have it done
quickly. See also con game(turning back the odometer).
con game(on the rack) - Mechanic puts your car up on a rack for repair work
and then tries to convince you he has "uncovered" other car problems needing
immediate attention. Such problems may include: worn ball joints, worn
shocks, worn brake linings, etc. See also con game(worn ball joints), con
game(worn shocks), and con game(worn brake linings).
con game(out of regular) - Service station advertising regular gasoline often
at cut-rate prices, then informing you they are out when you stop for a fill-
up. You are then given the sales pitch for the more expensive gas they do
have. See also con game(gas overcharging).
con game(padding the bill-1) - Repair business tries to convince you to allow
them to pad or unreasonably increase an insurance estimate. If you agree,
you may be held liable (with others) in a fraud conspiracy.
con game(padding the bill-2) - Repair business adds unnecessary, and/or phony
parts and/or labor charges to a repair bill to increase their profit. See
also con game(extra repair work) and con game(phony repair work).
con game(parts switching) - Car repairman removes good car parts from a car
without the owners knowledge and replaces them typically with parts purchased
from wrecking yards. Such parts include: high performance or other
profitable engines in good condition, generators, carburetors, starters, etc.
The purpose is to make money selling the original parts in good condition.
High performance engines are popular. The switch usually takes place without
the owner's knowledge. It may happen when a car is brought in for service,
left parked in a garage for an extended period, etc. Most car owners who
fall victim to this con game never make the discovery. Good defense
includes: working with a reputable repair shop, carefully inspecting the car
and engine block number before accepting the work done, putting an
identifying mark on easily substituted parts, and leaving your car in safe
areas.
con game(phone call repair work) - See con game(extra repair work).
con game(phony repair work) - Common scheme practiced where a repair shop
charges for work never done. If it's work you specify, the shop will do only
what is absolutely necessary cutting corners wherever possible to maximize

their profit. They may call you during the day to convince you there are additional problems you were not aware of. If you agree to the additional work, they may do nothing and still charge you for the work. One trick used here includes repainting or steam cleaning car parts to make it look like new parts have been installed. Another more risky approach is doing nothing but still charging you for parts and labor, hoping you won't check the work carefully enough to discover what their trying to pull on you. Good defense includes: having only specified work done, and insisting on seeing any used parts that were replaced. Putting an identifying mark on replaceable parts is very helpful.

con game(rear end collision) - One or more people in a car stage a rear end collision type accident with another car in order to collect insurance money. The con artist(s) usually drives a cheap car and seeks out an expensive one to hit. The con usually works the following way. An expensive car is spotted on the road. The cheap car is then maneuvered in front of the expensive car and stopped without warning, causing a rear end collision. The con artist(s) then claims injury and demands to be taken to a hospital. When the insurance adjuster arrives at the hospital, the injuries are faked and the aches and pains are emphasized. Once the adjuster disappears, the con artist(s) quickly recovers and leaves the hospital, usually to an out of state address, and presses the insurance company for a quick settlement. Elaborate rear end collision rings have been known to operate, just like car theft rings.

con game(repainting used parts) - Mechanic removes a used part, replaces part or none of it, repaints the part, and then charges you as if a new part had been installed. Large parts such as transmissions can be quite costly if a mechanic makes a minor adjustment or replaces a minor part and then repaints it and charges you for a new one. Insist on all the old parts when having repairs done. Good defense is locating a reputable repair shop, or scratching an "X" or painting a dot on all replaceable parts in an inconspicuous place. Ask to see the old part(s) and then look for your mark(s).

con game(repair order) - Common scheme practiced where a car repair business uses the leverage of a repair order to compel you to have the balance of initial work done at their business. It usually works in the following way. You bring your car in for repair work. They perform an inspection or cost estimate at low cost usually disassembling some part. You are then told an extensive amount of works needs to be done. If you choose to have the work done elsewhere, they will inform you that there is a charge for reassembling the part in question. Since you signed the repair order, you have given them the right to keep the car until the work is paid for.

A repair order works to their advantage. Even if you threaten legal action, they know they can keep the car until the matter is resolved. Such legal problems can drag out far longer then most people are willing to put up with. The shop, therefore, usually wins. If you simply have them reassemble the part, you must pay for that work and there could be worse problems with it when you get it back. The other alternative, which is the one the repair shop hopes you will go for, is to have them go ahead and do the repair work they say needs to be done.

A good defense against this practice includes: getting more than one estimate of the problem without tearing anything apart, locating a reputable repair shop, checking with the Better Business Bureau for any complaints filed on shops you are considering, insisting on a clear description and cost of work to be done on the repair order, carefully reading any repair order before you sign it, obtaining a signed copy of the work order before you leave your car, and allowing only the specified work on the repair order to be performed. If they aren't cooperative with you in the beginning, they probably won't be later on. See also repair order and mechanics lien.

con game(sawdust in the rear end) - Car dealer adds a small amount of sawdust to a worn and noisy rear end to quiet it down. It doesn't keep it quiet for long, but often long enough to make a sale.

con game(serial number plate switching) - Car thieves set up a repair business to work on cars for the sole purpose of obtaining legal serial number plates which they remove and switch with stolen ones. This is done to give their stolen cars a legitimate identity. The end result is car owners end up driving a car that, according to the serial plate, is stolen. This work has been done professionally enough that it's very difficult to determine if any tampering has taken place. Your best defense is to seek out reputable repair shops and to know your car's serial number before you leave it for repairs.

con game(short sticking) - Service station attendant gets a false low reading on your car's oil dipstick to convince you more oil is needed. If you fall for it, they will often pour an "empty" can of oil into your engine and charge you for a full one. He may also try to talk you into oil additives. Good defense is closely observing any checking a service station attendant does, and declining the need for extras such as additives.

con game(skinning the dude) - Slick service station attendant attempts to get business from you by: slashing tires, radiator hoses, and fan belts; short sticking the oil level to convince you to buy more oil; stealing the gas cap; trying to convince you tires and other car parts are on the verge of failing; etc. Good defense in this situation is to get out of the car and observe what they are doing which is what they hope you won't do, or doing any checking yourself. See also con game(honker) and con game(barbershopping).

con game(slashing) - Slick service station attendant punctures a tire or water hose, cuts a fan or other belt, etc. while you are not looking in order to sell you parts. Good defense is get out of the car and closely observe any checking they do, or perform your own checks. See also con game(skinning the dude) and con game(honker).

con game(sunshine treatment) - Car repair business charges for work never done to a car. The term "sunshine treatment" is derived from leaving a car to be worked on outside and unrepaired. See also con game(padding the bill-2), con game(phone repair work), and con game(repainting used parts).

con game(tow truck) - Tow truck operator listens to a police radio for car breakdowns in his area, arrives quickly on the scene, and tries persuading you into signing a contract and getting towed to a local repair garage. The contract usually gives the tow truck operator exclusive rights to repair your car. It is best not to sign such a document if the operator is working with a local garage. If they refuse to take you to another repair shop, you will know there is some deal worked out between the two businesses. In such a case, you are better off waiting for the police and a reputable tow truck. If you decide to have someone tow you, do the following: determine the towing charge in advance, sign a form that allows only towing and not repair to the destination of your choosing, and get the tow truck operator's business card.

con game(steal the registration) - Ruse practiced in the past where a car salesman would pressure a potential car customer into a sale by selling his existing car out from underneath him. It would work as follows. While the customer is distracted looking at cars, the registration of his existing car is stolen. The car salesman makes a quick deal selling the car to a wholesaler. The salesman then approaches the customer and pressures him into buying a car by claiming that he has just sold his existing car.

con game(tow truck and police collusion) - Police, at the scene of a car accident, will subtly threaten issuing a citation if the car owner does not agree to use a certain local tow truck operator. The policeman benefits by receiving a fee and/or a percentage of the repair costs for each tow job and the tow truck operator benefits by getting the business.

con game(trade vs. repair) - Car dealer body shop tries to convince a customer whose car requires several hundred dollars of repair work (usually $200 or more) to trade the car in for a new car rather than have the repair work done. The best defense is to take the car elsewhere for repairs.

con game(traffic trap) - Motorist is unfairly stopped due to overly strict enforcement of traffic laws. The motorist is often out of state and gets caught in an abrupt speed reduction zone, crossing over faded out double yellow lines, etc. Once stopped, the con usually works as follows. The driver is told he has broken a certain traffic law and must appear before a judge. He is instructed to follow the officer in. When the judge is found, the driver is asked to plead guilty or not guilty. Both the judge and the police officer know that most people will plead guilty to avoid staying over for a trial even if they are innocent. Once the fine has been paid, there is often a split between the judge and the police officer.

con game(transmission repair) - Transmission repair shop tries to convince you your transmission problem can only be determined by signing a repair order to take the transmission apart first. You are then assured of a repair work estimate. They usually offer to diagnose the problem for free or a very low price. If you decline the repairs after the transmission is torn apart, you must still pay to have it put back together. The repair shop knows that if there is a dispute, the car can be tied up legally until the matter is settled. Most people, therefore, give in and have the repairs done which is what the mechanic is hoping for all along. It has been estimated that up to 80 percent of all transmission repairs can be done with the transmission still in the car. Be very wary of someone who insists the only way to diagnose is by removal. The way they act toward you will reflect the way they do business. Get several opinions first, and ask friends if they know of a reputable establishment. The best transmission shops don't advertise. They don't have to.

con game(turning back the odometer) - Owner turns back the mileage reading of used car odometer to improve its salability. Often the work is done by specialists who are good at it and can often do such a job in ten to twenty minutes. See also con game(one owner rental car).

con game(used parts-1) - Repair shop tries convincing a customer certain used parts and/or supplies must be replaced with new parts to make the necessary repairs. In reality, some or most of the parts are not necessary or can be adjusted or cleaned, and reinstalled. Examples include: spark plugs, condenser, points, distributor cap, valve springs, piston rings, oil filter, fuel filter, brake fluid, brake cylinder, transmission fluid, rear end fluid, and brake linings.

con game(used parts-2) - Auto body shop installs used car parts usually obtained from wrecked cars, and then charges the customer for the parts at new prices.

con game(warranty work) - New car dealer uses various tactics to stall working on a car under warranty until it expires. Such tactics include doing no work on the car and having the car owner come back several times for the same problem, discouraging the owner by telling them it may take a week or two to get it fixed, putting the owner off by claiming to back order necessary parts, etc.

New car dealers usually don't like doing repair work on cars under warranty because the factory reimburses the dealer at a lower rate than he can make on non-warranty work. Shop income is maximized by keeping warranty work to a minimum when non-warranty work is plentiful. This is another situation illustrating the importance of thoroughly checking out a car before agreeing to buy it.

con game(white flash) - Car repair business tries to convince you part or all of your car's wiring system has to be rewired because of some "electrical flash" your car got exposed to. The only cars ever in need of an extensive rewire job are usually those suffering fire damage, or whose fuses have been bypassed or replaced with high amperage values. Getting two or more estimates will help confirm or deny this problem.

con game(white smoke) - Repairman pours a small amount meat curative or barbecue sauce (containing titanium tetrachloride) onto a generator, alternator, or hot engine surface creating a reaction causing a lot of white smoke to form. The repairman will usually also disconnect a battery cable and ask you to try and start the car. The car won't start and the pitch will then be made to sell you a new generator or alternator, battery, and any other related parts he can convince you are needed. Your tip-off should a properly running engine before you turned it off, and the red generator idiot light coming on or a constant discharge showing on an ammeter. If there is no light or reading, you can bank on the battery cable being loosened. Even if a generator or alternator has completely failed, your car will run until the battery becomes discharged. Good defense it to smell the smoke which won't smell like the smoke from a fire, and check the battery cables for tightness at the terminals. Carefully watching a repairman will usually eliminate this problem.

con game(worn ball joints) - Mechanic places your car on a rack to examine a steering problem and then "discovers" the ball joints in the front steering system are worn out. The mechanic will usually grab one wheel and shake it back and forth to show the worn ball joints are causing some slop or wobble in the steering linkage. You will then be told the condition is dangerous and must be corrected right away or the car will not steer safely. His final pitch will be that he can quickly correct the problem while it is on the rack.

Be very suspicious of this maneuver. All steering linkages have some play when the whole weight of the car is off them. The play is due to manufacturing tolerances, clearance, and the need to minimize stress in the linkage. The proper way to test ball joints is with the weight off the wheel and lifting the wheel straight up and down. If there is noticeable movement in this direction, the affected joints may need replacement. If you're not sure about the work, ask yourself if the car steers okay without excessive play in the steering wheel. If it does, decline to have this work done or get another estimate.

con game(worn brake linings) - Mechanic is usually doing work in the tire area and then "discovers" the brakes need repairing. Be wary of this maneuver. Try to remember when the brake system was last worked on and about how many miles might be on the brake linings. It is wise to decline the work, and have the brake system checked later by a qualified mechanic or shop you can trust.

con game(worn shocks) - Mechanic works in the tire area and then "discovers" the shock absorbers are worn out. A mechanic may even remove a shock and show you the fluid is leaking out. The oil should look dirty and caked. If not, fresh oil has probably been squirted on to give evidence of a leak. If you agree to have the work done and the shocks are okay, they may just remove them, repaint them, and place them back on the car. Decline to have the work done, unless you know they are worn out, and want the work done. Considerations at that moment will be price, brand name, shock life, guarantee, economics, and need. You can perform a simple test yourself to determine shock wear. Stand at one fender on your car and press the fender down firmly. If the car rebounds up and then stays in position, they are

okay. If a bouncing movement occurs, it's probably time to replace them.
congested traffic – Traffic slowed or stopped due to excess cars on the road, a car accident, or other delays.
Conklin Electric – American electric car produced in 1895.
con man – Person who gets money or property from another under false pretenses after gaining their confidence and trust.
Connecticut – American car produced in 1908.
connection – Transferring from one car, bus, train, etc. to another during the course of a journey.
connecting rod – Rigid metal arm used to link a piston and a crankshaft together for transferring power generated in an engine cylinder to a crankshaft.
connector block – Plastic plug designed to house one or more electrical connectors and connect them to other electrical connectors. All kinds of shapes are used depending on the application. A common connector block is the one plugging into the back of an alternator.
connector pipe – Exhaust system pipe used to connect a muffler to a tailpipe.
Connersville – American car produced in 1914.
Conoco, Inc – A U.S. petroleum company headquartered in Wilmington, Delaware. It was formerly called Continental Oil Company, and is a subsidiary of E.I. DuPont De Nemours & Co. See also petroleum company.
Conover – American car produced from 1906-1908 by Conover Motor Co. in New Jersey.
Conquest – A Japanese car imported from 1984 to date for Dodge Division of Chrysler Corp. in Michigan.
Conrad – American car produced from 1900-1904 by Conrad Motor Carriage Co. (1900-1903), and Lackawanna Motor Co. (1904), both in New York.
con rod – See connecting rod.
consign your car – To take your car to a car dealer in order to have him sell it. If the car sells, a specified fee goes to the dealer. Cars should be consigned for a specified period of time in writing. A time period of 2-4 weeks works to the owner's advantage. See also on consignment.
consignment – Property sent to an agent for the purpose of selling, shipping, or storing it.
consignment(net figure) – Consignment arranged so the agent selling the property and the owner agree to a selling price the owner will receive. A car dealer can make a substantial amount of money if he can sell it for much more than the agreed selling price. See also consignment(percentage).
consignment(percentage) – Consignment arranged so the agent selling the property receives a percentage of the actual selling price. Cars dealers usually get 10-12 percent. It is considered the best way for a car owner to consign. See also consignment(net figure).
consistency – The relative firmness or solidity of a material.
Console – Abbreviation for floor mounted shift.
Consolidated – American car produced in 1903-1906 and 1916.
constant depression carburetor – See carburetor(air valve).
constant mesh gears – Gears always remaining in contact with each other.
constant mesh transmission – See transmission(constant mesh).
constant vacuum carburetor – See carburetor(air valve).
constant velocity joint – See universal joint(constant velocity).
consumer protection – Legal protection provided to consumers against dishonest business practices, schemes, etc.
Consumer's Union – Consumer organization organized in 1938 by a handful of scientists, technicians, and writers. It publishes the well known Consumer Reports Magazine and an annual Auto Buying Guide. The organization was responsible for helping the Center for Auto Safety get off the ground (most of its funding) by establishing the Ralph Nader Auto Safety Fellowship.
Consumer Reports – Magazine published by Consumer's Union. It summarizes testing done on various consumer products and reports the product's safety, quality, and usefulness.
CONT – Abbreviation for Continental.
contact cement – Adhesive compound used to bond porous surfaces together. It is applied to both surfaces and allowed to dry. Both surfaces are then pressed together firmly forming an instant bond.
contact patch – See tire footprint.
contact pattern – Area located on a gear teeth's surface where opposing gear contact is made.
contact pattern(crossed) – Pattern created when two facing gear teeth surfaces show wear that is offset instead of opposite.
contact pattern(lame) – Pattern created when two facing gear teeth surfaces show wear that is opposite, but high on one side and low on the other.
contact point arcing – Electrical arcing created across the air gap between open contact points. It usually occurs only on distributor points where high voltage from the ignition coil bleeds off as a secondary effect of inducing very high voltage. Capacitor is usually placed in the circuit to absorb any

high voltage. Arcing indicates it is not working or is the wrong size.
contact points - See breaker points.
contemporary car - Car generally classified as built from 1968 to date. See also brass era car, vintage car, antique car, milestone car, special interest car, classic car, contemporary classic car, pre-war car, and post-war car.
contemporary classic car - Car generally classified as built after 1945 and in demand by car collectors. See also brass era car, vintage car, antique car, contemporary car, milestone car, special interest car, classic car, pre-war car, and post-war car.
Continental - American car produced in 1907-1914 and 1933-1934 by University Automobile Co. in Connecticut (1907-1909), Indiana Motor & Mfg. Co. in Indiana (1909-1914), and Continental Automobile Co. in Michigan (1933-1934). Also, an American car produced from 1958 to date by Lincoln Division of Ford Motor Co. in Michigan.
continental kit - Kit composed of necessary parts to mount a spare tire compartment on a car's trunk.
Continental Oil Co - See Conoco, Inc.
continuance - Delaying a trial date to a later time.
continuous braking - Brakes applied for an extended period of time. It usually occurs when descending a long steep grade, and can cause brake linings to burn and fail. It is better to shift to a lower gear letting the engine help brake the car and allow brakes to be used intermittently.
continuously variable transmission - See transmission(continuously variable).
Contessa Motor Hood - Popular hat worn around 1909 by women when traveling by car. It was made of silk and lace with a Mica face shield.
contract - Agreement made between two or more people in writing and enforceable by law to do something.
contract(finance) - Contract drawn up to specify terms of loaning money to a party. Anytime money is borrowed, the borrower signs such a contract.
contract(quasi) - Contract created between two parties based on mutual consent which is not expressed but implied or assumed by law.
contract(sales) - Contract signed by a purchaser specifying terms of a sale. New car buyer will sign some kind of sales contract when he takes delivery of a car. Before signing one of these contracts, do the following: purchase from a reputable dealer; read all the clauses carefully; make sure all the extras you want and all the contract modifications are in writing; do a careful inspection and road test the car; figure the approximate market value before negotiating; have dealer certify car is safe to operate, will pass any state inspection, and that he will repair or pay for repairs to make it so; be wary of public service cars (taxi, rental, police, etc.); verify any one-owner claims; avoid specific limits to dealers liability in contract; compare loan and insurance rates; and insist that all the car problems you find be corrected before you take delivery or get it in writing, signed by the sales manager, what items will be fixed without charge. See also warranty(new car).
contract(service) - Contract drawn up specifying servicing arrangements for a purchased product. It is often negotiated when a product is purchased.
contract(trade in) - Contract drawn up to specify terms of trading in a used car for a new car. It is usually a sales contract with a clause specifying the agreed upon trade-in allowance for a used car.
contraction - A reduction in size.
contributory negligence - Carelessness on the part of a driver, pedestrian, etc. that contributes to causing an accident.
control arm - See upper control arm and lower control arm.
control damper assembly - Hinge and plate assembly (air gate) positioned in an air inlet to control the flow of normal and preheated air into an air cleaner. The plate moves by means of linkage to a vacuum and/or temperature controlled diaphragm.
controlled access highway - Any roadway built where owners with adjoining property have no legal right to access except at specified points (intersections, on ramps, etc.).
controlled coupling unit - See fill and dump coupling.
controlled drift - See power slide.
controlled slide - See power slide.
control module - A car's on-board computer. It is commonly located behind one of the front seat kick panels. Exercise caution when installing accessories such as speakers in the panels. You could accidentally cut into the module, a costly move. See also black box.
control pressure regulator valve - Valve used in an automatic transmission to regulate hydraulic fluid pressure.
control pressure reducer valve - Valve used in an automatic transmission to reduce hydraulic fluid pressure when needed.
control unit - Solid state device used to interrupt current flow in an ignition coil's primary windings to induce a high voltage current flow in the secondary windings. It receives an amplified voltage signal from a magnetic

pickup coil located in the distributor, and uses a transistor (instead of points) to interrupt the primary current flow. Most units are sealed with an epoxy requiring replacement of the whole unit if it doesn't work. See also reluctor and pickup coil.

control valve body - Device designed to control the flow of fluid in an automatic transmission to the servos and oil clutches.

conv - Abbreviation for convertible.

Convaircar - American car produced in 1947. It was a prototype car and aircraft with separately attached wings and motor. Flight and road tests were conducted, but the vehicle was never produced in quantity.

convection - Transfer of heat by air currents.

convenience group - Specified list of convenience accessories offered in a package deal for installation on a new car. Such convenience items might include: intermittent wipers, tinted windshield, and retractable headlights.

conventional - Tractor built with the engine mounted in front of the cab. See also cabover.

conventional tire - See tire(conventional).

conversion work - Work performed by a dealer or independent to bring a nonconforming car into compliance with State and/or Federal regulations.

converter(1) - Electrical device designed to change alternating current to direct current. See also rectifier and diode.

converter(2) - Device used to convert LPG from a liquid to a gas. See also carburetor(adapter type).

converter(3) - See fluid coupling. See also torque converter and catalytic converter.

converter check valve - See drain-back valve.

converter cover - Outer cover or housing of a torque converter.

converter light-off - Combination of heat and catalyst action needed in a catalytic converter to cause emission reducing reactions to occur with exhaust gases.

converter pellets - Pellets used in a catalytic converter to reduce exhaust emissions. Most catalytic converters allow them to be replaced, and is a cheaper route to go than replacing the converter.

converter pressure relief valve - Valve used in an automatic transmission to keep hydraulic pressure in a converter from reaching a certain maximum value.

convertible - See body style(convertible).

convertible boot - Covering positioned over the folded down top of a convertible. It is typically held in place with snap fasteners.

convertible stack - Portion of a convertible top located above a car's beltline when the top is folded down.

convertible top - Car top designed to be retracted or removed.

conviction - Decision made in a court of law judging an accused party guilty.

Cook - American car produced in 1908-1909 and 1921.

cookies - See cookie cutters.

cookie cutters - Wheel cover design popular on Porsche 911. It is designed like a pie cut into 10 wedges with alternating black and polished aluminum finish.

coolant - Fluid used in an engine cooling system. Coolant in today's cars is a mixture of antifreeze and water. In earlier times, straight water or water and alcohol was used.

coolant condition - Quality and quantity of various coolant compounds contained in coolant solution. Continued safe use will depend on such factors as: antifreeze protection level, additive level and life expectancy, and contaminants in solution. Contaminants include: rust, scale, electrolysis of dissimilar metals, and automatic transmission fluid. Rust and scale occur when antifreeze level drops to a low percent of total solution. Rust will give coolant a chocolate color. It is usually caused by using straight water, and coolant with depleted rust inhibitors due to age and/or exhaust gas entering cooling system. Electrolysis occurs when metal is removed from interior coolant passageways. It commonly deposits itself in the radiator and can be seen as a whitish deposit on top of the tubes when removing the radiator cap and looking inside. Automatic transmission fluid will appear if an automatic transmission cooler, mounted inside the radiator, is leaking, and will cause coolant to take on a strawberry or red color. See also fluid leak(red oil in coolant) and fluid leak(engine oil in coolant).

coolant flushing adapter - T-shaped fitting placed in a heater hose line to introduce fresh water into a cooling system when it is being flushed. The fitting is usually designed to connect to a garden hose.

coolant jacket - Water passageways cast into the structure of an engine block to circulate water around the engine cylinders for cooling.

coolant recovery system - Part of a closed cooling system used to provide extra space for engine coolant to expand into when it gets hot, and minimize coolant loss and air infiltration. It consists of: a sealed radiator cap, overflow hose, and an overflow tank. When engine coolant gets hot, the radiator cap's pressure relief valve opens at 15 psi allowing some coolant to flow into the overflow tank. When the engine cools down, a vacuum is produced and the vented coolant is drawn back into the radiator. See also cooling system.

coolant sensor - See sensor(coolant temperature).

cooling fins - Blade-like projections on metal surfaces designed to increase heat dissipation. Such projections are found on alternator bodies, brake drums, radiator tubing, and heat sinks.

cooling system - An assemblage of parts used to keep a car engine from overheating. The cooling system parts typically include: a radiator, water pump, connecting hoses, thermostat, engine block water and cylinder head cooling passageways, and coolant recovery system. Without a cooling system, several internal combustion engine parts would melt from the heat generated or not move due to high friction from heat expansion. An engine's cooling system must remove about 1/3 of the heat generated by an engine. For a full size V-8 engine traveling at freeway speeds, it's equivalent to continuously removing as much heat as it takes to heat a 4-6 room home in cold weather.

cooling system condition - Ability of a cooling system to reliably cool an engine. Factors affecting its ability include: flow restrictions in radiator or cooling passageways, leaks, and stuck thermostat.

cooling system pressure test - See car service tip(cooling system pressure test).

Cooper - American line of tires produced by The Cooper Tire Co.

Cooperative Auto Shop of San Francisco - Cooperative organized in San Francisco in 1974 to provide its members with reliable low cost auto repair and maintenance services.

cop - Policeman.

Copley Minor - American car produced in 1907.

Coppock - American car produced from 1907-1912.

Corbett - American car produced in 1907.

Corbin - American car produced from 1903-1912 by Corbin Motor Vehicle Co. in Connecticut.

Corbitt - American car produced from 1912-1913 by Corbitt Auto Co. in North Carolina.

Cord - American car produced from 1929-1937 by Auburn Automobile Co. in Indiana. Also, an American car produced beginning in 1964 by Auburn-Cord-Duesenberg Co. in Oklahoma (1964-1967), and Elfman Motors in Pennsylvania (1967-1968), and SAMCO in Oklahoma (1968 on).

Cordoba - American car produced from 1975 to date by Chrysler Corp. in Michigan.

cords - Strands of heavy reinforcing material used in a tire body. Materials used include: polyester, nylon, and rayon.

core - Radiator section designed to do majority of water cooling. It consists of a series of vertical tubes finned for heat dissipation. Fluid is circulated through the tubes and cooled by a stream of air. A tank is soldered to the top and bottom of the core. Most cars have radiator and heater cores.

core charge - Additional payment made when brake shoes, clutch discs, and other rebuildable car parts are purchased. The payment is refunded when the old parts are returned for recycling.

core plug - See freeze plug.

core shift - Condition created when a casting such as an intake manifold has interior passageways that are not equally spaced from the outside casting walls. Such a defect can create thin walls, holes in water passageways, etc.

Corinthian - American car produced from 1922-1923 by Corinthian Motors Co. in Pennsylvania.

Corl - American car produced in 1911.

Corliss - American car produced in 1917.

Cornelian - American car produced from 1914-1915 by Blood Bros. Machine Co. in Michigan.

cornering - Ability to drive through a corner at higher speeds.

Cornish-Friedberg - American car produced from 1908-1909 by Cornish-Friedberg Motor Car Co. in Illinois.

corona - Electric field built up around a high voltage cable from the flow of current. It transforms oxygen into ozone within the field. Spark plug cables are made of rubber compounds designed to resist the deteriorating effects of corona.

Coronet - American car produced from 1957-1982 by Dodge Division of Chrysler Corp. in Michigan.

Correja - American car produced from 1908-1915 by Vandewater & Co. in New Jersey.

corrosion - Process defined as the eating or wearing away of metals and other compounds by the action of chemicals such as oil oxidation products, fuel combustion by-products, and water (rust). See also battery corrosion and rust.

corrosion inhibitor - See additive(corrosion inhibitor).

Cort - American car produced in 1914.

Cortland - American car produced in 1911.

Cortez - American car produced in 1947.

Cortina - American car produced from 1966-1970 by Ford Motor Co. in Michigan.

Corum, L L - He won the Indianapolis 500 Race in 1924 with Joe Boyer driving an average of 98.2 mph in a Deusenberg Special.

Corvair - American car produced from 1960-1972 by Chevrolet Division of General Motors Corp. in Michigan. It featured a lightweight aluminum air-cooled rear-mounted engine.

Corvette - American high performance car produced from 1953 to date by Chevrolet Division of General Motors Corp. in Michigan.

Corweg - American car produced in 1947.

Corwin - American car produced from 1905-1907.

co-sign - To sign a promissory note, in addition to the original signer, for the purpose of guaranteeing payment if the original signer defaults.

co-signer - A second person or party obligated to the terms of a contract in the event the first person or party defaults.

cosmetic work - Minor repair work needed in order to restore a car to good condition.

Cosmopolitan - American car produced from 1907-1910 by D.W. Haydock Automobile Mfg. Co. in Missouri.

cost of owning an automobile - Various costs associated with owning and operating an automobile. They include: depreciation, maintenance, repairs, parts, gas & oil, insurance, licensing & registration, and parking.

Cotay - American car produced from 1920-1921 Coffyn-Taylor Motor Co. in New York.

Cotta - American car produced from 1901-1903 Cotta Automobile Co. in Illinois.

cotter key - Small wedge-like piece of steel usually used to hold gears and other devices on a shaft without slipping. It rests in a slot cut into a shaft and protrudes a short distance above the shaft surface. See also keyway.

cotter pin - Split metal pin commonly used in shafts to hold bolts, washers, etc. in position. It is pronged on one end only. After insertion in a hole, the ends are bent to hold it in place.

Cougar - American car produced from 1966 to date by Mercury Division of Ford Motor Co. in Michigan.

counterbalance - Portion of a crankshaft cast opposite to a throw to balance the weight. The counter balance consists of two surfaces on both sides and opposite to a crank pin. Also, a weight attached to a moving part so the part will be balanced. A tire, balanced with lead weights, is an example.

counter clockwise - Circular rotation to the left or opposite to the normal movement of clock hands.

counter gears - See cluster gears.

counterman - See job(partsman).

countershaft - Shaft mounted in the lower portion of a manual transmission containing several non-sliding gears. The gears mesh with sliding gears of a transmission mainshaft to produce the various gears ratios. See also splined mainshaft, and transmission countershaft.

countershaft gear - See gear(transmission countershaft).

countersink - To enlarge the top part of a screw or bolt hole to recess a screw or bolt head below the surface.

Country Club - American car produced in 1904.

Country Squire - American car produced from 1957-1964 and 1980 to date by Ford Motor Co. in Michigan.

Country Wagon - American car produced from 1957-1964 by Ford Motor Co. in Michigan.

coupe - See body style(coupe).

Coupe de ville - See body style(town car).

cough an engine - To heavily damage an engine.

Couple-Gear - American car produced in 1905.

coupling - Device used to join two moving parts together. A universal joint is an example.

Courier - American car produced in 1904, 1909-1912, and 1922-1924 by Sandusky Automobile Co. (1904), Courier Car Co. and United States Motor Co. (1909-1912), and Courier Motor Co. (1922-1924), all in Ohio. Also, a Japanese truck imported by Ford Motor Co. in Michigan.

court - Place used to hold trials.

court costs - Costs charged usually to losers in courtroom litigation by the court.

courtesy discount - Fictional price discount offered on a car to a customer resisting a sales pitch.

courtesy light - See light(courtesy).

Covel Electric - American car produced in 1912.

coverage - One or more clauses in a contract, warranty, insurance policy, etc. used to specify what the issuer of the document will cover.

cover band – Flexible metal band used to cover a generator inspection opening for inspecting the brush and commutator area.

Covert – American car produced from 1901-1907 by Byron V. Covert & Co. (1901-1904), and Covert Motor Vehicle Co. (1904-1907), both in New York.

Covic – American car produced in 1930.

cowl – Car body structure used to attach the windshield, dashboard, and firewall. It runs across the car just in front of the windshield.

cowl hood – Hood with a raised center section. The section may be raised for cosmetic appearances or for gaining additional clearance above the carburetor and other engine parts.

cowl panel – Sheet metal panel positioned to run from the base of a windshield forward to a hood cut line and between the front fenders.

Coyote – American car produced from 1909-1910 by Redondo Beach Car Works in California.

CP(1) – American car produced in 1908.

CP(2) – Abbreviation for coupe.

Cpe – Abbreviation for coupe.

cpe – Abbreviation for coupe.

C pillar – Rear metal post in a car roof. It runs from each rear roof corner to a car's upper trunk lid area. All cars have two. See also A pillar, B pillar, and D pillar.

CPT – American car produced in 1906.

CP Truck – American truck produced from 1909-1914.

CR – Abbreviation for Costa Rica found usually on an international license plate.

cracked block – Engine block damaged due to high heat usually caused by lack of coolant or restricted coolant flow. High heat causes the metal to warp, crack, deform, or otherwise fail. Cracked blocks usually must be replaced.

cracked case – Cracked battery case.

cracked distributor cap – Distributor cap damaged with one or more hairline or larger cracks usually near the top. Crack may cause water to leak in or a carbon track to build up between terminals. If the crack is significant, a replacement is usually indicated.

cracked engine block – See cracked block.

cracked flywheel – Flywheel characterized by cracks in its structure. It is usually due to excessive heat build-up. Possible causes include: clutch plate slipping due to weak pressure plate springs or wrong size clutch plate or pressure plate, excessive clutch clipping due to poor driving habits, riding the clutch excessively, and using a clutch plate worn to the rivets.

cracking – Petroleum refining method characterized by heating heavier hydrocarbons under pressure to split their molecules into lighter ones.

cracking tower – Tall cylindrical tower used divide crude oil, heated to 800 degrees Fahrenheit, into its different fractions. The different boiling points of the various fractions cause them to condense out at different heights in the column.

cradle – Sub-frame commonly used on a unibody car to support an engine.

Cragar – American line of performance equipment.

Craig-Hunt – American car produced in 1920.

Craig-Toledo – American car produced from 1906-1907 by Craig-Toledo Motor Co. in Michigan and Ohio.

Crane – American car produced from 1912-1915 by Crane Motor Co. and Crane Motor Car Co., both in New Jersey.

Crane & Breed – American car produced from 1912-1917 by Crane & Breed Mfg. Co. in Ohio.

Crane-Simplex – American car produced in 1915-1924 by Simplex Automobile Co. in New Jersey. It was an outstanding prestige car in its time.

crank – Arm or lever connected to a shaft to transmit and change rotary motion into reciprocating motion or vice versa. See also crankshaft.

crank arm – Crankshaft throw. Journal surface on a crankshaft designed to receive the large end of a connecting rod. The arm length or throw determines the distance the piston will travel.

crankcase – Lower part of an engine block housing the crankshaft. The crankcase is not the oil pan.

crankcase dilution – Condition created when unburned fuel leaks past piston rings into the crankcase area to dilute oil in the oil pan.

crankcase emission control system – Assemblage of parts and controls used to regulate the emission of crankcase vapors into the atmosphere. Older engines simply had crankcase vent tubes or breather caps that allowed vapors to vent directly to the atmosphere. Today's engines route the vapors back into the engine for combustion. Though car manufacturers have created many different methods of controlling emissions, they are all similar. See also emission control system(crankcase).

crankcase flush – Liquid compound added to engine oil minutes before oil is to be drained for the purpose of removing accumulated sludge and varnish in the engine.

crankcase ventilation – Airflow pattern induced in a crankcase by one of several means for the purpose of minimizing the accumulation of water, fuel vapors, and sludge. Early engines vented crankcase fumes outside the engine while today's engines route them into the engine's intake manifold for combustion. A PCV valve usually controls the flow into the intake manifold.

crankcase ventilation system – Assemblage of parts designed to keep an engine's crankcase area ventilated and minimize the accumulation of vapors. Parts can include: PCV valve, tubes, hoses, vacuum controls, and vented or sealed oil filler caps.

crankcase vent tube – Vertical vent tube positioned to run from an engine valve train area to the underside of an engine block. As the car travels, air passing by the end of the tube creates a vacuum effect, drawing crankcase vapors from an engine. It was used on older engine designs, but was not that effective as it only removed vapors when the car was traveling at a good speed. See also road draft tube and emission control system(crankcase-road draft tube).

cranking voltage – Voltage used to operate a starter.

crank pin – Lower connecting rod bearing surface located on the crankshaft. Every crankshaft has the same number of crank pins as cylinders. They allow the up/down motion of pistons to be transmitted to a crankshaft through connecting rods to generate circular motion.

crankshaft – Heavy metal machined shaft designed to transfer power from engine cylinders to the drive train. It runs the length of an engine and is mounted in the bottom of an engine block. The shaft contains offset portions, called cranks, where the connecting rods are fastened. The cranks translate the up/down motion of pistons into rotary motion. The crankshaft is considered the backbone of the engine with most of the engine parts attached directly or indirectly to it.

crankshaft counterbalance – See crankshaft counterweights.

crankshaft counterweights – Series of weights attached to a crankshaft for balancing the weight of each piston, rod, and crank pin.

crankshaft gear – Gear mounted on the front of a crankshaft for driving a camshaft gear by means of a chain or belt.

crankshaft pulley(1) – Pulley mounted on a crankshaft outside an engine block. It is used to drive pulley driven accessories via one or more belts. Accessories include: fan/water pump, air conditioner, generator, alternator, and air pump.

crankshaft pulley(2) – Serrated pulley mounted on the front of a crankshaft inside a timing cover. A heavy duty serrated belt connects the pulley to a camshaft pulley to maintain the proper valve timing relationship during engine operation. See also crankshaft gear.

crankshaft socket – Socket built to fit over the end of a crankshaft and be operated by a socket wrench for easy rotating of crankshaft.

crankshaft sprocket – See crankshaft gear.

crankshaft torque – Torque developed by a crankshaft as a result of engine operation. Crankshaft torque is low at idling speed and increases rapidly as rpm increases.

crapper – Rough car or junker. See also rat.

crash – See accident.

crash helmet – Helmet worn to protect the head in the event of a crash. Race car drivers wear them.

crash sensor – Sensor designed to activate an air bag when a car stops abruptly. Mechanical and electronic sensor designs have been developed. Each is built to react to the force of deceleration.

Crawford – American car produced from 1905-1923 by Crawford Automobile Co. in Maryland.

cream puff – Used car maintained in good condition and easy to sell. It usually requires no repair work. Car salesmen rarely get them.

credit – Reputation built for being financially solvent and handling money well, entitling a person to be trusted in buying or borrowing.

credit bureau – Organization engaged in collecting consumer credit information for subsequent distribution to money lenders.

credit line – Amount of money available for borrowing from a lending institution.

creditor – Person engaged in extending credit. Also, it refers to a person owed money.

credit rating – The rating given to a person, business, etc. as to how well they have handled credit in the past.

creep – Condition created when a car with an automatic transmission, in drive, tends to move forward despite having a foot on the brake. It is usually caused when engine idle speed is a little too high. Creep can also be caused in a manual transmission car if the clutch drags while the pedal is fully depressed and transmission is in gear.

creeper – Low profile platform on casters or wheels used to allow a mechanic to lay horizontally on it and slide underneath a car readily.

creeping car - Car traveling well below the posted speed limit. Such cars are often maddening for people to trail behind. It is best to remain patient and pass when it is safe.

Crescent - American car produced in 1907 and from 1913-1914 by Crescent Motor Co. in Ohio (1907), and Michigan (1913-1914).

Cresson - American car produced in 1915.

Crestmobile - American car produced from 1900-1905 by Crest Mfg. Co. in Massachusetts.

Cricket - American car produced in 1914. Also, a Japanese car imported from 1978-1982 by Plymouth Division of Chrysler Corp. in Michigan.

criminal complaint - Charges filed with a local prosecutor alleging criminal intent. In the case of an auto repair shop, the contention is the car owner was defrauded or conned in some way. Such a complaint must usually claim the following: intent to do the work, knowledge the work was not done, owner accepted the repair shop's work, the shop received payment, the shop knows they mislead the owner.

Criterion - American car produced in 1912.

crm puf - Abbreviation for cream puff.

Croce - American car produced in 1914.

Crock - American car produced in 1909.

Croesus Jr - American car produced in 1907.

Crofton Bug - American car produced from 1959-1961 by Crofton Marine Engine Co. in California.

Crompton - American car produced in 1903-1905 by Crompton Motor Carriage Co. in Massachusetts.

crook lock - Anti-theft device constructed as a bar for attaching to a brake pedal and steering wheel. They can be effective since they are visible and may discourage a potential car thief.

Crosley - American car produced from 1939-1952 by Crosley Motors, Inc. in Ohio. Other models were produced during same period.

crossed flags - See flags(crossed).

crossed spark plug wires - Two or more spark plug wires connected to the wrong engine cylinders. This condition causes engine misfiring and sluggish performance.

crossfiring - Condition created when high voltage migrates from one spark plug cable into another, or from one distributor cap tower to another. It is minimized by using proper cables and keeping them properly separated. High voltage ignition systems producing more than 30-32,000 volts can cause ignition crossfiring.

crossing the tracks - Crossing railroad tracks.

cross member - See frame cross member.

cross shaft(pinion) - Shaft used to mount a differential pinion gear.

cross shaft(steering) - Shaft in a steering gearbox used to mesh with a steering shaft worm gear. One end is also splined to the pitman arm.

Cross Steam Carriage - American car produced in 1897.

cross walk - Area marked across a road surface legally requiring car traffic to slow down and stop if someone is within the markings. Signs are usually posted on both sides of the road notifying approaching cars of the crosswalk.

crosswind - Wind moving across a car's path. Wind can be natural or caused by vehicles on the road such as semi-trucks.

Crouch - American car produced from 1897-1900 by Crouch Automobile Mfg. & Trans. Co. in Pennsylvania.

Crow - Canadian car produced from 1915-1918 by Canadian Crow Motor Co. in Ontario.

Crow-Elkhart - American car produced from 1909-1924 by Crow-Elkhart Motor Car Co. in Indiana.

Crowdus - American car produced from 1901-1903 by Crowdus Automobile Co. in Illinois.

Crown - American car produced in 1905, 1907-1910, and from 1913-1914 by Detroit Auto Vehicle Co. in Michigan (1905), Crown Motor Vehicle Co. (1907-1909) and Graves & Congdon Co. (1909-1910) in Massachusetts, Crown Motor Car Co. in Kentucky (1913-1914), and Hercules Motor Car Co. in Indiana (1914).

Crown-Magnetic - American car produced in 1920.

Crowther-Duryea - American car produced from 1915-1916 by Crowther Motors Co. in New York.

Croxton - American car produced from 1911-1914 by Croxton Motor Co. in Ohio (1911-1912), and Pennsylvania (1912-1914).

Croxton-Keeton - American car produced from 1909-1910 by Croxton-Keeton Motor Co. in Ohio.

CRT - Abbreviation for cathode ray tube.

crude - See crude oil.

crude oil - Unrefined or unprocessed petroleum oil found in nature usually deep below the surface of the ground.

cruise(1) - Abbreviation for cruise control.

cruise(2) - To drive about from place to place for business and/or pleasure.

cruise control - See speed control system.
Cruise-O-Matic - Automatic transmission produced by Ford.
Cruiser - American car produced from 1917-1919 by Cruiser Motor Car Co. in Wisconsin.
cruise release brake switch - Electric switch activated by a brake pedal to disengage a speed control system.
Cruiso - See Cruise-O-Matic.
crumpled panel - Sheetmetal panel damaged from an impact.
Crusader - American car produced in 1923.
Crystal City - American car produced in 1914.
CS - Abbreviation for Czechoslvakia found usually on an international license plate.
C/S - Abbreviation for convertible sedan.
CSSA - Abbreviation for cold start spark advance.
CST - Abbreviation for Central Standard Time.
c tape - Abbreviation for cassette tape. See also cass.
CTO - Abbreviation for coolant temperature override. See also temperature override switch.
CTS - Abbreviation for coolant temperature sensor.
CTVS - Abbreviation for coolant thermostatic vacuum switch.
Cub - American car produced in 1914.
cube - Three dimensional representation used to specify dimensions of a vehicle being developed. Also, it refers to exterior die models grouped and positioned to checking different surface continuities.
cubes - Engine's cubic inch displacement.
cubic capacity - Volume of an enclosed space measured in cubic inches. Also, it refers to an individual engine cylinder's volume.
cubic centimeter - Volume formed by a measurement of one centimeter in three dimensions.
cubic inch - Volume formed by a measurement of one inch in three dimensions.
cubic measure - Method of measuring volume by using cubic units. English and metric units are the most common. See also cubic inch and cubic centimeter.
Cubster - American car produced in 1949 by Osborn Wheel Co. in Pennsylvania. It was a home-assembled 6.6 hp chain-driven car.
Cucmobile - American car produced in 1907.
Cuda - Plymouth Barracuda car.
Cugnot, Captain Nicholas - He was a Frenchman who constructed the first steam car in 1769. It had a top speed of three mph.
cu in - Abbreviation for cubic inch.
Cull - American car produced in 1901.
Culver - American car produced in 1905 and 1916.
Cummings, William - He won the Indianapolis 500 Race in 1934 driving an average of 104.9 mph in a Boyles Product Special.
Cummins - American car produced in 1930.
Cunningham - American car produced in 1907-1936 by James Cunningham Son & Co. in New York. Also, an American car produced from 1951-1955 by B.S. Cunningham Co. in Florida.
Cunningham Steamer - American steam car produced in 1901.
cupped tires - Tires worn in random areas of the tread usually due to wheel hopping. See also tire wear(cupped).
curb - Raised edge formed on the side of a road or sidewalk.
curb weight - Weight of a car measured with no passengers or loads and a full tank of gas.
curing - Stage required in the manufacture of some synthetic materials to prepare or harden the material after it has been formed.
Curran - American car produced in 1928.
current limit relay - Electrical relay designed to limit current flow to a specified maximum amount. When current becomes excessive, the relay opens the circuit. One is commonly found mounted between the battery and the car's lighting switch where it protects the lighting circuit and lighting switch from overloading.
current limit relay(lockout type) - Current limit relay designed to open a set of points, using a solenoid mechanism, when current flow becomes excessive. Small flow of current continues to flow keeping the points open.
current limit relay(thermal overload type) - Current limit relay designed to open a set of points when a bimetallic strip bends from the heat generated by excessive current flowing through it.
current limit relay(vibrating type) - Current limit relay designed to vibrate a set of points open and closed rapidly when current flow becomes excessive. The action slows the current flow.
current regulator - Electromagnetic switching device used to limit generator current to a maximum specified value in order to prevent generator damage. It is commonly found in regulators and consists of two contact points, separated by an air gap, opening and closing 20-60 times per second. Point movement is controlled by a solenoid mechanism mounted beneath the points.

See also cutout relay and voltage regulator.

Curtis - American car produced in 1921.

Curtis Steamer - American steam vehicle produced in 1866.

Curtis Truck - American truck produced from 1915-1916.

cushion springs - Series of steel springs mounted inside a car cushion to provide support and a comfort for a passenger.

Custer - American car produced in 1921.

Custom - American car produced from 1960-1977 by Mercury Division of Ford Motor Co. in Michigan.

Custoka - Austrian car line produced from 1971 to date by Custoka Kunststoffkarosserien.

Custom - American car produced from 1960-1963 by American Motors Corp. in Michigan. Also, an American car produced from 1957-1980 by Ford Motor Co. in Michigan.

custom - Stock car modified inside and/or out to suit a person's tastes. The outward appearance was commonly made to look lower, longer, and more streamlined than original.

custom auto - See custom.

Custom Cruiser - American car produced from 1980 to date by Oldsmobile Division of General Motors Corp. in Michigan.

custom interior - Car interior specially designed and built to suit an owner's desires.

custom paint job - Paint applied in a special way to suit an owner's desires.

customer rate - Hourly rate charged for non-warranty auto repair work.

customize - To make or build according to personal specifications.

customizer - Person skilled in modifying an original car to suit a person's individual tastes.

custom wheel - See alloy wheel.

cut - To eliminate another car from competition.

cut a fat one - To drive a car at top speed.

cutback valve - Valve used in an automatic transmission to reduce hydraulic pressure above a certain speed to certain hydraulic circuits.

cut in - To closely move a car in front of another moving car.

Cutlass - American car produced from 1962 to date by Oldsmobile Division of General Motors Corp. in Michigan.

cutline - Groove cut in a clay model to outline a hood, door, or decklid opening.

cutoff - Road leaving another road often to provide a shortcut.

cutout(1) - Device used to open or close an electrical circuit.

cutout(2) - Valve used in an exhaust system to divert exhaust gases directly to the atmosphere or to another pipe.

cutout relay - Electromagnetic switching device used to prevent battery current from flowing back into a generator and causing damage. It consists of two contact points separated by an air gap. Point movement is controlled by a solenoid mechanism mounted beneath the points. The points open and close when generator voltage is less than or greater than battery voltage. See also current regulator and voltage regulator.

cut rate - Price or rate below normal market price.

cut rate gas - Gas selling for less than normal market price.

cut rate operation - Business engaged in offering services and/or products for less than normal market prices.

cut rate prices - Prices less than normal market prices.

Cutting - American car produced from 1909-1912 by Clark-Carter Automobile Co. (1909-1911, and Cutting Motor Car Co. (1911-1912), both in Michigan.

cutting corners - See cutting the corner.

cutting in - See cut in.

cutting the corner - To drive around a corner on the inside shoulder. It is usually done to get around a corner quicker.

cutting the head - To enlarge the intake and exhaust valve seat diameters in a cylinder head in order to receive larger valves.

cut off - To disconnect or break.

Cugnot, Thomas - He was a Frenchman who built a steam powered gun carriage in 1770.

CV(1) - Abbreviation for constant velocity.

CV(2) - Abbreviation for convertible. See also Cvt.

CV boot - Flexible rubber covering placed over a constant velocity joint to protect it from outside contamination.

CVI - American car produced from 1907-1908 by CVI Motor Car Co. in Michigan.

CV joint - Constant velocity joint. See also universal joint(constant velocity).

CVT - Abbreviation for continuously variable transmission.

Cvt - Abbreviation for convertible. See also CV(2).

CV window - Controlled ventilation. Movable glass pane located directly aft of an "A" pillar and separate from a side window.

CY(1) - Abbreviation for cylinder. See also Cyl.

CY(2) - Abbreviation for Cyrrus found usually on an international license plate.

cycle - Series of repeated events.

cyclecar - See body style(cyclecar).

Cyclecar - American car produced in 1914.

Cycleplane - American car produced from 1914-1915 by Cycleplane Co. in Rhode Island.

Cyclomobile - American car produced in 1920.

cyclist - See motorcyclist.

Cyclone - American car produced in 1921.

cyl - Abbreviation for cylinder. See also CY.

cylinder - Circular hole with depth. In an engine block, each piston slides in a cylinder where combustion takes place. See also bore.

cylinder block - See engine block.

cylinder bore - See bore.

cylinder cam - Individual cam lobe on a distributor cam. The number of cam lobes equals the number of engine cylinders. Each cam opens and closes the distributor points when the point rubbing block contacts its surface. A four cylinder engine, for example, has four cylinder cams.

cylinder distortion - Cylinder condition created when its length warps or circumference becomes out of round. It is caused by poor engine block design, expansion and contraction, unequal tightening of bolts, etc.

cylinder gauge - See dial gauge.

cylinder glaze - Engine cylinder condition created when the wall surface becomes very smooth due to extended use. The fine hone scratches are gone. When a piston is fitted with new rings into an unreconditioned cylinder, it's a good idea to break the glaze with a hone. This puts small scratches on the wall surface which will help to seat the rings faster. It also helps prevent the ring surfaces from scoring since a lightly scratched wall retains an oil film better than a smooth one.

cylinder head - Metal unit bolted on top of an engine block to cover the top of the cylinders and form the combustion chamber tops. Modern cylinder heads usually contain the valves and camshaft, and are made of aluminum. Older heads were made of steel.

cylinder head(cross flow) - Cylinder head built with intake ports on one side and exhaust ports on the other. The design causes the air/fuel mixture to flow from one side of the combustion chamber to other during the combustion process. See also engine(hemi head).

cylinder head(F type) - See engine(F head).

cylinder head(hemi) - Cylinder head built with dome-shaped combustion chambers.

cylinder head(high swirl) - Cylinder head built so that the ports, combustion chambers, and piston domes work together to cause the air/fuel mixture to: swirl into the cylinders during intake, accelerate swirling at a controlled rate through the compression stroke until ignition occurs, and continue swirling through the remainder of the combustion cycle. The design allows lean fuel mixtures to be used. It is becoming very popular in racing. See also Widmar, Larry.

cylinder head(I type) - See engine(I head).

cylinder head(L type) - See engine(L head).

cylinder head(overhead valve) - See engine(overhead valve).

cylinder head(T type) - See engine(T head).

cylinder head(twin cam) - See engine(twin cam).

cylinder head cracks - Cracks formed usually between valve seats or elsewhere in the combustion chamber top. If the cracks are small, they can sometimes be peened closed with a peening hammer. If larger, they require careful welding (if they can even be welded), or else head replacement.

cylinder head gasket - Gasket placed between a cylinder head and an engine block. Its purpose is to maintain a gas and water tight seal. The gasket is cut to conform to the cylinder outlines and the various oil and water passageways that run from the engine block to the cylinder head. It is usually made of metal and a heat resistant material like asbestos, and is available in different thicknesses in order to alter the compression ratio. See also car service tip(cylinder head gasket failure).

cylinder head seat - See valve seat.

cylinder head temperature gauge - Gauge used to measure the temperature of a cylinder head.

cylinder hone - See hone(cylinder).

cylinder numbering - Numbers assigned to each engine cylinder for timing purposes. On an in-line engine, cylinders are numbered in ascending order from the front or fan area. On a V-8 engine, the cylinders are number 1 through 4 on the left side, and 5 through 8 on the right side with each side ascending from the fan area. The left side of the engine is determined by facing the engine compartment.

cylinder reconditioning - Process defined by the machining of one or more engine cylinders back to a round dimension of a specified size for fitting a new piston and its rings.

cylinder sleeve – Tube press fitted into a cylinder bore of an engine's block for the purpose of providing a new cylinder surface. Many engines do not have cylinder sleeves, but can employ them when the bore wears sufficiently. They are usually made of cast iron.

cylinder wall glazebreaker – Tool used for honing cylinder walls, usually with stones. See also cylinder hone.

cylinder wear – Amount of dimensional change measured from the original dimensions of a cylinder. The upper part of a cylinder typically shows greater wear due to poor lubrication and more prevalent corrosion. Cylinder wear, in general, mostly occurs during the first few miles of operation when an engine is started and warming up. Factors influencing wear include: type of lubricant, abrasive material in lubricant, degree of lubrication, engine temperature, fuel used, abrasive material in fuel, amount of water condensing in a cylinder, way an engine is run, pressure of piston rings against cylinder walls, composition of various metal parts, and length of time engine is not used before starting.

Cyclone – Experimental car built by Cadillac in 1959. It was equipped with a radar device for sensing objects in the path of the car and warning the driver. Also, an American car produced from 1960-1977 by Mercury Division of Ford Motor Co. in Michigan.

cyclops eye headlight – Car equipped with one headlight mounted in the center of the grille. The Briscoe car of 1915 featured such a headlight.

D

D – Abbreviation for West Germany found usually on an international license plate. See also DDR.

D1 – Abbreviation for Drive 1 range (second gear) on an automatic transmission shift selector.

D2 – Abbreviation for Drive 2 range (third gear) on automatic transmission shift selector.

D&V – American car produced in 1903.

DAC – American car produced from 1922-1923 by Detroit Air-Cooled Car Co. in Michigan.

Dagmar – American car produced from 1922-1927 by Crawford Automobile Co. in Maryland.

Daihatsu – Japanese car line produced from 1954 to date by Daihatsu Kogyo Co. Ltd. Recent models include: Charade, Charmont, Cuare, Delta, Mira, and Rugger.

Daimler – American car produced from 1900-1907. Also, a British car line produced from 1896 to date. The most recent company is Jaguar Cars Ltd. (1980 to date).

Dain – American car produced in 1912.

Daley Steam Wagon – American steam car produced in 1893.

Dalton – American car produced from 1911-1912 by Dalton Motor Car Co. in Michigan.

damage appraisal – Determination made by a body shop of the damage sustained by a car. It is sometimes attached to a bill as an extra charge when a car is towed in, providing another enticement for keeping a car there for repairs. Most body shops today provide free estimates of the repair cost.

damages – Out-of-pocket losses incurred in a contract or other legal dispute.

damper – See shock absorber.

damper coil – Strip of flat spring steel coiled into a spring shape and used to produce a dampening effect when placed in a valve spring. It is designed to remain in contact with the valve spring coil's inner surface. See also valve spring surge.

Daniels – American car produced from 1915-1924 by Daniels Motor Car Co. in Pennsylvania. It was a big expensive luxury car.

Danielson – American car produced in 1914.

Dan Patch – American car produced in 1911.

Darby – American car produced from 1909-1910 by Darby Motor Car Co. in Ohio.

Darling – American car produced in 1901 and 1917.

Darlington – Racing circuit built in Darlington, South Carolina. It was the first such raceway designed for stock cars. It has been called the Indianapolis of the South.

Darracq 4 Cylinder – French car driven by Paul Baras to a 1904 world land speed record of 104.5 mph at Ostend, Belgium.

Darracq V-8 – French car driven by Victor Hemery to a 1905 world land speed record of 109.6 mph at Aries-Salon, France.

Darrin – American car produced in 1946 and from 1953-1958 by Howard A. Darrin Automotive Design in California.

Darrow – American car produced from 1902-1903 by Darrow Motor Vehicle Co. in New York.

Dart – American car produced in 1914. Also, an American car produced from 1960-1980 by Dodge Division of Chrysler Corp. in Michigan.

Dart Truck – American truck produced in 1916.

Dartmobile – American car produced in 1922.

dash – See fire wall.

dash assembly – Assemblage of parts attached to a car's fire wall. They include: dashboard, heating/cooling/defrosting system, gauges and switches, glove compartment, and radio opening.

dashboard – Metal or plastic structure positioned behind the windshield to which a car's gauges, glove compartment, heating/defrosting system, etc. are attached. Also, it refers to: a board located on the forward part of a buggy or other vehicle to intercept water, mud, or snow; or sometimes to the car's instrument panel.

dash cover – Material used to cover a dashboard.

dash mat – Replacement mat used to cover the top portion of a car's dash. It is usually made out of molded plastic.

dashpot – Device used to slow or delay operation of moving parts. A dashpot is commonly employed on an automatic transmission equipped car to slow the return of the throttle linkage. See also anti-stall dashpot.

Datsun – Japanese car line produced by Nissan Motor Company Ltd. from 1961-1982. Popular models included: Lil Hustler (truck), B-210, and 240-280Z series sports cars. See also Nissan.

Dawson, Joe – He won the Indianapolis 500 Race in 1912 driving an average of 78.7 mph in a National.

Davenport – American car produced in 1902.

Davids – American car produced in 1902.

DaVinci – American car produced in 1925.

da Vinci, Leonardo – He was a scientist, philosopher, and inventor, in the 15th century, who drew sketches of a tanklike self-propelled vehicle.

Davis – American car produced from 1908-1930 by George W. Davis Motor Car Co. in Maryland. Also, an American car produced from 1947-1949 by Davis Motor Co. in California. The latter was a small three-wheeled car with an all-aluminum body. Only 17 cars were made.

Davis Cycle Car – American car produced in 1913.

Davis, Floyd – He won the Indianapolis 500 Race in 1941 with Mauri Rose driving an average of 115.1 mph in a Noc-Out Hose Clamp Special.

Dawson – American car produced from 1900-1902 and 1904-1905 by Dawson Mfg. Co. in Virginia, and J.H. Dawson Machinery Co. in Illinois respectively.

Day – American car produced from 1911-1914.

Dayco – American line of V belts produced by Dayco Corporation.

Day Elder truck – American truck produced in 1919.

daylighter – Drivers known for driving with headlights lights on during the day.

daylighting – Winning margin created at a finish line where there is an open gap between the tail of the winning car and the front end of the next one.

daylight opening – Area outlined through which light will pass in glazed areas.

Dayton(1) – American car produced from 1909-1911 and 1913-1915 by W.D. Dayton Machinery Co. (1909-1911), Dayton Cyclecar Co. (1913-1914), and Crusader Motor Car Co. (1914-1915), all in Illinois. Also, an American electric car produced from 1911-1915 by Dayton Electric Car Co. in Ohio.

Dayton(2) – American line of tires.

Daytona – American car produced in 1956. Also, an American car line produced from 1975 to date by Daytona Automotive Fiberglass in Florida. Also, an American car produced from 1980 to date by Dodge Division of Chrysler Corp. in Michigan.

Daytona 500 – Annual 500 mile race held at the Daytona International Speedway in Daytona Beach, Florida. The first race was held in 1959.

Daytona International Speedway – Two and one half-mile race track built with high banked turns in Daytona Beach, Florida. See also Daytona 500.

Day Utility – American car produced from 1911-1914 by Day Automobile Co. in Michigan.

DC(1) – Abbreviation for direct current.

DC(2) – Abbreviation for dual cowl.

DC generator – See generator(DC).

DC motor – See motor(DC).

DCP – Abbreviation for dual cowl phaeton. See also DC(2).

dd – Abbreviation for dealer development.

DDR – Abbreviation for East Germany found usually on an international license plate. See also D.

dead axle – See axle(dead).

dead battery – Battery completely discharged. It must be recharged or jumped in order to start a car.

dead center – Maximum upper or lower position of a piston in an engine cylinder.

dead cylinder – Engine cylinder whose spark plug is not firing.

dead in the water – Engine condition created when a car won't start due to excess water in an engine compartment or some other problem.

dead pedal – Pedal mounted in the far left corner of the driver's floorpan area for resting the left foot. It was used on older sports and racing cars so drivers could brace themselves going through turns fast. It has returned on some late model cars.

dead stop – To bring a car to a complete stop. See also rolling stop.

Deal – American car produced from 1905-1911 by Deal Motor Vehicle Co. in Michigan.

dealer – Individual or company engaged in buying and selling used cars with the emphasis on selling.

dealer consignment – Arrangement made between a car dealer and car seller where the dealer agrees to pay the seller a prearranged price for the car when it is sold. See also consignment.

dealer development – See dealer preparation.

dealer preparation – Time, labor, and parts put into readying a car for sale by a dealer. Factories usually pay dealers a certain amount to prepare each car when it is delivered. A dealer will sometimes pocket the money to increase profit, and not bother to prepare the car, assuming the factory has done everything necessary to make it ready for sale.

dealer preparation checklist – List of items to be done by a car dealer in order to make a new car ready for use after it has been shipped from the car manufacturer. When buying a new car, be sure the dealer signs this list.

dealer prep charges – Fee charged to a new car buyer to prepare a new car for use after it is received from the car manufacturer. See also dealer preparation.

dealership – Business or agency authorized to sell a commodity.

Dearborn – American car produced in 1910-1911 and 1919.

death trap – Car considered dangerous to the safety of the driver and passengers when driven.

decal – Transfer sheet used for wood graining, labeling, art work, etc.

decane – Liquid methane series hydrocarbon compound found in petroleum deposits with a boiling point of 345 degrees Fahrenheit. It is one of the ingredients of gasoline.

Decatur – American car produced in 1912.

Decauville – American car produced from 1909-1912.

deceleration – Slowing down or reducing speed.

deceleration valve – Valve used to bleed more air into an intake manifold when the fuel mixture becomes rich due to deceleration. When faulty, it can cause: rough idling and backfiring.

deceptive advertising practices – Advertising methods used to lure potential customers, through misleading or false statements, prices, guarantees, etc.

Decker – American car produced from 1902-1903 by Decker Automatic Telephone Exchange in New York.

deck – Flat area located behind a front car seat when a rear seat is folded down. Also, it refers to a car panel area behind the rear window and between the rear fenders.

decking – To machine a flat surface such as on a cylinder head. See also milled head.

decklid – Hinged panel used to provide access to a luggage compartment.

decked out – To furnish something with decorations, ornaments, accessories, good materials, etc.

De Cross – American car produced from 1913-1914 by De Cross Cyclecar Co. in Ohio.

De Dion – He was a rich French count who built light cars in the 1890s with the help of a partner named Bouton.

De Dion axle – See axle(De Dion).

De Dion-Bouton – American car built in 1898 with the fastest engine of its time, the De Dion engine. De Dion-Bouton cars were built from 1888-1904.

De Dion engine – Highest rpm (2000) gasoline engine produced in 1898.

De Dion Motorette – American car produced in 1900.

Deemotor – American car produced in 1923.

Deemster – American car produced in 1923.

deep cycling – Battery cycling from a charged to highly discharged state. Conventional automotive batteries are not designed for deep cycling and can fail after a few such drains.

Deere – American car produced in 1906.

Deere-Clark – American car produced from 1906.

Deering – American car produced in 1918.

Deering Magnetic – American car produced from 1918-1919 by Magnetic Motors Corp. in Illinois.

def – Abbreviation for defroster.

defective part – Part characterized as malfunctioning, broken, or unsafe to operate.

defects in materials and workmanship – Clause included in many warranties guaranteeing the quality and safe operation of a product for a specified period of time.

defendant – Person charged with committing a crime.

defensive driver – Car driver focused on paying attention to any condition that could cause an accident while driving. Such conditions include: road surface; movement of other traffic; foot traffic; animals near roads; possible improper operation of another car; cars running lights, stop signs, and right of way signs; etc.

defensive driving – To operate a car as a defensive driver.

defensive pedestrian – Pedestrian prepared to cross a road believing approaching cars do not see him.

Defiance – American car produced in 1919.

defoamant – See additive(foam inhibitor).

defog – Abbreviation for rear window defroster (air or electric).

defroster – Device used to blow heated air onto the inside surface of a window to evaporate condensed moisture. It typically consists of: blower (used also by heater), controls, ducting, and air gate controlling air flow.

defroster control – Lever, switch, button, etc. used to control the amount of

defrosting action.
defroster control outlets — Air discharge outlets used in a car's interior heating system to direct the flow of warm air onto a windshield.
defroster door — Mode-and-blend door used to control flow of warm air to defroster ducting.
defroster valve — Vacuum operated valve used in a climate control system to regulate the position of a mode-and-blend door controlling flow of warm air into defroster ducting.
degasser — Carburetor device used to correct a rich air/fuel mixture when a throttle is suddenly closed. Most devices work to restrict or stop fuel discharging from idle discharge ports until intake manifold vacuum decreases back to normal.
degreaser — Substance used to dissolve grease and oil.
degree(circle) — Smallest whole angular measurement of a complete circular turn. It is an angle found by dividing a circle into 360 pie-shaped pieces, and selecting one piece.
degree(Celsius) — See degree(Centigrade).
degree(Centigrade) — Scale used for measuring temperature. Water freezes and boils at 0 and 100 degrees respectively. See also Celsius.
degree(Fahrenheit) — Scale used for measuring temperature. Water freezes and boils at 32 and 212 degrees respectively. See also Fahrenheit.
degree in a cam — Process defined as installing a camshaft in an engine block and properly timing it with a crankshaft.
degree wheel — Wheel divided into 360 degree markings and used to set exact engine timing, valve settings, etc. It is bolted onto the front end of a crankshaft when in use.
de icer — Substance used to melt moisture frozen on a window surface.
DeKalb — American car produced in 1915.
Delage — American car produced in 1922.
Delage V-12 — Car driven by Rene Thomas to a 1924 world land speed record of 143.3 mph at Arpajon.
De LaVergne Motor Drag — American car produced in 1896.
delayer plate — See choke housing plate.
Delcar — American truck produced from 1947-1949 by American Motors in New York.
Delco-Remy — American line of batteries and electrical controls produced by Delco-Remy.
De Leon — American car produced from 1905-1906.
Delia Truck — American truck produced in 1916.
delivery satisfaction sheet — Document signed by a new car owner at the time of purchase stating the customer is satisfied with the condition of the car at the time of delivery. New car buyers should carefully check out a car before signing this document. Items such as front end wheel alignment, and wheel balancing are not covered in the warranty. If you are purchasing a new car, insist these two items be checked before you take delivery by putting it in writing in the document. There are too many opportunities for front ends to go out of alignment in the trip from the factory to the dealer, and it happens often.
Delling Steamer — American steam car produced from 1923-1927 by Delling Steam Motor Co. in New Jersey.
Del Mar — American car produced in 1949.
Delmore — American car produced in 1923.
Delorean — American car produced from 1980-1982 by Delorean Motors Ltd. in Ireland. It was a stainless steel safety sports car.
DeLorean, John — He was General Motors executive who left the company to produce his own unique stainless steel sports car with gull wing doors in the 1970s. Only a few were produced in Ireland before the venture failed..
Del Rio — American car produced from 1957-1964 by Ford Motor Co. in Michigan.
Deluxe — American car produced from 1906-1909. Also, an American car produced from 1960-1963 by American Motors Corp. in Michigan.
Delta — American car produced from 1923-1925. Also, an American car produced from 1955 to date by Oldsmobile Division of General Motors Corp. in Michigan.
Deltal — American car produced in 1914.
demagnetize — To remove magnetization from a magnetizable material.
De Mars — American electric car produced from 1905-1906 by De Mars Electric Vehicle Co. in Ohio.
DeMartini — American car produced in 1919.
Demats — American car produced in 1905.
demister — See defroster.
demo(1) — See demonstrator.
demo(2) — To take a prospective customer for a drive in a car he may want to buy.
demolition derby — Race held where used cars are repeatedly driven into each other until only one is left running (the winner).
demo model — See demonstrator.

Demon — American car produced from 1963-1977 by Dodge Division of Chrysler Corp. in Michigan.

demonstration ride — New car test drive made by prospective car buyers and the car salesman. It typically lasts 20-30 minutes.

demonstrator — New car used to give prospective new car buyers a demonstration ride. It is commonly driven by a dealer's car salesmen and other employees until sold and is not usually a good buy.

Demot — American car produced from 1909-1911 by Demot Car Co. in Michigan.

Demotte — American car produced in 1904.

demountable rim — Rim designed to be removed from a wheel.

denatured alcohol — Ethyl alcohol rendered unfit for human consumption by adding one or more substances to it.

Denby — American car produced in 1922.

Deneen — American car produced in 1917.

Denegre — American car produced in 1920.

density — Mass of an object compared to its volume.

Depalma, Ralph — He won the Indianapolis 500 Race in 1915 driving an average of 89.8 mph in a Mercedes. He also set a world land speed record of 149.9 mph in 1919 driving a Packard V-12.

DePaolo, Peter — He won the Indianapolis 500 Race in 1925 driving an average of 101.1 mph in a Deusenberg Special.

department of motor vehicles — Agency organzied to administer car licenses, registrations, title changes, conduct driver's tests, etc. Every state has one.

Department of Transportation — Federal agency formed in 1966 to insure the welfare, growth, and stability of the nation would benefit from policies encouraging safe, efficient, economic, and fast transportation.

Dependable — American car produced in 1919.

dependable mechanic — Honest mechanic skilled at doing good quality, reliable repair work.

depolarize — To remove the polarity of a magnetizable material. See also polarity.

depreciation — Value of an item decreased due to price drop, wear, tear, decay, etc.

depreciation surprise — New car purchased for a higher price then it is worth. This can happen due to depreciation of year end models or cars that have been updated. See also con game(model year updating) and con game(last year's model).

depth perception — Person's ability to see the difference in distance of objects before him. It is especially important in passing, following, and backing up. See also color perception.

Derain — American car produced from 1908-1911 by Simplex Mfg. Co. (1908-1910), and Derain Motor Co. (1910-1911), both in Ohio.

Derby — Canadian car produced from 1924-1926 by Derby Motor Cars in Saskatchewan.

derby — Race or contest open to all wishing to enter and offering a prize to the winner.

de Rochas, Alphonse Beau — He was a French engineer who patented a four cycle internal combustion engine design in 1862.

Desande — Netherland car line produced from 1979 to date by Desande Automobielen.

Desberon — American car produced from 1903-1904 by Desberon Motor Car Co. in New York.

Desert Flyer — American car produced in 1908.

Deschaum — American car produced from 1908-1910.

De Shaw — American car produced from 1906-1909 by Charles De Shaw (1906-1907), and De Shaw Motor Co. (1907-1909), both in New York.

De Soto — American car produced from 1913-1916 by De Soto Motor Car Co. in Indiana. Also, an American car produced from 1928-1960 by Chrysler Corp. in Michigan.

detail man — See job(car detailer).

De Tamble — American car produced from 1908-1913 by Speed Changing Pulley Co. (19081-1909), and De Tamble Motors Co. (1909-1913), both in Indiana.

detergent-dispersant — See additive(detergent-dispersant)

De Tomaso — Italian car line produced from 1965 to date by De Tomaso Automobili SpA. Recent models include: Longchamp (1973 to date) and Pantera (1971 to date).

De Tomaso, Allessandro — Italian known for designing, building, and marketing Pantera sports cars. See also De Tomaso and Pantera.

detonation — Uncontrolled self-ignition of part of an air/fuel mixture in a combustion chamber. It is caused when only part of a combustion chamber's fuel mixture burns before temperature and pressure build to cause spontaneous ignition of other unburned parts. End result is two or more flame fronts expand in the combustion chamber, colliding violently to cause cylinder head vibration (shock wave) which generates a knocking sound. It is heard as a rapid metallic jingling sound usually when an engine is under load or accelerated hard.

The sound is dangerous because the explosion generates shock waves which can be strong enough to rupture a piston head (creating a crack or hole), rupture cylinder walls, or crack heads. Secondary effects can include: broken spark plug ends, bearing overloading, engine overheating, high fuel consumption, power loss, blown head gasket, oil film breakdown between crankshaft bearing and journals, cylinder galling, piston melting, burned exhaust valves, and rod separation. The sound is often not audible at high speeds.

Factors contributing to detonation include: high compression ratio due to engine design or wrong gasket, excessive vacuum and/or centrifugal spark advance, low octane fuel, combustion chamber shape, sharp metal edge in combustion chamber acting as a glow plug, air and fuel temperature, leanness of air, lack of turbulence in fuel mixture, reduced exhaust gas recirculation due to faulty EGR valve, spark plug location causing long flame fronts, high engine operating temperature, rich or lean fuel mixture, excessive oil foaming, low or rapidly changing intake manifold vacuum, stuck exhaust manifold heat control valve, restricted exhaust system, faulty engine control system sensor(s), turbocharger overboost, and defective solid state timing controls on cars so equipped.

If an engine is designed properly and the right fuel used, a fuel mixture will resist detonation. The octane rating of a fuel determines how prone it is to detonation. Today's engines tend to ping (detonate) because of the emphasis placed on high gas mileage and low emissions. Their octane requirements are significantly higher than the fuel available. See also octane rating, preignition, exhaust(black smoke puffs), spark plug appearance(black specks), and exhaust(yellow colored flame).

detonation(turbo) – Detonation occurring in a turbocharged engine. It is more likely due to increased temperatures and pressures. It is controlled in one or more of the following ways: use of an intercooler, lowering engine's compression ratio, injecting water or alcohol during boost, and using a waste gate to prevent overboost.

Detroit – American car produced from 1899-1902, 1904-1908 and 1913-1914 by Detroit Automobile Co., Detroit Auto Vehicle Co., and Detroit Cyclecar Co. respectively, all in Michigan.

Detroit Air Cooled – American car produced in 1923.

Detroit-Chatham – American car produced in 1912.

Detroit-Dearborn – American car produced from 1910-1911 by Detroit-Dearborn Motor Car Co. in Michigan.

Detroit Electric – American electric car produced in 1907-1938 by Anderson Carriage Co. (1907-1910), Anderson Electric Car Co. (1911-1918), and Detroit Electric Car Co. (1919-1938), all in Michigan. It was one of the best known electric cars in the U.S. It was mostly successful due to demand by women for a simple urban car to use. Production averaged 1,000/year until World War I.

Detroiter – American car produced from 1912-1917 by Briggs-Detroiter Motor Car Co. in Michigan.

Detroit-Oxford – American car produced from 1905-1906 by Detroit-Oxford Mfg. Co. in Michigan.

Detroit Speedster – American car produced in 1914.

Detroit Steamer – American steam car produced from 1922-1923 by Detroit Steam Motors Corp. in Michigan.

detune an engine – Process used to minimize noxious exhaust emissions by altering the ignition and carburetion characteristics of an engine from optimum performance. Such engines often retard ignition timing under certain operating conditions to reduce pollutants.

Deuce – A 1932 Ford. It was a popular early car modified into a hot rod.

Deuce coupe – See Deuce.

De Vaux – American car produced from 1931-1932 by De Vaux-Hall Motor Corp. in California and Michigan.

device – Thing made for a specific working purpose.

Deville – American car produced from 1955 to date by Cadillac Motor Car Co. in Michigan.

De-Vo – American car produced in 1936.

Dewabout – American car produced in 1899.

DEXRON II – See equipment manufacturer's specification(DEXRON II).

Dey – American car produced in 1917.

Dey-Griswold – American car produced from 1895-1898 by Dey-Griswold & Co. in New York.

DH – Abbreviation for drop head.

d'Hautefeuille, Jean – He built a cylinder and piston assembly to pump water in 1678.

diagnosis – Process used to find the cause of a problem by determining its nature and circumstances.

diagnostic center – Car service business skilled in analyzing a car's operating condition by using elaborate testing and monitoring equipment. Good diagnostic center will have: a car hoist, front end alignment and headlight adjustment equipment, an oscilloscope for checking the ignition system, an exhaust gas analyzer, a brake analyzer, and a dynamometer for simulating road conditions.

diagonal pliers – Plier made with two cutting edges for cutting wire, etc.

Dial – American car produced in 1923.

dial a winner – Push button automatic transmission.

dial gauge – Gauge used commonly used to measure engine cylinder diameter and wear, wheel runout, etc.

dial indicator – Tool used to detect slight movement and display it on a circular gauge face.

diameter – Straight line located running through the center of a circle with both ends terminating at the intersection of a circle's circumference.

diametrical runout – See runout(radial).

Diamond – American car produced from 1910-1912 and 1914.

Diamond Arrow – American car produced in 1907.

diamond – Condition created when a car's frame has been knocked out of alignment from a front or rear impact at one corner. The net effect is the frame changes from a square outline to a parallelogram.

Diamond T Passenger – American car produced from 1905-1911 by Diamond T. Motor Car Co. in Delaware.

Diamond T Truck – Large American truck produced from 1911 to date.

Diana – American car produced from 1925-1928 by Diana Motors Co. in Missouri.

diaphragm – Flexible cloth or rubber-like sheet used to cover an area separating it into two different compartments. It is commonly used in fuel pumps where its back and forth movement pumps fuel.

Dickson Steamer Truck – American steam truck produced in 1865.

dicky – Rumble seat.

Dictator – American car produced in 1913.

die(1) – Tool used to make threads on bolts, screws, etc.

die(2) – Device used for molding, cutting, stamping, or shaping.

Diebel – American car produced from 1900-1901.

die casting – Process used to make a casting by injecting molten metal or other material under pressure into a fully finished mold. It is also the product of such a process.

diegoing – To replace a car's front axle with another one to lower the front end.

Diehlmobile – American car produced from 1962-1964 by H.L. Diehl Co. in Connecticut. It was a small three-wheeled spare car built to fold into a trunk.

dielectric – Non-conducting or insulated substance.

die model – Three dimensional representation of a car made from hard wood. It is built from engineering drawings and templates.

diesel(1) – See diesel fuel.

diesel(2) – Abbreviation for diesel engine.

diesel fuel – Fuel found suitable for burning in a diesel engine. Though diesels can burn a wide variety of fuels, the most common are the grade 1D fuels which range from Kerosene to intermediate distillates. These fuels minimize corrosion and formation of harmful engine deposits. One tradeoff in refining the impurities out of these fuels is a lower heat value and thus slightly lower power producing capability. A benefit is less maintenance to the engine. See also car service tip(dirty diesel fuel), and car service tip(diesel fuel bacteria).

diesel fuel grading – Classifications made by ASTM of different fuels suitable for use in diesel engine. Most common grades are 1D, 2D, and 4D. Grade 1D consists of those fuels with lower boiling points that have less impurities present. They are known as high-grade diesel fuels and range from Kerosene to intermediate distillates. Grades 2D and 4D represent fuel categories that have higher boiling points and more impurities.

diesel engine – See engine(diesel)

dieseling – Condition created when a shut off engine continues to run slowly due to fuel continuing to reach, ignite, and burn in the engine cylinders. It is usually due to a slightly cracked throttle and hot spots in the combustion chamber. Other possible causes include: idle speed too high, electrical leakage from car instruments feeding back to ignition coil (usually due to ground problem), combustion chamber carbon build-up, faulty fuel-cut solenoid, rich fuel mixture at idle, and faulty idle stop solenoid. A temporary halt to dieseling can be accomplished with the ignition switch off as follows: on manual transmission cars - press and hold brake pedal, put car in a gear and slowly release clutch until engine stops; and on automatic transmission cars - remove air cleaner top and cover carburetor air intake. See also car service tip(dieseling test), hot spot, and preignition.

diesel injection pump – Pump designed to inject a high pressure charge of diesel fuel into a combustion chamber at the proper time and in the proper quantity. A typical pump has many moving parts, precise fittings, and works at pressures of 1,500-2,000 psi. A distributor type arrangement of high pressure fuel lines routes the fuel charge from the pump to each cylinder. Diesel injection pumps are very vulnerable to water, dirt, and other fuel contaminants because of their highly precise and delicate parts. Such contaminants can quickly destroy a pump and the injectors. See also engine(diesel).

diesel lubricating oil - See oil(diesel lubricating), and car service tip(dirty diesel oil).

diesel timing - Point specified in a piston's compression stroke when combustion of diesel fuel occurs. Diesel timing is much more critical than ignition timing in a gas engine. The timing consists of sending a diesel fuel charge into a combustion chamber at the proper time and pressure and in the correct quantity. If the whole process is off even a few degrees, peak combustion temperatures can become very high and quickly destroy the engine. See also diesel injection pump.

difference - The monetary difference between the selling price of a new or used car and the actual wholesale value of a customer's trade-in.

difference buyer - Potential car buyer interested only in the difference between his present car and a newer one.

Differential - American car produced in 1921 and 1932.

differential - Gear assembly located in the rear end for transferring driveline rotation to both rear axles at the same time. It also allows one wheel to turn faster than another when going around a turn. It is one of the powertrain components. Four wheel drive cars also have a differential in the front.

differential(conventional) - Differential used to transmits most of its rotation to the wheel having the least traction. It is common on most cars and is actually a one wheel drive unit. When a car's drive wheels get stuck, the one with the least traction will start spinning.

differential(double reduction-helical gearing) - Differential used to provide two selectable speeds to rear axles. It typically consists of: a pinion drive, ring gear, and low and high speed helical gear sets. Rear axle rotation speed is changed by changing from one gear set to another.

differential(double reduction-planetary gearing) - Differential used to provide two selectable speeds to rear axles. It typically consists of: a pinion drive, ring gear, and planetary gear set. Speed change occurs by changing the gears that rotate in the planetary gear set.

differential(limited slip) - Differential used to transmit power to both wheels regardless of tire traction. The unit contains cone or wheel clutches that allow both wheels to spin most of the time, and to spin at different speeds when cornering. A vehicle with this type differential is a true two wheel drive car.

differential(planetary) - Differential used to transfer power to axles using a pinion gear, ring gear, and planetary gear set assembly.

differential(Torsion) - Differential used to transmit power to both wheels regardless of tire traction. Limited slip action is accomplished by using worm gears on the axle shafts (instead of side gears), and two or more pairs of dual worm wheels with spur gears (instead of differential pinion gears). Advantages over clutch type limited slip differentials include: no clutch plates, provides much better traction, traction is adjustable, uses conventional differential gear lubricant, limited slip mode works all the time, and weighs less.

differential(two speed) - See differential(double reduction).

differential case - Steel housing used to contain differential parts. Major parts include: ring, pinion, and axle shaft gears; axle and input shaft bearings.

differential gear - See differential.

differential gear ratio - A ratio expressed as the number of driveline revolutions needed for every revolution of a rear axle or differential unit. For example, a differential with a gear ratio of 3.10 will cause the driveline to turn 3.10 revolutions for every axle revolution. Lower ratios decrease engine rpm for a given speed. See also gas saving tip(changing rear end ratios).

differential noise - Condition created when a differential emits noise under use. The noise can also come from other areas due to noise telegraphing. Possible noise sources and causes include: worn or damaged differential gears or bearings, and front wheel or rear wheel bearings; rough road surface; tires that are studded, under-inflated, and unevenly worn; and problems in engine or transmission.

differential valve - Valve used to warn a car driver when either the front or rear brake lines have lost fluid pressure. It is mounted between the two brake line networks and measures the pressure difference between them. When it exceeds a certain value, a warning light comes on. See also proportioning

valve and metering valve.
digital multimeter – Electric measuring instrument designed to display
measurements with a liquid crystal display.
digger – Dragster.
Dile – American car produced from 1914-1916 by Dile Motor Car Co. in
Pennsylvania.
Dillon Steam – American car produced in 1920.
dilution – See crankcase dilution.
dimmer switch – Electrical switch used to turn a car's bright headlights on
and off. Today's cars mount this switch on the steering column. Earlier
cars used a foot operated switch.
dim your lights – To turn off the high headlight beam setting and operate with
lower beam headlights.
DIN – Abbreviation for Deutsche Industrie Normen. It is a German method of
determining horsepower similar to SAE net horsepower.
Dingfelder – American car produced from 1902-1903 by Dingfelder Motor Co. in
Michigan.
dinged – Dented.
dinging – Process used to straighten a dented car body area. Dented area is
restored to its original profile by applying pressure in the proper areas
with such tools as hammers, spoons, dollies, slide hammers, etc. In general,
damage is usually removed in the reverse order in which it was made. Any
damaged car panel can be restored to its original profile. In the case of
severely damaged panels, it's often cheaper and quicker to replace them.
Di-Noc – Trade name used for a decal, material consisting of three layers,
decal, glues and paper. Outer portion can be painted with a special
elasticized paint. When applied to the surface of a car model, Di-Noc
backing is first soaked in warm water. The wet paper backing is separated
from the decal, which takes the form of the clay surface and gives the model
the effect of a painted car.
dinosaur – Large heavy car with a V8 engine.
dings – Dents in the car body.
diode – See rectifier.
Diplomat – American car produced from 1976 to date by Dodge Division of
Chrysler Corp. in Michigan.
dipping – To arrange a down payment for a car customer from a small local loan
company. See also double-dipping.
dipstick – Slender removable metal rod formed with markings on one end for
measuring fluid levels. Fluids commonly measured include oil, automatic
transmission fluid, and power steering fluid. See also car service
tip(dipstick appearance).
dipstick heater – Slender metal rod used to keep a shut down engine warm in
cold weather by electrically heating oil in the oil pan. It is inserted
through a dipstick opening. Rod is made of a resistive material which heats
up when supplied with electricity and grounded to the oil pan. It works best
when inserted while oil is still warm.
direct current – Electric current flowing in one direction only.
Direct Drive – American car produced in 1907.
directional signals – See turn signals.
directional signal switch – See turn signal switch.
directional stability – Ability of a car to continue moving in a straight
line with a minimum of steering control. Such cars are not greatly affected
by rough roads or cross winds.
Disbrow – American car produced from 1917-1918 by Disbrow Motors Corp. in
Ohio.
disc – Thin flat circular plate or object. See also rotor.
disc brakes – See brake(disc).
disc brake caliper – See caliper assembly.
disc brake service – Service work performed on front wheel disc brakes. It
consists of: inspecting a front wheel disc brake system for proper operation,
locating possible problems, and performing certain repair, maintenance, and
replacement work. Most shops offer to do the following for a certain rate:
install new disc pads, resurface front rotors, and repack front wheel
bearings. Other problems like leaking brake cylinders, air in the brake
lines, and bad wheel bearings usually cost extra to remedy.
discharge – See battery discharge.
discharged battery – See battery(discharged).
discharging the system – See air conditioner(discharging the system).
disclaimer notice – Notice denying or rejecting responsibility for a product
service, etc.
discount house – Business engaged in offering products at less than full list
price. The tradeoff is such businesses usually do not offer much after sale
service.
disc pad – See brake pad.
disc rotor – Heavy circular steel plate attached to a front wheel assembly,

providing the braking surface for disc brakes.

Discs – Abbreviation for disc brakes on front wheels.

dismantler – Car business engaged in disassembling junked or totaled cars to sell the parts. There are currently about 14,000 in the United States. It is a legal chop shop. See also wrecking yard.

dismissal – Decision made by a court to drop charges.

Dispatch – American car produced from 1911-1922 by Displatch Motor Co. in Minnesota.

displaced area – Body damage in which the metal has been moved, but not damaged. See also simple bends, upsets, rolled buckles, and stretches.

displaced coolant – Engine coolant transferred to an overflow reservoir when cooling system volume and radiator cap pressure (usually 15 lbs) increase limits are exceeded. See also coolant recovery system.

displacement – Volume of air moved by a piston traveling from the bottom to top of its stroke. See also engine displacement.

disposition – Trial results.

DIST – Abbreviation for distributor. See also ignition coil terminal.

distillation range – Distillation characteristics of a diesel fuel specified by determining the temperature reached when 10 percent of a diesel fuel's vapors have been condensed and collected. The 10 percent recovery is called the 10 percent point. The boiling range of the 10 percent determines such fuel characteristics as: deposit formation, igniting ability, smooth engine operation, and exhaust odor. The boiling range of the remaining 90 percent determines combustion quality characteristics such as deposit formation and exhaust smoke.

Distribution Octane Number – On the road test used to determine the antiknock quality of a gasoline's more volatile compounds. Cars tested have manual transmissions with inefficient intake manifolds. It is an ASTM testing method that was developed by Mobil Research, and is more commonly used outside the United States. See also Research Octane Number, Motor Octane Number, DON, and R-100 Method.

distributor – Electrical switching device operated by a running engine, used to control flow of current in a primary ignition circuit, and distribute resultant secondary or high voltage to spark plugs at a certain time and in a certain sequence. Major parts of a distributor include: a geared shaft, distributor rotor, centrifugal and vacuum advance mechanisms, set of points or equivalent, and a distributor cap.

A distributor not operating properly can cause problems such as: backfiring, preignition, power loss, cutout at high speed, rough idling, misfiring, and hard starting of a warm engine. See also distributor part number.

distributor(double alternate) – Distributor constructed with two sets of points of that operate alternately. A distributor cam has half as many lobes as engine cylinders. Some designs use two ignition coils which permits longer coil saturation time.

distributor(dual advance) – Distributor constructed to use both vacuum and centrifugal advance mechanisms to adjust ignition timing. Also, it sometimes refers to a distributor using two vacuum diaphragms. One diaphragm controls ignition timing like a conventional vacuum advance unit. The other works to retard spark during idling and deceleration for improved emissions.

distributor(dual diaphragm) – See distributor(exhaust emission control).

distributor(dual point) – Distributor constructed with two sets of points to increase coil saturation time through increased dwell.

distributor(exhaust emission control) – Distributor constructed to use two vacuum controlled diaphragms for the control of exhaust emissions. One diaphragm is controlled by direct intake manifold vacuum while the other is controlled by vacuum developed as air rushes by an opening in the carburetor airway. The two diaphragms work together to keep the spark retarded during deceleration and idling, and advanced when accelerating. Such spark settings allow more complete combustion of the air/fuel mixture and minimize noxious exhaust. See also retard diaphragm and advance diaphragm.

distributor(external adjustment) – Distributor constructed to allow dwell angle adjustment outside the distributor housing.

distributor(pointless) – Distributor constructed to use a light emitting device in place of conventional distributor points.

distributor(twin ignition type) – Distributor constructed to actually drive two separate ignition systems. Components used include: two sets of points, two condensers, two ignition coils, and two spark plugs per cylinder. In most designs, both points open at the same time to fire the two spark plugs of a cylinder. Some designs offset the point opening slightly.

distributor advance curve kit – Assemblage of parts used allowing a standard distributor to advance its timing more rapidly for more power and acceleration. Kit usually consists of: necessary springs, weights, and bushings.

distributor breaker plate – See distributor point plate.

distributor cam - Multi-lobed circular surface mounted on a distributor shaft. It serves to open and close the distributor points as its shaft rotates. The number of individual cam lobes around the circumference equals the number of engine cylinders. See also dwell angle and cylinder cam.

distributor cam plate - Plate attached to distributor shaft and used to modify spark advance. One end of the centrifugal advance weight springs are attached to it. The centrifugal advance weights are usually mounted underneath the plate and move it depending on distributor shaft rotational speed.

distributor cap - Insulated top of a distributor. It contains: one center tower terminal receiving high voltage from an ignition coil, and several spark plug output terminals transferring high voltage through spark plug wires to spark plugs. Transfer of high voltage from the center to outer terminals is made by a rotor mounted on the end of the distributor shaft inside the cap. Misfiring can be due to distributor cap problems such as: cracks, carbon tracking between terminals, excessive dirt, eroded firing points, and corroded spark plug terminals. See also distributor rotor and firing point.

distributor cap clip - One of usually two spring steel clips used to hold a cap in place. They are anchored to the distributor body at one end and snap on the distributor cap at the other end.

distributor cap terminal - See spark plug terminal.

distributor cap tower - See center tower terminal and spark plug tower terminal.

distributor diaphragm - See advance mechanism(vacuum).

distributor housing - Body of a distributor. It contains various distributor parts including: point assembly, centrifugal advance mechanism, cap, and rotor. The vacuum advance mechanism and condenser are attached to the outside of the body.

distributor machine - Machine used to test different aspects of a distributor's advance mechanisms. The distributor is removed from the engine and mounted on the machine. It is rotated at different speeds to determine: amount of centrifugal and vacuum advance, and degrees of rotation between cylinder firing.

distributor modulator valve - See solenoid vacuum valve.

distributor part number - Number stamped on the housing of a distributor to indicate the advance curves being used. Specification books define the advance curve/part number relationship.

distributor point arcing - Condition created when conventional distributor points first open and an electrical arc occurs across the air gap. It is commonly caused by a defective condenser in the primary circuit which does not provide a place for high voltage current to flow until the contact points are wide open. Another possible cause is a defective ignition coil resistor. Point arcing shortens point life. It causes transfer of the point's tungsten metal from one contact surface to another. The metal will transfer to the negative or positive point depending on whether the condenser capacity is too high or too low respectively. See also distributor point pitting.

distributor point base - See distributor point plate.

distributor point contact support - Portion of a distributor point assembly used to contain the stationary point, point base, distributor lever shaft, and primary winding terminal.

distributor point float - See point bounce.

distributor point gap - Air gap located between distributor points when they are fully open. Gap width determines dwell angle. As it increases, dwell angle decreases. If the gap is too large, there will be insufficient time between two cylinder cams for current to flow through an ignition coil's primary windings resulting in a weak spark. If the gap is too small, the points will not open enough or long enough and misfiring will result. Point gap is adjusted with a thickness gauge or dwell meter. See also dwell angle and cylinder cam.

distributor point arm - Pivoting arm portion of a distributor point assembly. It is insulated from ground and contains a movable contact point and the rubbing block assembly. The rubbing block portion contacts the distributor cam surface.

distributor point arm spring tension - Tension exerted by a spring on a distributor point arm. If tension is weak, point arm will tend to chatter and float causing missing at higher engine rpm. If tension is high, excessive wear will occur on the points, distributor cam, and point rubbing block. The tension is checked with a spring gauge.

distributor point pitting - Condition created when points mounted in a distributor burn and/or pit. Possible causes include: bad or wrong size condenser, and oil on point surface. If the condenser is the wrong size, check the direction of material transfer. If tungsten is building up on the positive point surface (movable point on negative ground cars), the condenser is weak or must have a higher capacity. An over-capacity condenser will cause tungsten build-up on the negative point surface.

distributor point pivot post - Small shaft in a distributor point assembly used as a pivot point for a distributor point arm.

distributor point plate - Movable circular plate in a distributor housing mounted just underneath a distributor cam on the distributor point support plate. It contains distributor points, condenser, and cam felt. See also distributor point support plate.

distributor point rubbing block - Portion of a distributor point assembly used to touch a distributor cam surface for opening and closing points. It is typically made out of a plastic or resin material softer than the cam metal, but long wearing.

distributor points - Pair of electrical contacts used within a distributor to interrupt current flow in a primary ignition circuit. It consists of: a movable point arm and rubbing block assembly, stationary contact point base, insulation fittings, and primary circuit terminal. One point remains stationary while the other moves. Older cars pass more electric current across the points giving them a 5,000 to 10,000 mile life. In that span of time, they will open and close from 50-200 million times, depending on the average speed driven. Points on today's cars can last indefinitely because of low current flow. When the points aren't working right, your car will stall, miss, cutout, or not start. Point life can be extended by sanding the peak formed on one of the contacts and readjusting them to the proper gap setting. See also distributor point lever and distributor point contact support.

distributor point support plate - Stationary circular plate mounted just underneath the distributor cam for supporting the distributor point plate.

distributor rotor - See rotor(distributor).

distributor service - Service work done on a distributor restoring it to proper operating condition. It usually consists of inspecting the various parts and testing the distributor's operation. Defective or worn out parts are replaced. Such parts can include: points, condenser, distributor cap, distributor cam, distributor shaft bearings, vacuum and centrifugal advance mechanisms, and rotor.

distributor shaft - Shaft used in a distributor housing. Its rotation opens and closes distributor points, operates the centrifugal advance mechanism, and distributes high voltage in the distributor cap from the center tower terminal to the spark plug terminals. Shaft rotation is derived from a crankshaft via gearing, and is typically 1 revolution for every 2 crankshaft revolutions.

distributor springs - Small springs used to hold centrifugal weights in place. Spring strength determines amount of centrifugal advance.

distributor vacuum control switch - Switch built to incorporate the functions of a thermal vacuum valve, and a solenoid vacuum valve. It usually routes intake vacuum to a distributor's vacuum advance unit when an engine is overheating regardless of the transmission's gear. Advancing the timing increases engine rpm and helps engine run cooler.

distributor vacuum delay valve - See spark delay valve.

distributor wear - Wear found on distributor components.

distributor window - Removable small clear plastic window built into some distributor caps to allow adjustment of point dwell.

Ditzler - American line of automotive paint products produced by Ditzler Automotive Finishes.

Divco Truck - American truck produced in 1927.

dive - Condition created when a car's front end moves downward during braking.

diverter valve - See air bypass valve.

divided highway - Highway constructed with two traffic directions separated by a median of land. Freeways are divided highways.

dividers - Structures used to divide traffic lanes on a road.

diving tendency - Condition created when a car's front end is prone to noticeably dropping when brakes are applied. Possible causes include: worn front shocks and excessive brake friction.

Dixie Jr - American car produced from 1908-1909 by Southern Motor Car Factory in Texas.

Dixie Flyer - American car produced from 1916-1923 by Kentucky Wagon Mfg. Co. in Kentucky.

Dixie Tourist - American car produced from 1908-1910.

Dixon - American car produced in 1922.

DIY - Abbreviation for do it yourself.

DK - Abbreviation for Denmark found usually on an international license plate.

dk - Abbreviation for dark.

DL(1) - See service rating(DL).

DL(2) - Abbreviation for delivery.

DLG - American car produced from 1906-1907 by St. Louis Automobile & Supply Co. in Missouri.

dlo - Abbreviation for daylight opening. It is the distance between the top

and bottom of a window.
Dlr - Abbreviation for dealer.
DLX - Abbreviation for deluxe.
Dlx - Abbreviation for deluxe.
DMV - Abbreviation for Department of Motor Vehicles.
DNF - Abbreviation for race car not finishing a race.
Doane Truck - American truck produced in 1929.
Dobler, Abner - He formed Doble Steam Motors in 1920 in the San Francisco area after gaining support from Detroit with his prototype steam powered car. He built his first steam car at age 16. In later years, he worked abroad as a steam power consultant to locomotive manufacturers. He retired in the early 1950s because of poor health.
Doble Steam Car - American steam car produced from 1914-1931 by Abner Doble Motor Vehicle Co. in Massachusetts (1914-1915), General Engineering Co. in Michigan (1916-1918), and Doble Steam Motors Corp. in California (1924-1931). It was regarded as the finest steam car produced in the world.
doctored car - Used car temporarily repaired to make it drivable. It usually has serious safety problems and is potentially dangerous to drive. See also con game(doctored car).
doctored car racket - See con game(doctored car).
document citation - Traffic ticket issued for traffic law violation connected with a driver's license or car registration.
Doddsmobile - American three-wheeled car produced in 1947.
dodecane - Liquid methane series hydrocarbon compound found in petroleum deposits with a melting and boiling boiling point of 15 and 421 degrees Fahrenheit respectively. Its heating value is 20,350 btu/lb.
Dodge - American car line produced from 1914 to date by Chrysler Corp. (1928 to date) in Michigan. Also, an American car produced from 1914-1915 by A.M. Dodge Co. in Michigan.
Dodge-Graham - American car produced in 1929.
Dodge, John & Horace - They were brothers and skilled American mechanics who formed the Dodge Motor Company and manufactured Dodge cars.
Dodgeson Eight - American car produced in 1926.
Dodo - American car produced in 1909.
dog - Rough car or junker characterized as hard to drive.
dog clutch - See clutch(dog).
dogleg - Right angle bend.
dog show - Used car auction.
dog tracking - Condition created when a car, traveling in a straight line, wanders back and forth. It is usually an alignment problem.
DOHC - Abbreviation for double overhead camshaft.
dolly block - Tool used to remove dents and restore original curves or straight lines in car body panels. It is a piece of solid metal (usually steel) formed into a specific shape. Several types are made for working on different surfaces including: mushroom, wedge, toe, general purpose, utility, and heel.
Dolly Madison - American car produced in 1915.
Dolphin - American car produced in 1961.
Dolson - American car produced from 1904-1907 by J.F. Dolson & Sons, and Dolson Automobile Co., both in Michigan.
D'olt - American car produced from 1921-1926.
DOM - Abbreviation for Dominican Republic found usually on an international license plate.
dome light - See light(dome).
domestic model - Car produced in the United States.
Dominion - Canadian car produced in 1911 and 1914.
DON - Abbreviation for Distribution Octane Number.
Donohue, Mark - He won the Indianapolis 500 Race in 1972 driving an average of 163.0 mph in a Sunoco McLaren.
donut - Car maneuver performed by breaking traction with a car's rear wheels, and spinning a car in a complete circle keeping the front wheels in the circle's center area.
doodlebug - See midget racer.
door frames - Steel structural shape surrounding door opening.
door jam - Vertical support surface located just behind a rear door edge. It contains a door latch, provides a door stop, and forms part of a door's sealing surface.
door handle - Handle used to grasp and open a car door.
door lock - Lock used to prevent a car door from being opened. It is typically positioned near a door handle.
door panel - Sheet metal panel used to cover the outside of a car door.
door pull - Fabric strap or arm rest mounted inside a car door to provide a means for pulling a car door closed.
dope - See mouse milk.
doping - Any of several methods used to hide car problems.

Dorchester - American car produced from 1906-1907 by Hub Automobile Co. in Massachusetts.
Dormandy - American car produced from 1903-1905 by United Shirt & Collar Co., and Troy Carriage Works, both in New York.
Dorris - American car produced from 1905-1926 by St. Louis Motor Carriage Co. (1905-1906), and Dorris Motor Car Co. (1906-1926), both in Missouri.
Dorris Truck - American truck produced from 1919.
Dort - American car produced from 1915-1924 by Dort Motor Car Co. in Michigan.
dos-a-dos - See body style(dos-a-dos).
double barrel carburetor - See carburetor(double barrel).
double clutching - Down shifting practice employed on synchromesh transmissions to save wear on gears, and/or to shift into non-synchronized gears such as first while moving. Process occurs as follows: disengage clutch and shift to neutral, engage clutch and speed up transmission with accelerator, disengage clutch, release accelerator, and shift to next lower gear (or first gear when moving), and finally engage clutch. This process is repeated for each downshift.
double coding - See con game(double coding).
double contacts - Two sets of contact points fitted to work together. They are most commonly found in regulators where they are used to transfer higher current flows. See also regulator(double contact).
double dipping - See con game(double dipping).
Double Drive - American car produced in 1920.
double hocking through the mouth - See downstroke.
double panel - Sheetmetal panel constructed of two metal sheets separated by an air space.
double roller chain - Chain constructed with two parallel rows of rollers. They are used where increased power must be transferred.
double shocking - To use two shock absorbers on each wheel instead of one.
double talk - To speak in an evasive, vague, uncertain, etc. manner.
double yellow line - Line painted on a roadway to mark the center of a road and notify drivers it is illegal to pass.
Douglas - American car produced from 1918-1922 by Douglas Motors Corp. in Nebraska.
dove - See goose.
Dover - American car produced in 1929.
Dow - American line of sealants produced by Dow Corning Corporation.
Dowagiac - American car produced in 1908.
dowel - Pin made of wood, metal, etc. for sliding into two holes lining up together. Dowels keep parts in alignment and in some cases actually bind two surfaces together. For example, a transmission bell housing is accurately positioned onto the back of an engine block by dowels mounted around the outer surface and by corresponding holes in the rear of an engine block.
down draft - Air current flowing downward. See also carburetor(down draft).
downhill grade - Road characterized by sloping downward for a distance.
Downing - American car produced from 1913-1915 by Downing Cycle Car Co. in Michigan.
Downing-Detroit - American car produced from 1913-1915 by Dragon Automobile Co. in Pennsylvania
downshifting - Shifting done from a higher to a lower gear. It is primarily used in racing, as a braking maneuver, or to increase power to the drive wheels. Shifting to a lower gear increases engine rpm and compression which slows or dampens engine speed if the accelerator is not used. It does put a large amount of extra stress on many car components. Such stress can be minimized by decelerating early and using moderate braking before downshifting. See also double clutching and upshifting.
downshift valve - Valve used in an automatic transmission to cause shifting from current gear to next lower gear. It directs fluid under pressure to the proper location in a transmission. It is activated by: linkage to the carburetor throttle valve, a plunger operated electric switch, or a vacuum diaphragm unit (most popular).
downstroke - Car buyer's total down payment. It includes all cash and any equity from a trade-in.
downstroke - To finance or borrow for a downpayment twice by calling the loan in twice on the same day to a bank. It is not legal, but the deal is usually closed before the bank and finance company have a chance to check on it.
Doyle - American car produced in 1900.
D pillar - Fourth metal post used to support a car roof. It is found only on station wagons and certain special car bodies. See also A pillar, B pillar, and C pillar.
dr - Abbreviation for door.
drafting - See slipstream.
drag(1) - To drag race.
drag(2) - To shape the surface of a car clay model using a drag angle tool.
drag angle - A combination template and molding tool used to shape car clay

models.
drag coefficient - Value used to express the resistance of an object moving through an air, water, etc. stream.
dragging out - Starting characteristic used by dragsters where both wheels spin rapidly burning rubber to heat up and get extra traction.
draggin wagon - Car modified for drag racing.
drag link - Metal rod used in steering linkage for transferring side-to-side motion of a pitman arm to tie rods attached to each front wheel. Pitman arm is attached at one end while the other end is typically attached to an idler arm bolted to a side frame rail. Both arms give a drag link an even side-to-side movement.
drag meet - Racing event scheduled where drag racing takes place.
Dragon - American car produced in 1906-1908 by Dragon Automobile Co. (1906-1907), and Dragon Motor Co. (1908), both in Pennsylvania. Also, an American car produced in 1921.
drag race - Race held between two high performance cars. It is usually done on a short straight course at a race track designed for high speed driving.
drag racer - Person driving a dragster.
drag racing - Sport of racing dragsters.
dragster - High performance car designed strictly for accelerating quickly to high speed in a drag race. It is not legal for driving on the road.
drag strip - Short straight road used allowing two high performance cars to race against each other. Legal drag strips are found only at certain race tracks. Untraveled straight roads outside of towns are sometimes used for illegal drag racing.
drag strut - Metal rod used to hold a car's front wheel assembly in position. It is mounted as a movable brace between a car frame and a wheel assembly.
drag template - Cross sectional profile made of a particular body section portion. It is used to duplicate intricate shapes on car models or to develop dies for making actual parts.
drag tube - See crankcase vent tube.
drain-back - Flow of oil back into an oil pan when an engine is stopped from the oil filter, moving engine parts, etc. Some oil filters are constructed with check valves to reduce drain-back.
drain-back valve - Valve used in an automatic transmission to keep oil in a converter when engine is shut off.
drain plug - Threaded plug used to drain fluid from a reservoir. Cars drain plugs are used on: transmission, differential, radiator, oil pan, and engine block.
Drake - American car produced in 1921.
draw(1) - Electrical current used in operating an electrical device.
draw(2) - Method used to select racing opponents or racing lanes prior to the race.
draw filing - To file across a surface at right angles.
draw on the battery - Condition created when current is drawn from a battery.
Drednot - American car produced in 1913.
dress-up kit - Kit composed of various items used to improve the appearance of a car. Such items may include: chrome strips, chrome valve covers, hose and wire braids, etc.
Drexel - American car produced from 1916-1917 by Drexel Motor Car Co. in Illinois.
drift - See slide(car).
Driggs - American car produced from 1921-1923 by Driggs Ordance & Mfg. Co. in Connecticut.
Driggs-Seabury - American car produced from 1915-1916 by Driggs-Seabury Ordnance Corp. in Pennsylvania.
drill - Rotational tool used to make holes in various materials. Drills are powered in several ways including: hand, air, electric, and hydraulic.
drill bit - Shaft constructed with a cutting tip for boring a hole and spiral grooves for carrying cuttings away when rotated.
drilled rotor - Disc brake rotor constructed with holes drilled at regular intervals to increase heat dissipation. See also ventilated rotor.
d-ring - Ring pulled by a race car driver to open a safety chute at the end of a high speed run.
drinking and driving don't mix - Phrase used to emphasize that: drinking makes subsequent driving dangerous for the driver, other cars, and pedestrians. Alcohol decreases awareness and coordination, and increases response time to situations requiring quick judgement all of which contribute to the making of accidents.
drip molding - See drip rail.
drip rail - Small rain gutter mounted along the side of a car roof and used to direct water away from windows and cover roof welds.
drips - See drip molding.
drivability problem - Condition created when a car's engine does not operate well due to malfunctions in the air, fuel, and/or ignition circuit. Symptoms

may include: loss of power, poor fuel economy, hesitation, stalling, pinging, hard starting, rough idling, and dieseling.

drivable model - Full size car model fitted with a fiberglass body to evaluate it in motion.

drive - To operate a car controlling its direction and movement.

drive around - To catch up to and pass a race track opponent after starting a race late.

drive around the block - To drive a car around a block area and come back to the starting point. It is often done by drivers who can't find a place to park or who are waiting to pick up someone.

drive away - To drive a car away from its present location.

driveaway(1) - Business engaged in providing drivers to drive cars to and from anywhere.

driveaway(2) - Statement made to someone disliked.

drive belt - V-shaped belt used to transfer power from one shaft to another by means of pulleys. Common drive belts are fan and air conditioning belts. Some belts transfer power to two or more shafts. For example, a fan belt transfers power to a water pump and an alternator. Belts are usually composed of rubber, steel wires, cord, and fabric.

drive fit - To force a shaft into a hole of slightly smaller diameter.

drive in - Food service business engaged in serving food to parked cars by waitresses or waiters. Also, it refers to an outdoor movie theatre where cars park to watch a movie.

drive like there is an egg under your foot - To drive a car keeping light pressure on the gas pedal as much as possible for maximum fuel economy.

driveline - Heavy hollow metal shaft used to transfer power from a transmission to a differential. Primary components include: front yoke, front universal, drive shaft, rear universal, and companion flange. Front yoke is splined to mesh with a transmission output shaft. Universal joints allow flexing. Companion flange connects the output end of a driveline to a differential pinion shaft. Driveline must be carefully balanced like a tire to reduce vibration from its spinning action. See also torque tube drive.

driveline(open) - Driveline exposed from the transmission end to the differential. See also hotchkiss and torque tube.

driveline(two piece) - Driveline constructed of two pieces connected between a transmission and differential by three U-joints. The design allows a floorpan to be lowered.

driveline balancing - To balance a driveline about its center of rotation to minimize vibration.

driveline noise - Condition created when a driveline emits noise as it rotates. Possible causes include: worn universal joints, being out of balance, and worn transmission output shaft bearing. See also sound(clunking-1).

driveline safety loop - Metal loop placed around a driveline and attached to a car body at one or more locations to catch a driveline in the event one of the U-joints fails. U-joint failure is dangerous and has caused metal pieces to fly through a floorpan or a loose driveline to flip a car.

driveline vibration - Vibration created when a driveline becomes unbalanced. Possible causes include: balance weights missing, dent or bend in driveline, and bad universal joint.

driveline whip - Condition created when an engine operating at medium to high rpm is suddenly dropped to idle. Some engines with manual transmissions employ an anti-stall dashpot to minimize the effect.

driven plate - See clutch plate.

drive pinion - Gear and shaft assembly mounted at the input side of a differential housing. It transfers rotation from a drive shaft to a differential ring gear. Primary components consist of: pinion shaft, pinion gear, pinion flange, two tapered roller bearings, and oil seal.

drive pinion gear - See gear(drive pinion).

driver - Person driving a car.

drive range - Gearing arrangement used in an automatic transmission to permit a certain upper and lower car speed and load limit. A three speed automatic, for example, has three drive ranges.

driver efficiency - Level of driver alertness. It usually declines after about six hours at the wheel.

driver improvement program - Program used by certain states to assist drivers in improving their driving habits when they have committed too many traffic violations.

driver rating - Method used by insurance companies to rate a driver's driving record in order to determine the appropriate policy and fees to charge. Four categories are usually used: preferred, standard, substandard, and assigned risk. All ratings below preferred are usually charged a progressively higher rate.

driver's license - See license(driver).

drive shaft - See driveline. Also, it refers to a shaft used to transfer power from a power source to an end use.

drivetrain - See powertrain.

driveway - Short road built from a street to a building, garage, house, etc. Also, it refers to a road.

drive wheel - Wheel driven by power transmitted from an engine.

driving - To operate a car.

driving a long stretch - To drive an extended period of time and/or many miles.

driving against traffic - To drive a car in a traffic lane going opposite to designated traffic flow.

driving cost - Cost required to own and operate a car. It is usually expressed in cents per mile. Major costs include: gas and oil, repairs, tires, depreciation, insurance, taxes and registration, and parking.

driving defensively - To drive as a defensive driver.

driving instructor - Person skilled in teaching others how to drive a car.

driving on a suspended license - Situation created when a person continues driving even though his drivers license is suspended.

driving record - Record compiled of a person's driving history.

driving situation - See road situation. See also road situation tip.

driving test - Test taken to determine a person's driving ability.

driving tip - Useful information given to help someone operate their car more knowledgeably, economically, efficiently, and/or safely.

driving tip(downshifting) - Downshifting helps with braking on long down grades or increasing power when climbing hills. Downshifting should be carefully done on wet roads and never on ice (could start an uncontrollable skid).

driving tip(hills) - Driving up hills requires maintaining forward momentum, especially when slippery. If traction is lost, back the car down to the bottom of the hill and start over again. Driving down hills requires maintaining a slower speed, shifting to a gear providing some braking effort, and avoiding any hard braking which could start the car spinning or slidding.

driving tip(minimizing fuel consumption) - See gas saving tip.

driving tip(night driving) - When driving at night, the following tips will make the experience safer: minimize eye fatigue by dimming instrument panel lighting, adjusting rear view mirror to night setting or slightly different angle, and adjusting side mirror to a slightly different angle; use bright lights whenever possible; look to road shoulder when cars approach (especially if high beams are on); reduce speed; keep windshield and headlights clean; dim headlights when approaching other cars; and stay aware of your physical condition (pull over when you get drowsy).

driving tip(skidding) - If a car begins skidding, immediately let up on the gas (rear wheel drive cars) and gently steer in the direction the car is moving until control is regained. See also skid.

driving tip(sliding around turn) - See power slide.

driving tip(sliding on slippery roads) - If a car begins to slide, immediately let up on the gas pedal (rear wheel drive car), and gently steer in the direction the car is moving until traction is regained, then continue at a slower speed. If road conditions are bad (black ice, compact snow, etc.), traction devices such as chain may be required to continue driving. See also skid.

driving tip(snow or slush on road) - Roads covered with snow and/or slush provide an interesting challenge to maintaining control. It can be like constantly driving a car that is constantly losing traction and sliding a little. Short of installing chains, the following pointers will help provide control: keep extra distance between you and other cars, maintain forward momentum, keep a firm but relaxed grip on the steering wheel, avoid sharp steering wheel movements, keep steering the car in the direction of forward movement every time you start to slide, slow down when sliding begins, and find the speed you are most comfortable driving in.

driving tip(starting on snowy/icy road) - They key to getting a car moving on a slippery road surface is to avoid spinning the wheels. This is accomplished by slowly applying power to the drive wheels. If they start to spin, stop and start over. For automatic transmission cars, wheel spin can only be controlled by the gas pedal. For manual transmission cars, wheel spin can best be controlled by starting in second gear and slowly engaging the clutch.

driving tip(towing with a unit body car) - As a general rule, unit body cars can tow trailers weighing up to 2,000 lbs. The problem lies in spreading the trailer load over enough of the frame. For higher towing weights, a suitable regular frame car is needed.

driving tip(wheels stuck) - When the drive wheels get stuck, avoid spinning the tires as they will only get buried deeper. First, try rocking the car to get moving again as follows: place gear in forward and momentarily spin the drive wheels to get a slight forward motion, then quickly go into reverse gear and momentarily spin the wheels backwards. Repeating this action causes

the car to develop a back and forth motion that can get the car going again
if the rocking action becomes sufficient. If this approach doesn't work, the
tires can be jacked up and the holes filled in with large rocks, wood planks,
etc., or the path ahead of the wheels needs to be dug out for several feet
before attempting to move the car. Traction mats are sometimes effective.

driving under the influence - Condition created when a driver operates a car
with alcohol in his blood stream at a high enough concentration to impair
driving ability.

drop center rim - Ledge-like edge fabricated along each side of a wheel's
outer edge and used to hold a tire to a wheel. It was first used on steel
disc wheels in the 1930s and is still used on today's wheels. See also
wheel(steel disc).

drop forging - To shape a piece of hot steel between two dies.

drophead coupe - See body style(drophead coupe).

dropped axle - Solid front axle modified to lower a car's frame toward the
ground. It is usually done for a custom look.

dropping - See channeling.

dropping point - Temperature reached when grease changes from a solid or
semi-solid state to a liquid. It does not specify the maximum operating
temperature of the grease.

drop the hammer - To rapidly engage a car's clutch when a race begins.

drop the pan - To remove an oil pan from the bottom of an engine.

drop the transmission - Process used to remove a transmission from a car. It
consists of placing a transmission jack underneath a transmission for
support, removing all necessary linkage, removing engine attachment bolts,
removing frame support, sliding transmission backwards until input shaft is
free of flywheel, lowering it to the ground, and sliding it out from
underneath a car.

drowsiness - Driver condition created when it becomes difficult to stay awake.
The eyes keep wanting to close, and a driver's alertness is decreased. It is
dangerous to drive while drowsy. If turning on the radio, talking to a
passenger, cracking a window, etc. doesn't help, then stop and rest awhile.
The only real cure for drowsiness is sleep.

drum - See brake drum.

drum brake - See brake(drum).

Drummond - American car produced from 1915-1918 by Drummond Motor Car Co. in
Nebraska.

drunk - Temporary state of mental and physical impairment caused by drinking
too much alcohol in too short a time period.

drunk driver - Person driving after drinking too much alcohol.

drunk driving - To drive a car while drunk.

dry battery - See battery(dry).

dry grip - Condition exhibited by a tire maintaining good traction on dry
pavement.

dry sleeve - Metal cylinder pressed into an oversize bore of a cylinder to
form a piston bearing surface. Sleeves allow engine blocks to be rebuilt
several times regardless of cylinder wall damage. See also wet sleeve.

dry start - Engine condition caused when an engine runs briefly without oil
after first being started. This is due to a full flow oil filter mounted in
such a way oil flows back to an oil sump when a car stops. When the car is
restarted, the oil pump must first fill the oil filter with oil before any
oil proceeds on to the lubrication points. Oil filters with drainback valves
minimize this problem. Some manufacturers mount oil filters so they can stay
full of oil all the time. See also oil filter(full flow) and oil filter
drainback valve.

dry sump - Engine built to be lubricated using oil stored in a separate tank
or radiator instead of the normal oil pan. One or more pumps route the oil
to and from the engine. A dry sump often does a better job of keeping the
oil cool.

DS(1) - See service rating(DS).

DS(2) - Abbreviation for dual sidemount tires.

dual advance distributor - See distributor(dual advance).

dual brakes - Braking system constructed to provide an independent hydraulic
circuit for each pair of wheels. It is a safeguard preventing all brakes
from failing at once.

dual breaker points - Two sets of points used in a distributor to increase cam
angle or dwell so a satisfactory spark will be generated at high engine
speeds. Some dual point cars have two spark plugs for each cylinder.

dual diaphragm distributor - See distributor(dual diaphragm).

dual diaphragms - Advance and retard diaphragm assembly used in dual
diaphragm distributors for controlling exhaust emissions.

dual exhaust - See dual exhaust system.

dual exhaust system - Car exhaust system composed of two separate exhaust
systems due to two separate exhaust manifolds. It is most commonly found on
V8 engines. It's wise to steer away from cars with these systems for two

good reasons. First, the parts don't get hot enough to burn off the corrosive acids that accumulate. Secondly, there are twice as many parts to replace.

dual floats - Carburetor float bowl fitted with two floats.

Dual-Ghia - American car produced from 1955-1964 by Dual Motors Corp. in Michigan.

dual headlight system - Car equipped with headlights capable of producing low and high beams of light.

dual master cylinder - See brake dual master cylinder.

dual muffler system - Exhaust system built using two separate mufflers for routing gases out of the engine. Dual mufflers are usually installed on dual exhaust systems, but in some cases are used on single manifold engines to reduce backpressure.

dual plane manifold - See intake manifold(dual plane).

duals - See dual exhaust.

dual tailgate - Rear door of a station wagon built to open downward for loading cargo or sideways like a car door.

Duck - American car produced in 1913.

duct - Passageway made of metal, plastic, rubber, etc. for conducting air, gas, or fluids. A heat duct in a car, for example, routes warm air from a blower motor to respective outlets.

duct sensor - Temperature sensor mounted in a car's ductwork to regulate temperature output.

duct tape - Fabric tape used to seal sheet metal duct joints. It is also useful for temporarily patching hoses, seat cushions, holes in sheet metal, plastic windows, etc.

ductwork - Assemblage of ducts linked together for routing gases or fluids to and from various specified points.

Dudgeon Steam - American steam vehicle produced in 1857.

Dudley - American car produced from 1913-1915 by Dudly Tool Co. in Michigan.

Dudley Electric - American car produced in 1915.

Duer - American car produced from 1907-1908 by Chicago Coach & Carriage Co. in Illinois.

Duesenberg - American car produced from 1920-1937 by Duesenberg Motor Co. in Indiana, and in 1966 by Duesenberg Corp. in Indiana. The roadster version was a famous high performance sports car.

Duesenberg 16 - American car driven by Tommy Milton to a 1920 world land speed record of 156.0 mph at Daytona, Florida.

Duesenberg, Frederick Samuel - Man made famous by his racing experience, racing cars, and engines. He designed a famous horizontal valve engine, and organized the Duesenberg Motor Company to produce them. He and his brother, August, subsequently organized Duesenberg Brothers Company to manufacture the famous Duesenberg racing cars. The cars captured all the 1919 world racing records in engine displacement classes from 160-450 cubic inches.

Dumont - American car produced in 1902.

Dumore - American car produced in 1918.

Dunlop(1) - He was an Irishman who experimented with pneumatic tires in the 1890s and later went on to form the Dunlop Tire Company.

Dunlop(2) - American line of tires produced by Dunlop Tire & Rubber.

Dunn - American car produced from 1914-1918 by Dunn Motor Works in New York.

Duplex - American car produced from 1908-1909. Also, a Canadian car produced in 1923.

Dupont(1) - American car produced in 1915 and from 1920-1932 by Dupont Motors Inc. in Delaware.

Dupont(2) - American line of automotive paint products.

Duquesne - American car produced from 1903-1906 and 1912-1913 by Duquesne Construction Co. in New York, and Duquesne Motor Car Co. in Pennsylvania respectively.

Durable Dayton - American car produced in 1916.

Durant - American car line produced from 1921-1932 by Durant Motors in Michigan, New York, Indiana, and New Jersey.

Durey, Arthur - He set a world land speed record of 84.7 mph in 1903 driving a Gobron-Brille.

Durocar - American car produced from 1907-1909 by Durocar Mfg. Co. in California.

Duryea - American car produced from 1895-1915 by Duryea Motor Wagon in Massachusetts (1895-1898), Duryea Mfg. Co. in Illinois (1896-1898), Duryea Power Co. in Pennsylvania (1899-1908), and Duryea Motor Co. in Michigan (1908-1913), and Cresson-Morris Co. in Pennsylvania (1914-1915).

Duryea Brothers - They were two American brothers, both skilled mechanics, who developed the first simple car in the U.S. in 1893.

Duryea, Charles E - He built his first car in 1893 and formed the Duryea Motor Wagon Company with his brother J. Frank. He subsequently organized the Duryea Power Company to manufacture three cylinder cars. In subsequent years, he became an automotive textbook writer.

Duryea-Gem - American car produced in 1916.
Duryea Lightcar - American car produced in 1915.
Dusseau - American car produced in 1912.
Duster - American car produced from 1960-1981 by Plymouth Division of Chrysler Corp. in Michigan.
Dutch, Von - Car customizer regarded as one of the best pinstripers.
Duty - American car produced in 1920.
Duyo - American car produced in 1914.
DVB - Abbreviation for delay vacuum bypass.
DVDV - Abbreviation for distributor vacuum delay valve.
dwell - See dwell angle.
dwell angle - Number of degrees rotated by a distributor shaft from the instant distributor points close to when they open. During this period, the point rubbing block does not touch the cam surface. In one distributor shaft revolution, a dwell angle will occur as many times as there are engine cylinders. Angle is a function of point gap. As the gap decreases, the point block contacts an individual cylinder cam on the distributor cam fewer degrees of revolution and so the dwell angle between individual cams will increase. Dwell angle of an engine is around half of the distributor cam rotation that is allotted to each cylinder. Cam rotation for 4, 6, and 8 cylinder engines is 90, 60, and 45 degrees respectively. Typical dwell angles are 49, 28, and 24 respectively. See also distributor cam and cylinder cam.
dwell meter - Instrument used to measure an ignition system's dwell angle by electrically monitoring the opening and closing of distributor points. It is typically connected to the ground side of primary coil windings and the car frame.
dwell tachometer - Combination instrument used to measure dwell angle, engine rpm, and sometimes the condition of distributor points.
DWI - Abbreviation for driving while intoxicated.
Dyke - American car produced from 1901-1904 by A.L. Dyke Auto Supply Co. in Missouri.
dykes ring - Compression piston ring built into an L-shaped cross section.
Dymaxion - American car produced from 1933-1934.
dynamic balance - See balance(dynamic).
dynamic imbalance - See dynamic unbalance.
dynamic unbalance - Condition created when the mass of a tire and wheel assembly is not evenly distributed around its circumference, and/or the mass moves outside the plane of rotation swept out by the tire width. The former creates an up and down vibration while the latter creates a wobbling or sideways vibration. See also static unbalance and unbalanced tire.
dynamo - See generator.
dynamometer - Expensive sophisticated machine used to analyze a car's health and pinpoint problems by putting a car through different simulated road and driving conditions while it is stationary. A dynamometer has stationary rollers used to rest a car's wheels on. The rollers turn and other aspects of the machine come into play as it artificially creates various road conditions for a car to perform under. Various instruments are hooked up to a car to monitor its performance, and pinpoint any trouble spots.
dynamometer test - Test performed on a car using a dynamometer to analyze its operating condition.
DZ - Abbreviation for Algeria found usually on an international license plate.

E

E(1) – Abbreviation for Spain found usually on an international license plate.
E(2) – Auction car rating code used to specify a car in excellent condition.
Eagle – American car produced in 1904-1906, 1908-1909, and 1923-1924 by Eagle Auto Co. in New York (1904-1905), Eagle Automobile Co. in New Jersey (1905-1906), Eagle Motor Carriage Co. in New York (1908), Eagle Automobile Co. in Missouri (1909), Durant Motors in New York (1923-1924). Also, an American car produced from 1980 to date by American Motors in Michigan.
Eagle-Macomber – American car produced from 1914-1918 by Eagle-Macomber Motor Co. in Ohio.
Eagle Rotary – American car produced from 1917-1918.
EAK – Abbreviation for Kenya found usually on an international license plate.
Earl – American car produced in 1907-1908 and 1921-1923 by Earl Motor Car Co. in Wisconsin and Earl Motors in Michigan, respectively.
Earnhardt, Dale – He became the NASCAR Grand National Champion in 1980.
earth – See ground.
Eastern – American car produced in 1901.
Eastern Diaries – American car produced in 1925.
Eastman – American car produced in 1899-1902 by Eastman Automobile Co. in Ohio.
Easton – American car produced from 1907-1913.
easy credit – To obtain credit easily. Easy credit usually comes at a price. It usually consists of: lower monthly payments over more months and often a higher interest rate, or higher monthly payments at a lower interest rate.
easy mark – Unaware potential customer spotted by a con man or car salesman who can easily be cheated or conned.
Eaton – American car produced in 1898.
EC(1) – Abbreviation for excellent condition. See also FC and GC.
EC(2) – Abbreviation for Ecuador found usually on an international license plate.
eccentric – Two or more circles, one inside the other, having different centers of rotation.
eccentric adjusting screw – Screw commonly used in a distributor to adjust distributor point gap.
ECD – Abbreviation for emission control device.
Eck – American car produced in 1903.
Eclipse – American car produced from 1900-1903 and 1905 by Eclipse Automobile Co. in Massachusetts (1900-1903), and Kreuger Mfg. Co. in Wisconsin (1905).
ECM – Abbreviation for electronic control module.
Econoline – American car produced from 1968-1974 by Ford Motor Co. in Michigan.
economizer valve – Valve mechanism used to control flow of additional fuel into an engine when a throttle is wide open. It usually relies on intake manifold vacuum underneath a throttle plate. When a plate becomes fully open, vacuum is low and the valve opens to let additional fuel into the venturi area.
Economy – American car produced in 1906, 1908-1911, and 1914. Also, an American car produced from 1917-1921 by Economy Motor Co. in Ohio.
economy car(1) – Car built for economical operation. Its characteristics include: small size, light weight, small efficient engine, no air conditioning, and few accessories. Wheelbase is usually under 100 inches. Engine displacement is normally under 2500 cc.
economy car(2) – Subcompact car.
Economycar – American car produced from 1913-1914 by Economycar Co. in Rhode Island.
economy run – Specified course laid out on public roads where participating cars travel the maximum distance possible on a limited amount of fuel.
ECU – Abbreviation for electronic control unit. See also black box.
Eddy – American car produced in 1902.
Edelbrock – American line of performance automotive products.
Edelbrock, Vic – He founded the Edelbrock Corporation, manufacturer of performance car parts.
Edmond – American car produced in 1900.
Edsel – American car produced from 1957-1959 by Ford Motor Co. in Michigan. It was built to fill the gap between Ford and Mercury car lines and was based on customer research. It never caught on.
EDT – Abbreviation for Eastern Daylight Time.
educated guess – Guessing an answer to a question based on knowing some

related knowledge.

edwardian car – British car generally classified as built from 1905-1918. See also vintage car and veteran car.

Edwards – American car produced from 1953-1955 by E.H. Edwards Co. in California.

Edwards-Knight – American car produced from 1912-1914 by Edwards Motor Co. in New York.

EEC – Abbreviation for electronic engine controller. It usually refers to an on-board computer used to control various engine functions.

effective interest rate – Annual percentage rate based on inclusion of miscellaneous fees and charges.

EFI – Abbreviation for electronic fuel injection.

eggcrate – Intricate grillework made by intersecting metal strips at right angles. It creates more depth than can be obtained by stamping.

EGR – Abbreviation for exhaust gas recirculation.

EGR system – See emission control system(combustion-exhaust gas recirculation).

EGR system cutout switch – Switch designed to stop the recirculation of exhaust gases when a car's brakes are applied. It works by removing vacuum to the EGR valve. Cars equipped with this switch often produce trace detonation when the brakes are applied due to increased combustion chamber temperatures from decreased exhaust gas recirculation.

EGR valve – See exhaust gas recirculation valve.

EHV – American car produced from 1903-1906.

Eichstaedt – American car produced in 1902.

EIM – American car produced in 1915.

EIS – Abbreviation for electronic ignition system.

EIS control unit – See control unit.

Eisenhuth – American car produced in 1896.

Eisenhuth-Compound – American car produced in 1903.

EKE – Abbreviation for engine knock eliminator.

Eklhart – American car produced in 1908-1916 and 1922.

elapsed time – Time measured from the start of a race to its finish.

EL – Abbreviation for electric.

Elbert – American car produced in 1914 by Elbert Car Co. in Washington.

Elbert Cyclecar – American car produced from 1914-1915.

El Camino – American car produced from 1968 to date by Chevrolet Division of General Motors Corp. in Michigan.

Elcar – American car produced from 1915-1931 by Elkhart Carriage & Motor Car Co., and Elcar Motor Co., both in Indiana.

Elcar-Lever – American car produced in 1930.

Elco – American car produced in 1915-1916 by Bimel Buggy Co. in Ohio.

Elcurto – American car produced in 1921.

Eldorado – American car produced from 1955 to date by Cadillac Motor Car Co. in Michigan.

Eldredge – American car produced in 1903-1906 by National Sewing Machine Co. in Illinois.

Eldridge, Ernest – He set a world land speed record of 146.0 mph in 1924 driving a Fiat 6 Cylinder.

Eldridge Truck – American truck produced in 1913.

elec – Abbreviation for electric.

Electra – American electric car produced from 1913-1915 by Storage Battery Power Co. in Illinois. Also, an American car produced from 1955 to date by Buick Division of General Motors Corp. in Michigan.

Electra King – American electric car produced beginning in 1961 by B&Z Electric Car Co. in California. It was a small 3 or 4 wheeled vehicle used by handicapped people.

electrical circuit – Path taken when electricity flows from a source to an electrical device, then back to the source via a ground.

electrical current – Flow of electrons measured in a conductive medium like a copper wire. It is the flow of electrons that powers the headlights, runs the heater, provide high voltage sparks, etc.

electrical problem – Condition created when part of a car's electrical system fails to operate properly.

electrical problem(ammeter reading erratic) – Ammeter needle moves from a high charge to a low discharge rate. Magnitude is in proportion to engine speed. Possible causes include: faulty regulator relay winding, or a burned out resistor in regulator.

electrical problem(battery dead) – Battery has lost all of its stored electrical energy. Possible causes include: defective battery, battery cells low on water, short in electrical system; and no charging current flowing to battery due to defective alternator, dirty regulator contact points, and/or defective regulator.

electrical problem(battery intermittently charging) – Current flows irregularly to battery when engine is running. Possible causes are the same

as for electrical problem(battery not charging).
electrical problem(battery not charging) – No current flows to battery when engine is running. Possible causes include: defective alternator, battery charging wire disconnected or corroded, battery posts corroded, regulator contacts dirty or oxidized, regulator poorly grounded, regulator fuse wires melted, defective regulator, and defective alternator diode(s).
electrical problem(battery not taking a charge) – Battery does not store a charge despite flow of charging current. Possible causes include: defective battery, battery cells low on water, low charging current level due to defective regulator or dirty regulator contacts, and battery being drained due to short in electrical system.
electrical problem(battery overcharging) – Battery receives too much current or a constant current flow regardless of its state of charge. Possible causes include: alternator output not controlled by regulator due to defective regulator, improper calibration, contacts stuck or welded together, poor ground, or missing wiring.
electrical problem(battery slowly discharges) – Current flow to battery is too low to keep it charged. It is usually due to an improperly adjusted or defective regulator. Partial discharge is indicated by: dimming headlights and dashlights during starting, weak sounding horn, etc. See also **regulator**.
electrical problem(blower motor won't operate) – Heater motor doesn't work regardless of speed settings. Possible causes include: blown circuit fuse, defective speed switch, defective resistor(s), and open circuit between resistor(s) and motor power input terminal.
electrical problem(engine cranks but won't start) – See starting problem (engine cranks but won't start), and engine problem(cranks but won't start).
electrical problem(engine cranks slowly) – See starting problem(engine cranks slowly).
electrical problem(short circuit) – See short circuit.
electrical problem(starter won't operate) – See starting problem(starter won't operate).
electrical problem(starter won't disengage) – See starting problem(starter won't disengage).
electrical system – Assemblage of wires, electrical devices, and controls built into a car to meet its electrical requirements.
electric car – Car powered by electricity. It typically consists of a large bank of chemical batteries used to power an electric motor. Such cars are still experimental because of the inadequate amount of power storable in existing battery types. See also **hybrid electric car**.
electric fuel pump – Electrically powered pump used to move fuel to a carburetor. It is usually mounted near a gas tank. Some have adjustable pressure options. Some run continuously while others run according to pressure developed.
electricity – Flow of electrons occurring from atom to atom in conductive materials.
electric lamps – See electric lights.
electric light – Light generated from a bulb whose filament gets hot, then bright from current flow.
electric shock – The flow of electric current in a body. It doesn't take much to be deadly. For example, a shock of 120 volts at 3/10 amperes can kill a person in 1/10 of a second.
Electric Shopper – American electric car produced beginning in 1960 by Electric Shopper in California.
electric spark – Small bluish flame generated when electricity exists at a high enough potential to move across an air gap.
Electric Vehicle – American car produced in 1897.
Electric Wagon – American car produced in 1897.
electric winch – Winch powered by an electric motor. Cars with portable winches usually run directly off the battery or an auxiliary battery.
electric wiring – Conductive wiring used to transfer electricity from one point to another.
Electrobat – American car produced in 1895.
electrochemical – Chemical production of electricity. Batteries produce electricity chemically.
electrocution – Killing caused when too much electricity flows through a body.
electrode(center) – Small straight metal rod located in the center of the spark plug. It is used to conduct a high voltage spark to a spark plug tip.
electrode(side) – Small curved metal rod welded to the shoulder of a spark plug. It provides a ground for a high voltage spark to jump to.
electrode(spark plug) – One of two small metal rods located at a spark plug tip. They are separated by an air gap. High voltage current jumps the gap to create an electric spark. See also electrode(side) and electrode(center).
electrodes – See electrode(spark plug).
electrode gap – Air gap located between a spark plug's center and side electrodes.

electrolyte – Solution formulated to conduct electricity. Electrolyte conducts electricity by movement of its positive and negative ions to respective electrodes. A battery conducts electricity by immersing its positive and negative plates in an electrolytic solution of sulfuric acid and water.
   Electrolyte in a charged up lead-acid car battery contains about 35-37 percent sulfuric acid by weight corresponding to a specific gravity of around 1.27.

electrolyte level – Level of electrolyte in a battery. Lead acid battery should have about 1/4 - 1/2 inch of electrolyte covering the top of the plates. As the plates become exposed, the acid concentration builds, plates are eaten away, and exposed areas dry and harden.

electrolytic solution – See electrolyte.

electromagnet – Metal device built to become magnetic when current flows through a coil of conductive wire. Metal is iron or steel and remains magnetized as long as current continues to flow.

electromagnetic relay – See relay. See also solenoid switch.

Electromaster – American electric car produced beginning in 1962 by Nepa Mfg. Co. in California.

electron – Negatively charged particle forming part of an atom.

electronically tuned radio – Radio designed to locate radio stations with solid state controls and not tuning knobs.

electronic control module – On-board computer used to control various functions of a car engine upon receiving electric signals from various sensors. Such functions may include: timing, dwell, fuel metering, and radiator fan operation. It is usually a dependable unit not prone to failure, but is sensitive under certain conditions. See also black box, open loop mode, closed loop mode, limp-in mode, computer command control, engine control sensor, sensor, and EEC.

electronic ignition module – Solid state device used to control output of ignition coil. Certain models are sensitive to failure when: heat exceeds 125 degrees, ground is poor, connections become dirty or corroded, and current flow is wrong. See also black box, control unit, reluctor, and pickup coil.

Electronic LaSaetta – American electric car produced in 1955.

electronic part – Part usually defined as a solid state device.

electronics – Science defined as dealing with the development and application of devices and systems involving electron flow in gaseous media, semiconductors, or a vacuum.

electronic scattershield – Electronic circuit built into an onboard computer to prevent over-revving of an engine. It operates like a governor, and cuts fuel flow and/or ignition when a certain engine rpm is exceeded. See also idiot circuit.

electronic spark timing module – Electronic device used to control ignition coil output. It is usually triggered by a magnetic pickup in the distributor when the engine is cranking, and by an on-board computer when the engine is running. A faulty module is indicated, if the engine will crank but not start and fuel is being metered by a carburetor or injector. See also Hall switch.

Electronomic – American car produced in 1901.

Electruck – American truck produced in 1924.

element – See battery cell.

element(paper) – Paper filter material used in an air, oil, or fuel filter.

elephant – Plymouth or Dodge hemi engine with 426 cu.in. displacement.

elevation – Two dimensional drawing drawn to represent a front, side, or rear view of a plan view drawing.

elevation view – See elevation.

Elgin – American car produced from 1899-1901 and 1916-1925 by Elgin Automobile Co., and Elgin Motor Car Corp. respectively, both in Illinois.

ELI – Abbreviation for extended lubrication interval. See also grease(extended lubrication interval chassis).

eliminated – To get beat in a car race.

Elinore – American car produced in 1903.

Elite – American car produced in 1901, 1906, and 1909. Also, an American car produced from 1975-1980 by Ford Motor Co. in Michigan.

Elite Steamer – American steam car produced in 1901.

Elk – American car produced in 1913.

Elkhart – American car produced from 1908-1909 by Elkart Carriage & Mfg. Co. (1908), and Elkart Motor Car Co. (1908-1909), both in Indiana.

Elliot – American car produced in 1897 and 1902.

Elliot, Bill – He won the Daytona 500 Race in 1985 averaging 172.3 mph in a Ford.

Elliot steering knuckle – See axle(Elliot steering).

Ellis – American car produced in 1901.

Ellsworth – American car produced in 1907.

Elmira – American car produced in 1920.
Elmore – American car produced from 1900-1912 by Elmore Mfg. Co. in Ohio.
Elston – American car produced in 1895.
Elvick – American car produced in 1895.
Elwell-Parker – American car produced in 1909.
Elysee – American car produced in 1926.
Emancipator – American car produced in 1909.
Emblem – American car produced in 1910.
Embree-McLean – American car produced in 1910.
emergency brake – Assemblage of parts used to manually engage rear brakes of a car. Brake is used to keep a car from rolling when at rest, or stopping a moving car whose regular brake system has failed. Some older cars had an emergency brake mounted on the transmission output shaft.
emergency equipment – Various items carried in a car to handle the more common road situations. Items typically include: spare tire, empty gas can, extra water, wrenches and screwdrivers, pliers and wire cutters, pocket knife, manual tire pump, extra fan belt and radiator hoses, duct tape, extra hose clamps, bailing wire, gloves, tarp to lay on, rags, tire chains, flashlight, first aid kit, tire jack and lug wrench, flares and/or reflectors, jumper cables, extra engine oil, small shovel, starting fluid, extra points, and emery cloth.
emergency relief valve – Valve used in an automatic transmission to prevent hydraulic pressure from exceeding a certain maximum value.
emergency vehicle – Vehicle equipped to travel to the site of an emergency, render assistance, and transport injured people to a medical facility.
Emerson – American car produced from 1916-1917 by Emerson Motors Co. in New York. Also, an American car produced in 1907.
EMF(1) – Abbreviation for electromotive force or electric voltage.
EMF(2) – American car produced from 1908-1912 by Everitt-Metzger-Flanders Co. in Michigan.
emission control program – Program instituted in several states requiring all cars past a certain year of manufacture to be tested on an annual basis for the level of several exhaust gas compounds emitted. Engines falling outside an acceptable range must be brought up to minimum standards.
emission control system – Assemblage of parts and controls used on an engine to control the quantity of noxious gases produced during combustion and/or to control crankcase vapors.
emission control system(combustion) – System designed to control noxious gas emissions from an engine as a result of the combustion process in each engine cylinder.
emission control system(combustion-air injection) – System designed to control noxious exhaust gases by pumping air under pressure directly into the downstream side of each exhaust valve, or into a thermal reactor. The air helps gases, exiting the combustion chambers, burn more completely before reaching the atmosphere. Air injection can create problems like increased backpressure and backfiring due to increased burning of overrich exhaust mixtures on deceleration. Air bypass valves are used to minimize the problem. See also air pump.
emission control system(combustion-air pump) – See emission control system(combustion-air injection) and air pump.
emission control system(combustion-aspirator) – System designed to control noxious exhaust gases by routing fresh air from the air cleaner to the exhaust manifold through piping. Flow rate is controlled by an in-line aspirator valve. A faulty system can cause annoying noises such as rumbling, squealing, or knocking in the engine compartment area.
emission control system(combustion-catalytic converter) – System designed to control noxious exhaust gases by converting hydrocarbons and carbon monoxide into water vapor and carbon dioxide in a catalytic converter mounted between the exhaust manifold and the muffler. See also catalytic converter.
emission control system(combustion-combination emission control) – System designed to control noxious exhaust gases during deceleration by energizing a CEC valve. It opens to route vacuum to the vacuum advance unit while slightly opening the throttle valve to lean the fuel mixture.
emission control system(combustion-exhaust gas recirculation) – System designed to control NOx emission level by diluting incoming air and fuel mixture with rerouted exhaust gas. The diluted fuel mixture burns cooler lowering combustion temperature and resulting in a lower NOx emission level, since NOx formation is directly related to heat. Another benefit is reduced pinging tendency. An exhaust gas recirculation (EGR) valve and a thermal valve provide the primary controls.
   A faulty system can cause: excessive pinging when cold; hard starting; stalling when accelerating, decelerating, or stopping quickly; hesitation when accelerating; stumbling while cruising; rough idling; and power loss. System problems are usually a valve stuck open or closed, or a valve opening or closing at the wrong time. See also car service tip(EGR valve tip),

exhaust gas recirculation valve, and thermal valve.

emission control system(combustion-ignition/induction) - System designed to reduce noxious exhaust gases by running a carburetor lean at idle, opening the throttle a little at idle, and retarding the spark with a spark port and spark valve.

emission control system(combustion-improved combustion) - System designed to reduce hydrocarbon and carbon monoxide emissions by routing air preheated in the exhaust manifold area to the air cleaner. It allows a car to warm up faster and use leaner fuel mixtures.

emission control system(combustion-NOx) - System designed to control emissions of oxides of nitrogen by controlling vacuum to the vacuum advance unit. A spark delay valve is employed which delays vacuum reaching the vacuum advance unit when going from idle to a partly opened throttle. Some systems also use temperature sensors to operate the valve when outside air temperature is above 60-70 degrees.

emission control system(combustion-pulse air) - See emission control system(combustion-aspirator).

emission control system(combustion-thermal reactor) - System designed to control noxious exhaust gases by pumping air under pressure directly into a chamber built to replace an exhaust manifold. It allows continued high temperature burning of exhaust pollutants. The air helps gases, exiting the combustion chambers, burn more completely before reaching the atmosphere. Air injection can create problems like increased backpressure and backfiring due to increased burning of rich exhaust mixtures on deceleration. An air bypass valve is used to minimize the problem. See also emission control system(combustion-air injection), thermal reactor, and air pump.

emission control system(combustion-transmission controlled spark) - System designed to control oxides of nitrogen emissions by preventing vacuum advance in a transmission's lower gears. Vacuum advance works only when: car is in high gear or reverse, or when engine temperature is above or below specified values (typically 210-220 and 70-85). Three components usually control the vacuum. They include: solenoid vacuum valve, transmission switch, and a coolant temperature switch.

emission control system(crankcase) - System designed to control crankcase vapors. Advantages include: reduce crankcase emissions, and better fuel economy. Disadvantages include slight increase in intake valve and intake manifold deposits.

emission control system(crankcase-closed type) - System designed to control crankcase vapors by sealing crankcase from the outside with no ventilating air introduced into an engine. Crankcase and rocker arm vapors are routed into an engine by maintaining a slight vacuum on both areas. This is done by discharging the fumes into the air cleaner through the top of the rocker arm cover and/or directly into the intake manifold through a PCV valve or other controls. A sealed breather cap is used. Variations of this system are popular today.

emission control system(crankcase-modified road draft tube-1) - System designed to control crankcase vapors by routing vapors from a plugged existing road draft tube to an air cleaner via a vent tube. This method tends to enrich the air/fuel mixture, requiring carburetor adjustment for proper operation. It is a common method of changing over an old road draft tube setup.

emission control system(crankcase-modified road draft tube-2) - System designed to control crankcase vapors by routing vapors from a plugged existing road draft tube to an air cleaner via a vent tube fitted with a PCV valve. See also emission control system(crankcase-modified road draft tube-1).

emission control system(crankcase-open type) - System designed to control crankcase vapors by routing ventilating air into an engine, usually through a breather cap, down through the crankcase area, up to the rocker arm area, and then on to the intake manifold. You can tell if this type system is working by removing the breather cap and placing your hand over the opening. If you feel a slight suction, the system is probably working satisfactorily.

emission control system(crankcase-PCV) - First emission control system installed on cars (early 1960s) and designed to control crankcase vapors using a positive crankcase ventilation (PCV) valve. Unburned gases built up in a crankcase area are rerouted, via the valve, into an engine's combustion chambers for safe burning. A faulty system can cause: power loss, slow speed missing at high speed, drop in gas mileage, hard starting, rough idling, stalling, oil in air cleaner and around outside of oil filler cap, above normal water accumulation in engine oil, and rust or varnish film on dipstick. See also PCV valve, car service tip(PCV system test), and spark plug fouling(oil and carbon).

emission control system(crankcase-road draft tube) - Early system used to remove crankcase vapors before emission controls became common. Air enters through a ventilated oil filler cap and exhausts through a vertical metal tube when air is moving past its outlet. Tube inlet is mounted in lower crankcase area with outlet below the oil pan. See also road draft tube.

emission inspection - Inspection made to analyze exhaust output of a car to determine if several gas compounds fall within specified guidelines. Compounds commonly tested are carbon monoxide, hydrocarbons, and oxides of nitrogen.

emissions - Noxious gases produced in an engine during the combustion process and released to the atmosphere. The most common are unburned hydrocarbons, carbon monoxide, and oxides on Nitrogen. They are mostly produced when an engine idles, is driven at slow speed, or decelerates. A rich fuel mixture produces larger quantities of unburned hydrocarbons and carbon monoxide. A lean fuel mixture produces higher oxides of nitrogen. See also high speed gas and smog.

emissions analyzer - See exhaust gas analyzer.

Emmerson & Fisher Motor Wagon - American car produced in 1896.

Empire - American car produced from 1901-1902, 1904-1905, and 1909-1919 by Empire Mfg. Co. in Illinois (1901-1902), William Terwilliger & Co. in New York (1904-1905), Empire Motor Car Co. in Indiana (1909-1912), and Greenville Metal Products in Pennsylvania (1912-1919).

Empire State - American car produced from 1900-1901 by Empire State Automobile Co. in New York.

Empress - American car produced in 1906.

EMS - American car produced in 1908.

enamel - See paint(enamel).

enclosed running boards - Running boards located along bottom edge of car doors. They became popular in 1940.

end gases - Combustion gases formed at the end of an air/fuel mixture's combustion process. See also residual gases.

endless line painting - Custom painting technique used where a panel area is covered with a continuous line pattern weaving, intersecting, overlapping as desired. It is usually created by: using thin masking tape to create the pattern, spraying the area, and then removing the tape.

Endurance - American steam car produced from 1923-1924 by Endurance Steam Car Co. in California.

energy - Capacity for doing work.

Enger - American car produced from 1909-1917 by Enger Motor Car Co. in Ohio.

Englehardt - American car produced in 1901.

Engler - American car produced from 1914-1915 by W.B. Engler Cyclecar Co. in Ohio.

engine - Machine used to convert thermal energy into mechanical energy in order to produce rotation or motion. Most thermal engines use the principle of internal combustion to create mechanical energy.

engine(air cooled) - Engine built to be cooled with air instead of water. Engine block and cylinder head is usually finned to dissipate heat faster.

engine(atmospheric) - Engine designed to provide power from external heat. A steam engine is a typical example.

engine(canted) - Engine designed and/or installed to take less vertical space in order to reduce a car's hoodline.

engine(diesel) - Engine built to ignite diesel fuel solely by the heat of highly compressed air within its cylinders. A true diesel has no ignition system. It causes diesel fuel to ignite by injecting it into cylinders whose pistons have already compressed the air to a high enough pressure and temperature (over 800 degrees Centigrade) to ignite the fuel without a spark. Diesels differ from gasoline engines in the following way: slower acceleration, different starting characteristics, much higher compression, no spark plugs, noisier, different lubricating oil requirements, heavier duty bottom end, and better fuel economy (20-30%). Most car diesel engines are designed to have the same life expectancy as their gasoline counterparts. The reported 300-500,000 mile life expectancy of industrial diesels is based on much more rugged design, special features, good preventive maintenance, and skilled use of an engine to minimize wear.

engine(dual fuel) - Engine built to run on two different fuels such as gasoline and propane.

engine(dual overhead cam) - Overhead cam engine built using a separate cam for intake and exhaust valves.

engine(eight cylinder) - Gas or diesel engine built with eight pistons or cylinders. Cylinders can be in-line or a V-shape arrangement.

engine(F head) - Engine built with exhaust valves in the cylinder head opening downward, and intake valves in the engine block opening upward. The overhead and side valves operate off one camshaft located in the lower part of the engine block. An overhead rocker arm assembly controls the exhaust valve movement through push rods connected to the camshaft's exhaust cams. In this design, the intake and exhaust manifolds are usually mounted on opposite sides of the engine block. Valves and initial manifold passageways are built into the head and block. The F-head engine is actually a combination of the

L-head and I-head engine designs.

engine(flat) - Engine built with all cylinders arranged in two flat horizontally opposed banks. Volkswagen and other rear engine cars use this arrangement to save space.

engine(flathead) - See engine(L head).

engine(four cycle) - Engine built using four strokes of each piston to complete a power producing combustion cycle. Strokes are completed in two crankshaft revolutions. The first two, intake and compression, consist of a downward and upward piston stroke. The second two, power and exhaust, likewise consist of a downward and upward piston stroke.

engine(four stroke) - See engine(four cycle).

engine(flywheel) - Experimental engine built to store energy in a flywheel. In most designs, the flywheel receives and stores rotational energy from an engine and from decelerating. The engine may run constantly or kick in when flywheel rpm drops below a certain level.

engine(gas) - See engine(gasoline).

engine(gasoline) - Engine built to operate on gasoline fuel.

engine(hemi) - Engine built with hemispherical shaped combustion chambers.

engine(high compression) - Engine built with a high compression ratio usually over 8.5:1. Such an engine requires higher octane fuel, but also produces more power.

engine(high torque) - Engine built to generate high torque at low engine rpm. It also refers to an engine generating higher torque than other similar sized engines.

engine(horizontally opposed) - Engine built using horizontal cylinders mounted on opposite sides of a crankcase. It is designed to be flat, and fit under seats and floors. Volkswagen cars used them in the past.

engine(internal combustion) - Engine built to burn air/fuel vapors inside cylinders to develop power. The internal combustion engine works because gasoline in vapor form burns rapidly.

engine(I head) - Engine built with intake and exhaust valves in the cylinder head opening downward. An overhead rocker arm assembly controls the movement of the valves through push rods connected to a camshaft located in the lower portion of the engine block. Valves and initial manifold passageways are built into the head. This engine design was the forerunner to the overhead cam engine in common use today.

engine(in line) - Engine built with all its cylinders arranged in one straight row.

engine(laydown) - See engine(canted).

engine(leaded fuel) - Engine built to run on leaded gasoline. It usually has softer exhaust valves and valve seats than an engine designed to run on unleaded gasoline. Using unleaded gasoline will shorten the valve life. The lead acts as a lubricant. Some engines can be retrofitted with hard exhaust valves and valve seats. Top cylinder oiler and fuel additives can be used, but both increase pollution. About 10-15 percent of the car engines running today are built to run on leaded fuel.

engine(L head) - Engine built with both valves located in the engine block opening upward to one side of the cylinder. Valve movement is controlled by a camshaft located underneath the valves in the lower part of the engine block. The valve ports and initial manifold passageways are built into the block. The cylinder head is relatively thin since it contains no valves or ports, and is sometimes referred to as a flathead.

engine(liquid cooled) - See engine(water cooled).

engine(low compression) - Engine built to develop a lower compression ratio usually under 8.5:1. Such engines last longer with less stress on moving parts, run on lower octane fuel, and develop less power than high compression engines.

engine(Otto) - See engine(four stroke).

engine(overhead cam) - Engine built with the camshaft located above the cylinders. This type of engine design eliminates the need for push rods, allows good valve action at high speeds, makes the engine block stronger, allows the engine to rotate at higher rpms, and produces more horsepower then lower cam engines.

engine(overhead valve) - See engine(I head).

engine(over square) - Engine built with the cylinder bore greater in diameter than the stroke length. For example, an engine built with 3.5 inch diameter cylinder bore and 3 inch stroke length.

engine(pancake) - See engine(horizontally opposed).

engine(pre emission) - Engine built before specific exhaust emission controls were required.

engine(Rankine cycle) - External combustion engine built to drive pistons or a turbine by using the energy in expanding gases such as steam. A steam engine is an example.

engine(radial) - Engine built with cylinders arranged like spokes on a wheel. Airplanes use this type engine.

engine(RAM Z) — Experimental internal combustion engine designed by Charles Ramsey with the following features: no valves in cylinder head, 1/3 as many moving parts, and piston producing power 100% of the time.

engine(rotary) — Engine built with one or more triangular shaped rotors rotating in an elliptical shaped chamber. The rotor seals the chamber at its three apex points. With every revolution, each rotor side performs the intake, compression, power, and exhaust functions of a four cycle engine. The design eliminates the need for pistons, valves, and connecting rods. It runs smoothly, but is not as fuel efficient as a piston gas engine. Early models had spark plug and seal problems. Japan still produces a rotary engine car. See also Mazda.

engine(semi diesel) — Diesel engine built with an ignition system rather than depending only on fuel compression heat to cause ignition.

engine(side valve) — See engine(L head).

engine(six cylinder) — Gas or diesel engine built with six pistons or cylinders. The cylinders can be in-line or a V-shape arrangement.

engine(slanted) — See engine(canted).

engine(sleeve valve) — Engine built with metal sleeves positioned between pistons and cylinder walls to route gases through holes during their up and down movement. It was an early engine design.

engine(square) — Engine built with equal bore and stroke measurements. For example, an engine with a 3 inch stroke and 3 inch bore.

engine(steam) — Engine built to produce rotation by routing steam under pressure to its cylinders. Steam is generated separately by a boiler.

engine(Stirling cycle) — Engine built to produce rotation by externally heating a gas located in a sealed engine cylinder and piston assembly. Alternate heating and cooling causes piston movement. Advantages include: very quiet, long engine life, low vibration, low emissions, and use of different fuels. Disadvantages include: expensive to build, effective seal problem, and certain inflexibility in design.

engine(stratified charge) — Engine built with lean and rich fuel mixtures simultaneously supplied to each cylinder, usually through two respective intake valves.

engine(supercharged) — Engine built or modified with a supercharger.

engine(T head) — Engine built with the intake and exhaust valves located in the engine block on opposite sides of the cylinder moving upward. Valve movement is controlled by two camshafts located underneath the valves in the lower part of the engine block.

engine(tilted) — See engine(canted).

engine(transverse) — Engine block mounted perpendicular to a car's length. It is usually done to save space and is popular on small front wheel drive cars.

engine(turbine) — Engine built using a rotating a vaned wheel (fan-like device). The wheel rotates on its shaft when exposed to pressure. Pressure is created by burning an air/fuel mixture in a combustion chamber with the vaned wheel being the outlet or escape point for the pressure. A jet engine uses this same principle only it uses no vaned wheel at the exit point. Instead, it develops power or thrust by controlling the size of the exit opening. Turbine engines are still experimental in cars. Several aspects of their design, such as high temperature and rpm, need to be worked out before they can truly compete with today's gas engines.

engine(turbocharged) — Engine built or modified with a turbocharger.

engine(twin cam) — Engine built with two camshafts overhead in the cylinder head.

engine(two cycle) — Engine built using two strokes of each piston to complete its power producing combustion cycle. Strokes are completed in one crankshaft revolution. The first stroke performs intake and compression with an upward piston stroke. The second stroke generates power and exhausts gases with a downward piston stroke.

engine(two stroke) — See engine(two cycle).

engine(valve in head) — See engine(I head).

engine(V type) — Engine built with cylinders separated into two banks or lines and angled to each other in a V-shape when viewed head on.

engine(Wankel) — See engine(rotary).

engine(water cooled) — Engine built to dissipate generated heat by circulating water in passageways around the hot areas of an engine. The water, in turn, is cooled by circulating through a radiator that dissipates the heat to the atmosphere.

engine analyzer — Elaborate testing device used to monitor the operation of an engine and diagnose problems. Recent models are actually computers. Several probes are attached to an engine to get the information needed to gauge engine performance and diagnose problems. Items monitored include: high voltage output from ignition coil, and in No. 1 spark plug wire; battery voltage; current flowing through starter cable; top dead center position; engine and coolant temperatures; intake manifold vacuum and pressure; current flowing to points; and exhaust emissions.

engine assembly - Assemblage of parts used to construct an engine.
engine block - Steel casting used to form the central part of an internal combustion engine. It contains the combustion cylinders.
engine block(in line) - Block built with all combustion cylinders arranged in one vertical row. Four and six cylinder engines commonly have this configuration.
engine block(long) - Block assembled with all its bolt-on attachments except for engine accessories such as air conditioners, air pumps, alternators, carburetor, etc.
engine block(short) - Block fitted usually with new pistons, rings, and pins; camshaft bearings (where applicable); and freeze plugs. Items not included are usually: crankshaft; connecting rods; main/rod bearings; oil pump; gaskets; camshaft(s); cylinder head(s); manifolds; water pump; and engine accessories such as alternator or generator, carburetor, air pump, air conditioner.
engine block(V) - Block built with all combustion cylinders arranged in a 2 row V-shape arrangement. Most full-size and some mid-size American cars use this design in a V-8 or V-6 cylinder arrangement.
engine compartment - Enclosed area located in a car where an engine is mounted.
engine control sensor - Device used to monitor an aspect of engine operation and send an appropriate signal to an instrument for read-out and/or an on-board computer for controlling engine operation. Engine sensors are used to monitor such things as: oxygen content, barometric pressure, throttle position, coolant temperature, intake vacuum, car speed, engine rpm, air flow, air temperature, detonation, exhaust temperature, cylinder head temperature, fuel pressure, and fuel flow. See also sensor.
engine cylinder - Cylindrical tube located in an engine block where a piston slides up and down.
engine cylinder power balance test - See power balance test.
engine displacement - Combined volume of air moved by each piston in traveling from the bottom to the top of its stroke.
engine drownout - Condition created when water sprays or flows up into an engine compartment and grounds out high voltage wiring, stopping the engine.
engine efficiency - Ratio of engine power received to power generated. It is a measure of useful power. Gasoline engines lose a great deal of the power they generate. Losses occur from heat generated in the cooling and exhaust systems, and from various types of engine friction. The result is extraction of only a fraction of the power inherent in the fuel.
engine fire - See engine problem(fire).
engine fires up - Engine starts and continues to run.
engine froze up - See engine problem(seizure).
engine heater - Device used to keep an engine warm after it is stopped. It is usually used in winter time to keep an engine block from getting too cold. Popular types include dipstick heater and block heater.
engine is catching - Engine is turning over and starting to run.
engine is flooded - See engine problem(flooded).
engine is froze - See engine problem(seizure).
engine is misfiring - See engine problem(misfiring).
engine knock - See detonation.
engine louvres - Intake opening in a car body installed to allow fresh air into an engine compartment. The louvres usually consist of a series of parallel slits.
engine lubrication system - Assemblage of parts used to continuously lubricate the surfaces of an engine's moving parts with oil when it is running. Lubrication system parts include: oil pan, pickup tube screen, pickup tube, oil pump, oil filter, passageways, hoses, and pressure gauge. The majority of an engine's moving parts are pressure fed oil. Other parts receive oil by splashing, such as cylinder walls, where oil leaks out of the big end connecting rod bearing and is thrown onto the wall.
engine modification system - See emission control system(combustion-ignition/induction).
engine mount - See motor mount.
engine oil - Lubricating fluid used in an engine to coat moving parts in order to reduce friction, heat, and prolong the life of the parts. In addition to lubricating, engine oils are designed to minimize carbon and sludge formation, and resist oxidation. High quality oils resist foaming. See also oil.
engine overhaul - Process defined as restoring a worn out engine to new operating condition by: usually removing it from a car, disassembling it, replacing all worn parts with new ones and/or machining worn surfaces to new engine tolerances, reassembling it, and installing it back in a car.
engine peak - Engine rpm reached at maximum power. See also peak out.
engine power - Rate or speed work is performed. Power is generated from burning fuel in the cylinders. In general, energy in the fuel is converted

into about 1/3 usable power, 1/3 heat out the exhaust pipe, and 1/3 heat dissipated by the cooling system. Many factors determine engine power. They include: compression ratio; cylinder bore diameter; stroke length; valve size, timing, and lift; internal engine friction; condition of parts; engine rpm; number of cylinders; and fuel used.

engine problem - Condition created when an engine does not operate or perform in a satisfactory manner.

engine problem(acceleration causes cutout) - Engine runs OK at idle, but cuts out everytime it is accelerated. Cutting out is usually an ignition problem, and acts like the ignition switch is repeatedly turned on and off. Possible causes include: faulty pickup coil lead(s) break internally when pickup coil rotates due to vacuum advance unit receiving vacuum at open throttle setting, and faulty automatic choke setting when cold. See also engine problem(cuts out).

engine problem(acceleration causes hesitation) - Engine does not smoothly increase power when accelerated. Possible causes include: carburetor metering too a lean fuel mixture (most common), faulty accelerator pump circuit, low carburetor float level, faulty oxygen sensor, faulty EGR system, wrong size or type EGR valve, EGR or thermal valve improperly plumbed, fouled or worn spark plug(s), partially plugged fuel injector(s), excessively retarded or advanced ignition timing, weak ignition coil (gets worse as it gets hot), plugged or faulty intake manifold crossover passage, leaky vacuum hose, corroded wire connection, faulty warm air intake system, gas vapor canister improperly plumbed, and obstruction in exhaust system. Engines today are designed to run hot and very lean to meet emission standards. Only a minor change in settings can affect engine performance significantly. See also fuel injector deposit, engine problem(acceleration poor), and engine problem(stalling-4).

engine problem(acceleration causes pinging-1) - Engine pings when accelerated or placed under a light load. Full acceleration causes little pinging effect. It is often due to excessive vacuum spark advance. When the car is accelerated heavily, the vacuum falls close to zero retarding the timing sufficiently to minimize pinging. Possible causes include: vacuum advance is not dropping fast enough under load due to missing vacuum advance parts, faulty vacuum advance unit, faulty vacuum delay switch, faulty vacuum reducer valve, and/or faulty thermostatic vacuum switch; faulty centrifugal advance mechanism; faulty EGR system; and faulty warm air intake system causing hot air to enter carburetor. See also trapped spark and car service tip(pinging test).

engine problem(acceleration causes pinging-2) - Engine produces a rapid metallic jingling sound when: under load, driving at a constant speed, coasting to a slower speed, or accelerating hard (with pinging tapering off as speed increases or desired speed is reached). Possible causes include: high compression ratio due to engine design or wrong head gasket; excessive spark advance under load from improper vacuum and/or centrifugal settings, and faulty solid state timing controls (especially at low vacuum); low octane fuel; carbon build-up in combustion chambers; combustion chamber shape; reduced exhaust gas recirculation due to faulty EGR system; worn timing chain; camshaft running late; high engine operating temperature; high intake air temperature due to binding air gate and/or faulty air temperature sensor; lean fuel mixture; excessive oil foaming; stuck exhaust manifold heat control valve; restricted exhaust system; and faulty engine control system sensor(s). See also detonation and preignition.

engine problem(acceleration poor) - Engine increases speed slowly or when floored dies. Possible causes include: faulty distributor advance; retarded ignition timing; accelerator pump discharging little or no fuel; worn timing chain; lean fuel mixture; poor cylinder compression due to piston, piston ring, and cylinder wall wear; and poor engine and/or exhaust emission design. See also engine problem(acceleration causes hesitation).

engine problem(acceleration poor with low fuel level) - Engine accelerates poorly when gas tank gets less than 1/4 full, and seems to run OK when tank is full. Possible causes include: gas tank filter partially clogged, faulty fuel tank ventilation, and faulty charcoal canister in vapor recovery system.

engine problem(backfiring) - Fuel/air mixture ignites in an intake manifold creating explosive sounds while engine is running or attempting to get started. Possible causes include: leaky intake and/or exhaust valves, worn camshaft, improper camshaft timing, improper valve clearances, loose timing chain, sticky valves and/or lifters, missing exhaust cam lobe(s), induction firing, faulty deceleration valve, ignition cross firing, excessive backpressure, faulty PCV valve, and EGR valve stuck open. See also backfire, carburetor fire, and engine problem(carburetor fire).

engine problem(black smoke on startup-1) - Engine starts hard and belches black smoke on startup. It may require flooring gas pedal to start engine. It is usually due to an over rich fuel mixture. Possible causes include:

heat soak, fuel foaming, faulty vapor recovery system, fuel injector(s) leaking usually due to bad seals, carburetor float level high, excessive fuel pressure, carburetor needle valve damaged or leaking, ignition timing retarded, faulty accelerator pump circuit causing fuel to continuously flow into carburetor airway, dirt in the fuel delivery system, and low boiling point gas. See also oxygen sensor and air/fuel ratio.

engine problem(black smoke on startup-2) – Diesel engine starts, then tends to stall and belches lots of black smoke especially during cold weather. Possible causes include: rich fuel mixture, ignition timing retarded, faulty or too cool glow plugs, starter motor speed low, poor quality diesel fuel, and fuel gelling problems.

engine problem(burns oil) – Engine consumes excessive quantity of oil. Possible causes include: worn crankshaft, camshaft, and/or connecting rod bearings; worn and/or stuck piston rings; worn pistons and cylinder walls; worn valve guides; oil viscosity too low; and engine running too hot. See also oil consumption.

engine problem(carburetor fire) – Fire caused when an engine backfires through a carburetor and conditions are right. It usually occurs when a driver tries to start an engine. It can be put out, not by beating the flames, but by turning the engine off, pulling the ignition coil plug wire, and continuously spinning the engine with the starter while keeping your foot off the gas pedal. The vacuum created by the engine and the lack of fuel will extinguish the flame. See also backfire, engine problem(backfiring), induction firing, engine problem(fire), and car's on fire.

engine problem(carburetor flooding) – Carburetor meters too much fuel into an engine causing it to stall out. Possible causes include: float level too high, leaking carburetor gaskets, excessive fuel pressure, choke plate stuck, and a crack in the carburetor body. See also engine problem(flooded).

engine problem(carburetor icing) – Ice formed on a carburetor throttle plate. It most commonly occurs when: humidity is high (60-100%) temperature is near freezing (but can be up to 55 degrees), and an engine has just been started (rich fuel mixture) and is warming up. The ice forms because the atomized fuel: enters the air stream above the throttle plate, undergoes some evaporation absorbing heat from the air, lowers nearby metal parts temperatures, and condenses moisture in air onto cold surfaces where it freezes. The ice builds up on the closed portion of the throttle plate and can quickly cover the upper idle discharge port. If it ices up, the engine will stall out when the engine is idled. It can readily be restarted but will stall when idle speed is again reached. Most of today's carburetors minimize this condition by keeping the base area of the carburetor warm with coolant water or exhaust gases, and by controlling air intake temperature.

engine problem(carburetor squealing) – Carburetor emits a squealing sound when accelerated at moving speeds. The squealing-whistling sound is likely coming from some type of air leak into the intake portion of the engine. Possible causes include: cracked or leaking carburetor base gasket, loose carburetor hold-down bolts, improper base gasket, faulty EGR valve, cracked or burned EGR gasket, faulty air cleaner gasket, and ruptured intake manifold hose.

engine problem(carburetor throttle sticks) – Throttle shaft intermittently binds up when engine is running. Possible causes include: broken return springs, cable linkage kinked, throttle plate shaft binding, obstruction near linkage causing binding, and linkage parts binding.

engine problem(carburetor throttle sticks when cold) – Throttle shaft binds when engine is cold. It is usually due to gum and other deposits. Source of deposits include: cheap gasoline; gasoline with maximum alcohol content allowed; and excessive blowby gases routed to carburetor due to worn piston rings, cylinder walls, and/or valve guides.

engine problem(check engine light on) – See warning light(check engine).

engine problem(cranks but hard to start-1) – Engine turns over fast enough and intermittently fires the fuel mixture, but not enough to keep engine running. Possible causes include: lean fuel mixture due to low float level, idle circuit out of adjustment, vapor locking, heat soak, choke not operating, faulty fuel pump, low fuel pressure, fuel tank almost empty, and/or plugged fuel filter; fouling spark plugs; weak or non-existent spark due to grounding spark plug cables, faulty ignition coil, primary leads reversed on ignition coil, and/or low voltage in primary circuit during start mode; restricted air intake; faulty spark delay valve; faulty vacuum reducer valve; faulty thermostatic vacuum switch; large vacuum leak; faulty PCV system; EGR valve open at zero vacuum; faulty vapor recovery system; and arcing in distributor cap. See also car service tip(starting test) and car service tip(cranking vacuum test).

engine problem(cranks but hard to start-2) – Diesel engine turns over fast enough, but is hard to start after sitting awhile. When it does start, a great deal of black smoke is usually emitted. Possible causes include: faulty glow plug(s), faulty injector(s), and/or pump.

engine problem(cranks but hard to start-3) – Engine turns over fast enough, but doesn't catch until it has been cranked for 20-30 seconds. It is usually due to a carburetor whose float bowl is empty requiring cranking to fill it before the engine will fire. Possible causes include: internal leak in carburetor due to crack, casting defect in float bowl, and/or leaking bowl plugs, heat soak, and low fuel pressure during cranking.

engine problem(cranks but hard to start-4) - Engine turns over fast enough, but won't catch until gas pedal has been floored for a while. Possible causes include: engine flooded; rich fuel mixture due to choke stuck closed, high float level, and/or internal carburetor leak.

engine problem(cranks but won't start-1) - Cold engine turns over fast enough but won't run. The problem is not in the starting system, but is usually due to lack of fuel or no spark. An engine, firing spark plugs and receiving fuel and air, has to run unless there are major problems.

Lack of fuel problems can include: broken or leaking fuel lines, defective fuel pump, plugged carburetor jets, stuck needle valve, empty fuel tank, clogged fuel pickup filter, low float level, and choke not operating.

Spark problems can include: grounded or loose coil wire; fouled spark plugs; defective ignition coil; no current to ignition coil's primary windings; defective condenser; distributor points grounded, not separating (due to rubbing block wear or loose point adjustment screws), or remaining open; carbon tracking on ignition coil and/or distributor spark plug towers; electronic ignition magnetic pickup coil tooth broken due to reluctor contact; distributor cap loose or ajar; excessive current draw when starter engaged, and faulty black box.

Air problems can include: restricted air intake.

Other problems can include: camshaft and timing chain or belt reassembled wrong, and loose timing chain or belt that has jumped teeth on camshaft and/or crankshaft sprockets. Improper valve timing can cause low engine compression that can be detected by a cranking-vacuum test, and when a battery can turn an engine over for quite a while without running down. See also starting problem, car service tip(distributor cap loose), sound(popping), and car service tip(cranking vacuum test).

engine problem(cranks but won't start-2) - Hot engine turns over fast enough but won't run. It often occurs when a hot engine has been shutoff for 5-15 minutes. Fuel and/or ignition system troubles are usually to blame. An engine firing spark plugs, and receiving fuel and air has to run unless there are major problems.

Fuel problems can include: engine flooded due to heat soak, internal carburetor leak into intake manifold, and high float level; and lean fuel mixture due to broken or leaking fuel lines, defective fuel pump, plugged carburetor jets, stuck needle valve, empty fuel tank, clogged fuel pickup filter, vapor lock, EGR valve stuck open, and choke not operating.

Spark problems can include: grounded or loose coil wire; fouled spark plugs; high resistance in ignition coil or condenser due to heat; coil ballast resistor sensitive to heat; no current to ignition coil's primary windings; distributor points grounded, not separating (due to rubbing block wear or loose point adjustment screws), or remaining open; distributor cap loose or ajar; electronic ignition magnetic pickup coil tooth broken due to reluctor contact; excessive current draw when starter engaged causing low primary coil voltage; and faulty black box.

Air problems can include: restricted air intake. See also starting problem, car service tip(distributor cap loose), sound(popping), and car service tip(cranking vacuum test).

engine problem(cuts out-1) - Engine acts like ignition key has been switched off. It may occur after running a long time, driving up a long hill, accelerating hard, etc. Possible causes include: distributor sensitive to heat; faulty Hall switch, vapor locking, faulty fuel pump, ruptured fuel line, ignition module with poor connection, and wiring that is oxidized, damaged or has loose connections. See also engine problem(acceleration causes cutout).

engine problem(cuts out-2) - Engine acts like ignition key is repeatedly turned on and off. It usually occurs when placing an engine under a heavy load for awhile, and disappears shortly after the load is removed. Possible causes include: fuel mixture becomes lean due to emission and carburetion controls; fuel boiling and vapor locking in carburetor, fuel lines, and/or fuel pump; faulty fuel pump, clogged fuel pickup filter, clogged fuel filter; faulty venting of fuel tank; faulty engine controls sensitive to temperature; and excessive backpressure.

engine problem(dieseling) - Engine continues to run slowly after the ignition switch has been turned off. It is usually due to fuel continuing to reach, ignite, and burn in the engine cylinders without spark, hence the term dieseling. Possible causes include: idle speed too high, electrical leakage from car instruments, throttle plate not closing, combustion chamber carbon build-up, faulty fuel-cut solenoid, rich fuel mixture at idle, faulty idle stop solenoid, faulty spark delay valve, faulty thermostatic vacuum switch, and faulty vacuum reducer valve. See also dieseling and car service tip(dieseling test).

engine problem(fire) - Fire breaks out in an engine compartment. It is usually caused by leaking fuel. In the event of a fire stop the car quickly, get everyone out of the car, turn off the ignition, open the hood protecting your hands and body from flames, discharge a fire extinguisher near the base of the flames with repeated short bursts or smother the flames with a blanket. See also engine problem(carburetor fire), engine problem(backfiring), backfire, and induction firing.

engine problem(flooded) - Excessive amount of fuel reaches the cylinders, soaks the spark plugs with gasoline, and makes starting difficult or impossible. It is usually caused by a carburetor creating an overly rich air/fuel mixture. The remedy is to let the engine sit for a few minutes letting combustion chamber heat dry things out. The engine is then restarted with the throttle wide open and the choke held open, if necessary. This greatly increases the amount of air reaching the cylinders which further helps to dry the spark plugs. In some cases, a faulty ignition system will cause plugs to get soaked before they begin firing. Check for spark by grounding one or more plug wires as the engine is turned over. A blue spark indicates normal operation. See also engine problem(carburetor flooding).

engine problem(flywheel breakup) - Flywheel becomes damaged causing problems such as vibration, poor shifting, and bearing and seal failures. Possible causes include: flywheel not round, flywheel warped, flywheel out of alignment with respect to crankshaft and/or transmission input shaft, installation incorrect, transmission case warped, and defective torque converter.

engine problem(fuel economy poor) - Engine consumes excessive quantities of fuel for its size. Possible causes include: car underpowered yielding a low horsepower to weight ratio; poor engine design; carrying a heavy load; high rolling resistance due to low tire pressure, or muddy, slushy, or snowy road; dragging brakes; high internal engine friction due to galled surfaces, low oil level, and/or improper oil; oil too thick; leaks in gas tank, fuel lines, fuel filter, fuel pump, and/or carburetor; low cylinder compression due to worn piston/piston rings and cylinder wall, leaking valves, and/or worn cam; driving in lower gears, hilly terrain, stiff headwind, or on road with high rolling resistance; inefficient carburetor design; carburetor metering too much fuel due to faulty choke, high float level, improper adjustments, wrong size metering parts, dirty air filter, and/or faulty rebuild; retarded engine timing; need for a tune-up; poor intake manifold heating due to stuck or plugged heat riser valve; restriction in exhaust system; coolant temperature remains too low due to missing, stuck open, or low temperature thermostat; choke may stay partly on due improper adjustment, sticking, low coolant temperature, and/or faulty coolant sensor; faulty spark delay valve; faulty vacuum reducer valve; fouled spark plug(s); faulty choke vacuum break; faulty thermostatic vacuum switch; and faulty warm intake air system directing too much cool air to carburetor. See also gas mileage, gas saving tip, fuel economy, coolant sensor, and engine problem(black smoke after startup).

engine problem(gas smell when stopped) - Engine emits a strong gasoline smell when car comes to a stop. Possible causes include: fuel overheating in carburetor and fuel line area due to high engine compartment temperatures; fuel line leaking; small fuel leak in carburetor area (emits strong odor due to heat and lack of confinement); faulty exhaust manifold heat riser; and faulty vapor recovery system due to leaking charcoal canister, plugged return line, and/or broken return line.

engine problem(generator light on) - See warning light(generator).

engine problem(high rpm during shifting) - Engine races momentarily when an automatic transmission equipped car shifts gears. It is usually due to rings or bands being out of adjustment.

engine problem(idles poorly) - See engine problem(runs rough at idle).

engine problem(knocking) - Engine emits knocking sound under different driving conditions. See also sound(knocking).

engine problem(misfiring-1) - Spark plugs are not consistently firing at idle, low rpm, and/or when accelerating. Possible causes include: distributor points out of adjustment; fouling or worn spark plugs; defective, dirty, and/or wet interior distributor cap; spark plug wires grounding, crossed, or defective; spark plug cable boots split or oil soaked; corroded terminals on spark plug wire or spark plug terminal; induction firing; low voltage to ignition coil due to bad resistor; air leak into intake manifold; poor cylinder compression; water in the gas; faulty PCV system; and defective ECM causing low dwell and resultant weak spark. See also engine problem(misfiring-2) and engine problem(cuts out-2).

engine problem(misfiring-2) - Spark plugs are not consistently firing at higher engine rpm. Possible causes include: reversed ignition coil polarity, distributor point float, spark plug gap too wide, voltage to ignition coil marginal, spark plug cable resistance marginally excessive, faulty resistor spark plug(s), and partially fouled spark plug(s).

engine problem(oil consumption excessive) - Engine consumes an excessive quantity of oil when running. Possible causes include: worn pistons, piston rings, and cylinder walls; stuck piston rings due to residue build-up from wear, and/or too high or too low crankcase ventilation pressure; faulty PCV valve; wrong type oil; engine running too hot; and low oil level. See also oil consumption.

engine problem(oil pressure light flickers) - Engine reaches operating temperature and the oil pressure light flickers on and off at idle. It usually due to low oil pressure. Possible causes include: low oil level, faulty oil pressure sensor, crankshaft and camshaft bearing(s) worn and/or damaged (cannot maintain oil pressure due to excessive clearance), worn oil pump, plugged oil filter, wrong viscosity oil, plugged oil gallery, and oil gallery leak. If the light stays on even after an oil change, odds are wear damage has been done to the crankshaft and camshaft bearings. Such bearings get damaged when they don't receive adequate oil, the oil becomes severely contaminated and abrasive, emission control system fails, or when the engine overheats causing the oil to get too hot and lose its lubricating ability. See also engine problem(overheating) and oil pressure.

engine problem(overheating) - Engine temperature rises above normal operating temperature. Slight overheating can be caused by something as simple as driving a loaded car up a long grade in the summer with the air conditioning on. Severe overheating is probably due to a more serious problem. Possible causes include: reduced coolant flow due to stuck thermostat, clogged radiator passageways, clogged water jacket passageways, restriction in water pump, and/or collapsed lower radiator hose (due to deformed, missing, or improperly positioned internal reinforcement spring); radiator fins clogged with bugs and debris, or covered with a cold weather shield; fan shroud missing or damaged; low coolant level due to leaking head gasket, hoses, radiator, cylinder head crack, cylinder wall crack, water pump engine block crack, and radiator cap; coolant is pure antifreeze (less efficient in removing heat); inoperative fan due to broken belt, electrical malfunction, faulty radiator-fan thermostat, or clutching malfunction (depending on fan design); fan belt slipping due to cracks, splits, glazing, and/or oil soaking; fan shroud missing or improperly installed; oil level low; oil type wrong; brakes dragging; lean fuel mixture; compression leakage into coolant due to faulty head gasket, and /or engine block cracks; camshaft or timing chain worn; ignition timing too advanced due to setting and/or wrong electronic ignition module firing spark plugs too early or fast; and ignition timing too retarded. See also car service tip(cooling system pressure test) and car service tip(compression leakage into coolant test).

engine problem(power gradually lost) - Engine gradually loses power with lower and lower cruising speeds possible. At maximum speed attainable, engine acts like it's starved for fuel. Possible causes include: catalytic converter becoming progressively clogged. See also car service tip(clogged catalytic converter), and engine problem(speed unattainable).

engine problem(power lacking-1) - Engine power drops below normal right away or after warm up. Possible right away causes include: out of tune, insufficient spark advance at higher speed due to retarded timing, distributor advance springs too strong, and/or stuck distributor base plate; restricted throttle opening; restricted fuel and/or air flow; wrong electronic ignition module firing spark plugs too slowly; and low cylinder compression (engine worn out). Possible causes after warm-up include: lean or rich fuel metering; partially plugged fuel injector(s); excessive exhaust gas recirculation due to faulty EGR valve; faulty warm air intake system; restricted throttle opening; restricted fuel flow; faulty electronic spark control; low coolant temperature due to faulty thermostat and/or coolant sensor; wiring problem; gas vapor canister improperly plumbed; leaky vacuum hose; faulty PCV system; and partially clogged, poorly designed, or wrong type catalytic converter. See also fuel injector deposit and car service tip(vacuum advance test).

engine problem(power lacking-2) - Engine loses power after accelerating at highway speeds. Possible causes include: clogged fuel pickup filter, fuel tank under vacuum restricting fuel flow, ignition system sensitive to heat, fuel line near hot engine parts creating vapor locking when engine temperature builds, faulty needle float valve causing low float level, low fuel pressure, intake air restriction, faulty air preheat system causing hot air to continue to flow into carburetor, and excessive backpressure.

engine problem(runs cold) - Engine heats up to operating temperature slowly if at all. Possible causes include: thermostat missing or stuck open, and low temperature thermostat.

engine problem(runs fast at idle-1) - Warm engine idles too fast. Possible causes include: idle set too high, stuck fast idle cam, choke not fully opening, and improperly set idle stop solenoid.

engine problem(runs fast at idle-2) - Cold engine idles too fast. Possible causes include: improper choke setting, fast idle set too high, and leaking PCV system hose.

engine problem(runs on) - See engine problem(dieseling).

engine problem(runs rough-1) - Engine intermittently cuts out and backfires, then runs OK for awhile. Possible causes include: exhaust valve(s) remaining partially open during ignition due to burned valve seats and/or head, broken or weak valve spring(s), worn cam lobe(s), improper valve clearance adjustment, and/or improper valve timing; faulty spark plug wiring; cracked distributor cap; faulty ignition system causing spark to reach plugs at wrong times; spark plug(s) fouling; and induction firing.

engine problem(runs rough-2) - Engine cuts out, stumbles, and bucks when driven at a constant throttle setting. Possible causes include: excess fuel dumping into carburetor airway due to high float level, faulty needle float valve, excessive fuel pressure, and/or faulty accelerator pump circuit; faulty EGR valve; vapor locking; charcoal canister plumbed in backwards; ignition timing too advanced; water in the gas; exhaust system restriction; crossed spark plug wires; spark plugs fouling; and arcing in distributor cap. See also engine problem(stumbling), engine problem(acceleration causes cutout), and engine problem(cuts out-2).

engine problem(runs rough-3) - Engine cuts out, and jerks when it is decelerating. Possible causes include: ignition timing too advanced, faulty EGR valve causing excessive recirculation of exhaust gases, and improper air/fuel mixture.

engine problem(runs rough-4) - Engine jerks and misses when under full throttle. Possible causes include: restricted fuel flow due to vacuum in fuel tank, clogged fuel pickup filter, partially plugged fuel lines, vapor locking, faulty fuel pump, and/or faulty high speed circuit in carburetor; excessive advance; faulty EGR valve; and spark plugs fouling.

engine problem(runs rough at idle-1) - Engine idles poorly and may have noticeable car vibration. Possible causes include: faulty ignition timing due to excessive advance, loose distributor, loose timing belt or chain, worn distributor shaft bushing, distributor cap arcing, missing centrifugal advance springs, and/or loose breaker plate; rich or lean fuel mixture due to idle circuit improperly adjusted or dirty, faulty fuel-cut solenoid, faulty accelerator pump circuit continuously routing fuel to carburetor airway, float level too high (defective float, improper adjustment, and/or stuck needle valve), choke stuck closed, and fuel puddling; excess carbon and/or gum build-up in carburetor airway, intake manifold, and upper cylinders (more common on high mileage engines); faulty idle air control valve; faulty deceleration valve; faulty spark delay valve; faulty vacuum reducer valve; faulty vapor recovery system; faulty thermostatic vacuum switch; faulty PCV system; intermittent or no spark due to grounding plug wires, fouled plug(s), and/or misaligned rotor; water in the gas; idle set too high causing EGR valve to open prematurely; external vacuum leak(s); and internal vacuum leak(s) in carburetor (usually due to gasket leak).

engine problem(runs rough at idle-2) - Engine intermittently idles poorly. Possible causes include: fuel boiling due to low boiling point or high carburetor temperatures, vapor locking, faulty float bowl needle valve, water in the gas, and use of gasohol. See also heat soak and car service tip(boiling fuel test).

engine problem(runs rough at idle-3) - Engine idles and runs poorly when cold. Possible causes include: intake manifold not heating up properly due to faulty exhaust manifold heat control valve, improperly connected coolant hoses, faulty temperature sensor, and clogged hot air or water passageways; choke plate opening too fast; faulty air cleaner preheat system; retarded ignition timing; faulty EGR valve; vacuum leak; faulty accelerator pump circuit; wrong spark plug gap; and spark plug(s) fouling.

engine problem(runs rough at idle-4) - Diesel engine idles poorly at idle, but runs smoothly at higher rpm. Possible causes include: faulty injector pump due to internal air leak, faulty metering, and/or incorrect timing.

engine problem(runs rough at idle-5) - Engine idles poorly whenever it rains. Possible causes include: wiring getting wet and grounding.

engine problem(runs rough at idle-6) - Engine idles poorly after a long trip. Possible causes include: dirt or water in carburetor, and gum and varnish build-up in carburetor airway.

engine problem(runs rough at idle-7) - Engine suddenly begins to idle poorly. Possible causes include: spark plug wire loose, and spark plug(s) fouling.

engine problem(seizure) - Lubricated moving engine parts stop moving and get stuck due to high friction. Possible causes include: lack of lubrication, engine overheating, hot spots, wrong type oil, and ethylene glycol leaking from coolant into oil. See also freeze up.

engine problem(smoky exhaust) - See exhaust(blue smoke).

engine problem(speed unattainable) - Engine cannot maintain highway speeds when pulling loads or traveling in hilly terrain. Engine speed will drop to a lower speed than desired with possible stalling and subsequent hard

starting problems. This is usually a fuel foaming or vapor lock problem.
Conditions contributing to the problem include: driving at high altitude
(gasoline boils at a lower temperature), in hot weather, pulling a heavy
load, and/or using lots of engine accessories during heavy engine load; using
low boiling point gas such as winter gas in summertime; poor carburetor, fuel
pump, and fuel line layout causing overheating of fuel before it reaches
carburetor; engine underpowered for car size; and engine badly out of tune or
worn. See also engine problem(power gradually lost), engine
problem(stalling-1), fuel foaming, vapor lock, gasoline(summer), and
gasoline(winter).

engine problem(stalling-1) - Warm engine tends to stop running after it is
started, while driving, slowing down, or when stopped. An important fact to
remember here is: if an engine is getting spark, fuel, and air, it has to
start and run provided the engine's moving parts are operating properly and
not damaged. Possible causes include: idling too low; clutch released with
rpm too low; carburetor not metering enough fuel due to improper adjustments,
clogged carburetor passageways, loose or broken accelerator or main jet
metering rods, faulty fuel pump, restriction in fuel line, dirty fuel filter,
dirty tank filter, faulty float bowl needle valve, faulty fuel-cut solenoid,
vacuum formed in fuel tank (opening cap will create a whooshing sound due to
inrushing air), and/or vapor locking; fuel foaming; water in the gas; choke
stuck closed flooding out engine due to binding shaft or faulty vacuum
breaker diaphragm; engine badly out of tune; faulty choke vacuum break;
defective ignition coil and/or module when hot; engine controls such as
emissions, ECM, and/or carburetion out of adjustment in relation to each
other; loose or dirty ignition coil connections; faulty low voltage current
flow to distributor; carburetor icing up; vacuum leak(s); faulty EGR system;
faulty warm air intake system; poorly designed or wrong type catalytic
converter; and air intake restriction. See also engine problem(speed
unattainable) and heat soak.

engine problem(stalling-2) - Cold engine tends to stop running after it is
started. Possible causes include: fast idle set too low; choke not fully
closed; carburetor not metering enough fuel due to improper idle circuit
adjustments, faulty fuel pump, restriction in fuel line, dirty fuel filter,
dirty tank filter, faulty float bowl needle valve, vacuum in fuel tank
(opening cap will create a whooshing sound due to inrushing air), and/or
faulty fuel-cut solenoid; carburetor icing up; engine badly out of tune;
ignition problems due to faulty low voltage current flow to distributor,
faulty ignition coil, loose ignition coil connections, faulty coil ballast
resistor, faulty pickup coil lead(s) breaks internally when pickup coil
rotates due to vacuum advance unit receiving full vacuum at closed throttle
setting, fouled spark plugs, and/or grounded or faulty spark plug leads;
vacuum leak(s); and improper valve timing.

engine problem(stalling-3) - Cold engine starts, then stalls when accelerated.
Possible causes include: fuel mixture too lean due to improper idle speed
adjustment, faulty accelerator pump circuit, faulty choke, poor intake
manifold and carburetor base warming, and faulty EGR and/or thermal valves.

engine problem(stalling-4) - Warm engine starts, but hesitates or tends to
stall when accelerated. Possible causes include: fuel mixture too lean due
to improper idle speed adjustment, faulty accelerator pump circuit, intake
manifold not warming up due to faulty preheat system; and/or faulty air
silencer and/or reed valve in pulse-air emission control system.

engine problem(stalling-5) - Engine starts, runs momentarily, then tends to
idle poorly or stop. Possible causes include: excessive backpressure due to
exhaust system restriction, faulty fuel pump (works only in start mode or
pump cannot maintain pressure or flow rate), restriction and/or air in fuel
line, dirt in fuel delivery system, faulty float bowl needle valve, faulty
pickup coil lead(s) (on vacuum advance units receiving full vacuum at idle),
and improper valve timing. See also engine problem(black smoke on startup-
1).

engine problem(stalling-6) - Engine tends to stop when a load such as an air
conditioner is placed on engine. Possible causes include: idle set too low,
and faulty speed-up solenoid.

engine problem(stalling-7) - Warm engine left shutoff for 5-10 minutes starts
and stalls or won't fire at all unless allowed to cool down. Possible causes
include: ignition timing off; fuel delivery problems due to vapor lock, fuel
foaming, heat soak, leaking injectors, and/or leaking fuel pump check valve;
vacuum leaks in vacuum lines, and/or intake manifold gaskets; and EGR valve
open. See also engine problem(stalling-1).

engine problem(stalling-8) - Cold engine starts OK and runs OK when hot, but
tends to stumble or stall when partly warmed up. Possible causes include:
excess fuel entering intake manifold due to fuel foaming, high fuel pressure
and/or temperature in fuel line flooding float bowl, choke resetting, choke
unloading late, and/or leak in carburetor body.

engine problem(stops running) - See engine problem(cranks but won't start).

engine problem(stumbling) – Engine does not run smoothly and idles rough as though something is not being metered evenly. Possible causes include: EGR valve stuck open, accelerator pump circuit dumping a continuous stream of fuel into carburetor airway, vapor lock, fuel foaming, faulty fuel pump, fuel puddling, faulty warm air intake system, faulty or improperly sized PCV valve, intake manifold not warming up, faulty manifold pressure sensor, faulty barometric pressure sensor, heat sensitive ignition coil, and insufficient voltage to primary side of ignition coil. See also car service tip(EGR valve check).

engine problem(vibration) – Engine causes car body vibrations when running. Possible causes include: wrong size connecting rod and/or main bearings installed, unbalanced harmonic balancer, worn or broken motor mounts, unbalanced water pump, and misfiring.

engine problem(won't start) – Engine will not turn over when ignition switch is in start position. Possible causes include: dead or weak battery; break in starting circuit wiring; corroded terminal(s) on battery, and/or starter relay; faulty starter solenoid or starter relay; faulty ignition switch; melted fusible link in starting circuit; blown fuse(s); field or armature windings grounded in starter; faulty black box; and faulty neutral safety switch on automatic transmission equipped cars. See also car service tip(electrical connections) and car service tip(starting system test).

engine seized up – See engine problem(seizure).

engine shroud – Sheetmetal panels used to conceal engine compartment. Panels include: firewall, inner wheel panels, and hood.

engine sluggish – See engine problem(sluggish).

engine stalling – See engine problem(stalling).

engine stand – Device used for holding an entire engine off the ground in an upright position so it can easily be worked on. Engine is usually attached to the stand by using the flywheel bolt holes.

engine swapping – To remove a standard engine from a car and replace it with an engine from a different make car. The installed engine is usually more powerful and not as old.

engine thermostat – See thermostat.

engine torque – Torque produced by crankshaft rotation. One goal in engine design is keeping engine torque high throughout the engine speed range. Factors contributing include: large manifolds, large or multiple valves per cylinder, volumetric efficiency, compression ratio, large carburetors, and minimizing exhaust backpressure. See also torque.

engine torque strut – Small bar attached to the lower portion of an engine's block and to the car's frame. It is commonly used in front wheel drive cars where it is attached to the car frame just below the radiator. It is usually shaped like a large dog bone. See also sound(clunking-4).

engine tune-up – See tune-up.

engine varnish – See varnish deposit.

engine wear – Amount of change measured in an engine's metal surfaces subjected to wear. Wear is caused by several factors including: type of lubricant, abrasive material in lubricant, degree of lubrication, engine temperature, fuel used, abrasive material in fuel, the amount of water that condenses in the cylinder, the way the engine is run, the pressure of the piston rings against the cylinder walls, the composition of the various metal parts, and length of time engine is not used before starting.

engine won't start – See starting problem.

Enkel Truck – American truck produced in 1915.

entry exit ease – Determination made of how easy it is to enter or leave a car's interior. It is a common test element in a new car evaluation.

Entz – American car produced in 1914.

EP – Abbreviation for extreme pressure. See also grease(extreme pressure).

EPA – Abbreviation for the Environmental Protection Agency.

EPA fuel mileage – Fuel mileage tests performed by the Environmental Protection Agency to determine fuel economy of news cars in simulated city and highway driving.

EPA numbers – Fuel economy figures computed by the EPA as a by-product of testing a car's emission level. A city and highway figure is usually determined. They are estimates, and may not accurately express fuel economy. They are considered accurate if used to compare one car against another. The test is performed on a dynamometer, and is designed to simulate warm dry weather and a level road. Test cars are supplied by the manufacturers and are often stripped down to their minimum weight. The test has consisted of: driving for 23 minutes a distance of 7.5 miles at speeds from 0-56 mph and averaging 20 mph, and making 18 stops to simulate traffic lights in rush hour traffic. The time period is further divided into a cold-start and hot start segment to determine cold engine and a warm engine emissions. City and highway mileage figures have been more conservative since 1985 due to applying a respective 0.9 and 0.78 factor.

epicyclic gears – See gear(planetary).

epoxy resin - Material derived from polymerization of certain solid epoxy chemicals. It is used: as an adhesive, coating, and an insulative material; and in flux compounds and castings.

Epperson - American car produced in 1912.

EPR valve - Evaporator pressure regulator valve.

equalizer - Device used to transfer weight away from the hitch area of a trailer, and toward the front of a towing vehicle and the rear of a trailer.

Equa-lok - Tradename of a limited slip differential.

equipe - Race team.

equipment bay - Work area built large enough to hold a car or truck for servicing. The bay is often set up for doing specific work such as front end alignment, tune-ups, dropping transmissions, checking/adjusting car fluids, etc. Specialized equipment bays in large service areas are often manned by mechanics trained only for that work such as tune-ups.

equipment manufacturer's specification - Specification issued by an equipment manufacturers regarding the use of certain oils, fluids, etc. in their products.

equipment manufacturer's specification(DEXRON II) - Automatic transmission fluid specified for use in 1975 and later GM cars. It is suitable for use where Type A or DEXRON is specified.

equipment manufacturer's specification(Type F Fluid) - Automatic transmission fluid specified for use in 1980 and earlier Ford automatic transmissions and 1980 on Ford transaxles and power steering systems. It is also specified for use in Borg Warner automatics and certain industrial and agricultural hydraulic systems.

equipment violation - Traffic citation issued for non-operating or illegal equipment.

equity - The value of a used car after subtracting any remaining car debts from the actual wholesale value. See also negative equity.

Erbes - American car produced from 1915-1916.

Erie - American car produced from 1916-1919 by Erie Motor Co. in Ohio.

Erie & Sturgis - American car produced in 1897.

Ernst - American car produced in 1896.

Erskine - American car produced from 1926-1930 by Studebaker Corp. in Indiana.

Erving - American car produced from 1911-1913.

ES - Abbreviation for El Salvador found usually on an international license plate.

ESC - Abbreviation for electronic spark control.

Escort - American car produced from 1980 to date by Ford Motor Co. in Michigan.

escutcheon - Plate used to retain or cover another part. It is used to cover such items as: keyhole, door handle, and switch.

Eshelman Sportabout - American car produced from 1953-1958 and 1960 by the Eshelman Co. in Maryland.

Ess Eff - American car produced in 1912.

esses - Section of a race track built with a series of slight left and right turns.

Essex - American steam car produced in 1906. Also, an American car produced from 1918-1932 by Hudson Motor Car Co. in Michigan. The Essex, by Hudson, was the first cheap sedan car produced in the United States in 1922 that was suitable for passenger travel in all kinds of weather.

Essex Steam Car - American steam car produced in 1901.

EST(1) - Abbreviation for electronic spark timing.

EST(2) - Abbreviation for Eastern Standard Time.

EST module - See electronic spark timing module.

Estate - American car produced from 1980 to date by Buick Division of General Motors Corp. in Michigan.

estate wagon - Station wagon.

estimate - List prepared of estimated parts and labor cost required to do a specific repair to a car.

ET(1) - Abbreviation for elapsed time.

ET(2) - Abbreviation for Egypt found usually on an international license plate.

ETH - Abbreviation for Ethiopia found usually on an international license plate.

ethane - Gaseous methane series hydrocarbon compound derived from natural gas or produced in the process of refining pet products. It has a melting and boiling point of -298 and -127 degrees Fahrenheit respectively.

ethical standards - Rules for the proper conduct of a business, profession, individual, etc.

ethanol - Alcohol made primarily from corn or wheat. See also methanol, alcohol, and gasohol.

ethics - Body of moral beliefs used to govern or distinguish a particular group or culture.

ethylene glycol - Chemical solution added to cooling system water to lower its

freezing point for cold weather operation. It also increases temperature at
which coolant will vaporize when hot. In pure form, it freezes at -92
degrees Fahrenheit. If it leaks into an engine crankcase, it can plug up oil
lines and cause pistons to seize.

ethyl gasoline - See gasoline(ethyl) and gasoline(leaded).

Etnyre - American car produced from 1910-1911 by Etnyre Motor Car Co. in
Illinois.

Euclid - American car produced in 1904, 1907-1908, and 1914.

Eugol - American car produced in 1921.

Eureka - American car produced from 1907-1914 by Eureka Motor Buggy Co. in
Missouri (1907-1914), Eureka Motor Buggy Co. in Pennsylvania (1908-1909), and
Eureka Co. in Illinois (1909). Also, an American car produced in 1897.

European feel - Car handling characteristic typified by straight car tracking
and stiffer steering. It is usually accomplished by using a larger wheel
caster angle.

European lighting - Car equipped with separate lights for braking, backing up,
and signaling turns.

Evans - American car produced in 1904, 1912, and 1914.

Evansville - American car produced in 1907-1909 by Evansville Automobile Co.
in Indiana.

evacuating the system - See air conditioner(evacuating the system).

evaporation - Process defined as a substance changing from a liquid to a
vapor. It is the opposite of condensation.

evaporation control - Pollution control system built to use a vapor separator
to collect fumes from a fuel tank and a charcoal canister to store them for
burning in the engine.

evaporative emission control system - See vapor recovery system.

evaporator - Radiator-like device used in an air conditioning system to cool
air passing over its coils. Liquid refrigerant is changed into a cool vapor
coming from an expansion valve into the low pressure evaporator area. The
vapor cools the evaporator's coils which absorb heat from the air passing
over them. Vapor exits the evaporator flowing to the suction side of the
compressor. It is usually located behind the heater core or near it.

evaporator core - See evaporator.

Everitt - American car produced from 1909-1912 by Metzger Motor Car Co. in
Michigan.

Everybody's - American car produced from 1907-1909 by Everbody's Motor Car
Mfg. Co. in Illinois.

Ewing - American car produced from 1908-1910.

exc - Abbreviation for excellent.

Excalibur J - American car produced from 1952-1953 by Beassie Engineering Co.
in Wisconsin.

Excalibur SS - American car produced from 1964 to date by Excalibur Automotive
Corp. (1976 to date) in Wisconsin. It is a 1930 Mercedes-Benz SSK replica.

Excel - American car produced in 1914.

Excelsior - American car produced in 1910.

excessive fuel consumption - Engine condition created when too much fuel is
used to operate an engine. Possible causes include: low cylinder
compression, high backpressure, high internal engine friction, brakes
dragging, ignition system defect, poor driving habits such as high speed
driving and jack rabbit starts, leaks in fuel lines or connections, float
level incorrect, idle mixture adjustment screw incorrect, intake manifold not
properly heated, high fuel pressure, and retarded engine timing.

exchange - To trade a used auto part for another same part such as an
automatic transmission. It is commonly practiced at wrecking yards where a
price reduction is given if the existing part is turned in when another is
bought. It is most common on parts like transmissions, differentials, and
engines.

exclusions - One or more clauses in a contract, warranty, insurance policy,
etc. used to specify what is not covered.

exclusive agent - Agent employed to represent only one company's products,
policies, etc. See also captive agent.

Executive - American car produced from 1980 to date by Chrysler Corp. in
Michigan.

exhaust - By-products generated in a combustion chamber as a result of burning
of an air/fuel mixture under pressure. They include: water, unburned
hydrocarbons, carbon monoxide gas, oxides of nitrogen, acid compounds, and
carbon.

exhaust(black smoke) - See exhaust(black soot).

exhaust(black smoke puffs) - Brief puffs of black smoke produced in exhaust
indicating detonation. It is not the same as a steady black smoke or soot
resulting from an over-rich mixture. See also spark plug appearance(black
specks).

exhaust(black soot) - Substance produced in exhaust indicating excess unburned
hydrocarbons or an overly rich fuel mixture is being burned. End result is

some fuel is not completely burned causing soot to form with the exhaust fumes. Possible causes include: high float level, faulty float bowl needle valve, excessive fuel pressure, faulty accelerator pump circuit dumping continuous stream of fuel into airway, faulty EGR valve, retarded ignition timing, misfiring, heavy load on engine, low engine compression, and fouling spark plugs.

exhaust(blue colored flame) – Color generated by exhaust flames combusting normally. They are only visible with short exhaust stacks.

exhaust(blue smoke) – Heavy blue-tinted white smoke produced in exhaust when excessive quantities of oil are being burned in an engine's combustion chambers. Possible causes include: worn or stuck piston rings allowing too much oil to remain on the cylinder walls (common cause of smoking under acceleration), leaking valve stem guides due to bad valve stem seals (common cause of smoking under deceleration), faulty crankcase vent system, leaking supercharger intake shaft seals, and faulty PCV valve.

exhaust(cold smoke) – See exhaust(white smoke-1) and exhaust(white smoke-2).

exhaust(smoky) – See exhaust(blue smoke).

exhaust(white smoke-1) – Light white steamy smoke produced from water in exhaust. Some water is always present, since the combustion of one gallon of gasoline generates about one gallon of acidic water. If the white smoke is continuous, water is leaking into an engine's combustion chambers, usually from a leaking head gasket. If the smoke is present only during a cold startup, it is usually due to condensation of water in exhaust, a normal phenomenon.

exhaust(white smoke-2) – White colored smoke produced in exhaust when particles of liquid diesel fuel are present. It is usually due to an engine running cold, and disappears when the engine is warmed up. Possible causes include: faulty or missing thermostat causing overcooling, fuel with low volatility, low engine compression, low cetane rating, misfiring, and late injection of fuel.

exhaust(yellow colored flame) – Color (or traces of it) generated by exhaust flames when engine is in detonation range. They are only visible with short exhaust stacks. See also spark plug appearance(black specks) and exhaust(black smoke puffs).

exhaust cutout – Valve used to divert direction of exhaust gases to another pipe or the atmosphere.

exhaust efficiency – Degree to which exhaust gases flow freely and smoothly from an engine's exhaust valves to the tailpipe. See also backpressure, exhaust tuning, and headers.

exhaust emission control system – Assemblage of parts and controls used to regulate emission of noxious gases into the atmosphere from an exhaust system. Two approaches are used. One method regulates emission formation in the combustion chamber, while the other regulates emission formation in the exhaust system. Factors affecting creation of emissions include: ignition timing, air/fuel ratio, temperature of incoming air, octane rating of fuel, shape of combustion chamber, existing chamber deposits, intake vacuum, type of transmission, valve timing, cylinder displacement, backpressure, engine rpm, type of spark plug, fuel additives, compression ratio, and coolant temperature. See also emission control system.

exhaust emission control system(combustion chamber) – Exhaust emission control system used to control formation of harmful by-products in engine cylinders. Following areas help provide control: controlling ignition timing and air/fuel ratio, special combustion chamber shapes, dual spark plugs, and valve timing.

exhaust emission control system(exhaust system) – Exhaust emission control system used to control formation of harmful by-products outside a combustion chamber in different parts of an exhaust system. Some techniques used include: a catalyst muffler continuing the combustion process of gases on route to the tailpipe, and an air pump pumping air into the area just outside each exhaust valve to provide oxygen for assisting the more complete combustion of partly burned gases.

exhaust emissions – See exhaust.

exhaust flap – See exhaust manifold heat control valve.

exhaust fumes – See exhaust and exhaust gas.

exhaust gas – Gases formed in a combustion chamber as the result of burning an air/fuel mixture under pressure. Gases are primarily carbon monoxide, oxides of nitrogen, and unburned hydrocarbons. See also exhaust.

exhaust gas analyzer – Instrument used to analyze and determine amounts of certain exhaust gas compounds such as carbon monoxide and hydrocarbons. It uses a remote probe inserted into a tailpipe. The device can also be used to detect the presence of exhaust gas leaking into engine coolant by placing probe at radiator cap opening with cap removed.

exhaust gas recirculation – See emission control system(combustion-exhaust gas recirculation).

exhaust gas recirculation valve – Valve used to reroute a portion of the exhaust gases into an intake manifold to lower combustion temperatures, flame front speeds, and formation of oxides of nitrogen. It usually operates on vacuum controlled by a thermal valve, and is mounted on the intake manifold near the carburetor. The valve is normally closed when an engine is cold and intermittently open when warm depending on vacuum. A valve stuck open will cause the engine to stumble and idle rough while cold. A valve stuck closed will increase pinging tendency.

EGR valve sometimes builds up a white powdery deposit. It is due to fuel additives in certain brands of gasoline. See also car maintenance tip(EGR valve test), and emission control system(combustion-exhaust gas recirculation).

exhaust heat tube – See heat riser tube.

exhaust manifold – Cast iron device used to collect exhaust gas from cylinders, cool gases by expansion into a larger space, and route them to an exhaust pipe. Manifold contains a passageway for each cylinder with all merging into one outlet. Four cylinder engine has one manifold with four passageways. V-8 engines have two separate manifolds. It is the longest wearing part of the exhaust system. Performance of an exhaust manifold is enhanced by decreasing resistance to air flow. This is accomplished by increasing internal dimensions of passageways and smoothing their surfaces and corners. See also backpressure.

exhaust manifold heat control valve – Valve mounted on an exhaust manifold to control flow of hot gases into passageways around the carburetor base. If the valve does not open, the engine will: warm up slowly, ping, have poor fuel economy, and lose power due to increased backpressure (depending on design).

exhaust manifold heat riser valve – See exhaust manifold heat control valve.

exhaust manifold heat stove – See hot air stove.

exhaust pipe – Metal pipe used to route exhaust gases from an exhaust manifold to a muffler.

exhaust stack – Long vertical exhaust pipe mounted on one side of a truck's cab.

exhaust stroke – See stroke(exhaust).

exhaust system – Assemblage of parts used to transport exhaust gases safely and quietly from an engine to the atmosphere. Parts consist primarily of: an exhaust manifold, exhaust pipe, muffler, tailpipe, and optional resonator.

exhaust system corrosion – Corrosion created inside and outside an exhaust system. Outside corrosion is mainly due to rust from moisture in the form of rain, snow, humidity, etc. Inside corrosion is due to exhaust gases containing water, acids, and other corrosives. Most corrosion occurs on the inside. Combustion of fuel alone generates almost a gallon of water for every gallon of fuel burned. Mufflers corrode more rapidly when they are not run long enough (short trips) to get inside surfaces hot enough to evaporate accumulated water.

exhaust system leakage test – A simple test used to determine if an exhaust system is restricted, or leaking and where. The engine is started. A plug is then inserted into the tailpipe. This increases backpressure and will cause increased exhaust gas flow to any leak(s), making them easier to hear or feel. If the system is already restricted somewhere else, there will be little change in engine performance or flow of exhaust gases. If there are no other restrictions, the flow rate of exhaust gases will increase through the leak(s).

exhaust temperature gauge – Gauge used to measure exhaust gas temperature.

exhaust tuning – Adjustment made to a car's exhaust system to achieve optimum performance. It most cases, it is attained by decreasing backpressure and increasing exhaust gas scavenging. Most common modification involves the use of headers, larger diameter exhaust pipes, and low back pressure mufflers. Tuned exhaust will improve gas mileage, increase power, and remove weight from an engine (exhaust manifolds). See also intake tuning.

exhaust valve – Valve used to route exhaust gases from an engine cylinder to an exhaust manifold.

exit – Way to get off a road, freeway, etc.

EXP – American car produced from 1980 to date by Ford Motor Co. in Michigan.

exotic fuel – High performance fuels used primarily for racing. They include: alcohol, nitromethane, and nitrous oxide.

expander – Ring placed under a piston ring to increase ring pressure against a cylinder wall.

expansion – Increase in size. Almost all substances increase in size when heated. Expansion is the opposite of contraction.

expansion plug – See freeze plug.

expansion tank – Tank filled partly with coolant and connected to a radiator cap. It seals a cooling system, minimizes coolant loss, provides a place for coolant expansion.

expansion valve – Valve unit used in a car air conditioning system to receive pressurized liquid refrigerant from a receiver-drier, expand the refrigerant to a lower temperature and pressure, and regulate its flow into the low pressure side of an evaporator. Flow is usually controlled by a temperature sensing bulb located in an evaporator outlet.

experience – Knowledge and skills gained in a given field as a result of events happening in a person's life. Such events include studying, practicing, experimenting, making mistakes, trial and error efforts, on the job training, etc.

explosive range of a gas – Different proportions of fuel mixed with air capable of causing an explosion. Every combustible gas has a range of explosiveness. Outside the range, the fuel mixture is either too lean or too rich for an explosion to occur. If it's too rich, too much fuel vapor is present and not enough oxygen. If it's too lean, the opposite is true.

expressway – Highway built for high speed traffic. There are usually few intersections and a limited number of entrances and exits.

expunge – To remove all reference of traffic violations from a person's record.

extension – Bar of varying length used to extend the distance between a socket wrench and a ratchet. They are used to place a socket wrench in a restricted space and allow a ratchet to turn it where there is more freedom of movement.

extension pipe – Exhaust pipe positioned to receive hot gases from an exhaust manifold and transfer them to a muffler.

external bowl vent – Vent used to route any hot fuel vapors in a carburetor float bowl directly to the atmosphere. See also anti-percolator.

extractor – See header.

extras – Optional accessories added to a standard new car, usually at the customer's request, but sometimes added by the dealer to increase profit or cover lost finance charges.

extreme pressure lubricant – See oil(extreme pressure) and grease(extreme pressure).

extrusion – Part or component formed by pushing material through a die by pressure.

Exxon Corporation – A U.S. petroleum company headquartered in New York, New York. See also petroleum company.

eyeballing – To view a surface outline, spacing between parts, etc. with the eyes.

eyebrow – Cowl or visor located above a headlamp, instrument panel, or wheel opening.

eyes – Light beams used to start and stop electronic timers at a race track.

Eyston, Captain George – He set a world land speed record in 1937 and 1938 driving a Thunderbolt V-12. Speeds were 345.5 and 357.5 mph.

F

F(1) - Abbreviation for France found usually on an international license plate.
F(2) - Auction car rating code used to specify a car in fair condition that has been modified or which needs reconditioning.
fac - Abbreviation for factory installed.
facing the valves - To machine valve faces back to specifications. This is done when a valve job is performed. See also valve facer.
Facto - American car produced in 1920.
factor of safety - See safety factor.
factory - Buildings where products are manufactured.
factory experimental - Stock car produced in limited numbers.
factory outlet - Business setup to directly market a factory's products. It may or may not be owned by the factory.
factory sticker price - Selling price specified by the factory and posted on a sticker affixed to the product.
factory tolerance - Amount of difference in a dimension allowed in an item manufactured at a factory.
factory trained mechanic - See job(factory trained mechanic).
Fageol - American car produced from 1916-1917.
Fageolbus - American car produced in 1916.
Fahrenheit - Physicist named Gabriel Daniel Fahrenheit (1686-1736) who developed the Fahrenheit temperature scale. See also degree(Fahrenheit).
Fairbanks-Morse - American car produced in 1909.
fair car - See car classification(fair).
fair game - Potential customer.
fairy - Potential car buyer who understands the car-buying game and is not threatened by the sales tactics of car salesmen.
Fairlane - American car produced from 1957-1979 by Ford Motor Co. in Michigan.
Fairmont - American car produced by Ford from 1980 to date.
Fairmount - American car produced from 1906-1907.
faked injury - Non-existent injury. Most faked injuries are those hard to detect. They include: whiplash and headache injuries resulting from accidents. Such injuries are difficult to disprove. See also con game(rear end collision).
FAL - American car produced from 1909-1913 by Fal Motor Co. in Illinois.
Falcar - American car produced in 1909.
Falcon - American car produced in 1909, 1914, 1922, and 1938-1943. Also, an American car produced from 1960-1972 by Ford Motor Co. in Michigan.
Falcon Cycle Car - American car produced from 1913-1914.
Falcon-Knight - American car produced from 1927-1928 by Falcon Motor Corp. in Michigan.
falsing - False alerts triggered on a radar detector. They can be generated by: non-radar signals emitted from other radar detectors, microwave intrusion alarms, high voltage power lines, garage door openers, and airport radar.
family car - Car built to carry a family of four or more people depending on car size.
family chariot - See family car.
Famous - American car produced from 1908-1909 by Famous Mfg. Co. in Illinois. Also, an American car produced in 1917.
fan - Fan mounted on a water pump shaft. It pulls air through the radiator at low driving speeds.
fan belt - Rubber and cord composition belt used to drive a car's water pump, generator, and fan. It usually has a V-shaped cross section.
  Proper belt tension is very important. If the belt is too loose, it will slip, wear out prematurely, cause a battery to discharge, and overheat an engine. If it is too tight, generator and water pump bearings will wear out prematurely. As a general rule of thumb, a belt deflection of 1/2 to 3/4 of an inch between the water pump and generator is considered proper tension.
  A fan belt is worn when it shows signs of being frayed around the edges or has become so stretched no more tension adjustment is possible. Wear and friction can be significantly reduced by coating a new fan belt with silicone spray.
fan belt tension gauge - Instrument used to measure proper tension or belt tightness.
fan clutch - Clutch mounted on a fan to control fan speed, noise, and help minimize fan power requirements. The clutch usually uses some type of bimetallic strip to sense air temperature. When temperature rises and falls,

more and less silicone oil respectively flows into a fluid coupling that turns the fan. A fan clutch can reduce engine power loss. For example, a 16-18 inch fan requires 2-3 horsepower at 3,000 rpm, and considerably more at higher rpm. See also car service tip(fan clutch test).

Fangio, Juan Manuel - He was an Argentine racing mechanic for Alpha Romeo who began racing in 1948, and became the World Grand Prix champion in 1951, 1954, 1955, 1956, and 1957. Cars driven were an Alfa Romeo, Mercedes-Maserati, Mercedes, Ferrari, and Maserati. He retired in 1958 at age 47.

Fanning - American car produced from 1902-1903 by F.J. Fanning Mfg. Co. in Illinois.

fan pattern - Shape of a spray gun's paint pattern. Proper shape looks like eye turned sideways.

fan pulley - Pulley mounted on a fan to receive power from a fan belt.

fare amount - Amount charged for transportation in a taxicab, bus, plane, etc. Also, it refers to a person transported in a taxicab, bus, plane, etc.

Fargo - American car produced in 1913.

Farina, Giuseppe - He was an Italian who became the Grand Prix world champion in 1950 driving an Alfa Romeo.

Farmack - American car produced from 1915-1916 by Farmack Motor Car Co. in Illinois.

Farmer - American car produced in 1907.

Farmobile - American car produced in 1908.

Farner - American car produced from 1922-1923 by Farner Motor Car Co. in Illinois.

fast and loose pulleys - Early transmission used to transfer power from a countershaft to a car's rear axle. One loose and two fixed pulleys were mounted on a countershaft. Meshing with spur gears on the drive axle occurred by moving a belt from a loose to a fixed pulley.

fastback - Roofline constructed to slope directly down toward or to the rear bumper of a car.

fast get away - To leave an area quickly in a car.

fast idle - Engine rotational speed higher than a normal idle. It commonly occurs when the engine is cold and a carburetor choke mechanism is in use. See also fast idle cam.

fast idle cam - Cam-like semi-circular plate mounted on a choke shaft. It works with a fast idle screw to keep a cold engine running at higher rpm preventing it from stalling until it warms up.

fast idle cam link - Short rod used on some carburetors to link a fast idle cam to a choke lever on a choke shaft.

fast idle rod - Rod used to link a choke shaft with a throttle shaft. It allows the two shafts to work together properly when an engine is cold or warm.

fast idle rod pivot points - The maximum and minimum distance an idle rod can move in a slotted fitting mounted on the end of a choke lever shaft. It provides proper operation between a choke and a throttle shaft during fast idle or warm-up.

fast idle screw - Screw mounted on a carburetor body or linkage for controlling idle speed of an engine when cold. It operates only when a car's choke is in use. Cold idle speed is greater because the cold surfaces of an engine create poor fuel vaporization requiring an engine to run faster in order to keep running.

fast lane - Lane of traffic on a freeway or divided highway where faster traffic travels. It is usually the left lane.

fatigue - Property exhibited by a material when it breaks down in strength through a large amount of bending or flexing. Fatigue commonly first appears as small cracks subsequently developing into complete breaks.

Fauber Cycle Car - American car produced in 1914.

Faulkner-Blanchard - American car produced in 1910.

Faultless - American car produced in 1914.

faulty ignition wiring - Electric wiring in a car's ignition circuit characterized by not allowing current to flow consistently or at all. Possible causes include: poor connections, corroded battery terminals, grounding wire, partial break in a wire, and bad ignition coil resistor.

Fawick Flyer - American car produced from 1910-1912 by Fawick Motor Car Co. in South Dakota.

Fay - American car produced in 1912.

F/BK - Abbreviation for fastback.

FC - Abbreviation for fair condition. See also EC and GC.

featheredged - See feather the paint.

feather foot - Driving habit characterized by driving at or below posted speed limits, accelerating slowly, or otherwise gently using the gas pedal. See also lead foot.

feathering - Brake pedal applied lightly for an extended time period (like going down a hill). It can cause brake linings to glaze.

feather the paint - To gradually taper paint thickness to bare metal for the

purpose of creating a smooth surface or transition from paint to metal.
Fedelia - American car produced from 1913-1914 by J.H. Sizelan Co. in Ohio.
Federal - American car produced from 1901-1903 and 1907-1909 by Federal Motor
  Vehicle Co. in New York (1901-1903), Federal Motor Car Co. in Illinois
  (1907), Federal Automobile Co. in Illinois (1907-1908), and Rockford
  Automobile & Engine Co. in Illinois (1908-1909).
Federal-Mogul - American line of engine bearings produced by Federal-Mogul
  Corp.
Federal Steamer - American steam car produced in 1905.
Federal Truck - American truck produced in 1910.
federal version - Car built to comply with U.S. emission standards and not
  necessarily California's more restrictive standards.
Fee - American car produced from 1908-1909.
feedback carburetor - See carburetor(feedback).
feeler gauge - Tool used to measure air gaps between surfaces such as spark
  plug electrodes, contact points, and intake and exhaust valve tappet
  clearances. It consists of a series of different thickness hardened steel
  blades contained in a protective case.
fell asleep at the wheel - Driving condition created when a driver has fallen
  asleep while driving. It causes many traffic accidents.
felony - A major crime committed requiring a greater punishment than a
  misdemeanor. Felonies include: murder, arson, and rape.
female - Designation used to describe mechanical fitting with a hollow part
  for receiving a male fitting. Internal threads of nuts and pipes, the hole
  for a headphone jack, etc. are example of female fittings. See also male.
female connector - See female.
fender - On modern cars, the side part of a car body in front of or behind the
  doors. On older cars, it was the curved sections of metal that covered each
  wheel.
fender bender - Accident causing car body damage.
fender welting - Flexible vinyl or rubber material used along the inside edge
  of a fender to minimize rust and body to fender squeaks.
Fenton - American car produced in 1914.
f/equip - Abbreviation for fully equipped.
Fergus - American and British car produced from 1915-1921 by J.B. Ferguson in
  Ireland (1915-1921), and Fergus Motors of America in New Jersey (1921-1922).
  Also, an American car produced in 1949.
Ferrari - Italian car line produced briefly in 1940 and then from 1947 to date
  by Societa Esercizio Fabbriche Automobilie e Corse Ferrari Mraanello. Recent
  models include: Mondial, Testarossa, Berlinetta, Dino, and GTO. As of 1985,
  Ferrari racing machines accumulated more Grand Prix race victories (91), than
  any other make.
    The U.S. representative is Chinetti-Garthwaite Imports headquartered in
  Paoli, Pennsylvania. See also Lotus.
Ferrari, Enzio - Italian man born in 1898 and founder of the Ferrari car line.
Ferrer-VW-GT - American car produced beginning in 1966 by Ferrer Motor Corp.
  in Florida.
Ferris - American car produced from 1920-1922 Ohio Motor Vehicle Co. in Ohio.
ferrous metal - Metal containing iron or steel.
fg lmps - Abbreviation for fog lamps.
FH - Abbreviation for fixed head.
F-head engine - See engine(F-head).
FI - Abbreviation for fuel injected.
F/I - Abbreviation for fuel injected.
FIA - Abbreviation for Federation Internationale de l'Automobile. It is a
  world wide ruling body for car racing. Racing car clubs from all over the
  world are under its wings. AAA is a United States arm.
FIA race car group - Classification used specify what category a race car
  belongs in. Eight major groups are used.
FIA race car group 1 - Classification used for series-production touring
  cars. Cars are basic passenger cars meeting certain requirements.
FIA race car group 2 - Classification used for touring cars. Cars are basic
  passenger cars meeting certain requirements.
FIA race car group 3 - Classification used for the following GTs: series-
  production grand touring cars. Cars are basic luxury road cars meeting
  certain requirements.
FIA race car group 4 - Classification used for the following GTs: grand
  touring cars. Cars are basic luxury road cars meeting certain requirements.
FIA race car group 5 - Classification used for special competition cars
  derived from groups 1-4.
FIA race car group 6 - Classification used for two-seater racing cars. Cars
  are specially built for closed circuit racing only.
FIA race car group 7 - Classification used for formula single-seater racing
  cars. Cars are specially built single-seater cars used only for closed
  circuit racing. Three formula categories are used. Formula One is for Grand

Prix cars with engines up to 3,000 cc and up to 12 cylinders. Formula Two is for cars with non-supercharged engines up to 2,000 cc and up to 6 cylinders. Formula Three is for cars with engines up to 2,000 cc and up to 4 cylinders along with certain other restrictions.

FIA race car group 8 - Classification used for formula libre racing cars. Cars are specially built for closed circuit racing and don't qualify for any Formula category of group 7.

Fiat(1) - American car produced from 1910-1918 by Fiat Motor Co. in New York.

Fiat(2) - Italian car line produced from 1907 to date by Fiat SpA. Recent models include: Argenta, Campagnola, Panda, Regata, Ritmo, Uno, Spyder, and X1/9.

   The U.S. representative is Fiat Motors of North America, headquartered in Montvale, New Jersey.

Fiberglas - Trademark used for a textile material made by weaving finely spun filaments of glass. Fiberglas is a very strong material, not flammable, resists heat expansion, and is insulative. Its uses include: figerglass belts, car bodies, and car body repair material.

Fiat 6 - Car driven by Ernest Eldridge to a 1924 world land speed record of 146.0 mph at Arpajon.

fiberglass belt - Flexible belt material made of fiberglass and used beneath tire tread to give a tire added strength.

fiberglass belted tire - See tire(fiberglass belted).

fiberglass body - Car body constructed of fiberglass.

Fidelity - American car produced in 1909.

field - Area containing active magnetic or electric lines of force.

field(magnetic) - Area where a magnetic force occurs.

field magnets - Steel alloy material wound with conductive wire and positioned around the armature of a motor, generator, etc. for creating a magnetic field for an armature to spin in. Some motors have permanent field magnets, while others require power to become magnetized. Car alternator field magnets usually require power.

field of vision - Area seen by the eyes when looking straight ahead. People with good vision can see about 180 degrees. A person with poor field of vision must compensate by glancing to the side. See also peripheral vision.

field plate - Stationary circular plate used in a speedometer assembly to shield the speed cup and rotating magnet.

Field Steam - American steam car produced in 1887.

field windings - Windings of conductive wire located in a generator or alternator to create a magnetic field when current passes through them. Without field windings, no generator would generate current. A DC generator uses stationary outer field windings while an alternator uses field windings that rotate on a rotor. See also generator windings, rotor(alternator), generator(DC), and alternator.

Fiero - American car produced from 1980 to date by Pontiac Division of General Motors Corp. in Michigan.

Fiesta - American car produced from 1976-1980 by Ford Motor Co. in Michigan.

Fifth Avenue - American car produced from 1980 to date by Chrysler Corp. in Michigan.

Fifth Avenue Coach - American car produced in 1924.

fifty percenter - Service station attendant employed with the understanding he will receive a 50% cut of the profits for all parts and supplies sold to customers.

filament - Resistance material used in a light bulb to produce light by glowing when current flows through it.

file(1) - Metal tool constructed with hardened ridges for removing metal, wood, plastic, etc.

file(2) - To remove material from a metal, wood, plastic, etc. object.

filing a claim - To fill out a form requesting reimbursement for some loss covered on an insurance policy, homeowner policy, etc.

filing exaggerated claims - Claims filed where the stated loss is greater than the actual loss.

filing suit - To file a lawsuit with a court.

fill and empty coupling - Fluid coupling filled and emptied of automatic transmission fluid as needed.

filled axle - Lowered front axle filled with additional metal for increased strength.

filler - See solder(plastic).

filler cap - Cap used to cover an opening where fluid is added. Such caps include: radiator, valve cover, power steering reservoir, etc.

filler neck - Section of pipe positioned to transfer gas from the gas cap area to the gas tank.

fill er up - Statement made to a gas station attendant instructing him to add fuel to your fuel tank until it is full.

fillet - Curved filling used to blend or join two intersecting planes.

filter - Device used to remove foreign particles from air or from fluids.

filter bowl - Bowl used most commonly in a fuel filter for trapping water and providing housing space for a filter element. They are used on older cars.

filter sock - Filter mounted on a fuel pickup to prevent fuel tank contaminants from entering fuel line.

fill up - To add fuel to a car's fuel tank until full.

fin - Abbreviation for finish.

Fina-Sport - American car produced form 1953-1955 by Perry Fina in New York.

finance charge - All the loan charges a car buyer incurs when he chooses to finance a car instead of paying cash. Such charges include: credit fees, loan origination fees, interest, and insurance.

financed transaction - Process followed to outline and complete a procedure for payment of something such as a car, boat, trailer, motor home, etc.

finance reserve - Car dealer's portion of a car loan's carrying charges.

financing - To obtain credit or capital.

Finch - American car produced in 1902.

Findley - American car produced in 1910 and 1912.

fine lining - Custom painting technique used to apply small linework of contrasting color to a panel. Ink pens are normally used. Another method uses a sharp knife to scratch a design removing paint to reveal the undercoat.

fink - Race track cheater.

finner - Five dollars worth of money.

fire - Result of fuel combustion where heat and light are created. See also burn.

Firebird - Experimental gas turbine car produced by Ford. There have been several versions including: Firebird I, II, III, and IV. Also, an American car produced from 1967 to date by Pontiac Division of General Motors Corp. in Michigan.

fire extinguisher - Device filled with a chemical substance capable of putting out fires.

Firenza - American car produced from 1980 to date by Oldsmobile Division of General Motors Corp. in Michigan.

fireplace - Car's front grille.

Firestone - American line of tires produced by the Firestone Tire & Rubber Co.

Firestone-Columbus - American car produced from 1907-1915 by Columbus Buggy in Ohio.

fire suit - Fireproof suit worn by drag racers.

fire test - Test performed to determine temperature an oil ignites or burns. See also flash test.

fire wall - Metal partition used to separate the engine and passenger compartments.

firing on all cylinders - Engine operation characterized by all spark plugs firing properly.

firing order - Order in which engine cylinders receive a spark igniting the fuel mixture. Engines are designed not to fire in sequence, but in an alternating sort of order such as 1-4-3-2. Alternate firing ignites cylinder fuel mixtures, as much as possible, at opposite ends of a crankshaft. This works with engine design to balance the strain placed on an engine crankshaft which in turn causes an engine to run smoothly. A sequential firing order, such as 1-2-3-4, would cause excessive engine block vibration which in turn would place a great deal of stress on a crankshaft and an engine's motor mounts.

firing point - Lower protruding portion of a metal conductor in a spark plug terminal found inside a distributor cap. A cap has one firing point for each cylinder. The distributor rotor transfers high voltage current from the center terminal to each firing point it lines up with. Engine misfiring can be caused by corroded firing points.

first class running condition - Car with engine and drivetrain in good operating condition.

Fischer - American car produced in 1902-1904 and 1914.

Fish - American car produced in 1908.

Fisher - American car produced in 1924.

Fisher Brothers - They were five brothers whose father was a master carriage maker. Two of the brothers, Frederick and Charles, started the Fisher Body Company in 1908. In subsequent years, the other brothers - Lawrence, Alfred, and Howard - joined the business. The company eventually became a division of General Motors Corporation known as Fisher Body Division.

fishhook - Spear or arrowhead shaped ending to a decorative molding or paint stripe.

fish scaling - Custom painting technique used to apply a fishscale pattern to a panel typically by using a template consisting of a series of side-to-side half circles.

fishtail - Driving condition created by a side-to-side shifting or sliding of a car's rear section. It usually starts when a car skid is overcorrected and continues until repeated and opposite overcorrections are eliminated. See also skid.

fit – Degree of proper contact between two surfaces.

Fitch Phoenix – American car produced in 1966.

Fittipaldi, Emerson – He became the Grand Prix world champion in 1972 and 1974 driving a Lotus-Ford and McLaren-Ford.

Five Hundred Club – Association organized to recognize salesmen who have sold at least 500 cars.

five o'clock surprise – Car owner reaction created when a car repair bill is found to be much higher than anticipated.

fixit ticket – Traffic citation issued to a driver of a vehicle, requiring repairs to be made.

FL – Abbreviation for Liechtenstein found usually on an international license plate.

flag(black) – Black flag waved in a race to get a particular car into the pit.

flag(checkered) – Checkered flag waved in a race at each driver completing the required number of laps.

flag(green) – Green flag waved in a race to signal the start.

flag(red) – Red flag waved in a race to stop it.

flag(striped) – Blue flag with orange stripes waved in a race at a driver instructing him to move over and let a faster car pass freely. It is usually waved when one or more drivers are not driving fairly or according to rules.

flag(white) – White flag waved in a race to indicate the last lap.

flag(yellow) – Yellow flag waved in a race to signal a problem on the track. It temporarily stops a race instructing all cars to remain in their current position and drive at a uniform lower speed until the race resumes.

flags(crossed) – Two rolled up flags displayed in an "X" pattern when a race is half over.

Flagler – American car produced from 1914-1915 by Flagler Cyclecar Co. in Wisconsin.

Flaherty, Pat – He won the Indianapolis 500 Race in 1956 driving an average of 128.5 mph in a John Zink Special.

flame arrestor – Fine wire mesh used to stop the progression of a flame front.

flame front – Boundary formed in a combustion chamber between the burning and unburned portion of the air/fuel mixture. Flame fronts travel over 100 mph.

flame hardening – Process used to harden metal surfaces for increased wear life. Oxy-acetylene flame is used to bring metal surface to specified high temperature and then quench it quickly to produce hardness.

flames – Custom painting technique used to apply flame patterns onto various panels in various designs. Flames are also available as decals.

flame suit – See fire suit.

flame thrower – Car ignition system modified for increased performance.

Flanders – American car produced from 1909-1912 by Everitt-Metzger-Flanders Co. in Michigan.

Flanders Electric – American electric car produced from 1912-1915 by Flanders Mfg. Co. (1912-1913), Tiffany Electric Co. (1913-1914), and Flanders Electric Co. (1914-1915), all in Michigan.

flange – Projecting rim or collar used to give added strength to a metal fitting and often help hold it in place. Flanges can be found on pipes, shafts, wheels, etc. The projecting rim on the outside of a railroad car wheel is a good example of a flange.

flare(1) – Chemical light device used to produce bright light for distress, warnings, etc. It is usually in the form of a short stick.

flare(2) – See fender flare.

flared fender – Fender profiled to extend outward from a car body. It is usually done for show, to accommodate wide or larger diameter tires, or dropped suspensions. It is usually created by cutting out some of the existing fender and reshaping it with new metal riveted or welded in place.

flared tip – Pipe end enlarged for attachment to another pipe or fitting.

flaring tool – Tool used to form flared tubing connections.

flash between coats – See flashed off.

flashed off – Condition created when a primer coat of paint has sufficiently dried by evaporation of its solvent to allow sanding in preparation for a topcoat.

flasher – See flasher unit.

flasher unit – Electrical device used to interrupt current flow repeatedly for turning lights on and off. A bimetallic strip is used that opens and closes a set of contacts as the strip heats up from current flow, then cools. Flasher units are used for blinking turn signal and hazard lights.

flashing light – Vehicle light designed to go on and off repeatedly or rotate continuously. Flashing lights indicates danger, car problems, etc. A flashing red light on an emergency vehicle requires nearby vehicles to yield to it.

flash point – Lowest temperature measured where an oil vapor and air mixture will ignite when exposed to an open flame.

flash test – Test performed to determine ignition temperature of an oil's vapor. See also fire test.

flat - Tire condition created when air pressure is gone due to a leak in a tire casing.

flat battery - Completely discharged battery.

flatbed(1) - See flatbed truck.

flatbed(2) - See car transport(flatbed).

flatbed truck - Truck built with a large flat bed having removable sides or no sides at all.

flat deck - Car trunk lid area built generally flat.

flat engine - See engine(flat).

flathead engine - See engine(L-head).

flat out - To drive at a car's top speed.

flat rate - Method of charging for car repair and maintenance work based on specified work times. Car manufacturers publish flat rate books specifying the amount of time it takes to do every possible work item. A mechanic is usually paid a share of the time he works. Thus the incentive is there for the mechanic to speed up the work and get careless. Flat rates encourage shoddy workmanship and give the repair business a bad name. Customers are almost always charged according to flat rates.

flat rate book - Book produced by different manufacturers specifying the amount of time to do every conceivable repair job on their cars. See also flat rate.

flat rate manual - See flat rate book.

flat rate scale - Flat rate times listed in a flat rate book.

flat spot(1) - Carburetor condition created when an air/fuel mixture momentarily becomes lean during acceleration. It is usually caused by an inadequate supply of fuel squirted into a carburetor passageway upon acceleration, an improperly adjusted idle mixture screw, or fuel not readily vaporizing.

flat spot(2) - Area on a flywheel ring gear where teeth have been worn down. Such areas make it difficult for a starter to rotate an engine when the drive pinion gear engages. See also starting problem(starter won't engage).

flat tire - See tire(flat).

fleet - Large group of cars operated or moved together.

fleet owner - Person or company owning a large number of cars. Taxicab owners, private trucking firms, car rental agencies are examples.

Fleetruck - American car produced from 1926-1927.

Fleetwood - American car produced from 1963 to date by Cadillac Motor Car Co. in Michigan.

Flexbi - American car produced in 1904.

Flexible - American car produced in 1932.

flexi-flyer - Long wheelbase dragster built to keep its front wheels on the ground.

Flint - American car produced from 1902-1904 and 1923-1927 by Flint Automobile Co. in Michigan, and Locomobile Co. of America in New York respectively.

Flint-Lomax - American car produced in 1905.

flipped - Driving condition created when a car turns over on its roof. It is usually caused by: going over an embankment or by quickly turning a car on a roadway at a high rate of speed.

flippers - Hubcaps.

flip up shield - Windshield built to be raised allowing air to enter.

float(1) - Flotation device used in a carburetor float bowl with a needle valve to regulate fuel flow and level. See also float bowl.

float(2) - Driving condition created when a car traveling at higher speeds tends to lift in the front end due to air pressure underneath the car. See also spoiler.

float(3) - See valve float.

float bowl - Fuel reservoir located within a carburetor for receiving fuel from a fuel pump and storing it at a constant level. Fuel flow and level are maintained by using a float device and needle valve. As the bowl fills up with fuel, the float pushes against the needle valve to shut off the flow from the fuel pump. The float bowl contains primary and secondary jets for metering fuel to primary and secondary discharge nozzles. The fuel level in the bowl must be within a certain narrow range in order for a carburetor to function properly.

float circuit - See carburetor circuit(float).

float drop - Distance lowered by a carburetor float before the needle valve opens.

float gauge - Gauge used to measure a carburetor's float level.

floating bridge - Bridge built to carry traffic across a body of water by actually floating the bridge on the water. Such bridges typically use concrete caissons that are anchored in place.

floating power - Engine mounting or supporting system used so its center of gravity lies on a line between two mounting points, allowing the engine to float or move around that line.

---

float level - Height of gasoline maintained in a carburetor float bowl. Float level determines how easily fuel is drawn into a carburetor's primary or secondary airways when an engine is operating at off idle. If the float level is too low, an engine will be starved for fuel and run poorly. If the level is too high, excess fuel will be drawn into the engine. This will tend to cause: quicker deposit formation, possible engine stumbling and flooding, and poor fuel economy. See also heat soak.

float level gauge - Gauge used to check a carburetor's float level setting. See also float level.

floating bathtub - Full size car manufactured in Detroit.

floating power - Engine allowed to have some movement independent of a car by means of rubber engine mountings.

float the valves - See valve float.

Flock, Tim - He became the NASCAR Grand National Champion in 1952.

flooded - See engine problem(flooded).

flooded engine - See engine problem(flooded).

flooding - See engine problem(flooded).

flooding the engine - See engine problem(flooded).

floorboard - Car floor area located where driver and passenger feet rest.

floor console - Structure situated between front bucket seats and resting on a transmission hump. It is shaped to contain such items as a gear shift, parking brake lever, tray area, compartments, gauges, etc.

floored - To keep a car's accelerator pedal pushed all the way to the floor.

floor it - To push a gas pedal all the way to the floor to get maximum acceleration and speed.

floor jack - Hydraulic jack built to roll on a floor and hydraulically raise and lower part of a car.

floor linkage - Transmission linkage set up by using a floor shifter and rods running from the shifter base to the transmission.

floor mat - Removable mat placed in the foot area of a car's interior. It protects the underlying carpet from getting unnecessarily dirty and/or wet thereby lengthening its life.

floor outlets - Air discharge outlets used in a car's interior heating system to direct airflow down onto the floor area.

floorpan - Floor of a car's passenger compartment.

floor panning - Situation created when a dealer's cars are owned by a lending institution instead of a dealer. Most dealers floor-pan the cars they sell.

floor pedal - Pedal positioned near a drivers feet.

floor shift - Transmission shift lever mounted on the floor to the right of the driver.

floor shift control lever - See floor shift.

floor time - Time spent by a car salesman actually selling cars in a showroom or out on a lot. It does not include any non-selling activities such as phone calling, sitting in meetings, eating, etc.

floor whore - Car salesman working not by appointment, but by simply approaching any available potential car buyer on a lot.

flow bench - Shop area set up with appropriate equipment to measure air flow and distribution in intake manifolds, exhaust manifolds, carburetors, etc.

flow box - Box designed to duplicate one or more engine airways for the purpose of researching its airflow characteristics.

flow machine - Machine used to measure air flow and distribution in intake manifold and exhaust manifolds, carburetors, etc.

flow-out - Paint condition created when a newly sprayed paint spreads out evenly into a smooth coat.

flow pattern - Manner in which air or a liquid flows in a passageway. Non-turbulent laminar flow is desired in most cases as it increases flow velocity and volume.

flow through ventilation - Fresh air system used to direct fresh air into a car's interior and out through louvered openings near the rear window.

fluid - Any substance characterized by flowing readily and requiring a vessel to contain it. Gases and liquids are fluids.

fluid coupling - Device used to transmit power from one shaft to another by spinning fluid. It is most commonly found in an automatic transmission where it serves as a hydraulic clutch and cushions the transfer of engine power. Primary components consist of: a fluid filled housing, drive impeller, driven impeller, and input and output shaft connections. The engine turns one impeller which spins the fluid. The spinning fluid causes the other impeller to rotate and supply torque to an automatic transmission. At high rpm, speed loss in only a few percent, but at low rpm it can approach 100 percent. See also torque converter.

fluid drive - Impeller-like elements located within a fluid coupling to transmit engine power. See also fluid coupling.

fluid flywheel - Fluid type coupling, similar to a torque converter, used in early automatic and semi-automatic transmissions. It was mounted between the clutch assembly and the engine output shaft.

fluid leak – Condition created when fluid escapes from a container, sump, hose, etc. due to a crack, puncture, corrosion, loose bolts, loose drain plug, etc. The secret in finding many leak sources is looking for the path the fluid takes to reach its drip point.

fluid leak(clear stain) – If found under a wheel or on brake housing, it means brake fluid is leaking from a brake cylinder, or nearby brake lines. If found under an engine area, it may mean a master brake cylinder, nearby brake lines, or a clutch slave cylinder may be leaking.

fluid leak(engine coolant) – Coolant solution found escaping from an engine's cooling system. Depending on the cause, fluid can leak internally or externally. Possible leak locations include: radiator, heater core, hoses, head gasket, small crack(s) in cylinder head combustion chamber area, pressure cap, water pump seal, and core plugs. The leak's ground location will help determine the leak source. See also cooling system pressure test.

fluid leak(engine oil in coolant) – It indicates engine oil leaking into the cooling system and probably means coolant is leaking into the engine. Steam in the exhaust will be an indication. Possible causes include: leaky head gasket. See also car service tip(pressure leak into coolant test).

fluid leak(gas) – See fluid leak(reddish stain).

fluid leak(internal) – Internal fluid leaks are usually caused by a fluid in question somehow leaking into combustion chambers and burning or vaporizing. Brake fluid can sometimes leak via vacuum lines from a vacuum booster or other vacuum connection. Engine coolant can leak from: a leaking head gasket and/or carburetor base gasket, crack in a cylinder head's combustion chamber area, and an engine block crack.

fluid leak(oil) – If found under an engine, it usually means an oil leak somewhere on the engine block. The leak could be coming from a crankcase gasket, oil pan drain plug, oil filter, oil pressure sending unit, fuel pump gasket, etc. Another possibility in the engine area is leakage from a steering gear box. If the leak is found under a manual transmission, the transmission is leaking at the drain plug, input shaft seal, output shaft seal, from a crack, or from loose bolts (on some transmissions).

fluid leak(pale stain) – A pale stain usually indicates water. A water spot under a radiator or engine indicates a leaking radiator, water pump, water circulation hose, or removal of excess water by an engine's cooling system. If a water stain develops on the ground beyond the tail pipe after engine operating temperature is reached , it indicates water is leaking into an engine's combustion chambers. The most common cause is from a leaking head gasket.

fluid leak(pink oil) – See fluid leak(reddish oil).

fluid leak(power steering unit) – See fluid leak(reddish oil).

fluid leak(reddish oil) – If found under an engine area, power steering fluid is leaking. If found under a car's transmission area, automatic transmission fluid is the culprit, especially if it has a strong smell. Possible power steering fluid leak causes include: over filled reservoir, leaking reservoir, split hose, and bad pump or pitman shaft seals. Possible automatic transmission fluid leaks causes include: bad front and/or rear transmission seal; and leaky pump case bolts, pump to case gasket, front oil pump seal, pan, and/or pan gasket.

fluid leak(reddish stain) – It is usually gasoline if the spot(s) evaporates quickly. Gas leak causes include: loose fittings, cracked hoses, leaky tank seams, leaky fuel filter, leaky fuel pump, and leaky or cracked carburetor.

fluid leak(red oil in coolant) – It usually indicates automatic transmission fluid is leaking into the radiator from a leaky transmission oil cooler tank installed inside the radiator.

fluid leak(thick oil) – If found under a car's rear axle, it means the leak is coming from a differential seal, filler plug, or crack in the housing. If found under a manual transmission, it indicates a leak coming from a filler plug, vent, crack in the housing, loose bolts, and input or output shaft seal. If found on a rear wheel, it may be due to an overfilled differential. See also fluid leak(oil).

fluid leak(transaxle) – Oil escapes from within a transaxle. Possible causes include: excess play in axles exiting the housing, cracked housing, and leaking gaskets.

fluid leak(transmission) – Oil escapes from within a transmission. Possible causes include: damaged gaskets and oil seals, lubricant foaming too much, oil level too high, plugged vent, cracked case, loose drain plug, loose or missing filler plug, leaky speedometer cable connection, and loose or missing case bolts.

fluid leak(wet floor on front passenger side) – It usually indicates water leaking from a clogged air conditioner drain valve or broken drain hose. If the floor is carpeted, it will be wet and have a musty odor. Air conditioners condense moisture from the air onto the surface of the evaporator core. If the drain is plugged, the moisture will eventually overflow down to the floor area.

Another cause of wetness can be due to engine coolant leaking from a heater core or related hoses or valves.

fluid level – Level of fluid in a reservoir.

flushing adapter – See coolant flushing adapter.

flushing solution – Solution used to remove excess rust and scale from an engine's cooling system. It usually requires: draining the existing coolant, filling the system with the flushing solution, running the engine for 1/2 hour, draining the cooling system, adding a neutralizer solution, running engine for 5-10 minutes, draining the cooling system, refilling with fresh water, running engine for 5-10 minutes, draining the cooling system, and refilling with antifreeze mixture. Since all flushing solutions are not the same, make sure the one used is compatible with the car's radiator metal composition.

flush the brake system – Procedure followed to remove air, dirt, water, and other contaminants from brake lines.

flux(brazing) – Chemical used to clean a joint to be brazed of dirt and oxidation, keep oxygen away from the molten metal, and dissolve any oxides forming on the metal surface or in the molten metal. Different flux compounds are available for different applications. Borax is one of the most common. See also brazing.

flux(electric) – See flux(magnetic).

flux(magnetic) – Lines of magnetic force in a magnetic field.

flux(soldering) – Chemical used to clean a joint to be soldered of dirt and oxidation, keep oxygen away from the molten metal, and dissolve any oxides forming on the metal surface or in the molten metal. Corrosive and no-corrosive flux compounds are available for different applications. See also soldering.

flux(welding) – Chemical used to clean a joint to be welded of dirt and oxidation, keep oxygen away from the molten metal, and dissolve any oxides forming on the metal surface or in the molten metal. Welding rods are coated with flux compounds. See also welding.

flux paste – Flux composed of powder and liquid fractions mixed into a paste form. Some pastes use petroleum jelly as a base.

flyboy – Weekend drag racer.

fly by night dealer – Unreliable or irresponsible dealer.

Flyer – American car produced from 1913-1914 by Flyer Motor Car Co. in Michigan. Also, an American car produced in 1933.

Flying Auto – American car produced in 1947 and 1950.

Flying Cloud – American car produced from 1926-1936 by Reo Motor Car Co. in Michigan.

flying kilometer – Method used to time a car for average speed in a kilometer distance by passing a starting point at full speed.

flying mile – Method used to time a car for average speed in a mile distance by passing a starting point at full speed.

flying start – Start of a race characterized by race cars moving down a raceway past a starting line in a formation.

flywheel – Heavy flat disk attached to the end of a crankshaft. The mass of a flywheel acts as a shock absorber smoothing engine output into a less jerky spinning motion. A stock flywheel is usually made out of cast iron. It is not generally designed to rotate faster than 5,000 rpm. Cast steel is used for higher rpm typically in racing applications.

flywheel ring gear – See gear(flywheel ring).

FMVSS – Abbreviation for Federal Motor Vehicle Safety Standards.

foam inhibitor – See additive(foam inhibitor).

foam resistance – Property exhibited by an oil resisting foaming in an engine crankcase or other oil reservoir. Foam can cause oil to: oxidize more easily, leak, and interfere with lubrication. Today's oils use a foam inhibitor additive.

FOB – Abbreviation for free on board (you pay for freight).

fob – Abbreviation for free on board (you pay for freight).

fog – Cloudlike layer of minute water droplets or ice crystals located near the surface.

fogging the paint – Spray painting technique used to correct a small paint fault.

fog lights – See light(fog).

foil – To cover a car clay model with thin metal foil giving it a chrome look.

foiled bright surface – Bright aluminum foil applied over car clay model to simulate chrome plated look.

following too closely – Driving condition created when a driver positions his car too close behind another for the speed he is traveling. The rule of thumb is one car length for each 10 mph in good weather, and two car lengths in bad weather. See also tailgating.

FoMoCo – Abbreviation for Ford Motor Company.

Fool-Proof – American car produced in 1912.

Foos – American car produced in 1913.

foot brake - The brake pedal.
foot operated starter - See starter drive(foot operated).
foot pedal - Pedal located near a drivers foot.
foot pound - Unit of energy measurement equal to the work required to lift a one pound weight a one foot distance.
foot traffic - People walking on a sidewalk, near a roadway, in a mall, etc.
force fit - See drive fit.
Ford - American car line produced from 1903 to date by Ford Motor Co., headquartered in Detroit, Michigan.
Ford 4 Cylinder Arrow - American car driven by Henry Ford to a 1904 world land speed record of 91.4 mph at Lake St. Claire, Michigan.
Ford, Henry - He was a self-trained American engineer who founded the Ford Motor Company in 1903. He constructed a steam engine at age 15 and became an expert watch repairman by age 20. He introduced the light serviceable car, known as the Model T in 1908. Over 15 million were sold in 19 years. See also Tin Lizzie.
Fordmobile - American car produced in 1903.
Ford Motor Company - American car manufacturing company formed in 1903 by Henry Ford.
foreign car - Car made outside the United States of America.
foreign model - See foreign car.
Forest - American car produced from 1905-1906 by Forest Motor Car Co. in Massachusetts.
Forest City - American car produced from 1906-1909.
forfeit bail - To lose bail.
forge - To shape metal by hammering while still in a hot and plastic state.
forked eight - V-8 engine.
Formula - International rules made for production of all racing cars.
Formula Car - Racing car built according to international Grand Prix Formula rules. Characteristics typically include: one seat, exposed wheels, and open cockpit. There are generally three formula classifications: One, Two, and Three. See also FIA race car group.
forward brake shoe - See brake shoe(leading).
Forster Six - Canadian car produced from 1920-1922 by Forster Motor Mfg. Co. in Quebec.
Fort Pitt - American car produced from 1908-1909 by Fort Pitt Mfg. Co. in Pennsylvania.
Fort Wayne - American car produced in 1911.
Foster - American steam car produced from 1900-1905 by Foster Automobile Co. in New York.
Fostler - American car produced from 1904-1905 by Chicago Motorcycle Co. in Illinois.
Fostoria - American car produced from 1916-1917 by Fosteria Light Car Co. in Ohio.
foul - To leave a starting line prematurely.
fouled spark plug - See spark plug fouling.
fouling temperature - Temperature below which a spark plug will foul or no longer produce a spark. It is usually considered too be around 700 degrees Fahrenheit. See also spark plug fouling, and spark plug heat range.
four banger - Four cylinder engine.
four barrel carburetor - See carburetor(four barrel).
four cycle - See engine(four cycle).
four cycle engine - See engine(four cycle).
four door hardtop - See car style(four door hardtop).
four door sedan - See car style(four door sedan).
four lane highway - Highway built with two lanes of traffic for each direction. Most U.S. freeways are four lane highways separated by a median of land.
Fournier - American car produced in 1902.
Fournier, Henry - He set a world land speed record of 76.6 mph in 1902 driving a Mors 4 Cylinder.
four on the floor - Four speed transmission.
four speed - Four speed manual transmission.
four stroke engine - See engine(four cycle).
Four Traction - American car produced from 1907-1909.
four way flasher - Hazard warning light system employed on most cars today. It consists of a flasher switch and flasher unit wired to a cars front and rear turn signals. When activated, all signal lights flash on and off continuously.
four way stop - Intersection with stop signs erected for each of four approaching roads.
four wheel brakes - Car equipped with brakes on all four wheels.
four wheel drift - Common racing maneuver used in which a car is placed in a slight slide through a turn and continues sliding by using throttle control. It is actually a mild power slide and is usually done on curves with

pavement.
Four Wheel Drive – American car produced from 1902–1907.
four wheel drive – Drivetrain used on a car or truck to power front and rear
axles.
Fox – American car produced from 1921–1923 by Fox Motor Co. in Pennsylvania.
Foyt, A J – He won the Indianapolis 500 Race in 1961, 1964, 1967, and 1977.
Average speeds were 139.1, 147.4, 151.2, and 161.3 mph. Cars driven were a
Bowes Seal-Fast Special, Sheraton-Thompson Special (1964 and 1967), and
Gilmore Racing Team. In 1972, he won the Daytona 500 Race averaging 161.6
mph in a Mercury.
f/pwr – Abbreviation for full power.
fractionating tower – See cracking tower.
Fram – American line of air, oil, and gas filters produced by Fram
Corporation.
frame – Heavy steel reinforced structure used to attach all the chassis
components. Frame supports the body and power train components, and is
supported by wheels and a suspension system. It is the foundation of a car.
frame(backbone) – Elongated X-shaped frame built with triangular frame
portions for front and rear wheel axles. It is light with high torsional
rigidity.
frame(coke bottle) – Perimeter frame built with no cross members except for
transmission support.
frame(cruciform) – X-type frame built with adjustable length center section
for changing wheelbase length on different models.
frame(ladder) – Early frame constructed to resemble a ladder. It is similar
to a perimeter frame except the rails do not surround the passenger
compartment. Several cross members are used.
frame(monocoque) – Frame constructed with an outer skin and underlying support
members. Since, the skin provides the structural strength, the underlying
frame members are minimized. A monocoque frame is comparable to a boat hull
in the manner in which strength is achieved and loads are distributed. It is
used on racing cars, is expensive to build, but is very strong in almost all
directions. See also body style(monocoque) and tub.
frame(multi tube) – Tube frame constructed with usually four main tubes. Two
main tubes run down each side of the car with vertical and diagonal bracing
between them for strength and rigidity. Cross members are also tubes. It is
a popular design for drag racing machines.
frame(perimeter) – Frame constructed with rails surrounding the passenger
compartment, and front and rear extensions. Each corner has a torque box.
frame(platform) – Frame constructed similar to a unitized frame. It is square
in the back and tapers toward the front with front extensions to the wheels.
It is used on the Volkswagen Beetle car and original Mustangs.
frame(space) – Multi-tube frame constructed into a bridgelike structure for
high strength. Many small diameter tubes are used. It became popular in the
1950s.
frame(straight rail) – Frame constructed with straight side rails and cross
members. It was commonly used until the early 1930s.
frame(sub) – Partial frame attached to an existing car frame to provide
additional support or support for a new part.
frame(tube) – Frame constructed out of tubing and welded into a strong web-
like structure using triangular bracing for rigidity. It is an expensive
frame, but popular in racing type cars where weight must be kept to a
minimum.
frame(tubular) – See frame(tube).
frame(unitized construction) – Frame constructed in which all members are
interrelated and carrying loads.
frame(unitized construction with bolt on stub frame) – Unitized frame
constructed to use a stub frame for supporting all front end components. It
is commonly used front wheel drive cars.
frame(unibody) – Car built without a traditional frame, but with carefully
interlocking pieces all working together to support each other. Many late
model cars today use this type of construction.
frame(X type) – Frame constructed with main rails crossing and forming an X-
shaped pattern. Cross members are located at both ends. It allows low
floors, but little side protection from impacts.
frame centerline – Centerline established down the middle of a car for
separating a frame equally into left and right halves. It is used as a
reference to measure from, underneath a car, when an out of line frame must
be straightened.
frame checking – Method used to determine proper alignment of a car's frame.
It is done before, during, and after the damage has been repaired. See also
frame straightening.
frame cross member – Structural steel shape positioned to run between frame
side rails.
frame damage – Frame forced out of alignment usually due to an impact. It

can cause collapsed frame sections, twisting, bending, etc.
frame member - Structural steel shape used to form part of a car's chassis.
frame rail - See frame side rail.
frame side rail - Main structural steel shape located running down both sides of a car to form the backbone of a car's chassis.
frame straightener - Car rack equipped with frame straightening equipment.
frame straightening - Process used to restore a damaged car frame to its original profile. See also frame checking.
France - One of the six largest car producing countries in the world.
franchise - Business granted the right to market a product or service developed by another company. Franchises provide several advantages for a business including: a reputation that doesn't have to be earned, a steady flow of customers from advertising by parent company, and a working method of doing business.
franchised dealership - Dealership franchised by a larger dealership or a car manufacturer.
Frankfort - American car produced in 1922.
Franklin - American car produced from 1901-1934 by H.H. Franklin Mfg. Co. in New York (1901-1917), and Franklin Automobile Co. in New York (1917-1934). It was regarded as the world's most successful air-cooled car before the Volkswagen came into being.
Franklin Truck - American truck produced in 1907.
Frantz - American car produced from 1901-1902 by Reverend H.A. Frantz in Pennsylvania.
Fraser - American steam car produced in 1911.
fraud - Deception perpetrated on someone to gain a dishonest or unfair advantage.
Frayer-Miller - American car produced from 1904-1910 by Oscar-Lear Automobile Co. in Ohio.
Frazer - American car produced from 1946-1951 by Kaiser-Frazer Corp. in Michigan.
Frazer-Nash - English sports car produced from 1924-1957 by A.F.N. Ltd.
freak drop - Small blob of paint splattered onto a paint surface with radiating spikes or tentacles around the circumference. It is usually created using an airbrush to deposit paint, then using air to fan the paint into tentacles.
freak drop painting - Custom painting technique used to create a panel of freak drops in a specific design. See also blowup painting.
Frederickson - American car produced in 1914.
Fredonia - American car produced from 1902-1904 by Fredonia Mfg. Co. in Ohio.
free diagnosis con - See con game(free diagnosis).
free flowing cylinder head - Cylinder head built with low resistance to air flow in and out of the combustion chamber area.
Freeman - American car produced in 1901 and 1931.
free play - Amount of looseness in a linkage. It is measured as the amount of movement required from application to actual response. Steering wheels have varying amounts of free play before the wheels turn. The amount depends on the design, wear, etc. See also clutch free play.
free service - Service provided by a business at no charge.
free travel - Distance traveled by a floor pedal before making contact.
freeway - Divided highway built with limited access and for high speed travel.
freeway driving - To drive on a freeway.
freeway miles - Number of miles driven on freeways. It is often used to describe the type of driving a used car has had.
freeway runner - See con game(freeway runner).
freeway signs - Signs posted on freeways at various locations to inform drivers of needed highway information.
freeway trip - Trips taken by driving on one or more freeways.
free wheeling - Condition created when a car coasts freely with a transmission engaged by means of a free wheel unit. Also, it refers to a car coasting in neutral.
free wheel unit - Overrunning clutch used in an overdrive unit. It permits coasting when drive shaft speed becomes greater than transmission speed. It was introduced in 1930 by Studebaker.
freeze plug - Circular metal plugs used to seal circular opening in an engine block cooling system circuit. Most cars have several plugs on each side of the block. They are removed, when an engine block is rebuilt, to facilitate flushing of block passages, and then reinserted when the work is done, to seal up the block cooling passageways. They also provide pressure relief in the event the block coolant freezes. The holes exist so molten material can be removed from an engine block during the casting process to form the water passageways.
freeze up - Condition created when lubricated parts sliding against each other get stuck to each other. Freezing usually occurs when a lubricated area loses its lubricating ability due to lack of lubrication or excessive

temperature. When lubrication diminishes, parts heat up, friction increases, and parts surfaces start scratching each other until the friction becomes too great for movement to continue.

freezing(parts) – See freeze up.

freezing(water) – Phenomenon created when water changes from a liquid to a solid. It occurs when water temperature drops below 32 degrees Fahrenheit.

Freidberg – American car produced in 1908.

Freighter – American car produced in 1917.

Fremont – American car produced from 1921-1922 by Fremont Motors Corp. in Ohio.

French – American car produced in 1913.

frenching – Molding a headlamp deeper into a fender.

freon – Inert gas used as a refrigerant or propellant. Properties include: low boiling point, nontoxic, noninflammable, nonexplosive, odorless, and nontoxic. Freon is derived from methane or ethane compounds.

freon 12 – Type of freon gas used in automotive air conditioning systems. It is called Dichlorodifluoromethane.

freon 22 – Type of freon gas used in non-automotive refrigerating systems.

free wheel – See overrunning clutch.

frenched headlights – Headlights molded into a car fender.

fresh air duct – Air intake duct used to route fresh air from a car's front grille area to an air cleaner's air inlet. See also hot air duct.

friction – Resistance generated between two objects touching and moving by each other. Friction is largely caused by irregularities in the surface of the two bodies. Uneven surfaces tend to interlock and offer more resistance to motion, than smooth flat surfaces. Friction is also proportional to the pressure between the surfaces. It is very important. Without it, a car could not move or stop. See also coefficient of friction.

friction bearing – Bearing with no moving parts. Bearing surface is composed of babbit, a lead compound. Lubrication between babbit material and a bearing surface is what minimizes friction. This type bearing is used in low speed heavy load situations, such as supporting large shafts.

friction disc – See clutch disc.

friction drive – Method used to transfer power on earlier cars where a driving wheel bears against a driven wheel at a right angle.

friction facing – Flat friction material bonded or riveted to both sides of a clutch plate. It is installed along the outer half and is made of heat resisting material such as asbestos.

friction material – Metal and organic substances used to make friction linings used on brake pads, brake shoes, and clutch plates. Metals used include: iron, copper, tin, nickel, lead, and brass. Non-metallic inorganic materials include: graphite, alumina, moly sulfide, and silicon dioxide. Organic materials include: asbestos, powdered resins, rubber compounds, fillers, and cork and leather (older cars). See also brake lining.

friction material(copper based) – Material composed of powdered copper and other fillers. It is popular on clutch plates where a lot of slippage is important. Its smooth surface requires a pressure plate with heavier spring pressure.

friction material(iron based) – Material composed of powdered iron and other fillers. It is a popular on racing clutches, providing more grab and no need for a special pressure plate.

friction material(metallic) – Material composed of powdered metal and other fillers. Metal based linings are more expensive to produce. Advantages include: higher energy and friction heat absorption than organic materials, higher temperature and pressure operation, reduced wear rate, increased life of friction bearing surfaces, reduced heat distortion and/or scoring tendency, and more constant coefficient of friction.

friction pad – See brake pad.

friction transmission – See transmission(friction).

fridge – Abbreviation for refrigerator.

Friedman – American car produced from 1900-1903 by Friedman Automobile Co. in Illinois.

Friend – American car produced from 1920-1921 by Friend Motors Corp. in Michigan.

Frisbee – American car produced in 1921.

frisket paper – Adhesive-backed transparent paper used in applying lettering designs to panels.

Fritchle – American electric car produced from 1904-1917 by Fritchle Auto & Battery Co. in Colorado.

Front-Away – American car produced in 1917.

front band – See brake band(front).

front bumper – Car bumper mounted on the front end of a car.

front cluster gear – See gear(front countershaft).

front countershaft gear – See gear(front countershaft).

front directionals – Front turn signal lights. See also rear directionals and light(turn signal).

Front Drive - American car produced in 1906.

Frontenac - American car produced from 1906-1913 by Abendroth & Root Mfg. Co. in New York. Also, an American car produced from 1917-1922. Also, a Canadian car produced from 1931-1933 and 1959-1960.

front end - The forward portion of a car usually ahead of the firewall. It also refers to a car's front steering, wheel, and suspension system.

front end alignment - Adjustment to the various steering angles of front tires so they turn properly in relation to each other and contact the road properly. Adjusted angles include: castor, camber, toe-in, steering axis inclination, and toe-out during turning. Front end alignment requires a careful inspection of all car components affecting wheel alignment including suspension system, weight distribution in car, and frame straightness. See also wheel alignment.

front-end gross - Dealership profit made on the sale of a new or used car. See also back-end gross.

front end roll - Tendency of a car's front end to rise on the inside of a turn, when cornering, due to centrifugal force. Anti-sway bars are used to minimize it.

front facebar - Front bumper side.

front fender - Sheetmetal panel fitted to cover an area from the headlight to front door edge, and from the lower body edge to the hood edge. Every four wheel car has two.

front fender crown - Small sheetmetal panel located at the leading edge of a front fender.

front fender skirt - Front fender portion behind the wheel.

front grille - Decorative metal panel positioned by a car's headlights. It has an open architecture to permit relatively unrestricted air flow to the radiator.

front hanger - Device used to attach the front end of a leaf spring assembly to a car frame.

Frontmobile - American car produced from 1917-1918 by Bateman Mfg. Co. and Safety Motor Co. in New Jersey.

front propeller shaft - Front half of a two piece drive shaft.

front servo - Hydraulic piston and cylinder assembly used to control tightness of a brake band encircling a front planetary gear set drum in an automatic transmission.

front shock absorber - See shock absorber(front).

front shocks - See shock absorber(front).

front suspension - See suspension system(front).

front turn signals - Signal lights mounted at the front of a car on both sides. They are used to indicate a car's turning direction by flashing.

front wheel alignment - See front end alignment.

front wheel drive - Car built to transfer engine power to the front wheels.

front wheel wobble - Condition created when front wheels vibrate or oscillate back and forth. It is usually due to wear in steering linkage.

front yoke - Transmission end of a driveline. It consists of a short splined shaft and collar assembly. The shaft portion slides into a transmission extension housing. The collar forms part of a front universal joint.

frosted window - Car window sandblasted with an art design for a customizing effect.

frozen brake drum - Brake drum binding against brake shoes.

FRP - American car produced from 1914-1918 by the Finley-Robertson-Porter Co. in New York.

FS - American car produced from 1911-1912.

FTC - Federal Trade Commission.

fuel - Any substance characterized by readily burning (combusting) and furnishing heat. It liberates a large amount of heat. In general, most fuels are composed of carbon or carbon compounds with hydrogen. Fuel can be a solid, liquid, or gas.

fuel(gas) - Fuel characterized by not being solid or liquid. Examples of gaseous fuels include: natural gas or methane, hydrogen, propane, and acetylene.

fuel(liquid) - Fuel characterized by being between a solid and a gas. Examples of liquid fuels include: gasoline, kerosene, furnace oils, alcohol, and animal fats. Car most commonly operate on liquid fuels. Most of the liquid fuels in the United States are obtained from petroleum.

fuel(solid) - Fuel characterized by being neither liquid or gas. Examples of solid fuel include: coal, coke, lignite, wood, and charcoal. Cars do not run directly on these type fuels, but can run from the heat or gases they generate.

fuel additive - Compound added to gasoline or other fuel to enhance its operating characteristics. Several types are available to help: reduce chamber deposit accumulations, reduce detonation, absorb water in the fuel, and lubricate valve stems and the upper cylinder wall area. See also additive.

fuel burner - See fueler.

fuel cell - Electrochemical device used to convert chemical energy directly into electrical energy. Oxygen and hydrogen are usually used as the active materials with some type of solid ion-exchange membrane used as a solid electrolyte. The oxygen and hydrogen are introduced on opposite sides of the solid electrolyte when electrical power is required. Their flow rate determines the power generated.

fuel consumption - Amount of fuel consumed by a car's engine during driving. It is usually expressed as miles per gallon. See also fuel economy.

fuel cut solenoid - Electrically operated plunger used to stop fuel flow in a carburetor's idling circuit when a car's ignition is shut off. It is used to combat dieseling. It typically consists of a long slender rod that remains retracted as long as current flows to the solenoid. See also idle stop solenoid.

fuel dam - Shallow troughs located on the plenum floor of certain intake manifolds. There are usually several located directly underneath the carburetor for the purpose of minimizing fuel puddling.

fuel economy - Measure of a car's fuel consumption made by computing the number of miles driven and dividing it by the gallons of fuel consumed. Also, it refers to how stingy a car is in using gas. Fuel economy is affected by such factors as: driving habits; traffic conditions; car weight; rolling resistance; terrain and weather; type of transmission and gearing; carburetor design and adjustments; stuck or slow operating choke; engine design, temperature, timing, rpm, internal friction, and wear; fouled spark plug(s); fuel delivery system leaks; dragging brakes; plugged or stuck heat control valve; need for a tune-up; dirty air filter; poor engine compression; engine oil too thick; low transmission fluid; low tire pressure; horsepower to weight ratio; wheel bearing friction; front end alignment; tire size; type of exhaust system; air dams; and solid state and sensor controls used on some cars to monitor and regulate timing and carburetion. See also gas mileage, gas saving tip, and engine problem(fuel economy poor).

fueler - Car engine built to burn special racing fuels.

fuel evaporation control system - See vapor recovery system.

fuel filter - Filter used to remove dirt, rust particles, sludge, and water from fuel. Locations can include: fuel lines, fuel pump, carburetor fuel inlet. Filter materials include: paper element (most common), ceramic material, and fine wire mesh.

fuel foaming - Hot fuel transformed into foam in a carburetor's float bowl as a result of high temperatures in the engine compartment. The foam flows out of the bowl vent and into the carburetor airway increasing the air/fuel mixture's richness. Winter gas formulated with higher volatility (lower boiling point) is prone to this phenomenon when used on warm days. Fuel foaming differs from vapor lock in that foaming will force raw gasoline from the float bowl into the carburetor airway when the engine stalls, while vapor locking empties the float bowl and accelerator pump circuit of all liquid fuel so even the accelerator pump won't squirt fuel into the carburetor airway. Engines suffering from fuel foaming will tend to stall, lose power, and be hard to start when stopped until engine compartment cools down. See also heat soak, vapor lock, car service tip(fuel foaming), engine problem(speed unattainable), and engine problem(stalling-1).

fuel gauge - Gauge used to measure the amount of fuel in a fuel tank. It consists of two units: a gauge in the dashboard and a remote sensing unit in the fuel tank. The sensing unit consists of a lever with a float mounted at one end and a sliding resistance contact at the other. Different electrical resistance is registered depending on the position of the float. Resistance is translated electrically into fuel gauge readings you see at the dashboard.

fuel heater - Heater used in a diesel fuel line to warm diesel fuel. Its purpose is to help prevent wax build-up in cold diesel fuel that could plug and/or damage diesel injection pump.

fuelie - See fueler.

fuel injected - To inject or force fuel under pressure into an engine intake manifold or combustion chamber, usually through one or more injector nozzles.

fuel injection - Fuel forced under pressure directly into a combustion chamber or intake manifold. It is a more precise way of metering fuel to an engine, but is also much more expensive than carburetion. Fuel injection systems are used in both gas and diesel engines. They can operate electronically or mechanically and with or without the use of a computer. Advantages include: more power, better fuel economy, better cold engine starting, higher torque, quicker engine warm-ups, reduced intake airway heating requirements, lower intake air temperatures, lower emissions, no fuel flow on deceleration, more accurate fuel delivery, quicker engine response, and more resistant to vapor lock and fuel foaming. Disadvantages include: injector discharge tips prone to plugging with dirty or wrong type gasoline, and greater expense. See also fuel injector deposit.

fuel injection(diesel) - Fuel delivery system used to force diesel fuel into a diesel engine's combustion chambers. This is done because a diesel engine does not do as good job of developing vacuum as a gasoline engine does. The system typically consists of a pump, cylinder injectors, and necessary lines. The pump must generate pressures high enough to overcome the cylinder pressure at ignition time. Diesel fuel is injected at the time of ignition when high internal temperature causes ignition of a fuel mixture with compressed air. A properly functioning injection system must perform the following: meter the correct amount of fuel to each injector, time the injection, control the injection rate, atomize the fuel, and distribute the fuel in a chamber.

fuel injection(diesel-air injection) - Early diesel fuel injection system used using external air pressure blasts to force fuel into a cylinder.

fuel injection(diesel-solid injection) - Diesel fuel injection system used which exerts direct pressure on fuel to force it into a cylinder. Different types include: pressure-time, distributor, multiple unit, and unit injection.

fuel injection(gas) - Fuel delivery system used to eliminate the need for a carburetor by spraying a specified amount of fuel into the intake manifold entrance or near each intake valve. The two basic types are single and multipoint injection.

fuel injection(gas-constant) - Gasoline fuel injection system used to inject a small continuous amount of fuel into an intake manifold as long as an engine is running. Single point or throttle body injection uses this system.

fuel injection(gas-cylinder) - See fuel injection(gas-multi point).

fuel injection(gas-intermittent) - Gasoline fuel injection system used to inject fuel into an intake manifold when each cylinder is on its intake stroke. Multipoint injection uses this system.

fuel injection(gas-manifold) - Gasoline fuel injection system used to inject fuel into an intake manifold.

fuel injection(gas-multipoint) - Gasoline fuel injection system used to inject fuel to a fuel injector mounted outside each engine cylinder's intake valve. Fuel is injected onto a hot intake valve as the air enters the respective cylinder. This system uses the intake manifold only for routing air to the cylinders. Multipoint is a more expensive system, but offers better performance. It is commonly found on sports, luxury, and heavy late model cars.

fuel injection(gas-port) - See fuel injection(gas-multipoint).

fuel injection(gas-single point) - Gasoline fuel injection system used to inject fuel at the entrance to an intake manifold with a throttle body unit. Fuel is injected continuously through one injector with a second often used when engine demand is heavy. It is a common economy version of fuel injection.

fuel injection(gas-throttle body) - See fuel injection(gas-single point).

fuel injection(gas-timed) - See fuel injection(gas-intermittent).

fuel injection system - Assemblage of parts used to inject the proper amount of fuel into an engine at the proper time under different operating conditions. A typical gas fuel injection system consists primarily of: a pump, injector lines, and injectors.

fuel injector - Device used to meter fuel in an atomized form under pressure into an engine's intake system. Fuel injectors are prone to clogging if a proper fuel is not used. Low detergency fuel or water/alcohol mixtures can cause deposits to form at the tip as a result of evaporation. A clogged tip will result in: uneven spray pattern, loss of power, surging, and misfiring.

fuel injector deposit - Combustion by-products formed on the tip of an injector. Today's hot running engines using fuel injectors near the combustion chambers are prone to plugging up due to carbon and varnish deposits baking on after a hot engine is shut down. High detergent gasoline helps to minimize the deposit formation. If allowed to plug up, the engine will begin starving for fuel and exhibit lean fuel mixture engine problems.

fuel injector pintle - Movable pin located in a fuel injector body for metering fuel at the injector's discharge end.

fuel inlet - Fuel entry point on a carburetor body.

fuel knock - See detonation.

fuel level - Measurement made from some top part of a carburetor to the fuel level in the float bowl. See also float level.

fuel level gauge - Gauge used to register fuel level or quantity of fuel remaining in a fuel tank.

fuel line - Steel and/or rubber piping used to transport fuel from a cars fuel tank to a carburetor. A fuel pump bisects a line either at a tank or near a carburetor.

fuel mileage numbers - Fuel economy determined for a specified car under different driving conditions such as city driving and highway driving. See also EPA numbers, and EPA fuel mileage.

fuel mixture - Mixture of fuel and air used to power an engine. Fuel is usually gasoline, but can be propane, alcohol, etc. A mixture of 16 parts

air to one part fuel is common for gasoline. See also air/fuel ratio.
fuel mixture turbulence – Degree to which flow of an air/fuel mixture into a
combustion chamber becomes non-laminar. Advantages of turbulent mixture
include: more quicker and more complete burning process, reduced exposure of
end gases to pressure and heat, minimized fuel mixture boundary layer, and
more even distribution of residual gases in incoming fuel mixture.
   A nonturbulent mixture will not only negate the above advantages, but will
also tend to encourage detonation due to poorer ignition of fuel mixture.
fuel pickup – Inlet point in a car's fuel tank. A filter is often mounted
there.
fuel pickup pipe – Section of fuel line located in the fuel tank. It runs
from the fuel pickup to the top or exit point of the tank.
fuel pressure – Pressure exerted on fuel to pump it through fuel lines. A
pressure of 1-3 psi is typical when reaching a carburetor. Electric fuel
pumps push the fuel at somewhat higher pressure in order to overcome
resistance losses in lines and maintain desired output pressure at a
carburetor.
fuel pressure regulator – Device mounted in a fuel delivery system near a
carburetor to control fuel pressure to a set level.
fuel puddling – Condensation of fuel vapor into small puddles in an intake
manifold. It is caused by temperature drop and forcing fuel vapor around
sharp curves in the runners. An intake manifold prone to fuel puddling will
cause hard starting, and poor idle problems.
fuel pump – Pump used to move fuel from a fuel tank to an engine's carburetor.
A fuel pump can be powered manually or electrically. Vacuum is usually used
to draw fuel from a fuel tank, and pressure is used to push the fuel to a
carburetor or a fuel injection system. Pumps mounted near a gas tank are
more efficient because pumps work better pushing fluid, then pulling it.
Mechanical fuel pumps are mounted on an engine block and powered by the
engine's camshaft. Electrical pumps are almost always mounted near a fuel
tank. Some electrical pumps run continuously while others pump only when
fuel pressure drops below a specified level. Different type electric pumps
include: impeller, diaphragm, bellows, and plunger. A good quality fuel pump
should pump at least one quart of fuel per minute into an open container.
See also diesel injection pump.
fuel pump diaphragm – Circular rubber like membrane used to pump fuel when it
moves back and forth in a fuel pump.
fuel pump eccentric – Elliptical shaped surface mounted on a cam shaft for
driving a mechanical fuel pump lever.
fuel pump test – Test made to determine a cars fuel pumping capacity. If a
pump cannot keep up with a carburetors demand, an engine will starve for fuel
in all off idle carburetion modes.
fuel quantity governor – Device used on diesel injection pumps to regulate
fuel flow to the injectors.
fuel stability – Ability specified of a fuel to remain in stable condition
when stored for significant periods of time. Stability is determined by
resistance to formation of gums, lacquers, sediments, etc., and may be a
natural characteristic of a fuel or one gained through addition of certain
additives.
fuel strainer – Small fine wire mesh cylinder used to trap particles of debris
in fuel. It is commonly found in carburetor fuel inlets.
fuel surge – Extra fuel flowing into an engine for a brief period of time.
Possible causes include: carburetor float bowl needle valve stuck open due to
dirt particles, and rich fuel mixture due to electronic or vacuum controls
malfunction.
fuel switch – Anti-theft device designed to stop fuel flow into a carburetor.
fuel system cleaning – To clean all passageways responsible for moving fuel.
fuel tank vent line – Fuel vapor line running from a charcoal canister to the
fuel tank. It routes any gasoline vapors to a charcoal canister. See also
vapor recovery system, purge line, and carburetor fuel bowl vent line.
fulcrum – Support and pivot point located on a lever lifting an object.
full bore – To drive a car with the throttle wide open.
Fuller – American car produced from 1908-1910 by Angus Automobile Co. in
Nebraska (1908), and Fuller Buggy Co. in Michigan (1909-1910).
full floating axle – See axle(full floating).
full flow oil filter – See oil filter(full flow).
full house – Engine modified for the maximum attainable performance.
full mark – Indicator line used on an oil or transmission dipstick to show the
desired maximum oil level. If oil is filled above this mark, the crankshaft
will begin striking the oil pool as it rotates. Such a condition tends to:
increase oil temperature through agitation, cause oil foaming, throw more oil
on the cylinder walls increasing oil consumption, and cause possible oil
fouling of spark plugs. See also add mark.
full race – Engine modified and tuned for drag racing. It usually idles
poorly.

full retard – See basic timing.

full service – Car service offered at a service station usually including: filling the gas tank with fuel; washing windows; and checking engine fluids, belts, and tire pressures. Such service is usually added into the price of the fuel.

full tank of gas – Fuel tank filled completely with gas.

full time mechanic – Mechanic employed full time at an auto repair business.

Fulton – American car produced in 1908 and 1917.

full warranty – See warranty(full).

funny car – Stock car modified for racing and still resembling the original stock design. They look funny because of such differences as: a changed wheelbase, large tires, and altered body style.

Fury – American car produced from 1955-1985 by Plymouth Division of Chrysler Corp. in Michigan.

fuse – Protective device used in an electrical circuit to stop current flow when it becomes excessive. Typical fuse is a small glass tube with metal ends containing a small piece of low melting point wire. The size, thickness, and type of wire determines current carrying capacity of a fuse.

fuse block – Panel unit used to centralize the major car electrical circuits and equip them with fuses to protect each circuit from getting overloaded. The block assembly consists of: a mounting surface for the fuse holders, the fuse holders, terminals for routing the electric circuits to the fuses, and the fuses. A cover is usually supplied which also briefly describes each circuit.

fuse box – See fuse block.

fuse pack – Small container with assorted fuses.

fuse panel – See fuse block.

fusible link – High current fuse constructed to melt when a certain current flow is reached. It is used in high current circuits typically moving 50-100 amperes.

fusion – Phenomenon created when two metals reach their melting points and flow or weld together.

Futura – American car produced from 1960-1982 by Ford Motor Co. in Michigan.

fuzz – Policeman.

fwd – Front wheel drive.

FWD Car – American car produced in 1910.

FWD Truck – American truck produced in 1910.

Fwick – American car produced in 1912.

FX car – Factory experimental car.

G

G(1) – Unit of acceleration equal to the force of gravity, and used to measure a car's roadholding ability.

G(2) – Auction car rating code used to specify a car in good condition.

Gabelich, Gary – He set a world land speed record of 630.3 mph in 1970 driving a Blue Flame.

Gabriel(1) – American car produced in 1912.

Gabriel(2) – He raced a Mors car in the 1903 Paris-Madrid race averaging 65.3 mph to Bordeaux.

Gadabout – American car produced in 1915.

gadgetry – Mechanical or electrical device.

Gaeth – American car produced in 1898 and 1902-1911 by Gaeth Motor Car Co. in Ohio.

gage pressure – Pressure measured as a difference between atmospheric and absolute pressure. For example, a pressure of 8 psi gage would be 8 + 14.6 or 22.60 psi absolute. A pressure of -5 psi gage would be 14.6-5 or 9.6 psi absolute. Zero gage pressure is atmospheric pressure or 14.6 psi. Most automotive gauges; such as vacuum, oil pressure, turbo booster, etc.; measure gage pressure. See also absolute pressure.

gal – Abbreviation for gallon.

Galaxie – American car produced from 1957-1977 by Ford Motor Co. in Michigan.

Gale – American car produced from 1904-1910 by Western Tool Works in Illinois.

galling – Situation created when two rubbing surfaces damage each other because of excessive friction, bad alignment, etc. Damage usually appears in the form of chafing, scratches, chipping, etc.

Galloway – American car produced from 1908-1910 and 1915-1917 by the William Galloway Co. in Iowa.

Galt – Canadian car produced from 1911-1915 by Canadian Motors in Ontario.

galvanize – To plate or coat a metal surface with zinc to protect against rusting.

galvanometer – Instrument used to detect and measure small current flow.

gap – Intended physical break used to disrupt the continuity of an electrical circuit. Some remain fixed while others open and close. Examples include spark plug electrodes and contact points. Some gaps are used to interrupt the flow of current, while others are used generate high voltage sparks.

gap the plugs – See spark plug gapping.

gap setting – Air thickness specified between two points of an electrical circuit. Spark plugs and ignition contact points have certain air gap settings.

gar – Abbreviation for garaged.

garagable – Degree to which a car's size allows it to be parked in a normal sized garage.

garaged – Car condition created when a used car has spent a great deal of its time stored in a garage or kept there when parked.

garage goon – Dishonest and/or inexperienced car mechanic or repairman.

Gardner – American car produced from 1919-1931 by the Gardner Motor Co. in Missouri.

Gareau 35 – Canadian car produced in 1909-1910.

Garford – American car produced from 1906-1912 and 1916 by Garford Mfg. Co. in Ohio.

Garford Truck – American truck produced in 1907.

Garlits, Don – He was considered one of the first professional drag racers. He began working the drag racing circuit in the 1950s and became famous. He went by the name Big Daddy.

garnish molding – Inside door panel molding located above the armrest, composed usually of metal, and used as a retainer for a door trim panel. Also, it is found on "A" pillars, roof rails, and backlight.

Gary – American car produced from 1916-1917 by Gary Automobile Mfg. Co. in Indiana.

Gary Truck – American truck produced in 1915.

gas(1) – State of matter characterized by being less dense than a liquid and not having a definite shape or volume. When heated and cooled, gas greatly expands and contracts. Gas is regarded as a fluid in that it flows readily and requires a vessel to contain it.

gas(2) – Gasoline.

Gas-Au-Lec – American car produced from 1905-1906 by Vaughn Machine Co. and Corwin Mfg. Co. in Massachusetts.

gas buggy – Early term used to describe a car using a gas burning internal combustion engine.

gas-charged shock - Shock absorber constructed to use an inert gas under pressure for dampening action.

gas coupe - Racing car built to run on gasoline.

Gas Engine - American car produced from 1905-1906.

gas engine - See engine(gasoline).

gas explosion - Explosion caused when gas vapors ignite rapidly.

gas gauge - See fuel level gauge.

gas guzzler - Car characterized as having poor fuel economy.

gasket - Flexible sheet-like material placed between the flat metal surfaces of two parts to seal their connection. Gaskets are commonly needed because precise flatness or smoothness is almost impossible to achieve. Several types of materials are used including: cork, paper, and rubber. Some form into a shape when applied eliminating the need for actual precut gaskets. One such material is silicone.

gasket cement - Adhesive compound used to glue gasket material to parts being connected.

gas lamps - Headlights used on early cars powered by a gas such as acetylene.

Gaslight - American car produced from 1960-1961 by Gaslight Motors Corp. in Michigan. It was a replica of a 1902 Rambler.

gas line - See fuel line.

gas mileage - Number of miles traveled on a gallon of fuel. Gas mileage is usually expressed in terms of city or highway driving. Highway driving mileage in today's cars is often 50-75 percent greater than city driving. See also fuel economy.

gas mileage device - Device installed on a car to supposedly increase the number of miles traveled on a gallon of fuel. Some devices do work while others are just gimmicks to get your money. See also gas saving tip.

gas mizer - Car characterized by having good fuel economy.

Gasmobile - American car produced from 1900-1902 by Automobile Company of America in New Jersey.

gasohol - Fuel mixture composed of usually 90 percent gasoline and 10 percent alcohol (the maximum concentration allowed by law). Advantages include: higher octane rating (2-3 points at 10 percent blend), and lower carbon monoxide emissions. Disadvantages include: tendency of alcohol to attract water (when the two mix, alcohol often no longer remains mixed in gasoline), increased vapor pressure (1-3 pounds at 10 percent blend causing possible vapor lock problems in hot weather), corrosive nature of alcohol on many fuel system components. Gasohol mixed with more than 10 percent alcohol can cause the following problems for a non-alcohol designed engine including: rapid oxidation (corrosion) of steel, iron, pot metal, and aluminum surfaces coming in contact with the fuel vapor; dilution of engine oil; and plugging of small carburetor passages.

   Two types of alcohol are used: methanol and ethanol. Of the two, methanol is regarded as potentially far more damaging to fuel system components. Anticorrosive agents are added to methanol blends to supposedly counteract this problem. As a general rule, never use ethanol blends over 10 percent, methanol blends over 5 percent, or methanol blends without anticorrosive agents. See also alcohol.

gasoline - Volatile liquid hydrocarbon fuel used to power internal combustion engines. It is a petroleum product with no precise chemical formula because it is a mixture of various hydrocarbon compounds of the methane series. They include: pentane, hexane, heptane, undecane, decane, nonane, and octane. The boiling points of these compounds range from 100-400 degrees Fahrenheit with gasoline boiling from 40-225 degrees depending on composition.

   An ideal gasoline typically has the following properties: allows easy starting, permits engine to run smoothly with only trace detonation, resists vapor locking, minimizes deposits in fuel delivery system and combustion chambers, provides good fuel economy, and is the least expensive.

   Current gasoline consumption in the United States averages around 100 billion gallons annually.

gasoline(ethyl) - Gasoline formulated with tetraethyl lead, ethylene dichloride, and ethylene dibromide. The compounds slow down and control the air/fuel burning rate.

gasoline(gasohol) - Gasoline composed of up to 10 percent alcohol by volume. See also gasohol.

gasoline(half and half) - Gasoline mixture composed of equal parts leaded regular and unleaded super. It performs similar to unleaded super, yet provides adequate lead to lubricate soft exhaust valve engines.

gasoline(high detergent) - Gasoline formulated with certain compounds to help keep intake and combustion chamber portions of an engine from accumulating deposits. Fuel-injected cars benefit from an occasional tank of premium high detergent gasoline.

gasoline(leaded) - Gasoline formulated with tetraethyl lead, a poisonous lead compound added to boost octane rating and lubricate soft valves and valve seats. More and more cars are now running on unleaded gasoline. Leaded gasoline emits harmful contaminants into the air through the exhaust. The Environmental Protection Agency plans to phase this gasoline out in the next few years.

gasoline(leaded premium) - Gasoline formulated with tetraethyl lead and having an octane rating typically ranging from 88-90.

gasoline(leaded regular) - Gasoline formulated with tetraethyl lead with octane ratings typically ranging from 86-88.

gasoline(no name) - Surplus gasoline purchased from major refiners at a discount with savings usually passed on to motorists.

gasoline(premium) - Gasoline formulated with tetraethyl lead and having a higher octane rating than regular. Premium is popular with high performance engines, but is not widely sold anymore.

gasoline(regular) - See gasoline(leaded).

gasoline(summer) - Gasoline refined for use in the summer. It usually has a higher boiling point to help minimize vapor lock during hot weather. Different brands have different boiling points. See also gasoline(winter) and vapor lock.

gasoline(super unleaded) - See gasoline(unleaded premium).

gasoline(unleaded) - Gasoline formulated with essentially no lead. This type of gasoline is more expensive, but is supposedly cleaner burning.

gasoline(unleaded premium) - Gasoline formulated with no lead and an octane rating typically ranging from 87-89.

gasoline(unleaded regular) - Gasoline formulated with no lead and an octane rating typically ranging from 85-87.

gasoline(unleaded super) - See gasoline(unleaded premium).

gasoline(winter) - Gasoline refined for winter use. It has a lower boiling point so fuel vapors can be more readily created for easier starting. Different brands have different boiling points. See also gasoline(summer) and vapor lock.

gasoline alley - Race track location used for preparing and assembling race cars. See also paddock.

gasoline engine - See engine(gasoline).

Gasoline Motor Carriage - American car produced in 1897.

gasoline pipes - See fuel line.

gas pedal - See accelerator.

gas pedal sticking - Condition created when carburetor's throttle linkage binds. Possible causes include: broken return springs, cable linkage kinked, throttle plate shaft binding, obstruction near linkage causing binding, and linkage parts binding.

gas pump - Pumping device used to meter gasoline at service stations.

gas pumper - Person employed at a service station to pump gas and often do mechanic work as well. Their work experience may vary widely.

gas return lines - Fuel lines used to return gas vapors or liquid gas back to a fuel tank. Some fuel systems are designed to continuously pump fuel to a carburetor and allow whatever is not used to return to a fuel tank. See also vapor recovery system.

gas saving tip - An idea, method, technique, procedure, and/or device used to supposedly improve a car's fuel economy. Many tips do improve fuel economy while others are just gimmicks to get your money.

gas saving tip(advancing the timing) - Advancing ignition timing about 5 degrees over factory setting usually improves gas mileage on older cars with less elaborate timing controls. It increases power derived from each air/fuel mixture ignition. Spark plug gaps should be reduced slightly. Advancing the timing may cause the engine to ping or detonate under load if the fuel's octane rating is not high enough. Driving tests will determine where the limit is. Significant advance is not recommended if the car regularly performs the following: drives uphill grades, carries loads, and accelerates for power. See also advance(excessive).

gas saving tip(air bleed screw) - Idle mixture adjustment screw constructed with a hole drilled down the center. The idea behind the device is introduction of additional air into the idle air/fuel mixture to increase fuel economy. The same effect can be created by backing off on the existing screw or pulling an intake manifold hose. The device merely provides a vacuum leak into an engine and does not increase fuel economy.

gas saving tip(air conditioner) - A car air conditioner requires extra engine power to operate. When engaged, it typically removes 5-10 mph of speed from an engine. Depending on engine size, fuel consumption can increase 5-15 percent. A cutout switch can be installed to work with a throttle and stop an air conditioner when a car is climbing a hill or passing. A driver can also simply turn it off during those times. Another simple energy-saving technique is to remove the air conditioner belt during cooler times of the year. A belt will exert some drag on an engine even when an air conditioner is not engaged.

gas saving tip(air injector) - Device used to provide additional air to an intake manifold through a fitting in the manifold. It functions on manifold vacuum. When the vacuum becomes low, it opens to admit additional air into the manifold and help lean out the air/fuel mixture. The effect unbalances the mixture reaching the cylinders. No significant improvements in fuel economy have been verified.

gas saving tip(brakes) - Unnecessary brake dragging increases rotation resistance, lowering fuel economy. Warped drums or rotors can cause this. Also, brake shoes adjusted too close to a drum surface will drag.

gas saving tip(carburetor rebuild kit) - Often times a carburetor with 40-60,000 miles clogs up somewhat with gum and other debris. In that time, the float needle and seat can wear, the accelerator pump diaphragm can deteriorate, gaskets can begin leaking, passageways gum and clog up, etc. A rebuild kit and carburetor cleaning rectifies these problems allowing the carburetor to function efficiently, and therefore meter the proper amount of fuel under different engine loads. It also provides an opportunity to experiment with different main jet sizes. See also gas saving tip(smaller main jets).

gas saving tip(changing camshaft) - Camshafts are available with cam lobes profiled to increase fuel economy. Valve timing is usually changed so intake valves close sooner on the compression stroke resulting in less fuel consumption and more low-end torque. Cam manufacturers claim mileage increases of 1-3 mpg on larger engines. It may be a worthwhile investment if a car's cam needs replacing.

gas saving tip(changing carburetor) - Later model carburetors can often be retrofitted to older engines to increase fuel economy. Fuel calibration is more adjustable and precise. In addition, certain four barrel carburetor designs are actually more fuel efficient than two barrel types on larger engines. Mileage improvements of 20-30 percent have been achieved on some V-8 engines using a more efficient carburetor. Carburetors are best changed if the existing one provides poor fuel economy or is worn out. A carburetor rebuild or modification should be considered first.

gas saving tip(changing head) - The cylinder head of a car directly affects an engine's breathing characteristics. Gas mileage can increase significantly if the compression ratio is raised. Also, smaller valves and associated ports help. Certain engines can be swapped for heads that are 1-3 points higher in compression. Sometimes a head can be milled to increase the ratio. Mileage improvements of 3-6 mpg on large block engines have been attained through higher compression ratios once the carburetion and ignition timing has been reset. One drawback is a higher compression ratio requires use of a higher octane fuel.

gas saving tip(changing intake manifold) - Aftermarket intake manifolds are available for V-8 engines that: provide smooth low resistance air flow, significantly increase gas mileage, cause engine to run smoother, and provide increased power and low end torque. The decreased air flow resistance usually requires modifying carburetor fuel metering to obtain maximum mileage gain. Gas mileage has improved 30 percent on some installations where a manifold and tuned or special carburetor has been installed.

gas saving tip(changing rear end ratios) - A differential with a lower ratio will increase rear wheel rotation in each gear. Entire units can be bought or the pinion and ring gear set can be purchased. In the latter case, the gears will have to be properly installed. Not all cars have different rear end ratios available. A lower ratio will definitely increase fuel economy like an overdrive. For example, a differential that produces 25 percent faster rotation would provide as much as 25 percent better fuel economy at highway speeds. A lower ratio differential is cheaper than an overdrive unit, but it also decreases a cars acceleration and climbing ability in each gear.

gas saving tip(driving habits) - A number of driving techniques help to increase fuel economy. They include: avoid jack rabbit starts in city driving; keep engine rpm down as much as possible; cold start an engine properly; consolidate short trips; maintain even speeds; drive up hills with a steady throttle; reduce speed when carrying a heavy load, bucking a strong headwind, and driving in wet snow; drive with wind whenever possible; minimize shifting; shift from lower gears as soon as possible; avoid excess idling; minimize fast stopping; catch lights; brake gradually to a stop; avoid weaving in and out of traffic; and drive within speed limits (driving at 80 versus 50 mph can increase fuel consumption up to 50 percent).

gas saving tip(electronic ignition system) - An electronic ignition system, added to a conventional ignition system car, usually provides the following improvements: negligible point wear, precise timing, hotter and more consistent spark. The addition of such a device along with a properly functioning carburetor and spark plugs of a proper heat range can provide mileage increases of 1-3 mpg. A capacitative discharge unit is one of the more popular aftermarket add-ons.

gas saving tip(exhaust tuning) - A car's exhaust system can be modified to increase fuel economy and available power by decreasing backpressure and increasing exhaust gas scavenging. The most common modification involves the use of headers, larger diameter exhaust pipes, and low back pressure mufflers. An increase of 1-3 mpg on V-8 engines is common in city driving. See also exhaust tuning.

gas saving tip(fast idle) – Adjusting an engine's fast idle to 600-800 rpm will decrease gas consumption when it is cold. It may require experimenting to determine the lowest rpm possible without stalling.

gas saving tip(five speed transmission) – A car equipped with a five speed manual transmission can save 5-10 percent on fuel consumption over a four or three speed manual transmission.

gas saving tip(front end alignment) – Tires improperly aligned will have increased rolling resistance and shorter life. Front ends should be checked at least every time new tires are installed and as often as every year to maintain peak operation.

gas saving tip(fuel additives) – Fuel additives are available claiming to: lubricate an engine's upper end, cool an air/fuel mixture burn, increase octane rating, and remove moisture from fuel and a fuel system. Such additives don't increase fuel economy. Those used for moisture removal are helpful.

gas saving tip(gas to propane conversion) – Switching an engine from gasoline to propane usually lowers fuel economy significantly. Propane has a lower Btu content and a slower burn time than gasoline. Thus an engine will require more fuel under the same gas load and will have reduced power as well. To increase engine performance, an engine would have to be modified as follows: increase compression ratio, increase ignition advance, and increase propane and air flow into cylinders.

gas saving tip(Hydro Catalyst) – A carburetor to intake manifold gasket device constructed with two cone shaped screens mounted in the openings projecting toward the manifold. The screens supposedly have different polarities which electrically excite and make the air/fuel mixture more combustible. The end result is more efficient combustion, lower emissions, and better gas mileage. Certain test cars have shown a mileage increase up to 5 percent. Leaded gas appears to show the most favorable improvement.

gas saving tip(idle speed) – High idle speed causes greater fuel consumption. Tests have shown small rpm increases have lowered fuel economy 1-2 percent.

gas saving tip(ignition timing) – Late model cars with elaborate spark timing controls do not usually benefit from timing modification. Tests have shown that advancing or retarding such cars 5-6 degrees lowers fuel economy 3-5 percent. See also gas saving tip(advancing the timing).

gas saving tip(increasing air flow) – The air/fuel mixture ratio is controlled by the amount of air and fuel reaching a carburetor airway. Paper filter elements reduce airflow especially when dirty, and can lower fuel economy 1-2 percent. They should be cleaned frequently. Extra openings can be made in the top portion of an air cleaner outside the air filter which will increase the air supply somewhat and cause an engine to run a little leaner. Aftermarket polyurethane filter elements are effective in maintaining good airflow and can be cleaned with soap and water when dirty.

gas saving tip(lighter transmission oil) – Changing from a 80-90 weight oil down to a 40 weight oil in a transmission provides only a negligible increase in fuel economy. It is not worth the risk to a transmission since a lower weight oil will not adequately protect gears against heat and heavy load stresses.

gas saving tip(mini supercharger) – Device mounted on a carburetor base containing a small propeller-like blade for each venturi which spin in the air flow. It is suppose to improve fuel atomization by striking and mixing the fuel mixture. In reality, the propellers actually increase air stream resistance somewhat and nullifies any positive effect. The result is a device producing no noticeable improvement in gas mileage.

gas saving tip(overdrive unit) – Two speed transmission mounted behind a manual or automatic transmission to reduce engine rpm in each gear. Overdrive units definitely increase fuel economy. For example, a unit reducing engine rpms 15 percent could increase fuel economy at highway speeds up to 15 percent. It is, however, expensive at $400-700 and also requires modification of an existing driveline as well proper installation.

gas saving tip(preheating intake air) – Cars equipped without preheated air systems suffer in fuel economy especially in the winter. All preheat systems warm the air by drawing it from a heat stove around the exhaust manifold into the air cleaner. The best solution is to get an existing air cleaner with an air gate and temperature sensor already built in, and an existing heat stove. This will require some checking to determine what car make and model would best retrofit to your car. First, the size and shape air cleaner your car can handle is determined. The exhaust manifold is carefully observed to determine how to shroud part of it. A trip is then made to a good size wrecking yard to locate the parts needed by looking at different car makes and models. An exhaust shroud may have to be made for the car.

gas saving tip(pumping gas) - Gasoline losses due to evaporation and expansion can be minimized by following a few guidelines. They include: keep tank at least three quarter full when not in use, buy gas in the morning or late evening, and don't over fill.

gas saving tip(removing emission controls) - Removing emission controls on older engines can increase fuel economy and performance, but not on the more recent computer controlled ones. The case is moot anyway, since it is illegal to alter or remove emission control equipment.

gas saving tip(smaller main jets) - Main jet size can often be decreased several thousandths. Most carburetors are set to meter fuel at sea level air pressure and 70 degrees Fahrenheit. Main jet sizes can be decreased .002 inches in diameter for every 2,000 feet of elevation, and for every 35 degree increase in temperature. The opposite is true for colder temperatures. In addition to changes due to air pressure and temperature, jets can also get smaller as timing is advanced. Experimentation and driving tests will confirm the optimum settings.

gas saving tip(spark intensifier) - Small capacitor wired into a secondary circuit of an ignition system. The claim is that a brief hot spark is created each time the coil discharges boosting the spark at the spark plugs. In reality, no benefit is derived.

gas saving tip(spark plug gap) - Spark plug gaps should be narrower for highway driving and wider for city driving. The proper gap will lengthen the plug life and provide better fuel economy. Tests have shown spark plugs with gaps 0.020-30 larger or smaller than specified will lower fuel economy by 15-25 percent.

gas saving tip(spark plug intensifier) - Device usually mounted on top of a spark plug to supposedly increase the spark strength and improve fuel economy. It may decrease a spark plug's tendency to foul, but that is all. See also spark plug intensifier.

gas saving tip(spoiler) - Car wind resistance can be reduced somewhat by adding a front spoiler. It generates a downward force on the front end at higher speeds eliminating floating and reducing air turbulence and thus drag under a car. Mileage gains of 1-3 mpg have been reported depending on wind conditions and driving speeds.

gas saving tip(synthetic oil) - See gas saving tip(unusual lubricants) and oil(synthetic).

gas saving tip(thermostat) - Engines running cooler don't vaporize and burn fuel as completely as hotter engines. If an engine has a 160 degree or cooler thermostat, one rated at 180-190 degrees should increase fuel economy.

gas saving tip(tire pressure) - Tire pressure affects rolling resistance. Minimum rolling resistance is achieved by significantly overinflating tires. The ride, however, is harsh and tires wear prematurely in the center of the tread. Car manufacturers typically recommend pressures below tire manufacturers to achieve a softer ride. During fall, winter, and spring, cold tires can safely be inflated 4-6 pounds above car manufacturer's recommendations or 10 percent over maximum pressure specified on tire's sidewall. Such inflation will create a somewhat harsher ride, and will increase tire wear only slightly or reduce it significantly, depending on the tire's design. Studies have shown that boosting tire pressure 5 lbs over car manufacturer's recommendations can increase tire life over 15 percent. Higher tire pressure will also reduce rolling resistance, and often improve fuel economy 1-3 percent. Tires underinflated 5-10 lbs can lower fuel economy 1-3 percent, and wear out prematurely due to increased heat from sidewall flexing.

gas saving tip(tire selection) - Selecting tires with the right characteristics will affect rolling resistance and hence fuel economy. The following design features increase fuel economy: tread width matching rim width, fairly straight tread pattern lines, and radial tire design. See also tire(steel belted radial).

gas saving tip(using regular gas) - A car designed to run on leaded gasoline, can use regular gas for average driving unless its engine has a high compression ratio.

gas saving tip(unusual lubricants) - Many aftermarket lubrication products are available claiming to increase engine performance, fuel economy, reduce engine temperature, and/or engine life. Most are designed to reduce the coefficient of friction between moving surfaces. Products include: synthetic oil; teflon based oil; and oil additives to reduce oil temperature, reduce friction, improve viscosity at high temperature, resist oil breakdown at high temperature, and coat moving parts with low friction compounds. This is a very controversial area with claims made by both sides. Some of the special oils have produced small improvements in fuel economy and engine performance due to decreasing the coefficient of friction between moving parts. Synthetic oils are advantageous where their special properties are needed. Some additives actually lower automatic transmission oil temperature while others improve an existing oil's lubricating characteristics at higher temperatures. In most cases, improving conventional oil characteristics with additives is preferable to using special or synthetic oils. See also oil(synthetic).

gas saving tip(vacuum gauge) - Gauge used to measure an engine's intake manifold vacuum. It does not change an engine's performance in any way. It can, however, improve fuel economy by making the driver more aware of how he drives. Vacuum is directly related to fuel consumption. The lower the vacuum reading the more fuel and air are being drawn into an engine. By keeping the vacuum reading as high and steady as possible, fuel consumption is minimized. See also gauge(vacuum).

gas saving tip(vacuum hose leaks) - Extra air leaking into the intake manifold can cause an engine to run rough, stumble, and increase fuel consumption. Tests have shown leaking or disconnected hoses can reduce fuel economy up to 10 percent.

gas saving tip(valve body kit) - Parts kit used to change the fluid movement characteristics of certain automatic transmissions by modifying how the valve body unit behaves. Installations have resulted in better shifting, shifting at more appropriate rpms, and better kickdown action. Improvements of 1-2 mpg have been achieved.

gas saving tip(vapor injector) - See vapor injector.

gas saving tip(wheel bearings) - Growling, tight, or loose wheel bearings will increase resistance to rotation. Bearing noise requires immediate attention. Bearings should be repacked every 25-30,000 miles with good quality wheel bearing grease to insure long life.

gasser - Racing car built to run on gas.

gassing - Battery condition created when electrolyte bubbles due to charging a battery. It is actually the water portion of an electrolyte solution breaking down into oxygen and hydrogen gas.

gas tank - Tank used to contain gasoline.

gas tank straps - Metal straps used to attach a fuel tank securely to a car.

gas treatment - Additive added to fuel to improve certain fuel characteristics. See also additive(fuel).

gas turbine engine - Turbine engine built to power a car with gasoline. It is still considered experimental.

gas up - To add gasoline to a car's fuel tank.

gas volume - Space occupied between a spark plug's insulator in the firing tip area, and the interior plug shell surface. In general, plugs with the same insulator nose length and smaller or larger gas volumes will run colder and hotter respectively.

gas welding - See welding(gas).

Gates - American line of tires produced by The Gates Rubber Co.

Gatts Horseless Carriage - American car produced in 1905.

gauge - Device used to measure and/or register measurements.

gauge(ammeter) - Gauge used to measure the amount and direction of electric current flow. In a car, it is usually wired in ahead of all electrical accessories, except the starter, to record the amount of current entering or leaving a battery.

gauge(clinometer) - Picture-type gauge used mostly on four wheel drive cars to measure forward and sideways tipping angles. It is designed to provide roll-over protection by warning drivers when angles are too high.

gauge(cylinder temperature) - Gauge used to measure cylinder head temperature in the combustion chamber area by means of a thermocouple sensor usually placed at the base of a spark plug. See also sensor(cylinder head temperature).

gauge(fuel level) - Gauge used to measure fuel level in a fuel tank usually by means of an internally mounted float type sensor.

gauge(fuel pressure) - Gauge used to measure fuel pressure usually on the output side of a fuel pump. See also sensor(fuel pressure).

gauge(hourmeter) - Gauge used to measure the cumulative number of hours an engine has been operated.

gauge(odometer) - Gauge used to measure cumulative miles driven by a car. It is usually housed inside a speedometer.

gauge(oil level) - Gauge used to measure when engine oil level falls below a certain level by means of a sensor mounted on an oil pan. See also sensor(oil level).

gauge(oil pressure) - Gauge used to measure the amount of oil pressure developed in a running engine. It is typically measured near the output side of the oil filter. Cars use mechanical and electrical types. The mechanical type uses high pressure plastic or copper tubing to route a small stream of pressurized oil to a dash mounted gauge. The electrical type uses a remote pressure sensing unit, mounted on the engine block, that varies a resistance value according to oil pressure. The resistance varies the voltage reaching a dash mounted gauge, and hence the displayed oil pressure value.

gauge(oil temperature) - Gauge used to measure oil temperature in an engine,

manual transmission, automatic transmission, or differential.
gauge(speedometer) – Gauge used to measure forward car movement in miles per hour.
gauge(tachometer) – Gauge used to measure engine rotational speed in revolutions per minute.
gauge(trip odometer) – Gauge used to indicate miles driven on a trip. It is resetable and is usually housed inside a speedometer.
gauge(turbo boost) – Gauge used to indicate intake vacuum and pressure.
gauge(vacuum) – See vacuum gauge.
gauge(voltmeter) – Gauge used to measure a car's battery voltage. It gives a better indication of battery condition than an ammeter.
gauge(water temperature) – Gauge used to measure coolant temperature by means of a sensor usually mounted near the thermostat.
gauge number – American Wire Gauge number used to determine the size of a wire. Each number represents a specific cross sectional area of a wire in circular mils. Each area also equates to a wire diameter. A circular mil is equal to the area of a circle one mil in diameter. One mil is 1/1,000 of an inch. A wire, for example, with a gauge of 16 has a circular mil area of 2583 square mils and a diameter of .0508 inches.
   American Wire Gauge numbers typically range from 0000 to 36. The corresponding circular mil areas and wire diameters range from 211,600 to 25.0 square mils and .4600 to .0050 inches respectively.
Gawley – American car produced in 1895.
GAWR – Abbreviation for gross axle weight rating.
Gay – American car produced in 1915.
Gaylord – American car produced from 1910-1913 and 1955-1956 by Gaylord Motor Car Co. in Michigan (1910-1913), and Gaylord Cars in Illinois (1955-1956).
GB – Abbreviation for Great Britain found usually on an international license plate.
GBM – Abbreviation for Isle of Man found usually on an international license plate.
GBZ – Abbreviation for Gibraltar found usually on an international license plate.
GC – Abbreviation for good condition. See also FC and EC.
GCW – Abbreviation for gross combination weight.
gd – Abbreviation for good.
gear – Toothed wheel built to mesh with another so motion from one is passed to another.
gear(annulus) – See gear(planet ring).
gear(axle shaft) – See gear(side).
gear(bevel cut) – Gear built with a taper, like a truncated cone. It is commonly used with another bevel gear to transfer power from one shaft to another at angles of less than 180 degrees.
gear(differential pinion) – See gear(spider).
gear(differential ring) – Large ring gear mounted in a differential carrier for rotating differential side gears which rotate rear axle shafts.
gear(differential ring-hypoid) – Differential ring gear built with gear teeth cut similar to a spiral bevel, but which allows a pinion gear to contact a ring gear below its centerline. It allows a drive shaft to be lowered permitting a lower floor body.
gear(differential ring-spiral bevel) – Differential ring gear built with spiral bevel cut gear teeth. The sliding contact of the teeth make a differential run quieter and stronger.
gear(differential ring-straight bevel) – Differential ring gear built with straight bevel cut gear teeth. It was used on earlier differentials.
gear(drive) – Set of gears in a transmission used to produce output shaft rotation when they are meshed.
gear(drive pinion) – Small gear mounted on a starter motor shaft to engage a flywheel ring gear when a starter rotates.
gear(fifth) – An arrangement of transmission gears used to provide a fifth forward speed when meshed.
gear(first) – See gear(low).
gear(flywheel ring) – Large ring gear mounted on the rim of a flywheel. It is used to rotate an engine when a starter motor pinion gear engages it.
gear(fourth) – Arrangement of transmission gears used to provide a fourth forward speed when meshed.
gear(front countershaft) – Gear mounted on the front of a transmission countershaft gear meshing with the transmission's main drive gear.
gear(Granny) – Low gear in a transmission designed to pull heavy loads at a very low speed.
gear(helical) – Gear built with teeth cut at an angle to the gear's centerline.
gear(high) – Arrangement of gears used to provide the fastest driveline rotation. Generally higher gearing, means less power available to rapidly change rotational speed. A car, for example, can accelerate rapidly in first

gear, but not in fourth.

gear(hypoid) - Gear used with a pinion gear to allow the pinion to make contact below the centerline. Gear teeth are cut similar to a spiral bevel gear. It is a common design for differential ring and pinion gears.

gear(idler) - Gear used to transfer power between gears.

gear(intermediate) - Any gears in a transmission between first and final drive gear.

gear(internal) - See gear(planet ring).

gear(low) - Arrangement of transmission gears used to provide the lowest driveline rotation and highest power response when meshed.

gear(pinion) - Small gear used to fit into a larger gear, or between two gears as in a differential.

gear(planet) - One of several gears located between the sun and ring gears in a planetary gear set. It is also referred to as a pinion gear.

gear(planet ring) - Ring gear used in a planet gear set. See also gear(planet).

gear(rack) - Bar gear cut with gear toothed surface for meshing with another gear. See also gear(rack and pinion).

gear(rack and pinion) - Gear combination commonly used in steering systems. The rotation of the pinion gear moves the rack gear. Like the worm and sector gear combination, rotation is transferred 90 degrees from the pinion gear to the rack gear.

gear(reverse) - Arrangement of transmission gears used to provide driveline rotation in the opposite direction when meshed. Most cars have reverse in one speed only.

gear(reverse idler) - Gear constantly meshed with a rear countershaft gear. Reverse gear on a transmission's mainshaft meshes with this gear to create reverse rotation in the transmission output shaft.

gear(ring) - Large ring shaped gear. Depending on the design, the gear's teeth may be on the inner or outer circumference, or one side. See also gear(flywheel ring), gear(differential ring), and gear(planet ring).

gear(second) - Arrangement of transmission gears used to provide a second forward speed when meshed.

gear(side) - Gear used in the differential to drive an axle shaft. There are usually two of these gears in a differential, one for each wheel.

gear(spider) - Small gear used in a differential to turn both side gears at the same or different speeds. Spider gears are the heart of a differential and the key to how it works. Differentials usually have four of these gears, each on their own shafts.

gear(spiral bevel) - Gear built with curved and tapered teeth cut at angle to a ring and pinion gear centerline. It is used with a pinion gear. The gear teeth meshing is quieter and stronger than a straight bevel gear. It is widely used in car differentials.

gear(spur) - Gear built with teeth parallel to the shaft it rides on. It is also known as a straight cut gear.

gear(starter pinion) - Small gear mounted on a starter drive shaft. It engages a flywheel ring gear when a starter is rotated.

gear(steering) - Gear combination used to transmit turning of a steering wheel shaft to steering linkage through a steering gear box. See also gear(rack and pinion) and gear(worm and sector).

gear(straight cut) - Gear built with teeth cut perpendicular to the gear plane.

gear(sun) - Central gear used in a planetary gear set.

gear(third) - Arrangement of transmission gears used to provide a third forward speed when meshed.

gear(timing) - One of two or more gears used to provide a means of operating different engine parts at the proper time of an engine cycle. The most common timing gears are mounted on the camshaft and crankshaft. They are connected by a timing chain or belt and control the opening and closing of valves in relation to crankshaft position.

gear(transmission countershaft) - Series of gears cut on one long gear blank. Countershaft gears are usually found in the bottom of a manual transmission. There they provide a connection for the transmission input and output shafts. The transmission's main drive gear constantly remains in contact with one countershaft gear rotating it anytime the clutch is engaged regardless of whether the transmission is in a gear or not.

gear(worm) - Coarse spiral-shaped gear usually found on a shaft. It is designed to work with a geared wheel. It is commonly found in a steering box where it engages and drives another gear.

gear(worm and sector) - Gear combination commonly used in steering gear boxes to transfer steering wheel shaft rotation 90 degrees to another shaft controlling movement of steering linkage via a pitman arm.

gear action - Rolling and sliding action occurring between gear teeth.

gear arrangement - The relationship of gears to each other.

gearbox - Case or housing used to enclose gears, protect them from contamination, keep them lubricated, and provide a means of transferring power reliably. A manual transmission has a gearbox as does a steering system. See also transmission(manual).

gear clashing - Condition created when gears do not mesh well during transmission shifting creating a grinding sound. It is due to either poor shifting habits or a transmission prone to gear clashing. See also transmission(sliding gear).

gear clutch - See synchronizer clutch.

gear cone - Cone-shaped surface located on the side of a gear and used to mesh with a synchronizer ring.

gear face - Lower surface of a gear tooth. See also gear flank, gear toe, and gear heel.

gear flank - Upper surface of a gear tooth. See also gear face, gear toe, and gear heel.

gear grinding - Condition created when gear teeth do not properly mesh or lack lubrication, causing excessive wear or broken teeth.

gear heel - Outer edge of a gear tooth cut in the plane of rotation such as a differential ring gear. See also gear toe, gear flank, and gear face.

gearing - Assemblage of gears and related parts used in a transmission, differential, steering gearbox, etc.

gearing down - To readjust a gear arrangement in a transmission so the input (engine) goes faster and the output (driveline) goes slower.

gearing up - To readjust a gear arrangement in a transmission so the input (engine) goes slower and the output (driveline) goes faster.

gear jamming - To quickly shift from one gear to another often without the use of a clutch. Such a practice is hard on gears.

Gearless - American car produced from 1907-1909 by Gearless Transmission Co. (1907-1908), and Gearless Motor Car Co. (1908-1909), both in New York.

Gearless Steamer - American steam car produced from 1921-1923 by Gearless Motor Corp. in Pennsylvania.

gear lever - See gear shift.

gear lube - See oil(gear).

gear lubricant - See oil(gear).

gear meshing - To align two or more gears together for the purpose of transferring rotation from one to another.

gear oil - See oil(gear).

gear puller - Tool used to remove a gear from a shaft.

gear ratio - Ratio defined as the number of turns a driving gear makes to one turn of a driven gear. For example, a 3:1 differential means the driveline (pinion gear) would turn three times for every revolution of the axle shafts (sun gear). A 3:1 gear ratio is defined as a lower ratio then 2:1. In a manual transmission, for example, a 12 and 24 tooth driving and driven gear set has a gear ratio of 2:1. The driving gear (12) must make two revolutions before the driven gear (24) makes one revolution. In other words, the engine must turn two revolutions for every single transmission output shaft revolution. See also overall gear ratio.

gears are stripped - Condition created when each gear's toothed surfaces have worn away, preventing rotation from being transferred from one gear to another.

gear shift - Hand operated lever connected to a transmission's linkage allowing shifting of gears. Cars typically have either a floor or steering column mounted gearshift.

gear shifting - To change from one gear arrangement to another as in shifting from first to second.

gear toe - Inner edge of a gear tooth cut in the plane of rotation such as a differential ring gear. See also gear heel, gear flank, and gear face.

gear train - Assemblage of gears and related components used in a transmission, differential, steering gearbox, etc.

GEC - American car produced in 1898 and 1902.

Gem - American car produced from 1917-1919 by Gem Motor Car Co. in Michigan.

General(1) - American car produced in 1903-1904 and 1912.

General(2) - American line of tires.

General Cab - American car produced in 1929.

General Electric - American electric car produced from 1898-1899.

General Motors Corporation - Company formed in 1908 by combining the Buick, Cadillac, Oldsmobile, and Oakland companies into one company that would produce a variety of cars. Today, cars produced include: Buick, Cadillac, Chevrolet, Oldsmobile, and Pontiac. It is regarded as the biggest car manufacturer in the world today, and is headquartered in Detroit, Michigan.

General Motors XP883 - Prototype city car built by General Motors in the 1960s. It had a fiberglass body, an electric motor, and a gas motor. The two motors could work separately or together.

General Tire - U.S. tire manufacturing company.

General Vehicle - American car produced from 1906-1919.

generator - Electric device used to convert mechanical energy into electrical energy. All car generators produce alternating current that must be converted into direct current before it can be used by a cars electrical system. The two main types of generators are the alternating current generator or alternator, and the direct current generator or DC generator. See also DC generator and alternator.

generator(AC) - See alternator.

generator(bucking field) - Direct current generator built to use a bucking field coil concept to control generator voltage. See also bucking field coil.

generator(DC) - Generator built to generate alternating current, then transform it into direct current. Alternating current is generated by rotating many separate coils of wire, bundled together to form an armature, inside a circular field of stationary magnets, known as field magnets. The field magnets are also coils of wire energized when a car is started to produce a magnetic effect. If field magnets were not energized, armature coils would produce no electricity when they rotate. All of an armature's individual coils begin and terminate at separate insulated areas on the commutator which is a segmented ring-like area, mounted at one end of an armature core. Current flows in and out of the armature via brushes resting on a commutator surface. A commutator and brush arrangement extracts only the positive portion of each coil's electricity. Generator output or voltage depends on such factors as: field magnet strength, armature speed, and the number of loops in each individual armature coil. DC generators are not generally used on todays cars due to the advantages of alternators.

generator(interpole) - Direct current generator built using an interpole to minimize arcing of generator brushes. See also interpole.

generator(shunt wound) - Direct current generator built with field coil leads directly connected to an armature's brushes. Current flows independently to field coils instead of through armature. It was an early generator that had improved low speed generating characteristics, was a successor to the third brush generator, and is still common.

generator(split field) - Direct current generator built with two separate field coil circuits used to increase field strength for better power generation at low rpm. They were popular on buses, cabs, and other vehicles subjected to extended idling periods or low speed driving.

generator(third brush) - Direct current generator built utilizing the principle of armature reaction to control a generator's output. Three brushes are used. The first two function as in a normal generator. The third brush is adjustable and regulates current flow through field windings and thus the voltage the generator produces. This early generator design did not provide adequate current at low speed or idling.

generator bearing condition - Degree of generator bearing wear or life left.

generator brush length - Length left on carbon brushes riding on a generators commutator or an alternators slip ring surface.

generator noise - Noise produced in a generator by worn, defective, or loose components. Problems include: bad bearing or bushing, worn commutator, poorly seated brushes, loose drive pulley, and loose body mounting bolts.

generator output - Amount of voltage and current produced by a generator at different rpms. No output is usually due to a faulty ground in a generator somewhere before reaching field or generator windings. Excessive output is often caused when field winding resistance is removed or bypassed creating a stronger magnetic field than needed.

generator windings - Windings of conductive wire in a generator or alternator used to generate the voltage and current necessary to operate a car's electrical system. A DC generator uses generator windings rotating on a shaft while an alternator uses stationary outer windings. See also field windings, stator(alternator), DC generator, and alternator.

Genesse - American car produced from 1911-1912.

Geneva - American car produced from 1901-1904 and 1916-1917 by Geneva Automobile & Mfg. Co. in Ohio, and Schoeneck Co. in Illinois respectively. Also, an American car produced in 1911.

Genie - American car produced beginning in 1962 by British Motor Car Importers in California. Cars were primarily small rear-engine formula junior racers.

genuine racer - Experienced drag racer.

German-American - American car produced in 1902.

Geronimo - American car produced from 1917-1920 by Geronimo Motor Co. in Oklahoma. It was named after the famous American Indian chief.

Gersix - American car produced in 1915.

get a horse - Phrase first uttered by spectators at the first car track race in Narragansett Park in Cranston, Rhode Island in 1896. Spectators were reacting to the slow speed of the vehicles over the one mile course. The average speed was 26.8 miles per hour.

get-away - To quickly leave an area in a car.

get behind the wheel - To sit in the drivers seat of a car and prepare to drive.

get on it - To accelerate a car rapidly.
get rich quick artist - Person interested in making a lot of money in short
period of time usually by dishonest means. See also con man.
get the brakes fixed - To restore a brake system to good operating condition.
getting a firm grip - To grasp the steering wheel firmly with both hands.
getting a tow - See slipstream.
getting air out of the lines - To remove air in a brake systems lines. See
also bleeding the brakes.
getting bit - To get an electric shock.
getting out of it - To back off on the accelerator pedal.
GH - Abbreviation for Ghana found usually on an international license plate.
Ghent - American car produced from 1917-1918 by Ghent Motor Co. in Illinois.
Giant Truck - American truck produced in 1915.
Gibbs - American car produced from 1903-1905.
Gibson - American car produced in 1899.
Gifford-Pettit - American car produced from 1907-1908.
Gillette - American car produced in 1916.
Gilson - Canadian car produced in 1921.
give the engine a bath - To clean an engine and often its compartment area of
grease, oil, dirt, etc.
GJG - American car produced from 1909-1911 by GJG Motor Car Co. in New York.
glare resistance - Ability possessed by a person's eyes to refocus and see
after being exposed to bright lights. A simple test is to look at a bright
light in semi-darkness for 5-10 seconds. Within 5-7 seconds, you should be
able to read a page of printed material.
glass - See fiberglass.
glass belted tire - See tire(fiberglass belted).
glass cloth - Thin fiberglass matting used to form the base of a fiberglass
shape. It is also used with plastic filler to cover a rusted out hole in a
car body.
glass eye - Opening located at the back of a headlamp to let a driver know if
a headlamp is on. The feature was introduced on some cars in 1926.
Glassic - American car produced from 1966-1968 by Glassic Industries in
Florida. It was a replica similar to a Ford Model A.
glassing - To fill car body holes with fiberglass.
glass pack muffler - See muffler(glass pack).
glass pack - See muffler(glass pack).
glass tint - Window characterized by having a tinted surface. Some windows
have only the upper portion tinted. Tint is available as an aftermarket add-
on in the form of a spray or a plastic sheet.
glass wrapped - Fiberglass body car.
glaze - Smooth glassy finish. An example is a cylinder wall becoming glazed
over a long period of time due to piston ring friction.
glaze breaker - Tool used to remove the glossy surface on an engine cylinder
wall.
glazing compound - Thick primer-like compound used to fill very small areas or
low spots on car body surfaces. It requires no catalyst, and works best when
applied after a primer has been applied.
glazing putty - See glazing compound.
Gleason - American car produced from 1909-1914 by Kansas City Vehicle Co. in
Missouri.
Glen - Canadian car produced in 1921.
Glide - American car produced from 1903-1920 by the Bartholomew Co. in
Illinois.
Glidden, Charles - He was affiliated with Bell Telephone in his early years,
and made the first auto journey around the world in 1904.
Globe - American car produced from 1921-1922 by Globe Motors Co. in Ohio.
Also, an American car produced in 1917.
glove compartment - Small storage compartment located on the passengers side
of the dashboard.
Glover - American car produced in 1917 and 1920-1921.
glow plug - Spark plug like device mounted in the cylinder head of a diesel
engine to ignite diesel fuel in an engine cylinder. It is recessed into a
small alcove above a combustion chamber with the injector nozzle. Glow plugs
are necessary to start cold diesel engines because compression temperatures
are not initially high enough to ignite the fuel. The plugs have an electric
filament that gets hot. It runs off a battery and is disconnected when an
engine starts. A glow plug will last 40-60,000 miles if used properly. For
maximum life: use as little as possible, keep "on" time to a minimum, and
avoid leaving them on accidentally. Excessive use can cause metal pieces to
fall into combustion chambers causing damage.
GM - Abbreviation for General Motors Corporation.
GMC - Abbreviation for General Motors Corporation.
GMC Truck - American truck produced from 1912 to date by General Motors in
Michigan.

goat – Older racing car.
Gobron-Brille 4 Cylinder – French car driven by Arthur Duray to a 1903 world land speed record of 84.7 mph at Dourdan, France. Also, a car driven by Louis Rigolly to a 1904 world land speed record of 103.6 mph at Ostend, Belgium.
Goethemobile – American car produced in 1902.
go for a drive – To take a drive in a car usually just for pleasure.
goggles – Large spectacles equipped with safety type lenses and rims to protect eyes from flying debris, wind, light, etc.
gold – Trophy.
Golden Eagle – American car produced in 1906.
Golden Gate – American car produced from 1894-1895 by A. Schilling & Sons in California.
Golden Rod V-8 – American car driven by Bob Summers to a 1965 world land speed record of 409.3 mph at Bonneville, Utah.
Golden Slate – American car produced in 1902.
Golden State – American car produced in 1928.
Golden West – American car produced in 1919.
gold leaf lettering – Custom lettering technique used to apply gold leaf letters on a panel. See also size.
good deal – Happy customer.
goodies – Extra trim and ornaments added to give a car a custom look. Also, it refers added engine equipment.
Good Maxwell – American car produced from 1921-1923 by Maxwell Motor Corp. in Michigan.
good mechanical condition – Used car characterized by having a powertrain in good operating condition.
Goodspeed – American car produced in 1922.
Goodwin – American car produced in 1923.
Goodyear – American line of tires produced by Goodyear Tire & Rubber Co.
gooker – Mechanically stock car with many accessories, chrome parts, etc.
gook wagon – See gooker.
goose – Potential car customer who is easily manipulated.
gooseneck – Hitch area of a trailer.
Gopher – American car produced in 1911.
got a flat – Car condition created when a car has a flat tire.
got cited – To get a traffic citation.
Gotfredson Truck – American truck produced in 1921.
Gottlieb Daimler – He was a German engineer who successfully tested and patented a motorized bicycle in 1885, and a motorized carriage in 1886.
got took – To get cheated on a trade or sale.
gourd guard – Safety helmet.
Goux, Jules – He won the Indianapolis 500 Race in 1913 driving an average of 75.9 mph in a Peugeot.
Gove – American car produced in 1921.
governor(1) – Mechanical device used to automatically control the speed of a rotating part.
governor(2) – Valve mechanism used in an automatic transmission to control hydraulic pressure according to speed. It usually progressively opens according to transmission output shaft rpm.
governor weights – See centrifugal weights.
gow – See moxie.
GP – Abbreviation for Grand Prix.
GR – abbreviation for Greece found usually on an international license plate.
Grabowsky – American car produced from 1908-1913.
Graham Motorette – American car produced from 1902-1903 by Charles Serfin & Co. in New York.
Graham-Fox – American car produced in 1903.
Graham-Paige – American car produced from 1927-1941 by Graham-Paige Motors Corp. in Michigan.
grain alcohol – See ethanol.
gram – Metric measurement of weight. One gram equals 0.03527 ounces.
Gramm – Canadian car produced in 1913.
Gramm Truck – American truck produced in 1911.
Gramm-Berstein – American car produced in 1912.
Gramm-Logan – American car produced from 1908-1910.
Granada – American car produced from 1975 to date by Ford Motor Co. in Michigan.
Grand – American car produced in 1912.
Grand Am – American car produced from 1964 to date by Pontiac Division of General Motors Corp. in Michigan.
grande epreuve – Major test.
Grand Le Mans – American car produced from 1964 to date by Pontiac Division of General Motors Corp. in Michigan.
Grand Marquis – American car produced by Ford from 1983-1986.

Grand Prix(1) - American car produced from 1961 to date by Pontiac Division of General Motors Corp. in Michigan.

Grand Prix(2) - One of a series of races conducted annually in Europe and the United States. Drivers earn points in each race. Cars must be built according to rules. The first race was held in 1906 on a 64 mile circuit near Le Mans, France.

grand prix - Highest award given in a competition.

Grand Rapids - American car produced in 1913.

Grand Touring - See Grand Turismo.

Grand Turismo - Car style originated in Italy. In general, it is characterized as a high performance sports type car, with high speed, good road handling and holding ability, good braking and quick steering ability, stiff clutch, and four speed manual gearbox. Also, an American car produced from 1954-1964 by Studebaker-Packard Corp. in Indiana.

Grandville - American car produced from 1965-1976 by Pontiac Division of General Motors Corp. in Michigan.

Gran Fury - American car produced from 1955 to date by Plymouth Division of Chrysler Corp. in Michigan.

Granite Falls - American car produced in 1912.

granny gear - See gear(granny).

Gran Sport - American car produced from 1964-1977 by Buick Division of General Motors Corp. in Michigan.

Grant - American car produced from 1913-1922 by Grant Motor Car Corp. in Ohio.

Grant-Ferris - American car produced in 1901.

grape - Customer characterized as easy to manipulate and therefore swindle. It is used in the car repair business to describe a potential customer to employees.

graphite - Soft native carbon used as a lubricant.

graphite oil - See oil(graphite).

Grass-Premier - American car produced in 1923.

grater - Coarse body file resembling a cheese grater. It is commonly used for removing plastic filler.

gravel deflector - Metal plate mounted between a front or rear bumper and a car body.

Graves-Condon - American car produced in 1899.

Gray - American car produced in 1916 and 1920. Also, an American car produced from 1922-1926 by Gray Motor Corp. in Michigan.

Gray-Dort - Canadian car produced from 1915-1925 by Gray-Dort Motors in Ontario.

graying - Paint condition created when newly applied paint tends to dull the gloss of existing paint. See also compounding.

gray market car - Cars unfairly introduced into the market place. Such cars include: one-of-a-kind imports that have avoided EPA testing, and cars totaled by insurance companies and returned to service.

grays - Gray market cars.

grease - Moldable solid or semi-solid oily substance used for various types of lubrication.

grease(chassis) - Grease formulated for use in car chassis parts requiring periodic lubrication.

grease(extended lubrication interval chassis) - Grease formulated for use in car chassis parts sealed for life. Certain types are regarded as multipurpose greases.

grease(extreme pressure) - Grease formulated for use where high loads or pressures are encountered. The extreme pressure property is sometimes incorporated in one of the other type greases.

grease(multipurpose) - Grease formulated for use where: chassis, wheel bearing, and universal grease is used; and other miscellaneous car uses.

grease(wheel bearing) - Grease formulated for long term use in antifriction wheel bearings. Properties include: resistance to high temperature, softening, and separating effects of centrifugal action; and protection against rust.

grease(universal joint) - Grease formulated for use in universal joints.

greaseball mechanic - See job(backyard mechanic).

grease fitting - See zerc fitting.

grease job - Car service work performed adding grease to all: car suspension, steering system, and universal joint parts requiring grease on a periodic basis.

grease monkey - See job(auto mechanic). Also, it refers to an employee who does unskilled work while learning the repair trade.

grease seal - Seal used to contain grease in car parts, housings, etc.

Great - American car produced in 1903.

Great-Arrow - American car produced in 1903.

Great Eagle - American car produced from 1910-1918 by U.S. Carriage Co. in Ohio.

Great Smith - American car produced from 1905-1911 by Smith Automobile Co. in

Kansas. It was an overly expensive and reportedly was the first car to climb Pike's Peak with its own power. See also Smith.

Great Southern – American car produced from 1910-1914 by the Great Southern Automobile in Alabama.

Great Western – American car produced from 1908-1916 by Model Automobile Co. (1908-1909), and Great Western Automobile Co. (1909-1916), both in Indiana.

Greeley – American car produced in 1903.

Green Bay Steamer – An American steam vehicle produced in 1877.

green flag – See flag(green).

greenhouse – Upper part of a car located above the beltline. It includes the glass, roof, and supporting members.

Greenleaf – American car produced in 1902.

Green Monster – See Green Monster J-79 Jet.

Green Monster J-79 Jet – American car driven by Art Arfons to a world land speed record in 1964 and 1965 at Bonneville, Utah. Speeds were 434.0 and 576.6 mph.

green poultice – Money settlement made in insurance cases that, when awarded, seems to cause rapid recovery of such illnesses as whiplash.

Green, Tom – He set a world land speed record of 413.2 mph in 1964 driving a Wingfoot Express J-46 Jet.

Greenville – American car produced in 1925.

Great Britain – One of the six largest car producing countries in the world.

Gregory – American car produced in 1922, 1949, and 1952.

Gregory Front Drive – American car produced from 1918-1922 by Front Drive Motor Co. in Missouri.

Gremlin – American car produced from 1970-1978 by American Motors Corp. in Michigan.

Grensfelder – American car produced in 1901.

Greuter – American car produced in 1899.

Greyhound – American car produced in 1914-1915, 1921-1923, and 1929.

grid – See battery grid.

Gride – American car produced in 1903.

Griffith – American car produced from 1964-1968 by Griffith Motors in New York.

grille – Lattice-like metal trim panel used to cover a car area between the front headlights and in front of a radiator.

grille shell – Car body area surrounding a cars grille.

grind(1) – To remove a portion of a metal surface by using an abrasive wheel.

grind(2) – See grind 'em down.

grind 'em down – To talk a customer into paying more money for a car.

grinding noise – Noise characterized by harsh rubbing or grating. It is commonly made when moving metal surfaces lose lubrication in between. See also sound(grinding).

grind the gears – Transmission shifting done from one gear set to another without completely disengaging the clutch. The end result is gear teeth grinding against other gear teeth causing potential transmission damage.

Grinnell – American electric car produced from 1912-1913 by Grinnell Electric Car Co. in Michigan. It reportedly had a 90 mile charge range.

Griswold – American car produced in 1907.

gross axle weight rating – Maximum support weight allowed for an axle. See also GAWR.

gross combination weight – Maximum weight combined weight of a vehicle and trailer. See also GCW.

gross duration – Cam duration derived from a .004 inch cam lobe lift. See also net duration and hydraulic intensity.

gross vehicle weight rating – Maximum total weight a car is designed to move. See also GVWR.

ground – Electrically conductive body taken as zero potential and to which an electrical circuit can be connected. A ground is a return path for an electrical circuit. In a car, the frame is used as the ground. All electrical circuits form a complete path by starting from a battery, connecting to a car frame, and returning to a battery's negative or ground terminal via a ground strap.

ground clearance – Vertical distance measured from the lowest chassis part to the ground.

ground electrode – See spark plug electrode(side).

ground strap – Heavy metal conductor cable used to connect the negative terminal of a battery to the frame of a car.

Grout – American car produced from 1899-1912 by Grout Bros. and Grout Automobile Co. in Massachusetts.

Grout Steamer – American steam car produced in 1906.

growler – Electrical device used for testing generator or electric motor armatures.

GT – Abbreviation for Grand Turismo.

GT coupe – Grand Turismo coupe car.

GTBA – Cosolvent, known as gasoline-grade tertiary butyl alcohol, used in some alcohol-blended gasolines to minimize the separation problem. See also alcohol and gasohol.

GTO – American car produced from 1964-1971 by Pontiac Division of General Motors Corp. in Michigan.

GTS – Abbreviation for Grand Turismo Sport.

GTX – American car produced from 1962-1977 by Plymouth Division of Chrysler Corp. in Michigan.

guarantee – Promise or assurance given that a product or service is of a specified quality, content, and/or benefit; or that it will perform satisfactorily for a specified period of time. To be effective, it should be in writing.

guarantee(30 day) – Guarantee good for 30 days.

guarantee(50/50 30 day) – Guarantee used by many auto repair businesses stipulating if work done is defective within a time period, usually 30 days, they will agree to pay for half of the corrective work needed. Such a guarantee encourages incompetence since the business will get more money no matter what the quality of their work was. You pay for their mistakes. Businesses will often try to get out of this problem by stalling you past the 30 days. If they go ahead and do the repair work again, they may likely charge you the full list price for everything.

guarantee(lifetime service) – Guarantee offered by certain auto repair businesses specifying covered repair parts will be fixed or replaced if they wear out or fail for the life of the car. There is usually no labor or parts charge.

guarantee(pro rata) – Guarantee used to cover an item declining in value during the guarantee period.

guarantee(repair work) – Guarantee offered by many repair shops guaranteeing only the parts installed. It doesn't amount to much, since most car parts are already guaranteed by a manufacturer's warranty.

guarantee(unconditional) – Guarantee defined as placing no conditions on standing behind a product or service. It is a misleading way of describing of a guarantee since virtually all of them have conditions.

guarantee(used car) – Guarantee given by some dealers specifying how they stand behind a used car sold to a buyer. Without a guarantee in writing, the buyer is purchasing "as is". See also sales contract.

guard rail – Protective fence located on a road's shoulder around curves, along drop-offs, over bridges, etc.

gudgeon pin – See piston pin.

Guilder Truck – American truck produced in 1922.

guilty – To be judged as: having done a wrong, committing an offense, breaking a law, etc.

Guinness, Kenelm – He set a world land speed record of 133.8 mph in 1922 driving a 350 hp Sunbeam V-12.

Gulf Corporation – A U.S. petroleum company headquartered in Pittsburgh, Pennsylvania. It is now part of the Chevron Corp. See also petroleum company.

gum – Oxidized resin-like compound in gasoline deposited in a fuel system, carburetor, and certain engine areas. It forms when gasoline is exposed to heat.

gunning the engine – Speeding up an engine momentarily to a high rpm.

Gurley – American car produced in 1901.

gust – Sudden increase in wind velocity.

gutted – Car interior removed except for instruments and necessary equipment.

gutter – See drip rail.

Guy – Canadian car produced in 1911.

Guy-Vaughan – American car produced from 1910-1913 by Vaughan Car Co. in New York.

GVWR – Abbreviation for gross vehicle weight rating.

GWW – American car produced in 1919.

gymkhana – Any contest involving the use of skill such as an auto race.

gyp – See con.

gyp mechanic – Dishonest mechanic.

gypster – Car repairman characterized by trying to obtain more than a normal amount of money for little or no work.

gypsy service station – Isolated, out of the way service station setup for the purpose of hustling travelers by claiming it is their last chance for gas, tires, batteries, oil, etc. Major oil companies often provide products for these stations.

Gyron – Experimental two-wheeled vehicle controlled by a gyroscope. Ford built it in 1961.

Gyroscope – American car produced from 1908-1909 by Blomstrom Mfg. Co. (1908), and Lion Motor Car Co. (1909), both in Michigan. Also, an American car produced in 1917.

H

H – Abbreviation for Hungary found usually on an international license plate.
h – Abbreviation for heater.
Haase – American car produced in 1904.
hack – Hot rod.
Hackett – American car produced from 1916-1919 by Hackett Motor Car Co. in Michigan.
Hackley – American car produced from 1905-1906.
Hahn Truck – American truck produced in 1914.
HAI – Abbreviation for hot air intake.
hailing a taxi – To motion a taxicab to stop for a ride.
hairpin – Sharp 180 degree turn.
hairy canary – Lousy car dealer.
HAL – American car produced from 1916-1918 by HAL Motor Car Co. in Ohio.
Hale – American car produced in 1917.
half axle – Swinging half axle.
half breed – Car made by welding the opposite ends of two same model cars together. It is considered an unsafe car. See also con game(half breed car).
half shaft – Rotating shaft used to transfer power from a differential to a wheel. It usually refers to those shafts used in front wheel and independent suspension cars.
half ton – Pickup truck rated at 1000 lb. carrying capacity.
Hal-Fur – American car produced in 1919.
Hall – American car produced in 1904 and 1914-1915 by Hall Motor Vehicle Co. in New Jersey, and Hall Cyclecar Mfg. Co. and Hall Motor Car Co. in Texas respectively.
Hall effect – Voltage induced when a rectangular metal plate goes through a magnetic field. Induced voltage is independent of plate speed. The principle is used in some engine control sensors to send signals to an on-board computer. See also sensor(camshaft) and sensor(crankshaft).
Hall Gasoline Trap – American car produced in 1895.
Halladay – American car produced in 1907-1916 and 1918-1922 by Streator Motor Car Co. and Barley Mfg. Co. in Illinois (1907-1913;1913-1916), and Halladay Motors Corp. in Ohio (1918-1922).
Hall switch – Electric switch used in some computer equipped cars to control spark advance and fuel injection. It is usually housed inside the distributor. A faulty switch is indicated if cranking the engine produce no fuel flow at the injector tip. See also EST module.
halogen headlamp – See quartz halogen headlamp.
halo roof – Car roof built to provide rollover protection.
Halsey – American car produced from 1901-1909.
Halton – American car produced in 1901.
Halverson – American car produced in 1908.
Hambrick – American car produced in 1908.
Hamilton – American car produced in 1909.
Hamilton, Pete – He won the Daytona 500 Race in 1970 averaging 149.6 mph in a Plymouth.
Hamely – American car produced in 1903.
Hamlin-Holmes – American car produced from 1909-1930 by Hamlin Motor Co. and Hamlin Holmes Motor Co. in Illinois.
Hammer – American car produced from 1905-1906 by Hammer Motor Co. in Michigan.
hammer-on technique – Technique use to straighten a sheetmetal panel by using a hammer and dolly. The dolly is placed behind the panel and a hammer strikes where the dolly is. The hammering is done sparingly to minimize metal stretching. See also stretch.
Hammer-Sommer – American car produced from 1902-1904 by Hammer-Sommer Auto Carriage Co. in Michigan.
hammer welding – Gas welding technique used in conjunction with hammer and dolly work to produce smooth and even welded seams. It is used for replacing rusted out panel areas or adding new metal without using plastic filler.
handicap – Headstart given to a slower racing car. It is usually done when cars of different classes race against each other.
hand job – Semi-interested car customer wasting a car salesman's time.
handler – Drag-racing car driver.
Handley-Knight – American car produced from 1921-1923 by Handley Motors in Michigan.
handling – Response of a car to different road maneuvers.

handling test - Test performed by car evaluators to determine how a car responds at a certain speed when making certain abrupt maneuvers.

hand rubbed finish - Protective car finish created by applying a wax to a paint surface and rubbing it out by hand.

hand signals - Lower left arm positions used by a driver to indicate the turning direction of a car. Hand signals are used when turn signals don't work. There are three major positions: horizontal - to indicate a left turn, vertically up - to indicate a right turn; and vertically down - to indicate slowing down or stopping.

Hanes - Line of automotive repair manuals. See also Chilton, Motor, and Mitchell(2).

Hanger - American car produced in 1915.

hang it out - To jump a start before the green light flashes.

hang out the laundry - To open a parachute brake.

Hanks, Sam - He won the Indianapolis 500 Race in 1957 driving an average of 135.6 mph in a Belond Exhaust Special.

Hannay Truck - American truck produced in 1917.

Hanover - American car produced from 1921-1924 by Hanover Motor Car Co. in Pennsylvania. It was intended primarily for export.

Hansen - American car produced in 1902.

Hansen-Whitman - American car produced in 1907.

Hanson - American car produced from 1917-1923 by Hanson Motor Co. in Georgia.

Harberer - American car produced from 1910-1913.

hard - Characteristic of a car selling well. Such cars usually have few listings in newspaper car ads. See also soft and hot.

hard braking - To apply brakes hard enough to lock the wheels and cause skidding. This type of braking invites an accident. If you must slow down quickly, pump the brakes. See also pumping the brakes.

hard chrome plating - See chrome plating.

Harder - American car produced in 1911.

Harding - Canadian car produced in 1911. Also, an American car produced from 1916-1917.

hard packed snow - Snow deposited on a roadway and compacted by traffic into hard snow bordering on ice.

hard pedal - Brake pedal condition created when it must be applied hard to brake a car. It is usually caused by wet, oily, and/or worn brake linings. Some metallic brake linings have a low coefficient of friction by design which gives a hard pedal effect.

hard sell - Tactic employed by salesmen to compel you into buying a product or service by using several kinds of pressure selling techniques.

hard solder - See solder(hard).

hard starting - Engine condition created when an engine is difficult to start. Possible causes include: low compression, defective ignition system, weak battery, bad starter, poor contact in starter solenoid, bad choke, incorrect choke adjustment, float level incorrect, insufficient fuel pressure, oil too heavy for weather conditions, and high moving part friction due to lack of oil or wrong size parts. See also engine problem(cranks but hard to start).

hardtop - See body style(hardtop). Also, it refers to any stationary car roof using no middle pillar and built around retracting window glass. See also car roof.

hard to steer - Car characterized by having a steering system which does not operate well or easy.

hard trim - Interior passenger compartment parts characterized as not being soft trim. Such parts include: garnish moldings, script, ornaments, and appliques.

Hardy - American car produced in 1903.

Hare - American car produced in 1918.

harmonic balancer - Weighted circular disc or pulley device used to reduce the torsional and twisting vibration of a crankshaft in multi-cylinder engines. It is usually mounted on the front end of a crankshaft.

Harper - American car produced from 1907-1908 by Harper Buggy Co. in Indiana.

Harrie - American car produced in 1925.

Harrigan - American car produced in 1922.

Harris - American car produced in 1893 and 1898.

Harris Six - American car produced in 1923.

Harrisburg - American car produced in 1922.

Harrison - American car produced in 1905-1907 by Harrison Wagon Co. and Harrison Motor CarCo. in Michigan. Also, an American car produced in 1912.

Harroun - American car produced from 1917-1922 by Harroun Motor Sales Corp. in Michigan.

Harroun, Ray - He won the Indianapolis 500 Race in 1911 driving an average of 74.6 mph in a Marmon Wasp.

Hart-Kraft - American car produced in 1908.

Hartley - American car produced in 1898.

Hartman - American car produced in 1914.

Harvard – American car produced from 1915-1920 by Pioneer Motor Car Co. and Adirondack Motor Car Co. in New York, and Harvard Motor Car Co. in Maryland.
Harvey – American car produced in 1914.
Hasbrouck – American car produced from 1899-1901 by Hasbrouck Motor Co. in New Jersey.
Haseltine – American car produced in 1916.
Hassler – American car produced in 1917.
hatchback – See body style(hatchback).
Hatfield – American car produced from 1906-1908 and 1917-1924 by Hatfield Vehicle Co. in Ohio, and Cortland Car & Carriage Co. in New York respectively.
Hathaway – American car produced in 1924.
hauled in – To get arrested.
hauler – Very fast car or driver.
Haupt – American car produced in 1909.
Haven – American car produced in 1917.
Havers – American car produced from 1908-1914 by Havers Motor Car Co. in Michigan.
Haviland – American car produced in 1895.
Havoc – American car produced by Rochester in 1914.
Hawk – American car produced in 1914. Also, an American car produced from 1955-1963 by Studebaker-Packard Corp. in Indiana.
hawk – Potential car customer who is hard to close a deal on.
Hawkeye – American car produced in 1917 and 1923.
Hawkins – American car produced in 1915.
Hawley – American car produced in 1907.
Hawthorn, Mike – He became the Grand Prix world champion in 1958 driving a Ferrari.
Hay-Berg – American car produced from 1907-1908 by Hay Berg Motor Car Co. in Wisconsin.
Haydock – American car produced from 1907-1910.
Hayes – American line of performance automotive products.
Hayes-Anderson – American car produced in 1928.
Haynes – American car produced from 1894-1924 by Haynes Apperson Co. and Haynes Automobile Co. in Indiana.
Haynes-Apperson – American car produced from 1898-1904 by Haynes-Apperson Co. in Indiana.
Haynes, Elwood – He was a well known metallurgist who developed important structural alloys for car use. He was an early advocate of using aluminum in cars, built one of the first successful cars in 1894, and went on to form the Haynes Automobile Company on 1898.
Hayward – American car produced in 1913.
Hazard – American car produced in 1914.
hazard a guess – To make a guess.
HB – American car produced in 1908.
h'back – Abbreviation for hatchback.
HC(1) – American car produced in 1916.
HC(2) – Abbreviation for high compression.
HC(3) – Abbreviation for hydrocarbons.
HCS – American car produced from 1920-1925 by H.C.S. Motor Co. in Indiana.
HD – Abbreviation for heavy duty.
HDLA – Abbreviation for high-density low-alloy steel. It is also known as high strength steel.
hdtp – Abbreviation for hardtop.
head – See cylinder head.
header – Structural member located at the juncture of a windshield top with the forward edge of a roof.
headers – Arrangement of exhaust pipes used to allow each cylinder to separately exhaust gases into an exhaust pipe system. Headers replace an exhaust manifold and bolt up to the exhaust pipe under a car in the transmission area. They aid in reducing backpressure, improving gas mileage, and increasing power available. See also exhaust tuning, backpressure, acoustical tuning, and inertia tuning..
headers(acoustical) – See headers(individual pipes). See also acoustical tuning.
headers(collector) – Headers designed to funnel together into a collector box for connecting to a car's exhaust piping.
headers(individual pipes) – Headers designed so each cylinder individually exhausts to the atmosphere. It is used in racing.
head gasket – See cylinder head gasket.
head gasket leak – Condition created when a head gasket has lost part of it seal and leaks water and or exhaust fumes. See also blown head gasket.
headlamp – See headlight.
headlight – One of usually two or four powerful lights mounted in a cars grille area and used to illuminate the road area in front of a car. Most are

sealed beam units.
headlight covers - Plastic lens mounted in front of headlights to protect them
from flying rocks and other debris. They are usually used on cars using
recessed headlights.
headlight door - Retractable door used to cover headlights when they are not
in use.
headlight focus - Point located in front of a car where the headlight beam is
focused to its smallest point.
headlight retaining ring - Removable metal ring fitted around the edge of a
car headlight to hold it in place.
headlight switch - Electrical switch used to control current flow to
headlights, parking lights, tail lights, and turn signal lights.
headliner - Interior roof panel usually made of vinyl.
headlining - See headliner.
head mechanic - Mechanic employed in an auto repair business who either has
the most experience or is in charge of other mechanics.
head on collision - Car accident created when two cars strike each other in
the front end traveling in opposite directions.
head porting - See porting.
head rest - Support mounted on top of a car seat to provide a resting place
for a head and protect it against whiplash from rear end collisions.
head restraint - See head rest.
head room - Vertical passenger compartment dimension measured from the floor
to the ceiling.
Healey - American car produced in 1951.
Healey Electric - American car produced in 1911.
heap - Car characterized as worn out, broke down a lot, junked, or lying
somewhere rusting away.
heat - Degree of hotness or high temperature measured.
heat baffle - Sheet metal plate mounted around the base of a carburetor to
deflect intake and/or exhaust manifold heat away from carburetor to minimize
vapor lock, fuel foaming, and heat soak.
heat content - Energy contained in a fuel per unit of volume (gallon,
liter, etc.). It is typically expressed in BTU units. See also BTU.
heat control valve(1) - Valve used to divert flow of some exhaust gases to an
intake manifold heating chamber when an engine is cold.
heat control valve(2) - See heater control valve.
heater - Mechanical device used to keep a car's interior warm. Main
components include: a heater core and motorized blower for circulating warm
air.
heater blower motor - See heater motor.
heater control - Lever, button, switch, etc. used to control a heater control
valve.
heater control valve - Valve used to control the flow of hot water to the
heater core to regulate interior air temperature.
heater core - Small radiator mounted inside a car to radiate heat. Warm water
circulates through the core by diverting part of a cooling systems water.
See also car service tip(condensation on windshield).
heater hose - Rubber hose used to convey hot water to a heater core inside a
car.
heater inlet line - Rubber hose used to move hot engine coolant to the heater
core. See also heater return line.
heater motor - Motor used to drive a fan blowing air across a heater core and
thereby circulating warm air in a car.
heater problem - Condition created when a car's heater does not perform
properly.
heater problem(blower motor inoperative) - Heater's blower motor does not work
on any setting. Possible causes include: blown fuse due to wrong size or a
short in circuit, faulty blower motor, faulty motor speed switch, and motor
not grounded.
heater problem(condensation on windshield) - Moisture condenses on windshield
when heater is operated. It is usually due to a leaking heater core.
heater problem(coolant leaking from heater area) - Coolant leaks around the
lower heat outlets onto or under the front seat carpet. Possible causes
include: leaking heater core, heater control valve, and/or heater hoses
inside firewall.
heater problem(no heat) - Heater with functioning blower produces little or no
heat regardless of heat temperature control lever setting. Possible causes
include: restricted coolant flow due to clogged heater core, clogged heater
control valve, and/or clogged or kinked heater hose; low coolant level;
faulty heater control valve; faulty heater vacuum valve; engine coolant not
warming up; inoperative mode-and-blend door; and disconnected or leaking
vacuum line running from intake manifold to heater vacuum valve.
heater return line - Rubber hose used to return hot engine coolant from the
heater core back to the engine block.

heater switch – Electric switch used to control the fan speed of a heater motor and thus the amount of warm air circulated inside a car. Also, it sometimes refers to a switch controlling a valve regulating warm water flow rate in a heater core.

heater vacuum valve – Valve used to control vacuum to a vacuum operated heater control valve. It is activated by a heater temperature control lever.

heat exchanger – Device used to transfer heat from a warmer area to a cooler one such as a car radiator.

heat jacket – Chamber cast into an intake manifold to receive exhaust gases which help heat it. The exhaust manifold commonly bolts directly underneath such an intake manifold to facilitate the transfer.

heat range – See spark plug heat range.

heat riser – See exhaust manifold heat control valve.

heat riser tube – See hot air tube.

heat riser valve – See heat control valve(1).

heat sink – Device used to dissipate heat generated by semiconductor devices. It is usually a finned metal plate or block made out of aluminum. Alternators use heat sinks to dissipate heat generated by diodes.

heat soak – Condition created when a hot engine is stopped long enough for the engine heat to raise the fuel temperature to its boiling point in the fuel pump, carburetor, and fuel lines. End result is: fuel vaporizes, carburetor float bowl needle valve is forced open, and fuel expands in float bowl filling main fuel wells and creating thermosiphoning effect which floods the intake manifold with fuel. Additionally, vapor locking occurs in fuel pump and/or fuel lines. Engines prone to this problem need to isolate engine heat as much as possible so the fuel delivery system components don't reach the typical 100-120 degree boiling range of gas. Possible solutions include: heat baffles between carburetor and manifolds, fresh outside air routed to carburetor area, electric fan used to blow air at carburetor during high engine compartment temperatures, changing from metal to rubber and fabric fuel lines, and insulating components. Engines suffering from heat soak are hard to restart due to vapor locking, and/or lack of liquid fuel in fuel delivery system. See also fuel foaming.

heat stove – See hot air stove.

heat treatment – Process defined as heating and cooling a solid metal in specific ways to impart certain desired properties.

heat wave – Hot weather condition created when a high temperature air mass covers a large area and moves slowly through it.

heavy traffic – Condition created when large numbers of cars are traveling on roadways causing cars to move slower than usual.

Hebb – American car produced in 1918.

heel – Larger half or base of a gear tooth. See also toe.

heel and toe system – Right foot maneuvering practice used mostly by race car drivers in combination with double clutching to decelerate quickly during downshifting. The driver usually shifts into neutral, and then prepares to depress the accelerator with the heel while braking with the toe.

HEI – Abbreviation for high energy ignition.

Heifner – American car produced in 1921.

Heilman – American car produced in 1908.

Heine-Velox – American car produced from 1906-1909 and 1921 by Heine-Velox Motor Co., and Heine-Velox Engineering Co. respectively, both in California.

helical – Shape formed like a coil or threads.

helical gear – See gear(helical).

Helicoil – Threaded insert product used to restore damaged threads by: drilling them out, retapping the new hole, and then screwing a springlike set of threads into the newly tapped hole.

helmet – Head covering worn to protect a head against injury due to impact, fire, flying objects, etc.

HELP – See Highway Emergency Locating Plan.

helper spring – Single leaf spring attached to one side of a car's leaf spring to boost carrying capacity or help restore original suspension.

Hemery, Victor – He set a world land speed record in 1905 and 1909 driving a Darracq V-8 and Benz 4 Cylinder Blitzen Benz. Speeds were 109.7 and 126.0 mph.

hemi – Dome-shaped combustion chamber. Also, it refers to an engine equipped with such chambers.

hemi head – See cylinder head(hemi)

Hendel – American car produced in 1904.

Henderson – American car produced from 1912-1915 by Henderson Motor Car Co. in Indiana.

Hendrickson Truck – American truck produced in 1916.

Henley – American car produced in 1899.

Henney Hearse – American car produced from 1921-1931 by Henney Motor Car Co. in Illinois.

Hennigan – American car produced from 1908.

Henrietta – American car produced in 1901.
Henry(1) – Ford Motor Company product.
Henry(2) – American car produced from 1910-1912 by Henry Motor Car Co. in Michigan.
Henry J – American car produced from 1950-1954 by Kaiser-Frazer Corp. in Michigan.
Henrylee – American car produced in 1912.
heptane – Liquid methane series hydrocarbon compound found in petroleum deposits with a melting and boiling point of -131 and 209 degrees Fahrenheit respectively. It is a gasoline ingredient with a heating value of 20,600 btu/lb.
Hercules – American car produced in 1914.
Hercules Electric – American electric car produced in 1907.
Herff-Brooks – American car produced from 1914-1916 by Herff-Brooks Corp. in Indiana.
Hermes – American car produced in 1920.
Herreshoff – American car produced from 1909-1914 by Herreshoff Motor Co. in Michigan (1909-1914), and Herreshoff Light Car Co. in New York (1914).
Herreschoff-Spillman – American car produced from 1904-1907 by Herschell-Spillman Co. in New York.
herringbone gear – Pair of helical gears built to intersect at an angle less than 90 degrees.
Herschmann – American car produced in 1904.
Hertel – American car produced from 1895-1900 by Max Hertzel in Illinois, and Oakman Motor Vehicle Co. in Pennsylvania and Massachusetts.
Hertz – American car produced from 1925-1928 by Yellow Cab Mfg. Co. in Illinois.
Heseltine – American car produced from 1916-1917 by Heseltine Motor Corp. in New York.
hesitation – Condition created when an engine does not immediately respond to a gas pedal movement, causing a momentary stalling effect. It is usually due to a very lean fuel mixture. Other causes include: retarded ignition timing, faulty low voltage wire inside distributor.
Hess Steam – American steam car produced in 1902.
Hewitt – American car produced from 1906-1907 by Hewitt Motor Co. in New York.
Hewitt-Lindstrom – American electric car produced from 1900-1901 by Hewitt-Lindstrom Electric Co. in Illinois.
hexane – Liquid methane series hydrocarbon compound found in petroleum deposits with a melting and boiling point of -140 and 156 degrees Fahrenheit respectively. It is one of the ingredients of gasoline with a heating value of 20,700 btu/lb.
hex head – See screw head(hex)
Heymann – American car produced in 1898 and 1904.
Hg – Chemical symbol for mercury. Intake manifold vacuum is measured in inches of mercury.
hiawatha appraisal – Ploy used by a car salesman to subtly put off looking over a customer's potential trade-in car. He looks at it from a distance with his hand above his eyes (like a salute) and is reluctant to get a closer look.
Hickenhull – American car produced in 1904.
Hicks – American car produced in 1900.
hidden headlights – See retractable headlights.
hides – Tires.
Hidley – American car produced in 1901.
Higdon & Higdon Horseless Carriage – American car produced in 1896.
high altitude – Elevation way above sea level.
high altitude jetting kit – Package of carburetor parts produced by a car manufacturer for changing carburetor jet sizes according to prevailing elevation where a carburetor operates.
highball – Trade-in tactic used to sell a potential customer a car. It usually works one of two ways: the customer is given an above average trade-in value for his used car in the hopes of gaining repeat business in the future, or a car purchase is brought close to closing before "a big mistake" or some other ploy is used to lower the trade-in price. See also low ball, con game(bargain advertising), and con game(high ball).
highballing – See high ball.
high beam – Car headlight beam used to produce long range lighting of a road. It is primarily used outside of urban areas. On two headlight cars, a high beam setting activates a higher wattage filament in each headlight. On four headlight cars, the two outside headlights produce the high beams. See also low beam.
high beam diagram – Vertical wall surface marked with various referencing lines relevant to a car in order to properly adjust the horizontal and vertical position of a cars high headlight beams. See also low beam diagram.
highboy – Car body at stock height.

high centered — Situation created when the underside of a car contacts the ground enough to cause the drive tires to lose traction.

high cog — Type of drag racing axle.

high combustion swirl — Induction technique used to speed up flow of an air/fuel mixture in a combustion chamber. Advantages include: better mixing and burning of fuel mixture, better distribution of recirculated exhaust gases, and ability to raise engine compression ratio.

high compression — Condition created when an air/fuel mixture is compressed to a high compression ratio in a combustion chamber.

high compression head — Cylinder head built with combustion chamber areas smaller than normal to raise the compression ratio. High compression heads can be made by machining down standard heads or from custom built heads. Thin head gaskets also increase compression ratios.

high crown — Car body panel shape curving rapidly away in all directions. See also low crown, combination crown, and reverse crown.

high-density low-alloy steel — See high strength steel and HDLA.

high discharge voltage check — Test made on individual battery cells to determine their health. Test involves use of a high discharge battery voltmeter which discharges a cell at a high rate. If the cell voltage falls below a certain value (usually 1.5) in 10-15 seconds, the cell is judged in poor condition. See also battery voltmeter.

high discharge voltmeter — See battery voltmeter.

high energy ignition — Electronic ignition system.

Highlander — American car produced in 1921.

high lift cam — See camshaft(high lift).

highlight — Area located on a reflective surface where light is the brightest.

high mileage — Condition created when a car has been driven a lot of miles.

high octane premium — Gasoline with a significantly higher octane rating than regular.

high performance — Description of a car, car part, etc. built to exceed standard performance characteristics.

high performance coil — Ignition coil built to produce higher voltage output than a stock coil. It can often eliminate high speed missing.

high performance options — Optional high performance equipment, modifications, parts, etc. added to a car.

high rise manifold — See intake manifold(high rise).

high speed chase — Road situation created when one or more police cars chase a car driving illegally at high speed in an attempt to stop it.

high speed circuit — See main circuit.

high speed gas — Fuel traveling at a higher speed in an air stream. As the speed of an air/fuel mixture increases, it enters a combustion chamber faster. End result is fuel burns more completely due to faster flame front and reduces emissions.

high speed jet — Jet mounted in a carburetor float bowl to meter additional fuel to an engine when a carburetor throttle is wide open. It usually works with a tapered metering rod positioned in a jet and slowly withdrawn as a throttle is opened.

high speed run — See drag race.

high speed shimmy — See wheel tramp and wheel alignment problem(wheel shimmy).

high speed tuning — Tuning an engine for maximum performance and speed. This type of tuning can involve extensive modifications to an engine including: increasing compression ratio, balancing and blueprinting engine, enlarging valves, multiple valves per cylinder, increasing bore and stroke, high lift cams, low resistance intake and exhaust manifolds, and turbo or supercharging.

high spot — Panel area lying above a desired surface contour.

high strength steel — Steel used in late model cars. Advantages include: thinner and lighter than regular steel but with equal strength. Disadvantages include: low tolerance to bending or stress, weldable only with a MIG welder, loses strength when damaged, and readily rusts. See also HDLA, and HSS.

high temperature enamel — See paint(high temperature-enamel).

high tension wiring — See high voltage cable.

high test — Premium or high octane gasoline.

high torque engine — See engine(high torque).

high torque starter — Starter motor built to generate higher than normal amounts of torque for improved engine starting ability.

high traction compound — Tire tread rubber compound formulated to improve traction between the tread and the road surface.

high voltage — Electrical voltage characterized by being much higher than usual. On a car, it usually refers to voltage generated by an ignition coil.

high voltage cable — Insulated electrical wire used to carry high voltage electricity. It consists of an electric conductor and surrounding insulation. Typical conductor materials include: solid copper wire and graphite impregnated material. Copper is the best conductor, but it

generates static interference with radios and TVs and has caused accidental
detonations at construction sites where explosive charges were detonated
electrically. Graphite, therefore, is commonly used. It does a good job of
suppressing static, but it has a high resistance per foot of cable which
increases every time the cable is flexed. The insulator material prevents
grounding of electricity and is designed to resist deterioration from: hot
and cold; chemicals such as oil, water, dirt, grease; abrasion; and corona.
High voltage cables are commonly found in a car ignition system where they
transfer high voltage current from the ignition coil to the spark plugs. See
also spark plug cables, Mag-wire, and corona.
high voltage capacitor system - Car spark plug ignition system introduced in
1966 by Oldsmobile. It could fire fouled plugs, increase their life 3 to 4
times, and eliminate tune ups for at least 25,000 miles. See also ignition
system(transistor) and ignition system(capacitor discharge).
high voltage terminal - Central terminal on an ignition coil used to discharge
high voltage current. A high voltage wire transfers current from the
terminal to the center tower terminal of a distributor cap.
high volume business - Marketing concept defined as selling large numbers of
cars at a lower profit in order to increase sales.
highway - Any public or main road.
Highway Emergency Locating Plan - Plan announced by the American Manufacturers
Association to establish a nationwide communications network to assist
stranded motorists. Motorists were to use CB radio equipment. Channel 9
would be used and monitoring stations would listen in around the clock within
the 10-20 mile equipment range.
highway hypnosis - Condition of reduced alertness created by looking at
unchanging or repetitive images, quietness, inactivity, etc., especially at
night. To fight the condition change what you are doing frequently.
Highway King - See Austin.
Highway-Knight - American car produced in 1920.
highway justice - Justice dispensed in small towns to motorists charged with a
local traffic violation. The violation is usually due to an obscure speed
zone. The motorist is usually required to appear before a judge right away,
plead guilty, and pay a fine; or face a subsequent trial and the need to
return to the small town. Most motorists pay the fine.
highwayman - Thief skilled in robbing people on public roads.
highway patrol - State law enforcement agency mandated to patrol a state's
highways in patrol cars to enforce traffic laws and render assistance to
travelers in need.
highway safety inspections - Road inspections conducted by highway patrol or
state police agencies on cars they suspect are unsafe to drive. If you get
pulled over for such an inspection and your car is not safe to drive, you
will be told to drive it home or to a garage right away. If your car is
dangerous to drive (poor brakes, etc.), an officer may impound your car on
the spot, requiring you to have it towed home or to a repair shop.
highway sign - See road sign.
high wheeler - Early car built to look like a motorized buggy. It was popular
in the United States and Canada from 1907-1912 with over 70 different makes
available.
Higrade - American car produced in 1919.
Hill - American car produced from 1907-1908.
hill climb - Competitive event scheduled for motorcycles or four wheel drive
vehicles to climb a steep hill in the shortest period of time.
Hill, Graham - He started working for Lotus as a mechanic and went on to
became the Grand Prix world champion in 1962 and 1968 driving a BRM and a
Lotus-Ford. Graham also won the Indianapolis 500 Race in 1966 driving an
average of 144.3 mph in an American Red Ball Special.
hill holder - Device used to prevent a car from rolling backwards by
automatically engaging and disengaging car brakes according to the car angle
and clutch pedal position.
hill holding - Driving technique used with an automatic transmission to keep a
car from rolling backwards on a hill without using the brakes. It is done by
accelerating the engine slightly until the automatic grabs enough to keep the
car stationary. It is not a good habit, since it increases wear and tear on
the transmission.
Hillman - British car line produced from 1907-1978 by Chrysler United Kingdom
Ltd. (1970-1978). Popular models included: Minx (1950-1970) and Hunter
(1967-1978)
Hill, Phil - He became the Grand Prix world champion in 1961 driving a
Ferrari.
Hill's Locomotor - American car produced in 1895.
Hillsdale - American car produced in 1908.
Hilton - American car produced in 1921.
Hinde & Dauch - American car produced from 1906-1908.
Hindustan - Indian car line produced from 1946 to date by Hindustan Motors

Ltd. in West Bengal.

Hines — American car produced from 1908-1910 by National Screw & Track Co. in Ohio.

hinge cap oiler — See cap oiler.

Hinkel — American car produced in 1925.

history — To be defeated.

hit and run — Accident situation created when a car or person is hit by another vehicle which then abruptly leaves the scene to avoid getting caught.

hitch(1) — Device welded or bolted to a car frame for attaching a trailer.

hitch(2) — To hitchhike.

hitch a ride — See hitchhiking.

Hitchcock — American car produced in 1909.

hitchhiking — Traveling done by getting free car rides when possible and walking otherwise.

Hitler, Adolph — He backed Ferdinand Porsche financially to get the Volkswagen industry started before World War II broke out.

hit the brakes — To rapidly apply the brakes.

hit the button — To engage a nitrous oxide injection system.

hit the gas — To rapidly depress a gas pedal to accelerate a car quickly.

hit the road — To leave or go away.

hi-top — Roof extension mounted on certain vans to increase headroom and/or provide extra sleeping quarters.

HKJ — Abbreviation for Jordan found usually on an international license plate.

h'lts — Abbreviation for highlights.

Hobbie — American car produced from 1908-1909 by Hobbie Automobile Co. in Iowa.

Hodge Steamer Fire Engine — American fire engine produced in 1840.

Hodgson — American car produced in 1902.

Hoffman — American car produced in 1903 and 1931.

Hoffman Gas — American car produced in 1901.

Hoffman Steam — American steam car produced from 1902-1904.

Holden — American car produced in 1915.

holdback — Profit included in each new-car's selling price that is regarded as a dealer's cost.

hold-in winding — Extra winding of wire in a solenoid used to keep contacts together once they have been pulled together by a solenoid's pull-in winding. It is used to lower current flow in a solenoid, since it takes less current to hold contacts together than to pull them together.

hole shot — To beat opponents away from a starting line.

Holland — American car produced from 1902-1905 by Holland Automobile Co. in New Jersey.

Holland, Bill — He won the Indianapolis 500 Race in 1949 driving an average of 121.3 mph in a Blue Crown Spark Plug Special.

Holland Steam — American steam car produced in 1905.

Holley(1) — American car produced from 1903-1904 by Holley Motor Co. in Pennsyvlania.

Holley(2) — American line of carburetor, ignition, and other automotive products.

Hollier — American car produced from 1915-1921 by Lewis Spring & Axle Co. in Michigan.

Holly — American car produced from 1914-1917 by Holly Motor Co. in New Jersey.

Hollywoods — Fancy exhaust system.

Holmes — American car produced in 1906-1907 and 1918-1923 by Holmes Motor Vehicle Co. in Massachusetts, and Holmes Automobile Co. in Ohio respectively.

Holmes Gastricycle — American car produced in 1895.

Holsman-Autobuggy — American car produced from 1902-1909 by Holsman Automobile Co. in Illinois.

Hol-Tan — American car produced in 1908.

Holton — American car produced in 1921.

Holtzer-Cabot — American car produced in 1895.

Holyoke — American car produced from 1901-1903 by Holyoke Automobile Co. in Massachusetts.

Holyoke-Steam — American steam car produced from 1899-1903.

Homer — American car produced in 1908.

Homer-Laughlin — American car produced in 1916.

Honda — Japanese car and motorcycle line produced from 1967 to date by Honda Motor Co. Ltd. Some models are now produced in the United States. Popular car models include: Accord (1976 to date), Ballade (1981 to date), City (1982 to date), Civic (1973-1983), Prelude (1980 to date), Quintet (1981 to date), and Acura (1986 to date).

The U.S. representative is known as American Honda Motor Co., headquartered in Gardena, California.

Honda Motor Company Ltd — Japanese car manufacturing company formed in 1948 by Soichiro Honda. It began by producing motorcycles. Car production began in the early 1960s.

Honda, Soichiro – He formed the Honda Motor Company in 1948. Besides being known as a race driver and mechanic, his other attributes included: inventor, leader, philosopher, and folk hero.

hone – Rotating tool built with three or more stones and used for machining the inside surface of a cylinder to smooth surface irregularities, remove glazing, or increase bore diameter. The stones can be adjusted to machine different diameters. If the metal to be removed is significant, it is usually removed with a boring bar.

hone(brake) – Small honing tool built with three flat grinding stones and used for lightly sanding and smoothing the inside walls of wheel and master brake cylinders. It usually works in an electric drill, and has a flexible shaft with the stones bearing against the cylinder wall surface by adjustment or by centrifugal force.

hone(cylinder) – Honing tool for machining engine cylinders.

hone(dry) – Honing done without fluid. Cuttings are usually collected with a vacuum attachment.

hone(wet) – Honing done with fluid such as water. Wet honing keeps a cylinder at a lower temperature.

Hong Qi – Chinese car line produced from 1958-1981 by Number One Automobile Plant.

honk – To run a car fast.

honker(1) – Very fast car.

honker(2) – Sharp instrument used by dishonest car repairmen to cut or puncture tires, rubber hoses, belts, etc. See also con game(honker).

Hood – American car produced from 1900-1901 by Simplex Motor Vehicle Co. in Massachusetts.

hood(1) – Hinged car panel used to cover and provide access to an engine compartment.

hood(2) – Car top.

hood cut – Line separating a car hood from adjacent car panels.

hood gap – Gap or opening located between the edge of a hood and a front fender panel.

hood latch – Latch used to keep a hood closed. Today's cars usually have a two-stage latch. The first stage is opened by means of a remote cable from inside a car. The second stage is then opened by hand at the front of the hood.

hood ornament – Ornament located on a hood for decoration.

hood protector – See bra.

hood release – Lever or pull device mounted inside a car and used to release a car hood latch.

hood scoop – Air scoop mounted on a hood to direct additional fresh air into an engine's air intake.

hood ventilator – Adjustable vent opening in a car hood used help cool an engine during hot weather and allow fumes to escape.

Hoosier Scout – American car produced in 1914.

Hoover – American car produced in 1917.

Hopkins – American car produced in 1902.

hopped up – Car modified to have higher engine performance than stock.

Hoppenstand – American car produced from 1948-1949 by Hoppenstand Motors in Pennsylvania.

hop up – Upward change of direction in a line or surface.

Horizon – American car produced from 1978 to date by Plymouth Division of Chrysler Corp. in Michigan.

horizontal aiming screw – Screw used in a car headlight assembly to adjust the side to side position of a headlight beam.

horizontally opposed engine – See engine(horizontally opposed).

horn – Electromagnetic device used for generating a loud sound. The primary components of a horn are: a set of points, a field coil, a diaphragm, and housing. A car horn is used to warn pedestrians and other cars of your presence.

Horner – American car produced in 1917.

Hornet – American car produced from 1969 to date by American Motors Corp. in Michigan.

horn relay – Electromagnetic switch used to transfer a heavy current flow to a horn when a horn button is pushed.

Hornsted, L G – He set a world land speed record of 124.1 mph in 1914 driving a Benz 4 Cylinder.

horse car – Any of the Ford Mustang cars.

horseless carriage – Early term used for a self-propelled vehicle.

horsepower – Measurement of an engine's rate of doing work. One horsepower is defined as the unit of energy needed to lift 550 pounds a distance of one foot in one second, or 33,000 pounds a distance of one foot per minute. It was originated by an engineer, named Watt, who determined that a strong horse could lift 366 pounds of coal up a mine shaft at the rate of one foot per second. It was equivalent to raising 21,960 pounds one foot per minute.

Watt arbitrarily raised the figure to 33,000 pounds, the rate used today.

horsepower(AMA) — See horsepower(rated).

horsepower(brake) — Actual horsepower delivered at the crankshaft of an engine. It takes into account losses due to friction, power required to run the water pump, fan belt, and generator. The term is derived from the equipment originally used to determine engine power. Engines today are usually tested for brake horsepower by connecting the engine crankshaft to the shaft of a dynamometer. See also Prony brake.

horsepower(double figure) — Early method used to specify horsepower where two figures were quoted such as 20/25. The first figure referred to power developed at 1,000 rpm, and the second to power at maximum rpm.

horsepower(friction) — Power required to overcome the friction within an engine. It increases with speed and size of an engine. All moving parts inside an engine create some friction. They include: pistons and rings against the cylinder walls, bearing surfaces, oil pump, water pump, valve train assembly, camshaft cams, etc.

horsepower(indicated) — Horsepower developed within engine cylinders.

horsepower(rated) — Early method used for determining engine horsepower based on using a mean effective pressure of 67.2 psi and a piston speed of 1,000 fpm. Today's engines exceed both these values considerably and hence the test is no longer applies. It is also known as AMA horsepower.

horsepower to weight ratio — Ratio of the total weight of the car to the horsepower available. It determines the weight one horsepower must move. This ratio has a large effect on gas mileage, acceleration, top speed, and all around performance.

horse trader — Person skilled in bargaining who can spot other people's strengths and weaknesses, and use that information along with his various sales tricks to make a deal to his advantage. Horse traders were popular before the advent of the car, and used their skills to sell horses. Many of a horse trader's techniques are employed by car salesmen today.

horse trading — Bargaining session conducted where all parties involved employ the techniques of a horse trader to close a deal to their advantage.

Horsey Horseless Carriage — American car produced in 1899.

hose brakes — Hydraulic brakes.

Hoskins — American car produced in 1921.

hot — See hard.

hot air duct — See hot air inlet.

hot air inlet — Separate air intake attached to the air inlet of an air cleaner, for receiving preheated air from an exhaust manifold area. The preheated air is usually collected by a metal shroud surrounding an exhaust manifold known as a hot air stove, and a duct running to a hot air inlet. The flow of normal and preheated air is controlled by a temperature and/or vacuum sensitive diaphragm used to open and close an air gate in an air inlet. The thermostat sensor controls the flow of preheated air to a carburetor when the outside air is cold. The vacuum sensor controls the flow of additional air through an air inlet when a car is accelerating, operating at high speed, etc. A malfunctioning hot air inlet may cause: pinging if too much hot air enters a warm engine, or reduced power and fuel economy if too much cold air enters. See also control damper assembly and fresh air duct.

hot air pipe — See hot air tube.

hot air tube — Tube used to carry warm air collected from a hot air stove to an air cleaner intake. It is usually made of a heat resistant paper or aluminum, and is effective in increasing fuel economy in the winter and preventing carburetor icing as well. See also vacuum motor and hot air inlet.

hot air stove — Light gauge metal shroud used to surround some or all of an exhaust manifold for the purpose of ducting warm air to an air cleaner. Most cars have them today for improving gas mileage in cold weather. See also hot air inlet.

hot car drop — Repair shop set up to also act as a front for receiving stolen cars and/or routing them to their final destination.

hotchkiss — Driveline exposed from the transmission end to the differential.

hot dog — Show off driver. Also, it refers to a hard-to-beat driver.

hot idle compensator — Carburetor device used to admit extra air to an intake manifold in order to combat an over rich air/fuel mixture condition at idle. The condition develops when an engine gets hot from extended idling and causes some of the float bowl fuel to vaporize and find its way into the air passageway along with the metered liquid fuel.

hot lacquer — See paint(hot lacquer).

hot plug — See spark plug(hot).

hot prospect — See live one.

hot rod — Stock car modified for high performance. Modifications typically involve: greatly increasing engine horsepower, using racing wheels, improving traction characteristics, lightening overall weight, using more powerful fuel, etc.

hot rodder - Person experienced in building and/or driving hot rods.
hot rodding - Driving characterized by high speed, fast acceleration, burning rubber, racing, etc. Such maneuvers are usually legal at race tracks only.
Hot Rod Magazine - See magazine(Hot Rod Magazine).
hot soak - See heat soak.
hot shoe - Hard to beat driver.
hot shutdown - To stop an engine when it is at operating temperature.
hot smoke - See exhaust(black smoke).
hot spot - One or more areas located in a combustion chamber where heat builds up. Hot spot can include: spark plug tip with too hot a heat range, and sharp edges or carbon build-up in combustion chamber. It often causes dieseling.
  Also, it refers to one or more areas located in a water jacket where circulation slows or stops, usually due to scale deposits. It causes the affected area to locally overheat and distort. If close to a cylinder wall, it can cause a piston skirt to bind, galling the cylinder wall and slowing starter cranking speed. The best way to prevent this from occurring is to flush the cooling system regularly, and use antifreeze with rust and corrosion inhibitors. See also scale deposit, dieseling, and preignition.
hot tank - Tank filled with hot water and certain other cleaning compounds, or a suitable solvent. It is commonly used to clean cylinder heads and engine blocks.
hot tank the block - To put an engine block in a hot tank for cleaning.
hot tank the head - To put a cylinder head in a hot tank for cleaning.
hot tapper - Engine with noisy valve lifters.
hot tube ignition - Early ignition system built with small platinum tubes inserted where spark plugs go. The tube was heated to a high enough temperature by an external gas burner to cause ignition when a fuel mixture entered the tube. It was outdated by 1900.
hot wire - Electrical wire used to carry a measurable electrical voltage.
hot wire a car - Method used to bypass a car's ignition switch run and start modes to start and run the engine. A wire is usually connected to an active 12 volt line and run past the ignition switch to the starter relay. This approach eliminates the need for a key, and is commonly used by thieves attempting to steal a car.
hot wire sensor - Electric device used to measure mass airflow into an engine.
Houghton Steamer - American steam car produced from 1900-1901.
Houk - American car produced in 1917.
Houpt - American car produced from 1909-1910 by Harry S. Houpt Mfg. Co. in Connecticut.
Houpt-Rockwell - American car produced in 1910-1912 by New Departure Mfg. Co. in Connecticut.
House - American car produced in 1920.
house - Dealership business or its management.
house car - Car purchased, serviced, and traded in on another car at the same dealership.
House-Steamer - American car produced in 1901.
Howard - American car produced in 1901, 1903-1905, 1913-1918, and 1929-1930 by Howard Automobile Co. in New Jersey, Howard Automobile Co. in New York, A Howard Co. in Ohio, Lexington-Howard Co. in Indiana, and Howard Motor Int. Corp. in New York respectively.
Howard Gasoline Wagon - American car produced in 1895.
Howe - American car produced in 1907.
Howey - American car produced in 1903.
hp - Abbreviation for horsepower.
H point - Reference point in a person's lower hip area used for making body-position measurements.
HRL - American car produced in 1921.
HSC - Abbreviation for high combustion swirl.
H Slot - The gearshift pattern commonly used today on four speed transmissions. Packard was granted the patent in 1902.
HSS - Abbreviation for high strength steel.
HT - Abbreviation for hard top.
Hub - American car produced from 1899-1900 and 1907 by Hub Motor Co. in Illinois, and Hub Automobile Co. in Massachusetts respectively.
hub - Circular metal plate fitted with mounting studs for attaching a wheel to a car. Lug nuts holds a wheel on the studs. On rear wheels, the hub is welded to the end of the rear axle shaft and is separate from the brake drum. On front wheels using drum brakes, the hub is welded to the brake drum. On front wheels using disc brakes, the hub is welded to the rotor.
hub and rotor assembly - A rotating assembly used mostly on front wheels to provide a braking surface for the brake pads and a mounting point for a wheel. The hub and rotor are usually welded together. See also hub.
hub cap - Stylish circular metal cover for the outer wheel side of a tire.
Huber - American car produced in 1894.

Hudson – American car produced from 1901-1902 by Beau-Chamberlain Mfg. Co. in Michigan. Also, an American car produced from 1909-1957 by Hudson Motor Car Co. in Michigan and American Motors Corp. in Wisconsin.
Hudson Steam – American car produced in 1904.
Hudson Steam Car – American steam car produced in 1901.
Huebner – American car produced in 1914.
huffer – See supercharger.
Huffman – American car produced from 1920-1925 by Huffman Bros. Motor Co. in Indiana.
Hug Truck – American car produced in 1922.
Hughes – American car produced from 1899-1900 by Hughes & Atkin in Rhode Island.
Hulme, Denny – He was a New Zealand race car driver who became the Grand Prix world champion in 1967 driving a Brabham-Repco.
Hummingbird – American car produced in 1946.
hump – Center part of a car's floorpan raised to allow passage of a driveshaft from a transmission to a differential.
Hunt – American car produced in 1905.
Hunter – American car produced in 1921.
Huntington – American car produced in 1907.
Huntington-Buckboard – American car produced in 1889.
Hunt, James – He became the Grand Prix world champion in 1976 driving a McLaren-Ford.
Hupmobile – American car produced from 1908-1940 by Hupp Motor Car Corp. in Michigan and Ohio.
Hupp-Yeats – American electric car produced from 1911-1918 by R.C.H. Corp. in Michigan (1911-1912), and Hupp-Yeats Electric Car Co. in Michigan (1912-1918).
Hurlburt – American car produced in 1922.
Huron – American car produced in 1921.
Hurryton – American car produced in 1922.
Hurst – American line of transmission shifters produced by Hurst Performance, Inc.
Huselton – American car produced in 1914.
hustler – Person skilled in swindling others to obtain money. See also con man.
Hustler Power Car – American car produced in 1911.
Huygens, Charles – He built the first explosion engine utilizing gunpowder in 1678.
hwy – Abbreviation for highway.
hybrid electric car – Car powered by an electric motor receiving its electrical energy from two sources: a bank of chemical batteries and/or a small gasoline or diesel powered engine driving a high output alternator. Such cars are still experimental, but are designed to run indefinitely up to a certain speed when the engine is operating. See also electric car.
Hydra-Matic – Popular automatic transmission produced by Cadillac beginning in 1949, and used in Cadillac, Pontiac and Oldsmobile cars until 1963.
hydraulic – To operate by the movement and force of liquid.
hydraulic brake – See brake hydraulic.
hydraulic brake system – Assemblage of parts and hydraulic brake fluid used to operate brake shoes and/or pad by hydraulic pressure. The system consists primarily of a master cylinder, brake lines, and brake cylinders.
hydraulic clutch – Clutch release mechanism comprised of a hydraulic cylinder and linkage to depress a clutch pressure plate instead of a straight mechanical linkage.
hydraulic intensity – Difference measured between a cam's gross and net duration or .004 and .050 inch cam lobe lift. It is an important factor in determining low speed performance characteristics. See also gross duration and net duration.
hydraulic lifter – Valve lifter built to use hydraulic pressure from an engine's oil to keep it in constant contact with a camshaft and a valve stem. Hydraulic lifter automatically adjusts to variations in valve stem length. It does not increase a valve's life, but makes it run quieter and with less maintenance.
hydraulic pressure – Pressure created in a hydraulic system.
hydraulics – Branch of physics concerned with mechanical properties and application of those properties to water and other liquids in motion.
hydraulic steering stabilizer – Shock absorber type cylinder fastened to a car frame and the steering linkage to provide stability and minimize vibration.
hydraulic system – Assemblage of parts and hydraulic fluid used to perform work by forcing fluid under pressure through lines. The brake system on cars is a hydraulic system.
hydraulic valve lifter – See hydraulic lifter.
hydro – Automatic transmission.
Hydro-Car – American car produced in 1901.

hydrocarbon – Organic compound composed of only hydrogen and carbon. Hydrocarbons occur naturally as solids, liquids, and gases. Over 2,000 compounds have been identified. Solids include hexacontane and hexadecane. Liquids include pentane, hexane, heptane, and octane. Gases include methane, ethane, propane, and butane. All petroleum fuels are composed of hydrocarbons. See also fuel.

hydrocarbon engine – See engine(hydrocarbon).

hydrogen – Gas characterized by being colorless, odorless, flammable, and the lightest of the known elements. Experimental cars have been built powered by hydrogen.

hydrogenation – Process used for increasing the gas yield from crude oil by adding hydrogen molecules to oil molecules in the presence of a catalyst.

hydrometer – Instrument designed for measuring the specific gravities of liquids. See also antifreeze hydrometer, battery hydrometer, and built-in eye.

Hydrometor – American car produced in 1917 by Automobile Boat Mfg. Co. in Washington.

hydroplaning – Driving condition created when a car's tires ride up on a wedge of water and thereby lose contact with a road surface.

hydropneumatic suspension – Car suspension system built where bladders filled with gas and liquid control the amount of springing and car height.

hydrostatic gauge – Gauge used to measure a fluid level like gasoline by means of a calibrated vertical clear tube connected to the top and bottom of the tank.

Hylander – American car produced in 1922.

hypoid gear – See gear(hypoid).

Hyslop – American car produced in 1915.

Hyundai – Korean car line produced from 1974 to date by Hyundai Motor Co. Ltd. Recent models include: Pony Excel and Giugiaro.

I

I – Abbreviation for Italy found usually on an international license plate.

Iacocca, Lee – Chairman of Chrysler Corporation credited for saving Chrysler from bankruptcy in 1980.

icy spot – Area located on a roadway where ice has formed.

ID – Abbreviation for inside diameter.

Ideal – American car produced from 1902-1903 by B&P Co. in Wisconsin. Also, an American electric car produced from 1909-1914 by Ideal Electric Co. in Illinois.

Ideal Motor Company – Company organized in 1911 by Harry Stutz to manufacture Stutz cars.

idiot circuit – See electronic scattershield.

idiot light – Warning light installed in an instrument panel that lights red when a certain malfunction occurs in an engine such as low oil pressure and coolant overheating. It is referred to as an idiot light because it gives no indication of an impending problem. See also warning light.

idle – See idle speed.

idle adjusting needle – See idle mixture adjustment screw.

idle adjustment screw – Screw mounted on the carburetor's body to adjust the closed position of a carburetor's throttle plate and thus the idle speed of a car. Turning the screw in opens a throttle plate a little, admitting more fuel and air into the intake manifold and raising the engine rpm. Unscrewing does the opposite.

idle air bleed – See idle by-pass air bleed.

idle air by-pass adjustment screw – Adjustable screw used in certain carburetor designs to control the flow of air around a throttle plate during idle. It permits a throttle plate to be almost completely closed at idle, and helps eliminate rough idling by preventing formation of carbon deposits around throttle plate.

idle air control valve – Valve used in electronic fuel injection unit to control engine idle by regulating amount of air bypassing throttle plate.

idle bleed – Small opening made off an idle by-pass air bleed passageway into a carburetor airway. It is used in certain carburetor low speed circuits.

idle by-pass air bleed – Small air passageway used to route air usually from above a choke plate to an idle mixture adjustment screw when a car is idling.

idle circuit – See carburetor circuit(low speed).

idle circuit nozzle – Small opening used to transport fuel from an idle circuit to a carburetor barrel.

idle discharge hole – See idle discharge port.

idle discharge port – Small port located beneath the throttle plate where low speed circuit fuel is discharged during idle and slight off-idle conditions. Fuel discharges from this port as long as there is a strong vacuum, caused by the throttle plate remaining closed or mostly so. See also low speed port.

idle fuel – Fuel located within a carburetor flowing through an idle or low speed circuit.

idle fuel economizer – See idle restriction.

idle jet – Calibrated opening at one end of an idle tube used to meter the amount of fuel entering an idle tube.

idle limiter – Needle-like device installed in an idle circuit to limit enrichment of an air/fuel mixture at idle. It is usually located close to the idle mixture adjusting screw.

idle mixture screw – See idle mixture adjustment screw.

idle mixture adjustment screw – Adjustable screw mounted near the base of the carburetor for metering an air/fuel mixture into the airway just below a throttle plate. When screwed out and in, more and less mixture is allowed to enter an engine respectively. Air bleeds are located in the passageways leading to the screw to help vaporize fuel before entering a carburetor airway. This is necessary because the air moving past the throttle plate is moving slowly and introducing unvaporized fuel into the air passageway would cause it to settle on the intake manifold walls. See also air bleeds and idle jet.

idle needle valve – See idle mixture adjustment screw.

idle passage plug – Screw used to close an idle circuit passageway usually housing an idle jet.

idle port – Idle circuit exit opening located in carburetor airway near edge of throttle valve in idle position. See also off-idle ports.

idle port plug – Screw or plugging device used to seal idle circuit openings near an idle mixture adjustment screw.

idler arm – Pivoting arm used in steering linkage to support the other end of a drag link. It is mounted on the passenger side of a car. The pivoting center of the arm is strategically mounted on a car chassis.

idle restriction – Narrower passageway section located in an idle circuit. It is typically used to restrict fuel and/or air flow rate when a throttle plate opens.

idler pulley – Pulley positioned to keep a belt tight against other pulleys. It is often adjustable and drives nothing.

idle speed – Engine rotation speed set when an engine is running, carburetor throttle plate is closed, and no load is placed on an engine. It is the speed at which many carburetor and ignition adjustments are made. A car idling too low will tend to stall. Most cars idle at 600-900 rpm range. Idle speed on a new engine increases as it breaks in and friction is reduced.

idle speed screw – See idle speed adjustment screw.

idle speed adjustment screw – See idle adjustment screw.

idle stop solenoid – Solenoid used on emission carburetors to completely close a throttle plate when the ignition is turned off. It is designed to suppress dieseling. See also dieseling, fuel cut solenoid, and speed up solenoid.

idle tube – Tube used to pick up fuel from a float bowl for the low speed carburetor circuit.

ignite – To set on fire.

igniter – Distributor.

ignition – Process used to start combustion of an air/fuel mixture in a gas engine. It occurs when an electric spark is delivered to a combustion chamber.

ignition advance – See advance(spark).

ignition cable – See spark plug cable and high voltage cable.

ignition coil – Electrical device, also known as a pulse transformer, used to increase 6 or 12 volt battery voltage to a high enough voltage (20,000 or more) so a spark of electricity can jump a spark plug gap and fire an air/fuel mixture. The heat of a spark is what ignites the mixture. The coil consists of: a primary low voltage winding, secondary high voltage winding, low voltage electrical terminals, high voltage electrical terminal, iron core, internal or external resistance unit, and housing. The iron core is usually covered first with the secondary winding, then the primary. It serves to concentrate the magnetic field, and momentarily prolong current flow when the points open. The primary winding carries the battery voltage. The secondary winding carries the high voltage created when battery voltage is abruptly dropped by breaking the primary circuit with contact points or other suitable switch located in a distributor. A burned out coil is commonly caused by a bad ignition coil resistor. See also primary coil winding winding, secondary coil winding, iron core, and car service tip(ignition coil test).

ignition coil(vibrator type) – Ignition coil built with a set of contact points mounted near the coil's iron core, opening and closing according to the magnetic field developed. Points are wired in series with the primary windings. It was a popular design with early cars and became known as the Model T coil. It has been used on more recent cars using diesel engines.

ignition coil output – High voltage value generated by an ignition coil's secondary windings.

ignition coil polarity – Direction of current flow in a coil. Also, it refers to the N-S direction of a coil's magnetic field.

ignition coil resistor – Resistor connected in series with the primary windings of an ignition coil. The main purpose of a coil resistor is to control the voltage reaching the ignition coil's primary windings, and thus spark strength. An engine requires a stronger spark when it is started. Such a spark is created when a resistor is bypassed and an ignition coil temporarily receives full battery voltage generating a hotter spark. When the engine is running, a hotter spark is not necessary so the ignition switch, in the run position, pass current through the resistor dropping the voltage level. This is important since most ignition coils are designed to operate continuously at less than battery voltage. If the resistor were not used, the ignition coil would quickly burn out. The resistor usually drops voltage to 5-7 volts. On 12 volt systems, a common resistance value is 1.5 ohms. Some designs use a resistance wire while others use a resistor mounted near an ignition coil. The latter is more popular today.

ignition coil terminal – Primary voltage connection points on an ignition coil. One receives current from the ignition switch, while the other routes the flow of current out of the primary windings and on to the distributor points or switching device. Input terminals will have a marking such as: +, SW, or BATT. Output terminals will have a marking such as: -, CB, or DIST.

ignition condenser – See condenser.

ignition control module – See electronic control module.

ignition cross fire – Spark plug cable(s) receives high voltage at the wrong time. It can cause an engine to stumble, jerk, and backfire. Possible causes include: cables too close together or crossing each other; arcing in distributor cap due to moisture, oil, and/or crack; wrong coil voltage; and cables installed in wrong sequence.

ignition-induction system - See emission control system(combustion-ignition/induction).

ignition key - Key used to operate a car's ignition switch.

ignition module - See electronic ignition module.

ignition point - See contact points.

ignition point condition - Degree of wear and corrosion indicated on a set of distributor points.

ignition pulse amplifier - Solid state electronic device used in a transistor ignition system to increase the strength of a signal from a distributor point mechanism for controlling the flow of primary current in an ignition coil. Components consist of: resistors, transistors, capacitors, diodes, and printed circuits. See also magnetic pulse distributor.

ignition switch - A multi-position switch used to connect and disconnect various car accessories, and start or stop an engine. It usually operates with a key and has five positions known usually as: OFF, ACC (accessories), LOCK, ON (or run), and START. OFF position opens all switch circuits. ACC position closes circuits running certain accessories, but keeps steering wheel and certain automatic transmissions locked. LOCK position opens all circuits and usually locks steering wheel so it cannot be moved. The key is inserted and removed in this position, and cannot be removed on certain automatic transmission cars unless transmission is in park. ON position closes all accessory circuits, and closes an additional circuit energizing an ignition system through an ignition coil ballast resistor. START position closes the engine starting circuit and bypasses a ballast resistor to temporarily increase coil primary voltage and resulting secondary voltage.

ignition system - Assemblage of parts and controls used to produce and distribute high voltage sparks to ignite a fuel mixture in the engine cylinders. The primary components consist of: a battery, ignition switch, low voltage wiring and resistors, ignition coil, distributor, points and condenser, spark plugs, and high voltage wiring.

ignition system(capacitor discharge) - Electronic ignition system constructed to create a rapid rise and fall in an ignition coil's primary windings by discharging a capacitor. The pulse triggers the secondary windings to produce high voltage current. Capacitive discharge provides considerably higher voltage to the primary windings (usually 300 volts), resulting in higher secondary voltage. It allows for short dwell periods which means high rpm driving without missing.

Aftermarket CD ignition systems usually retain use of the car's existing points. Point life is greatly extended due to reduced current flow (1 amp vs. 3-5 for conventional) reducing arcing and burning, but the car still retains some of the problems associated with points such as point float and rubbing block wear. Other stock ignition components can still be used. See also ignition system(contact controlled capacitor discharge) and ignition system(magnetic controlled capacitor discharge).

ignition system(contact controlled capacitor discharge) - Electronic ignition system constructed with the primary current flow controlled through a capacitor-diode-oscillator assembly by means of conventional distributor points.

ignition system(contact controlled transistor) - Electronic ignition system constructed with the primary current flow controlled through a transistor by means of conventional distributor points.

ignition system(conventional) - Ignition system constructed to create and distribute high voltage electricity to spark plugs by disrupting current flow in an ignition coil's primary windings with a set of movable contact points mounted inside a distributor. The high voltage capacity of the system is limited to the amount of current allowed to flow through the points. A typical limit is 5 amps.

ignition system(direct capacitative) - New experimental ignition system constructed with each spark plug having its own small ignition coil and condenser mounted directly above. It eliminates a distributor, high voltage wiring, and a central ignition coil. Additionally, hotter sparks firing at 40,000 volts rather than 25,000 volts are created allowing plugs to have larger gaps. Hotter longer sparks means more reliable firing of even lean fuel mixtures.

ignition system(electronic) - See ignition system(solid state).

ignition system(magnetic controlled capacitor discharge) - Electronic ignition system constructed with the primary current flow controlled through a transistor by a pulse generator. Distributor points are eliminated.

ignition system(magnetic controlled transistor) - See ignition system(magnetic controlled capacitor discharge).

ignition system(magnetic pulse breakerless) - Electronic ignition system constructed with primary current flow controlled by a reluctor and magnetic pickup coil assembly in the distributor. Distributor points are eliminated. As a result, no points or condensers wear out, and dwell angle is fixed.

ignition system(solid state) – Ignition system constructed to use solid state electronic components (transistors, magnetic devices, etc.) to switch current flows on and off in an ignition coil eliminating the use of conventional points. It began appearing on cars in the late 1960s with conventional points being eliminated on almost all cars by 1975. Benefits over conventional systems include: higher primary voltage and resultant secondary voltage, spark plugs run cleaner and last longer, voltage higher at high rpm, reduced misfiring tendency at high rpm, and lower emissions. See also ignition system(transistor), ignition system(capacitor discharge), and multiple spark discharge.

ignition system(transistor) – Ignition system constructed to use a solid state electronic component for switching large current flows on and off through the action of a set of movable points located in a distributor housing. In this system, distributor points carry only a small portion of the primary current flow. When they open, they trigger the transistor to interrupt the primary winding current flow. The distributor points last indefinitely because of the low current flow. If a car is retrofitted with a transistor ignition system, the original ballast resistor should be bypassed. Advantages of this system include: stable voltage, long distributor point life, less frequent tune-ups, and high engine rpm without missing.

ignition timing – Point specified in a piston's compression stroke when a spark occurs at a spark plug's electrodes to ignite a compressed air/fuel mixture. See also advance(spark).

IGOA – Independent Garage Owners of America.

IHC – American car produced in 1911. Also, an American car line produced from 1961-1980 by International Harvester Corp. in Illinois.

I-head engine – See engine(I-head).

ihp – Abbreviation for indicated horsepower.

IL – Abbreviation for Israel found usually on an international license plate.

Illinois – American car produced from 1910-1914 by Overholt Co. in Illinois.

Illinois Electric – American electric car produced in 1901 and 1909-1914.

IMCO – Abbreviation for improved combustion. See also emission control system(combustion-improved combustion).

immaculate condition – Very clean used car.

IMP – American car produced from 1913-1914 and 1955 by W.H. McIntyre Co. in Indiana, and Int. Motor Products in California respectively.

impact angle – Angle of impact measured between a body surface and the direction of impact.

impact wrench – Air, electric, or hand driven wrench used to tighten or loosen, nuts, screws, etc. by delivering sharp rotational blows at a specified rate.

Impala – American car produced from 1955 to date by Chevrolet Division of General Motors Corp. in Michigan.

impeller – Circular, rotating, fan-like device used to pump air or fluid.

Imperial – American car produced in 1903-1904, and 1906-1916 by Rodgers & Co. in Ohio (1903-1904), Imperial Motor Car Co. in Pennsylvania (1906-1907), and Imperial Automobile Co. in Michigan (1907-1916). Also, an American luxury car line produced from 1926 to date by Chrysler Corp. in Michigan. Also, an American car produced from 1954 to date by Chrysler Corp. in Michigan.

implied consent law – Law enacted in most states giving law enforcement agencies the right to test you for intoxification while driving, if you apply for and receive a valid driver's license. If you refuse the test when you are requested to take it, your license can be suspended or revoked whether you are later proved guilty or not. Every driver who obtains a driver's license under this law agrees to be checked for intoxification. See also breath test.

implied warranty – See warranty(implied).

import – Merchandise brought in from a foreign country usually to sell.

imported car – Car produced in a foreign country, and brought into the U.S. usually for sale.

impulse coupling – Device used on magnetos for strengthening high voltage and retarding ignition timing during engine starting. It is mounted on one end of the magneto's rotor shaft.

IMSA – Abbreviation for International Motor Sports Association, Inc.

in(1) – Abbreviation for inch.

in(2) – Piece of knowledge obtained about a potential car customer that helps make a sale. Such knowledge could be: the type of car he owns, where he works, his interests, and/or his personality.

in-and-out box – See transmission(in-and-out box).

inboard brake pad – Disc brake pad positioned to bear against the inside rotor braking surface.

incentive system – Method of payment made to an individual based on performance, jobs completed, etc., rather than an hourly wage.

incl - Abbreviation for including.
included angle - See wheel alignment angle(included).
IND - Abbreviation for India found usually on an international license plate.
Independence - American car produced in 1912.
Independent - American car produced in 1915-1916, 1920, and 1927.
independent - Car repair business not owned by another company.
independent agent - Agent engaged in selling several different brands of products, policies, etc. See also exclusive agent.
independent front end - Front end of a car equipped with independent front suspension. See also suspension system(independent).
independent front suspension - See suspension system(independent).
independent garage owner - Small businessman engaged in repairing cars. Most have built their business through hard work, personalized service, honesty, and usually lower rates than larger car repair operations.
independent suspension - See suspension system(independent).
Indian - American car produced from 1928-1929 by Indian Motorcycle Co. in Massachusetts. Only three cars were built.
Indiana - American car produced in 1910 and 1921.
Indiana Truck - American truck produced in 1909.
Indianapolis - American car produced in 1899.
Indianapolis 500 - Annual 500 mile race conducted in Indianapolis, Indiana. The first race was held on the track in 1909.
Indianapolis of the South - See Darlington.
induced voltage - Voltage generated in an electrical conductor as a result of the conductor moving through a magnetic field.
induction(electric) - Process defined as the production of an electric or magnetic effect in an object when the object is exposed to an electric or magnetic field.
induction(fuel) - Movement of an air/fuel mixture from a carburetor to the cylinders of an engine.
induction firing - High voltage current generated in a spark plug cable by an adjacent cable carrying current, running parallel, and too close. The current in one cable induces current in the other which sometimes causes two spark plugs to fire at once. Induction firing has been known to cause such problems as carburetor fire, backfiring, rough running, and engine damage. Induction firing can be minimized by: not running spark plug cables parallel for long distances, not using metal tubular wire looms, and keeping wires separated as much as possible.
induction manifold - See intake manifold(induction).
induction system - Assemblage of parts used to deliver an air/fuel mixture to an engine's cylinders. Parts include: air cleaner, carburetor or fuel injection parts, intake manifold, and intake valves.
inductive timing light - See timing light(inductive).
Indy - Abbreviation for Indianapolis Race Track.
inertia - Tendency exerted by matter to remain in its state of motion. A moving body will tend to move and a stationary body will tend to remain stationary.
inertia drive - See starter drive(Bendix).
inertia tuning - Exhaust tuning done to a racing or non-racing engine's header exhaust system by determining individual pipe lengths necessary to allow the exhaust gas mass to blend properly together creating proper scavenging of each cylinder. Pipe diameters used are the same as the port diameters. See also acoustical tuning.
inexperienced driver - Car driver not skilled in driving a car.
inferior workmanship - Product poorly made or constructed.
infraction - A law violation.
in-frame job - Work done on an engine without having to remove it.
Ingersoll-Rand - American car produced in 1921.
Ingram-Hatch - American car produced from 1917-1918 by Ingram-Hatch Motor Corp. in New York.
injected - Engine fuel system built to inject fuel.
injector - See injector nozzle.
injector line - High pressure fuel line located running from an injector pump to an injector nozzle.
injector nozzle(diesel) - Device mounted in an engine cylinder head for metering high pressure diesel fuel into an engine cylinder. The fuel is usually injected into a little chamber off a main combustion chamber where a glow plug tip is also located. See also fuel injector.
injector nozzle(gas) - Device mounted in an intake manifold of an engine for metering and atomizing gasoline. There can be more than one injector, depending on the design of an intake manifold. See also fuel injector.
injector pump - Pump used to pressurize and distribute diesel or gas fuel to appropriate injector lines for injection into combustion chambers or an intake manifold.
Inland - American car produced in 1920.

inlet over exhaust – Intake and exhaust valve arrangement found in an F-head engine.

in-line engine – See engine(in line).

inner caliper half – Half of a disc brake caliper housing positioned on the inside of a rotor. See also outside caliper half and caliper assembly.

inner pad and plate – Disc brake pad and cover plate assembly mounted next to the inside caliper piston. See also outer pad and plate.

inner tube – Flexible doughnut-shaped tube installed and inflated in a tire carcass to support it. Most car tires today are tubeless.

Innes – American car produced in 1921.

input shaft – Shaft used to delivers power to a mechanism. The input shaft of a manual transmission receives power from an engine and transfers it to the transmission.

inspection certificate – Document issued certifying a car has been inspected and found to be in safe driving condition. Certain states require dealers to furnish these certificates to buyers of used cars, or guarantee in writing they can pass such an inspection.

installment plan – Loan payment plan used specifying payment of a debt in fixed amounts at specified intervals for a specified period of time.

instruction permit – Permit issued to allow a non-licensed person to practice driving for a specific time period under certain conditions.

instrument panel – Portion of a car interior located directly in front of a driver and containing primary gauges and controls for operating a car.

insulation(electrical) – Substance characterized by not conducting electricity. It is used to keep electricity flowing in the wires of electrical circuits. Insulation is usually a plastic coating on wires, with other coatings being enamel, shellac, etc., depending on the application.

insulation(temperature) – Material used to isolate and maintain temperature differences between two nearby surfaces. Common insulation materials are fiberglass, foam, and ceramic wool.

insulator – Electrically nonconductive device used to hold electric wires in place. Insulators are typically made out of glass, porcelain, bakelite, plastic, etc.

insurance – Contract used to guarantee compensation for specified losses due to fire, accident, death, etc.

insurance(25/50/10) – Common insurance policy used to provide liability coverage. The figures refer to the maximum amount of money, in thousands, an insurance company will pay for each person hurt, the total medical payout, and the property damaged by the insurance holder in an accident.

insurance(bodily injury liability) – Insurance used to financially protect a driver of a car who injures or kills passengers in his own car, people riding in other cars, and/or pedestrians. Coverage usually applies to the driver, family members, and people having permission to drive the car. It usually provides legal defense and pay damages up to specified limits.

insurance(collision) – Insurance used to financially protect a car investment if it collides with another car or object. Damage to the vehicle is paid regardless of fault and is usually on some kind of deductible basis. This insurance does not cover damaging other people's property or injuries to people. See also insurance(deductible).

insurance(comprehensive) – Insurance used to financially protect a car investment if damage results from unforeseen circumstances such as car theft, broken glass, earthquake, fire, flood, vandalism, riots, hitting animals, etc. Comprehensive does not usually cover the inside contents of the car.

insurance(deductible) – Insurance based on insured person paying for specified cost of a claim before remaining damages are paid by insurance company. Typically, a car owner will pay for the first $50-500 worth of a car's damage depending on desired coverage. Deductible insurance clauses are often found in more than one place in insurance policies.

insurance(emergency road service) – Insurance used to pay for car towing in the event of a breakdown while on the road. It may also provide other coverage such as money advances, reimbursement for motels, etc.

insurance(liability) – Insurance used to financially protect a driver of a car from being liable for damage to other property and injury to other people as the result of an accident. See also insurance(bodily injury liability) and insurance(property damage liability).

insurance(liability-single limit) – Liabililty insurance written to set one coverage limit on: bodily injury to one person, bodily injury to two or more people, and property damage. See also insurance(liability-split limit).

insurance(liability-split limit) – Liability insurance written to set coverage limits on: bodily injury to one person, bodily injury to two or more people, and property damage. It is a common automotive insurance policy. See also insurance(liability-single limit).

insurance(medical) – Insurance used to pay for medical expenses arising from injuries to a driver and his passengers while in a car. It also pays for injuries to a driver and his immediate family members in other cars or while walking. Coverage does not depend on who is at fault in an accident. Medical coverage is an important part of a car insurance policy.

insurance(minimum) - Minimum liability insurance.

insurance(no fault) - Insurance used to financially cover damages to a person's car by the person's insurance agency regardless of fault. It is used primarily to speed up car repair payments to people involved in accidents.

insurance(package) - Insurance used to provide relatively complete coverage. Parts of such a policy consist of: liability, collision, comprehensive, medical, etc.

insurance(property damage liability) - Insurance used to protect the driver of a car damaging another person's property. The property is commonly a car, but can also be a building, parking meter, etc. The coverage is generally the same as for bodily injury insurance.

insurance(theft) - Insurance used to financially protect against theft of a car or its contents.

insurance(uninsured motorist) - Insurance used to pay for medical expenses in the same way medical insurance does, but which provides the protection against hit and run drivers or uninsured motorists. The coverage is intended to act as if the offenders actually carried insurance.

insurance adjuster - Person employed by an insurance company to settle claims.

insurance claim - Document filed with an insurance company to receive monetary compensation for an insured loss.

insurance commission - Fee paid to dealers by insurance companies for the insurance portion of a car loan. Every car bought on time must be insured to protect a car from any damage. Insurance companies will often make arrangements for dealers to receive a certain fee each time a car loan is made stipulating their insurance company as the car insurer. Dealers will try to talk the prospective car buyer into the insurance policy and may even offer some discount. It is best to check the policy offered with others available before making a decision. If you go with the dealer's recommendation, make sure the policy has liability protection. See also con game(dealer insurance).

insurance coverage - Insurance policies issued by an insurance company to insure against specific conditions. Automotive insurance coverage is usually divided into three broad categories: liability, physical damage, and medical payments. See also driver rating.

insurance policy - See insurance.

insurance policy(floater) - Policy issued to cover property frequently moved from one place to another against damage, theft, etc.

insurance policy(rider) - Addition or amendment to an insurance policy.

insurance premiums - Insurance payments made monthly, yearly, etc.

insurance rates - Rates established by an insurance company for the various coverages offered. There are many insurance rate cost saving measures available. They include: safe driver policies, small car discounts, non-smoker discounts, package insurance discounts, multiple car discounts, yearly vs. semi-annual payments, driver education discounts, etc.

int - Abbreviation for interior.

intake - Opening in a surface created to allow an air inflow, usually to cool brakes, an engine, or occupants for passenger comfort.

intake manifold - Steel or aluminum casting used to route an air/fuel mixture from the base of a carburetor to an engine's intake valves. The primary components are a flat surface for mounting a carburetor, a series of passageways equaling the number of cylinders accessed, a flat surface for attaching each passageway to its respective intake valve, and a water jacket for keeping the passageways warm to improve fuel vaporization for better fuel economy.

intake manifold(cross ram) - Manifold built with long passageways and a low profile. It usually utilizes two offset carburetors.

intake manifold(dual plane) - Manifold built with two separate sets of passageways. The carburetor feeds an air/fuel mixture into each side during primary and secondary operation.

intake manifold(double level) - See intake manifold(dual plane).

intake manifold(dual quad) - Manifold built to use two four barrel carburetors.

intake manifold(high ram) - See intake manifold(ram).

intake manifold(high rise) - Manifold built with a raised carburetor mounting flange in order to make the runners or passageways taller and more gently curved for reduced flow restrictions. Most are the dual plane type.

intake manifold(individual runner) - See intake manifold(ram).

intake manifold(induction) - Manifold built with separate primary and secondary ports and passageways. It is used to increase the efficiency of getting an air/fuel mixture to the engine cylinders.

intake manifold(IR) - See intake manifold(ram).

intake manifold(performance) - Manifold built with improved air flow characteristics over a stock design.

intake manifold(ram) – Manifold built like a high-rise, but with relatively straight individual passages running down into each cylinder. A plenum chamber is mounted on top in some designs to evenly distribute the air/fuel mixture to all cylinders, and allow for flexibility in carburetor selection. It is popular in racing and produces a slight air ramming or pressurizing effect.

intake manifold(ram log) – See intake manifold(cross ram).

intake manifold(single plane) – Manifold built with one set of passageways. The carburetor feeds an air/fuel mixture into the same openings during primary and secondary operation. This is the most common manifold.

intake manifold(Tarantula) – See intake manifold(vertical ram).

intake manifold(triplet) – Intake manifold built with runners cast in groups of two for use on straight six engines.

intake manifold(vertical ram) – Manifold built with long runners on a single plane meeting at a central plenum chamber. Runners display an X-shape pattern when viewed from above. It allows good mixing of the air/fuel mixture, flexibility in carburetors used, and high efficiency at higher rpm.

intake manifold(Y) – Manifold built in a Y shape to allow two carburetors to be mounted where there was one. It is a popular performance setup for a Volkswagen Beetle engine.

intake manifold crossover passage – Passageway built into the intake manifold casting to permit circulation of hot coolant or exhaust gases to keep the area around the carburetor base warm for good fuel vaporization. A plugged passageway can cause hesitation, poor startup in cold weather, and poor fuel economy. If the crossover area is cool or just warm to the touch when the engine has reached operating temperature, it is probably plugged.

intake reversion – Condition created in an intake manifold where reverse pressure or back-flow occurs during valve overlap period (when intake valve is just opening and exhaust valve is almost shut), and when intake valve slams shut (abrupt stop in air flow). A pulsing effect is created that is more readily dissipated on two-plane manifolds than on single plane.

intake reversion pulsation – See intake reversion.

intake stroke – See stroke(intake).

intake tuning – Adjusting an engine's intake system to achieve optimum performance. Most of it centers around the design of the intake manifold. See also exhaust tuning.

intake valve – Valve used to admit a liquid or gas mixture into a chamber and then seal it.

intercooler – Radiator device used to cool pressurized air flowing from a turbocharger's output before it enters an engine's intake manifold. Cooler air is more dense and allows more air and fuel to be introduced into a combustion chamber for increased power. Intercoolers permit the use of higher boost pressures and compression ratios, and yet still minimize detonation. Power output of a turbocharged engine can usually be increased at least 10 percent with the addition of a properly sized and installed intercooler.

interest – Money paid by a borrower to use money or borrow it.

interest charges – See interest.

interest rate – The amount of money paid on a regular basis for money borrowed, saved, etc.

interior trim – Car's interior surfaces except for carpeting and upholstery.

interlocking seat belt ignition system – Ignition system characterized by not allowing a car to be started unless driver and passenger seat belts are used. It typically works with a sensor detecting whether someone is sitting in each seat.

interlock switch – Switch designed to prevent another car part from operating unless the switch is closed or opened depending on application.

intermediate – See mid-size.

intermediate gear – See gear(intermediate).

intermediate band – See brake band(front).

intermediate pressure plate – See clutch pressure plate(intermediate).

intermittent – Action starting and stopping at intervals.

intermittent wipers – Windshield wipers set to wait between wiping cycles a short period of time. The setting is handy when rain is coming down slowly.

internal balance vent – See balance vent tube.

internal combustion – Combustion taking place in an enclosed space.

internal combustion engine – See engine(internal combustion).

International-Auto Wagon – American car produced in 1900.

International – American car produced from 1907-1911 and 1961 to date by International Harvester Co. in Ohio and Illinois respectively.

international license plate letters – Letter codes used on international license plates to denote the car's home country. Letters used include: A, AL, AND, AUS, B, BG, BOL, BR, BS, C, CDN, CH, CI, CL, CO, CR, CS, CY, D, DDR, DK, DOM, DZ, E, EAK, EC, ES, ET, ETH, F, FL, GB, GBM, GBZ, GH, GR, H, HKJ, I,

IL, IND, IR, IRL, IS, J, KWT, L, LOA, LT, M, MA, MAL, MC, MEX, N, NL, NZ, P, PAK, PE, PI, PL, PY, R, RA, RC, RGH, RI, RL, RM, ROK, RSM, RSR, S, SF, SN, SU, SYR, T, TN, TO, TR, TT, U, USA, VN, YU, Z, ZA, and ZAÍ.

International Truck – American truck produced in 1901.

interpole – Device used in a generator to help reduce arcing of generator brushes. It is a small pole piece mounted inside a generator housing between the two regular pole pieces. It is coiled with heavy wire in series with the armature coils. It reduces brush arcing by neutralizing the magnetic effect of armature coils which helps eliminate neutral point shift. When neutral points are shifted, armature coils are still generating voltage when brushes contact them. This tends to short out the brushes.

intersection – Meeting point created when two or more roads come together.

Inter-State – American car produced from 1909–1918 by Inter-State Automobile Co. in Indiana (1909–1914), and Inter-State Motor Co. in Indiana (1914–1918).

interstate – Major highway built to run from one state into or through another.

Interurban – American car produced in 1905.

in the bucket – Situation created when a car buyer's net payoff is higher than the car's actual wholesale value.

in the chute – Car positioned at a starting line or in a staging area and ready to race.

Intrepid – American car produced in 1904.

Invicta – American car produced from 1959–1964 by Buick Division of General Motors Corp. in Michigan.

ioe – Abbreviation for inlet over exhaust.

Iowa – American car produced in 1908–1909 and 1919.

IR – Abbreviation for Iran found usually on an international license plate.

IRL – Abbreviation for Ireland found usually on an international license plate.

IROC – Abbreviation for International Race of Champions.

irreversibility – Measure of a car steering system's ability to insulate road bumps and jerks from reaching the steering wheel.

iridescent – Quality exhibited by a material displaying a rainbow of colors.

iron – Rough car or junker.

iron monger – Used car dealer engaged in selling poor used cars.

iron peddler – See mouse house(2).

Iroquois-Buffalo – American car produced from 1906–1908 by Iroquois Motor Car Co. in New York.

Iroquois-Seneca – American car produced from 1905–1908 by Iroquois Motor Car Co. in New York.

Irvin – American car produced in 1902.

Irving-Napier Golden Arrow – English car driven by Major Henry Segrave to a 1929 world land speed record of 231.4 mph at Daytona, Florida.

Irvington Izzer – American car produced in 1910.

IS – Abbreviation for Iceland found usually on an international license plate.

island – Platform used to divide portions of a street, provide a place for pedestrians to stand, etc.

Issac, Bobby – He became the NASCAR Grand National Champion in 1970.

issued a ticket – To get a traffic citation.

Italy – One of the six big car producing countries. Their biggest firm is Fiat.

itemized bill – Bill made out detailing all charges for parts, labor, etc.

Ivanhoe – Canadian car produced in 1903.

Iverson – American car produced in 1908.

Izuzu – Japanese car line produced from 1953 to date by Izuzu Motors Ltd. Recent models include: Aska, FLorian, Gemini (I-Mark), Piazza (Impulse), P'up, Rodeo, and Trooper II. Izuzu cars imported for General Motors (part owner since 1971) have included: Chevrolet LUV pickup, Buick Opel, and Chevrolet Spectrum.

Izuzu Motors Ltd. – Japanese car manufacturer known for producing Izuzu cars. It entered the car business in 1938 as Ishikawajima Shipbuilding Company Ltd. The firm name was changed to Izuzu Motors Ltd. in 1949. General Motors became part owner of the firm in 1971.

Izzer – American car produced in 1911.

J

J – Abbreviation for Japan found usually on an international license plate.
jacked up – Condition created when a car's body and/or suspension has been elevated in the front, back, or both areas.
jack knifed – Condition created when a car pulling a trailer or other two piece vehicle loses control on a road, bends at its pivot point, and skids or turns over.
jackpoint – Specific location(s) used on a unibody or front-wheel drive car to jack it up. Using a jack in other locations can damage a car body/frame.
jack rabbit start – To accelerate a stationary car quickly.
jack shaft – See transmission input shaft.
Jackson – American car produced in 1899. Also, an American car produced from 1902-1923 by Jackson Automobile Co. in Michigan.
Jacks Runabout – American car produced in 1900.
jack stands – Stationary adjustable support devices used to keep heavy objects elevated. They are commonly used to support a car's rear end.
Jacquet Flyer – American car produced in 1921.
Jaeger – American car produced from 1932-1933 by Jaeger Motor Car Co. in Michigan.
Jaguar – British car line produced from 1954 to date by Jaguar Cars Ltd. (1980 to date). Popular models include: Sovereign, XKE (1961-1977), XJ6, and XJS. The U.S. representative is Jaguar MG Rover Triumph, headquartered in Leonia, New Jersey.
jail – Prison used for detaining people awaiting trial or convicted of minor offenses.
jalopy – Rough car or junker.
jam a transmission – To force a transmission from neutral into a gear without using a clutch or using a clutch at high engine rpm.
James – American car produced in 1909.
Jamison – American car produced in 1902.
Janney – American car produced from 1906-1907.
Japan – One of the six largest car producing countries in the world.
Jarrett, Ned – He became the NASCAR Grand National Champion in 1961 and 1965.
Jarrott, Charles – He won the Circuit of Ardennes race in Belgium in 1902 averaging 54 mph in a 1902 Panhard.
Jarvis-Huntington – American car produced in 1912.
Jarvis Truck – American truck produced in 1906.
Javelin – American car produced from 1968-1975 by American Motors Corp. in Michigan.
Jaxon – American car produced in 1903.
Jay – American car produced from 1907-1909.
Jay-Eye-See – American car produced in 1921.
J C Whitney – Large U.S. mail-order car parts firm headquartered in Chicago, Illinois.
Jeannin – American car produced from 1908-1909 by Jeannin Automobile Mfg. Co. in Missouri.
Jeantaud Electric – French car driven by Comte Gaston de Chasseloup-Laubat to a world land speed record in 1898 and 1899 of 39.2 and 43.7 mph at Acheres, France.
Jeep – American car produced from 1941-1963 by Willys-Overland Co. in Ohio (1941-1963). Also, an American car line produced from 1963 to date by Kaiser-Jeep Corp. in Ohio (1963-1970), and American Motors Corp. in Ohio (1970 to date). Popular models include: Cherokee (1963 to date), CJ (1963 to date), Commando (1967-1973), Jeepster, Scrambler, and Wagoneer (1963 to date). See also Bantam.
Jeffery – American car produced from 1914-1917 by Thos. B. Jeffrey Co. in Wisconsin.
Jeffrey, Thomas – He invented the clincher tire in 1881, and began manufacturing G&J cars in 1902.
Jeffries, Dean – Popular car customizer known for his pinstriping skills.
Jem Specia – American car produced in 1922.
Jenatzy, Camille – He set a world land speed record of 65.7 mph in 1899 driving a Jenatzy Electric.
Jenatzy Electric – Belgian car driven by Camille Jenatzy to a world land speed record in 1899 of 65.7 mph at Acheres, France.
Jenkins – American car produced from 1907-1912 by J.W. Jenkins (1907), and Jenkins Motor Car Co. (1908-1912), both in New York.
jerk – See difference buyer.

Jersey City - American car produced in 1919.

Jesse James - Poorly liked used car salesman.

jet - Mechanical device used for controlling fuel flow in various parts of a carburetor. It is usually: shaped like a small bolt, threaded on one end, bored to a specified hole diameter in the middle, and made of brass.

jet black - Glossy black.

jet drilling - Process defined as drilling out carburetor main jets to a larger size.

Jetmobile - Three-wheeled American car produced in 1952.

Jewel - American car produced from 1906-1909 by Forest City Motor Co. in Ohio.

Jewett - American car produced in 1906. Also, an American car produced from 1923-1926 by Paige-Detroit Motor Car Co. in Michigan.

Jewett, Harry - He assumed control of the Paige-Detroit Motor Company in 1910, and ran it until 1927 when the Graham brothers acquired his interests.

Jimmy - GMC truck engine modified for racing.

jitney - Small bus used to pick up passengers along a regular route at varying hours. Also, it refers to a small bus or car that become popular in 1915 due to transit strikes.

jitterbug - An oscillating air powered sander.

job - Work performed usually for money.

job(automotive engineer) - Work performed designing and constructing automobiles.

job(backyard mechanic) - Auto mechanic work performed by a person having little or no formalized training. A lot of the person's skills are self-taught through working on cars, trial and error, and reading. Many independents have this kind of background.

job(car designer) - Work performed designing cars.

job(car mechanic) - Work performed doing a broad range of light and heavy duty repair work on cars. Responsibilities typically include: diagnosing and locating troubles, making proper adjustments to different car systems, and properly installing and removing car parts.

job(car restorer) - Work performed restoring used cars to their original condition.

job(car salesman) - Work performed selling new and/or used cars and trucks. Most of the salesman's income is usually derived from commissions on cars sold. As a result, he can be very pushy and employ all kinds of high pressure sales tactics to close a deal. A skilled salesman should like selling, understand car mechanics, get along well with people, be able to communicate well, be able to demonstrate cars, and be knowledgeable of strengths and weaknesses of cars for sale as well as competing cars.

job(car stylist) - Work performed designing a car's appearance. The job involves creating and designing, with the cooperation of engineers, all of a car's interior and exterior shapes.

job(car detailer) - Work performed cleaning, protecting, and/or making various car items look like new on new or used cars. Detailing typically includes: waxing car body; cleaning all rubber material, engine, upholstery, and carpeting; repainting certain areas; fixing upholstery tears; and dying carpeting. A detailer may also be skilled in fixing minor car problems.

job(factory parts manager) - Work performed managing the distribution of parts to new car dealerships. The person is employed by the car manufacturer.

job(factory service instructor) - Work performed instructing service employees of new car dealerships on different aspects of proper car servicing. The person is employed by the car manufacturer.

job(factory service manager) - Work performed managing service business between the manufacturer and new car dealers. The person is employed by the car manufacturer.

job(factory service representative) - Work performed handling service business between a car manufacturer and new car dealers in a specified territory. The person is employed by the car manufacturer and usually under the supervision of a factory service manager.

job(factory trained mechanic) - Auto mechanic work performed on specific cars. The person is usually employed by a dealership and trained to work on specific cars by attending and completing a factory training program. European and other foreign countries usually have extensive factory training programs, while U.S. programs may only last a week at a factory.

job(jobber salesman) - Work performed selling parts for a wholesale parts warehouse. The job usually has a defined territory and entails calling on many different auto repair, supply, and sales business.

job(lot manager) - Work performed managing a car lot.

job(mechanic) - Work performed repairing and/or maintaining cars and trucks.

job(motor vehicle salesman) - See job(car salesman).

job(parts chaser) - Work performed picking up and delivering car parts and supplies for such businesses as: wrecking yards, car parts stores, car dealers, etc.

job(parts man) - See job(parts salesman).

job(parts manager) – Work performed heading up a parts department. The job usually requires a background in service work and selling parts. Responsibilities typically include: supervising parts salesmen; and ordering, stocking, inventorying, and replacing parts and accessories. See also parts department.

job(parts salesman) – Work performed selling parts. Job skills include: understanding car mechanics; having a talent for organizing; being aware of parts inventory at all times and recommend adjustments in a timely manner; and being able to read and understand car manuals, spec sheets, etc. pertaining to car parts. See also parts department.

job(sales manager) – Work performed heading up a sales department. Job skills include: being a skilled salesman with a demonstrated managing ability. Responsibilities typically include: supervising all salesmen, and supervising sales activity in service department. See also sales department.

job(service manager) – Work performed heading up a service department. Responsibilities typically include: supervising all service workers, maintaining customer satisfaction, and building up shop business. See also service department.

job(shop foreman) – Work performed supervising auto mechanics at an auto repair business. It is usually someone who is an expert mechanic who has been promoted. Responsibilities typically include: supervising mechanics, scheduling repair work, inspecting finished work, maintaining shop work quality and efficiency.

job(specialty mechanic) – Specialized auto mechanic work performed in a particular area such as: tune-ups, body work, transmissions, front end alignments, electrical work, etc.

jobber – Person or business engaged in buying goods from manufacturers in quantity and then reselling them to dealer or retailers. A wholesaler or middleman.

jobber salesman – See job(jobber salesman).

job description – Detailed description made of a job's work responsibilities. It may also specify desired and/or required qualifications such as: degree in a specific field, training, certification, specified years of experience, etc.

Joerns – American car produced in 1911.

Johncock, Gordon – He won the Indianapolis 500 Race in 1973 and 1982. Average speeds were 159.0 and 162.0 mph. Cars driven were an STP Double Oil Filter, and STP Oil Treatment.

Johnson – American car produced from 1905-1912 by Johnson Service Co. in Wisconsin.

Johnson, Junior – He won the Daytona 500 Race in 1960 averaging 124.7 mph in a Chevrolet.

Johnsonmobile – American car produced in 1959.

Johnson Steamer – American steam car produced in 1901.

Joliet – American car produced in 1912.

Joly & Lambert – American car produced in 1916.

Jomar – American car produced from 1954-1955 by Ray Saidel in New Hampshire.

Jones – American car produced from 1915-1920 by Jones Motor Car Co. in Kansas.

Jones, Alan – He became the Grand Prix world champion in 1980 driving a Williams-Ford.

Jones-Corbin – American car produced from 1902-1907 by Jones-Corbin Co. (1902-1904), and Jones-Corbin Automobile Co. (1904-1907), both in Pennsylvania.

Jones, Parnelli – He won the Indianapolis 500 Race in 1963 driving an average of 143.1 mph in a Agajanian-Willard Battery Special.

Jones Steam Car – American steam car produced in 1898.

Jonz – American car produced from 1908-1911.

Jonz-Kansas City – American car produced in 1911.

Jonz-New Albany – American car produced in 1911.

Jordan – American car produced from 1916-1931 by Jordan Motor Car Co. in Ohio.

Jordan, Edward S – He was the man remembered for changing car advertising from a specifications appeal to an emotional one. He also ran the Jordan Motor Car Company producing Jordan cars.

jounce clearance – Clearance measured between a wheel and wheelhouse.

journal – Bearing surface.

journey – Trip.

journeyman – Trade worker characterized by having completed his apprenticeship to become a qualified worker in his field. See also apprenticeship.

journeyman card – Card carried by a journeyman specifying how much training and experience he has.

Joy, Henry – President of Packard in 1901.

joyrider – Person who steals a car just to take it for a ride and then abandons it.

JPL – American car produced in 1913.

Juergens – American car produced in 1908.

jug – Carburetor.

juice – Special racing fuel. See also moxie.
juice brakes – Hydraulic brakes.
Jules – Canadian car produced from 1911-1912.
Julian – American car produced in 1922.
Julian-Brown – American car produced in 1925.
Jumgo – American car produced in 1918.
jump – To leave a starting line prematurely. See also jump start.
jump bail – Situation caused by a person free on bail suddenly leaving to allude law enforcement authorities.
jumper cables – Pair of heavy gauge insulated electrical wires used to transfer electricity from one battery to another. They are primarily used to start a car with a weak or dead battery. See also jump start.
jumper wire – Length of wire used to transfer electricity temporarily from one terminal to another. Terminals or alligator clips are often attached to each end. It is commonly used to bypass certain switches and/or circuits to determine if they are defective.
jump spark – High voltage electrical current forced to move across an air space from one terminal to another.
jump start – Procedure used to start a car with a weak or dead battery by drawing electricity from a strong or charged battery. The following steps will insure a safe jump start: move both batteries close together without bumpers touching; shut off engine of good battery; disconnect weak battery ground strap on late model cars (to prevent current surging); use jumper cables in good condition; connect red jumpers to positive post of good battery, then weak one; connect black jumpers to negative post of good battery, then engine ground of weak one (to minimize sparks igniting battery gases); leave strong battery engine off; start weak battery engine for a maximum of 20-30 seconds; and remove jumper cables promptly when engine starts, in reverse order.
    As a rule, attach positive cables first, then negative. Remove negative cables first.
    Late model alternators can sometimes be damaged (burned out diodes and/or ruined internal regulators) if cables are not promptly removed. To prevent such problems: pull the wiring plug on the back of the alternator, or disconnect the battery terminal cables before starting the weak battery engine.
Junior – American car produced in 1925.
junked out – Disposal made of a used part because it is not worth saving.
junker – Car characterized as worn out, in need of many repairs, and running poorly if at all.
junk heap – A junker. Also, it refers to a car that no longer operates, is rusted out, has been gutted, etc.
junk ring – Flexible ring used to seal an inner sleeve valve.
junk yard – Salvage yard used to store miscellaneous items of possible resale value.
Juno Truck – American truck produced in 1911.
Junz – American car produced in 1902.
jury trial – Trial held in a court of law where a defendant's guilt or innocence is decided by a group of citizens who hear the case.
justice of the peace – Local public officer usually authorized to do the following: to try people in minor civil and criminal cases, determine penalties in such cases, conduct preliminary examinations of people accused of serious crimes, and administer oaths and marriages. A local judge in a small town.
Juvenile – American car produced from 1906-1907.

K

K – Abbreviation for thousand.
K&M – American car produced in 1908.
Kadix – American car produced in 1913.
Kaiser – American car produced from 1946-1955 by Kaiser-Frazer Corp. in Michigan (1946-1955), Willys Motors in Michigan 1953-1954), and Willys Motors in Ohio (1954-1955).
Kaiser Darrin – American car produced from 1952-1954.
Kaiser, Henry J – He was a millionaire shipbuilder who organized the Kaiser-Frazer Corporation with Joseph Frazer. It was considered the last real attempt by a new car manufacturer to break into the "closed" American car industry.
Kalamazoo – American car produced in 1914 and 1922.
Kamm tail – Sharp car body tail section truncation found on racing cars. It is used to minimize weight and air drag.
Kane-Pennington – American car produced in 1894.
Kansas City – American car produced from 1905-1909 by Kansas City Motor Car Co. in Missouri.
Karavan Truck – American truck produced from 1920-1922.
Karbach – American car produced from 1908-1909.
Kardell – American car produced in 1918.
Karl Benz – He was a German engineer who successfully tested and patented a motorized tricycle in 1886.
Karmann Ghia – See Volkswagen.
Kato – American car produced from 1907-1908 by Four Traction Auto Co. in Minnesota.
Kauffman – American car produced from 1909-1912 by Advance Motor Vehicle Co. in Ohio.
Kavan – American car produced in 1905.
Kaws – American car produced in 1922.
K band – A radar frequency. See also X band.
KD – American car produced in 1912.
Kdf-Wagen – The 1937 Volkswagen prototype. Only 210 were built by 1939 when Hitler shifted production at the factory to produce military vehicles.
Kearns – American car produced from 1909-1915 by Kearns Motor Buggy Co. in Pennsylvania.
Keasler – American car produced in 1922.
Keech, Ray – He won the Indianapolis 500 Race in 1929 driving an average of 97.6 mph in a Simplex Piston Ring Special. He also set a world land speed record of 207.6 mph in 1928 driving a White triplex V-12.
Keene – American car produced from 1900-1902.
Keeton – American car produced from 1910-1914 by Keeton Motor Co. in Michigan. Also, an American car produced in 1908.
Keldon – American car produced in 1920.
Keller – American car produced from 1948-1950 by George D. Keller Motors in Alabama.
Keller Kar – American car produced from 1914-1915 by Keller Cyclecar Corp. in Illinois.
Kellogg – American car produced in 1903.
Kelly – American car produced in 1911.
Kelly Blue Book – A bi-monthly publication containing wholesale and retail pricing guidelines for used cars. It usually goes back about seven years, and is an official guide for car dealers, banks, etc. on used car prices. See also NADA Official Used Car Guide.
Kelly Blue Book Auto Market Report – See Kelly Blue Book.
Kelly-Springfield(1) – American line of tires.
Kelly-Springfield(2) – American car produced in 1918.
Kelsey – American car produced from 1913-1914 and 1921-1924 by Kelsey Car Corp. in Illinois, and Kelsey Motor Co. in New Jersey respectively. Also, an American car produced in 1909.
Kelsey & Tilney – American car produced in 1899.
Kelsey Friction – American car produced from 1921-1924.
Kelsey Motorette – American car produced from 1910-1913.
Kendle – American car produced in 1912.
Kenilworth – American car produced in 1923.
Kenmore – American car produced from 1909-1912 by Kenmore Mfg. Co. in Illinois.
Kennedy – Canadian car produced in 1909-1910. Also, an American car produced

from 1915-1918 by W.J. Kennedy in California.

Kensington – American car line produced from 1899-1904 by Kensington Automobile Co. in New York. They produced steam, electric, and gasoline cars.

Kent – American car produced from 1916-1917.

Kentucky – American car produced from 1915-1924.

Kenworth Truck – American truck produced from 1923 to date.

Kenworthy – American car produced from 1920-1922 by Kenworthy Motor Co. in Indiana.

Kermath – American car produced from 1907-1908 by Kermath Motor Car Co. in Michigan.

Kermet – American car produced in 1900.

Kerns – American car produced in 1914.

kerosene – Mixture of liquid hydrocarbons obtained from distilling petroleum, bituminous shale, or similar materials. The boiling point ranges from 175-300 degrees Fahrenheit. It is used: in avaition fuels, for lighting, and heating.

Kerosene Surrey – American car produced in 1900.

Kessler – American car produced from 1921-1922 by Kesseler Motor Car Co. in Michigan.

Kettering, Charles – He was an engineer who organized Delco laboratories to develop an ignition system. Later, he became head of General Motors research laboratories.

key(1) – Small metal block inserted in a shaft slot to prevent shaft mounted parts from turning. See also keyway.

key(2) – Device used to rotate a tumbler in a lock. Keys are primarily used in car locks to: lock or unlock doors and trunks, and close various electrical circuits in an ignition switch.

key in the ignition – Car key inserted into an ignition switch usually mounted on a steering column.

Keystone – American car produced from 1899-1900, 1909-1910, and 1915 by Keystone Motor & Mfg. Co., Munch-Allen Motor Car Co., and H.C. Cook & Bros. respectively, all in Pennsylvania.

Keystone-Motorette – American car produced in 1896.

Keystone Steamer – American car produced in 1909.

keyway – Groove cut for the insertion of a key.

Kiblinger – American car produced from 1907-1909 by W.H. Kiblinger Co. Indiana.

kickdown switch – Electrical switch used on automatic transmissions to cause a transmission to drop one gear when a gas pedal is pushed down and until it is eased off.

kickpad – Area located along the bottom of a door interior where scuffing is likely due to people getting in and out of a car.

kick the choke down – To rapidly depress the gas pedal in an attempt to get the choke plate to open up further. It is commonly done when a cold engine has been started and left to warm up for awhile. Without movement of the throttle linkage, a choke plate will often stay in one position. This can cause excessive fuel consumption during warm-up, unless the choke plate is allowed to open by periodically depressing the gas pedal.

Kidder – American car produced from 1900-1901 by Kidder Motor Vehicle Co. in Connecticut.

Kidney – American car produced in 1910.

killer bleed – Air bleed(s) used to weaken vacuum in a carburetor airway allowing secondary throttle plate(s) to open more slowly.

kill switch – Anti-theft device used to prevent a car from starting. It usually consists of a switch wired into a car's starting circuit preventing a car from starting unless it is turned on. Some switches plug in to work and are removed when a driver leaves a car. It is considered highly effective.

kill the engine – To stop an engine from rotating.

kilometer – Metric measurement equal to 1,000 meters. One kilometer is equal to 0.62 miles.

kilowatt – Measure of electrical energy equal to 1,000 watts.

Kimball – American car produced in 1922.

Kimball Electric – American electric car produced from 1910-1912 by C.M. Kimball & Co. in Illinois.

King – American car produced in 1896 and 1909. Also, an American car produced from 1910-1924 by King Motor Car Co. in Michigan (1910-1923), and New York (1923-1924).

King, Charles – He designed the Silent Northern car and organized the King Motor Car Company in 1910.

King Midget – American car produced beginning in 1946. It was the only survivor of the Post World War II minicar boom in the U.S.

King of the Belgians – See body style(King of the Belgians).

King of the Kustomizers – See Barris, George.

kingpin – Long bolt used in front suspension systems to attach a wheel spindle

to a front axle. A wheel pivots on a king pin.
kingpin inclination – Caster of a kingpin.
King Remick – American car produced in 1910.
Kingston – American car produced from 1907-1908.
King Zeitler – American car produced from 1919.
Kinnear – American car produced in 1913.
Kinney – American car produced in 1922.
Kirk – American car produced from 1903-1905.
Kirkham – American car produced in 1906.
Kirksell – American car produced in 1907.
Kissel – American car produced from 1906-1931 by Kissel Motor Co. in
Wisconsin.
kit – Tools, supplies, instructions, etc. assembled for a specific purpose.
Examples include: carburetor rebuild kit, first aid kit, gasket set, etc.
kit car – Collection of car components sold to replace the body and interior
parts of an existing car. The engine and chassis of the existing car is
usually used.
kiting – To specify a speed on a traffic citation higher than was actually
observed.
Kleibar – American car produced from 1924-1929 by Kleibar Motor Truck Co. in
California. The company was well known for its commercial vehicles on the
U.S. west coast.
Kleiber Truck – American truck produced in 1910.
Klemm – American car produced in 1917.
Kline Kar – American car produced from 1909-1923 by B.C.K. Motor Co. in
Pennsylvania (1910-1911), and Kline Motor Car Corp. in Pennsylvania (1911-
1912), and Virginia (1912-1923).
Kling – American car produced in 1907.
Klink – American car produced from 1906-1909 by Klink Motor Car Mfg. Co. in
New York.
Klock – American car produced in 1900.
Klondike – American car produced in 1918.
K mi – Abbreviation for thousand miles.
Knee Action – The first independent front wheel suspension system built. It
was introduced by GM in 1933.
Knickerbocker – American car produced from 1901-1903 by Ward Leonard
Electrical Co. in New York. Also, an American car produced in 1912.
Knight & Kilborne – American car produced from 1906-1909.
Knight Special – American car produced in 1917.
knocking – See detonation.
knock off – Quickly removable lug nut.
knock offs – See knock off hub.
knock off hub – Hub designed for quick attachment and removal of wheels
especially in racing. Large wing nuts or levers are typically used.
knock off wheel hub – See knock off hub.
knock the clock – To turn back an odometer in a speedometer to register fewer
miles and thus make a used car more attractive to sell. It is an illegal
practice.
Know – American car produced in 1900.
Knox – American car produced from 1900-1915 by Knox Automobile Co. in
Massachusetts.
Knox-Landsen – American car produced in 1904.
Knox Truck – American truck produced from 1904-1907.
Knudson – American car produced in 1899.
knurl – Process used to create a raised thread pattern surface with a sharp
wheel or other device. The device pushes or rolls metal outward as it
penetrates into the surface. Knurling is sometimes done to valve guides to
prolong their life. See also knurling valve guides.
knurler – Tool built to knurl surfaces.
knurling valve guides – Process used to reduce the inside diameter of valve
guides, using a knurling tool. It is done to increase the life of a guide by
decreasing the guide to valve stem clearance. Most of the wear usually
occurs in the guide.
KO – American car produced in 1921.
Kobusch – American car produced in 1906.
Koeb-Thompson – American car produced from 1910-1911 by Koeb-Thompson Motors
Co. in Ohio.
Koehler – American car produced from 1910-1914 by H.J. Koehler Co. in New
Jersey.
Komet – American car produced in 1911.
Koningslow – American car produced from 1903-1904.
kooky – Bobtail roadster.
Kopp – American car produced in 1911.
Koppin – American car produced in 1915.
Kph – Abbreviation for kilometers per hour.

Kraft Steam – American steam car produced in 1901.
Kramer – American car produced in 1915.
Krastin – American car produced from 1902–1903 by Krastin Automobile Co. in Ohio.
Krebs – American car produced in 1913.
Krebs Truck – American truck produced in 1922.
Kreuger – American car produced from 1904–1905 by Kreuger Manufacturing Co. in Wisconsin.
Krim-Ghia – American car produced beginning in 1966 by Krim-Ghia Import Co. in Michigan.
KRIT – American car produced from 1909–1916 by Krit Motor Co. in Michigan.
Kron – American car produced in 1915.
Kuhn – American car produced in 1918.
Kunz – American car produced from 1902–1906 by J.L. Kunz Machinery Co. in Wisconsin.
Kurtis – American car produced from 1949–1955 by Kurtis-Kraft (1949–1950), and Kurtis Sports Car Corp. (1953–1955), both in California.
Kurtis-Kraft – American car produced from 1949–1955.
Kurtz – American car produced from 1921–1923 by Kurtz Motor Car Co. in Ohio.
KWT – Abbreviation for Kuwait found usually on an international license plate.

L

L(1) – Abbreviation for Low range (first gear) on automatic transmission shift selectors.

L(2) – Abbreviation for Luxembourg found usually on an international license plate.

L&E – American car produced from 1922-1931 by Lundelius & Eccleston in California.

Labonte, Terry – He became the NASCAR Grand National Champion in 1984.

labor time – Time required by a mechanic to remove, and repair or replace one or more parts.

lace painting – Custom painting technique used to apply a lace pattern on a car body surface by placing a piece of lace in a desired location, spraying over it, and then removing it. Lace painting is sometimes used alone or in conjunction with other painting effects.

Laconia – American car produced in 1914.

lacquer – See paint(lacquer).

lacquer deposit – See varnish deposit.

Lad's Car – American car produced from 1912-1914 by Niagara Motor Corp. in New York.

LaFayette – American car produced from 1920-1924 by Lafayette Motors Co. in Indiana and Wisconsin. It was a luxurious V-8 car. Also, an American car produced by Nash from 1934-1939.

La France – American car produced in 1910.

La France-Republic – American car produced in 1925.

Laguna – American car produced from 1964 to date by Chevrolet Division of General Motors Corp. in Michigan.

lakes pipes – Long side ehxaust pipes.

La Marne – American car produced in 1920.

La Marne Jr – American car produced in 1919.

Lambert – American car produced in 1891 and 1904-1917 by Buckeye Mfg. Co. in Indiana.

Lamborghini – Italian car line produced from 1963 to date by Nuova Automobili Ferruccio Lamborghini SpA (1980 to date). Popular models include: Countach, Jalpa, and Cheetah.

Lamborghini, Ferrucio – He was an Italian tractor manufacturer who began manufacturing high performance race cars in 1963.

laminated – Object covered with one or more layers of material.

laminated windshield – See safety glass.

Lamphen – American car produced in 1904.

Lamson – American car produced in 1917.

Lamphor – American car produced in 1909.

Lancamobile – American car produced from 1899-1901 by J.H. Lancaster Co. in New York.

Lancaster – American car produced in 1900-1901.

Lancer – American car produced from 1960-1962 and 1980 to date by Dodge Division of Chrysler Corp. in Michigan.

Lancia – Italian car line produced from 1906 to date by Fabbrica Automobili e Cia. Popular models include: Beta, Delta, Prisma, and Thema.

Lancia Aprilla – Italian Lancia car produced in 1939. It had several features making it a car ahead of its time. They included: independent suspension, low profile and streamlined, and an engine made largely of aluminum. Its top speed was 80 mph and fuel consumption averaged 28 mpg with normal driving.

Lancia Lambda – Italian Lancia car produced in the 1920s. It was an expensive car with large wheels, high seats, and a top speed of more than 70 mph. It became one of the first cars to introduce welded body-chassis construction.

landau – Carriage made with a top in two pieces each of which separately fold down. See also body style(landau).

landau bar – Decorative S-shaped ornament located on a "C" pillar surface. Originally, it was a functional S-curved hinge used to fold down the rear part of a horse drawn carriage roof.

landaulet – See body style(landaulet).

landaulet body – See body style(landaulet).

landaulette – See body style(landaulet).

landau top – Stationary car roof built with the rear half appearing like a convertible top. See also body style(landau).

Landover – American car produced from 1917-1918.

lands – Ridges created from the cutting of ring grooves in a piston.

Landshaft – American car produced in 1913.

Lane – American car produced from 1899-1910 by Lane Motor Vehicle Co. in New York.

lane – Portion of a highway built wide enough to accommodate one vehicle.

lane change – To move from one lane of traffic to another on a one way street.

lane control signal – Traffic light used to control traffic flow for one or more lanes of traffic.

Lane Steam Wagon – American steam car produced in 1900.

Langan – American car produced in 1898.

Langan Truck – American truck produced in 1921.

Langer – American car produced in 1896.

Lanpher – American car produced from 1900-1912 by Lanpher Motor Buggy Co. in Missouri.

Lansden – American electric car produced from 1906-1908 by Lansden Co. in New Jersey.

La Petite – American car produced in 1905.

lap – One complete trip around a race track. See also to lap.

lap joint – Overlapping joint.

lapping – Process defined as fitting two surfaces together by placing an abrasive material between them and then rubbing or moving the surfaces against each other. See also valve lapping.

lapping the valves – See valve lapping.

Larchment – American car produced in 1900.

Lark – American car produced from 1958-1963 by Studebaker-Packard Corp. in Indiana.

large block – Engine block characterized by displacing over 350 cubic inches. See also small block.

large independent – Large car repair business characterized by employing many people and not owned by another company. It is usually a successful outgrowth of a small independent business. Most of them still offer reasonable prices and good dependable work. In dealing with them, ask for satisfied customers you can contact before you commit to major work.

large size car – Standard size car of the past. It is still produced today, and appeals to people who want room, comfort, and are not very concerned about gas mileage. Prices range from $9,000 to 13,000 with weight in excess of 3,500 lbs.

Larre-Bee Deyo – American car produced in 1920.

Larsen – American car produced in 1908.

Larson – American car produced in 1910.

La Salle – American car produced from 1927-1940 by Cadillac Motor Car Co. in Michigan.

La Salle Niagara – American car produced in 1906.

Laser – American car produced from 1980 to date by Chrysler Corp. in Michigan.

Lasky – American car produced in 1916.

last year's model – See con game(last year's model).

late model – Car model recently produced. It is usually new to a few years old.

lateral point blades – Grooves cut in tire tread elements at an angle to the centerline of tire tread. They are used to improve water channeling, increase the number of tread biting edges, and decrease centerline stiffness of a tread to improve the tire footprint.

lateral arm – See transverse arm.

lateral runout – See runout(lateral).

Lauda, Niki – He became the Grand Prix world champion in 1975, 1977, and 1984 driving a Ferrari (1975 and 1977) and McLaren-Porsche.

Laughlin – American car produced from 1916-1918.

Laurel – American car produced from 1916-1920 by Laurel Motors Corp. in Indiana.

Lauth-Juergens – American car produced from 1907-1910 by Lauth-Jergens Co. in Illinois and Ohio.

Lavigne – American car produced in 1914.

Lavoie – Canadian car produced in 1923.

Law – American car produced in 1902, 1905, and 1912.

Lawson – American car produced in 1900.

lawsuit – Legal action filed in a court of law in which an injured party seeks to recover damages that are too high, extensive, and/or complex for a small claims court to handle. A lawyer is usually retained to handle the case. Often the threat of a lawsuit from an attorney's office will prod the offending party to settle the dispute.

lawsuit(class action) – Lawsuit filed in which consumers with similar complaints ban together as a group (class) to consolidate the complaints and the damages incurred. In practice, just a few of the injured parties file the suit on behalf of the others. If the suit is won, the defendant must pay the damages incurred by each injured party to the court. Injured parties then recover their damages from the court-held fund by filing a claim. A class action suit is an effective way of getting lawyer representation for

small individual damage claims incurred by many.
Lawter - American car produced in 1909.
lay rubber - To burn rubber.
lay claim to - To assert your right to property, products, services, etc.
laygear - See transmission countershaft gear.
lb - Abbreviation for pound.
lc - Abbreviation for low compression.
LCE - American car produced in 1914.
LD - Abbreviation for landau.
Leach - American car produced from 1899-1901 and 1920-1923 by Leach Motor Vehicle Co. in Massachusetts, and Leach Motor Car Co. in California respectively.
Leach-Biltwell - American car produced from 1920-1923.
lead acid type - Battery type characterized by the use of lead plates and an acid electrolyte.
lead burning - Process defined as the joining of two pieces of lead together by melting or fusing the joint.
leaded gas - Gasoline mixed with a tetraethyl lead additive to increase the octane rating and help lubricate the valves.
Leader - American car produced from 1905-1912 by Columbia Electric Co. (1905-1906), and Leader Mfg. Co. in Ohio (1906-1912).
lead foot - Driving habit characterized by driving fast, accelerating fast, or otherwise keeping a foot hard down on a throttle. See also feather foot.
leading driver - Driver of a car located at the front of a group of cars.
lead(1) - Metal characterized as soft, malleable, heavy, and bluish-gray. It is used with other compounds in lead acid batteries.
lead(2) - Flexible and insulated electrical conductor used to transfer electricity. Examples include: jumper cables, battery to starter lead, welding cable, and electrical wire segment.
lead sled(1) - Poorly finished custom car.
lead sled(2) - Car built to run on leaded gasoline.
leaf spring - See spring(leaf).
leak - See fluid leak.
leak check - Test performed on a system carrying fluid or vapor to determine if there are any leaks in the lines, coupling, seals, etc. Leaks are usually detected by pressurizing a system. Systems commonly checked for leaks include: air conditioner, cooling, fuel, and brake. See also fluid leak.
leak-down tester - Instrument used to measure pressure leakage of engine cylinders to determine sealing ability of rings and thus wear in engine cylinders. The tester gives best results on a warm engine with reading taken at TDC and no crank movement.
lean mixture - Air/fuel mixture characterized as having a high air-to-fuel ratio or not containing enough fuel to properly burn in a combustion chamber.
Lear - American car produced from 1903-1909.
learner's permit - A temporary driver's license issued to a young person allowing practice driving usually during the day with a licensed driver. It serves as practice for later taking a driving test. Knowledge of driving is not required, but the applicant will be required to show a knowledge of traffic laws and safety rules.
lease - Contract used by a car owner to loan a car for profit. It usually gives the user use and possession of a car for a specified time at fixed payments. See also residual value.
lease(closed end) - Lease used to specify that the lessee pays: the initial complete cost of the car over a period of time along with an adequate additional amount to cover the residual car value. It is more popular than the open end lease, since the lessee can walk away from the car when the last lease payment is made. It is usually more expensive, but there are few uncertainties which makes it attractive. See also lease(straight), lease(walk away), lease(net rental), and lease(open end).
lease(equity) - See lease(open end).
lease(finance) - See lease(open end).
lease(net rental) - See lease(closed end).
lease(open end) - Lease used to specify that the lessee pays: the initial complete cost of the car over a period of time, and the residual value of the car when the lease is terminated. If the residual value is different from the original estimate, the lessee will pay either more or less. Depending on the car leased, this type of lease can be the cheapest or the most expensive. The car can usually be sold at any time, as long as the lessor is paid in full. It is not as popular as close-end leases. See also lease(equity), lease(finance), and lease(closed end).
lease(straight) - See lease(closed end).
lease(walk away) - See lease(closed end).
leasing - To lease a car. Most leasing agencies contract to do repair and maintenance work on a leased car. Leasing costs more than buying on time, because at the expiration of the lease you have nothing. Car leasing appeals

to those people who have the following needs: don't want to bother with repair and maintenance; need a car for a limited period of time; want to invest money in other investments than a car; want new car with lower monthly payments; need car for business and can deduct it as a business expense; and want a luxury car.

leasing agreement – Contract used to specify the terms under which you will use someone else's car. The two most common agreements are open-end and close-end. Leases are usually close-end, specifying a period of use from 36 to 60 months. See also lease(open end) and lease(close end).

leather belt – Wide flat belt made of leather. It was used to transfer power from engines to wheels in early cars.

Le Baron – American car produced from 1976 to date by Chrysler Corp. in Michigan.

Lebgett – American car produced in 1903.

LED – Abbreviation for light emitting diode.

Lee Diamond – American car produced in 1911.

leeway – See margin of profit.

left hand drive car – Car built with the driver's seat and steering wheel on the left side. American cars are built this way. See also right hand drive car.

left hand rule – Rule used to indicate direction of magnetic flux movement. The movement of current in the direction of the fingers indicates magnetic flux movement in the direction of the thumb.

legal action – Action taken legally to solve a problem.

legal aid society – Organization engaged in providing free consultation and representation to people who cannot afford legal services.

legal document – Document written and agreed to in such a manner that it is legally enforceable.

Leganon – American car produced from 1906-1907.

leg room – Front horizontal passenger compartment dimension measured from the front of the seat back to the lower firewall area underneath the pedals.

Lehigh – American car produced in 1926.

Lehr – American car produced in 1908.

Leland, Henry – Enterprising man involved with Ford and Cadillac companies who was instrumental in introducing parts interchangeability, electric starting, and ignition advance concepts. He subsequently organized the Lincoln Motor Company which was bought out by Ford in 1922.

Le Mans – City located in N.W. France where car racing is popular. It is only one of two racing circuits left in the world where cars race in the streets around the town. The course is 8.34 miles. As of 1985, over 63 annual races have been held.

LeMans – American car produced from 1961-1981 by Pontiac Division of General Motors Corp. in Michigan.

lemon – Car or product characterized as being inferior, unsatisfactory, prone to malfunction, etc.

lemon law – Law enacted to protect the purchaser of a new car. Over 33 states have enacted such laws following the lead of California and Connecticut. Often, the law extends the warranty of a car to 2 years or more. The owner is given specific legal rights in resolving car defects by reporting them to a manufacturer. The dispute is then settled through an arbitration program. If the issue does not get settled, the owner has the right to sue for a refund or for a new car. See also warranty of serviceability.

Le Moon Truck – American truck produced in 1917.

Lenawee – American car produced from 1903-1904 by Church Manufacturing Co. in Michigan.

Lende – American car produced from 1908-1909 by Lende Automobile Mfg. Co. in Minnesota.

lender – Person or agency engaged in lending or loaning money to qualified people or businesses.

lending institution – Business engaged in lending money.

Lengert – American car produced in 1896.

Lennon – American car produced in 1909.

Lenot – American car produced from 1912-1922.

Lenox – American car produced from 1911-1918 by Lenox Motor Car Co. in Massachusetts.

Lenox Electric – American electric car produced from 1908-1909.

Leon Mendel – American car produced in 1890.

Leon Rubay – American car produced in 1923.

leper – New or used car shunned by a car salesman because of poor overall condition or because it has been on the lot a long time.

Leroy – Canadian car produced from 1899-1902 by Good Brothers in Ontario.

LeSabre – American car produced from 1955 to date by Buick Division of General Motors Corp. in Michigan.

Lescina – American car produced in 1916.

Leslie – American car produced in 1918.

Lesperance – American car produced in 1911.
lessee – Person or business agreeing to the terms of a lease.
lessor – Person or business issuing a lease.
let out the clutch – To engage a disengaged clutch.
lettering – Custom painting technique used to apply lettering designs to panels.
let the buyer beware – To warn a potential buyer of a product to be aware of possible fraudulent practices, inferior products, non-existent guarantees, etc.
Lethbridge – American car produced in 1907.
Levacar – Experimental car built by Ford in 1959 that floated on a cushion of air and moved by using bursts of compressed air.
Levassor, Emile – He was the inventor of the Panhard et Levassor car. He also won the first French Grand Prix race in 1894 by driving 732 miles in 48 hours with an average speed of 15 mph.
Lever – American car produced in 1930.
lever – Mechanical device constructed as a bar or arm and capable of turning about a fixed point in order to lift or twist something. There are many lever examples in a car. Whenever you use clutch, brake or gas pedals, you are moving linkages using levers to perform their work.
lever strut – Metal piece used to anchor and change the pivot location of a lever.
Lewis – American car produced from 1898-1902 and 1913-1916 by Lewis Cycle Co. in Pennsylvania (1898-1902), and Lewis Motor Co. (1913) and LPC Motor Car Co. (1914-1916) in Wisconsin.
Lewis Airomobile – American car produced in 1937.
Lexington – American car produced from 1909-1928 by Lexington Motor Co. in Kentucky (1909-1913), Lexington-Howard Co. in Indiana (1914-1918), and Lexington Motor Co. in Indiana (1918-1928).
L-head engine – See engine(L-head).
Lf – Abbreviation for left front.
Lh – Abbreviation for left hand.
LHD – Abreviation for left hand drive.
Lhd – Abreviation for left hand drive.
liability insurance – See insurance(liability).
Liberty – American car produced in 1914. Also, an American car produced from 1916-1924 by Liberty Motor Car Co. in Michigan.
Liberty-Brush – American car produced in 1912.
license – Certificate or permit granting authority to do something.
license(chauffeurs) – License issued to a person employed to drive for another person or business. Chauffeur must usually know the safety requirements of the U.S. Department of Transportation, Bureau of Motor Carrier, and the respective state driving laws pertaining to commercial vehicles.
license(drivers) – License issued to every person, other than a chauffeur, controlling a motor vehicle on a highway.
license(operators) – See license(drivers).
license(suspended) – License rendered invalid for a specified length of time due to a violation of certain driving rules and regulations.
licensed driver – Car driver with a valid driver's license.
license holder(1) – See licensed driver.
license holder(2) – Bracket used to attach a car's license plate.
license plate – Flat rectangular metal plate imprinted with a sequence of letters and numbers to identify the registered owner of a car. All cars must have a license plate in order to operate legally on public roads. Each state has its own license plate design. Cars require a front and rear plate while motorcycles require only a rear plate. See also validation sticker.
lid – See cylinder head.
lien – Claim made on someone else's property, as security, in order to receive payment of a legitimate debt.
lien holder – Person, business, etc. authorized to retain title of or a claim to a piece of property until a debt owed has been paid off. A bank, for example, is the lien holder of a car it finances until the loan is paid off.
lien sale – Car sale conducted when a car's repair bills have not been paid by the owner. In many states, a car repair business can start a lien sale within 10 days of failure to pay. A legal notice is usually required in the local newspaper. The car is sold to the highest bidder. If the proceeds don't pay for the repair debt owed, the owner can then be taken to court for the balance. See also mechanics lien.
lifetime tire rotation – Free service offered by certain tire sales businesses where a tire purchaser may bring in his car and have the tires rotated at no charge. It is usually offered free after a minimum number of miles have been driven.
lift – Condition created when a car body's: rear end moves upward during braking, or front end moves upward due to sudden acceleration or air rushing underneath car (high speed driving).

liftback - See body style(liftback).
lifter - See valve lifter.
lifter is sticking - Valve lifter problem created when it does not return to it resting position. Sticking is usually caused by dirty oil, varnish deposits, etc.
lifter pump-up - Condition created at high engine rpm where valve lifters tend to float like valves due to rapid direction changes. It is often associated with hydraulic lifters. Lifter floating contributes to valve floating. Stock cams are good for up to 5,000 rpm before lifter pump-up and **valve float** set in. See also valve float.
liftgate - Rear station wagon door. It opens sideways, down, or up depending on the car. The window retracts into some doors and is part of others. Also, it sometimes refers to a liftback door. See also tailgate.
liftgate wiper-washer - Rear window windshield wiper and washer unit.
lift kit - See body lift kit.
liftover height - Height measured to the edge of a car's trunk edge or the top surface of a tailgate in down position.
Light - American car produced in 1914.
light - Electrical device used to emit light usually by means of a metal filament that glows when current flows through it.
light(backup) - One of two lights located on the back of a car and activated when a car is placed in reverse. It is usually covered with a clear or white plastic lens.
light(caution) - Traffic signal light used at an intersection where traffic does not stop in two or all four of the opposing directions. It emits a flashing yellow light in the non-stop directions to alert approaching drivers to proceed cautiously through the intersection.
light(clearance) - Light mounted on the fender of a truck.
light(courtesy) - Small white light mounted in a car's interior to provide interior lighting. It is usually mounted in the middle of the ceiling or by the windshield mirror.
light(dome) - See light(courtesy).
light(flashing) - Traffic signal light used at an intersection to caution drivers about approaching traffic and how they are to proceed through the intersection. If yellow, it means to proceed with caution. If red, it means to stop and then proceed with caution. Also, it refers to any light flashing to indicate caution such as a malfunctioning traffic light, road barricades, police car lights, hazard lights, etc.
light(fog) - Two or more amber or yellow colored lights mounted low and in front of a car to provide extra illumination when foggy. They are typically used with low beam headlights to minimize snow, rain, or fog reflections.
light(glove compartment) - Small light mounted inside a glove compartment box which activates when the box is opened.
light(green) - Traffic signal light activated when traffic is to proceed.
light(hazard) - Light mounted on a car and used to indicate a car problem or signal other cars of a road hazard. The turn signal lights are usually wired to flash when a hazard switch is pulled.
light(head) - Sealed beam light mounted in the front of a car to provide illumination for night driving or during bad weather. Cars usually have two or four headlights.
light(high beam) - One of two headlights mounted in the front of a car to provide long range illumination. It may be incorporated into a low beam headlight or mounted as a separate light. A high beam switch activates it.
light(license plate) - Small light mounted near a license plate to illuminate it at night.
light(low beam) - One of two headlights mounted in the front of a car to provide short range illumination of roads and is used chiefly in towns or busy road traffic. It may be incorporated into a high beam headlight or mounted as a separate headlight.
light(map) - Small light mounted in a car's ceiling or dashboard to provide a concentrated light for reading a map, book, etc. without disturbing a driver.
light(marker) - One of several lights mounted on the front roofline of a truck's cab.
light(parking) - One of usually four lights mounted at each corner of a car. It is usually also function as a car's turn signal lights.
light(parking) - One of usually four lights mounted at each corner of a car. It is activated when a light switch turns it and/or the headlights on. It also usually functions as a car turn signal light.
light(red) - Traffic signal light activated when traffic is to stop.
light(reverse) - One of two lights mounted on the back of a car and activated when a car is placed in reverse gear. White lens usually cover the lights.
light(road hazard) - Flashing light mounted on road barricades. A yellow lens is usually used. Also, it refers to a car's hazard lights.
light(sealed beam head) - A headlight sealed against the elements.
light(spot) - Movable high candlepower light used to direct light to a

specific spot. Some are mounted on cars or trucks while others are plugged into a cigarette lighter.

light(tail) – One of two lights mounted in the outside rear of a car to provide illumination at night for following cars. They also emit a brighter light when the brakes are applied, and are usually covered with a red lens.

light(third brake) – Extra eye-level brake light mounted at the base of a car's rear window. It is reportedly effective in reducing rear end collisions.

light(turn signal) – One of four lights mounted at each corner of a car to signal the direction a car intends to move or turn. Each is usually covered with an amber or yellow lens, and operated by a turn signal switch mounted on a steering wheel column. When the switch is used a flasher device is activated causing the left or right lights to flash until the turn it completed or the switch is deactivated. Turn signal lights also function as parking lights.

light(yellow) – Traffic signal light activated to indicate to traffic that the signal is changing from green to red.

light group – Specified non-essential accessory lights offered in a single package deal with a new car. Such lights might include: map light, detachable engine compartment light, glove box light, trunk light, detachable interior light, etc.

lighting circuit – Electrical circuit(s) used in a car to power various lights.

lighting relay – Electrical relay used to send current to the main lighting circuit. It performs the following functions: controls the flow of current, minimizes voltage drop, and eliminates need to pass heavy current through a lighting switch. There is usually one lighting relay for every two headlights.

lighting system – Assemblage of components used to house and operate the various lights. Primary components include: electrical lighting circuits, headlights, tail and backup lights, turn signal lights, parking lights, interior light, instrumentation lights, and light control switches.

lights – Lights used to start an electronic timing system at the beginning of a race and to stop timing clocks at the finish.

lights are dim – Condition created when a car's headlights are producing less light than they should be. Possible causes include: weak battery, dirty battery terminals, and loose or corroded lighting circuit connections.

light switch – Switch used to control a car's outside lights and inside instrumentation lighting. Other separate switches may exist to control a dome light, map light, fog lights, etc.

light the rugs – To accelerate a car so the tires smoke.

light the tires – See light the rugs.

light turned green – Traffic light changed from red to green.

Lima – American car produced in 1915.

limitations – One or more clauses written in a contract, insurance policy, warranty, etc., specifying the limits of coverage.

Limited – American car produced in 1911. Also, an American car produced from 1977 to date by Buick Division of General Motors Corp. in Michigan.

limited slip differential – Differential unit used to keep rotational power going to both wheels all the time. This is accomplished by the use of clutch discs, clutch plates, or side gear rings. If one wheel loses traction, rotational power is transferred to the drive wheel with the best traction. It is used by drag racers, four wheel drive cars, and other vehicles that need to control individual wheel spin. See also differential.

limited warranty – See warranty(limited).

Limo – Abbreviation for limousine.

limousine – See body style(limousine).

limp-in mode – Electronic ignition system mode built into an on-board computer and activated when it malfunctions, allowing an engine to continue running until the car can get to a repair facility.

linch pin – Pin used to go through a hole in the end of an axle outside a wheel in order to keep a wheel from falling off. Linch pins were used in cars years ago with rear axles prone to coming loose. They are also used in machinery using wheels and axles of all types.

Lincoln – American car produced in 1909 and 1911-1914 by Lincoln Motor Vehicle Co. and Lincoln Motor Car Works respectively, both in Illinois. Also, an American car line produced from 1920 to date by Lincoln Division of Ford Motor Co. in Michigan.

Lincoln Continental – American car produced in 1939-1948 and 1957 to date.

Lincoln Highway – It was the first transcontinental highway built in the U.S. It ran from New York to San Francisco. Construction began in 1914 and was completed in 1925.

Lincoln Truck – American truck produced in 1917.

Lincoln Zephyr – American car produced from 1935-1942.

Lindsley – American car produced from 1907-1908 by J.V. Lindsley in Indiana and Michigan.

line - Car path chosen when cornering.

line boring - Machining process defined as the boring of several circular holes in a straight line and separated from each other by air space. For example, Volkswagen Beetle air cooled engines have non-removable journal caps which must be bored when they need to be enlarged for oversize bearings.

line of cars - Cars lined up behind each other. It usually refers to cars stopped waiting: one behind the other for a traffic light, to get off a freeway off ramp, to get gas at a gas station, etc.

liner - Section of material attached to an existing surface. Examples include: brake lining and cylinder liner.

lining contamination - Oil, grease, grit, dirt, etc. found on brake linings. Contamination causes a decrease in the performance of the lining.

linkage - Assemblage of metal rods and levers connected together to transmit motion or force. For example, when a gas or clutch pedal is moved, a linkage is being operated.

link and slot - Linkage mechanism used on some carburetors to provide a means of positively closing open secondary throttle plates.

Linn - American car produced in 1929.

Linscott - American car produced in 1916.

Lion - American car produced from 1909-1912 by Lion Motor Car Co. in Michigan.

lip molding - Bright molding applied to the sheetmetal around the edge of a wheel opening.

Lippard - American car produced in 1912.

liquid - State of matter characterized as neither gaseous or solid. Liquids have a definite volume, but an indefinite shape. It is known as a fluid. See also fluid.

Liquid Air - American steam car produced from 1901-1902 by Liquid Air Power & Automobile Co. in Massachusetts.

liquid withdrawl system - LPG carburetion system used to remove liquid fuel from the bottom of an LPG tank. See also vapor withdrawl system.

list - See list price.

listing agent - Agency engaged in placing cars offered for sale on listings sent to interested buyers. A fee is usually collected from the seller usually when the car is sold.

list price - Retail selling price specified. In the case of a car, it is the asking or beginning price in a car dealing situation. From that figure, the customer and salesman dicker for the best price each can obtain. See also at cost and margin of profit.

liter - Metric measure of volume. It is the volume of one kilogram of distilled water at four degrees centigrade. One liter is equal to 1.057 liquid quarts.

litre - Metric volume measurement. One liter equals 1,000 cc.

Little - American car produced from 1912-1915 by Little Motor Car Co. in Michigan.

Little Detroit Speedster - American car produced from 1913-1914 by Detroit Cyclecar Co. in Michigan.

little end - Piston end of a connecting rod. See also big end.

Little Giant Truck - American truck produced in 1910.

Littemac - American car produced from 1930-1931 by Thompson Motor Corp. in Iowa.

Little Princess - American car produced from 1913-1914 by Princess Cyclecar Co. in Michigan.

live - Electrical part characterized as having an electric potential or voltage.

live axle - See axle(live).

live one - Good potential customer.

live wire - See hot wire.

LM - Abbreviation for limousine. See also Limo.

LMC - American car produced in 1919.

LN - Abbreviation for like new.

LN7 - American car produced from 1980 to date by Mercury Division of Ford Motor Co. in Michigan.

Lo - Abbreviation for low.

LOA - Abbreviation for Laos found usually on an international license plate.

loaded - Condition of a car characterized by having many extra car accessories and/or high quality parts.

loaded model - Car built with many extra accessories and/or high quality parts installed. Such a car usually holds it resale value better.

loading the deal - See con game(loading the deal).

load levelers - Extra suspension springs used to help keep a car body level when loaded. Springs used include: coil springs mounted on shock absorbers, air bags inside coil springs, and helper leaf springs.

load range - System of letters found on tires indicating a specific tire load and inflation limit. Also, it refers to the carrying capacity of a car.

loan cash - The actual amount of money an installment loan gives a borrower.
loaner - Used car owned by a car repair businesses and loaned to customers whose cars are tied up with repair work. The work usually has to take more than one day before many businesses will agree to give you one.
loan fee - Additional fee paid to a lender in advance in order to secure a loan. It is usually based on a specified number of points. See also points.
loan fell through - Loan applied for, but not approved.
loan tie-in - Practice followed by some lenders in which a potential borrower agrees to open a savings or checking account at the lending business in order to get a loan.
loan value - The average money amount a finance company will lend on a specific car, truck, etc. It usually refers to the value of used cars.
lobe - Rounded projection. See also cam lobe.
lobe displacement angle - See cam lobe displacement angle.
local car - Car owned and driven locally.
locked rear end - Rear end modified to eliminate differential action and provide power to both wheels regardless of traction.
Locke Steamer - American steam car produced in 1902.
Lockhart, Frank - He won the Indianapolis 500 Race in 1926 driving an average of 95.9 mph in a Miller Special.
locking differential - See differential(limited slip).
locking hubs - Wheel hubs built to connect and disconnect from drive axles by means of devices mounted on the axle ends. On older cars, they were manually operated. Today's cars typically use hubs operated remotely.
locking pliers - See vise grip pliers.
lock out - Feature used on certain overdrive units to provide solid connection between transmission output shaft and driveline. It usually immobilized the planet gears in the overdrive's planetary unit so all rotation between the sun and ring gear stopped. It was actuated by pulling a knob or flipping a switch.
lock out knob - Push-pull type knob used to lock out an overdrive unit.
lockout lever - Lever used in carburetors with mechanically operated secondary throttle plates to prevent secondary throttle from opening until engine is warmed up. It is positioned between a choke and the secondary throttle plate shaft, or between the choke and the air valve(s) on carburetors so equipped. See also air valve.
lock out switch - Switch used on older overdrive units to eliminate electrical current drain from a constantly energized overdrive solenoid when overdrive was locked out. It was never very successful and lost its usefulness when current drain was found not to be a problem.
lockup pressure - Pressure exerted by a pressure plate against a clutch plate sufficient to prevent slippage. It can range from 2-5,000 lbs., depending on rotation speed and design. See also bob-weight.
lock up the brakes - Situation created when brake linings bear against a braking surface hard enough to prevent the wheel(s) from turning. This usually happens when a driver must stop suddenly. The affected car tires skid on the road surface because the tire to road surface friction is overcome by the forward momentum of a car. Skidding distance is determined by a car's speed, and friction between the tires and road surface. See also skidding, brakes are locking, and brakes locked.
lock washer - Washer designed to prevent a nut or bolt head from becoming loose.
Locomobile - American car produced from 1899-1929 by Locomobile Co. of America in Massachusetts and Connecticut.
Locomobile Steamer - American steam car produced in 1899.
locomotive - Early term used for a heavy, steam-driven car.
Logan - American car produced from 1903-1908 by Logan Construction Co. in Ohio. Also an American car produced in 1914.
Lomax - American car produced in 1913.
Lomgard - American car produced in 1921.
London Six - Canadian car produced from 1921-1924 by London Motors in Ontario.
Lone Star - American car produced from 1920-1922 by Lone Star Motor Truck and Tractor Corp. in Texas.
Long - American car produced in 1923.
long and short arm suspension - Suspension system constructed using an upper and lower control arm. The upper arm is shorter. This is done to allow wheel deflection in a vertical direction with a minimum change in camber.
long bed - See truck bed(long).
long block - See engine block(long).
Long Distance - American car produced in 1900.
Longest - American car produced in 1912.
longitudinal leaf spring - Leaf spring mounted parallel to a car's length.
longitudinal torsion bar - Torsion bars mounted parallel to a car's length.
long nose pliers - Pliers built with long and tapered jaws. It is used to get into tight places or hold small objects.

long wearing tread compound - Tire tread compound formulated to wear a long time.

looker - Semi-interested car customer characterized by having no immediate buying plans. He is usually in the process of visiting several car lots searching for the best deal and/or lowest price.

Loomis - American car produced from 1896-1904 by G.L. Loomis (1896-1897), Loomis Automobile Co. (1901-1903), and Loomis Auto Car Co. (1903-1904), all in Massachusetts.

loophole - Means or opportunity found to get around a law, rule, etc.

loose track - Wet race track.

Lord Baltimore - American car produced in 1913.

Lorenzen, Fred - He won the Daytona 500 Race in 1965 averaging 141.5 mph in a Ford.

Lorraine - American car produced in 1907-1908 and 1920-1922 by Lorraine Automobile Mfg. Co. in Illinois, and Lorraine Motors Corp. in Michigan respectively.

lorrie - A truck.

lorry - See lorrie.

Los Angeles - American car produced from 1913-1915 by Los Angeles Cycle Car Co. in New York.

lose the fire - To stall an engine.

loser's leave - Race car starting system built with an amber light and a go light.

loss experience - Total value of claims filed in a given territory resulting from car accidents over a certain period of time. The value would include all bodily injury, car damage, etc. expenses incurred. See also rating territories.

Lost Cause - American car produced from 1963-1964 by Lost Cause Motors in Kentucky. It was a custom Corvair.

lost foam casting - Casting process using polystyrene patterns packed in sand-filled pouring boxes. The polystyrene vaporizes when molten metal is poured on it leaving an exact replica of the pattern in the sand box.

lost motion - Motion generated between driving and driven parts that does not cause motion of the driven parts. An example is gear backlash.

Lotus - British car line produced from 1952 to date by Lotus Cars Ltd. (1966 to date). Popular models include: Espirit, Excel, and Europa. As of 1985, Lotus racing machines accumulated 73 Grand Prix race victories. See also Ferrari.

loud pedal - Gas pedal.

Louisiana - American car produced in 1900.

louver - Opening or vent used to control air flow. Vents are used to regulate air flow into a car's interior and/or an engine compartment.

louvering - To create louvers in a car body panel.

louver cover - Cover placed over a louver.

low ball - Selling tactic used to attract a customer back for future sales. The customer is offered an attractive below average price for a car he is interested in buying. It also refers to putting low figures in a sales contract, then changing them upwards at the last moment usually under the guise of the car buyer misunderstanding. See also high ball and con game(bargain advertising).

low balling - See low ball.

low beam - Car headlight beam used to produce short range lighting of a road. It is primarily used in towns and busy traffic. On two headlight cars, the low beam setting activates the lower wattage filament in each headlight. On four headlight cars, the two inside headlights produce the low beams. See also light(low beam) and light(high beam).

low beam diagram - Vertical wall surface marked with various referencing lines relevant to a car in order to properly adjust the horizontal and vertical position of a car's low light beams. See also high beam diagram.

low brake pedal - See low pedal.

low compression - Engine cylinder compression below minimum specifications. Possible causes include: worn pistons, rings, and/or cylinder walls; burned valves; and late valve timing due to improperly timed camshaft or loose timing chain or belt. See also engine problem(cranks but won't start), car service tip(cranking vacuum test), and sound(popping).

low crown - Car body panel shape curving slowly away in all directions. See also high crown, reverse crown, and combination crown.

Lowell - American car produced in 1908.

Lowell-American - American car produced from 1908-1909.

low end - Engine built with good low speed torque.

low end power - Engine power available at low rpm.

lower back panel - Car body panel located below the rear edge of a decklid and above a rear bumper.

lower control arm - Heavy steel pivoting arm assembly used with other components to provide support and steering ability to a wheel. It is most commonly used with front wheels. It differs from an A-arm in that lateral support is required due to only one mounting point or two mounting points closely spaced together (equivalent to one). Lateral support is provided by a strut rod attached to the lower control arm. It works in conjunction with an upper control arm (on older cars), coil spring, and steering knuckle-wheel spindle assembly to support and cushion a portion of a car's body, provide a place to securely attach a wheel to a car, and provide a pivoting point for a wheel turning left or right.

On today's cars, the coil spring, steering knuckle and wheel spindle assembly are usually integrated into a MacPherson strut and wheel spindle assembly. The lower control arm attaches to the bottom of it. The upper control arm is actually a part of the car frame. See also upper control arm, strut rod, and A-arm.

lower control arm bushing – Bushing used to provide a rotation point for the lower portion of a steering knuckle.

lower control arm rubber bumper – Rubber block used to limit the upward travel of a lower control arm.

lower control link – See lower control arm.

lower idle air bleed – Idle bleed usually located a short distance above off-idle port(s).

lower idle discharge port – See idle discharge port.

lower mode door – Mode-and-blend door used to control air flow to lower heating and air conditioning ducts.

low miles – Used car condition created when the number of miles driven is below average, considering the year it was produced.

low oil pressure – Engine condition created when oil pressure stays low during the operation of an engine. If a cold engine starts up with low pressure, check to see how low the oil is. If adequate pressure if maintained until the engine is warmed up, then excessive clearances exist usually in bearings. This happens because warm oil thins out and flows faster than the oil pump can keep up. In the latter case, the only remedy is to tear down the engine to find the source of the problem.

low on oil – Engine condition created when an engine has lost a substantial amount of oil.

low pedal – Condition created when a pedal can be pushed almost to the floor before it begins to work. See also brake pedal problem.

low pivot swing axle – See axle(low pivot swing).

low production – Car model or part produced in small quantities by the manufacturer.

low rider truck – Truck built with its body lower to the ground than stock.

low speed – See low gear.

low speed circuit – See carburetor circuit(low speed).

low speed port – Small fuel discharge port located near the idle discharge port on the top side of a throttle plate. Fuel flows only when the throttle plate is opened a little, exposing the port to a vacuum. Its function is to provide additional fuel to an engine in off-idle conditions until the discharge nozzle in the venturi can take over. It is also known as the upper idle discharge port.

low spot – Panel area located below a desired surface contour.

low visibility – Driver's inability to see much beyond the front of a car caused by adverse weather conditions such as snow, sleet, heavy rain, fog, etc.

Loyal – American car produced in 1920.

Lozier – American car produced from 1905-1917 by Lozier Motor Co. in New York. It was considered one of the highest quality cars in its time.

Lozier Steamer – American steam car produced in 1901.

LPC – American car produced from 1914-1916.

LPG – Abbreviation for liquefied petroleum gas.

LP gas – Liquefied petroleum gas. Mixture of gaseous hydrocarbon compounds composed of propane, butane, and smaller quantities of other gases. It is much more volatile than gasoline, as all the compounds have lower boiling points. In mild temperatures, the fuel is vapor since the average boiling point approximates that of propane at minus 44 degrees Fahrenheit. Trucks, cars, and tractors have been fitted with special carburetors to use this fuel. It is stored and transported by pressurizing the gas. In mild temperatures, 250 gallons of gaseous LP gas compresses into 1 gallon of liquid. LP gas is a clean burning fuel with the following advantages: high octane rating (93-100), no carbon deposits formed in engine, no engine oil dilution since gas is dry, reduced engine maintenance, longer oil change intervals, good cold weather starting, and relatively clean smelling exhaust.

LR – Abbreviation for Lorrie.

Lr – Abbreviation for left rear.

LT – Abbreviation for Libya found usually on an international license plate.

LTD(1) – American car produced from 1955 to date by Ford Motor Co. in Michigan.

LTD(2) – Abbreviation for laundalet.

Lthr – Abbreviation for leather.
lube – To lubricate.
lube chassis – To lubricate chassis components requiring periodic greasing.
lube job – Lubrication work done to all car components requiring periodic greasing. Many components requiring periodic greasing on older cars are sealed on today's models. See also grease job.
lube man – Person skilled in lubricating cars.
lube, oil and filter – Service work done to a car's fluids and lubrication points. It usually includes: changing oil and oil filter, lubricating all chassis points with zerc grease fittings, and checking fluid levels in differential, transmission, master brake cylinders, radiator, windshield washer reservoir, and power steering reservoir.
lubricant – Substance used to reduce friction between two moving parts by covering both surfaces with a smooth film. Good lubricant possesses the following desired qualities: body, fluidity or viscosity, absence of acidity, freedom from gumming, stability under temperature changes, and absence of foreign matter. Today's lubricants are usually of petroleum origin. Grease and oil are the two most common lubricants used in cars. Without lubrication, an engine would not work and wheels would not turn.
lubrication – Process defined as applying lubricant to specified moving parts of a car to reduce coefficient of friction and reduce wear and temperature.
lubricator – Device used to supply lubricant. An oil pump is an example.
Lucas – British line of automotive parts.
Luck Utility – American car produced in 1913.
Ludlow – American car produced in 1915.
Luedinghaus-Espenschied – American car produced in 1919.
lubrafiner – External oil filter mounted on one side of a tractor.
lug – Projection used to hold or support a part such as a wheel.
luggage boot – See trunk.
luggage rack – Rack mounted on the trunk or roof of a car to carry cargo in addition to what is carried inside.
luggage space – Space made available in a car to carry cargo. It usually refers to a car's trunk or rear deck space.
lugging the engine – Driving an engine at too low an rpm. Lugging strains engine parts because they are pulling a load and moving slowly. See also over-revving the engine.
lug nut – One of several nuts used to hold a wheel on a hub. A wheel typically has four or five lug nuts. The nut is flat on one end and coned shaped at the other. The cone shape provides additional friction area to keep the nut from working loose.
lug tires – See tire(lug).
lug wrench – Large L-shaped bar fitted with a socket wrench at one end for removing wheel lug nuts.
Luitwieler – American car produced in 1919.
Lu-Lu – American car produced in 1914.
lunch an engine – To destroy an engine.
Lund, Tiny – He won the Daytona 500 Race in 1963 averaging 151.6 mph in a Ford.
lung – See supercharger.
Lunkenheimer – American car produced in 1902.
lure trick – See con game(bargain advertising).
lush – Potential car customer characterized as easy to close a deal on.
Lutz – American car produced in 1917.
Luv – American truck imported from 1972-1981 for Chevrolet Division of General Motors Corp. in Michigan.
Luverne – American car produced from 1903-1918 by Luverne Automobile Co. in Michigan.
Luxor Cab – American car produced from 1920-1926.
luxury car – Car built where no expense has been spared to make it as desirable as possible. It is usually a well-built car with many add-ons. Wheelbase is usually over 119 inches. Price typically begins at $10,000. Some domestic models include: Chevrolet Corvette, Cadillacs, and Chrysler Executive.
luxury equipment package – Package of quality options available for a car. Such options may include: leather seat upholstery; special paint; tinted windows; car phone; wet bar; TV; special engine; and electric windows, doors, seats, and locks.
LWC – American car produced in 1916.
Lyman – American car produced from 1903-1904 and 1909.
Lyman & Burnham – American car produced from 1903-1904 by Lyman & Burnham in Massachusetts.
Lynx – American car produced from 1980 to date by Mercury Division of Ford Motor Co. in Michigan.
Lyon – American car produced in 1911.
Lyons-Atlas – American car produced from 1912-1915 by by Lyons-Atlas Co. in

Indiana.
Lyons-Knight – See Lyons-Atlas.

M

M(1) - Abbreviation for thousand. See also K.
M(2) - Abbreviation for Malta found usually on an international license plate.
M(3) - Auction car rating code used to specify a car in mint condition.
MA - Abbreviation for Morocco found usually on an international license plate.
Maccar - American car produced in 1914.
MacDonald Bobcat - American steam car produced from 1921-1924 by MacDonald Steam Automobile Corp. in Ohio.
Mack Truck - American truck produced in 1905.
machine(1) - Apparatus composed of interrelated parts and used to perform work of some kind.
machine(2) - To prepare, finish, alter, make, etc. with a machine.
machine(3) - Hot rod.
Mackenzie - American car produced in 1914.
Mackle-Thompson - American car produced in 1903.
MacNaughton - American car produced in 1907.
Macomber - American car produced in 1913.
Macon - American car produced from 1915-1917 by All Steel Car Co. in Missouri.
Macpherson, Earle - He designed the Macpherson Strut. It was introduced on a British Ford car in 1959.
Macpherson Strut - Shock absorber, suspension spring, and wheel spindle assembly mounted on each front wheel. It is very popular on today's cars.
Macy-Roger - American car produced in 1895.
Madison - American car produced from 1915-1918 by Madison Motors Co. in Indiana.
mag - See magneto.
MAG - Abbreviation for magnesium.
magazine - Publication produced with a paper back at regular intervals (monthly, bi-monthly, quarterly, etc.); and containing articles, product reviews, advertisements, etc. on a specific subject. There are many different magazines available covering the automotive field.
magazine(4 Wheel & Off-Road) - American magazine published monthly, covering different aspects of four wheel drive vehicles in off-road environments.
magazine(4X4's And Off Road Vehicles) - American magazine published monthly, covering different aspects of four wheel drive vehicles in off-road environments.
magazine(1101 Truck And Van Ideas) - American magazine published monthly, covering customizing information on trucks and vans.
magazine(Antique Automobile) - American magazine published bi-monthly for all members of the Antique Automobile Club of America.
magazine(Antique Motor News) - American magazine published monthly; covering antique, old, and imported cars.
magazine(Autocar) - English magazine published monthly, covering performance testing of cars and general automotive information.
magazine(Automobile Quarterly Magazine) - American magazine published quarterly, covering the historical side of older automobiles.
magazine(Automotive Age) - American magazine published monthly since 1966, covering the management and operation of automobile dealerships in the U.S.
magazine(Automotive Engineering) - American magazine published monthly since 1917, covering the technical aspects of the automotive field, products, technology, news, standards, legislation, etc.
magazine(Automotive Industries) - See magazine(Chilton's Automotive Industries).
magazine(Automotive News) - Newspaper style magazine published weekly since 1925, covering all aspects of the automotive industry including: products, sales, research, legislation, and company news.
magazine(Auto Racing Digest) - American magazine published bi-monthly since 1973, covering all types of racing throughout the world.
magazine(Autoweek) - American newspaper style magazine published weekly since 1958, covering auto racing.
magazine(Boy's Life) - Magazine published monthly, covering general automotive topics.
magazine(Car) - English magazine published monthly since 1962, covering cars and sports/performance car reviews.
magazine(Car And Driver) - American magazine published monthly since 1955, covering general interest domestic, foreign, and sports car topics, and road tests.
magazine(Car Care News) - American magazine published monthly since 1983,

covering car maintenance information for mechanically inclined and those learning.

magazine(Car Collector and Car Classics) – American magazine published monthly since 1966, covering investment information on antique and collector cars. It appeals to car enthusiats, collectors, and mechanics.

magazine(Car Craft) – American magazine published monthly since 1953, covering information on car performance, racing, how-to, classic, and new cars.

magazine(Car Exchange) – American magazine published monthly since 1979, covering antique and special interest cars.

magazine(Car) – English magazine published monthly, covering general interest automotive information and sports/performance car reviews.

magazine(Cars & Parts) – American magazine published monthly since 1957, covering restoration and selling of old cars.

magazine(Chilton's Automotive Industries) – American magazine published monthly since 1895, covering automotive business in depth.

magazine(Classic & Special Interest Cars) – See magazine(High Performance Kit Cars).

magazine(Coast Car Collector) – American magazine published monthly, covering collector cars for the western U.S.

magazine(Collectible Automobile) – American magazine published bi-monthly since 1984, covering classic U.S. cars.

magazine(Deals On Wheels) – American magazine published monthly covering general automotive interest information of a technical and entertaining nature.

magazine(Four Wheeler) – American magazine published monthly since 1962, covering use of and information on four wheel drive vehicles.

magazine(Hemming Motor News) – American magazine published monthly since 1954, covering the buying and selling of antique and classic cars, car parts, and books.

magazine(High Performance Kit Cars) – American magazine published monthly since 1983, covering all aspects of kit cars including road tests and evaluations.

magazine(Home Mechanix) – American magazine published monthly since 1929, covering do-it-yourself repair and maintenance information for home and car. Emphasis is more on cars. It was formerly called Mechanix Illustrated.

magazine(Hot Rod Magazine) – American magazine published monthly since January 1948. It covers: hot rod, custom, and drag racing information; products; news; etc.

magazine(Kit Cars) – American magazine published monthly, covering different aspects of kit car building.

magazine(Mechanix Illustrated) – See magazine(Home Mechanix).

magazine(Minnesota AAA Motorist) – American magazine published monthly, covering general automotive interest topics.

magazine(Montgomery Ward Auto Club News) – American magazine published monthly for its members, covering general automotive news.

magazine(Motor) – American magazine published monthly since 1903, covering the latest in repair and maintenance techniques for cars and light trucks. It is geared toward mechanics.

magazine(Motorhome) – American magazine published monthly since 1968, covering the owning and operating of motorhomes.

magazine(Motor Trend) – American magazine published monthly since 1949, covering general interest automotive information.

magazine(Mustang Monthly) – American magazine published monthly for Mustang enthusiats.

magazine(National Dragster) – American magazine published weekly since 1960, covering drag racing: statistics, events, rules, products, tools, equipment, cars, etc.

magazine(National Speed Sports News) – American magazine published weekly, covering all aspects of racing news.

magazine(New Driver) – American magazine published quarterly since 1977, covering car: purchase, maintenance, driving skills, energy conservation, etc. It is geared toward high school students.

magazine(Off Road) – American magazine published monthly, covering off-road information.

magazine(Off Road Travel) – American magazine published monthly, covering different aspects of traveling off-road.

magazine(Old Cars Weekly) – American magazine published weekly since 1971; covering old car sales, products, shows, personalities, repair, reconditioning, auctions, etc.

magazine(Owner Operator) – American magazine published monthly for independent truck drivers.

magazine(Peterson's Circle Track) – American magazine published monthly since 1982, covering oval track racing.

magazine(Peterson's Pickup and Mini Trucks) – American magazine published monthly since 1972, covering light truck: testing, customizing, modifying, selecting, personalities, events, etc.

magazine(Pickup, Van & 4WD) – American magazine published monthly, covering performance testing and buying of pickups, vans, and 4WD vehicles.

magazine(Popular Car) – American magazine published monthly since 1979, covering classic cars of the 1950s and 60s pertaining to repair, maintenance, product news, racing events, personalities, tests, etc.

magazine(Popular Hot Rodding) – American magazine published monthly since 1962, covering racing: events, accessories, car parts, new products, styling, repairs, etc.

magazine(Popular Off Roading) – American magazine published monthly, covering the off-road driving sport.

magazine(Popular Science) – American magazine published monthly since 1872, covering scientific, do-it-yourself, and automotive: developments, products, ideas, do-it-yourself, tests, etc.

magazine(Racecar) – American magazine published monthly for the racing crowd.

magazine(Racing Pictorial) – American magazine published monthly for auto racing enthusiasts.

magazine(Restoration) – American magazine published bi-monthly since 1984, covering old cars.

magazine(Road & Track) – American magazine published monthly since 1947, covering general auto topics, road tests, cars, racing, etc.

magazine(Road King) – American magazine published monthly for truck drivers.

magazine(Rod Action) – American magazine published monthly for performance car enthusiasts.

magazine(Scholastic Wheels) – American magazine published monthly for students enrolled in driver education programs.

magazine(Special Interest Autos) – American magazine published bi-monthly since 1970, covering old cars.

magazine(Sports Car) – American magazine published monthly, covering the interests of Sports Car Club members.

magazine(Sports Car Graphic) – American magazine published monthly since 1959, covering sports car: racing, production, and design.

magazine(Sport Trucking) – American magazine published monthly, covering trucks and vans.

magazine(Stock Car Racing) – American magazine published monthly since 1966, covering stock car: racing, drivers, and their careers.

magazine(Street Machine) – American magazine published monthly, covering recent model performance cars.

magazine(Street Rodder) – American magazine published monthly since 1972, covering high performance cars.

magazine(Street Rodding Illustrated) – American magazine published bi-monthly since 1980; covering races, shows, events, personalities, product information, information on manufacturers producing specific products, etc.

magazine(Super Chevy) – American magazine published monthly since 1973, covering Chevy car: buying, customizing, and modifying for performance.

magazine(Super Customs & Rods) – American magazine published bi-monthly since 1985, covering stock customized cars, trucks, and vans, events, restoration, history, and design.

magazine(Super Stock Cars) – American magazine published monthly, covering stock car racing.

magazine(The Automobile) – English magazine published monthly since 1982; covering veteran, vintage, and pre-1950s cars.

magazine(The Robb Report) – American magazine published monthly, covering Rolls-Royce and Bentley cars.

magazine(Thoroughbred And Classic Cars) – English magazine published monthly, covering collector cars.

magazine(Traffic Safety) – American magazine published monthly since 1901, covering safety aspects of driving.

magazine(Trailer Life) – American magazine published monthly since 1941, covering living in trailers.

magazine(Travelin' Vans, Mini Trucks & Pickups) – American magazine published monthly, covering customizing and how-to information pertaining to vans, mini trucks, and pickups.

magazine(Truckin') – American magazine published monthly since 1975, covering light truck: models, parts, how-to, accessories, etc.

magazine(Van Pickup And Off Road World) – American magazine published monthly for van enthusiasts.

magazine(Veteran And Vintage) – English magazine published monthly, covering collector cars.

magazine(Vette Vues Magazine) – American magazine published monthly, covering Corvettes.

magazine(VW & Porsche) – American magazine published bi-monthly since 1970, covering tests, racing, technical information, etc. pertaining to VWs and Porsches.

magazine(Ward Auto World) – American magazine published monthly since 1964, covering news on all aspects of the automotive industry.

Magic - American car produced in 1922.

magnaflux - Process defined as the detection of small crack in metal parts through the use of magnetic equipment and chemical compounds.

magnafluxing - Checking for small and invisible cracks in metal parts with magnaflux equipment.

Magnaquench - Tradename used for a GM high performance permanent magnet. It is made of iron, and boron and neodymium rare earths. Material has higher magnetic strength and coercivity.

magnet(electro) - Soft iron structure coiled with electric wire. It becomes magnetic when electric current passes through the wire. The field coils in an alternator are an example.

magnet(permanent) - Piece of alloy steel characterized by being permanently magnetized. It will attract all ferrous material without the need of electricity. Such steel retains its electricity for a long period of time.

magnetic - Property exhibited in certain iron and steel materials allowing them to be attracted to each other.

magnetic drain plug - Oil drain plug fitted with a permanent magnet for attracting steel particles held in suspension in oil.

magnetic field - Area defined where magnetic force exists.

magnetic force - Attracting or repelling force exhibited between two magnetic materials.

magnetic pickup - Solid state assembly used in a distributor housing to replace conventional distributor points and condenser. It consists primarily of: a permanent ceramic magnet, pickup coil, and pole piece. It generates weak magnetic signals for each cylinder which are detected and amplified by an ignition pulse amplifier for controlling the primary winding current flow in an ignition coil.

magnetic pulse system - See ignition system(magnetic pulse).

magnetic pulse distributor - Distributor used in transistor ignition systems with solid state components substituting for distributor points. The components include: a rotating timer core and magnetic pickup assembly. See also magnetic pickup.

magnetic rotor - Shaft-mounted permanent magnet device used in a magneto to generate electricity. It typically has two permanent magnets. Electricity is created when the magnetic field of the rotating permanent magnets moves through a stationary magnetic field.

magnetic switch - See relay. See also solenoid switch.

magneto - Electrical device used to generate and distribute current to a car's electrical system without need of a battery. In general, there are two magneto types, low voltage and high voltage. The low voltage type generates battery voltage current which is stepped up to high voltage through an ignition coil. The high voltage type directly generates voltage high enough to jump a spark plug gap. The primary parts typically consist of: a two pole rotating magnet, a stationary magnet, U-shaped magnetic steel laminations, and low or high voltage windings. It was used extensively in early cars for producing electrical sparks, but was largely replaced in the 1920s by the modern battery ignition system in use today. It is still used in racing cars where weight is a major consideration and a conventional battery is not needed.

magneto(flywheel) - Inductor magneto built with a moving permanent ring magnet, mounted on the outer edge of the flywheel, and a stationary ignition coil, points, and condenser. It is most commonly used on small one cylinder engines.

magneto(high voltage) - Magneto built to generate high voltage current for spark plugs. An ignition coil is incorporated into the magneto. Some designs place the ignition coil's primary and secondary windings in the rotating armature while others locate them in a stationary position at one end of the U-shaped frame laminations. A typical high voltage magneto system consists of: a two-pole permanent magnet rotor, U-shaped frame laminations, stationary ignition coil, and rotor shaft activated distributor points.

magneto(inductor) - Magneto built with stationary generator or high voltage windings and permanent magnets, surrounding a rotating armature equipped with permanent magnets. The armature rotation causes one magnetic field to cut another inducing a magnetic field in nearby magnetic steel laminations which in turn induces current flow in the generator windings.

magneto(low voltage) - Magneto built to generate low voltage current. An external ignition coil is used to generate high voltage current for the spark plugs.

magneto(revolving magnet) - Magneto built very similar to an inductor type magneto.

magneto(rotary inductor) - See magneto(inductor).

magneto(rotating magnet) - See magneto(inductor).

magneto(shuttle wound) - Magneto built with generator or high voltage windings built into an armature rotating in a magnetic field created by permanent

magnets.
magneto coil – Generator or high voltage windings of a magneto.
magneto ignition system – Ignition system constructed to use a magneto for generating electrical current. Advantages include: no battery needed, voltage maintained at low speed. Disadvantages include: higher starting rotation usually needed to generate sufficient voltage. Most cars today use a battery ignition system, but magneto ignition is still popular on small engines, tractors, trucks, motorcycles, and engines with no electrical accessories.
Magnolia – American car produced in 1903.
Magnum – American car produced from 1962-1982 by Dodge Division of Chrysler Corp. in Michigan.
Mags – Mag wheels.
Mag wheel – See wheel(Mag).
Mag wire – See spark plug cable(Mag-wire).
Mahoning – American car produced from 1904-1905 by Mahoning Motor Car Co. in Ohio.
Maibohm – American car produced from 1916-1922 by Maibohm Motors Co. in Wisconsin (1916-1919) and Ohio (1919-1922).
main bearing cap – Bridge type device used to hold a crankshaft main bearing journal and bearing assembly in place. Crankshafts have several.
main bearing journal – Main bearing surface on a crankshaft located between each of the crank pins.
main bearings – Bearings used to support a crankshaft. Four and eight cylinder engines usually have three and five main bearings respectively. The number of main bearings determines the degree of crankshaft flexing, and cylinder distortion.
main circuit – See carburetor circuit(main).
main discharge jet – Metering device mounted in the fuel passageway leading to the main discharge nozzle. It serves to introduce a small amount of air into incoming fuel for the following purposes: reduce surface tension of fuel, assist fuel flow at low pressures, and restrict fuel flow when main jets are exposed to a high vacuum.
main discharge nozzle – See primary discharge nozzle.
main drag – Main street.
main drive gear – See transmission main drive gear.
Maine – American car produced from 1915-1918.
main fuel well – Carburetor fuel passageway located leading from a float bowl to a primary discharge nozzle.
main input shaft – See transmission input shaft.
main jet – Small threaded brass fitting with a specified hole size installed in the bottom of a carburetor float bowl for metering fuel into a carburetor airway through most of an engine's power range. The jet opening also receives a movable tapered fuel metering rod on some carburetor designs to control fuel flow through the jet.
main metering jet – See main jet.
mains – Main bearings.
maintaining speed at minimum throttle – To drive a car at a specified speed with the least amount of gas pedal deflection.
maintenance schedule – Schedule made indicating dates or mileage points at which maintenance work is advised for a car.
maintenance work – Work performed to maintain a car, part, machine, etc. in good operating condition.
main venturi – Venturi located in a carburetor's primary airway. See also boost venturi.
main well – See carburetor(primary).
Mais – American car produced in 1911.
Maja – American car produced in 1908.
Majestic – American car produced in 1913, 1917-1918, and 1925.
major repairs – Repairs made to a car or machine requiring extensive rebuilding, replacing many parts or expensive parts, and or extensive labor.
make – Producer or manufacturer of a product. Examples of car makes include: Toyota, Ford, Dodge, Pontiac, etc. See also model, sub-model, and body type.
make and color – Car producer and car color.
make and model – Car producer and the model produced. For example, a Ford Mustang.
make and break ignition – Early ignition system built to generate low voltage for firing air/fuel mixtures in combustion chambers.
make a pile – To make a lot of money.
make out – To make a good deal.
make ready – See dealer preparation. See also con game(make ready).
making a bead – To form a weld along a metal surface.
MAL – Abbreviation for Malaya found usually on an international license plate.
malice – Desire to inflict suffering or injury on another person.
Malcom – American car produced from 1914-1915 by Malcolm Jones Cyclecar Co. in

Michigan.

Malcomson – American car produced in 1906.

Malden Steam – American steam car produced in 1898.

male – Designation made of a mechanical fitting having a part shaped to fit into a hollow part or female fitting. External threads of machine screws and pipes, a headphone jack, electric cord plug ends, etc. are examples of male fittings.

male connector – See male.

malfeasance – An act performed by a public official characterized as contrary or damaging to existing law, or legally unjustified.

Malibu – American car produced from 1964 to date by Chevrolet Division of General Motors Corp. in Michigan.

malleable casting – Casting made tough by annealing.

Mallory – American line of performance ignition systems and other automotive products produced by Mallory Electric.

Malvern – American car produced in 1905.

man – Abbreviation for manual transmission.

Manexall – American car produced in 1921.

maneuverability – Ability exhibited by a person, machine, device, etc. to perform a movement or procedure to achieve some objective. For example, the maneuverability of a car would be its ability to turn quickly and in small circles.

maneuverability test – Test performed by a car evaluator to determine how well a car handles over a specified course.

manganese bronze – Metal alloy composed of manganese, copper, and zinc.

Manhattan – American car produced in 1907 and 1921.

Manic – Canadian car produced beginning in 1970 by Les Automobiles Manic in Quebec.

manifold – Steel or aluminum casting constructed with multiple pipes radiating from a common opening and connecting to multiple openings on an engine block. The openings are either the intake or exhaust valve port openings. See also intake manifold and exhaust manifold.

manifold flange – Flat surface located at the inlet or outlet of an intake or exhaust manifold. It is where the connection is made to an engine block, exhaust pipe, carburetor, etc.

manifold gauge set – Set of gauges, valves, and hoses used to test the operation of an air conditioner system and introduce or bleed off freon gas. It connects to the discharge and suction side of a compressor.

manifold heat control valve – Valve located in an exhaust pipe or manifold to redirect some of the exhaust gases near the carburetor area to warm it and improve fuel vaporization.

manifold heat riser system – Assemblage of parts and controls used to direct heated air from an exhaust manifold area to an air cleaner depending on outside air temperature. Major components include: manifold heat shroud, heat riser tube, air temperature sensor, and vacuum controlled air gate.

Manistee – American car produced in 1912.

Manlius – American car produced in 1910.

Manly – American car produced in 1919.

Mann – American car produced in 1895.

manometer – Instrument used to measure vacuum. It is a U-shaped tube filled partially with mercury. One end is open to the atmosphere and the other is connected to a vacuum source. The difference in mercury levels in the two legs determines the vacuum.

Mansfield – American car produced in 1919.

Mansur – American car produced in 1914.

manual – Book written to describe how to work on, maintain, and/or repair a car, truck, part, etc.

manual choke – Choke built to be manually controlled by the driver of a car.

manual fuel pump – See mechanical fuel pump.

manual low valve – Valve used in an automatic transmission to regulate a backout valve when manually shifting into low gear.

manual transmission – See transmission(manual).

manual valve – Valve used in an automatic transmission to control which gear is engaged. It is operated by a transmission shift lever.

manufacturer's liability – Responsibility required by a car manufacturer to correct a defective or malfunctioning new car or truck. It is usually spelled out in the new car warranty.

manufacturer's representative – Car manufacturer representative.

manufacturer's warranty – See warranty(manufacturer's).

M&P Electric – American car produced from 1912-1913.

MAP – Abbreviation for manifold absolute pressure. See also sensor(manifold absolute pressure).

Maple-Leaf – American car produced in 1921.

Maplebay – American car produced in 1908.

map light – See light(map).

Marathon - American car produced from 1908-1915 by Southern Motor Works in Tennessee (1908-1910), and Marathon Motor Works in Tennessee (1910-1915).

Marble-Swift - American car produced from 1903-1905 by Marble-Swift Automobile Co. in Illinois.

marbling - See cobwebbing.

Marcus - Austrian car built in 1874.

Marcus, Siegfried - He was a Viennese chemist and engineer who developed a method for mixing liquid fuel and air in 1860. The mixture was called carburated air.

margin - See margin of profit.

margin of profit - Money made by a car salesman selling a new or used car. It is the difference between a dealer's asking price (his car cost plus expenses) and what a buyer is willing to pay. The margin of profit for a car salesman and a dealer won't necessarily be viewed the same.

Marion - American car produced from 1904-1914 by Marion Motor Car Co. in Indiana.

Marion-Handley - American car produced from 1916-1919 by Mutual Motors Co. in Michigan.

Marion-Overland - American car produced in 1910.

Maritime Six - Canadian car produced from 1913-1914 by Maritime Motors Ltd. in New Brunswick.

mark - Person characterized as suitable for conning by a con artist.

marked car - Police car equipped with visible police-type identification markings such as: flashing lights, car decals on side body panels, and license plates. See also unmarked car.

marked crosswalk - Crosswalk marked on a roadway with paint or other markings along with accompanying road signs.

Mark Electric - American car produced in 1897.

marker light - See light(marker).

Marketour - American car produced beginning in 1964 by Marketour Electric Cars in California. It was a small electric car used to run errands.

mark-up - Percentage of a wholesale or base price added to an item to yield its list price. Mark-ups are usually a hot debate item between car buyers and sellers.

Mark VI - American car produced by Lincoln from 1980 to date.

Marlan - American car produced in 1920.

Marlboro - American car produced from 1899-1902 by Marlboro Motor & Carriage Co. in Massachusetts.

Marlin - American car produced by Rambler from 1964-1967. Also, an American car produced from 1965-1972 by American Motors Corp. in Michigan.

Marmon - American car produced from 1902-1933 by Nordyke and Marmon Co. in Indiana (1902-1925), and Marmon Motor Car Co. in Indiana (1926-1933). The first cars were considered advanced for their time employing an air-cooled V-4 engine, mechanical overhead valves, pressure lubrication, and an almost independent front suspension.

Marmon, Howard - He designed the Marmon car, invented the duplex downdraft manifold, and was an early advocate of using aluminum in engines to save weight.

Marmon-Herrington - American car produced in 1932.

Marquette - American car produced in 1912. Also, an American car produced from 1929-1931 by the Buick Motor Co. in Michigan.

Marquis - American car produced from 1955 to date by Mercury Division of Ford Motor Co. in Michigan.

Marr - American car produced from 1903-1904 by Marr Auto Car Co. in Michigan.

Marriot, Fred - He set a world land speed record of 121.6 mph in 1906 driving a Stanley Steam Rocket.

Marron - American car produced in 1903.

Marsh - American car produced in 1898-1899, 1905-1906, and 1919-1921 by Marsh Motor Carriage Co. in Massachusetts, American Motor Co. in Massachusetts, and Marsh Motors Co. in Ohio respectively.

Marshall - American car produced from 1919-1921 by Marshall Mfg. Co. in Illinois.

marshall - Officer of the law authorized to carry out court orders.

marsh gas - See methane gas.

Martin - American car produced from 1920-1922 and 1928-1932 by Martin Motor Co in Massachusetts (1920-1922), Martin Aeroplane Co. in New York (1928-1932), and Martin Motors in Washington D.C. (1929-1932). It was a three-wheeled two passenger midget car with 40 mph top speed and 75 mpg fuel economy.

Martin Stationette - American car produced in 1954 by Commonwealth Research Corp. in New York. It was a three wheeled commuter car designed by James V. Martin, the originator of the earlier Martin car.

Martin-Wasp - American car produced from 1919-1924.

Marvel(1) - American car produced in 1907.

Marvel(2) - American line of additives produced by Marvel Oil Company, Inc.

Marwin Truck - American truck produced in 1918.

Maryland – American car produced from 1900-1901 and 1907-1910 by Sinclair Scott Co. in Maryland.

Maryland Electric – American electric car produced in 1914.

Mascotte – American car produced in 1911.

Maserati – Italian car line produced from 1926 to date by Officine Alfieri Maserati SpA. Popular models include: Quattroporte, Biturbo, Khamsin, and Merak.

   The U.S. representative is Maserati Automobiles, Inc., headquartered in Baltimore, Maryland.

Mason – American steam car produced from 1898-1899 by William B. Mason. Also, an American car produced from 1906-1910 by Mason Motor Car Co. in Iowa (1906-1908), and Mason Automobile Co. in Iowa (1908-1910). Also, an American car produced in 1922.

Mason, George – First president of American Motors Corporation in 1954.

Mason Steamer – American steam car produced in 1898.

Massachusetts – American car produced in 1901.

Massillon – American car produced in 1909.

Master – American car produced from 1917-1918 by Master Motor Car Co. in Ohio.

master cylinder – Device used in a hydraulic brake system to store brake fluid and force it to wheel cylinders when a brake pedal is pushed.

Matador – American car produced from 1971-1978 by American Motors Corp. in Michigan. Also, an American car produced from 1960-1961 by Dodge Division of Chrysler Corp. in Michigan.

match race – Race run where two out of three, or three out of five victories wins the race.

Mather – American car produced in 1901.

Matheson – American car produced from 1903-1912 by Matheson Motor Car Co. in Michigan, Massachusetts, and Pennsylvania.

Mathews – American car produced in 1907.

Mathewson – American car produced in 1904.

Mathis – American car produced from 1930-1931.

Matilda – American car produced in 1894.

Matra – French car manufacturer formed in 1965 to make race cars.

Maumee – American car produced in 1906.

Maverick – American car produced from 1969-1979 by Ford Motor Co. in Michigan.

Maxfer – American car produced in 1919.

Maxim – American car produced in 1912, 1920, and 1928.

Maxima – Cloud 9 car model produced by Ford in the 1960s. It was to be a jet propelled three-wheeled car with projected speeds faster than the speed of sound.

Maxim-Goodridge – American car produced in 1908.

Maxim Motortricycle – American car produced in 1895.

maximum rpm – Highest rpm an engine can safely be operated.

Maxwell – American car produced from 1904-1925 by Maxwell-Brisoce Motor Co. in New York (1904-1913) and Maxwell Motor Corp. in Michigan (1913-1925).

Maxwell-Briscoe – See Maxwell (1904-1913).

Maxwell, Jonathan – Inventor/organizer involved in the design of the Oldsmobile and Northern cars, and the organization of the Maxwell-Briscoe Company that produced a $500 two cylinder engine car.

May – American car produced in 1912.

Mayflower – Plymouth car.

Mayer – American car produced in 1899 and 1913.

Mayfair – American car produced in 1925.

mayhem – Crime defined as willfully injuring another person in order to: make him less able to defend himself, cripple, and/or mutilate him.

Maytag – American car produced from 1910-1915 by Maytag-Mason Motor Co. in Iowa.

Mazda – Japanese car line produced from 1960 to date by Toyo Kogyo Group. Popular models include: RX (1963 to date), Capella, Cosmo, Familia, Luce, and Savanna. Mazda became famous for using a rotary engine.

   The U.S. representative is Mazda Motors of America, Inc., headquartered in Compton, California.

Mazda Motors Corporation – Japanese car manufacturer known for producing Mazda cars. The firm was called Toyo Kogyo Company Ltd. until 1984.

MB – American car produced in 1910.

MC – Abbreviation for Monaco found usually on an international license plate.

McCarron – American car produced in 1929.

McCormick – American car produced in 1899.

McCrea – American car produced from 1906-1908.

McCue – American car produced from 1909-1911 by McCue Co. in Connecticut.

McCullough – American car produced from 1899-1900 by Backbay Cycle & Motor Co. in Massachusetts.

McCurdy – American car produced in 1922.

McDonald – American car produced in 1923.

McDonald, Arthur – He set a world land speed record of 104.7 mph in 1905

driving a Napier 6 Cylinder.
McFarlan – American car produced from 1910-1928 by McFarlan Motor Car Co. in Indiana.
McGee Steamer – American steam car produced in 1937.
McGill – American car produced in 1922.
McIntyre – American car produced from 1909-1915 by W.H. McIntyre Co. in Indiana.
McKay – American steam car produced from 1900-1902 by Stanley Mfg. Co. in Massachusetts. It was essentially a Stanley design modified to avoid patent infringement. Also, a Canadian car produced from 1911-1914.
McLaughlin – Canadian car produced from 1908-1922 by McLaughlin Motor Car Co. in Ontario. It was coined "Canada's Standard Car".
McLean – American car produced in 1910.
McNabb – American car produced in 1910.
McNamara, Robert – He was one of Ford Motor Company's presidents who resigned to becomes Secretary of Defense during the Kennedy administration.
MDT – Abbreviation for Mountain Daylight Time.
Mead – American car produced in 1912.
mean effective pressure – Average cylinder pressure developed during a power stroke minus the cylinder pressure developed during the intake, compression, and exhaust strokes. It is a value used in determining indicated horsepower.
mean motor scooter – High performance engine.
Mearo – American car produced in 1909.
Mears, Rich – He won the Indianapolis 500 Race in 1979 and 1984. Average speeds were 158.9 and 163.6 mph. Cars driven were The Gould Charge and Pennzoil Z-7.
Mecca – American car produced from 1914-1916 by Mecca Motor Car Co. in New Jersey (1914-1915), and Times Square Automobile Co. in Michigan (1915-1916).
mechanic – Person skilled in using tools and in repairing machines. Almost anyone can call himself a mechanic. No trade test or license is required in most states. See also job(car mechanic).
mechanical advance – See centrifugal advance.
mechanical brakes – See brake(mechanical).
mechanical efficiency – Measure made of an engine's mechanical efficiency by determining the ratio of brake horsepower to indicated horsepower, or power produced by the pistons divided by power available at the flywheel.
mechanical failure – Mechanical device or assemblage of parts characterized by its failure to continue working. For example, a starter has mechanically failed when it is no longer able to start a car.
mechanical fuel pump – Pump built to move fuel to an engine's carburetor via a lever operated by an engine's cam. The lever is attached to a flexible diaphragm in the pump body which pumps the fuel by its up and down movement. A mechanical fuel pump relies on engine rotation to function, while an electric fuel pump relies on electricity. See also electric fuel pump.
mechanically sound – Used car condition characterized by the powertrain and other mechanical components being in good operating condition.
mechanical noise – Sound generated from moving parts. See also sound.
mechanical trouble – Car problem(s) determined to be mechanical in nature.
mechanic apprentice – Person enrolled in a car trade school and working under the strict supervision of a skilled mechanic in order to learn his trade.
mechanic on duty – Mechanic scheduled to be working at a car repair business during a certain time or shift.
Mechanics – American car produced in 1925.
mechanic's lien – Claim agreed to, usually when signing a repair order, that puts your car up as security for the repair work debt to be incurred. The lien is lifted when you pay for the repairs. A lien is usually in fine print on the front or back of the repair order bill. Be sure to read it carefully before signing. With a mechanic's lien, you are placing yourself at the complete mercy of a repair shop. If you are not careful, they can bill you for any amount they decide on, and hold your car until you pay the bill. If you refuse to pay, even for a valid reason, the mechanic can legally sell your car to pay off the repair costs. The sale of your car can begin in a few days after a notice appears in a newspaper. If the sale of the car does not pay off the debt, the mechanic can take you to court for the balance. If you decide to take the shop to court, you will likely lose two ways: first it's your word against theirs and they are the "experts", and secondly you will have your car tied up until the case comes to court which is often months away.
    A mechanic's lien works for the mechanic. You are safe from this type lien if you don't own the car and are still making payments on it, since a new owner must be provided with a certificate of title. If you own the car and the shop is already working on it, you could pay and then stop payment on your check or simply take your car back physically until the dispute is settled. If your dispute is legitimate, this approach should hold up in court.

You can avoid getting into the above problems with liens if you follow some guidelines. They include: modifying the repair order to include an estimate of labor and parts in writing, initialing all the estimate items, adding a clause that only initialed items are to be done or installed, crossing out any remaining blank lines, and stating that all used parts are to be saved for inspection. Once this is done, you know what it's going to cost and the mechanic is forced to call and get your approval for any additional work. If you leave the repair order blank, it's like giving someone a blank check where they can fill in what they want. See also lien sale.

mechanic's pride - High opinion held by a mechanic of his work.

mechanic's skills - Talents possessed by a mechanic for doing good repair work on cars.

mechanic's special - Car with lots of mechanical problems and usually not a good buy.

mechanic's stethoscope - Sensitive listening tool used to detect abnormal noises or listen to the inner operation of moving parts. It looks similar to a doctor's stethoscope except for its long metal probe.

mechanic's time - See labor time.

Med-Bow - American car produced from 1907-1908.

Medcraft - American car produced from 1907-1908.

Media - American car produced in 1900 and 1907.

median - See median strip.

median strip - Center of a highway used to divide opposing traffic. It can be a barrier, or strip of land (usually landscaped or naturally covered).

Meech-Stoddard - American car produced in 1924.

Meislbach - American car produced from 1904-1909.

Melbourne - American car produced in 1904.

Mel Special - American car produced in 1923.

melting point - Temperature reached when a solid substance changes to a liquid.

MEMA - Abbreviation for Motor and Equipment Manufacturers Association.

Menard - Canadian car produced from 1908-1910 by Windsor Carriage & Wagon Works in Ontario. Also, an American car produced in 1921.

Menges - American car produced in 1908.

Menominee - American car produced in 1915.

Menominee Truck - American truck produced in 1920.

Merc - Abbreviation for a Mercury car.

Mercedes - American car produced in 1902.

Mercedes 4 Cylinder - Car driven by William Vanderbilt to a 1904 world land speed record of 92.3 mph at Daytona, Florida.

Mercedes Benz - West German car produced from 1926 to date by Daimler Benz AG. The U.S. representative is Mercedes-Benz of North America, headquartered in Montvale, New Jersey.

Mercedes C111 - Prototype car built in the 1960s by the German Mercedes car company to research and develop the possibilities of the Wankel engine. The car had a fiberglass body, gull wing doors, and a top speed of 187 mph.

Mercer - American car produced in 1909-1925 and 1931 by Mercer Automobile Co. in New Jersey, and Elcar Motor Car Co. in Indiana respectively.

Merchant - American car produced in 1914.

Merciless - American car produced in 1907.

Mercu - American car produced from 1909-1929.

Mercur - American car produced from 1985 to date by Mercury Division of Ford Motor Co. in Michigan.

mercury - Metal element characterized as heavy, silver-white, and fluid at room temperatures. It melts and boils at -38 and 674 degrees Fahrenheit.

Mercury - An American car produced in 1904, 1914, 1918-1920, 1922, and 1930. Also, an American car line produced from 1938 to date by Mercury Division of Ford Motor Co. in Michigan.

mercury column - One of the legs in a manometer.

Mercury Special - American car produced in 1946 by Paul Omohundro in California. It was an aluminum body car.

merging - The union of two separate traffic flows into one.

merging traffic - Driving maneuver performed where two roadways converge into one such as a freeway on ramp. Cars in both converging lanes are required to adjust their speed and proximity to each other to avoid a collision.

Merit - American car produced from 1920-1923 by Merit Motor Co. in Ohio.

Merkel - American car produced from 1905-1906 and 1914 by Merkel Mfg. Co. in Wisconsin, and J.F. Merkel in Ohio respectively.

Merry 'Ol - American car produced from 1958-1962 by American Air Products Corp. in Florida. It was a steel and plywood replica of the Oldsmobile curved dash runabout. A 4 hp air cooled Clinton engine was used. Top speed was 35 mph with a claimed 60 mpg fuel economy.

Merz - American car produced from 1914-1915 by Merz Cyclecar Co. in Indiana.

Meserve - American car produced in 1904.

meshing gears - To engage two or more rotating gears together in order to

transfer rotation from one to another.
mesh pattern - See contact pattern.
Messerer - American car produced in 1901.
met - Abbreviation for metallic or metal.
metal conditioner - Solvent used on bare metal to etch it for paint adhesion.
   See also prepcoat and paint(undercoat).
metallic paint - See paint(metallic).
Metcar - American car produced in 1901.
Meteor - American car produced from 1900-1903, 1905-1910, and 1914-1930 by
   Springfield Cornice Works in Massachusetts (1900), Meteor Engineering in
   Pennsylvania (1902-1903), Worthington Automobile in New York (1905-1906),
   Meteor Motor Car Co. in Iowa (1907-1910), Meteor Motor Car Co. in Indiana and
   Ohio (1914-1930), and Meteor Motors in Pennsylvania (1919-1922). Also, a
   Canadian car produced from 1949-1970 by Ford Motor Co. of Canada in Ontario.
   Also, an American car produced from 1955-1972 by Mercury Division of Ford
   Motor Co. in Michigan.
meter - Metric measurement of length. One meter equals 39.37 inches.
metering rod - Tapered movable rod located in a carburetor's main jet opening.
   When it is withdrawn, the rod gets smaller in diameter and fuel flow
   increases. This system is used on some carburetors instead of a power jet
   and power valve assembly.
metering valve - Valve used in a brake system to control pressure to the front
   disc brakes. It is usually mounted where the front brake line splits to each
   wheel. A faulty valve can cause the front end to pull one way or another.
   See also proportioning valve and differential valve.
methane - Gaseous methane series hydrocarbon compound. It occurs as the
   primary ingredient in natural gas. It is the simplest hydrocarbon, existing
   as a colorless, odorless, tasteless gas with a melting and boiling point of -
   296 and -259 degrees Fahrenheit respectively. Cars run well on methane, but
   the very low boiling point makes the gas difficult to economically compress
   into a liquid for storage and transportation. See also marsh gas.
methane series - Classification assigned to group a series of chemically
   related solid, liquid, and gaseous hydrocarbon compounds together. Methane
   is the light member of the group with the lowest boiling point. It is also
   sometimes known as the paraffin series.
methanol - Alcohol characterized as colorless, odorless, inflammable, water
   soluble, volatile, and poisonous. It is commonly produced by the
   destructive distillation of wood, or from garbage, natural gas, or coal. It
   is the alcohol commonly used in car engines. See also ethanol, gasohol, and
   alcohol.
metric size - Item built to metric dimensions.
Metropol - American car produced from 1913-1914 by Metrol Motors Corp. in New
   York.
Metropolitan - American car produced from 1922-1923 by Metropolitan Motors in
   Missouri. Also, an American car produced from 1954-1961 by Austin Motor Co.
   in Britain for American Motors Corp. in Wisconsin. It was a small three
   passenger coupe.
metropolitan area - Large busy city area.
Metz - American car produced from 1908-1922 by Waltham Mfg. Co. (1908-1909),
   and Metz Co. (1909-1922), both in Massachusetts.
Metzcar - American car produced from 1909-1912.
Metz, Charles - He manufactured the low priced Metz 22, and was an advocate of
   smaller, low priced cars.
Metzger - American car produced in 1909.
MEWA - Abbreviation for Motor and Equipment Wholesalers Association.
MEX - Abbreviation for Mexico found usually on an international license plate.
Meyer - American car produced in 1919.
Meyer, Louis - He won the Indianapolis 500 Race in 1928, 1933, and 1936.
   Average driving speeds were 99.5, 104.2, 109.1 mph. Cars driven were a
   Miller Special, Tydol Special, and Ring Free Special.
MG - British car line produced from 1924-1980 by Jaguar Rover Triumph (1978-
   1980). The MG designation originally stood for Morris Garages located in
   Oxford, England.
MG Midget - Low priced British sports car first produced in the 1930s.
mi - Abbreviation for miles.
Michelet - American car produced in 1921.
Michelin - Line of tires originally produced in France, but now also produced
   in the United States and Canada by the Michelin Tire Corporation.
Michigan - American car produced from 1903-1914 by Michigan Automobile Co.
   (1903-1908), and Michigan Buggy Co. (1908-1914), both in Michigan.
Michigan Hearse - American car produced in 1914.
Michigan Steamer - American steam car produced from 1908-1909.
mickey - Loan secured in order to make a car downpayment.
mickey mouse - See downstroke.
micrometer - Precision tool used for measuring dimensions to 1/1000 of an

inch.

Midas – Car repair business chain engaged in installing mufflers, entire exhaust systems, shock absorbers, and brakes.

Middleby – American car produced from 1908-1913 by Middleby Auto Co. in Pennsylvania.

middleman – See jobber.

Middletown – American car produced from 1909-1911 by Middletown Buggy Co. in Ohio.

midget racer – Small racing car built with a wheel base under 76 inches.

Midgley – American car produced in 1905.

Midland – American car produced from 1908-1913 by Midland Motor Co. in Illinois.

midnight auto parts – Parts stolen from legal cars.

midrange power – Engine power available at 50 percent of an engine's maximum allowable rpm.

mid-size – Medium size car characterized by offering room and reasonable gas mileage. It represents a good family car choice. Price usually ranges from $6,500-9,500. It usually weighs less than 3,500 lbs. Wheelbase ranges from 112-118 inches.

Midwest Tractor – American car produced in 1918.

Mier – American car produced from 1908-1909.

Miesusset – American car produced in 1907.

MIG – Abbreviation for Metal Inert Gas. See also welding(MIG).

Mighty Michigan – American car produced in 1913.

MIG torch – Torch body used to MIG weld.

MIG welding – See welding(MIG).

Mikuni – Line of carburetors.

mil – Unit of length equal to 1/1,000 of an inch. See also circular mil.

Mil – Abbreviation for milestone car.

Milac – American car produced in 1916.

Milburn Electric – American electric car produced from 1915-1924. It was one of the most popular American electric cars with over 7,000 being made. Several were used by the Secret Service under President Wilson.

mile post – Post located on a road indicating the number of miles from a certain point. The reference point is often a state line. See also road sign(milepost).

miles on a car – The number of miles a car has been driven since it was new.

milestone car – Car generally classified as built from 1945-1967. See also brass era car, vintage car, antique car, contemporary car, special interest car, classic car, contemporary classic car, pre-war car, and post-war car.

mill(1) – To cut, grind, and/or shape parts with a milling machine.

mill(2) – An engine.

milled head – Cylinder head's flat surface machined to increase flatness or increase an engine's compression ratio. It has the same effect as lengthening the piston stroke.

Mille Miglia – Italian race run from the town of Brescia to Rome and back. It covered 1009.5 miles. The races were held from 1926 to 1955.

Miller – American car produced in 1903 and 1907-1908. Also, an American car produced from 1912-1913 and 1915-1932 by Miller Car Co. in Michigan, and Harry A. Miller and Rellimah in California respectively.

Miller Special – American car produced from 1907-1908.

millimeter – Metric measurement equal to 1/1000 of a meter. It is also equivalent to 0.03937 inches.

Mills Milwaukee – American car produced in 1900.

Milton, Tommy – He won the Indianapolis 500 Race in 1921 and 1923 driving an average of 89.6 and 100.0 mph in a Frontenac and HCS Special respectively. He also set a world land speed record of 156.0 mph in 1920 driving a Duesenberg 16.

Milwaukee – American steam car produced from 1900-1902 by Milkwaukee Automobile Co. in Wisconsin. Also, an American car produced in 1906.

mineral oil – See oil(mineral).

mini deal – Alternate dealing method to low balling used where only a minimum profit is desired.

mini service – Service offered at service stations where gas is pumped for for but no car checks are made.

Ministry of International Trade and Industry – Japanese regulatory agency similar to the USA's Department of Commerce and the Interstate Commerce Commission.

mini-van – Smaller version of a full size van.

Minneapolis – American car produced in 1919.

Mino – American car produced in 1914.

minor – Person under legal age. In most states, legal age is 18.

mint condition – Condition of a used car created when it has been very well taken care of.

Mirada – American car produced from 1980 to date by Dodge Division of Chrysler

Corp. in Michigan.

Miranda card — Card used by certain police departments, containing the constitutional rights a suspect is to be informed of before arrest. Arresting officers will either read from the card or have the suspect: read it aloud, ask if he understands his rights, then sign it.

Miranda decision — Court decision made requiring law enforcement officers to inform suspected criminals of their constitutional rights.

misdemeanor — Any minor offense characterized as requiring a lesser punishment than for a felony. Punishment is usually less than one year in jail.

misfeasance — See malfeasance.

misfiring — Condition created when a spark plug does not generate a spark to ignite a fuel/air mixture in an engine cylinder. Possible causes include: fouled spark plug, faulty ignition coil, excessive resistance in high voltage wiring, and high voltage requirements at plug gap too great. See also spark plug voltage, engine problem(misfiring), and induction firing.

mismatched tires — Tires installed on a car that have different overall tire diameters. Mismatching creates speedometer and car handling problems, and loss in performance.

miss — Spark plug condition created when it receives no spark, and thus does not ignite an air/fuel mixture in a combustion chamber.

missed the exit — Condition created when a driver passes a road exit he intended to use.

missing — Engine condition created when one or more spark plugs are unable to ignite an air/fuel mixture in a combustion chamber. Missing is caused by lack of spark. Possible causes include: fouled spark plug(s); wet secondary wires, distributor, and/or ignition coil; faulty ignition coil; faulty low voltage distributor wire; carbon tracking in distributor cap; and broken or high resistance secondary wire(s). See also fouled spark plugs.

Mission — American car produced in 1914.

mistrial — Trial made void by: an error in the proceedings, lack of jurisdiction by a court, and/or inability of a jury to reach a verdict.

Mitchell(1) — American car produced from 1903-1923 by Mitchell Motor Car Co. in Wisconsin (1903-1910), Mitchell-Lewis Motor Co. in Wisconsin (1910-1916), and Mitchell Motors Co. in Wisconsin (1916-1923).

Mitchell(2) — Line of automotive repair manuals. See also Chilton, Hanes, and Motor.

MITI — Abbreviation for Japan's Ministry of International Trade and Industry.

Mitsubishi — Japanese car line produced from 1917-1921 and 1959 to date by Mitsubishi Motors Corp. Ltd. Popular models include: Chariot, Cordia, Debonair, Galant, Jeep, Lancer, Minica, Mirage, Pajero, Starion, and Tredia.

Miura — Lamborghini sports car named after Spanish fighting bulls.

mixed base oil — See oil(mixed base).

Mixit — See Porsche-Lohner Chaise.

mixture control solenoid — Solenoid device used to control the amount of fuel metered into a carburetor airway. See also carburetor(feedback).

ML — See service rating(ML).

mldg — Abbreviation for molding.

MM — See service rating(MM).

MME — Device built to allow a car trailer to operate double filament lights and a car to operate single filament. It is used on cars with European lighting (separate brake, tail, and turn signal lights).

M mi — Abbreviation for thousand miles. See also K mi.

Mobil 1 — Tradename used by Mobil Oil Corporation for a synthetic motor oil.

Mobile — American steam car produced from 1899-1903 by Mobile Company of America in New York.

Mobilette — American car produced from 1913-1915. Also, an American electric car produced beginning in 1965 by Mobilette Electric Cars in California.

Mobil Oil Corporation — A U.S. petroleum company headquartered in New York, New York. See also petroleum company.

Mock — American car produced in 1906.

mode-and-blend door — Small door used in a car's heating and air conditioning duct system to regulate the flow of warm and/or cool air to certain ducts. Most cars equipped with climate control systems use several. They are usually controlled by vacuum solenoid valves. When one or more malfunctions, the doors remain shut or open and can be the reason why no warm or cold air circulates regardless of control settings.

mode door — See recirculating door.

Model — American car produced from 1903-1909 by Model Gas Engine Co. (1903-1906), and Model Automobile Co. (1906-1909), both in Indiana.

model — Car's name following the make such as Colt, Celica, Escort, Firebird, etc. See also sub-model, make, and body type.

Model A — The car built to succeed the Model T, produced by the Ford Motor Company.

Model T — First successful car produced by the Ford Motor Company in 1908. It became the most popular car in America by 1911 selling at a rate of 50,000 per year. By 1927, it cost 1/3 the 1908 price. No major changes were made in the design during all those years. It was nicknamed the "Tin Lizzie". The engine ran at only 1500 rpms and the vehicle had a top speed of 40 mph. It was the first real "drive anywhere car".

Model T coil – See ignition coil(vibrator type).

model year – Year a given model car is produced.

model year updating – Shady practice used by many car dealers in which last year's models are updated so a 1984, for example, becomes a 1985. A prospective buyer should determine the actual car year before purchasing just to be safe. This can be done with serial numbers, etc. See also con game(last year's model) and con game(model year updating).

Modern – American car produced in 1907-1910 and 1912.

modesty panel – Car panel located below bumpers to conceal car chassis members. It is also called a modesty skirt.

Modoc – American car produced in 1913.

modulator – See transmission modulator.

modulator pipe – Vacuum line running from the intake manifold to a transmission modulator mounted on an automatic transmission.

modulator valve – See throttle valve(2).

modus operandi – A way of doing or making something.

Moehn – American car produced in 1895.

Moeller – American car produced in 1911.

Mogul – American car produced in 1912.

Mohawk – American car produced from 1903-1904 and 1914-1915 by Mohawk Auto & Cycle Co. in Indiana, and Mohawk Motor Co. in Massachusetts respectively.

Mohler – American car produced in 1901.

Mohler & DeGress – American car produced from 1901-1905.

molding – Strip of material used to decorate, accent a car body line, conceal construction joints, or protect a surface.

Mohs – American car produced beginning in 1968 by Mohs Seaplane Corp. in Wisconsin. It was a very unusual and expensive car. Features included: rear entry, cantilever seats, and refrigerator.

moisture build-up – Accumulation of moisture in an engine. Moisture will accumulate on metal surfaces and usually finds its way to the oil pan. Possible causes include: crankcase ventilation system venting too much or little, excessive short driving trips, and internal cooling system leak.

Moligan – American car produced in 1920.

Moline – American car produced from 1904-1913 by Moline Automobile Co. in Illinois.

Moline-Knight – American car produced from 1914-1919 by Moline Automobile Co. in Illinois.

Moller – American car produced from 1920-1921 by Moller Motor Car Co. in Pennsylvania.

MON – Abbreviation for Motor Octane Number.

Monaco – American car produced from 1962 to date by Dodge Division of Chrysler Corp. in Michigan.

Monarch – American car produced from 1905-1909 and 1914-1917 by Monarch Motor Car Co. in Illinois (1905-1909), Monarch Machine Co. in Iowa (1908), Monarch Motor Car Co. in Michigan (1914-1917). Also, a Canadian car produced from 1946-1961 by Ford Motor Co. of Canada in Ontario. Also, an American car produced from 1965 to date by Mercury Division of Ford Motor Co. in Michigan.

Moncrieff – American car produced from 1901-1902 by J.A. Moncrieff Co. in Rhode Island.

Mondex-Magic – American car produced in 1914.

monger – Lousy car dealer or car.

Monitor – American car produced in 1909 and 1915-1922 by Monitor Automobile Works in Wisconsin, and Cummins Monitor Co. and Monitor Motor Car Co. in Ohio respectively.

monkey wrench – Adjustable open end wrench built to open by moving one side of the opening down the wrench handle.

mono block – Engine block built with all cylinders contained in one casting.

monocar – See body style(cyclecar).

monocoque – See body style(monocoque).

Monroe(1) – American car produced from 1914-1924 by Monroe Motor Co. in Michigan (1914-1918), W. Small Co. in Michigan (1918-1922), and Premier Motor Corp. in Indiana (1923-1924).

Monroe(2) – American line of shock absorbers produced by Monroe Auto Equipment Co.

Monsen – American car produced from 1908-1909.

Montclair – American car produced from 1910-1914 by H.J. Koehler Co. in New Jersey.

Monte Carlo – American car produced from 1962 to date by Chevrolet Division of General Motors Corp. in Michigan.

Montego – American car produced from 1968-1977 by Mercury Division of Ford Motor Co. in Michigan.

Monterey – American car produced from 1955–1977 by Mercury Division of Ford Motor Co. in Michigan.

Montgomery Ward Auto Club – Large U.S. auto brokerage organization.

Monza – American car produced from 1971–1980 by Chevrolet Division of General Motors Corp. in Michigan.

Moody – American car produced in 1900.

Mooers – American car produced in 1900.

Moon – American car produced from 1905–1930 by Moon Motor Car Co. in Missouri.

moon – Solid spun aluminum wheel covers.

moonlighting – To work at another job after a regular full time job.

moonroof – Round sunroof mounted in a car's roof.

Moore – American car produced in 1902–1903. Also, an American car produced in 1906 and 1916–1921 by Moore Automobile Co. in Washington, and Moore Motor Vehicle Co. in Minnesota respectively.

Moorespring Vehicle Steam – American vehicle produced in 1888.

Moose Jaw Standard – Canadian car produced from 1916–1918 by Canadian Standard Auto & Tractor Co. in Saskatchewan.

MoPar – Abbreviation for Chrysler Corporation.

Mora – American car produced from 1906–1910 by Mora Motor Car Co. in New York.

Moreland Truck – American truck produced from 1910–1912.

Morlock – American car produced in 1903.

Morgan – American car produced in 1897 and 1908–1909. Also, a British car line produced from 1910 to date by Morgan Motor Co. Ltd.

Morgan – British sports car.

Morlock – American car produced in 1903.

Mor-Power – American car produced in 1921.

Morris – British car line produced from 1913 to date by Light Medium Cars Division, BL Cars Ltd. A popular model was the Morris Minor (1950–1971).

Morris-London – American car produced in 1922.

Morris Salom Electrobat – American electric car produced from 1895–1897.

Morrison – American electric car produced from 1890–1896. It was the second American built electric car and the first sold commercially.

Morrissey – American car produced in 1925.

Morriss-London – American car produced from 1919–1925 by Crow-Elkart Motor Car Co. in Indiana, and Century Motor Co. in Indiana.

Mors – American car produced in 1901 and 1906.

Mors 4 Cylinder – French car driven by Augieres to a 1902 world land speed record of 77.1 mph at Dourdan, France.

Morse – American car produced from 1904–1917 by Morse Motor Vehicle Co. in Massachusetts (1904–1909), Easton Machine Co. in Massachusetts (1909–1916), and Morse Cyclecar Co. in Pennsylvania (1914–1917).

Morse Steam Car – American steam car produced from 1904–1906 by Morse Motor Vehicle Co. in Massachusetts.

Mort – American car produced in 1925.

motel – Roadside hotel built to provide road travelers with lodging and nearby parking space.

Motor – Line of automotive repair manuals. See also Chilton, Hanes, and Mitchell(2).

motor – Device built to produce motion or rotation. Also, it refers to an engine.

motor(AC) – Machine built to use alternating electrical current to create mechanical energy.

motor(DC) – Machine built to use direct electrical current to create mechanical energy. The direction of rotation can be reversed by reversing current polarity.

motor(DC-compensated compound wound) – Shunt wound motor built with several light series windings. It is used for fixed load and even speed applications with high initial inertia to overcome (turning heavy wheels, etc.). It is not commonly used in car.

motor(DC-compound wound) – Motor built with series and shunt type windings. It is used where heavy starting loads are encountered with the subsequent need for even power at different speeds. It is commonly used in automotive accessories requiring multi-speeds (heater, windshield wiper, etc.).

motor(DC-lightly compounded) – Compound wound motor with a minor amount of shunt type windings.

motor(DC-permanent magnet) – Motor built with permanent magnets in place of field windings. It operates similar to a shunt wound motor. It is used as a windshield wiper motor, and is commonly used as a generator on motorcycles.

motor(DC-series wound) – Motor built with field windings connected to armature brushes. Current passes through field windings before reaching armature. It is well suited for heavy loads such as starting, raising/lowering convertible tops, and radio antennas. It can overspeed without a load.

motor(DC-shunt wound) – Motor built with current flowing separately to field windings and armature. It is commonly used where constant speed is needed under varying loads.

motor(electric) – Machine used to transform electrical energy into mechanical energy.

motor(external combustion) – Machine used to transform the heat of a fuel burned externally in mechanical energy. See also motor(internal combustion).

motor(internal combustion) – Machine used to transform the heat and pressure of a fuel burned inside a confined space into mechanical energy. See also engine.

motor buggy – See high wheeler.

Motor Buggy – American car produced from 1908-1910.

motorcade – Parade or procession of cars.

Motorcar – American car produced from 1906-1908.

motorcar – See car.

motor coach – Passenger bus powered by an engine.

motor court – See motel.

Motorcraft – Line of U.S. car products.

motorcycle – Two-wheeled powered vehicle similar to a bicycle.

motorcyclist – Person skilled in riding a motorcycle.

motor drome – Race course built rounded for cars or motorcycles.

Motorette – American car produced in 1906, 1910-1912, and 1946.

motor home – Small bus constructed with small apartment-like living quarters behind the driver's area.

motor horn – See horn.

motoring – To travel or drive in a car.

motoring public – Those people characterized as travelers by car.

motorist – Person driving a car.

motorize – To furnish with a motor.

motor lodge – See motel.

motor lorry – See truck. Also, it refers to an open sided truck.

motorman – Person engaged in operating an electrically powered vehicle such as a bus or subway.

motor minded – Person inclined to see his environment in mechanical or muscular activity terms.

motor mount – Molded rubber pad designed with metal brackets on both sides that attach it to an engine and a car frame. It is used to support an engine and dampen its vibrations. Two are usually installed, one on each side of the engine block.

Motor Octane Number Method – Laboratory engine test method used to evaluate the antiknock quality of gasoline in a standard single cylinder engine subjected to higher rpm, higher fuel mixture temperatures, and more severe operating conditions than in the RON test. MON numbers typically average 8-10 less than RON numbers. See also Research Octane Number Method, MON, R-100 Method, Distribution Octane Method, and Antiknock Index.

motor oil – See oil(motor).

motor pulls easily – Car engine condition created when it produces enough power to accelerate quickly and climb steep hills.

motor scooter – See motorcycle.

Motor Trend magazine – Magazine devoted to stock and custom car information, products, research, tests, etc. It first reached the newsstands in 1948.

Motor Truck – American truck produced in 1902.

motor truck – See truck.

motor vehicle – Car, truck, bus, etc. equipped with a motor and tires, and driven on roads.

motor vehicle liability insurance – See insurance(liability).

motorway – See expressway.

Motown – The city of Detroit, Michigan.

mountain driving – To drive a car or other vehicle in mountainous terrain.

Mountain Road – American car produced in 1917.

mount the tire – To place a tire casing on a wheel. Specialized equipment is used to perform the task.

mouse house(1) – See blood bank.

mouse house(2) – Car dealer characterized by selling older cars at high prices to people with low incomes. See also iron peddler.

mouse milk – Special gasoline or oil additive regarded as being of little value.

movable breaker plate – See distributor point plate.

Mover – American car produced in 1902.

moving core – Movable magnetic core used in a solenoid switch.

moving violation – Traffic law violation made by a driver when operating a car in motion such as speeding. If noticed by a policeman, a traffic citation is often issued.

moxie – Additional horsepower added to an engine.

Moyea – American car produced from 1902-1904 by Moyea Automobile Co. in New York.

Moyer – American car produced from 1911-1915 by H.A. Moyer in New York.

MPC – American car produced in 1925.

mpg - Abbreviation for miles per gallon.
mpg gauge - Gauge used to measure actual flow rate of fuel to a carburetor.
mpg rating - Rated mpg of a car exhibited under certain driving conditions.
Today's cars are mpg rated for city and highway driving.
mph - Abbreviation for miles per hour. It is a measurement of car speed.
MPM - American car produced from 1914-1915 by Mount Pleasant Motor Co. in
Michigan.
MS - See service rating(MS).
MST - Abbreviation for Mountain Standard Time.
M/T - Abbreviation for manual transmission. See also A/T and T/M.
Mt Pleasant - American car produced from 1914-1916.
mud - See solder(plastic).
mud apron - Cover mounted underneath an engine to prevent rocks, debris, mud,
etc. from getting into an engine compartment.
mud flaps - Metal or rubber flaps mounted behind wheels to catch mud flying
off tires and minimize build-up on a car body.
mudguard(1) - Set mud flaps.
mudguard(2) - Fender.
Mueller - American car produced in 1895-1900 by Meuller & Co. in Illinois.
Mueller-Benz - American car produced in 1895.
Mueller-Trap - American car produced in 1901.
muffler - Chambered metal enclosure constructed of various materials to cool
exhaust gases and help quiet their roaring sound as they explode out of the
engine cylinders. It is placed between an exhaust pipe and a tailpipe.
Mufflers wear out because a by product of the combustion process is water
which condenses in an exhaust system and mixes with acids and other compounds
to cause corrosion and rust. Most mufflers on the market today are not
designed to last a long time. If they were, the muffler business would not
make a very good living. Today's mufflers are usually lightly coated with
zinc. Long lasting stainless steel and ceramic coated mufflers are usually
hard to get.
muffler(bullet) - See muffler(glass pack).
muffler(ceramic) - Muffler built with the interior surfaces coated with
ceramic material to resist corrosion.
muffler(glass pack) - Low restriction performance muffler built for straight
through flow of exhaust gases. It uses uses fiberglass strands to muffle
exhaust noise. Shaped like a bullet, they are cheap mufflers and get noisy
after a short period of time due to the fiberglass shifting around and
packing together.
muffler(low restriction) - Muffler built to minimize resistance to exhaust gas
flow.
muffler(reverse flow) - Muffler built to reverse exhaust gas flow direction
twice before exiting. It is used to conserve space.
muffler(stainless steel) - Muffler built of stainless steel. Such mufflers
are highly resistant to corrosion.
muffler(straight through) - Muffler built for straight through gas flow from
front to back. The central pipe is perforated. A muffler shell surrounds
the pipe. The air space between the shell and pipe can be open or filled
with a material for sound deadening.
muffler(turbo) - Performance muffler built for low back pressure and noise.
muffler is shot - Muffler condition created when it can no longer contain
exhaust gases coming from an engine. Usually, the muffler has rusted or
corroded out in places due to the nature of the exhaust gases. A quick
method of determining if the muffler is causing the rumbling noise is to
start a car, let the engine idle for a few minutes, then stuff a rag into the
tailpipe. If the engine quits, there are no sizable leaks in the exhaust
system. If the engine continues to run, the gases are leaking out somewhere
else.
muffler pusher - Car repairman skilled in pressuring people to buy mufflers
for their cars as a solution to their current car problem.
muffler rubber insulator - One of two or more rubber strips used to mount a
muffler, cushion it from road irregularities, and isolate its vibration from
a car body.
muffler shop - Business engaged in installing exhaust systems on cars and
trucks. They may also install shocks, brakes, etc., depending on the
business.
Mulford - American car produced in 1909.
multilane freeway - Freeway with several lanes in each direction.
multimeter - Instrument used to measure voltage, amperage, and resistance in
electrical circuits.
multiple disc clutch - See clutch(multiple disc).
multiple spark discharge - Electronic device designed to send several sparks
in rapid succession when triggered by conventional distributor points. Such
devices claim: lower emissions due to more complete combustion, better fuel
economy, and improved engine performance.

Multiplex – American car produced from 1912–1913 by Multiplex Mfg. Co. in Pennsylvania. Also, an American car produced in 1954.
multi–point injection – See fuel injection(gas–multi point).
multi–port injection – See fuel injection(gas–multi point).
multi–stall garage – Car repair business equipped with two or more stalls for working on cars or trucks.
multi–viscosity oil – See oil(multi viscosity).
Munch Allen – American car produced in 1910.
Muncie – American car produced in 1903 and 1906.
municipal court – Court empowered to represent a local government.
Munsing – American car produced in 1908 and 1913.
Munson – American car produced from 1899–1902 by Munson Electric Motor Co. in Indiana.
Muntz Jet – American car produced from 1950–1955 by Muntz Car Co. in Indiana (1950–1951), and Illinois (1951–1955).
mural – Picture painted or decaled onto a car panel.
Murdaugh – American car produced in 1901.
Murena – American car produced beginning in 1969 by Murena Motors in New York. It was a luxury station wagon.
Murphy, Jimmy – He won the Indianapolis 500 Race in 1922 driving an average of 94.5 mph in a Murphy Special.
Murray – American car produced from 1902–1903, and 1916–1918 by Church Mfg. Co. in Michigan, and Murray Motor Car Co. in Pennsylvania respectively.
Murray–Max – American car produced from 1921–1928 by Murray Motor Car Co. in Massachusetts.
muscle car – High performance car.
music and air – Radio and air conditioning options installed in a car.
Muskegon – American car produced in 1918.
Mustang – American car produced from 1964 to date by Ford Motor Co. in Michigan. Also, an American car produced in 1948.
Mutual – American car produced in 1919.
Myer B&F – American car produced in 1912.
Myers – American car produced in 1904.

N

N(1) – Abbreviation for neutral position on automatic transmission shift selectors.

N(2) – Abbreviation for Norway found usually on an international license plate.

NACA duct – Air inlet duct used to direct air into an enclosed area for cooling. It is commonly used on rear engine race cars and some stock cars. It is usually located behind the rear side windows. The duct is named after the agency that did extensive research on it, the National Advisory Committee for Aeronautics.

NACCA – Abbreviation for National Association of Claimants Compensation Attorneys.

NADA – Abbreviation for National Automobile Dealers Association.

NADA Official Used Car Guide – Monthly publication containing wholesale and retail pricing guidelines for used cars. It usually goes back about seven years, and is an official guide for car dealers, banks, etc. on used car prices. See also Kelly Blue Book.

Nader, Ralph – He is a lawyer working as a popular consumer advocate. He started the Center for Auto Safety in 1967 to pressure the Department of Transportation into strengthening safety standards. See also Center for Auto Safety.

Nadig – American car produced in 1889.

Nance – American car produced from 1911-1912.

NAPA – Abbreviation for National Automotive Parts Association.

Napier – American car produced from 1904-1912.

Napier 6 Cylinder – English car driven by Arthur E. McDonald to a 1905 world land speed record of 104.7 mph at Daytona, Florida.

Napier-Campbell Bluebird – English car driven by Malcom Campbell to a 1928 world land speed record of 207.0 mph in Daytona, Florida.

Napier V-12 Bluebird – English car driven by Malcom Campbell to a 1927 world land speed record of 174.9 mph in Pendine, Wales.

Napolean – American car produced from 1916-1917 by Napoleon Auto Mfg. Co. in Ohio.

Narragansett – American car produced in 1915.

NASCAR – Abbreviation for National Association for Stock Car Auto Racing. It is a large racing group that supports many of the United States stock car races.

Nash – American car line produced from 1917-1957 by Nash Motor Co. in Wisconsin (1917-1954), and American Motors Corp. in Wisconsin (1954-1957).

Nash, Charles – He became president of General Motors in 1912. He developed the straight-line conveyor belt, and, in 1917, purchased the Thomas B. Jeffrey Company to begin producing Nash cars.

Nash Healy – American car produced from 1951-1954.

NATB – Abbreviation for National Auto Theft Bureau.

NATCB – Abbreviation for National Automotive Technicians Certification Board.

Natco – American car produced in 1912.

National – American car produced from 1900-1924 by National Motor Vehicle Co. in Indiana (1900-1916), and National Motor Car & Vehicle Corp. in Indiana from 1916-1924.

National Association of Claimants Compensation Attorneys – Association formed in the 1950s for the purpose of teaching it members how to better protect clients injured in accidents.

National Automobile Dealers Association – Organization known for producing a used car value guide popular with dealers, and for conducting mechanic's qualification tests. Passing qualifies a mechanic as a Certified General Automobile Mechanic (GAM) through the NIASE. Mechanics must have two years of work experience before testing. See also NADA Official Use Car Guide.

National Automotive Technicians Board – Board organized to conduct qualification tests for mechanics. Passing eight of the first ten classifications gives a mechanic a rating as a master technician. Mechanics must have two years of experience before testing.

National Driver's Register – Agency established by Congress to provide information on all drivers who licenses have been suspended, revoked, or denied.

National Electric – American car produced in 1900.

National Highway Traffic Safety Administration – Federal agency created to enforce Traffic and Motor vehicle legislation passed by Congress. Their work includes: road planning and building, and car importation and recalls.

National Sextet – American car produced in 1920.
Nationwide Auto Brokers – Large U.S. auto brokerage organization.
natural gas – Naturally occurring mixture of gases commonly associated with petroleum and coal deposits. It is largely composed of methane, ethane, nitrogen, and carbon dioxide with smaller quantities of propane, butane, hexane, pentane, and helium.
Naugahyde – Trademark used for imitation leather fabric.
Navajo – American car produced from 1953-1955 by Navajo Motor Car Co. in New York.
Navarre – American car produced in 1921.
NCPR – Abbreviation for National Congress of Petroleum Refiners.
Nebraska – American car produced in 1926.
needle and seat valve – See needle valve.
needle bearing – See bearing(needle).
needle nose pliers – See long nose pliers.
needle valve – Valve used to control fuel flow into a carburetor float bowl.
negative equity – To owe more on a car than its actual wholesale value. See also equity.
negative ground – Ground used as the negative side of an electrical circuit. See also negative ground system.
negative ground system – Direct current electrical system built to use the negative side as ground and the positive side as the potential. In a negative ground car, the negative terminal of the battery is connected to the car frame or ground. Today's cars mostly use this grounding system. See also positive ground system.
negative ground wire – Battery cable used to connect the negative battery terminal to an engine chassis or ground.
negative offset steering – Steering system characteristic defined by the ball joint centerline intersecting the tread outside its centerline on the road surface. The gap is known as the scrub radius. It helps reduce brake grabbing due to unequal road friction thereby helping a car to stop in a straight line.
negative pole – See negative terminal.
negative terminal – Terminal or connection located in an electrical circuit from which current (electrons) flows on its path to the positive terminal. The negative terminal on a battery is usually grounded to a car frame. See also battery posts.
negligent driving – To drive recklessly endangering the safety of other cars and people on a road.
Neilson – American car produced in 1907.
Nelson – American car produced from 1917-1921 by E.A. Nelson Motor Car. Co. in Michigan. Also, an American car produced in 1905.
Nelson & Le Moon – American car produced from 1915-1920.
Nelson-Brennen Peterson – American car produced from 1914-1915.
neoprene – Synthetic rubber produced by the polymerization of chloroprene that is highly resistant to petroleum products, oxidation, light, and heat. It is used to make fuel lines, spark plug cable insulation, etc.
nerf bar – Car bumper.
Netco Truck – American truck produced in 1916.
net duration – Cam duration derived from a .050 inch cam lobe lift. See also gross duration and hydraulic intensity.
net payoff – The money debt ramaining on a car after subtracting any prepaid insurance premiums or loan interest.
net profit – Actual profit made in a sale.
Neustadt – American car produced in 1912.
Neustadt-Perry – American car produced from 1902-1907 by Neustadt Motor Car Co. in Missouri.
neutral clutch – See clutch(neutral).
neutralizer solution – Solution used to stop the cleaning process started by a flushing solution in an engine cooling system.
neutral point – Position found in a magnetic field where a rotating generator coil generates no voltage.
neutral position – Transmission selector position used to disengage an engine from a transmission. All transmission gearing is disengaged between its input and output shafts with the result that no power is transmitted to a car's drive wheels.
neutral safety switch – Switch mounted on an automatic transmission and used to prevent starter operation, if the shift lever is in a drive gear. The switch allows starting in neutral and park (depending on transmission), by grounding the starting circuit running from the ignition switch to the starter relay. See also car service tip(neutral switch test).
neutral steer – Car handling condition created when all tires tend to lose traction at the same time when rounding a turn.
neutral switch – See neutral safety switch.
Nevada – American car produced in 1908.

Newark – American car produced in 1912.
new car – Newly produced and unused car shipped from a car manufacturer to a new car dealer unused. It has no previous owners. When buying a new car, follow these guidelines: shop carefully and don't buy on impulse; if possible wait until just before the new models come out, a time when dealers will want to move last year's models; go with a reliable dealer with a good reputation; read the new car warranty carefully; insist that the car's invoice provide a detailed description; and insist that the sales contract contain the following before signing – the selling price, description of trade in and allowance if applicable, down payment, any credit allowances, the net cost (selling price – trade in allowance – credit allowances), details on insurance requirements pertaining to financing (should include costs, coverage, classification), cost and brand name of any extras, front end alignment checked and OK, and total amount to be financed (including the number of payments, pre payment details, and late payment details).
new car dealer – Business engaged in selling new and used cars. Carefully select the dealer you do business with. If they don't put effort into carefully checking over the new cars they receive, it is an indication the dealer is more interested in getting your money than in making sure you are a satisfied customer. Such a dealer will only cause you problems if you need warranty work done. When selecting a dealer, take the following into consideration: integrity, overall car quality, after sales service, and interest in making you a satisfied customer.
new car dealership – Business authorized to sell new cars.
new car dealership mechanic – In general, mechanic relatively unskilled, and who knows only how to remove a few parts and replace them with new ones.
new car manufacturer – Manufacturer engaged in producing new cars.
new car warranty – See warranty(new car).
Newcomb – American car produced in 1921.
Newcomen, Thomas – He built a steam engine in 1705 to pump water from mines.
New Departure – American car produced from 1909-1910.
New England – American steam car produced from 1898-1900 by New England Motor Carriage Co. in Massachusetts. Also, an American electric car produced from 1899-1901 by New England Electric Vehicle Co. in Massachusetts.
New England Truck – American truck produced in 1914.
New Era – American car produced in 1902 and 1916-1917 by Automobile & Marine Power Co. in New Jersey, and New Era Motors and New Era Engineering in Illinois respectively. Also, an American car produced from 1929-1931.
New Haven – American car produced in 1899 and 1911.
New Home – American car produced in 1901.
New Orleans – American car produced in 1920.
new paint – Fresh paint recently applied over old paint.
new paint job – Used car recently painted with new paint.
New Perry – American car produced in 1903.
Newport – American car produced in 1916. Also, an American car produced from 1955 to date by Chrysler Corp. in Michigan.
new rubber – New car tires.
New Way – American car produced in 1907.
new vehicle warranty – See warranty(new car).
New York – American car produced in 1900, 1907, and 1926.
New Yorker – American car produced from 1955 to date by Chrysler Corp. in Michigan.
New York Six – American car produced from 1928-1929 by Automotive Corp. of America and New York Motors Corp. in Illinois.
NGK – Japanese line of spark plugs imported by NGK Spark Plugs USA.
NHRA – Abbreviation for National Hot Rod Association. It serves to help in the formation of hot rod clubs and publishes Hod Rod Magazine.
NHTSA – Abbreviation for National Highway Traffic Safety Administration.
Niagara – American car produced from 1903-1907 and 1915-1916 by Wilson Auto Mfg. Co. and Mutual Motor Car Co. respectively, both in New York.
NIASE – National Institute for Automotive Service Excellence.
nibbler – Tool used to remove small amounts of material such as sheetmetal typically from around an opening.
Nichols-Shephard – American car produced in 1912.
nickel – Five hundred dollars.
nickels – Small scratches and dents found on car body panels.
nickel steel – Steel alloyed with nickel to give it heat and corrosion resistance properties.
night driving – To drive at night. Only a fraction of the daily traffic flow occurs at night, yet more than half of all fatal accidents occur then. Night driving presents additional hazards such as: reduced field of vision, glare from on coming headlights, sleepiness, etc.
night vision – Ability to see at night.
Nielson – American car produced in 1907.
Niles – American car produced in 1916 and 1921.

nipple – Lubrication fitting.

Nissan – Japanese car line produced from 1960 to date by Nissan Motor Co. Ltd. Popular models include: Auster, Bluebird, Cedric, Gazelle, Gloria, Fairlady, King Cab, Langley, Laurel, Leopard, Liberta, March, Maxima, Prairie, President, Pulsar, Safari, Santana, Sentra, Silva, Skyline, Stanza, SX, ZX, and Sunny. Datsun cars were also produced by Nissan with the Datsun name until the early 1980s.

The U.S. representative is Nissan Motors Corp., USA, headquartered in Carson, California.

Nissan Motor Company Ltd – Firm merged with Kwaishinsha Motor Car Works (Datsun car producers) in 1933. Cars were produced under the Datsun label until the early 1980s. Today it is the fourth largest producer of cars in the world.

nitro – Powerful racing fuel formulated usually as a mixture of methyl alcohol, water, gasoline, and nitromethane. A mixture is used to avoid the high temperatures produced by pure nitromethane. Also, it refers to nitromethane.

nitromethane – Highly explosive fuel characterized as very corrosive to internal engine metals. Cars running on nitromethane are often flushed with proper solvents afterward. See also nitro.

nitrous oxide – Colorless gas used as laughing gas and in nitrous oxide injection systems. It is about 1.5 times as heavy as air, supports combustion almost as well as oxygen, and has a slightly sweet taste and odor.

nitrous oxide injection – Method of greatly increasing engine horsepower on demand through injection of nitrous oxide into the air stream of an engine along with additional fuel. It is the extra fuel and oxygen to burn it that creates the extra horsepower. The gas is usually introduced into the base of a carburetor through a special base plate gasket.

NL – Abbreviation for Netherlands found usually on an international license plate.

Noble, Richard – He set a world land speed record of 633.5 mph in 1983 driving a Thrust 2 Jet Car.

nobody pays list – Selling situation created where most people seldom get talked into paying list price for an item such as a car. See also list price.

no cash deal – Car sale made to the dealer's advantage. It is usually made by allowing a low down payment or none at all. The dealer usually makes a profit in several areas which can include: sale of the car itself, car insurance, financing arrangements, and pocketing dealer preparation fee.

no draft ventilation – Method used to ventilate a car interior without causing a significant movement or draft of air. One method was the use of side windows introduced in 1933 by Fisher.

no fault insurance – See insurance(no fault).

Noble – American car produced in 1902.

Noble Truck – American truck produced in 1917.

Nolan – American car produced in 1924.

no-load test – Test made on a starter motor to determine if a manufacturer's specified rpm is achieved when a specified voltage, current, and resistance are introduced into a starter motor circuit. Low rpm and high current flow may indicate: bearing or bushings that are worn or tight, and a dragging armature. Low rpm and low current flow usually indicates excessive resistance in starter motor. Possible causes include: break in a field winding, broken brush springs, worn out brushes, and dirty/oily commutator. High rpm and high current flow usually indicate shorted field windings. See also stall test, armature and field open circuit test, and armature and field grounded circuit test.

nolo contendere – Plea entered by a defendant in a criminal case which is not an admission of guilt but subjects the defendant to punishment as if he were guilty. It often results in a less severe penalty than admitting guilt, and saves the state the expense of a jury trial.

Noma – American car produced from 1919-1923 by Noma Motors Corp. in New York.

Nomad – American car produced from 1955-1960 by Chevrolet Division of General Motors Corp. in Michigan.

Nomex – Flame resistant fabric used to make race car driver clothing.

non-age – Any age in a person's life under legal age.

nonane – Liquid methane series hydrocarbon compound found in petroleum deposits with a melting and boiling point of -64 and 303 degrees Fahrenheit respectively. It is an ingredient of gasoline.

non ferrous metal – Metal composed of little or no iron. It does not rust.

Nonpareil – American car produced in 1913.

non-runner – Used car characterized as not in running condition.

non stock – New item or part manufactured in a modified form from its stock counterpart.

Non-Use Affidavit – See Certificate of Non-Operation.

nonwarranty work – Repair or maintenance work done to a car after the warranty has expired. When this work is done, the customer is usually charged the full shop rate with a tendency for unnecessary work or parts items to get added to the bill. See also repair bill.

no passing zone - Zone designated on a road where passing is usually dangerous. It is usually marked with signs and/or double yellow lines separating the traffic lanes.

Norcross - American car produced in 1907.

Nordhoff, Professor Heinz - He who took over the demolished Volkswagen factory at the end of World War II, and through British encouragement rebuilt the business.

normally aspirated - Aspect of an engine built to draw air into its cylinders without the use of a supercharger or turbocharger.

NORS - Abbreviation for new old replacement stock. See also NOS.

Northern - American car produced from 1902-1909 by Northern Mfg. Co. (1902-1905), and Northern Motor Car Co. (1906-1909), both in Michigan.

north pole - Magnetic pole emitting magnetic lines of force to a south pole.

Northway - American car produced in 1921.

Northwestern - American car produced in 1904.

Norton - American car produced from 1901-1902.

Norwalk - American car produced from 1910-1922 by Norwalk Motor Car Co. in Ohio (1910-1911), and Norwalk Motor Car Co. in West Virginia (1911-1922).

NOS - Abbreviation for new old stock. See also NORS.

nosed - Modification made to the front end of a car.

no-shift condition - See transmission(manual-difficult to shift).

No-Spin - Tradename used for a limited slip differential.

nostalgia rod - Car produced in an earlier time that has been changed into a hot rod.

notary public - Public officer authorized to witness various acts and certify their occurrence by observation and/or attesting so in writing.

notchback - See body style(notchback).

note - Paper written to acknowledge a debt and promise its payment.

not guilty - Verdict issued by a court dismissing charges against a defendant because the charges could not be proven.

Notice of Transfer - Document used in most states to provide notification to the Department of Motor Vehicles of an ownership transfer. See also Change of Ownership and Statement of Transfer.

no-tow - See car transport(flatbed).

no trade-in price - Selling price of an item if a used one is not surrendered to a seller. Prices of new items such as cars, batteries, starters, tires, etc. are often somewhat lower if you give the seller a used ones when you purchase.

Nova - American car produced from 1962 to date by Chevrolet Division of General Motors Corp. in Michigan.

Novara - American car produced in 1917.

no wax finish - Car topcoat applied that requires little or no waxing in order to maintain a high gloss.

NOx - Oxides of nitrogen. Any chemical compound composed of one part nitrogen and one or more parts oxygen. It is produced when gasoline is burned under pressure as in an internal combustion engine. Oxide formation can be reduced by lowering combustion temperatures through lower compression ratios and by recirculating exhaust gases. It is minimal at idle and increases when a car is accelerated. Oxides of nitrogen are one of the ingredients in smog.

NOx valve - See spark delay valve.

NR - Abbreviation for needs repair.

NSU - German car manufacturer responsible for producing the first prototype Wankel (rotary) engine in 1951.

Nucar - American car produced in 1929.

nut - Money amount added to the wholesale book price of a used car, by a dealer, to determine the minimum price at which it will be sold.

nut lock - Cap built to sit on top of a nut and prevent it from turning by means of a cotter key inserted through the nut lock and the bolt shaft. It used on front wheel hubs to keep the hub mounting nut from turning and thereby maintaining a desired torque on the wheel bearings.

Nuvolari, Tazio - He was the winning driver of the 1938 Italian Grand Prix, driving a 1938 Auto-Union race car.

Nyberg - American car produced from 1912-1914 by Nyberg Automobile Works in Indiana.

nylon belt - One or more layers of nylon material placed underneath a tire tread area.

nylon overlay - See nylon belt.

NZ - Abbreviation for New Zealand found usually on an international license plate.

O

OAC – Abbreviation for on approved credit.
OAH – Abbreviation for overall height of car.
Oakland – American car produced from 1907-1931 by Oakland Motor Car Co. in Michigan.
Oakland Motor Company – American car manufacturing company founded in 1907 in Pontiac, Michigan.
Oakman – American car produced from 1898-1900.
OAL – Abbreviation for overall length of car.
OAW – Abbreviation for overall width of car.
oasis – Refreshment stand.
Obertine – American car produced in 1915.
OBO – Abbreviation for or best offer.
observation area – Roadside stop developed for viewing local scenery.
obstacle course run – Closed driving course used to test driver skills.
OB Truck – American truck produced in 1928.
Occidental Petroleum Corp – A U.S. petroleum company headquartered in Los Angeles, California. See also petroleum company and Cities Service Company.
occupied car – Car carrying people.
O'Connell – American car produced in 1928.
O'Connor – American car produced in 1916.
octadecane – Solid methane series hydrocarbon compound found in petroleum deposits with a melting and boiling point of 83 and 601 degrees Fahrenheit respectively.
octane – Liquid methane series hydrocarbon compound found in petroleum deposits with a melting and boiling point of -70 and 258 degrees Fahrenheit respectively. It is an ingredient of gasoline where is serves to to suppress detonation in high compression engines. Heat value is 20,500 btu/lb.
octane booster – See additive(octane booster).
octane number – See octane rating.
octane number requirement – The minimum octane rating required for a specified engine to run without appreciable detonation.
octane number requirement increase – Increase in an engine's octane number requirement caused principally by build-up of combustion chamber deposits. Engines driven short distances increase build-up faster and to a higher level before leveling off.
octane rating – Number scale used to rate a particular gasoline's ability to resist detonation. The number represents the percentage of iso-octane needed in a heptane and iso-octane mixture to generate the same antiknock characteristics as the gasoline being tested. For example, if a mixture of 88 percent iso-octane and 12 percent heptane produced the same antiknock characteristics as the gasoline being tested, the gasoline would be assigned an octane rating of 88. The higher the number the greater the ability to resist detonation. Octane rating is not a measure of a fuel's inherent power, volatility, or ability to start an engine. Crude oil commonly exhibits an octane rating of 70 before refining. Today's cost of raising one octane number averages 4 cents per gallon. See also Research Octane Number, Motor Octane Number, Distribution Octane Number, R-100 Method, and Antiknock Index.
octane selector – Device used to adjust ignition timing according to fuel characteristics. Also, it refers to a gasoline pump equipped with a selector that allows a customer to blend different grades of gasoline, like regular and premium.
OD(1) – Abbreviation for outside diameter.
Od(2) – Abbreviation for overdrive.
od – Abbreviation for overdrive.
odd change type of close – Closing the sale tactic designed to impress a car customer he is getting a good deal by giving him the impression the profit margin is so small it is being figured to fractions of a dollar.
Odelot – American car produced in 1915.
odometer – Device used in the speedometer to measure and display the total distance traveled by a car. See also trip odometer and gauge(odometer).
OEM – Abbreviation for original equipment manufacturer.
Ofeldt – American car produced from 1899-1902 by F.W. Ofeldt & Sons in New York.
Offenhauser – American car produced in 1934.
off idle operation – Carburetor metering mode created when throttle plate begins to open.

off-idle ports - Additional ports used in certain carburetor designs to feed additional fuel to an engine as the throttle starts to open. They are positioned just above the main idle port.

off road - Off of public roads or in a roadless area.

off the bottle - To run the engine of a nitrous oxide equipped car without the use of nitrous oxide.

off the line - To leave a race track starting line.

off the trailer run - Good run made after unloading a car and before making any adjustments.

Offy - Abbreviation for the Offenhauser engine.

Ogden Truck - American truck produced in 1918.

ogee - Long S-shaped curve.

Ogren - American car produced in 1907. Also, an American car produced from 1915-1923 by Ogren Motor Car Co. in Illinois (1915), Ogren Motor WOrks in Illinois (1916-1918), and Ogren Motor Car Co. in Wisconsin (1919-1923).

OHC - Abbreviation for overhead camshaft.

ohc - Abbreviation for overhead camshaft.

OHV - Abbreviation for overhead valve.

Ohio - American car produced from 1899-1902. Also, an American car produced from 1909-1913 by Jewel Carriage Co. in Ohio. Also, an American electric car produced from 1910-1918 by Ohio Electric Car Co. in Ohio.

Ohio Falls - American car produced from 1911-1915.

ohm - One unit of resistance. It is used to measure resistance of current flowing through a conductor.

ohmmeter - Instrument used to measure the amount of electrical resistance in a length of wire, a component, or a circuit.

ohm's law - Electrical law based on observed electrical behavior that explains the relationship between voltage, resistance, and amperes. The law reads as follows: it requires a pressure of one volt to force 1 ampere through a resistance of 1 ohm. The equation is: volts = amperes x resistance.

oil - Combustible liquid substance derived from animal, vegetable, and mineral sources. It is usually liquid at mild temperature, soluble in organic solvents, and doesn't mix with water. Oil, used in engines, is primarily mineral in origin. See also petroleum, crude oil, and gasoline.

oil(artifical) - See oil(synthetic).

oil(asphalt base) - Oil derived from crude oil containing asphalt and almost no paraffin wax. Gulf Coast and California crude oils are of this type.

oil(automatic transmission) - Oil formulated for use in an automatic transmission and torque converter. See also DEXRON and Type F Fluid.

oil(break in) - Oil used in a new car during its break-in period.

oil(CD) - Car diesel oil.

oil(combination) - Oil formulated as a mixture of mineral and synthetic oil.

oil(detergent/dispersant) - Oil formulated with detergent/dispersant qualities. See also additive(detergent/dispersant-1).

oil(differential) - Heavy oil formulated for use in a car's differential housing. See also oil(gear).

oil(extreme pressure) - Oil formulated to withstand high pressures developed between surfaces such as gear teeth.

oil(gear) - Heavy oil formulated for lubricating enclosed gears in manual transmissions, differentials, steering boxes, etc. It can be a preferable replacement for a heavy engine oil since it usually has a lower pour point.

oil(graphite) - Oil mixed with graphite. Certain engine graphite oils are sold claiming decreased friction between moving parts.

oil(HD) - See oil(detergent/dispersant).

oil(heavy) - High viscosity oil. See also viscosity.

oil(heavy duty) - See oil(detergent/dispersant).

oil(light) - Low viscosity oil. See also viscosity.

oil(manual transmission) - See oil(gear).

oil(mineral) - Oil derived from petroleum deposits.

oil(mixed base) - Oil derived from crude oil containing paraffin wax and asphalt. United States mid-continent oils are of this type.

oil(monograde) - See oil(straight weight).

oil(motor) - Engine oil formulated to lubricate moving engine parts, help cool the engine, and collect contaminants such as combustion by-products, condensates, etc.

oil(motor light) - See service rating(ML).

oil(motor medium) - See service rating(MM).

oil(motor severe) - See service rating(MS).

oil(multi viscosity) - Engine oil formulated to meet SAE requirements for adequate lubrication and flow at both high and low temperatures. SAE 10W-30 is an example. Multi-viscosity oil will not properly lubricate as long as a single grade oil, because oil heating and cooling depletes additives providing multi-viscosity characteristics.

oil(paraffin base) - Oil derived from crude oil containing large amounts of paraffin wax and no asphalt. Pennsylvania crudes are of this type.

oil(racing) - Oil formulated to provide proper lubrication for the greater heat and pressure racing engines develop. More extreme pressure additive is used.
oil(rear end) - See oil(differential).
oil(SAE 5W) - Winter grade engine oil formulated to operate where outside air temperatures remain below -10 degree Fahrenheit.
oil(SAE 5W-30) - Engine oil formulated to operate where outside air temperatures range from -10 to 100 degrees Fahrenheit.
oil(SAE 10W) - Winter grade engine oil formulated to operate where outside air temperatures range from -10 to 30 degrees Fahrenheit.
oil(SAE 10W-30) - Engine oil formulated to operate where outside temperatures range from -10 to 90 degrees Fahrenheit. Higher maximum temperature oils (100+ degrees) have also been formulated in this category.
oil(SAE 15W-40) - Engine oil formulated to operate where outside air temperatures range from 0 to over 110 degrees Fahrenheit.
oil(SAE 20) - Engine oil formulated to operate where outside air temperatures range from 30-80 degrees Fahrenheit.
oil(SAE 20W) - Winter grade engine oil formulated to operate where outside air temperatures range from 10-80 degrees Fahrenheit.
oil(SAE 20W-50) - Engine oil formulated to operate where outside air temperatures range from 20 to over 110 degrees Fahrenheit.
oil(SAE 30) - Summer grade engine oil formulated to operate where outside air temperatures range from 30-100 degrees Fahrenheit.
oil(SAE 40) - Summer grade engine oil formulated to operate where outside air temperatures range from 60 to over 110 degrees Fahrenheit.
oil(SAE 80W-140) - Gear oil formulated to operate from -20 to over 250 degrees Fahrenheit.
oil(single grade) - See oil(straight weight).
oil(straight weight) - Oil formulated to meet SAE requirements for adequate lubrication and flow at a specific oil weight. SAE 30 is an example. Straight weight oil is usually a little better to use than multi-viscosity in warm climates, but frequent oil changes are far more important to maximum engine life.
oil(synthetic) - Special oil derived from petroleum and non-petroleum sources and synthesized to produce improved oil properties. Advantages to synthetic oil include: decreased engine friction, better high and low temperature viscosity, resistance to oil breakdown at high temperature, and cleaning action. Disadvantages include: cost, increased oil consumption in worn engines, and availability. See also gas saving tip(unusual lubricants).
oil(top) - Upper cylinder lubricant added to gasoline to help lubricate an engine's upper cylinder area. See also additive(upper cylinder lubricant).
oil(transmission) - See oil(manual transmission) and oil(automatic transmission).
oil(turbo) - Oil formulated to provide lubrication under greater heat in such areas as turbocharger bearings during operation and shutdown. It usually contains an extreme pressure additive to lubricate bearings effectively under heavy loads encountered in racing or turbocharged engines.
oil and water extractor - See air dryer.
oil bath air cleaner - See air cleaner(oil bath).
oil burner - See smoker.
oil cartel - An international organization formed to regulate the oil prices and production of oil producing countries. OPEC is the organization regulating Middle East oil.
oil change - Procedure followed to remove existing oil and install fresh oil. A good approach to effectively removing dirty oil consists of the following: warm engine up to operating temperature, place drain pan under oil drain plug, get drain plug wrench handy, put gloves on, stop engine, remove drain plug draining oil in pan, position pan underneath oil filter, remove filter by hand or with oil filter wrench (will be hot), let oil drain until 10-20 seconds elapses between drips (around 10 minutes) in order to effectively remove old sludge and other impurities, clean drain plug and opening, replace drain plug to proper tightness, clean oil filter mounting surface, install new filter to proper tightness, add oil through oil filler cap until full mark is reached, start and idle engine for a few minutes, look for any oil leaking around drain plug or oil filter, stop engine, check oil level and adjust till it reaches full mark (don't overfill).
   As a rule, it is considered wise not to mix different brands or types of lubricants, since some will not be compatible with each other. To do so can cause such problems as: poor mixing, destruction and/or inactivity of certain additives, and premature oil deterioration. See also oil change interval.
oil change interval - The distance traveled or time elapsed before engine, transmission, differential, etc. oil is changed.
   Most engines and their oils are subjected to hard service because the majority of driving is short trips (usually 10 miles or less). Since it typically takes 5-10 miles to warm an engine up to operating temperature,

engine oil should be changed more frequently than for highway driving. Manufacturers recommend change intervals ranging from 1,000-7,500 miles. In general, many experts advise changing oil every three months, or so many miles whichever occurs first to insure long engine life. Mileage recommendations include: every 2,000-3,000 miles for short trip driving, every 1-2,000 miles for very short trip driving (averaging five miles or less), and every 1,000 miles if temperature remains below zero.

Gear oil used in transmissions, differentials, etc. is usually designed for extended change intervals of 25,000 or more miles.

Delaying oil changes only shortens the life of affected moving parts. Contaminated oil accumulates fine metal particles, sludge, gasoline, water, etc. which can corrode metal parts and act like "liquid abrasive" quickly wearing out moving part surfaces. The small added expense of more frequent oil change intervals pays for itself in longer engine life, smoother and/or minimal wear on moving parts, and cheaper rebuilding of affected parts. See also oil change.

oil change kit - Kit composed of all items necessary to change oil. It typically includes: oil, oil filter, and storage container for used oil.

oil consumption - Consumption rate of engine oil measured in car miles driven. Consumption can vary widely from 500-5,000 miles per quart and still be considered normal depending on the engine. The optimum consumption is 2-3,000 miles per quart. Factors affecting oil consumption include: wear on engine moving parts, type of oil, water temperature, timing, amount of oil in crankcase, and driving habits.

oil cooler - Radiator used to cool engine or transmission oil. It helps in situations where oil gets hotter than 250 degrees Fahrenheit.

oil cooler pipes - Oil lines used to route oil to and from an oil cooler and oil pan.

oiler - See cap oiler.

oil field - Geographical area containing valuable oil deposits.

oil filler tube - Tube mounted on an engine block to facilitate addition of engine oil.

oil filter - Filtering device used to strain and remove foreign particles from circulating oil. Considerations in filter design include: retaining oil after engine stops, minimizing removal of oil additives, fineness of contaminant filtering, and flow rate.

oil filter(bypass) - Filter built to handle part of a oil pump's output. It is connected in parallel with other oil lubrication circuits. This filtering method is not considered effective in keeping foreign particles away from critical wear surfaces. Bypass filters were used on older engines and are no longer popular.

oil filter(drainback) - Filter built to retain oil when engine stops. It minimizes dry starts. See also oil filter drainback valve.

oil filter(full flow) - Oil filter built to filter all oil reaching an engine except when oil is cold or the filter gets plugged. Under the exception, a bypass valve routes the oil around the filter.

oil filter(single stage) - Filter built with one filtering medium.

oil filter(two stage) - Filter built with two filtering mediums.

oil filter drainback valve - Valve mounted in an oil filter to keep oil from emptying when oil pressure falls to zero. This type filter is used to minimize dry starts in cars that have sat for a few days.

oil foaming - Condition created when oil changes into a froth like soap bubbles. Most quality oils today have anti-foaming additives. Oil foaming can occur in an engine or transmission when too much oil has been added. It occurs because the oil is agitated by too many moving surfaces and also gets hotter. See also full mark.

oil gallery - Pipes or bored passageways located in an engine block for routing oil to all the moving engine parts.

oil grade - See viscosity rating. See also oil.

oiling - To cover metal with certain types of oil to prevent rust. It is quite popular in Canada and is considered much more effective than tar and/or wax compounds.

oil intake screen - Screen attached to the pickup tube end in an oil pan. It acts as a preliminary filter preventing large particles or pieces of debris from entering the oil gallery.

oil is too thin - Oil condition created when oil has lost too much of its viscosity usually due to high temperature. Thin oil does not keep moving parts very well lubricated and can lead to galling.

oil leak - Loss of oil condition created in an oil reservoir such as an oil pan, transmission, differential, steering box, etc. Possible causes include: loose drain plugs, cracked case, bad gaskets, loose bolts, fluid overfilled, and bad seals.

oil level monitor gauge - Gauge used to monitor oil level usually in an oil pan.

oilman - Person characterized as owning or operating oil wells. Also, it refers to a person selling or delivering oil.

oil pan – Metal reservoir bolted to the bottom of a crankcase or automatic transmission to hold oil.

oil pan gasket – Gasket used to seal an oil pan mounting surface.

oil pressure – Pressure developed by oil after leaving an engine's oil pump. It is usually measured near the pump's output side. As a general rule of thumb, 10 pounds oil pressure for every 1,000 rpm is considered adequate for lubrication requirements when using the type of oil recommended by the manufacturer. A lower pressure indicates oil system problems.

oil pressure gauge – See gauge(oil pressure).

oil pressure relief valve – Spring-loaded valve incorporated inside or near an oil pump to maintain an engine's oil pressure within specified limits. It opens to release some of an oil pump's output directly back to an oil sump when oil is cold and viscous. Most oil lubrication systems have one.

oil pressure sending unit – See sensor(oil pressure-1), sensor(oil pressure-2), and sensor(oil pressure-3).

oil pressure switch – See sensor(oil pressure-2).

oil pump – Mechanical device used to pump lubricating oil, under pressure, to various moving parts of an engine. It usually pumps with gears or a rotor and is driven by a gear on a camshaft or crankshaft.

oil pumping – Engine condition created when an excessive quantity of oil leaks past piston rings and gets burned in the combustion chamber. The condition is usually caused by excessive clearance between pistons and cylinder walls, but can also be caused by oil leaking out excessively from pressure lubricated bearings and being splashed and thrown up onto cylinder walls in large quantities. It causes fouling of spark plugs, excess carbon deposits, exhaust smoke, and excess oil consumption. The only remedy is reconditioning the engine cylinders or restoring the proper bearing clearances.

oil pump primer – Device used to operate an oil pump prior to starting an engine to prelubricate engine bearings. It is usually a shaft inserted into a distributor shaft hole and rotated with a drill.

oil relief valve – See oil pressure relief valve.

oil seal – Device used to stop oil from leaking past a certain area.

oil separator – Screen used to separate heavy oil in crankcase vapors and route it back into the crankcase. The separator is usually mounted on the air cleaner body.

oil side lamps – Lamps powered by oil. They were used to provide lighting near the doors of cars in the early 1900s.

oil slick – A film of oil floating on a body of water.

oil slinger – Cone-shaped collar used on a shaft to deflect oil away and prevent leakage along the shaft.

oil strainer – Screen filter located in an oil sump. It prevents large particulate matter in oil from getting into an oil lubrication system.

oil temperature – Temperature of oil used in a car. Mineral based oils should be kept below 260 degrees Fahrenheit for maximum life and to minimize oxidation. Synthetic oils are capable of operating effectively at 300 degrees on up depending on type.

oil temperature gauge – See gauge(oil temperature).

oil viscosity – See viscosity rating. See also oil.

oil well – A well drilled through layers of rock until it intersects a petroleum deposit yielding crude oil.

Okay – American car produced in 1907.

Okey – American car produced from 1907-1908 by Okey Motor Car Co. in Ohio.

OK Truck – American truck produced in 1917 and 1925.

old car shakes – Car handling condition created when a car drives like it's old and worn out.

old enough to vote – Characterization of an old used car still in use.

Oldfield – American car produced in 1917.

Oldfield, Barney – He set a world land speed record of 131.3 mph in 1910 driving a Benz 4 Cylinder Blitzen Benz. He also test drove Peerless's racing cars in the early 1900s.

old fogey driving – Driving habit characterized by driving a car much slower than the rest of the traffic, making slow turns, slowing down for a stop way ahead of stopping point, reacting slowly to signal light change, and accelerating very slowly from a stop.

Old Hickory – American car produced in 1915.

Old Reliable – American car produced in 1912 and 1926.

Old Pacific – Name of a single cylinder Packard car driven by Tom Fetch from San Francisco to New York in 53 days in 1903.

Oldsmobile – American car produced from 1896 to date by Olds Motors Works (1896-1943), and General Motors Corp. (1943 to date), both in Michigan.

Olds Motor Vehicle Company – Company organized in 1897 by Ransom E. Olds. It was reorganized in 1899 as the Olds Motor Works which developed the first really low priced car at $650. The company later became the Olds division of General Motors.

Olds Motor Works - See Olds Motor Vehicle Company.
Olds, Ransom E - He was an American automotive pioneer who manufactured a very successful car called the Oldsmobile in 1901. He organized the Olds Motor Works and later the Reo Motor Car Company.
Olds Steam Car - American steam car produced in 1896.
Old Steady - Name used for an Oldsmobile car that made a transcontinental trip in 1905 from New York to Portland in 44 days.
old time craftsman - Skilled worker recognized for taking pride in his work, and checking and rechecking his work before releasing back to a customer.
old timer vehicle - Older vehicle manufactured before a certain specified time and not used for general transportation.
Oliver - American car produced in 1905, 1911, and 1935.
Olympian - American car produced from 1917-1921 by Olympian Motors Co. in Michigan.
Olympic - American car produced in 1913 and 1922.
Omaha - American car produced from 1912-1913 by Omaha Motor Car Co. in Nebraska.
Omar - American car produced from 1908-1910.
Omega - American car produced beginning in 1968 by Suspensions International Corp. in North Carolina. It was a high performance car with a 150 mph top speed. Also, an American car produced from 1973 to date by Oldsmobile Division of General Motors Corp. in Michigan.
Omni - Japanese car imported from 1978 to date for Dodge Division of Chrysler Corp. in Michigan.
Omort - American car produced in 1927.
on-board computer - Computer installed on a car to monitor and/or regulate certain engine and related functions. See also engine control sensor, computer command control, CCC tester, sensor, ECM, PROM, open loop mode, closed mode, self-diagnostic mode, trouble code, and black box.
on-car spin balance - See tire balance(on-car spin).
on coming traffic - Traffic approaching a person or car.
on consignment - Condition created when a piece of property is sent to an agent to sell it. The owner of the property retains title to it until sold. See also consign your car.
Oneida Truck - American truck produced in 1917.
one man top - Early term for fabric car tops.
one-of - Custom car.
one owner - Characteristic of a car owned by one person since new.
one shot deal - Deal made by a salesman with no interest in customer satisfaction and hence repeat business.
one way clutch - See clutch(overrunning).
one way sign - Traffic sign used to indicate direction of traffic flow in all lanes of a road.
one way street - Street set up to permit traffic flow in one direction only.
on foot - To travel by walking. Also, it refers to being stranded with a broke down car.
Only - American car produced from 1909-1915 by Only Motor Car Co. in New York. The engine consisted of one large cylinder, 206 cu.in. in displacement.
ONR - Abbreviation for octane number requirement.
ONRI - Abbreviation for octane number requirement increase.
on the job training - Job training provided by employing a person and teaching him while he works.
on the money - Car traded in at the wholesaler's price.
on the rack - Car elevated by a car hoist.
on the road - To travel by road.
on the side - Person engaged in making money doing work after hours at other than his place of employment. See also moonlighting.
on the take - To accept money earned illegally. In dealer service departments, employees are often encouraged to convince a car owner other repairs are needed. The higher the owner's bill the more money an employees make. This practice of money enticement only encourages dishonesty.
on the wood - To drive a car at full throttle.
OO&O - Abbreviation for original owner and operator.
OPEC - Abbreviation for Organization of Petroleum Exporting Countries.
Opel - West German car line produced from 1898 to date by Adam Opel AG. Popular models include: Ascona, Corsa, Kadett, Manta, Monza, Rekford, and Senator.
open circuit - Electrical circuit characterized as not carrying current due to a break or excessive resistance in a conductor or associated fittings.
open end wrench - Wrench constructed with U-shaped openings at one or both ends for turning a nut or bolt.
open loop mode - On-board computer mode used when a car's engine is cold. It sets the fuel metering system up for a rich fuel mixture and interprets the various engine sensors accordingly until the engine warms up. It can also be used to sense certain engine problems, and partly shut itself down. See also

closed loop mode and limp-in mode.

operating temperature - Temperature reached by engine coolant when it gets warm enough to open the thermostat. It is the temperature at which an engine operates most efficiently.

operating temperature range - See spark plug heat range.

operator - Any person controlling the the physical operation of a car on a road.

Ophir - American car produced in 1901.

opposite lock - To turn wheels opposite to the direction of travel. It is used to control rear wheel skids by always steering a car in the direction the rear end is moving.

options - Extra accessories added to a vehicle at the time of purchase or later. They include: stereo cassette players, power steering, power brakes, better upholstery, special engine, air conditioning, etc.

opts - Abbreviation for options.

orange peel - See paint coat problem(orange peel).

orange triangle - Orange colored sign built in the shape of a triangle and mounted on the back of a slowing moving vehicle.

order - Written agreement signed by a customer to purchase a car.

Oregon - American car produced in 1916.

Orient-Auto-Go - American car produced in 1900.

orig - Abbreviation for original.

original condition - Used car condition characterized as looking like new. It is a phrase commonly used to attract attention in a classified ad.

original miles - Number of miles a car has been driven since new.

original obligation - Total amount of money to be loaned. For example, the original obligation of a $4,800 car loan is $4,800. The amount to be paid off is the unpaid balance. See also unpaid balance.

o-ringed - To place or install o-rings on a shaft, in an opening, etc.

Oriole - American car produced in 1927.

Orion - American car produced in 1900.

Orleans - American car produced in 1920.

Orlo - American car produced in 1904.

Ormond - American steam car produced from 1904-1905 by United Motor & Vehicle Co. in Massachusetts. It was an expensive car made in limited numbers.

Orson - American car produced from 1908-1909 by Brightwood Mfg. Co. in Massachusetts. It was coined "the bankers car" by the press. Only 100 were built, and they were never offered for sale to the public.

OSAC - Abbreviation for orifice spark advance control.

OSAC valve - See spark delay valve.

Oscar - Two dimensional adjustable manikin used by car designers and engineers to represent a person's size, shape, and movement limitations. It is used to properly design and size a car interior.

Oscarlear - American car produced in 1905.

oscillation - Regular back and forth movement.

oscilloscope - Electronic testing instrument used to measure and display instantaneous voltage, and voltage polarity on a cathode ray tube. The oscilloscope is used in more expensive ignition system analyzers where it can detect the following conditions: condenser behavior; ignition coil - voltage, polarity, shorting, and behavior; spark plug - firing voltage, electrode wear, fouling, and voltage change with engine load; primary circuit resistance and grounding; secondary resistance and grounding; and distributor - rotor with excessive gap or poor contact, breaker point behavior, and dwell angle.

Oshkosh - American car produced in 1926.

Oshkosh Truck - American truck produced in 1917.

Oso - Japanese line of tires.

Ostich, Nathan - He was a surgeon known for making the first attempt at a land speed record in a jet-powered car. It occurred in 1960 at the Bonneville Salt Flats in Utah. He was not able to exceed 250 mph.

Otto - American car produced from 1909-1912 by Otto Gas Works (1909-1911), and Ottomobile Co. (1912), both in Pennsylvania.

Otto cycle - Four stroke cycle of an engine's internal combustion process named after the man who developed the principle of four piston strokes for each engine cylinder explosion.

Otto engine - See engine(four stroke).

Ottokar - American car produced from 1903-1904 by Otto Konigslow in Ohio.

Ottomobile - American car produced from 1911-1912 by Ottomobile Co. in Pennsylvania.

Otto, Nicholas - He was a German manufacturer who developed a stationary four cycle internal combustion engine for light industrial use that was compact, quiet, and economical.

outboard brake pad - Disc brake pad positioned to bear against the outside rotor braking surface.

outer caliper half - Half of a disc brake caliper housing positioned on the outside of a rotor. See also inside caliper half and caliper assembly.

outer pad and plate - Disc brake pad and cover plate assembly mounted next to the outside caliper piston. See also inner pad and plate.

outer pivot - End of a tie rod attached to a wheel's steering knuckle arm. It is the point at which the side-to-side motion of the tie rod and drag link assembly is transferred to the pivoting motion of the steering knuckle arm which turns the wheel left or right. See also tie rod end.

out of control - Car or person characterized as not controllable. For example, a car sliding and spinning on an icy road is out of control.

out of court settlement - Settlement made between two parties before the litigation reaches court.

out of gear - Transmission condition created when the gears are arranged so power is not transmitted through the gearbox. A car is out of gear when it is in neutral.

out of line - Car frame out of alignment. It is usually caused by an accident, but can also be caused by sagging, broken springs, and other mechanical defects. A frame must be in alignment before a steering system can be properly aligned. This means such things as: frame rails must be the same height on both sides at respective locations, frame rails are the same distance apart where specified, and cross members are perpendicular to the frame centerline and frame rails.

out of pocket expenses - Expenses incurred that a person had to pay with his own money or were not otherwise covered. For example, such an expense would be buying a gift for a child during a business trip.

out of regular - See con game(out of regular).

out of round wear - A condition most commonly observed in worn engine cylinders in which the bore wears to an oval shape. It results from greater side pressure exerted by the piston on the power stroke.

out of the gate - See off the line.

out of the groove - To get out of a racing car path when racing speed cannot be maintained. It is a common courtesy in race car driving.

out of the hole - See off the line.

out of town - To be away from a place of residence.

out on bail - Criminal suspect released from jail until a court appearance due to posting of a bail bond.

output shaft - Shaft, inside a drive train unit, used to receive power and transfer it outside. Examples include transmission output shaft, and rear axle shafts.

outside air door - Mode-and-blend door used to control flow of air from outside into heating ducts.

outstanding condition - Auto condition code word used to specify a restored or original car. Only minor work separates it from a concours condition.

oval track - Race track shaped like an oval circle.

Ovenden - American car produced in 1899.

overall gear ratio - The gear ratio created between an engine and the drive wheels. Two gear ratios come into play, the transmission and the differential. The overall gear ratio is obtained by multiplying the transmission gear ratio by the differential gear ratio. For example, suppose a transmission's first gear ratio is 4:1 and the differential's gear ratio is 3:1. The overall gear ratio is then 4 times 3 or 12:1. It means the engine in first gear will turn 12 revolutions for every single revolution of the rear wheels. See also gear ratio.

overall ratio - See overall gear ratio.

overall steering ratio - See steering overall ratio.

over assessment - Estimate of repair work made showing more costs than necessary.

overboost - Condition created when a turbocharger increases intake manifold pressure too much. Overboost causes: detonation, overheating, and added stress on turbocharger components. Boost is usually controlled by a wastegate on the exhaust side of the turbocharger.

over-bore - Engine modified to larger than stock cylinder diameters.

overcarburetion - Condition created when an engine is fitted with a carburetor designed for an engine requiring larger air and fuel flows, or a carburetor metering more air and/or fuel than needed at various engine rpm.

overcooling - Condition created when the coolant circulating in an engine remains at a lower than desirable temperature. It decreases fuel economy, increase emissions due to lower combustion chamber temperature, and encourages the formation of sludge and acids in the engine oil. See also overheating.

overcorrecting - Driver steering situation created when a steering wheel is turned too far in the opposite direction to correct a car turn.

overdrive - External gear unit or a gear built into some manual transmissions (like 5 speeds) that, when actuated, allows an engine to turn slower than a transmission output shaft. The result is higher speeds with less engine effort and lower fuel consumption.

overdriving the headlights – Condition created when a driver drives a car too fast for the distance he can see. To be safe, driving speed should be reduced 10 or more mph over daytime speed limit.

over evaluation – Evaluation made of a repair estimate, insurance claim, etc., recommending a higher return to the claimee than is fair.

overflow tank – See radiator overflow tank.

overhang – Distance measured from wheel axle centerline to rearmost (or foremost) part of car.

overhanging load – Items carried on a vehicle extending beyond the front or back of its body.

overhaul – To rebuild a part, engine, brake system, etc.

overhauled engine – Rebuilt engine.

overhead cam – Camshaft located above the engine cylinders. See engine(overhead cam) and engine(dual overhead cam).

overhead cam engine – See engine(overhead cam).

overhead console – Raised panel located in a car ceiling between the two front passenger seats containing various accessories such as gauges, light, switches, etc.

overhead valve engine – See engine(overhead valve).

overheating – Condition created when the coolant circulating in an engine approaches its boiling point. Overheating stresses various metal components and can cause a warped or cracked block or head, especially when coolant level is low. Today's cars use pressurized systems which increase the boiling point up to 265 degrees for a 50-50 water-antifreeze concentration. See also overcooling and engine problem(overheating).

Overholt – American car produced in 1909 and 1912.

Overholt Steam – American steam car produced in 1912.

overinflation – Tire condition created when a tire's air pressure is higher than recommended. It makes a tire run hard, subjects it to impact damage, weakens the tire casing, and causes increased wear in the center of the tread. An overinflated tire does have less rolling resistance which increases gas mileage somewhat. See also underinflation.

Overland – American car produced from 1903-1929 and 1939 by Standard Wheel Co. in Indiana (1903-1905), Overland Co. in Indiana (1905-1907), and Willys-Overland Co. in Ohio (1908-1939).

overlap – See valve overlap.

overlay – Sheet of translucent paper placed over an original drawing. It is used to make copies of the underlying drawing, sketch alternate designs, provide additional detail, and/or make comparisons.

overload relay – See current limit relay.

overload spring – Heavy coil spring fitted around a shock absorber. It increases carrying capacity, improves overall stability, and eliminates bottoming out.

Overman – American car produced from 1899-1904 by Overman Wheel Co. (1899-1900), and Overman Automobile Co. (1901-1904), both in Massachusetts.

overpass – Highway, railroad, or pedestrian bridge over a roadway.

over-revving the engine – Driving an engine at too high an rpm. Over-revving strains engine parts because of high speed, rapid direction reversal, heat build-up, lubrication breakdown, parts getting in each other's way (pistons and valves for example), vibrations, etc. See also lugging the engine and valve float.

overrider – See bumper guard.

overrun brake band – Brake band used in conjunction with an overrun clutch to control engine braking effects in automatic transmission.

overrunning clutch – See clutch(overrunning).

oversize pistons – Pistons cast with larger than stock outside diameters.

oversize tires – Tires sized larger than stock size for a car.

overspray – Condition created when paint being sprayed dries before reaching the surface to be painted. Some overspray (also called dry spray) occurs in most spray painting conditions. Possible causes of excessive overspray include: thinner too fast, air pressure too high, spray gun held too far from surface. See also paint coat problem(rough/dull).

over-square – See engine(over square).

overstage – To move a race car's front wheels past the starting line.

overstating the case – To exaggerate or state a case too strongly.

oversteer – Tendency exhibited by a car rounding a corner, to turn more sharply than intended. Also, it refers to a car losing traction with the rear tires first when rounding a corner. It is caused by the rear wheels tracking at larger slip angles than the front tires. Oversteer can suddenly appear when only one end of a car's suspension has been softened. The following changes will reduce oversteer: increase rear and decrease front tire pressure, make front wheel camber more positive, put more weight toward the front of the car, use softer rear and stiffer front springs, and use smaller diameter front and larger diameter rear tires. See also understeer and neutral steer.

overworking the metal — To excessively hammer a metal shape back to return it to its original contour. Hammering increases and decreases metal thickness causing distortion. See also upset and stretch.

Owatonna — American car produced in 1903.

O-We-Go — American car produced from 1914-1915 by O-We-Go Car Co. in New York.

Owen — American car produced in 1899. Also, an American car produced from 1910-1914 by Owen Motor Car Co. in Michigan.

Owen Magnetic — American car produced from 1914-1921 by Baker, Rauch & Lang Co. in Ohio and Pennsylvania (1914-1919), and Owen Magnetic Motor Car Corp. in Pennsylvania (1919-1922). It was a luxury car using a 6 cylinder gas engine to generate electric power for operating a gearless magnetic transmission.

Owen Schoenieck — American car produced from 1915-1916 by Owen-Schoeneck Co. in Wisconsin.

Owen-Thomas — American car produced in 1909.

owner — Person registered as holding the legal title to a car.

owner's handbook — See owner's manual.

owner's manual — Brief manual supplied with each car. It contains important information on mechanical aspects and advice on caring for the car. Topics covered include starting, operating, driving, fluid levels and types to use, proper tire inflation, etc.

owner responsibility — Clause written in a document, such as a contract, warranty, insurance policy, etc., specifying what conditions a document holder must meet for a document to remain valid.

Owosso — American car produced in 1911.

Oxford — American car produced in 1905. Also, a Canadian car produced from 1913-1915.

oxidation — Chemical union of oxygen with any substance. Oxidation usually creates heat and increases the weight of a substance. Fuels, which oxidize faster, create heat in a shorter period of time, and are thus more powerful. Examples of oxidation compounds include: carbon and oxygen combining in a combustion chamber to form carbon dioxide and carbon monoxide, and iron and oxygen to form iron oxide or rust.

oxidation inhibitor — See additive(oxidation inhibitor).

oxidation resistance — Property exhibited by an oil resisting oxidation at high operating temperatures. It helps prevent formation of oil-derived deposits, and engine corrosion from oxyacids. Most engine oils today use an additive to minimize oxidation.

oxides of nitrogen — See NOx.

oxy-acetylene outfit — Equipment used to weld metals with oxygen and acetylene gases. It primarily consists of: an oxygen tank, an acetylene tank, gas regulators, gas hose, welding and cutting torch, assorted torch tips, goggles, and gas igniter.

oxygen sensing wire — Specially developed wire able to perform the same functions as an oxygen sensor.

oxygen sensor — See sensor(oxygen).

P

/P - Abbreviation for all power.

P(1) - Abbreviation for park position on automatic transmission shift selectors.

P(2) - Abbreviation for power.

P(3) - Abbreviation for Poland found usually on an international license plate.

P(4) - Auction car rating code used to specify a car in poor condition needing repair work such as tire replacement, painting, engine work, and interior reconditioning.

Pacer - American car produced from 1975-1980 by American Motors Corp. in Michigan.

Pacesetter - American car produced from 1962-1964 by Chrysler Corp. in Michigan.

Pacific - American car produced in 1914.

Pacific Special - American car produced in 1914.

pack - Extra charges included in a finance contract to increase profit. It is popular in car finance contracts. People with poor credit usually pay more. Rate charts are used to determine what the buyer should pay in extra charges. Some finance companies will offer kickbacks to those dealers who can get buyers to agree to higher extra charges. See also rate charts.

package - Car concept or organization with accompanying dimensions.

package drawing - Guide used by car designers and engineers in finishing a car design.

package tray - Shelf-like portion of a car interior located between the top of a rear seat and a backlight.

Packard - American car produced from 1898-1958 by New York & Ohio Co. in Ohio (1899-1901), Ohio Automobile Co. in Ohio (1901-1902), Packard Motor Car Co. in Ohio (1902-1903), Packard Motor Car Co. in Michigan (1903-1955), and Studebaker-Packard Corp. in Michigan (1955-1958).

Packard, James Ward - He was an early automotive pioneer who organized the Packard Electric Company in 1890 and introduced his first car in 1899. In 1900, he organized the New York and Ohio Automobile Company. It became successful and moved to Detroit in 1903 as the Packard Motor Company.

Packard V-12 - American car driven by Ralph DePalma to a 1919 world land speed record of 149.9 mph at Daytona, Florida.

Packers - American car produced in 1911.

Packet - American car produced from 1916-1917 by Packet Motor Car Mfg. in Minnesota.

packing - Material compressed inside a groove to prevent leakage around a moving shaft of an engine, pump, or valve. It is usually fibrous and impregnated with grease.

Paco - American car produced in 1908.

pad - Cushion-like soft material used for comfort, protection, or stuffing.

padded repair bill - Repair bill tabulated with charges for unnecessary or non-existent parts and labor work. See also con game(padding the bill).

padding the bill - To add charges to a repair bill for unnecessary labor and/or parts, labor not done, and/or parts never installed. See also con game(padding the bill).

paddock - Race track area used to store, repair, and prepare cars.

Page - American car produced from 1906-1907 and 1921-1924 by Page Motor Vehicle Co. in Rhode Island, and Victor W. Page Motors Corp. in Connecticut respectively.

Page-Toledo - American car produced in 1910.

Paige - American car produced in 1910.

Paige-Detroit - American car produced from 1908-1927 by Paige-Detroit Motor Car Co. in Michigan.

Paige-Detroit Motor Company - Company organized in 1909 by Fred Paige to produce two-cycle cars. In 1927, the Graham Brothers acquired control and changed the name to Graham-Paige.

Paige, Fred O - He was a man who organized the Paige-Detroit Motor Company in 1909 to produce two-cycle cars. He served as president until 1910.

paint - Liquid chemical compound applied as a thin coating to a surface and drying to a hard solid finish. Basic ingredients include: pigment, binder, and solvent. It is used to protect a surface from the elements as well as add beauty.

paint(acrylic enamel) - Enamel formulated to have the following advantages over regular enamel: increased resistance to effects of sun and weather, maintain high gloss with no waxing, hard finish, faster drying time, and highly resistant to oil and gasoline staining. Advantages over lacquer include: no rubbing required, tougher finish, and requires fewer coats. Disadvantages include: no polishing or waxing for two months, use of special solvents for removing road tar, not advisable to use over conventional lacquer, and much longer drying time than lacquer. Acrylic paints dry from evaporation of solvent.

paint(acrylic enamel with catalyst) - Two-part paint composed of acrylic enamel and an added catalyst. It creates a topcoat with properties between an acrylic enamel and a polyurethane paint. One big advantage is the much broader color selection range than with a polyurethane.

paint(acrylic lacquer) - Lacquer formulated to have the same advantages and disadvantages as acrylic enamel. It is a plastic-based material.

paint(acrylic resin) - Paint commonly used on new cars. It is sprayed and baked on at the factory and produces a hard finish resistant to oxidation for a few years.

paint(base coat) - Paint coating used to form the base for other subsequent paints applied over it. A base coat can be an undercoat or a coating designed not to be completely covered. For example, a light blue base coat of paint is applied and then different areas of a car body are shaded with a dark blue topcoat.

paint(candy) - Translucent custom paint applied over a special base coat to give an appearance of depth.

paint(clear coat) - Coating of clear paint. Clear coats are usually applied over new paint to protect the finish and give it extra sheen. Paints used include: polyurethane and lacquer.

paint(enamel) - Paint formulated with a base made from varnishes, alcohol, turpentine, and/or amyl acetates. Enamel is a more durable paint than lacquer and can be applied directly over it. It dries slower than lacquer by first evaporating the solvent and then oxidizing the binder with the air. Two coats of enamel are equivalent to 5-6 coats of lacquer. See also baked enamel finish.

paint(epoxy) - Two-part paint used to form an extremely hard and durable finish. Other characteristics include: fills well, doesn't shrink with age, can be applied over enamel or lacquer if a sealer is used, can be mixed with certain custom paints, highly resistant to chipping, takes a couple hours to dry to a touch, and not as fade-resistant as polyurethane paint.

paint(high temperature-enamel) - Enamel paint formulated to resist high temperatures. It is typically used on exhaust manifolds, engine blocks, mufflers, etc.

paint(hot lacquer) - Lacquer paint heated, typically to around 160 degrees, to improve painting results. Advantages include: lower paint viscosity requiring less thinning; less chance of drying before reaching surface; quicker drying time; tougher finish; less rubbing; elimination of blushing; less dirt in finish; reduced tendency for sag, orange peel, and overspray; and higher and more uniform gloss.

paint(lacquer) - Quick drying paint formulated with a base made from cellulose, resin, and Lac. It dries from the inside out. A deep shine requires rubbing and color sanding. Lacquer cannot be applied over enamel unless a sealer coat separates them.

paint(metallic) - Custom paint formulated with powdered metal whose many sides reflect light brightly in many directions.

paint(pearl) - Iridescent custom paint sprayed over a base coat.

paint(polyurethane) - Expensive paint composed of pure polyurethane compound. It forms an excellent impervious topcoat for demanding conditions. Characteristics include: fade resistance, good durability, very tough and flexible, very high gloss, resistance to corrosive liquids and fuels, hard to remove, and smaller color selection. See also paint(acrylic enamel with catalyst).

paint(primer) - See paint(undercoat).

paint(primer/sealer) - Paint formulated with primer and sealer properties.

paint(sealer) - Coating material formulated usually from resins for sealing underlying paint and preventing any chemicals in a topcoat from attacking it. Any paint, not totally compatible with an existing car paint, must go on after a sealer coat or cracking, blistering, flaking, peeling, etc. will occur.

paint(spatter) - Paint used to produce a mottled finish. It is commonly used in car trunks.

paint(surfacer) - See paint(undercoat).

paint(topcoat) - Outermost paint coating applied to a car. It typically consists of powder and liquid compounds known as pigment and binder respectively. A topcoat adheres to a rough or sticky surface, but not usually to metal. An adhesive surface is created by roughing up an existing paint surface and/or applying an undercoat.

paint(touch up) - Paint matched to a car's existing topcoat and used to fill chips and scratches. It is usually sold in a small container with an applicator brush.

paint(trunk) - See paint(spatter).

paint(two part) - Paint composed of two compounds sold separately, then later mixed together. One compound is a pigment/binder, while the other is a catalyst. Examples of two part paints include: epoxy, urethane, polyurethane, and two part enamel. It has the following characteristics: durable, resistant to corrosion, tricky to apply, harden quickly, mistakes can be sanded out and resprayed.

paint(undercoat) - Paint coating formulated to form an adhesive base between an existing metal and/or paint surface and a subsequently applied topcoat. Other characteristics include: fast drying time, good sealing effect, resistance to pigment settling, and ability to fill minor surface flaws. It is available in lacquer-based and enamel-based varieties that dry quickly and more slowly respectively as well as for other paint materials such as acrylics, epoxies, urethanes, etc. See also metal conditioner, prepcoat, and tack rag.

paint(vinyl) - Paint formulated to cover vinyl fabric materials.

paint(wrinkle) - Paint formulated to produce a crackled or grainy finish. It is used to protect certain metal surfaces and for customizing.

paint blemish - Stain, spot, mark, etc., marring a paint surface.

paint blushing - See paint coat problem(blushing).

paint coat problem - Condition created when the paint surface of a car does not have the proper finish. This can apply to new or existing paint.

paint coat problem(bleeding) - Condition created when underlying paint or body filler reacts with a newly applied paint to form surface blemishes on the new paint. Possible causes include: old paint pigment dissolving in new paint solvent, and filler not completely cured. Bleeding is usually prevented by letting all plastic filler cure and applying a good coat of primer or sealer over the old paint. See also paint(sealer).

paint coat problem(blistering) - Condition created when existing paint lifts between coats. It is most commonly due to rust. Other possible causes include: moisture, oil, grease, or foreign particles. The only solution is to properly sand the surface, clean it, and repaint.

paint coat problem(blushing) - Condition created when a newly applied paint finish becomes milky or dull. It is usually caused by: moisture condensing on wet paint due to humid weather, humid spraying area, high air pressure, damp paint surface, and/or water in air lines. It can also be caused by excessive evaporation of solvents. Adding retarder or a slower reducer to the paint will usually cure the problem. It is best to avoid spray painting during humid weather.

paint coat problem(bruising/chipping) - Condition created when an existing paint surface is chipped or softened to the metal. It is usually caused by small rocks hitting the paint finish. The chips can be touched up, but the only permanent solution is to properly sand the surface, clean it, and repaint.

paint coat problem(chalking) - Condition created when existing paint has a dull oxidized powdery appearance. It is usually caused exposure to sunlight and weather. If the condition is not severe, the chalking can be removed by using a rubbing or polishing compound and then waxing the surface.

paint coat problem(checking) - Condition created when newly applied paint separates into crowfoot-like lines. Possible problem causes are similar to those caused when paint cracks. See also paint coat problem(cracking).

paint coat problem(cracking) - Condition created when newly applied paint develops random cracks penetrating to metal or an undercoated surface. Possible causes include: bending of body panels, applying second coat before first one is dry, temperature differences (such as painting a hot surface then allowing it to cool rapidly), poorly mixed paint, primer or top coats too thick, incompatible paint products, too much catalyst in two-part type paints, and painting over areas showing signs of damage. Removing the cracks requires properly sanding to metal, cleaning, and repainting.

paint coat problem(craters) - See paint coat problem(fisheyes).

paint coat problem(crazing) - See paint coat problem(lifting) and paint coat problem(blistering).

paint coat problem(drips) - See paint coat problem(sagging).

paint coat problem(fish eyes) - Condition created when newly applied paint causes little eyes or bubbles to form. Possible causes include: contamination of surface with wax, grease, and oil. Correcting the problem requires properly sanding the surface; removing all traces of surface contamination with a wax and grease remover, resanding (if needed), and repainting.

paint coat problem(lifting) - Condition created when newly applied paint puckers and wrinkles. Possible causes include: paint with strong solvents applied to a partially oxidized surface, surface contamination such as wax, dirt, and water. Correcting the problem requires properly sanding the

surface, cleaning it, and repainting. with proper solvent.
paint coat problem(mottled) - Condition created when newly applied paint takes on a blotchy, streaked, and/or spotted texture. It is usually caused by painting a surface covered with a polished silicone wax. Correcting the appearance requires properly sanding the surface, removing all traces of wax and other contaminants, and repainting. See also paint coat problem(streaking).
paint coat problem(orange peel) - Condition created when newly applied paint takes on a texture like the skin of an orange peel. Possible causes include: paint not reduced enough, wrong thinner, thinner drying too fast, surface temperature too warm, wrong air pressure at gun, gun too close, too much overlap, air nozzle dirty, and slow gun movement.
paint coat problem(overspray) - See paint coat problem(rough/dull).
paint coat problem(pinholing) - Condition created when small pinholes begin appearing in newly applied paint usually over areas that have been body filled. It is usually caused by improper use of body filler. Possible causes include: too much hardener, mixing filler too vigorously (traps air bubbles in filler), filler not thoroughly mixed, and hardener not completely mixed with filler. If pinholes appear: 1 - sand down the affected area, and reapply filler, or 2 - apply successive coats of primer-surfacer to fill holes or use a light coat of body putty.
paint coat problem(ripples) - See paint coat problem(sagging).
paint coat problem(rough/dull) - Condition created when newly applied paint is sprayed on thinly and dries to a rough sandpaper-like finish with little or no sheen. It is usually caused by paint drying before it reaches the surface. Possible causes include: spray gun too far from surface; too much air in mixture; fast spray gun movement; no paint overlap; and wrong air nozzle; air pressure too high; thinned paint drying too quickly due to too little thinner, poor quality thinner, and thinner evaporating too fast for weather conditions. See also overspray.
paint coat problem(runs) - See paint coat problem(sagging).
paint coat problem(sagging) - Condition created when newly applied paint is sprayed on heavily and sags or runs. Possible causes include: gun too close, slow gun movement, paint too thin, too much overlap, air nozzle dirty, and low air pressure.
paint coat problem(sand scratching) - Condition created when scratches appear under newly applied paint that has dried. It is primarily caused by scratches that were not been sanded out with fine sandpaper.
paint coat problem(separations) - See paint coat problem(fisheyes).
paint coat problem(streaking) - Condition created when newly applied paint color is uneven with light and dark areas. Possible causes include: paint passes not properly overlapped, spray pattern not properly adjusted, base coat not properly applied, and partially plugged spray gun nozzle.
paint coat problem(surface blemishes) - Condition when dirt, dust, bugs, and other airborne contaminants land on a freshly painted surface. To avoid blemishes: keep the paint area and car as clean as possible, strain paint carefully, and use a paint cup strainer. Bodywork should be done in a location separate from where the painting will be done. Prepare the car by: blowing dust and other particles off all car surfaces and crevices away from the paint area, move car to the paint area, and go over surfaces again with a tack rag just before painting.
paint coat problem(swelling) - Condition created when newly applied lacquer paint causes underlying lacquer paint to swell. It is usually due to sanding the existing paint surface. The solvents in the new paints penetrate the old finish and swell. Lacquer paints jobs must first be sealed if the original surface is sanded.
paint coat problem(water spotting) - Condition created when an existing paint finish develops water spots. It is usually caused by washing a car in bright sunlight on a hot day.
paint coat problem(wrinkling) - Condition created when a newly applied paint wrinkles. It is usually caused by applying synthetic enamel in heavy coats. Warm temperatures aggravate the situation.
painted line - Paint line applied to the center of a roadway to keep traffic properly divided.
paint reducer - Solvent used to reduce the viscosity of enamel-based paint making it suitable for spraying. The amount of reducer used depends primarily on the paint type and temperature. In general, as the room temperature increases paint viscosity lowers and so less reducer is needed.
paint retarder - Solvent used to reduce the evaporation rate of a solvent-based paint.
paint scratch - Scratch located on a paint surface.
paint solvent - Liquid chemical compound formulated to thin paint down into a sprayable consistency and then evaporate after the paint is deposited onto the surface. The two main types of paint solvents are lacquer thinner, and enamel reducer. Both are are sometimes erroneously referred to as thinners.

Thinner solvents are used only with lacquer and acrylic lacquer paints.
Enamel reducers are used only with enamel paints.
paint sprayer - See spray gun.
paint stripping - Process used to remove all paint from a surface. Processes include: sandblasting and chemical removers.
paint thinner - Solvent used to reduce the viscosity of lacquer-based paint making it suitable for spraying. All-purpose types are suitable for most conditions, except hot weather where a slow thinner (retarder) is needed to slow the paint drying process. The amount of thinner used depends primarily on the paint type and temperature, and is often 2-3 times the amount of paint used.
As a general rule of thumb, increasing room temperature means paint viscosity lowers and so less thinner is needed.
PAIR - Abbreviation for pulse-air injection reactor.
PAK - Abbreviation for Pakistan found usually on an international license plate.
Pak-Age-Car - American car produced in 1925.
Palace - American car produced in 1912.
Palm - Canadian car produced from 1918-1919.
Palmer - American car produced in 1906.
Palmer-Moore - American car produced in 1905.
Palmer-Singer - American car produced from 1907-1914 by Palmer & Singer Mfg. Co. in New York.
Pan - American car produced from 1918-1922 by Pan Motor Co. in Minnesota.
pan - See oil pan.
Pan American - American car produced in 1902. Also, an American car produced from 1917-1922 by Pan-American Motor Corp. in Illinois.
pancake engine - See engine(horizontally opposed).
Panch, Marvin - He won the Daytona 500 Race in 1961 averaging 149.6 mph in a Pontiac.
Panda - American car produced from 1955-1956 by Small Cars in Missouri.
panel(1) - Specific area on car body surface painted a contrasting color to separate it from the car's topcoat. A panel can be most any defined shape. See also scallop and panel painting.
panel(2) - Section of sheetmetal used to cover a portion of a car body surface. For example, a door panel covers the outer portion of a door structure.
panel painting - Custom painting technique used to paint a car panel a contrasting color or design separating it from the rest of a car body surface.
panel truck - Truck built with an enclosed cargo area.
pan gasket - Gasket used to seal an oil pan to the bottom of a crankcase or automatic transmission housing.
Panhard et Levassor - French manufacturing company known for producing the first automobile of classic design (engine in front supplying power to a gearbox behind) in 1892. It was called a Panhard et Lavassor.
Panhard rod - Rod positioned perpendicular to a car's length and attached to a car frame. It is typically used to prevent lateral axle movement. It is also known as an anti-sway bar.
Panhard Truck - American truck produced from 1917-1918.
panic stop - Suddenly and quickly stopping a car. The brakes are often applied so hard the wheels lock up and cause skidding.
panning - Condition created when a radar device reads background instead of a target vehicle. It generally produces an inaccurate reading of the vehicle's speed.
Pantera - High performance sports car imported from Italy by Ford from 1971-1974. See also De Tomaso and De Tomaso, Allessandro.
Panther - American car produced in 1908. Also, an American car produced from 1962-1963 by Panther Automobile Co. in New York. It was a fiberglass sports car with a reported 150 mph top speed.
pant - Rear fender cover.
paper - See tissue.
paper down - Sales tactic used to close a car sale where a dealer makes a car downpayment for the customer on paper. The dealer doesn't actually pay anything and simply adds it to the total price of the car.
paper man - Used car dealer who finances his own cars regardless of a car buyer's credit.
Paragon - American car produced from 1905-1907 and 1921-1922 by Detroit Automobile Mfg. Co. in Michigan, and Paragon Motor Car Co. in Pennsylvania respectively.
paraffin(1) - Substance characterized as solid, white, waxy, tasteless, and odorless. It is derived from the distillation of petroleum.
paraffin(2) - Kerosene.
paraffin base oil - See oil(paraffin base).
paraffin series - See methane series.

parallel circuit - See circuit(parallel).
parallelogram steering linkage - Steering system constructed utilizing two short tie rods connected to steering arms and a long center link. The link is supported on one end by an idler arm and attached directly to a pitman arm at the other end. The arrangement forms a parallelogram shape.
Paramount Cab - American car produced in 1924.
parent company - Company engaged in supplying products to franchises or subsidiaries it owns.
Parenti - American car produced from 1920-1922 by Parenti Motors Corp. in New York.
park-and-sell lot - Car selling lot engaged in renting space to car sellers usually on a daily basis.
Park Avenue - American car produced from 1985 to date by Buick Division of General Motors Corp. in Michigan.
parked car - Car positioned in a parking spot.
Parker - Canadian car produced from 1921-1923 by Parker Motor Car Co. in Quebec.
Parkin - American car produced from 1903-1909 by Parkin & Son in Pennsylvania.
parking brake - See brake(emergency).
parking garage - Enclosed multi-level structure built to house parked cars.
parking lights - See light(parking).
parking lot - Area set aside for parking cars.
parking meter - Meter used to charge money for the use of a parking space. It contains a timer and is usually situated on busy city streets.
Park Lane - American car produced from 1957-1977 by Mercury Division of Ford Motor Co. in Michigan.
park position - Automatic transmission selector position used to prevent a transmission output shaft from turning. Some designs lock a shaft to a transmission case.
parole - Conditional release made of a person serving time in prison before the end of his maximum imposed sentence.
Parry - American car produced from 1910-1912 Parry Auto Co. in Indiana (1910-1911), and Motor Car Mfg. Co. in Indiana (1912).
Parsienne - American car produced from 1980 to date by Pontiac Division of General Motors Corp. in Michigan.
Parsons - American electric car produced from 1905-1906 by Parsons Electric Motor Carriage Co. in Ohio.
Parsons, Benny - He won the Daytona 500 Race in 1975 averaging 153.6 mph in a Chevrolet. He also became the NASCAR Grand National Champion in 1973.
Parsons, Johnnie - He won the Indianapolis 500 Race in 1950 driving an average of 124.0 mph in a Wynn's Friction Proofing Special.
partial flow filter - Oil filter designed to filter part of the oil output from an oil pump. See also full flow oil filter and bypass oil filter.
Partin - American car produced in 1913.
Partin-Palmer - American car produced from 1913-1917 by Partin Mfg. Co. (1913-1915), and Commonwealth Motors Co. (1913-1915), both in Illinois.
parting out - To retire a car from service and sell it in parts rather than as maintain high gloss with no waxing, hard finish, faster drying time, and one complete unit.
parts are frozen - Moving engine parts binding against each other and unable to move. See also freeze up.
parts car - Car purchased as a source of parts for keeping another car of the same make and model running. Also, it refers to a car not easily restorable due to: major missing parts, poor modifications, extensive rusting, serious damage, etc.
parts changing syndrome - Approach taken by car repairmen to remove and replace a part that could be repaired.
parts chaser - See job(parts chaser).
parts cleaner - Chemical compound used to clean car parts. Also, it refers to a tank or container where car parts are cleaned.
parts department - Department found at a car repair or sales business that orders, stocks, and sell car parts and accessories. At a car dealership, the department sells parts to the service department, local independent garages, and the public.
parts guarantee - Guarantee given by a manufacturer that parts produced will not be defective in materials and workmanship.
parts list - List of parts specified in a car repair. Also, it refers to a listing of car parts in various shop manuals, parts manuals, etc.
parts man - See job(parts man).
parts manual - Manual issued by car manufacturers to dealers detailing all the parts of various cars produced.
parts pushers - People in the car repair business engaged in pressuring you into getting parts for your car that may not be necessary. Often times, they are not mechanics.
Pasco - American car produced in 1908.

pass - Abbreviation for passenger.
passenger - Person traveling with the driver of a car.
passenger car - Car built to carry passengers besides a driver.
passenger car tire standards - Set of standards a car's tires should meet for safety. Manufacturers can legally sell tires not meeting a car's requirements. Such tires may not even be suitable for highway driving, so buy tires carefully.
passenger compartment - Portion of a car body where passengers sit.
passing - Driving maneuver used to get around and in front of a car being followed. Passing is a risky maneuver that often saves little time.
passing gear - Lower automatic or manual transmission gear engaged to provide more power when passing another car.
passive restraint - Device used to prevent forward movement of a car passenger in a seat only when a specified impact force occurs to a car's front end. Devices used include: seat belts and air bags.
Pastora - American car produced in 1913.
patent - Government grant given to an inventor or to another he specifies for the exclusive privilege to make, use, license, sell his invention for a specified period of time.
Paterson - American car produced from 1908-1923 by W.A. Paterson Co. in Michigan.
Pathfinder - American car produced from 1911-1918 by Motor Car Mfg. Co. (1911-1915), and Pathfinder Co. (1916-1918), both in Indiana.
Patrician - American car produced in 1917.
Patriot - American car produced in 1922.
patrol - To maintain order and security in specific areas either on foot or in a patrol car by watching for: any odd behavior, something out of place, or someone in trouble. Areas patrolled include: downtown areas, along roadways, and around buildings.
patrol car - Car used by law enforcement agencies to travel on public roads and enforce the law.
patrolman - Policeman assigned to patrol a certain area.
patrol wagon - Enclosed car, van, or truck used to transport prisoners.
Patterson-Greenfield - American car produced from 1916-1918 by C.R. Patterson & Sons in Ohio.
paved highway - Road covered with pavement.
paved road - See paved highway.
pavement - Asphalt, concrete, or other material used to cover a road surface.
pavement markings - Paint, circular mounds, etc. applied to pavement for marking lanes of traffic.
pavement markings(crosswalk lines) - Solid parallel lines spaced about three feet apart and applied across roads at intersection corners or sometimes at other locations.
pavement markings(edge lines) - Solid paint lines used along a roadway's edge. White lines are used along the outside, and yellow lines are usually used along the inside when roadway traffic lanes are separated by a median strip.
pavement markings(two way left turn lane) - Closely spaced solid and dashed yellow lines applied on both sides of a continuous left turn lane, located usually in the middle of a multi-lane highway. The solid lines appears along the outside edge of the lane.
pavement markings(no passing line) - Solid yellow line used on two lane roadways to denote when and in what direction passing is not allowed. Passing is not permitted from the lane in which the line appears for as long as it appears.
pavement markings(railroad crossing) - Several markings used to alert traffic to a railroad crossing and help control traffic flow. Markings usually consist of: a large white X sandwiched between two R letters, a yellow center line extending some distance from the crossing (to prevent passing), and a white stop line perpendicular to the road direction and a safe distance from the railroad tracks.
pavement markings(reversible lanes) - Closely spaced dashed yellow lines applied on both sides of a traffic lane used for reversible traffic flow. It is usually a center lane of a multi-lane highway.
pavement markings(stop line) - Solid white line used to indicate the stopping position of traffic at an intersection. It is applied perpendicular to the road direction.
pavement markings(yellow) - Yellow line(s) applied to the center and/or edge of traffic lanes to: separate opposing traffic lanes, control passing, mark two-way left turn lanes, and/or mark reversible lanes. Solid lines are usually used to restrict passing when applied between opposing lanes, or to designate an inside shoulder of a multi-lane highway separated by a median strip. Dashed lines are used to separate opposing traffic lanes, yet permit passing when safe.
pavement markings(white line) - White line painted between lanes of traffic going in the same direction (dashed), or along a roadway edge (solid).

pavement markings(yellow center lines) — Two solid yellow lines usually used to separate multi-lane traffic moving in opposite directions without a center median strip.

pavement markings(white) — White paint applied to a road surface to define two or more traffic lanes flowing in the same direction, or outside roadway edges. Freeways are a typical example. It is usually applied as a single dashed line.

pawl — Stud, pin, or bar moved or pivoted into engagement with teeth cut on another part. An example is a parking pawl in an automatic transmission sliding to contact teeth on another part to lock the rear wheels.

Pawtucket — American steam car produced from 1900-1901 by Pawtucket Steam Boat Co. in Rhode Island. It was a small one passenger car.

payload — Rated carrying capacity of a vehicle.

payment buyer — Potential car buyer interested only in the monthly payment amount. See also sucker.

Payne-Modern — American car produced from 1907-1909 by Modern Tool Co. in Pennsylvania.

payoff — See payola.

payola — Money paid to police officers for protecting a business or steering car business their way. A common example is a tow truck business paying police officers a fee each time they are given a tow job.

PB — Abbreviation for power brakes.

pb — Abbreviation for power brakes.

PCV — Abbreviation for positive crankcase ventilation. See also PCV valve.

PCV filter — Filter installed usually in an air cleaner to filter heavy crankcase vapors before entering the intake air stream.

PCV hose — Hose used to route crankcase vapors from the PCV valve to the PCV filter.

PCV system — See emission control system(crankcase-PCV).

PCV valve — Positive crankcase ventilation valve used to reroute unburned gases built up in a crankcase area into an engine's combustion chambers for safe burning. The valve eventually clogs from residue in the gases. Once clogged, blow-by gases begin condensing in the crankcase diluting the oil and forming sludge and acids. A clogged valve can cause hard starting, rough and/or lower idling, stalling, and lower fuel economy (due to restriction of designed-in vacuum leak). One way to check for a clogged valve is to start the engine, then remove the oil filler cap. Cover the opening with your hand or a piece of paper. If there is a vacuum, you'll feel it on your hand or see the paper get pulled down. A vacuum indicates a working valve. The valve should be checked on a regular basis and replaced every 12,000 miles or when indicated. When replacing, be sure to get the correct valve as it is calibrated according to the carburetor it works with. An incorrect valve can cause problems similar to a clogged valve and also a lean fuel/air mixture. See also emission control system(crankcase-PCV), emission control system(crankcase-closed type-2), car service tip(PCV system test), and pollution control valve.

PDB — Abbreviation for power disc brakes.

p disc — Abbreviation for power disc brakes.
maintain high gloss with no waxing, hard finish, faster drying time, and

PDL — Abbreviation for power door locks.

PDT — Abbreviation for Pacific Daylight Time.

PE — Abbreviation for Peru found usually on an international license plate.

Peabody — American car produced in 1907.

peacock — Car buyer compelled to purchase and drive one of the newest cars regardless of the extra cost involved.

peak line — Line formed by the intersection of two planes. Also, it refers to a sharply defined ridge in a metal surface.

peak out — Engine rpm reached when an engine is at maximum power.

Pearson, David — He won the Daytona 500 Race in 1976 averaging 152.2 mph in a Mercury. He also became the NASCAR Grand National Champion in 1966, 1968, and 1969.

Peck — American car produced in 1897. Also, a Canadian car produced in 1913.

pedal — Foot operated lever used to control a car's brakes, clutch, speed, parking brake, etc.

pedal pressure — Amount of pressure applied to a gas, brake, clutch, or parking brake pedal.

pedal reserve — Amount of pedal distance left pedal and the floor when applied. It usually refers to a brake pedal.

Pedersen — American car produced in 1922.

pedestrian — Person traveling on foot.

pedestrian crossing — See crosswalk.

pedestrian overpass — Foot bridge built over a busy roadway to allow people on foot to safely walk from one side to another.

pedestrian underpass — Tunnel built underneath a busy roadway to allow people on foot to safely walk from one side to another.

peen - To flatten, stretch, or clinch a piece of metal over by pounding with the round hammer head.

Peerless - American car produced from 1900-1931 by Peerless Motor Car Co. in Ohio. It was called "one of the three P's" in its time with the other two being Packard and Pierce-Arrow. The three formed a great trio in the car industry.

Peerles Steam - American steam car produced from 1902-1909.

Peet - American car produced from 1923-1926.

Pelletier - American car produced in 1906.

Pendleton - American car produced in 1905.

penetrating oil - Special oil used to help remove rusted parts by penetrating and dissolving the rust.

Penford - American car produced in 1924.

Peninsular - American car produced in 1915.

Penn - American car produced from 1911-1913 by Penn Motor Car Co. in Pennsylvania.

Penn-Unit - American car produced in 1911.

Pennant - American car produced in 1923.

Pennington - American car produced in 1894-1902.

Pennsy - American car produced from 1916-1919 by Pennsy Motors Co. in Pennsylvania.

Pennsylvania - American car produced in 1907-1911 by Pennsylvania Auto-Motor Co. in Pennsylvania.

Pennsylvania Turnpike - It was the first modern long distance road in the U.S., opening in 1940.

Pennzoil - American line of engine oils produced by Pennzoil Company.

Pennzoil Company - A U.S. petroleum company headquartered in Houston, Texas. See also petroleum company.

pentane - Liquid methane series hydrocarbon compound found in petroleum deposits with a melting and boiling point of -201 and 97 degrees Fahrenheit respectively. It is one of the ingredients in gasoline.

People's - American car produced from 1900-1902 by People's Automobile Co. in Ohio.

percentage - Racing fuel mixture composed of nitromethane and alcohol. For example, a car using 60 percent would be using a fuel containing 60 percent nitromethane and 40 percent alcohol.

percent cut - Splitting of the money received from the sales of parts and equipment. A 50 percent cut is a common split in many car repair businesses. Unfortunately, it only encourages mechanics, service station attendants, and others to sell unnecessary parts.

perception time - Time required by a driver to notice a possible hazard. If the driver is paying attention to road conditions and cars around him, it will be near zero. It can be several seconds if the hazard occurs when a driver is looking away. See also reaction time.

Perego-Clarkston Truck - American truck produced in 1920.

Perfection - American car produced from 1906-1908 by Perfection Automobile Works in Indiana.

Perfex - American car produced from 1912-1914 by Perfex Co. in California.

peripheral vision - Amount of side vision possessed by the eyes when looking straight ahead. People with good peripheral vision can see about 90 degrees to the side. Your peripheral vision is poor, if you must move an arm extended from your side more than 20 degrees toward the center of your vision.

periphery - Outer edge or circumference of a circle.

perjury - To knowingly tell a lie when under oath in a court of law to tell the truth.

Permatex - Line of adhesive and gasket type products.

Perry - American car produced in 1895.

personal recognizance - Obligation recorded in a court of law requiring a person to do some act such as: reappear in court, pay a debt, etc. It is similar to a bond, but differs in that it acknowledges some prior recorded debt.

Peru - American car produced in 1938.

PET - American car produced in 1914.

petcock - Small valve commonly used in fuel and water circuits to regulate flow or permit drainage.

Peter Pan - American car produced from 1914-1915 by Randall Co. in Massachusetts.

Peters - American car produced from 1921-1922 by Peters Autocar Co. in New Jersey.

Peters-Walton-Ludlow - American car produced in 1915.

Peterson Publishing Company - Publisher of a line of automotive self-help books and several car magazines.

Petillo, Kelly - He won the Indianapolis 500 Race in 1935 driving an average of 106.2 mph in a Gilmore Speedway Special.

Petrel – American car produced from 1908-1912 by Petrel Motor Car Co. (1908-1909), and Petrol Motor Car Co. (1910-1912), both in WIsconsin.

petrol – Gasoline.

petroleum – Complex naturally occurring mixture of solid, liquid, and gaseous hydrocarbons composed of compounds of hydrogen and carbon, and small amounts of sulfur, nitrogen, and oxygen. Products made from petroleum include: gasoline, diesel fuel, jet fuel, kerosene, lubricants, greases, waxes, soaps, asphalt, fertilizers, fuel coke, coke products, and various solvents and plastics.

petroleum asphalt – See asphalt.

petroleum company – Business engaged in extracting petroleum, refining it into various products, and marketing those products. United States companies include: Ashland Oil, Inc.; Atlantic Richfield Co.; Chevron Corporation; Cities Service Company; Conoco, Inc.; Exxon Corporation; Gulf Corporation; Mobil Oil Corporation; Occidental Petroleum Corp.; Pennzoil Company; Phillips Petroleum Co.; Shell Oil Company; AMOCO; Standard Oil Company; Sun Company, Inc.; Texaco,Inc.; and Unocal Corporation.

petroleum product – A product made from processed and/or unprocessed petroleum. See also petroleum.

petrol pump – See fuel pump.

Petty, Lee – He won the Daytona 500 race in 1959 averaging 135.5 mph in an Oldsmobile. He also became the NASCAR Grand National Champion in 1954, 1958 and 1959.

Petty, Richard – He is the son of Lee Petty and won the Daytona 500 race in 1964, 1966, 1971, 1973, 1974, 1979, and 1981. Average speeds were 154.3, 160.6, 144.5, 157.2, 140.9, and 144.0 mph. Cars driven were a Plymouth (1964, 1966, 1971), Dodge (1973 and 1974), Oldsmobile, and Buick. He became the NASCAR Grand National Champion in 1964, 1967, 1971, 1972, 1974, 1975, and 1979; and has won over 200 NASCAR races to date.

Peugeot – Car built in 1896. Also, a French car line produced from 1889 to date by SA des Automobiles Peugeot.
   The U.S. representative of currently built Peugot cars is Peugeot Motors of America, Inc., headquartered in Lyndhurst, New Jersey.

Peugeot Quadrilette – French car made in the 1920s with a 40 mph maximum speed.

PH – Abbreviation for phaeton. See also PHA.

PHA – Abbreviation for phaeton. See also PH.

phaeton – See body style(phaeton).

phase the driveline – Process defined as the alignment of a transmission's output shaft with a differential's pinion gear shaft. It is often required when a different engine and/or transmission are installed in a car. If not properly aligned, vibrations will occur shortening the life of various components.

phasing the drivetrain – Engine and transmission installed so that transmission output shaft is parallel to the differential's pinion gear shaft in both the horizontal and vertical plane.

Phelps – American car produced from 1903-1905 by Phelps Motor Co. in Massachusetts.

Phianna – American car produced from 1916-1922 by Phianna Motors Co. in New Jersey (1916-1918), and M.H. Carpenter in New York (1919-1922). It was one of the finest American prestige cars and built in limited numbers.

Philadelphia – American car in 1924.from 1910-1912.

Philion – American car produced in 1892.

phillips – See screw(phillips).

Phillips Petroleum Co – A U.S. petroleum company headquartered in Bartlesville, Oklahoma. See also petroleum company.

phillips screwdriver – Screwdriver used to turn phillip screws.

Phipps-Grinnell – American electric car produced from 1901-1912 by Phipps-Grinnell Automobile Co. in Michigan.

Phipps-Johnston – American car produced in 1909.

Phoenix – American car produced in 1900. Also, an American car produced from 1960-1961 by Dodge Division of Chrysler Corp. in Michigan. Also, an American car produced from 1975 to date by Pontiac Division of General Motors Corp. in Michigan.

phony claim – Insurance claim made for exaggerated or non-existent property damage or personal injury.

phosphor-bronze – Metal alloy composed of copper, tin, and lead elements. It is used in some heavy duty bearing applications.

PI – Abbreviation for Philippines found usually on an international license plate.

Pickard – American car produced from 1908-1912 by Pickard Bros. in Massachusetts.

pickup coil – Small permanent magnet used in an electronic ignition system in conjunction with a reluctor to generate a small voltage for each engine cylinder, amplify it, and send it to a control unit that triggers high voltage current in an ignition coil's secondary windings. It is mounted inside the distributor housing on a breaker plate near the rotating reluctor. See also ignition system and control unit.

pickup truck – Truck built with an open bed.

pickup tube – Tube positioned to extend from an oil pump down into the bottom of an oil pan to suck oil. An oil intake screen is fitted to the oil pan end.

pickup tires – Tires used on a pickup truck.

pickup tube screen – See oil intake screen.

pickup unit – Pivoting device used in fuel tanks to immerse a fuel line in the fuel regardless of its level. It also usually sends information to a fuel gauge indicating amount of fuel.

Pickwick – American car produced in 1930.

piece of iron – Rough car or junker.

piece of junk – See piece of iron.

Piedmont – American car produced from 1917-1922 by Piedmont Motor Car Co. in Virginia.

Pierce – American car produced in 1903.

Pierce Arrow – American car produced from 1901-1938 by George N. Pierce and Pierce-Arrow Motor Car Co. in New York. It was a prestige car for a long period of time.

Pierce Great Arrow – American car produced from 1904-1909 by Pierce-Arrow Motor Car Co. in New York.

Pierce Motorette – American car produced in 1901.

Pierce-Racine – American car produced from 1904-1909 by Pierce Engine Co. in Wisconsin.

Pierce-Stanhope – American car produced in 1903.

pig – See policeman.

pig farm – Used car dealer engaged in selling rough cars or junkers.

Piggins – American car produced in 1909-1910 and 1912.

pigment – Coloring matter mixed with water, oil, and/or other compounds to make paint. It is usually in powder form. A particular pigment color absorbs all the light rays except those reflecting back to the eye in the color observed.

pileup – Traffic accident characterized by large numbers of cars impacting each other usually going in the same direction. For example, pileups occur on freeways when weather is real foggy or visibility is otherwise very poor.

Pilgram – American car produced from 1914-1918 by Pilgrim Motor Car Co. in Michigan.

pillar – Vertical structural member used to connect a car roof with the lower body.

Pilliod – American car produced from 1915-1918 by Pilliod Motor Co. in Ohio.

Pilot – American car produced from 1909-1924 by Pilot Motor Car Co. in Indiana.

pilot bearing – Small bearing positioned in a flywheel or end of a crankshaft to support the end of a manual transmission input shaft. The bearing is typically a bronze bushing or a sealed roller bearing depending on the car.

pilot jet – Small brass fitting built with a specified hole size and mounted on in a carburetor to meter a small amount of fuel into a carburetor's venturi area so an engine can idle.

pilot valve – Small valve used to control a larger valve's action.

Pioneer – American car produced in 1909-1911, 1914-1915, 1917, and 1920. Also, an American electric car produced in 1959.

ping control module – Electronic device used to adjust ignition timing when pinging occurs. Some units automatically retard timing while others permit a driver to manually adjust.

pinging – See detonation.

ping point – Ignition timing setting reached where pinging increases.

pin holes – Tiny holes found in newly applied paint covering plastic filler areas. Possible causes include: improper sanding, too much hardener, hardener not adequately mixed into filler, air bubbles in filler through vigorous mixing, and wrong type hardener.

pinion – See gear(pinion).

pinion carrier – Bracket or mounting used to support and contain the pinion gears, shafts, and bearings. In a differential, it usually refers to the four pinion gears used to connect the two differential side gears.

pinion drive flange – Fitting used to attach a universal to the input end of a differential pinion shaft. It forms the final half of a driveline to differential universal joint.

pinion flange – See pinion drive flange.

pinion gear – See gear(pinion).

pinion stop – Sleeve mounted on a starter motor shaft for limiting the travel of a drive pinion gear.

pinking – See pinging.

pinstripes – Thin lines of paint or tape used to create unique designs on car

body panels. See also pinstriping.
pinstriping – Paint customizing technique used to apply thin lines of paint or special pinstriping tape in unique patterns to create, accent, highlight, and/or contrast trick painting designs. Pinstripes are also commonly used to setoff car body lines.
pinstriping brush – Small paint brush designed for applying pinstripe designs to a car body surface.
pinstriping tape – Narrow tape specially formulated to adhere to and set off car body lines.
pinstriping tool – Pen-like device used to apply paint to a car body surface with a rolling wheel. The line width is adjusted by using different rolling wheels. It contains a small paint reservoir.
Pinto – American car produced from 1971 to date by Ford Motor Co. in Michigan.
Pioneer – American car produced from 1960-1961 by Dodge Division of Chrysler Corp. in Michigan.
pipe wrench – Adjustable open end wrench used to tighten or loosen pipes or other circular surfaces. The jaws are usually serrated to provide a better grip. It is not used much in automotive work except to remove damaged bolts or nuts.
pipes – Custom exhaust system.
Piquet, Nelson – He became the Grand Prix world champion in 1981 and 1983 driving a Brabham-Ford and Brabham-BMW.
Pirate – American car produced in 1907.
Pirelli – Italian line of tires imported by the Pirelli Tire Corporation.
Pirsch – American car produced in 1910.
Piscorski – American car produced in 1901.
piston – Hollow cast or forged cylinder device capped at one end and built to move up and down inside an engine cylinder. It transmits the pushing force generated by ignition of an air/fuel mixture to a crankshaft through a connecting rod. A piston consists primarily of a hollow capped cylinder shape, grooves for piston rings along the top skirt of the piston, and a short shaft inside the piston for connection to a connecting rod.
piston(autothermic) – Aluminum piston built with steel or alloy inserts to control piston skirt expansion.
piston(belted) – Piston built with a continuous band of steel in the skirt area to control skirt expansion.
piston(cam ground) – Piston built to a slight oval shape. It becomes round when hot, allows smaller clearances, and reduces blowby gas and cylinder and piston scuffing.
piston(cast) – Piston built for average to moderate high performance. Most production cars use them. See also piston(forged).
piston(cup head) – Piston built with a slightly concave top surface to reduce an engine's compression ratio.
piston(dished) – See piston(cup head).
piston(domed) – Piston built with a raised head. Depending on the purpose served, different profiles are used. They include: gabled roof, step roof, and pent roof. It serves to increase compression ratio.
piston(flat top) – Piston built with a flat head.
piston(forged) – Piston built to withstand constant high rpm use. It is a racing type piston. For street use, disadvantages over cast pistons include: shorter ring-groove life, looser fit, less heat conductivity, and more expensive than cast pistons.
piston(slipper) – Piston built with its skirt cut away on the two non-thrusting side. Advantages include: lighter weight, better piston acceleration and deceleration, less power wasted, and longer bearing life.
piston(step) – See piston(domed).
piston(reverse deflector) – Piston built with a stepped head surface for enhancing the squish of an air/fuel mixture. It is popular in a supercharged engine.
piston(wedge) – Piston built with a raised wedge head profile.
piston collapse – Condition created when a piston skirt's diameter reduces due to stress or heat.
piston damage – Condition created when a piston becomes structurally damaged due to overheating. Possible causes include: stuck or broken rings, continued detonation, and poor quality.
piston displacement – Volume swept by a piston moving from the top to the bottom of its stroke.
piston groove – One of several grooves cut around the circumference of piston to receive a piston ring.
piston groove cleaner – Tool used to clean piston ring grooves.
piston head – Portion of a piston located above the piston rings.
piston lands – Portions of the piston's outer surface located between the rings.
piston pin – Short steel shaft mounted inside a piston. It attaches a piston to the upper end of a connecting rod.

piston pin(floating) - Piston pin built to turn freely in a connecting rod and piston.
piston pin spring - See spring(piston pin).
piston ring - Large split ring used to fit into one of the circular grooves cut around a piston. It provides a tight seal between a piston and a cylinder wall, keeping the combustion process above a piston. There are usually three rings mounted on a piston, two compression rings and one oil ring. See also piston ring(oil) and piston ring(compression).
piston ring(compression) - Ring used to keep the combustion process above the piston from leaking by. Most pistons have two of these type rings.
piston ring(oil) - Ring used to scrape oil from a cylinder wall. The ring is designed to allow oil to pass into the ring and then through holes or slots in the groove. In this way, oil is returned to the oil pan. There are many shapes and special designs used on oil control rings. Most pistons use one of these rings.
piston ring compressor - Tool used to compress piston rings in order to insert a piston into a cylinder.
piston ring expander - Spring used with a piston ring to help expand it against the cylinder wall.
piston ring gap - Clearance measured between piston ring ends when compressed in an engine cylinder. It is important to measure whenever new rings are installed, and is done by placing the ring in the the lowest position it will travel. Too small a gap may cause: rings to break and cylinder walls to score. Too large a gap may cause: oil blowby and oil burning.
piston ring groove - One of two or more channels cut around the outer circumference of a piston near the top to retain piston rings.
piston ring side clearance - Space measured between piston ring sides and lands.
piston seizure - Condition created when a piston stops moving and binds in an engine cylinder. It is usually due to a large increase in the coefficient of friction due to lack of lubrication.
piston skirt - Outer surface of a piston located below the piston rings.
piston skirt expander - Device used to expand a piston skirt from the inside to compensate for a decrease in diameter.
piston slap - Condition created when there is excessive clearance between the piston and the cylinder wall. It is most prominent when an engine is cold.
pit - Race track area located across from the main stands where cars are directed, repaired, and refueled during a race.
pitch - Rocking motion produced in the long direction of a car.
Pitcher - American car produced in 1920.
pitman arm - Short metal rod attached to a steering box and to the front tire tie rods. It moves the rods when the steering wheel is turned.
pitot tube - Instrument used to measure fluid velocity by detecting pressure differences in an opening.
pits - Individual areas assigned at a race track pit for servicing each race car.
pit stop - See pit. Also, a place where a car stops for service, refueling, resting on a long trip, to eat, etc.
Pittsburgh - American car produced in 1896-1899. Also, an American car produced from 1909-1911 by Fort Pitt Motor Mfg. Co. in Pennsylvania.
Pittsburgher - American car produced in 1919.
Pittsfield - American car produced in 1907.
pivot post - See distributor point pivot post.
pivot ring - One of two large rings used to pivot a diaphragm spring and thus a pressure plate in a clutch pressure plate assembly.
pivot window panels - Small triangular shaped windows inset in front car door windows. They are used to provide inside ventilation.
pkg - Abbreviation for package.
PL - Abbreviation for Poland found usually on an international license plate.
place of business - Location or address of a business.
plaintiff - Person or party filing a complaint in a legal matter.
Planche - American car produced in 1906.
planet gear - See gear(planet).
planetary gear band - See brake band.
planetary gear set - Gear set built similar in appearance to the solar system, hence the name. It is most common in automatic transmissions and overdrives. It usually consists of: an outer ring gear, two or more pinion (planet) gears, and a central sun gear. All the gears are constantly meshed. The gears can be controlled in many ways to provide different output speeds. In an automatic transmission, a planetary gear set is divided into three different gear units known as: the sun gear, planet gears and drum, and ring gear and drum. The rotation of each is controlled by brake bands applied to different drums.
planetary pinions - Pinion gears in a planetary gear set.
planetary transmission - See transmission(planetary).

plant it – To drive a car at full throttle.
plan view – View made looking down on an object. See also side view, elevation view, and section view.
Plass Motor Sleigh – American car produced in 1895.
plastic filler – See solder(plastic).
plastic wrap painting – Custom painting technique used to create a wrinkled effect. It usually works as follows. A slow drying paint is applied to a panel. Plastic wrap is then placed over the paint, rubbed and/or wrinkled with a hand, and then removed. The paint is then allowed to dry.
plastigage – Soft plastic material placed between two surfaces to measure the clearance between them. The width of the deformed material specifies the thickness. It is commonly employed for measuring the clearance between rod and main bearing caps and shafts.
plateau – Surface extended above a neighboring car body surface.
plates – See license plate and set of plates.
plates are shot – Battery condition created when positive and negative plates become worn out.
platinum – Metallic element characterized as gray, malleable, ductile, highly resistant to corrosion, and a good electrical conductor. It melts at 3,224 degrees Fahrenheit.
play – Movement between two parts.
Playboy – American car produced from 1946-1951 by Playboy Motor Car Corp. in New York.
play in the steering wheel – Amount of free movement in a steering wheel before the front steering wheels actually move. See also free play.
Plaza – American car produced from 1957-1959 by Plymouth Division of Chrysler Corp. in Michigan.
plea – Defendant's response to a charge made by a plaintiff in a court of law.
plenum – Space located in an intake manifold. Some manifolds use two separate plenums to increase air flow efficiency.
plenum volume – Open chamber volume located beneath the carburetor throttle plate and outside the manifold runners. Plenum volume and carburetor flow capacity have a general relationship that seems to hold: as carburetor flow capacity increase plenum volume needed decreases and vice versa.
plies – See tire plies.
p/locks – Abbreviation for power door locks.
plowing – See understeer.
plow truck – Truck equipped to remove snow and ice from roadways while traveling at significant speed. It is often equipped to apply sand as well. See also sand truck.
plug – Spark plug.
plug scope – See spark plug scope.
plug firing cup – See spark plug firing cup.
plug gap – See spark plug gap.
plug gapper – See spark plug gapper.
plugging – See plug the engine.
plug the engine – To install new or cleaned and regapped spark plugs in an engine.
plug wire – Spark plug cable.
plug wires are crossed – See crossed spark plug wires.
Plymouth – American car produced from 1908-1910. Also, an American car line produced from 1928 to date by Chrysler Corp. in Michigan.
Plymouth Truck – American car produced in 1908.
ply rating – Rating used to specify the number of rubber layers underneath a tire's tread area.
PMC Buggyabout – American car produced in 1908.
pneumatic – Pertaining to wind, air, or gas.
pneumatic trail – See self-aligning torque.
Pneumobile – American car produced from 1915.
pnt – Abbreviation for paint.
PO – Abbreviation for post office.
POA valve – Pilot operated absolute valve.
pod – Compartment built to house different mechanical devices such as lights, dials, gauges, etc. It is usually round or elliptical.
Pogue carburetor – Vapor phase carburetor invented by Charles Pogue in the 1930s. The design used exhaust heat to vaporize fuel before it entered the intake manifold. It reportedly produced high gas mileage.
Pogue, Charles Nelson – Inventor of the Pogue carburetor.
point – One percent of the amount borrowed from a lender. One or more points are often specified as a loan fee in order to secure a loan. See also loan fee.
point bounce – Condition created when a distributor point's open and close cycle is so fast that points do not fully close before next open cycle begins. Stronger point springs minimize the problem, but at the expense of increased distributor cam wear. It occurs at high engine rpm and often

causes misfiring. Electronic ignition systems don't have this problem.
point face – Contacting surface of a contact point.
point float – See point bounce.
point gap – See distributor point gap.
point rubbing block – See distributor point rubbing block.
points(1) – See distributor points.
points(2) – Exact locations on a model specified on a car model. They are usually derived from a blueprint or from the model itself. They are typically used to duplicate the opposite side of a car model surface.
point system – Method used by many state law enforcement agencies (motor vehicle division) to rate a driver convicted of driving violations. In general, 1-2 points are assessed for serious traffic violations. Many states can use 4, 6, or 8 points in a 1, 2, or 3 year period as grounds for license suspension. The points usually remain on a driving record for three years unless serious.
   It is also used by certain insurance companies to determine if you should pay more than the basic premium rate with each company defining how the points are to be applied. In general, you accumulate points for accidents and traffic violations. The more points the more you pay.
Pokorney – American car produced in 1905.
Polara – American car produced from 1960-1982 by Dodge Division of Chrysler Corp. in Michigan.
polarity – Reference point or condition characterized as having a positive or negative attribute. For example, an electric motor has electrical polarity with positive and negative magnetic fields. Another example, the circuit between a battery, and a generator or alternator must remain polarized at all times. If not, the current drain on a battery won't be replaced when an engine is running. The key is the voltage regulator which must be polarized when installed for the charging circuit to work properly. An auto repair business can take advantage of your ignorance here and sell you a new battery, alternator, and voltage regulator when you may only need one if at all. See also polarizing the generator.
polarizing the generator – Procedure employed to properly orient the magnetic fields in a DC generator with a battery. It is done every time a DC generator is removed and repaired, and every time a new regulator is installed. If it is not done, the generator or regulator may burn out from excessive current flow after a few minutes of operation. Type "A" circuit generators are polarized by momentarily touching a jumper wire from the regulator's generator armature terminal to the regulator's battery terminal. Type "B" circuit generators are polarized by removing the regulator field lead and momentarily touching it to the regulator's battery terminal.
   In general, all generators are "A" circuit, except Ford generators which are "B" circuit. All alternators are "B" circuit, except those equipped with internal regulators which usually use an "A" circuit.
   Alternators do not need to be polarized as their polarity cannot be lost or changed.
pole – Electromagnet mounted inside a generator or starter. It is also known as a field winding. Most generators and starters have two poles. See also pole shoe.
pole piece – See pole shoe.
pole position – Race car starting position located on the inside of a race track nearest the starting line. It is considered the most favorable starting position, and is usually occupied by the car with the fastest qualifying time.
poles – Ends of a magnet, positive and negative battery terminals, etc.
pole shoe – Steel alloy shape used to form the base for a field coil. Field windings are wounds around the shape. The steel alloy is made of special highly magnetic material to enhance the magnetic field generated when current flows through the coil windings. It is held against the inside of a generator or starter housing by one or more large screws.
police car – Patrol car.
police cruiser – Patrol car.
police dog – Dog trained to assist police.
policeman – Male member of a police force.
police officer – Member of a police force.
police patrol – See patrol.
police station – Police headquarters for a particular district. Officers are dispatched from the station and arrested people are brought to it.
police woman – Female member of a police force.
polishing compound – Paste compound used to remove light paint oxidation from car body surfaces. See also rubbing compound.
pollution control valve – See PCV valve.
Polo – American car produced in 1927.
polyester – Resin material formed primarily by condensing polyhydric alcohol with dibasic acids. It is used in the manufacture of textiles, resins,

plastics, fibers, etc.

polyester fiber cord – Tire cord material made of polyester which exhibits the best features of rayon and nylon. Goodyear introduced it in 1962.

polytetrafluoroethylene – Compound used in certain lubricating oils to further reduce friction between moving parts.

polyurethane – Synthetic rubber polymer used to make insulation and padding, molded products, adhesives, fillers, paint.

Pomeroy – American car produced in 1902. Also, an American car produced from 1920-1924 by Aluminum Co. of America in Ohio (1920-1922), and Pierce-Arrow Motor Car Co. in New York (1923-1924). It was made of 85% aluminum parts.

Ponder – American car produced in 1916 and 1923.

ponies – Amount of horsepower.

Pontiac – American car produced in 1907-1908 and 1915. Also, an American car line produced from 1926 to date by Oakland Motor Car Co. in Michigan (1926-1932), and Pontiac Division of General Motors in Michigan (1933 to date).

pony car – Any car of the Ford Mustang series.

poncho – High performance Pontiac car.

poor acceleration – Engine condition created when an engine is not able to adequately accelerate a car when needed. Possible causes include: accelerator pump defective or not operating, accelerator circuit clogged, float level incorrect, retarded ignition timing, excessive backpressure, and faulty low voltage wire inside distributor.

poor idling – Engine condition created when an engine does not idle smoothly. Possible causes include: uneven or low cylinder compression, leaking cylinder valves, ignition system problems, idle mixture adjustment screw incorrect, float level incorrect, inadequate fuel delivery, leaking carburetor gaskets, carburetor attaching bolts loose, clogged idle discharge ports, bad choke, loose or worn carburetor jets, vacuum leaks, leaking accelerator pump diaphragm, and clogged air cleaner.

poor quality – Quality of an item characterized as made of inferior materials, poorly assembled, etc.

poor visibility – To see only for a short distance or hardly at all.

pop – Nitromethane fuel additive.

Pope – American car produced from 1895-1899.

Pope, Albert Augustus – He is regarded as the father of the American bicycle industries. He began manufacturing electric cars through the Columbia Electric Company in 1896. In a short period of time, he controlled the Pope-Harford, Pope-Toledo, and Pope-Waverly companies. The success of his car ventures forced his original bicycle company, Pope Manufacturing Company, out of business.

Pope Columbia – American car produced in 1897.

Pope-Hartford – American car produced from 1903-1914 by Pope Mfg. Co. in Connecticut. It was considered a reliable car and was one of the best known in its time.

Pope Motor – American car produced from 1903-1908.

Pope-Robinson – See Robinson.

Pope-Toledo – American car produced from 1903-1909 by Pope Motor Car Co. in Ohio.

Pope Tribune – American car produced from 1904-1907 by Pope Mfg. Co. in Maryland.

Pope-Waverly – American car produced from 1903-1907 by Pope Motor Car Co. in Indiana.

popeye – Car operating with one good headlight.

poppet valve – See valve(poppet).

popping a brake cylinder piston – Condition created when a brake cylinder piston slides or is forced out of a cylinder bore.

Poppy Car – American car produced in 1917.

pop the clutch – To quickly engage a clutch usually to spin the drive wheels on pavement.

porcelain – Hard, white, nonporous variety of ceramic.

porcelain insulator – Insulator made of porcelain. It is used to form the central core of a spark plug, allowing a high voltage spark to be transferred from a spark wire to an electrode tip without grounding out.

pork chop – An instrument panel shape extending onto the interior of a front car door.

Porsche – West German car line produced from 1948 to date by Dr. Ing. h.c. F. Porsche KG. Popular models include: 911, 924, 928, and 944.

Porsche, Ferdinand – He was an Austrian engineer, born in 1875, who believed in a cheap people's car in the 1920s. Through Hitler's backing in the late 1930s, he started the Volkswagen industry.

Porsche-Lohner Chaise – Experimental car introduced at the Paris Exposition in 1900 by Ferdinand Prosche and Ludwig Lohner. It used a gasoline engine to drive a generator which powered electric motors contained in the hubs of each wheel. The car had no transmission, belts, chains, differential, etc.

port – Opening in a cylinder head. Intake ports are conduits for fuel mixture and exhaust ports convey waste gases.

porta power – Portable hydraulically powered tool used to lengthen or shorten distances between objects. In body shops, four and ten ton units are the most popular. Such a tool typically consists of: a pump cylinder, rams, and various pipe lengths and fittings.

ported vacuum switch(1) – Switch designed to open when vacuum in a carburetor airway reaches a certain level. It is common in EGR systems.

ported vacuum switch(2) – See thermal valve(2).

Porter – American car produced from 1900-1901 and 1919-1922 by Porter Automobile Co. in Massachusetts, and American & British Mfg. Corp. in Connecticut respectively.

Port Huron – American car produced in 1918.

porting and polishing – Process used to improve air flow in intake and exhaust manifolds by enlarging ports, and smoothing the passageway surfaces. It produces minimal power increases for engines running at low rpm, but is popular with racing engines where low air flow restrictions and high rpm are factors.

Portland – American car produced in 1914.

port type injection – See fuel injection(gas-port).

Posi – Abbreviation for positraction rear end.

positive crankcase ventilation – See emission control system(crankcase-closed type-2), emission control system(crankcase-PCV), and PCV valve.

positive ground – See positive ground system.

positive ground system – Direct current electrical system constructed where the positive side acts as ground and the negative side as the potential. In a positive ground car, the positive terminal of the battery is connected to the car frame or ground. It was used on earlier model cars, and is used on most English cars. Today's cars primarily use a negative ground system.

positive ground wire – Battery cable wire used to connect the positive terminal of a battery to the car's ground.

positive pole – See positive terminal.

positive terminal – Terminal of a battery, generator, or other electrical circuit from which current flows. See also battery posts.

Positraction – Tradename used for a limited slip differential.

Poss – American car produced in 1912.

post(battery) – Stub shaft located extending through a battery top and attaching to positive battery plates.

Postal – American car produced from 1907-1908 by Postal Auto & Engine Co. in Indiana.

post bail – To put up bail to release an arrested person.

post brush – Brush used to clean battery posts and terminals.

post-combustion device – Device used to control exhaust emissions after leaving the combustion chamber. Such devices include: catalytic converter and air pump. See also pre-combustion device.

posted speed limit – Speed limit of a road posted on signs.

post mortem – Examination made of a dead body by a coroner.

post type terminals – Electrical terminals such as those mounted on top of a battery.

post-war car – Car generally classified as built after World War II. See also brass era car, vintage car, antique car, contemporary car, milestone car, special interest car, classic car, contemporary classic car, and pre-war car.

pot – Carburetor.

potential – See voltage.

potential difference – See voltage drop.

pothole – Hole formed in a road or sidewalk pavement from excess use or weather extremes.

pounce wheel – Small wheel tool used to leave tiny perforations in a surface it rolls over. The wheel contains pointed projections around its circumference.

pour point – Temperature reached when a fluid congeals and will no longer flow.

Powell – American car produced in 1912.

Powell Sport Wagon – American car produced from 1954-1956 by Powell Sport Wagons in California. It was made from earlier recycled and rebuilt Plymouth parts.

power assisted brakes – Car brakes made more powerful by using a vacuum operated device which adds additional force to a brake pedal when applied.

power balance test – See car service tip(power balance test).

power band – Engine rpm range specified where maximum horsepower is generated.

power brakes – See brake(power)

power brake unit – See brake unit(power).

Power Car – American car produced from 1909-1912 by Powercar Auto Co. in Ohio.

Power Car Special – American electric car produced from 1953-1954 by Mystic River Sales in Connecticut.

power circuit – See carburetor circuit(power).

power drop - Drop exhibited in engine horsepower. Engine horsepower can drop is most commonly caused when a normally aspirated engine climbs in altitude. This is due to air being less dense at higher altitudes causing less oxygen to be available for combustion. Other causes include: high air temperatures, out of tune engine, low engine compression, restriction in exhaust system, blown head gasket, and carburetor improperly metering fuel.

Power-Flite - Two speed automatic transmission made by Chrysler.

power flow - The path followed in transferring power from one point to another. Power flow in a manual transmission is often not in a straight line.

Powerglide - Automatic transmission introduced by Chevrolet in 1955.

power impulse - Pressure created when a air/fuel mixture ignites to push a piston down. Two, four, six, and eight cylinder engines have power impulses every 1, 1/2, 1/3, and 1/4 revolution respectively.

power jet - Device used to meter additional fuel to an engine when a throttle is wide open. Fuel flows through the jet when a power valve opens due to low vacuum underneath the throttle plate. See also economizer valve.

Power of Attorney - Document used to authorize another person to act on your behalf in signing official documents or performing other specified legal duties in your absence.

power plant - Car engine.

Power Punch - American line of oil additives.

power seat - Front car seat built with positioning controlled by an electric motor. Directions of movement usually include: up, down, forward, back, and sometimes tilting.

power shifting - Shifting done rapidly from one gear to another by popping the clutch and maintaining high engine rpm. Stock transmission are not built for it.

power slide - Racing maneuver used to get around a turn quicker by placing a car in a deliberate skid while going through a turn. The skid is controlled with throttle action and the steering wheel is used only for making corrections. More throttle moves the car to the outside of the curve and less to the inside.

power steering - Steering system built to use hydraulic pressure for minimizing steering wheel turning effort. Hydraulic pressure acts either in a steering gear box or on a hydraulic cylinder attached to the steering linkage. It became popular in the 1950s after being introduced and used on military vehicles in World War II. Power steering units of today allow drivers to steer manually if the pump malfunctions or an engine is not operating.

power steering(integral) - Power steering system built with a power cylinder, control valve assembly, and power steering box all forming one unit.

power steering(linkage booster) - Power steering system built with a power cylinder operating the steering linkage. Primary components consist of: an engine driven hydraulic pump, control valve assembly linked to the steering shaft, and necessary hoses and fittings.

power steering box - Gearbox used to transfer turning motion in a power steering system into wheel motion.

power steering problem - Condition created when there is difficulty in operating or maintaining a car's power steering. It is important to check the steering linkage and wheel alignment for proper operation since power steering can mask binding and looseness problems causing serious damage if ignored. See also car handling problem.

power steering pump - Hydraulic belt-driven pump used to supply the necessary hydraulic fluid pressure to a power steering gearbox.

power stroke - See stroke(power).

power take-off - Accessory mounted onto a transmission allowing power to be transferred outside the transmission to a shaft or driveline. The accessory was usually either a small gearbox with an external shaft, or a short shaft with a driveline yoke assembly for attaching an external driveline. The transmission has to be designed for a power take-off in order to use it. Such transmissions have cover plates where the device is mounted.

power timing - Modification made to a distributor's centrifugal and vacuum spark advance curves in order to improve performance.

power top - Car top raised and lowered electrically.

power to weight ratio - Ratio used to classify a car's performance. It is derived by dividing a car's weight by its horsepower. For example, a car weighing 2,500 pounds and producing 100 horsepower would have a ratio of 25. A car with a ratio below 20 is considered well designed.

powertrain - Those car parts used to transmit power from an engine to the drive wheels. They include: transmission, driveline, differential, and rear axle. See also drivetrain.

power unit - Vacuum operated device used to open and close a throttle valve a small amount when a car's set speed is over or under exceeded. It is controlled by a speed transducer.

power valve – See economizer valve.
power window – Window built to move up and down with an electric motor.
Poyer – American car produced in 1913.
P/P – Abbreviation for private party.
p/p – Abbreviation for private party.
pp – Abbreviation for private party.
ppd – Abbreviation for postpaid.
Practical – American car produced from 1906-1911.
Prado – American car produced from 1920-1922 by Prado Motor Corp. in New York.
Pratt – American car produced in 1907. Also, an American car produced from
 1911-1917 by Elkart Carriage & Harness Mfg. Co. in Indiana (1911-1915), and
 Pratt Motor Car Co. in Indiana (1916-1917).
Praul – American car produced in 1895.
precedent – Legal decision used to serve as a guide in deciding other similar
 cases.
pre-combustion device – Device used to control exhaust emissions as they are
 generated in the combustion chamber. Such devices include: vacuum advance,
 exhaust gas recirculation, spark delay valve, PCV valve, and throttle
 position solenoid. See also post-combustion device.
Preferred – American car produced in 1920.
preferred interest rate – Interest rate made available to specified customers.
preheated-intake air system – Assemblage of parts and controls used to keep
 warm air flowing to a carburetor regardless of outside temperature. Warm air
 minimizes emissions since it allows a leaner fuel mixture. Faulty system can
 cause: pinging, stumbling, loss of power, poor fuel economy, stalling, and
 hesitation.
pre heater tube – See heat riser tube.
preheating – To apply heat to an area or object before using it or subjecting
 it to another process.
preignition – Preignition is similar to detonation, but differs in that
 spontaneous ignition of a fuel mixture occurs before a spark plug fires. It
 can be caused by: high compression ratio, low octane fuel, hot spot such as a
 hot glowing carbon deposit or hot spark plug end, advanced timing, and an
 overheating engine transferring too much heat to incoming air/fuel mixture.
 End result is the preignition flame front collides violently with the spark
 ignited flame front to produce a cylinder head vibration or knocking sound
 easily confused with detonation.
   Preignition is dangerous to the continued health of an engine, and can lead
 to major engine damage if not corrected. Damage can include: generation of
 hot spots on aluminum piston heads causing the areas to vaporize aluminum and
 form holes if the temperature is high enough, pistons seizing, and burned
 exhaust valves. Vaporized aluminum deposits on spark plug tip and can gall
 cylinder wall and piston skirt surfaces. See also detonation, trace
 detonation, spark plug appearance(aluminum throw off), hot spot, and
 dieseling.
preload – Load imposed on a bearing before actual loads are applied. For
 front wheel bearings, it is accomplished with an adjustable spindle nut which
 varies the pressure applied to the bearing surfaces.
prem – Abbreviation for premium.
Premier – American car produced from 1903-1925 by Premier Motor Corp. and
 Premier Motor Mfg. Co. in Indiana. Also, an Indian car line produced from
 1955 to date by Premier Automobiles Ltd.
premium – See gasoline(premium).
premium rates – See insurance rates.
Premocar – American car produced from 1921-1923 by Preston Motor Corp. in
 Alabama.
pre-owned car – Used car previously owned by one or more owners.
prepayment penalty – Additional loan charge assessed if a borrower pays a loan
 off before the final due date.
prepcoat – Solvent substance sprayed or rubbed onto a prepared paint surface
 to remove remaining dirt, wax, grease, and oxidation, and neutralize acids
 and other compounds. It is not to be used on car surfaces containing plastic
 filler due to its porous nature. See also tacking.
prepping the block – Process followed before rebuilding an engine block. It
 consists of: disassembling the components in an engine block, cleaning all
 the surfaces, and checking various clearances and diameters.
prep solvent – See prepcoat.
Prescott – American car produced from 1901-1905 by Prescott Automobile Mfg. in
 New York.
presentment – Written statement made by a grand jury of an offense determined
 from its own knowledge and observation and without the submission of any bill
 of indictment.
press fit – See drive fit.
pressure – Exertion of force upon a surface, fluid, gas, etc.
pressure bleeder – Device used to force brake fluid, under pressure, into a

master cylinder so bleeder screws can be opened at wheel cylinders, and all air removed from the brake system.

pressure cap - See radiator cap.

pressure crankcase ventilation system - See crankcase emission control system.

pressure plate - See clutch pressure plate.

pressure pot - Remote spray gun system used where a paint cup or pot is separate from a spray head. It is used where larger quantities of paint need to be sprayed at one time, and where more spray head flexibility is desired.

pressure relief valve - Valve built to open at a specific pressure. It is used to keep pressures from exceeding certain limits. Most oil lubrication systems have a relief valve. See also oil pressure relief valve.

pressure booster valve - Valve used in an automatic transmission to increase hydraulic fluid pressure when needed.

Prestolite - American line of automotive products.

Preston - American car produced from 1921-1923.

preventive maintenance - Regular maintenance done to a car to: keep it in top running condition, prevent trouble, extend its life, and keep a car warranty valid. Such maintenance includes performing the following regularly: changing oil and filter, tune-up, flushing cooling system and adding new antifreeze, checking and adjusting brakes, checking and adjusting fluid levels, greasing all necessary chassis points, checking and adjusting front end, etc. Car repair businesses are kept busy because of a lack of preventive maintenance.
  Following a good preventive maintenance program will often double or triple the life of a car.

pre-war car - Car generally classified as built after World War I. See also brass era car, vintage car, antique car, contemporary car, milestone car, special interest car, classic car, contemporary classic car, and post-war car.

price spread - See margin of profit.

price war - Intense price competition between businesses selling the same products.

Pridemore - American car produced from 1914-1915 by Pridemore Machine Works in Minnesota.

Prigg - American car produced in 1915.

prima facie evidence - Evidence established at first sight to establish a fact.

primary(carburetor) - Main carburetor airway. It is used to send the proper amount of fuel and air into an engine for idling, modest acceleration, and steady driving. Some cars have four barrel carburetors with two primaries. See also secondary(carburetor).

primary(electrical) - See primary circuit.

primary(ignition coil) - See primary coil winding.

primary brake shoe - See brake shoe(leading).

primary circuit - Electrical part of a car's ignition system used to carry low voltage battery current. See also secondary circuit.

primary coil winding - Heavy electric wire wound around an ignition coil's iron core to carry low voltage current. It typically consists of some 200 turns of relatively heavy wire such as 18 gauge, and is usually wound on top of the secondary winding.

primary cup - Rubber cup mounted at the pressure end of a master brake cylinder's primary piston. It serves to seal the chamber ahead of the moving primary piston, allowing hydraulic pressure to build in the drum brake portion of the system and against the back of the secondary piston. See also secondary cup.

primary current - Low voltage (12V) current flowing from a battery to an ignition coil and other electrical car loads. See also secondary current.

primary discharge nozzle - Nozzle device used to discharge fuel into a small boost venturi located in a primary carburetor airway. The fuel is drawn from a float bowl to a nozzle by means of a slight vacuum created by a boost venturi. See also venturi.

primary governor valve - Valve used in an automatic transmission to control hydraulic pressure from a governor below certain speeds in order to prevent certain gear shifts.

primary piston - One of two pistons used in a dual master brake cylinder. Its purpose is to pressurize hydraulic fluid used to operate the drum brakes, and to force movement of a secondary piston which pressurizes hydraulic fluid for the brakes. See also primary cup.

primary terminal - One of two low voltage terminals mounted on an ignition coil and used to route low voltage battery current in and out of a coil. See also primary coil winding.

primary throttle plate - See throttle plate(primary).

primary throttle pressure valve - Valve used in an automatic transmission to receive hydraulic fluid pressure from pump, and modify it according to carburetor throttle valve operation or intake manifold vacuum. See also

secondary throttle valve.
primary wires - Electrical wires of a primary circuit.
primary winding - See primary coil winding.
prime - To spray a metal surface with a base or preliminary coat of paint.
See also paint(primer).
primer - See paint(primer).
Primo - American car produced in 1906. Also, an American car produced from
1910-1912 by Primo Motor Co. in Georgia.
Prince - American car produced in 1902.
Princess - American car produced in 1905. Also, an American car produced from
1914-1918 by Princess Motor Car Co. in Michigan.
Princeton - American car produced from 1923-1924 by Durant Motors in Indiana.
private consignment lot - Non-dealer car lot engaged in displaying and selling
cars owned by private parties. Sale of a car usually gets the lot owner an
agreed commission or the difference between the agreed price and the actual
selling price.
probable cause - Reasonable grounds established that a suspect committed a
crime.
production - Mass produced car built for the general public.
production engine rebuilder - Auto business engaged in rebuilding engines
using production line techniques. Some are franchised while others are
factory authorized businesses. Engines produced are usually cheaper than
from independents.
professional driver - Driver skilled in: operating a car under many different
conditions, anticipating and recognizing dangerous driving situations, and
reacting to danger in the safest possible manner for all concerned.
professionally trained mechanic - Mechanic thoroughly trained and then tested
in order to become expert in doing all repairs on cars.
Progress - American car produced in 1912.
progressive linkage - Carburetor linkage used to open the throttle valves of
multiple carburetors. It opens one to start with and when a certain point is
reached, it starts opening the others.
progressive transmission - See transmission(progressive).
project car - Used car determined to be sound enough for rebuilding into good
working condition.
PROM - Read-only memory chip used to store information on specific engine
calibrations. Is is usually mounted inside an ECM. The car's on-board
computer makes timing, fuel, and other adjustments adjustments according to
the engine's sensors and the PROM's information.
Prony brake - First piece of equipment developed for determining engine power.
It consisted of a large drum connected directly to an engine crankshaft.
Around the drum was fitted a band type brake with an arm attached to a scale.
The test would be made by tightening the brake and thus deflecting the arm
until engine speed dropped off. The scale reading was noted. The test was
repeated at different engine rpms to develop a graph of an engine's brake
horsepower vs. engine speed.
propane - Gaseous methane series hydrocarbon compound derived from natural gas
or produced in the process of refining petroleum products. It has a melting
and boiling point of -305 and -44 degrees Fahrenheit respectively. Since it
is a vapor at ambient temperatures, it is compressed in order to store and
transport it economically. Propane is the primary ingredient in LP gas.
propeller shaft - See drive shaft.
proper inflation - Tire inflated to an air pressure falling within a
manufacturer's recommendations. A properly inflated tire, combined with
careful driving, and tire rotation, will maximize the life of the tire. See
also gas saving tip(tire pressure).
proper maintenance - Maintenance work done to a car at proper time or mileage
intervals to keep it safe for driving.
proportioning valve - Valve used to limit hydraulic fluid pressure to the rear
wheel brake cylinders. It is mounted somewhere in the rear brake trunk line.
Without it, rear wheels would brake harder than the front. A clogged
proportioning valve will cause a car's front end to dive every time the
brakes are applied. An open valve will cause a car's rear end to skid when
brakes are applied strongly. See also metering valve and differential valve.
prop shaft - Drive shaft.
pro race driver - Professional racer driving for money.
pro rata guarantee - See guarantee(pro rata)
pro rate - To proportionately determine.
prosecution - Legal proceedings held in a court of law against a person
accused of a crime.
Prospect - American car produced in 1902.
prospecting - Searching for potential customers.
prototype - Original car never before built.
proveout model - Car clay model built to make sure its design conforms with
the appearance originally approved by management. A record cast is

subsequently made in fiberglass. See also record model.
Prudence - American car produced in 1912.
PS(1) - Abbreviation for power steering.
PS(2) - Abbreviation for European horsepower rating.
Ps - Abbreviation for passenger. See also Pss.
p seats - Abbreviation for power seats.
psi - Abbreviation for pounds per square inch.
Pss - Abbreviation for passenger. See also Ps.
PST - Abbreviation for Pacific Standard Time.
PTFE - Abbreviation for polytetrafluoroethylene.
PU - Abbreviation for pickup truck.
public defender - Public official authorized to defend a person accused of a crime who lacks the funds necessary to hire his own counsel.
public transportation - Transportation provided for the public to travel on such as buses, trains, subways, and taxis. A fee is usually charged.
Publix - Canadian car produced from 1947-1948.
puffer - Supercharger.
pull - Tendency of a car to drift or veer to the right especially when brakes are applied. See also brakes are pulling to the right.
pulley - Circular grooved wheel mounted on a shaft and used to transmit shaft rotation to other devices via a belt riding in the groove.
pulling a grade - Driving a road inclining upward for some distance.
pulling a hill - See pulling a grade.
pulling out a dent - To remove a dent in a car panel by pulling it back to its original surface contour.
pulling the engine - To remove an engine from an engine compartment with or without the transmission attached.
pulling wrinkles - To remove sheetmetal damage by pulling out dents.
pull-in winding - Winding of wire used in a solenoid device to bring two contacts together. See also hold-in winding.
Pullman - American car produced from 1907-1908. Also, an American car produced from 1903-1917 by Broomell, Schmidt & Steacy (1903-1905), York Motor Car Co. (1905-1909), and Pullman Motor Car Co. (1909-1917), all in Pennsylvania. The 1903 model had six wheels.
pull rod(body repair) - Tool used to pull dents from a car body. It consists of a handle and thin metal shaft with a hook at the end. Small holes are drilled in the car body in the deepest part of the crease. One or more rods are inserted and the dent pulled. When the crease has been removed, the holes are then filled.
pull rod assembly - Rod, spring, and plate assembly attached to a diaphragm. It is commonly used to transfer motion from a rocker arm in a fuel pump to a diaphragm.
pulls to the left - Tendency of a car to veer to the left when brakes are applied. It is usually due to left side brakes having a greater coefficient of friction.
pull the engine - To remove an engine from a car, usually for rebuilding.
pulsation damper - Device used to smooth fuel surges from a fuel pump to a carburetor.
pulse-air - See emission control system(combustion-pulse air).
pulse-air injection reactor - See emission control system(combustion-pulse air).
pump(1) - Mechanical device used to move a liquid or gas through suction and pressure.
pump(2) - Supercharger.
pump cavitation - Condition created when a partial vacuum forms around impeller or fan blades. An oil pump cavitates when it starts drawing air instead of oil.
pump in - Dealer characterized by having customers buy from him that live out of town or in another area of town. See also pump out.
pumping gas - To fill a gas tank or gas container.
pumping the brakes - To repeatedly apply and release a brake pedal. It is used to quickly slow down without losing traction, especially on icy roads.
pumping the gas - To repeatedly depress and release a gas pedal to get extra gas to the engine cylinders. It is usually done to start a cold engine. Each time the pedal is depressed, the accelerator pump on the carubretor squirts a small amount of fuel into the carburetor airway.
pump jet - Small passageway used in an accelerator pump circuit to control the flow rate of fuel pumped into a carburetor airway. It is usually located where the fuel exits.
pump jet air bleed - See accelerator pump vent.
pump operating rod - Rod used to transfer motion from a throttle shaft to the accelerator pump linkage every time the throttle shaft is rotated.
pump out - Car dealer characterized by having potential customers buy elsewhere in another town or area of town. See also pump in.
pump stuff - Gasoline.

pump the gas - See pumping the gas.

pump weight - Small barrel shaped weight located in an accelerator pump circuit. It rests on top of a small bb-size check valve for the purpose of restraining fuel flow from an accelerator pump until pressure has built up.

pump your own gas - To fill your gas tank or other gas container without assistance.

Pungs-Finch - American car produced from 1904-1910 by Pungs-Finch Auto & Gas Engine Co. in Michigan.

punitive damages - Damages awarded by a court of law to a plaintiff in excess of due injury compensation in order to punish the defendant for the thoughtless or reckless behavior which caused the injury.

Pup - American car produced in 1947 by Pup Motor Car Co. in Wisconsin. It was a small two passenger car with a rear mounted 7.5 or 10 hp engine.

puppy dog selling - Car selling tactic used where a potential customer is allowed to take a car home overnight in the hopes it will grow on him like a puppy dog and he will want to keep it.

purge line - Fuel vapor vent line running from a charcoal canister to a carburetor airway. It routes fuel vapors from a charcoal canister to an intake manifold when an engine starts. See also vapor recovery system, carburetor fuel bowl vent line, and fuel tank vent line.

Puritan - American steam car produced from 1902-1903 by Locke Regulator Co. in Massachusetts. Also, an American car produced from 1913-1914 by Puritan Motor Co. in Illinois.

Purolator - American line of oil and air filters.

push car - Car used to start race cars that are not equipped with starters.

pushing - See understeer.

pushrod - Metal rod used to connect a valve lifter to one end of a rocker arm in an internal combustion engine. Pushrods are used in engines having camshafts mounted outside an cylinder head.

pushover - See lush.

push-start - Method used to start a car without a starter. The car is pushed on a flat road or rolled down a hill until 5 or more mph is attained. Pushing can be done by another car or by several people. It can be done in forward or reverse, but forward is preferable. When the car reaches 5 or more mph: turn the ignition switch to "on", depress and hold clutch, put transmission in second gear, and rapidly release clutch. The car should start. If done in reverse, put transmission in reverse and depress clutch before rolling begins. Automatic transmission cars must be push-started 25 or mph before the converter will spin engine fast enough in low gear. This can be accomplished by pushing with another car or rolling down a good incline.

put - To get a potential car customer interested in a particular car.

put in the can - To operate a race car with the highest allowable percentage of nitromethane.

put it in drive - To shift a car's automatic transmission from neutral to the drive position.

put it in first - To shift a car's transmission into first gear.

put it in gear - To shift a car's transmission from neutral to one of the drive gears.

put it in low - To shift a car's transmission into low gear.

put it in reverse - To shift a car's transmission into reverse gear.

put it in the can - Top operate a race car with the largest allowable percentage of nitromethane in the fuel.

put to the wood - To open a car's throttle wide open.

put the guy on paper - Sales tactic used where a potential customer's interest in a car is written up on a sales contract as a subtle way of getting him to feel like he's committed even though he has not yet signed it.

PVS - Abbreviation for ported vacuum switch.

PW - Abbreviation for power windows.

pw - Abbreviation for power windows.

Pwr - Abbreviation for power. See also P.

PY - Abbreviation for Paraguay found usually on an international license plate.

Pyramid - American car produced in 1902.

Pyroil - American line of additives produced by Pyroil Company.

Q

Quadra-Link – Tradename used for a Jeep front suspension system.

Quadra-Trac – Tradename used for a Jeep power transfer system to front and rear differentials. See also Select-Trac.

Quaker State – American line of engine oils produced by Quaker State Oil Refining Corporation.

Quaker State Oil Refining Corp – A U.S. petroleum lubricants company headquartered in Oil City, Pennsylvania.

Quakertown – American car produced in 1915.

qualify – To separate customers interested in buying form those interested in just looking. It also means introducing a car salesman to a potential customer.

quality control – Program followed to insure the quality of a product produced.

quarter panel – Sheetmetal panel used to cover an area from the rear door edge to the taillight, and from the lower body edge up to base of the roof and the edge of the trunk opening. Every car has a quarter panel on each side.

quartz halogen bulb – Bulb used to produce greater light per watt. It is made of quartz, a tungsten filament, and filled with inert gases. The inert gases consist of iodine and one or more halogen gases. The gases recycle any tungsten deposits on the bulb wall back on the tungsten filament. This prevents the inner bulb surface from darkening and lowering light output. High filament temperatures are required for this process and necessitate the use of quartz as opposed to normal glass.

quartz halogen headlamp – Car headlight built with a quartz halogen bulb.

quasi contract – See contract(quasi).

Queen – Canadian car produced from 1901-1903 by Queen City Cycle & Motor Works in Ontario. Also, an American car produced from 1904-1907 by C.H. Blomstrom Motor Co. in Michigan.

quench – Cooling of remaining gases in a combustion chamber created by contact with a piston and combustion chamber metal. It helps to reduce a fuel mixture's tendency to detonate. See also squish.

quenching – Process defined as immersing hot metal in a gas, liquid, or solid for rapid cooling in order to impart certain desired properties to the metal.

Quick – American car produced from 1899-1900.

quick change rear end – Differential built with a quickly changeable gear ratio. The back of the unit is removed and spur gears are quickly exchanged. It permits a racing car to operate at different peak efficiency speeds.

quick steering – Type of steering system built where steering wheel movement closely matches wheel movement. Such a system typically turns from full left to right in 2 to 2 1/2 turns. An average car uses around 5 turns.

quietness – Degree of silence within a car under different driving conditions. It is a common test made when a new car is evaluated.

quill bearing – See bearing(needle).

Quinlan – American car produced in 1904.

Quinsler – American car produced in 1904.

quitclaim – To transfer a person's title, interest, right, etc. to something to another.

quitclaim deed – Deed used to specify a quitclaim.

quota of tickets – Share or portion of total tickets desired or required from a particular district, area, etc.

R

R — Abbreviation for Romania found usually on an international license plate.

r — Abbreviation for radio.

R12 — See freon(12).

R22 — See freon(22).

R-100 Method — European testing method used to evaluate the antiknock quality of a gasoline's compounds boiling below 212 degrees Fahrenheit. The Research Octane Number Method is used. It is used as an alternative to the Distribution Octane Number Method since it also indicates the antiknock quality of gasoline not efficiently distributed. See also Motor Octane Number Method.

R&L Electric — American car produced in 1920.

R&R — Abbreviation commonly used on repair bills referring to removing and repairing a part, and not remove and replace.

R&V Knight — American car produced from 1920-1924 by R&V Division of Root & Vandervoort Engineering Co. in Illinois. It was considered a good quality car.

RA — Abbreviation for Argentina found usually on an international license plate.

Rabbit — See Volkswagen.

RAC — American car produced from 1911-1912.

race(1) — Contest of speed held where race car, motorcycle, etc. drivers compete.

race(2) — Inner and/or outer contact surface of a bearing assembly used to contain balls or rollers and provide a surface for them to roll on.

race cam — See camshaft(high lift).

race car — High performance car built or modified from a stock car to run in races.

racer — Person engaged in racing cars, motorcycles, etc.

race run — Race held on an oval race track.

race track — Course laid out for racing.

race track circuit — See race track.

race way — Race track used for dragsters, stock cars, etc.

Racine — American car produced in 1895.

racing — To race.

racing cam — See camshaft(high lift).

racing crank kit — Performance crankshaft and related parts sold in kit form. Parts typically include: crankshaft; connecting rods; main and rod bearings; and pistons, rings, and pins.

racing engine kit — Complete performance engine block and related parts sold in kit form. A short block kit typically includes: engine block; pistons, rings, and pins; connecting rods; crankshaft; main and rod bearings; timing chain and gearing; and camshaft. A long block kit typically includes: short block kit parts, cylinder heads, valve lifters, push rods, high volume oil pump, and gaskets.

racing the engine — Speeding an engine up to a high rpm momentarily.

racing stripes — Large decorative stripes painted or glued on a car body.

rack and pinion box — See rack and pinion gearbox.

rack and pinion gearbox — Housing located at the end of a steering shaft containing a rack and pinion gear arrangement. The pinion engages a long rack (bar with a row of teeth cut along one edge).

rack and pinion steering — Steering system usually found on smaller cars where an input shaft (pinion) is geared directly to an output shaft (rack). It is found on sports cars where a tight responsive steering system is desirable.

radar — See radar detector.

radar detector — Electronic device used to detect radio type waves being beamed to it from radar guns used by law enforcement agencies.

radial — Moving straight out in all directions from a common center. Spokes of a wheel are an example of radial design. See also radial tire.

radial runout — See runout(radial).

radials — Abbreviation for radial tires.

radial tire — See tire(radial).

radiation — Energy sent out into space as rays of light, heat, etc. resulting from atomic and molecular changes.

radiator — Tank-like device mounted directly in front of an engine and used to transfer heat in engine coolant to the outside air by circulating coolant through finned tubes. Radiator parts typically include: a top tank with a coolant inlet, radiator core where vertical finned tubes are located, and a bottom tank with a radiator outlet and drain plug. The parts are made of metals resistant to corrosion with good heat transfer ability. Brass, aluminum, and copper are the most common. A radiator's heat transfer capacity is determined by the fins per inch on each tube, the tubes per inch, and the tube's length, width, and height.

The process of cooling the engine coolant begins when it flows from the top of the engine into the top radiator tank. There it spreads out and flows into the tubes. As the coolant flows downward, it radiates heat to the tube fins which lose heat to air passing through them. Cooled water then flows into a lower tank for routing back to the engine via the water pump.

radiator(cross flow) - Radiator built with two side tanks and horizontal finned tubes. Coolant flows into one side tank, through the tubes, and out the other side tank.

radiator(down flow) - Radiator built with a top and bottom tank, and vertical finned tubes. Coolant flows in the top, down through the tubes, and out the bottom. This is the most common type radiator in use today.

radiator cap - Pressure relief valve used on a radiator to contain and pressurize coolant in a cooling system. It is designed to remain sealed up to a predetermined coolant pressure (usually 12-15 psi). Pressurizing coolant allows it to run at a higher temperature in liquid form before boiling (each pound of pressure raises the boiling temperature three degrees Fahrenheit). When the pressure is exceeded, the cap releases and coolant flows through an outlet tube to the ground or to an overflow tank. Using a cap rated at too low a pressure will cause accelerated coolant loss and subsequent engine overheating. A cap rated at too high a pressure will cause hoses and radiator parts to rupture. Some caps are equipped with a manual pressure relief valve. Be very careful when removing a cap. Temperatures can exceed 200 degrees Fahrenheit. A sudden release of steam and coolant can burn you. If the upper radiator hose is hot and firm, the system is under pressure and the cap should not be removed. Wait for it to cool down. See also boiling point and antifreeze concentration.

radiator core - Main part of a radiator constructed as a series of vertical parallel finned rectangular tubes through which coolant flows in order to cool. Air passes around the tubes to cool coolant. When a car is stopped or moving slowly, the fan pulls air through the core. When moving down the road, air is forced through the fins. The size of radiator cores is smaller on today's engines, because of better heat transfer and the pressurization of coolant systems which more efficiently reject heat.

radiator corrosion - See car service tip(radiator corrosion).

radiator cover - Removable covering placed in front of a radiator to reduce air flow. Covers are commonly used in the winter time to keep coolant warmer. Some covers are made of fabric while others can be a simple as a piece of cardboard.

radiator drain tap - Small threaded plug or brass valve mounted at the base of the radiator. When removed or opened, it drains engine coolant.

radiator fan thermostat - Heat sensor used to start and a stop an electric fan, depending on air temperature. It is usually located near the top of the radiator on either side of the electric fan housing. It may be malfunctioning, if engine gauges indicate overheating, and fan is not operating. See also engine problem(overheating).

radiator fins - Thin aluminum projections attached to radiator tubes which help dissipate heat to the air.

radiator flush - Chemical compound used to help flush contaminants from an engine cooling system. Also, it refers to the process of flushing out a radiator or cooling system.

radiator grille - Car body grille located in front of a radiator.

radiator hose - One of two short lengths of hose attached to a radiator for routing coolant flow into and out of an engine's water jacket. The upper hose routes coolant from the top of the engine block to the upper radiator tank while the lower hose routes coolant from the lower tank to the water pump. The lower hose usually contains an internal spring to help hold the shape of the hose and resist collapse from the water pump suction. When the hoses become brittle, they should be replaced. Hoses can collapse under certain conditions. It can happen to an upper radiator hose when an engine cools if the radiator cap vent valve is plugged. It can happen to a lower radiator hose, if the internal spring is missing, damaged, broken, or out of place. See also engine problem(overheating).

radiator leak - See fluid leak(engine coolant).

radiator needs to be rodded out - Radiator condition created when radiator tubes become partially plugged restricting coolant flow. The tubes get plugged in time due to rust, scale, other deposits, and infrequent radiator fluid changes.

radiator overflow tank - Tank used on sealed engine cooling systems to allow for expansion, contraction, extra cooling fluid, and to minimize loss of coolant through evaporation.

radiator tank – Metal trough soldered to a radiator core. A radiator has a
top and bottom tank. The top tank channels incoming coolant to the core, and
the bottom tank channels coolant to a water pump for recirculation in an
engine.

radiator tubes – Vertical rectangular tubes in a radiator core where coolant
is circulated for cooling.

radio antenna – Metal rod or wire used to receive radio signals.

radio frequency interference – Electrical by product of high voltage cables
carrying current. It creates static interference on radio and stereo
equipment mounted in cars unless shielded.

radio reception – The clarity a radio exhibits in picking up and amplifying
radio signals. Poor reception can be due to a faulty radio antenna and cable
assembly with high resistance.

radius – Distance from the center of a circle to the edge.

radius rods – Rods attached from an axle to frame for keeping axle
perpendicular to frame centerline.

Rae – American car produced in 1909.

Rae Electric – American car produced in 1898.

rag top – Convertible.

rail – Dragster. Also, it refers to a frame rail.

rail job – Car modified for drag racing.

railroad crossing – Intersection of a road and railroad.

Railsbach – American car produced in 1914.

Railton W-12 Mobil Special – English car driven by John Cobb to a world land
speed record in 1938, 1939, and 1947 at Bonneville, Utah. Speeds were 350.2,
369.7, and 394.2 mph.

Rainier – American car produced from 1905-1911 by Rainier Co. in Ohio and
Michigan (1905-1907), and Rainier Motor Car Co. in Michigan (1907-1911).

rain molding – See drip rail.

raised hood – Signal used to indicate a car stopped along a roadside is broke
down.

raise the hood – To prop open a hood.

raising – See bumping.

raked – Car with its front end lower than the rear end.

raking – See diegoing.

Ralco – American car produced in 1904.

Raleigh – American car produced from 1920-1922 by Raleigh Motors in
Pennsylvania and New Jersey.

rally – Organized car run held on public roads to test different driver
skills. See also reliability run.

rallycross – Racing event held at a race track whose surface is partly sealed.

rallye – Long distance car race held on public roads unfamiliar to drivers and
marked off by numerous checkpoints. It is usually not a speed race but
rather a contest to see which car can maintain various road speed limits the
closest.

ram air – See ramming effect.

Rambler – American car produced from 1900-1913 and 1950-1970 by Rockaway
Bicycle Works in New York (1900-1903), Thos. B. Jeffrey Co. in Wisconsin
(1902-1913), Nash Motors Co. in Wisconsin (1950-1954), and American Motors
Corp. in Wisconsin (1954-1970). The Rambler became a car line at American
Motors from 1958-1970.

Ramcharger – American truck produced from 1972 to date by Dodge Division of
Chrysler Corp. in Michigan.

ramming effect – Slight supercharging effect created when air is forced into
an air cleaner's intake from a car's forward movement into an air stream.
Higher speed generates more pressure. Some cars use hood scoops directly
over a carburetor while others use air scoops running from a carburetor to
the car grille area.

ramp(freeway) – Sloping road built to provide an entrance to or exit from a
freeway.

ramp(support) – See car ramp.

Rampage – American car produced from 1982 to date by Dodge Division of
Chrysler Corp. in Michigan.

Ranchero – American car produced from 1957-1979 by Ford Motor Co. in Michigan.

Ranch Wagon – American car produced from 1957-1964 by Ford Motor Co. in
Michigan.

Rand & Harvey – American steam car produced from 1899-1900 by Rand & Harvey in
Maine.

Randall – American car produced in 1904.

Randall Steamer – American steam car produced from 1902-1903.

Randall Steam – American steam car produced from 1908-1910.

Ranger – American car produced from 1908-1910, and 1920-1922 by Ranger Motor
Works in Illinois, and Southern Motor Mfg. Assoc. in Texas respectively.
Also, an American car produced from 1982 to date by Ford Motor Co. in
Michigan.

Ranier – American car produced in 1911.
Rankine cycle engine – See engine(Rankine cycle).
Rapid Truck – American truck produced from 1902-1913.
Rassel – American car produced in 1911.
Rassler – American car produced in 1907.
rat – Rough car, junker, or wreck.
ratchet jaw – Person characterized as talking a lot without saying much.
rate charts – Interest rate charts used to specify the various interest costs
  for different purchase prices. Some rates may include insurance coverage and
  other optional items. Car dealers will generally try to negotiate the
  highest rate they can. Different charts are used for different situations.
rate of interest – Interest used in a loan.
Rathmann, John – He won the Indianapolis 500 Race in 1960 driving an average
  of 138.8 mph in a Ken-Paul Special.
rating territory – Area designated for determining rates for car insurance.
  Insurance companies break the country up into different areas and analyze
  accident statistics for those areas in order to arrive at insurance rates for
  each one. Territories can range in size from part of a city to an entire
  state. See also loss experience.
rat motor – Chevrolet engine with 427 cu.in. displacement.
rattle – Rapid succession of short sharp sounds.
rattle trap – Car characterized by lots of rattles, squeaks, and vibrations.
rat trap – Engine cylinder head.
Rauch & Lang – American electric car produced from 1905-1922 by Rauch & Lang
  Carriage Co. (1905-1916), and Baker, Rauch & Lang Co. (1916-1922), both in
  Ohio.
Raulang – American electric car produced from 1922-1928 by Rauch & Lang
  Electric Car Mfg. Co. in Massachusetts.
raunchy – Car with a poor paint job or appearance.
Raybestos – American line of brake linings.
Rayfield – American car produced from 1911-1915 by Rayfield Motor Car Co. in
  Illinois.
Ray Graham – He and his brothers Robert and Joseph formed the Graham Brothers
  Truck Company to manufacture light weight trucks in the 1920s.
Raymond – American car produced from 1912-1913 by Raymond Engineering Co. in
  Massachusetts.
rblt – Abbreviation for rebuilt.
RC(1) – Abbreviation for racing car.
RC(2) – Abbreviation for China found usually on an international license
  plate.
RCH – American car produced from 1912-1916 by Hupp Corp. in Michigan.
r defog – Abbreviation for rear defroster.
rdstr – Abbreviation for roadster. See also RDT.
RDT – Abbreviation for roadster. See also rdstr.
reach – To offer above wholesale price for a trade-in. It is usually done if
  a car salesman knows it will sell quickly and he can still make a profit.
reaction time – Time required by a driver to react to a situation after a
  decision has been made. For most drivers it is about 3/4 of a second. An
  example would be applying the brakes.
Read – American car produced from 1913-1914 by Read Motor Co. in Michigan.
Reading – American steam car produced from 1900-1903 by Steam Vehicle Co. of
  America (1900-1902), and Meteor Engineering Co. (1902-1903), both in
  Pennsylvania. Also, an American car produced from 1910-1913 by Middleby Auto
  Co. in Pennsylvania.
readout – The observed or displayed value of an instrument, gauge, etc.
ready to go – Abbreviation for car in reasonably good driving condition.
Real – American car produced from 1914-1915 by H. Paul Prigg Co. in Indiana.
ream – To enlarge a hole with a reamer or coned-shaped file.
reamer – Cone-shaped filing tool used to enlarge a hole.
rear axle – Metal rod used to transfer power from a differential to a rear
  wheel. Rear wheel drive cars have one for each wheel. It is one of the
  powertrain components and is housed in a rear end.
rear axle(high ratio) – Rear axle built with a high differential gear ratio.
  See also gear ratio.
rear axle ratio – See differential gear ratio.
rear band – Brake band used to encircle the rear planetary gear set drum of
  an automatic transmission.
rear bed – Bed built into the back of a van.
rear bumper – Car bumper mounted on the rear of a car.
rear countershaft gear – Gear mounted on the back of a transmission
  countershaft gear usually meshing with a transmission's reverse idler gear.
  See also gear(reverse idler).
rear deck – Flat open area located behind the back seat of a car. Hatchback,
  liftback and station wagon cars have this area.
rear deck lid – Trunk used on sedans. Also, it refers to the rear door on

hatchback or liftback cars.

rear defogger - See rear window defogger.

rear directionals - Rear turn signal lights. See also front directionals.

rear end - Assemblage of parts used to transfer power from a driveline to the wheels of a rear wheel drive car. It is a cast steel housing lying between the two rear wheels and primarily contains two axles, and a differential unit.

rear end collision - Accident created between two cars when a lead car is struck in the rear by a trailing car. It usually occurs when the lead car stops abruptly or is otherwise at rest on a road.

rear ended - Condition created when a car is struck in the rear area by another car.

rear ender - See rear end collision.

rear facebar - Rear bumper side.

rear fender - See quarter panel.

rear fender cover - See rear fender skirt.

rear fender skirt - Half-circle shaped sheetmetal insert used to cover the upper half of a wheel opening. It is used on some rear wheels.

rear louvers - Horizontal louvered structure mounted on the rear window of a car providing a clear view out the back, but shields the interior from sunlight. It consists of a series of horizontal slats mounted in a frame, and overlapping each other like venetian blinds. Some designs can be lifted up for easy cleaning. See also shade kit.

rear luggage compartment - Open storage area located behind the back seat of an automobile.

rear main bearing - Crankshaft journal bearing located closest to the flywheel.

rear number plate - Plate used to attach the rear license plate.

rear servo - Hydraulic piston and cylinder assembly used to control the tightness of a brake band encircling a rear planetary gear set drum in an automatic transmission.

rear shackle - Device used to attach the rear end of a leaf spring to a car frame.

rear shocks - See shock absorber(rear).

rear shock absorber - See shock absorber(rear).

rear slider - Abbreviation for horizontal sliding window used as a pickup truck back window.

rear spoiler - Spoiler mounted on the rear deck or trunk of a car.

rear springs - Springs used to support a car's rear axle or wheels.

rear suspension - Suspension system used to support the rear portion of a car's body and chassis.

rear suspension out of line - Condition created when the rear end suspension and, thus the rear axle axis, becomes out of line with the frame centerline. Possible causes include: frame and/or underbody is out of line, front spring hanger in wrong location, broken leaf spring or coil spring, and rear axle housing bent.

rear view mirror - Mirror mounted inside a car at the top middle of a car windshield to allow a driver to view traffic behind him.

rear wheel bearings - Roller bearings used to support rear wheel axles.

rear wheel track - Road contact relationship of rear wheels to each other.

rear window - Window opposite a car windshield.

rear window defogger - Rear window heating device designed to keep window from fogging up. It usually consists of several electric resistance wires glued to the inside window surface. When energized, the wires heat up transferring heat to the window to drive off condensed moisture. Also, it refers to a rear-mounted defogger similar to one used for a car's windshield.

rear window defroster - See rear window defogger.

rear window louver - See rear louvers.

Rebel - American car produced from 1964-1977 by American Motors Corp. in Michigan.

Reber - American car produced from 1902-1903 by Reber Mfg. Co. in Pennsylvania.

re bondo - To cover part or all of a car body panel again with plastic filler.

rebored - Engine block machine work done where the cylinders have been enlarged to house larger pistons. It is usually done to overhaul an engine or increase its performance.

rebound - Return action of a suspension spring after it has been compressed.

rebuild - Process defined as restoring an item to original operating condition by dismantling its parts and reassembling it with new parts or restoring the used parts to a new condition. For example, an engine rebuild.

rebuilt engine - Engine restored to a new operating condition. See also engine overhaul.

rebuilt part - Car part restored to new condition.

rebuilt transmission - Manual or automatic transmission restored to a new operating condition.

rebuttal – Denial made of a charge in a court of law through the introduction of contradictory evidence.

recall – Notification made to affected car owners of a car defect. Owners are usually instructed to bring the car into a dealer at their convenience at which time the defect will be corrected.

recall letter – Letter sent out by a car manufacturer notifying specific car owners of possible defects. It usually instructs an owner to take the car to the nearest dealer for a free correction of the problem.

recall notice – See recall letter.

Recaro – Brand of bucket seats.

recap – See tire(recap).

receiver – See receiver-drier.

receiver-dehydrator – See receiver-drier.

receiver-drier – Device used in an air conditioning system to receive liquid refrigerant from a condenser, store it, and remove moisture. Components typically consist of: housing, filter and screen assembly, drying agent, and inlet/outlet fittings. It should replaced if left open to the atmosphere for five or more hours, and if system has become contaminated.

reception – See radio reception.

recessed windshield wipers – Windshield wipers built to retract into a recessed area at the bottom of a car's windshield when not in use.

recharge – To add freon to a car's air conditioner until it hold the recommended quantity.

reciprocating action – Back and forth movement like a piston in a cylinder.

recirculated air – Cool or warm air discharged into a passenger compartment and forced to flow back into heating and air conditioning intake ducting. Air is usually recirculated when outside temperature is hot or cold. Recirculated air requires less energy than outside air to heat and cool a car's interior during cold and warm weather.

recirculating ball steering box – Steering device used to transmit turning motion and reduce friction by using a series of steel balls mounted in a worm gear groove.

recirculating door – Movable door located in a car's heating/cooling ductwork for controlling the amount of outside air passing over heater and/or evaporator coils.

reckless driving – Driver habits characterized as dangerous to the safety of himself, pedestrians, and other cars. Dangerous habits include: tailgating, driving fast in slow speed zones, not stopping at stop signs, cutting in front of cars, weaving in and out of traffic, and stopping without warning.

reclining seat – Seat built to tilt backwards.

Recond – Abbreviation for a recent car subjected to major repairs.

reconditioned car – Car inspected and repaired sufficient to make it operate more safely.

record model – Fiberglass or plaster reproduction of a car designer's original approved car clay model. See also proveout model.

recourse – Right of a lender to collect on a loan.

recoverable – Auto code word used to specify a car in one piece, but requiring a complete restoration job.

recreational vehicle – Vehicle used by people for play, amusement, relaxation, etc. It usually refers to a motor home, but can also include such other vehicles as: truck/camper combination, snowmobile, and off-road motorcycle.

rectangular sign – See road sign(rectangular).

rectifier – Electric device used to permit current flow in one direction only. Rectifiers are used to change alternating current into direct current in an alternator.

reed valve – See valve(reed).

Red Arrow – American car produced in 1915.

Red Ball – American car produced in 1924.

red book – See blue book.

Red Bug – American electric car produced from 1923-1928 by Automotive Electrical Service Co., and Standard Automobile Corp., both in New Jersey.

red flag – See flag(red).

Red Flag Law – Law passed in England in 1875 forbidding any self propelled vehicle from traveling on public roads unless a man walked in front of the vehicle carrying a red warning flag.

Red Jacket – American car produced in 1904.

red light(1) – See traffic light(3 light signal).

red light(2) – To leave a starting line before a green light flashes. To foul.

redline(1) – Maximum recommended safe engine rpm. Beyond such a limit risks engine damage due to rapidly moving parts getting in each other's way, and inadequate lubrication. Cars equipped with tachometers usually have a red mark or line indicating the rpm limit. After market tachometers usually have an adjustable red line arm.

redline(2) – Minimum price accepted by a dealer for a car. It is usually

determined before the car is offered for sale on the lot.
Redpath - Canadian car produced in 1903.
Red Shield - American car produced in 1911.
reduced speed - To drive slower than the posted speed limit.
reducer - See paint reducer.
Red Wing - American car produced in 1928.
Reed - American car produced in 1909.
reed valve - One way valve built in the shape of a flat strip. It is used on some two cycle engines and on air compressors.
Rees - American car produced in 1921.
Reeves - American car produced from 1896-1898 and 1905-1912 by Reeves Pulley Co. (1896-1898; 1905-1910), and Reeves Sexto-Octo Co. (1911-1912), both in Indiana.
refill brake system - To add brake fluid to a brake system until the proper master brake cylinder reservoir level has been reached.
refinance - To finance a loan again or obtain a new one.
reflector - Object made of reflective material to reflect and direct light.
reforming - Petroleum refining process used to increase high octane gasoline yield from a barrel of crude oil. It combines specified light molecules to yield more complex high octane molecules. The process lowers the yield of high octane unleaded gasoline from a barrel of crude oil. The lower yield is the main reason for the slightly higher cost of unleaded fuel. Reformed gas is also more volatile due to the incorporation of butane and other light fraction by-products which raise octane slightly.
refrigerant - Chemical compound used in mechanical refrigeration systems to remove or add heat to an enclosed environment. R-12 freon is the common refrigerant used in automotive air conditioners. It is a liquid with a low boiling point.
refrigerate - To cool or make cold.
refrigeration system - Assemblage of interdependent mechanical devices used to provide heating or cooling to an enclosed environment. A car air conditioner is a refrigeration system providing cooling to a car's interior. A refrigeration system primarily consists of a compressor, low and high pressure piping, a condenser, an evaporator, a heat transfer coil, and the freon.
Regal - American car produced from 1907-1920 by Regal Motor Car Co. in Michigan (1907-1920). Also, a Canadian car produced from 1914-1917 by Canadian Regal Motor Car Co. in Ontario. Also, an American car produced from 1973 to date by Buick Division of General Motors Corp. in Michigan.
regapping - Checking and adjusting, if necessary, the space between spark plug electrodes, contact points, etc.
Regas - American car produced from 1903-1905 by Regas Automobile Co. in New York.
Regent - American car produced in 1917.
registered owner - Legal owner of a car, boat, trailer, etc.
registration - Certificate issued to serve as proof that someone or something has been registered. Examples include: boat, car, motorcycle, motor home, and trailer registration.
regrinding the camshaft - Process defined as machining a camshaft's intake and exhaust cam lobes to new profile shapes to increase engine horsepower. See also cam(racing).
regroover - See tire regroover.
reground - To grind a machined surface again.
reground camshaft - Camshaft reworked by grinding intake and exhaust cam lobes to new profiles for increasing engine horsepower. See also cam(racing).
regular - See gasoline(leaded).
regular maintenance program - Maintenance program followed at regular time or mileage intervals.
regulator(1) - Electric switching device used to control a generator's voltage and current output to keep a battery charged and prevent damage to the battery, generator, and car's electrical system. It typically consists of: a base, cover, one or more sets of electromagnetically operated points, bimetallic springs to compensate for effect of temperature rise on control units, and one or more resistance circuits. The regulator controls generator output by automatically adding or removing additional resistance to the current flow in the generator's field windings. This decreases or increases the field magnetic strength. See also cutout relay, current regulator, and voltage regulator.
  A defective regulator usually causes either too little or too much battery charging. Symptoms of too little charging include: dim lights at idle increasing with engine speed, slow flashing of turn signal lights speeding up with engine speed, and battery requires charging up every couple weeks. Too much charging causes: rapid loss of battery water.
regulator(1-carbon pile) - Alternator regulator used in heavy duty, high current output applications.

regulator(1-cutout relay) – DC generator regulator used with third brush generators that had only a cutout relay.

regulator(1-double contact) – DC generator and alternator regulator built with double sets of points for each control unit. Designs are available with one to three units. It is commonly used on cars with heavier electrical loads.

regulator(1-three unit DC) – DC generator regulator built with three relays. The relays are a cutout relay, a current limiter or regulator, and a voltage limiter or regulator.

regulator(1-transistor) – Solid state regulator used with alternators. It has no moving parts. The parts consist of: transistors, diodes, resistors, and capacitors.

regulator(2) – Valve used to reduce pressure to a set level.

regulator polarity – Direction of current flow through the contact points and circuits of a regulator. The wrong polarity can cause a regulator's points to burn and pit rapidly.

regulatory sign – See road sign(regulatory).

Rehberger Truck – American truck produced in 1924.

Reid – American car produced from 1903-1905.

Reiland & Bree – American car produced in 1928.

Reinertsen – American car produced in 1902.

rejection and revoction of acceptance – Legal maneuver used to return a car to a seller and obtain a refund of the purchase price because of serious defects which lower the car's value and violate a warranty or other right the buyer has arising from the sale. It is wise to consult an attorney if you follow this approach as the matter may wind up in court and the steps in the maneuver must be carefully followed. The rejection part of the maneuver allows you to cancel the sale. This must occur shortly after you take possession of the car. The revocation part allows you to return a defective car even if it has been driven awhile. The seller must be given a reasonable time to repair the defect. To start this whole process, the car must be returned to the seller along with an offer to surrender the keys and the Certificate of Title.

relative distance – See depth perception.

Relay – American car produced in 1904.

relay – Switching device used to open or close a set of electric contact points by using a moderate flow of battery voltage current. Some relays close points using an electromagnetic action while others are closed using the heat generated by the current flow. Electromagnetic relays usually employ a fixed magnetic core and a movable coil, or a fixed core and coil. Heat type relays usually consist of a thin metal strip composed of two dissimilar metals. When the strip heats, the two metals expand at different rates causing it to bend in one direction or another. Cars usually have several relays. They include: turn signal (heat type), lighting, starter, air conditioning, regulator, electric fan, and defroster.
 In general, the difference between relays and solenoids can be stated as follows: relays have fixed magnetic cores and movable or fixed coils, and solenoids have movable magnetic cores and fixed coils. See also solenoid switch.

relay rod – See drag link.

Relay Truck – American truck produced in 1921.

relay winding – Wire wound around an iron core in a relay device.

reliability run – Driving contest held where cars drive over a designated course with observers at check points. See also rally.

Reliable Dayton – American car produced from 1906-1909 by Dayton & Mashey Automobile Works in Illinois.

Reliance – American car produced in 1903-1907 by Reliance Auto & Motor Co. in New York. Also, an American car produced in 1917.

Reliant – British car line produced from 1952 to date by Reliant Motors Co. Ltd. Also, an American car produced from 1981 to date by Plymouth Division of Chrysler Corp. in Michigan.

relief – Difference in height between two surfaces.

relieving – Process defined as the removal of metal from engine valves and the valve area to increase flow of combustion chamber gases. Also, it refers to the removal of any ridge between a valve seat and the block surface. It is mostly done on racing engines.

reluctor – Device used in an electronic ignition system with a magnetic pickup coil to trigger high voltage current in an ignition coil. It is mounted on a distributor shaft in place of a cam. Around its circumference are ridges corresponding to the number of engine cylinders. Each ridge triggers a small current flow which is amplified in the pickup coil and sent on to a control unit. The control unit contains a transistor that opens the primary circuit just like conventional points do, inducing high voltage in the ignition coil's secondary winding. See also ignition system and control unit.

remanufactured – Item rebuilt to new operating condition. Examples of remanufactured car parts include: clutch plate, pressure plate, brake shoes, starter, and alternator.

Remel-Vincent Steam - American steam car produced in 1923.

Remington - American car produced in 1900-1904 and 1914-1915 by Remington Motor Vehicle Co. in New York, and Remington Motor Co. in New Jersey respectively.

remote starter switch - Switch with long leads used to bypass an ignition switch and engage a starter from an engine compartment.

remove and repair - Car repair practice defined as removing a part from a car, and taking it apart, and repairing it if possible. Part replacement is done only as a last resort. Repair of used parts is not a popular practice anymore because more money can be made by replacing parts.

remove and replace - Car repair practice defined as removing a part from a car, and simply replacing it with a new one rather than repairing the old one. This is the common practice of today's repair shops.

Renault - French car distributed from 1978 to date by American Motors Corp. in Michigan. Also, a French car line produced from 1898 to date by Regie Nationale des Usines Renault. Popular models include: Alliance, Espace, and Fuego.

The U.S. representative is Renault USA, Inc., headquartered in Englewood Cliffs, New Jersey.

Renault, Marcel - He won a 620 mile race, in 1902, averaging 40 mph in his Renault car.

rendering - Detailed illustration.

Rennoc - American car produced in 1918.

Reno - American car produced in 1908.

rental car lot - Business engaged in renting cars.

Renville - American car produced in 1911.

Reo - American car produced from 1904-1936 by Reo Car Co. (1904), and Reo Motor Car Co. (1904-1936), both in Michigan.

Reo Truck - American truck produced from 1908 to date by White Motor Co. in Michigan.

repack the front wheel bearings - To clean the front wheel bearings and install new new grease. On most cars, this work is done every 25-30,000 miles to insure a long bearing life. It removes dirt, debris, and/or water that may accumulate in the bearings and cause damage. The work usually proceeds as follows. Each tire is removed. The bearings are removed. The bearings and the races on which they ride are inspected for wear, scratches, cracks, and broken or missing rollers. If necessary, the bearings are cleaned in a suitable solvent. The old grease is removed from between the two bearing races in the wheel hub assembly. The area is thoroughly cleaned and then new grease is installed. Existing bearings are relubricated and installed. The wheel hub is installed with the bearings. The wheel hub retaining nut is installed to about 10-15 lbs of torque while rotating the wheel by hand. The nut is then loosened till free, then retightened to 20-25 lbs of torque. It is then finally loosened one more time till just free and tightened only to the nearest slot in the nut for inserting the cotter pin. In general, the nut should have a snug feel.

Repair - See Recond.

repair and tune-up guide - Publication designed to provide detailed repair and tune-up information for one or more car makes.

repair bill - Bill used by car repair shop listing the charges for the repair work done to a car. It's a good idea before paying a repair bill to have the service manager go with you on a short test drive so you are satisfied with the work done before paying for it. See also repair order, mechanic's lien, and con game(repair order).

repair facility - Business engaged in repairing cars.

repair gyp - See con game.

repair job - Repair work done to correct a car malfunction.

repair order - Document signed by a car owner giving a car repair business the right to do specified work on a car and obligate the owner to pay the charges in full before he can get possession of his car back. See also con game(repair order), repair bill, and mechanic's lien.

repair order fraud - See con game(repair order).

repair plug - Small solid rubber stem used to patch punctures in tires bodies. The repair process consists of: cleaning and roughening the puncture hole, applying cement to the hole and the plug, inserting the plug into the hole, letting the plug set, and trimming off the excess on the outside.

repair work - See repair job.

repair work guarantee - See guarantee(repair work).

repeat - Previous car customer returning to buy another car from a car salesman. Repeats are an important source of future income for a car salesman.

repo - Repossessed car.

repossession - Car taken back from a buyer by an owner, usually because the buyer has been delinquent on payments.

repossession fee - Fee charged, by a finance company owning a car, to people attempting to retrieve their repossessed car back.

repossessor - Person engaged in repossessing cars.

Republic - American car produced from 1911-1916 by Republic Motor Car Co. in Ohio (1911-1912), and New York (1913-1916).

Republic Truck - American truck produced from 1914-1931.

reputable garage - Car repair shop known for doing good work and treating a customer fairly.

re-ring kit - Assemblage of parts used when new piston rings are installed in an engine. It usually consists of: piston rings, rod bearings, and various replacement gaskets.

resale value - Value of an item if it were sold.

Research Octane Number Method - Laboratory engine test method used to evaluate the antiknock quality of gasoline subjected to mild operating conditions at low rpm. A standard single cylinder engine is used. It is run at low speeds, moderate loads, and with a cool air/fuel mixture temperature. See also RON, Motor Octane Number Method, Distribution Octane Number Method, R-100 Method, and Antiknock Index.

reserve alkalinity - Indicator used to specify an oil's ability to neutralize acids and lengthen its protection time against engine wear and deposit formation. See also additive(detergent/dispersant-1).

residence district - Territory comprised primarily of residential dwellings fronting on the roads within the district.

residual gases - Combustion gases left in an engine cylinder after an exhaust valve has closed and an intake valve begins opening.

residual value - Estimated value of a leased car when its lease expires. See also bring back.

resin - Substance characterized as viscous, clear or translucent, yellowish or brownish, and organic or manmade. It is used in medicine, plastics, paints, and as one part of epoxy glue.

resistance - Property exhibited by an electrical conductor where current flow is reduced or prevented. Resistance usually generates heat.

resistor - Device placed in an electrical circuit to limit current flow at a specified voltage.

resistor spark plug - See spark plug(resistor).

resonator - Secondary muffler installed behind a main muffler in an exhaust pipe system to help further quiet exhaust sound.

Resta, Dario - He won the Indianapolis 500 Race in 1916 driving an average of 84.0 mph in a Peugeot.

rest area - Roadside stop built where drivers and passengers can stop and rest safely off a road. It usually has rest rooms, water, places to walk animals, telephones, and trash or RV sewage disposal.

restricted tires - Tires not meeting passenger car tire standards. Such tires are often not designed or constructed for highway use.

resurface drums - To machine the braking surface of brake drums to proper dimensions.

resurfacing cylinder head - To machine the cylinder block mating surface of a head until it is considered flat.

retail value - Suggested selling price of a car. It is a car's wholesale value plus the profit desired by a car dealer.

retainer(1) - Device used to hold parts together. See also valve keeper.

retainer(2) - Down payment made by a client to an attorney for legal services.

retard - To decrease an ignition timing setting so a spark fires later. It usually translates to a spark occurring at TDC or on the downward portion of a power stroke. It is measured in degrees. An excessively retarded spark will cause an engine to lose power, waste fuel, and cause possible preignition (due to overworking engine). See also advance(ignition) and retarding the spark.

retard diaphragm - Vacuum operated diaphragm mounted on a distributor to retard timing when an engine is idling or decelerating. See also advance diaphragm.

retarding the spark - Adjustment of ignition timing made to cause a spark generation later in a piston's cycle.

retard solenoid - Solenoid used to control exhaust emissions when engine is idling and at normal operating temperature by retarding ignition timing. It is usually made a part of the vacuum advance unit. A faulty solenoid will not increase idling speed when grounded. See also car service tip(retard solenoid test).

retard stop - Device in a vacuum advance mechanism used to limit movement of a retard diaphragm. See also advance stop.

retractable headlights - Car headlights protected by a movable cover.

retread - See tire(retread).

return line - See gas return line.

reveal molding - Metal frame or molding used to outline an opening or depression.

Revere – American car produced from 1917-1926 by Revere Motor Car Corp. (1917-1922), and Revere Motor Co. (1922-1926), both in Indiana. It was a luxury car best remembered for its roadster model.

reverse – Transmission shift lever and gear setup used to permit a car to move backwards. Most cars have only one speed in reverse.

reverse band – Brake band used to control rotation of an automatic transmission drum controlling reverse gearing.

reverse brake shoe – See brake shoe(trailing).

reverse charge – Charging a battery by running the current through backwards. It can be done, but ruins the plates of most batteries. Cars hooked up to a reversed charged battery will exhibit the following symptoms: starter will work, ignition may or may not work depending on design, polarized gauges will read backwards, non-polarized gauges will read OK such as an ammeter, and solid state devices such as computers and transistors won't work.

reverse crown – Shape with an inside curvature. See also high crown, low crown, and combination crown.

reversed coil polarity – Condition created when primary leads on an ignition coil are connected in reverse. It causes the spark voltage to have positive polarity. Polarity should always be negative whether the car has a positive or negative ground. Reversed polarity will cause: weak spark, missing at higher speed, hard starting, and/or dishing of spark plug side electrodes. See also car service tip(ignition coil reversed polarity test) and spark plug appearance(dished side electrode).

reverse field winding – Field coil winding found in generator field coil windings where current flows in the opposite direction. The purpose is to control current in a generator by creating a magnetic field opposing the regular one. It is usually an auxiliary winding on a regular field winding. See also bucking field coil and generator(bucking field).

reverse flush – Process defined cleaning a cooling system by pumping water or other compounds in the opposite direction to normal flow. It helps wash out accumulated sediment, scale, and other particles.

reverse idler gear – Gear used in a manual transmission to reverse the rotation of a transmission output shaft. It is usually mounted separately from all other gears on its own shaft.

reverse lights – See light(reverse).

reverse lockout – Feature found on certain transmission shifters preventing reverse from being accidentally engaged when shifting through the forward gears.

reverse lockout switch – See lock out switch.

reverses – Wheel rims turned around to provide wider car tracking.

reversing relay – Relay designed to close when another relay or switch opens and vice versa. It is used to produce certain effects in emission control systems.

reversion pulsation – See intake reversion.

reversion reducer – Exhaust pipe fitting used to equalize pressure between dual exhausts or headers.

revving it – To rapidly increase engine rpm and hold it momentarily.

revving the engine – See revving it.

revoke your license – To lose a driver's license temporarily or permanently due usually to some violation of traffic law.

revs – Engine rotational speed in revolutions per minute.

Rex – American car produced in 1914.

Rex Buckboard – American car produced in 1902.

Rexford, Bill – He became the NASCAR Grand National Champion in 1950.

Reya – American car produced in 1918.

Reynolds – American car produced in 1920.

rf – Abbreviation for right front.

RFI – Abbreviation for radio frequency interference.

RGH – Abbreviation for Chile found usually on an international license plate.

rh – Abbreviation for right hand.

RHD – Abbreviation for right hand drive.

rhd – Abbreviation for right hand drive.

Rhodes – American car produced in 1908.

RI – Abbreviation for Indonesia found usually on an international license plate.

ribbon painting – Custom painting technique used to apply a free-flowing ribbon outline to a car panel often with a three dimensional effect.

Richard – American car produced from 1914-1917 by Richard Automobile Mfg. Co. in Ohio.

Richelieu – American car produced from 1922-1923 by Richelieu Motor Car Corp. in New Jersey.

rich mixture – Air/fuel mixture used containing too much fuel for the amount of air it is mixed with. A rich mixture leaves excess fuel unvaporized. It then seeps by piston rings and flows into a crankcase. Once there, it dilutes oil, reduces the oil's lubricating ability, and combines with water and other foreign compounds to form sludge. The heat in a cylinder area also tends to make excess gas deposit varnish and resin by-products on pistons and cylinder walls.

Richmond - American car produced from 1902-1903 and 1908-1917 by Richmond Automobile & Cycle Co. in Indiana (1902-1903), and Wayne Works in Indiana (1908-1917).

Rickenbacker - American car produced from 1922-1927 by Rickenbacker Motor Co. in Michigan. The 1923 model was the first low priced car offered with front wheel brakes.

Ricketts - American car produced from 1908-1909 by Ricketts Auto Works in Indiana.

Rickmobile - American car produced in 1948.

Riddle - American car produced from 1916-1926 by Riddle Mfg. Co. in Ohio. It was one of the first cars built for people in wheel chairs.

ride comfort - Determination made of driver and passenger comfort while sitting and traveling inside a car. It is a common test element in a new car evaluation.

rider - See insurance policy(rider).

Rider-Lewis - American car produced from 1908-1910 by Rider-Lewis Motor Car. Co. in Indiana.

ride the brakes - To keep the brakes engaged continuously through constant foot pressure on the brake pedal. Such a driving habit causes: brake linings and braking surfaces to overheat, deform, and wear out prematurely; and fuel economy to decrease due to reduced power transmitted to the drive wheels.

ridge reamer - Tool used to remove carbon deposits from the ridge at the top of an engine cylinder.

riding the clutch - Condition created when a driver keeps his foot on a clutch pedal after shifting gears. It is a bad habit since pressure on a clutch pedal causes a throw out bearing to contact a pressure plate and spin unnecessarily. The result is usually premature wearout of a throw out bearing whose replacement requires dropping the transmission.

Riess-Royal - American car produced in 1922.

right hand drive car - Car built with the driver's seat and steering wheel on the right side. English cars are built this way. See also left hand drive car.

right of offset - Right given to some lenders in a loan to withdraw money from a borrower's checking or savings account any amount that is due.

right-of-way - Right established by law of one car to cross in front of another. For example, at four-way stops, a car to your right has the right-of-way if you both stop at the same time.

Rigolly, Louis Emile - He was the first man to break the 100 mph barrier in a car. He accomplished the feat in 1904 at Ostead in Belgium driving a 100 hp Gobron-Brille car 103.6 mph.

Rigs-That-Run - American car produced in 1899.

Riker - American electric car produced from 1896-1902 by Riker Electric Motor Co. in New York (1896-1899), Riker Electric Vehicle Co. in New Jersey (1899-1900), and Riker Motor Vehicle Co. in New Jersey (1901-1902).

Riley & Cowley - American car produced in 1902.

rim bead seat - Outer portion of a wheel used to make contact with a tire bead to form an air tight seal.

rim leakage - Tire condition created when a wheel rim leaks air. Possible causes include: rough surface, cracks, or other defects or irregularities.

rims - See wheel.

Rindt, Jochen - He was an Austrian who became the 1970 Grand Prix world champion driving a Lotus-Ford.

ring and pinion - Differential drive pinion and ring gear.

ring gear - See gear(ring)

ring grooves - Square grooves cut into the top part of a piston's outer surface for piston rings.

ring groove tool - Tool used to scrape carbon from piston ring grooves.

ring job - Repair job performed where pistons are removed, cleaned, and reinstalled with new rings. It is considered a poor man's overhaul job since rings account for only part of engine wear in the cylinder area. A ring job can extend an engine's life by 50 percent.

ring pressure - Pressure exerted by piston rings against a cylinder wall.

ring side clearance - Gap measured between the top edge of a piston ring and the edge of its respective piston ring groove. A feeler gauge is used to determine the gap size. Excess gap can cause: oil burning, excessive blowby, and lower cylinder compression.

ring section - Piston area containing piston rings.

Rinker Electric - American electric car produced in 1898.

Riper - American car produced in 1917.

rip-off artist - Person engaged in cheating, robbing, stealing, and/or exploiting people. The world has an abundance of these kind of people. See also con man and con game.

rise time - Time requires for ignition coil to generate a high voltage current from its secondary windings when distributor points are separated or its equivalent is triggered. Conventional point systems have rise times ranging from 75-125 microseconds while capacitative discharge systems average 20 microseconds. Rapid rise time allows fouled plugs to be fired and electrode erosion to be minimized due to decreased spark duration.

rising rate suspension - Suspension system built with springs that increase in their spring rate when compressed. It is used to create consistent ride characteristics under different loads, keep the ride soft, and resist body roll when cornering.

Ritter - American car produced in 1912.

Ritz - American car produced from 1914-1915 by Ritz Cyclecar Co. in New York 1914), and Driggs-Seabury Ordnance Corp. in Pennsylvania (1915).

Riveria - American car produced from 1962 to date by Buick Division of General Motors Corp. in Michigan.

rivet - Metal pin used to hold two objects together. One end of the pin has a head and the other end must be set or peened over.

RL - Abbreviation for Lebanon found usually on an international license plate.

RM - Abbreviation for Malagasy Republic found usually on an international license plate.

RMA - Abbreviation for Rubber Manufacturer's Association.

RMC - American car produced in 1908.

RN - Abbreviation for runabout.

RO - American car produced in 1911.

Roach - American car produced in 1899.

road - Ground surface built for cars to travel on. Typical surfaces include: dirt, gravel, blacktop, and concrete.

roadability - Ability exhibited by a car to handle up and down motion from a bumpy irregular road, and side to side motion when cornering.

Roadable - American car produced in 1946.

road agent - See highwayman.

road bar - See roll bar.

roadbed - The surface and foundation of a road.

road block - An obstruction on a road used to stop car movement.

Road Cart - American car produced by R. S. Scott in 1896.

road cruise - Organized trip using a group of cars for transportation.

road cut - Excavation made into a hillside to allow a road to pass through at a specified grade.

road draft tube - Vertical metal tube used to draw crankcase vapors from an engine. Air enters through a ventilated oil filler cap and exhausts through a road draft tube when air is moving past its outlet. Tube inlet is mounted in lower crankcase area with outlet below the oil pan. Before emission controls, it was a common method of circulating air through a crankcase area to breathe. It is no longer used. See also emission control system(crankcase-road draft tube).

road emergency - Circumstance or event encountered suddenly while driving requiring immediate action to avoid danger. Such an emergency could be: flat tire, car sliding on icy road, tree fallen over road, someone trying to force you off the road, etc. See also road situation and road situation tip.

Roader - American car produced from 1911-1913 by Roader Car Co. in Massachusetts.

road hazard - Danger located on or near a road. Examples include: roadslide, accident blocking traffic, chemicals spilled on road, and icy road with fog.

road hazard warranty - See warranty(road hazard).

road hog(1) - Driver who obstructs traffic by driving too slow, taking up more than one lane, etc.

road hog(2) - Used car wholesaler. He plies his trade by calling upon each used car dealer in his area in an attempt to sell his inventory of cars.

road house - Tavern, nightclub, restaurant, etc. located on a country road.

road is slick - Road surface characterized as offering poor tire traction. Examples include roads covered with: snow, ice, and heavy rain.

Road King - American car produced in 1922.

road map - Map made of an area detailing roads, towns, points of interest, rivers, national forests, etc.

road metal - Materials used to build and/or repair roadbeds. Such materials include: cinders, crushed rock, sand, etc.

Road Plane - American car produced in 1945.

road race - Race conducted on a public road, or a racing circuit simulating a road.

Roadrunner - American car produced from 1962-1980 by Plymouth Division of Chrysler Corp. in Michigan.

road shoulder - Road area located immediately beyond edge of pavement or road surface.

roadside - Side of a road.

roadside park - See rest area.

roadside pumps – Early term used for gasoline pumps that began appearing in the early 1920s for dispensing fuel into cars. They were usually located outside grocery and drug stores.

road sign – Sign mounted near a road. There are many different types of signs serving different purposes. In general, they provide information and regulate traffic flow. Today's sign communicates more with symbols and less with words. It is also identified by color-coding and shape.

road sign(construction and maintenance warning) – Sign used to alert a driver to dangers ahead and permit adequate time to adjust speed.

road sign(destination) – Sign used to inform a driver of distance and direction to a destination.

road sign(diamond shape) – Sign used warning of existing or possible hazards on or near a road. Yellow background is for general warning. Orange background is for construction and maintenance.

road sign(distance) – Sign used to inform a driver of distance to other points.

road sign(guide) – Sign used to inform a driver of various types of helpful information such as location, road number, how to get somewhere, etc.

road sign(horizontal rectangle shape) – Sign used generally as guide sign showing location, direction, and other pertinent information.

road sign(inverted triangle shape) – See road sign(triangular shape).

road sign(milepost) – Sign used to designate distance in miles from where the route begins. Mile zero usually starts at southern and western borders of the route, or where the route begins.

road sign(octagon shape) – Sign used meaning stop. It usually has a red background and the word STOP.

road sign(location) – Sign used to inform a driver of direction to go to reach other points.

road sign(park and recreation area) – Sign used to guide a driver to a recreation area or park.

road sign(pentagon shape) – Sign used meaning a school zone or school crossing. It usually has a yellow background.

road sign(rectangular shape) – See road sign(horizontal rectangle shape) and road sign(vertical rectangle shape).

road sign(rectangular) – See road sign(horizontal rectangle shape) and road sign(vertical rectangle shape).

road sign(regulatory) – Sign used to tell a driver what to do. Examples include: stop, wrong way, and do not enter.

road sign(round shape) – Sign used to indicate a road is crossing a railroad.

road sign(school) – Sign used to warn of school area and/or crossing.

road sign(service) – Sign used to indicate nearby services or facilities along a road such as telephone, rest area, camping, hospital, etc.

road sign(triangular shape) – Sign used meaning slow down and yield to right of way traffic. Some have red backgrounds whiles others are yellow.

road sign(vertical rectangle shape) – Sign used generally as regulatory signs telling drivers what they must do.

road sign(warning) – Sign used to alert driver to conditions lying immediately ahead or for something to watch out for.

road sign classification – Signs are classified into three general groups: regulatory, warning, and guide. The groups use seven basic sign shapes and eight basic colors.

road sign color – Background color of a road sign. Eight major colors are used each with their own meaning.

road sign color(black) – Color used on one way and information signs.

road sign color(blue) – Color used on driver services guidance signs.

road sign color(brown) – Color used on public recreation area and park signs.

road sign color(green) – Color used on distance, direction, and information signs.

road sign color(orange) – Color used on construction and road maintenance signs.

road sign color(red) – Color used on stop, yield, wrong way, and do not enter signs.

road sign color(white) – Color used on regulatory signs.

road sign color(yellow) – Color used for general warning signs.

road situation – Any circumstance or event encountered while driving or stopped on a road that affects passenger safety, interferes with driving, indicates potential car trouble, or disables a car. Such circumstances or events include: flat tire; engine, car handling, transmission, etc. problem; out of gas; bad weather; icy and/snowy road surface; hitchhiker; people flagging you down; getting in an accident; approaching another accident, car theft; and road block.

road situation tip – Useful information given to help someone deal with a road situation more knowledgeably, economically, efficiently, and/or safely. See also car service tip, driving tip, engine problem, car handling problem, transmission problem, clutch problem, sound, vibration, brake problem,

electrical problem, and emergency equipment.
road situation tip(accelerator stuck) – See accelerator's stuck.
road situation tip(accident-first at scene) – When arriving at the scene of an accident before anyone else, it is important to remember to do the following: park car some distance away from accident off the road, locate victims and minimize moving them unless their life is in danger, shut off any running cars, have someone call the police, have others get up and down the roadway with flares or flashlights to warn approaching traffic, apply basic first aid to injured – stop any bleeding with pressure bandage, and keep them warm.
road situation tip(accident-your own) – If you get involved in an accident, remember to do the following: don't leave the area, shut off your car, find out who is injured, move injured if their present location is dangerous, cover them and stop any bleeding, apply other first aid if qualified, set up warnings for approaching traffic, get name, address, and license number of witnesses to accident, exchange information with other drivers (name, address, license number) but don't discuss accident, get names of passengers in other cars, observe physical condition of all affected people, report accident to police unless it is minor, if police arrive get name and badge number of officers, answer all police questions put to you unless results of accident appears serious and you do not want say anything without legal representation, observe damage done to other car(s) and note any other damage on car(s) not related to accident, record details of the accident site (time, place, weather conditions, your speed, picture of how you believe accident happened, nearby traffic control devices, etc.), file accident report, contact insurance agent as soon as possible, and don't allow anyone to take your car away from the immediate scene of the accident unless you agree.
road situation tip(animal jumps onto roadway) – As soon as the animal is sighted, brake the car to a stop as quickly as possible. Sometimes hitting the horn or lights will scare them off. If a wild animal is struck, be considerate of the animal and move it well off the roadway. If a dog, cat, or cow is hit, make an effort to locate the owner or call the police.
road situation tip(automatic transmission overheating) – In stop and go traffic during hot weather, an automatic transmission's fluid can overheat if constantly kept in drive, hastening fluid breakdown and subsequent mechanical damage. Shifting into neutral will minimize the problem when stopping. See also transmission problem(automatic-overheating).
road situation tip(brakes fail) – Loss of braking power is a dangerous situation requiring immediate action. To stop without regular brakes, first try pumping the brakes. If they don't work, proceed as follows: fasten seat belt, gear car down as much as possible (use engine compression to slow car down), and start engaging emergency brake slowly bringing car to a stop. To stop with no regular or emergency brakes proceed as follows: fasten seat belt; gear transmission down as much as possible; turn ignition switch to off position; look ahead for a safe obstruction to slow car to down such as a roadside guard rail, loose dirt on shoulder, a hill, snowbank, bushes, etc.; and move into obstruction as safely as possible until car is stopped. See also brake problem(brakes weak).
road situation tip(carbon tracking) – An engine can misfire or not run at all if the distributor cap and/or ignition coil tower have carbon tracks. Scraping or filing a wide channel through a crack will often temporarily eliminate the conductive path to ground formed by the carbon.
road situation tip(car fire) – Any car fire is dangerous. As soon as a fire is noticed, pull off the road to a stop. Everyone should get safely away from the car except for those putting out the fire. There are usually three types of fires: engine, car interior, and car exterior.
An engine fire is usually due to fuel leaking onto a hot engine surface such as an exhaust manifold and igniting. It can be extinguished by smothering the fire with a fire extinguisher, baking soda, or a blanket. Be careful when opening the hood, to avoid getting face burns. If the fire is not coming from the carburetor, stop the engine, before extinguishing.
A car interior fire can be caused by cigarettes, short in electrical wiring, matches, etc. If small, it can extinguished like any normal fire. If extensive, it may require getting and keeping everyone away from the car until the fire department arrives.
A car exterior fire can be very dangerous if near the gas tank. If near the tank, get and keep everyone safely away from the car until the fire department is contacted and arrives. Other car areas can be extinguished like a normal fire (if not extensive). See also engine problem(carburetor fire) and engine problem(fire).
road situation tip(car bumpers locked) – To free the bumpers, proceed as follows: have two or more people stand on the lower bumper, and try back the other car slowly away. If this approach is not successful, jack the higher bumper up until it clears the lower bumper.
road situation tip(car plunges into deep water) – If you find yourself

conscious and sinking with a car in deep water, proceed as follows: open one or more windows immediately (don't bother with the doors unless car is full of water), and climb out as soon as possible. If the car has power windows, open one or more before they short out. If the windows can't be opened, break one with a heavy object (hard to do), or wait until car is filled with water, open a door, and swim to surface. If you must wait until car is full of water, position yourself in the back (with front engine cars). There will be an air pocket there for awhile, allowing you to breathe (hopefully) until you can open one of the doors.

road situation tip(car stalled in water) – Engine quits because water has gotten the high voltage wiring wet and is grounding it out. If the water is not dangerous, let the car sit for awhile to dry out, or get out and dry the wiring. If the water is dangerous (a rising stream flowing across a roadway, etc.), you may have to leave the car where it is for your own safety and get out of the water.

A manual transmission car can be moved a short distance by placing the transmission in second gear, removing the emergency brake, and using the starter to move the car.

road situation tip(check engine light on) – See warning light(check engine).

road situation tip(clutch fails) – When the clutch of a manual transmission equipped no longer operates, there are three options: tow the car, drive it in one gear, or drive it shifting from one gear to another. If the car is stopped, put the car in second gear, start the engine, and drive in this gear. If you are more daring, you can shift to a higher gear, but it requires skill or else transmission damage will result.

road situation tip(driveline fails) – A driveline usually fails at the front or rear universal joint. A rear joint failure is not dangerous. It only prevents the car from being driven. A front joint failure is dangerous as it can cause metal metal pieces to fly through a floorpan or flip the flip a car. Since, you cannot immediately diagnose such a failure from inside a moving car, assume the worst. The car must be slowed down quickly. Loose road surfaces are to be avoided before stopping since the driveline could become buried and flip the car. See also driveline safety loop.

road situation tip(engine overheats) – When an engine overheats, the car should be stopped immediately and allowed to cool or engine damage may result. Don't try to remove the radiator cap for at least 1/2 hour or hot coolant and steam may escape injuring you and causing valuable coolant loss. After the engine cools down, check the coolant level by checking the overflow reservoir level or by removing the radiator cap.

A number of problems can cause overheating, but the most common are: pulling too heavy a load in hot weather often with air conditioning and other engine accessories on; low coolant level; poor coolant circulation due to clogged water passageways, radiator, etc.; and/or engine timing excessively advanced or retarded. If everything checks out, the engine is probably overheating due to a heavy load and hot weather. The load and/or speed will have to be reduced with periodic stopping if overheating starts again. Running a car heater on full can often help reduce overheating tendency somewhat since the heater radiator removes heats from coolant like an engine radiator only on a smaller scale. See also engine problem(overheating).

road situation tip(engine won't start) – See engine problem(cranks but won't start), car service tip(slow starting test), car service tip(starting system test), and car service tip(starting test).

road situation tip(fan belt breaks) – Cars have several belts running such accessories as water pumps, alternators, air conditioners, power steering pumps, and air pumps. A car can still be driven if the broken belt drives any of the previous accessories except for a water pump. A car can usually be driven at least one-half hour without an alternator operating. A non-operating power steering pump just makes for hard turning. A non-spinning air pump may cause some exhaust backfiring. A water pump, however, must rotate or else an engine will overheat and become damaged. Broken water pump belts require replacement with a new one or use of an emergency substitute such as panty hose, rope, etc.

road situation tip(flat tire) – A flat tire is a common road mishap. When it is occurs, slow down quickly and get off the road so a spare can be safely installed. If necessary, drive on the flat, until you reach such a place.

To replace a flat with a spare proceed as follows: remove spare tire; loosen lug nuts slightly; position jack and raise car; remove lug nuts; remove tire; mount spare tire; install lug nuts until slightly tight; lower car and remove jack; tighten lug nuts firmly; and put spare tire, jack, lug wrench, etc. away.

road situation tip(foggy weather) – When driving in fog day or night, turn on the low beam lights only, reduce speed, and turn on the defroster. High beam lights usually reflect too much light off the fog water particles back into the driver's eyes.

road situation tip(generator light on) – See warning light(generator).

road situation tip(heater quits) – A heater can quit for a number of reasons. It it suddenly stops blowing air, the motor has lost power or is grounding the current. Check the fuse and the speed switch. If the blower is working, but the air is cool, possible causes include: clogged heater core, heat control valve stuck or clogged, and engine thermostat stuck open.
road situation tip(hood flies up) – If a car hood suddenly opens up and blocks your view, proceed as follows: turn on emergency flashing lights, roll down the driver's window, determine traffic situation ahead and behind you, slow down and pull off the road as quickly as possible, and determine and fix hood problem before proceeding.
road situation tip(horn stuck on) – If the horn cannot be stopped, pull the car over, and proceed as follows: raise the hood, locate the horn fuse and pull it, or locate the horn relay and tap it. If the horn is still stuck, then pull each horn lead wire, or else cut them.
road situation tip(identification papers lost) – If a wallet, traveler's checks, credit cards, etc. get lost, the loss should be reported immediately to police. As soon as possible, notify the bank to stop payment on the checks, contact the credit card institutions to issue replacements, get a duplicate driver's license. Many people get emergency money by having relatives wire it to them.
road situation tip(insect in car) – To safely get rid of an insect when driving proceed as follows: slow down quickly remaining calm, pull off the road to a safe spot, open all the car doors and windows, wait for the insect to escape or else encourage it with a stick, paper, etc.
road situation tip(keys lost) – If you lose your car keys and there is no spare hidden on the car, call the police unless you can jimmy open the car yourself or a same make car dealer is nearby (can often supply a key). Once entry is gained, a car even with no key can often be successfully started and driven by bypassing a non-locking ignition switch. One good habit is to keep an extra car key in your wallet or purse, and an extra one at home.
road situation tip(lights fail) – Non-functioning car headlights are usually due to a blown fuse located in the fuse panel or block. A flashlight will be needed for a careful inspection. The fuse panel cover usually describes what the fuses are used for. If there is no description, look for a fuse whose filament is burned or cracked, and carefully remove and replace it with the right size and amperage.
road situation tip(lock frozen) – One of the easiest ways to unfreeze a frozen lock is to heat the key with a match or cigarette lighter, then insert it while hot. It may have to be repeated a few times. To prevent frozen locks, periodically squirt a lightweight oil such as WD-40, into the tumbler.
road situation tip(low on gas) – When gas level becomes low, reduce speed to 25-30 mph and maintain a very steady foot on the accelerator. This will greatly improve mileage if car was traveling at highway speeds.
road situation tip(muffler dragging) – Mufflers come loose and drag on the ground when they corrode and/or support fittings fail. The muffler must be allowed to cool before handling it. When cool, either try to wire or refit it temporarily back in position, or remove it and put up with the noise until you can get a replacement. If it's removed, keep some windows cracked to avoid possible carbon monoxide build-up.
road situation tip(out of gas) – If the engine stops running and an empty fuel tank is suspected, a few simple tests will verify the problem. First, check for fuel in the carburetor by removing the air cleaner, and watching for fuel squirting into the carburetor airway when the linkage is operated. Next, check for fuel in the tank by bouncing the back of the car up and down while listening for gas sloshing around. If both tests show no fuel and no extra fuel is around, your choices are: flagging down a motorist for some extra fuel, waiting for the state police to stop by, or traveling to the nearest town to get extra fuel.
road situation tip(points corroded) – Corroded points can cause little or no spark to be generated. They can be cleaned up with: an emery board, penknife, fingernail file, screw driver blade, etc. Be sure the points are adjusted to separate after they are filed. A temporary gap can be set using a thick piece of paper. See also car service tip(distributor point test).
road situation tip(pulling off the road) – When it becomes necessary to pull off the road, proceed as follows: check for traffic behind you, pull off (as far as possible) onto a paved road shoulder at traffic speed or an unpaved one at a safe speed, stop as quickly and safely as possible, turn on at least your emergency lights, and place warning devices (flares, reflectors, etc.) a few hundred feet behind car. If possible, avoid stopping in dangerous spots such as on curves, crests of hills, tunnels, etc. If you need help, tie a white cloth to the antenna or other conspicuous place, raise the hood, get in the car, lock it, and wait for assistance. If a stranger arrives and you prefer not to risk dealing with him, ask them to notify the state patrol by phone of your predicament when they reach the next town.
road situation tip(rotor worn) – Excessive distributor rotor wear can stop

high voltage current from reliably reaching the spark plugs. A new temporary tip can be made by using a paper clip or other piece of metal taped to the end of the rotor.

road situation tip(starting with a weak battery) – An engine can often be started if the battery is not too weak and it is the only problem. The trick is to increase the cranking speed and sparking at the spark plugs. Before starting again: check and clean all battery cable and starter relay connections to minimize resistance, check electrolyte level in cells adding water if necessary (rain water is best for improvising), and let battery rest for 10-15 minutes.

If the car has a manual transmission, the engine can be push-started. It's easiest to start on an incline, but the car can be pushed by another car or by several people. Moving the cart in a forward direction is best, but it can be done in reverse. Put the car in second or reverse, turn the ignition switch to on, push the clutch in and hold it, get the car moving 5-10 mph, and then quickly release the clutch. It should start.

If the car has an automatic transmission, a speed of at least 25 mph will be needed to start it when low gear is engaged. This eliminates push starting unless another car can push or the car is parked on a good incline.

If the car must be started at rest, the following maneuver will increase the cranking speed, and improve the spark through increased coil saturation: turn off all accessories, remove every other spark plug in the distributor's firing sequence (remove 2, 3, and 4 spark plugs in 4, 6, and 8 cylinder engines respectively), place disconnected spark plug cable ends where they will ground the spark, and start engine. Once the engine is running, the spark plugs can be screwed back in and the cables reconnected. Spark plugs can also fire better on lower voltage by decreasing their gaps.

road situation tip(steering fails) – Loss of steering requires immediate action to avoid an accident. Proceed as follows: fasten seat belt, turn on emergency flashers, and stop car as quickly as possible. When stopped, try to get the car off the road onto the shoulder.

road situation tip(timing setting) – An engine with conventional points can be timed accurately without a timing light as follows: locate firing position of number one cylinder (see car service tip(cylinder firing position)), line up timing mark with pointer, remove distributor cap, loosen distributor, place a piece of thin paper between points, rotate distributor opposite to distributor cam movement while maintaining a light upward pull on the paper, stop distributor rotation as soon as paper pulls free, tighten distributor, and replace distributor cap.

road situation tip(throttle stuck) – See accelerator's stuck.

road situation tip(wheel loose) – A loose wheel is usually caused by loose and/or missing lug nuts. The car will vibrate and produce a rattling sound. If the lug nuts are loose, tighten them. If several are missing, take one from each unaffected wheel until the loose tire has most of its lug nuts. The car should then be driven carefully to the nearest service station or parts store to replace the missing nuts.

road situation tip(windshield wipers fail) – Non-functioning wipers are only a problem in rainy or snowy weather. Possible causes include: blown fuse, poor ground, bad connection, stuck blade(s), stripped splines on wiper shaft, and/or faulty linkage. If the problem cannot be located, you'll have to drive without them (at a slower speed), wait for the weather to clear, or wait for help to arrive.

road situation tip(windshield wipers smear) – Wiper blades do not cleanly remove water or cleaning fluid from window. It is usually due to worn blades. New ones are the best cure.

road slush – Partially melted snow on a roadway.

Roadster – American car produced in 1903 and 1915.

roadster – See body style(roadster).

road test – To drive a new car or a used car after repair work has been done to make sure it operates properly. When making a road test, listen carefully and watch for any mechanical problems such as shaking, wandering, jerking, etc. If you know a reliable mechanic friend, get him to come along. Also, take a pencil and pad to jot down your observations. If possible, drive the car in stop and go traffic, and on the freeway. Most road testing is done by the customer today so the mechanic can get on to his next job.

road test(new car) – Procedure followed for evaluating how well a new car operates by actually driving the car under different conditions. When road testing a new car, your evaluation will be less complete than for a used car. If you have a mechanic friend, talk him into coming along and take a pencil and pad with you. Drive the car, during the day, in stop and go traffic and on the freeway. As you drive, observe the following: all the car accessories such as light, heater, windshield wipers, air conditioning, radio, seat and window adjustments; operation of the transmission and brakes; smoothness and sound of the engine; how the car steers; any funny noises; etc. After driving, stop the car somewhere where you've got access to water and check the following: look at the body from several directions to see if there are scratches, dents, nicks, etc.; run water (a hose or a car wash) over the car with someone inside to check for leaks. This type of road test can be done in less than an hour. When you return to the dealer, explain what the problems are. If a satisfied customer is important to them, they will try to correct the problems. If the dealer won't correct the problems or allow you to road test a new car, take your business elsewhere.

road test(used car) – Procedure followed for evaluating how well a used car operates by actually driving the car under different conditions. The road test would be the same as for a new car, but more thorough because of the wear and tear put on the vehicle. When the car is parked it requires a more careful overall inspection than a new car. See also car inspection.

road tractor – Motor vehicle designed to pull other vehicles, but not carry their weight.

road walk – Back and forth movement or wandering of a car's front end while driving. Amount of movement will vary depending on the road surface. Possible causes include: mismatched and/or unbalanced tires; steering linkage loose, out of adjustment, or improperly assembled; steering geometry improper; roll steer excessive; and worn steering gear box.

roadway – Portion of a road built and maintained for use of vehicular traffic.

Roamer – American car produced from 1916-1925.

roaring into a curve – To speed a car into a turn.

Robe – American car produced in 1914.

Roberts – American car produced in 1904.

Roberts, Fireball – He won the Daytona 500 Race in 1962 averaging 152.5 mph in a Pontiac. His accomplishments in stock car racing made him a legend.

Roberts, Floyd – He won the Indianapolis 500 Race in 1938 driving an average of 117.2 mph in a Burd Piston Ring Special.

Roberts Six – Canadian car produced in 1921.

Robie – American car produced in 1914.

Robinson – American car produced in 1900-1904 by John T. Robinson & Co. (1900-1902), and Pope-Robinson Co. (1902-1904), both in Massachusetts. It was a well-built expensive car.

Robson – American car produced from 1908-1909 by Robson Mfg. Co. in Illinois.

Roche – American car produced from 1920-1926.

Rochester(1) – American car produced from 1901-1902 by Rochester Cycle Mfg. Co. in New York.

Rochester(2) – American line of carburetors.

Rockaway – American car produced in 1904.

rock bottom – To get a price to the lowest level feasibly attainable.

Rockcliff – American car produced in 1905.

rock deflector – Screen or plexiglass panel mounted at the front edge of a car's hood to protect the hood and/or radiator area from flying objects such as rocks. See also bug deflector.

Rockefeller Yankee – American car produced from 1949-1950 by Rockefeller Sports Car Corp. in Long Island. It was a fiberglass body sports car using many Ford components.

rocker – See rocker arm.

rocker arm – Pivoting arm used to transmit camshaft motion, directly or via push rods, to an engine valve. Rocker arms are used in engines with one or more valve assemblies overhead.

rocker arm adjusting screw – Adjustable screw used to regulate the clearance between a valve stem base and its associated cam. Depending on engine type, the screw is part of a valve lifter or part of a rocker arm. An engine has one for each valve.

rocker arm adjustment – Adjustment made to regulate valve clearance. Rocker arm adjusters include an adjustable screw for the center of the rocker arm or an adjustable screw mounted on one end of the rocker arm. Some older models had no adjustment at all, requiring the installation of new push rods in order to adjust valve clearance. See also rocker arm.

rocker arm assembly – Assemblage of parts used to transfer motion from an engine camshaft, directly or via push rods, to the valves. The parts typically consist of: rockers, rocker shaft, rocker springs, and shaft support blocks. Some rockers pivot on individual studs rather than from a common shaft.

rocker arm cover – See valve cover.

rocker arm shaft – Shaft on which rocker arms are mounted.

rocker arm tip – Tilt of a rocker arm in relation to valve stem. If rockerarm radius does not coincide with valve stem centerline, it can cause valve guide to quickly wear into an egg shape, causing increased oil consumption, fouled spark plugs, and decreased engine performance.

rocker panel – Section of a car body located between the front and rear wheel wells and beneath the doors.

rocker panel moldings – Metal strips attached to rocker panels for corrosion protection.

rockers – See rocker arm.
rocker shaft – See rocker arm shaft.
rocker spring – Spring mounted on a rocker shaft to keep a rocker centered over its cam.
Rocket – American car produced in 1913, 1924, and 1948.
Rockette – American car produced in 1946.
Rock Falls – American car produced from 1919–1925 by Rock Falls Mfg. Co. in Illinois.
Rockford – American car produced in 1908.
Rock Hill – American car produced in 1910.
Rockne – American car produced from 1931–1933 by Rockne Motors Corp. in Michigan. It was named after Knute Rockne, the famous American football coach of Notre Dame University.
Rockwell – American car produced in 1908.
rockwell hardness – Scale used to designate the hardness of a substance.
rod(1) – See hot rod.
rod(2) – To modify a car into a performance car.
rod bearing – See bearing(rod).
rod builder – Person engaged in building rods.
rodder – Person characterized as a builder and driver of fast cars. See also hot rodder.
rodding the radiator – Process used to clean a clogged radiator. It consists of: immersing the radiator in a cleaning solution, removing the top and bottom tanks, forcing thin rods of the proper size through the radiator tubes to remove the loosened scale, resoldering tanks back onto a radiator core, and pressure testing the radiator for any leaks.
rod end – Joint located at end of tie rod.
Rodgers – American car produced in 1903–1905 and 1921.
Roebling-Planche – American car produced from 1906–1909 by Walter Automobile Co. in New Jersey.
Roger – American car produced in 1903.
Rogers – American car produced in 1895 and 1911–1912
Rogers & Hanford – American car produced from 1901–1902.
Rogers Steamer – American steam car produced in 1899.
Rogue – American car produced from 1964–1972 by American Motors Corp. in Michigan.
ROK – Abbreviation for South Korea found usually on an international license plate.
roll – Rotating motion created about a car's length when the suspension springs compress on one side and expand on the other.
roll back – See car transport(flatbed).
roll bar – Heavy metal bar structure located behind a driver's seat to protect a driver in the event of a roll-over. It is most commonly used on race cars and pickup trucks.
rolled buckle – Body panel damage created when metal is bent back over itself. See also displaced area, upset, simple bend, and stretch.
roll cage – Tubular steel structure built with a roll bar and additional bars in the doors and roof to protect a driver in the event of a roll-over.
roll center – Centerline of car body rotation when cornering. It is usually higher in the back of the car. See also roll stiffness.
roller – Camshaft used with roller tappets.
roller bearing – See bearing(roller).
roller clutch – See clutch(roller).
roller tappets – See valve lifter(roller).
Rollin – American car produced from 1923–1925 by Rollin Motor Co. in Ohio.
rolling radius – Distance measured from the center of the tread contact to the wheel rim center.
rolling resistance – Resistance to tire rotation caused by the contact of tire tread with a road surface. Rolling resistance is controlled by the following: tire pressure, tire footprint, tread wear, rubber compound, tire construction, and road surface smoothness. It increases with larger tire footprint, lower tire pressure, and rough road surface. It decreases with smaller tire footprint, higher tire pressure, and smooth road surface. Rolling resistance affects car steering. For example, if one front tire has a greater rolling resistance, the tendency will be for the car to pull to the higher resistance side. See also overinflation and underinflation.
rolling stock – All of the vehicular equipment used by a company. For example, a trucking company's rolling stock would consist of all its trucks, tractors, trailers, and cars.
rolling stop – To bring a car almost to a complete stop, moving slowly, before starting up again.
roll-over – Condition created when a car rolls over onto its roof due to losing control on a roadway or going over an embankment.
roll resistance – See roll stiffness.
Rolls Royce(1) – American car produced from 1921–1931 by Rolls-Royce of

America in Massachusetts. The company was formed to build the famous British cars in America to avoid paying high import duties.

The U.S. representative of currently built Rolls Royce cars is Rolls Royce Motors, Inc., headquartered in Paramus, New Jersey.

Rolls Royce(2) – British car line produced from 1904 to date by Rolls Royce Motors (171 to date). It quickly gained the reputation of being the best and most expensive car in the world. It is still, to this day regarded as one of the best cars money can buy, and remains very expensive. The early cars had large engines and were very powerful. Current popular models include: Camargue, Corniche, Phantom, Silver Spirit, and Silver Spur.

Rollsmobile – American car produced beginning in 1958 by Starts Mfg. Co. (1958-1960), and Horseless Carriage Corp. (1960 on) both in Florida. The car was made as a 3/4 scale replica of a 1901 Oldsmobile and 1901 Ford. Top speed was reported to be 30 mph with a fuel economy of 100 mpg.

roll steer – Car handling characteristic defined as a slight steering effect created when a car body rolls.

roll stiffness – Resistance exhibited to rotation about a car's length when cornering. See also roll center.

Roman – American car produced in 1909.

Romanelli – Canadian car produced beginning in 1970 by Romanelli Motors in Quebec. It was a high performance sport car with: fiberglass body, V-12 engine, and top speed over 200 mph.

Romer – American car produced in 1921.

RON – Abbreviation for Research Octane Number.

roof – See car roof.

roof rails – Structural members built into each side of a roof providing support.

roominess – Determinaton made regarding the amount, arrangement, and efficient use of space in a car's interior. It is a common test element in a new car evaluation.

Roosevelt – American car produced from 1929-1931 by Marmon Motor Co. in Indiana. It was named after President Theodore Roosevelt.

Root and Van Dervort – American car produced in 1904.

Rootes – British car.

Rootes type blower – See supercharger(rootes type).

Roper Steam Vehicle – American steam car produced in 1894.

Rosberg, Keke – He became the Grand Prix world champion in 1982 driving a Williams-Ford.

Rose, Mauri – He won the Indianapolis 500 Race in 1941 (with Floyd Davis), 1947, and 1948. Average speeds were 115.1, 116.3, and 119.8 mph. Cars driven were a Noc-Out Hose Clamp Special, and Blue Crown Spark Plug Special (1947 and 1948).

Ross – American car produced in 1905-1909 and 1915-1918 by Louis S. Ross in Massachusetts (1905-1909), Ross & Young Machine Co. in Michigan (1915), and Ross Automobile Co. in Michigan (1915-1918).

Rossler – American car produced in 1907.

Rotarian – American car produced in 1921.

Rotary – American car produced in 1904-1905 and 1922-1923 by Rotary Motor Vehicle Co. in Massachusetts, and Bournonville Motors Co. in New Jersey respectively.

rotary engine – See engine(rotary).

rotary valve – See valve(rotary).

rotating the wheels – To change wheel locations on a car to prolong their life. Rotating tires supposedly evens out tire wear. The more common rotation is left front to right rear, and right front to left rear.

rotor(alternator) – Shaft-mounted device used to generate a moving magnetic field in an alternator. The rotor consists of: a shaft, a field wound around the shaft, two multi-pole end pieces enclosing the field coil, and two slip rings for transferring current to and from the field coil.

rotor(brake) – See brake rotor.

rotor(engine) – Revolving triangular shaped device used in a rotary engine to perform the same functions as a piston.

rotor(distributor) – T-shaped insulated device mounted on top of a distributor shaft for transferring high voltage current from a distributor's center tower terminal to the spark plug terminal's firing points. It is in constant contact with the center tower terminal. Some designs integrate a resistor to suppress static. Most rotors fit on a distributor shaft end with a press fit. Some screw onto an existing plate.

rotor parallelism – See brake rotor parallelism.

rotten egg smell – See smell(rotten egg).

rough – See car classification(rough).

rough car – See car classification(rough).

rough edged – Car construction typified by annoying sounds and/or vibrations, cheap construction materials, underpowered, etc.

rough idling – Engine condition created when an engine does not idle smoothly.

It is usually caused by one or more of the following: worn distributor points, worn and/or fouled spark plugs, improperly adjusted carburetor, partially closed choke, excess fuel entering engine, and worn out engine with low compression and burned valves.

roughing the metal into shape – To use various body work tools to restore a sheetmetal panel to its original contour.

route – Road designated for travel. Also, it refers to a specified road or series of roads used to get from one location to another.

routine maintenance – Normal maintenance work done on a car such as changing oil and filter.

Rovan – American car produced in 1914.

Rovena-Front Drive – American car produced in 1926.

Rover – British car line produced from 1904 to date by Light Medium Cars Division, BL Cars Ltd. Popular models include: Vitesse and Land Rover.

Rover Company – British car manufacturer. It produced the world's first experimental turbine gas car.

Rover gas turbine car – World's first gas turbine car produced in the 1960s by the British Rover car company. It was a two seater with a top speed of 152 mph, and could accelerate from 0-100 mph in just 13.2 seconds.

row a transmission – To shift a transmission.

Rowe – American car produced in 1911.

Rowe-Stuart – American car produced in 1922.

Royal – American electric car produced in 1905 and 1914. Also, an American car produced from 1957-1959 by Dodge Division of Chrysler Corp. in Michigan.

Royal Princess – American car produced in 1905.

Royal Tourist – American car produced from 1904-1911 by Royal Motor Car Co. (1904-1908), and Royal Tourist Car Co. (1908-1911), both in Ohio.

royalty – Specified monetary amount paid to an patent owner, author, etc. for the right to use, manufacture, and/or sell a patented or copywrighted item.

RP – Abbreviation for replica.

rpm – Abbreviation for revolutions per minute.

rr – Abbreviation for right rear.

r rack – Abbreviation for roof rack.

RS – Abbreviation for rumble seat.

RSC – Abbreviation for rumble seat coupe.

RSM – Abbreviation for San Marino found usually on an international license plate.

RSR – Abbreviation for Rhodesia found usually on an international license plate.

Rubay – American car produced from 1922-1924 by Rubay Co. in Ohio.

rubber – Elastic substance made from natural latex or synthetically. It is used extensively in cars to absorb vibration.

rubber coil spring – Experimental spring used to replace conventional metal coil springs. It is typically shaped like a spring, but solid. Advantages include: long life, light weight, absorption of noise, accurate tensioning, and easy handling.

rubber isolator – Piece of rubber material formed into a particular shape for isolating car vibrations. It is typically used in the following areas: top and bottom of shock absorbers, front and back mounting locations of leaf springs, engine mounting plates, and various steering system joints.

rubbing block – Small plastic block mounted on a distributor point assembly. It is attached to the movable point arm and opens the points every time it contacts one of the distributor cam lobes.

rubbing compound – Mildly abrasive paste-like compound used to remove paint oxidation from a car body surface. It is more abrasive than polishing compound.

rubbing out – See rubbing out the paint.

rubbing out the paint – Process used to polish newly applied lacquer-based paint. Lacquer-based paints require polishing to achieve a gloss or sheen because spray gun air pressure and rapid paint drying time causes the paint surface to mottle or not flow out into a smooth surface. Polishing usually proceeds as follows after the paint dries: apply fine-grit rubbing compound to new paint surface by hand and carefully polish, remove all residue, polish surface with buffing wheel and cornstarch, and then go over surface with polishing compound.

rub it out – See rubbing out the paint.

rubout – See rubbing out the paint.

Rugar – American car produced beginning in 1969 by Sturm, Rugar & Co. in Connecticut. It was a Bentley replica.

Rugby Truck – American truck produced in 1927.

Ruggles – American car produced in 1905.

Ruggles Truck – American truck produced in 1921.

rug kit – Kit composed of the necessary pre-cut carpet pieces to cover the entire inside floor area of a car.

Ruler – American car produced in 1917.

rumble(1) - Street fight between rival teen-age gangs.

rumble(2) - Space located in the back of a car for luggage, an extra seat, etc.

rumble seat - Seat contained in the trunk area of earlier model coupes or roadsters. The trunk lid folds back to form the seat back. It was used to carry additional passengers in a two passenger car.

rumble strip - Strip containing closely spaced parallel grooves cut into the surface of a road's paved shoulders. A strip is usually a foot wide running perpendicular from the edge of the roadway to the edge of the shoulder. A series of strips are usually installed, spaced 5-10 feet apart. Car tires running over the strips make a noticeable sound like driving on a steel decked bridge. They help alert drowsy drivers whose cars begin drifting off the road.

Rumley - American car produced in 1920.

run - To drive a race car once through the traps. Also, it refers to taking trip, delivering products, etc.

Runabout - American car produced in 1902.

runabout - See body style(runabout).

runaway - Dangerous condition created when a car or truck begins moving down a road without a driver or one that cannot easily be stopped due to a mechanical malfunction such as a brake system failure or sticking accelerator.

run-flat - Tire's ability to continue running when flat a specified distance and speed. See also tire(run-flat).

Runner - American car produced in 1913.

runner(1) - Air passageway in an intake manifold used to route a fuel mixture from a carburetor to an engine cylinder.

runner(2) - Car driven at high speeds on public roads usually by a skilled driver.

runner(3) - Person who smuggles cars or illegal commodities such as alcohol with a car.

running a red light - To drive into a intersection after the traffic light has turned red. It creates a very dangerous situation inviting an accident since stopped traffic begins moving into the intersection.

running board - Step mounted on a car's body under the door to help passengers get in and out. On older cars, it ran from the back edge of a front fender to the front edge of a rear fender. On later cars, it receded inside and underneath the car doors where it is today.

running fit - Shaft and journal surface joined with sufficient clearance for rotation without overheating.

running gear - Working components of a car. They include: wheels, axles, springs, and frame.

running lights - See light(parking).

running order - Car's running condition.

running out of gas - To use up all the gas in a car's gas tank.

running the battery down - To discharge a car's battery.

running time(1) - Time required for a vehicle to get from one place to another.

running time(2) - Hours or miles an engine has been operated since it was new or rebuilt.

run-on - See dieseling.

runout - Radial or lateral movement measured on a circular part surface when rotated. It is usually measured with a dial indicator.

runout(diametrical) - See runout(radial).

runout(lateral) - Runout measurement made perpendicular to the plane of rotation. For example, a wheel's rim is measured for lateral runout to determine any sideways movement or wobbling.

runout(radial) - Runout measurement made to determine a circle's out of roundness or the difference between its high and low spots. It's often made on the outside diameter of tires and wheels to determine the cause of tire balance problems.

runs good - Characteristic of a car with an engine in good running condition.

run-up - Accelerating part of car driving or engine rpm. See also coast-down.

run whatcha brung - Car race with no rules.

rural area - Area located in the country away from large towns.

Rush - American car produced in 1918.

rush hour - Time of day characterized by large numbers of people in transit going to or from work in cars, buses, trains, etc. A period of heavy traffic.

Rushmobile - American car produced in 1902.

Russell - American car produced in 1902-1904 by Russell Motor Vehicle Co. in Ohio (1902-1904). Also, a Canadian car produced from 1905-1915 by Canada Cycle and Motor Co. in Ontario.

Russell-Knight - American car produced in 1914.

rust - Reddish brown coating formed on steel or iron by the process of

oxidation. Rust occurs when oxygen and moisture are present on the surface
of the steel or iron.
    Rust tends to occur on cars more often in certain places. Rust-prone areas
include: inner fenders, trunk lid, rocker panels, door bottoms, lower rear
quarter panel, and roof along gutters.
rustbucket - Used car in poor shape with lots of rust.
rust inhibitor - See additive(rust inhibitor).
rut - Groove or track made in a road usually by the repeated passage of cars.
Rutenber - American car produced in 1903.
Rutherford, Johnny - He won the Indianapolis 500 Race in 1974, 1976, and 1980.
Average speeds were 158.6, 148.7, and 142.9 mph. Cars driven were a McLaren,
Hy-Gain McLaren, and Pennzoil Chaparral.
Ruttman, Troy - He won the Indianapolis 500 Race in 1952 driving an average
of 128.9 mph in a Agajanian Special.
Ruxton - American car produced from 1929-1931 by New Era Motors in New York.
RV - Abbreviation for recreational vehicle.
r wiper - Abbreviation for rear windshield wiper.
RX7 - See Mazda.
Ryder - American car produced from 1908-1911.
Rylander - American car produced in 1914.

S

S(1) - Abbreviation for seats.
S(2) - Abbreviation for Sweden found usually on an international license plate.
S&M - American car produced from 1913-1914 by S&M Motors Co. in Wisconsin.
S&M Simplex - American car produced from 1904-1907 by Smith & Mabley Mfg. Co. in New York.
S&S - American car produced from 1924-1930 by Sayers & Scovill Co. in Ohio.
S&S Hearse - American car produced in 1907.
SA - See API service category(SA).
Saab - Swedish car line produced from 1950 to date by SAAB Scania Aktiebolag Ltd.
    The U.S. representative is Saab-Scania of America, Inc., headquartered in Orange, Connecticut.
Sable - American car produced from 1980 to date by Ford Motor Co. in Michigan.
saddle tanks - See auxiliary tanks.
saddle tank valve - Valve used to connect two or three gas tanks together.
SAE - Abbreviation for Society of Automotive Engineers.
SAE steels - Number indexing system used to specify the composition of SAE steel. It consists of a four digit number. The first digit refers to the type of steel. The second digit specifies the approximate percentage of major alloying element. The remaining two digits specify approximate carbon content in hundredths of 1 percent. For example, a SAE 2250 steel specifies a nickel steel, with 2 percent nickel, and 0.50 percent carbon.
SAE threads - Thread per inch values set up by the SAE.
SAE viscosity numbers - Numbers used to classify lubricants according to viscosity or fluidity.
Safari - American car produced from 1955-1964 by Pontiac Division of General Motors Corp. in Michigan.
safe driver - Driver recognized as proficient in safely operating a car.
Safety - American car produced in 1901, 1909, and 1917.
safety blanket - Fabric shield placed around a transmission's bell housing to contain flying debris in the event rotating parts disintegrate. It is usually a multi-layered material such as nylon with adjustable straps. See also safety shield and scattershield bellhousing.
safety chains - Set of chains attached to a car and trailer as a backup connection in the event the trailer hitch malfunctions.
safety conscious - To be aware of the importance of safety.
safety factor - Ratio figured as the maximum strength of a material divided by the maximum anticipated load applied to it. A safety factor specifies how strong a part must be. For example, a shaft with a safety factor of 2 would be designed to withstand twice the anticipated maximum load. The higher the safety factor the stronger the part must be. Strength can be attained by increasing the thickness or going to a higher strength material. Most parts are designed with safety factors greater than one.
safety hub - Device installed on a rear axle to keep a rear wheel attached to a car if the axle breaks.
safety relief valve - Valve designed to open at a predetermined pressure preventing excessive pressure build-up in a device. The valve is usually spring-loaded.
safety rim wheel - Wheel designed with small humps on a rim's inner edge to keep a tire on a rim in the event of a blowout. Chrysler introduced the concept in 1940.
safety shield - Liner placed around the inside of a transmission's bell housing to prevent disintegrating parts from destroying bell housing and causing dangerous flying debris to escape. See also safety blanket and scattershield bellhousing.
safety valve - See pressure relief valve.
safety zone - Area marked off on a roadway and with signs for the exclusive use of pedestrians.
Safeway - American car produced in 1925.
Saf-T-Cab - American car produced in 1926.
Sager - Canadian car produced in 1910.
sagging spring - Coil or leaf spring compressed more than the specified amount for the amount of weight it is supporting. See also car service tip(spring sag adjustment).
Saginaw - American car produced from 1914-1916 by Valley Boat & Engine Co. (1914-1915), and Lehr Motor Co. (1916), both in Michigan.

sail panel – Sheetmetal panel used to form the rear vertical side portion of a roof and also support one corner. Every roof has a sail panel on each side.

sales contract – See contract(sales).

sales department – Department charged with handling sale of products at a car repair, dealer, or parts store. At a car dealership, it is the department responsible for selling cars and service. See also job(car salesman) and job(sales manager).

sales pitch – Line of talk used by a car salesman to persuade a potential car buyer to purchase a car.

salesman's bible – See blue book.

sales quota – Specified number of items to be sold in a given period of time.

sales manager – See job(sales manager).

Salmson – French sports car produced in the 1920s. It was light weight and sat two people.

salon body – Car body interior built to look like a study, drawing room, parlor, etc.

saloon – Sedan. See also body style(sedan).

Salter – American car produced from 1909-1912 by Salter Motor Co. in Missouri.

salt the roads – To sprinkle ice or snow-covered roads with salt to lower the freezing point of water and thereby help melt snow or ice for improved traction. Salt is corrosive to car bodies. See also sand the roads.

Salvador – American car produced in 1914.

Sampson – American car produced in 1904 and 1911.

Sampson Electric Truck – American electric truck produced in 1907.

Samson – An American car/truck combination produced from 1922-1923 by Samson Tractor Co. in Wisconsin.

Sanbert – American car produced in 1911.

sand back paint – See feather the paint.

sandbagger – Race car driver who slows down in a staging area to pick the opponents he wants to eliminate.

sandblast – Process used to clean a surface by mixing sand with compressed air and directing the mixture to the surface.

sandblaster – Equipment used to sandblast surfaces. It typically consists of: a sand hopper, sand, spray gun with ceramic nozzle, air compressor, and necessary hoses and fittings.

sand the roads – To sprinkle ice or snow-covered roads with sand to provide increased traction. See also salt the roads.

Sandow Cab – American car produced in 1925.

Sandow Truck – American truck produced in 1915.

sand truck – Truck used to apply sand to roads in wintertime.

Sanford-Herbert – American car produced in 1911.

Sanford Truck – American truck produced in 1918.

Sandusky – American car produced from 1902-1903 by Sandusky Automobile Co. in Ohio. Also, an American car produced in 1911.

Santos Dumont – American car produced from 1902-1904 by Columbus Motor Vehicle Co. in Ohio.

Sapporo – American car produced from 1978-1983 by Plymouth Division of Chrysler Corp. in Michigan.

Saratoga – American car produced from 1957-1964 by Chrysler Corp. in Michigan.

SASE – Abbreviation for self-addressed stamped envelope.

Satellite – American car produced from 1962-1977 by Plymouth Division of Chrysler Corp. in Michigan.

sauce – Racing fuel.

Savage – American car produced in 1912.

Saviano Scat – American car produced in 1960.

SAVM – Abbreviation for spark advance vacuum modulator.

Savoy – American car produced from 1957-1977 by Plymouth Division of Chrysler Corp. in Michigan.

saw dust in the rear end – See con game(saw dust in the rear end).

Sawyer – American car produced in 1913.

Saxon – American car produced from 1913-1923 by Saxon Motor Car Co. in Michigan.

Saxon-Duplex – American car produced in 1920.

Sayer – American car produced from 1917-1923 by Sayers & Scovill Co. in Ohio.

Sayers & Scoville – American car produced from 1907-1924.

Sbarro – Swiss car produced from 1971 to date by Ateliers de Construction Automobile Sbarro sari. Popular models include: Fura, Ibiza, Panda, Replica, Rhonda, Royale, Stash, and Windhound.

SC(1) – See API service category(SC).

SC(2) – Abbreviation for supercharged.

S/C – Abbreviation for supercharged.

scale deposit – Coating of rust, lime, and other mineral deposits formed within a cooling system.

scallop – Narrow, tapering panel used to follow a car contour. Some run in a long line tapering at one or both ends while others form a U-shape tapering

at the tips. It is usually a single color. See also panel.
scallop painting – Custom painting technique used to apply different scallop designs on a car body surface.
Scamp – American car produced from 1962-1981 by Plymouth Division of Chrysler Corp. in Michigan.
Scarab – American car produced from 1934-1939 and 1946 by Stout Engineering Co. in Michigan.
scare tactic – Ploy used to frighten a car owner into the urgency for immediate repairs.
scattershield – See scattershield bellhousing.
scattershield bellhousing – Transmission bell housing usually made out of thick steel (1/4") to prevent rotating disintegrating parts from escaping. See also safety shield and safety blanket.
scavenger – High performance car able to outrun everything on the road.
scavenger pipe – Straight length of exhaust pipe installed at the end of an exhaust pipe system usually for looks. It is usually chrome plated.
SCCA – Abbreviation for Sports Car Club of America. It sponsors, organizes, and oversees many of the different road races in the United States.
scenic highway – Highway located passing through beautiful natural surroundings.
Schacht – American car produced from 1905-1913 by Schacht Mfg. Co. (1905-1909), and Schacht Motor Car Co. (1909-1913), both in Ohio.
Schaefer – American car produced in 1910.
Scharf Gearless – American car produced in 1914.
Schauer – Line of battery chargers.
Schaum – American car produced in 1901.
Schebler – American car produced in 1908.
Scheckter, Jody – He became the Grand Prix world champion in 1979 driving a Ferrari.
scheduled maintenance – Maintenance done according to a manufacturer's recommendations, service manuals, etc.
schematic diagram – Detailed drawing made of a car's electrical system.
Schleicher – American car produced in 1895.
Schloemer – American car produced in 1889.
Schlosser – American car produced from 1912-1913.
Schlotterback – American car produced in 1912.
Schmidt – American car produced in 1910.
Schnader – American car produced in 1907.
Schneider, Louis – He won the Indianapolis 500 Race in 1931 driving an average of 96.1 mph in a Bowes Seal Fast Special.
Schoeneck – American car produced in 1917.
Schoening – American car produced in 1895.
school bus – Vehicle built for transporting students to and from school.
school zone – Area located around a school. Roads inside the area are usually marked for reduced speed.
Schram – American car produced in 1913.
Schwartz – American car produced in 1920.
Scientific – American car produced in 1921.
Scioto – American car produced in 1911.
scoop(1) – Device used to collect. It may be either functional or merely ornamental. See also hood scoop and ram air.
scoop(2) – See spoiler.
Scoot-Mobile – American car produced in 1946 by Norman Anderson in Michigan. It was a three wheeler with a top speed of 40 mph.
scope – See oscilloscope.
score – Scratch or mark made on a finished surface.
scored cylinder – Engine cylinder wall damaged with cuts or scratches usually due to broken piston rings, lack of oil lubrication, or metal from a ventilated piston.
Scott – American electric car produced from 1899-1901 by St. Louis Electric Automobile Co. (1899-1900), and Scott Automobile Co. (1900-1901), both in Missouri. Also, an American car produced in 1921.
Scout – American car produced from 1961 to date by International Harvester Co. in Illinois. It was a popular car that could be converted from an enclosed runabout, to a small pickup, to a convertible with no top windows or doors.
scout – Tow truck operator engaged in locating or tracking down a specific car to be towed. See also con game(tow truck) and con game(tow truck and police collusion).
scouting system – Communication method used by tow truck operators to locate cars needing a tow to a repair shop or service station. Such methods include: having people drive the highways; and listening to CB radio, police scanner, etc. transmissions.
scraper – Clay modeling tool used to roughly shape a model surface. It is shaped like a short handled rake. A straight or curved blade is mounted crosswise to the handle, ranging from 1-6 inches wide. Blades are doubled

edged, one with serrations and the other with a smooth edge.

screamer - Hot rod.

screeching - Harsh shrill high pitched sound. Tires emit such a sound when they lose traction on dry pavement and leave part of the tire rubber on the road.

screw - Mechanical device used to fasten things together. It consists of a circular-shaped threaded metal rod with a head mounted at one end for turning. Screws come in a variety of head and thread configurations.

screw(hex) - Screw built with a six-sided head. Hex shape is common to bolt heads and can be turned with socket tools.

screw(lag) - Heavy duty wood screw built with large course threads and usually a hex head for turning.

screw(machine) - Screw built with a straight shank and threaded to receive a nut. The head of the screw and the nut sandwich things together.

screw(phillips) - Screw built with a cross shaped slot in the head for turning.

screw(sheet metal) - Screw built with course threads for joining pieces of sheet metal together.

screw(slot) - Screw built with a single straight groove in the head for turning.

screw(wood) - Screw built with a tapered shank to hold wood together.

screwdriver - Tool used to turn screws. Different types include: slot, phillips, and clutch.

screw extractor - Tool built with counter clockwise threads and used to remove screws and bolts broken off. The procedure consists of: drilling a specified hole size in the broken screw or bolt, inserting an extractor, and rotating it counter clockwise until the broken piece is removed.

screw head - Driving end of a screw. See also screw.

screw head(hex) - Screw head built with a flat six sided shape for turning with a wrench or socket tool.

screw head(phillips) - Screw head built with a cross-shaped slot for turning with a phillips screwdriver.

screw head(slot) - Screw head built with a single straight groove for turning with a blade screwdriver.

screwshaft - Portion of a starter drive shaft constructed with threads cut for moving a pinion gear assembly back and forth.

Scripps - American car produced in 1911.

Scripps-Booth - American car produced from 1913-1922 by Scripps-Booth Co. in Michigan.

scrolling - See ribbon painting.

scroll work - Custom painting technique used to apply scrolls and/or lettering designs to panels. Scrolls are designs that spiral.

SCSA - Abbreviation for speed control spark advance.

scuderia - Race team.

scuffing - See skidding and spinning.

scuffing action - Tendency of a tire to skid on a road surface. Older steering systems caused front wheels to scuff when they were turned.

scuff plate - Cover placed along the lower inside of a door panel. It is usually made of rubber, metal, or carpeting. See also kickpad.

scuttle - See air intake vent.

SD(1) - See API service category(SD).

SD(2) - Abbreviation for sedan. See also sed.

SE(1) - Abbreviation used on some spark plug cables to specify their use on hot running engines. See also SS.

SE(2) - See API service category(SE).

Seagrave - American car produced in 1912, 1921, and 1960.

Seagrave, Major Henry - He set a world land speed record in 1926, 1927, and 1929 driving a Sunbeam V-12 (1926 and 1927), and Irving-Napier Golden Arrow. Speeds were 152.3, 203.8, and 231.4 mph.

seagull - Constant complainer.

seal - Device used to prevent leakage. Examples include: pan gasket, O-rings, bearing seals, valve cover gasket, etc.

sealant - Substance used for sealing. Examples include: silicone, thread compound, gasket adhesives, etc.

sealed beam - See light(sealed beam head).

sealed beam headlight - Car headlight lamp built with the lens, filament and reflector parts sealed into a single unit.

sealed beam unit - See light(sealed beam head).

sealed bearing - Bearing filled with grease lubricant and then sealed to contain the lubricant.

sealed components - Components sealed to prevent leakage of a fluid or gas out or dust, water, air, etc. in.

sealing compound - Material used to seal a battery cover to a battery case. It is acid-proof, melts easily, and is not a conductor.

Searchmont - American car produced from 1900-1903 by Searchmont Motor Co.

(1900-1902), and Fournier-Searchmont Co. (1902-1903), both in Pennsylvania.
Sears - American car produced from 1906-1911 by Sears Motor Car Works in Illinois. It was built for the Sears, Roebuck mail order company. Over 3,500 cars were sold. See also Allstate.
seat - Surface used by another part to rests. See valve seat.
seat adjuster - Mechanism used to slide a seat forward or backward. It is mounted underneath a seat and usually controlled by a lever located along the side of a seat. See also power seat.
seat belt - Detachable belt attached to a car's frame and used to keep a car passenger in a seat in the event of a rapid stop or impact. A seat belt consists primarily of: left and right web straps, frame attachments, and belt buckle. There are four major types of seat belts. They are: lap belt, diagonal belt, lap and diagonal belt, and lap belt and harness. The lap and diagonal belt is common in many cars today.
seat belt anchor - Device used to attach a seat belt to a car's frame.
seat cover - Cover placed or a car seat to protect it from wear, keep it warmer, or cover worn seat upholstery. Also, it refers to the original seat upholstery.
seating - Gradual wearing in of new moving parts for proper fit. For example, piston rings in a new engine must be used for a period of time before they properly conform to a cylinder wall shape and provide a tight seal.
seating buck - Car interior mockup used to evaluate dimensions and space needs. Items evaluated include: arrangement of interior components, comfort, passenger entrance and exit, sitting room, head room, instrument accessibility, etc. Dimensions are usually very accurate. See also trim buck.
seat side shield - Molding or applique located on the outer edge of a seat cushion.
Seattle-ite XXI - Cloud 9 car model produced by Ford in the 1960s. It was a front wheel drive car with four of wheels in front and gull wing doors.
Sebring - American car produced from 1910-1911 by Sebring Motor Car Co. (1910), and Sebring Automobile Co. (1911), both in Ohio.
secondary(carburetor) - Auxiliary carburetor airway. It is used to send more fuel and air into an engine for faster acceleration, passing, attaining top speed, etc. Some cars have four barrel carburetors using two secondaries.
secondary(electrical) - See secondary circuit.
secondary(ignition coil) - See secondary coil winding.
secondary brake shoe - See brake shoe(trailing).
secondary circuit - Electrical part of an ignition system used to carry high voltage current from an ignition coil's secondary windings to the spark plugs.
secondary coil winding - Electric wire wound around an ignition coil's iron core to carry induced high voltage current. It typically consists of some 22,000 turns of fine wire such as 38 gauge, wound around an iron core first. The winding is connected to a grounded primary terminal and a high voltage terminal. A condenser is used to help prevent the high voltage current from jumping across the distributor points in conventional ignition systems. See also primary coil winding, ignition coil, and condenser.
secondary collector - Short pipe reducer section used to bolt a header's collector box to a car's exhaust pipe.
secondary cup - Rubber cup mounted at the pressure end of a master brake cylinder's secondary piston. It serves to seal the chamber ahead of the moving piston, allowing hydraulic pressure to build in the disc brake portion of the system. See also primary cup.
secondary current - High voltage direct current flowing in spark plug cables. See also primary current.
secondary discharge nozzle - Nozzle device used to discharge fuel into a small boost venturi located in a secondary airway of a carburetor. Fuel is drawn from a float bowl to the nozzle by means of a slight vacuum created by a boost venturi. See also venturi.
secondary governor valve - Valve used in an automatic transmission to change hydraulic pressure reaching primary governor valve.
secondary piston - One of two pistons used in a dual master brake cylinder. Its purpose is to pressurize hydraulic fluid used to operate the disc brakes. It is acted upon by hydraulic pressure generated from the brake cylinder's primary piston. See also secondary cup.
secondary resistance - Electrical resistance built into any part of the ignition system conducting high voltage current. It limits current flow and extends plug life.
secondary road - Road connected to or providing access between primary roads.
secondary throttle plate - See throttle plate(secondary).
secondary throttle valve - Valve used in an automatic transmission to receive hydraulic pressure from primary throttle valve and reduce it.
secondary winding - High voltage heavily insulated wire wound inside an ignition coil. It is used to conduct high voltage current generated inside

an ignition coil to the coil's output tower.

secondary wiring - High voltage heavily insulated wiring used to carry high voltage current from an ignition coil to the spark plugs.

second car - Extra car.

secret par time - Time taken to complete a measured course on public roads when adhering to posted speeds and other traffic flow controls. Car rallies are typically run this way. The winner is the car getting closest to this time which is announced when all the cars have completed the course.

section(1) - Car chopping process defined as shortening, narrowing, or lowering a car body on its frame. See also chop.

section(2) - See section view.

section view - View made of an object at 90 degrees to a plane cut through the object.

sed - Abbreviation for sedan. See also SD(2).

sedan - See body style(sedan).

Sedanca de Ville - See body style(town car).

sediment(battery) - Active plate material gradually lost and accumulated below battery plates.

see to appreciate - Car advertising phrase commonly used to indicate a car must be seen to appreciate its condition.

Segrave, Sir Henry - He was the first man to break the 200 mph barrier in 1927 by driving his 1000 hp Sunbeam 203.8 mph at Daytona.

Seiberling - American line of tires produced by The Seiberling Tire & Rubber Co.

Seitz - American car produced in 1911.

seize - To interlock or stop movement of two surfaces moving against each other such as a piston and engine cylinder.

Sekine - American car produced in 1923.

Selden - American car produced from 1906-1914 by Selden Motor Vehicle Co. in New York.

Selden, George - He was a patent attorney who developed a three cylinder Brayton type engine in 1877, and patented a road locomotive design using the engine in 1895.

Selden Truck - American truck produced in 1913.

selective transmission - See transmission(selective).

selector - Automatic transmission shifter.

selector fork - Device used to move a synchronizer clutch in a transmission. Most transmissions have several mounted on shafts.

Select-Trac - Tradename used for a Jeep power transfer system to front and rear differentials. See also Quadra-Trac.

self-adjuster - See brake adjuster.

self-aligning torque - Torque created when cornering due to a front tire generating torque at a point behind its tire footprint area.

self-diagnostic mode - On-board computer mode activated to automatically display one or more trouble codes if there is an engine problem, sensor problem, on-board computer problem, etc., depending on the systems design.

self-energization - Process defined as increasing brake shoe to drum friction by designing a braking mechanism to drag shoes into a wedging action with the anchor pins.

self-engaging drive - See starter drive(Bendix).

self service - To serve oneself.

Sellers - American car produced from 1909-1912 by Sellers Motor Car Co. in Kansas.

seller's disclaimer - Denial made by a seller for any responsibility as to a product's quality, operating condition, expected life, etc.

Sellew-Royce - American car produced in 1909.

sell or starve pay plan - Total commission payment plan used by certain businesses to pay their salesmen. Under the plan, a salesman's total income is a percentage of sales made. Such payment plans encourage dishonesty. For example, a service man, honest in assessing each potential customer's car repair needs, would not make enough to live on and would quickly lose his job.

sell up - To talk a potential car customer into a higher priced car.

SEMA - Abbreviation for Specialty Equipment Manufacturers Association.

semi - Semitruck and trailer vehicle.

semidiesel - See engine(semidiesel).

semi-elliptic spring - See spring(leaf).

Seminole - American car produced in 1928.

semitrailer - Any vehicle: built without power, designed for carrying people or property, towed by a motor vehicle, and designed to transfer part of its weight onto the towing vehicle.

Senator - American car produced from 1906-1910 by Victor Auto Co. in Indiana.

sending unit - Device installed at a sensing site and usually designed to control current flow through a gauge by varying electrical resistance. See also sensor(oil pressure).

Seneca – American car produced from 1917-1924 by Seneca Motor Car Co. in Ohio. Also, an American car produced from 1960-1961 by Dodge Division of Chrysler Corp. in Michigan.

sensor – Device used to determine an aspect of engine or car operation.

sensor(air flow) – Device used to determine the air flow rate into an intake manifold. It is commonly used on fuel injected engines where it relays information to an on-board computer for maintaining a proper air/fuel ratio. The device is usually mounted upstream from the throttle plate. Single point injection systems usually incorporate this device with the fuel injector(s).

sensor(air temperature-1) – Device used to determine air temperature near the carburetor airway in an air cleaner. It is used to control a vacuum motor operated gate valve built into an air cleaner's snorkel. The position of the gate valve determines how much air is unheated and how much is drawn from the exhaust manifold area.

sensor(air temperature-2) – Device mounted in an air flow meter and used to determine air temperature in a fuel injected car. Signals are sent to an on-board computer to help determine the proper air/fuel mixture to use at any given moment.

sensor(altitude) – Device used to determine when a preset altitude has been reached, and close a switch. It is commonly used on fuel injected cars to slightly decrease the amount of fuel injected under all loads to compensate for the thinner air.

sensor(anti lock) – See sensor(wheel speed).

sensor(backup) – See sensor(reverse).

sensor(barometric pressure) – Device used to determine atmospheric pressure.

sensor(brake pad wear) – Device used to determine when a brake pad reaches a certain minimum thickness. It then grounds an electrical circuit to a rotor surface.

sensor(camshaft) – Device used on some late model fuel injected cars to determine when No. 1 cylinder is at top dead center of its compression or exhaust stroke. It is usually mounted in an unused distributor bore. Signals are generated using the Hall effect, and are transmitted to an on-board computer.

sensor(car speed) – Device usually mounted near a driveline to determine its rotational speed and hence car speed.

sensor(coolant level) – Switch type device used to determine fluid level in an overflow reservoir. It closes an electrical circuit when the level falls below a certain point and illuminates a warning light.

sensor(coolant temperature-1) – Device mounted in the water passageways near the water thermostat to determine coolant temperature.

sensor(coolant temperature-2) – Device mounted in an engine's water jacket to detect water temperature, and use the temperature reading to control certain operations of an on-board computer such as air/fuel mixture, idling speed, and spark advance. In the latter case, a faulty sensor may not properly send signals to an on-board computer causing a drop in fuel economy and/or engine power.

sensor(crankshaft) – Device used on some late model fuel injected cars to determine when pistons reach top dead center. It picks up a signal from the crankshaft pulley. Signals are generated using the Hall effect, and are transmitted to an on-board computer.

sensor(cylinder head temperature) – Electric thermocouple device used to determine high temperatures generated in an engine's cylinder head. It is usually mounted at the base of a spark plug. Different current values are produced depending on the temperature and sent to a cylinder head temperature gauge for read-out.

sensor(differential pressure) – Device used to detect an air pressure difference between intake manifold and atmosphere. It may be a specific value or a range of values.

sensor(detonation) – Device used to detect detonation of a fuel mixture. It is mounted into an intake manifold or cylinder head threaded hole as close as possible to a combustion chamber. It detects high frequency sound vibrations (around 6,000 Hz) emitted when detonation or spark knock occurs. The sound is converted into an electric signal and sent to an on-board computer which retards ignition advance according to the knocking sound strength. It is commonly used in a turbocharged engine to control detonation by instructing an on-board computer to either retard ignition timing or open a turbocharger's wastegate to reduce boost.

sensor(engine rpm) – Device used to determine the rotating speed of an engine's crankshaft.

sensor(exhaust temperature) – Electric thermocouple device used to determine high temperatures generated in exhaust systems. It is usually mounted on an outside surface. Different current values are produced depending on the temperature and sent to an exhaust temperature gauge for read-out.

sensor(front height) – Device used to determine front height of a car body in relation to car axles. It is usually mounted next to a shock absorber or

coil spring.
sensor(fuel flow) – Metering device mounted in a fuel line to determine the flow rate of fuel being delivered to the engine.
sensor(fuel pressure) – Electric resistance unit used to determine fuel pressure at some point in a fuel delivery system. Different current values are produced in the unit depending on the fuel pressure, and sent to a fuel pressure gauge for read-out.
sensor(high altitude) – See sensor(altitude).
sensor(ignition) – Device used to determine when a car's ignition system is energized.
sensor(manifold absolute pressure) – Device used to determine absolute pressure in an intake manifold. It is common on fuel injected engines where it is usually mounted just upstream from the throttle plate.
sensor(oil level) – Switch type device used to detect presence of fluid at a certain level in an oil pan. It closes an electrical circuit when the level falls below a certain point and activates a warning light.
sensor(oil pressure-1) – Fitting mounted near the output side of an oil filter, and used to route a small stream of oil to a mechanical oil pressure gauge. It provides the most accurate oil pressure reading.
sensor(oil pressure-2) – Electrical switch unit used to determine oil pressure. It is usually mounted near the output side of an oil filter. The switch type closes a contact when pressure falls close to zero (usually under 5 lbs.) illuminating an oil pressure warning light.
sensor(oil pressure-3) – Electrical resistance unit used to determine oil pressure. It is usually mounted near the output side of an oil filter. It registers different resistance values, depending on the oil pressure, which are sent to an oil pressure gauge for read-out.
sensor(oil temperature) – Electrical resistance or thermocouple unit used to determine engine, transmission, or differential oil temperature. It is usually mounted in the respective oil pan or housing. Different current values are produced in both units depending on oil temperature, and sent to an oil temperature gauge for read-out.
sensor(oxygen) – Sensor mounted on an exhaust manifold to determine oxygen content in exhaust gas. The sensor generates a voltage signal from the difference in atmospheric and exhaust gas oxygen content. Oxygen content rises as the fuel mixtures becomes lean with the voltage signal dropping close to zero. The signal is sent to an on-board computer to control an engine's air/fuel ratio for most efficient combustion. If the ratio stays low (rich fuel mixture) for several minutes, it will usually send a signal to the on-board computer to illuminate a check engine type warning light.
sensor(rear height) – Device used to determine rear height of a car body in relation to car axles. It is usually mounted next to a shock absorber or coil spring.
sensor(reverse) – Device mounted in a transmission and used to detect when reverse gear has been engaged. It triggers backup lights and other car features associated with driving in reverse.
sensor(temperature) – See sensor(air temperature), sensor(water temperature), and sensor(oil temperature).
sensor(throttle position) – Device used to determine the angular position of the throttle valve shaft. It is commonly used in fuel injected engines where throttle position information is relayed to an on-board computer for maintaining the proper air/fuel ratio.
sensor(water) – Device used to detect the presence of water in diesel fuel. It is usually mounted in the fuel tank, and triggers a warning light.
sensor(water temperature) – Device mounted near the thermostat and used to determine engine coolant temperature. It sends a signal to a water temperature gauge for read-out.
sensor(wheel speed) – Device used to determine wheel acceleration and deceleration rates and relay information back to an on-board computer in an anti-lock braking system. It is mounted in the wheel area and/or in the differential housing.
separator – See battery separator.
Sepentina – American car produced in 1915.
series winding – Armature and field windings of a motor or generator connected in series.
serpentine – See V-belt.
Serpollet, Leon – He set a world land speed record of 75.1 mph in 1902 driving a Serpollet Steam.
Serpollet Steam – French steam car driven by Leon Serpollet to a 1902 world land speed record of 75.1 mph at Nice, France.
Serrifile – American car produced in 1921.
service advisor – See service salesman.
service contract – See contract(service).
service department – Department charged with performing repair work on cars at a repair shop or dealer. See also job(service manager).

service manager – See job(service manager).
service rating – Letter designation assigned to an oil to classify what kind of operating conditions the oil is suitable for. See also viscosity rating.
service rating(DL) – Letter designation assigned to an oil suitable for use in diesel engines operating under light to normal conditions. Those conditions include: trucking and farm tractor driving.
service rating(DS) – Letter designation assigned to an oil suitable for use in diesel engines operating under the most severe conditions. Those conditions include: continuous light loads and low temperatures, continuous heavy loads and high temperatures, use of high sulfur fuels, and use of abnormally volatile fuel.
service rating(ML) – Letter designation assigned to an oil suitable for use in gasoline engines operating under light duty service and favorable operating conditions. Those conditions include: trips longer than 10 miles at medium speeds with no temperature extremes.
service rating(MM) – Letter designation assigned to an oil suitable for use in gasoline engines operating under moderate duty service and infrequent high rpm conditions. Those conditions include: long trips at moderate speeds, and summer temperatures.
service rating(MS) – Letter designation assigned to an oil suitable for use in gasoline engines operating under severe conditions. Those conditions include: short trips with stop and go driving, continuous high speed driving, and continuous heavy load driving.
service repair order – See repair order.
service salesman – Salesman employed in a service department to sell repairs and replacement parts to customers. Most operate on commission so they tend to sell you as much as they can get away with. See also sell or starve pay plan.
Service Truck – American truck produced in 1919.
service writer – See service salesman.
Servitor – American car produced in 1907.
servo – Hydraulically operated piston and cylinder assembly used to control the tightness of a brake band encircling a planetary gear set drum in an automatic transmission. See also front servo and rear servo.
servo action – Method used to increase braking power with brake shoes. When the brakes are applied, the leading shoe is designed to bear or push against the trailing shoe increasing its braking ability. This lessens brake pedal pressure required. Servo action is a popular brake construction concept. See also self-energization.
set of plates – Two license plates mounted on the front and back of a car for identification. See also license plate.
set of points – Distributor point assembly. Also, it refers to any movable points assembly.
set of rims – Wheels needed for a car. Four are usually required.
set of tools – Tools needed to perform mechanic, electrical, plumbing, or other type work.
set of tires – Car tires needed for all wheels. Four are usually required.
setting bail – To determine bail amount for an arrested person.
settle out of court – To settle differences between two litigating parties outside of a courtroom.
set up – Carburetor and intake manifold arrangement. Also, it refers to the various changes that can be made to modify a race car's suspension.
Seven-Little-Buffalos – American car produced in 1908.
Severin – American car produced from 1920-1922 by Severin Motor Car Co. in Missouri.
Seville – American car produced from 1967 to date by Cadillac Motor Car Co. in Michigan.
sewing machine – Small foreign car.
SF(1) – See API service category(SF).
SF(2) – Abbreviation for Finland found usually on an international license plate.
SG Gay – American car produced in 1915.
SGV – American car produced from 1911-1915 by Acme Motor Car Co. (1911-1902), and SGC Co. (1913-1915), both in Pennsylvania.
Sha – American car produced in 1920.
shackle – Swinging support used to attach one end of a leaf spring to a car frame.
shackle bolt – Heavy bolt used to attach the end of a car leaf spring assembly to a shackle and thus to a car's frame.
shackle kit – Assemblage of parts used to make up a spring shackle. See shackle.
Shadburn – American car produced from 1917-1918.
shade kit – Rear window louver assembly. It is used to keep a window clear in bad weather and minimize the entry of sunlight.
shading – Custom painting technique used where certain panel colors are made

progressively darker or lighter. Airbrushes are normally used to create the effect. See also blending.

Shad-Wyck - American car produced from 1917-1923 by Shadburne Brothers in Illinois and Indiana.

shaft - Round straight bar used for transmitting motion and torque.

Shain - American car produced from 1902-1903.

shale oil - Dark mineral oil produced when oil shale or brown coal is destructively distilled.

Shamrock - American car produced in 1917.

Shanghai - Chinese car produced from 1965 to date by Shanghai Motor Vehicle Plant.

Sharon - American car produced in 1915.

Sharp - American car produced from 1914-1915 by Sharp Engineering & Mfg. Co. in Michigan.

sharp - To offer a better deal than another salesman. It is considered in poor taste by most salesmen.

Sharp-Arrow - American car produced from 1908-1910 by William H. Sharp (1908), and Sharp-Arrow Automobile Co. (1908-1910), both in New Jersey.

sharp car - See car classification(sharp).

sharp curve - Curve with a short turning radius. Examples include: road curve, curve on a car body panel, etc.

Shatswell - American car produced from 1901-1903 by H.K. Shatswell & Co. in Massachusetts.

Shaum - American car produced from 1905-1908.

shave - To cut or scrape a surface away with a sharp cutting tool.

Shavers Steam Buggy - American car produced in 1895.

shaving - To remove car body trim to achieve a custom look.

Shaw - American car produced in 1900. Also, an American car produced from 1920-1921 and 1924-1930 by Waldron W. Shaw Livery Co. in Illinois, and Shaw Mfg. Co. in Kansas respectively.

Shawmut - American car produced from 1905-1909 by Shawmut Motor Co. in Massachusetts.

shear - To cut material between two blades.

Shaw, Wilbur - He won the Indianapolis 500 Race in 1937, 1939, and 1940. Average speeds were 113.6, 115.0, 114.3 mph. Cars driven were a Shaw-Gilmore Special, Boyle Special, and Boyle Special.

sheetmetal - Metal panel areas located on a car. It includes: hood, fenders, doors, roof, quarter panels, instrument panel, decklid, etc. It excludes: glass, bumpers, grille, lights, nonmetal trim, etc.

Shelby - American car produced in 1902-1903 by Shelby Motor Car Co. in Ohio. Also, an American car produced from 1910-1912, and 1917.

Shelby Charger - American car produced from 1980 to date by Dodge Division of Chrysler Corp. in Michigan.

Shelby Cobra - American car produced from 1962-1970 by Shelby-American in California (1962-1967), Shelby Automotive in Michigan (1967-1968), and Ford Motor Co. in Michigan (1968-1970). It was a high performance sports car. Pre-1965 models were built around a modified British AC chassis. Post-1965 models were modified Ford Mustangs.

Shelby Charger - American car produced from 1980 to present by Dodge a division of Chrysler Corp. in Michigan.

Shelby GT - American car produced from 1965-1970 by the makers of the Shelby Cobra. It was a high performance modified version of a Ford Mustang Fastback. Almost 15,000 were produced.

Sheldon - American car produced in 1905.

Shell Oil Company - A U.S. petroleum company headquartered in Houston, Texas. See also petroleum company.

Sheridan - American car produced from 1920-1921 by Sheridan Motor Car Co. in Illinois.

sheriff - Law enforcement officer of a state county entrusted to preserve the peace and uphold the law of the land.

Sherwin-Williams - American line of automotive paint products.

shift(1) - To change from one transmission gear arrangement to another.

shift(2) - See gear shift.

shifter - See gear shift.

shift collar - See shift fork.

shift fork - Fork-like device used to slide back and forth on a shifting shaft and extend outward to contact and move gears on a transmission's mainshaft to mesh with countershaft gears. The number of forks depends on the number of gears and the transmission design. The fork movement is controlled by a gearshift.

shifter shaft - See shifting shaft.

shifting shaft - One of two or more shafts used to transfer gearshift motion into sliding different gears sets together in a manual transmission. Two shafts are typically used. Shift forks are mounted on shifting shafts. They slide back and forth to mesh different gear sets together, producing the

different transmission speeds. The shifting mechanism is designed so
shifting forks move on only one shaft at a time in order to avoid engaging
two sets of gears at one time.
shift kit – Assemblage of parts used to install a different shifter and
linkage setup on a car.
shift lever – Lever located in a starter for moving a starter pinion gear into
a flywheel ring gear to spin an engine. Lever movement is controlled by a
solenoid mounted outside a starter.
shift linkage – Assemblage of parts used to transmit shift lever motion into
moving gears to their proper positions.
shift pattern – Various transmission shift lever positions used to engage the
different gears. Today's four and five speed transmissions typically use H
and double H shift patterns respectively.
shift point – Optimum point found in road speed or engine rpm when a
transmission should be shifted from one gear to the next.
shift valve – Hydraulic fluid flow valve used in an automatic transmission to
control shifting from one gear to another. Usually more than one is used.
shim(1) – Small thin sheet of material used as a spacer to adjust the distance
between two parts. Precise spacing often requires several shims. Shims can
be metal, wood, plastic, etc.
shim(2) – Somewhat dishonest car wholesaler.
shimmy – Vibration condition created when front wheels move side-to-side,
shake, or wobble during driving. Shimmy usually transmits itself up the
steering wheel column as an oscillating motion. Possible causes include:
unbalanced, defective, or improperly inflated tires; worn or damaged front
wheel drive parts such as CV joints and struts; steering gearbox out of
adjustment, loose, or out of alignment; loose, worn, leaking, or damaged
shock absorbers; worn or loose steering linkage; loose or bent wheels; bad
wheel bearing(s); and front end parts binding or interfering. See also car
handling problem(wheel shimmy), and car service tip(wheel shimmy test).
shim stock – Very thin metal pieces used as dividers in mold making.
shit box – Rough car or junker.
shive – See shive wheel.
shive wheel – Groove wheel used to support a hoist rope.
shock absorber – Hydraulic mechanism used to dampen the up and down movement
of a spring. A shock absorber is installed near a spring at each wheel
location. There are different types, but they all serve the same purpose.
shock absorber(front) – Shock absorber mounted near one of the front springs.
shock absorber(rear) – Shock absorber mounted near one of the rear springs.
shock absorber(telescoping) – Shock absorber built to extend or telescope in
length. It typically consists of: an outer shell, inner shell, piston rod,
pressure and reservoir tubes, seals, intake and compression valves, hydraulic
fluid, and mounting brackets. It opens and closes under load by forcing
fluid through a respective valve opening. The valve openings are restricted
enough that a car's rapid spring action is slowed down and controlled. This
shock absorber is the one most commonly used on cars today.
shock absorber action – Operation of a shock absorber. Shock absorbers are
installed to minimize sudden loading and unloading demands made on a car's
suspension springs. In so doing, they minimize wheel bounce.
shock absorber test – See car service tip(shock absorber test).
shocks – See shock absorber.
shocks are worn out – Shock absorbers have lost their ability to dampen the up
and down movement of a car's suspension springs. See also car service
tip(shock absorber test).
shoddy repair job – Unacceptable or poor repair work done to a car.
shoe – Driver.
Shoemaker – American car produced from 1907-1909 by Shoemaker Automobile Co.
in Illinois.
shoes – Tires.
shooting brake – Station wagon.
shop(1) – Car repair business.
shop(2) – To check around for the best deal. Also, it refers to a car
salesman checking around to find a person or place to sell trade-ins to.
shop foreman – See job(shop foreman).
shop manual – Manual produced by a car manufacturer providing information on a
specific car's the workings of the various systems, specifications,
maintenance, repair, adjustments, inspection procedures, tolerances, assembly
and disassembly procedures, etc.
shopper – See looker.
shopping for credit – To check different establishments to find the best
credit arrangements.
short – See short circuit.
short bed – See truck bed(short).
shortbed truck – Truck built with a shorter than normal truck bed.
short block – See engine block(short).

short circuit — Electrical circuit problem caused by current reaching ground before the circuit has been completed. Short circuits are usually caused by: torn, worn, or melted insulation; loose connections; broken wires; etc.

short long arm system — See suspension(short long arm).

short sticking — See con game(short sticking).

short trip — Journey by car defined as covering a short distance or period of time. The majority of driving done in cars usually averages 10 miles or less.

shoulder room — Horizontal passenger compartment dimension measured from the left front door panel to the right.

shoulder slots — See tire shoulder slots.

show car — Car displayed at auto shows.

showroom — Room used to display merchandise.

showroom condition — Appearance exhibited by a used car looking like a new one. It is a common advertising phrase seen in classified ads.

showroom look — See showroom condition.

showroom model — New car displayed in a car dealer's showroom.

shrink fit — Tight fit created between two parts. It usually requires heating one of the parts to create enough expansion for the other part to fit in or on. For example, a flywheel ring gear is fitted to a flywheel by heating the gear, placing it on the flywheel, and allowing it to cool. Another example, is a shaft going into a hole. The hole area is heated, the shaft inserted, and the assembly allowed to cool.

shrinking — Procedure followed to restore an elongated car panel contour back to its original size.

shroud — Device used to cover, conceal, or contain something.

shunt(1) — Alternate current path in an electrical circuit.

shunt(2) — Racing accident.

shunt winding — Windings in an electric motor or generator wound in such a way the field and armature circuits are connected in parallel.

shut down — To beat a race car opponent.

shut off — To slow down before finishing a run.

SI — Abbreviation for special interest car.

siamesed — Ports cast in pairs in cylinders heads. Also, it refers to engine cylinder cast with no intervening water jacket passageways.

Sibley — American car produced from 1910-1911 by Sibley Motor Car Co. in Michigan.

Sibley-Curtis — American car produced in 1912.

side curtains — Curtains used to cover the side windows of a car.

side draft — Air current flowing horizontally. See also carburetor(side draft).

side electrode — See spark plug electrode(side).

side mirror — Driving mirror mounted on the left and/or right front car door to assist a driver in seeing the roadway behind and to the side.

side mounted spare wheel — Spare tire carried in an upright position behind one of the front fenders or just ahead of one of the rear fenders. It was a common location on older cars.

side play — Amount of side-to-side movement in a car's steering linkage while the tires remain stationary. Most cars have a small amount. See also car service tip(wheel side play test).

side rail — See frame side rail.

side street — Street leading away from a main street.

sideswipe — To impact the side of one car with another at a very small impact angle.

side valve engine — See engine(L-head).

side valve — See valve(side).

side view — View made of an object at 90 degrees to a plan view.

side view mirror — See side mirror.

sidewall — See tire sidewall.

sidewall stock — See tire sidewall stock.

side window — Small triangular shaped window located in the forward part of front seat windows. It pivots on a vertical axis, and is used to control air flow inside a car. They were introduced by Fisher in 1933, but are not popular on today's cars.

side window catch — Locking lever latch combination used to open side windows a limited distance and close and lock them.

Siebert — American car produced from 1907-1909.

Sierra — American car produced from 1957-1959 by Dodge Division of Chrysler Corp. in Michigan.

sight gauge — See site glass.

sight glass(air conditioner) — Small glass or plastic window used in an air conditioning system to check the refrigerant level. It is usually located in the high pressure side between the evaporator and condenser, but is sometimes integrated with the expansion valve. When the air conditioner is operating, the appearance of bubbles or foam usually indicates a low level of refrigerant. No bubbles indicates the level is full or empty. In the latter case, cycling the magnetic clutch on and off will show bubbles if the system is full.

sight glass(carburetor) - Small glass or plastic window mounted in a carburetor body for observing gasoline level in a float bowl. It usually has a mark to indicate the proper level.

sight plug - See sight gauge.

Sigma - American car produced in 1914.

Signal - American car produced in 1915.

signal flasher - Flash unit used to make turn signal lights flash.

signaling - Process defined as using a car's turn signaling device or using hand signals to notify other cars or pedestrians of your intent to make a turn or move from one lane to another.

signals - See turn signals.

Signet - American car produced from 1913-1914 by Fenton Engineering Co. in Michigan. Also, an American car produced from 1962-1981 by Plymouth Division of Chrysler Corp. in Michigan.

silencer - Muffler.

Silent Knight - American car produced from 1906-1909 by Knight & Kilbourne Co. in Illinois.

Silent Northern - American car produced by Charles King in 1902. Its features included three-point suspension and an integrated engine transmission assembly.

Silent Sioux - American car produced from 1909-1912 by Sioux Auto Mfg. Co. in South Dakota (1909-1910), and Wisconsin (1910-1912).

silicone - See silicone rubber.

silicone rubber - Rubber-like silicone polymer formulated to maintain elasticity over a wide temperature range. It is used commonly on cars: in place of certain gaskets, and in insulating spark plug cables.

silicon steel - Steel alloyed with silicon and chromium. Its properties include: resistance to burning and oxidation and not warping easily. Exhaust valves in today's engines are usually made of this steel.

sillment seals - Two seals in a spark plug. One is between the porcelain insulator and the spark plug shell. The other is between the porcelain insulator and the center electrode. The seals are made of a highly heat resistant material.

Silver Arrow - American car produced in 1933 by Pierce-Arrow Motor Co. in New York. It was special show car priced at $10,000. Only five were made. Features included: no running boards, 12 cylinder engine, concealed spare tire, and split rear window. It was exhibited at the 1933 World's fair in Chicago.

silver brazing - To braze using a silver brazing alloy. It is a process popular in many industries.

silver brazing alloy - Alloy composed of silver and other chemical elements and used to braze metals together. Typical elements include: gold, copper, cadmium, phosphorus, and zinc. Many alloys have been formulated to join different metals together.

Silver Ghost - Early Rolls Royce car model known for being very quiet.

Silver Knight - American car produced in 1906.

silver solder - See solder(silver).

silver soldering - See silver brazing.

Simca - French car line produced from 1935-1980 by Automobiles Talbot (1980).

Simmons - American car produced in 1910.

Simms - American car produced from 1920-1921 by Simms Motor Car Corp. in Georgia.

Simonds Steam Wagon - American steam car produced in 1895.

simple bend - Body damage produced when metal is bent, but not back over itself. See also rolled buckle, displaced area, upset, and stretch.

Simplex - American car produced from 1907-1917 by Simplex Automobile Co. in New Jersey. The 1914 model was supposedly the last chain-driven car produced in America.

Simplex-Crane - American car produced from 1915-1917 by Simplex Automobile Co. in New Jersey.

Simplicities - American car produced in 1905.

Simplicity - American car produced from 1906-1911 by Evansville Automobile Co. in Indiana.

Simplo - American car produced from 1908-1909 by Cook Motor Vehicle Co. in Missouri.

Sinclair - American car produced in 1921.

Sinclair-Scott - American car produced from 1906-1907.

Singer - American car produced from 1915-1920 by Singer Motor Co. in New York. Also, a British car line produced from 1905-1970 by Singer Motors Ltd.

single barrel carburetor - See carbruetor(single barrel).

Single-Center - American car produced from 1906-1908 by Single-Center Buggy Co. in Indiana.

single plane manifold - See intake manifold(single plane).
Sintz - American car produced from 1903-1904.
siping - Tire tread cutting process designed to improve tread life and traction. It does improve traction on snow and ice.
siren - Device used to produce a loud often wailing sound.
six holder - Six cylinder engine.
six pack - Six cylinder engine.
six position technique - Car selling technique used where a car salesman will stand at six different locations around a car and explain specific features.
Six Wheel Truck - American truck produced in 1921.
size - Adhesive compound used to hold gold and silver leaf to a surface. The leaf material is rubbed onto the covered area and adheres only where the size is.
Sizer - American car produced in 1911.
SJR - American car produced from 1915-1916 by SJR Motor Co. in Massachusetts.
skate - To take a potential car customer from another car salesman. It also means to change a deal on an unsuspecting customer. Both are considered in poor taste.
Skelton - American car produced from 1920-1922 by Skelton Motor Car Co. in Missouri.
Skene - American car produced from 1900-1901 by J.W. Skene Cycle & Automobile Co. in Maine.
skid - Driving condition created when tires lose traction on a road surface during braking. Skidding occurs on slippery surfaces or when attempting to stop quickly by locking up the brakes. When a car skids, it's often difficult to predict how it will behave.
  Front and rear wheel drive cars behave differently when skidding occurs. When a rear wheel skid begins, most experts agree it is usually best stopped by backing off the gas pedal: quickly if it is a front engine-rear wheel drive car, and slowly if it is a front engine-front wheel drive car.
skid(oversteer) - Car continues to swing in one direction despite turning of the front wheels in the skid direction. It is common on ice.
skid(pendulum) - See skid(oversteer).
skid(rebound) - See skid(reverse).
skid(reverse) - Over-correction of a skid usually causes a car to skid in the opposite direction. Fishtailing is a good example of repeated reverse skidding.
skid(spinning oversteer) - Uncontrolled spinning of a car caused usually when front wheels lose traction and then rear wheels are locked up and lose traction.
skid(trailing throttle) - Front wheels lose traction when foot is quickly removed from the gas pedal of a front wheel drive car.
skid(understeer) - Front wheels lose traction. It usually happens when rounding a turn (car continues in a straight line), or from hydroplaning. It is a dangerous skid and usually occurs on wet or icy roads. Cars more prone to this skid have rear engine-rear wheel drive or front engine-front wheel drive.
skid marks - Tire rubber marks left on a road surface as a result of tires losing traction.
skid pad - Area set up for testing how a car handles in different skid situations.
skid plate - Protective metal panel mounted underneath a car engine and/or transmission area to shield against ground obstructions.
skilled mechanic - Car mechanic known for being good at the car repair work he does and having a good reputation.
skin - Sheetmetal covering of a car.
skin game - See con game.
skinned - To cover a car body area, such as a door frame, with a sheetmetal or fiberglass panel.
skinning - To remove a car's upholstery and replace with a custom material.
skinning the dude - See con game(skinning the dude).
skins - Worn out or bald tires. Also, it refers to tires in general.
skirt - See piston skirt.
skirted fender - Fender built to curve downward along its length to help cover a wheel more completely.
Skoda - Czechoslovakian car line produced from 1923 to date by Skoda np (1945 to date).
Skyhawk - American car produced from 1975 to date by Buick Division of General Motors Corp. in Michigan.
Skylark - American car produced from 1961 to date by Buick Division of General Motors Corp. in Michigan.
SL - Abbreviation for saloon sedan.
slalom - Racing event held usually on a paved surface with a course forcing reduced car speed due to many temporary obstacles.
slander - To make false, defamatory, malicious statements damaging to another

person.
slanted windshield - Windshield built with a slope to it.
slashed tire - Tire cut usually through the sidewall with a knife or other cutting tool. It usually ruins the tire.
slasher - Ring worn by some service station con artists containing a knife like cutting edge or puncturing projection. It is used to quickly damage a tire so repairs are needed. See also con game(skinning the dude).
slashing - See con game(slashing).
slave cylinder - Hydraulic cylinder used to transfer motion from a remote master cylinder via a high pressure fluid line. Many cars use them to move clutch release forks, instead of using a more elaborate linkage.
sled - Rough car or junker.
sleeper(1) - High performance car disguised as a stock car.
sleeper(2) - Compartment built behind the back of a conventional truck cab to provide a sleep area for the driver.
sleepiness - See drowsiness.
sleeve - Tubelike part used to fit in, over, or around another part. For example, some engine blocks use cylinder sleeves press fitted into each cylinder bore.
sleeve valve - See valve(sleeve).
sleeve valve engine - See engine(sleeve valve).
slick(1) - Plastic or metal tool used to smooth car clay model surfaces.
slick(2) - Racing tire built with smooth tread for maximum traction on pavement.
Slick 50 - Tradename used by PetroLon Corporation for a polytetrafluorethylene impregnated oil.
slicks - See slick(2).
slickshift - See transmission(slickshift).
slick surface - Slippery surface.
slide(1) - Mass of rock, snow, mud, etc., moved from its original position on a slope.
slide(2) - A maneuver commonly employed by race car drivers on turns in which all four wheels are induced to break traction and thereby cause the car to slip throughout the turn. Such a maneuver can be initiated by quickly hitting the brakes and then the accelerator. See also power slide.
slide area - Area covered by a slide.
slide hammer - Tool used to pull severe dents out of car body panels. It consists of: shaft and handle, sliding weight, and shaft end attachment.
sliding fit - See running fit.
sliding rear window - Rear window equipped with an inner horizontal sliding window. It is commonly found on pickup trucks.
slingshot - Dragster built to carry a driver behind the rear wheels. It better distributes weight and maximizes traction.
slip angle - Angle measured between the direction of wheel travel and the tread direction.
slip joint - Splined shaft coupling used to transfer rotation from one shaft to another and allow movement between the two shafts as well. It is most commonly used on the transmission side of a driveline.
slip joint pliers - Pliers built to allow the hinge point to be offset for gripping larger diameters. It is a common type of pliers found in many toolboxes.
slippery - Streamlined.
slip ring - Insulated metal ring mounted at one edge of an alternator rotor. Its surface provides a continuous rotating contact surface for brushes transferring current to the rotor windings. Alternators have two slip rings, mounted side by side and providing a complete circuit for current flow in the rotor windings.
slipshod - Careless or sloppy.
slipshod workmanship - Careless or sloppy work.
slipstream - Area of little air movement found immediately behind a moving car. Race cars often closely follow a lead car to stay in it, since it allows a trailing car to run an engine under less strain.
slip yoke - See front yoke.
slow moving vehicle - Vehicle traveling well below posted speed limits.
slowpoke - See slow moving vehicle.
sludge - Thick black slimy material deposited in various parts of an engine. It is created when moving parts mix oil, water, dust, gas, oxidized petroleum products, and other compounds together. It forms more quickly in car engines repeatedly driven short distances at low speeds. Engines, operated this way, seldom get hot enough to rid a crankcase of accumulating water and water vapor. It typically deposits in the bottom of an oil pan, in the valve train area, on valve covers, etc. If allowed to accumulate excessively, it can plug oil passageways, the oil intake screen, etc. which may block the flow of oil to an engine. Sludge formation can be minimized by using detergent oils, high temperature water thermostats, changing oil and filter frequently,

keeping the crankcase ventilated, and avoiding repeated short distance driving.

sluff-off – Downward slant in a hood or trunk decklid design.

slug – Piston.

slush – Snow or ice partially melted.

slush car – Automatic transmission equipped car.

slush pump – Automatic transmission.

SM – Abbreviation for sidemount.

Small – American car produced in 1915 and 1919-1922.

small block – Engine block displacing under 350 cubic inches. See also large block.

Small Claims Court – Court created in 1938 to provide an inexpensive and informal way for people to recover small amounts of money. The amount you can recover ranges from $100 to $5,000 depending on the state. The procedure is simple enough that an attorney is not necessary and in certain states they are not allowed. The proceeding is like a three-way conversation between you, the judge, and the party you are suing. Technicalities are ignored and each party tells their side of the story in their own words. A small filing fee is charged. To file a suit, a short form is filled out at the Clerk of the Small Claims Court office. On the form, you will be asked to provide information such as: the party names, amount of money being disputed, and the circumstances of the situation. When the form is signed, a court date is set, usually within a few weeks to a month, and a summons goes to the party you are suing, notifying them they must appear in court to answer the charges you have alleged. Simply filing the suit ends the matter in many cases, because the offending party will take you seriously and settle. If the party does not show up in court, it is usually ruled in your favor by default. The default cannot be set aside unless the party had good reason for not being there.

small independent – Small auto repair business characterized by employing a few people and not owned by another company.

smash-up – Car with extensive body damage.

SMD – Abbreviation for surface mounted device.

smell – Presence of one or more odors in the air detected by a person's nose and olfactory nerves. Cars can emit a variety of smells that can be normal or abnormal.

smell(burnt oil) – Smell produced when oil gets too hot. Possible causes include: low transmission fluid level, clogged crankcase ventilation system, oil leaking onto engine block, exhaust manifold, or exhaust pipe, and excess blow-by. Transmission oil has a totally unique smell.

smell(burnt rag) – Smell (like burning rags) produced usually by dragging brakes (such as emergency brake on) or burned wiring insulation from a short circuit.

smell(burnt rubber) – Smell produced from rubber that has become scorched. Possible causes include: spinning the tires, skidding, low tire pressure, and rubber hose to close to manifold.

smell(burnt wiring) – Smell produced when plastic insulation on wires melts.

smell(exhaust fumes) – Smell produced due to exhaust system leaks caused by corrosion, bad gaskets, and/or a clogged muffler. It is usually more noticeable when a car is idling or driven slowly.

smell(gasoline) – Smell produced when gasoline leaks. Possible causes include: flooded engine; leaking fuel lines, filter, pump, carburetor, and/or charcoal canister; and overfilled gas tank.

smell(rot) – Pungent and/or mildewy odor produced by carpeting and underpad which has rotted due to water.

smell(rotten egg) – Bad odor similar to rotten eggs found emanating from catalyst equipped cars. It is commonly due to sulfur compounds, found in some gasolines, contacting hot surfaces in a catalytic converter and muffler. Low sulfur gas will minimize the problem. Other possible causes include: plugged catalytic converter becomes too hot as residual gases pass through it, certain converters generate smell during warm-up period, poor converter design, rich air/fuel mixture, and driving short distances.

Smith – American car produced from 1898-1905 by Smith Automobile Co. in Kansas. See also Great Smith.

Smith & Mabley – American car produced from 1905-1907.

Smith Flyer – American car produced from 1917-1920 by A.O. Smith in Wisconsin.

Smith Motor Wheel – American car produced in 1909.

Smith Spring Motor – American car produced in 1896.

smitty – See muffler(glass pack).

smog – Haze found hanging over geographical areas with high traffic flows and/or industrialization accompanied by poor air flow movement. It is formed by exhaust smoke, moisture, and various combustion products. Hydrocarbons and oxides of nitrogen are major ingredients in smog. Sunlight increases smog by reacting with various airborne pollutants to form more pollutants. Smog directly affects people's health. In low concentrations, it burns the

eyes and may affect the respiratory system of certain people. In high
concentrations, it can cause death. California was the first state to limit
carbon monoxide and hydrocarbon emissions from cars.
smog control system – See emission control system.
smog device – Device used on a car engine to limit exhaust and/or crankcase
emissions.
smog motor head – Engine cylinder head designed to handle some of an engine's
emission control requirements.
smog pump – See air pump.
smog valve – See PCV valve.
smoke – See exhaust.
smoke off – To leave the starting line first.
smoker – Car characterized by burning an excessive amount of oil, exhausting a
great deal of smoke into the air. See also oil pumping.
smoke screen – Trail of smoky exhaust fumes left by a car burning excessive
quantities of oil.
SN(1) – American car produced in 1921.
SN(2) – Abbreviation for Senegal found usually on an international license
plate.
Snap-On – Line of tools produced by Snap-On Tools Corporation.
snap ring pliers – Plier used to remove snaps rings.
Sneva, Tom – He won the Indianapolis 500 Race in 1983 driving an average of
162.1 mph in a Texaco Star.
snorkel tube – See air inlet.
snowball – Whitewall tire.
snowbank – Large mound or mass of snow.
snow job – Attempt made to deceive or persuade someone on the merits of
something by flattery, exaggeration, etc.
snowmobile – Vehicle built to travel over snow. It steers with skis or
runners.
snowplow – Vehicle built to remove large accumulations of snow from a road and
discharge it off the road via a chute arrangement.
snows – Abbreviation for snow tires.
snow tire – See tire(snow).
snrf – Abbreviation for sunroof.
Snyder – American car produced from 1906-1908 by D.D. Synder Motor & Mfg Co.
in Ohio.
sociable body – See body style(sociable).
Society of Automotive Engineers – Organization formed to set standards for the
automotive industry. It also publishes research papers. See also SAE.
socket – See socket wrench.
socket(deep) – Socket wrench built with a long cylinder length for longer
reach.
socket wrench – Cylinder built to receive a nut or bolt at one end, and a
detachable handle at the other end.
socket wrench handle – Handle used to attach to a socket, permitting it to be
turned. Different types include: ratchet, spinner, extension, and flex bar.
soft – Characteristic of a car selling poorly. Such cars often have several
listings in newspaper car ads. See also hard and cold.
soft credit – Credit made easy to obtain and which is usually structured to a
lender's advantage.
soft engagement – Method used to more readily engage a clutch plate by
building the plate with a slight warp.
soft solder – See solder(soft).
soft trim – Soft or yielding portions located in a car's interior such as
seats, door panels, carpets, headlining, armrest, padding, etc.
SOHC – Abbreviation for single overhead camshaft.
solder – Metal or other type alloy used to join or patch two metal surfaces
together. Metal solders melt at under 800 degrees Fahrenheit. Several
different metals are used to make the various solder alloys. They include
lead, tin, antimony, bismuth, indium, zinc, cadmium, copper, and silver with
lead and tin being the most common. Metals joined with solder include: sheet
steel and iron, copper, brass, tin, and bronze. Non-metal solders are
primarily plastic compounds designed to replace lead as a filler. They apply
without heat. See also solder alloy and lead alloy.
solder(aluminum) – Metal solder alloy formulated from such metals as tin,
zinc, copper, and cadmium.
solder(brazing) – See solder(hard).
solder(hard) – Metal solder alloy formulated to melt at higher temperatures.
It usually contains copper and zinc compounds. Silver solder is considered a
hard solder. See also solder(soft).
solder(plastic) – Non-metal material used to fill dented areas of a car body
without heat. The most common types consist of a resin material that becomes
hard when mixed with a catalyst. Drying time is usually 20-30 minutes with a
5-10 minute application time. Once hard, the material forms a strong bond

with the underlying metal despite temperature extremes. It has a hard finish, and does not shrink or crack with age. The material is usually filed and sanded while still somewhat soft.

solder(lead) – Lead alloy solder. The most common is a 70-30 mixture of lead and tin. It melts at just under 500 degrees Fahrenheit. See also solder alloy.

solder(silver) – Solder composed of lead and silver. It typically melts and flows at temperatures of 570-590 degrees Fahrenheit. The silver content is usually 2-3 percent. See also silver brazing alloy.

solder(soft) – Metal solder alloy formulated to melt at lower temperatures. It usually contains tin and lead elements. Electrical solder is considered soft solder.

solder alloy – Solder composed of two or more metals. Lead and tin alloys are most common. Composition ranges from 95-5 to 38-62 expressed as percentages of lead and tin respectively. The liquid temperature of solder ranges from 361-595 degrees as the respective percentage of lead rises from 38-95 percent. Antimony is added to solder to increase its strength, but does the opposite on metals such as cadmium, zinc, and galvanized metals. Bismuth and silver improve a solder's tinning action and lower and raise melting temperatures respectively. Cadmium is used in certain high temperature solders. Indium is used to combat corrosion problems.

solder flux – See flux(soldering).

soldering – Process defined as joining two pieces of metal together without melting them, using a material with a melting point below 800 degrees Fahrenheit. The bond occurs when molten solder molecules intertwine with those of the parent metals. The joint is not as strong as a brazed or welded joint. It is used when the following is desired: neatness, sanitation, and leakproof or low electrical resistance joint. See also brazing, joining metal, and tinning.

soldering gun – Gun-shaped soldering device used to melt and apply solder with an electrically heated tip. The tip is smaller than on a rod-shaped soldering iron.

soldering iron – See soldering gun. Also, a rod-shaped iron with an electrically heated tip. The tip melts and smoothes or irons solder along a joint.

solder torch – Torch built to solder using acetylene, natural gas, propane, or mapp gas to heat the tip and melt the solder.

sole warranty – See warranty(sole).

solenoid – See solenoid switch.

solenoid switch – Heavy duty electromagnetic switch used to close high current flow contacts. It contains a movable magnetic core, surrounded by a stationary electric coil. The core moves when current passes through the coil closing electric contacts which remain closed only as long as current passes through the coil. A solenoid switch is used on cars to send a high current flow to a starter for rotating an engine.

Another switch design sometimes referred to as a solenoid switch is a starter relay built to move the electric coil along a stationary magnetic core until it closes heavy contacts. See also relay.

solenoid vacuum valve – Electrically operated valve used to control vacuum reaching distributor's vacuum advance unit. It usually operates according to an air temperature sensor in the air cleaner, and a transmission switch or speed switch. When air intake temperature is above 70 degrees, the valve lowers or stops intake vacuum to the vacuum advance unit, retarding timing in all transmission gears except high (if transmission switch is used), or until a certain speed, commonly 30 mph, is reached (if speed switch used). When temperature is below 70, the valve allows full intake vacuum, permitting normal vacuum advance. See also vacuum switching valve.

Solex – Line of carburetors.

solid injection – Fuel injection system used in diesel and semidiesel engines where liquid fuel without air is injected into engine cylinders.

solid rubber tire – See tire(solid rubber).

solids – Mechanical valve lifters.

solid state – Designation used to describe electronic devices that control current without moving parts, heated filament wires, etc. See also ignition system(solid state).

solid state ignition – See ignition system(solid state).

solo – Single run.

solvent – Substance used to dissolve another substance. Most solvents are liquids.

Somerset – American car produced 1985 to date by Buick Division of General Motors Corp. in Michigan.

Sommer – American car produced from 1904-1907 by Sommer Motor Co. in Michigan.

Souders, George – He won the Indianapolis 500 Race in 1927 driving an average of 97.5 mph in a Deusenberg.

Soules – American car produced from 1905-1908.

sound – Vibrations found occurring in air, water, and other mediums which stimulate a person's auditory nerves causing a person to hear a specific sound. Cars emit a variety of sounds that can be normal or abnormal. They can be grouped into five categories: intake, exhaust, mechanical, body, and aerodynamic.

Also, it refers to an auto condition code word used to specify a restored or authentic original car requiring work to make it roadworthy.

sound(banging-1) – Sharp loud pounding or hammering sound produced in the front end when braking or turning. It is usually caused by a strut rod with worn and/or torn bushings.

sound(banging-2) – Sound produced when an engine backfires.

sound(banging-3) – Sound produced when metal parts are too close to each other. If the sound comes from inside the engine, a serious problem exists.

sound(bell) – Bell-like or clanking sound produced when hitting a bump in the road. It is usually caused by a worn out shock absorber.

sound(bumping-1) – Sound produced by a loose main bearing. It makes a deeper heavier sound than a connecting rod. It is most audible when the engine is lugging. The sound can be isolated by shorting out spark plugs.

sound(bumping-2) – Sound produced by a starter motor when cranking. It is due to a loose pole shoe dragging against a turning armature.

sound(bumping-intermittent) – Sound produced by a loose flywheel. The noise may tend to fade in and out. Shorting out the spark plugs will not effect the sound. One way to isolate the problem is to turn the ignition off, then back to ON position when the engine has just about stopped. This action induces a sudden twist to an engine and will produce a noticeable knock if the flywheel is loose.

sound(buzzing-high pitched) – Sound produced in an automatic transmission due to a plugged filter. Changing the filter and fluid should cure the sound.

sound(chattering-1) – Rapid rattling, clicking, vibrating sound produced when a clutch plate is engaged. Possible causes include: clutch plate and pressure plate combination poor (most common); clutch plate facing that is oily, greasy, glazed, worn, and/or warped; splines on clutch plate hub or transmission shaft worn, broken, and/or loose; splined hub binding; pressure plate binding; pressure plate release levers binding or out of adjustment; pressure plate springs worn or wrong length; clutch housing or clutch plate assembly out of alignment; universal joints worn or loose; engine mounts worn, loose, broken, and/or soaked with oil; drive axle or differential worn or loose; and bent transmission input shaft.

sound(chattering-2) – Sound produced when brakes are applied. Possible causes include: loose brake linings, brake drum scored or machined poorly, brake shoes not centered, and warped brake drum and/or rotor.

sound(chirping-1) – Short shrill sound similar to what birds make. It commonly occurs when a power steering fan belt gets a little loose and will be heard when turning the steering wheel. Another possibility is a rear axle pinion bearing getting too dry.

sound(chirping-2) – Sound produced in the front of a car by a water pump whose bushings or bearings are starting to go out. It will need to replaced right away.

sound(chirping-3) – Rapid sound produced by faulty EGR check valve.

sound(chirping-4) – Sound produced by a faulty AIR or PAIR system.

sound(chirping-5) – Sound produced in a car's front wheel area at higher speeds that gets louder when turning the wheels one way and quieter the other. Possible causes include: wheel covers, cracked wheel, broken wheel weld, noise generated at wheel-tire contact surface, faulty suspension component(s), and faulty body component(s).

sound(clanking) – See sound(bell).

sound(clattering-1) – Sound produced in the front of an engine due to a bad bearing in one of the belt-driven components. Belts can be removed one at a time to locate faulty component.

sound(clattering-2) – Sound produced in the front of an engine due to belt wear. Sound is due to slipping and/or riding in the bottom of the pulley groove. Belt may be cracked, glazed, covered with oil or grease, or worn unevenly.

sound(clattering-3) – See sound(rattling-4).

sound(clattering-4) – See sound(rattling-5)

sound(clicking-1) – See sound(tapping-muffled).

sound(clicking-2) – Slight sharp repetitive sound produced by a piston with excessive wall clearance, a loose piston pin, or an old piston with new tight piston pins. An indicator of piston slap is a decrease in engine noise as the engine warms up. A loose piston pin will often produce a click at the bottom and top of each stroke. It is usually loudest at idling speed, and becomes louder if the affected spark plug is shorted out, or the timing advanced. Tight pins will produce a piston slap type sound that usually disappears after an engine is run a few hundred miles and loosens up the piston pins.

sound(clicking-3) - Sound produced by piston rings with excess clearance in their grooves. The sound is similar to the tapping sound of a loose valve tappet, except that a loose tappet clicks every other revolution and loose piston rings click twice per revolution.

sound(clicking-4) - Common subtle sound produced by a speedometer cable in need of lubrication. It clicks according to the speed of the car and not the engine.

sound(clicking-5) - Sound produced when one or more hydraulic lifters are sticking or low on oil. If the sound disappears after a few minutes of starting, the hydraulic lifters were just low on oil. If the sound remains, one or more stuck lifters may be to blame. A mechanic's stethoscope is commonly used to locate them. Stuck lifters usually need to be replaced.

sound(clicking-6) - Clicking sound produced in an automatic transmission. Possible causes include: worn bushings, gears, and clutch hub; low oil level; and damaged gear teeth.

sound(clicking-7) - See sound(clattering).

sound(clicking-8) - Loud sound produced by one or more broken valve springs.

sound(clicking-9) - Sound produced when a tire has picked up a nail, rock, etc. The sound is strictly a function of tire speed.

sound(clicking-10) - Sound produced in wheel area due to a bad wheel bearing, or loose or damaged brake part.

sound(clunking-1) - Sound produced in a stationary car when a transmission is engaged, or when load is applied with car in motion. It indicates one or more worn universal joints. Depending on car design, such joints are located on drivelines, and front and/or rear axles. If wear is not excessive and joints can be lubricated, lubrication will often correct the problem. If not, the affected joint will have to be replaced.

sound(clunking-2) - Loud sound produced when car stops, or when car is shifted: from reverse to forward, or park to reverse. It may also be accompanied by a momentary sensation of brakes dragging when car first moves. It is commonly due to a drive yoke binding on a transmission output shaft spline surface. Yoke moves in or out due to phenomenon called axle windup. It is created when torque is applied to wheels. Yoke binding causes yoke to suddenly give way and clunk. Lubrication of yoke splines and bushings of torque arms controlling axle windup helps.

sound(clunking-3) - Loud sound made when an automatic transmission kicks down the transmission gearing as the car is brought to a stop. It is usually a vacuum leak which requires adjusting the vacuum modulator or replacing it.

sound(clunking-4) - Sound produced on certain front wheel drive cars when transmission is shifted. It is often due to worn bushings in a torque strut connecting the lower engine block to the front car frame. Bushing condition can be checked by rocking engine back and forth. See also engine torque strut.

sound(clunking-5) - See sound(banging-1).

sound(clunking-6) - Sound produced by an automatic transmission due to a vacuum leak. Check the vacuum modulator and adjust or replace as necessary.

sound(clunking-7) - Sound produced by a loose or worn MacPherson strut when an engine load is applied or when a car slows down.

sound(clunking-8) - Sound produced by a loose wheel nut when an engine load is applied or a car slows down.

sound(coast down) - Sound produced when a car in motion slows down without braking by closing the carburetor throttle plate. Possible abnormal causes include: worn or loose wheel bearing, and/or MacPherson strut; and worn differential.

sound(cracking) - Sharp sudden sound produced in engine compartment when a high voltage spark jumps to ground from spark plug wires, ignition coil tower, distributor cap. Arcs are more noticeable when it gets dark.

sound(droning-1) - Continuous monotonous humming or buzzing sound produced from resonance in an exhaust system. Possible causes include: loose or broken brackets, fasteners, and hangers; loose muffler and/or catalytic converter parts; and loose belt-driven accessories such as alternators or air pumps.

sound(droning-2) - Sound produced in engine compartment area due to faulty bearing(s), and/or support bracket of alternator, air pump, air conditioner, power steering pump, etc.

sound(droning-3) - Sound produced by improperly installed or tightened motor mounts when an engine load is applied and/or during acceleration.

sound(droning-4) - Sound produced by improperly routed or loose fuel line, throttle linkage, air conditioner line, etc. when an engine placed under load and/or during acceleration.

sound(engine) - Sound produced in the engine area. If the sound does do not cause a noticeable change in engine performance, it is often correctable at low cost.

sound(explosive) - Sudden loud sound produced when fuel accumulates in an oil pan, oil and metal parts get hot, and fuel ignites. Possible fuel accumulation causes include: internal carburetor leak, carburetor flooding, heat soak, and choke stuck closed.

sound(grinding-1) – Harsh grating sound produced in an automatic transmission. Possible causes include: park position causing restricted servo valve movement. See also sound(clicking-6).

sound(grinding-2) – Sound produced in a differential or transaxle when the oil has become contaminated with metal or dirt fragments. It is often most noticeable when load is applied.

sound(grinding-3) – Sound produced in the clutch area when the clutch pedal is depressed. It is usually caused by a bad clutch release bearing.

sound(grinding-4) – Sound produced by a starter motor when cranking. It is due to a loose pole shoe dragging against a turning armature.

sound(grinding-5) – Sound produced by a starter motor when cranking. It may or may be turning the engine over. It is usually due to a faulty starter drive unit (broken spring, pinion gear, or overrunning clutch), and/or stripped flywheel ring gear.

sound(grinding-6) – Sound produced by a starter motor when cranking. It is due to the pinion gear engaging too far from the flywheel ring gear. Pinion teeth may skip over the flywheel teeth. It is a serious problem that will damage both gears in short order. Possible causes include: bad starter drive bearing, missing starter to engine block shims, and wrong type starter.

sound(grinding-7) – Sound produced whenever a manual transmission is shifted from one gear to another. It occurs on older non-synchromesh transmissions using sliding type gears. See also gear clashing.

sound(grinding/whining-constant) – Constant grinding and/or whining sound found to increase with car speed. The sound usually decreases when the car is turned in either direction. The steering wheel often will generate a slight vibration when the sound occurs. It is usually caused by a wheel bearing going out due to crushed or broken rollers or balls. Immediate replacement is necessary or other parts will also be damaged.
    If the sound is muffled, one or more inner axle bearings and differential pinion bearings may be going out.

sound(growling/humming-1) – Low rumbling or droning sound produced when a manual transmission is running in neutral. It can often times be stopped when a clutch pedal is depressed. Since the main shaft does not rotate in neutral, the only defects associated with it is a worn or damaged pilot bearing or bushing. Possible causes include: worn or damaged pilot bearing or bushing, pinion gear, pinion shaft bearing, countershaft drive gear, reverse gear, and reverse idler gear; excessive end play in countershaft, pinion shaft, or reverse idler gear; bent or misaligned countershaft; and transmission out of alignment.

sound(growling/humming-2) – Rumbling or droning sound produced when a manual transmission is running in gear. It is usually heard in neutral as well. Possible causes include those under sound(growling/humming-1) as well as the following: worn or damaged sliding gears, main shaft rear bearing, and speedometer gears; and excessive main shaft end play.

sound(growling/humming-3) – Rumbling or droning sound produced when an automatic transmission is rotating. Possible causes include: brake bands dragging; oil level too low; and excessive wear in shafts, gear teeth, and/or gear bushings.

sound(growling/humming-4) – Rumbling or droning sound produced in a rotating differential during engine load. Possible causes include: scored gear teeth, pinion and ring gear improperly meshing, and wrong type gear lubricant.

sound(gurgling-1) – Bubbling/rippling sound produced by aspirator valve on a running engine. It is mounted in piping that runs from an engine's air cleaner to the exhaust manifold. The sound indicates that it is operating. See also emission control system(combustion-aspirator).

sound(gurgling-2) – Sound produced by an air conditioning system low on refrigerant. Sound is often most noticeable when engine is idling, blower is off, and temperature control is at its coldest setting.

sound(hammering-rapid) – It usually indicates a loose connecting rod or crankshaft bearing. The sound increases with the speed of an engine and not the car. Stop your car immediately if you hear such a sound to avoid any further engine damage.

sound(hissing-1) – Sound emitted at an air conditioner's expansion valve when the charge is too high.

sound(hissing-2) – Sound produced in an engine compartment from a vacuum leak.

sound(howling) – Sound produced in the clutch area of a manual transmission. It is usually caused by metal to metal contact of the clutch disc and pressure plate. The sound is often most noticeable when the car begins moving. Replacement of the two parts and inspection of the clutching mechanism for proper operation is usually required to eliminate the noise.

sound(humming-1) – Sound produced by snow tires, especially at higher speeds.

sound(humming-2) – Sound produced by a differential with worn parts. See also sound(growling/humming-4).

sound(knocking-1) - Sound produced by oversize pistons striking a protruding head gasket or new piston rings striking an uncleaned cylinder ridge.

sound(knocking-2) - Sound produced by worn timing gears. The intensity of the sound remains regardless of engine use. Shorting out spark plugs will not affect the sound. A stethoscope is useful in pinpointing this sound.

sound(knocking-3) - Sound produced in a rebuilt or inspected engine by parts that are misaligned, have excessive end play, and/or have excessive side clearance.

sound(knocking-4) - Sound produced in an operating air conditioner compressor when the discharge valve gets stuck closed.

sound(knocking-5) - Intermittent sound produced by excessive end play in a crankshaft. It is usually a sharper sound than the bumping sound made by a loose main bearing. If the car has a manual transmission, disengaging the clutch will affect the noise.

sound(knocking-6) - Intermittent sound produced by rubber engine motor mounts that have either deteriorated or been bolted down enough that there is not much clearance between metal mounting points. When the car is accelerated, the twisting action of the engine is not absorbed sufficiently by the rubber mounts, and the net result is metal to metal contact or a knocking sound.

sound(knocking-7) - Loud intermittent sound commonly produced by a slightly loose connecting rod. It usually gets loud around 30-50 mph, and loudest just when the driver removes his foot from the gas pedal (engine changing from pulling to coasting). This sound is often confused with piston slap and/or loose piston pins. Experience is needed to tell the sounds apart, but the difference can sometimes be verified by listening with a stethoscope at the cylinder head and crankcase areas. Loose rods often sound loudest at the crankcase, and piston slap or loose piston pins loudest at the cylinder head. Affected cylinders can often be isolated by shorting out the spark plug. This tends to lessen or eliminate the sound. In the end, these sounds require that the engine be taken apart and carefully inspected to determine the actual problem. See also sound(knocking-9), and car service tip(cylinder knock test).

sound(knocking-8) - Momentary sound produced by an engine when it is first started. It is usually due to bearings without sufficient oil pressure. Possible causes include: excess bearing wear, filter without a built-in check valve, and oil changed and empty oil filter installed (oil must fill filter before bearings receive oil).

sound(knocking-9) - Intermittent sound produced by one or more loose piston pins. It is loudest when the engine is decelerating. See also car service tip(cylinder knock test).

sound(knocking-10) - Sound produced by a faulty AIR or PAIR system.

sound(knocking-11) - Sound produced by an engine when it is accelerated or when it is decelerated from a high speed. It is typical of a connecting rod in danger of separating from a piston. If you suspect a bad rod, drive the car gently home, then plan on engine repair work.

sound(knocking-12) - Sound produced when an engine is idling or accelerated. It is due one or more exhaust system parts too close to other metal parts.

sound(knocking-13) - Sound produced when an engine is accelerated hard or run at high speed. It is due to valve float and can cause serious engine damage.

sound(knocking-14) - Momentary sound produced when a warm engine is restarted after 15-30 minutes. It is usually caused by preignition due to fuel flowing into intake manifold during brief shutdown due to heat soak. The temporary rich fuel condition coupled with the hot engine cylinder metal creates the condition.

sound(knocking-15) - Sound produced by a broken drive axle. Car will lose all drive power unless it is equipped with a limited slip differential. Possible causes include: overloading car, bad driving habits such as popping the clutch at high rpm, and wheel bearing or housing out of alignment.

sound(knocking-16) - Sound produced by a fan out of alignment hitting components near it when rotating.

sound(metallic) - Sharp sound created by a loose differential ring gear when changing from reverse to a forward transmission gear.

sound(muffled bell) - Sound created when there is excessive clearance between the piston and the cylinder wall. It is most prominent when an engine is cold.

sound(noisy distributor) - Abnormal sound(s) produced by a distributor. Possible causes include: worn distributor shaft bushing, missing or stuck centrifugal weights, loose breaker plate, rotor and cap contact, and reluctor and pickup coil contact.

sound(noisy front end) - Abnormal sound(s) produced in a car's front suspension or steering system when it is being driven. An indication is the noise does not seem to be related to engine rpm. Possible causes include: loose or worn steering gear, shock absorbers, spring shackles, stabilizer bushings, steering linkage joints, and control arm bushings; loose steering gear box and tie strut bushings; and lack of lubrication in ball joints.

Possible causes in power steering equipped cars include the previous as well as the following: fluid low and/or mixed with air, improperly attached pressure hoses, and loose drive belt.

sound(noisy timing chain cover) – Abnormal sound(s) produced in the timing chain cover area. Possible causes include: loose timing chain, faulty chain tensioner, and loose camshaft gear.

sound(noisy valve train) – Abnormal sound(s) produced in the valve train area. Possible causes include: faulty spring, rocker arm, lifter, and push rod.

sound(popping-1) – Short light explosive sound produced through a carburetor when an engine is cranked and valves are out of time with pistons. Possible causes include: camshaft and timing chain or belt reassembled wrong, and loose timing chain or belt that has jumped teeth on camshaft and/or crankshaft sprockets.

sound(popping-2) – Sound produced in an exhaust system due to afterburn.

sound(popping-3) – Sound produced when an engine misfires.

sound(rattling-1) – Succession of sharp short sounds produced in a clutch and transmission area due to loose, broken, worn, or damaged parts. Possible causes include: worn hub or shaft splines, pressure plate pivot points, release bearing, pilot bearing, transmission bearings, transmission parts, and driveline; loose clutch plate hub; loose or broken clutch plate springs; out of alignment clutch pressure plate release levers, clutch housing, and clutch assembly; and bent input transmission shaft.

sound(rattling-2) – Sound produced by a defective sway bar link. The link is either missing or the rubber bushings at each link end are torn, cracked, or distorted.

sound(rattling-3) – Sound produced in the front end of a car by a front sway bar with loose joints or joint fittings. It is usually more noticeable when the road surface is rougher.

sound(rattling-4) – Sound produced when one or more connecting rods are loose or about to separate from a piston. It occurs under idle as well as load conditions. Pressure lubricated engines will usually use excessive amounts of oil before the rods ever become this noisy. It indicates the cap screws have somehow gotten loose. The engine will have to be taken apart promptly to determine the actual cause. See also sound(knocking-11).

sound(rattling-5) – Rapid metallic jingling type sound produced when the engine is under load or accelerated hard. It is caused by detonation.

sound(rattling-6) – Sound produced in certain recent manual transmissions due to engine vibration. It is usually louder at idle, and more pronounced with four cylinder engines. Disengaging the clutch will usually stop the noise. It is caused by certain transmission parts rattling from the engine vibration. It is usually harmless.

sound(rattling-7) – Sound produced in an engine compartment at different speeds. Possible causes include: faulty thermostatic vacuum switch, broken or disconnected brackets, loose air cleaner, and timing chain. See also sound(banging-3).

sound(rattling-8) – Sound produced by unused front disc brakes that disappears when the brakes are applied. The sound increases on rough road surfaces. Possible causes include: sticking caliper piston(s), caliper assembly not centering, worn disc pads, worn or damaged pad retainers, and improper mating between caliper piston and pad backing plate.

sound(rattling-9) – Sound produced when an engine is idling or accelerated. It is due to one or more exhaust system parts too close to other metal parts.

sound(rattling-10) – Sound produced by a wheel with loose lug nuts.

sound(rattling-11) – Sound produced by one or more small rocks inside a hubcap.

sound(roaring-1) – Throaty sound produced that seems to fluctuate in loudness with engine speed. It is usually caused by a hole in a muffler or exhaust pipe system, or a worn out or loose gasket at an exhaust pipe or manifold connection. A sudden throaty sound can also be caused from an actual break in the exhaust pipe system.

sound(roaring-2) – Sound produced by certain automatic transmissions that increases in volume with speed usually starting at 30 or more mph. Possible causes include: low fluid level causing clutch problems, and converter vibration.

sound(roaring-3) – Sound produced when an electric or clutch equipped fan starts operating.

sound(rubbing) – Sound produced by a starter motor when cranking. It is due to a loose pole shoe dragging against a turning armature.

sound(rumbling-1) – Common sound produced when an exhaust system has a leak in the muffler, at a joint, the exhaust manifold, etc.

sound(rumbling-2) – Sound produced when an air conditioner is operating. It is usually due to too much refrigerant in the system.

sound(rumbling-3) – Sound produced in a high compression engine due to bending or flexing of a crankshaft. It is caused by high pressure rise rates when a piston approaches top dead center, and when the mixture burns.

sound(rumbling-4) - Sound produced by a faulty AIR or PAIR system.

sound(run up) - Sound produced when a car is accelerated, sometimes at a certain engine rpm or car speed. Possible abnormal causes include: loose or worn fan belt, and/or timing belt; faulty engine accessory and/or support bracket; loose sheet metal such as air cleaner parts, pinging; and bad connecting rod.

sound(scraping/dragging) - Sound produced when something under a car has broken loose and is dragging on the ground. Mufflers, exhaust pipes, drivelines, and sticks are most common. If it's the driveline, you will notice that racing the engine does not move the car, but makes an awful dragging scrapping racket under the car. See also driveline safety loop and road situation tip(driveline fails).

sound(screech) - Harsh high-pitched sound produced every time brakes are applied. It is usually caused when brake linings, worn away to the metal backing plates, contact the braking surfaces. Linings in this condition need to be replaced immediately and rotors and drum checked to see if they need resurfacing.

sound(slapping) - Dull, sharp sound produced by a piston with excessive clearance between itself and the cylinder wall due to wear. It is most noticeable when an engine is cold and idling. Such an engine usually burns oil, is not safe to drive, and needs to be rebuilt.

sound(squeaking-1) - Sharp high pitched sound produced in the suspension and/or steering system sounding like rusty springs. It commonly occurs when suspension and/or steering parts dry out and need lubrication.

sound(squeaking-2) - Sound produced in a clutch area during engine and/or clutch operation. Possible causes include: lack of lubrication in clutch release bearing, pilot bearing, release bearing retainer, and pressure plate pivot points; and out of alignment clutch housing and/or clutch assembly.

sound(squeaking-3) - Sound produced in a car's driveline area during acceleration or deceleration. It is often due to worn or binding universal joints on the driveline. To check remove the driveline. If a joint is loose or doesn't pivot freely, it should be replaced.

sound(squeaking-4) - Intermittent sound produced in a front brake area. Applying brakes and/or turning wheel will stop sound for awhile. Possible causes include: warped rotor due to overheating, and/or overtightening of lug nuts; warped wheel due to overtightened lug nuts; and interference between wheel and caliper assembly, dust cover and disc, and caliper and disc.

sound(squealing-1) - High pitched shrill sound commonly produced when wet brakes shoes are applied. It disappears shortly when the brakes dry out. It commonly happens when driving through water deep enough to soak the brake drums.

sound(squealing-2) - Sound produced by a faulty AIR or PAIR system.

sound(squealing-3) - Intermittent sound produced by glazed brake linings. It can also be caused by brake pads if: backing plates rub against the disc piston, lining material is cheap, rotor surface is not smooth, and/or rotor is slightly warped. Applying a high temperature grease or gasket compound to brake pad backing plates often helps.

sound(squealing-4) - Loud sound produced everytime the brakes are applied. It is usually due to worn out brake linings which should be immediately replaced to minimize damage to the braking surfaces.

sound(squealing-5) - Intermittent sound produced in the engine area by a loose or worn fan belt. When the car lights are turned on, the belt will usually squeal worse due to increased slippage. Possible causes include: loose or worn belt, wrong type belt with angle not matching pulley angle, and overloaded belt due to too many accessories.

sound(squealing-6) - Prolonged sound produced when brakes are applied. Possible causes include: grease soaked linings, glazed linings, linings worn down to metal mounting surface, spring steel wear sensors contacting braking surface due to worn pads or shoes, brake component(s) improperly installed, brake drum and shoe diameters different, and pads vibrating (front disc).

sound(sucking) - Sound produced in an engine compartment from a vacuum leak.

sound(swishing) - A sharp hissing sound produced when a steering wheel is turned. Possible causes include: faulty power steering pump, steering shaft coupling contacting steering column surface, and horn brush contacting ring terminal behind steering wheel.

sound(tapping-1) - Repetitive muffled tapping or clicking sound quieted down by insulation, other components, etc., and varying with engine rpm. Sticking valve lifters commonly emit this type sound, which at idle may only be one click per second. Sticking lifters are usually caused by dirty oil. An oil change and addition of a top cylinder lubricant will often cure the problem after driving 50 miles or so.

sound tapping-2) - Sound produced by one or more valve lifters with excessive tappet bore clearances. It is often caused by oil not adequately lubricating the lifter due to excess heat and bubbles in the oil. Cooling the oil down with an oil cooler, oil pan baffle, etc. will often eliminate the problem.

Also make sure the proper oil is being used. A heavier oil will quiet even worn lifters somewhat.

sound(tapping-3) - Sharp repetitive tapping sound produced in an engine compartment and varying with engine rpm. If the engine is idling roughly or unevenly, one of the spark plugs may be grounding out. What frequently happens is that in wet weather moisture gets on the spark plug's outside insulator causing the spark to jump to the base of the spark plug rather than the electrodes inside. The problem is cured by drying the affected plug and cap area. Also, a disconnected spark plug wire will produce the same result. The remedy in this case is simple, just reconnect the wire.

sound(tapping-4) - Sound produced near the top front portion of the engine due to a broken rocker arm return spring in a mechanical fuel pump. It is loudest when idling due to low fuel consumption.

sound(ticking-1) - A light clicking tapping sound produced in an engine's combustion chambers due to trace detonation.

sound(ticking-2) - Sound produced when a starter relay closes and the battery is almost dead.

sound(thumping-1) - Dull heavy pounding sound produced by loose or worn shock absorber bushing. It is most noticeable when driving over a rough bumpy road at slow speed. Affected shock absorber can often be located by bouncing each corner of a car and listening for a thump.

sound(thumping-2) - Sound produced by an axle with excessive end-play when cornering or driving on a rough road.

sound(thumping-3) - Sound produced by a broken or rough differential side gear when cornering.

sound(thumping-4) - Sound produced by a cold tire with a flat spot, a flat tire, or a tire with a loose belt.

sound(thunking) - Abrupt muffled sound (like an axe blade striking a tree trunk) produced when shifting into gear. Possible causes include: worn CV joint(s) on front wheel drive car, and worn U-joints on rear wheel drive car.

sound(torque sensitive) - Sound produced by a car when load is applied to an engine. Possible abnormal causes include: differential or transaxle worn or low on fluid, worn or damaged U-joint or CV joint, etc.

sound(whining-1) - High pitched sound produced in an automatic transmission low on fluid. It can also exhibit this sound when the fluid gets worn out due to carrying heavy loads. Low fluid is one of the most common causes of automatic transmission malfunction.

sound(whining-2) - Quiet constant sound produced only when a car is moving. It increases with speed, and is usually an indication of a worn wheel bearing and needs immediate attention.

sound(whining-3) - Loud sound produced at higher speeds when slowing down or coasting. It usually indicates trouble with differential gears such as: out of adjustment pinion gear, and/or scored gear teeth due to excessive pinion bearing end-play. Running low on fluid in the rear end can cause this to happen.

sound(whining-4) - Sound produced by a rear end when car is traveling at speeds higher speeds (over 40 mph) until pressure is let off the gas pedal. Possible causes include: worn rear axle bearing(s), and ring and pinion gear set. Whining sound increasing and decreasing with speed usually points to a worn ring and pinion gear set. Worn parts must be replaced to eliminate whine.

sound(whining-5) - Sound produced in an automatic or manual transmission by gears worn or installed outside of allowable specifications.

sound(whistling-1) - Clear shrill sound produced in an engine compartment from a vacuum leak. It usually varies with engine speed.

sound(whistling-2) - Sound produced when an automatic transmission downshifts. It is usually due to a noisy planetary gear set caused by worn, roughly finished, or damaged gears.

sound(whistling/rumbling) - High clear shrill sound produced and followed by an intermittent rumbling sound from the front of a car when it is slowed down at the end of a long trip. It is usually caused by overheating due to very low coolant level, or by a broken fan belt. If you are low on water, pull over and stop the car for at least 30-45 minutes with the hood up. Add more water before starting the engine back up.

sound(whooshing) - Sound produced around car windows not adequately sealed against rubber gasket.

sound deadening material - Substance applied to a surface for absorbing vibrations and insulating against noise.

soup - See moxie.

soup box - Power robbing transmission.

souped up - To have increased an engine's performance. See also full house.

South Bend - American car produced in 1914 and 1919.

Southern - American car produced in 1906 and 1909.

Southern Six - American car produced from 1921-1922 by Southern Automobile Manufacturing Co. in Tennessee. It was a well built car.

Southern stocker - See Carolina stocker.
south pole - Magnetic pole receiving magnetic lines of force from a north pole.
Sovereign - American car produced from 1906-1907 by Matthews Motor Co. in New Jersey.
SP - Abbreviation for sport.
space buck - See seating buck.
spacer - Sheet of material mounted between two surfaces to adjust clearance.
spacer washer - Washer built to perform the function of a spacer.
Spacke - See Brook-Spacke.
spaghetti - Too much chrome on a car.
spanner - See spanner wrench.
spanner wrench - Wrench used to tighten or loosen round nuts.
spare - Extra tire carried in a car.
spare parts - Extra parts.
spare tire - See spare.
spare tire in a can - Spray can filled under pressure with sealant material and used to inflate a flat tire. The sealant material is injected into a tire through a valve stem. It flows into any small leak and seals it. The can contains enough pressure to fill most tires to about 25 lbs pressure. It is considered a temporary repair.
spare tire sealer - See spare tire in a can.
spark - Electrical discharge created between two separated points in an electric circuit. When electric voltage is great enough, the resistance of the open air gap is overcome and electricity flows in the form of a spark. The voltage required to produce a spark at a spark plug gap depends on: air/fuel mixture, compression pressure, gap width, and engine rpm. Voltage requirements are highest when an engine is at low rpm and being moderately accelerated (momentary lean mixture).
spark advance - See advance(ignition).
spark advance vacuum modulator - Vacuum operated valve used to control the type of vacuum reaching the vacuum advance unit under different engine conditions such as steady speed, accelerating, decelerating, and idling. It usually monitors both spark ported vacuum and manifold vacuum. When both vacuums add up to more than a certain value (usually 6-8 inches), spark ported vacuum is routed to the vacuum advance unit. When both vacuums are less, manifold vacuum is routed. The modulator functions like a dual diaphragm distributor. It is mounted with appropriate hosing between the vacuum advance unit and the two vacuum sources.
spark control computer - See on-board computer.
spark controls - Any controls used to regulate when a spark plug receives its spark.
spark curve - Graph used to show spark advance versus engine rpm. See also advance curve.
spark delay valve - Device used to control emissions by temporarily delaying vacuum (usually 15-20 seconds) to the vacuum advance unit under different engine conditions such as steady speed, accelerating, decelerating, and idling. It is mounted in the line between the vacuum advance unit and the vacuum source (usually just above the throttle plate). The valve delays vacuum by means of a tiny orifice. Faulty operation can lead to such engine problems as: stumbling, pinging, rough idling, poor fuel economy, hesitation when accelerating, hard starting, and power loss. See also OSAC valve, NOx valve, and spark ported vacuum.
spark duration - Time elapsed maintaining a spark across a spark plug's electrodes. Conventional point systems maintain a spark 6 times as long as CD ignition systems. Short spark duration can cause rough idling on engines burning lean air/fuel mixtures. Ignition systems with short durations get around the problem by allowing a variable duration depending on engine conditions. See also rise time.
spark gap - See spark plug gap.
spark knock - See detonation.
spark plug - Device used to conduct high voltage electricity between two separated electrodes to ignite a fuel mixture. A normal spark plug consists primarily of: a threaded mounting base, a porcelain insulated nickel alloy center electrode, and a side electrode welded to the base.
spark plug(booster) - See spark plug(series gap).
spark plug(booster gap) - See spark plug(series gap).
spark plug(centerfire) - Spark plug with one center electrode and several side electrodes mounted around the base of the plug. Benefits claimed include: more than one spark, less prone to fouling, and more complete fuel combustion.
spark plug(copper core) - Spark plug constructed with a longer insulator nose and a center electrode containing copper core. The longer nose reduces fouling at low speeds, and the copper electrode dissipates heat better at high speeds. A copper core plug runs hotter at low speeds and cooler at

highway speeds than a normal spark plug. It is designed to better resist fouling and overheating in today's car engines which run cooler at low speeds and hotter at high speeds. It is a good choice for cars driven short distances that are prone to plug fouling.

spark plug(cold) - Spark plug constructed with a low heat range. A short insulator tip is used for quickly transferring heat to the cylinder head. It is very efficient in high heat and temperature conditions like those encountered in freeway driving or racing. Small engines running hot commonly use them. They tend to foul in engines driven short distances. See also spark plug(hot), spark plug heat range, and gas volume.

spark plug(cut back) - Spark plug built similar to a J-gap plug except that the side electrode tip is cut back farther until a gap between it and the center electrode appears when viewed on end. The spark tends to flow across the air gap at angle rather than sideways (retracted gap) or vertically standard gap). The design allows the side electrode to be lowered in height while still allowing a projected nose to be used.

spark plug(hot) - Spark plug constructed with a high heat range. A long insulator tip is used to retain heat longer, and burn off deposits accumulated from short stop and go driving. It is used for city driving, and cars prone to oil fouling. Hot plugs can cause preignition at highway speeds due to higher combustion chamber temperatures. See also spark plug(cold), spark plug heat range, and gas volume.

spark plug(J gap) - Spark plug built like a standard plug except for the side electrode end covering only half of the center electrode tip when viewed on end. Advantages of this plug include: less voltage required to fire due to sharp edge of side electrode, better higher rpm firing, and less prone to grounding out due to flying carbon particles. It is popular with performance and racing cars.

spark plug(multiple gap) - Spark plug built similar to a surface gap plug except the opening is segmented like a cut pie into two or more separate side electrodes. Advantages include: works well in aircraft engines which tend to run at constant rpm, and resistant to gap growth. Disadvantages include: tends to foul in car engines because the restricted insulator tip exposure prevents it from getting hot enough during low speed driving to burn off accumulating deposits, and insulator tip deposits are difficult to completely remove.

spark plug(platinum) - Spark plug built with a platinum center electrode. The insulator is usually also raised. Benefits claimed include: lower spark voltage needed, wider plug heat range, improved starting, minimal missing on acceleration, and relatively maintenance-free.

spark plug(projected nose) - Spark plug built with its firing tip projecting beyond the bottom edge of the spark plug. It allows the plug to run hot enough at low speed to avoid fouling, and cool enough at high speed to avoid preignition. At low speed, the tip maintains a higher temperature by being more directly exposed to the flame front in the combustion chamber. At high speed, the tip stays cooler due to the cool incoming fuel charge. Advantages include: greater heat range than standard plugs, fuel mixture more efficiently burned, and resistance to low speed fouling. Disadvantages include: use restricted in some engines due to extra tip length, and tends to advance timing due to quicker flame front formation (may require 1-4 degrees retard on standard plug engines). Where space is not a problem, it will perform about as well as a platinum plug and is considerably less expensive.

spark plug(push wire) - See spark plug(retracted gap).

spark plug(resistor) - Spark plug built with a resistor in the center electrode. It is designed to reduce: TV and radio interference, electrode erosion, current flow, and capacitive and inductive phases of a spark. Typical resistance will vary from 5-10,000 ohms. A faulty plug will show resistance that is infinite or varies as the plug is shaken.

spark plug(retracted gap) - Spark plug built with the side electrode mounted perpendicular to the center electrode. It is usually fitted as a pin in a hole drilled through the threaded portion of the spark plug shell. It is designed to be a very cold racing plug used only in engines running at high rpm. It is very prone to fouling at lower rpm making it totally unsuitable in a car doing city driving.

spark plug(series gap) - Spark plug built with an extra air gap inside the ceramic insulator midway between both ends of the center electrode. It is designed to keep firing, despite a build-up of semiconductive deposits on the plug's firing tip, by allowing high voltage to build up before it jumps the first gap and then the second. It is a somewhat more expensive plug, but can help in certain situations where plugs are prone to fouling.

spark plug(surface gap) - Spark plug built with its firing end covered by a metal plate except for a small hole in the middle where the center electrode is located. A small fixed circular air gap exists around the circumference of the electrode. The plug fires across the gap where there is the least resistance. Advantages include: more stable voltage requirement under high

pressure than a standard plug.
spark plug(tapered seat) - Spark plug built with a tapered seat on the shell base where the threads meet. It eliminates the need for a compressible gasket. Proper spark plug torque is important to avoid seat damage.
spark plug appearance - Visual appearance of a spark plug in the firing tip area. It is a good indicator of internal engine conditions. See also spark plug deposit.
spark plug appearance(aluminum throw off) - Firing tip area covered with varying amounts of once molten aluminum. Possible causes include: preignition due to spark plug being too hot or wrong reach, excessive ignition advance, and low octane fuel. See also preignition.
spark plug appearance(bent electrode) - Side electrode bent into a semi-question mark shape when viewed from the side. Possible causes include: side electrode deformed by using pliers or similar type gapping tool to adjust air gap.
spark plug appearance(black carbon deposit) - Dry fluffy black carbon deposits cover firing tip area. Too much fuel is reaching the spark plug. If all plugs have this appearance, it indicates: high float level, internal carburetor leak, faulty accelerator pump circuit dumping continuous stream of fuel into airway, choke sticking closed or adjusted to stay closed too much, clogged air filter, excessive short distance driving, low secondary voltage, and/or a too cold plug. If only one plug has this appearance, the spark plug wire may be bad which will cause the fuel entering the cylinder to remain mostly unburned. Possible engine symptoms include: misfiring and poor idling.
spark plug appearance(black oily deposit) - Too much oil is getting to a combustion chamber. It is usually caused by excess clearance between a piston and a cylinder wall due to engine wear. The piston rings wear as well and are not able to keep oil on a cylinder wall from building up. The only remedy in this case is to rebuild the engine. If an isolated cylinder shows this condition, the affected cylinder's piston may have broken piston rings or perhaps a leaky valve stem seal. Other possible causes include: leaking oil bath air cleaner, spark plug too cold, clogged crankcase ventilation tube, and faulty PCV system. Possible engine symptoms include: misfiring and rough idling. A booster gap plug will resist fouling in an oil rich environment.
spark plug appearance(black sooty deposit) - See spark plug appearance(black carbon deposit).
spark plug appearance(black specks) - Small pin-point size black specks deposited on the ceramic material around the center electrode. It is indicative of detonation. See also exhaust(black smoke puffs).
spark plug appearance(broken side electrode) - Side electrode has snapped off with carbon coating the surrounding surfaces. There is no obvious indication of overheating. Possible causes include: detonation due to overheated combustion chamber carbon deposits or sharp metal projections.
spark plug appearance(burned electrodes) - Electrodes are burned away with insulator nose tip melted and deformed. Possible causes include: preignition due to excessive spark advance, low octane fuel, and/or spark plug too hot.
spark plug appearance(core bridging) - Deposits have built up between insulator nose and interior spark plug shell surface. Possible causes include: excessive build-up of carbon, repeated long idling followed by rapid acceleration, poor grade of oil, and excess oil reaching combustion chamber.
spark plug appearance(cracked insulator) - Ignition timing is incorrect. See also spark plug appearance(mechanical damage).
spark plug appearance(dished side electrodes) - On standard plugs, the underside of the side electrode wears into a concave shape. It is due to reversed coil polarity caused when the primary terminal leads on the coil are reversed.
spark plug appearance(gap bridging) - Deposits become lodged between center and side electrodes. Possible causes include: excessive carbon build-up in cylinders, small gap, excess oil reaching combustion chamber, and long idling period followed by heavy acceleration.
spark plug appearance(glazed deposits) - Electrode and insulator nose covered with hard glassy conductive coating, usually brown in color. Possible causes include: hard acceleration after extended idling or low speed driving. It can be avoided by slowly accelerating engine after such driving.
spark plug appearance(reddish brown color deposit) - See spark plug appearance(light blue green deposit).
spark plug appearance(light blue green deposit) - A clean looking plug with the colored coating deposited on the ceramic material. It is usually due to excess water reaching the combustion chamber.
spark plug appearance(light brown dry deposit) - Normal combustion is taking place with a proper air/fuel mixture and no excessive oil consumption. It is an indication of an engine in good operating condition.
spark plug appearance(mechanical damage) - Firing tip area components are

damaged such as bent electrode, fractured insulator ceramic, and displaced center electrode. Possible causes include: plug reach wrong causing collision with piston head and/or valve, excessive valve opening, loose or wrong size piston, and wrong size head gasket.

spark plug appearance(normal deposits) - Light tan, brown, or gray deposits found lightly covering insulator tip. It indicates a spark plug of the proper heat range operating in a mechanically sound engine with proper fuel mixture metering.

spark plug appearance(silica deposits) - Hard conductive deposits cover side electrode and/or insulator tip area. Possible causes include: unfiltered air entering intake system bringing in dirt, sand, and other airborne contaminants. Leakage could be due to: ruptured air filter, poor seal around air filter, cracked or missing vacuum hose, and bad intake manifold gaskets.

spark plug appearance(splashed deposits) - Insulator nose covered with dark splotches. Possible causes include: existing combustion chamber deposits are being removed and splashed onto nose due to recent tune up.

spark plug appearance(white blistered end) - Engine is running too hot or a spark plug's heat range is too high causing it to get too hot. If the plug gets too hot, the end of the electrodes burn. If the plug's heat range is okay, then the excess engine heat can be due to poor engine cooling, excessive ignition advance timing, or use of low octane fuel which is pre-igniting.

spark plug appearance(white crusty deposit) - Combustion is normal. Color is due to certain fuels compounded to change the nature of spark plug deposits so they don't adhere and build up thereby lessening spark plug misfiring. It can also be due to slow driving habits causing deposit build-up.

spark plug appearance(wide gap) - Air gap between electrodes larger than specifications. Possible causes include: wrong gap set, electrode wear due to long plug running time, excessive high voltage due to minimal secondary circuit resistance, and high combustion chamber pressure and temperature.

spark plug appearance(worn components) - Spark plug firing tip end shows signs of extensive wear such as rounded electrodes, thinner electrodes, pitted or chipped insulator nose. Possible causes include: spark plugs in use for extended period of time. Worn spark plugs should be replaced. See also spark plug life.

spark plug appearance(yellow crusty deposit) - See spark plug appearance(white deposit).

spark plug blowout - Condition created when a spark plug is not seated properly causing the high combustion chamber temperatures and pressures to leak out eating a hole in the spark plug shell in the process. Also, it refers to a spark plug, loosely installed, that works its way out of the hole until pressure sends it out like a projectile.

spark plug cable - Insulated electric wire used to transfer high voltage current from an ignition system's distributor to a spark plug. See also high voltage cable.

spark plug cable(carbon impregnated) - High voltage plug wire built with carbon particles in the core of the insulator jacket.

spark plug cable(carbon string) - See spark plug cable(resistor type).

spark plug cable(inductor) - See spark plug cable(Mag wire).

spark plug cable(magnetic suppression) - See spark plug cable(Mag wire).

spark plug cable(Mag wire) - High voltage spark plug wire built to use magnetic inductance to suppress static. It consists of fine solid copper wire wound around a flexible magnetic core. The advantages include: solid metal conductor, low resistance, no resistance increase with cable flexing, and low static interference (minimal TV and radio interference) due to core inductance. Resistance averages 150-1,000 ohms per foot.

spark plug cable(metallic core) - See spark plug cable(solid conductor).

spark plug cable(metallic resistance) - See spark plug cable(Mag-wire).

spark plug cable(resistor) - High voltage spark plug wire used to suppress radio and TV interference through resistance in the core. The conductor consists of a material like rayon, linen, or polyester thread that is impregnated with graphite. The disadvantage of this conductor is the likelihood of resistance increasing every time the cable is flexed. Original resistance is 4,000 ohms per foot.

spark plug cable(solid conductor) - High voltage spark plug wire built with a copper core. It transmits current with the least loss, but creates the greatest amount of static. It is the most reliable wire to use.

spark plug deposit - Substance bonded onto the various surfaces located in the firing tip area of a spark plug. See also spark plug appearance, and car service tip(spark plug deposit removal).

spark plug electrode - Conductive lead on a spark plug used in conjunction with another electrode for transferring a spark. The ends of the two electrodes are separated by a small air gap.

spark plug electrode(center) - Metal electrode positioned running down the center of a spark plug. It transfers high voltage current from a spark plug

wire to a spark gap located at the end of the electrode.
spark plug electrode(ground) - See spark plug electrode(side).
spark plug electrode(side) - L-shaped metal electrode mounted on the bottom of
a spark plug shell. Its end serves as the other side of a spark gap, and the
ground for a high voltage circuit. The electrode can be bent to adjust the
spark gap.
spark plug electrode erosion - Condition created when a spark plug's electrode
surfaces become rounded and farther apart from long usage or high spark plug
temperature. The heat range should be checked to make sure it is proper for
the type of driving.
spark plug firing cup - Threaded spark plug extender used to make plugs run
hot and resist fouling from oil. It is sometimes used in engines burning oil
until the engine can be rebuilt. It is shaped like a cup with threads at the
base. A spark plug screws into the cup and the cup screws into a spark plug
hole just like a spark plug.
spark plug fouling - Condition created when a spark plug no longer produces a
spark at the firing end because the area has become coated with carbon, oil,
fuel, and/or and other combustion products. The products create a path of
lower resistance to ground than across the spark plug gap. A fouled plug
must usually be removed and cleaned. An exception is plugs fouled by
flooding an engine. In this case, the plugs are left to dry a few minutes
from the residual heat in the engine cylinders. The engine is then restarted
with the throttle wide open to increase airflow to the plugs for further
drying.
 General causes of plug fouling include: excess oil, weak and/or
intermittent spark, rich or lean fuel mixture, wrong plug heat range, certain
fuel additives, and low engine compression. Excess oil causes include:
faulty PCV valve, worn pistons, piston rings, cylinder walls, and/or valve
stem guides. Weak spark causes include: low primary voltage, faulty ignition
coil, excess resistance in high voltage cable(s), high resistance in coil
ballast resistor, and/or wide plug gap. Intermittent spark causes include:
faulty black box, cracked distributor cap, cracked rotor, ignition coil
sensitive to heat, and point float at high rpm. Rich fuel mixture causes
include: high float level, excess fuel pressure, internal carburetor leak,
air restriction, and choke plate not opening fully. Lean fuel mixture causes
include: clogged fuel pickup filter, clogged fuel filter, fuel line
obstruction, low float level, and/or low fuel pressure. See also spark plug
voltage.
spark plug fouling(carbon) - Spark plug fouls due to carbon build-up from
running at low speeds or from an overly-rich air/fuel mixture. Engine
symptoms include: misfiring and rough idling.
spark plug fouling(gas) - Spark plug fouls due to excessive gasoline reaching
plug. It most commonly occurs in large high horsepower engines using
carburetors. Possible causes include: excess fuel pressure, high float
level, faulty accelerator pump circuit, idle circuit adjusted rich, EGR not
operating, spark plugs too cold, rich fuel mixture, internal carburetor leak,
and fuel foaming.
spark plug fouling(ignition related) - Spark plug fouls due to weak,
inconsistent, or non-existent high voltage reaching spark plug tip. Possible
causes include: excessive resistance in spark plug wire and/or ignition coil
wire, arcing in distributor, crossed wires, faulty rotor, faulty ignition
coil, bad ballast resistor, and faulty point mechanism.
spark plug fouling(oil and carbon) - Spark plug fouls due to excess oil
reaching the combustion chamber. Engine symptoms include: misfiring and
rough idling. Possible causes include: worn piston, piston rings, and
cylinder wall; broken piston rings; leaking valve stem guide seals; and PCV
system routing too much oil vapor into air cleaner.
spark plug fouling(tetraethyl lead) - Spark plug fouls due to lead compounds
in fuel. The deposited compounds become conductive at higher temperatures.
Engine symptoms include: adequate low speed idling, but missing under full
load or high combustion chamber temperatures.
spark plug gap - Open space located between a spark plug's two electrodes. It
determines the characteristics of an electrical spark jumping across the
electrodes. It is usually set with a thickness gauge. Today's spark plugs
use gaps ranging from .030-.065 inches. Factors affecting gap width include:
combustion chamber shape, fuel characteristics, compression ratio, and
ignition system components. Gap width gradually increases (averages .001 per
1-2,000 miles of driving) as a spark plug is used and is due to: miles used,
fuel characteristics, combustion chamber temperatures, high voltage capacity
of ignition system, and action of electric spark moving across the
electrodes. Wide gaps can make starting easier, but also shorten plug life,
erode electrodes faster, and cause misfiring under load. Small gaps can
cause rough idling and increased fouling tendency.
spark plug gapper - Tool used to set the air gap between a spark plug's center
and side electrode to a specified thickness. See also feeler gauge.

spark plug gapping – Adjustment made to the air gap between spark plug electrodes by moving the side electrode. It also usually refers to filing the electrode surfaces flat.

spark plug gasket – Metal gasket located at the spark plug seat and used to prevent combustion chamber pressure leaks.

spark plug heat flow path – Various areas of a spark plug where a portion of combustion chamber heat is dissipated. It is not evenly dissipated with a substantial portion being dissipated by the gasket and threaded portion.

spark plug heat range – Temperature maintained at a spark plug firing end. Plugs are made to operate at different temperatures to suit different combustion chamber conditions. Factors affecting heat range include: porcelain insulator length/thickness, gas volume, insulator composition, air/fuel ratio, compression ratio, combustion chamber design, combustion chamber temperature (400-3000 degree Fahrenheit range), cylinder heat dissipation, emission controls, turbocharger or supercharger boost, backpressure, and fuel characteristics.
A plug with the proper heat range will stay just hot enough to burn the wet fuel mixture off the center electrode and insulator tip, keeping carbon deposits from accumulating on its firing end. If the heat range is too high (tip stays hotter than 1600-1750 degrees), the spark plug tip stays hot enough to ignite the next fuel charge entering the combustion chamber causing preignition with resultant pinging. Also, rapid deterioration of electrodes and porcelain insulation may occur. If the heat range is too low (tip stays colder than 700 degrees), deposits are: not burned off, begin accumulating, and eventually become a lower resistance ground for high voltage electricity than the air gap. The end result is a spark plug that no longer fires.
A general rule of thumb is: cold engines need hot plugs and hot engines need cold plugs. A cold engine is one used mostly for city driving where warming up, taking short trips, and doing lots of idling is the norm. It is hard on plugs because the combustion chamber temperatures don't get hot enough. A hot engine is one used mostly for highway driving where combustion chamber temperatures get and stay hot. See also spark plug(cold), spark plug(hot), and spark plug fouling.

spark plug insulator – White ceramic material used to surround and insulate a spark plug's center electrode.

spark plug insulator seal – Seal located between the insulator tip base and the inside surface of the spark plug shell threaded portion.

spark plug insulator tip – Ceramic material surrounding the center electrode near its firing tip. The material needs to maintain a temperature above 700 degrees Fahrenheit to avoid plug fouling and below 1600 degrees to avoid preignition. See also spark plug heat range.

spark plug intensifier – Device usually mounted on top of a spark plug to improve its firing ability. It simply adds an electrical resistance or air gap to the spark plug making it operate like a booster gap spark plug. It is often advertised as a mileage improver, but only serves to make plugs less prone to fouling.

spark plug life – Number of miles a spark plug will operate satisfactorily. Under normal driving conditions today, a spark plug will last 15-30,000 miles before replacement is necessary. Cleaning, filing, and regapping the electrodes during that time can extend the plug life.

spark plug nose – The exposed lower insulator portion of a spark plug housed inside the spark plug shell.

spark plug numbers – Number and/or letter sequence used to specify the various design aspects of a spark plug, including its heat range, gap arrangement, thread size, reach, booster gap use, internal resistor use, firing tip construction, and side electrode configuration. American companies tend to use low and high numbers for cold and hot plugs respectively, while foreign companies use the opposite.

spark plug reach – Length used to form a spark plug shell's threaded portion. Correct reach is important. If the reach is too long, the electrodes may protrude into a combustion chamber far enough to strike a piston head or valve. If the reach is too short, the plug may not protrude far enough into the combustion chamber to properly fire the air/fuel mixture causing rough engine idling or misfiring.

spark plug resistor – Resistor built into a spark plug to help suppress static.

spark plug sandblaster – Small sandblasting device used to clean spark plug tip deposits by spraying the area with sand particles at high speed. It is usually a small self-contained unit.

spark plug scavenging area – Open space located between the insulator tip and the threaded body wall of a spark plug. Deposits build up in this area according to the plug's heat range and driving habits.

spark plug scope – An oscilloscope or other device setup to visually display spark plug voltages.

spark plug seat – Flat area located at the spark plug shell's base where the threads begin. It is used to provide a pressure tight seal. A gasket may or may not be used. See also spark plug(tapered seat).

spark plug shell - Outer metal portion of a spark plug.

spark plug side electrode - Electrode used to provide a ground for high voltage current. It is attached to the spark plug shell and positioned so its tip is located close to the center electrode with an intervening air gap. High voltage current, traveling down the center electrode, jumps the air gap to the side electrode which is grounded. The thickness and composition of the side electrode affect how prone it is to causing engine preignition. If it is thin or the metal composition slows heat conduction away from the area, the electrode will tend to overheat and become an ignition point for a fuel mixture before the plug actually fires.

spark plug terminal(1) - One of several terminals located on a distributor cap where high voltage is transferred to a spark plug cable. It consists of a molded plastic tower on top of a distributor cap and a metal conductor protruding inside a distributor cap. See also center tower terminal and firing point.

spark plug terminal(2) - Electric terminal end of a spark plug used to connect a spark plug wire. It consists of a threaded stud that may or may not use a threaded cap, depending on the type of spark plug wire used.

spark plug terminal stud - See spark plug electrode(center).

spark plug tower - See spark plug terminal.

spark plug voltage - Voltage required to jump a spark plug's air gap. Voltage requirements increase when: gap width increases, sharp edge of both electrodes become rounded, deposits build-up on tip, electrodes overheat, fuel mixture is lean (lower gas conductivity between electrodes), combustion chamber pressure is high, air temperature is low, and car is accelerated. Plug misfiring most often occurs under acceleration due to one or more of the following factors: rounded electrodes, increased gap, decreased coil voltage output with speed, and increased voltage requirements in acceleration mode. Plugs misfiring under acceleration will tend to run smoothly when the gas pedal is backed off due to decreased voltage requirements.

In general, spark plug voltage requirements double at high speed, and triple under hard acceleration.

Under normal driving conditions, a gap width range of .010-.060 inches requires a respective voltage range of 2,000-12,000 volts to jump the gap.

spark plug wire - See spark plug cable.

spark plug wires are crossed - See crossed spark plug wires.

spark port - Small hole located in a carburetor airway immediately above or below the throttle plate near the idle port, and used to transfer vacuum to a distributor's vacuum advance unit. A spark port located below the throttle generates full vacuum when the throttle is closed. The vacuum drops off rapidly as the throttle is opened. A spark port located above the throttle plate generates no vacuum at idle, high vacuum when the throttle slightly opens, and low vacuum when more fully open. Some carburetor designs also use an additional spark port located in the venturi area. See also spark valve and vacuum spark controls.

spark ported vacuum - Intake manifold vacuum source used to control a vacuum advance unit on a distributor by creating a low vacuum when throttle plate is closed and a higher vacuum when open, just the opposite of intake manifold vacuum. The highest value is reached at full throttle. The port is located just above the throttle plate. See also spark delay valve and vacuum spark controls.

spark retard controller - Device used to retard ignition timing when detonation begins occurring.

spark valve - Valve mounted on a carburetor body and used to control the vacuum advance of a distributor by controlling vacuum coming from spark ports located at the throttle valve and venturi. When intake manifold vacuum is high, the valve stays open and maintains the vacuum advance portion of a spark advance. When vacuum drops, such as under acceleration or full load, the vacuum advance is retarded. The venturi opening prevents the circuit from causing excessive spark retard. At high speed, the valve is closed and the venturi opening maintains a high vacuum advance. See also spark port and vacuum spark controls.

spark voltage - See spark plug voltage.

Spartan - American car produced in 1907 and 1911.

spastic - Person who falls prey to double-dipping.

Spaulding - American car produced from 1902-1903 and 1910-1916 by Spaulding Motor & Auto Co. in New York, and Spaulding Mfg. Co. in Iowa respectively.

spd - Abbreviation for speed.

SPD - Abbreviation for speedster.

SP DLX - Abbreviation for special deluxe.

Sp Dlx - Abbreviation for special deluxe.

speaker - Device used to convert electric current to sound waves or amplifying sound to a desired level. Examples include: radio speakers, door buzzer, and

horn.
SPEC – Abbreviation for special. See also Spl.
Special – American car produced in 1906. Also, an American car produced 1962-1980 by Buick Division of General Motors Corp. in Michigan.
special interest car – Car generally classified as built after 1935 and valued according to styling, performance, features, etc. See also brass era car, vintage car, antique car, contemporary car, milestone car, classic car, contemporary classic car, pre-war car, and post-war car.
Specialty – American car produced in 1898.
specialty mechanic – See job(specialty mechanic).
specific gravity – Ratio expressed as the density of a substance divided by the density of water.
spec – See specification.
specification – Detailed description made of parts of a whole unit covering such details as: size, shape, weight, quantity, construction method, material, assembly method, torque requirements, performance, quality, etc.
speed – See speeding.
Speedatron – American line of performance automotive products.
speed cheating – See speeding.
speed clock – One of two or more clocking devices used to measure elapsed time and determine speed from one point to another. Cars racing a 1/4 mile will finish by driving through a trap fitted with speed clocks at both ends to record speed.
speed control system – Assemblage of components used to regulate car speed by controlling a throttle. In general, a speed control system is engaged by accelerating a car to a desired speed, then activating a speed control switch. It is disengaged by braking to a slower speed or turning the speed control switch off.
speed cup – Circular device used in a speedometer assembly to display car speed. The cup contains an attached speed pointer that deflects according to the rotational speed of a magnetic field.
speed handle – Socket wrench handle shaped like a carpenter's brace and used to quickly turn a socket wrench.
speeding – To drive a car faster than a posted speed limit.
speed limit – Maximum speed allowed on a road. It is usually posted along a roadside at regular intervals.
speedo – Abbreviation for speedometer.
speedometer – Instrument used to determine and display the speed of a car by measuring transmission output shaft rotation. The speed is indicated in miles per hour or kilometers per hour. The primary components include: a dial, speed pointer, speed pointer hair spring, odometer, trip odometer, field plate, speed cup, magnet and shaft, housing, and cable. The speedometer works by rotating a permanent magnet near a speed cup. As the magnet rotates, it creates a rotating magnetic field that deflects the speed cup according to rpm. The deflection is indicated by the speed pointer and dial.
speedometer cable – Flexible cable assembly used to transfer rotation from a transmission or a front wheel to a speedometer. It consists of: a protective jacket, internal metal cable, and fittings at both cable ends.
speedometer calibration – Procedure followed for mechanically balancing a magnet shaft's torque with a speed pointer hair spring at three different points on a speedometer scale.
speedometer problem – Condition created when a speedometer is not operating properly. Most problems pertain to a speed pointer not operating properly, or a malfunctioning odometer. The speed pointer may move erratically, not return to zero, and/or read too low or too high. The odometer may not operate at all or display incorrect mileage. Possible speed pointer problems include: kinked speedometer cable; worn magnet shaft bearings; excessive end play in magnet shaft; dirt or grease in magnet-speed cup area; rusted or damaged to speed cup; improperly positioned field plate, a weak, broken, binding, or out of adjustment hair spring; and unbalanced speed pointer. Possible odometer problems include: stripped gearing in odometer assembly and wrong tire size.
speed pointer – Movable needle in a speedometer used to indicate car speed.
speed shift – To shift gears rapidly without letting off on the accelerator.
speed shop – Business engaged in selling performance automotive equipment such as high rise intake manifolds, high lift cam kits, high cfm carburetors, special pistons, ignition systems, racing clutch components, etc.
speed switch – Electrical switch designed to close when a certain speed is exceeded. It usually senses speed by speedometer cable or driveline rotation speed. See also solenoid vacuum valve.
speed transducer – Device used in a speed control system to sense when a car is traveling faster or slower than a speed control setting, and make the necessary adjustments to a throttle to return a car to the desired speed. See also power unit.

speed trap – Stretch of road used by police to carefully check traffic speeds and strictly enforce traffic laws. Tactics used include: hidden police cars, radar, using chase cars or motorcycles, setting up just inside reduced speed zones, setting up where speed violations are common, and citing offenders only slightly exceeding a speed limit.

speed tuning – Minor modifications made to ignition and fuel delivery systems to improve performance.

speed-up solenoid – Solenoid operated plunger used to slightly open a throttle plate when an engine load such as an air conditioner is turned on. It helps to prevent stalling. See also idle stop solenoid.

Speedwagon – American car produced in 1918.

Speedway – American car produced from 1904-1905 by Gas Engine & Power Co. in New York.

speedway – See race track.

Speedway Special – American car produced in 1918.

Speedwell – American car produced from 1907-1914 by Speedwell Motor Car Co. in Ohio.

Spencer – American car produced in 1914. Also, an American car produced from 1921-1922 by Research Engineering Co. in Ohio.

Spencer Steamer – American steam vehicle produced in 1862 and 1901.

Spenny – American car produced from 1914-1915 by Spenny Motor Car Co. in Illinois.

Sperling – American car produced from 1921-1923 by Associated Motors Corp. in Indiana.

Sperry – American car produced in 1901.

Sphinx – American car produced from 1914-1915 by Sphinx Motor Car Co. in Pennsylvania.

Spicer – American car produced in 1903.

spider – X-shaped fitting built with bearing caps on each end to permit rotation about each shaft. It forms the core of a universal joint.

spider gear – See gear(spider).

spiderwebbing – See cobwebbing.

spiff – Tax-free cash bonus paid to a car salesman.

Spiller – American car produced in 1900.

Spillman – American car produced in 1907.

spin balance – See tire balancer(dynamic) and balance(dynamic).

spindle – Shaft or pin used to carry a rotating part. Each front wheel of a car is mounted on a spindle.

spindle bolt – Long bolt used in front suspension systems to attach a wheel spindle to a front axle. The wheel pivots on the spindle bolt.

spindle shaft – See wheel spindle.

spinner – Custom hubcap.

spin on filter – Filter built with a threaded hole for screwing onto a base. Today's oil filters are installed this way.

spin out – Driving condition created when a car skids on all four wheels and swings out of control spinning one or more turns before coming to a halt.

spin the tires – See burning out.

spiral bevel gear – See gear(sprial bevel).

Spirit – American car produced from 1979 to date by American Motors Corp. in Michigan.

Spirit of America J-47 Jet – American car driven by Craig Breedlove to a world land speed record in 1963 and 1964 at Bonneville, Utah. Speeds were 407.5 and 526.3 mph.

Spirit of America Sonic 1 – American car driven by Craig Breedlove to a 1965 world land speed record of 600.6 mph at Bonneville, Utah.

spkr – Abbreviation for speaker.

Spl – Abbreviation for special. See also SPEC.

splash blending – Cost cutting maneuver performed by some unscrupulous gas companies where a one tank truck partially fills a service station tank with good gasoline, and another truck later tops off the tank with alcohol or a cheaper more highly volatile gas. Often, the first truck will make a delivery in the daytime with the second truck stopping by at night.

spline(1) – Straight stick or board built with various widths and thicknesses ranging from a 1-12 feet in length. It is used to help find high or low spots on the surface of a model.

spline(2) – Groove or slot cut into a shaft and parallel to its centerline. Shafts commonly have many splines cut around their circumference for transmitting shaft rotation to gears sliding along the splines.

splined mainshaft – Main input/output transmission shaft splined along different portions of its length for gears to slide. Gears on the main shaft typically slide to mesh with different non-sliding gears on a lower countershaft to produce the different gear ratios.

spline joint – Two parts splined around their surface to join together and prevent rotation but allow longitudinal movement. Such a joint is used on the transmission end of a driveline.

splines – Grooves cut into shafts or holes parallel to their centerlines. They keep parts rotating together. Splined shafts are common on cars. They include the transmission input and output shafts, and the rear axle shafts. Clutch discs have splined holes that mesh with the splines on a transmission input shaft.

split manifold – Exhaust manifold partitioned near its outlet for routing gases to two separate exhaust pipes.

split system master cylinder – See brake dual master cylinder.

splitter – Small lever mounted near the top of a shift stick and used to engage an overdrive.

splitting a shift – To change gear ratios by shifting an auxiliary transmission before shifting a main transmission.

split windshield – Windshield built using two separate pieces of glass separated by a center support post. Some windshields were split horizontally with the upper half able to tilt outward for improved ventilation. Both types were used in earlier cars.

Spoerer – American car produced from 1907-1914 by Carl Spoerer's Sons Co. in Maryland.

spoiler – Air deflector used on racing cars to control lift tendencies. Street cars employ them below the front grille and on the rear deck or trunk area. Rear spoilers are more cosmetic while the front spoiler can help keep a car grounded at higher speeds.

spokes – Wire wheels.

spongy pedal – Brake pedal condition created when it does not feel firm but gives as it is applied. It is usually due to air in the brake fluid. The remedy is bleeding the brake system. On older designs and older brake fluids, this effect can be caused by a vapor lock in the brake system.

spook(1) – Spoiler.

spook(2) – Car leaving a starting line too soon.

spooking – Driving with no particular destination in mind.

spool valve – Valve used in certain power steering units to control fluid flow in the unit's valve body.

spoon – Tool used to remove dents in car body panels. It consists of a handle with a broad flat or curved surface. The surface spreads the blow of a striking hammer. The spoon is placed between the dent and the hammer. Different types include: flat, elbow, and straight.

spoon brake – Early brake used on hard rubber tires. It was a curved metal plate looking much like the brake shoes of today. The brake would slow the car by contacting the tire and creating friction.

Sport – American car produced in 1921.

sports car – Low profile car built with two seats and a high performance engine. Other characteristics often include: quick acceleration, highly maneuverable, good roadability, tight steering system, and stiff suspension.

Sportsman – American car produced by Cord from 1965-1966.

sportster – Car with sports car-like features.

Sport Wagon – American car produced from 1961-1972 by Buick Division of General Motors Corp. in Michigan.

spot disc brake – See brake(disc).

spotlight – Light built to generate a strong focused light beam.

spot putty – See glazing compound.

spot welding – Welding process defined as joining a small spot of two metal surfaces together by fusing the spot with electric current. A spot weld is typically around 1/4 to 1/2 inch in diameter. Spot welds are commonly used to join metals together where warping is a problem. It minimizes heat going into metals being joined.

Spracke – American car produced in 1921.

Sprague – American car produced in 1896.

sprague clutch – See clutch(sprague).

spray gun – Handheld device used to mix liquid paint with air and discharge the mixture in atomized form. It consists of: a paint cup, and paint head assembly.

spray gun(combination) – Spray gun built to incorporate two or more features of other spray guns. For example, some guns have internal and external mix capabilities as well as pressure or siphon feed.

spray gun(external mix) – Spray gun built to atomize paint and air outside an air cap. It is the most common spray gun used for painting cars. It is the only really suitable gun for spraying fast drying paint such as lacquer.

spray gun(gravity feed) – Spray gun built with an overhead paint cup for moving paint to the paint head by means of gravity.

spray gun(internal mix) – Spray gun built to atomize paint and air inside an air cap. It works well for slow drying paints and consumes less air than an external mix gun.

spray gun(pressure feed) – Spray gun built to move paint from a paint cup to the paint head by applying air pressure into the top of the cup.

spray gun(suction feed) – Spray gun built to move paint from a paint cup to a paint head by a partial vacuum. The vacuum is created by a stream of compressed air moving at right angles to an opening, creating a pressure drop that allows atmospheric pressure to move paint.

spray gun(touch up) – Smaller spray gun built to paint small repair areas or do custom painting. It is somewhat larger than an airbrush and is usually an external-mix siphon-feed type.

spray mask – Transparent water-soluble spray formulated to dry to a rubber-like film and be removable. It is used to create different trick painting effects.

spray nozzle – See injector nozzle.

spread – See margin of profit.

spreading the bead – Process defined as compressing the circumference of a tire in order to force the bead surfaces of a tire against a wheel's rims. Today's shops use compressed air to quickly force the tire beads against the wheel rims. See also breaking the bead.

spring – Elastic device built to yield when pressure is applied and return to its original shape when pressure is removed. Springs come in many sizes and shapes. They can expand, contract, and bend. Springs are usually made of spring steel.

spring(anti rattle) – Spring clip used in disc brake calipers to hold brake pads in a specified position. See also brake pad retainer.

spring(Bendix) – Heavy spring mounted at the end of a starter drive shaft and used to absorb the impact of flywheel and starter engagement.

spring(bimetallic) – Spring composed of two different metals coiled to wind and unwind as temperature changes. Winding effect is created from the two metals having different expansion and contraction rates. It is commonly used in automatic chokes and electric relays.

spring(coil) – Heavy spring steel rod shaped in a spiral and used to provide support between a car body and a wheel. Some cars have coil springs supporting all wheels, while others support only front or rear wheels. Coil springs, in front suspension systems, are installed between the upper and lower control arms on some cars, and or on top of upper control arm in others.

spring(compression) – Spiral spring built with its coils in an expanded position. Compression springs are used as suspension coil springs, valve springs, etc.

spring(diaphragm) – Large flat plate shaped spring with radial fingers. It is commonly found in clutch pressure plates.

spring(expansion) – Spiral spring built with its coils in a compressed position. Expansion springs are commonly used in linkages for returning shafts, arms, etc. to their original positions.

spring(helical) – Spring formed in the shape of a spiral. They are used for intake and exhaust valve springs, and independent wheel suspension. See also spring(expansion) and spring(compression).

spring(helper) – Leaf spring attached to one half of a car's existing leaf spring to provide additional load capacity and lift.

spring(leaf) – Spring built in the shape of a long flat curved bar with a rectangular cross section. A leaf spring is one method of providing support and cushioning between a wheel axle and a car body. A series of leaves are commonly stacked on top each other to provide the necessary load capacity for supporting a car's sprung weight at the affected wheel. Leaf springs are most commonly found on rear axles, one for each wheel. The leaves are held in place by attaching them at three points: the front and back to the car frame, and the middle to the wheel axle. See also front hanger and rear shackle.

spring(pedal return) – Expansion spring used to return a clutch, brake, or parking brake pedal to its original position.

spring(piston pin) – See wrist pin retainer.

spring(semi elliptic) – See spring(leaf).

spring(suspension) – Spring located near one of a car's wheels. Suspension springs allow a car to encounter significant road irregularities without severely jarring the chassis or passengers. Shock absorbers are used to dampen their up/down movement.

spring(torsional) – Compression springs used to soften abrupt changes in rotation of components. A common use is on clutch plates where several small springs are mounted to smooth plate rotation changes during shifting.

spring booster – Device used to strengthen sagged springs or to increase the load capacity of standard springs.

spring compressor – Tool used to compress helical compression springs. It is used to remove valve springs from valve stems, coil springs from MacPherson strut assemblies, etc.

Springer – American car produced from 1904-1906 by Springer Motor Vehicle Co. in New York.

Springfield – American car produced in 1900, 1904, and 1907. Also, an American car produced from 1908-1911 by Springfield Motor Car Co. in

Illinois.

spring hammering - Process defined as lightly and repeatedly hammering a spoon on a metal surface to restore its contour.

springing cookies - Car maneuver performed by breaking rear wheel traction and spinning the rear end in circles. Large circles are left on the road surface either as tire marks on pavement or ruts on non-paved roads.

spring loaded - Object held in position by one or more springs.

spring steel - Type of steel built with enough elasticity to withstand a great deal of bending and return back to its original shape.

Sprint - Chevrolet car imported by General Motors from Suzuki Motors Company Ltd.

sprinter - See mag wheel.

Sprite - American car produced in 1914.

Sprite - Low priced British sports car.

sprt - Abbreviation for sport.

sprung weight - Weight of all car parts supported by a suspension system. Supported parts include: car frame, body, and power train. See also unsprung weight.

Spyder - Alpha Romeo car.

spud - Tool constructed over 2 feet long with a flat steel chisel edge, and used for heavy digging or removal of clay on a car model.

spud-in connection - Connection made by drilling, cutting, etc. an opening. For example, a hole drilled into a pipe where another pipe is inserted.

spur gear - See gear(spur).

spurt hole - Hole located in a connecting rod and its bearing to permit pressurized oil to be sprayed onto a cylinder wall for additional lubrication.

squad car - See patrol car.

square engine - See engine(square).

square hit - Car body area struck at a 90 degree impact angle or head on.

sq ft - Abbreviation for square feet.

sq in - Abbreviation for square inch.

squeal the tires - See burning out.

Squier Steam - American steam car produced in 1899.

squirrel - Driver known for racing an engine and burning rubber.

squish - Swirling of an air/fuel mixture created in a combustion chamber when a piston reaches the top of its compression stroke. Squish moves the air/fuel mixture past the spark plug to help the flame front move quickly throughout the chamber. Good squish helps reduce detonation tendency. See also quench.

springing the valve - To install a spring on a valve. It also refers to the process of selecting the right kind of valve spring to use.

SS(1) - Abbreviation used on some spark plug cables to specify their use on a cool running engine. See also SE.

SS(2) - Abbreviation for super sport.

ss - Abbreviation for stick shift.

SSE - American car produced from 1916-1917 by SSE Co. in Pennsylvania.

SSI - Abbreviation for solid state ignition.

ST - Abbreviation for standard (manual) transmission. See also AT.

stabbing the brakes - To hit the brakes sharply but briefly one or more times depending on the reason.

stab braking - Emergency braking method used to quickly slow a car down without losing traction. The brake pedal is rapidly pumped with a series of sharp brief stamps.

stabilizer - Large shock absorber.

stabilizer bar - See anti-sway bar.

stabilizer link - See anti-sway link.

stack - Short intake or exhaust pipe.

stack fire - See carburetor fire.

stacks - Custom exhaust system.

Stafford - American car produced from 1910-1915 by Stafford Motor Car Co. in Kansas and Missouri.

stage - To lineup race cars properly at the starting line.

staging area - Race track area located between the pit area and the starting line. It is where cars are placed in their respective groups just prior to a race.

Stahl - American car produced in 1910.

stainless steel - Steel alloyed with four or more percent chromium to prevent rusting and increase resistance to corrosion.

stale gasoline - Gasoline stored in a tank too long.

stalk - Slender shaft. It usually refers to a turn signal, windshield wiper, or other steering wheel mounted shaft.

stall - See equipment bay.

stalled car - Car unable to move due to problems such as flat tire, flooded engine, no gas, etc.

stalled engine – Engine dies and/or cannot be started due to problems such as: flooding, no gas, overheating, and faulty low voltage wire inside distributor.

stalling – To come to a rest or stop.

stall test – Electric test made to determine if a starting motor's voltage and current readings at a specified resistance match a manufacturer's specifications. It is done by preventing an armature from turning, applying battery voltage to a starter motor circuit through a variable resistor at its highest setting, and then adjusting the resistance until a manufacturer's voltage and current readings are obtained. See also no-load test, armature and field open circuit test, and armature and field grounded circuit test.

stamping – Process defined as using dies to cut and shape a piece of sheet metal.

standard – Car built with a wheelbase over 119 inches.

Standard – American car produced from 1903-1907, 1909-1910, and 1912-1923 by Standard Motor Construction Co. in Kansas and Missouri (1903-1907), St. Louis Motor Car Co. in Missouri (1909-1910), Standard Engineering Co. in Illinois (1914), and Standard Steel Car Co. in Pennsylvania (1912-1923). Also, an American car produced from 1960-1972 by Ford Motor Co. in Michigan.

Standard Electric – American electric car produced from 1912-1915 by Standard Electric Car Co. in Michigan. It reportedly had a top speed of 20 mph and a 110 mile range per charge.

Standard Electrique – American electric car produced in 1903.

standard of quality – Level of quality specified for a part, service work, etc.

Standard Oil Company – A U.S. petroleum company headquartered in Cleveland, Ohio. See also petroleum company.

Standard Oil Company of California – See Chevron Corporation.

Standard Oil of Indiana – See AMOCO Corporation.

Standard Six – American car produced from 1910-1911.

Standard Steam Car – American steam car produced from 1920-1921 by Standard Engineering in Missouri. It reportedly could build up a head of steam in less than one minute.

Standard Steamer – American steam car produced in 1900.

standard thread – Thread pitch measured in english units of threads per inch.

standard transmission – See transmission(manual).

stand bail – To provide bail for a person in jail accused of an offense.

standing kilometer – Method used to time a car for average speed in a kilometer distance by starting from rest at the starting point. It is used for making acceleration runs. See also flying kilometer.

standing mile – Method used to time a car for average speed in a mile distance by starting from rest at the starting point. It is used for making acceleration runs. See also flying mile.

standing 1/4 mile – Same as a standing mile except for a 1/4 mile distance. It is a popular drag racing distance as race tracks.

Standish – American car produced from 1924-1925 by Luxor Cab Mfg. Co. in Massachusetts.

stand on it – To drive a car at full throttle.

Stanhope – American car produced in 1903 and 1905.

Stanley – American steam car produced from 1897-1927 by Stanley Dry Plate Co. (1897-1899), Stanley Mfg. Co. (1899-1901), Stanley Motor Carriage Co. (1901-1924), and Steam Vehicle Corp. (1924-1927), all in Massachusetts. It was a very popular steam car in America. Also, an American car produced from 1907-1909 by Stanley Automobile Mfg. Co. in Indiana (1907), and Troy Automobile & Buggy Co. in (1908-1910).

Stanley Brothers – They were twin brothers, Freelan and Francis, who organized the Stanley Motor Company in the 1890s, and ran it until retiring in 1917. They both designed the Stanley Steamer, producing the first model in 1897. In 1906, they built a racing steam powered car that set a world's record of 127.66 mph.

Stanley Steamer – American steam car produced from 1897-1924.

Stanley Steam Rocket – Car driven by Fred Marriot to a 1906 world land speed record of 121.6 mph at Daytona, Florida.

Stanley-Whitney – American car produced from 1899-1902.

Stanmobile – American car produced in 1901.

Stanton-Steam – American car produced in 1910.

Stanwood – American car produced from 1920-1922 by Stanwood Motor Car Co. in Missouri.

Star – American car produced from 1903-1904, 1908, 1914, and 1917. Also, an American produced from 1922-1928 by Durant Motor Co. in New Jersey, Michigan, and California.

Starbird, Daryl – Car customizer known for producing futuristic cars.

Starbuck – American car produced in 1914.

Starchief – American car produced from 1955 to date by Pontiac Division of General Motors Corp. in Michigan.

Starfire – American car produced from 1965-1980 by Oldsmobile Division of
General Motors Corp. in Michigan. Also, an American car produced from 1965-
1976 by Pontiac Division of General Motors Corp. in Michigan.
Star-Fleet Truck – American truck produced in 1927.
Starin – American car produced from 1903-1904 by Starin Co. in New York.
starter – See starting motor.
starter drive – Device attached to a starter for rotates an engine for
starting. There are several methods used. In general, the rotation of the
starting motor activates a starter drive attached to the end of the motor
shaft. The rotation pushes a drive pinion gear outward to meet a flywheel
ring gear. When the two make contact, the engine begins rotating. When the
starter is disengaged, the drive pinion gear retracts away from the flywheel
gear. See also Bendix drive and overrunning clutch.
starter drive(barrel) – Starter drive built with a barrel and drive pinion
assembly that moves toward a starter to engage a flywheel ring gear when it
is rotating.
starter drive(Bendix) – Starter drive built to provide an automatic means of
engaging a drive pinion gear with a flywheel gear for rotating an engine, and
an automatic means of disengaging it when an engine starts. It consists of a
drive head, drive spring, and pinion and shaft assembly.
    It was almost universally used years ago. Advantages include: no solenoid
required to engage starter drive reducing current flow somewhat, economical
to build and service, and compact size. Primary disadvantage is: the drive
is prone to breaking in large high horsepower engines.
starter drive(foot operated) – Starter drive built to engage starter pinion by
depressing a starter pedal mounted on the floorboard on the driver's side.
The pedal mechanically moved the starter pinion into position. It was the
original positive engagement type starter drive.
starter drive(friction clutch) – Starter drive built with a clutching
mechanism composed of a series of spring-loaded clutch plates. The plates
allow momentary slippage when a drive pinion gear engages a flywheel ring
gear. It is used in certain heavy duty cranking applications.
starter drive(inboard) – Starter drive built with a drive pinion gear moving
toward a starter motor when engaging a flywheel ring gear.
starter drive(inertia) – See starter drive(Bendix).
starter drive(movable pole shoe) – Positive engagement type starter drive
built without a separate solenoid. Current flows through one of the field
coils attracting a movable pole shoe into its core. The pole shoe is
attached to the starter drive and pivots it into engagement. When the pole
is seated, current flows through the rest of the field windings spinning the
starter.
starter drive(overrunning clutch) – See starter drive(positive action).
starter drive(positive action) – Starter drive built with a drive pinion gear
moving into a flywheel gear by means of a pivoting lever. The lever is
usually moved by a solenoid mounted on top of a starter. Starter over-
speeding is prevented by mounting an overrunning clutch on the drive.
    This drive is commonly used on most cars today. Primary advantage is
reduced starter motor bearing load due to extra bearing mounted at end of
drive shaft. Primary disadvantage is increased current requirement due to
solenoid.
starter drive(positive engagement) – See starter drive(positive action).
starter drive(self engaging) – See starter drive(Bendix).
starter motor – See starting motor.
starter relay – See solenoid switch.
starter pedal – Pedal used in older cars to activate a starter. When the
pedal is depressed, a heavy duty switch is closed sending current from a
battery to a starter, and a drive pinion gear is also meshed with a flywheel
ring gear. The pedal is mounted on the floor in the driver's area.
starter switch – See solenoid switch.
starting circuit – Electrical circuit used in a car to activate a starter
motor.
starting figure – See list price.
starting motor – Electric motor designed to rotate an internal combustion
engine at rpms sufficient to permit starting. The parts typically consist
of: the motor housing, armature and commutator assembly, brushes, field
coils, starter drive, support bearings or bushings, electrical terminals, and
starter-mounted solenoid and shift lever.
    Starters typically draw from 100-500 amps at 12 volts depending on outside
temperature, design, and engine size.
starting point – See list price.
starting problem – Condition created when an engine cannot be started or
starts with difficulty. The problem lies in the starter motor, the starting
circuit, the ignition system, or the fuel system. In general, if an engine
turns over adequately, is receiving fuel, and getting spark, it has to start.
Eliminating the motor as a problem requires careful diagnosis and possible

motor testing. The starter motor can usually be eliminated as the problem if motor testing shows: a manufacturer's specifications for current flow and rpm are met at a certain specified voltage and resistance. See no-load test, stall test, armature and field grounded circuit test, and armature and field open circuit test.

starting problem(engine cranks but won't start) – Starting problem created when a starter turns an engine over fast enough, but it won't run. This is usually not a starter motor or starting system problem. It is usually due to lack of fuel or no spark. An engine firing spark plugs, and receiving fuel and air has to run unless there are major problems. Fuel problems can include: broken or leaking fuel lines, defective fuel pump, plugged carburetor jets, stuck needle valve, empty fuel tank, vapor lock, and flooded engine. Spark problems can include: grounded or loose coil wire; fouled spark plugs; defective ignition coil; no current to ignition coil's primary windings; defective condenser; distributor points grounded, not separating, or remaining open; excessive current draw when starter engaged, and faulty black box. Air problems include: restricted air intake.

starting problem(engine cranks slowly) – Starting problem created when an engine turns too slowly to easily start. In this case, the starter is partially functional, but something is still wrong. Possible causes include: a discharged or defective battery; excessive electrical resistance in the starter, starter relay, or wiring leading to a starter; loose pole shoe in starter dragging against turning armature; corroded battery terminals; oil viscosity too high; excessive engine friction due to wrong oil, low oil level, plugged oil passageways, pressure relief valve stuck open, or ethylene glycol leaking into oil; ignition timing too advanced; overheated engine causing tight clearances between certain moving parts; cylinder wall hot spots developing after engine is run hot causing piston skirt and cylinder wall friction to remain high; starter too hot due to excess cranking or engine compartment temperature; and excessive carbon build-up causing preignition. See also car service tip(starting system test), and car service tip(starter draw test).

starting problem(starter won't operate) – Starting problem created when turning ignition switch to start position causes no starter response. Possible causes include: dead or weak battery; break in starting circuit wiring; corroded terminal(s) on battery, and/or starter relay; faulty starter solenoid or starter relay; faulty ignition switch, field or armature windings grounded in starter, and faulty neutral safety switch on automatic transmission equipped cars. See also car service tip(electrical connections), car service tip(starting system test), and engine problem(won't start).

starting problem(starter won't disengage) – Starting problem created when a starter engages and rotates an engine, but is not able to disengage a drive pinion gear from a flywheel ring gear. Possible causes include: malfunctioning starter relay or solenoid, sticking solenoid plunger, broken solenoid spring, broken starter drive spring, sticking screwshaft, and malfunctioning ignition switch.

starting problem(starter won't engage) – Starting problem created when a starter spins, but does not engage a flywheel ring gear to rotate an engine. Possible causes include: drive pinion gear teeth stripped, flywheel ring gear teeth broken in places, and malfunctioning starter drive. Often the flywheel ring gear teeth wear down in places causing "flat spots" where a drive pinion gear engages, but there are no teeth to mesh with. In this case, turning a flywheel a little will provide an undamaged ring gear section and allow a starter to operate.

star wheel – Adjusting wheel mounted on a brake adjuster (star wheel adjuster) and used to lengthen or shorten the gap between brake shoes at one end.

star wheel adjuster – Brake shoe gap adjuster. It consists of: a threaded rod with one end containing a gear wheel and brake shoe slot, and a threaded tube with a slotted end. The rod screws into the tube to move the slotted ends closer or farther apart adjusting for brake clearance. Some are designed to be self-adjusting. When the gear teeth wear or break, the adjuster can stop working and cause the brakes to go out of adjustment. See also brake adjuster.

state licensing board – State agency authorized to license various businesses to operate. Writing to these agencies is often an effective tool for threatening an uncooperative repair shop into settling a dispute with you. The possible loss of a business license is a serious matter for a business. State licensing boards need to know what businesses to scrutinize.

Statement of Transfer – See Notice of Transfer.

States – American car produced from 1915-1919 by States Cyclecar Co. (1915-1916), and States Motor Car Co. (1917-1919), both in Michigan.

Static – American car produced in 1923.

static balance – See balance(static).

static electricity – Stationary electrical charges created by friction.

Lightening is an example of static electricity.
static imbalance – See static unbalance.
static shield – Plastic cover placed over the distributor point assembly inside the distributor cap to protect points from high voltage current, and to cut down on radio interference from condenser wire.
static timing – Ignition timing of an engine made with the engine shut off. A simple test light operating at car voltage is used. See also car service tip(static timing) and basic timing.
static pressure – Pressure created in brake lines when a brake pedal is released. A check valve maintains the pressure.
static unbalance – Tire condition created when the mass of a tire and wheel assembly is not evenly distributed around its circumference, but lies within a plane of rotation swept out by the tire width. It causes a back and forth vibration making a tire hop. Tires can also have a dynamic unbalance as well. See also dynamic unbalance and unbalanced tire.
station wagon – See body style(station wagon).
stator(alternator) – Windings of wire located in an alternator to generate voltage. The stator is mounted around the inside edge of an alternator housing. It consists of three separate sets of windings. They are connected to each other at one end. The other end of each winding is connected to two diodes, one positive and one negative. The alternating current generated in each winding passes through appropriate rectifiers or diodes to transform it into DC current.
stator(transmission) – Vaned ring used in a torque converter to direct oil from a driven member back to a driving member. A stator helps prevent fluid leaving torque converter from flowing backward and retarding impeller movement.
stator assembly – Assemblage of parts used to form an alternator's generator windings. It consists of three generator windings, necessary fittings, and the outer winding retainer shell.
status location – Selling tactic used by a car salesman to impress a potential customer with the origin of a car. The customer is told it was parked at an important place or driven by an important person.
statute of limitations – Law specifying periods of time beyond which certain actions cannot be taken.
Staver – American car produced from 1907-1914 by Staver Carriage Co. in Illinois.
St Cloud – American car produced in 1921.
std – Abbreviation for standard.
std ignition – Abbreviation for standard ignition. It is the ignition system furnished with a car when it is produced.
steady state driving – Driving a car at a constant speed. Freeway driving at 55 mph is an example. In terms of constant speed, the faster a car is driven, the worse the fuel economy. The primary reason is air drag which increases with the square of the car's speed.
steal – To get a car or other item for much less than expected.
steam cleaning the engine – To clean the outer surfaces of an engine with steam.
steam engine – See engine(Rankine cycle).
Steamobile – American steam car produced from 1900-1902 by Keene Automobile Co. in New Hampshire.
Steam Vehicle – American car produced from 1900-1903.
Stearns – American car produced from 1899-1930 by F.B. Stearns Co. in Ohio.
Stearns-Electric – American electric car produced from 1900-1904.
Stearns-Knight – American car produced in 1911.
Stearns Steam Car – American steam car produced from 1900-1904 by Stearns Steam Carriage Co. in New York.
Steco – American car produced in 1914.
steel – Metal composed of iron, alloyed with small percentages of carbon, and artifically produced.
steel belt – Fabric interwoven with steel wire. Steel belts are commonly used to make durable tires. See also tire(steel belted).
steel casting – Cast iron composed of varying amounts of scrap steel.
steel cord belt – See steel belt.
Steele – American car produced in 1915.
Steele Swallow – American car produced from 1907-1908 by Steele Swallow Auto Co. in Michigan.
steep grade – Road built with a steep slope either up or down.
steering – Directing the movement of a car. Also, it refers to the gearing method used to control the turning motion of the front tires.
steering(air power) – Power steering method designed to use air instead of hydraulic fluid to reduce steering effort.
steering(drag link) – See steering box(draglink).
steering(power) – Steering method designed to use hydraulic fluid under pressure to reduce steering effort. The pressure is maintained by an engine

driven pump.
steering(rack and pinion) – See steering box(rack and pinion).
steering(recirculating ball) –See steering box(recirculating-ball).
steering(Ross) – See steering box(Ross).
steering(worm and roller) – See steering box(worm and roller).
steering(worm and sector) – See steering box(worm and sector).
steering(worm and wheel) – See steering box(worm and wheel).
steering alignment – See front end alignment.
steering arms – Short metal rods used to transfer turning motion from tie rods
  to steering knuckles, causing the front wheels to pivot. Each one is either
  bolted to or forged with a steering knuckle.
steering axis – Axis about which a front wheel turns. It is usually not
  vertical and tilts backward somewhat.
steering axis inclination – See wheel alignment angle(steering axis
  inclination).
steering balance – See front end alignment.
steering box – Housing located at the lower end of a steering column which
  contains gearing for translating steering wheel rotation into linear motion
  to turn the front wheels. The gearing is designed to achieve good handling,
  ease of use, and low friction. See also gear(rack and pinion), gear(worm and
  sector), gear(steering), and irreversibility.
steering box(drag link) – Steering controlled by a pitman arm and draglink
  assembly linked to a pivot arm on the left front wheel. The pitman arm
  attaches to the base of the steering box's cross shaft to provide relatively
  horizontal rotation as the steering wheel is turned. The draglink runs
  parallel to the car's length and connects the pitman arm to a pivot arm on
  the left front wheel. The two front wheels steer together by means of a tie
  rod connecting the two together.
steering box(rack and pinion) – Gearing method designed with the gearbox
  mounted parallel to the axle. A worm gear is mounted on the end of the
  steering wheel shaft. It meshes with a rack gear built in the center of a
  shaft. As the steering is turned the rack gear shaft moves. This design
  eliminates the need for a pitman arm and a drag link. It is popular in race
  and other small cars because of its simplicity, fast action, and good road
  feedback. It does not, however, have a high degree of irreversibility and is
  not used in large cars because of increased driving effort.
steering box(recirculating ball) – Gearing method introduced by Cadillac in
  1940. It is the most commonly used steering box today. A worm gear is
  mounted on the shaft end. A sleeve-like device called a ball nut rides on
  the worm gear like a nut threaded on a shaft. The ball nut is built with
  coarse worm like threads and has gear teeth mounted on one side that mesh
  with a sector gear on the pitman shaft. Small steel balls ride between the
  worm gear and the ball nut in the grooves to reduce friction, allow high gear
  ratio, and absorb gear loads. As the steering wheel is turned, the ball nut
  moves up or down causing the pitman shaft to rotate.
steering box(Ross) – Gearing method introduced in 1923 using a worm like
  groove meshing with a pin mounted on an arm projecting from the pitman arm.
  As the pin moved up and down the groove, the Pitman arm would move. This
  design reduced friction and wear more than other gearbox designs of the time.
steering box(worm and roller) – Gearing method designed using a rounded
  surface worm gear on the steering wheel shaft with a single tooth rounded
  gear offset mounted on one end of the pitman arm. As the worm gear rotated,
  the single tooth gear would move up or down causing the pitman arm to rotate.
  This design is still used in some cars today.
steering box(worm and sector) – Early gearing method designed using a worm
  gear mounted on the steering wheel shaft and meshing with a 1/4 circle wheel
  gear mounted on the cross shaft. Only part of a complete wheel gear's
  circumference is needed because of the restricted turning of the car's
  wheels.
steering box(worm and wheel) – Early gearing method designed using a worm gear
  mounted on the steering wheel shaft and meshing with a wheel gear mounted on
  the cross shaft.
steering column – Shaft used to connect a steering wheel with a steering gear
  box.
steering effort – Amount of effort required by a driver to turn a steering
  wheel. When checking, a driver should check for the following: binding, hard
  turning, excessive free play, noise, and inconsistent turning effort.
  Possible causes lie in one or more of the following areas: steering gear box,
  steering linkage, wheel alignment angles, and tire wear.
steering gear – See gear(steering).
steering gearbox – See steering box.
steering geometry – Various angles assumed by the components making up a front
  wheel turning arrangement. The angles include: castor, camber, and toe-in.
  Also, it refers to the related angles assumed by front wheels when a car is
  negotiating a curve.

steering idler arm – See idler arm.
steering knuckle – Inner portion of the wheel spindle attached to an upper and lower control arm via ball joints, and pivoted by the steering mechanism, causing the wheels to turn.
steering knuckle arm – Metal arm used to pivot a wheel about its steering axis. It is firmly attached to a steering knuckle at one end. The open end is attached to a tie rod end. There, it receives the side-to-side motion of a steering's draglink and tie rod assembly, and transfers it into a pivoting motion to turn a wheel.
steering linkage – Assemblage of rods, levers, arms, gears, etc. used to transmit the turning motion of a steering wheel to the front wheels for turning.
steering lock – Maximum angle front wheels can be turned from straight ahead.
steering overall ratio – Ratio expressed as steering wheel degrees turned divided by wheel degrees turned.
steering post – See steering column.
steering pull – Driving condition created when a car tends to pull or drift to one side of the road. Possible causes include: improper wheel alignment angles, wrong size tires, brake linings dragging, and different tire pressures.
steering rack – Assemblage of parts used to connect a car's two front wheels together and allow them both to be turned in either direction.
steering shaft – See steering column.
steering spindle – See wheel spindle.
steering system – Assemblage of parts used to control the direction of a car's front wheels. Parts primarily consist of: a steering wheel and column, steering box, and steering linkage between the two wheels. See also steering box.
steering system(Ackerman) – First practical steering system introduced by Rudolph Ackerman. It consisted of stationary axle with pivoting wheels at each end. Also, it refers to each wheel turned according to its turning radius.
steering the car – To guide the direction of a car when driving.
steering tiller – Bar or handle used to steer early cars.
steering wheel – Circular wheel mounted on the end of a steering shaft and rotated to transmit turning motion to a car's front wheels.
steering wheel cover – Material used to cover the outer hand grip portion of a steering wheel.
Stegeman – American car produced in 1911.
Steinhart-Jensen – American car produced in 1908.
Stein-Koenig – American car produced in 1926.
Steinmetz – American car produced in 1920.
stellite – Metal alloy composed of chrome, cobalt, and tungsten and used for exhaust valve seat inserts. It is hard, has a high melting point, and good corrosion resistance.
stencil painting – Custom painting technique used where stencils are used to produce unique designs and accents to other custom painting.
Stephens – American car produced from 1916-1924 by Moline Plow Co. (1916-1921), and Stephens Motor Car Co. (1922-1924), both in Illinois.
Step-N-Drive – American car produced in 1929.
stepped frame – Frame lowered just ahead of the rear axle bumps.
step-up jet – Jet used in a vacuum step-up carburetor circuit to control the flow of additional fuel into an engine when a throttle is wide open. See also step-up metering rod, step-up piston, and vacuum step-up.
step-up metering rod – Fuel metering rod used in conjunction with a step-up jet and step-up piston to control the flow of additional fuel into an engine under different throttle settings. The lower portion of the rod "steps" down to smaller diameters for progressively higher flow rates. See also step-up jet, step-up piston, and vacuum step-up.
step-up piston – Vacuum controlled piston assembly used in a carburetor to control the up-down movement of a step-up metering rod which regulates the flow of fuel through a step-up jet. See also step-up jet, step-up metering rod, and vacuum step-up.
step-up rod – See step-up metering rod.
Stephens – American car produced from 1916-1924.
Stephenson – American car produced in 1910.
Sterling – American car produced in 1909-1911, 1914-1923 by Elkhart Carriage & Motor Co. in Indiana (1909-1911), Sterling Motor Car Co. in Massachusetts (1914-1916), Sterling Automobile Mfg. Co. in New Jersey and Connecticut (1915-1917), and Consolidated Car Co. in Connecticut (1917-1923).
Sterling-Knight – American car produced from 1923-1925 by Sterling-Knight Motors Co. in Ohio.
Sterkenburg – American car produced in 1931.
Sternberg – American car produced in 1909.
stethoscope – Instrument used to locate different sounds in moving parts. It

magnifies the intensity of a sound when placed near its source. The
instrument is very similar to a doctor's stethoscope except for a long metal
probe attached to the end.

Stetson - American car produced in 1917.

Stevens - American car produced in 1915.

Steven-Duryea - American car produced from 1902-1927 by J. Stevens Arms & Tool
Co. (1902-1906), Stevens-Duryea Co. (1906-1923), and Stevens-Duryea Motors
(1923-1927), all in Massachusetts.

Steward Truck - American truck produced in 1912.

Stewart - American car produced in 1895 and 1915.

Stewart-Coates - American car produced in 1922.

Stewart, Jackie - He was a Scottish driver who became the Grand Prix world
champion in 1969, 1971, and 1973 driving a Matra-Ford and Tyrell-Ford (1971
and 1973). He is largely credited with starting an era of safety
consciousness in racing.

Stewart-Warner - American line of instrument gauges produced by Stewart-Warner
Corporation.

stick - Manual transmission equipped car.

sticker price - List price of a car. It is usually posted on a car's window.

Stickney Motorette - American car produced in 1914.

stick shift - Gearshift used for a manually shifted transmission. It usually
refers to a floor shift lever.

stiff - Potential customer mainly interested in looking. Also, a potential
customer who is difficult to get financing for.

stiff shift - Condition created in a manual transmission car when a clutch
does not properly disengage, causing gear grinding upon shifting from one
gear to another. Possible causes include: clutch plate installed backwards,
warped clutch plate, warped pressure plate, and binding spline shaft.

stiff suspension - Suspension system on a car modified for increased stiffness
and improved handling by using stronger springs and shock absorbers. Race
cars have stiff suspensions.

Still - Canadian car produced from 1899-1903 by Canadian Motor Syndicate in
Ontario.

stillson wrench - See pipe wrench.

Stilson - American car produced from 1907-1910 by Stilson Motor Car Co. in
Massachusetts.

Stimula - French car line produced from 1978 to date by Automobiles Stimula.

stinger - Heavy duty extendible steel tube used in a wheel lift towing system.
It is fitted with a T-bar containing a claw at each end. The assembly slides
underneath a car, the claws attach to the wheels, and the stinger is raised
off the ground by a hydraulic cylinder. See also towing system(wheel lift).

Stingray - Corvette sports car model first produced in 1965 as a coupe or open
two-seater.

Stirling engine - See engine(Stirling cycle).

Stirling Moss - He was a British race car driver who won the British Grand
Prix in a Vanwall car in 1957.

St Joe - American car produced in 1909.

St John - American car produced in 1903.

St Louis - American car produced from 1898-1907 by St. Louis Motor Carriage
Co. in Missouri. Also, an American car produced in 1922.

stock car - Car produced by a manufacturer with no subsequent modifications.
Also, it refers to a stock car, used in racing, where only minor
modifications have been allowed.

stock coil - Standard ignition coil specified for car. See also high
performance coil.

stocker - See stock car.

Stoddard-Dayton - American car produced from 1904-1913 by Stoddard Mfg. Co.
(1904-1905), Dayton Motor Car Co. (1905-1912), and U.S. Motor Co (1912-1913),
all in Ohio.

Stoddard-Knight - American car produced in 1911.

stolen car - Car stolen from its owner. The following tips will help prevent
losing the car when you leave it: remove ignition keys, roll up all windows,
lock doors and trunk, leave any valuables out of sight in trunk or under
seat, park on busy and lighted streets, remove registration papers from car,
put a paper or business card identifying yourself in one of the door jambs,
put your initials or other identifying mark in several obscure places on the
car, inscribe your name on any expensive equipment in your car, and remove
the distributor cap and/or rotor.

stolen car business - Large illegal underground industry engaged in stealing
cars to resell intact or in parts. It averages over 5 billion annually. A
car is stolen an average of once every 30 seconds with almost half never
being recovered. See also chop shop and con game(chop shop).

stolen plates - License plates removed from one car and put on another car
that is usually stolen.

stop and go traffic - Traffic characterized as repeatedly moving and stopping

due to several stop lights, stop signs, congestion, etc.
stop leak – Compound mixed with a liquid to stop small leaks by filling them from the inside. It is most commonly used in engine coolant water to plug radiator leaks.
stoplight switch – See brake light switch.
stopping distance – See braking distance.
storage charge – Daily fee charged for keeping a towed car at a repair shop facility until arrangements for releasing and/or repairing the car are made.
Storck – American car produced from 1901-1903 by Frank C. Storck in New Jersey.
store – Car dealership.
Stork Kar – American car produced from 1919-1921 by Stork Kar Sales Co. in West Virginia.
Storm – American car produced in 1954.
stormer – Hot rod.
Storms – American car produced in 1915.
Stoughton – American car produced in 1919.
Stout – American car produced in 1946.
Stout Scarab – American car produced in 1935.
stovebolt – Chevrolet car or engine. See also bent stovebolt.
STP – Abbreviation for a popular oil additive. Also, it refers to an American line of automotive products produced by STP Corporation. Products include: gas and oil additives, motor oil, oil filters, and antifreeze.
straight – Characteristic exhibited by a car frame that has not been structurally damaged. Also, a car that does not wander on the road when driven because the steering system and front end alignment are in good shape.
straightening a panel – To restore a damaged car panel to its original shape.
straightening equipment – Equipment used to straighten a damaged car body. The most common equipment is a hydraulic porta-power device.
straight weight oil – See oil(straight weight).
strap – See battery strap.
Strathmore – American car produced from 1899-1902 by Strathmore Automobile Co. in Massachusetts.
stratified charge engine – See engine(stratified charge).
Stratton – American car produced in 1901-1902, 1908-1909, and 1923.
Streater – American car produced from 1905-1915.
street – Portion of a road built for the movement of motor vehicles.
street machine – Racing car set up for normal driving on public roads.
street machining – To modify cars for increased performance outside of manufacturing or auto repair facilities.
street race – Illegal race held on a public road.
street rod – High performance car built to be legally operated on public roads.
St Regis – American car produced from 1965 to date by Dodge Division of Chrysler Corp. in Michigan.
stressed body – Car body built to transfer some of the frame loads to the outer body panels.
stretch(1) – Selling tactic used to close a car sale in which a potential customer is given incentives such as high trade-in allowance, car discount, car options, etc.
stretch(2) – Body damage sustained where metal is stretched thinner. Restoring the surface to its original contour requires shrinking and other techniques to eliminate the excess metal surface area caused by stretch. See also simple bend, rolled buckle, upset, and displaced area.
strides – Pants worn when doing messy car work.
Stringer Steam – American steam car produced in 1901.
stripes – Abbreviation for car striping and/or pinstriping.
stripped – Characteristic of a car equipped with no optional equipment.
stripping – See shaving.
Strobel & Martin – American car produced in 1910.
Strobel & Rogers – American car produced in 1900.
strobe light – See timing light.
strobe timing light – See timing light.
stroboscope – See timing light.
stroke – Distance moved by a piston in a cylinder from top dead center to bottom dead center. Each stroke is one half revolution of a crankshaft.
stroke(four) – Engine combustion cycle designed to produce power and engine rotation by using four piston strokes. Each stroke is one half revolution of an engine crankshaft. The strokes, in order of occurrence, are: intake, compression, power, and exhaust. Because of continuous piston movement, the various strokes change from one to another without stopping. Almost all car engines today use the four stroke cycle in their design. See also stroke(intake), stroke(compression), stroke(power), stroke(exhaust), and engine(four cycle).
stroke(compression) – Second stroke of a four stroke combustion cycle used to

compress an air/fuel mixture for ignition. It is an upward piston movement from its lowest cylinder position to the top, and immediately follows the intake stroke. As the piston moves upward, the intake and exhaust valves remain closed. The air/fuel mixture has no choice but to become compressed as the piston travels upward. The stroke is completed when the piston approaches the top of the cylinder.

stroke(exhaust) - Fourth stroke of a four stroke combustion cycle used to expel hot gases created by the combustion process from an engine cylinder. It is an upward piston movement from its lowest cylinder position to the top, and immediately follows the power stroke. As the piston moves upward, the intake valve remains closed and the exhaust valve opens. Exhaust gases are expelled until the piston reaches the top of its movement at which point the exhaust valve closes. The intake stroke immediately follows to repeat the entire four stroke process.

stroke(intake) - First stroke of a four stroke combustion cycle used to pull an air/fuel mixture into an engine cylinder. It is a downward piston movement from its highest cylinder position to the bottom. As the piston moves downward, the exhaust valve remains closed, but the intake valve opens. The air/fuel mixture rushes in due to the vacuum created by the downward movement. The intake valve closes when the piston approaches the bottom of the cylinder.

stroke(intake and compression) - First stroke of a two stroke combustion cycle used to perform the intake and compression of the fuel mixture. As the piston begins moving up from its lowest cylinder position, the air/fuel mixture rushes in from an intake port located near the bottom of the cylinder wall. As the piston moves upward, the port disappears, and the air/fuel mixture is compressed. When the piston gets near the top of it stroke, the mixture is ignited.

stroke(power) - Third stroke of a four stroke combustion cycle used to ignite a fuel mixture and create high pressure in an engine cylinder for driving a piston downwards. It is a downward piston movement from its highest cylinder position to the bottom, and immediately follows the compression stroke. The air/fuel mixture is ignited by a spark when the piston is at the top. The combustion process causes a rapid expansion of pressure which forces the piston downward. The stroke is completed when the piston approaches the bottom of the cylinder. During this stroke the intake and exhaust valves remain closed.

stroke(power and exhaust) - Second and final stroke of a two stroke combustion cycle used to generate power and expel exhaust gases. With the piston beginning at the highest cylinder position, the fuel mixture ignites and pressure rapidly builds to push the piston downward. As the piston nears the bottom of its stroke, exhaust gases are allowed to escape through an exhaust port in the the cylinder wall.

stroke(two) - Engine combustion cycle designed to produce power and engine rotation by using two piston strokes. Each stroke is one half revolution of the engine crankshaft. A two stroke engine produces its power in one engine revolution combining four strokes into two. The strokes, in order of occurrence, are: intake and compression, and power and exhaust. Because of the continuous movement of the pistons, the various strokes change from one to another without stopping. Two stroke engines produce more power at lower engine rpm and are most common in small engine applications such as motorcycles. See also stroke(intake and compression), stroke(power and exhaust), and two cycle.

stroker - Engine modified to increase its stroke length. It is used to boost performance by raising the compression ratio.

stroking - To modify an engine's piston stroke length by machining crankshaft throws.

stroking an engine - See stroking.

stroke it - To take it easy.

Stromberg - Line of carburetors produced until 1967.

Strong & Rogers - American electric car produced from 1900-1901 by Strong & Rogers in Ohio.

Strouse - American car produced in 1915.

structure - See texture.

Struss - American car produced in 1897.

strut rod - Rod attached at the apex of a lower control arm and running diagonally forward or backward to the car's frame. It is used to strengthen the lower control arm and reduce vibration. Strut bushings are used at the car frame to allow some give in the rod. When they become worn, the front end may vibrate and/or generate clunking sounds during braking or turning.
    Strut rods are also used on certain rear ends (especially U-joint types) to minimize side-to-side movement. See also strut rod bushing.

strut rod bushing - Circular donut-like bushing used to allow slight movement of a strut rod. Two are used, one on each side of the frame attaching point. See also strut rod.

Stuart – American electric car produced in 1961.
stub pillar – Pillar used to hinge a rear door and latch a front one. It extends only from a rocker panel to a beltline.
stuck behind slow moving traffic – To drive behind a slow moving car or group of cars with no opportunity for safely passing.
stuck in freeway traffic – To be in a car on a freeway surrounded by slow moving or stopped traffic.
stuck in park – Car condition created when an automatic transmission gearshift is stuck in the park position preventing a car from being used. It is usually due to a linkage problem where something is binding.
stud – Metal rod threaded at both ends with one end screwed into a surface. It is used to provide a method of attaching one part to another. For example, car wheels are held on with the lug nuts threaded onto studs which are screwed into a wheel hub.
Studebaker – American car produced from 1902-1964 by Studebaker Corp. (1902-1954), and Studebaker-Packard Corp. (1954-1964), both in Indiana. It was manufactured in Canada from 1964-1966 by Studebaker Corp. of Canada in Ontario.
Studebaker Brothers – American car produced from 1902-1912.
Studebaker Electric – American car produced in 1902.
Studebaker EMF – American car produced in 1909.
Studebaker-Garford – American car produced in 1908.
Studebaker, John – He organized the Studebaker Brothers Wagon Company with his brother Henry in the 1850s. He bought out Henry's interest in 1858. His company, C. & J.M. Studebaker Company, started as a body maker in 1899, then produced its first vehicle, an electric car, in 1902. His company merged with EMF Company in 1911 to form the Studebaker Corporation. The first Studebaker car was produced in 1912. John was chairman of the corporation until he died.
stuffer – See supercharger.
stumble – Severe form of hesitation.
stunt driver – Driver skilled in performing dangerous maneuvers with cars. Examples include: flipping a car, spinning out, going over an embankment or into water, etc.
Sturgis – American car produced in 1895.
Sturges – American car produced in 1898.
Sturtevant – American car produced from 1904-1908 by Sturtevant Mill Co. in Massachusetts.
Stutz – American car produced from 1911-1935 by Ideal Motor Car Co. (1911-1913), and Stutz Motor Car Co. of America (1913-1935), both in Indiana. The 1914 Bearcat speedster became one of the most popular sports cars. Also, an American car produced from 1970 to date by Stutz Motor Car of America in New York. Recent models include: Bearcat, Blackhawk, Royale Limousine, and Victoria.
Stutz, Harry – He invented an improved rear axle and worked for several companies before organizing the Ideal Motor Company in 1911 to manufacture Stutz cars. In 1913, the company merged with Stutz Motor Parts Company to become Stutz Motor Car Company. Harry served as president.
Stutz Motor Car Company – Company formed in 1913 by the merger of Stutz Motor Parts Company and Ideal Motor Company. See also Harry Stutz.
Stuyvesant – American car produced from 1911-1912 by Stuyvescent Motor Car Co. in Ohio.
styled wheels – Mag or custom designed wheels.
stylist – See job(car stylist).
SU – Abbreviation for U.S.S.R. found usually on an international license plate.
Subaru of America – American car marketing company responsible for importing Subaru cars from a Japanese car manufacturer, Fuji Heavy Industries, and selling them to its dealers.
subcompact – Car built with a narrower wheelbase and shorter body than a compact car. It usually represents the smallest production car with the highest fuel economy. Prices can range from $5-9,000, with weight generally under 2,500 lbs. See also compact and economy car.
sub frame – See frame(sub).
sub model – Specific designation of a car model such as Limited, Supreme, GLX, etc. See also model, make, and body type.
Suburban – American car produced from 1910-1912. Also, an American car produced from 1963 to date by Chevrolet Division of General Motors Corp. in Michigan. Also, an American car produced from 1957-1959 by Dodge Division of Chrysler Corp. in Michigan. Also, an American car produced from 1957-1961 by Plymouth Division of Chrysler Corp. in Michigan.
Suburban Limited – American car produced in 1912.
Suburu – Japanese car line produced from 1958 to date by Fuji Heavy Industries Ltd. Popular models include: Brat, Domingo, Justy, Leone, and Rex. The U.S. representative is Suburu of America, Inc., headquartered in

Pennsauken, New Jersey.
Success - American car produced from 1906-1909 by Success Auto-Buggy Mfg. Co. in Missouri. Also, an American car produced in 1920.
sucker - See payment buyer.
sucking everybody up his exhaust pipe - Fast driver characterized by speeding his car down the road, passing all the cars, and often skidding around turns.
suction - See vacuum.
sue - To begin legal proceedings against another party for some perpetrated wrong.
sugar in the gas - Vandal trick played on a car by putting sugar in a car's gas tank. It usually plugs the tank and otherwise renders the fuel unusable requiring a partial or complete cleaning of the fuel system.
sugar scoop - Depressed surface leading to an air scoop.
suggested price - See list price.
suit - Legal proceeding held in a court of law to recover a right, make a claim, etc.
sulfur content - Amount of sulfur contained in a fuel. Crude oil contains sulfur compounds in amounts depending on the crude oil. Most is removed in the refining process. Depending on the concentration, the remaining amount can: impart a foul odor to exhaust and gasoline, corrode and form deposits on copper and brass parts in the fuel delivery system, and cause corroded deposits to plug up small orifices such as carburetor jets or fuel injector tips.
Sullivan - American car produced in 1904.
Sullivan, Danny - He won the Indianapolis 500 Race in 1985 driving an average of 153.0 mph in a Miller American.
Sullivan Truck - American truck produced in 1904.
sulfated - Battery condition created when the plates become coated with an excessive amount of lead sulfate. It can be due to a battery being improperly charged or to being discharged for an extended period of time.
Sultan - American car produced from 1909-1912 by Sultan Motor Co. in Massachusetts.
Sultanic - American car produced in 1913.
summer gas - See gasoline(summer).
Summers, Bob - He set a world land speed record of 409.3 mph in 1969 driving a Golden Rod V-8.
Summit(1) - American car produced in 1907.
Summit(2) - American line of tires produced by the manufacturers of Kelly-Springfield tires.
summons - Written court order requiring a defendant or witness to appear in court.
sump - See oil pan.
Sun - American line of car gauges and testing equipment.
Sun - American car produced from 1915-1918 and 1921-1924 by Sun Motor Car Co. in New York and Indiana, and Automotive Corp. in Ohio respectively.
Sunbeam - British car line produced from 1899-1937 and 1953-1976 by Chrysler United Kingdom Ltd. (1953-1976). Popular models included: Tiger, Apline, and Rapier.
Sunbeam V-12 - English car driven to a world land speed record in 1922, 1924, 1925, 1926, and 1927. Speeds were 133.8, 146.2, 150.8, 152.3 and 203.8 mph. Locations were Brooklands, England; Pendine, Wales (1924 and 1925); Southport, England; and Daytona, Florida. Drivers were Kenelm Lee Guiness, Malcom Campbell (1924 and 1925), and Major Henry Segrave (1926 and 1927).
Sunbird - American car produced from 1975-1986 by Pontiac Division of General Motors Corp. in Michigan.
Sun Company, Inc - A U.S. petroleum company headquartered in Radnor, Pennsylvania. See also petroleum company.
sun gear - See gear(sun).
sunday drive - Car trip made on a sunday for pleasure.
sun gear - See gear(sun).
sunroof - Movable tinted window mounted in the roof of a car. Movement designs include: pivoting open, sliding open, and removing it entirely.
Sunset - American steam car produced from 1901-1904 by Sunset Automobile Co. in California.
sunshine treatment - See con game(sunshine treatment).
sun visor - Pivoting sun shield mounted inside a passenger compartment at the inside intersection of a car roof and windshield. Two are usually installed, one on each side. It swings up out of the way, down to partially shade sunlight coming through the windshield, or down to partially shade sunlight coming through an adjacent side window.
Super - American car produced from 1960-1963 by American Motors Corp. in Michigan.
Superba - American car produced in 1959 by Checker Motors.
supercharged - Engine performance modification made by installing a supercharger.

supercharged engine - See engine(supercharged).

supercharger - Engine run blower or compressor used to pump air into an air/fuel mixture and on into engine cylinders. It is usually mounted between the carburetor and the intake manifold. Advantages include: provides instantaneous power boost at low rpm for fast low speed response (turbochargers don't), helps overcome friction losses in intake manifolds, improves exhaust gas scavenging, boosts engine horsepower, and usually less expensive than a turbocharger. Disadvantages include: increased detonation tendency requiring higher octane fuel, rapid rise in power requirement as air flow increases, more fuel consumed when supercharging, and power increase not proportional to fuel consumption increase. Air pressures developed typically range from 3 to 20 lbs depending on the model. It is one of the most effective ways of increasing engine power. See also turbocharger and intercooler.

supercharger(centrifugal) - Supercharger built using an impeller rotating at speeds up to five times the engine rpm to pump air into the engine. The impeller blades heat the air which is usually cooled with coolers. The coolers are typically lengths of finned tubing. The air delivery rate increases with the square of impeller rpm. Supercharging is much more variable than with a rootes type supercharger and carburetion is more difficult.

supercharger(rootes type) - Supercharger built using twin rotors, working together like egg beaters to pump air into an engine. Some rotors use two lobes while others have three. The rotors rotate at one to two times the engine rpm. The somewhat faster than engine rpm air delivery rate and minor air leakage allow supercharging to remain constant at different engine rpm.

supercharger(turbine type) - Supercharger built using a turbine engine design.

Superchief - American car produced from 1955-1960 by Pontiac Division of General Motors Corp. in Michigan.

Super Cooled - American car produced in 1923.

superheterodyne circuit - Electric circuit used in radar detectors to amplify incoming radar signals several hundred times and ignore signals outside police radar bands. The circuitry also includes a signal generator known as a Gunn oscillator that actually broadcasts a signal in the police radar band. Poorly designed detectors don't adequately shield this signal and cause other radar detectors to be tripped.

Superior - American car produced in 1908, 1914, and 1918. Also a Canadian car produced in 1910.

Super Kar - American car produced in 1946 by Louis Elrad in Ohio. It was three wheeled midget using a 15 hp air-cooled engine.

superspeedway - Race track built with high-banked turns for stock car racing.

superstructure - See body superstructure.

Super Traction - American car produced in 1923.

Super Truck - American truck produced from 1920-1928.

subpoena - Court document issued to a witness requiring his appearance in court.

Supreme - American car produced in 1917, 1922, and 1930.

Sure-Grip - Tradename of a limited slip differential.

surface plate - Flat cast iron plate used in car design work. It is covered with a pattern of five inch grid lines used as a measuring reference.

surface prep - See body prep.

surfacer - See paint(undercoat).

surface vaporizer - Early carburetor used in the 1890s. Fuel is heated with hot water from an engine's cooling system. Warm vapor is then mixed with air and routed into engine cylinders through a valve.

surge - Condition created when an engine does not deliver even power. It is usually caused by lean fuel mixtures and/or retarded timing.

surge brakes - Brake system commonly found on trailers which engages when car brakes are applied.

surpanel - Extra panel located next to a main panel. An example is a panel underneath the front bumper and between the fenders. See also modesty panel.

surrey - See body style(surrey).

Surrey'03 - American car produced from 1958-1959 by E.W. Bliss Co. in Ohio. It was similar in appearance to a 1903 Curved Dash Olds. It was powered by an 8 hp air-cooled engine and had a top speed of 35mph.

Surtees, John - He was a British driver who won the 1964 Grand Prix world championship driving a Ferrari.

suspended license - See license(suspended).

suspension - See suspension system.

suspension crossmember - Frame member located perpendicular to the length of a car and used to provide support for suspension components.

suspension height - Height of a car chassis above the ground. It is measured at the points specified by the car manufacturer. If must be even all around before the front wheel alignment angles can be checked and adjusted. Before making the measurements, the following should be done: put car on level

ground, bounce car up and down a few times both front and rear to equalize
suspension, equalize tire pressure, fill gas tank, allow no passengers
inside, and remove any excess weight from inside the car. If height is below
the minimum allowed, the affected springs and/or frame will need to be
adjusted or replaced. Weak coil springs are usually replaced. Leaf springs
can be resprung to their original curvature. Frame sag or damage should be
restored to its original shape by realignment or replacing the affected
member. Realignment requires restoring the affected frame member to its
original location in the frame and making sure it retains its original
strength.

suspension system – Entire system of springs and associated devices used to
support a car body on axles and cushion the ride. The parts consist of a
leaf or coil spring, a shock absorber, and necessary fittings, located at
each wheel. The suspension system prevents the car from getting excessive
vibration and jarring impacts which can dramatically shorten the life of many
car parts.

suspension system – Assemblage of parts used to suspend a car's frame, body,
and power train above the wheels.

suspension system(A arm) – Suspension system used to suspend front wheels
independently using an upper and lower control arm assembly for each wheel.

suspension system(double wishbone) – Suspension system used to suspend the
rear wheels independently using a lower and upper wishbone shape control arm
for each wheel. A swing axle is usually employed.

suspension system(front) – Suspension system used to suspend the front end of
a car above the wheels. There are two main types known as independent and
solid axle.

suspension system(independent) – Suspension system used to suspend wheels
independently. It is commonly used on the two front wheels, and gives a car
good road handling ability. The primary parts include: upper and lower
control arms, coil springs, shock absorbers, upper and lower ball joints,
wheel spindles, and upper and lower control arm shafts.

suspension system(MacPherson strut) – Suspension system used to suspend
each front wheel or all four wheels with an integral shock absorber-coil
spring assembly. See also Macpherson strut.

suspension system(semi independent) – Suspension system used on the rear
wheels of late model front wheel drive cars. Each wheel is suspended by a
coil spring on a trailing arm. The arms are linked together by a
crossmember.

suspension system(short long arm) – Front suspension system used allowing the
up and down movement of a wheel to remain vertical. It is done by making the
upper and lower control arms different lengths and by locating the control
arm pivot points strategically.

suspension system(solid axle) – Suspension system used between the front, rear
or both sets of wheels in which the wheels are linked together by an axle
shaft. It is most common on the rear wheels of rear wheel drive cars. The
primary parts typically include: rear axle, leaf springs and fittings, front
hangers, rear shackles, and shock absorbers. Four wheel drive vehicles
commonly use this type of suspension on the front and rear wheels.

suspension system(solid axle beam and leaf spring) – Suspension system used
between the front, rear or both sets of wheels in which the wheels are linked
together by an axle beam. It is used on older cars and medium to heavy duty
trucks. The primary parts of a front mounted system typically include: a
front axle, spindle shafts, spindle bolts, spindle bolt bearings, spindle
arm, shock absorbers, and coil springs.

suspension system(torsion bar) – Suspension system designed to use torsion
bars in place of leaf or coil springs. On front suspensions, some car
designs use torsion bars attached to the lower control arms at one end and a
mid section cross member at the other. Other designs, such as the Volkswagen
Bettle, use torsion bars between the front wheels.

Suzuki – Japanese car line produced from 1961 to date by Suzuki Motor Co. Ltd.
Popular models include: Alto, Cervo, Cultus, Fronte, and Jimmy.

Suzuki Motor Company Ltd – Japanese car and motorcycle manufacturer noted for
producing Suzuki cars. Car production began in 1954 after some years of
producing motorcycles. Models include the SA310. The SA310 is imported by
General Motors and called the Chevrolet Sprint.

SV – Abbreviation for side valve.

SVO – Abbreviation for special vehicle operations.

SW(1) – Abbreviation for switch. See also ignition coil terminal.

SW(2) – Abbreviation for station wagon.

Swanson – American car produced in 1911.

sway bar – See anti-roll bar.

S/W/C – Abbreviation for split window coupe.

Sweany – American steam car produced in 1895. It was very unique with a
separate 3 hp single-cylinder engine used to drive each wheel.

sweat – To join two metal surfaces together by applying solder to the internal joint, clamping it, and then applying heat. In plumbing, pipes are sweated together by heating a pipe joint, applying solder to it, and letting capillary action draw the solder into the joint.

sweep - Guide used in drawing irregular contours.

Sweikert, Bob - He won the Indianapolis 500 Race in 1955 driving an average of 128.2 mph in a John Zink Special.

swerve - To turn abruptly offset a car sideways from a forward direction or movement to avoid something.

Swift - American car line produced in 1959 by Swift Mfg. Co. in California. Replicas were built of a 1910 Ford, 1903 Cadillac, and a Stutz Bearcat in 5/8 scale. They were known as the Swift-T, Swifter, and Swift-Cat respectively.

swindle - To get money or property from another person by lying, cheating, deceiving, etc. See also con man and con game.

swindler - Person who swindles others.

swing axle - See axle(swing).

Swinger - American car produced from 1963-1977 by Dodge Division of Chrysler Corp. in Michigan.

swinging half axle - See axle(swinging half).

swing pedals - Pivoting pedals such as a clutch or brake pedal.

switch - Device used to start or stop flow of electrical current.

switchback - Race track or road area containing hairpin turns.

switching - Sales tactic used to convince a potential car buyer to purchase a car with a larger profit margin or one that gives a car salesman a bonus.

switching plugs - To remove and reinstall new or cleaned spark plugs.

swivel buckets - Bucket seats built to rotate.

syalon - Ceramic silicon nitride compound. It is composed of silicon, aluminum, oxygen, and nitrogen. Properties include: easily formed into any shape; highly resistant to wear; thermal shock, and heat; stronger than steel, harder than diamond, and lighter than aluminum.

Sylvania - American line of sealed headlights.

synchro - See synchronizing clutch.

synchromesh - Device used to bring gears to be meshed up to the same rotational speed before they engage. See also synchronizer clutch.

synchromesh transmission - See transmission(synchromesh).

synchronize - To make two or more events occur at the same time. Examples include: intake valves opening at the same time, two pistons at TDC at the same time, two gears rotating at the same speed, etc.

synchronizer - See synchronizer clutch.

synchronizer ring - Ring with a cone shaped surface used in a synchronizer clutch. It works like a clutch plate to bring up the speed of a driven gear to that of a driving gear. See also synchronizing clutch.

synchronizer hub - Gear hub with spacer bars used in a synchronizer clutch. It is the core of the clutch, encircling and rotating with a transmission shaft. A splined surface is used to allow a synchronizer sleeve or outer shell to slide over it.

synchronizer hub inserts - Small movable metal bars used in a synchronizer hub to push synchronizer rings against a gear's cone area, speeding up a gear before the synchronizer sleeve slides over them to lock the gear into position. The weight of the inserts can make a difference at high rpm in how difficult shifting will be.

synchronizer hub insert springs - Piston ring-like springs mounted underneath the synchronizer hub inserts inside the synchronizer hub.

synchronizer keys - See synchronizer hub inserts.

synchronizer shift plates - See synchronizer hub inserts.

synchronizer sleeve - Short cylinder-like device built with a splined inner surface, and used to cause engagement and lock a specific gear ratio into position. It slides over the splined surface of a synchronizer hub. It may or may not have an integral transmission gear depending on design.

synchronizing clutch - Clutching device used in synchromesh transmissions to speed up or slow down a gear to match the mainshaft rotation speed to avoid gear clashing. It consists primarily of: a splined hub with synchronizer ring spacers, splined sleeve, and synchronizer rings. The clutch rotates with the main shaft at all times and usually sits between two gears. The "clutch plate" of a synchronizing clutch is the synchronizer ring. There are usually two. In the first part of a gear shift, the clutch slides the ring until it contacts a projecting cone shaped surface on a nearby gear, causing them both to rotate at the same speed. As the shift is completed, the clutch sleeve slides, locking the gear, ring, and clutch hub together. The number of synchronizing clutches in a transmission depends on the number of gears and design. Most have at least two.

Two different type of synchronizing clutches are used today, the pin and block type. The block type has become the most popular.

synchronizer clutch gear - See synchronizer hub.

synchronizer clutch sleeve - See synchronizer sleeve.

synchronizer stop ring - See synchronizer ring.

synchro ring – See synchronizer ring.
Synnestvedt – American electric car produced from 1904-1908 by Synnestvedt Machine Co. in Pennsylvania.
synthetic oil – See oil(synthetic).
SYR – Abbreviation for Syria found usually on an international license plate.
Syracuse – American car produced from 1899-1903 by Syracuse Automobile Co. in New York.

T

T – Abbreviation for Thailand found usually on an international license plate.
tabs – Adhesive decals attached to license plates to denote the year of registration.
TAC – Abbreviation for thermostatic air cleaner.
tach – Abbreviation for tachometer.
tachometer – Instrument used measure an engine's rotating speed in revolutions per minute.
tack rag – Lintless rag used to remove any residual surface dust from a car body just before painting.
tacking – Process defined as using a tack rag and prep solvent to clean a car body surface just prior to painting it.
tack weld – Small weld bead made to a joint to temporarily hold it together.
TACS – Abbreviation for thermostatic air cleaner switch.
Taft Steam – American steam car produced in 1901.
tail – Animal tail tied to a car's antenna or elsewhere.
tailgate – See liftgate.
tailgater – Driver following closely behind another car. See also tailgating.
tailgating – Situation created when a car follows closely behind another car. It is a dangerous habit usually done to intimidate the lead car driver into moving out of the way or speeding up.
tail lights – See light(tail).
tailpipe – Final section of an exhaust pipe system used, extending out the back of a car. Some tailpipes are attached directly to a muffler mounted near the rear of the car. Others are attached to a connector pipe spanning the distance between a tailpipe and a mid-car-mounted muffler.
tailpipe coloration – Color of coating material inside a tailpipe. The color usually agrees with spark plug coloration in indicating an engine's behavior and condition. A slight difference will be the effect of a very lean fuel mixture which will tend to cause a light brown, gray or white coating. Also, a black coloration can indicate excessive backpressure if a car's ignition and carburetor settings are according to the factory. The latter requires tracking down the cause of the excessive backpressure (muffler restriction, tailpipe dents, etc.). See also backpressure.
tailpipe extension – Short pipe section installed at the very end of a car's exhaust system strictly for appearance sake. It is usually chrome plated and has one or two pipe outlets in a variety of configurations.
tailshaft – See transmission output shaft.
Tait – American car produced in 1901.
take – See on the take.
take delivery – To order or purchase a car or truck from a dealer and pick it up when it arrives. See also delivery satisfaction sheet.
takeoff – Extra transmission output coupling designed to allow other equipment to take advantage of a transmission's rotation to perform useful work. Some cars run a separate driveline from the transmission takeoff to a takeoff located at the front or rear of the car. Some winches on trucks are powered this way.
take over – Situation created when a potential car buyer is subtly turned over to another car dealer salesman experienced in closing a sale and/or raising the sale profit. See also TO man and TO.
take the wheel – To drive a car. Also, it refers to a front seat passenger holding a steering wheel momentarily while a driver uses both hands for something else.
take to the road – To begin traveling.
taking a bath – To lose money selling a car.
taking a drive – To drive a car to a specific destination.
taking a spin – See taking a drive.
Talbot – British car line produced from 1903–1938 and 1980 to date by Talbot Motor Co. Ltd. Popular models include: Horizon, Minx, and Rapier.
tall gear ratio – A gear ratio requiring a fewer number of input turns for every output turn. For example, a 2.6:1 differential ratio is considered a taller ratio than 3:1, since it requires only 2.6 driveline revolutions for every axle revolution.
tall rear end – Car differential built with a low gear ratio such as 2.65:1. It provides higher top speeds at the expense of poorer acceleration.
Tallyo – American car produced in 1914.
tandem – One behind the other. An example would be a tandem axle which would be one rear axle in front of another.

tank – Large full size car like a station wagon or sedan unpopular because of its size and/or poor fuel economy. See also dinosaur.

tanker truck – Large truck equipped with a large tank for carrying gasoline, diesel fuel, or other liquid.

tank it – Process used to clean a cylinder head, engine block, radiator, etc. by soaking it in a special solution formulated to remove deposits and prepare it for machine work.

tank the head – See hot tank the head.

tank up – To fill a gas tank with gasoline.

tap(1) – Tool used to cut threads in a hole.

tap(2) – Drain cock.

tape – Abbreviation for tape deck.

tape drawing – Drawing made of a car using black, pressure sensitive tape. It can easily be removed and changed.

tapered roller bearing – See bearing(tapered roller).

tappet – See valve lifter.

tappet clearance – See valve lifter clearance.

tapping the brakes – Method used to warn cars behind that a driver plans to slow down or stop. It is also used to discourage a car from tailgating. Sudden stopping without warning can cause a rear end collision.

Tarantula – Tradename used by Edelbrock for a vertical ram intake manifold. See also intake manifold(vertical ram).

Tarkington – American car produced from 1922-1923 by Tarkington Motor Co. in Illinois.

Tarrytown – American car produced in 1914.

Tasco – American car produced in 1948.

Tate – Canadian electric car produced from 1912-1913 by Tate Electrics in Ontario.

Tatra – Czechoslovakian car line produced from 1923 to date by Tatra.

Taunton – American car produced from 1901-1904 by Taunton Motor Carriage Co. in Massachusetts.

Taurus – American car produced from 1980 to date by Ford Motor Co. in Michigan.

taxi – See taxicab.

taxicab – Car used to transport people for money.

taxicab fleet – Large number of taxicabs owned by a taxicab company.

taximeter – Device used in a taxicab to compute and display fare owed.

Taylor – American car produced in 1921.

T bird – Abbreviation for Ford Thunderbird car.

T-bone(1) – Model T Ford car.

T-bone(2) – To broadside another car in a race.

T-bucket – Lightweight hot rod.

TC – Abbreviation for town car.

TCS – Abbreviation for transmission controlled spark. See also emission control system(combustion-transmission controlled spark).

T-cup – Small oil filter used on late model small engine cars. It is about the size of a large tea cup.

TDC – Abbreviation for top dead center. It is the highest point a piston travels in a cylinder.

TE – Abbreviation for top eliminator or drag race winner.

tear down the engine – To disassemble an engine to repair or rebuild it.

tear in the seat – Cut in a car's upholstery.

tech – Technical inspection made of race cars to ensure safety and properly classify them.

Teel – American car produced in 1913.

telescoping gauge – Gauge used to measure small internal diameters.

temper – Degree of hardness and resiliency imparted in a metal.

temperature door – Mode-and-blend door used in heating and air conditioning ductwork to control air flow around heater core.

temperature override switch – Electrical switch designed to sense coolant temperature and operate in three modes in an emission control system. The settings consist of: cold (usually below 80 degrees), neutral (usually from 80-230), and hot (over 230 degrees). The cold setting closes a switch, neutral opens it, and hot closes another switch to activate a hot engine warning light.

temperature sensor vacuum valve – See thermal valve.

temperature vacuum switch – See thermal valve.

tempering – Process defined as imparting strength and toughness to steel or cast iron by heating the metal to a specified temperature, keeping it there for a specified period of time, and cooling it in a specified manner.

Tempest – American car produced from 1961-1981 by Pontiac Division of General Motors Corp. in Michigan.

Templar – American car produced from 1917-1924 by Templar Motors Corp. in Ohio.

template – Pattern made of a surface profile. Different materials are used depending on the use and include: cardboard, plastic, masonite, plywood, and metal.

Temple - American car produced in 1899.

Temple-Dubrie - American car produced in 1910.

Temple-Westcott - American car produced from 1921-1922.

Tempo - American car produced from 1980 to date by Ford Motor Co. in Michigan.

Tennant - American car produced from 1914-1915 by Tennant Motors Co. in Illinois.

tension - Stress induced in a material produced by pulling or twisting forces.

terminal - Fitting used in an electric circuit for making a connection.

terminal post - See terminal and battery post.

terminal speed - Speed attained at the end of a 1/4 mile race.

terminal stud - Top portion of a spark plug. Spark plug wire is attached there.

terms and conditions of a warranty - Verbage written in a warranty specifying what is covered, excluded, and/or limited.

Terraplane - American car produced from 1932-1937 by Hudson Motor Car Co. in Michigan.

Terwilliger Steam - American steam car produced in 1904.

test drive - To drive a car for the purpose of determining how well it operates. If a dealer will not let you drive a new or used car you are considering, don't buy it.

test probe - Device inserted into an environment to measure voltage, heat, resistance, etc. For example, an electric tester has two probes used for measuring voltage, current, and resistance in an electrical circuit.

test the armature - To test a generator's armature to determine if there are short circuits in any of its coils. Coils grounded to an armature shaft are tested by measuring the resistance between each commutator bar and the armature shaft. No resistance indicates a ground. Grounding between windings of an individual armature coil are determined using a device called a growler. It indicates a short by causing a thin strip of steel to vibrate over the affected coil.

tetradecane - Liquid methane series hydrocarbon compound found in petroleum deposits with a melting and boiling point of 43 and 488 degrees Fahrenheit respectively.

Tex - American car produced in 1915.

Texaco, Inc - A U.S. petroleum company headquartered in White Plains, New York. See also petroleum company.

Texan - American car produced from 1918-1922 by Texas Motor Car Assoc. in Texas.

Texmobile - American car produced from 1921-1922 by Little Motors Kar Co. in Texas.

texture - Characteristic look or feel of a plastic material. For example, a grease may look or feel fibrous, smooth, rubbery, etc.

T-head engine - See engine(T-head).

the close - Point reached in a car salesman's pitch when a potential car buyer agrees to sign a sales contract or buyer's order.

theme sketch - Quick sketch made to put an idea down on paper.

thermactor system - See emission control system(combustion-air injection).

thermal efficiency - Ratio figured as energy created divided by the total heat energy contained in fuel. An internal combustion engine converts part of the fuel it burns into usable energy and part of it into heat. For example, an engine with a 40 percent thermal efficiency converts 40 percent of a fuel's heat energy into usable energy or power. The rest is lost as heat.

thermal ignition control valve - See spark delay valve.

thermal overload relay - See current limit relay.

thermal reactor - Chamber built to replace an exhaust manifold and allow high temperature continued burning of exhaust pollutants.

thermal vacuum switch - See thermal valve(2).

thermal valve(1) - Air conditioning valve actuated by intake manifold vacuum.

thermal valve(2) - Vacuum operated valve built to open an unobstructed intake vacuum path when coolant temperature reaches a specified point. Thermal valves are typically used to control EGR valves and to bypass certain spark advance controls when an engine overheats. It contains three ports: one connected to a spark ported vacuum source, one to the vacuum advance unit on the distributor, and one to manifold vacuum.

For EGR valves: when the thermal valve opens, vacuum originating from a carburetor airway point is extended to the EGR valve causing it to open and route a portion of the engine's exhaust gases into the intake manifold. A valve stuck open or closed can cause the EGR valve to open early, and stay open, or remain closed respectively.

For bypassing spark controls: the thermal valve opens to route manifold vacuum when an engine overheats (usually around 210-220 degrees Fahrenheit) permitting an engine to run cooler due to a faster idle (faster water pump and fan operation) at full vacuum advance, and less engine cylinder wall exposure to heat. A valve stuck open in the manifold position will cause increased emissions and possible excessive advance during low to medium speed driving. A valve stuck closed will continue to cause an engine to overheat with reduced power.

thermo-siphon – Engine cooling method used to circulate water without pumping by relying on the difference in specific gravity of hot and cold water. Larger water passages are used, than in a pump circulation system, to minimize resistance to flow. Today's cars circulate coolant with a pump.

thermostat – Temperature-activated valve used to control coolant flow according to its temperature. If the valve sticks closed, an engine will overheat. If the valve remains stuck in the open position, it may prevent water from getting warm enough which will affect the fuel economy. Generally, a hotter thermostat provides better fuel economy and power. Engine life running warmer or cooler coolant is about the same.

thermostatic air cleaner – Air cleaner built to control air intake temperature by controlling ambient and warm air flow from the engine compartment and exhaust manifold heat stove respectively.

thermostatic air cleaner switch – Temperature operated vacuum valve designed to route manifold vacuum to a vacuum motor controlling an air cleaner's air gate, when air temperature is below a certain value.

thermostatic spring – Temperature-sensitive spring mechanism. Cars use such springs in several places to do such work as: control coolant flow, control preheat air flowing into an air cleaner, control choke plate movement, and control exhaust manifold heat reaching intake manifold. See also thermostat and choke coil.

thermostatic vacuum switch – See thermal valve(2).

thermostatic vacuum switching valve – See thermal valve(2).

Thermot Monohan – American car produced in 1919.

thickness gauge – See feeler gauge.

thin deal – Car deal made where a car salesman makes a very small profit.

thingie – Car modified for drag racing.

thinner – See paint thinner.

third brush – Brush used in a generator to control current output. See also generator(third brush).

Thomart – American car produced in 1921.

Thomas – American car produced from 1902-1905 by E.R. Thomas Motor Co. in New York. See also Thomas Flyer.

Thomas-Detroit – American car produced from 1906-1908 by E.R. Thomas-Detroit Co. in Michigan.

Thomas, Edwin – He was a successful auto maker who designed and built the famous Thomas Flyer. It won the 1908 New York to Paris race.

Thomas, Herb – He became the NASCAR Grand National Champion in 1951 and 1953.

Thomas, J G Parry – He set a world land speed record of 171.0 mph in 1926 driving a Babs V-12.

Thomas, Rene – He won the Indianapolis 500 Race in 1914 driving an average of 82.5 mph in a Delage. He also set a world land speed record of 143.3 mph in 1924 driving a Delage V-12.

Thomas Flyer – American car produced from 1905-1919 by E.R. Thomas Motor Co. in New York. Also, a car designed and built by Edwin Thomas that won the 1908 New York to Paris race. See also Thomas.

Thomas Truck – American truck produced in 1907.

Thompson – American car produced in 1901-1902 and 1906.

Thomson – American car produced from 1900-1902 by Thomson Automobile Co. in Pennsylvania.

Thorne – American car produced in 1929.

Thornycroft – American car produced from 1901-1903.

Thorobred – American car produced in 1901.

three dimensional – To have three dimensions which are height, width, and depth.

three door hatchback – See body style(three door hatchback).

three lane highway – Areas of a two lane highway enlarged to three lanes usually on uphill grades. It allows traffic in either direction to pass.

three quarter race – Car modified for high performance and still street drivable.

three way combination valve – Valve used to receive brake fluid from a master brake cylinder and meter it separately to the front and rear brakes.

Thresher – American car produced in 1900.

Thrif-T – American car produced in 1955.

throttle – See throttle plate.

throttle body(1) – Flat cast plate mounted under the carburetor. It typically consists of: throttle valves, throttle shaft, idle mixture adjustment screws, and hot air or hot water passageways for keeping throttle valves warm in cold weather.

throttle body(2) – Fuel and/or air metering device mounted at the entrance to an intake manifold setup for fuel injection.

throttle body(2-multi point) - Air metering unit mounted in place of a carburetor on an intake manifold. It meters air into an intake manifold, and sends information to an on-board computer regarding air flow rates so fuel injectors can inject the proper amount of fuel and thereby allow the most efficient air/fuel ratio to be maintained. Primary components usually include: throttle body casting, throttle plate, idle speed control motor, and air flow sensor. See also throttle body(single-point), and fuel injection(gas-single point).

throttle body(2-single point) - Fuel and air metering unit mounted in place of a carburetor on an intake manifold. It injects fuel into the manifold at a specified rate to control the air/fuel ratio entering the engine cylinders. Primary components usually include: throttle body casting, one or two injectors, idle speed control motor, fuel pressure regulator, and throttle position sensor. See also throttle body(multi-point), and fuel injection(gas-single point).

throttle body injection - See fuel injection(gas-single point).

throttle body injector - See throttle body(single-point), and throttle body(multi-point).

throttle booster valve - Valve used in automatic transmission to increase hydraulic pressure to primary throttle pressure valve.

throttle bore - Carburetor airway.

throttle freeze - See accelerator's stuck.

throttle lever - Lever mounted on a throttle shaft and operated by gas pedal linkage.

throttle modulator valve - Valve used in an automatic transmission to reduce hydraulic pressure when shifting from one gear to another.

throttle plate - Circular metal disk mounted on a movable shaft below a carburetor venturi. A carburetor has as many plates as venturis. It acts as a butterfly valve controlling the air/fuel mixture amount reaching the cylinders. Primary throttle valves are controlled by linkage to a gas pedal. Secondary plates are usually controlled by vacuum.

throttle plate(primary) - Throttle plate located in a carburetor primary airway. Four barrel carburetors have two primary throttle plates. See also primary(carburetor).

throttle plate(secondary) - Throttle plate located in a carburetor secondary airway. It is usually controlled in one of three ways. One method uses a mechanical linkage opening a secondary throttle valve when a primary throttle valve is opened a certain amount (commonly 50 degrees). A second method uses a vacuum diaphragm opening a secondary throttle valve when intake manifold drops close to zero. A third method uses a combination of the first two. See also primary(carburetor) and secondary(carburetor).

throttle position solenoid - Electrically operated solenoid used to keep a throttle plate slightly open when engine rpm is above a certain value. When rpm falls below the value (usually 2-3000 rpm), the throttle returns to normal idle. An engine speed sensor activates it. The solenoid helps reduce the level of unburned hydrocarbons which serves to protect and extend the life of a catalytic converter.

throttle position transducer - See throttle position solenoid. See also transducer.

throttle stop screw - See idle adjustment screw.

throttle valve(1) - See throttle plate.

throttle valve(2) - Valve used in an automatic transmission to control amount of hydraulic fluid pressure available to other control valves, clutches, and brake bands. The valve is controlled by: linkage to a carburetor throttle valve, or a vacuum diaphragm unit mounted on the intake manifold (more popular). See also TV rod.

throttle valve linkage - Springs, shafts, cables, etc. used to connect a throttle valve to a gas pedal.

throw - Offset portion or distance measured from a crankshaft centerline to a connecting rod shaft or crank pin centerline. A crankshaft has as many throws as cylinders. See also counterbalance.

throw a shift - To shift from one gear to another. The time required is an important consideration in drag racing.

throw out bearing - See clutch throw out bearing.

Thrush - Line of performance mufflers.

Thrust 2 Jet Car - American car driven by Richard Noble to a 1983 world land speed record of 633.5 mph at Blackrock, Nevada.

thrust bearing - Bearing built to withstand side pressures.

thrust washer - Washer used to provide a bearing surface for the thrusting surfaces of part. It is commonly made of hardened steel or bronze.

Thunderbird - American car produced from 1957 to date by Ford Motor Co. in Michigan.

Thunderbolt V-12 - English car driven by Captain George Eyston to a world land speed record in 1937 and 1938 at Bonneville, Utah. Speeds were 312.0 and 357.5 mph.

thunderbug — See midget racer.

TIC — Abbreviation for thermal ignition control.

ticket — Summons to court for a traffic violation.

tick over — See idle speed.

tie down — Hook or other attachment device located on a truck's bed or side walls, a car's roof, etc.

tie 'em in close — Selling tactic used to make a potential customer feel committed to a sale. See also put a guy on paper.

tie rod — Small metal rod used in a steering system to connect front wheels to a steering mechanism. Some cars have one long adjustable tie rod while others use two that are separately adjustable. Tie rods control the amount of toe-in or toe-out when the wheels are pointed straight ahead. See also wheel alignment angle(toe in), wheel alignment angle(toe out), and wheel alignment angle(toe out on turns).

tie rod end — Short fitting located on the wheel end of a tie rod. One end contains an outer pivot for attaching to a steering knuckle arm and the other end is threaded for attaching to an adjuster tube on a tie rod.

tie strut — Short adjustable bar attached to the lower portion of a steering knuckle in order to control a tire's caster angle. See also wheel alignment angle(caster).

TIG — Abbreviation for Tungsten Inert Gas. See also welding(TIG).

TIG torch — Torch body used perform TIG welding.

TIG welding — See welding(TIG).

Tiffany — American electric car produced from 1913-1914 by Tiffany Electric Car Co. in Michigan.

Tiffin — American car produced in 1914.

Tiger — American car produced in 1914.

tight steering — See quick steering.

Tiley — American car produced from 1904-1906 and 1908-1913 by Tiley Pratt Co. in Connecticut.

Tilicum — American car produced in 1914.

tiller steering — Steering system guided by use of a tiller rather than a steering wheel.

tilt — Abbreviation for tilting steering wheel.

tilt bed — See car transport(flatbed).

tilt bed car trailer — Car trailer bed built to tilt up for easy loading of a car. See also car transport(flatbed).

tilt type steering wheel — Steering wheel built to pivot for facilitating entering and leaving a driver's seat, and for adjusting a steering wheel position for individual comfort.

tilt wheel — Steering wheel built to move up and down a certain distance for driver comfort.

timer core — Small circular vaned device mounted on a distributor shaft in place of a distributor cam. It is used with a magnetic pickup in a magnetic pulse ignition system to replace distributor points. The two devices work together to send electrical signals to an ignition pulse amplifier which controls primary current flow in an ignition coil.

time the engine — To check and set an engine's ignition timing.

timer — See distributor.

time trap — Short distance located just before a drag strip's finish line where a car's speed is recorded.

time trial — Race held where a racing car races against a clock instead of other cars. Cars with the fastest times then go on to other races.

timing — See ignition timing.

timing belt — Reinforced rubber belt used to rotate a camshaft by linking drive sprockets on a camshaft and crankshaft. It is usually completely enclosed as it is sensitive to wear and breakage from foreign substances getting sandwiched between it and the drive gears. It will also wear faster at higher engine speeds. Good preventive maintenance on timing belts suggests replacement after 50-75,000 miles, or sooner if engine is driven hard. Belt appearance can be deceiving regarding wear and life left. Some engines can be extensively damaged when a belt breaks due to piston and valve collisions.

timing card — Diagram used to specify a camshaft's valve overlap, valve duration, valve lift, etc.

timing chain — Drive chain used to rotate a camshaft by linking drive sprockets on a camshaft and crankshaft. It keeps the valves properly timed by maintaining a correct relationship between the camshaft and crankshaft. A loose chain can produce a slapping sound hitting the inside of a timing cover case, and can also affect valve timing causing rough idling.

timing cover — Plate or housing used to cover an engine's timing gear area. It is usually made of aluminum, and serves to protect the timing gears and belt or chain from dirt, water, and other outside contaminants.

timing gears — See gear(timing).

timing light — Electric light tool used to set engine timing. The light

usually has three leads. Two leads go to the battery terminals, and the
third one attaches between the number one spark plug cable boot and the top
of the spark plug. While the engine is running, the light is aimed at timing
marks located on a crankshaft pulley. The light flashes each time the number
one plug fires, "freezing" the timing mark position for easy reading and
adjustment.

timing light(inductive) – Timing light built to detect magnetic inductance
generated by high voltage current flowing in a spark plug wire and generate
light impulses as a result of the inductance. The inductive pickup typically
clips around the number one spark plug wire. It is the most common and
popular type of timing light.

timing light(strobe) – See timing light.

timing marks – Series of lines or notches made on a crankshaft pulley for
noting the degree position of the number one piston in relation to the top of
its stroke. Also, marks on a crankshaft and camshaft timing chain sprockets
used to specify their relationship to each other when a timing chain is
attached.

timing pointer – Pointer attached to an engine block near a crankshaft pulley
that acts as a reference for crankshaft timing marks.

timing the ignition – Tune up procedure followed where spark plug firing is
adjusted to occur at the correct instant of a given piston's cycle.

timing setback – Retarding ignition timing from its current setting.

Timmis – Canadian car line produced from 1979 to date by Timmis Motor Co. in
British Columbia.

Tin Box Age – Brief time period begun following the onset of the Depression in
1930, when car manufacturers concentrated on making cheap cars with
lightweight bodies.

tin can – Rough car or junker.

Tincher – American car produced from 1904-1907 by Chicago Coach & Carriage Co.
in Illinois, and Tincher Motor Car Co. in Indiana.

Tinkham – American car produced in 1899.

Tin Lizzie – Popular nickname for the Model T Ford car. Also, an American car
produced beginning in 1960 by McDonough Power Equipment Co. in Georgia (1960-
1965), and Crue Cut Mfg. Co. in Missouri (1965 on). It was a 1/2 scale
replica.

tinning – To coat or plate a metal surface with a thin layer of another metal
usually with a lower melting point. When done on car panels, the surface is
usually tinned with a lead-based solder. See also solder.

tinning flux – See soldering flux and brazing flux.

tipping the gas – To fill up a gas tank.

tip the can – To increase a racing fuel's percentage of nitromethane.

tire – Rubber casing mounted onto a car wheel and pressurized with air.
Tires provide a cushioned ride and traction for a wheel. Most car tires
today are tubeless. Early tires were solid rubber. See also tire(belted
bias), tire(bias ply), and tire(radial).

tire(all season) – Tire built to operate satisfactorily in summer and
winter weather.

tire(all season performance radial) – All season steel belted radial tire
built for high speed driving on dry pavement, and good performance on wet or
icy road surfaces.

tire(all terrain) – See tire(lug).

tire(bald) – Tire condition created when tread is worn away leaving a smooth
surface with little traction.

tire(belted) – See tire(radial).

tire(belted bias ply) – Tire built with the basic body structure of a bias-ply
tire, but with important differences. It has two or more extra layers (or
belts) of material located between the body plies and the tread. The layers
are usually reinforced with steel or fabric.

tire(bias ply) – Tire built using reinforcing cords in the body plies which
run in alternating directions at an angle (or bias) to the center line of the
tread.

tire(clincher) – One of the first inflatable tires used. It was clamped to
the wheel rim and was difficult to change.

tire(conventional) – Non-radial or bias-ply tire.

tire(dual) – Two tire casings mounted onto a single special wheel. It is an
experimental tire design with the following advantages: minimal hydroplaning
due to large deep center gutter, reduced wear, run-flat capability, and good
cornering stability.

tire(eight ply) – Tire casing built with eight plies of cord material running
across the tire from bead to bead. This type of tire is commonly found on
cars and trucks carrying heavy loads. See also tire(four ply).

tire(fiberglass belted) – Tire built with one or more fiberglass belts under
the tire tread area.

tire(flat) – Tire condition created when a tire has lost its air pressure.
Possible causes include: punctures, cuts, bad seals around the tire rims, and

leaky tire valves. Do not drive on flat tires as surveys have shown two out of three flat tires driven short distances are too damaged to repair. Cuts and punctures can only be permanently repaired by applying patches from inside the tire. All other repairs should be considered temporary.

tire(four ply) - Tire casing built with four plies of cord material running across the tire from bead to bead. Each ply is separated by a layer of rubber. If the cord material direction runs diagonally across the tire, it is known as bias ply tire. If it runs perpendicular to the tread centerline, it is known as a radial ply tire.

tire (four ply rating two ply) - Tire built with two cords instead of four. Each is twice as strong as those used in a normal 4-ply tire. These type tires have also been referred to as 70-series.

tire(glass belted) - See tire(fiberglass belted).

tire(high performance) - A radial tire built with the following features: speed rated to at least 130 mph, low tire profile of 45-60, excellent traction and handling capabilities, and good tread life.

tire(high profile) - Tire built with narrower tread width and higher bead-to-tread height.

tire(low profile) - Tire built with the entire tread area closer to a wheel rim than a conventional tire. Wider designs give the tire better cornering ability at high speeds.

tire(lug) - Tire built with a deep tread design to provide traction in sand, soft earth, snow, mud, etc. It is not generally regarded as a highway tire, but as an off road tire.

tire(mini spare) - Smaller spare tire used in some late model cars. They are used primarily to save storage space. The smaller tire should only be used for driving short distances (under 25 miles) if mounted on a differential axle or else the differential could be damaged.

tire(off road) - See tire(lug).

tire(performance radial) - Radial tire built to hold up against high speed driving on dry road pavement.

tire(plastic) - Experimental tire casing made out of injection molded polyurethane. Advantages over rubber tires include: cheaper to make, no plies needed, runs cooler, weighs less, and long wearing.

tire(radial) - Tires casing built with its plies of cord material running across the tire, bead to bead, perpendicular to the direction of the tread centerline. Most radial tires use just two cord plies, and two or more belts under the tread. Radial advantages include: stronger tire than bias ply, reduced tread squirming, reduced skidding tendencies due to better road traction, sidewalls more flexible allowing tread to stay flatter when cornering, less heat build-up, better fuel economy from reduced rolling resistance, and reduced internal friction between cord plies when deflected.

tire(recap) - Used tire recovered with new tread. Worn tread area is cut down smooth and sanded to roughen the surface. New rubber with a tread pattern is bonded to the old tread surface. Bonding area is limited to the tread area. It is not as durable as retread tires due to less bonding area.

tire(retread) - Used tire recovered with new tread. Worn tread area is covered with full width new tire tread. In addition, new tread shoulders are wider than on recap providing more area to bond to tire. Net result is a more durable tire than a recap.

tire(run flat) - Tire casing built to mount on a special wheel and permit continued driving if casing goes flat. Tire is rated for a specified maximum speed and distance. See also run-flat.

tire(six ply) - Tire casing built with six plies of cord material running across the tire from bead to bead. It is commonly used for light to medium truck applications. See also tire(four ply).

tire(snow) - Tire built with an open tread pattern, deep grooves, and a softer rubber compound to produce traction on snowing road surfaces.

tire(solid rubber) - Tire built of solid rubber. It was used on early cars, and was quickly replaced with pneumatic tires.

tire(spare) - Extra tire carried in most cars in case a tire goes flat. See also tire(mini spare).

tire(steel belted radial) - Radial tire built with one or more steel belts underneath the tire tread area.

tire(studded) - Tire built with a tread pattern containing hardened metal studs at regular intervals for the purpose of providing extra traction on icy road surfaces. The tire tread is molded with stud pin holes. A stud gun is used to insert them into the tread. The studs are designed to wear at the same rate as the tread. Tire studding is usually done only on snow tires. Studded snow tires perform almost as well on packed snow or ice as tire chains.

tire(super sport) - Performance tire built with the following characteristics: lower and wider profile, better cornering and steering response, less flexing and subsequent heat build-up, and somewhat harsher ride.

tire(truck) - See tire(six ply) and tire(eight ply).

tire(tube) - Tire built to maintain air pressure by using an inner tube within its casing.

tire(tubeless) - Tire built to maintain air pressure by forming an air tight seal with a tire bead and wheel rim. No inner tube is required. Today's tires are primarily tubeless.

tire(twin) - See tire(dual).

tire(two ply) - Tire casing built with two plies of cord material running across the tire from bead to bead. Each ply is separated by a layer of rubber. If the cord material direction runs diagonally across the tire, it is known as a bias ply tire. If it runs perpendicular to the tread centerline, it is known as a radial ply tire.

tire(wide oval) - Tire built with tread closer to a wheel rim and wider than a standard tire. It provides better traction and reduced skidding tendencies.

tire(winter) - See tire(snow).

tire(wire cord) - Tire built with cord material composed of wire instead of nylon, rayon, or polyester. Such tires are designed for heavy duty use on buses, trucks, etc.

tire aspect number - Number used to express a tire's aspect ratio. It is computed by converting the fractional value of a tire's aspect ratio into a whole number. For example, an aspect ratio of 6:10 equals 60 percent or 60. As the number decreases, tire height decreases and/or tread width increases. See also tire profile and tire series.

tire aspect ratio - Ratio expressed as a tire's tread-to-bead height divided by its sidewall to sidewall width. It specifies a tire's cross sectional area (profile) and appearance. A low aspect ratio tire is typically a low and wide tire. See also tire aspect number, tire profile, and tire series.

tire balancer - Device used to equalize the distribution of mass around a car's tire and wheel assembly.

tire balancer(bubble) - See tire balancer(static).

tire balancer(static) - Machine used to balance a tire using a flat circular platform suspended underneath on a pointed shaft at the center. A central circular bubble level is mounted to determine equal distribution of mass on the platform. The tire is laid on the plate and the necessary lead weights are positioned around the rim of the tire until a level condition is achieved. The lead weights are then fastened securely to the rim. Static balance is not as popular today as the more accurate dynamic balancing. It sometimes used in conjunction with on-car spin balancing to achieve good overall balance.

tire balancer(dynamic) - Machine used to balance a tire while it rotates off the car. A tire and wheel assembly is mounted on the machine, and then spun until specified locations and weight amounts are determined. Weights are then installed at the tire rim locations. The tire is respun to check the balance and adjusted if needed. This balancing method is superior to static balancing and is the popular one in use today.

tire balancer(on car spin) - Dynamic tire balancer used to balance tires left on the car and off the ground. It is a more accurate method of balancing tires because the brake and suspension components become involved in equalizing the mass distribution.

tire balancer(spin) - See tire balancer(dynamic) and tire balancer(on-car spin).

tire balancer(wheel) - See tire balancer(static) and tire balancer(dynamic).

tire balancer(wheelspin) - See tire balancer(dynamic).

tire balancing - Process used to equalize the distribution of a tire's mass around its circumference and from side to side in order to minimize vibration when tire rotates fast. A tire out of balance around its circumference will vibrate up and down causing wheel hop. A tire out of balance along it axis will create a back and forth or wobbling vibration. See also tire balancer.

tire bead - Reinforced inner tire edge used to hold a tire on a wheel rim, and provide an airtight seal. The bead is reinforced with steel wire for strength.

tire bead bundle - Flexible steel wires encased in rubber and molded into the inner edge of a tire. See also tire bead.

tire belt - Layer of material reinforced with steel or fabric and used to strengthen the tread area and resist puncturing by sharp objects. It is located directly underneath the tire tread. See also tire cord.

tire belt wedge - Wedge of specially compounded rubber built into a tire at the tread edge. It is used to modify sidewall flexing and the behavior of shoulder tire tread on cornering.

tire body plies - See tire plies.

tire break-in - Tires require a proper break in just like a new engine in order to achieve maximum life. They take a "set" or certain shape within the first 50 miles. Maximum speed should be limited to 50 mph during those miles. New tires may also lose air at a higher rate until set, requiring more frequent initial inspection of tire pressure.

tire buffing - Removal of tire tread done to produce a tire with an even radius. The result is an evenly spinning tire. Even though some tread is removed, the tire's life is actually increased because it rolls smoothly. The procedure is not common today, since most tire irregularities are handled by spin balancing tires and adding appropriate balance weights.

tire buffing rib - Projection of rubber molded into a tire's widest point in a sidewall. It is designed to protect a sidewall from tire scuffing when curb parking, etc.

tire carcass - Body of a tire. It excludes the tread.

tire carcass plies - Layers of polyester or other material used to help make up the body of a tire. They are sandwiched between the tire liner, the sidewalls, and tire tread.

tire casing - See tire carcass.

tire center ribs - Tire tread channels located running around a tire's circumference and between its shoulder tread.

tire checking - Small cracks developed on the outer sidewall surface of a tire due to exposure to the elements.

tire cleaner - Substance formulated to clean and renew the appearance of a used tire.

tire concentricity - Degree of tire roundness.

tire condition - Amount of life left in a tire.

tire construction technique - Technique used to fabricate a tire casing.

tire cord - Fiber material used to make up the structure of a tire belt. Rayon, nylon, and polyester are the most popular. Steel belts consist of fiber material reinforced with steel.

tire defect - Faulty or defective tire construction. Defects can originate when the tire is produced or during the tire's life. They include: tread separation, ruptured cords, and broken bead. Defective tires are not safe to drive on.

tire eccentricity - Measure made of a tire's even distribution of mass when rotated. A tire will be eccentric or wobble if its mass is not evenly distributed around the circumference of a wheel. The mass can be uneven vertically and/or horizontally. Also, there can be eccentricity in the wheel as well. Finding the cause requires checking the wheel first. If the wheel runs true, tire eccentricity is minimized by balance weights or by tire buffing. See also wheel eccentricity.

tire footprint - Tread pattern contact area made on a road surface. Its size and shape is influenced by many of the variables affecting tire to road contact. Low profile tires have a short and wide footprint, while high profile tires have long and narrow footprints. At high speeds, long footprints change into a crescent shape, squirm a great deal, and actually lift portions of the tread off the road. Short and wide footprints maintain their shape resisting distortion and squirm forces. See also tire to road contact.

tire friction - Friction developed between tire tread and a road surface. The fastest stopping is achieved by maintaining tire friction or traction and not skidding.

tire gauge - Hand-held pencil-shaped gauge used to measure tire air pressure.

tire grade - Tire quality specified within a tire manufacturer's line. A top grade tire may be called a premium, first line, deluxe, etc.

tire grooves - Grooves or channels cut into the tread of a tire. Many different groove patterns are available. Pattern design considerations include: enhancing road traction, limiting hydroplaning, improving tire life, reducing squirm, and decreasing rolling resistance.

tire inflation - See tire pressure.

tire iron - Specially designed steel bar used on a tire changer to move a tire bead from the inside to the outside of a rim. The bead end must be smooth to avoid damaging the tire bead.

tire level - Tire price specified within a tire manufacturer's line.

tire life - Number of miles driven on a tire before it needs to be replaced. A tire's life is over when the tread is worn away, or there is some defect or weakness in the tire body that cannot be fixed. Tire tread needs to be replaced when the body cords start showing in the rubber or the tread wear indicators show replacement is needed. To maximize your tire life remember the following: buy the right size tires for your car; buy heavy duty tires if you plan to travel a lot; get in the habit of checking tire pressure and appearance frequently; rotate tires on a regular basis, check wheel alignment; watch for excessive wear along a tire's outer edges (underinflation); watch for excessive wear in the middle of tire tread (overinflation); avoid hitting, scraping, or climbing curbs; and minimize overloading tires. See also car service tip(tire rotation-radial).

tire liner - Layer of rubber material used to line the inside of a tire surface.

tire make - Tire manufacturer.

tire marks - Tread material left on a paved road surface due to fast starts, stops, or cornering. See also tire tracks.

tire plies - Layers of rubber-coated fabric used to make a tire body. They lie between the tire liner and the tire belts and tire sidewall stock.

tire pressure - Pressure of air contained inside a tire body. Specified tire pressure is based on a tire that has not been driven for a few hours or one which has only been driven a short distance. Warm tires will typically have 4-8 pounds higher pressure depending on conditions. For this reason, tire pressure can only be accurately adjusted when a tire is cool. See also overinflation, underinflation, proper inflation, gas saving tip(tire pressure), and car service tip(tire rotation-radial).

tire pressure sensing system - Assemblage of parts and controls used to monitor car tire pressure and activate sensors when pressure drops below a safe level.

tire profile - Tire cross section specified by a tire's aspect ratio. Low profile tires are typically low with wide tread. See also tire series.

tire regroover - Tool used to regroove a used or worn out tire with a tread pattern. It uses heat and a cutting blade. Some car repair shops will regroove tires and try to sell them as new. Driving on regrooved tires is a dangerous practice and should be avoided. The condition of a tire body will usually be a giveaway.

tire rotation - Periodic rearrangement made of tires on different wheels to even out irregular wear and prolong tread life. If a spare tire is rotated on a regular basis (5,000 mile average) with the others, tire life is extended 20 percent. On some rear wheel drive cars, rear tires can last almost twice as long, making tire rotation very important.

tires are bald - See tire(bald).

tire sealant - Material pumped into a tire casing under pressure to seal up tire leaks or prevent new ones. There are two types: temporary and permanent. Temporary sealants are used one time to inflate and temporarily seal a punctured tire. In most cases, it does the job, and will last enough miles to get the car to a repair facility. Permanent sealants are used to seal persistent rim leaks, and prevent tires from going flat when punctured (by sealing puncture as it occurs). Both types will accentuate unbalancing of an unbalanced tire.

tire series - Tire specified according to its aspect number. For example, a tire with a 70 aspect number would be called a 70 series tire. See also tire aspect number.

tire sidewall - Portion of a tire located between the tread and the bead.

tire sidewall stock - Rubber portion of a tire used to form the exterior sidewalls. See also tire tread stock.

tire size - Specific tire dimensions designed to place a tire in a specific category.

tire shoulder slots - Tire grooves cut in a tire tread's shoulder.

tire shredding - Condition created when different portions of a tire start coming apart in pieces. It can be due to a number of problems including: under inflation, excessive heat build-up, hard driving, poor recap quality, tread worn out, blowout, and driving on a flat tire.

tire to road contact - Amount of solid contact exhibited by a tire traveling on a road surface. It is influenced by: tire pressure, tread pattern, tire composition, tire balance, weight on wheel, wheel alignment angles, shock absorber behavior, and suspension spring behavior. See also tire footprint.

tire tracks - Tire tread pattern left on a road surface. See also tire marks.

tire tread - Tire portion molded onto the outer surface of a tire casing in a certain tread pattern. It is the only part of a tire contacting a road surface. Its composition and thickness determine the life expectancy of a tire. See also tread pattern.

tire tread(asymmetrical) - Tire tread design built with a variation in groove shape and size from one side to another. It is used to provide the best blend of wet/dry driving, braking, and ride characteristics.

tire tread element - Repeatable tire tread pattern. Every tire has one or more basic patterns in use. Each shoulder or center rib has a tread element pattern. The center ribs may have one design and the shoulder ribs another. The element pattern for each rib repeats itself around the circumference of a tire.

tire tread squirm - Condition created when tread twists somewhat while contacting a road surface. Different tread designs and other methods like steel belts minimize the condition.

tire tread stock - Rubber portion of a tire used to form the tread pattern and its base. See also tire sidewall stock.

tire trick - See con game(check your tires).

tire type - Tire model.

tire valve - Slender check valve mounted in a valve stem to regulate air flow into and out of a tire. Valves should be sealed with valve caps since tire valves slowly lose air causing tires to become underinflated.

tire wear - Amount of tire tread worn away from a tire's original tread profile. Factors affecting the type and amount of tire wear include:

driving habits, tire pressure, wheels out of alignment or unbalanced, loose or worn suspension and/or steering systems, and road surfaces.

tire wear(camber) – See tire wear(side).

tire wear(center) – See tire wear(middle).

tire wear(cornering) – Front or rear tire wear caused by taking turns at speeds high enough to cause loss of traction. The wear shows up as a rounded tread shoulder and a rough scratchy surface on one or both sides of the tread depending on the frequency and direction of turning.

tire wear(cupped) – Front or rear tire tread worn abnormally with several circular concave wear marks. It is usually due to loose front end components which allow a tire to bounce up and down when road bumps are encountered. The bouncing tends to gouge the tire. Possible causes include: worn ball joints, shock absorbers (due to loss of dampening action), tie-rod ends, and control arm bushings; bent axle; and unbalanced tire.

tire wear(excessive on one side) – Front tires excessively worn on the inside or outside due to a wrong camber setting. When out of adjustment, the tires tilt excessively inward or outward. It is corrected by adjustment.

tire wear(feathered edge) – Front tires worn to a smooth wavy thin edge along the inside or outside. It is caused by front wheels being out of alignment with either too much toe-out or toe-in respectively.

tire wear(irregular) – Front and/or back tires wearing out prematurely and in an irregular way. It is usually due to being unbalanced. Out of balance front tires will often transmit vibration up the steering column. Sometimes worn steering idler arms are to blame.

tire wear(middle) – Front or back tires prematurely worn in the middle due to over inflation. Be sure to check air pressure when tires are cool. They can increase as much as six pounds when hot from driving.

tire wear(normal) – Front and/or back tires wearing normally for the miles traveled. The car is usually in good alignment, and the tire tread is wearing evenly.

tire wear(patchy on one side) – Front or rear tire worn with irregular patchy areas on one side of a tire. It is usually due to out of balance tires.

tire wear(sawtooth) – Front tire wear characterized by each tire element being worn at an angle creating a tread profile that looks like the cutting edge of a handsaw. It is caused by excessive toe-in or toe-out, depending on the direction of wear.

tire wear(shoulder) – Front or back tires worn evenly but prematurely on both sides. It is caused by underinflation. Keep tires at or a few pounds above a manufacturer's recommendations. Underinflated tires have a much shorter life due to increased flexing, rolling resistance, and associated heat.

tire wear(side) – Front tires worn excessively on one side. It is most commonly caused by an excessive camber angle. Positive or negative angles cause outside or inside wear respectively.

tire wear(spotty) – Front tires worn on both outer portions of the tread with cupping marks on one side. It is usually due to more than one problem. The most common causes are: underinflation, incorrect camber, and excessive toe-in or toe-out.

tire wear indicator – See tread wear indicator.

Tischer – American car produced in 1914.

tissue(1) – Car deal with very little profit.

tissue(2) – The actual dealer cost of a new car.

tissue paper – See tissue.

Titan – American car produced in 1916 and 1919.

Titan Truck – American truck produced in 1917.

Titan Vim – American car produced in 1925.

Tjarda – American car produced in 1934.

TK – Abbreviation for truck.

T/M – Abbreviation for transmission.

TMF – American car produced in 1909.

TN(1) – Abbreviation for tonneau.

TN(2) – Abbreviation for Tunisia found usually on an international license plate.

TO(1) – Abbreviation for take over. See also TO Man.

TO(2) – Abbreviation for United Arab Emirates found usually on an international license plate.

toe – Smaller half or top of a gear tooth. See also heel.

toe-in – See wheel alignment angle(toe-in).

toe-in toe-out adjuster – Spring-loaded rod tool used to align front wheels so they are parallel to each other.

toe-out – See wheel alignment angle(toe-out).

toe-out on turns – See wheel alignment angle(toe-out on turns).

to lap – To lead another race car by one or more laps of a race track.

Toledo – American car produced from 1900-1903, 1910, 1913, and 1915.

Toledo Steamer – American steam car produced in 1900-1902 by American Bicycle Co. in Ohio.

tolerance – Allowable maximum and minimum size difference of a part from a specified dimension.

toll booth – Booth located at the entrance to a toll road or bridge to collect use fees.

toll bridge – Bridge set up to charge fees for crossing it.

toll gate – Gate on a road or bridge located where use fees are collected.

toll road – Road set up to charge fees for traveling on it.

toll way – See toll road.

TO man – Experienced salesman used to take over a pending deal. He is usually a sales manager.

tommy bar – T handle.

Tonawanda – American car produced in 1900.

tongue weight – A trailer's weight located in front of the wheels. It is usually 10 percent of the trailer's weight whether it is loaded or not.

tonneau – Rear compartment or part of a car. It may or may not contain seats. See also body style(tonneau).

tonneau cover – Cover used to conceal a car's rear compartment area, especially in hatchback cars. Also, it refers to a cover used to cover the interior of a convertible car when the top is down.

tool man – Slick service station attendant experienced at quickly sizing up a customer to determine if he is a good prospect for a con game.

too worn to patch – Inside tire surface wear characterized as too thin or split to hold a patch well.

Topaz – American car produced from 1980 to date by Mercury Division of Ford Motor Co. in Michigan.

top – Top eliminator. See also TE.

top chop – To lower the roof on a car.

topcoat – See paint(topcoat).

top cylinder lubricant – Lubricating additive added to gasoline to help lubricate valve heads and seats, and the top portions of the piston and cylinder wall.

top cylinder oiler – Device used to meter top cylinder lubricant into fuel.

top dead center – Highest piston position reached in a cylinder.

top dollar – Highest value feasibly attainable when selling a product.

top eliminator – Only race car left after elimination runs have been held.

top end(1) – Engine components located above the block.

top end(2) – Second half of a quarter mile race.

top end(3) – Highest speed attainable by a car.

top flight mechanic – Experienced mechanic with a good reputation.

top hatter – Car salesman experienced at keeping prices high for a good profit margin.

top it off – See fill up.

top time – Maximum speed attained during a 1/4 mile drag race.

top up – See fill up.

Toquet – American car produced in 1905.

Torbensen – American car produced from 1906-1908.

Torino – American car produced from 1960-1979 by Ford Motor Co. in Michigan.

Toronado – American car produced from 1965 to date by Oldsmobile Division of General Motor Corp. in Michigan. It was the first American car produced with front wheel drive since 1937.

torpedo – See body style(torpedo).

torque – Force characterized by exerting a turning or twisting effort. Torque does not necessarily produce motion. An example would be torque used to tighten bolts or nuts. Torque producing motion is commonly associated with rotating shafts, such as an engine crankshaft, driveline, rear wheel axle, etc. It is measured in foot-pounds or inch-pounds.

torque converter – Fluid coupling used to transfer engine torque to an automatic transmission. It differs from a normal fluid coupling or converter in that engine torque can be increased or multiplied, and a stator is used to reduce backflow of fluid against impeller. It is located in a transmission bell housing and is usually bolted to a flywheel. The converter consists: of a housing, driving member or pump vane, a driven member or turbine vane, a reaction member or stator vane, and transmission fluid. Torque is transferred when an engine spins one of the vanes in the fluid which spins the fluid and thus the other vane.

Torque-Flite – Three speed automatic transmission made by Chrysler. See also Power-Flite and Clutch-Flite.

torque multiplication – Increasing engine torque.

torque multiplier – Fluid coupling used in an automatic transmission built to fill and empty fluid as needed. See also fill and empty coupling.

torque rod – Metal rod used to control oscillating motion of an engine. It is most commonly used on transverse mounted engines in front wheel drive cars. One end is fastened to the lower engine block with the other end to a car frame crossmember. More than one may be used. Rubber bushings are used at both ends to dampen vibration.

torque steer – Condition created on certain late model front-wheel drive cars where the front end tends to squirm back and forth under hard acceleration.

torque tube – Non-rotating steel tube used to house a driveline. It bolts around a differential input opening and is supported at the transmission end.

torque tube drive – Driveline system built using a torque tube with an internal shaft to transfer power from a transmission to a differential. The tube does not rotate. The internal drive shaft uses only one universal joint at the transmission end.

torque wrench – Wrench used to tighten nuts or bolts to a specified torque value.

Torsen – See differential(Torsen).

torsional vibration – Twisting and untwisting action developed in a shaft when power or loads are applied.

torsion bar – Spring steel rod built to exert resistance when twisted. It is used in car suspension systems to provide spring-like action in different ways. See also suspension(torsion bar).

torsion bar spring – Long straight bar attached to a car frame at one end and a control arm at the other. Spring action is produced when the bar is twisted.

torsion bar suspension – See suspension system(torsion bar).

torsion gear rattle – See sound(rattling-6).

torus – Donut-shaped part in an automatic transmission used to transfer power from an engine to a transmission. It is filled with hydraulic fluid. See also converter.

torx – Sunken six-point socket-like screw head.

Total – American car line produced from 1977 to date by Total Performance in Connecticut.

total advance – Actual spark advance. At any given moment in the operation of an engine, spark advance is a total of three advance components: static, centrifugal, and vacuum.

totaled – Car damaged extensively enough that the repair cost exceeds its current undamaged value. Totaled cars are usually sold to dismantlers.

total odometer – See odometer.

total stopping distance – Distance required to stop a vehicle safely once a driver has made the decision. It equals reaction time distance plus braking distance. See also reaction time and braking distance.

touch up – Small paint job made on a portion of a car body to cover scratches, a small dents, etc. The object is to apply paint to the small area and get it to blend with the surrounding paint.

touch up kit – Small paint container filled with paint matched to a car's color. It comes with a small applicator brush and is used to fill surface chips.

tough – Something nice.

tough customer – Potential customer experienced in negotiating a deal or who is difficult to close a sale on.

Touraine – American car produced from 1912-1915 by Nance Motor Car Co. (1912-1913), and Touraine Co. (1913-1915), both in Pennsylvania.

touring – Traveling from place to place.

touring car – See body style(touring car).

tourism – Practice of touring.

Tourist – American car produced from 1902-1909 by Auto Vehicle Co. in California. It was a well known car on the West Coast in its time.

tourist – Person traveling from place to place.

tourist class – Least expensive class of travel on a train, airplane, etc.

tourist court – See motel.

tourist season – Time of year regarded as popular for traveling. In the U.S., it is usually the summertime.

tourist trap – Business engaged in taking advantage of tourists usually by overcharging.

tow – To transport a non-operational car to a repair shop or service station where repairs can be made.

Towanda – American car produced in 1904.

towbar – Flexible triangular-shaped structural member used to pull a vehicle. It is portable, mounts to the front bumper of a vehicle, and attaches to a ball mounted on the rear of the towing vehicle.

tow charges – See towing charges.

towed away – Car removed from its parked location while the owner was away.

Tower – American car produced in 1918.

towing a trailer – To pull a trailer behind a car or truck.

towing charges – Charges levied against a car or truck towed away to a towing yard or business location. A towed vehicle is not released to an owner until the charges are paid.

towing hub – One of two freewheeling hubs bolted between each drive wheel and its wheel hub to prevent the differential from turning. They are typically used to protect a differential when towing a car.

towing system – Method used by a towing vehicle to attach and pull a disabled car. See also towing tip.

towing system(flatbed) – Movable flat metal deck mounted on a towing vehicle. It is designed to slide backwards, tip to the ground, winch a car onto itself, and slide forward back into a horizontal position. It is probably the best method of transporting a car, but is also the most expensive.

towing system(no tow) – See towing system(flatbed).

towing system(roll back) – See towing system(flatbed).

towing system(sling type) – Extendible pivoting T-shaped bar(s) elevated with a boom and retractable sling mounted on the back of a towing vehicle. Different fittings such as chains, J-hooks, crossbeams, spacer blocks, etc. are often used. It is the most common method in use today (over 90 percent) for lifting the front or rear end of a car off the ground when towing. It can adequately tow older cars and many of today's cars. It is, however, losing favor to the wheel-lift and flatbed towing systems because more and more of the new cars: have soft front or rear ends, have lightweight chassis components, and need special sling attachments and fittings to tow safely.

towing system(tilt bed) – See towing system(flatbed).

towing system(wheel lift) – Extendible T-bar hitch-like arrangement with movable claws mounted at each end of the T-bar for grabbing the tires. It slides under the vehicle, clamps the tires, then elevates the car off the ground by means of a hydraulic cylinder in the vehicle's bed.

towing tip – Useful information given to help tow a car safely.

towing tip(driveline) – Any time the drive wheels remain on the ground, the driveline should be removed if: towing distance exceeds 15 miles, and towing speed exceeds 30 mph. When removing the driveline, mark the relative position of the components to avoid vibration problems when reassembling. Driveline components are carefully balanced to minimize vibration.

towing tip(drive wheels) – If the car is to be towed with only two of the wheels off the ground, it is preferable that they be the drive wheels. If they must stay on the road, make sure: the parking brake is off, the transmission is in neutral, towing speed does not exceed 30 mph, towing distance does not exceed 15 miles, clamping devices are used to lock front wheels straight ahead, elevated tires are at least 4-6 inches off the ground, and rear frame and other car components have adequate clearance. See also towing tip(driveline) and towing tip(wheeled dolly).

towing tip(high speed tow) – Towing a car at high speed (highway speed) requires the disconnection of the driveline if the drive wheels are on the ground.

towing tip(long distance tow) – Towing a car over 15 miles necessitates disconnection of the driveline if the drive wheels are on the ground.

towing tip(wheeled dolly) – Some towing operators have a wheeled dolly they use underneath the drive wheels to prevent them from turning. If this is used there is no need to remove the driveline even for long distance or high speed towing.

towing vehicle – See tow truck.

Town & Country – American car produced from 1957 to date by Chrysler Corp. in Michigan.

Town Car – American car produced in 1909. Also, an American car produced from 1980 to date by Lincoln Division of Ford Motor Co. in Michigan.

town car – See body style(town car).

Towne Shopper – American car produced in 1948.

tow truck – Truck built to tow disabled or illegally parked vehicles. See also towing system.

tow truck operator – Person experienced in driving a tow truck and towing vehicles safely.

toy – Race car.

Toyo – Japanese line of tires.

Toyo Kogyo Company Ltd – Japanese car company noted for producing Mazda cars. It was founded in 1920 as Toyo Cork Kogyo producing corks. The name changed to Toyo Kogyo Company Ltd. in 1927. Three-wheeled truck production began in 1931. The first Mazda car was produced in 1961 with the first rotary in 1967. The company was renamed Mazda Motors Corporation in 1984.

Toyota – Japanese car line produced from 1936 to date by Toyota Motor Co. Ltd. Popular car models include: Blizzard, Camry, Carina, Celica (1971 to date), Century, Chaser, Corolla, Corona, Corsa, Cresta, Crown, Hi Lux, Land Cruiser (1960 to date), Mark II, MRZ, Soarer, Sprinter, Starlet, Tercel, and Vista. The U.S. representative is Toyota Motor Sales, U.S.A., headquartered in Torrance, California.

TR(1) – Abbreviation for touring car.

TR(2) – Abbreviation for Turkey found usually on an international license plate.

tr – Abbreviation for transmission. See also trans.

Trabant – East German car line produced from 1959 to date by VEB Sachsenring Automobilwerk.

Trabold - American car produced in 1921.

trace detonation - Slight detonation considered harmless to engine parts. It is usually heard as a faint pinging or ticking sound under the following conditions: cold engine, wide open throttle driving, rapid throttle opening or closing, braking on an EGR equipped car. Higher octane fuel will further minimize trace detonation. Trace detonation indicates an acceptable grade of gasoline is being used. See also detonation, preignition, and EGR system cutout switch.

trace knock - See trace detonation.

track(1) - Distance measured between the two front wheels or the two rear wheels of a car.

track(2) - Straightness and smoothness a car exhibits when moving down a road.

track(3) - Tire tread.

track bar - See anti sway bar.

track brake - Brake built to slow down a car by generating friction with the road surface.

tracking - Lineup of rear wheel tracks directly in the front wheel tracks.

track race - Race held on a course built for racing.

track rod - Steel rod used to form part of a car's front wheel steering linkage, and assist in turning the wheels when a steering wheel is turned. Also, a rod used to limit lateral axle movement. See also Panhard rod.

traction - Friction between tires and the road surface.

Traction Avant - French Citroen car introduced in 1934 and considered ahead of its time. It had front wheel drive and a body construction technique employing pressed steel sections welded into a box form. The body construction was stronger than other cars at the time, and is still used by some car manufacturers today.

traction bar - One of two bars attached to a rear axle (one near each rear wheel) and to the chassis frame side rails. It prevents rear axle windup.

traction device - Device installed on or used by a wheel to increase its traction ability. Tire chain is an example.

Tractobile - American steam car is produced from 1900-1902 by Pennsylvania Steam Vehicle Co. in Pennsylvania.

tractor - The cab-engine-towing unit of a semitruck. See also tractor-trailer and trailer(2).

tractor fuel - Fuel formulated to be much less volatile than gasoline. It is similar to kerosene and diesel fuel.

tractor-trailer - Semitruck.

trade examination - Test taken by an individual training to work on cars to determine his grasp of the subject.

trade in - Item given to a seller at the time of purchase usually to lower a selling price. Trade-ins include: car, battery, tires, alternators, starters, and brake linings.

trade in allowance - Monetary amount promised to a customer trading in an item toward purchase of another item. It commonly refers to trading in a used car to lower the purchase price of another used car or new car.

trade in car - Car traded in for another used or new car.

trade in contract - See contract(trade in).

trademark - A slogan, sign, device, mark, label, etc. adopted by a manufacturer to designate his own goods from others.

trades and terms - Advertising offer indicating a willingness to sell a car by trading for something else or by negotiating some financial arrangement.

trading down - To buy an older, less expensive, or smaller car than the one currently owned.

Traffic - American car produced in 1914.

traffic - Vehicles, animals, pedestrians, etc. traveling over roads.

traffic accident - See accident.

traffic citation - Form issued by a traffic officer to a driver for an observed violation of a traffic law. Though the driver must sign the form, it is not an admission of guilt, but merely a promise to appear in court on the assigned date and time. Failure to do so generally results in a warrant being issued for the driver's arrest. It contains information on: the violation, time, date, place, license number, etc. If the violation is not a serious one, most traffic citations offer you the option of settling the matter out of court by admitting guilt and paying a fine. If you feel you are innocent, the only way to clear the charge is to appear in court and state your case before a judge.

  Traffic citations always specify a traffic law violation in one or more of the following areas: moving, equipment, parking, and pedestrian. See also warning, kiting, document citation, equipment violation, and fixit ticket.

traffic control signal - Any mechanical, electrical, or manual device used to control traffic flow.

traffic court - Court authorized to hear traffic violation cases and render judgements.

traffic is backed up for miles - One or more lines of cars stretched out for one or more miles and moving slowly or not at all. Possible causes include: accident, rush hour, bad weather, road damage or blockage.

traffic is blocked - Traffic prevented from moving due to an accident, malfunctioning traffic light, road problems, etc.

traffic is moving at a snail's pace - Slow traffic movement due to an accident, rush hour, bad weather, etc.

traffic jam - Traffic stopped or slowed due to rush hour, malfunctioning traffic light, accident, bad weather, drivers slowing down to look at something, slow moving cars, one or more cars stopping to pick up people, detour, etc.

traffic lane - Area of a roadway designated as one car width. Freeways have multiple lanes going in one direction. Two lane roadways have one in each direction. All lanes are separated from each other by some type of pavement markings.

traffic laws - Laws passed to regulate traffic.

traffic light - Light used to regulate flow of traffic.

traffic light(2 way stop) - Four-way multi-flashing light device equipped with two opposing red and two opposing yellow lights. It is used at dangerous intersections to stop traffic in two opposing directions and caution traffic in the other two opposing directions.

traffic light(3 light signal) - Multi-light device used to control traffic flow. It consists of 3 lights: red, yellow, and green. The illuminated red light requires traffic to stop at marked stop lines until the green light is activated. The illuminated yellow light warns drivers the traffic light is changing from green to red. When the red light activates, drivers are prohibited from entering the intersection. The green illuminated light permits drivers to proceed if it is safe to do so. If the green light contains an arrow, drivers are allowed to proceed only in the arrow's direction.

traffic light(4 way stop) - Four-way multi-flashing light device equipped with four red lights to control traffic flow in all four directions of an intersection.

traffic light(flashing red) - Flashing red light used at dangerous intersections usually to reinforce the effect of an existing stop sign. It is treated by drivers as a stop sign.

traffic light(flashing yellow) - Flashing yellow light used at dangerous intersections or with warning signs to inform drivers to proceed cautiously.

traffic light(lane signal) - Light used mostly on freeways or expressways to control traffic in individual traffic lanes. It is mounted directly over a lane. A red X means traffic is not allowed in the lane. A yellow X means traffic will not be allowed in the lane shortly. A green arrow means the lane can be used.

traffic light(pedestrian) - Illuminated signs used to control pedestrian traffic across streets.

traffic light(railroad crossing) - Flashing red lights activated at a railroad crossing to stop traffic until an approaching train passes by.

traffic officer - Law officer assigned to stand in an intersection and direct traffic flow.

traffic pattern - Flow of traffic in an area.

traffic regulation - See traffic laws.

traffic school - Driver education program run by some courts often as an alternative to a conviction.

traffic sign - See road sign.

traffic snarl - See traffic jam.

traffic ticket - See traffic citation.

traffic trap - See con game(traffic trap).

traffic violation - Traffic law broken usually by a car driver.

traffic violator - Person violating a traffic law.

traffic volume - Amount of traffic found on one or more specified roads.

trailer(1) - A vehicle: built without motive power, and designed to be pulled by a car or truck. There are two main types. Open trailers are used primarily for hauling cargo. Enclosed trailers are built to provide portable sleeping, eating, and bathing facilities.

trailer(2) - The rear or back section of a semitruck. It couples to a tractor. See also tractor-trailer.

trailer camp - See trailer park.

trailer court - See trailer park.

trailer hitch - Structural device mounted on the front of a trailer for attaching it to a towing vehicle.

trailer hook up mirror - One of two mirrors mounted on a car or truck to provide a rear line of sight around a trailer. They are mounted on both front doors a foot or more away.

trailer park - An area built to accommodate trailers, motor homes, and/or mobile homes on a temporary or permanent basis. Utilities such as electricity, sewer disposal, and water are piped to each space.

trailing arm – Pivoting arm used to connect a steering knuckle to a torsion bar. Two arms are used to connect the top and bottom of a steering knuckle. The Volkswagen Bug uses trailing arms in its front suspension system. Also, it refers to an independent suspension system built to allow wheels to lean with a car body when a car corners. It is popular on rear wheels of front wheel drive cars.

tranny – Abbreviation for transmission.

tramp – Vibration and oscillating motion created when front wheels turn.

trans – Abbreviation for transmission. See also tr.

Trans AM – American car produced from 1967 to date by Pontiac Division of General Motors Corp. in Michigan.

transaxle – Drive unit built containing a transmission and differential assembly. It usually bolts directly to the flywheel end of an engine. Its advantages include: strong engine and drive train unit, compactness, decreased possibility of misalignment, and unit mounted to frame and supported by car suspension system. See also axle(trans).

transducer – Device used to transform one form of energy into another. A solenoid is an example of a transducer. It transforms electrical energy into mechanical energy (movement).

transfer case – Gear unit used to transfer power from a transmission to both axles or just to the rear. It mounts behind or on the side of a transmission, depending on design.

transfer panel – Large durable decal used to cover a car body panel such as a door.

transfer tube – Short brake line used on a disc brake caliper assembly to route brake fluid to a second brake cylinder. Today's caliper assemblies have the fluid transfer built into the housing.

transformer – Electrical device used to change the characteristics of electrical current. Transformers typically increase or decrease voltage available to an electrical circuit. This can be done with AC or DC current. AC voltage in homes, for example, has been decreased from a nearby transformer from several hundred volts to 110 or 220 volts. DC voltage in a car ignition coil (transformer), for example, is increased from 12 volts to several thousand volts. All transformers have primary and secondary windings that are insulated from each other. The primary winding carries the input voltage. The secondary winding carries the output voltage.

transistor – Solid state electronic component used to switch a specified current flow according to a small current flow through an auxiliary circuit in the transistor.

transistor ignition – See ignition system(transistor).

Transit – American car produced in 1912.

transmission – Gear unit used to transfer power from an engine to drive wheels. It uses gears or torque conversion to create different engine to drive wheel rpm ratios for driving at different speeds.

transmission(automatic) – Transmission built to automatically make gear changes according to varying road and load conditions. Primary components include: a fluid coupling (torque converter); one or more planetary gear sets with associated drum, brake band, and clutch; mainshaft; and fluid control parts. Each gear set is controlled through fluid pressure which regulates brake band clamping and engages or disengages a respective clutch.
   An automatic transmission uses at least 10-15 percent more fuel than a manual.

transmission(automatic overdrive) – Automatic transmission built with four forward gears.

transmission(auxiliary) – Auxiliary manual transmission used with a car's main manual transmission to provide more gear ratios than are possible from the main transmission alone. For example, a three speed auxiliary transmission would give a five speed main transmission fifteen different gear ratios.

transmission(close ratio) – Transmission built with gear ratios having a smaller overall spread between low and high gear. It is popular in racing for keeping an engine in the upper part of its power band at all times.

transmission(constant mesh) – Manual transmission built where all gears remain in contact or meshed at all times. Synchronizer clutches are used to engage the gears.

transmission(continuously variable) – Transmission built to allow a continuous range of gear ratio changes. Pulleys with variable diameters are commonly used.

transmission(CVT) – See transmission(continuously variable).

transmission(friction) – Early transmission built with two discs rotating at right angles to each other. Different gear ratios are achieved by moving the edge of one disc along the face of another.

transmission(fully synchronized) – Manual transmission built with all the forward gears in contact with each other at all times. Synchronizing clutches are used to create the different transmission speeds. Reverse is not usually synchronized.

transmission(helical gear synchromesh) - Manual synchromesh transmission built with the gears cut at an angle rather than straight.

transmission(hydramatic) - Automatic transmission used for many years on many different types of older cars.

transmission(in and out box) - Device used to eliminate a clutch and transmission by providing a means for engaging and disengaging a car's drive wheels to and from an engine. It must be operated when the car is stopped and the engine off. The car is then push-started. It is used on race cars traveling at speeds always within the usable power band of the engine. Primary advantage is removing the weight of a transmission and clutch assembly.

transmission(manual) - Transmission built with gear sets mounted on two or more shafts and engaged in different combinations through the use of a gear shifter and an engine clutch. The different gear combinations create different driveline rotational speeds.

transmission(overdrive) - Two speed transmission located behind a main transmission, and used to increase driveline speed and double the number of main transmission speeds. It consists of a planetary gear unit and overrunning clutch. It is used primarily to increase top speed and fuel economy. See also gas saving tip(overdrive unit).

transmission(planetary) - Transmission built out of one or more planetary gear sets. Early Model T Fords used them. Today's automatic transmissions use them.

transmission(progressive) - Transmission used in early cars which required shifting through all the intermediate gears when shifting from low to high gear and vice versa.

transmission(selective) - Transmission built to allow the shifting mechanism to go directly from neutral to any gear. Sliding gear and constant mesh transmissions are this type.

transmission(slickshift) - Transmission built for power shifting.

transmission(sliding gear) - Early predecessor to today's synchromesh transmission. It consisted of two parallel shafts with splined gears sliding along the shafts to create different gear ratios. It was difficult to operate without clashing the gears.

transmission(standard) - See transmission(manual).

transmission(stepless) - See transmission(continuously variable).

transmission(synchromesh) - Manual transmission built with two or more gear ratios in constant contact with each other. The different gear ratios are engaged by synchronizing clutches. In some transmissions, all the gear ratios are synchromesh, while in other first and reverse are not.

transmission(two stick) - Main and auxiliary transmission built to operate together. One stick is used to operate each transmission. See also transmission(auxiliary).

transmission adjustment - Adjustment made to a transmission to make it operate properly.

transmission band - See brake band.

transmission bearings - Various ball, roller, and needle bearings used in a transmission to support shafts, gear sets, and synchronizer clutches.

transmission case - Housing used to contain all of a manual or automatic transmission's components.

transmission case cover plate - Plate attached to the top of a transmission housing. It provides access to the shift linkage and other components.

transmission cluster gear - See gear(transmission countershaft).

transmission cooler - See transmission oil cooler.

transmission countershaft - Shaft used in a transmission to carry various gears which are meshed with gears mounted on the transmission's main shaft to create various gear sets. It is offset and parallel to the main shaft.

transmission countershaft gear - See gear(transmission countershaft).

transmission fluid - Special oil formulated for use in automatic transmissions. It should be changed every 20-25,000 miles in most cars and sooner if heavy loads are often carried.

transmission governor - Device used in an automatic transmission to regulate fluid pressure according to car speed.

transmission jack - Hydraulic jack built to facilitate installation and removal of transmissions from cars and trucks.

transmission input shaft - Shaft used to transfer power from the engine through the clutch to the transmission's main shaft. One end rests in the pilot bearing in the flywheel area. The other end contains the main drive gear and rests behind an oil seal just inside the transmission housing.

transmission lever - See transmission shifter.

transmission lubrication - Lubricating fluid used to reduce the friction of moving parts in a transmission. Parts lubricated include: gear teeth, shaft bearings, shaft splines, synchronizers, etc. A heavier oil (SAE80-90) is used in manual transmissions while automatic transmissions use lighter oil. See also oil(gear).

transmission main shaft - Central shaft used in a manual transmission to carry various gears which are meshed with gears mounted on a countershaft to create various gear sets or ratios.

transmission modulator - Vacuum operated valve used to regulate hydraulic pressure in an automatic transmission so the clutches, bands, and other valves work together for smooth shifting and no slipping. A vacuum line runs from the intake manifold to the modulator. See also car service tip(transmission modulator test).

transmission oil cooler - Small tank installed inside the existing radiator for cooling transmission oil. It may also be a small separate radiator mounted usually near the front bottom of a water radiator to circulate transmission oil for cooling. Two lines run between the transmission and the radiator to circulate the fluid. See also fluid leak(red oil in coolant).

transmission oil leak - See fluid leak(transmission) and fluid leak(red oil in coolant).

transmission oil pan - Pan attached to the bottom of a transmission housing. It is usually found only on automatic transmissions.

transmission output shaft - Shaft used in a transmission to receive the rotation derived by a certain gear set ratio and transfer that rotation to a driveline. It is usually coupled directly behind the transmission's main shaft.

transmission overhaul - Process defined as restoring a worn out transmission to new operating condition by: removing it from a car, disassembling it, replacing all worn parts and/or machining worn surfaces to new tolerances, reassembling it, and installing it back in a car.

transmission problem - Condition created when a transmission does not sound right or is not operating properly.

transmission problem(automatic-excessive shifting) - Transmission repeatedly shifts back and forth between two gears. Possible causes include: lockup clutch locking and unlocking due to high vacuum level (requires more engine load to keep it locked.

transmission problem(automatic-jerky shifting) - Transmission causes car to jerk or buck when shifting from one gear to another. Possible causes include: vacuum components controlling shifting leaking, and transmission/throttle linkage out of adjustment.

transmission problem(automatic-noisy) - See sound(growling/humming-3), sound(clicking-6), and sound(grinding).

transmission problem(automatic-overheating) - Automatic transmission oil overheats causing one or more of the following symptoms to occur: slipping in gear, shifting erratically or not at all, not going into gear, and emitting burned oil smells. Possible causes include: low fluid level, wrong type fluid, and excessive stop and go driving in hot weather.
   Overheating is the number one cause of automatic transmission failure. High temperatures can create the following internal problems: bake oil seals causing leakage, break down oil's lubricating ability, cause gum and resin deposits to form in the various passageways causing moving parts to stick, burn clutch plates and brake band linings. See also road situation tip(automatic transmission overheating).

transmission problem(automatic-rough engagement) - Gears engage roughly in an automatic transmission. Possible causes include: oil viscosity too low, scored drums, burned clutch plates and brake band linings, bands out of adjustment, and throttle valve linkage out of adjustment.

transmission problem(automatic-slow engagement) - Gears engage slowly in an automatic transmission. Possible causes include: burned or scratched drum, brake band linings, and/or clutch plates; loose brake bands; bands out of adjustment; and binding clutch plates.

transmission problem(bearing noise) - Grinding or grating noise emanates from transmission bearings when the engine is running. Possible causes include: worn input shaft bearing, clutch release bearing, pilot bearing, main shaft bearings, counter shaft bearings, and output shaft bearings. The input shaft and clutch release bearings can often be diagnosed by performing a simple test. With the engine running, depress the clutch. If the noise is gone, a bad input shaft bearing is suspect. If the noise continues, the clutch release bearing is probably bad and was adjusted to spin continuously. Any bad shaft bearings require immediate replacement or the various gear sets, synchronizer clutches, and other bearings will be damaged resulting in a complete transmission replacement.

transmission problem(manual-difficult to shift-1) - Transmission is difficult to shift from one gear to another. Possible causes include: clutch not releasing; worn, binding, or damaged main shaft splines; bent or broken shift fork(s); and shift linkage out of adjustment.

transmission problem(manual-difficult to shift-2) - Transmission is difficult to shift from one gear to another in cold weather. Possible causes include: oil viscosity too high, and transmission never gets warm due to extreme cold temperature and or lack of use.

transmission problem(manual-gear grinding) — Gears grind against each other when transmission is shifted from one gear set to another. Possible causes include: warped clutch plate or pressure plate, clutch release fork out of adjustment, and hydraulic clutch linkage low on fluid or containing air.
transmission problem(manual-noisy in neutral) — See sound(growling/humming-1).
transmission problem(manual-noisy in gear) — See sound(growling/humming-2).
transmission problem(manual-slips out of first gear) — Engaged first gear in a manual transmission slips back into neutral. Possible causes include: worn or damaged first gear set, transmission bearings, shaft splines, and shift forks; shift linkage out of adjustment; and excessive end play of mainshaft, countershaft, and/or reverse idler shaft.
transmission problem(manual-slips out of high gear) — Engaged high gear in a manual transmission slips back into neutral. Possible causes include: worn or damaged pinion gear bearing, pinion gear teeth, and shift forks; shift linkage out of adjustment, worn, or missing parts; and transmission out of alignment.
transmission problem(manual-slips out of second gear) — Engaged second gear in a manual transmission slips back into neutral. Possible causes include: worn or damaged transmission bearings, shift forks, and second gear set; shift linkage out of adjustment; and excessive endplay of mainshaft or countershaft.
transmission problem(manual-slips out of reverse gear) — See transmission problem(manual-slips out of first gear).
transmission rebuild — See transmission overhaul.
transmission repair — Repair work done to an automatic or manual transmission is order to return the unit to operating condition. When repairs seem necessary take the following advice. Never go to a transmission shop unless you have been sent there by a mechanic you trust. If the job appears major, get several estimates, before making any commitments. See also transmission overhaul.
transmission replacement — Another transmission installed in place of the existing transmission.
transmission seal — Seal located on the input and/or output shaft to prevent transmission oil from leaking out along the shafts. Also, it refers to any other seals, gaskets, etc. used to keep oil from leaking out of a transmission housing.
transmission shaft — One of several shafts located within a transmission. Different types include: input shaft, output shaft, main shaft, and countershaft.
transmission shift point — Point reached in engine rpm when it is most efficient to shift to the next higher or lower gear.
transmission shift rods — Rods used to link a transmission shift lever to its shift forks.
transmission shifter — Hand operated shift arm used to select the different gears of a transmission. The two common mounting locations include directly above the transmission on the floor and on the steering column.
transmission shift lever — See transmission shifter.
transmission shop — Business engaged in removing, installing, and rebuilding automatic and manual transmissions in car and trucks.
transmission selector — See transmission shifter.
transmission selector position — Gear or drive range engaged by a transmission shifter.
transmission switch — Electrical switch designed to close when high gear is used in a manual or automatic transmission. See also solenoid vacuum valve.
transmission temperature gauge — See gauge(transmission temperature).
transmission vacuum modulator — See transmission modulator.
Transport Truck — American truck produced in 1923.
transportation car — See work car.
Trans Sport — Experimental van built by Pontiac Division of General Motors in 1986. Features include: rakish glass covered front nose, TV camera and monitor used in place of rear view mirror, and range finder to detect distance to car behind you.
transverse arm — Suspension arm used to keep the bottom of a Macpherson strut suspension system from moving laterally.
transverse engine — See engine(transverse).
transverse leaf spring — Leaf spring mounted at right angles to a car's length.
trapped spark — Ignition spark advance held in an advanced setting due to a vacuum delay or related type switch. The switch either opens after a short period of time or air bleeds the vacuum off. When the delay becomes excessive, pinging is the result especially under light to heavy acceleration.
traps — Race track area located at the finish line where a three light system records a car's top speed and stops elapsed time clocks.
Trask-Detroit — American car produced in 1922.

Travelall - American car produced from 1961 to date by International
  Harvester. It is a nine passenger four door station wagon.
Traveler - American car produced from 1906-1915 by Traveler Motor Car Co. in
  Indiana (1906-1910), Traveler Auto Co. in Indiana (1911-1913), Traveler Motor
  Car Co. in Michigan (1914-1915). Also, an American car produced in 1924.
traveler's advisory - Driving hazard information made available to travelers
  for specified areas. Such hazards include: flooding, storms, snow, sleet,
  ice, slides, bad accident, and traffic jam.
Travelette - American car produced from 1961 to date by International
  Harvester. It is a four door six passenger pickup truck.
Traverse City - American car produced in 1918.
Traylor - American car produced in 1920.
tread(1) - Distance measured between the centerline of front or rear tires
  measured at the ground. See also track(1).
tread(2) - See tire tread.
tread contact - Tread width contacting a road surface. An over inflated tire
  will have less tread contact.
tread cupping - See tire wear(cupped).
tread face - Tire tread area outlined when a tire rests on a road surface.
tread marks - See tire marks.
tread pattern - Overall configuration of tire tread elements. The type of
  tread pattern determines the type of driving a tire is suited for. Tire
  treads have been designed for the following road conditions: paved highways,
  snow and ice, off the road, on and off road use, soft earth, racing, rocky
  surface, and sand.
tread stock - See tire tread stock.
tread wear indicators - Strip area molded into a tire tread pattern in several
  places creating a solid rubber band across tread grooves when a minimum safe
  amount of tread rubber remains.
tread width - Distance measured from a frame centerline to the center of a
  tire tread. It should be the same for the left and right front, and the left
  and right rear.
Trebert - American car produced in 1907.
trembler coil ignition - Early ignition coil built with an internal
  electromagnetic vibrator for interrupting the primary current flow so as to
  induce high voltage in the secondary windings. It was invented in 1895 by
  Georges Bouton.
trial date - Date set by a court of law when a case is to be heard.
Triangle - American car produced in 1918.
Tribune - American car produced from 1913-1914 by Tribune Motor Co. in
  Michigan.
Tri-Car - American car produced in 1907 and 1955.
trick engine - Special engine.
trick finish - Paint finish made to sparkle, glitter, and/or be iridescent.
  It is achieved by adding compounds, such as powdered aluminum or steel, to an
  existing paint.
trick out - To customize part or all of a car.
trick painting - Custom painting techniques used to produce special designs or
  effects. See also airbrush.
trick panel - Panel painted with trick painting techniques for a custom
  effect.
Tricolet - American car produced in 1905.
tridecane - Liquid methane series hydrocarbon compound found in petroleum
  deposits with a melting and boiling point of 22 and 456 degrees Fahrenheit
  respectively.
trim - Finish items located inside a car such as door knobs, door handles,
  upholstery, carpeting, etc. Also, it refers to finish items used to cover or
  highlight different portions of a car's exterior. They include: chrome
  fittings, hood ornament, chrome car name insignia, chrome plated license
  plate holders, and chrome moldings around certain seams.
trim buck - Full size car interior built to show how it will look. Exact
  dimensions are secondary. See also seating buck.
trim panel - Trim used to cover a portion of car.
Tri-Moto - American car produced from 1900-1901 by Western Wheel Works in
  Illinois.
Trinity Steam - American car produced in 1900.
trip - To go from one place to another and back.
trip computer - See car computer.
Triple A - See AAA.
triple carb setup - Engine equipped with three carburetors. The carburetors
  usually open up in stages as follows: first the center primaries, the rear
  primaries, the front primaries, and then all the secondaries (typically after
  3/4 throttle).
Triple Truck - American truck produced in 1909.
Triplex - American car produced in 1905.

trip odometer – Resettable device used to measure and display the number of miles traveled. It is located in the speedometer.

trip plan – Plan made to gather necessary information and make necessary arrangements for a safe and enjoyable trip. Information gathered includes: routes traveled, maps, destination brochures, weather conditions, any detours, availability of accommodations, local customs, food and water available along trip route, etc. Arrangements made include: hotel or motel reservations, transportation reservations, tickets or reservations for certain events, necessary permits, exchange of domestic for foreign money, etc.

Triumph(1) – American car produced from 1900-1901 and 1906-1909 by Triumph Motor Vehicle Co., and Triumph Motor Car Co. respectively, both in Illinois.

Triumph(2) – British car line produced from 1923 to date by Light Medium Cars Division, BL Cars Ltd. The TR 1 through 8 sport car series were produced from 1949-1981.

Trojan – American car produced in 1916.

Trombly – American car produced in 1911.

trophy run – Final race in a class.

trouble code – Numerical value displayed by an on-board computer when put in a self-diagnostic mode. The number displayed represents a specific engine problem, test result, etc. The value is usually displayed by flashing the check engine light in two flash sequences. For example, a double flash, a pause, then a single flash would indicate a trouble code value of 21. A car's shop manual describes what the different values represent.

troubleshooter – Person experienced in locating and eliminating the cause of a problem.

troubleshooting – Procedure defined as locating a problem and determining the item(s) needing replacement by observation and testing. The approach is the same for most problems. In the case of cars, it consists of: identifying the car symptoms; matching car symptoms and associated problems; reviewing each problem area to narrow down the cause; determining the problem area; and repairing or replacing the part(s) causing the problem.

trouble with the brakes – See brake problem.

Troy – American car produced in 1908-1909.

TRS – Abbreviation for transmission controlled spark.

trs – Abbreviation for tires.

truck – See body style(truck).

truck bed – Cargo platform mounted on a truck's chassis behind the cab. Some trucks have a flat bed while most have a boxed-in bed with a tailgate.

truck bed(long) – Truck bed built seven to eight feet long.

truck bed(short) – Truck bed built usually averaging six feet.

truck bed mat – Durable material placed on the floor of a truck bed to protect it.

truck step – Step located underneath a truck door to facilitate entry into a cab. It is usually found or installed on trucks with a high ground clearance or high cabs.

True – American car produced in 1914.

Trumbull – American car produced from 1913-1915 by American Cyclecar Co. (1913-1914), and Trumbull Motor Car Co. (1915), both in Connecticut.

trumpets – Tailpipe extensions.

trunk – Large enclosed compartment built in a car for carrying luggage, spare tire, cargo, etc.

trunk key – Key used to lock and/or unlock a car's trunk.

trunk volume – The volume contained in a car's trunk space.

trunnion – One of four short shafts found on a universal joint. It is machined to act as a race surface for bearing needles to roll against.

TRW – American line of automotive performance products produced by TRW, Inc.

TSB – Abbreviation for technical service bulletin.

TT – Abbreviation for Trinidad found usually on an international license plate.

T top – Car roof built with two removable roof sections above each front seat, separated by a center section of roof. The design keeps a roof's structure stronger.

TTW – Abbreviation for total trailer weight.

tub – Main section of a monocoque frame.

tube – Hollow cylindrical body. Also, it refers to an inner tube.

tubeless tire – See tire(tubeless).

tube steak – Hot dog.

Tuck – American car produced from 1904-1905 by Tuck Petroleum Motor Co. in New York.

Tucker – American car produced from 1900-1903 and 1946-1948 by William Tucker in California, and Tucker Corp. in Illinois respectively.

Tucker Mobile – American car produced in 1900.

Tucker Torpedo – American car produced in 1946.

Tudhope – Canadian car produced from 1906-1913 by Tudhope Motor Car Co. in

Ontario.

Tulcar – American car produced in 1915.

Tulsa – American car produced in 1917–1923 by Tulsa Automobile Corp. in Oklahoma.

tumblehome – Angle or slant from vertical created by a car's side window glass when looking down the car length.

tuned exhaust – See exhaust tuning.

tuned exhaust manifold – Exhaust manifold carefully constructed to minimize pressure build-up from adjacent cylinders exhausting gases. Result is each cylinder more completely discharges exhaust gases during exhaust stroke allowing a larger more undiluted fuel mixture charge to enter which increases engine efficiency and power. See also headers and tuned intake manifold.

tuned intake manifold – Intake manifold carefully constructed to minimize air flow resistance and work with air pulsation created by the opening and closing of intake valves to create a slight supercharging effect. Proper design includes size, shape, and length considerations for the manifold's plenum chamber and runners. See also tuned exhaust manifold.

tune-up – Process defined as checking, adjusting, and/or repairing the various ignition and fuel system components to obtain maximum performance from an engine.

A minor tune-up usually consists of: installing new spark plugs, points, and condenser; setting the dwell angle or point gap; timing the engine; inspecting parts for wear, cleanliness, and replacement such as the distributor cap, rotor, ignition cables, PCV valve, air filter, crankcase vent filter, and vapor canister; checking and adjusting belts; checking and adjusting carburetor idle speed and mixture settings; checking the battery and charging system; and checking cooling system in winter time.

A major tune-up usually consists of: the work performed in a minor tune-up, compression check, vacuum testing, adjusting valves, and performing a combustion analysis.

tune-up in a can – Additive added to engine oil to improve an engine's performance. Such additives claim to reduce friction, engine heat build-up, deposit accumulation, etc. See also mouse milk.

tuning – Work performed on an engine to obtain maximum power and reliability.

tuning specs – Specifications unique to a particular engine used to set such engine controls as: ignition timing, carburetor settings, emission control settings, spark plug gaps, point gap, etc.

tuning specs label – Metal label mounted in the engine compartment of most cars indicating tuning specs relevant to the car.

tunnel – See hump.

turbine – See engine(turbine).

turbo – See turbocharger.

turbo boost gauge – See gauge(turbo boost).

turbocharged – Engine performance modification made by installing a turbocharger.

turbocharged engine – See engine(turbocharged).

turbocharger – Supercharger built to rotate from the force of moving exhaust gases. It is considered a more efficient method of pressurizing an incoming air/fuel mixture than shaft or belt driven superchargers because it utilizes energy already generated and expelled by an engine in the form of heat (exhaust). Air injection and rotation are provided by a respective compressor wheel and a turbine wheel mounted on a common shaft. The compressor wheel is mounted near the entrance to the intake manifold. The turbine wheel is mounted near the exhaust manifold outlet. The shaft and turbocharger housing is cooled by the incoming air and circulating engine oil. Life expectancy is directly related to how hot a turbocharger gets. Restrictions in intake air or exhaust, and inadequate cool down after a hard run will shorten its life.

Turbochargers were first used in Grand Prix racing in 1977 by Renault. By 1985, most grand Prix racing machines were using them. See also supercharger, intercooler, detonation(turbo), overboost, and sensor(detonation).

Turbo Cruiser No 2 – Turbine powered bus built by General Motors in 1964.

turbo diesel – Turbocharged diesel engine.

Turboflite – Experimental gas turbine powered car built by Chrysler in 1961.

turbo muffler – See muffler(turbo).

turbo power – Engine power enhanced by a turbocharger system.

Turbo Titan – Experimental gas turbine powered truck built by General Motors in 1956.

Turbo Titan II – Experimental gas turbine powered truck built by General Motors in 1959.

turbulence – Condition created when a fluid or gas flow is not laminar but mixed up or irregular.

turn – Tactic used by a car salesman to gain a potential customer's trust by referring him to another car salesman to confirm what he has been saying. He

usually refers them to the sales manager.
Turnbull - American car produced in 1918.
turn diameter - Diameter of the smallest circle a car can generate when turning full left or right.
turned back speedometer - Speedometer odometer reading modified by turning the speedometer cable backwards or resetting the tumblers. It is usually done on high mileage cars to increase their saleability and is illegal. See also con game(turning back the odometer).
Turner - American car produced from 1900-1901.
turning back the speedometer - See con game(turning back the odometer).
turning lane - Lane built on a roadway to permit cars to turn left or right without obstructing the flow of traffic.
turning radius - Distance used to represent the smallest circle a car can turn in. It is measured from the center of a circle to its edge. See also turn diameter.
turning the brake drum - See brake drum reconditioning.
turn on the ignition - To turn an ignition switch so it activates an accessory circuit or a starter circuit (but does not start engine).
turn off - Road exit or intersection.
turn out - Widened road shoulder used to permit slower moving traffic to pull over safely and allow faster traffic to pass by. It is common on winding narrow roads.
turnpike - Freeway or high speed highway. Also, it refers to a barrier placed across a roadway until a toll is paid. See also tollgate.
turn signals - See light(turn signal).
turn signal indicator - One of two indicator lights located in an instrument panel. It flashes when the appropriate turn signal lights are flashing.
turn signal switch - Electrical switch mounted on a steering column as a movable arm for energizing the left or right hand turn signal lights on a car depending on the direction the arm is moved. The switch is also wired in series with a flasher unit causing the lights to blink.
turn the brake drum - Process used to reface the scored or otherwise damaged braking surface of a brake drum. It is machined on a metal lathe with metal cutting tools.
turn the drum - See turn the brake drum.
turn the rotor - Process used to reface the scored or otherwise damaged braking surface of brake rotor. It is usually machined on a metal lathe with metal cutting tools.
turn turtle - Flipped or turned over racing car.
turnunder - Car body panel area located along a car side where it sweeps down or in from a car's widest point to the rocker panel area.
turret top - See hardtop.
TVR - British car line produced from 1954 to date by TVR Engineering Ltd. (1965 to date).
TV rod - Throttle valve rod used on older automatic transmissions to control a transmission throttle valve. It is connected between the transmission and a carburetor throttle valve. When the carburetor throttle valve opens, it opens the transmission throttle valve to regulate slippage and shift points. See also throttle valve(2).
TVS - Abbreviation for thermostatic vacuum switch.
TVSV - Abbreviation for thermostatic vacuum switching valve.
T-Wagon - American car produced from 1984 to date by Chrysler Corp. in Michigan.
T/whl - Abbreviation for tilt wheel.
twilight - Time of day marked by a setting sun and a sky still bright.
twilight zone - Racing speeds over 200 mph.
twin balancing shafts - Two rotating shafts mounted in an engine block to cancel out shake and vibration. It is used in certain larger displacement four cylinder engines to provide smoother low and high rpm speeds. Some designs mount both shafts low, while others mount one high and one low. Shafts typically rotate opposite crankshaft rotation and at higher rpm.
twin cam engine - See engine(twin cam).
Twin City - American car produced in 1914.
Twin Coach - American car produced in 1927.
Twister - Cloud 9 car model (3/8 scale) produced by Ford in the 1960s. It was an experimental dragster shaped car with twin engines designed to produce 950 horsepower.
two barrel carburetor - See carburetor(double barrel).
two cycle engine - See engine(two cycle).
two door hardtop - See body style(two door hardtop).
two door sedan - See body style(two door sedan).
two cycle - See stroke(two).
two lane highway - Road built with two traffic lanes separated by one or two painted lines in the center. See also pavement markings.
Twombly - American car produced from 1910-1911 and 1913-1915 by Twombly Motors

Co. in New York, and Twombly Car Corp. in New Jersey respectively.
two part paint — See paint(two part).
two plus two — See body style(2+2).
two stick transmission — See transmission(two stick).
two stroke cycle engine — See engine(two stroke).
two tone paint — Car paint applied in two different colors.
two wheel drive — Drivetrain used on a car or truck to provide power to a front or rear axle. Most are built this way.
Twyford — American car produced from 1902-1908 by Twyford Motor Car Co. in Pennsylvania.
Type F Fluid — See equipment manufacturer's specification(Type F Fluid).
typewriter — Push button automatic transmission car.

U

U(1) - Abbreviation for Uruguay found usually on an international license plate.

U(2) - Auction car rating code used to specify an unrestored car.

UAZ - Soviet car line produced from 1961 to date by Ulyanovsk Automobile Works.

U bolt - Metal rod bent into a U-shape and threaded at both ends. It is used in exhaust systems to clamp pipes.

UF02 - Experimental fuel economy car built by British Ford in 1984. It set a record 3,803 mpg with its low slung 49 lb. weight and 15cc engine driving one rear wheel by chain.

UIO - Abbreviation for unit in operation. It usually refers to the number of cars a dealer has ordered.

U joint - See universal joint.

Ultimate - American car produced in 1920.

ultimate cornering force - Maximum cornering or sideways force generated before tires lose traction.

Ultra - American car produced in 1908-1911 and 1918.

unattended vehicle - Vehicle left alone on a street or highway.

unbalanced tire - Tire condition created when distribution of mass around its circumference is not equal. The mass consists of any components rotating with a tire including: wheel, brake drum or rotor, and wheel hub. An unbalanced tire may appear fine and rotate smoothly when spinning slowly. At higher speeds, however, centrifugal force comes into play and any uneven weight distribution will cause tire vibration. This happens because greater centrifugal force is exerted where the mass is heaviest.
   The mass of an unbalanced tire can occur within a tire's plane of rotation and/or outside it. If the mass remains within the plane, a vertical oscillation occurs. It can cause wheel hop and abnormal tire wear. If it is outside, a wheel will create a wobbling or back and forth vibration. Vibration increases with increased rotational speed due to the effects of centrifugal force.
   Unbalanced tires make driving more dangerous and wear various car parts out faster. Danger usually occurs at higher speed from reduced road traction due to wheel hop. Parts worn out faster include: tire tread, ball joints and tie rod ends, shock absorbers, and steering gears. See also static unbalance and dynamic unbalance.

Uncle Daniel - See sleeper.

undecane - Liquid methane series hydrocarbon compound found in petroleum deposits with a melting and boiling point of -14 and 384 degrees Fahrenheit respectively. It is one of gasoline's ingredients with a heat value of 20,375 btu/lb.

underbody - Car structure used to attach a car body.

under car inspection - Inspection made of the condition of a car's components located underneath.

undercoat - See paint(undercoat).

undercoating(1) - Rubbery material used to coat wheel wells, car underside, hood, trunk lid, etc. It is used to deaden sound and protect the underlying metal from rusting.

undercoating(2) - See paint(undercoat).

under hood inspection - Inspection made of an engine. It usually includes: checking fluid levels, condition of belts and hoses, looking for possible leaks, and listening for any abnormal noises.

underinflation - Tire condition created when a tire's air pressure is lower than recommended. It causes overflexing of tire sidewalls which builds up excessive heat, increases rolling resistance, and increases outer tread wear. Heat is one of the primary destroyers of tires. A front tire with less pressure than its counterpart can cause: hard steering, pulling to one side, and road handling problems. See also overinflation and proper inflation.

underpass - Passageway built underneath a road, railroad, etc. for cars and/or pedestrians.

underpowered - To lack sufficient power to perform adequately.

understeer - Condition created when a car rounding a corner tends to resist a driver-applied turning force to the front wheels and continue in a straight line. Understeer can suddenly appear when a car's suspension has been softened at only one end. The following changes will reduce understeer: increase front and decrease rear tire pressure, make front wheel camber more negative, put more weight toward the back of the car, use softer front and stiffer rear springs, and use larger diameter front and smaller diameter rear tires. See also oversteer and neutral steer.

under the rack – Area located underneath a garage hoist. It is one way for a mechanic to do repair work on the underside of a car.

under warranty – Car still covered by a manufacturer's warranty.

unequalized brakes – Condition created when car brakes do not all grab with the same braking force. It causes a car to pull to the left or right making a car dangerous to drive.

unequalized tires – Condition created when car tires have different air pressures, treads, and/or tire types. It will create unstable road traction and will be most noticeable when braking and cornering.

uneven tread wear – Condition created when a car's tire tread has not worn evenly. Possible causes include: different tire pressures; tires not rotated; incorrect camber and toe-in wheel alignment angles; excessive wheel runout; driving too fast especially on turns; loose, worn, and/or damaged suspension parts; bent wheel spindle shaft, steering knuckle, steering knuckle arm, and/or control arm; and brakes grabbing.

unglue – To ruin an engine.

unhorse – To persuade a customer to leave his car for repair work.

Uniform Commercial Code – Body of laws governing businesses. The implied warranty provision of this code is generally accepted by the non-automotive industry and covers products without warranties or guarantees. It means a manufacturer will live up to all promises and stand behind his product even if it means replacing it.

Uniform Tire Quality Grading Scale – Scale devised to judge a tire's different specifications and construction characteristics and arrive at an overall expression of quality. Generally, the higher the number the longer the tire will last. One rough rule of thumb equates each 10 points to 3,000 miles of tread life.

Uniform Vehicle Code – Body of general motor vehicle regulations written to provide guidelines to states for enacting their own regulations. It is responsible for keeping the traffic laws very uniform throughout most of the states.

Union – American car produced from 1902-1905 and 1911-1914 by Union Automobile Co. in Indiana, and Union Sales Co. in Ohio respectively.

Union Oil of California – See Unocal Corporation.

Union Truck – American truck produced from 1902-1904.

union – Group of people, businesses, states, etc. joined together for a common purpose.

union labor – Laborers belonging to a union.

union shop – Business run where employee wages, benefits, rules, regulation, etc. are fixed by an agreement between the business and a union.

union wages – Wages earned by union members.

Uniroyal – American line of tires produced by Uniroyal.

unit body – See body style(unit body)

unit construction – Type of car building used since the 1930s in which separate parts of the car body and chassis are welded together to make a metal box.

United – American car produced in 1902-1904, 1914, and 1916.

United Auto Brokers – Large U.S. auto brokerage organization.

United Auto Workers – Large union of automotive industry workers.

United Motor – American car produced in 1902.

United States Motor Company – Car company formed in 1912 by Benjamin Briscoe. It consisted of over 130 different firms, but remained in business just a short period of time.

Unito – American car produced in 1908.

unit power plant – Power train assembly built combining an engine, clutch, and transmission into one unit.

Universal – American car produced in 1912, 1914, 1917, and 1919.

universal – Cross shaped device used to form the core of a universal joint. Each of its four stub shafts contains a roller bearing cap permitting rotation.

universal joint – Flexible coupling used between two rotating shafts that permits changes in the angle between them. Primary components include: central spider with bearings, seals, and snap rings; collar attachment points; and U-bolts for securing a universal. It is found at both ends of a driveline, on floating rear axles of cars, and in steering linkages. It also refers to a flexible socket joint used to allow socket turning at an angle. See also constant velocity joint and trunnion.

universal joint(ball and trunnion) – Flexible coupling built using balls instead of needles for a bearing.

universal joint(constant velocity) – Flexible coupling built with two universal joints to cancel out vibrations at high rpm. It is commonly used in two-piece drivelines to lower a floorpan, and on front transaxle shafts. A protective housing usually surrounds it. See also CV boot.

universal joint(fluctuation canceler) - See universal joint(constant velocity).

University - American car produced in 1907.

unleaded - See gasoline(unleaded).

unleaded gas - See gasoline(unleaded).

unloader - See carburetor unloader.

unlocked car - Car parked with its doors unlocked.

unmarked car - Police car disguised to appear as an ordinary car. No visible police identification markings are used such as: flashing light unit, police type plates, and decals on side body panels. See also marked car.

Unocal Corporation - A U.S. petroleum corporation headquartered in Los Angeles, California. It was formerly called Union Oil of California. See also petroleum company.

unpaid balance - Amount of money unpaid on a loan after paying the down payment and closing costs.

unpaid obligation - See unpaid balance.

unreal - Car performing very well.

Unser, Al - He won the Indianapolis 500 Race in 1970, 1971, and 1978. Average speeds were 155.7, 157.7, 161.4 mph. Cars driven were a Johnny Lightning Special (1970 and 1971), and F.N.C.T.C. Chaparral Lola.

Unser, Bobby - He won the Indianapolis 500 Race in 1968, 1975, and 1981. Average speeds were 152.9, 149.2, and 139.1 mph. Cars driven were a Rislone Special, Jorgensen Eagle, and Norton Spirit Penske PC-9B.

unsprung weight - Weight composed of all car parts not supported by a suspension system. The parts include: tires, wheels, brake assemblies, rear axle, and lower control arms. Keeping this weight to a minimum maintains good road holding ability. See also sprung weight.

understeer - Car handling situation created when front tires tend to lose traction first when rounding a turn. It happens because the front tires track at larger slip angles than the rear tires. See also oversteer and neutral steer.

Unwin - American car produced in 1907.

up - Opportunity offered to a car salesman to close a sale on a potential customer walking into a showroom or onto a car lot. Car salesmen generally wait their turn. See also walk-in, walk-out, and up system.

updating(1) - Making an older car look newer by replacing lights, trim, and other car parts with those on newer car models.

updating(2) - See updating the model year.

updating the model year - Practice engaged at new car dealerships where last year model cars are updated and sold as current year models. See con game(last year's model).

updraft - See carburetor(up draft).

upgrade - To increase a trade-in from one car classification to another to improve its value and increase the chances of selling it. See also car classification.

uph - Abbreviation for upholstery.

uphol - Abbreviation for upholstery.

upholstery - Material used to cushion and cover car seats.

upper back panel - Car body panel located between a backlight and decklid.

upper control arm - Heavy steel pivoting arm assembly used with other components to provide support and steering ability to a wheel. It is commonly used with the front wheels of older cars. It differs from an A-arm in that lateral support is required due to only one mounting point or two mounting points closely spaced together (equivalent to one). Lateral support is provided by a strut rod attached to a lower control arm. It works in conjunction with a lower control arm, coil spring, and steering knuckle-wheel spindle assembly to support and cushion a portion of a car's body, provide a place to securely attach a wheel to a car, and provide a pivoting point for a wheel turning left or right. Most cars today use a Macpherson strut which eliminates the need for an upper control arm. See also lower control arm.

upper control arm bushing - Bushing used to provide a rotation point for the upper portion of a steering knuckle.

upper control arm rubber bumpers - Rubber blocks mounted on a frame member and positioned to limit the upward movement of an upper control arm.

upper control link - See upper control arm.

upper cylinder lubrication - Lubrication made of upper internal engine areas not well lubricated by an engine's oil lubrication system. Such areas include: upper cylinder walls, valve guides, etc. Lubricant is usually introduced into the fuel or intake manifold. See also additive(upper cylinder lubricant).

upper mode door - Mode-and-blend door used to control flow of air in upper heating and air conditioning ducts. See also lower mode door.

upset - Process defined as shortening and thickening a metal piece by compressing or hammering the ends. Also, body damage caused when a metal shape such as a high crown depresses and thickens an affected panel area.

See also simple bend, displaced area, stretch, and rolled buckle.

upshifting - Shifting from a lower gear to a higher gear. See also downshifting and double clutching.

upshift light - Indicator light used on certain cars to indicate when a manual transmission should be shifted to the next higher gear for improved gas mileage.

up system - Method used to assign potential car buyers to car salesman by number, seniority, etc. See also up.

Upton - American car produced from 1900-1907 by Upton Machinery Co. (1900-1905), and Beverly Mfg. Co. (1905-1907), both in Massachusetts.

urban area - Any unincorporated or incorporated area developed primarily for business and/or residential use.

Urgan - American car produced in 1913.

US(1) - American car produced in 1908.

US(2) - Abbreviation for United States.

USA(1) - Abbreviation for United States of America. It is one of the six largest car producing countries in the world.

USA(2) - Abbreviation for United States of America found usually on an international license plate.

USAC - Abbreviation for United States Automobile Club.

US Auto - American car produced from 1899-1918.

US Carriage - American car produced from 1910-1918.

used car - Car purchased and driven a period of time sufficient to wear various car parts. It may have had several owners prior to the current one. Two or more of today's used cars are sold for every new one purchased. Complaints on used car purchases run three or more to one, which is a clear signal for a prospective buyer to beware and shop carefully.

The best chance of getting a good used car will come from having a qualified mechanic examine it before deciding to buy. If the examination is done yourself, carefully examine the car for the following: even engine cylinder compression; cracks in engine block, and intake and exhaust manifolds; leaks around main bearing seals, water pump, radiator, radiator hoses, power steering unit, valve covers, transmission, air conditioner unit, heater core, shock absorbers, master and wheel brake cylinders, and differential; worn brakes, universal joints, steering linkage, tires, upholstery, carpeting, interior trim, and exterior paint finish; unusual noises during test drive in engine, transmission, brake system, rear end, front end, and wheels; unusual vibrations during test drive; uneven tire wear; pulling left or right when car is braked; rusted and/or dented body surfaces and exhaust system components; proper functioning of windshield wipers, turn signal indicator, alternator, heater, front and rear defrosters, air conditioner unit, and all lights; cracks in windows; blue exhaust smoke; broken headlight, taillight, and parking light lens; previous damage to body panels and/or frame; existence of spare tire, jacks, and lug wrench; smoothness of gear shifts; battery condition; review of car maintenance records to date; and careful inspection of car identification numbers. The car should be test driven preferably by someone experienced with cars.

used car auction - Auction selling used cars.

used car lot - Business engaged in displaying and selling used cars on a parking type lot. Lot may be owned privately or by a dealer.

used car shopper - Person interested in buying a used car.

US Electric - American electric car produced from 1899-1901 by U.S. Automobile Co. in Massachusetts.

US Long Distance - American car produced from 1901-1903 by United States Long Distance Automobile Co. in New Jersey.

use of the car - To have a car available for your use.

using oil - Condition created when a car's engine consumes too much oil. It is usually due to excessive piston to cylinder wall clearances. Other causes include: bad valve guide seals; and leaking main crankshaft seals, head gasket, valve cover gasket, oil pan, oil filter, and oil gauge supply line.

The type of leak can be determined by watching the exhaust. If the oil is leaking internally into the cylinders, blue exhaust smoke will be observed when accelerating, driving at a constant speed, and/or decelerating. Lack of blue smoke indicates a leak outside the cylinder area.

US Long Distance - American car produced from 1900-1904.

US Motor Car - American car produced in 1908.

US Motor Vehicle - American car produced from 1899-1901.

Utility - American car produced in 1910 and 1918. Also, an American car produced from 1921-1922 by Victor W. Page Motors Corp. in Connecticut.

UTL - Abbreviation for utility.

U turn - To turn a car around and head in the opposite direction.

V

V6 — V6 engine.
V8 — V8 engine.
vacuum — Condition created inside an enclosed area (such as a pipe or chamber) when air or other gas pressure is less than the surrounding atmosphere.
vacuum advance — See advance(vacuum).
vacuum advance unit — Diaphragm device used to control spark advance during normal driving and acceleration through the use of intake manifold vacuum. It is mounted on a distributor body with an arm extending from a diaphragm to a distributor point plate. The change in vacuum causes the diaphragm to move the point plate back and forth.
vacuum assist unit — See brake booster unit.
vacuum booster — Diaphragm assembly built to increase an applied force through the use of intake vacuum. It is commonly used with a master brake cylinder operating disc brakes. Without a booster, disc brakes would not brake as strongly as drum brakes. See also brake unit(vacuum suspended type).
vacuum booster pump — Pump used to provide a steady source of vacuum for operating accessories like windshield wipers, etc. It was common on older engine designs, and was usually mounted on top of a mechanical fuel pump.
vacuum break — See choke vacuum break.
vacuum breaker diaphragm — Diaphragm mounted on a carburetor to control full choke opening. It is designed to open a choke in closed position slightly to prevent a cold engine from stalling out due to lack of air.
vacuum bypass valve — See solenoid vacuum valve.
vacuum check valve — Valve built to open under vacuum. It is commonly used in vapor recovery systems to meter collected gas vapors into an engine only when it is running.
vacuum control — See vacuum advance.
vacuum delay switch — Switch used to control vacuum ignition advance by temporarily retaining vacuum. When it sticks, it can cause pinging, by carrying excessive vacuum advance into a high load situation where little such advance is desired.
vacuum diaphragm — Diaphragm operated by intake manifold vacuum. Cars use several of these devices to perform such duties as: boost braking action, control spark advance, regulate hot air inlet opening on air cleaner, etc. See also air gate, car service tip(air cleaner warm air test), vacuum override control, vacuum pump, vacuum pump diaphragm, and vacuum motor.
vacuum gauge — Gauge used to measure intake manifold vacuum. It can provide important information on an engine's operating condition. If used properly, the gauge can pinpoint problems in the following areas: ignition timing, carburetor adjustments, ignition system, backpressure, valves, cylinder leakage, and intake manifold leakage.
vacuum gauge reading — Value displayed by a vacuum gauge sensing intake manifold vacuum beneath a carburetor throttle plate of a running engine. An engine idling in good running condition will produce a steady reading of 16-21 inches at sea level. For every 1,000 foot increase in elevation, the reading will drop about one point. Engines with more cylinders tend to have higher readings. A vacuum reading should be made when an engine is at operating temperature.
vacuum gauge reading(carburetor-poorly adjusted) — Reading drifts back and forth 4-7 points between 12-19 inches vacuum. It indicates the carburetor is poorly adjusted at idle.
vacuum gauge reading(exhaust-restricted) — Reading is normal when the engine is started, drops steadily toward zero when engine is run at 2-3,000 rpm, then slowly rises to a below normal reading. It indicates excessive backpressure in an exhaust system due to a plugged muffler, kinked pipe, clogged catalytic converter, or other obstruction. See also car service tip(restricted exhaust test).
vacuum gauge reading(fluctuation-drifting) — Reading drifts back and forth slowly. It usually indicates a rich air/fuel mixture.
vacuum gauge reading(fluctuation-intermittent) — Reading drops 3-4 points intermittently. It usually indicates sticky valves.
vacuum gauge reading(fluctuation-rapid at idle) — Reading fluctuates rapidly when engine is idling. Possible causes include: worn valve guides, cracked or wet distributor cap, and burned exhaust valve(s).
vacuum gauge reading(fluctuation-rapid during acceleration) — Reading fluctuates rapidly when engine is accelerated. It indicates weak valve springs.

vacuum gauge reading(gap-improper spark plug/point) - Reading drifts back and forth 1-2 points. It indicates spark plugs gapped too close together or ignition points not operating properly.

vacuum gauge reading(leakage-cylinder head gasket) - Reading registered when two or more cylinders are leaking between each other due to a leaking head gasket. The reading will drift back and forth.

vacuum gauge reading(leakage-intake manifold) - Reading registered when air is leaking into an intake manifold. It will usually be steady, but 3-10 points below normal. Possible causes include: leaks around a carburetor, throttle plate not fully closing, gaskets leaks, hose leaks, defective leaky manifold emission accessories, and manifold cracks.

vacuum gauge reading(leakage-ring) - Reading fairly steady, but 3-4 points below normal. It indicates excess leakage of cylinder pressure past piston rings. A quick open and close throttle maneuver will typically bring a low and high response of near 0 and around 22 inches. See also vacuum gauge reading(pistons, cylinders-wall).

vacuum gauge reading(lower and steady) - Reading is steady, but lower than normal. Possible causes include: retarded ignition timing, intake manifold or other air leaks, and low compression.

vacuum gauge reading(normal) - Reading is steady between 16-21 inches. If the throttle is quickly opened and closed, the vacuum should drop to less than 5 and increase to around 25 before stabilizing back at 16-21 inches. See also vacuum gauge reading(pistons and cylinder walls-worn).

vacuum gauge reading(timing-retarded ignition) - Reading is steady and lower than normal (14-16). It indicates retarded ignition timing, especially if cylinder compression is good and a carburetor cannot be adjusted to bring vacuum back to normal.

vacuum gauge reading(timing-retarded valve) - Reading is steady, but considerably lower than normal (8-14). It indicates retarded valve timing, especially if a carburetor cannot be adjusted to bring vacuum back to normal.

vacuum gauge reading(valve guides-worn) - Reading fluctuates rapidly between 14 and 19 when engine is idling. It indicates worn valve guides.

vacuum gauge reading(valve sticking) - Reading is normal, drops 3-5 points, then returns to normal repeatedly. It indicates one more valves are sticking.

vacuum gauge reading(valve springs-worn) - Reading fluctuates rapidly when a car is accelerated, increasing with engine speed. It indicates weak or broken valve springs.

vacuum gauge reading(pistons and cylinder walls-worn) - Reading registers around 0, then jumps to around 22 inches when throttle is opened and closed quickly. It indicates worn pistons, piston rings, and/or cylinder walls. See also vacuum gauge reading(normal).

vacuum modulator - Device used in an automatic transmission to operate a valve controlling fluid pressure to various locations according to engine intake manifold vacuum.

vacuum motor - Device built to rotate or move other mechanical components through the use of intake manifold vacuum. Older cars had vacuum motors that operated the windshield wipers.

vacuum override control - Vacuum controlled diaphragm used to regulate an air gate controlling the air flow into an air cleaner's air inlet under full throttle openings.

vacuum pump - See vacuum booster pump.

vacuum pump diaphragm - Circular rubber like membrane used to generates vacuum when it moves back and forth in a vacuum pump.

vacuum reducer valve - Valve used to reduce vacuum by a specified amount to the vacuum advance unit and any other components in the circuit under different engine conditions such as steady speed, accelerating, decelerating, and idling. It is mounted in the line between the vacuum advance unit and the vacuum source. Faulty operation can lead to such engine problems as: stumbling, pinging, rough idling, poor fuel economy, hesitation when accelerating, hard starting, and power loss. See also spark delay valve.

vacuum solenoid valve - See solenoid vacuum valve.

vacuum spark controls - Parts and devices used to control an engine's spark advance according to vacuum readings at specified points in a carburetor airway. They include: spark port(s), spark valve, distributor vacuum advance unit, and connecting hoses.
    Vacuum control of spark advance happens primarily when the carburetor is in part open throttle position. For normal cars, it is important. For racing cars, vacuum controls are usually not necessary. See also spark port and spark ported vacuum.

vacuum step up - Carburetor circuit built to supply additional fuel to an engine under full throttle, like a power jet. It consists of a step-up metering rod and step-up piston assembly that increase fuel flow through a step-up jet into an engine when intake manifold vacuum drops.

vacuum suction disc - Disc used in body work to remove certain minor dents.

It is built in a circular shape with a handle and has the ability to adhere
to a surface temporarily by creating a suction or vacuum on its underside.
vacuum switch - Switch used to prevent a starter from being engaged while an
engine is running by sensing intake manifold vacuum. It is usually mounted
on or near the carburetor.
vacuum switch(ball type) - Vacuum switch built to regulate the use of a
starter motor. It consists of a ball, throttle shaft, and intake manifold
vacuum arrangement that open and close electrical contacts.
vacuum switch(diaphragm type) - Vacuum switch built to control use of a
starter by using a diaphragm to open and close electrical contacts.
vacuum switching valve - Electrically operated vacuum valve with multiple
outlets. It is usually controlled by a computer to regulate which outlet(s)
receive vacuum. Vacuum is typically routed to: EGR valve, EGR port, thermal
valve(s), air switching valve, air bypass valve, and throttle position
solenoid.
valid driver's license - Legal unexpired driver's license.
Valiant - American car produced from 1960-1977 by Plymouth Division of
Chrysler Corp. in Michigan.
Valkyrie - American car produced beginning in 1967 by Velocidad in California.
It is a high performance rear engine sports car with a reported top speed of
180 mph.
Valley Dispatch - American car produced in 1927.
valve - Device used to open and close an aperture. Car engines use intake and
exhaust valves. Its structure consists of a circular valve stem joined to
a flat circular valve head.
valve(burned) - Valve condition created when hot gases and high combustion
temperature raise the temperature of a valve face surface high enough to
partially melt it. When this happens, the valve can no longer provide a good
seal and must be reground or replaced.
valve(exhaust) - Valve used to route exhaust gases from an engine cylinder.
The valve head and seat are typically made of heat resistant alloy steel
known as stellite.
valve(inclined) - Valve positioned at an angle instead of vertically to reduce
bends and restrictions at the port area. Most engines use this approach
today.
valve(intake) - Valve used to admit an air/fuel mixture into an engine
cylinder.
valve(poppet) - Valve commonly used in today's car engines. It is noisy and
doesn't cool well, but provides good sealing. The valve consists of a
circular head attached to an elongated valve stem. It is designed to open
and close a circular hole or port.
valve(rotary) - Rotating disc built with one section cutout to produce a
valving action when passing by a port opening. It is commonly used as an
intake valve on two stroke engines.
valve(side) - Valve mounted at the side of a combustion chamber in an engine
block.
valve(sleeve) - Metal sleeve positioned between a piston and cylinder wall.
Holes are strategically placed in the sleeve to line up during up and down
movement for passage of gases.
valve(sodium filled) - Exhaust valve built with a hollow stem half filled with
metallic sodium. It melts at 207 degrees Fahrenheit and helps increase heat
transfer. Valve head temperatures are typically reduced from 10-25 percent
depending on the amount of stem and valve head made hollow.
valve(sticky) - Valve movement interrupted due to friction, or a weak or
broken spring.
valve adjusting screw - Adjustable screw mounted on the top of a valve lifter
and used to control valve lifter to valve stem clearance. See also valve
tappet.
valve body - Cast aluminum housing used to control fluid flow in an automatic
transmission.
valve cap - Screw on cap used on a valve stem to prevent leakage of air from
inside the tire.
valve clearance - Gap measured between the end of a valve stem and a rocker
arm or valve lifter. If valve lifters are used, the clearance is adjusted
there. If rocker arms are used, the adjustment is made with an adjustable
screw mounted on the rocker arm. If the clearance is wide, the affected
valves open late and close early decreasing engine performance. If the
clearance is too narrow, the valves open too early and close too late
decreasing engine performance. See also tappet.
valve cooling - Cooling of a valve stem and head. Valves are not directly
cooled by water. Cooling comes from dissipating heat to a valve seat and up
a valve stem to a valve guide. Most heat dissipates through the valve seat.
Valve head temperatures can range from 1,000 to 1,400 degrees.
valve core - See tire valve.
valve cover - Cover used to enclose a valve train assembly protecting it from

dirt, debris, water, etc., and to keep lubricating oils from leaking out onto
an engine block. F-head and L-head engines have side valve covers. Overhead
valves have a valve cover bolting onto a cylinder head.

valve damper - Cup-like device mounted at the base of a valve spring in order
to reduce spring surge. See also valve spring surge.

valve duration - Amount of time a valve remains open.

valve face - Beveled edge of a valve head used to contact a valve seat and
provide a seal.

valve facer - Tool used to grind the correct factory angle on a valve face.

valve facing - Process defined as machining valve faces back to factory
specifications.

valve float - Condition created, usually at high engine rpm, when the inertia
of reciprocating valve parts prevents the valve springs from keeping the
valve lifter (or rocker arm) in constant constant contact with the cam. It
is not a flaw in engine design, but simply the way moving parts behave in a
non-racing engine at high speed. Weak or improper valve springs can
contribute to valve float, especially at lower rpm, by causing valves to open
and close slower than normal. Heavier springs will often decrease valve
float, but increase wear on the entire valve train. Valve float is a serious
problem and can cause valve and/or piston damage due to collisions especially
at higher engine rpm. See also lifter pump-up and valve spring surge.

valve grinder - See valve facer.

valve grinding - See valve lapping.

valve guide - Lubricated metal sleeve used to keep a valve centered when
opening and closing. Every valve uses one. When a guide become worn or its
oil seals wear out, it allows excess oil to flow into a combustion chamber.

valve head - Enlarged circular portion of a valve mounted on a valve stem. A
valve face is cut around the outside of a valve head.

valve in head engine - See engine(valve in head) and engine(overhead valve).

valve interference angle - Small angle created during a valve job between a
valve seat and valve face. It is usually one degree or less, and helps both
surfaces to seal tightly until they wear in together.

valve job - Work done on engine valves to return them to proper operating
condition. It is usually required when valves have run 70-100,000 miles.
Symptoms indicating valve wear include: rough running engine even if tuned
up, engine noises, and a noticeable drop in power. A compression check of an
engine will quickly determine the need for a valve job. Watch to make sure a
mechanic does it properly.

A valve job usually proceeds as follows. The cylinder head is removed from
an engine. The head is tanked to remove deposits and clean it up for machine
work. All parts subject to movement are checked for wear such as valves,
valve seats, valve guides, valve springs, cam lobes, and cam bearing
surfaces, and replaced as necessary. The cylinder head is checked for
flatness and milled, if necessary. Valves and their seats are reground or
replaced. When the machine work is completed, the component parts of a head
are assembled. Preliminary valve clearances are set. The head is then ready
to reinstall on an engine. Once reinstalled, the engine is warmed up, the
valve clearances are rechecked and set, and the head bolts are retorqued.

valve keepers - Two small semi-circular cone-shaped devices used to keep a
valve spring compressed and fixed to the end of a valve stem. The valve stem
has a groove cut near its base to receive the keepers. They fit into a
groove and bear against a valve spring cup mounted on the top of a valve
spring.

valve key - See valve keepers.

valve lapping - Process used to create a smooth even surface between a
machined valve face and corresponding valve seat in order to insure a good
seal. Lapping is done by placing a fine grinding compound between the two
surfaces, letting them contact each other, and rotating the valve stem until
the desired seal is attained. One disadvantage is some of the lapping
compounds become embedded in the valve seat and face metal.

valve lash - Valve clearance.

valve lift - Distance a valve moves from its resting position.

valve lifter - Device situated between a cam and valve or push rod of an
engine. It transmits cam movement to a valve. The two primary lifter types
are mechanical and hydraulic. See also rocker arm.

valve lifter(hydraulic) - Lifter built to use oil for maintaining zero valve
clearance. It is a quieter type of lifter.

valve lifter(mechanical) - Valve lifter built in the shape of a mushroom with
an adjusting screw at one end for controlling valve clearance.

valve lifter(roller type) - Mechanical lifter built with a roller mounted on
its base to reduce friction.

valve lifter(solid) - See valve lifter(mechanical).

valve lifter clearance - Clearance measured between valve lifter base and
associated cam. See also rocker arm adjusting screw.

valve lock - See valve keeper.

valve margin - Distance measured between the edge of a valve head and the outer surface edge of a valve face. The margin determines if a valve can be reground.

valve overlap - Number of degrees measured where an intake and exhaust valve of an engine cylinder stay open at the same time. See also cam lobe displacement angle.

valve plate - See air gate.

valve port - Opening in a engine block or cylinder head opened or closed by an intake or exhaust valve.

valve refacer - See valve facer.

valve retainers - See valve keepers.

valve seat - Circular metal surface built into an engine block or cylinder head and used to provide a seal surface for a valve face. Today's engines have valve seat inserts made of hard material for long wear.

valve seat angle - Angle specified on a valve face's machined area which contacts valve seat. It is usually measured from the valve's flat top surface. The two most common angles are 45 and 30 degrees.

valve spring - Spring mounted near the base of a valve and used to keep a valve closed when not in use. Valve keepers attach a valve to a spring. Most cars use a single spring. Some high performance engines use a spring within a spring. A spring 10 percent shorter than its original length should be replaced.

valve spring(damper) - Damper coil used inside a valve spring to provide a dampening effect reducing valve spring surge. It is used in single and double spring arrangements.

valve spring(double spring) - Two springs used in place of one. One is placed inside the other and may have the same or a reverse wound coil.

valve spring(stock) - Spring used in stock engine.

valve spring compressor - Tool used to compress a valve spring in order to remove it from a valve train assembly.

valve spring locks - See valve keepers.

valve spring surge - Condition created when valve springs reduce their expansion rate at certain high engine rpms. Vibrations, created by a cam moving at certain rpms, stimulate the natural frequency of the springs which tends to slow down their expansion rates. Different spring designs are used to minimize this phenomenon.

valve stem(1) - Shaft portion of an intake or exhaust valve body built to slide within a valve guide.
    Some intake or exhaust valve stems are built with a hollow core. The core is usually filled with a material formulated to liquefy when hot, such as sodium. Its purpose is to help transfer heat away from a valve head to a valve stem.

valve stem(2) - Device mounted in a wheel rim for regulating air pressure in a tire. It consists of: a rubber cone shaped housing, threaded shaft, valve core, and valve cap.

valve stem guide - Short lubricated tube used to restrict a valve stem's movement to an up and down motion insuring proper seating of a valve face and seat.

valve stem seal - Small oil ring type seal mounted on a valve stem guide, and designed to keep oil from leaking down a valve stem into a combustion chamber.

valve tappet - See valve lifter.

valve timing - Relationship created between opening and closing of intake and exhaust valves, and up and down movement of pistons. Valve timing is maintained by means of a timing chain or belt connecting a camshaft and crankshaft. Changes in valve timing are made by adjusting valve clearances, changing the relationship of the timing chain or belt linkup marks, or installing a different cam.

valve train - Assemblage of parts used to operate intake and exhaust valves when an engine is running. The parts typically include: valves, springs, pushrods, rocker arms, tappets, retainers, cam, and cam bearings. The valve train is a significant source of engine noise due to the many moving parts. It is located in the cylinder head of most car engines today.

valve train valley - Area on V-8 engines located underneath the intake manifold and between the two valve train assemblies.

Valvoline - American line of engine oils and other lubricants produced by Valvoline Oil Co.

Valvoline Oil Co - A U.S. petroleum lubricants company headquartered in Lexington, Kentucky. It is a subsidiary of Ashland Oil, Inc.

Van - American car produced from 1910-1911 by Van Motor Car Co. in Michigan.

van - See body style(van).

Van Auken - American car produced in 1914.

Vandergrift - American car produced in 1907.

Van Dyke - American car produced in 1912.

vane - One of several flat or curved metal blades attached radially to a shaft, drum, cylinder, etc., and used to move gas or liquid.

Vanderbilt, William – He set a world land speed record in 1902 and 1904 driving a Mors 4 Cylinder and a Mercedes 4 Cylinder. Speeds were 76.1 and 92.3 mph.

Vandewater – American car produced from 1908-1914.

Van L – American car produced in 1911.

Vannell Steam Carriage – American steam car produced in 1895.

Van Wagoner – American car produced in 1900.

Vanwall – British race car manufactured from 1954 to 1958. The cars were the last successful front engine racing cars used.

vapor – Gaseous state of a liquid. A fuel begins rapidly transforming into vapor when it reaches its boiling point.

vapor injector – Device used to lower the flash point and extend the burning rate of an air/fuel mixture in a combustion chamber by introducing certain fluids into a car's intake manifold. The injector usually consists of a container, tubing, air intake control, and carburetor or manifold fitting. Vapor is injected into the engine by: sucking air into the container, bubbling the fluid to create vapor, and drawing the vapor into the intake manifold. A typical fluid mixture consists of alcohol and water. A vapor injector is a proven gas mileage enhancer with improvements ranging from 10-25 percent if properly set up and depending on engine design. See also gas saving tip and water injection system.

vaporization – Process defined as the changing of a liquid, like gasoline, into a gaseous mixture. In a carburetor, this occurs when liquid fuel is atomized in the air passageway and sucked into a warm intake manifold where its temperature is raised. The only fuels completely burned in a combustion chamber are those in vapor form. Liquid portions of fuel mixtures find their way, in varying amounts, down the cylinder walls and into the crankcase contributing to deposits and harmful sludge formation respectively. The degree of vaporization is directly regulated by a fuel's boiling point.

vaporizer(1) – Device used to transform high pressure liquid LPG and allow it to expand into a gas at low pressure before introducing it into an engine. See also regulator.

vaporizer(2) – Device used to help change a liquid into a vapor.

vapor lock – Condition created when the flow of liquid fuel to a carburetor airway is disrupted by the formation of fuel vapors somewhere in fuel lines, and/or fuel pump. A car's fuel delivery system is designed to transport and meter liquid fuel, not vapor, to an intake manifold. Fuel vapor is generated when fuel reaches its boiling point. Vapor then tends to occupy the affected area, displacing the liquid and reducing its flow. The amount of vapor generated will depend on the fuel's vapor pressure and temperature. Gasoline boils at a lower temperature if it is more volatile (winter gas) or used at higher altitudes (can boil at 100 degrees Fahrenheit at 5,000 feet).

Vapor lock usually occurs when: driving in hot summer weather, using winter gas in warm to hot weather, driving at high altitudes under load, and/or allowing engine compartment temperatures to get too high (can reach 200 degrees when idling during hot weather).

Vapor lock is usually created by fuel vaporizing somewhere in the engine compartment portion of the fuel line leading up to an engine-mounted fuel pump. When vapor reaches a fuel pump, liquid fuel flow stops since the pump is designed to pump fluid and not vapor.

Vapor lock causes include: high engine compartment heat; high heat source (such as an exhaust manifold) near the fuel line and/or fuel pump; use of low boiling point gasoline; engine running hot or overheating due to clogged radiator core or fins, faulty thermostat, faulty radiator cap, and restrictions in water passageways.

Vapor lock symptoms include: engine starving for fuel, loss in power, missing, and engine stalling when bad. The symptoms will go away for awhile when an engine has been allowed to cool, or when cool water is poured on the fuel pump and lines.

Fuel delivery systems are designed to remain as cool as possible by doing such things as: using carburetor vents, insulating carburetor base from intake manifold heat, shielding fuel delivery system components from exhaust heat, insulating exhaust components, using fabric and rubber lines instead of metal (absorb less heat), placing fuel pumps that pull fuel in an air stream for better cooling, using fuel pumps that push fuel, and using extra lines to collect and route fuel vapors back to a fuel tank. See also gasoline(winter), gasoline(summer), heat soak, and fuel foaming.

vapor pressure – Pressure developed by a liquid's vapor portion over a liquid surface in a closed chamber. It largely depends on a liquid's boiling point.

vapor recovery system – Assemblage of parts used to prevent gasoline vapors in the carburetor and fuel tank from escaping into the atmosphere. Components primarily consist of: activated charcoal canister and gas tank return fuel lines. Vapors are trapped in the canister. Intake manifold vacuum draws the vapors into an engine when it starts. A faulty system can cause: a hot engine to idle rough, hard starting, and gas odors inside the car.

vapor separator - Device used to help prevent vapor lock by feeding vapors back to a gas tank by means of a separate line.

vapor separator tank - Tank used to temporarily store fuel vapors being routed back to a gas tank.

vapor withdrawl system - LPG carburetion system used to extract vapor from the top of an LPG tank. See also liquid withdrawl system.

variable venturi carburetor - See carburetor(air valve).

varnish - See varnish deposits.

varnish deposits - Varnish-like substance deposited in an engine and/or carburetor area. Engine deposits result from running an engine hot and hard for extended time periods. The heat breaks down oil, causing varnish-like elements to separate out and deposit on engine surfaces. These deposits can be minimized by changing oil regularly and making sure the cooling system works properly. Carburetor deposits occur primarily in the air passageway where fuel is mixed with air. Heat causes gasoline varnish and resin compounds to start separating out and slowly build up.

Vaughn - American car produced in 1905, 1913-1914, and 1923.

Vauxhall - British car line produced from 1903 to date by Vauxhall Motors Ltd. Popular models include: Astra, Carlton, Cavalier, Nova, and Senator.

VAZ - Soviet car line produced from 1969 to date by Volzhsky Automobilny Zavod.

V belt - Reinforced rubber belt built usually with a V-shaped cross section. It is used to drive pulleys located on fans, alternators, air compressors, water pumps, and air pumps.

VDO - Line of gauges.

VEC - American car produced from 1903-1905 by Vehicle Equipment Co. in New York.

Veerac - American car produced in 1913.

Vega - American car produced from 1971-1979 by Chevrolet Division of General Motors Corp. in Michigan.

vehicle - Device used to transport or convey. Examples include: car, boat, truck, plane, sled, wagon, trailer, etc.

vehicle emission control information - Information specified to allow proper setting of various engine emission control systems. See also tuning specs label.

vehicle identification number - Number used to uniquely identify a car, truck, etc. It is stamped onto a car body or on a tag mounted somewhere on the body. The sequence of numbers and characters refer to such car details as: date of manufacture, construction location, make, model, body type, engine type, restraint equipment, etc.

vehicular manslaughter - Unlawful killing of another person with a vehicle and without any desire to inflict injury or harm on another. It can be voluntary or involuntary.

vel - Abbreviation for velvet or velour.

Velie - American car produced from 1908-1929 by Velie Motor Vehicle Co. (1908-1916), and Velie Motor Corp. (1916-1928), both in Illinois.

velocity stack - Air funnel mounted over a carburetor intake. It eliminates an air cleaner, minimizes airflow resistance, and eases the transition of air into a carburetor. Disadvantages include: no air filtration, and no air pre-heat system.

vendor - Person selling products.

vent - Small triangular-shaped window located in the front portion of a car's forward window and used to permit ventilation of air with a direct draft.

ventilated disc - See ventilated rotor.

ventilated piston - Aluminum piston head damaged by excess heat causing the aluminum metal to melt and vaporize until a hole is made. Possible causes include: excessive ignition advance due to improper setting and/or wrong electronic ignition module, engine overheating, preignition, and detonation. See also piston damage and engine problem(overheating).

ventilated rotor - Disc brake rotor constructed with air vanes between the two rotor surfaces to increase rotor heat dissipation. Also, it refers to a rotor that has been drilled with numerous holes to increase heat dissipation. See also drilled rotor.

ventilate the block - To force a connecting rod out through the engine block or oil pan.

Ventura - American car produced from 1961-1980 by Pontiac Division of General Motors Corp. in Michigan.

venturi - Portion of a channel, tube, pipe, etc. built tapering to a smaller diameter. A liquid or a gas flowing through such an area will speed up and cause a partial vacuum to be formed. The taper is much steeper facing the flow of air. A venturi is used as a carburetor intake bore to properly meter liquid fuel. See also venturi principle.

venturi effect - See venturi principle.

venturi principle - Method used to create a partial vacuum in a moving air stream by constricting and then expanding the air flow. At the constriction, air speed increases and air pressure decreases. Vacuum in a venturi is greatest at the throat or point of highest air speed.

venturi tube – Tube built with a restricted cross section in order to induce the venturi principle.

vent wings – Small triangular-shaped windows mounted at the leading edge of front seat side windows. They were used on older cars to improve interior ventilation.

Vera – American car produced in 1912.

Veracity – See Smith.

Vernon – American car produced from 1915-1920 by Vernon Automobile Corp. in New York.

Verrett Motor Wagon – American car produced in 1896.

Versailles – American car produced by Lincoln from 1980 to date by Lincoln Division of Ford Motor Co. in Michigan.

Versare – American car produced in 1928.

vertical aiming screw – Screw used in a car headlight assembly to adjust the up and down position of a headlight beam.

Vestal – American car produced in 1914.

Veteran – American car produced in 1921.

veteran car – British car generally classified as built before 1905. See also edwardian car and vintage car.

Vetta Ventura – American car produced from 1964-1966 by Apollo International Corp. in California.

Vette – Chevrolet Corvette sports car.

V front grille – Grille shaped in the form of a V.

vg – Abbreviation for very good.

VI – Abbreviation for viscosity index.

viaduct – Bridge or elevated roadway built to carry traffic over water, other streets, etc. It usually consists of a series of short spans.

Viall – American car produced in 1917.

vibration – Back and forth or oscillating movement of an object.

vibration(car) – Vibration located somewhere in the structure of a car. Car vibrations usually occur in the chassis or the drivetrain. A drivetrain vibration occurs at a certain rpm whether a car is moving or not. A chassis vibration will occur only when a car is traveling at a certain speed. Chassis vibration is the most common vibration. It includes: unbalanced tires, worn ball joints, bad wheel bearings, broken springs, worn shock absorbers, and worn steering linkage parts.

vibration(chassis) – Vibration created by one or more worn chassis parts. See also vibration(car).

vibration(clutch/transmission) – Vibration created by an unbalanced condition in the clutch/transmission area. Possible causes include: bad bearings, broken or chipped gears, loose transmission parts, low transmission oil, unbalanced or wrong type clutch plate, loose pressure plate, bent transmission input shaft, out of alignment clutch housing and/or clutch assembly, and different pressure plate springs. The problem can be further diagnosed by observing the vibration when the clutch is engaged and disengaged.

vibration(differential) – Vibration created in a car's differential. Possible causes include: excess backlash between ring and pinion gears, pinion gear meshing out of adjustment, bad pinion gear input bearing, and excess U-joint angle at differential end of driveline. Worn differentials are most often noisiest when decelerating.

vibration(drive axle) – Vibration created by a bent axle. Vibration will usually occur at higher speeds (over 55 mph).

vibration(driveline) – Common drivetrain vibration created when a driveline becomes unbalanced. It can happen if: driveline gets slightly bent or dented, balance weights break loose, or universal joints are worn. This vibration is easy to spot because it vibrates according to the speed of rear wheels. See also vibration(universal joint) and car service tip(car vibration test).

vibration(engine) – Vibration created in the engine compartment area. It can be isolated from chassis vibrations by simply operating the engine at different rpms while the car is stationary. It is not as common as chassis vibrations, since an engine is designed to remain balanced during its operating life. Most engine vibrations are caused by components supporting the engine or controlling its movement. Possible causes include: faulty engine motor mounts, loose or damaged crossmember, loose or too tight engine mount bolts, worn or damaged torque rod, one or more missing engine mount and/or crossmember bolts, and misfiring. See also mechanic's stethoscope, car service tip(car vibration test), and vibration(engine motor mount).

vibration(engine motor mount) – Vibration created when loose or damaged motor mount(s) allows engine and transmission unit to get out of alignment with car's driveline. Vibration occurs when car is moving especially at low speed. See also vibration(transmission mount) and car service tip(car vibration test).

vibration(exhaust system) - Vibration created when loose exhaust system parts resonate due usually to drivetrain vibration. See also car service tip(car vibration test).

vibration(fan) - Engine vibration created by an unbalanced fan. Possible causes include: bent blade(s), loose mounting screws, missing blade(s), and part of blade(s) missing. The vibration can be narrowed down to the fan-water pump area by simply disconnecting the fan belt and running the engine briefly to see if the vibration still exists. If there is no vibration, remove the fan and replace the fan belt. If the vibration occurs, it indicates a bad water pump. See also vibration(water pump).

vibration(generator) - Engine vibration created when a generator becomes unbalanced. Possible causes include: bad bearings or bushings, loose generator mounts, and loose generator pulley. To isolate the generator as a cause, follow the same procedure outlined in vibration(water pump).

vibration(steering) - Chassis vibration created by worn parts in a car's steering system. Possible causes include: worn ball joints, front end out of alignment, and steering box low on oil. Steering vibration is usually transmitted up the steering column shaft so that the driver feels the steering wheel vibrate in his hands. See also vibration(steering wheel).

vibration(steering wheel) - Front end vibration transmitted up a car's steering column. The direction of the vibration often indicates the problem. Possible causes of side-to-side vibration (actually an oscillation) include: wheel damage, lateral tire runout (wobbling), unbalanced tire-wheel assembly, non-parallelism of rotor surfaces. Possible causes of up-and-down vibration with car at rest include: engine shaking due to low idle speed. Possible causes in motion include: loose, tight, or damaged drive belts; loose accessory mounting bolts; broken accessory mounting brackets; faulty engine support components such as engine motor mount, motor mount bolts (too loose or tight), torque rod, and/or cross member; and faulty transmission-driveline components such as unbalanced or bent driveline, wrong length drive shaft (front wheel drive), and loose transmission crossmember. See also car service tip(car vibration test).

vibration(transaxle) - Vibration created when one or more transaxle components is worn, damaged, or unbalanced. The vibration is usually apparent only when the car is in motion. Possible causes include: wrong size drive shaft, loose bolts at shaft flange, and worn or rusted CV joints due to outside contamination. See also car service tip(car vibration test).

vibration(transmission mount) - Vibration created when loose or damaged transmission crossmember support mount allows engine and transmission unit to get out of alignment with car's driveline. Vibration occurs when car is moving especially at low speed. See also vibration(engine motor mount).

vibration(universal joint) - Common drivetrain vibration created by one or more worn universal joints. Wear is usually due to: lack of lubrication, bad needles in the bearing, or a galled bearing surface. A worn joint can be moved by hand. It usually exhibits a tell tale clunking sound when a car is put in gear, especially an automatic. It will also make a cracking sound when driving and will cause vibration according to the speed of rear wheels (for rear wheel drive cars).

vibration(water pump) - Engine vibration created by an unbalanced water pump. Possible causes include: missing impeller pieces, and bad bearing or bushing. In the water pump area, the fan, water pump, or generator can be the vibration source since they are all linked by the fan belt. To isolate the water pump as a cause, remove the fan, run the engine, remove the fan belt, and run the engine. If the vibration persists with the fan removed, the problem lies in either the generator or the pump. Rotate the water pump and then the generator carefully by hand. Listen for any cracking-grinding noise. Feel if it turns freely or like the bearing or bushing has sand in it. If you are still not sure, a mechanic's stethoscope will reveal the noise when turning.

vibration(wheel-1) - Vibration created by an unbalanced wheel and/or tire. Possible causes include: unbalanced tires, bent wheel, tread or belt separation, loose brake drum parts, warped brake drums, etc. Tire vibration can be eliminated or spotted by spin balancing. Other possible problems are handled by visual inspection. See also car handling problem(wheel shimmy).

vibration(wheel-2) - Vibration created by loose or broken wheel related parts. Possible causes include: bent or broken wheel, loose hubcap or lug nuts, excessive axle end-play, and missing or worn on drive axle.

vibration damper - See harmonic balancer.

vice grip pliers - Pliers built with serrated jaws and a locking mechanism for maintaining a tight grip. It is a common tool in a mechanics tool box.

vice grips - See vice grip pliers.

victim - Person involved in a situation where he has been deceived, cheated, injured, etc.

victimize - To swindle, cheat, con, etc.

Victor - American car produced from 1907-1911 and 1913-1915 by Victor Automobile Mfg. Co. in Missouri (1907-1911), Victor Motor Car Co. in Pennsylvania (1913-1914), and Richmond Cycle Car Mfg. Co. in Virginia (1914-1915).

Victoria - American car produced in 1900. Also, an American car produced from 1957-1961 by Ford Motor Co. in Michigan.

victoria - See body style(victoria).

Victors - American car produced in 1923.

Victor Steamer - American steam car produced in 1900.

Victory - American car produced in 1920.

Viking - American car produced in 1908. Also, an American car produced from 1929-1930 by Olds Motor Works in Michigan.

Vim Cyclecar - American car produced in 1915.

VI Modifier - Additive used to make oil thicker. See also VI.

Vim Truck - American truck produced in 1914.

VIN - Abbreviation for vehicle identification number.

Vincent Bendix - He organized an Auto company in 1907 that manufactured over 7,000 Bendix cars. He developed a starter drive and named it after himself. See also starter drive(Bendix).

vintage - Dating from a period long ago.

vintage car(1) - Car generally classified as built before 1912. See also brass era car, antique car, contemporary car, milestone car, special interest car, classic car, contemporary classic car, pre-war car, and post-war car.

vintage car(2) - British car generally classified as built from 1919-1930. See also edwardian car and veteran car.

vinyl top - Car top covered partially or completely with a vinyl material.

Viqueot - American car produced in 1905.

Virginian - American car produced from 1911-1912 by Richmond Iron Works in Virginia.

vis-a-vis - See body style(vis-a-vis).

viscosimeter - Instrument used to determine oil viscosity by measuring the time it takes a specified quantity of oil to flow through a specified opening at a certain temperature.

viscosity - Value used to represent an oil's ability to flow. It is the internal friction of a fluid caused by molecular attraction. A low viscosity oil flows more easily than a high viscosity oil. Low and high viscosity oil is sometimes referred to as light and heavy oil respectively.
    Viscosity has a direct effect on the following aspects of engine operation: engine cranking speed, sealing ability of pistons, coefficient of friction, gear movement, power loss, heat build-up in moving parts, load carrying ability of oil film, and consumption rate of oil. See also pour point.

viscosity index - Number series used to rate an oil's ability to resist changes in viscosity at different temperatures. High and low viscosity index oils change little and a lot respectively. Engine oils typically have a high index since they have such desirable characteristics as: increased engine cranking speed due to reduced viscous drag; reduced wear on moving parts due to better distribution and flow of oil at low temperatures, and less thinning out at high temperatures; and decreased oil consumption.

viscosity index improver - See additive(viscosity index improver).

viscosity rating - One or more numbers assigned by the Society of Automotive Engineers to designate the flow characteristics or thickness of an oil over a temperature range. The number(s) are assigned with the SAE prefix, i.e., SAE 10W-30. A low number indicates low viscosity (thinner oil). A high number indicates an oil able to maintain proper thickness under higher temperature conditions. A dual number indicates an oil able to maintain proper thickness from the lower number to the upper one. A "W" letter designation is assigned to oils able to remain fluid and flow over a wider range of temperatures. A viscosity rating gives no indication of an oil's quality. See also oil.

visibility - Ability to see under prevailing conditions of light, distance, and clearness of air.

vision - Degree of outward visibility in all directions from within a car's interior. It is a common test element in a new car evaluation.

visor - See sunvisor.

Vista Cruiser - American car produced from 1965 to date by Oldsmobile Division of General Motors Corp. in Michigan.

Vixen - American car produced in 1914. Also, an experimental car produced in 1966 by American Motors. It had a landau type roof and canted vents in the rear.

Vixen Cyclecar - American car produced from 1914-1916.

VN - Abbreviation for South Vietnam found usually on an international license plate.

Vogel - American car produced in 1909.

Vogue - American car produced from 1917-1923 by Vogue Motor Car Co. in Ohio.

Vogul - American car produced in 1918.

voiding the warranty – To invalidate a warranty. For example, new car warranties often require regular scheduled maintenance during the warranty period. If the maintenance is not followed, the warranty is no longer valid.

Voiture Legere – Lightweight racing cars built before 1914.

Voiturette – American car produced in 1914.

voiturette – See body style(voiturette).

Volare – American car produced from 1976 to date by Plymouth Division of Chrysler Corp. in Michigan.

volatile – Property of a liquid characterized by rapid evaporation or change from a liquid to a vapor state.

volatile fuel – Fuel characterized by rapid evaporation. Gasoline contains a certain percentage of volatile fuel. The volatility of fuel determines the ease of starting, how long to warm up an engine, and engine performance. In winter time, gasoline is marketed with a higher percentage of volatile fuel to help starting in cold weather. Gasoline, containing too high a percentage of volatile fuel, is prone to vapor locking. See also vapor lock.

volatility – Tendency a fluid has to form vapors.

Volkswagen – West German car line produced from 1936 to date by Volkwagenwerk AG (1960 to date). Popular models include: Beetle (1936-1979), Dasher (1973-1979), Fastback (1961-1973), Golf (1974 to date), Jetta (1974 to date), Karmann Ghia (1956-1974), Rabbit (1974 to date), Polo, Scirocco (1974 to date), Squareback (1961-1973), Thing (1973-1974), Transporter (1954 to date), Santana (1982 to date), and Passat(1974 to date).
  The U.S. representative is Volkswagen of America, Inc., headquartered in Warren, Michigan.

volt – Unit of electrical force or pressure. It moves a current of one ampere through a resistance of one ohm.

Volta, Alexander – He proved the concept that explosive gases could be ignited by an electric spark in 1776.

voltage – Electrical pressure found in an electrical circuit causing current to flow. It is analogous to water pressure.

voltage converter – Device used to raise or lower voltage. Resistors and transformers perform this task.

voltage drop – Difference in electrical voltage measured on both sides of a resistance. It is the resistance in an electrical circuit that causes a voltage drop.

voltage drop test – Common electrical test used to detect excessive resistance and breaks in an electrical circuit. It is performed by touching two voltmeter leads to two different parts of an electrical circuit where a voltage drop is to be measured. The reading will determine if there is a problem.

voltage limiter – Device used to maintain steady current flow to car instruments.

voltage regulator – Electromagnetic switching device used to prevent generator voltage from exceeding a specified value and to keep voltage at a constant level. It consists of two contact points, separated by an air gap, that open and close 50-200 times per second. Point movement is controlled by a solenoid mechanism mounted beneath the points. See also current regulator, cutout relay, and regulator.

voltmeter – Instrument used to measure voltage in an electrical circuit. See also multimeter.

voltmeter gauge – See gauge(voltmeter).

Voltra – American car produced in 1917.

Voltz – American car produced in 1915.

volume – Amount of three dimensional space occupied by an object or area.

volume selling – Practice followed of selling large numbers of cars by reducing the margin of profit per car.

volumetric efficiency – Ratio determined by dividing the theoretical amount of fuel charge by the actual fuel charge received in a combustion chamber. No engine can be 100 percent efficient. Several factors influence how effective an engine design is in getting a theoretical charge of fuel to a combustion chamber. Those factors include: intake manifold restrictions, valve timing, outside temperature, manifold temperature, combustion chamber shape, etc. Volumetric efficiency drops with altitude since outside air pressure drops, decreasing the pressure difference between a combustion chamber and the outside. Volumetric efficiency can be increased by using a supercharger.

Volvo – Swedish car line produced from 1927 to date by AB Volvo.
  The U.S. representative is Volvo of America Corporation, headquartered in Rockleigh, New Jersey.

VOM – Abbreviation for volt/ohm meter.

vortex – Swirling mass of liquid or gas.

VOX – Abbreviation for voice activated circuit.

Voyager – American car produced from 1984 to date by Plymouth Division of Chrysler Corp. in Michigan. Also, an American car produced from 1974-1982 by Plymouth Division of Chrysler Corp.

V-ribbed belt — Belt with a V-shaped cross section.
Vreeland — American car produced in 1920.
v/rf — Abbreviation for vinyl roof.
VRV — Abbreviation for vacuum reducer valve.
VSV — Abbreviation for vacuum switching valve.
VT — Abbreviation for voiturette.
V-top — Abbreviation for vinyl top.
V-type engine — See engine(V type).
Vukovich, Bill — He won the Indianapolis 500 Race in 1953 and 1954. Average speeds were 128.7 and 130.8 mph. The car driven in both races was a Fuel Injection Special.
Vulcan — American car produced in 1913-1915 by Vulcan Motor Car Co. (1913), and Vulcan Mfg. Co. (1913-1914), both in Ohio. Also, an American car produced in 1920.
vulcanize — Process used to change rubber from a plastic to an elastic state by treating rubber with sulfur compounds under heat.
vulcanized rubber — Crude rubber treated with sulfur and heat to give it more desirable properties.
VW — Abbreviation for Volkswagen.

W

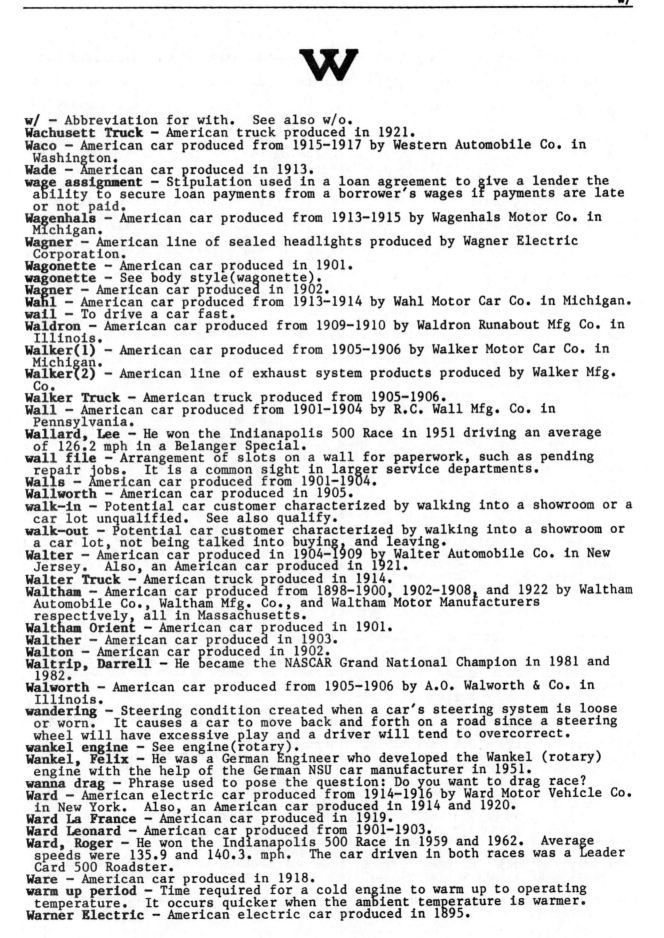

w/ – Abbreviation for with. See also w/o.
Wachusett Truck – American truck produced in 1921.
Waco – American car produced from 1915-1917 by Western Automobile Co. in Washington.
Wade – American car produced in 1913.
wage assignment – Stipulation used in a loan agreement to give a lender the ability to secure loan payments from a borrower's wages if payments are late or not paid.
Wagenhals – American car produced from 1913-1915 by Wagenhals Motor Co. in Michigan.
Wagner – American line of sealed headlights produced by Wagner Electric Corporation.
Wagonette – American car produced in 1901.
wagonette – See body style(wagonette).
Wagner – American car produced in 1902.
Wahl – American car produced from 1913-1914 by Wahl Motor Car Co. in Michigan.
wail – To drive a car fast.
Waldron – American car produced from 1909-1910 by Waldron Runabout Mfg Co. in Illinois.
Walker(1) – American car produced from 1905-1906 by Walker Motor Car Co. in Michigan.
Walker(2) – American line of exhaust system products produced by Walker Mfg. Co.
Walker Truck – American truck produced from 1905-1906.
Wall – American car produced from 1901-1904 by R.C. Wall Mfg. Co. in Pennsylvania.
Wallard, Lee – He won the Indianapolis 500 Race in 1951 driving an average of 126.2 mph in a Belanger Special.
wall file – Arrangement of slots on a wall for paperwork, such as pending repair jobs. It is a common sight in larger service departments.
Walls – American car produced from 1901-1904.
Wallworth – American car produced in 1905.
walk-in – Potential car customer characterized by walking into a showroom or a car lot unqualified. See also qualify.
walk-out – Potential car customer characterized by walking into a showroom or a car lot, not being talked into buying, and leaving.
Walter – American car produced in 1904-1909 by Walter Automobile Co. in New Jersey. Also, an American car produced in 1921.
Walter Truck – American truck produced in 1914.
Waltham – American car produced from 1898-1900, 1902-1908, and 1922 by Waltham Automobile Co., Waltham Mfg. Co., and Waltham Motor Manufacturers respectively, all in Massachusetts.
Waltham Orient – American car produced in 1901.
Walther – American car produced in 1903.
Walton – American car produced in 1902.
Waltrip, Darrell – He became the NASCAR Grand National Champion in 1981 and 1982.
Walworth – American car produced from 1905-1906 by A.O. Walworth & Co. in Illinois.
wandering – Steering condition created when a car's steering system is loose or worn. It causes a car to move back and forth on a road since a steering wheel will have excessive play and a driver will tend to overcorrect.
wankel engine – See engine(rotary).
Wankel, Felix – He was a German Engineer who developed the Wankel (rotary) engine with the help of the German NSU car manufacturer in 1951.
wanna drag – Phrase used to pose the question: Do you want to drag race?
Ward – American electric car produced from 1914-1916 by Ward Motor Vehicle Co. in New York. Also, an American car produced in 1914 and 1920.
Ward La France – American car produced in 1919.
Ward Leonard – American car produced from 1901-1903.
Ward, Roger – He won the Indianapolis 500 Race in 1959 and 1962. Average speeds were 135.9 and 140.3. mph. The car driven in both races was a Leader Card 500 Roadster.
Ware – American car produced in 1918.
warm up period – Time required for a cold engine to warm up to operating temperature. It occurs quicker when the ambient temperature is warmer.
Warner Electric – American electric car produced in 1895.

warning – Form issued by a traffic officer to inform a driver of a suspected or actual traffic law violation. It usually requires no: court appearance, payment of a fine, or admission of guilt. It is used at the discretion of the officer when it is felt that writing up a citation is not necessary but a warning is. See also traffic citation.

warning light – Dash light used to indicate a particular engine or car problem when illuminated. See also sensor.

warning light(check engine) – Light used to indicate a malfunction usually in the emission control system. It does not indicate imminent engine damage, and is part of a car's self-diagnostic system. Fixing the problem usually requires a visit to the dealer. The light can be triggered by: faulty on-board computer; and faulty sensors such as oxygen, coolant temperature, air flow, coolant level, manifold absolute pressure.

warning light(fuel level) – Light used to indicate a low fuel level usually less than 1/4 tank.

warning light(generator) – Light used to indicate battery is not receiving enough charging current and is therefore discharging. Some only come on when discharge is as high as 10-15 amperes. It is wise to get to a service station or other service facility as quick as possible. A weak battery can power an ignition system for awhile (turn off all electrical accessories). If the engine is turned off, you may not get it started.

warning light(oil pressure) – Light used to indicate engine oil pressure has dropped to 5-7 psi. The engine should be stopped immediately if it comes on when driving.

warning light(upshift) – See upshift light.

warning light(water temperature) – Light used to indicate coolant temperature is too high (usually close to boiling). The engine should be stopped immediately if it comes on during driving.

warped block – Engine block damaged when its dimensions become distorted due to overheating, loose engine parts, etc. It is usually serious and often requires replacement.

warped brake drum – Brake drum damaged when its dimensions become distorted due to overheating. It requires replacement.

warped head – Cylinder head damaged when its dimensions become distorted due to overheating, improper tightening or loosening of head bolts, and head bolts that become loose. If the head is not severely warped, the block mating surface can sometimes be milled back to a flat surface.

warped rotor – Wheel rotor damaged when its dimensions become distorted due to overheating. It requires replacement. A rotor can also become warped if the wheel lug nuts are put on too tight.

warr – Abbreviation for warranty.

warrant – Authorization issued by a court to arrest a person.

warranty – Guarantee made of the quality, quantity, and condition of goods sold to a purchaser. Warranties are suppose to protect purchasers by assuring them of a product's quality and a manufacturer's integrity. In reality, their real purpose is to limit the business's responsibility.

warranty(90 day) – Written warranty used to guarantee free repair or replacement of a product found defective in materials or workmanship within 90 days.

warranty(advertising) – Written warranty created by claims made in the advertising of a car. Such a warranty is created if the following can be proven: the seller promised something or made a statement of fact; the tendency of an ad was to induce a person to buy a car; untrue promises, or statements of fact were made in an ad; the car is worth the amount claimed; and the purchaser relied on an ad, promises, or facts stated in an ad when purchasing a car.

warranty(express) – Written warranty.

warranty(extended) – Written warranty used to extend an existing warranty when it expires. Extended warranties are often available at additional cost to a purchaser.

warranty(factory) – See warranty(manufacturer's).

warranty(full) – Written warranty made meeting certain minimum Federal standards. It includes such provisions as: prompt no-charge repair or replacement; a refund if repeated attempts have been made to repair a faulty unit unsuccessfully; clearly specified time limits, if any; and applies to owner and anyone else who uses the product.

warranty(full 90 day) – Full warranty good for a 90 day duration.

warranty(full 1 year) – Full warranty good for a 1 year duration.

warranty(implied) – Pledge made by a the seller, which may not be in writing, that a product will work as claimed by a manufacturer.

warranty(limited) – Written warranty made not meeting the minimum Federal standards of a full warranty. Limited warranty must be conspicuously labeled.

warranty(manufacturer's) – Written warranty furnished by a manufacturer guaranteeing the quality of his products and specifying his obligations to

correct defects.
warranty(new car) – Written warranty used to protect each new car against defects in materials and workmanship for a specified period of time. It is backed by a car manufacturer, and is usually honored by the dealer selling the car. The trouble with this warranty is that it's up to a dealer to determine if there is a defect in materials or workmanship, meaning they have the edge in a dispute. Generally, when you sign a sales contract you are accepting a car in the condition in which it is received. A dealer, therefore, is legally free to charge you for any parts or work not covered by a manufacturer's warranty. A smart car buyer will carefully inspect and road test a new car before accepting it. Dealers know that very few people go to this trouble. See also terms and conditions of a new car warranty.
warranty(road hazard) – Written warranty supplied usually with new tires specifying tire dealer coverage for tire damage due to road hazards such as punctures and flats.
warranty(service) – Written warranty used to specify service work coverage for a particular product.
warranty(sole) – Clause written in a warranty specifying the warranty as the only one covering a specified product.
warranty claim – Formal request or demand made that certain provisions of a warranty are being violated and amends are to be made.
warranty formula – Recompensation rate paid by car manufacturers to dealers who do service work on new cars under warranty.
warranty limitation – Provision made in a warranty specifying limits to a product guarantee. Warranties are generally so full of limitations the burden is placed on the consumer to make sure a product is okay. In the case of a new car, be sure to carefully inspect and road test it before signing any document, such as a sales contract, which acknowledges your acceptance of it. Also, read over the limitations carefully.
warranty of serviceability – Written warranty used to cover the operating ability of a used car sold by a dealer. It requires a dealer to inspect a car before offering it for sale and making sure it can operate safely on the road. Also, the following parts of a car must be in good operating condition or as specified: lights, directional signals, brakes, steering, muffler, defroster, windshield wipers, odometer, mirrors, seat belts (if made after 1963), front wheels aligned, tires with tread over 2/32 inch, and unimpaired visibility through all glass. This warranty cannot be bypassed even if a dealer gets you to sign a contract saying you bought a car "as is". The warranty is violated if a car was defective when sold. It is used in most states.
warranty rate – Hourly rate charged for warranty work.
warranty work – Repair or maintenance work done to a car within a warranty period. Manufacturers usually reimburse car dealers for such work at a lower flat rate than they can get for non-warranty work. Dealers tend to exchange parts rather than do actual repair, or stall on doing the work until the warranty expires.
Warren – American car produced from 1909-1914 by Warren Motor Car Co. in Michigan.
Warren-Detroit – See Warren.
Wartburg – East German car line produced from 1956 to date by VEB Automobilwerk.
Warwick – American car produced from 1903-1904 by Warwick Cycle & Automobile Co. in Massachusetts.
washboard road – Road with narrow trench-like ruts in road surface perpendicular to the road direction.
washer fluid – Fluid used to wash a car windshield. It is usually a mixture of alcohol and water. The alcohol prevents the solution from freezing.
washer pump – See windshield washer pump.
washer reservoir – Small tank used in an engine compartment to store fluid used to wash a car windshield.
washing the windshield – Process defined as activating a windshield washer system to apply washer fluid to a car's windshield. Also, it refers to washing a car's windshield with soap and water when a car is being washed.
Washington – American car produced from 1909-1911 and 1921-1924 by Carter Motor Car Corp. in Washington D.C. and Maryland, and Washington Motor Co. in Ohio respectively.
wash-out – Car dealer tactic used to hide profit on a car sold by using an identification number for a trade-in car that in turn is used on a car being sold.
Wasp – American car produced from 1919-1925 by Martin-Wasp Corp. in Vermont.
wastegate(1) – Louvers or textured grille used to exhaust air. It can be ornamental and/or functional.
wastegate(2) – Valve built into the exhaust side of a turbocharger housing for bypassing exhaust gases around the exhaust turbine wheel in order to prevent overboost. See also detonation(turbo).

waste mold – Negative mold destroyed when freeing a positive cast.

watch commander – Person responsible for running a business or agency for a specified time period.

water – A car value loss determined between the amount a seller has put into a car and its actual wholesale value. For example, a seller is considered in the water $1,500, if he has put $5,000 in a car and its wholesale value is only $3,500.

water beads up – Condition created when water tends to form into droplets on a car paint surface. It is usually due to special paint compounds or a wax-like coating.

water channeling – Water movement located underneath a tire footprint area. Higher water channeling makes a tire more resistant to hydroplaning. Channeling is affected by the shape and number of tread elements, and the number of grooves cut along with their depth and direction.

water injection system – An assemblage of parts and controls used to introduce water into an engine's intake manifold to mix with gasoline. Different injection methods are used, but the purpose is the same. Water serves to: control and slow a fuel mixture's burning rate, and minimize detonation and preignition by essentially raising the octane level of the fuel used. Drawbacks include: lubrication of moving parts reduced somewhat, oxidation of certain metals, and chemical reactions with metal and lubricant.

water in the gas – Gas condition created when water gets into a car's fuel system. Small amounts of water are almost always present in the bottom of most service station tanks since water is more dense than gas. It collects there from tanker trucks and from condensation. Water in a car's gas is derived from pumping gas from near empty service station station tanks, and from condensation in the car fuel tank usually when it is only partly full. When water gets into gas, the best solution is to drain the fuel tank, fuel lines, and carburetor. Next best is adding an alcohol-based water absorption additive, cleaning or changing the fuel filter, and driving the car until the water is gone. Chemical coated test sticks are available to test for the presence of water in a tank.

Water can corrode various engine parts. It reacts with fuel tank metal to form rust and scale. It reacts with carburetor metal to form a yellow scale that can quickly corrode it.

water jacket – Passageway located around certain engine components for circulating water to remove heat. Water jackets surround engine cylinders and combustion chamber areas to dissipate heat generated from the combustion process. Water jackets are also commonly found in intake manifolds where hot water is used to heat a manifold for better fuel vaporization.

water leak – Condition created when water penetrates into a car's interior because of torn gaskets, worn weather-stripping, missing gutters, rust, etc. No cars are totally waterproof.

Waterloo-Duryea – American car produced from 1904-1905 by Waterloo Motor Works in Iowa.

water outlet – Aluminum fitting mounted near the top of an engine block or intake manifold. It is used as a water exit point from an engine block, and is usually where an engine's thermostat is installed.

water passage – See water jacket.

water pump – Centrifugal pump used to circulate water in an engine for cooling. It is usually driven by an engine's main crank pulley via a fan belt. It draws water from the bottom of a radiator, and works whenever an engine is running.

water temperature – Temperature of coolant water.

water temperature gauge – See gauge(water temperature).

water temperature sensor – See sensor(coolant temperature-1).

water thermostat – Bimetallic valve placed in an engine's water cooling circuit to control water temperature. Today's cars use high temperature thermostats in the 180-190 degree range. Higher temperature water minimizes sludge formation, increases fuel economy, and reduces hydrocarbon and carbon monoxide exhaust emissions. It is usually located near an intake manifold around the top of an engine block.

water vapor injection – Device used to inject varying amounts of water vapor into an engine's intake manifold. Some devices rely on intake manifold vacuum to draw in a water mist while others actually pump varying amounts of water into an intake manifold depending on engine demand. See also vapor injector.

Waterville – American car produced in 1911.

watery fuel – See water in the gas.

Watrous – American car produced from 1905-1907 by Watrous Automobile Co. in New York.

Watson – American car produced in 1907 and 1916.

Watson, Larry – Car customizer known for his skills in custom paint work such as scalloping, pinstriping, and pearl.

watt – Unit of measurement for electrical power. One watt of power is generated when one volt flows at the rate of one ampere.

Watt, James – He was a Scotsman who developed the steam engine in 1780. He is considered largely responsibile for triggering the Industrial Revolution.

Watt – American car produced in 1910.

watt linkage – Three bar linkage arrangement used on a car's rear axle housing to limit lateral movement.

Waukesha – American car produced in 1908.

Waverly – American electric car produced from 1898-1903 and 1908-1907 by Waverley Co. (1896-1901), International Motor Car Co. (1901-1903), Pope Motor Car Co. (1903-1907), and Waverley Co. (1908-1916), all in Indiana.

wax – Substance characterized as plastic, easily molded, hard when cold, and soft when warm. Its uses include: candles, modeling, molds, coating surfaces.

Wayne – American car produced from 1904-1910 by Wayne Automobile Co. in Michigan (1904-1908), and Wayne Works in Indiana (1905-1910).

WB – Abbreviation for wheelbase.

WD40 – Low viscosity utility oil sold in a spray can.

wear and tear – Damage or deterioration sustained from ordinary use.

wear pattern – Manner in which a surface wears. Surface wear examples include: tire tread, cylinder wall, gear teeth, cam lobe, valve face, valve stem, and main bearing surface.

Weatherly, Joe – He became the NASCAR Grand National Champion in 1962 and 1963.

weather stripping – Narrow strip material used to minimize or exclude the flow of air, water, heat, cold, etc. Materials used include: felt, metal, rubber, and wood.

weaving in and out of traffic – To repeatedly move a car from one lane to another in heavy traffic to arrive at a destination more quickly. When done to extremes with no regard for other cars, it is considered negligent driving.

Webb – American car produced in 1904.

Webberville – American car produced in 1920.

Webb-Jay – American steam car produced in 1908.

Weber – American car produced in 1905.

Weber – Line of Italian carburetors and other automotive products.

wedge block – Combustion chamber and piston top formed in a wedge shape.

weekend warrior – Person racing dragsters on weekends only.

Weeks – American car produced in 1908.

Wege – American car produced in 1917.

Weier-Smith – American car produced in 1917.

weigh station – Roadside truck weighing facility operated by a state agency to enforce maximum weight limits allowable on trucks and other heavy cargo carrying vehicles. When open, all large trucks are required to stop and get weighed.

weight base – Flat rotating circular plate typically mounted underneath a distributor point plate. It supports a distributor's centrifugal advance mechanism. See also advance mechanism(centrifugal).

weight rating – See viscosity rating.

weight springs – Small springs used to control the movement of a distributor's centrifugal weights. Different spring strengths are sometimes used to change the centrifugal advance characteristics of a distributor.

weight transfer effect – Condition created when a car's weight distribution shifts more to the front wheels or to one side during braking or cornering respectively. It occurs because the car's center of gravity is somewhere above the wheels.

Welch – American car produced from 1903-1911 by Chelsea Mfg. Co. (1903-1904), and Welch Motor Car Co. (1904-1911), both in Michigan.

Welch and Lawson – American car produced in 1895.

Welch-Detroit – American car produced from 1909-1911 by Welch Motor Car Co. in Michigan.

Welch-Merquette – American car produced in 1904.

welch plug – See freeze plug.

Welch-Pontiac – American car produced in 1911.

weld – Seam joining two metal pieces together. Also, it refers to welding metal together.

weld broke – Broken weld joint.

welded together – Two pieces of metal joined together by welding.

welder – Person experienced in welding.

welding – Process defined as joining two materials together by fusing, hammering, compressing, gluing, etc. It usually refers to heating two metal pieces to their melting points along a seam and adding a filler metal. See also brazing and soldering.

welding(arc) – Welding process created by forcing electric current to jump an air gap at the end of a welding rod which generates intense heat, melts the welding rod, and fuses a metal seam together. See also welding rod.

welding(gas) – Welding process created by burning a mixture oxygen and a combustible gas to heat and fuse metal seams together. Acetylene is the most common combustible gas used.

welding(heliarc) – Arc welding process created by using aluminum welding rod surrounded by inert gas to weld two aluminum pieces together. The process is usually done with a MIG welder.

welding(MIG) – Arc welding process created by using a semi-portable torch-like body which feeds electrode wire, energizes an electric arc, and floods welding area with an inert gas when a trigger is squeezed.

welding(TIG) – Arc welding process created by using a semi-portable torch-like body which contains a fixed-length tungsten electrode and a means to flood a welding area with inert gas. The tungsten electrode is used to create an arc once struck and resist being consumed. It acts like an gas welder in that the arc is provided to supply heat only. Various metal rods and inert gases are used depending on the metal being welded.

weld it up – To weld metal together.

Wel-Doer – Canadian car produced in 1914.

Werner Truck – American truck produced in 1926.

West & Burgett – American car produced in 1899.

Westcott – American car produced from 1912-1925 by Westcott Motor Car Co. in Indiana and Ohio.

Western – American steam car produced from 1902-1903 C.G. Moore Mfg. Co. in Massachusetts.

Westfield Steam – American steam car produced in 1910.

West Gasoline Vehicle – American car produced in 1895.

West Germany – One of the six largest car producing countries in the world.

Westinghouse – American car produced in 1901.

Westman – American car produced in 1912.

Weston – American car produced in 1896.

West Steamer – American steam car produced in 1897.

wet brakes – Brake linings soaked with water due to traveling through water or driving on a wet road. They dry out fast when the brakes are applied.

wet out – Condition created when fuel vapor separates from the air to condense into droplets on: intake manifold walls, port areas, and combustion chamber walls. Maintaining air/fuel mixture turbulence and warm metal surfaces helps keep the fuel suspended.

wet sanding – To sand a surface with sandpaper and water.

wet sleeve – Metal cylinder pressed into an oversize cylinder bore to form a piston bearing surface. This type sleeve also replaces a cylinder wall and allows water to circulate around the outside of the sleeve itself. Sleeves allow engine blocks to be rebuilt several times regardless of cylinder wall damage. See also dry sleeve.

Weyher – American car produced in 1910.

WFS – American car produced from 1911-1913 by W.F.S. Motor Car Co. in Pennsylvania.

wgn – Abbreviation for wagon.

Whaley-Henriette – American car produced in 1900.

Wharton – American car produced from 1921-1922 by Wharton Motors Co. in Texas.

what kind of condition it's in – Condition of a product.

Wheel – American car produced in 1902.

wheel – The entire circular steel frame used to support and mount a tire to a car axle shaft.

wheel(Mag) – Lightweight cast alloy wheel. It is used primarily on racing cars because of its light weight, but is also used to add a racy appearance to stock cars. Original wheels were made of magnesium, but most today are made of aluminum or steel. Mag wheel now relates more to appearance than composition.

wheel(steel) – Wheel built out of steel parts welded together. Most cars today use this type wheel.

wheel(steel disc) – Wheel built out of steel in the shape of a disc. It was popular in the 1930s. Its drop center rim design allowed lower pressure tires to be used. Today's wheels still use this rim concept for keeping tires on the wheels.

wheel(steel wire) – See wheel(wire).

wheel(wire) – Wheel built to support the outer wheel surface using radiating steel spokes.

wheel(wood spoke) – Early wheel built to support the outer wheel surface using radiating wood spokes.

wheel adapter – Plate mounted on a wheel hub with a different lug pattern in order to mount a different type of tire.

wheel aligner – Tool used to check caster, camber, and toe-in.

wheel alignment – Relationship exhibited by a car's wheels to each other and a road surface when straight and turned. Since rear wheels are fixed, most alignment adjustments are made to front wheels. Properly aligned wheels permit a car to steer a true course with the least effort and reduce tire wear to a minimum. Correct front wheel alignment is achieved when the proper relationship between the suspension system, steering system, and wheel alignment angles exists.

Because wheel alignment angles are interrelated, a proper wheel alignment inspection must be done before parts are replaced and adjustments made. The inspection is a three step process.

The first inspection is a stationary examination of all factors contributing to overall alignment. They include: frame straightness; proper curb height and weight; tire tread wear pattern; tire pressure evenness; wheel lug looseness or incorrect installation; steering wheel turning effort in both directions; wheel bearing looseness; steering system linkage looseness and/or wear at all pivot points, bolts, and ball joints; and steering gear box looseness.

The second inspection is a road test. The following is done: determining and marking the straight line position of steering wheel; checking front and rear wheel tracking by driving car on wet pavement and observing relationship of tread marks left; checking car for drifting left or right; checking for vibration at different speeds; and checking turning effort required, abnormal noises, and vibration.

The third inspection is a stationary test examining the following settings in the order listed: suspension height, caster angle, camber angle, toe-in, steering axis inclination, and toe-out in turns. Adjustments need to be made when: steering linkage adjustment points change; new steering linkage parts are added; steering linkage parts are damaged, worn, or bent; ball joints are worn; and Macpherson strut assembly becomes bent or damaged. In the case of damaged or worn out parts, they must be replaced before any adjustments can be made. See also car handling problem.

wheel alignment angle – Angle checked and adjusted during a front end alignment to control contact and movement of a car's front tires. Several angles are checked. They include caster, camber, toe in or toe-out, and steering axis inclination. Some cannot be modified while others are adjustable. The angles refers to the tilting of the wheels and the steering axis. They control the manner in which front wheels behave when a car is driven. Most angles are interrelated meaning changing one will change others. See also wheel plane and steering axis.

wheel alignment angle(camber) – Small angle measured between a vertical plane and wheel plane of a wheel. It is the tilt of a wheel inward or outward at the top (negative or positive camber), and measures how close a wheel is to being perpendicular to a road surface. All wheels, attached to a pivoting suspension type system such as to a full floating axle, have some type of camber setting. On the front wheels of today's cars, this angle often cannot be adjusted because of an integral wheel spindle and strut assembly. See also wheel alignment angle(caster).

wheel alignment angle(caster) – Small angle measured between a steering wheel axis and a vertical axis. Wheels can have a negative or positive caster with most cars having positive. Positive caster is what allows a car to track in a straight line or allows it to be towed without having someone steer it. On many cars, this angle cannot be adjusted because of an integral wheel spindle and strut assembly, such as a Macpherson strut.

wheel alignment angle(included) – Angle identified as the sum of the camber and steering axis inclination angles.

wheel alignment angle(steering axis inclination) – Angle measured between the vertical plane of a wheel and a steering axis formed by a line running through upper and lower ball joints. It usually tilts inward. Like caster and camber, this angle cannot be adjusted on many newer cars because of an integral wheel spindle and strut assembly. On older cars, the steering axis was vertical, but it caused the car to pull and wheels to scuff excessively especially on rough roads.

wheel alignment angle(toe in) – Horizontal angle formed when wheel planes are no longer parallel to each other due to front half of front tires pointing toward each other. Most cars have a slight toe-in to help keep wheels parallel and counteract other forces tending to cause a toe-out condition. If the toe-in is too much, the front tires will scuff or skid as they rotate and the tread will featheredge along the outside. Toe-in is adjusted by shortening tie rod length. The tie rod links the two front wheels so they turn together.

wheel alignment angle(toe out) – Opposite of the toe-in wheel alignment angle. The front half of front tires point away from each other. Toe-out is adjusted by increasing tie rod length.

wheel alignment angle(toe out on turns) – Amount of toe-out created when front wheels are turned. The two front tires must toe-out somewhat during turning because one is turning about a shorter radius than another. Without a slight toe-out on turning, the inside tire would scuff and slip. The toe-out condition is created in the steering linkage by designing the steering arms of each wheel to angle inward. The net effect is the outside tire turns less sharply than the inside tire. For example, an inside tire turning 25 degrees would typically have the outside tire turn 22 degrees off a car centerline.

wheel alignment problem – Condition created when front wheels do not track properly when a car is driven.

wheel arches – See fender.

wheel balance – See balance(wheel).

wheel balancer – See tire balancer.

wheelbase – Distance measured between centers of front and rear wheels on one side of a car. If the distance on the left side is different from the right, car weight will not be balanced over the wheels and a car will not track properly.

wheel bearing – See bearing(wheel).

wheel bearing(front) – Wheel bearing used to support and allow rotation about a wheel spindle shaft. Most front wheels are mounted with two tapered roller bearings to handle side thrust when tires turn. See also repack the front wheel bearings.

wheel bearing(rear) – Wheel bearing used to support and allow rotation of a rear axle shaft. One is mounted at each end with the bearing located at the wheel hub usually press fitted onto the shaft.

wheel bearing grease – See grease(wheel bearing).

wheel chocks – Triangular-shaped blocks used to slide under tires and prevent a car from moving.

wheel covers – See hub cap.

wheel cylinder – See brake cylinder.

Wheeler – American car produced from 1900-1902 by Wheeler Automobile Mfg. Co. in Massachusetts.

wheelhouse – Enclosure around front and rear wheels.

wheel housing cover – Cover used to seal the lower inner fender wells. It minimizes a tire splashing water up onto engine causing stalling problems, and help to keep air flowing properly through the engine compartment.

wheel hub – See hub.

wheelie – To lift the front wheels of a race car off the ground when leaving a starting line.

wheel lug – See lug nut.

wheel packing – Grease placed in a cavity acting as a reservoir for greasing wheel bearings. It is usually only done to front wheel bearings. See also repack the front wheel bearings.

wheel plane – Plane located passing through the middle of a tire tread to the center of a wheel. The wheel plane becomes a vertical plane when wheel camber angle drops to zero.

wheel puller – Tool used to remove a wheel hub. It attaches to a wheel and exerts a pulling pressure by means of a sliding hammer.

wheel rim – Metal flange located around the outside circumference of a wheel upon which a tire is mounted. A wheel has an inside and an outside rim.

wheel runout – Degree of even lateral and radial movement measured when a wheel is rotated.

wheel shimmy – See car handling problem(wheel shimmy).

wheelspin balancer – See tire balancer(wheelspin).

wheel spindle – Shaft used to support a wheel and tire assembly and allow it to rotate. It extends outward from a steering knuckle. The inner and outer wheel bearings ride on the spindle shaft.

wheel stand – See wheelie.

wheel stud nut – See lug nut.

wheel tramp – Condition created when a wheel tends to move up and down so it repeatedly bears hard, or tramps, on a road surface. It is sometimes called high speed shimmy. See also car handling problem(wheel shimmy).

wheel well – Area located on the underside of a car body surrounding a wheel.

whiplash – Medical ailment caused by a rear end collision that injures a person's neck. The ailment is usually classified as a cervical strain and is caused by the rapid backward movement of a head when impact occurs. Whiplash is a very controversial ailment believed to be contrived in many car accidents.

Whippet – American car produced from 1926-1931.

Whitcomb – American car produced in 1928.

White – American steam car produced from 1900-1918 by White Sewing Machine Co. (1900-1906), and White Co. (1906-1918), both in Ohio. Also, an American car produced in 1914.

White Brothers – They were three brothers, Windsor-Rollin-Walter, who began their automotive careers while working for their father's company, White Sewing Machine Company. Rollin and Windsor produced a steam powered car in 1900. They organized the White Company in 1906.

white coated specialist – Professional experienced in a particular field of study or work.

White Company – Company organized by the White brothers in 1906. The first car and truck were produced in 1910 and 1915 respectfully.

white flag — See flag(white).
white flash trick — See con game(white flash).
White Hall — American car produced in 1911.
White Hickory — American car produced in 1906 and 1917.
white letters — Raised letters formed on the sidewall of a tire casing. They are usually raised and colored white to stand out for a custom look.
white metal — Metal alloy composed of tin, antimony, and lead. It has a low melting point and coefficient of friction. Pewter is a white metal.
White, Rex — He became the NASCAR Grand National Champion in 1960.
Whiteside — American car produced in 1911.
white smoke trick — See con game(white smoke).
White Star — American car produced from 1908-1910 by White Star Co. in Georgia.
White Triplex V-12 — American car driven by Ray Keech to a 1928 world land speed record of 207.6 mph at Daytona, Florida.
whitewall — Black tire built with a circular white strip on the outside sidewall surface. The width of the strip depends on the tire make.
Whiting — American car produced from 1910-1912 by Flint Motor Wagon Works (1910), and Whiting Motor Car. Co. (1911-1912), both in Michigan.
Whitman — American car produced from 1908-1909.
Whitney — American car produced from 1895-1898 by G.E. Whitney Motor Wagon Co. in Massachusetts (1895-1897), and Whitney Motor Wagon Co. in Maine (1897-1898).
wholesaler — See jobber.
wholesale value — Used car's value to an individual or business planning to resell it.
Wichita — American car produced in 1914.
Wichita Truck — American truck produced in 1918.
Wick — American car produced from 1902-1903 by Wick Co. in Ohio.
Widmar, Larry — He is known in racing circles for developing a high-swirl, lean-burn cylinder head design that generates high horsepower, low exhaust temperatures, and low fuel consumption. It received attention in 1985 when the Daytona 500 and NHRA Winternationals (Pro Stock category) were won with engines using such heads. See also cylinder head(high swirl).
wienie — See allowance buyer.
Wilcox — American car produced from 1907-1912.
Wilcox, Howard — He won the Indianapolis 500 Race in 1919 driving an average of 88.1 mph in a Peugeot.
Wilcox Truck — American truck produced from 1910-1927.
Wildcat — American car produced from 1962-1970 by Buick Division of General Motors Corp. in Michigan.
Wildfire — American car produced in 1953.
Wildman — American car produced in 1902.
Willard — American car produced in 1905.
Willet — American car produced in 1912.
Williams — American car produced in 1905. Also, an American steam car produced from 1957-1968 by Williams Engine Co. in Pennsylvania.
Willingham — American car produced in 1916.
Wills, Childe — He was an engineer who initiated use of vanadium steel and molybdenum steel into car construction. He left Ford Motor Company in 1919 as a millionaire and organized his own company, Wills-St. Claire. In 1933, he became chief metallurgist for Chrysler where he remained until death.
Wills St Clair — American car produced from 1921-1927 by Wills Sainte Claire Co. in Michigan.
Will Truck — American truck produced in 1928.
Willys — American car produced in 1909, 1916-1918, and 1930-1963 by Willys-Overland Co. in Ohio (1908-1963).
Willys Jeep — See Jeep.
Willys, John North — He organized the American Motor Car Sales Company in 1906 to sell the car output of the Overland Company. By 1908, he was made president of Willys-Overland. He boosted sales of the cars from 4,000 in 1908 to 94,500 in 1915.
Willys-Knight — American car produced from 1914-1932 by Willy-Overland Co. in Ohio.
Willys-Overland — American car produced from 1908-1951.
Willy-Overland Company — Company organized in 1908 to produce the Willys-Overland car. The company prospered until 1933 when it went into receivership. The firm became part of Kaiser Industries Corporation in 1953.
Wilson — American car produced from 1903-1905.
Wilson Truck — American truck produced in 1915.
winch — Mechanical device used to hoist or pull by winding a wire or rope around a drum. The drum is rotated through gearing by a hand crank or by an electric motor.
windcord — Narrow cord material used to outline a door opening, finish the edge, and close any gaps.

wind deflector – Fiberglass panel mounted on the roof of a truck's cab or sleeper to lower a truck's air resistance.
Windfield, Gene – Popular car customizer known for building radical looking cars with custom paint jobs.
winding road – Road characterized by few straight sections and many curves, switchbacks, etc.
windjammer – Supercharger.
windmill – Supercharger.
window deflector – Small metal shield mounted along the leading vertical edge of a car's front side window to deflect air and water away.
wind resistance – Amount of force exerted by the wind against a car body when a car is moving. The shape of a car has a large effect on this value.
windscreen – Windshield.
windshield – Section of glass mounted above and across a car's dashboard.
windshield(five ply) – See windshield(LOF).
windshield(LOF) – Recent safety windshield installed on limited numbers of cars in the U.S. It consists of: an outer glass, polyvinyl butyral liner, inner glass, polyvinyl butyral liner, and anti-lacerative polyester film.
windshield(safety) – Windshield constructed to resist shattering of glass in the event of impact from inside or outside the car.
windshield(Saint Gobain) – Recent safety windshield used extensively in Europe since 1977, and now becoming more popular in the U.S. It consists of: an outer glass, polyvinyl butyral liner, inner glass, and anti-lacerative polyurethane film.
windshield(Securiflex) – See windshield(Saint-Gobain).
windshield(standard) – See windshield(three ply).
windshield(three ply) – Most common safety windshield constructed with an outer glass, an energy absorbing polyvinyl butyral liner, and an inner glass.
windshield pillar – Support post located between a cowling and roof at a windshield's midpoint. It was common on two-piece windshields.
windshield washer – Assemblage of parts used to spray a car's outside windshield surface with fluid. The primary parts consist of: a fluid reservoir, pump, necessary hoses and fittings, and a control switch. Most systems operate by simply pressing a button which pumps water from a reservoir through hoses to discharge nozzles positioned below the bottom of a windshield on the passenger and driver's sides.
windshield washer pump – Small pump mounted near or under a washer reservoir for pumping washer fluid to a car's windshield.
windshield wax – Wax-like product applied to a windshield. Advantages claimed include: reduced icing, better visibility in the rain, reduced friction for wipers. Disadvantages include: usually expensive, often hard to apply, and requires reapplication at regular intervals.
windshield wiper – Pivoting mechanical arm and flat rubber blade assembly used to sweep the surface of a car windshield in a back and forth arcing motion to keep it clean. It is most commonly used to remove water when it rains. The wiper arm pivots on a shaft usually located just below the bottom of a windshield. The wiper arm typically sweeps a 90 degree path or 1/4 pie shape on a car windshield. Cars today use two electrically operated windshield wipers.
windshield wiper action – Speed attained and area swept by windshield wipers.
windshield wiper arm – Metal arm assembly that: holds a wiper blade, presses it against a car windshield, and sweeps it back and forth through an arc of around 90 degrees. The rotation motion is supplied by an electric or vacuum motor.
windshield wiper motor – Motor used to operate a car's windshield wipers. Two types have been developed: vacuum and electric. Vacuum motors were used on older cars. Today's cars use electric motors. The motor uses gearing, cams and other components to translate circular motion into a back and forth motion for the wiper arms.
windshield wiper problem – Condition created when the windshield wipers are not operating properly. Common problems include: wiper arms not moving, moving too slowly, sweeping too small an arc, operating at one speed only, sweeping too fast, and not parking; and noisy operation. Possible causes of these problems lie in one or more of the following areas: worn wiper motor brushes and bearings, shorted or grounded field or armature windings in the wiper motor, corroded and/or worn wiper motor control contacts, malfunctioning wiper control switch, defective circuit resistors, malfunctioning wiper relay switch, binding wiper linkage, stripped wiper arm shaft, improper wiper arm positioning, excessive end play of motor armature, and blown fuse.
windshield wiper system – Assemblage of parts used to operate a car's windshield wipers. The primary parts used include: wiper motor, motor to wiper arm linkage, wiper arms, wiper arm shafts, wiper blades, wiper relay, and wiper control switch.
windshield wiper system(electric) – Common windshield wiper system used today.

It is powered by an electric motor.
windshield wiper system(electropneumatic) — Windshield wiper system powered by a vacuum motor in such a way the wipers can operate at a constant or intermittent speed.
windshield wiper system(vacuum) — Windshield wiper system powered by a vacuum motor. It was used on older cars.
Windsor — American car produced in 1906 and 1929. Also, an American car produced from 1960-1961 by Chrysler Corp. in Michigan.
windup — To rapidly increase engine rpm to its peak. Also, it refers to accelerating a car to a high rate of speed.
wind wings — See vent wings.
Winfield — American car produced in 1921.
wing — Fender. Also, it refers to a spoiler.
Wing — American car produced in 1896.
Wingfoot Express J-46 Jet — American car driven by Tom Green to a 1964 world land speed record of 413.2 mph at Bonneville, Utah.
Wing Midget — American car produced in 1922 by H.C. Wing & Sons in Massachusetts. It was a small one passenger car with a reported top speed of 80 mph and fuel economy of 50 mpg.
Winkler — American car produced in 1911.
Winner — American car produced in 1899 and 1907.
Winnipeg — Canadian car produced in 1921.
winter gas — See gasoline(winter).
winterizing a car — Procedure followed to prepare a car for winter operation. It usually refers to: draining a car's cooling system, flushing it, and adding the proper amount of antifreeze solution for low temperature cooling system protection; checking battery and cleaning all terminals; installing snow tires; covering radiator opening somewhat; and checking proper operation of choke and air preheat system.
Winther — American car produced from 1920-1923 by Winther Motor Truck Co. in Wisconsin.
Winther Truck — American truck produced in 1917.
Winton — American car produced from 1897-1924 by Winton Motor Carriage Co. in Ohio.
Winton, Alexander — He built his first car in 1896. Other credits include: organizing the Winton Motor Carriage Company in 1897, producing the first 8 cylinder car in 1905, developing a workable storage battery, designing a speed governor, designing an aircraft engine that burned lightweight oil, serving as president of his company until 1924, and organizing the Winton Engine Company.
Winton Engine Company — Company organized in 1925, by Alexander Winton, to produce marine, rail, and industrial diesel engines. It was purchased by General Motors in 1930 and became their Cleveland Diesel Division.
wipers — See windshield wiper.
wiper blades — See windshield wiper blade.
wiper rod — See windshield wiper arm.
wire gauge(1) — Instrument used to measure the diameter of a metal conductor as a gauge number. See also gauge number.
wire gauge(2) — See gauge number.
wire divider — Bracket used to separate spark plug wires running from the distributor to the various spark plugs. It prevents cable crossfiring and helps keeps them from getting too close to an exhaust manifold.
wire loom — See wire loom. Also, it refers to a tube used to contain wires like a wire harness. Tubular wire looms are usually not a good idea since they encourage cable overheating, electrical interference, and induction firing.
wires — Wire wheels. Also, it refers to wheel covers simulating wire wheels in appearance.
wire size — Diameter of an electric cable's wire conductor. It is usually expressed as a gauge size. The outside diameter of an electrical cable is not a measure of its current carrying capacity since insulation can vary greatly in thickness. Wire size is important. If it is too small, the following can occur in an affected circuit: excessive resistance and voltage drop, overheating, and poor operation of electrical accessories. As wire size increases, current carrying capacity increases and voltage drop decreases.
   Car wire size usually ranges from 10-18 gauge. Ten gauge is the heaviest and is used for supplying current to a fuse block, headlights, or charging of a battery. Twelve gauge is commonly used between a fuse block and high current headlights, and accessories. Fourteen gauge is commonly used for horns, radios, cigarette lighters, etc. Sixteen gauge is commonly used for running lights, backup lights, dome lights, etc. Eighteen gauge wire is commonly used for car instruments. See also American Wire Gauge and wire gauge.
wire spoke wheels — Wheels built with radiating spokes for looks and to

provide support.

wire wheel covers — Hub caps built with a wire spoke appearance.

wiring — Assemblage of electrical wires used to form the various electrical circuits in: a car's electrical system, radio, cassette player, etc.

wiring diagram — Detailed drawing made showing all the details of a car's electrical system including: wiring, connections, and electrical devices.

wiring diagram symbol — Picture, number(s), character(s), etc. used to assign a specific meaning to an item on a wiring diagram. For example, BLK 16 shown next to a wire indicates the wire is black and has a gauge thickness of 16.

wiring diagram symbol(+) — It is used to indicate positive.

wiring diagram symbol(-) — It is used to indicate negative.

wiring diagram symbol(BLK) — It usually designates a black wire.

wiring diagram symbol(BLK 16) — It usually indicates a black wire with a thickness of 16 gauge. Other gauges are similarly represented.

wiring diagram symbol(BR) — It usually designates a black wire with a red stripe.

wiring diagram symbol(BRN) — It usually designates a brown wire.

wiring diagram symbol(BW) — It usually designates a black wire with a white stripe. Other combination colors are similarly represented with primary color first and stripe color second.

wiring diagram symbol(DK GRN) — It usually designates a dark green wire.

wiring diagram symbol(LT GRN) — It usually designates a light green wire.

wiring diagram symbol(G) — It usually designates a green wire.

wiring diagram symbol(L) — It usually designates a blue wire.

wiring diagram symbol(LW) — It usually designates a blue wire with a white stripe.

wiring diagram symbol(O) — It usually designates an orange wire.

wiring diagram symbol(R) — It usually designates a red wire.

wiring diagram symbol(W) — It usually designates a white wire.

wiring diagram symbol(Y) — It usually designates a yellow wire.

wiring harness — Large number of wires bundled together and forming the major electrical circuits of a car.

Wisco — American car produced in 1910.

Wisconsin — American car produced in 1899 and 1910-1911.

Wisconsin Truck — American truck produced in 1921.

wishbone — See center pivot radius rod.

with all its faults — See as is.

Witt Will — American car produced in 1917.

Witt Thompson — American car produced from 1921-1923.

Wizard — American car produced in 1914. Also, an American car produced from 1921-1922 by Wizard Automobile Co. in North Carolina.

w/o — Abbreviation for without. See also w/.

Wolfe — American car produced from 1907-1909 by H.E. Wilcox Motor Car Co. in Minnesota.

Wolfsburg — Town located in Germany where the Volkswagen car manufacturing plant was built.

Wolseley — British car produced by Herbert Austin, in 1898. It was his first.

Wolverine — American car produced in 1896 and 1913. Also, an American car produced from 1904-1906, 1917-1920, and 1927-1928 by Reid Mfg. Co. (1904-1905), Wolverine Automobile & Commercial Vehicle Co. (1905-1906), Wolverine Motors (1917-1920), and Reo Motor Car Co. (1927-1928), all in Michigan.

Wolverine-Detroit — American car produced in 1912.

Wonder — American car produced in 1909 and 1917.

Wood — American steam car produced from 1902-1903 by Wood Vapor Vehicle Co. in New York.

wood alcohol — See methanol.

wood body — Car body built mostly out of wood.

Woodburn — American car produced in 1912.

wooden body — Early car body built with wooden framework and covered with thin metal panels.

wood graining — Custom painting technique used to simulate wood grain patterns. The effect can be created with a wood grain squeegee scraped across a wet paint surface. Another method calls for applying a slow drying base coat, letting it partially dry, and then applying a contrasting wood color with a brush. The brush will mix the two paints yielding a wood grain effect.

Woodill Wildfire — American car produced from 1952-1958 by Woodhill Fiberglass Body Corp. in California.

woodie — Early car built with a body substantially or completely out of wood. Also, a steel-bodied car covered with wood.

Wood-Loco — American car produced from 1901-1902 by Wood-Loco Vehicle Co. in New York.

Woodruff — American car produced in 1904.

Woods — American electric car produced from 1899-1919 by Woods Motor Vehicle Co. in Illinois. It was one of the longest selling electric cars in America.

The 1917 model offered dual power using a gasoline engine as a back up to an electric motor.

Woods Magnetic – American car produced in 1917.

Woods Mobilette – American car produced from 1914-1916 by Woods Mobilette Co. in Illinois.

Wood Truck – American truck produced in 1905.

word of mouth – To make a product, service, idea, etc. known through verbal communication of one person to another. Many small businesses have become successful this way.

work – To get a potential car customer to accept a car salesman's terms.

work car – Car used for driving to and from work. Also, it refers to a used car suitable for work transportation.

work hardening – Metal altered to become less ductile due to upset.

working hubcap – Loose hubcap.

working tight – Car dealer business tactic used to increase sales by spreading the cost of selling cars over the entire car lot inventory. This allows some cars to be sold for less money than the dealer has invested in it.

workmanship – Skill or quality of a worker or a product.

works car – Race car sponsored and maintained by the manufacturer.

Worldmobile – American car produced in 1928.

World Truck – American car produced in 1927.

worm gear – See gear(worm)

worn bearings – Bearings worn sufficiently to create excessive clearances between a bearing and bearing surface, or internal bearing parts depending on the bearing type.

worn out suspension – Suspension system worn sufficiently to require replacement of certain suspension parts for continued safe operation.

Worth – American car produced from 1909-1910 by Worth Motor Car Mfg. Co. in Illinois.

Worthington Bollee – American car produced from 1904.

wrap a car – To wreck a car.

wraparound – Linear surface found going around a corner such as a wraparound windshield, bumper, or taillight.

wraparound bumper – Car bumper built with ends curving around the corners of a car body.

wreck – Car ruined or destroyed beyond reasonable repair.

wreckage – Remains of something wrecked.

wrecked – Status of a car damaged beyond reasonable repair. See also totaled.

wrecker – See tow truck. Also, it refers to a person experienced in removing wreckage or debris.

wrecking car – Car equipped as a wrecker.

wrecking yard – Business engaged in collecting, dismantling, and selling car parts found on totaled or non-operating cars. See also dismantler.

Wright – Canadian car produced in 1929.

wringing fit – Fit made with less clearance than a running fit. For example, a shaft goes into a respective hole by pushing and twisting it by hand.

wrist pin – See piston pin.

wrist pin retainer – Circular device positioned in a slot at each piston pin end to restrain lateral piston pin movement. Several different devices have been designed including: spring clips, continuous rings, spring locks, and buttons.

writ – Judicial instrument issued by a court to command the performance of a specified act by a person.

write down – The lowering of a used car's value on a car dealers books.

written authorization – Approval or justification made in writing.

written estimate – Estimate written up by a repair shop of the cost of doing repair work to a car. It usually includes parts and labor charges. It is your best defense against a padded repair bill. A repair shop is bound to charge no more than the estimate unless you approve additional work. See also con game(repair order) and mechanic's lien.

wrong way driver – Driver characterized by operating a car in a traffic lane opposite to the normal traffic flow direction.

WS – Abbreviation for windshield.

ww – Abbreviation for white wall tires.

www – Abbreviation for wide white wall.

Wyeth – American car produced in 1913.

Wynn – American line of additives produced by Wynn's Friction Proofing, Inc.

X

X7 – Experimental car produced in 1960 by Chrysler with a gas turbine engine.
X band – A radar frequency used by police. It is broadcast between 10.500-10.550 GHz. See also K band.
X car – Experimental car.
Xenia – American car produced from 1914-1915 by Hawkins Cyclecar Co. in Ohio.
Xint – Abbreviation for excellent interior.
XKE – See Jaguar.
XR7 – American car produced from 1967-1974 by Mercury Division of Ford Motor Co. in Michigan.

Y

Yale – American car produced from 1903–1907 and 1916–1918 by Kirk Mfg. Co. in Ohio (1903), Consolidated Mfg. Co. in Ohio (1903–1907), and Saginaw Motor Car Co. in Michigan (1916–1918). Also, an American car produced in 1921.

Yank – American car produced in 1950.

Yankee – American car produced in 1910.

Yankee Cyclecar – American car produced in 1914.

Yarborough, Cale – He won the Daytona 500 Race in 1968, 1977, 1983, and 1984. Average speeds were 143.3, 153.2, 156.0, and 151.0 mph. Cars driven were a Mercury, Chevrolet, Pontiac, and Chevrolet. He also became the NASCAR Grand National Champion in 1976–1978.

Yarbrough, LeeRoy – He won the Daytona 500 Race in 1969 averaging 158.0 mph in a Ford.

year-round performance – Aspect of a product characterized by its ability to perform during any time of the year. Examples include: all season tire, cooling systems protected from low temperature and high temperature, and multi-viscosity oil.

yech – Rough car or junker.

Yellow Cab – American car produced in 1921.

Yellow Coach – American car produced in 1921.

yellow flag – See flag(yellow).

Yellow Knight – American car produced in 1928.

Yenko – American car produced from 1965–1969 by Yenko Sportscars in Pennsylvania. It was a modified Chevrolet Corvair Corsa.

yield – To give way to.

YLN – Taiwan car line produced from 1958 to date by Yue Loong Co. Ltd.

Yokohama – Japanese line of tires.

York – American car produced from 1905–1907 by York Automobile Co. in Pennsylvania.

York-Pullman – American car produced from 1908–1917.

Young – American car produced in 1921.

Yugo – See Zastava.

YU – Abbreviation for Yugoslavia found usually on an international license plate.

yump – Road bump large enough to force a fast car off the ground.

Z

Z28 – American car produced from 1976 to date by Chevrolet Division of General Motors Corp. in Michigan. It is a Camaro model.
Z – Abbreviation for Zambia found usually on an international license plate.
ZA – Abbreviation for South Africa found usually on an international license plate.
ZAI – Abbreviation for Zaire found usually on an international license plate.
Zastava – Yugoslavian car line produced by Zavodi Crvena Zastava. Recent model includes the Yugo.
Z-car – Japanese sports car produced by Nissan. It was introduced into the U.S. in 1969 as a Datsun, and evolved from 240Z to a 300ZX. The car name was changed in the early 1980s to Nissan, the parent Japanese auto manufacturer. Through the years, it has become the biggest selling sports car in automotive history.
Zeitler & Lamson – American car produced in 1917.
Zent – American car produced from 1902-1907 by Zent Automobile Mfg. Co. in Ohio.
Zephyr – American car produced from 1936-1940. Also, an American car produced from 1978 to date by Mercury Division of Ford Motor Co. in Michigan.
zerc – See zerk.
zerk – Grease gun fitting found on steering knuckles, universal joints, A-arms, steering linkage joints, older rear wheel bearing housings, etc.
zero line – Horizontal and/or vertical base line used in a drawing to make measurements from.
Ziebel – American car produced from 1914-1915 by A.C. Ziebel in Wisconsin.
ZIL – Soviet car line produced from 1956 to date by Zavod Imieni Likhacheva.
Zimmerman – American car produced from 1908-1914 by Zimmerman Mfg. Co. in Indiana.
zinc – Bluish white metallic element commonly used to galvanize iron or steel to protect against rust and other corrosion.
Z-ing – To lower a car by cutting notches in the frame.
Zip – American car produced from 1913-1914 by Zip Cyclecar Co. in Iowa.
zirc – See zerk.
zombie gauge – Any instrument gauge characterized by its needle staying in the same position it was left in just before an engine is shut off and afterwards.
zone of safety – Distance left between you and an object to be avoided after you safely stop.
zone rep – Regional representative of a company.
zoomies – Dragster exhaust headers built to sweep upward. The configuration helps exert downward pressure on the tires, and keeps smoke away from a drivers face.

APPENDIX

AUTOMOTIVE TIME LINE

13th Cent – CARS POWERED WITHOUT ANIMALS – Believed by Roger Bacon, an English philosopher and scientist in the 13th century. He also believed such vehicles existed in ancient times.

15th Cent – TANKLIKE SELF-PROPELLED VEHICLE – Sketched in the 15th century by Leonardo da Vinci, an Italian: painter, sculpter, architect, musician, engineer, mathematician, and scientist.

1678 – CYLINDER AND PISTON ASSEMBLY – Used by Jean d'Hautefeuille to pump water.
– FIRST EXPLOSION ENGINE – Built by Charles Huygens using gunpowder.

1688 – STEAM ENGINE – Built by Dennis Papin in Kassel, Germany.

1705 – STEAM ENGINE – Built by Thomas Newcomen to pump water from mines.

1770 – STEAM POWERED GUN CARRIAGE – Built by Nicholas Cugnot.

1776 – EXPLOSIVE GAS – Concept of igniting combustible gas with an electric spark proven by Alexander Volta.

1782 – ENGINE CRANK – Introduced by an Englishman named James Watt.

1792 – FIRST U.S. TOLL ROADS – Open in Connecticut and Pennsylvania.

1801 – FIRST STEAM POWERED COACH – Built by an Englishman named Richard Trevithick.

1805 – FIRST U.S. SELF-PROPELLED VEHICLE – Steam Dredge built by Oliver Evans and known as Orukter Amphibolos.

1815 – FIRST SUCCESSFUL STEAM LOCOMOTIVE – Built by George Stephenson.
– BROKEN STONE ROAD – Introduced in England by John Macadam.

1844 – RUBBER VULCANIZATION PROCESS – Patented by Charles Goodyear.

1855 – FIRST US SELF-PROPELLED STEAM FIRE ENGINE – Patented by A.B. Latta.

1856 – MAKING STEEL – Discovered by Henry Bessemer in England.

1859 – WORLD'S FIRST OIL WELL – Drilled by E.L. Drake in Titusville, Pennsylvania.

1863 – SELF-PROPELLED VEHICLE – Built and driven 9 kilometers in Paris by a Belgian named Jean-Joseph Etienne Lenoir.

1876 – FOUR STROKE ENGINE – Patented by Nicholas Otto in Germany.

1878 – FIRST CAR RACE – Ran from Green Bay to Madison, Wisconsin. It was won by two men, J. Carhart and A. Farrand, driving an Oshkosh steam car.

1879 – SELDEN PATENT – Filed by George Selden for a car using a one-cylinder Brayton engine.

1886 – FIRST USEABLE MOTORCAR – Patented by Carl Benz.

1889 – FIRST PNEUMATIC TIRE – Patented by John Dunlop in Ireland.

1893 – U.S. OFFICE OF ROAD INQUIRY – Established under the department of Agriculture to begin addressing the need for roads in the U.S.

1894 – RURAL BRICK ROAD – First one built near Cleveland, Ohio. Four miles of brick pavement were laid.
– FIRST MOTORSPORTS EVENT – Held in Paris and known as the Paris-Rouen Trial.

1895 – AUTOMOTIVE MAGAZINES – First publications started. They included: The Horseless Age, The Motorcycle, and Autocar.
– FIRST MAJOR CAR RACE – Held in Illinois and ran 50 miles from Chicago to Evanston. It was won by Frank Dureya.
– FIRST U.S. CAR COMPANY – Organized by Duryea brothers.

AUTOMOTIVE TIME LINE

1895 – FIRST PNEUMATIC TIRE USAGE – In Paris-Bordeaux race by Michelin Brothers.
- FIRST AUTOMOTIVE ASSOCIATION – American Motor League is organized in Chicago.
- FIRST RACING ACCIDENT – Dog hit by Prevost's Panhard car in Paris-Bordeaux race.
- SELDEN PATENT – Granted on his Road engine.

1896 – FIRST CAR PURCHASED – The first known purchase of an American car. One of the Duryea cars is sold.
- FIRST CAR IN DETROIT – Driven by Charles Brady King.
- FIRST TRACK RACE IN U.S. – Car race over one mile course at Narragansett Park in Cranston, Rhode Island.
- FIRST 4 CYLINDER ENGINE – Produced by Panhard et Levassor.
- USE OF WORD AUTOMOBILE – The French word begins appearing in references to cars in U.S.
- HENRY FORD – Builds his first gasoline car. It didn't work.
- DUREYA HORSELESS CARRIAGE – Displayed by Barnum & Bailey Circus in street parade.

1897 – FIRST CAR INSURANCE POLICY – Gilbert Loomis takes out $1,000 liability coverage on his one cylinder car in Westfield, Massachusetts. The premium is $7.50.
- STEAM CAR COMPANY – Established by Stanley Brothers.
- CARS EXPORTED TO JAPAN – Several steam cars shipped from U.S.
- OLDS MOTOR VEHICLE COMPANY – Gets organized and builds first Oldsmobile car.

1898 – FIRST INDEPENDENT CAR DEALERSHIP – Set up by William Metzger of Detroit.
- FIRST FRANCHISED U.S. CAR DEALERSHIP – Set up by H.O. Koller in Reading, Pennsylvania to sell Winton Cars.
- FIRST SHAFT DRIVE – Introduced by Renault.
- FIRST USE OF ALUMINUM ALLOY IN CAR – Haynes begins using metal in cars he manufactures.
- FIRST AIR COOLED CAR – Produced by H.H. Franklin.

1899 – COLLECTING MAIL – U.S. Post Office conducts mail delivery experiments with cars in Washington D.C., Buffalo, and Cleveland.
- U.S. ARMY CAR PURCHASE – U.S. Army makes first major purchase of electric vehicles.
- CLEVELAND TO NEW YORK TRIP – Alexander Winton drives one of his cars one way in 47 hours 37 minutes of driving time.
- FIRST U.S. CAR FACTORY – Opened by Ransom Olds.
- FIRST CAR PARTS AND SUPPLY BUSINESS – Set up by A.L. Dyke in St. Louis, Missouri.
- FIRST U.S. WOMAN'S DRIVER LICENSE – By Mrs. John Phillips of Chicago.
- AUTO REPAIR GARAGE – One of the first gets staffed by mechanics in New York City.
- FIRST AUTOMOBILE SALESROOM – Opened in New York City by Percy Owen. He sold Winton cars.
- PITTSBURGH MOTOR VEHICLE COMPANY – Becomes Autocar Company.
- OLDS MOTOR WORKS – Get organized by R.E. Olds and moves from Lansing to Detroit.
- RENAULT COMPANY – Organized in France.
- STANLEY STEAMER RUN – Climbs Mt. Washington in New Hampshire.
- STANLEY STEAMER CAR RIGHTS – Get sold to Mobile and Locomobile.
- MOTOR AGE MAGAZINE – First issue published.

1900 – FIRST NATIONAL CAR SHOW – Held in New York City at Madison Square Gardens. Over 300 vehicles are exhibited, ranging in price from $280 to 4,000.
- FIRST BUS – Introduced by Mack.
- FIRST PRESIDENT IN A CAR – President McKinley.
- FIRST CAR AMBULANCE – In New York City.
- FIRST CAR ADVERTISING – Appears in the Saturday Evening Post.
- ENGINES UNDER HOODS – Several U.S. Manufacturers move engines under hoods.
- KEROSENE LAMPS – Introduced by R.E. Dietz Company. They had 20 candle power, could cast a beam 200 feet, and produced steady light over even rough roads.

AUTOMOTIVE TIME LINE

1900 – GAS VS. ELECTRIC CAR RACE – Gas powered car defeats electric car at
Washington Park race in Chicago.
  – STEAM CAR TO TOP OF PIKES PEAK – John Walker drives his steam car.
  – NATIONAL ASSOCIATION OF AUTOMOTIVE MANUFACTURERS – Gets organized.
  – ENGINE SPEED GOVERNORS – Several manufactuers begin using them.
  – FLOATLESS CARBURETOR – Several manufacturers begin using carburetors
that don't require floats to regulate fuel flow.
  – STEERING WHEEL – Used on Ohio car built by Packard instead of a tiller.

1901 – PETROLEUM PRICE – Price drops to under 5 cents per barrel due to big
oil find near Beaumont, Texas known as the Spindletop gusher.
  – DETROIT FACTORY FIRE – Olds Motor Works destroyed by fire. Only one
experimental car is saved with a curved dash.
  – ROAD TOURING SIGNS – Placed from New York to Boston.
  – SPEED LIMIT AND REGISTRATION LAWS – Passed in Connecticut.
  – STEERING WHEEL – Becomes the accepted method of steering car.
  – FIRST SPEEDOMETERS – Used on Oldsmobiles.
  – FIRST MOTOR VEHICLE LAW – Passed in Connecticut.
  – FIRST U.S. CAR SOLD IN LARGE NUMBERS – Oldsmobile Curved-Dash Runabout.
  – MAGNETO GENERATOR – Becomes more popular.
  – REMOVABLE TIRES – Become more popular.
  – GAS STATION – A place for storing and dispensing fuel, storing cars,
and repairing them is set up in New York City.
  – LICENSING CARS – New York state begins.

1902 – AMERICAN AUTOMOBILE ASSOCIATION – Gets organized in Chicago.
  – CAR GUARANTEE – Sixty day guarantee accepted by National Association of
Automobile Manufacturers.
  – FIRST PORCELAIN INSULATED SPARK PLUG – Designed by Louis Clarke.
  – FIRST 8 CYLINDER ENGINE – Introduced in Paris.
  – SPEEDING VIOLATION – A man is arrested and fined $10 for speeding in
excess of 10 miles per hour in Minneapolis.
  – CADILLAC AUTOMOBILE COMPANY – Gets organized and starts producing cars.
  – FIRST FOUR CYLINDER WATER COOLED CAR – Locomobile builds car with gas
engine in front.
  – RUNNING BOARDS – First used on Silent Northern car produced by J.D.
Maxwell and Charles D. King.
  – FIRST FRONT MOUNTED ENGINE CAR IN U.S. – Installed on Locomobile car.

1903 – FORD MOTOR COMPANY – Gets organized.
  – FIRST TRANSCONTINENTAL CAR TRIP – Dr. Nelson Jackson and Sewall Croker
drive a two cylinder Winton from San Francisco to New York in 63 days.
Tom Fetch drives "Old Pacific" Packard car from San Francisco to New
York in 61 days.
  – FIRST 6 CYLINDER ENGINE – Introduced in Amsterdam.
  – FIRST ALL STEEL BODY CAR – Introduced by Vauxhall.
  – ASSOCIATION OF LICENSED AUTOMOBILE MANUFACTURERS – Gets organized.
  – MOTOR MAGAZINE – Begins publication.
  – PRESSED STEEL FRAME CONSTRUCTION – Adopted by Peerless.
  – BUICK MOTOR COMPANY – Gets organized.
  – POWER TAKE OFF COUPLING – Developed by B. Gramm.
  – SLIDING GEAR TRANSMISSIONS – Become popular.
  – SHOCK ABSORBERS – Become popular.
  – T HEAD CYLINDERS – Become popular.
  – INTAKE VALVES – Mechanical operation becomes popular.
  – WINDSHIELD – Introduced.
  – CANOPY TOP – Introduced.
  – SHOCK ABSORBERS – Introduced.
  – CADILLAC CAR – Introduced.

1904 – FIRST STUDEBAKER – Sold.
  – SCHOOL FOR AUTO MECHANICS – Established by the Detroit YMCA.
  – PREST-O-LITE COMPANY – Gets organized.
  – MERGER – Leland & Faulconer Manufacturing Company merge with Cadillac
Automobile Company to form the Cadillac Motor Car Company.
  – FIRE AT CADILLAC PLANT – Costly and delays production.
  – FIRST BUS – Manufactured by White.
  – NATIONAL ASSOCIATION OF RETAIL AUTOMOBILE DEALERS – Gets formed.
  – WORLD SPEED RECORD – Set by Henry Ford driving his 999 car 91.37 mph,
then broke by M Rigolly in his Gobron-Brille car in Ostend, Belgium at
103.55 mpg.

AUTOMOTIVE TIME LINE

1904 – FIRST AUTOMATIC TRANSMISSION – Sturtevant car using a centrifugal clutch.
  – FIRST MAN TO EXCEED 100 MPH – M. Rigolly.
  – FIRST JAPANESE CAR PRODUCED – Steam car manufactured by Yamaha Torao in Okayama.

1905 – FOLDING CAR TOPS – Get introduced.
  – SOCIETY OF AUTOMOBILE ENGINEERS – Gets formed.
  – BUS ROUTE – Started in New York City.
  – AMERICAN MOTOR CAR MANUFACTURERS ASSOCIATION – Gets organized.
  – WATER/AIR COOLED CAR – Ariel car built for air cooling in winter and water cooling in summer.
  – TRUCKS – Several types introduced. Manufacturers included Packard, Mitchell, and Maxwell.
  – UNIVERSAL RIMS – Introduced by Goodyear to allow clincher or straight type tire usage.
  – IGNITION LOCK – Introduced.
  – TONNEAUS WITH SIDE ENTRANCE – Introduced.
  – FIRST STOLEN CAR – Reported in St. Louis.
  – FIRST INSTALLMENT PLAN CAR SALE – Reported.
  – FIRST FRONT WHEEL DRIVE CAR – Introduced in Holland by Spyker.
  – TIRE CHAINS – Introduced.
  – SPARE TIRE – Introduced.
  – IGNITION LOCK – Introduced.

1906 – WORLD RECORD SPEED – Stanley Steamer reaches 126.77 mph at Ormand, Beach Florida.
  – STORAGE BATTERY – Included as standard equipment on a Buick car.
  – SIX CYLINDER ENGINES – Become popular.
  – FIRST GRAND PRIX – Held near Le Mans, France. Ferenc Szisz won driving a 90 hp Renault 770 miles at an speed of 65 mph.
  – CARAVAN OF TRUCKS – A fleet of White trucks was assembled to transport supplies from Los Angeles to San Francisco after the 1906 earthquake.
  – FIRST REMOVABLE TIRE RIM – Introduced by Michelin brothers.
  – FRONT BUMPERS – Began appearing on some cars.

1907 – FIRST MOTOR TRUCK SHOW – Held in Chicago.
  – FIRST GAS-POWERED JAPANESE CAR – Produced by Jidosha Seisakusho Company.
  – INTERNATIONAL HARVESTER COMPANY – Begins producing cars.
  – EIGHT CYLINDER CAR – First V-8 touring car built by Hewitt.
  – NICKEL PLATING – Oldsmobile begins plating brass parts.
  – FIRST WHITE HOUSE CAR – President Taft gets White Steamer car.
  – NEW YORK TO CHICAGO RUN – Completed the 1,060 mile distance in 39 hours 36 minutes in a Franklin car.
  – SPEED BUMPS – Installed in the streets of Glencoe, Illinois to discourage speeders.
  – FOUR CYLINDER ENGINE – Adopted by Buick.

1908 – FOUR CYLINDER ENGINE – Becomes the most common car engine type.
  – GENERAL MOTORS – Gets organized in New Jersey.
  – DEWAR TROPHY – Cadillac become first U.S. car manufacturer to win for greatest contribution toward advancement of car industry.
  – FIRST USE OF INTERCHANGEABLE CAR PARTS – Introduced on Cadillac car.
  – THOMAS FLYER – Wins the New York to Paris Race going around the world in 170 days. The car was driven 13,341 miles in 88 days.
  – VANADIUM STEEL – Incorporated into Ford car parts by C. Wills.
  – FISHER BODY COMPANY – Organized by the Fisher brothers.
  – MODEL T FORD CAR – Introduced at $850.
  – FOUR WHEEL DRIVE – Invented.
  – FIRST CONCRETE PAVEMENT – Laid in Detroit.
  – FISHER BODY COMPANY – Organized.
  – MAGNETIC SPEEDOMETER – Introduced.
  – SLEEVE VALVE ENGINE – Introduced.
  – SILENT TIMING CHAIN – Introduced.
  – MOTOR DRIVEN HORN – Introduced.

1909 – AIR POWERED SELF STARTERS – Introduced on several cars.
  – FIRST WOMAN TO DRIVE ACROSS U.S. – Mrs. John Ramsey drove from New York to San Francisco in a Maxwell car in 53 days with 3 other women companions.

AUTOMOTIVE TIME LINE

1909 – FIRST U.S. CONCRETE ROAD – Built in Wayne County, Michigan.
- FIRST CAR BODY – Built by W.S. Seaman & Company in Milwaukee.
- HUDSON MOTOR COMPANY – Gets organized.
- OVERDRIVE TRANSMISSION – Introduced on Gramm trucks.
- SELDEN PATENT – Determined valid and ruled infringed upon by Ford.
- INDIANAPOLIS SPEEDWAY – Completed by Carl Fisher and associates.
- YEARLY CAR PRODUCTION – Exceeds 100,000.
- CADILLAC – Becomes part of General Motors.
- HIGH VOLTAGE IGNITION SYSTEMS – Now common.
- CELLULAR RADIATORS – Become more popular.
- ONE MAN CAR TOPS – Introduced.
- USE OF CHROME NICKEL AND VANADIUM STEEL – Increases significantly.
- ENGINE BLOCK CASTING – The casting of the entire engine block in one unit becomes more common.
- CAR MAKES AVAILABLE – Almost 300 different makes are available. They are produced in 24 states. Detroit leads with the greatest number for a city followed by Chicago.

1910 – TORPEDO BODY STYLE – New body style, resembling a bathtub on wheels, appears.
- MODEL 38 – First car, produced by Overland, to sell for $1,000 and offer as standard equipment a windshield, top, magneto, and lamps.
- DELIVERY TRUCK – Reo introduces a light-weight low-priced truck.
- FIRST FOUR WHEEL DRIVE CAR – Introduced by Four Wheel Drive Auto Company.
- FIRST V-8 ENGINE – Introduced by DeDion.
- FIRST INDIANAPOLIS RACE – Three day racing meet held.
- FIRE FIGHTING VEHICLE – Introduced by American La France Fire engine Company.
- LINE OF TRUCKS – Introduced by G.A. Schacht. Sizes ranged from 1/2 to 3 ton carrying capacity.
- DRIVE IN GAS STATION WITH ISLAND – Introduced in Detroit by Central Oil Company.

1911 – FOUR DOOR CARS – Become popular.
- FIRST SEMI-TRANSCONTINENTAL TRUCK TRIP – Made in a Saurer truck.
- FIVE TON TRUCK – Introduced by Pierce-Arrow.
- YEARLY TRUCK PRODUCTION – Exceeds 10,000.
- GENERAL MOTORS TRUCK COMPANY – Gets organized.
- SELDEN PATENT – Litigation upholds it as valid, but Ford cleared of infringement.
- PAINTED CENTERLINES ON ROADS – Concept introduced by Edward Hines in Detroit, Michigan.
- CHEVROLET MOTOR COMPANY – Gets organized.
- FIRST USE OF REARVIEW MIRROR IN U.S. – Introduced at the first Indianapolis 500 mile race by Ray Harroun in his Marmon Wasp racing car.
- FIRST SELF STARTER – Introduced by Cadillac.
- INDIANAPOLIS 500 RACE – First year. It was won by Ray Harroun in a Marmon Wasp.
- FIRST MONTE CARLO RALLY – Held.
- AUTOMOBILE COMPANY SECURITIES – Get listed on New York Stock Exchange.
- STUDEBAKER CORPORATION – Gets organized.
- ELECTRIC STARTER – Introduced by Cadillac.
- ELECTRIC LIGHTS – Introduced by Cadillac.
- CAR MANUFACTURER STOCKS – Listed on New York Stock Exchange.
- ORIGINAL DATSUN COMPANY – Formed as Kwaishinsha Motor Car Works. They produced DAT cars, changing name to Datson, and then Datsun.

1912 – CAR SELF-STARTER – Becomes popular. Types included acetylene, compressed air, gasoline, mechanical, and electrical.
- FIRST TRANSCONTINENTAL TRUCK TRIP – Packard truck with 3 ton load drives from New York to San Francisco in 46 days.
- FIRST WHITE TRAFFIC LINE – Appears in Redlands, California.
- TRUCK DUMP BED – Introduced on a 5-ton Sampson coal truck. The device was powered by compressed air.
- ENGINE TEMPERATURE INDICATOR – Introduced by Boyce Moto-Meter.
- SAE STANDARDS – Made for screw threads and other parts.
- YEARLY U.S. CAR PRODUCTION – Exceeds 356,000.
- YEARLY U.S. TRUCK PRODUCTION – Exceeds 22,000.
- ELECTRIC CAR MAKERS – Get organized.

AUTOMOTIVE TIME LINE

1912 - ALL STEEL BODY - Introduced.

1913 - MASS PRODUCTION - Ford uses various techniques to speed up production due to the popularity of the Model T, attaining a production rate of 1,000 cars per day.
- CHEVROLET - Moves to Flint, Michigan and merges with Little Motor Company.
- DEWAR TROPHY - Cadillac wins it a second time.
- BENDIX STARTER DRIVE - Introduced.
- WIRE WHEELS - Introduced as standard equipment on several cars.
- YEARLY U.S. CAR PRODUCTION - Exceeds 461,000.
- FOUR WHEEL DRIVE TRUCK - Introduced by Thomas B. Jeffrey.
- WRAP-AROUND WINDSHIELD - Introduced on several Kissel Kars.
- FORCED FEED LUBRICATION - Introduced by Packard.
- WORM BEVEL GEARS - Introduced by Packard.
- FIRST CHEVROLET ASSEMBLY PLANT - Opened.
- FIRST FOUR WHEEL DRIVE QUAD TRUCK - Introduced by the Thomas B. Jeffrey Company.
- FIRST FREE ROAD MAPS - Distributed by Gulf Oil Company.
- FIRST INSTALLMENT PLAN - Used to sell cars.

1914 - FIRST STOP SIGN - Introduced in Detroit.
- WAGE & WORK BENEFITS - The following benefits were announced by Henry Ford for employees over 22 years of age: 5 dollar/day minimum wage, profit sharing, and an 8 hour work day.
- HIGH SPEED V-8 ENGINE - Introduced by Cadillac.
- YEARLY U.S. CAR PRODUCTION - Exceeds 500,000.
- V-8 ENGINE - Introduced by Cadillac.
- RAMBLER - Changes name to Jeffrey.
- FIRST TRANSCONTINENTAL ROAD - Construction begins on Lincoln Highway running from New York to San Francisco.
- FIRST TRAFFIC LIGHT - Introduced in Cleveland. It was electric.
- DODGE AUTOMOBILE - Production begins.
- SPIRAL BEVEL GEAR - Introduced by Packard.
- HEADLIGHTS - Appear built into fenders.
- ADJUSTABLE DRIVER SEAT - Introduced by Maxwell.
- GASOLINE PUMPS - Barred from curbside location in Detroit, Michigan.

1915 - EIGHT CYLINDER ENGINE - Becomes popular.
- FIRST TWELVE CYLINDER ENGINE - Packard introduces its Twin Six.
- FIRST ALUMINUM PISTONS - Introduced by Packard.
- YEARLY U.S. CAR PRODUCTION - Exceeds 895,000.
- SPARE TIRE IN TRUNK - Introduced in Franklin car.
- FIRST SOLID METAL WHEEL - Introduced on White truck.
- REMOUNTABLE RIMS - Replace Clincher type wheels.
- TILT BEAM HEADLIGHTS - Offered by Cadillac.
- SINGLE HEADLIGHT CAR - Introduced by Briscoe.
- TRUCK PRODUCTION - Gains in importance due to World War I.
- MATERIAL SHORTAGES - Develop due to war in Europe.
- JITNEYS - Become popular due to transit strikes.
- PRISM HEADLIGHT LENSES - Introduced.

1916 - SLANTED WINDSHIELDS - Introduced.
- ALUMINUM CAR - Marmom 34 car introduced. It had a number of aluminum parts including: engine castings, body, fender, and trim parts.
- YEARLY U.S. CAR PRODUCTION - Exceeds 1,500,000.
- FORD FACTORY SITE - Purchased on banks of Rogue River.
- FLEET OF TRUCKS - Used by Army in Mexico.
- FEDERAL ROAD AID ACT - Passed to start a nationwide system of interstate highways.
- HAND OPERATED WINDSHIELD WIPERS - Introduced.
- REAR VIEW MIRROR - Introduced.

1917 - NASH CAR - Introduced.
- LINCOLN MOTOR COMPANY - Gets organized.
- IMPROVED FUEL VAPORIZTION - Studebaker introduces better vaporization of fuel by heating a portion of the intake manifold with exhaust gases.
- YEARLY U.S. CAR PRODUCTION - Exceeds 1,745,000.
- YEARLY U.S. TRUCK/BUS PRODUCTION - Exceeds 125,000.
- RADIATOR SHUTTERS - Introduced.
- V-SHAPED WINDSHIELD - Introduced.

AUTOMOTIVE TIME LINE

1917 – MILITARY AIRCRAFT ENGINES – Produced by several car manufacturers.
- COUPE CAR – Introduced by Paige with rumble seat.
- CAR HEATERS – Introduced on several of the enclosed cars.

1918 – FUEL SHORTAGES – Coal and petroleum in short supply due to nation's dependence on railroads for transportation. Railroads were burdened with war time priorities.
- WASHINGTON POSITION – Cars still regarded as luxuries.
- UNIQUE CARBURETORS – Introduced to burn low grade fuel and kerosene.
- YEARLY U.S. CAR PRODUCTION – Exceeds 950,000.
- YEARLY U.S. TRUCK/BUS PRODUCTION – Exceeds 227,000.
- CAR FACTORIES – Gear up for war work producing such items as aircraft engines, tanks, tractors, military vehicles, anti-aircraft guns, shell casings, etc.
- CAR APPEARANCE – Take on war like look due to steel wheels, and straight lines.
- GLASS AREA – Increases on enclosed cars.
- FOUR WHEEL HYDRAULIC BRAKES – Developed by Malcom Longhead.
- 100 MPH AVERAGE SPEED AT INDIANAPOLIS – Exceeded by Rene Thomas.
- STEEL ALLOCATION – Controlled by Government for passenger car production.
- CHEVROLET – Becomes part of General Motors.
- WHITE COMPANY – Stops producing cars and concentrates on trucks.
- LARGEST PRODUCER OF TRUCKS – Nash builds 11,494 units for the Army.
- NATIONAL AUTOMOBILE DEALERS ASSOCIATION – Gets organized.
- PRELUDE TO FIRST DATSUN CAR – Produced by Kwaishinsha Motor Car Works as a Datson.

1919 – ESSEX CAR – Introduced by Hudson as a four cylinder low priced car.
- FLAT RATE REPAIR SYSTEM – Introduced.
- FIRST GAS TAX – Introduced in Oregon.
- TWO RANGE TRUCK TRANSMISSION – Introduced by G.A. Schacht. It had 8 forward speeds and 2 reverse speeds.
- YEARLY U.S. CAR PRODUCTION – Exceeds 1,650,000.
- YEARLY U.S. TRUCK/BUS PRODUCTION – Exceeds 250,000.
- FORD MOTOR COMPANY YEARLY CAR PRODUCTION – Exceeds 750,000.
- GENERAL MOTORS ACCEPTANCE CORPORATION – Organized to handle cars sold on installment plan.
- FRONT AND REAR BUMPERS – Introduced as standard equipment on the Wescott car.
- FIRST POWER BRAKES – Introduced by Hispano-Suiza.
- HENRY FORD – Becomes sole owner of Ford Motor Company.
- ENGINE UNDER TRUCK SEAT – Introduced on Autocar trucks.
- FIRST THREE COLOR TRAFFIC LIGHT – Installed in Detroit.
- INSTRUMENTATION BACKLIGHTING – Introduced on some cars.

1920 – CONVERTIBLE CARS – Becoming uncommon.
- METAL WHEELS – Offered on cars by Buick and McFarlan.
- GENERAL MOTORS RESEARCH CORPORATION – Gets organized.
- DUESENBERG CAR – Introduced. It had an eight cylinder engine and was the first car to use four wheel hydraulic brakes.
- VIBRATION DAMPENER – Introduced by Packard.
- SHIPPING FREIGHT BY TRUCK – Becomes more popular due to railway strikes.

1921 – CAR SALES – Drop dramatically due to post war depression.
- NICKEL MOLYBDENUM STEEL – Developed by Studebaker.
- NICKEL PLATING – Began appearing on headlamps and radiators.
- FIRST DRIVE-IN RESTAURANT – Opens in Dallas.
- HYDRAULIC BRAKES – Become popular.
- YEARLY U.S. CAR PRODUCTION – Exceeds 1,500,000.
- YEARLY U.S. TRUCK/BUS PRODUCTION – Exceeds 150,000.
- LINCOLN CARS – Introduced.
- ADJUSTABLE FRONT SEAT – Introduced by Hudson.
- CARBURETION CONTROL – Based on water temperature. It was introduced by Cadillac.
- FIRST INAUGURATION RIDE – By President Warren Harding in a Packard Twin-Six.
- FIRST ADJUSTABLE FRONT SEAT – Introduced by Hudson.
- BACKUP LAMP – Introduced by Wills-St. Claire.
- RUBBER MOTOR MOUNTS – Introduced.

AUTOMOTIVE TIME LINE

1921 - SPRING SHACKLES - Introduced by Mack.

1922 - AIR CLEANERS - Introduced on cars.
- ROADSTER COUPE BODY - Becomes popular.
- BALLOON TIRES - Introduced on cars.
- YEARLY U.S. CAR PRODUCTION - Exceeds 2,274,000.
- YEARLY U.S. TRUCK/BUS PRODUCTION - Exceeds 270,000.
- LINCOLN MOTOR COMPANY - Bought by Ford.
- GAS GAUGE - Introduced on several cars.
- SYNCHRONIZED TRAFFIC LIGHT SYSTEM - Installed in Houston, Texas.
- ELWOOD HAYNES - Receives John Scott medal for his metallurgical achievements in chrome iron, stainless steel, and stellite.
- MOTOR DRIVEN SNOW REMOVAL EQUIPMENT - First year of heavy use nationwide.

1923 - L-HEAD ENGINES - Eight cylinder versions mass produced by Packard.
- RADIO - Offered as an accessory by Springfield Body Corporation.
- FOOT HEADLAMP DIMMER SWITCH - Becomes standard equipment on many cars.
- FIRST 24 HOUR RACE - Held in Le Mans, France for production cars.
- POWERED WINDSHIELD WIPERS - Becomes standard equipment on many cars.
- FOUR WHEEL BRAKES - Becomes standard equipment on many cars.
- ETHYL GASOLINE - Introduced by General Motors Research Corporation.

1924 - NO ELECTRIC OR STEAM CARS - Displayed at the 24th National Automobile Show.
- BAKED ENAMEL FINISH - Appears on economy cars.
- GENERAL MOTORS PROVING GROUND - Completed.
- TEN MILLIONTH CAR - Produced by Ford.
- FIRST HIGH SPEED TOLL ROAD - Opened from Milan to Como, Italy.
- TRANSCONTINENTAL BUS TRIP - Made by Reo bus.
- FIRST STEEL BODY ENCLOSED CAR - Introduced by Dodge.
- DUAL BEAM HEADLAMPS - Headlamps introduced with two filament bulbs.
- SAE STANDARDS - Adopted by U.S. manufacturers.

1925 - EASIER STEERING SYSTEMS - Appear to allow better handling of balloon tires.
- ONE PIECE WINDSHIELDS - Become common.
- MOHAIR UPHOLSTERY - Becomes common.
- CRANK TYPE WINDOW LIFTS - Become common.
- TOTAL U.S. CAR PRODUCTION TO DATE - Reaches 25 million.
- CAR PAINT COLORS - Increase substantially due to quick drying pyroxylin finishes that can be sprayed on and baked.
- AVAILABLE ACCESSORIES - Include tire jacks, cigar lighters, weather tight enclosure, mirrors, trunk racks, etc.
- CHROMIUM PLATING - Introduced by Oldsmobile.
- FORD MOTOR COMPANY PRODUCTION RATE - Exceeds 9,000 per day.
- MAXWELL-CHALMERS - Reorganized into Chrysler Corporation.
- TOTAL U.S. CAR PRODUCTION TO DATE - 25 million.
- LINCOLN HIGHWAY - Opens.
- FRONT/REAR BUMPERS - Become standard on many cars.
- NATIONWIDE CHAIN OF GAS STATIONS - Established.
- FEDERAL AID HIGHWAY MARKINGS - Standards adopted. East-west roads assigned even numbers and north-south roads get odd numbers.

1926 - SAFETY TYPE GLASS - Introduced by Cadillac.
- MODEL T - Ford announces plans to stop production.
- FISHER BODY CORPORATION - Gets bought by General Motors Corporation.
- FIVE DAY WORK WEEK - Begins at Ford Motor Company.
- PONTIAC CAR - Introduced.
- OCTANE SCALE FOR GASOLINE - Developed by Dr. Graham Edgar.
- HOT WATER CAR HEATERS - Introduced in U.S.
- TRANSCONTINENTAL TRUCK RUN - Truck is driven by Cannonball Baker from New York to San Francisco in under 6 days.
- CHANGE IN AUTO ADVERTISING - Started by Jordon Motor Company. It shifted emphasis away from technical details and more toward driving pleasures.
- REO - Introduces Flying Cloud model cars.

1927 - SMALL CAR TREND - Developing.
- COMMON ACCESSORIES - Included gas, oil, air filters; balloon tires; rear view mirrors; crankcase ventilators; etc.

AUTOMOTIVE TIME LINE

1927 - MODEL A - Ford introduces successor to Model T car near end of year.
- HYPOID REAR AXLES - Used by Packard and Marmon to lower their cars.
- VACUUM BRAKE BOOSTER - Introduced by Mack.
- AERODYNAMICS - Relation to body design studied by Carl Breer.
- PACKARD PROVING GROUND - Two and one half mile track built at Utica, Michigan.
- MODEL T CAR DISCONTINUED - Ford announces end. A total of 15,007,033 were produced.
- INTERNAL EXPANDING HYDRAULIC BRAKE SYSTEM - Introduced by Lockheed.
- CONCRETE MIXER TRUCKS - Introduced by White.

1928 - COMPRESSION RATIOS - Increased to over 5.0:1.
- SYNCHROMESH TRANSMISSION - Introduced by Cadillac.
- CHRYSLER- Bought out Dodge Brothers, Inc.
- SAFETY GLASS - Offered on Fords as standard equipment.
- CAR RADIOS - Introduced.
- FLEET OWNER MAGAZINE - Began publication.
- TRANSCONTINENTAL BUS SERVICE - Began.

1929 - TAIL LAMPS - Introduced on both sides of cars.
- MINIMUM WAGE - Raised to $7/day by Ford Motor Company.
- TRAVEL TRAILER - Introduced by Aerocar.
- PASSENGER CAR BODIES - Over 90 percent of those built are now enclosed.
- FRONT WHEEL DRIVE - Introduced by Cord.
- RADIOS - Become more popular as optional car equipment.
- DOWN DRAFT CARBURETOR - Introduced by Chrysler to increase fuel economy and fuel distribution efficiency.
- FOOT OPERATED HEADLIGHT DIMMER SWITCH - Introduced.
- NASH - Introduced its first eight cylinder car.
- CARS SOLD - Most are now closed models.

1930 - V-12/V-16 ENGINES - Introduced by Cadillac.
- CHRYSLER - Introduced its first eight cylinder car.
- CARBURETOR INTAKE SILENCER - Introduced by Studebaker.
- FREE WHEELING - Introduced by Studebaker.
- YEARLY CAR PRODUCTION - Exceeds 2,900,000.
- TOTAL U.S. CAR PRODUCTION TO DATE - Reaches 50 million.
- WIRING FOR RADIOS - More cars sold with wiring in-place for radios.
- TIN PLATED PISTONS - Introduced by Pontiac.
- POLICE CARS WITH RADIOS - Introduced.

1931 - OAKLAND CARS - Discontinued.
- CAR INTRODUCTION - Changed to November/December period to help stimulate car buying in winter.
- REFRIGERATED TRUCK HAULING - GMC truck delivers 21 tons of fruit from California to New York in 117 hours driving time.
- YEARLY CAR PRODUCTION - Exceeds 1,900,000.
- BUICK - Introduced an eight cylinder car.
- TOTAL U.S. CAR PRODUCTION TO DATE - 50 million.
- STANDARD WARRANTY - 90 day/4,000 mile warranty recommended by National Automobile Chamber of Commerce.

1932 - AUTO PRODUCTION - Poorest since 1918 due to deepening depression.
- FULL SKIRTED FENDERS - Introduced on a Graham.
- HYDRAULIC VALVE LIFTERS - Introduced by Pierce-Arrow.
- YEARLY U.S. CAR PRODUCTION - Exceeds 1,000,000.
- FORD MODEL A MOTOR - Changes to V-8.
- FREE WHEELING - Introduced by several car manufacturers.
- VISORS - Move inside on several cars.
- FENDER SKIRTS - Introduced.
- VACUUM CLUTCHES - Introduced by several car manufacturers.
- OUTSIDE WINDSHIELD SHADES - Lose popularity to inside visors.
- AUTOMATIC CHOKE - Introduced on Oldsmobile and Packard cars.
- FIRST DATSUN JAPANESE CAR - Produced under Datsun name.

1933 - GAS MILEAGE ADVERTISING - Promoted by several car manufacturers.
- POWER BRAKES - Become available on several cars.
- SIDE WINDOWS - Introduced on Fisher car bodies.
- STARTER PEDAL CHANGE - The accelerator pedal is used to start engines on some cars in order to eliminate the separate starter pedal.
- INDEPENDENT WHEEL SUSPENSION - Introduced by GM.

AUTOMOTIVE TIME LINE

1933 – NEW BUS DESIGN – Introduced by White with flat 12 cylinder engine under the floor.
- VALVE SEAT INSERTS – Introduced.
- FIRST DRIVE IN THEATRE – Opened in Camden, New Jersey.
- DATSUN AND NISSAN MERGER – Kwaishinsha Motor Car Works (Datsun car producer) and Nissan Motor Company Ltd. merge.
- TOYOTA CAR COMPANY – Got off the ground when Toyoda Loom Works formed an automotive department.

1934 – STREAMLINING – Becomes important with introduction of DeSoto Airflow car.
- INDEPENDENT FRONT WHEEL SUSPENSION – Becomes popular.
- AUTOMATIC TRANSMISSION – Complete automatic introduced by Reo.
- SUPERCHARGER – Mechanical type introduced by Graham.
- CHEVROLET PRODUCTION TO DATE – 10 million cars.
- AUTOMATIC TRANSMISSION OVERDRIVE – Introduced on Chrysler & Desoto Airflow cars.
- YEARLY U.S. CAR PRODUCTION – Exceeds 2,000,000.
- NATIONAL AUTOMOBILE CHAMBER OF COMMERCE – Changed name to Automobile Manufacturers Association.
- HIGH OUTPUT GENERATOR – Introduced by Cadillac.
- DASH MOUNTED GEARSHIFT – Introduced by Reo.
- BUILT IN RADIOS – Introduced.
- STEEL TURRET TOP – Introduced on General Motor cars.

1935 – STATION WAGON BODY – Introduced by Chevrolet.
- LINCOLN-ZEPHYR CAR – Introduced by Ford.
- YEARLY CAR PRODUCTION – Exceeds 3,000,000.
- NASH MOTOR – Introduced motor with manifold inside block.
- FIRST PARKING METER – Installed in Oklahoma City.
- FIRST TOYOTA CAR – Prototype A-1 built by Toyoda Loom Works.
- FIRST TOYOTA TRUCK – Prototype G-1 built by Toyota Loom Works.
- CAR RADIOS IN USE – Over 3 million.
- HAND BRAKE – Becomes common on the left side of the driver.

1936 – CAR OWNERSHIP – 54% of U.S. families own cars.
- CAR WHOLESALE PRICE – Almost all cars sell for less than $750.
- REO – Stopped producing cars to concentrate on commercial vehicles.
- DIESEL POWERED TRUCK – Introduced by Diamond.
- FIRST PRODUCTION DIESEL CAR – Introduced by Mercedes.
- BACKUP BRAKING SYSTEM – Introduced on Hudson cars.
- DEFROSTERS – Introduced on many cars.
- NASH MOTORS COMPANY – Merges with Kelvinator Corporation to form Nash-Kelvinator Corporation.

1937 – STEERING COLUMN GEARSHIFTS – Become common on several cars.
- WINDSHIELD WASHERS – Introduced by Studebaker.
- FIRST AUTOMATIC TRANSMISSION – Introduced by Oldsmobile.
- YEARLY CAR PRODUCTION – Exceeds 3,900,000.
- UNIONIZATION OF U.S. CAR PLANTS – Occurs nationwide.
- TOYOTA CAR COMPANY FORMED – Toyoda Loom Works changes name to Toyota Motor Company.

1938 – INDUSTRY SLUMP – Production declined 40 percent to about 2,000,000.
- MERCURY CARS – Introduced by Ford.
- CONDITIONED AIR – Nash introduced a concept of filtering and heating air from the outside before it enters the car interior.
- REAR COIL SUSPENSION – Introduced on several cars.
- VACUUM OPERATED GEARSHIFT – Introduced by Chevrolet.
- FLUID DRIVE TRANSMISSION – Introduced by Chrysler.
- VACUUM OPERATED CONVERTIBLE TOP – Introduced by Plymouth.
- DIRECTIONAL SIGNALS – Introduced by Buick.

1939 – TOTAL U.S. CAR PRODUCTION TO DATE – 75 million.
- HOOD LOCK RELEASE UNDER DASH – Introduced by Hudson.
- CROSLEY CAR – Introduced.
- SEALED BEAM HEADLAMPS – Become common.
- FLASHING TURN SIGNALS – Introduced by Buick.
- PUSH BUTTON RADIOS – Introduced.
- CAR WITH NO RUNNING BOARDS – Introduced on Lincoln-Zephyr car.
- AUTOMATIC OVERDRIVE – Becomes common.

AUTOMOTIVE TIME LINE

1939 – TAXI CABS – Introduced by Pontiac.
    – AIR CONDITIONING – Introduced by Packard and Nash.
    – FOUR WHEEL COIL SPRING SUSPENSION – Introduced by Oldsmobile.

1940 – WAR PREPARATIONS – Many automobile plants gear up for military production for the duration of the war.
    – SAFETY RIM WHEEL – Introduced by Chrysler.
    – TWO SPEED ELECTRIC WINDSHIELD WIPERS – Introduced by Chrysler.
    – PENNSYLVANIA TURNPIKE – Opens.
    – UNITIZED BODY – Introduced by Nash.
    – ROLLS ROYCE AIRCRAFT ENGINES – Packard began producing.
    – PRATT & WHITNEY AIRCRAFT ENGINES – Ford began producing.
    – ARMY TRUCKS – Dodge built 20,000.
    – LASALLE CAR – Discontinued by Cadillac.
    – RUNNING BOARDS – Become enclosed inside door on most cars.
    – COMPOUND CARBURETOR – Introduced by Buick. It caused a second carburetor to function when the accelerator pedal is pushed to the floor.

1941 – FRONT FENDERS – Extend to middle of front doors on some cars.
    – SEMI AUTOMATIC TRANSMISSION – Introduced by Hudson. Manual or semi-automatic could be selected by pushing buttons on the dash.
    – IRON ALLOY PISTONS – Introduced to decrease weight.
    – AVIATION ENGINE PLANT – Built by Buick.
    – SHELLS FOR THE U.S. ARMY – Produced by Oldsmobile.
    – TANKS AND GUNS – Produced by Chrysler.
    – YEARLY U.S. CAR PRODUCTION – Exceeds 4,000,000.
    – YEARLY U.S. TRUCK/BUS PRODUCTION – Exceeds 1,000,000.
    – INDIANAPOLIS SPEEDWAY – Closed for the duration of the war.
    – COMBAT CARS – Produced by Ford.
    – ANTI AIRCRAFT GUNS – Produced by Pontiac.
    – MACHINE GUNS – Produced by General Motors.
    – AIRCRAFT ENGINES – Produced by Studebaker.
    – JEEP – Introduced by Willys.
    – HALF TRACKS/TANK DESTROYERS/CARGO TRUCKS – Produced by White.
    – AUTOMOTIVE COUNCIL FOR WAR PRODUCTION – Gets organized to gear Automotive industry up for wartime production.

1942 – CAR PRODUCTION HALTED – Due to war. Before halt, over 220,000 produced.
    – CAR RATIONING – Began.
    – CIVILIAN TRUCK PRODUCTION HALT – Production stopped due to war.
    – NATIONAL SPEED LIMIT – Reduced to 40 than 35 mph to conserve fuel.
    – GASOLINE SUPPLIES – Cut 50 percent in 17 eastern states.
    – WILLOW RUN BOMBER PLANT – Built and opened by Ford to produce bombers.
    – NATIONWIDE GASOLINE RATIONING – Ordered by President Roosevelt to conserve petroleum and rubber products.
    – AMPHIBIAN TANKS – Produced by Graham-Paige.
    – PRATT & WHITNEY ENGINES – Produced by Nash-Kelvinator.
    – SIKORSKY HELICOPTERS – Produced by Nash-Kelvinator.
    – AIRCRAFT ENGINE PLANT – Chrysler built large aircraft engine plant in Chicago.
    – AUTO INDUSTRY ARMS PRODUCTION VALUE – Over 4.5 billion dollars.

1943 – NON ESSENTIAL DRIVING – Banned in 17 eastern states by the Office Of Price Administration.
    – GASOLINE RATION BOOKS – 25 million issued.
    – YEARLY U.S. CAR PRODUCTION – Exceeds 135.
    – YEARLY U.S. TRUCK/BUS PRODUCTION – Exceeds 660,000.
    – AUTO INDUSTRY EMPLOYMENT – Reaches 1.25 million but begins to taper off due to demand of armed services.
    – FLYING AUTOMOBILE – After war production announced by William Stout.
    – AUTOMOTIVE PLANTS PRODUCING WARTIME MATERIALS – Reached 1,038.
    – AUTO INDUSTRY ARMS PRODUCTION VALUE – Reached 13 billion.

1944 – WAR PRODUCTION BOARD – Authorized a production of 1,000,000 civilian and military trucks.
    – CIVILIAN JEEP VERSION – Announced by Willys.
    – GASOLINE RATIONING – Reduced to 2 gallons per week.
    – OFFICE OF WAR INFORMATION – Released statistic that over 4,000 used cars were being scrapped each day.

AUTOMOTIVE TIME LINE

1944 - U.S. VEHICLES SUPPLIED TO U.S.S.R. TO DATE - Almost 350,000.
- AUTO INDUSTRY ARMS PRODUCTIONS VALUE - Reached 9 billion.
- AUTO INDUSTRY PRODUCTION EFFICIENCY - Improved to drop costs by 1/3 since 1941.

1945 - YEARLY U.S. CAR PRODUCTION - Exceeds 69,000.
- WILLOW RUN PLANT - Closed after producing almost 8,700 bombers.
- KAISER-FRAZER CORPORATION - Formation announced.
- FORD CIVILIAN CAR PRODUCTION - Resumed.
- EXISTING PASSENGER CARS - Almost 50 percent now at least 7 years old.
- WAR PRODUCTION BOARD - Authorizes transition to civilian car production after V-E day, then announced reconversion to begin in July.
- REPLACEMENT PARTS RESTRICTIONS - Lifted.
- GASOLINE RATIONING - Ended the day after Japan surrendered.
- TRUCK PRODUCTION RESTRICTIONS - Lifted.
- AUTOMOTIVE COUNCIL FOR WAR PRODUCTION - Dissolved.
- NEW CAR MODELS ANNOUNCED - By Pontiac, Chevrolet, Cadillac, Oldsmobile, Nash, Hudson, Packard, Studebaker, and others.
- TOTAL WAR PRODUCTION TO DATE - Automotive industry produced 92% of vehicles, 87% of aircraft bombs, 85% of helmets, 50% of engines, 56% of tanks, 47% of machine guns, 10% of torpedoes, 10% of aircraft, and 3% of sea mines.
- TOTAL WAR PRODUCTION VALUE TO DATE - The automotive industry produced almost 29 billion dollars worth of war products.

1946 - TOTAL CAR PRODUCTION SINCE THE WAR - Reached 1 million.
- RADIO TELEPHONES - Introduced in cars.
- POWER WINDOWS - Introduced.
- YEARLY U.S. CAR PRODUCTION - Exceeds 2,000,000.
- YEARLY U.S. TRUCK/BUS PRODUCTION - Exceeds 940,000.
- FIRST FIBERGLASS CAR BODY - Introduced on Stout 46 car.
- INDIANAPOLIS RACE TRACK - Opens back up.
- NETWORK TELEVISION CAR ADVERTISING - Started by Chevrolet.
- FIRST FERRARI CAR - Introduced. It was the Type 125 Corsa V-12.
- CAR INDUSTRY WAGE-PRICE RESTRICTIONS - Lifted.
- SELF-ADJUSTING BRAKES - Introduced by Studebaker.
- JEEP WAGON - Introduced by Willys-Overland Motors.

1947 - NEW GENERAL MOTORS ASSEMBLY PLANT - Opened in Wilmington, Delaware.
- CHEVROLET ASSEMBLY PLANT - Opened in Flint, Michigan and Van Nuys, California.
- DRIVER EDUCATION COURSES - Introduced in many high schools.
- HENRY FORD - Dies.
- THREE WHEELED CAR - Davis car introduced.
- DRIVER EDUCATION COURSES - Introduced in many high schools.
- WORLD LAND SPEED RECORD - Set by John Cobb's Railton Racer with speed of 394.16 mph on Utah Salt Flats.
- TORPEDO - Introduced by Tucker Corporation.

1948 - TUBELESS TIRES - Introduced by Goodrich.
- HIGH COMPRESSION ENGINE - Introduced by General Motors and designed to use high octane gasoline.
- TOTAL CAR PRODUCTION TO DATE - Reached 100 million.
- HONDA MOTOR COMPANY - Established.
- FIRST CAR TAILFINS - Introduced by Cadillac.
- HYDRAULIC TORQUE CONVERTER - Introduced by Buick.
- FIRST ELECTRIC WINDOWS - Introduced in England by Daimler.
- NEW ASSEMBLY PLANTS - Several opened.
- FIRST NASCAR RACE - Held at Dayton Beach, Florida. It was won by Red Byron in a Ford.
- DUAL CONTROL CARS - Over 1,000 loaned to high schools for driving training from car manufacturers.

1949 - BONDED BRAKES - Introduced.
- NINE PASSENGER STATION WAGON - Introduced by DeSoto.
- NEW ENGINE STARTING SYSTEM - Chrysler introduced method of starting a car using ignition key only.
- HOTSHOT SPORTS CAR - Introduced by Crosley.
- COMPRESSION RATIOS - Reach 7.5:1.
- HARDTOP CONVERTIBLES - Become popular.
- FALL INTRODUCTION OF NEW CARS - Began for many car manufacturers.

AUTOMOTIVE TIME LINE

1949 - SELF-ENERGIZING BRAKES - Introduced.

1950 - PUNCTURE SEALING TUBELESS TIRES - Introduced by Goodrich.
 - MILITARY CONTRACTS - Awarded to most car manufacturers as a result of Korean conflict.
 - NUMBER TWO CAR MAKER IN U.S. - Ford edges out Chrysler.

1951 - POWER STEERING - Introduced by Buick and Chrysler.
 - USE OF NICKEL, ZINC, AND TIN CUTBACK - Ordered by Federal Government.
 - SIX CYLINDER ENGINE WITH OVERHEAD VALVES - Introduced by Ford.
 - EXCISE TAX INCREASES - From 7 to 10% on cars, 5 to 8% on trucks, and 5 to 8% on automotive parts.
 - ALLSTATE CAR - Introduced by Sears.
 - HEMISPHERICAL COMBUSTION CHAMBERS - Introduced by Chrysler.

1952 - 100TH ANNIVERSARY - For Studebaker.
 - 50TH ANNIVERSARY - For American Automobile Association.
 - SUSPENDED BRAKE PEDAL - Introduced by Oldsmobile and Ford.
 - SUSPENDED CLUTCH PEDAL - Introduced by Ford.
 - 12 VOLT ELECTRICAL SYSTEM - Introduced by Chrysler.
 - FOUR WAY SEAT ADJUSTMENT - Introduced by Packard.
 - FRONT WHEEL SUSPENSION USING BALL JOINTS - Introduced by Ford.
 - LPG POWERED TRUCKS - Introduced by Reo and International Harvester.
 - DIESEL TRUCK - 2.5 ton 3 cylinder truck introduced by GMC.
 - CROSLEY CAR - Production stops after General Tire and Rubber buyout.
 - CHRYSLER PROVING GROUND - Construction began at Chelsa, Michigan on 3,800 acres.

1953 - WILLYS-OVERLAND - Purchased by Kaiser Motors Corporation.
 - KAISER-FRAZER - Changed its name to Kaiser Motors Corporation.
 - FIBERGLASS BODY CAR - Experimental version introduced by Ford.
 - GENERAL MOTORS PLANT FIRE - Transmission plant in Livonia, Michigan is destroyed.
 - CORVETTE SPORTS CAR - Introduced by Chevrolet with Fiberglass body.
 - AIR CONDITIONING - Becomes common.
 - FIRST RADIAL PLY TIRE - Introduced by Michelin.
 - 12 VOLT ELECTRICAL SYSTEM - Becomes common.
 - FIRST DISC BRAKE SYSTEM - Used at Le Mans by winning C-Jaguar car.
 - OIL PRESSURE AND GENERATOR IDIOT LIGHTS - Introduced to replace gauges.
 - EIGHT CYLINDER ENGINES - Become more popular.

1954 - NASH-KELVINATOR AND HUDSON COMPANY MERGER - American Motors Corporation formed.
 - STUDEBAKER AND PACKARD COMPANY MERGER - Studebaker-Packard Corporation formed.
 - TUBELESS TIRES - Become standard on most cars.
 - GAS TURBINE - Successfully tested by Chrysler Corporation.
 - THUNDERBIRD CAR - Introduced by Ford.
 - FORD PROVING GROUND - Construction began at 4,000 acre Romeo, Michigan site.
 - FIRST GAS INJECTION SYSTEM - Introduced on Mercedes 300SL car.
 - SAFETY PADDING ON DASHBOARDS - Introduced by car manufacturers.
 - COWL VENTILATION INTAKES - Introduced by car manufacturers.
 - FOUR HEADLAMPS - Introduced on Cadillac.
 - REMOTE CHASSIS AND SUSPENSION LUBRICATION SYSTEM - Introduced on some Ford cars.

1955 - KAISER AND WILLYS - Announced end of car production with emphasis on Jeep production.
 - SLICK AIRWAYS - Introduced overnight freight deliveries using trucks and airplanes.
 - IMPROVED SEALED BEAM HEADLAMPS - Installed in most cars.
 - SAFETY DOOR LATCHES - Become standard equipment on most cars.
 - EMPHASIS ON SEAT BELTS - Increased.
 - LE MANS RACING DISASTER - 82 people killed.
 - REQUIREMENT FOR DRIVER EDUCATION COURSE - Required before issuing driver's license in Michigan.
 - EXPERIMENTAL FIREBIRD II TURBINE CAR - Introduced by General Motors.
 - REMOTE TRUNK LID LOCK - Introduced by Cadillac.
 - PUSH BUTTON AUTOMATIC TRANSMISSION SELECTOR - Introduced on several cars.

AUTOMOTIVE TIME LINE

1956 - CHEVROLET - Began producing heavy duty trucks.
   - EXPERIMENTAL FREE PISTON ENGINE - Introduced by General Motors that would burn any fuel. Fuels used included gasoline, vegetable fats, and peanut oil.
   - FEDERAL GAS AND DIESEL TAXES INCREASED - To support construction of Interstate Highway System.
   - TORSION BAR SUSPENSION - Introduced on Chrysler cars.
   - INTERSTATE HIGHWAY ACT - Passed.
   - INTERSTATE HIGHWAY SYSTEM - Approved after passage of Highway Act. Program required Federal Government to cover 90 percent of cost of 41,000 mile highway system.
   - FORD MOTOR COMPANY STOCK - Goes public.
   - TRANSCONTINENTAL EXPERIMENTAL GAS TURBINE CAR TRIP - Chrysler car driven from New York to Los Angeles.
   - NATIONAL AUTOMOBILE SHOW - First show since 1940 is held in New York's coliseum.
   - FUEL INJECTION - Introduced as an option on some cars.
   - RETRACTABLE REAR WINDOW - Introduced on Mercury.
   - ELECTRIC DOOR LOCKS - Introduced on several luxury cars.
   - SPEEDOMETER WARNING BUZZER - Introduced.
   - NON SLIP DIFFERENTIAL - Introduced by several car manufacturers.
   - PUSH BUTTON AUTOMATIC TRANSMISSION - Introduced by Chrysler.

1957 - RETRACTABLE HARD TOP - Introduced by Ford.
   - TOURING LUXURY BUS - Introduced by Mack.
   - FORD THUNDERBIRD - Two passenger model production stopped. Four passenger model production began.
   - NASH AND HUDSON NAMES - No longer used by American Motors cars.
   - EXPERIMENTAL TURBINE TRUCK - Introduced by Chevrolet and Ford.
   - DUAL HEADLAMP SYSTEM - Now used by most cars.
   - PAPER AIR CLEANERS - Become common.
   - CRUISE CONTROL DEVICE - Introduced by Chrysler.

1958 - FORD MOTOR COMPANY PRODUCTION TO DATE - Reached 50 million.
   - CHRYSLER CORPORATION PRODUCTION TO DATE - Reached 25 million.
   - INTERSTATE HIGHWAY SYSTEM CONSTRUCTION - Speeded up with additional funding.
   - END OF PACKARD CAR - Announced by Studebaker-Packard Corporation.
   - PIGGY BACK SERVICE - Railroads began transporting semi-trailers on flat cars.
   - EXPERIMENTAL GLIDEAIR CAR - Model introduced by Ford that floated on a thin cushion of air.
   - EXPERIMENTAL FIREBIRD III CAR - Introduced by General Motors Corporation. The car used a single stick to control steering, braking, and accelerating. It was guided down a road with a wire buried in the roadway. A separate power plant was used to power accessories.
   - AUTOMOBILE INFORMATION INFORMATION DISCLOSURE ACT - Passed to require that car manufacturers affix an identification label on each car including such information as make, model, serial number, retail price, etc.
   - FIBERGLASS TRUCK CAB - Introduced by White.
   - FIRST DATSUN CARS - Exported to U.S.
   - SWIVEL FRONT SEATS - Introduced by Chrysler.
   - FIRST CONTINUOUSLY VARIABLE TRANSMISSION - Introduced on the DAF Daffodil.
   - REMOTE SIDE VIEW MIRROR CONTROL - Introduced on several cars.
   - DAY AND NIGHT REAR VIEW MIRROR - Introduced on Chrysler cars.
   - ELECTRIC TRUNK LID RELEASE - Introduced on Ford cars.
   - INDIVIDUAL ADJUSTABLE RECLINING SEATS - Introduced on Rambler.
   - ELECTRONIC FUEL INJECTION - Introduced by Chrysler.

1959 - EXPERIMENTAL CELLA I CAR - Introduced by DeSoto. It was an electrochemical scale model that converted liquid fuel directly into electrical energy used to power the car.
   - EXPERIMENTAL CYCLONE CAR - Introduced by Cadillac. It was equipped with a radar device for sensing objects in the path of the car.
   - EXPERIMENTAL LEVACAR - Introduced by Ford. It was designed to float on an air cushion and be propelled by compressed air.
   - EXPERIMENTAL AIR-CAR CAR - Introduced by Curtis-Wright Corporation. A 300 horsepower car designed to travel on a 6-12 inch cushion of air.
   - SEVEN INCH HEADLAMP - Introduced.

AUTOMOTIVE TIME LINE

1959 – EXPERIMENTAL TITAN II TRUCK – Introduced by Chevrolet. It was a
further refinement of the Titan I gas turbine truck.
– HOMESTEAD CARAVAN TO ALASKA – Caravan of 16 vehicles known as the
'59ers drove 4,239 miles from Detroit to Anchorage, Alaska area in 25
days to homestead. The party consisted of 39 men, women, and children.
– CORVAIR CAR – Introduced by Chevrolet. It featured a lightweight
– AC GENERATOR SYSTEM – Introduced by Plymouth.
– MAVERICK SPECIAL CAR – Willys introduced deluxe Jeep station wagon.
– FEDERAL GASOLINE TAX – Increased from 3 TO 4 cents per gallon.
aluminum air-cooled rear mounted engine.
– ELECTROLUMINESCENT DASH LIGHTING DISPLAY – Introduced by Chrysler.
– DUAL CHAMBERED WATER PUMP – Introduced on Pontiac.
– MACPHERSON STRUT – Introduced on British Ford car.
– SINGLE REAR HINGED DOOR – Introduced on Rambler.
– ANTI-THEFT IGNITION SWITCH – Introduced on Ford cars.
– FOUR LIGHT EMERGENCY FLASHING SYSTEM – Introduced on Chrysler.
– EDSEL CAR – Discontinued.

1960 – ALUMINUM V-8 ENGINE – Introduced by Buick and Oldsmobile.
– ALL WEATHER ANTIFREEZE COOLANT – Introduced by several manufacturers.
– FIRST DAYTONA 500 RACE – Held at Daytona International Speedway. Lee
Petty wins.
– FIRST TOYOTA CARS – Exported to U.S.
– INTERCONTINENTAL PIGGY-BACK SERVICE – Introduced by U.S. Freight
Company using trucks, railroads, and steamships.
– DE SOTO CAR – Discontinued by Chrysler.
– U.S. ARM OF NISSAN MOTOR CORPORATION – Formed.
– FIRST DATSUN CARS – Exported to U.S.

1961 – EXPERIMENTAL TURBOFLITE CAR – Chrysler introduced a gas turbine powered
car.
– EXPERIMENTAL X7 CAR – Chrysler introduced a gas turbine powered car.
– EXPERIMENTAL GYRON VEHICLE – Ford introduced a two wheeled gyroscope
controlled vehicle.
– THREE SEAT STATION WAGON – Introduced by Oldsmobile.
– DUAL BRAKE SYSTEMS – Become standard on most cars.
– CLUTCH INTERLOCK – Introduced by Ford.
– FIRST U.S. V-6 ENGINE – Offered by Buick.
– SCOUT CAR – Introduced by International Harvester.
– TRAVELALL CAR – Introduced by International Harvester.
– JEEP FLEETVAN CAR – Introduced by Willys Motors.
– FIRST AMERICAN WORLD CHAMPION DRIVER – Awarded to Phil Hill.
– ENGINE CONVERSION KITS – Offered by Detroit Diesel of General Motors
for changing diesel engines into multi-fuel engines.
– BUDENE SYNTHETIC RUBBER – Introduced by Goodyear.

1962 – GENERAL MOTORS CAR PRODUCTION TO DATE – Reached 75 million.
– STUDEBAKER-PACKARD CORPORATION – Dropped Packard name from company
title.
– AMBER FRONT TURN SIGNAL LIGHTS – Adopted by industry.
– COBRA CAR – Shelby American introduced a high performance sports car.
– CORVAIR SPYDER CAR – Introduced by Chevrolet.
– CORVAIR MONZA CONVERTIBLE – Introduced by Chevrolet.
– FUEL INJECTED TURBO CHARGED V-8 ENGINE – Introduced in Oldsmobile's
Jetfire car.
– AVANTI CAR – Introduced by Studebaker.
– POLYESTER FIBER TIRE CORD – Introduced by Goodyear.
– 50,000 MILE TIRE – Introduced by General Tire.
– TIRE TREAD BONDING AGENT – Introduced by U.S. Rubber. The chemical
solved the tread and ply separation problem.
– FRONT WHEEL DISC BRAKES – Introduced on Studebaker's Avanti as standard
equipment, and other cars as a option.
– SELF-ADJUSTING BRAKES – Become common on most cars.
– TRANSISTORIZED IGNITION SYSTEM – Offered on Pontiac as an option.
– POSITIVE CRANKCASE VENTILATION SYSTEM – Becomes common.
– TURBINE CARS – Produced by Chrysler and distributed to 50 motorists.
– GULL WING DOORS – Appear on Ford's experimental Cougar 406 sports car.
They are electrically operated.
– MAGNESIUM WHEELS – Introduced by Pontiac.
– MOTOR HOMES AND CAMPERS – Rise in popularity.
– CHAMP CAMPER VEHICLE – Introduced by Studebaker.

AUTOMOTIVE TIME LINE

1962 – CONDOR MOTORHOME – Introduced by Ford.
- TRAVILLE MOTORHOME – Introduced by Traville Corporation.
- SOLAR POWERED ELECTRIC CAR – Introduced by International Rectifier Company. A 1912 Baker electric car was used. The roof was fitted with over 10,000 solar cells.
- V-6 ENGINE – Introduced by General Motors.
- GLADIATOR TRUCKS – Four wheel drive units introduced by Willys.

1963 – STUDEBAKER CORPORATION – Stopped U.S. production of cars and moved company to Hamilton, Ontario.
- MARMON-HERRINGTON COMPANY – Retired after 31 years in business.
- WILLYS MOTORS COMPANY – Becomes Kaiser Jeep Corporation and moves from Toledo, Ohio to Oakland, California.
- METEOR CARS – Discontinued by Lincoln-Mercury.
- RETRACTABLE HEADLIGHTS – Introduced.
- FRONT SEAT BELTS – Introduced on Studebaker cars as standard equipment.
- FIBERGLASS TRUCK BODIES – Introduced by Studebaker on their 1/2 and 3/4 ton models.
- FLOATING MOTORHOME – Introduced by Stewart Coach Industries.
- SAFETY TIRE – Goodyear introduced a tire with an inner tire which could be driven 100 miles after an outside tire flat.
- FIRST 5 YEAR/50,000 MILE WARRANTY – Introduced by Chrysler covering engine and powertrain parts.

1964 – MUSTANG CAR – Introduced by Ford.
- BARRACUDA CAR – Introduced by Chrysler.
- MARLIN CAR – Introduced by American Motors.
- FRITZ DUESENBERG – Announced a new company for building luxury car based on the famous old Duesenberg cars.
- AUTOMATIC TRANSMISSION SELECTOR PATTERN – Gets standardized.
- FIRST ROTARY ENGINE CAR – NSU Sports Prinz car.
- ELECTROCOATING PROCESS – Used by Ford for applying paint primer.
- 2 YEAR/24,000 MILE WARRANTY – Introduced by American Motors, Ford, and General Motors. It covered all parts except tires.
- 5 YEAR/50,000 MILE WARRANTY – Introduced by Chrysler. It covered the engine, transmission, driveline, and rear axle.
- I BEAM AXLES – Introduced by General Motors on light trucks.
- TURBO CRUISER NO 2 TURBINE BUS – Built by General Motors.

1965 – AUTOMOTIVE PRODUCTS TRADE ACT – Removed tariffs on new cars and parts.
- HIGHWAY EMERGENCY LOCATING PLAN – American Manufacturers Association announced plan to aid motorists in distress that used CB radio equipment.
- MOTOR VEHICLE AIR POLLUTION CONTROL ACT – Passed.
- REAR SEAT BELTS – Become standard on most cars.
- DUAL STATION WAGON TAILGATES – Introduced on all Ford station wagons.
- RAMBLER NAME – Dropped by American Motors.
- AVANTI II CAR – Introduced by Avanti Motor Corporation.
- WORLD LAND SPEED RECORD – Achieved by Craig Breedlove in the Spirit of America Sonic 1 at the Bonneville Salt Flats. Speed was 600.6 mph.
- CORD CAR – Cord Automobile Company introduced a smaller version of the classic 1930s Cord known as the Sportsman.
- FRONT WHEEL DRIVE – Introduced by Oldsmobile on its 1966 Toronado.
- BRONCO CAR – Introduced by Ford.
- CHARGER CAR – Introduced by Dodge.
- SHELBY GT 350 CAR – Introduced by Shelby American.

1966 – NATIONAL TRAFFIC AND MOTOR VEHICLE SAFETY ACT – Enacted to provide a national safety program and establish safety standards for cars.
- U.S. DEPARTMENT OF TRANSPORTATION – Formed.
- STUDEBAKER CORPORATION – Stopped producing cars.
- UNSAFE AT ANY SPEED BOOK – Authored by Ralph Nader and released.
- EXPERIMENTAL ELECTROVAN CAR – A fuel cell van built by General Motors.
- EXPERIMENTAL ELECTROVAIR II CAR – A battery powered Corvair built by General Motors.
- SEALED SODIUM-SULFUR BATTERY – A lifetime battery for electric cars was developed by Ford.
- COLLAPSIBLE STEERING COLUMNS – Introduced by several manufacturers.
- ENGINE PREHEATER – Offered as an option on some Oldsmobile cars. Device kept carburetor inlet temperature at 100 degrees allowing for easier cold weather starting.

AUTOMOTIVE TIME LINE

1966 - HIGH VOLTAGE CAPACITOR SYSTEM - Offered as an option on Oldsmobile cars.
- COUGAR CAR - Introduced by Lincoln-Mercury.
- CAMARO CAR - Introduced by Chevrolet.
- SHELBY GT 500 CAR - Introduced by Shelby American.
- CORD CAR - Discontinued. Less than 100 cars built. Company goes under.
- 5 YEAR/50,000 MILE WARRANTY - Adopted by most car manufacturers following Chrysler's lead in 1964. It covered the engine, transmission, driveline, and rear axle.
- CORROSION RESISTANT UNDERBODY - Many 1967 models made of galvanized steel for rust protection.

1967 - FIRST ROTARY ENGINE PRODUCTION - Mazda introduced the 110S car.

1969 - DATSUN 240Z CAR - Introduced in U.S.
QUARTZ HALOGEN DRIVING LIGHTS - Begin appearing as auxiliary driving lights.

1970 - CLEAN AIR ACT - Passed.

1973 - VOLKSWAGEN BEETLE - Discontinued in Wolfsberg, Germany after 16.2 million cars had been produced over a 25 year period.
- FIRST U.S. OIL EMBARGO - Oil exports to U.S. banned by Arab oil producers. It causes fuel shortages, gas lines at service stations, etc.

1974 - NATIONWIDE 55 MPH SPEED LIMIT - Enacted to conserve fuel.
BLACK BOXES - Begin appearing on cars.

1975 - CONVENTIONAL POINTS - Replaced on most cars by solid state components.

1976 - ELECTRONIC SPARK ADVANCE CONTROL - Introduced by Chrysler.

1977 - INDIANAPOLIS 200 MPH AVERAGE SPEED - Exceeded by Tom Sneva.
- FIRST 4 TIME WINNER OF INDIANAPOLIS 500 RACE - Achieved by A.J. Foyt.

1978 - U.S. VOLKSWAGEN PRODUCTION - Begins.
- FIRST PLASTIC BODY CAR - Introduced on Lotus Elite.
- FIRST AMERICAN FWD/TRANSVERSE ENGINE CAR - Introduced by Chrysler.

1979 - GAS SHORTAGE - Creates gas lines at service stations nationwide.

1980 - CHRYSLER GOVERNMENT LOAN - Chrysler receives large loan from Federal Government to avert bankruptcy.

1981 - FIRST 6-PASSENGER FWD STATION WAGON - Introduced by Chrysler.

1983 - GENERAL MOTORS AND TOYOTA JOINT VENTURE - Approved by Federal Trade Commission. Joint venture cars will be built in California.
- CHRYSLER GOVERNMENT LOAN - Paid off.
- WORLD LAND SPEED RECORD - Achieved by Richard Noble in the Thrust 2 Jet Car at Blackroc, Nevada. Speed was 633.5 mph.
- FIRST 5 YEAR/50,000 MILE WARRANTY - Introduced by Chrysler to protect against outer body rust on passenger cars.
- COPPER-CORE SPARK PLUGS - Installed on a mass production basis by Chrysler.

1984 - FIRST MANDATORY SEAT BELT LAW - Passed in New York.
- FIRST 5 YEAR/100,000 MILE WARRANTY - Introduced by Chrysler to protect against outer body rust on pickup trucks.
- FIRST VAN WITH FWD - Introduced by Chrysler.

1985 - NEW GENERAL MOTORS PLANT - Saturn car plant located in Tennessee.
- FIRST 5 YEAR/50,000 MILE WARRANTY - Introduced by Chrysler protecting truck powertrains.

1986 - 100TH ANNIVERSARY OF CAR - Recognized.

BOOK ORGANIZATION

1.0 ORGANIZATION

In this book, a unique method of entering terms alphabetically was developed to efficiently define, organize, and locate information. In addition, extensive cross referencing has been included to direct the reader to more detailed and/or related information.

Each term is a separate entry, and may or may not be related to neighboring terms, depending on its format. Several general formats are used.

In many cases, terms contain much more than a basic definition. Examples and/or further detailed information are often provided to deepen the reader's understanding.

2.0 TERM FORMAT

Term format refers to the way a term is presented for definition. Four basic formats have been developed for use in this book. They have proven sufficient to group all the terms in the desired manner. Each one is shown below. In general, term formats become more precise in defining a term as more specified descriptors (primary, secondary, and tertiary subject) are used. Each descriptor to the right further defines the one on its left.

- term –
- term(primary subject) –
- term(primary subject-secondary subject) –
- term(primary subject-secondary subject-tertiary subject) –

Descriptors are often used among the various term formats to help further differentiate one term from another. The descriptors used are: ( ), primary subject, secondary subject, tertiary subject, –, /, and n.

Each term is completely boldfaced to stand out from surrounding text, and entered according to the normally accepted usage. Accepted usage includes: use of lower and/or upper case characters where appropriate; capitalizing the first letter of proper nouns; and entering people's names as last name, first name.

2.1 Individual Term Formats

2.1.1 term –

The format, term –, is the most common. It is used to define a term having only one meaning, and is usually unrelated to any other neighboring terms. The following are examples of this format:

    bullnosing –
    bum a ride –
    bumblebee –

2.1.2 term(primary subject) –

The format, term(primary subject) –, is used when a term has two or more different meanings. The primary subject descriptor can be a number, word, or phrase. The examples that follow illustrate each type.

    Grand Prix(1) –
    Grand Prix(2) –

    sound(chirping) –
    sound(clunking) –
    sound(knocking) –

BOOK ORGANIZATION

```
engine(air cooled) -
engine(dual fuel) -
engine(F head) -
```

2.1.3   term(primary subject-secondary subject) -

The format, term(primary subject-secondary subject) -, is used to further divide any term with two or more primary subject meanings into secondary subjects. The primary and secondary subject descriptors can be numbers, words, or phrases.

The following two examples illustrate using numbers as primary or secondary subjects. In the first example, the term, regulator, has two different primary subject meanings, regulator(1) and regulator(2). Regulator(1) is further divided into the different secondary subjects shown. In the second example, the term, sound(knocking) is further divided into the different secondary subjects shown.

```
regulator(1) -
regulator(1-carbon pile) -
regulator(1-cutout relay) -
regulator(1-double contact) -
regulator(2) -

sound(knocking-1) -
sound(knocking-2) -
sound(knocking-3) -
```

In the next two examples, the terms shown illustrate the use of phrases and words only for primary and secondary subjects.

```
emission control system(combustion-improved combustion) -
emission control system(combustion-NOx) -
emission control system(combustion-pulse air) -
emission control system(combustion-thermal reactor) -

car service tip(free play test-brake pedal) -
car service tip(free play test-clutch pedal) -
car service tip(free play test-fan belt) -
car service tip(free play test-parking brake) -
```

2.1.4   term(primary subject-secondary subject-tertiary subject) -

The format, term(primary subject-secondary subject-tertiary subject) -, is used to further divide any term with two or more secondary subject meanings into subsequent tertiary subject meanings. Primary, secondary, and tertiary descriptors can be numbers, words, or phrases. In general, number descriptors are either preceded or followed by a word or phrase, when used. The examples below illustrate the different usage. In the following example, the term, sound, has two different primary subject meanings: sound(1) and sound(2). Sound(2) is further divided into subsequent secondary and tertiary subject meanings.

```
sound(1) -
sound(2) -
sound(2-banging-1) -
sound(2-banging-2) -
sound(2-banging-3) -
sound(2-growling-1) -
sound(2-growling-2) -
```

In the following example, two different types of crankcase emission control systems are defined that use a modified road draft tube.

```
emission control system(crankcase-modified road draft tube-1) -
emission control system(crankcase-modified road draft tube-2) -
```

BOOK ORGANIZATION

2.2   Descriptors

Descriptors are notations used to help group and further differentiate one term from another. When used, they are always bracketed by parentheses, i.e. ( ). The descriptors used are: ( ), primary subject, secondary subject, tertiary subject, -, /, and n.

2.2.1   descriptor: ( )

The descriptor, ( ), is used to contain all other descriptors and to specify a term requiring more refinement to be clearly defined. For example, the term "engine" is not adequate to define the various types of engines, so terms such as the following are used:

    engine(F head)
    engine(L head)
    engine(V-8)

2.2.2   descriptor: primary subject

The descriptor, primary subject, is used within the descriptor, ( ), when a term has more than one meaning. It can be in the form of a number, word, or phrase. In the first example, words and phrases are used to define and group together different types of engines. In the second example, numbers are used to define and group together different meanings of "Grand Prix".

    engine(air cooled) -
    engine(diesel) -
    engine(dual fuel) -
    engine(F head) -

    Grand Prix(1) -
    Grand Prix(2) -

2.2.3   descriptor: secondary subject

The descriptor, secondary subject, is used within the descriptor, ( ), when a primary subject has more than one meaning. It can be in the form of a number, word, or phrase. In the first example, words and phrases are used to define and group together different types of "emission control system(combustion)" terms. In the second example, numbers are used to define and group together different types of "sound(knocking)" terms.

    emission control system(combustion-improved combustion) -
    emission control system(combustion-NOx) -
    emission control system(combustion-pulse air) -
    emission control system(combustion-thermal reactor) -

    sound(knocking-1) -
    sound(knocking-2) -
    sound(knocking-3) -
    sound(knocking-4) -

2.2.4   descriptor: tertiary subject

The descriptor, tertiary subject, is used within the descriptor, ( ), when a secondary subject has more than one meaning. It can be in the form of a number, word, or phrase. In the first example, words are used to define and group together different types of "sound(2-banging)" and "sound(2-growling)" terms. In second example, numbers are used to define and group together different types of "emission control system(crankcase-modified road draft tube)" terms.

BOOK ORGANIZATION

```
sound(1) -
sound(2) -
sound(2-banging-intermittent) -
sound(2-banging-loud) -
sound(2-banging-constant) -
sound(2-growling-constant) -
sound(2-growling-intermittent) -

emission control system(crankcase-modified road draft tube-1) -
emission control system(crankcase-modified road draft tube-2) -
```

2.2.5 descriptor: -

The descriptor, -, is used within the descriptor, ( ), to separate: primary, secondary, and tertiary subject descriptors. In some cases, it is used to hyphenate a word. In the first example, "-" is used to separate the primary subject, combustion, from the secondary subjects shown. In the second example, "-" is used to hyphenate the words used to describe different types of oil.

```
emission control system(combustion-improved combustion) -
emission control system(combustion-NOx) -
emission control system(combustion-pulse air) -
emission control system(combustion-thermal reactor) -

oil(10W-30) -
oil(10W-40) -
oil(20W-50) -
```

2.2.6 descriptor: /

The descriptor, /, is used within the descriptor, ( ), to denote "and/or". In the following example, "/" is used to specify a growling and/or humming type of sound.

```
sound(growling/humming) -
```

2.2.7 descriptor: n

The descriptor, n, is used within the descriptor, ( ), to denote a number. It is used as a primary, secondary, and/or tertiary subject. Numbers are used when suitable words or phrases are deemed unnecessary or not readily definable. The following examples illustrate using numbers as primary, secondary, and tertiary subjects.

```
P(1) -
P(2) -
P(3) -
P(4) -

sound(knocking-1) -
sound(knocking-2) -
sound(knocking-3) -

sound(1) -
sound(2) -
sound(2-banging-1) -
sound(2-banging-2) -
sound(2-banging-3) -
sound(2-growling-1) -
sound(2-growling-2) -
```

BOOK ORGANIZATION

3.0 Cross Referencing

Cross referencing from one term to another is done at the end of the term. Two general formats are used as shown below. The first format refers the reader to another term for a detailed meaning of the current one. The second format refers the reader to other related terms providing more detailed related information.

    See term
    See also term, term, ... and term.

TERM SUMMARY

The following list summarizes those terms in the book for which there are two or more types. The number of types are shown under the occurrence column. For example, the term, engine, shows 57 different types of engines entered in this book. Also listed are general terms scattered throughout the book under their own special term names such as different car makes, car models, products, oil companies, etc. For example, some of the different car makes would be listed as: Ford, Buick, Toyota, Pontiac, etc.

TERM	OCCURRENCE
additive	36
advance	5
advance mechanism	2
air tool	7
auction	2
auction car rating code letter	*
auto condition code word	*
automotive product	*
axle	12
battery	17
body style	61
brake	13
brake lining	3
brake master cylinder	2
brake pedal problem	3
brake problem	25
brake shoe	5
cam	5
camshaft	11
carburetor	20
carburetor circuit	9
car classification	4
car handling problem	19
car make	*
car manufacturer	*
car model	*
car part	*
car service tip	193
car transport	5
catalytic converter	3
choke	7
choking	2
circuit	4
Class	10
climate control setting	6
clutch	17
clutch plate	2
clutch problem	10
compression check	2
compressor	2
condenser	2
con game	88
consignment	2
contact pattern	2
contract	5
cross shaft	2
current limit relay	3
custom paint technique	*
Daytona 500 champion	*
differential	7
distributor	8
driveline	2
driving tip	11
electrical problem	13
emission control system	20
engine	57
engine block	4
engine problem	73
equipment manufacturer's specification	2
exhaust	10

TERM SUMMARY

TERM	OCCURRENCE
famous race car	*
FIA race car group	8
flag	8
fluid leak	16
flux	5
frame	17
freezing	2
friction material	3
fuel	3
fuel injection	13
gasoline	17
gas saving tip	45
gauge	17
gear	45
generator	7
Grand Prix champion	*
grease	6
guarantee	7
heater problem	4
ignition system	11
induction	2
injector nozzle	2
insulation	2
Indianapolis 500 Champion	*
insurance	16
insurance policy	2
intake manifold	17
international license plate letter	*
job	25
lease	7
license	4
light	27
magazine	84
magnet	2
magneto	8
motor	10
muffler	7
NASCAR champion	*
oil	44
oil filter	5
paint	27
paint coat problem	27
pavement markings	10
people	*
petroleum company	*
petroleum compound	*
petroleum product	*
place	2
radiator	5
regulator	21
road sign	8
road sign color	41
road situation tip	2
road test	4
rotor	3
runout	3
screw	3
screw head	3
secondary	38
sensor	4
service rating	3
shock absorber	2
sight glass	7
skid	8
smell	7
solder	146
sound	17
spark plug	25
spark plug appearance	

TERM SUMMARY

TERM	OCCURRENCE
spark plug cable	9
spark plug electrode	3
spark plug fouling	5
special language term - American	*
special language term - British	*
special language term - car advertising	*
special language term - car auctioneers	*
special language term - car customizers	*
special language term - car dealers	*
special language term - car historians	*
special language term - car salesmen	*
special language term - con men	*
special language term - French	*
special language term - insurance industry	*
special language term - Italian	*
special language term - law enforcement	*
special language term - mechanics	*
special language term - oil industry	*
special language term - racers	*
special language term - radar industry	*
special language term - repairmen	*
special language term - Scandinavian	*
special language term - tire industry	7
spray gun	15
spring	11
starter drive	5
starting problem	2
stator	8
steering	7
steering box	8
stroke	3
supercharger	10
suspension system	2
throttle body	2
throttle plate	2
timing light	43
tire	7
tire balancer	14
tire wear	6
towing system	5
towing tip	8
traffic light	23
transmission	16
transmission problem	2
truck bed	3
universal joint	18
vacuum gauge reading	2
vacuum switch	10
valve	4
valve lifter	3
valve spring	2
valve stem	19
vibration	5
warning light	15
warranty	5
welding	6
wheel	7
wheel alignment angle	2
wheel bearing	7
windshield	3
windshield wiper system	16
wiring diagram symbol	*
world land speed record holder	

Note:
1. * - The asterisk indicates a general term whose different types are entered
   throughout the book according to specific names. For example, "car make"
   is entered as Dodge, Ford, Chrysler, Pontiac, Toyota, Honda, etc.

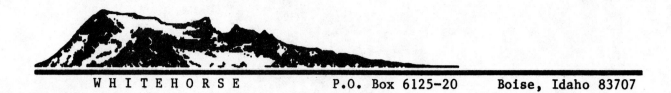

ORDER FORM

Please send me the following books published by Whitehorse:

Qty	Book Title	Binding	Unit Cost	Total Cost
___	Automotive Reference - 1987 Edition	Softcover	$19.95	_____
___	Automotive Reference - 1987 Edition	Hardcover	$29.95	_____
		Subtotal		_____
		State Tax (see notes)		_____
		Shipping (see notes)		_____
		Total		_____

Please PRINT the following clearly:

Name _____   Shipping Method Number ____

Shipping Address _____

City _____   State _____   Zipcode _____ - _____

Book subject interests _____

Check if you want to be notified of new book releases _____

Notes:

- PRICING - Prices are subject to change without notice.
- GUARANTEE - 30 day money back. If not satisfied, return the book in resaleable condition for a full refund.
- SALES TAX - Idahoans add 5% of the subtotal.
- SHIPPING METHOD/COST (United States):
  - #1 - UPS Ground (Stateside): $3/1st book; $1.50/each additional book
  - #2 - UPS 2nd Day Air (Stateside): $6/1st book; $4/each additional book
  - #3 - UPS 2nd Day Air (Alaska/Hawaii): $9/1st book; $4.50/each add. book
  - #4 - 4th Class Book Rate: $2.50/1st book; $1/each additional book
- METHOD OF PAYMENT:
  - Personal Check / Cashier's Check / Money Order
  - No CODs or Credit Cards